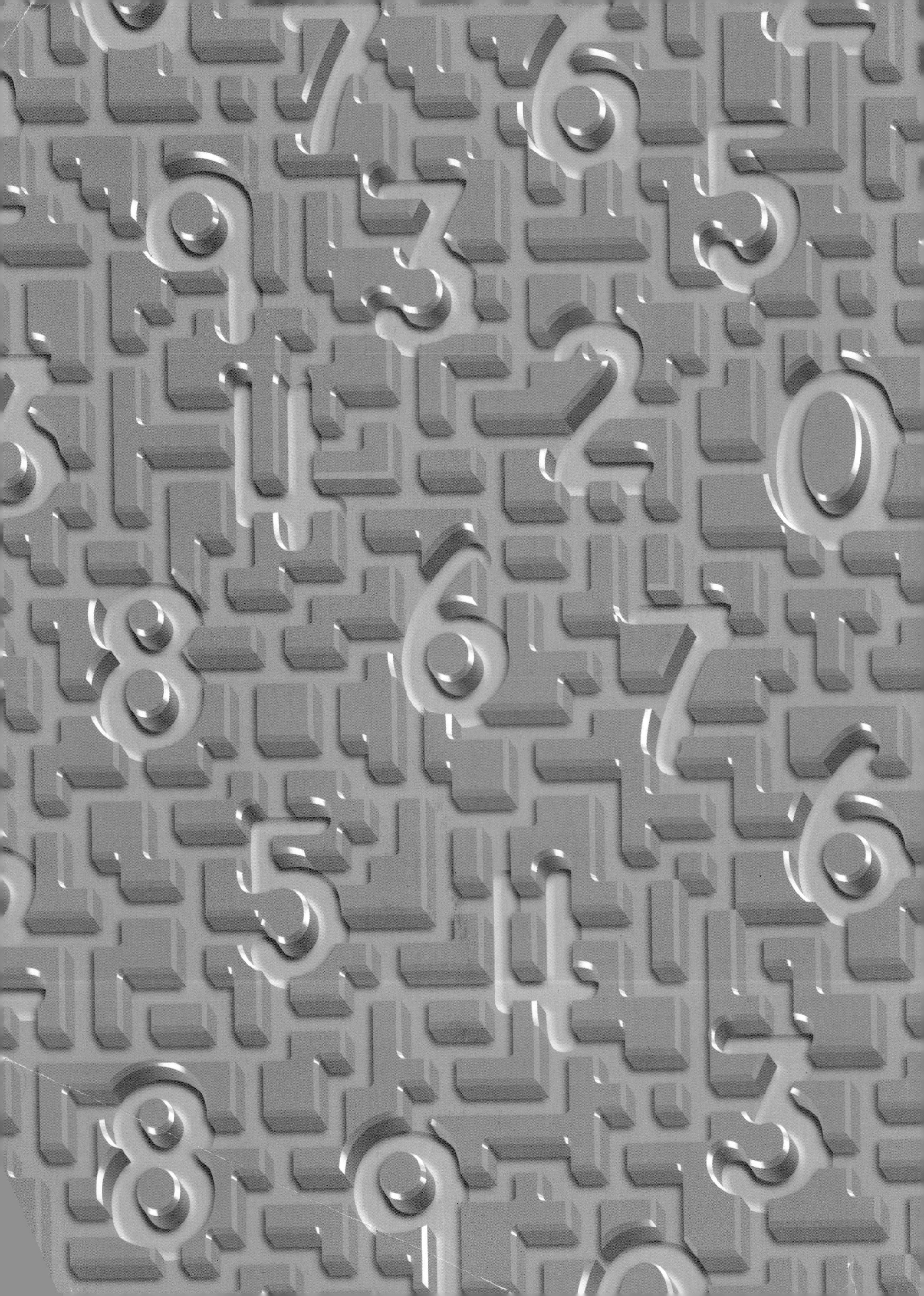

Harcourt

Orlando Austin Chicago New York Toronto London San Diego

Visit *The Learning Site!*
www.harcourtschool.com

Printed in the United States of America

ISBN 0-15-334742-2

4 5 6 7 8 9 10 032 10 09 08 07 06 05

Senior Author

Evan M. Maletsky
Professor of Mathematics
Montclair State University
Upper Montclair, New Jersey

Mathematics Advisor

David Singer
Professor of Mathematics
Case Western Reserve University
Cleveland, Ohio

Authors

Angela Giglio Andrews
Math Teacher, Scott School
Naperville District #203
Naperville, Illinois

Jennie M. Bennett
Houston Independent School District
Houston, Texas

Grace M. Burton
Professor, Watson School of Education
University of North Carolina at Wilmington
Wilmington, North Carolina

Lynda A. Luckie
K–12 Mathematics Coordinator
Gwinnett County Public Schools
Lawrenceville, Georgia

Joyce C. McLeod
Visiting Professor
Rollins College
Winter Park, Florida

Vicki Newman
Classroom Teacher
McGaugh Elementary School
Los Alamitos Unified School District
Seal Beach, California

Tom Roby
Associate Professor of Mathematics
California State University
Hayward, California

Janet K. Scheer
Executive Director
Create A Vision
Foster City, California

Program Consultants and Specialist

Janet S. Abbott
Mathematics Consultant
California

Lois Harrison-Jones
Education and Management Consultant
Dallas, Texas

Elsie Babcock
Director, Mathematics and Science Center
Mathematics Consultant
Wayne Regional Educational Service Agency
Wayne, Michigan

William J. Driscoll
Professor of Mathematics
Department of Mathematical Sciences
Central Connecticut State University
New Britain, Connecticut

Rebecca Valbuena
Language Development Specialist
Stanton Elementary School
Glendora, California

UNIT 1
CHAPTERS 1-3

Understand Numbers and Operations

Why Learn Math? xxii

1 GETTING READY: ADDITION AND SUBTRACTION CONCEPTS

Check What You Know 1
1 ALGEBRA Fact Families 2
2 ALGEBRA Missing Addends 4
3 ALGEBRA Properties 6
4 Two-Digit Addition 8
5 Two-Digit Subtraction 10
6 **Problem Solving Skill:** Choose the Operation 12
Extra Practice 14
Review/Test 15
Standardized Test Prep 16

2 PLACE VALUE AND NUMBER SENSE 18

Check What You Know 19
1 HANDS ON Even and Odd 20
2 Place Value: 3-Digit Numbers 22
3 HANDS ON Place Value: 4-Digit Numbers 24
Problem Solving: Thinker's Corner
4 **Problem Solving Strategy:** Use Logical Reasoning . . 28
5 ALGEBRA Number Patterns 30
6 Place Value: 5- and 6-Digit Numbers 32
Extra Practice 34
Review/Test 35
Standardized Test Prep 36

3 COMPARE, ORDER, AND ROUND NUMBERS . . 38

Check What You Know 39
1 Benchmark Numbers 40
2 ALGEBRA Compare Numbers .42
Problem Solving: Thinker's Corner
3 Order Numbers 46
4 Problem Solving Skill: Use a Bar Graph 48
5 Round to Nearest 10 and 100 50
6 Round to Nearest 1,000 52
Extra Practice 54
Review/Test 55
Standardized Test Prep 56

UNIT WRAPUP

It's in the Bag: Pocket Place Value 58
Challenge: Roman Numerals 59
Study Guide and Review 60
Performance Assessment 62
Technology Linkup: Number Patterns 63
Problem Solving on Location in New York 64

Technology Link

Harcourt Mega Math
Chapter 1: pp. 2, 8; Chapter 2: pp. 22, 25
Chapter 3: p. 43
The Harcourt Learning Site:
www.harcourtschool.com
Multimedia Math Glossary:
www.harcourtschool.com/mathglossary

UNIT 2
CHAPTERS 4-7

Addition, Subtraction, Money, and Time

4 ADDITION .66

Check What You Know .67
1 Estimate Sums .68
2 HANDS ON Addition with Regrouping .70
3 Add 3- and 4-Digit Numbers .72
4 **Problem Solving Strategy:** Predict and Test .74
5 Choose a Method .76
Problem Solving: Thinker's Corner
6 ALGEBRA Expressions and Number Sentences .80
Extra Practice .82
Review/Test .83
Standardized Test Prep .84

5 SUBTRACTION .86

Check What You Know .87
1 Estimate Differences .88
2 HANDS ON Subtraction with Regrouping .90
3 Subtract Across Zeros .92
Problem Solving: Linkup to Science
4 Subtract 3- and 4-Digit Numbers .96
5 Choose a Method .98
Problem Solving: Thinker's Corner
6 **Problem Solving Skill:** Estimate or Exact Answer .102
Extra Practice .104
Review/Test .105
Standardized Test Prep .106

Technology Link

Harcourt Mega Math
Chapter 4: pp. 70, 77; Chapter 5: p. 91
Chapter 6: pp. 111, 119; Chapter 7: pp. 134, 139
The Harcourt Learning Site: www.harcourtschool.com
Multimedia Math Glossary:
www.harcourtschool.com/mathglossary

6 USE MONEY 108

Check What You Know 109
1 Count Bills and Coins 110
Problem Solving: Linkup to Social Studies
2 **Problem Solving Strategy:** Make a Table 114
3 Compare Money Amounts 116
4 HANDS ON Make Change 118
5 Add and Subtract Money 120
Extra Practice 122
Review/Test 123
Standardized Test Prep 124

7 UNDERSTAND TIME 126

Check What You Know 127
1 Tell Time 128
Problem Solving: Thinker's Corner
2 A.M. and P.M. 132
3 HANDS ON Elapsed Time 134
4 Use a Schedule 136
5 Use a Calendar 138
Problem Solving: Thinker's Corner
6 **Problem Solving Skill:** Sequence Events 142
Extra Practice 144
Review/Test 145
Standardized Test Prep 146

UNIT WRAPUP

It's in the Bag: My Coin Keeper 148
Challenge: Money Amounts to $100 149
Study Guide and Review 150
Performance Assessment 152
Technology Linkup: Add and Subtract Money 153
Problem Solving on Location in Washington, D.C. . . 154

UNIT 3
CHAPTERS 8-11

Multiplication Concepts and Facts

8

UNDERSTAND MULTIPLICATION 156

Check What You Know 157
1 ALGEBRA Connect Addition and Multiplication 158
2 Multiply with 2 and 5 160
3 HANDS ON Arrays 162
4 Multiply with 3 164
Problem Solving: Thinker's Corner
5 **Problem Solving Skill:**
Too Much/Too Little Information 168
Extra Practice 170
Review/Test 171
Standardized Test Prep 172

9

MULTIPLICATION FACTS THROUGH 5 174

Check What You Know 175
1 Multiply with 1 and 0 176
2 Multiply with 4 on a Multiplication Table 178
3 **Problem Solving Strategy:** Find a Pattern 180
4 Practice Multiplication 182
Problem Solving: Thinker's Corner
5 ALGEBRA Missing Factors 186
Extra Practice 188
Review/Test 189
Standardized Test Prep 190

Technology Link

Harcourt Mega Math
Chapter 8: pp. 158, 162; Chapter 9: p. 182
Chapter 10: p. 200; Chapter 11: pp. 213, 216
The Harcourt Learning Site:
www.harcourtschool.com
Multimedia Math Glossary:
www.harcourtschool.com/mathglossary

10 MULTIPLICATION FACTS AND STRATEGIES . . 192

Check What You Know 193
1 Multiply with 6 194
2 Multiply with 8 196
3 **Problem Solving Skill:** Use a Pictograph 198
4 Multiply with 7 200
5 ALGEBRA Practice the Facts .202
Problem Solving: Thinker's Corner
Extra Practice 206
Review/Test 207
Standardized Test Prep 208

11 MULTIPLICATION FACTS AND PATTERNS 210

Check What You Know 211
1 Multiply with 9 and 10 212
Problem Solving: Linkup to Reading
2 ALGEBRA Find a Rule 216
3 ALGEBRA Multiply with 3 Factors 218
4 ALGEBRA Multiplication Properties 220
5 **Problem Solving Skill:** Multistep Problems 222
Extra Practice 224
Review/Test 225
Standardized Test Prep 226

UNIT WRAPUP

It's in the Bag: Multiplication Rocks 228
Challenge: Multiply with 11 and 12 229
Study Guide and Review 230
Performance Assessment 232
Technology Linkup: Multiplication Mystery 233
Problem Solving on Location in New Jersey and Pennsylvania 234

UNIT 4 Division Concepts and Facts

CHAPTERS 12-14

UNDERSTAND DIVISION .236

Check What You Know .237
1 HANDS ON The Meaning of Division .238
2 Subtraction and Division .240
3 ALGEBRA Multiplication and Division .242
Problem Solving: Thinker's Corner
4 ALGEBRA Fact Families HANDS ON .246
Problem Solving: Thinker's Corner
5 **Problem Solving Strategy:**
Write a Number Sentence .250
Extra Practice .252
Review/Test .253
Standardized Test Prep .254

DIVISION FACTS THROUGH 5 .256

Check What You Know .257
1 Divide by 2 and 5 .258
2 Divide by 3 and 4 .260
3 Divide with 1 and 0 .262
4 ALGEBRA Expressions and Equations .264
5 **Problem Solving Skill:** Choose the Operation .266
Extra Practice .268
Review/Test .269
Standardized Test Prep .270

Technology Link

Harcourt Mega Math
Chapter 12: pp. 242, 247; Chapter 13: p. 261
Chapter 14: pp. 274, 281
The Harcourt Learning Site:
www.harcourtschool.com
Multimedia Math Glossary:
www.harcourtschool.com/mathglossary

DIVISION FACTS THROUGH 10 ... 272

Check What You Know ... 273
1 Divide by 6, 7, and 8 ... 274
Problem Solving: Linkup to Reading
2 Divide by 9 and 10 ... 278
3 Practice Division Facts ... 280
Problem Solving: Thinker's Corner
4 ALGEBRA Find the Cost ... 284
5 Problem Solving Strategy: Work Backward ... 286
Extra Practice ... 288
Review/Test ... 289
Standardized Test Prep ... 290

UNIT WRAPUP

It's in the Bag: Candy Bar Division ... 292
Challenge: Divide by 11 and 12 ... 293
Study Guide and Review ... 294
Performance Assessment ... 296
Technology Linkup: Find the Unit Cost ... 297
Problem Solving on Location in Illinois ... 298

UNIT 5 Data and Measurement

CHAPTERS 15-18

15 COLLECT AND RECORD DATA .... .300

Check What You Know .... .301
1 HANDS ON Collect Data .... .302
2 Use Data from a Survey .... .304
3 Classify Data .... .306
4 **Problem Solving Strategy:** Make a Table .... .308
5 HANDS ON Line Plots .... .310
Problem Solving: Linkup to Reading
6 HANDS ON Mean and Median .... .314
Extra Practice .... .316
Review/Test .... .317
Standardized Test Prep .... .318

16 ANALYZE AND GRAPH DATA .... .320

Check What You Know .... .321
1 **Problem Solving Strategy:** Make a Graph .... .322
2 Bar Graphs .... .324
3 HANDS ON Make Bar Graphs .... .326
4 ALGEBRA Ordered Pairs .... .328
5 Line Graphs .... .330
Extra Practice .... .332
Review/Test .... .333
Standardized Test Prep .... .334

Technology Link

Harcourt Mega Math
Chapter 15: pp. 311, 315; Chapter 16: pp. 325, 330
Chapter 17: p. 348; Chapter 18: p. 359
The Harcourt Learning Site:
www.harcourtschool.com
Multimedia Math Glossary:
www.harcourtschool.com/mathglossary

17 CUSTOMARY UNITS .336

Check What You Know .337
1 HANDS ON Length .338
Problem Solving: Thinker's Corner
2 Inch, Foot, Yard, and Mile .342
3 HANDS ON Capacity .344
4 HANDS ON Weight .346
5 Ways to Change Units .348
6 **Problem Solving Skill:** Estimate or Measure .350
Extra Practice .352
Review/Test .353
Standardized Test Prep .354

18 METRIC UNITS AND TEMPERATURE .356

Check What You Know .357
1 HANDS ON Length .358
Problem Solving: Thinker's Corner
2 **Problem Solving Strategy:** Make a Table .362
3 HANDS ON Capacity .364
4 HANDS ON Mass .366
5 HANDS ON Fahrenheit and Celsius .368
Extra Practice .370
Review/Test .371
Standardized Test Prep .372

UNIT WRAPUP

It's in the Bag: Stamp-o-Graph Math .374
Challenge: Read a Circle Graph .375
Study Guide and Review .376
Performance Assessment .378
Technology Linkup: Enter Data on a Spreadsheet .379
Problem Solving on Location in Wisconsin .380

UNIT 6 Geometry

CHAPTERS 19-22

19 GEOMETRIC FIGURES .382

Check What You Know .383
1 Line Segments and Angles .384
Problem Solving: Thinker's Corner
2 Types of Lines .388
3 Plane Figures .390
4 Triangles .392
Problem Solving: Linkup to Art
5 Quadrilaterals .396
Problem Solving: Linkup to Reading
6 **Problem Solving Strategy:** Draw a Diagram .400
Extra Practice .402
Review/Test .403
Standardized Test Prep .404

20 CONGRUENCE AND SYMMETRY .406

Check What You Know .407
1 HANDS ON Congruent Figures .408
2 HANDS ON Symmetry .410
3 HANDS ON Similar Figures .412
4 HANDS ON Slides, Flips, and Turns .414
5 **Problem Solving Strategy:** Make a Model .416
Extra Practice .418
Review/Test .419
Standardized Test Prep .420

Harcourt Mega Math
Chapter 19: p. 396; Chapter 20: pp. 408, 414
Chapter 21: p. 424; Chapter 22: p. 452
The Harcourt Learning Site:
www.harcourtschool.com
Multimedia Math Glossary:
www.harcourtschool.com/mathglossary

21 SOLID AND PLANE FIGURES 422

Check What You Know 423

1 HANDS ON Solid Figures .424

Problem Solving: Thinker's Corner

2 Combine Solid Figures 428

3 Tessellations 430

4 HANDS ON Draw Figures .432

Problem Solving: Linkup to Social Studies

5 **Problem Solving Skill:** Identify Relationships 436

Extra Practice 438

Review/Test 439

Standardized Test Prep 440

22 PERIMETER, AREA, AND VOLUME 442

Check What You Know 443

1 HANDS ON Perimeter 444

Problem Solving: Linkup to Social Studies

2 HANDS ON Area 448

3 **Problem Solving Skill:** Make Generalizations 450

4 HANDS ON Volume 452

Problem Solving: Linkup to Reading

Extra Practice 456

Review/Test 457

Standardized Test Prep 458

UNIT WRAPUP

It's in the Bag: Pocketful of Polygons 460

Challenge: Measure with Degrees 461

Study Guide and Review 462

Performance Assessment 464

Technology Linkup: Symmetry .465

Problem Solving on Location in Illinois and Pennsylvania 466

UNIT 7 Patterns and Probability

CHAPTERS 23-24

23 ALGEBRA PATTERNS

ALGEBRA PATTERNS 468
Check What You Know 469
1 Geometric Patterns 470
Problem Solving: Thinker's Corner
2 Visual Patterns 474
3 Number Patterns 476
4 HANDS ON Make Patterns 478
5 Problem Solving Strategy: Find a Pattern 480
Extra Practice 482
Review/Test 483
Standardized Test Prep 484

Technology Link

Harcourt Mega Math
Chapter 23: p. 476
Chapter 24: pp. 489, 493
The Harcourt Learning Site:
www.harcourtschool.com
Multimedia Math Glossary:
www.harcourtschool.com/mathglossary

PROBABILITY ... 486

Check What You Know ... 487
1 Probability ... 488
2 HANDS ON Outcomes ... 490
3 HANDS ON Experiments ... 492
Problem Solving: Linkup to Science
4 HANDS ON Predict Outcomes ... 496
5 Combinations ... 498
6 **Problem Solving Strategy:** Make an Organized List ... 500
Extra Practice ... 502
Review/Test ... 503
Standardized Test Prep ... 504

UNIT WRAPUP

It's in the Bag: Probability Clues ... 506
Challenge: Color Patterns ... 507
Study Guide and Review ... 508
Performance Assessment ... 510
Technology Linkup: Make a Graph ... 511
Problem Solving on Location in Tennessee ... 512

UNIT 8 Fractions and Decimals

CHAPTERS 25-28

25 UNDERSTAND FRACTIONS .514

Check What You Know .515
1 Parts of a Whole .516
Problem Solving: Linkup to Social Studies
2 Parts of a Group .520
3 HANDS ON Equivalent Fractions .522
Problem Solving: Linkup to Science
4 Compare and Order Fractions .526
Problem Solving: Linkup to Social Studies
5 **Problem Solving Strategy:** Make a Model .530
6 Mixed Numbers .532
Extra Practice .534
Review/Test .535
Standardized Test Prep .536

26 ADD AND SUBTRACT LIKE FRACTIONS .538

Check What You Know .539
1 HANDS ON Add Fractions .540
2 Add Fractions .542
3 HANDS ON Subtract Fractions .544
4 Subtract Fractions .546
Problem Solving: Linkup to Geography
5 **Problem Solving Skill:** Reasonable Answers .550
Extra Practice .552
Review/Test .553
Standardized Test Prep .554

Technology Link

Harcourt Mega Math
Chapter 25: p. 527; Chapter 26: p. 547
Chapter 27: pp. 560, 562; Chapter 28: p. 580
The Harcourt Learning Site:
www.harcourtschool.com
Multimedia Math Glossary: www.harcourtschool.com/mathglossary

27 FRACTIONS AND DECIMALS 556

Check What You Know 557
1 Fractions and Decimals 558
2 HANDS ON Tenths 560
3 HANDS ON Hundredths 562
4 Decimals Greater Than One 564
5 Compare and Order Decimals 566
6 **Problem Solving Skill:**
Too Much/Too Little Information 568
Extra Practice 570
Review/Test 571
Standardized Test Prep 572

28 DECIMALS AND MONEY 574

Check What You Know 575
1 Fractions and Money 576
2 HANDS ON Decimals and Money 578
3 Add and Subtract Decimals and Money 580
Problem Solving: Linkup to Reading
4 **Problem Solving Strategy:**
Solve a Simpler Problem 584
Extra Practice 586
Review/Test 587
Standardized Test Prep 588

UNIT WRAPUP

It's in the Bag: Fraction Trade Game 590
Challenge: Fractions and Decimals on a Number Line 591
Study Guide and Review 592
Performance Assessment 594
Technology Linkup: Fractions and Decimals 595
Problem Solving on Location in Virginia 596

UNIT 9

CHAPTERS 29-30

Multiply and Divide by 1-Digit Numbers

MULTIPLY BY 1-DIGIT NUMBERS 598

Check What You Know 599

1 ALGEBRA Multiply Multiples of 10 and 100 HANDS ON 600

2 Multiply 2-Digit Numbers 602

Problem Solving: Linkup to Art

3 Problem Solving Skill: Choose the Operation 606

4 Choose a Method 608

Problem Solving: Linkup to Math History

Extra Practice 612

Review/Test 613

Standardized Test Prep 614

DIVIDE BY 1-DIGIT NUMBERS 616

Check What You Know 617

1 HANDS ON Divide with Remainders 618

2 HANDS ON Divide 2-Digit Numbers 620

Problem Solving: Linkup to Reading

3 Problem Solving Skill: Interpret the Remainder 624

4 Divide 3-Digit Numbers 626

5 Estimate Quotients 628

Extra Practice 630

Review/Test 631

Standardized Test Prep 632

Technology Link

Harcourt Mega Math
Chapter 29: p. 603
Chapter 30: p. 619
The Harcourt Learning Site:
www.harcourtschool.com
Multimedia Math Glossary:
www.harcourtschool.com/mathglossary

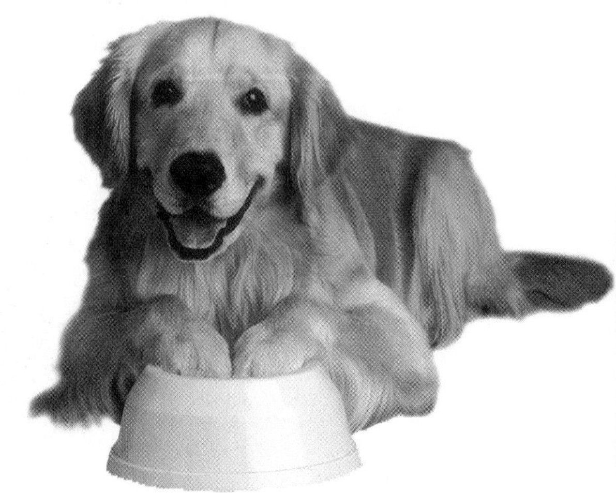

UNIT WRAPUP

It's in the Bag: Multiply and Divide Start to Finish 634
Challenge: Multiply 3-Digit Numbers 635
Study Guide and Review 636
Performance Assessment 638
Technology Linkup: Multiply and Divide 639
Problem Solving on Location in Indiana 640

STUDENT HANDBOOK

Table of Contents H1
Troubleshooting H2
Sharpen Your Test-Taking Skills H32
Basic Facts Tests H36
Table of Measures H41
Glossary H42
Index H55

Why Learn Math?

Building Success Now

You use math when you participate in sporting events. ▼

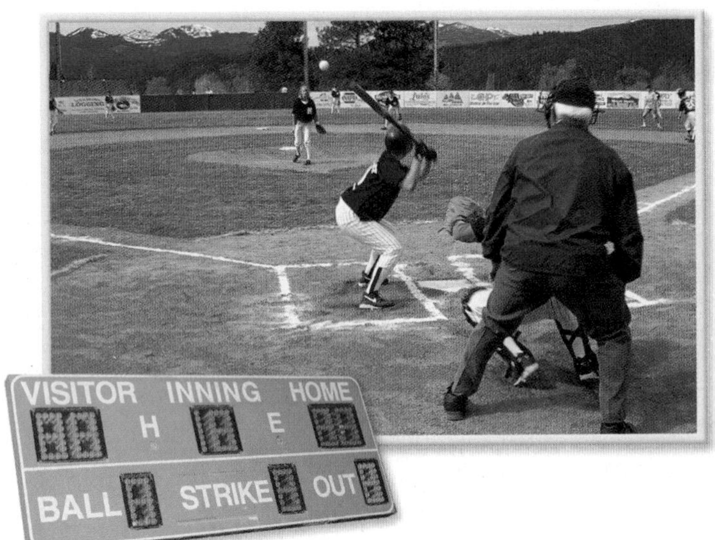

▲ You use math when you measure pieces of wood to build a tree house.

You use patterns in math when you play games or work with arts and crafts. ▶

You will use the mathematics that you learn in **Harcourt Math** every day. The skills you learn will help you **build success** both now and in the future.

Building Success for the Future

◀ If you become a civil engineer, math skills will help you build bridges.

▼ If you become an astronaut, you will use math skills during space missions.

▲ If you become a scientist, math skills will help you conduct experiments.

Have a great year and enjoy learning Math!

PRACTICE WHAT YOU LEARN

It's in the Bag

PROJECT Make a pouch to hold unit activities throughout the year.

Materials

- Large grocery bag
- Scissors
- Tape
- Plastic bag with zip closure
- 2 3-inch strips of Velcro (with adhesive backing)
- Markers or crayons

Directions

1. Open the bag so that one of the large sides faces you. Cut along the 2 folds down to the bottom. Then cut a 3-inch strip off the top of this cut side. (*Picture A*) Stand the bag up and fold the cut side into the bag. Crease at the back of the bag along the bottom. Tape the top of the cut side to the back of the bag.
2. Stand the bag with the larger side facing you. Starting at the top of the bag, cut along the folds until you get to the edge of the taped-down flap. (*Picture B*) Cut across the side flaps and remove them. The sides should now be about $7\frac{1}{2}$ inches tall.
3. Fold up the bottom of the bag to lay flat. In the center of the top flap, cut out a 4-inch square. Center the plastic bag over the window. Tape the sides and bottom of the plastic bag to the flap.
4. Attach the Velcro strips along the sides of the top and bottom flaps. (*Picture C*) Fold the bag in half. Decorate the outside of the pouch.

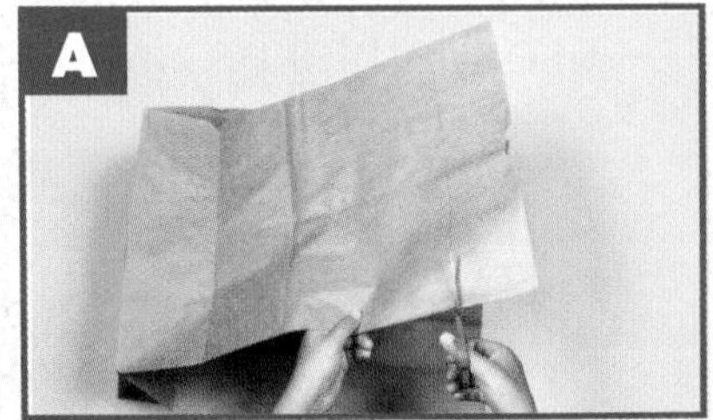
A

B

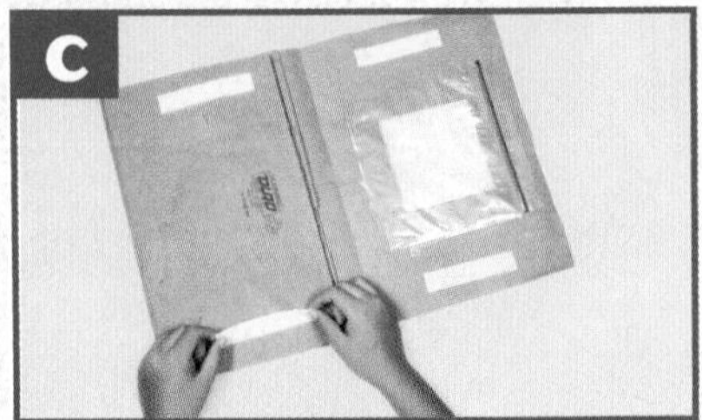
C

SHOW WHAT YOU LEARN

Taking a test is one way to show what you've learned. Being a good test taker is like being a good problem solver. When you answer test questions, you are solving problems.

Each time you take a test, remember to:

- Listen carefully to your teacher's instructions.
- Read all the directions.
- Pay attention to where and how to mark the test.
- Read the problems carefully.
- If you don't understand a problem, read it again.
- Mark or write your answers clearly.
- Answer questions you are sure about first.
- Work quickly but carefully.
- If you finish early, go back and check your work.
- Relax and do the best that you can.

CHAPTER 1

Getting Ready: Addition and Subtraction Concepts

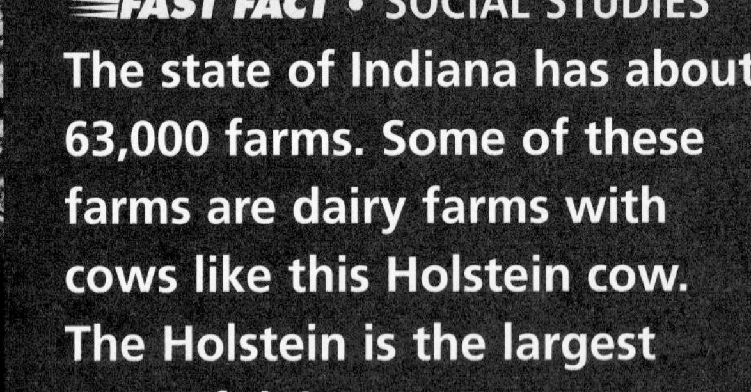

FAST FACT • SOCIAL STUDIES
The state of Indiana has about 63,000 farms. Some of these farms are dairy farms with cows like this Holstein cow. The Holstein is the largest type of dairy cow.

PROBLEM SOLVING **The pictograph shows the number of animals on one Indiana farm. How many animals are there in all?**

ANIMALS ON AN INDIANA FARM

Sheep	
Cows	
Goats	
Chickens	

Key: Each = 2 animals.

CHECK WHAT YOU KNOW

Use this page to help you review and remember important skills needed for Chapter 1.

ADDITION FACTS

Find the sum.

1. $\begin{array}{r} 8 \\ +2 \\ \hline \end{array}$	**2.** $\begin{array}{r} 7 \\ +3 \\ \hline \end{array}$	**3.** $\begin{array}{r} 1 \\ +6 \\ \hline \end{array}$	**4.** $\begin{array}{r} 6 \\ +5 \\ \hline \end{array}$	**5.** $\begin{array}{r} 3 \\ +4 \\ \hline \end{array}$
6. $\begin{array}{r} 7 \\ +7 \\ \hline \end{array}$	**7.** $\begin{array}{r} 4 \\ +8 \\ \hline \end{array}$	**8.** $\begin{array}{r} 9 \\ +5 \\ \hline \end{array}$	**9.** $\begin{array}{r} 8 \\ +6 \\ \hline \end{array}$	**10.** $\begin{array}{r} 8 \\ +9 \\ \hline \end{array}$
11. $\begin{array}{r} 5 \\ +4 \\ \hline \end{array}$	**12.** $\begin{array}{r} 3 \\ +6 \\ \hline \end{array}$	**13.** $\begin{array}{r} 4 \\ +7 \\ \hline \end{array}$	**14.** $\begin{array}{r} 8 \\ +1 \\ \hline \end{array}$	**15.** $\begin{array}{r} 6 \\ +7 \\ \hline \end{array}$

SUBTRACTION FACTS

Find the difference.

16. $\begin{array}{r} 7 \\ -2 \\ \hline \end{array}$	**17.** $\begin{array}{r} 9 \\ -3 \\ \hline \end{array}$	**18.** $\begin{array}{r} 8 \\ -1 \\ \hline \end{array}$	**19.** $\begin{array}{r} 10 \\ -\ 5 \\ \hline \end{array}$	**20.** $\begin{array}{r} 9 \\ -6 \\ \hline \end{array}$
21. $\begin{array}{r} 12 \\ -\ 7 \\ \hline \end{array}$	**22.** $\begin{array}{r} 13 \\ -\ 5 \\ \hline \end{array}$	**23.** $\begin{array}{r} 11 \\ -\ 5 \\ \hline \end{array}$	**24.** $\begin{array}{r} 14 \\ -\ 6 \\ \hline \end{array}$	**25.** $\begin{array}{r} 15 \\ -\ 8 \\ \hline \end{array}$

VOCABULARY POWER

REVIEW

addend [a′dend] *noun*

Addend comes from the Latin word *addendum*. By the end of the 1600s, *addends* meant all the numbers being added. In the number sentence $8 + 5 = 13$, what numbers are the addends?

PREVIEW

fact family

inverse operations

Order Property of Addition

Identity Property of Addition

Grouping Property of Addition

www.harcourtschool.com/mathglossary

LESSON 1

Algebra: Fact Families

Learn

FARM ANIMALS The pictograph shows some of the animals on Brittany's farm.

ANIMALS ON BRITTANY'S FARM	
Chickens	🚜 🚜 🚜
Cows	🚜 🚜 🚜 🚜 🚜
Ducks	🚜 🚜 🚜 🚜
Sheep	🚜 🚜 🚜
Key: Each 🚜 = 2 animals.	

How many ducks and chickens are there?

Look at the pictograph. Find the symbols for ducks. Then skip-count by twos. There are 8 ducks. Now skip-count the symbols for chickens. There are 6 chickens.

$$8 + 6 = 14 \text{ or } 6 + 8 = 14$$

So, there are 14 ducks and chickens in all.

The numbers 6, 8, and 14 can be used to make a fact family. A **fact family** is a set of related addition and subtraction number sentences that use the same numbers.

$8 + 6 = 14$ $\quad$ $6 + 8 = 14$

$14 - 6 = 8$ $\quad$ $14 - 8 = 6$

- Write another fact family that uses the number 8.
- What is the fact family for 6, 6, and 12? Why are there only two facts?

MATH IDEA Addition and subtraction are opposite or **inverse operations**. Fact families are examples of inverse operations.

$5 + 7 = 12$ $\quad$ $7 + 5 = 12$

$12 - 7 = 5$ $\quad$ $12 - 5 = 7$

Quick Review

1. $9 + 4 = \square$
2. $12 - 5 = \square$
3. $8 + 6 = \square$
4. $14 - 9 = \square$
5. $6 + 9 = \square$

Vocabulary

fact family
inverse operations

Technology Link

More Practice: Harcourt Mega Math Country Countdown, *Counting Critters*, Level U

Check

1. Explain why 7, 9, and 16 can be used to make a fact family.

Complete.

2. $6 + 7 = 13$, so $13 - ■ = 7$.
3. $15 - 7 = 8$, so $■ + ■ = 15$.

Write the fact family for each set of numbers.

4. 4, 7, 11
5. 7, 7, 14
6. 5, 9, 14
7. 6, 9, 15

Practice and Problem Solving

Extra Practice, page 14, Set A

Complete.

8. $5 + 8 = 13$, so $13 - 5 = ■$.
9. $16 - 8 = 8$, so $8 + ■ = 16$.
10. $12 - 8 = 4$, so $■ + 8 = 12$.
11. $4 + 9 = 13$, so $13 - ■ = 9$.
12. $9 + 9 = 18$, so $18 - ■ = ■$.
13. $17 - 9 = 8$, so $■ + ■ = 17$.

Write the fact family for each set of numbers.

14. 5, 6, 11
15. 8, 8, 16
16. 7, 9, 16
17. 5, 7, 12
18. Write a problem using the number sentence $9 + 3 = 12$.
19. **Write About It** Write two fact families using the number 7.
20. **Vocabulary Power** Left is the opposite of right. Addition and subtraction are opposite operations. What other math words do you know that are opposites?
21. Jared had 6 red marbles, 7 blue marbles, and 3 green marbles. He lost 4 blue marbles. How many marbles does Jared have now?

Mixed Review and Test Prep

Find the sum.

22. $4 + 0 = ■$
23. $7 + 3 = ■$
24. $6 + 5 = ■$
25. $4 + 5 = ■$

26. What number does the model show?

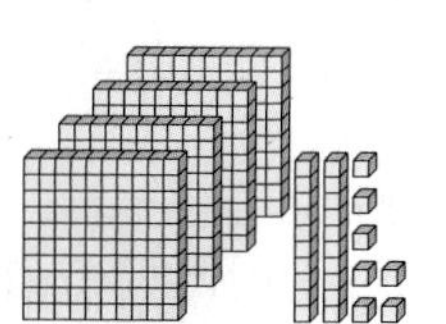

A 317
B 325
C 421
D 427

LESSON 2

Algebra: Missing Addends

Quick Review

1. 5 + 6 = ■
2. 7 + 8 = ■
3. 6 + 9 = ■
4. 8 + 8 = ■
5. 5 + 7 = ■

Learn

HORSEBACK RIDING Aaron's family went horseback riding in the Greene-Sullivan State Forest in Dugger, Indiana. They rode on two trails that are a total of 14 miles long. The Yellow Loop trail is 9 miles long. How long is the Orange Loop trail?

One Way Use an addition fact to find the missing addend.

9	+	■	=	14
↑		↑		↑
addend Yellow Loop trail		missing addend Orange Loop trail		sum Total miles ridden

9 + 5 = 14

Another Way Use a related subtraction fact to find the missing addend.

14	−	9	=	■
↑		↑		↑
sum Total miles ridden		addend Yellow Loop trail		missing addend Orange Loop trail

14 − 9 = 5

Since 9 + 5 = 14 and 14 − 9 = 5, the Orange Loop trail is 5 miles long.

MATH IDEA You can think of an addition fact or a related subtraction fact to find a missing addend.

Check

1. **Explain** how you can use a related subtraction fact to find $\square + 8 = 17$.

Find the missing addend.

2. $5 + \square = 11$
3. $\square + 3 = 12$
4. $4 + \square = 10$
5. $\square + 5 = 13$

Practice and Problem Solving

Extra Practice, page 14, Set B

Find the missing addend.

6. $8 + \square = 15$
7. $\square + 3 = 11$
8. $\square + 6 = 13$
9. $\square + 6 = 14$
10. $\square + 8 = 8$
11. $5 + \square = 13$
12. $7 + \square = 14$
13. $\square + 9 = 15$
14. $9 + \square = 16$
15. $\square + 7 = 13$
16. $7 + \square = 15$
17. $8 + \square = 17$

18. James had 9 video games. He received more games as birthday gifts. Now James has 16 games. Use counters and an addition sentence to show how many games James received as gifts.

19. **FAST FACT** • SOCIAL STUDIES Indiana's Ghost Town Trail got its name from a railroad line running between old mining towns. The trail is 16 miles long. Four miles were added to the trail in 1993. How long was the trail in 1992?

20. **REASONING** How many pairs of missing addends are there for $\square + \square = 8$? List the pairs.

21. I am a number less than 50. My tens digit is 4. The sum of my digits is 4. What number am I?

22. I am a number less than 100. My tens digit is 7 more than my ones digit. My ones digit is 2. What number am I?

23. **? What's the Error?** Jenna wrote $12 - 4 = 7$ to help her find $4 + \square = 12$. Describe and correct her error.

Mixed Review and Test Prep

Complete. (p. 2)

24. $5 + 7 = 12$, so $12 - 5 = \square$.
25. $6 + 8 = 14$, so $14 - \square = 8$.
26. $18 - 9 = 9$, so $\square + 9 = 18$.
27. $15 - 6 = 9$, so $6 + \square = 15$.

28. **TEST PREP** Which sentence is *not* in the fact family for 6, 9, and 15? (p. 2)

A $6 + 6 = 12$
B $6 + 9 = 15$
C $9 + 6 = 15$
D $15 - 9 = 6$

LESSON

3 Algebra: Properties

Learn

Special rules, called properties, can help you add.

IN THE PARK Olivia saw 6 monarch butterflies and 7 swallowtails. Courtney saw 7 monarchs and 6 swallowtails. How many butterflies did each girl see in all?

Quick Review

1. 4 + 9 = ■
2. 8 + 6 = ■
3. 8 + 7 = ■
4. 6 + 9 = ■
5. 9 + 7 = ■

Vocabulary

Order Property of Addition
Identity Property of Addition
Grouping Property of Addition

Order Property of Addition

You can add two or more numbers in any order and get the same sum.

6	+	7	=	13	7	+	6	=	13
↑		↑		↑	↑		↑		↑
addend	+	addend	=	sum	addend	+	addend	=	sum

So, 6 + 7 = 7 + 6. Olivia and Courtney each saw 13 butterflies.

Identity Property of Addition

Courtney saw 12 tulips in a garden. Olivia didn't see any. How many tulips did the girls see in all?

When you add zero to a number, the sum is that number.

12 + 0 = 12

So, the girls saw 12 tulips in all.

Grouping Property of Addition

Olivia saw 9 birds, 1 rabbit, and 4 squirrels in a meadow. How many animals did she see in all?

You can group addends in different ways and still get the same sum.

$$(9 + 1) + 4 = 9 + (1 + 4)$$
$$10 + 4 = 9 + 5$$
$$14 = 14$$

Hint: The ( ) symbols tell you which numbers to add first.

So, Olivia saw 14 animals in all.

Check

1. **Explain** how the Grouping Property of Addition can help you find $2 + (8 + 4)$.

Find each sum.

2. $15 + 0 = ■$

3. $8 + 6 = ■$
   $6 + 8 = ■$

4. $4 + (6 + 5) = ■$
   $(4 + 6) + 5 = ■$

Practice and Problem Solving

Extra Practice, page 14, Set C

Find each sum.

5. $7 + 4 = ■$
   $4 + 7 = ■$

6. $(3 + 7) + 8 = ■$
   $3 + (7 + 8) = ■$

7. $8 + 9 = ■$
   $9 + 8 = ■$

8. $8 + (1 + 9) = ■$
   $(8 + 1) + 9 = ■$

9. $6 + 11 = ■$
   $11 + 6 = ■$

10. $8 + (5 + 6) = ■$
    $(8 + 5) + 6 = ■$

11. $13 + 0 = ■$

12. $(6 + 8) + 3 = ■$
    $6 + (8 + 3) = ■$

13. $8 + 5 = ■$
    $5 + 8 = ■$

14. Jake has 4 cats. Matthew has 5 birds and 2 dogs. Draw a picture to show how many pets they have in all.

15. The sum of two numbers is 14. One of the numbers is 5 less than the sum. What are the two numbers?

16. **REASONING** $3 + 9 = 12$ and $9 + 3 = 12$ shows the Order Property of Addition. Can you use the Order Property to subtract? Why or why not?

17. Anna picked 7 roses, 7 tulips, and 3 daisies. Then she gave her mother 8 of the flowers. How many flowers did she have left?

Mixed Review and Test Prep

Find the sum.

18. $8 + 7 = ■$

19. $6 + 9 = ■$

Find the difference.

20. $16 - 8 = ■$

21. $17 - 9 = ■$

22. **TEST PREP** Josh saw 3 butterflies in his yard on Saturday. On Sunday he saw 2 more than he saw on Saturday. How many butterflies did he see in all?

A 5 **B** 6 **C** 7 **D** 8

LESSON 4

Two-Digit Addition

Quick Review

1. 9 + 7 = ■
2. 8 + 5 = ■
3. 6 + 9 = ■
4. 7 + 6 = ■
5. 3 + 8 + 7 = ■

Learn

TILL THE COWS COME HOME Zack counted 36 cows in the barn. Then he counted 48 cows grazing in the pasture. How many cows did Zack count in all?

36 + 48 = ■

Example 1

STEP 1

Add the ones.
6 + 8 = 14 ones

$$\begin{array}{r} {}^{1}\\ 36 \\ +48 \\ \hline 4 \end{array}$$

Regroup 14 ones as 1 ten 4 ones.

STEP 2

Add the tens.
1 + 3 + 4 = 8 tens

$$\begin{array}{r} {}^{1}\\ 36 \\ +48 \\ \hline 84 \end{array}$$

So, Zack counted 84 cows in all.

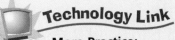

Technology Link
More Practice:
Harcourt Mega Math Country Countdown, *Block Busters,* Level M

Example 2

One cow drank 46 gallons of water. A second cow drank 37 gallons, and a third cow drank 53 gallons. How many gallons of water did the three cows drink in all?

46 + 37 + 53 = ■

STEP 1

Add the ones.
6 + 7 + 3 = 16 ones

$$\begin{array}{r} {}^{1}\\ 46 \\ 37 \\ +53 \\ \hline 6 \end{array}$$

Make a ten.

Regroup 16 ones as 1 ten 6 ones.

STEP 2

Add the tens.
1 + 4 + 3 + 5 = 13 tens

$$\begin{array}{r} {}^{1}\\ 46 \\ 37 \\ +53 \\ \hline 136 \end{array}$$

Regroup 13 tens as 1 hundred 3 tens.

So, the cows drank 136 gallons of water in all.

Check

1. **Explain** when you need to regroup ones as tens. Give an example.

Find the sum.

2. $\begin{array}{r} 32 \\ +\ 6 \\ \hline \end{array}$

3. $\begin{array}{r} 28 \\ +51 \\ \hline \end{array}$

4. $\begin{array}{r} 88 \\ +\ 7 \\ \hline \end{array}$

5. $\begin{array}{r} 49 \\ 6 \\ +12 \\ \hline \end{array}$

6. $\begin{array}{r} 79 \\ 64 \\ +22 \\ \hline \end{array}$

Practice and Problem Solving

Extra Practice, page 14, Set D

Find the sum.

7. $\begin{array}{r} 47 \\ +22 \\ \hline \end{array}$

8. $\begin{array}{r} 72 \\ +\ 9 \\ \hline \end{array}$

9. $\begin{array}{r} 18 \\ +69 \\ \hline \end{array}$

10. $\begin{array}{r} 78 \\ +87 \\ \hline \end{array}$

11. $\begin{array}{r} 56 \\ 98 \\ +\ 4 \\ \hline \end{array}$

Copy and complete each table.

	Add 10.	
12.	71	
13.	43	
14.	8	

	Add 25.	
15.	25	
16.	7	
17.	49	

	Add 58.	
18.	30	
19.	65	
20.	78	

21. What related subtraction fact can you write to find the missing addend for 7 + ■ = 15?

22. **REASONING** I am a two-digit number. My ones and tens digits are the same. The sum of my digits is 8. What number am I?

23. The third-grade classes went on a field trip. One bus took 29 students. A second bus took 34 students. How many students went on the field trip?

24. Sara and her father went fishing. Sara caught 12 fish. Her father caught 9 fish. They threw back 4 small fish. How many fish did they have left?

Mixed Review and Test Prep

Write the fact family for each set of numbers. (p. 2)

25. 8, 9, 17

26. 5, 7, 12

Find the missing addend. (p. 4)

27. 8 + ■ = 13

28. ■ + 9 = 15

29. **TEST PREP** Jordan has a fish tank with 6 goldfish, 3 black mollies, and 4 guppies. How many fish does she have in all? (p. 6)

A 10
B 13
C 14
D 16

LESSON 5

Two-Digit Subtraction

Quick Review

1. 15 − 7 = ■
2. 16 − 8 = ■
3. 14 − 9 = ■
4. 15 − 6 = ■
5. 13 − 8 = ■

Learn

GLOWING IN THE DARK Emma and her brother Colin enjoy catching fireflies. They place them in two glass jars so they can count them before letting them go. One night Emma caught 32 fireflies. Colin caught 18 fireflies. How many more fireflies did Emma catch than Colin?

32 − 18 = ■

STEP 1

Since 8 > 2, regroup 32 as 2 tens 12 ones.

$$\begin{array}{r} \overset{2\,12}{\not{3}\not{2}} \\ -18 \\ \hline \end{array}$$

STEP 2

Subtract the ones.
12 − 8 = 4 ones.

$$\begin{array}{r} \overset{2\,12}{\not{3}\not{2}} \\ -18 \\ \hline 4 \end{array}$$

STEP 3

Subtract the tens.
2 − 1 = 1 ten

$$\begin{array}{r} \overset{2\,12}{\not{3}\not{2}} \\ -18 \\ \hline 14 \end{array}$$

So, Emma caught 14 more fireflies than Colin.

Since addition and subtraction are opposite or inverse operations, you can use addition to check subtraction.

Example 1

$$\begin{array}{r} 32 \\ -18 \\ \hline 14 \end{array} \qquad \begin{array}{r} 14 \\ +18 \\ \hline 32 \end{array}$$

Example 2

$$\begin{array}{r} 65 \\ -29 \\ \hline 36 \end{array} \qquad \begin{array}{r} 36 \\ +29 \\ \hline 65 \end{array}$$

Check

1. **Explain** how you can use an inverse operation to check 62 − 37 = 25.

2. $\begin{array}{r} 67 \\ -\ 3 \\ \hline \end{array}$ 3. $\begin{array}{r} 82 \\ -40 \\ \hline \end{array}$ 4. $\begin{array}{r} 91 \\ -23 \\ \hline \end{array}$ 5. $\begin{array}{r} 74 \\ -\ 8 \\ \hline \end{array}$ 6. $\begin{array}{r} 50 \\ -37 \\ \hline \end{array}$

Practice and Problem Solving

Extra Practice, page 14, Set E

Find the difference. Use addition to check.

7. $77 - 4$
8. $96 - 51$
9. $50 - 20$
10. $48 - 16$
11. $52 - 9$
12. $23 - 14$
13. $44 - 25$
14. $71 - 38$
15. $66 - 7$
16. $80 - 53$
17. $56 - 29$
18. $60 - 8$
19. $83 - 67$
20. $95 - 78$
21. $55 - 27$

Copy and complete each table.

	Subtract 20.	
22.	54	
23.	70	
24.	35	

	Subtract 35.	
25.	64	
26.	72	
27.	86	

	Subtract 47.	
28.	71	
29.	69	
30.	94	

USE DATA For 31–32, use the table.

31. The greater the number of miles per hour, the faster the insects fly. The West Indian butterfly flies how many miles per hour faster than the honeybee?

32. The difference between the speed of the dragonfly and the honeybee is the same speed as which other insect?

FASTEST INSECT FLYERS	
Insect	**Miles per Hour**
Dragonfly	18
Bumblebee	11
West Indian butterfly	30
Hornet	13
Honeybee	7

Mixed Review and Test Prep

Find the sum. (p. 8)

33. $52 + 27$
34. $30 + 58$
35. $43 + 9$
36. $71 + 19$

37. TEST PREP Eric's puppy gained 4 pounds the first month, 2 pounds the second month, and 6 pounds the third month. How many pounds did it gain in all? (p. 6)

A 8 B 10 C 12 D 14

LESSON 6

Problem Solving Skill
Choose the Operation

UNDERSTAND › PLAN › SOLVE › CHECK

Quick Review

1. 15 + 4 = ■
2. 24 − 3 = ■
3. 18 + 2 = ■
4. 36 − 6 = ■
5. 47 − 5 = ■

THE 19TH STATE The state flag of Indiana has 19 gold stars and a flaming torch. There are 13 stars in an outer circle representing the 13 original states. How many stars are in the inner circle?

Before you solve a problem, you need to decide what the problem asks you to find.

Use addition to find how many in all, or the total.	Use subtraction to find how many are left, to compare, or to find a missing part.

Since you need to find the part that is missing, you subtract.

19	−	13	=	6
↑		↑		↑
total number of stars		number of stars in outer circle		number of stars in inner circle

So, there are 6 stars in the inner circle.

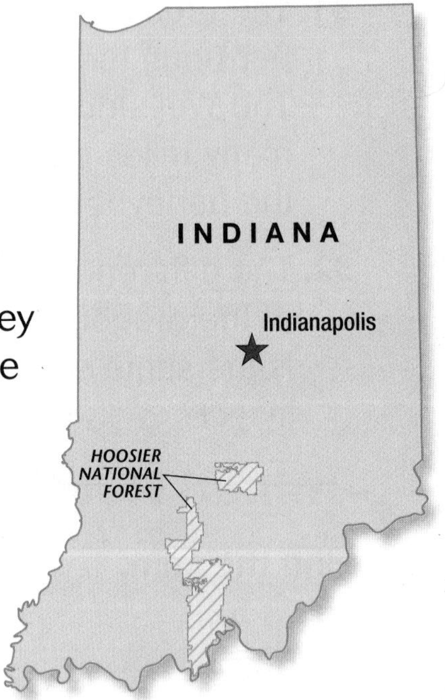

Andrew's family camped in the Hoosier National Forest. They hiked the 15-mile Two Lakes Loop and the 12-mile Birdseye trail. How many miles did they hike?

Since you need to find how many in all, you add.

$$15 + 12 = 27$$

So, they hiked 27 miles in all.

Talk About It

- Write a number sentence that shows the total number of stars on the Indiana state flag.
- Give an example of a problem in which you would subtract to compare.

Problem Solving Practice

Choose the operation. Write a number sentence. Then solve.

1. There were 48 children on the playground. Then 34 children went inside. How many children were left on the playground?
2. Cardinals' eggs hatch in about 13 days. Baby cardinals fly about 12 days after they hatch. About how many days after the female lays her eggs do baby cardinals fly?

▲ Indiana's state bird is the cardinal.

From Indianapolis, Indiana, Emily's family drove 65 miles on Saturday to visit friends in Richmond. On Sunday they drove 91 miles to Fort Wayne. How many more miles did they drive on Sunday than on Saturday?

3. Which number sentence can you use to solve the problem?

   A $65 + 91 = 156$
   B $91 - 65 = 26$
   C $65 - 65 = 0$
   D $91 + 91 = 182$

4. How many miles did Emily's family drive in the two days?

   F 126
   G 151
   H 156
   J 165

Mixed Applications

For 5–7, use the pictograph.

5. How many more third-grade students at Joel's school like soccer than basketball?
6. How many fewer students like football than soccer?
7. **What's the Question?** The answer is 6 students.

THIRD-GRADE FAVORITE SPORTS

Basketball	⚽ ⚽ ⚽ ⚽
Soccer	⚽ ⚽ ⚽ ⚽ ⚽ ⚽
Football	⚽ ⚽
Baseball	⚽ ⚽ ⚽

Key: Each ⚽ = 2 students.

Extra Practice

Set A (pp. 2–3)

Complete.

1. $14 - 5 = 9$, so $9 + \blacksquare = 14$.
2. $9 + 7 = 16$, so $16 - \blacksquare = 7$.

Write the fact family for each set of numbers.

3. 5, 8, 13
4. 6, 8, 14
5. 7, 8, 15
6. 7, 7, 14

Set B (pp. 4–5)

Find the missing addend.

1. $5 + \blacksquare = 13$
2. $\blacksquare + 6 = 15$
3. $6 + \blacksquare = 14$
4. $\blacksquare + 5 = 14$
5. $\blacksquare + 8 = 17$
6. $8 + \blacksquare = 15$
7. $7 + \blacksquare = 13$
8. $7 + \blacksquare = 16$

Set C (pp. 6–7)

Find each sum.

1. $8 + 9 = \blacksquare$
   $9 + 8 = \blacksquare$
2. $9 + 5 = \blacksquare$
   $5 + 9 = \blacksquare$
3. $8 + (3 + 7) = \blacksquare$
   $(8 + 3) + 7 = \blacksquare$
4. $7 + 8 = \blacksquare$
   $8 + 7 = \blacksquare$
5. The pet store sold 8 hamsters, 2 guinea pigs, and 5 ferrets. How many animals did it sell in all?
6. Liz planted 7 daisies and 4 roses. Audrey planted 4 pansies and 7 tulips. How many flowers did each girl plant in all?

Set D (pp. 8–9)

Find the sum.

1. $\begin{array}{r} 53 \\ +21 \\ \hline \end{array}$
2. $\begin{array}{r} 72 \\ +\ 8 \\ \hline \end{array}$
3. $\begin{array}{r} 28 \\ +64 \\ \hline \end{array}$
4. $\begin{array}{r} 56 \\ +19 \\ \hline \end{array}$
5. $\begin{array}{r} 67 \\ +25 \\ \hline \end{array}$

Set E (pp. 10–11)

Find the difference. Use addition to check.

1. $\begin{array}{r} 48 \\ -\ 6 \\ \hline \end{array}$
2. $\begin{array}{r} 86 \\ -50 \\ \hline \end{array}$
3. $\begin{array}{r} 75 \\ -38 \\ \hline \end{array}$
4. $\begin{array}{r} 92 \\ -66 \\ \hline \end{array}$
5. $\begin{array}{r} 62 \\ -27 \\ \hline \end{array}$

Review/Test

✓ CHECK VOCABULARY

Choose the best term from the box.

Order Property of Addition
Identity Property of Addition
Grouping Property of Addition
fact family
inverse operations
addend

1. $(6 + 4) + 7 = 6 + (4 + 7)$ is an example of the __?__. (p. 6)
2. A set of related addition and subtraction number sentences that use the same numbers is called a __?__. (p. 2)
3. $7 + 8 = 8 + 7$ is an example of the __?__. (p. 6)
4. Addition and subtraction are __?__. (p. 2)
5. $12 + 0 = 12$ is an example of the __?__. (p. 6)

✓ CHECK SKILLS

Write the fact family for each set of numbers. (pp. 2–3)

6. 6, 9, 15
7. 8, 8, 16
8. 5, 7, 12
9. 8, 9, 17

Find the missing addend. (pp. 4–5)

10. $6 + \blacksquare = 13$
11. $\blacksquare + 9 = 16$
12. $7 + \blacksquare = 15$
13. $9 + \blacksquare = 14$

Find the sum or difference. (pp. 8–9, 10–11)

14. $35 + 24$
15. $77 - 43$
16. $63 + 8$
17. $71 - 44$
18. $59 + 47$

✓ CHECK PROBLEM SOLVING

Solve. (pp. 12–13)

19. Jonathan read 36 library books during the school year. His sister Kara read 48 books. How many books did the children read in all?

20. Abby and Jack collected 72 shells in all while on vacation at the seashore. Abby collected 37 shells. How many shells did Jack collect?

CHAPTER 1

Standardized Test Prep

NUMBER SENSE, CONCEPTS, AND OPERATIONS

1. Luke wrote these addition sentences.

$8 + 9 = 17 \quad 9 + 8 = 17$

Which subtraction sentence belongs to the same fact family?

A $9 - 8 = 1$
B $17 - 9 = 8$
C $17 - 7 = 10$
D $9 - 1 = 8$

2. What is the value of the digit 5 in 547?

F 5
G 50
H 500
J 5,000

3. Tobey found the sum of two addends. Neither addend is zero. What is true about this sum?

A It is less than either addend.
B It is less than one addend but greater than the other addend.
C It is greater than either addend.
D It is equal to one of the addends.

4. Explain It Liz has 23 stickers. Mary has 42 more stickers than Liz. Tell how to use estimation to find about how many stickers Mary has.

MEASUREMENT

5. Carly wants to measure the length of her baby gerbil. What units of measure would be the most appropriate for her to use?

F yards
G feet
H inches
J miles

6. Which temperature does the thermometer show?

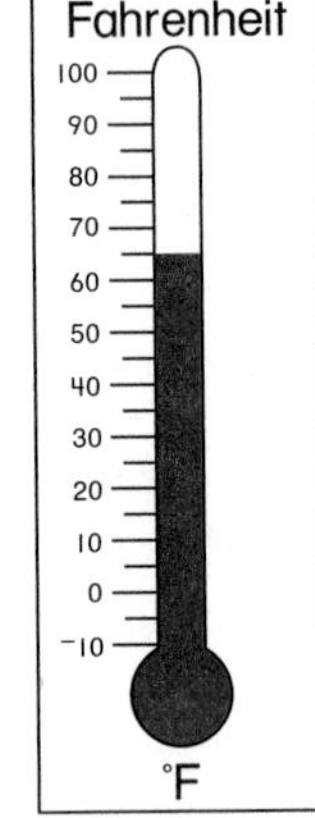

A 55°F
B 60°F
C 65°F
D 70°F

TIP **Eliminate choices.** See item 7. Find the answer choices that weigh **more or less** than 1 pound.

7. Kara names an item that weighs about 1 pound. Which item does she name?

F a chair
G a soccer ball
H a pencil
J a bicycle

8. Explain It Dee made a sketch of her square yard. She wants to put a fence around it. How can Dee decide about how much fencing she should buy?

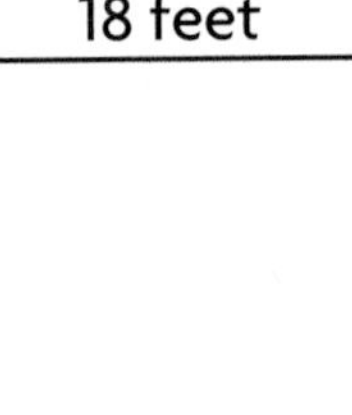

GEOMETRY AND SPATIAL SENSE

9. Akira flipped this arrow over the line. Which figure did he form?

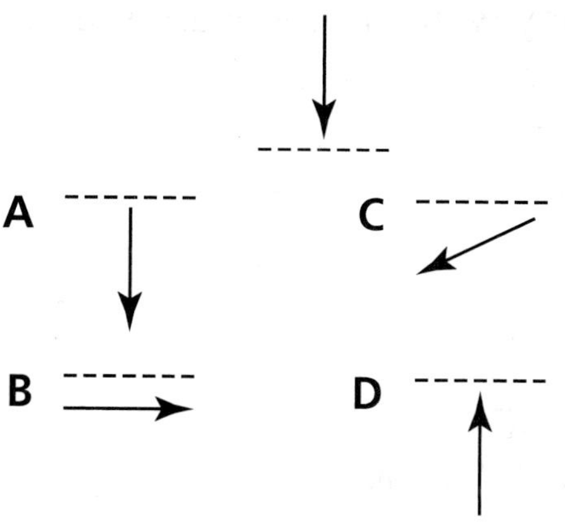

10. Which of these figures is NOT a triangle?

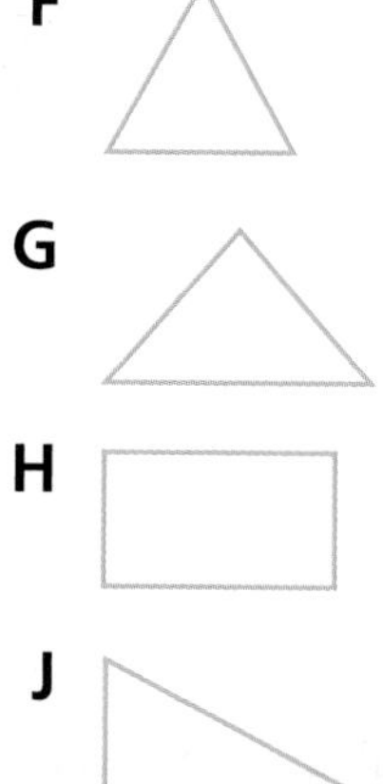

11. Explain It Tell how the two shapes are alike and how they are different.

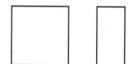

DATA ANALYSIS AND PROBABILITY

12. Jason and Amy are using this spinner to play a game. What color is Amy most likely to spin?

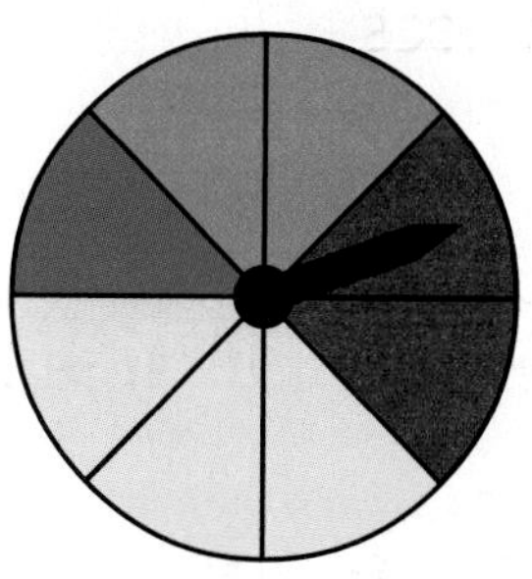

A green
B blue
C yellow
D red

13. The graph shows the number of animals at Frank's farm. How many cows are at Frank's farm?

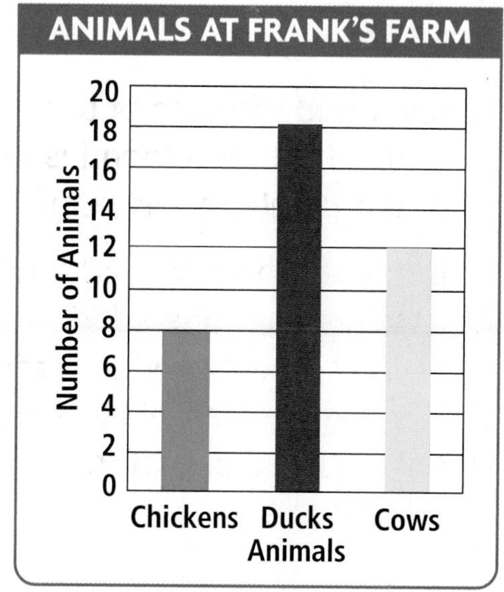

F 8
G 12
H 16
J 18

14. Explain It Look at the bar graph above. Tell how to find the range.

CHAPTER 2

Place Value and Number Sense

FAST FACT • SCIENCE Horses have the largest eyes of any land mammal. Their large eyes help horses see almost directly behind themselves while facing forward. Horses need hay, oats, and fresh water to stay healthy.

PROBLEM SOLVING Use the pictograph. Skip-count to find how much water a horse needs each week and each month.

HOW MUCH WATER A HORSE NEEDS

Time	Water
1 day	🪣
1 week	🪣🪣🪣🪣🪣🪣🪣
1 month	🪣🪣🪣🪣🪣🪣🪣🪣🪣🪣🪣🪣🪣🪣🪣 🪣🪣🪣🪣🪣🪣🪣🪣🪣🪣🪣🪣🪣🪣🪣

Key: Each 🪣 = 10 gallons.

Check What You Know

Use this page to help you review and remember important skills needed for Chapter 2.

Place Value: 2-Digit Numbers

Write the value of the blue digit.

1. 40
2. 73
3. 65
4. 39
5. 28
6. 19
7. 32
8. 76
9. 27
10. 84

Model 3-Digit Numbers

Write the number that matches the model.

11. 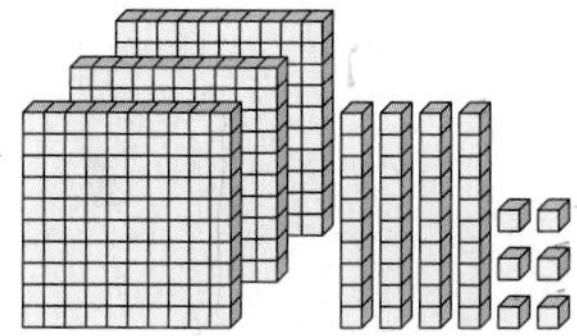

12. 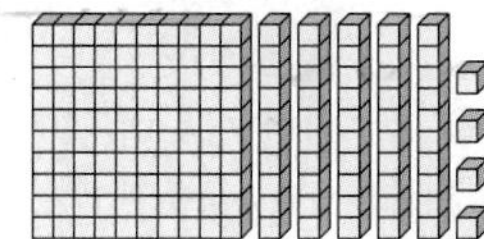

13. 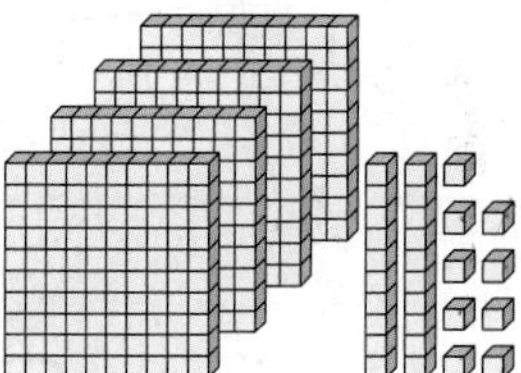

14. 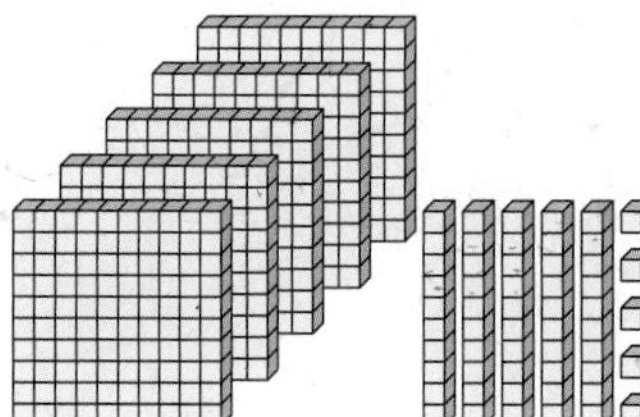

15. 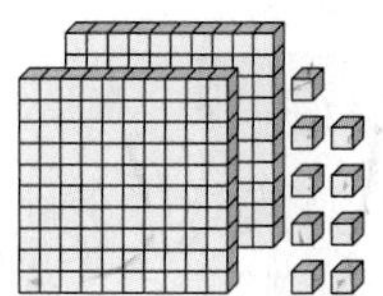

16. 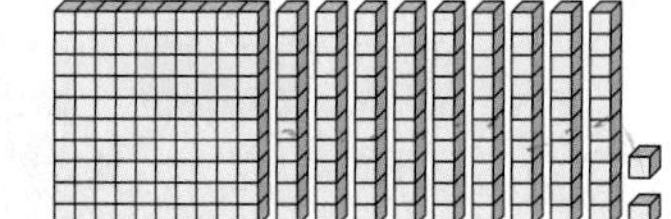

Vocabulary Power

REVIEW

number [num′bər] *noun*

A number tells you how many or how much. A number can be shown with words or symbols. Fifteen and 15 show the same number. Choose a number and write a word and a symbol to show it.

PREVIEW

even
odd
digits
standard form
expanded form
word form
pattern

www.harcourtschool.com/mathglossary

LESSON 1

Even and Odd

Quick Review

1. 8 + 2
2. 6 + 3
3. 9 + 3
4. 10 + 5
5. 25 + 5

VOCABULARY

even odd

MATERIALS

connecting cubes, hundred chart, crayons

Explore

You can use cubes to find odd and even numbers.

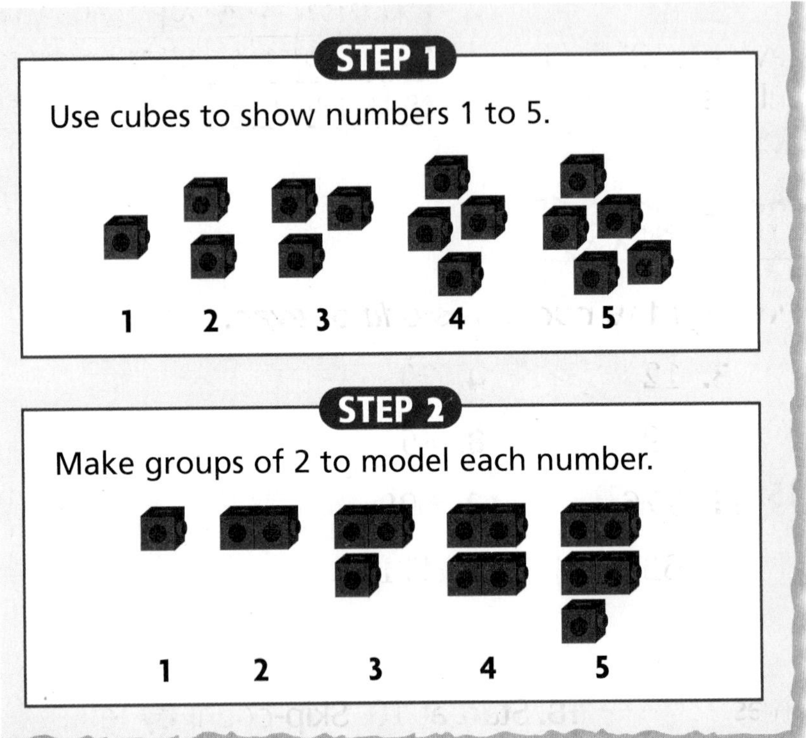

STEP 1
Use cubes to show numbers 1 to 5.
1
2
3
4
5
STEP 2
Make groups of 2 to model each number.
1
2
3
4
5

Even numbers show pairs of cubes with no cubes left over.

Odd numbers show pairs of cubes with one cube left over.

- How do you know which numbers are even?
- Is 3 an even or odd number? Explain.
- What pattern do you see?

Try It

a. Make models of the numbers 6 to 20. How are the models of even and odd numbers different?

b. Choose five other numbers to model. Are they even or odd? How do you know?

REASONING The numbers 6 and 16 are even. Are 26, 36, 46, 56, and 66 even or odd? Explain.

Connect

You can use a hundred chart to find odd and even numbers.

- Start at 2. Shade that box.
- Skip-count by twos and shade each box you land on.
- Look at your shaded chart. What pattern do you see?

1	2	3	4	5	6	7	8	9	10
11	12	13	14	15	16	17	18	19	20
21	22	23	24	25	26	27	28	29	30
31	32	33	34	35	36	37	38	39	40
41	42	43	44	45	46	47	48	49	50
51	52	53	54	55	56	57	58	59	60
61	62	63	64	65	66	67	68	69	70
71	72	73	74	75	76	77	78	79	80
81	82	83	84	85	86	87	88	89	90
91	92	93	94	95	96	97	98	99	100

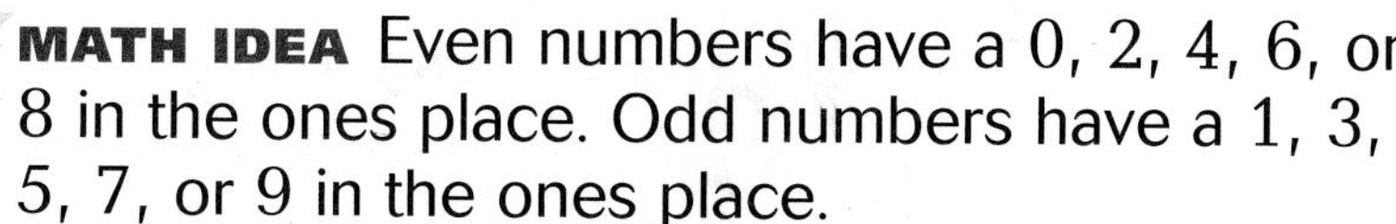

MATH IDEA Even numbers have a 0, 2, 4, 6, or 8 in the ones place. Odd numbers have a 1, 3, 5, 7, or 9 in the ones place.

Practice and Problem Solving

Look at each number. Tell whether the number is *odd* or *even*.

1. 3 **2.** 6 **3.** 12 **4.** 30

5. 27 **6.** 98 **7.** 19 **8.** 45

9. 344 **10.** 281 **11.** 776 **12.** 998

13. 173 **14.** 832 **15.** 620 **16.** 411

Use the hundred chart.

17. Start at 5. Skip-count by fives. Move 4 skips. What number do you land on? Is it odd or even?

18. Start at 10. Skip-count by tens. Move 6 skips. What number do you land on? Is it odd or even?

19. The first five houses on Quinn's street are numbered 4, 8, 12, 16, and 20. What are the next three house numbers? Explain.

20. **REASONING** Marcos skip-counted. He started at 2. He landed on 15. Could he be skip-counting by twos? Why or why not?

Mixed Review and Test Prep

21. $\begin{array}{r} 64 \\ +21 \\ \hline \end{array}$ (p. 8)

22. $\begin{array}{r} 78 \\ -54 \\ \hline \end{array}$ (p. 10)

23. 25 + 11 = ■ (p. 8)

24. 37 − 10 = ■ (p. 10)

25. **TEST PREP** Jon had 12 red marbles and 17 blue marbles. How many marbles did he have in all? (p. 8)

A 30 **B** 29 **C** 19 **D** 5

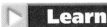

LESSON 2

Place Value: 3-Digit Numbers

FARM FACTS The symbols 0, 1, 2, 3, 4, 5, 6, 7, 8, and 9 are **digits**. Numbers are made up of digits.

On Mr. Sam's farm there are 248 chickens. What does the number 248 mean?

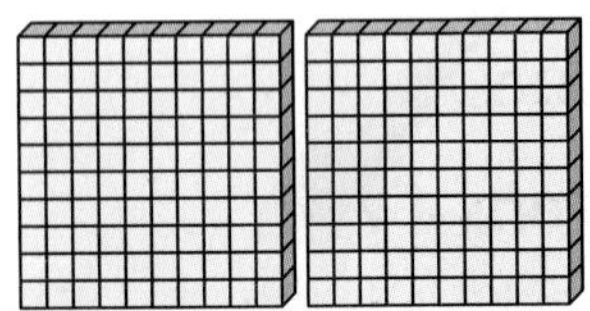

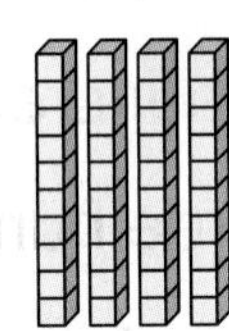

HUNDREDS	TENS	ONES
2	4	8

So, 248 means 2 hundreds + 4 tens + 8 ones or 200 + 40 + 8.

MATH IDEA You can write a number in different ways: standard form, expanded form, and word form.

Standard form: 248

Expanded form: 200 + 40 + 8

Word form: two hundred forty-eight

- In the number 408, what is the meaning of the zero in the tens place?

Quick Review

Write the number.

1. 5 tens 1 one
2. 4 tens 3 ones
3. 7 tens 0 ones
4. 1 ten 9 ones
5. 2 hundreds 6 tens 8 ones

VOCABULARY

digits
standard form
expanded form
word form

Extra Practice:
Harcourt Mega Math Country Countdown, *Block Busters*, Level S

Check

USE DATA For 1–2, use the table.

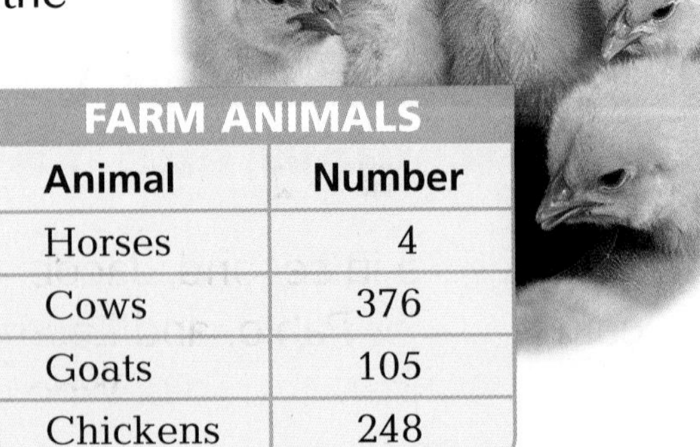

FARM ANIMALS	
Animal	**Number**
Horses	4
Cows	376
Goats	105
Chickens	248

1. **Explain** why the value of the digit 3 is 300 in the number of cows on the farm.
2. Write the expanded form for the number of goats on the farm.

Write each number in standard form.

3. 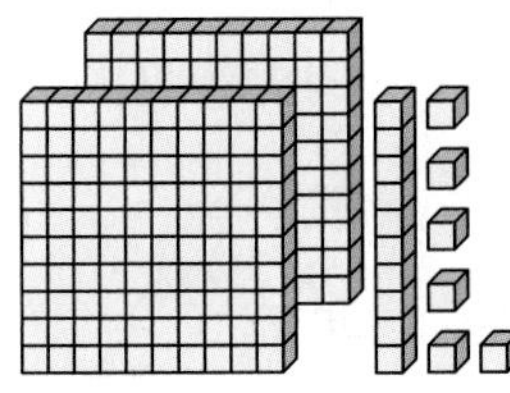

4. 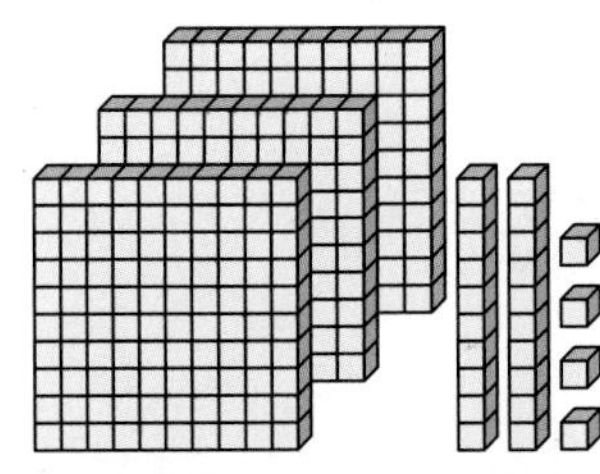

5. 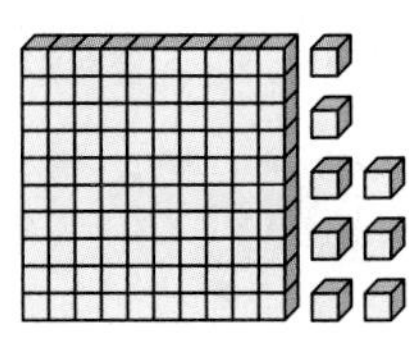

Practice and Problem Solving

Extra Practice, page 34, Set A

Write each number in standard form.

6. 100 + 50 + 3
7. 400 + 70 + 6
8. 600 + 30 + 9
9. 900 + 2
10. 4 hundreds 2 tens 1 one
11. 6 hundreds 8 tens 3 ones
12. 7 hundreds 2 tens 3 ones
13. 4 hundreds 5 ones
14. one hundred three
15. three hundred forty-five
16. six hundred eleven
17. nine hundred seventy-one

Write the value of the blue digit.

18. 846
19. 267
20. 493
21. 923

22. Mr. Sam put 297 bales of hay in one barn. There are still 86 bales of hay in the field. How many more bales of hay are in the barn than in the field?

23. **FAST FACT** • SCIENCE There are about 210 kinds of horses in the world. What is the value of the digit 2 in the number 210?

24. **Vocabulary Power** *Value* means "what something is worth." Use this meaning to describe the digit 5 in 527.

25. **REASONING** I am a digit in each of the numbers 312, 213, and 132. My value is different in all three numbers. What digit am I? What is my value in each number?

Mixed Review and Test Prep

26. 24 + 35 = ■ (p. 8)

27. 48 − 17 = ■ (p. 10)

28. Pablo came in second, Jacob came in after Pablo, and Lauren came in ahead of Pablo. Who won the race?

29. What number continues the pattern? (p. 20)

3, 5, 7, 9, 11, ■

30. **TEST PREP** Which number is greater than 54?

A 37 B 45 C 53 D 55

LESSON 3

Place Value: 4-Digit Numbers

Quick Review

Write the value of the blue digit.

1. 246 **2.** 394

3. 714 **4.** 502

5. 802

Learn

HORSE SENSE The largest horse on record is a Belgian that stood 18 hands—or 6 feet—tall and weighed 3,174 pounds. You can use base-ten blocks to show the number of pounds.

HANDS ON

Activity

Materials: base-ten blocks

Make a model to show 3,174.

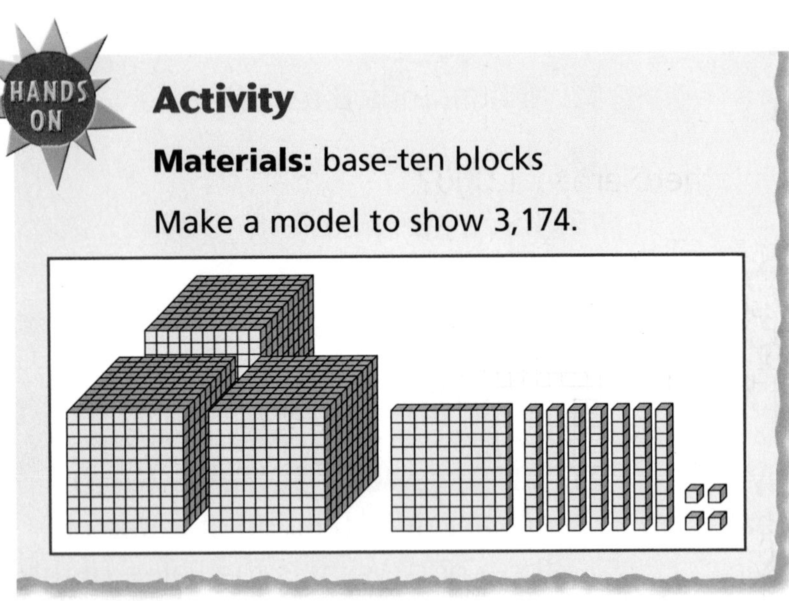

A place-value chart can help you understand the value of each digit in a number.

THOUSANDS	HUNDREDS	TENS	ONES
3,	1	7	4
↑ Value is 3,000.	↑ Value is 100.	↑ Value is 70.	↑ Value is 4.

Standard form: 3,174

↑ A comma is used to separate the thousands and hundreds.

Expanded form: 3,000 + 100 + 70 + 4

Word form: three thousand, one hundred seventy-four

- What is the value of the digit 4 in 4,618?

Understanding Thousands

You can use place-value blocks to help you understand thousands.

There are 10 ones in 10.

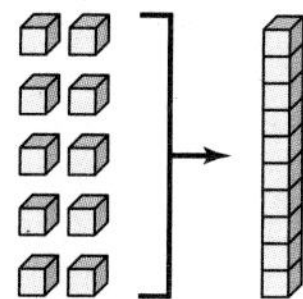

There are 10 tens in 100.

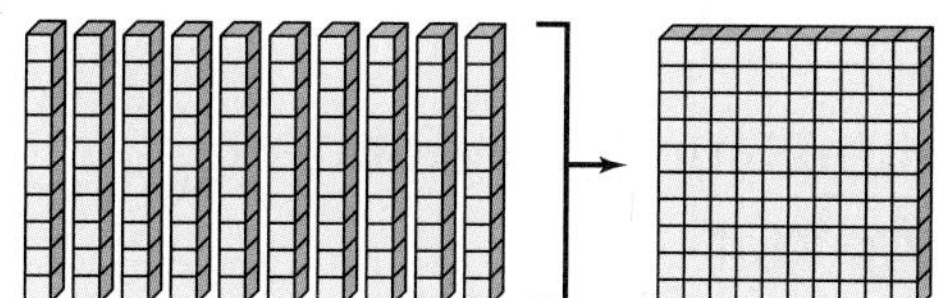

How many hundreds do you think there are in 1,000?

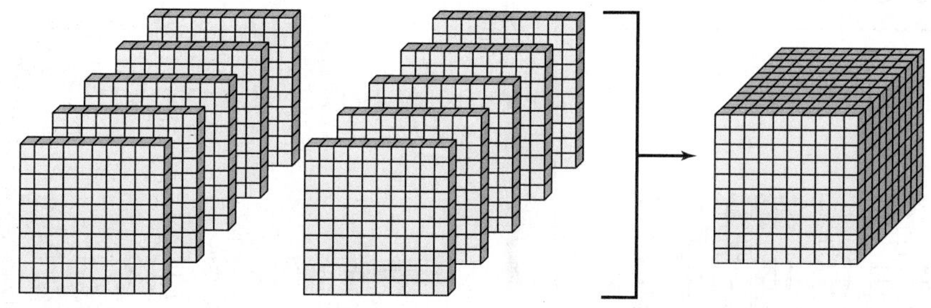

There are 10 hundreds in 1,000.

- How many hundreds do you think there are in 2,000?

Check

1. **Explain** the value of each digit in 5,403.

Write in standard form.

2. 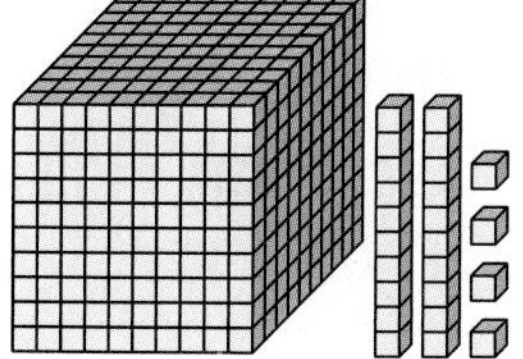

3. 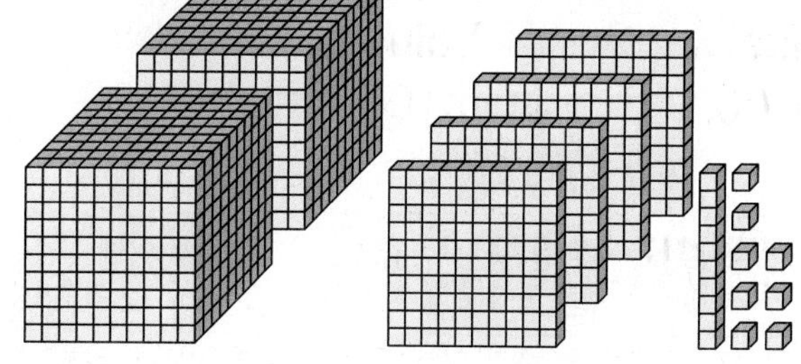

Write in expanded form.

4. 5,632 5. 7,401 6. 8,011 7. 3,462

8. How many tens are in 100? How many tens are in 200?

LESSON CONTINUES

Practice and Problem Solving

Extra Practice, page 34, Set B

Write in standard form.

9.

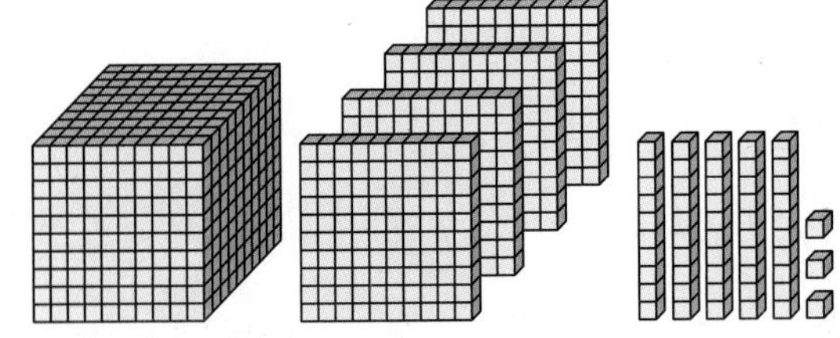

10.

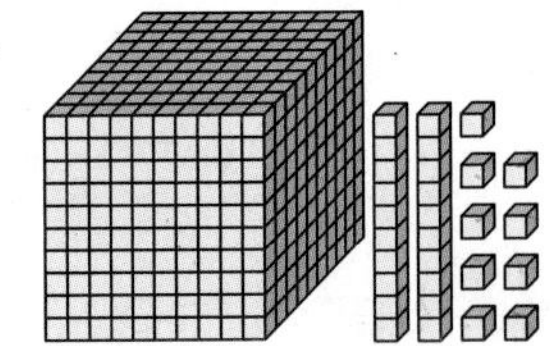

11. 5,000 + 400 + 50

12. 4,000 + 300 + 90 + 7

13. 9,000 + 700 + 20 + 3

14. 1,000 + 10 + 8

15. two thousand, four hundred eighty-three

16. six thousand, one hundred ninety-four

For 17–20, write in expanded form.

17. 1,234

18. 4,321

19. 3,016

20. 8,367

21. How many tens are in 400?

22. How many hundreds are in 3,000?

Complete.

23. 1,000 + 500 + ■ + 8 = 1,548

24. 3,000 + ■ + 90 + 7 = 3,897

25. USE DATA The pictograph shows what Molly saw at the farm. How many animals did Molly see in all?

FARM ANIMALS

Horses	
Chickens	
Cows	

Key: Each = 10 animals.

26. REASONING I am a 4-digit number. My thousands digit is 4 less than my tens digit. My hundreds digit equals the sum of my tens digit and my ones digit. My tens digit is 4 more than my ones digit. My ones digit is 1. What number am I?

27. What is the least possible number you can write with the digits 2, 9, 4, and 7? Use each digit only once.

28. Write About It Why do you have to use a zero when you write one thousand, six hundred four in standard form?

29. The number 124 is an even number. Write 5 more even numbers including one with 4 digits.

30. Show that each of the even numbers 6, 8, 10, and 12 can be written as the sum of a group of twos.

Mixed Review and Test Prep

Tell whether the number is *even* or *odd*. (p. 20)

31. 61 **32.** 18 **33.** 58

34. 97 **35.** 102 **36.** 183

Find the sum.

37. 6 + 3 **38.** 4 + 7 **39.** 12 + 4

40. 9 + 8 **41.** 10 + 5 **42.** 11 + 10

Find the difference.

43. 14 − 5 **44.** 16 − 8 **45.** 13 − 7

46. 17 − 7 **47.** 18 − 6 **48.** 11 − 6

Find the sum.

49. $\begin{array}{r} 6 \\ 5 \\ +3 \\ \hline \end{array}$ **50.** $\begin{array}{r} 9 \\ 7 \\ +1 \\ \hline \end{array}$ **51.** $\begin{array}{r} 8 \\ 3 \\ +7 \\ \hline \end{array}$

52. **TEST PREP** Which number is eight hundred four in standard form? (p. 22)

A 940 **C** 804
B 840 **D** 84

53. **TEST PREP** Which number is the expanded form for 432? (p. 22)

F 200 + 30 + 4 **H** 400 + 30
G 400 + 2 **J** 400 + 30 + 2

Problem Solving Thinker's Corner

NAMES FOR NUMBERS You can name any number in different ways. Here are different names for 78 and 152.

78	**152**
70 + 8	100 + 50 + 2
25 + 25 + 25 + 3	50 + 50 + 52
80 − 2	155 − 3
100 − 22	200 − 48

Write two other names for each number.

1. 45 **2.** 215 **3.** 698 **4.** 1,523

LESSON 4

Problem Solving Strategy
Use Logical Reasoning

Quick Review

1. 400 + ■ + 9 = 499
2. ■ + 700 + 5 = 8,705
3. ■ + 60 + 3 = 763
4. 900 + 30 + ■ = 936
5. ■ + 400 + 7 = 1,407

PROBLEM Todd used base-ten blocks to model 243. He used 2 hundreds, 4 tens, 3 ones. What is another way he can show 243 with base-ten blocks?

UNDERSTAND

- What are you asked to find?
- Is there information you will not use? If so, what?

PLAN

- What strategy can you use to solve the problem?

You can use *logical reasoning*.

SOLVE

- How can you use the strategy to solve the problem?

Begin with 2 hundreds, 4 tens, 3 ones.

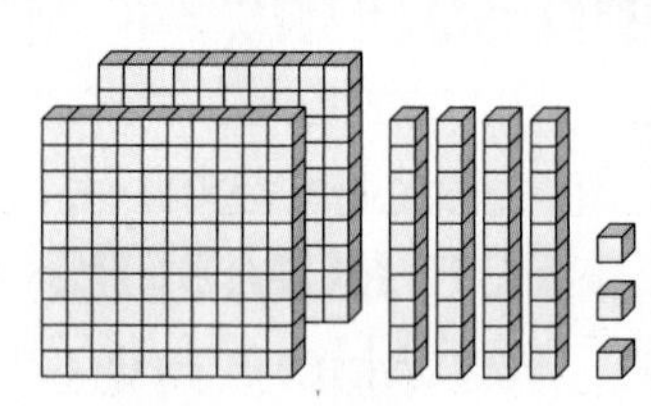

Trade one of the hundreds for 10 tens. Add the 10 tens and the 4 tens. You now have 1 hundred, 14 tens, 3 ones.

So, another way to show 243 is with 1 hundred, 14 tens, 3 ones.

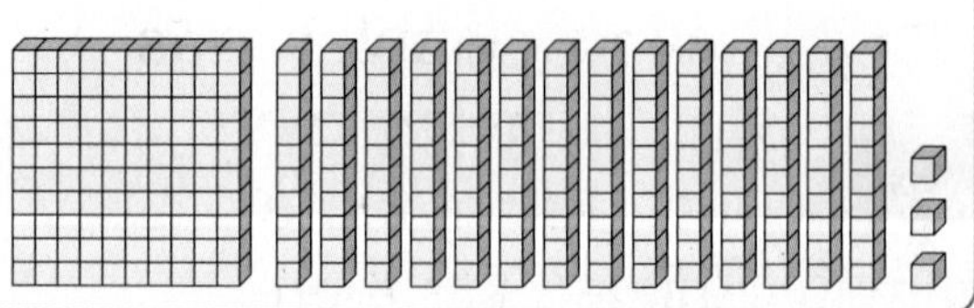

CHECK

- Look at the problem. Does your answer make sense? Explain.
- Explain how to model 243 with base-ten blocks a third way.

Problem Solving Practice

Use logical reasoning and solve.

1. **What if** Todd doesn't have any tens? How can he model 243 without using any tens?

2. Emily made a model for 156 using 1 hundred, 5 tens, 6 ones. What are two other ways she can show 156 using base-ten blocks?

3. Sage used 34 tens, 2 ones to model a number. What other way can she model the same number?

   A 3 hundreds, 4 tens
   B 3 tens, 2 ones
   C 3 hundreds, 2 ones
   D 3 hundreds, 4 tens, 2 ones

4. Louis used 1 thousand, 2 hundreds, 4 tens, 3 ones to model a number. What number did he model?

   F 143 **H** 1,423
   G 1,243 **J** 2,143

Strategies

- Draw a Diagram or Picture
- Make a Model or Act It Out
- Make an Organized List
- Find a Pattern
- Make a Table or Graph
- Predict and Test
- Work Backward
- Solve a Simpler Problem
- Write a Number Sentence
- **Use Logical Reasoning**

Problem Solving

Mixed Strategy Practice

5. Write the greatest possible 4-digit number using the digits 3, 4, 5, and 6. Write the least possible 4-digit number.

6. **Reasoning** A 3-digit number has the same number of ones, tens, and hundreds. If the sum of the digits is 9, what is the number?

7. **Use Data** The pictograph shows farm animals. How many more sheep than horses are there? How many animals are there in all?

8. **Write a problem** about 8 hundreds, 4 tens, 6 ones. Tell how to solve the problem.

FARM ANIMALS

Horses	∩∩
Cows	∩
Sheep	∩∩∩∩∩∩∩∩ ∩∩∩∩∩∩∩∩

Key: Each ∩ = 5 animals.

LESSON 5

Algebra: Number Patterns

Learn

WHAT'S NEXT? A **pattern** is an ordered set of numbers or objects. The order helps you predict what will come next.

Examples

Predict the next number in each pattern.

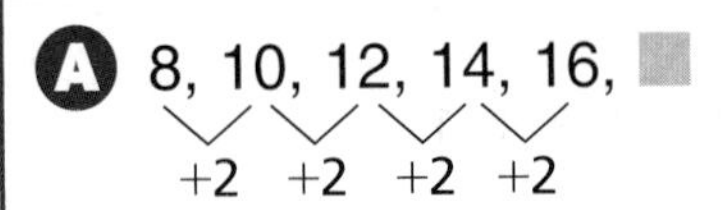

The next number will be 16 + 2, or 18.

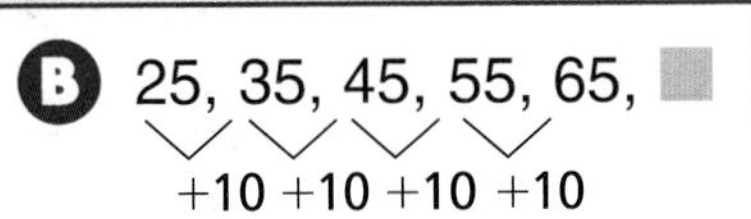

The next number will be 65 + 10, or 75.

C

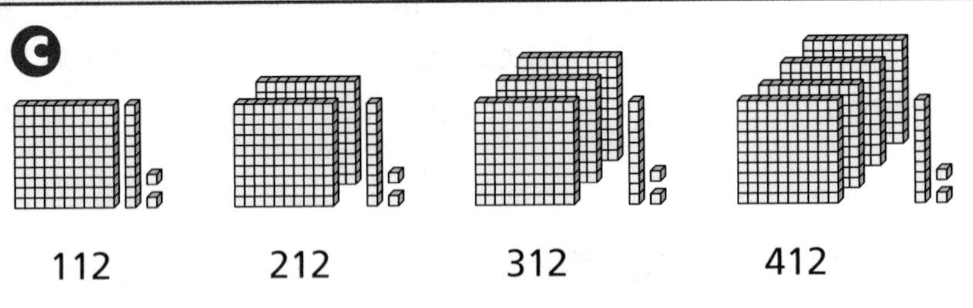

112 212 312 412

The numbers increase by 100, so the next number will be 412 + 100, or 512.

- **REASONING** What is the next number in the pattern 923, 823, 723, 623? Explain.

Quick Review

Find each missing number.

1. 17 + ■ = 21
2. 24 + ■ = 32
3. 55 + ■ = 65
4. 8 + ■ = 28
5. 393 – ■ = 293

VOCABULARY
pattern

Check

1. **Explain** what base-ten blocks are needed for the sixth number of the pattern in Example C.

Predict the next number in each pattern. Explain.

2.  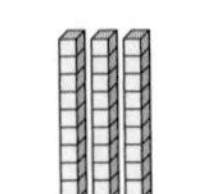 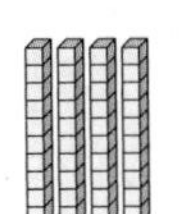 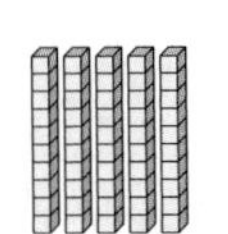

3. 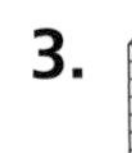 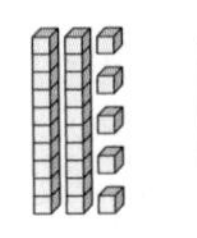 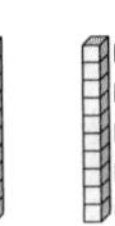

4. 30, 35, 40, 45, ■

5. 58, 68, 78, 88, ■

6. 13, 17, 21, 25, ■

Practice and Problem Solving

Extra Practice, page 34, Set C

Predict the next number in each pattern. Explain.

7\. 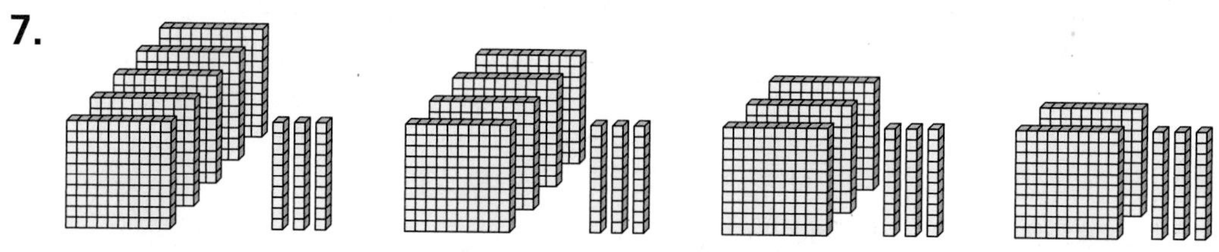

8\. 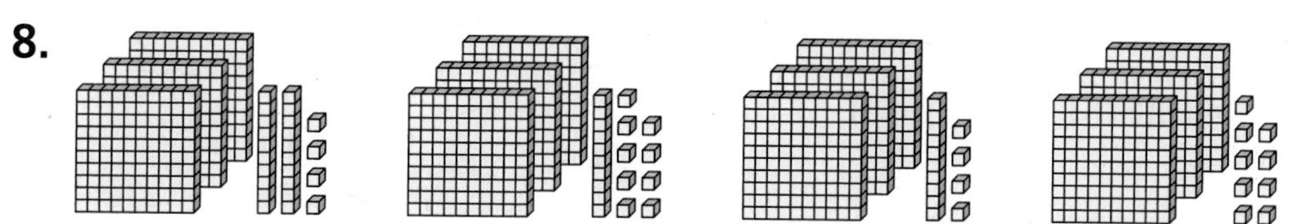

9\. 50, 70, 90, 110, ■

10\. 110, 105, 100, 95, ■

11\. 580, 590, 600, 610, ■

12\. 235, 335, 435, 535, ■

13\. 657, 667, 677, 687, ■

14\. 712, 715, 718, 721, ■

15\. Adam skip-counts by thousands to write a number pattern. The first number is 1,495. The second number is 2,495. What are the third and fourth numbers?

16\. Drew rented 4 movies and 5 video games. Phillip rented 5 movies and 3 video games. Who rented more items? Explain.

17\. **What's the Question?** Hans wrote the following number pattern.

432, 434, 436, 438

The answer is 446.

18\. **Write a problem** about a number pattern. Exchange problems with a classmate and solve.

Mixed Review and Test Prep

Find each sum. (p. 8)

19\.
```
  25
  18
+ 42
```

20\.
```
  34
   7
+ 56
```

21\.
```
  19
  60
+ 12
```

22\. 49 + 27 = ■ (p. 8)

23\. **TEST PREP** Nancy has a box of 52 crayons. She takes out 24 crayons to draw a picture. How many crayons are left in the box? (p. 10)

A 22
B 24
C 28
D 38

LESSON 6

Place Value: 5- and 6-Digit Numbers

Quick Review

Write in expanded form.

1. 384 **2.** 51

3. 677 **4.** 9,240

5. 3,818

Learn

THE SOONER STATE Oklahoma has an area of 69,903 square miles. You can use a place-value chart to help you understand each digit in the number.

TEN THOUSANDS	THOUSANDS	HUNDREDS	TENS	ONES
6	9,	9	0	3

Remember

Put a comma between the thousands place and the hundreds place.

69,903
↑
comma

You can write this number in three ways:

Standard form: 69,903

Expanded form: 60,000 + 9,000 + 900 + 3

Word form: sixty-nine thousand, nine hundred three

- How many ten thousands are in 69,903?

In 2000, there were 506,132 residents in Oklahoma City, the state capital. Look at this number in the place-value chart.

HUNDRED THOUSANDS	TEN THOUSANDS	THOUSANDS	HUNDREDS	TENS	ONES
5	0	6,	1	3	2

You can write this number in three ways:

Standard form: 506,132

Expanded form: 500,000 + 6,000 + 100 + 30 + 2

Word form: five hundred six thousand, one hundred thirty-two

- What is the value of the digit 5 in 506,132?

OKLAHOMA

Oklahoma City

Check

1. Explain the value of each digit in 21,694.

Write in standard form.

2. 500,000 + 20,000 + 6,000 + 700 + 30 + 4
3. thirty-five thousand, nine hundred forty-seven

Write in expanded form.

4. 16,723
5. 52,019
6. 238,605

Practice and Problem Solving

Extra Practice, page 34, Set D

Write in standard form.

7. 20,000 + 6,000 + 700 + 30 + 4
8. 400,000 + 10,000 + 400 + 8
9. forty-two thousand, three hundred fifteen
10. six hundred eighteen thousand, nine hundred

Write in expanded form.

11. 316,723
12. 55,119
13. 11,012
14. 749,207

Write the value of the blue digit.

15. 81,465
16. 262,817
17. 843,912
18. 19,273

Complete.

19. 100,000 + ■ + 2,000 + 600 + 50 + 1 = 112,651
20. 60,000 + ■ + 300 + 10 + 9 = 62,319

21. **REASONING** I am an even number between 51,680 and 51,700. The sum of my digits is 23. What number am I?

22. **What's the Error?** Karla wrote eleven thousand, forty-five as 1,145. Explain her error. Write the number correctly in standard form.

Mixed Review and Test Prep

23. 98 − 52 (p. 10)

24. 72 + 19 (p. 8)

25. 25 + ■ = 29 (p. 4)

26. 43 + ■ = 49 (p. 4)

27. **TEST PREP** What is the value of the blue digit in 5,789? (p. 24)

A 7
B 70
C 700
D 7,000

Extra Practice

Set A (pp. 22–23)

Write each number in standard form.

1. 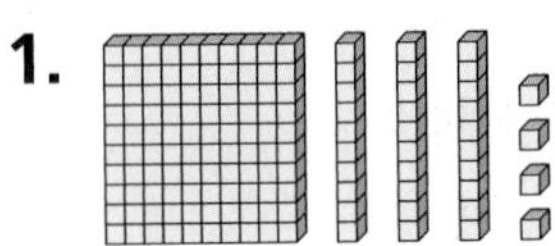
2. 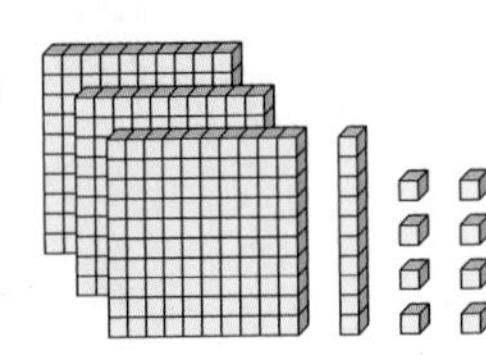
3. 500 + 60 + 6
4. 700 + 4
5. four hundred seventy-six
6. nine hundred ninety-one

Write the value of the blue digit.

7. 346
8. 872
9. 13
10. 554

Set B (pp. 24–27)

Write in standard form.

1. 1,000 + 900 + 40 + 2
2. 5,000 + 700 + 80 + 3
3. two thousand, four hundred sixty-seven
4. eight thousand, eighteen

Write in expanded form.

5. 5,487
6. 6,055
7. 6,170
8. 7,796

Set C (pp. 30–31)

Predict the next number in each pattern. Explain.

1. 310, 410, 510, 610, ■
2. 75, 70, 65, 60, ■
3. 503, 506, 509, 512, ■
4. 8,324, 7,324, 6,324, 5,324, ■

Set D (pp. 32–33)

Write in standard form.

1. 10,000 + 6,000 + 900 + 60 + 5
2. 600,000 + 50,000 + 3,000 + 6
3. fifty-one thousand, four hundred
4. twenty-two thousand, eighteen

Write in expanded form.

5. 65,487
6. 376,055
7. 536,173
8. 47,796

Review/Test

✓ CHECK VOCABULARY

Choose the best term from the box.

odd
even
digits
expanded form

1. A number with a 0, 2, 4, 6, or 8 in the ones place is an ? number. (p. 20)
2. The symbols 0, 1, 2, 3, 4, 5, 6, 7, 8, and 9 are called ? . (p. 22)

✓ CHECK SKILLS

Write whether the number is *odd* or *even*. (pp. 20–21)

3. 31
4. 74
5. 348
6. 929

Write in standard form. (pp. 22–27, 32–33)

7. 800 + 60 + 9
8. 3,000 + 700 + 10 + 1
9. 8,000 + 500 + 20 + 2
10. 30,000 + 4,000 + 700 + 5
11. 200,000 + 90,000 + 4,000 + 600 + 50 + 5
12. fifty-three thousand, eight hundred nineteen

Predict the next number in each pattern. (pp. 30–31)

13. 135, 235, 335, 435, ■
14. 250, 230, 210, 190, ■

Write the value of the blue digit. (pp. 22–27, 32–33)

15. 863
16. 9,845
17. 12,053
18. 372,859

✓ CHECK PROBLEM SOLVING

Solve. (pp. 28–29)

19. Katie made a model using base-ten blocks. She used 3 hundreds, 12 tens, 8 ones. What number did she model?
20. Randy modeled 257 with base-ten blocks. He used 2 hundreds, 4 tens. How many ones did he use?

Standardized Test Prep

NUMBER SENSE, CONCEPTS, AND OPERATIONS

1. Sara rolled a number cube 3 times. She rolled these numbers. What is the **least** number Sara can write?

A 245 C 425
B 254 D 542

2. Which number makes the number sentence true?

7,000 + 300 + ■ + 6 = 7,396

F 9 H 900
G 90 J 9,000

3. You are playing a game with numbered tiles. In order to play, you draw four tiles from the pile.

8 6 3 9

The winner is the player who makes the greatest 4-digit number from the tiles. What is the **greatest** number that can be made from these four tiles?

A 9,863 C 8,639
B 9,368 D 3,689

4. **Explain It** Eric had 37 marbles. Kevin gave him some more. Now Eric has 62 marbles. How can you use estimation to find about how many marbles Kevin gave Eric?

MEASUREMENT

5. Juan has been reading for 1 hour. This clock shows the time it is now. At what time did Juan start reading?

F 3:15 H 4:00
G 3:45 J 5:45

6. Don stayed at his grandmother's house for 3 weeks. How many days did Don spend at his grandmother's house?

June						
Sun	Mon	Tue	Wed	Thu	Fri	Sat
		1	2	3	4	5
6	7	8	9	10	11	12
13	14	15	16	17	18	19
20	21	22	23	24	25	26
27	28	29	30			

A 7 days C 21 days
B 14 days D 28 days

7. Shannon has some yarn. Which is the best unit to measure the length of the yarn?

F cups H inches
G pounds J gallons

8. **Explain It** Jon has 2 quarters and 2 pennies. Rita has 4 dimes, 2 nickels, and 3 pennies. Who has more money? Tell how you found your answer.

ALGEBRAIC THINKING

9. Rosa has 43 stickers. She buys a new pack of stickers. Now she has 55 stickers. Which number sentence could be used to find how many stickers are in the new pack?

A $55 - 43 = \blacksquare$
B $55 + 43 = \blacksquare$
C $55 \times 43 = \blacksquare$
D $55 \div 43 = \blacksquare$

10. Which of the following will help you find the missing addend in this number sentence?

$13 + \blacksquare = 21$

F $20 - 7 = 13$
G $21 - 13 = 8$
H $21 - 9 = 12$
J $22 - 8 = 14$

11. What is the next number in the pattern?

858, 758, 658, ■

A 657
B 648
C 558
D 458

12. **Explain It** Rico wrote this number pattern.

400, 403, 406, 409

What rule did Rico use to make his pattern? Explain how you know. What are the next three numbers in the pattern?

GEOMETRY AND SPATIAL SENSE

13. Which shape describes this photograph?

F hexagon
G rectangle
H square
J trapezoid

TIP **Eliminate choices.** See item 14. You can eliminate the sphere, which has no flat surfaces, and the cone, which has only one flat surface. You can also eliminate the rectangular prism because the six figures Todd used are squares and not rectangles.

14. Todd tapes six paper squares together to make a solid figure. Which solid figure does he make?

A sphere
B cone
C rectangular prism
D cube

15. Are the two figures congruent? Explain how you know.

CHAPTER 3

Compare, Order, and Round Numbers

FAST FACT • SOCIAL STUDIES The five Great Lakes are on or near the border between the United States and Canada. Lake Superior is the largest and the deepest of the five lakes.

PROBLEM SOLVING The graph shows the depths of the Great Lakes. Which lakes have depths that round to 800 feet?

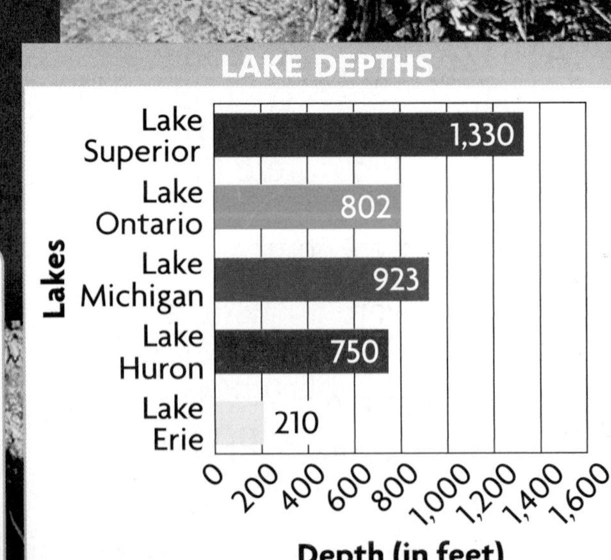

CHECK WHAT YOU KNOW

Use this page to help you review and remember important skills needed for Chapter 3.

COMPARE 2- AND 3-DIGIT NUMBERS

Write <, >, or = for each ●.

1. 34 ● 25

2. 45 ● 56

3. 239 ● 293

4. 67 ● 76

5. 342 ● 342

6. 706 ● 760

ORDER NUMBERS

Write the numbers in order from least to greatest.

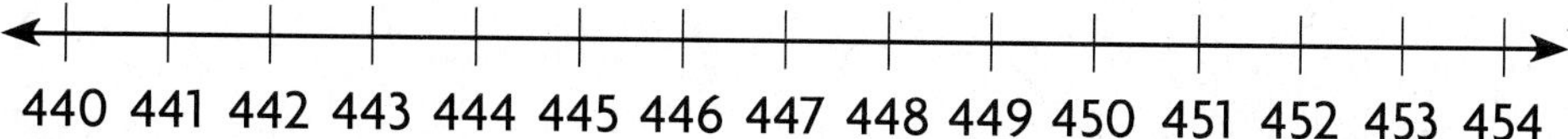

440 441 442 443 444 445 446 447 448 449 450 451 452 453 454

7. 451 442 448

8. 450 444 440

9. 452 441 449

10. 446 453 443

VOCABULARY POWER

REVIEW

hundred [hun′drəd] *noun*

The German word for hundred is *hundert*. Its value and meaning have changed over time. Its value is now 100. How many hundreds are in 672?

PREVIEW

benchmark numbers

greater than >

equal to =

compare

less than <

rounding

www.harcourtschool.com/mathglossary

LESSON 1

Benchmark Numbers

 **Learn**

HOW MANY? Numbers that help you estimate the number of objects without counting them are called **benchmark numbers**. Any useful number can be a benchmark.

About how many jellybeans are in Jar B? You can use 25 as a benchmark to estimate.

Quick Review

Which is greater?

1. 29 or 92
2. 101 or 1,001
3. 523 or 498
4. 7 or 70
5. 64 or 65

VOCABULARY

benchmark numbers

There are 25 jellybeans in Jar A.

There are about ■ jellybeans in Jar B.

B

There are about twice as many jellybeans in Jar B.

So, there are about 50 jellybeans in Jar B.

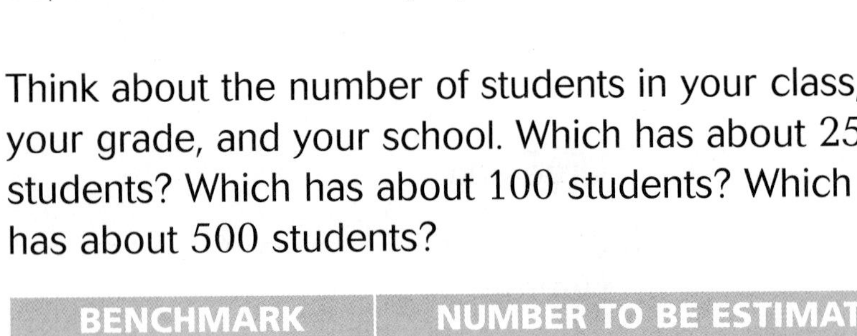

Think about the number of students in your class, your grade, and your school. Which has about 25 students? Which has about 100 students? Which has about 500 students?

BENCHMARK	NUMBER TO BE ESTIMATED
25	students in your class
100	students in your grade
500	students in your school

- Suppose all the third and fourth-grade classes went on a field trip. About how many students went? What benchmark can you use?

Check

1. **Explain** how a benchmark could help you estimate the number of girls in your grade.

Estimate the number of jellybeans in each jar. Use Jars A and B as benchmarks.

Jar A has 10 jellybeans.

Jar B has about 50 jellybeans.

2. 

10 or 50?

3. 

25 or 50?

4. 

100 or 200?

Practice and Problem Solving

Extra Practice, page 54, Set A

5. Estimate the number of jellybeans in the jar at the right. Use Jars A and B above as benchmarks.

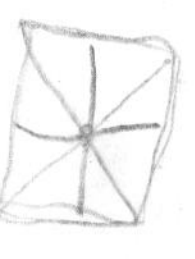

For 6–9, choose a benchmark of 10, 100, or 500 to estimate.

6. the number of players on a soccer team
7. the number of pretzels in a large bag
8. the number of sheets in a package of notebook paper
9. the number of leaves on a tree in summer
10. Juan had 30 blocks. He gave 18 to Rick but got 14 from Ron. How many blocks does Juan have now?
11. **Write a problem** in which a benchmark is used to estimate. Solve.

Mixed Review and Test Prep

Write each number in expanded form. (pp. 22, 24)

12. 268 **13.** 354 **14.** 420 **15.** 8,679

16. **TEST PREP** Choose the value of the blue digit in 15,688. (p. 32)

A 6 **B** 60 **C** 600 **D** 700

LESSON 2

Algebra: Compare Numbers

Learn

HOW NEAR? HOW FAR? Beth lives 262 miles from Homer and 245 miles from Lakewood. Which city does she live closer to?

Compare numbers to decide which of two numbers is greater. Use these symbols.

greater than > **less than <** **equal to =**

Quick Review

Write how many tens each number has.

1. 15 **2.** 20 **3.** 54
4. 37 **5.** 82

VOCABULARY

compare
greater than >
less than <
equal to =

One Way Use base-ten blocks.

Show 262 and 245. Compare from left to right.

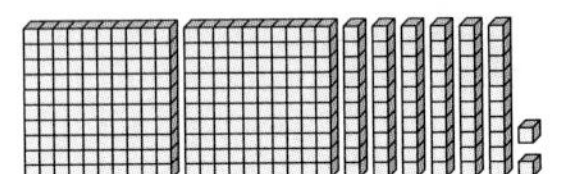

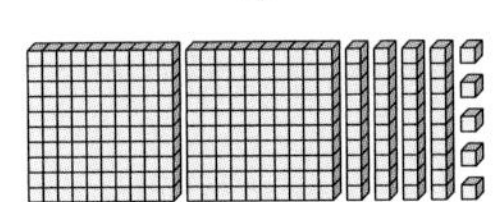

The hundreds are the same, so compare the tens. 6 tens is greater than 4 tens. So, 262 is greater than 245.

262 > 245
262 is **greater than** 245.

245 < 262
245 is **less than** 262.

So, Beth lives closer to Lakewood.

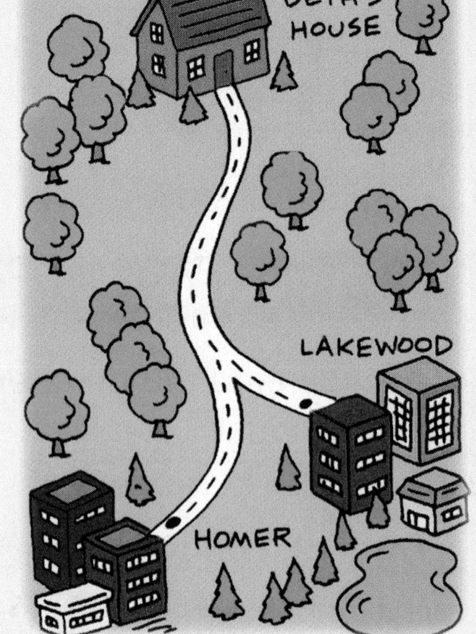

Another Way Use a number line.

From left to right, the numbers on a number line are in order from least to greatest.

A Compare 3,710 and 3,855.

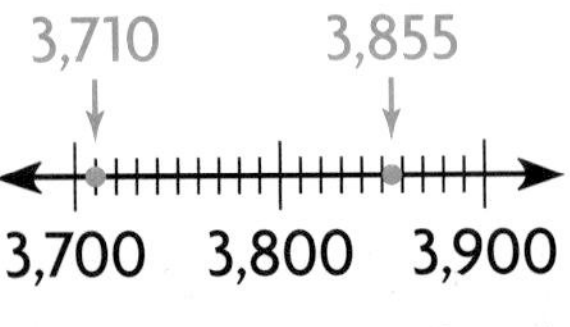

3,710 is to the left of 3,855, so it is less than 3,855.

3,710 < 3,855

B Compare 14,360 and 14,295.

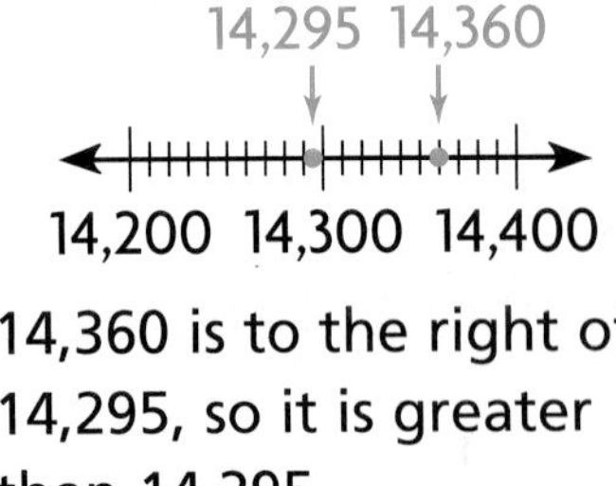

14,360 is to the right of 14,295, so it is greater than 14,295.

14,360 > 14,295

C Compare 65,730 and 65,730.

65,730 is only one point on the number line, so it is equal to 65,730.

65,730 = 65,730

Use a Place-Value Chart

A place-value chart can help you compare greater numbers.

Compare 413,165 and 413,271, starting from the left.

HUNDRED THOUSANDS	TEN THOUSANDS	THOUSANDS	HUNDREDS	TENS	ONES
4	1	3,	1	6	5
4	1	3,	2	7	1
↑ Hundred thousands are the same.	↑ Ten thousands are the same.	↑ Thousands are the same.	↑ 200 > 100		

So, 413,271 > 413,165 and 413,165 < 413,271.

MATH IDEA Compare numbers by using base-ten blocks, a number line, or a place-value chart.

More Practice:
Harcourt Mega Math Country Countdown, *Harrison's Comparisons*, Levels L and M; *Fraction Action*, Number Line Mine, Level B

Check

1. **Explain** how to use base-ten blocks to compare 341 and 300 + 40 + 1. What do you notice?

2. Use the number line in Example A on page 42 to compare 3,820 and 3,780. Which number is greater? Explain.

Compare the numbers. Write <, >, or = for each ●.

3.

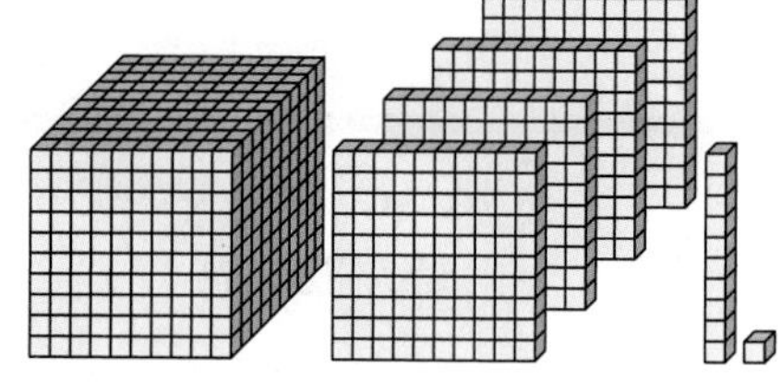

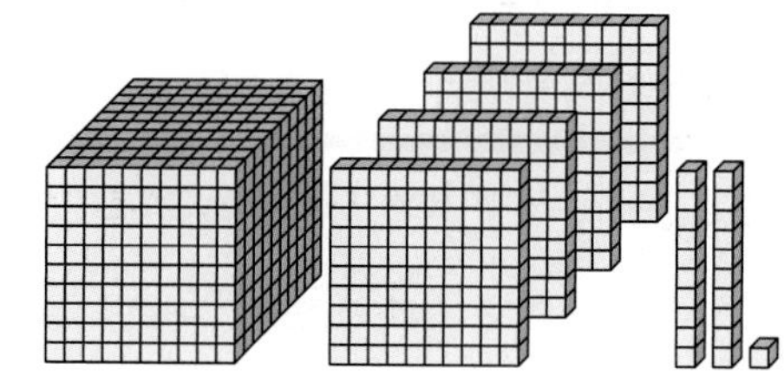

1,411 ● 1,421

4.

T	O
9	2
8	3

92 ● 83

5.

H	T	O
1	0	1
1	1	0

101 ● 110

6.

TH	H	T	O
2,	4	2	8
2,	4	3	8

2,428 ● 2,438

Practice and Problem Solving

Extra Practice, page 54, Set B

Compare the numbers. Write <, >, or = for each ●.

7.

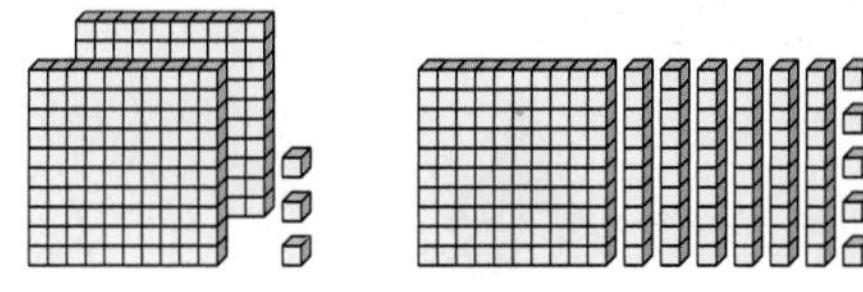

203 ● 165

8.

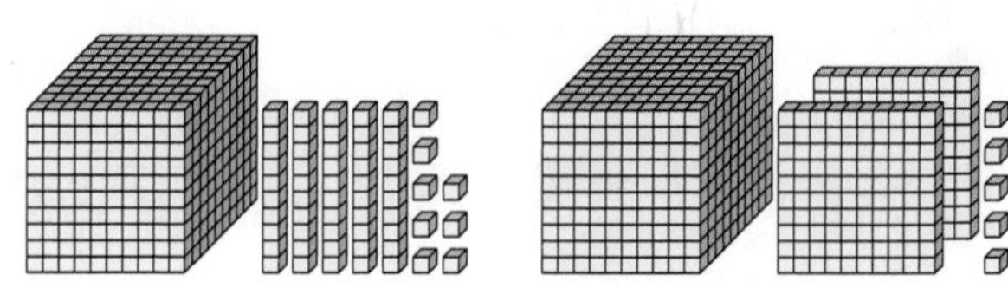

1,058 ● 1,205

9.

H	T	O
6	2	1
6	2	1

621 ● 621

10.

H	T	O
8	1	6
8	2	3

816 ● 823

11.

TH	H	T	O
4,	8	0	5
4,	8	1	9

4,805 ● 4,819

12. 629 ● 631 **13.** 5,712 ● 5,412 **14.** 102,412 ● 102,421

15. 1,894 ● 2,139 **16.** 10,348 ● 10,348 **17.** 437,393 ● 473,396

18. 151 + 200 ● 350 **19.** 696 − 418 ● 296 **20.** 475 + 72 ● 537

ALGEBRA Write the missing number that makes the number sentence true.

21. 341 = 34■ **22.** 887 < 8■4 **23.** 1,196 > 1,■98

24. What is the greatest place-value position in which the digits of 5,831 and 5,819 are different? Compare the numbers.

25. Compare the numbers 5,361 and 3,974. Which number is less? Draw a picture to show how you know.

For 26–28, use the numbers on the box.

26. List all the numbers that are less than 575.

27. List all the numbers that are greater than 830.

28. List all the numbers that are greater than 326 and less than 748.

29. **What's the Question?** Louis read 125 pages. Tom read 137 pages. The answer is 12.

30. **Write About It** You have 3 four-digit numbers. The digits in the thousands, hundreds, and ones places are the same. Which digits would you use to compare the numbers? Explain.

31. The numbers 456 and 564 have the same digits in a different order. Do they both have the same value? Explain.

32. The sum of three addends is 24. One addend is 5. Another addend is 3 more than 7. What is the missing addend?

Mixed Review and Test Prep

Tell whether the number is odd or even. (p. 20)

33. 13 **34.** 46 **35.** 187

36. 35 **37.** 2,721 **38.** 544

39. 736 **40.** 4,922 **41.** 26,571

Write the number in standard form. (p. 32)

42. 50,000 + 8,000 + 300

43. 30,000 + 700 + 5

Choose the letter for the number in standard form. (p. 32)

44. TEST PREP fifty-three thousand, six hundred seventy-two

A 53,072 C 53,627
B 53,602 D 53,672

45. TEST PREP seven hundred thirty-four thousand, five hundred twenty

F 73,452 H 734,502
G 734,052 J 734,520

Problem Solving Thinker's Corner

MANY USES OF NUMBERS Numbers tell how much or how many. They also tell the order of things. Numbers are even used to name things.

1. Give at least two examples for each.
   a. a number used to tell how much or how many
   b. a number used to tell the order of things
   c. a number used to name things

2. **REASONING** Give an example of numbers you would compare. Give an example of numbers that it wouldn't make sense to compare. Explain.

LESSON 3

Order Numbers

Quick Review

Tell which number is greater.

1. 37 or 29
2. 21 or 32
3. 58 or 65
4. 120 or 99
5. 235 or 253

Learn

MOUNTAIN HIGH The table lists the heights of three mountains in the United States. Which is the tallest?

Use a number line to order the numbers.

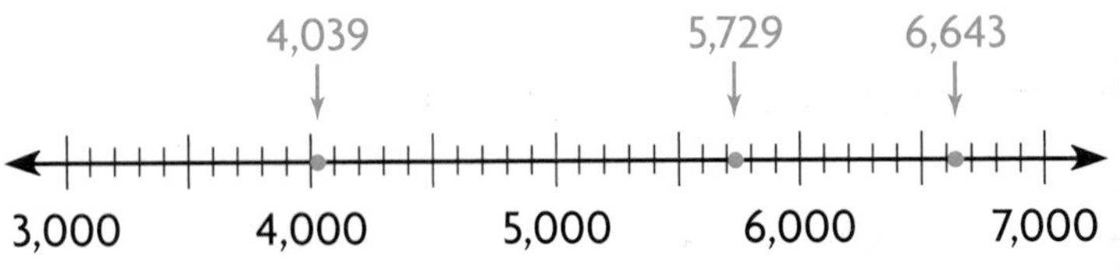

$4{,}039 < 5{,}729 < 6{,}643$

So, Clingmans Dome is the tallest.

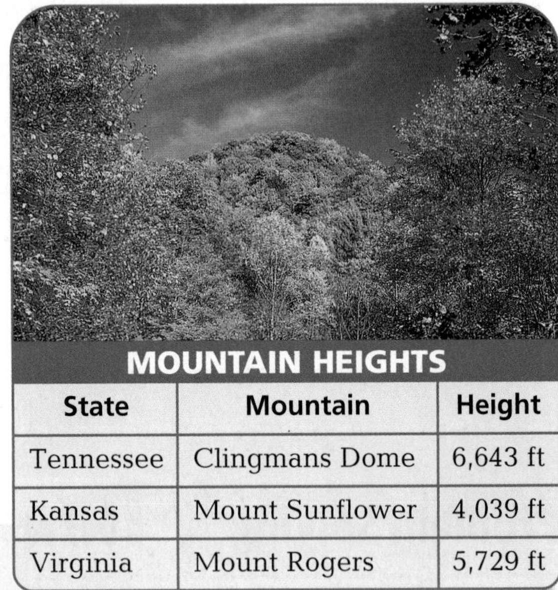

MOUNTAIN HEIGHTS

State	Mountain	Height
Tennessee	Clingmans Dome	6,643 ft
Kansas	Mount Sunflower	4,039 ft
Virginia	Mount Rogers	5,729 ft

You can order numbers by comparing the digits in the same place-value position from left to right.

Example

Order 47,613; 45,435; and 46,551.

STEP 1

Compare ten thousands.

47,613
45,435
46,551

The digits are the same.

STEP 2

Compare thousands.

47,613
45,435
46,551

They are not the same.
$7 > 6 > 5$

STEP 3

Write the numbers in order from greatest to least.

$47{,}613 > 46{,}551 > 45{,}435$

Check

1. **Explain** how you can order the numbers 251,432; 251,438; and 251,463 from greatest to least.

Write the numbers in order from least to greatest.

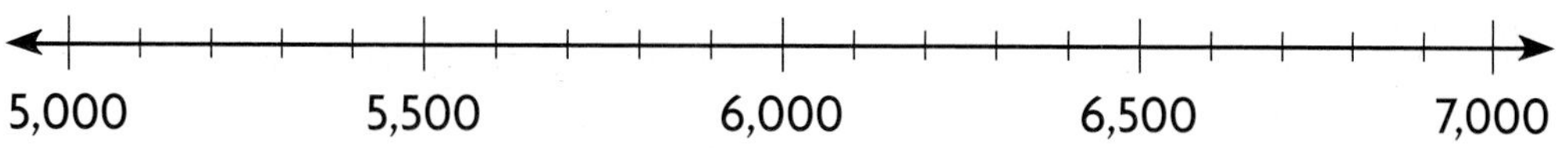

2. 5,200; 6,500; 5,900

3. 6,750; 6,125; 6,500

Practice and Problem Solving

Extra Practice, page 54, Set C

Write the numbers in order from least to greatest.

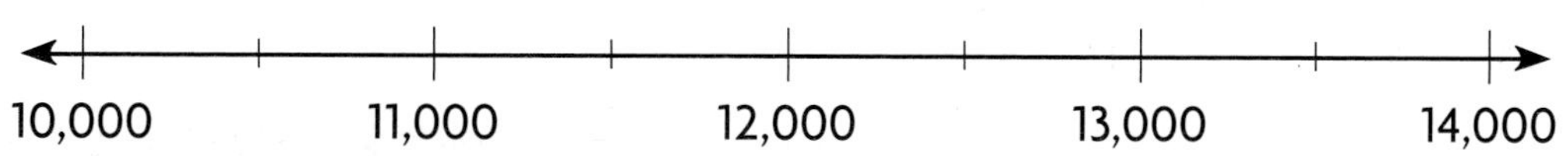

4. 10,500; 13,000; 12,500

5. 12,240; 11,845; 13,156

6.

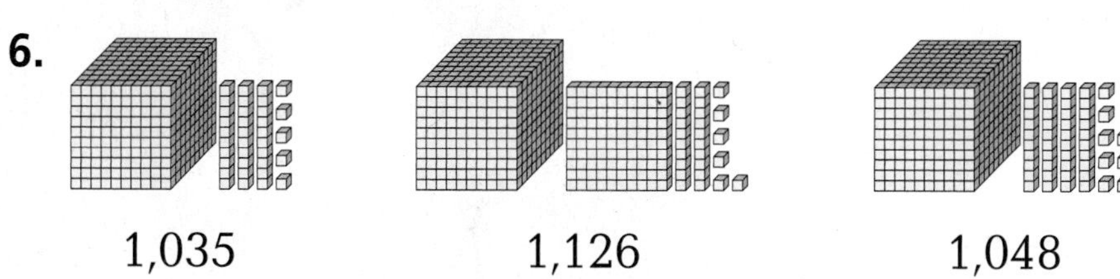

1,035 1,126 1,048

Write the numbers in order from greatest to least.

7. 7,837; 5,126; 3,541

8. 2,793; 2,728; 2,756

9. 32,603; 28,497; 90,050

10. 17,655; 22,600; 9,860

11. 493,849; 515,260; 504,316

12. 110,421; 109,863; 119,540

13. **REASONING** Write in order from least to greatest the six numbers whose digits are 2, 8, and 9.

14. Draw a picture that shows how to order 1,098; 1,126; and 973 from least to greatest.

15. **Vocabulary Power** The word *order* comes from the Latin word *ordo*, which means "a row or a line." How does this meaning relate to ordering numbers?

16. **? What's the Error?** Jason said that the numbers 3,545; 3,556; and 3,554 were in order from least to greatest. What is his error?

Mixed Review and Test Prep

17. Predict the next number in the pattern. Explain. 27, 23, 19, 15, ■ (p. 30)

18. Write the standard form for 60,000 + 500 + 9. (p. 32)

19. 45 + 10 (p. 8)

20. 56 + 20 (p. 8)

21. **TEST PREP** Which number is greater than 567? (p. 42)

A 549
B 560
C 562
D 575

LESSON 4

Problem Solving Skill
Use a Bar Graph

UNDERSTAND › PLAN › SOLVE › CHECK

Quick Review

Compare. Write $<$, $>$, or $=$ for each ●.

1. 124 ● 118
2. 229 ● 232
3. 244 ● 244
4. 3,156 ● 3,165
5. 4,371 ● 4,372

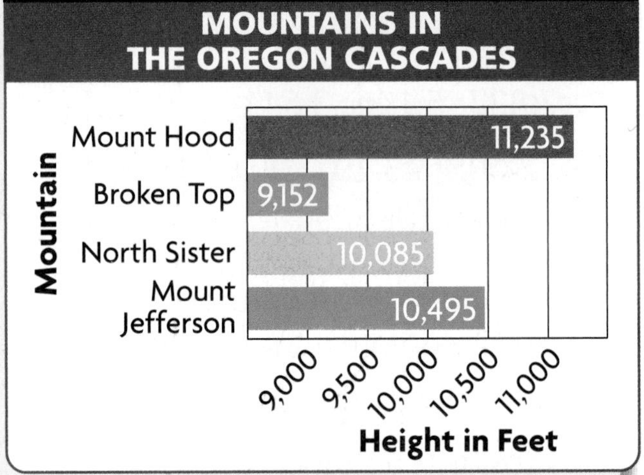

FOLLOW THE TRAIL Nancy and Emilio are studying the Oregon Cascade Mountains. They want to hike to the mountain that is higher than North Sister but not as high as Mount Hood. Which one should they choose?

Sometimes a bar graph can help you solve a problem.

Example

STEP 1

Look at the lengths of the bars in the graph. List the 4 mountains from highest to lowest.

Mount Hood, Mount Jefferson, North Sister, and Broken Top

STEP 2

Find all the mountains that are higher than North Sister.

Mount Jefferson and Mount Hood

STEP 3

Find all the mountains that are not as high as Mount Hood.

Mount Jefferson, North Sister, and Broken Top

MOUNTAINS IN THE OREGON CASCADES

Mountain
Mount Hood 11,235
Broken Top 9,152
North Sister 10,085
Mount Jefferson 10,495
9,000 9,500 10,000 10,500 11,000
Height in Feet

STEP 4

Find the mountain that is listed in both Step 2 and Step 3.

Mount Jefferson is the only mountain listed in both steps.

So, Nancy and Emilio chose Mount Jefferson.

Talk About It

- How does the height of Broken Top compare to that of North Sister?

Problem Solving Practice

1. **What if** Emilio and Nancy hiked to the mountain that is higher than Broken Top but not as high as Mount Jefferson? To which mountain did they hike?
2. What is the highest mountain under 11,000 feet that Emilio and Nancy studied?
3. **What if** the mountains were listed in order of height from least to greatest? What would be the order of the mountains?

USE DATA For 4–5, use the bar graph at the right.

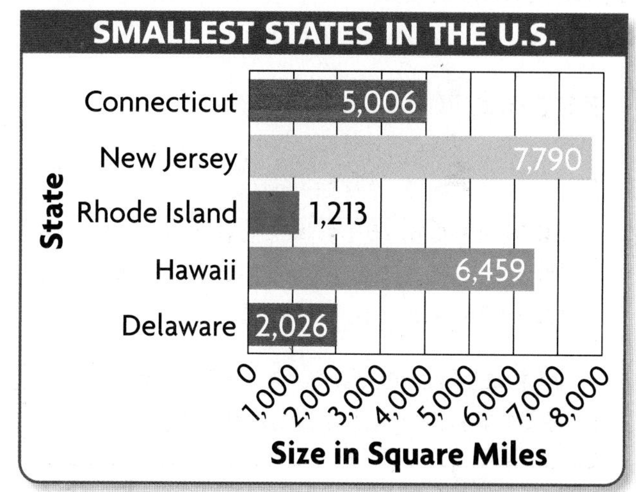

4. Which state is larger than Connecticut but smaller than New Jersey?
   - **A** Hawaii
   - **B** Rhode Island
   - **C** New Jersey
   - **D** Delaware
5. Name the three smallest states.
   - **F** Delaware, Rhode Island, Hawaii
   - **G** New Jersey, Hawaii, Connecticut
   - **H** Hawaii, Rhode Island, New Jersey
   - **J** Rhode Island, Delaware, Connecticut

Mixed Applications

6. Louis had base-ten blocks that showed 6 hundreds, 7 tens, 3 ones. Tom gave him 2 hundreds, 1 ten, 5 ones. Using standard form, write the number that shows the value of Louis's blocks now.
7. Celia lives in a town with a population of 12,346. Last year there were 1,000 fewer people living in the town. How many people lived in the town last year?
8. Tony had 128 postcards. Arlo gave him some more postcards. Now Tony has 152 postcards. How many postcards did Arlo give to Tony?
9. There were 253 students that went to the Science Museum. Of them, 127 were girls. How many were boys?
10. **Write About It** Explain how you would compare 4,291; 4,921; and 4,129 to put them in order from greatest to least.

LESSON 5

Round to Nearest 10 and 100

Quick Review

Write the numbers in order from least to greatest.

1. 23, 19, 16 **2.** 37, 31, 23

3. 29, 33, 32 **4.** 59, 57, 58

5. 218, 287, 278

VOCABULARY

rounding

Learn

HOW CLOSE? There are 43 third graders and 47 fourth graders going on a field trip to the zoo. About how many students in each grade are going to the zoo?

Rounding is one way to estimate when you want to know *about how many.*

A number line can help you.

Example 1

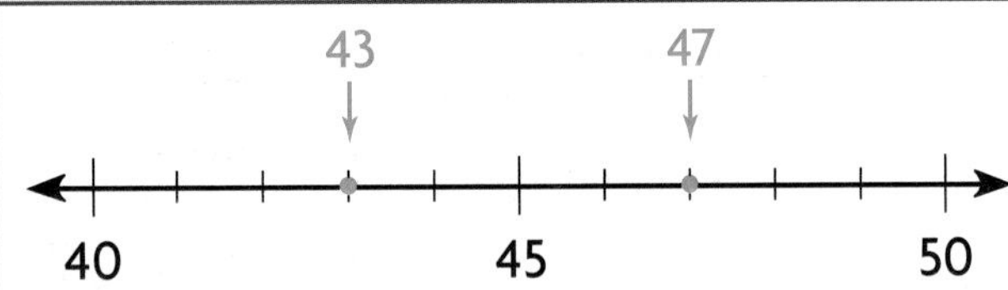

43 is closer to 40 than to 50.
43 rounds to 40.

47 is closer to 50 than to 40.
47 rounds to 50.

45 is halfway between 40 and 50. If a number is halfway between two tens, round to the greater ten. 45 rounds to 50.

So, about 40 third graders and about 50 fourth graders are going to the zoo.

Example 2

Round 3-digit numbers to the nearest ten and the nearest hundred.

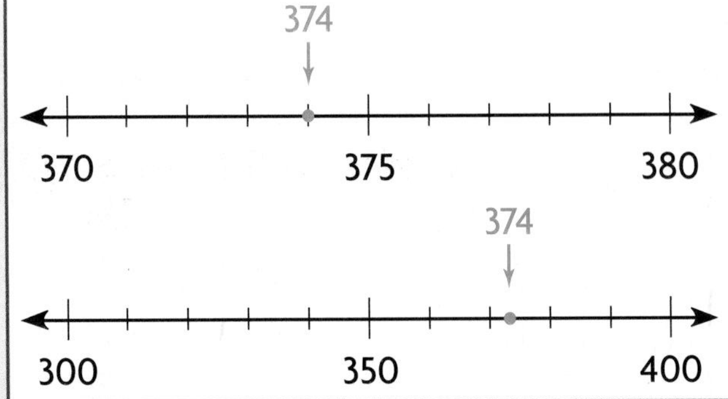

Round to the nearest ten.
374 is closer to 370 than to 380.
374 rounds to 370.

Round to the nearest hundred.
374 is closer to 400 than to 300.
374 rounds to 400.

Check

1. **Explain** how you can round 350 to the nearest hundred using the number line below.

Round to the nearest hundred and the nearest ten.

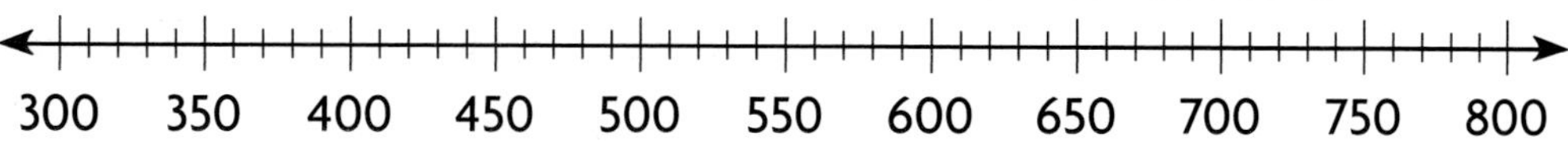

2. 643 **3.** 377 **4.** 445 **5.** 518 **6.** 750

Practice and Problem Solving

Extra Practice, page 54, Set D

Round to the nearest ten.

7. 16 **8.** 72 **9.** 53 **10.** 5 **11.** 78

12. 37 **13.** 44 **14.** 66 **15.** 94 **16.** 95

Round to the nearest hundred and the nearest ten.

17. 363 **18.** 405 **19.** 115 **20.** 165 **21.** 952

22. 698 **23.** 917 **24.** 385 **25.** 456 **26.** 883

USE DATA For 27–28, use the table.

ZOO ANIMALS	
Type	**Number**
Mammals	214
Birds	428
Reptiles	174

27. To the nearest hundred, about how many kinds of birds does the zoo have?

28. REASONING The number of _?_ + the number of _?_ $<$ the number of _?_ .

29. Kim rounded 348 to the nearest ten and said it was 350. She rounded 348 to the nearest hundred and said it was 400. Was this correct? Explain.

30. **Write a problem about animals. Use rounding to the nearest ten or to the nearest hundred in your problem.**

Mixed Review and Test Prep

31. 63 + 20 = ▇ (p. 8)

32. 32 + 14 = ▇ (p. 8)

33. 57 – 30 = ▇ (p. 10)

34. 48 – 17 = ▇ (p. 10)

35. **TEST PREP** What is the value of the blue digit in 16,230? (p. 32)

A 10 **C** 1,000

B 100 **D** 10,000

LESSON 6

Round to Nearest 1,000

Quick Review

Round to the nearest ten.

1. 52 **2.** 15 **3.** 27

4. 68 **5.** 76

Learn

ABOUT HOW MANY? When the Bronx Zoo in New York City first opened in 1899, it had 843 animals. In the spring of 2002, the Bronx Zoo had 4,405 animals.

To the nearest thousand, how many animals are in the zoo?

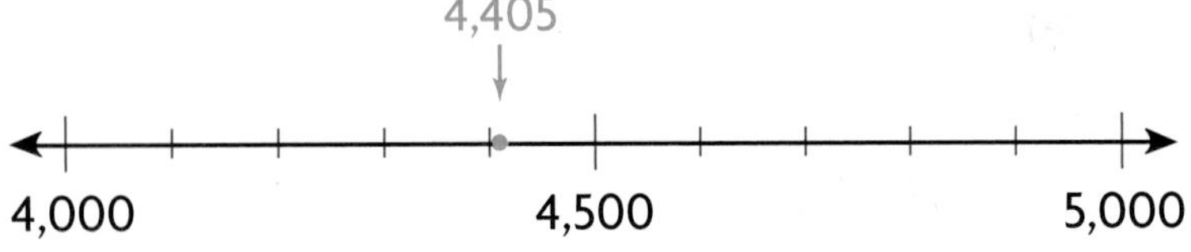

4,405 is closer to 4,000 than to 5,000.
4,405 rounds to 4,000.

So, there are about 4,000 animals in the zoo.

You can use rounding rules to round numbers.

Examples

A Round 2,641 to the nearest *thousand*.

2,641
↑

Look at the hundreds digit. Since 6 > 5, the 2 thousands digit rounds to 3 thousands. So, 2,641 rounds to 3,000.

B Round 2,641 to the nearest *hundred*.

2,641
↑

Look at the tens digit. Since 4 < 5, the 6 hundreds digit stays the same. So, 2,641 rounds to 2,600.

Rounding Rules

- Find the place to which you want to round.
- Look at the digit to its right.
- If the digit is less than 5, the digit in the rounding place stays the same.
- If the digit is 5 or more, the digit in the rounding place increases by 1.

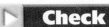

Check

1. **Explain** how you would use the rounding rules to round 3,728 to the nearest thousand.

Round to the nearest thousand.

2. 6,427
3. 2,500
4. 4,526
5. 1,670

Practice and Problem Solving

Extra Practice, page 54, Set E

Round to the nearest thousand.

6. 8,312
7. 4,500
8. 674
9. 9,478
10. 1,611
11. 5,920
12. 2,543
13. 4,444

Round each to the nearest thousand, the nearest hundred, and the nearest ten.

14. 3,581
15. 6,318
16. 2,350
17. 8,914
18. 4,624
19. 5,337
20. 1,273
21. 2,845

USE DATA For 22–23, use the table.

22. Round the weights of the giraffe and rhinoceros to the nearest thousand pounds. About how many giraffes would it take to equal the weight of the rhinoceros?

23. **Write About It** Tell how to round the weight of the hippopotamus to the nearest thousand, hundred, and ten.

24. **FAST FACT** • SCIENCE Asian elephants weigh less than African elephants. One Asian elephant weighed 7,586 pounds. What is 7,586 rounded to the nearest thousand?

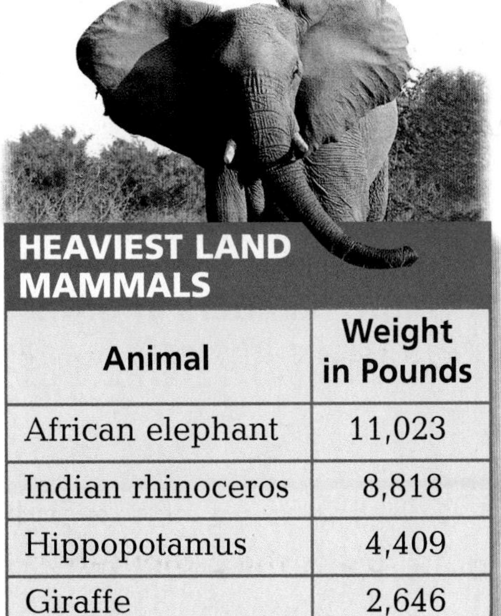

HEAVIEST LAND MAMMALS

Animal	Weight in Pounds
African elephant	11,023
Indian rhinoceros	8,818
Hippopotamus	4,409
Giraffe	2,646

Mixed Review and Test Prep

Write the value of the blue digit. (pp. 24, 32)

25. 8,251
26. 87,668

Write in expanded form. (pp. 22, 32)

27. 337
28. 12,982

29. **TEST PREP** 68 + 42 + 36 = ■ (p. 8)

A 136
B 138
C 142
D 146

Extra Practice

Set A (pp. 40–41)

For 1–2, choose a benchmark of 10, 100, or 500 to estimate.

1. the number of pieces in a small bag of dog food
2. the number of teeth in your mouth
3. There are 25 students in Ken's third-grade class. There are 4 third-grade classes. About how many students are in the third grade?

Set B (pp. 42–45)

Compare the numbers. Write <, >, or = for each ●.

1. 400 ● 12
2. 646 ● 600
3. 741 ● 741
4. 57 ● 75
5. 4,701 ● 4,071
6. 10,313 ● 10,515

Set C (pp. 46–47)

Write the numbers in order from least to greatest.

1. 124; 562; 347
2. 102; 89; 157
3. 1,466; 1,365; 1,988

Write the numbers in order from greatest to least.

4. 42,218; 43,010; 42,115
5. 610,100; 615,010; 605,310

Set D (pp. 50–51)

Round to the nearest hundred and the nearest ten.

1. 414
2. 888
3. 502
4. 635
5. 157
6. 733
7. 374
8. 498

Set E (pp. 52–53)

Round to the nearest thousand.

1. 3,345
2. 8,866
3. 5,533
4. 6,500
5. 9,457
6. 1,168
7. 7,662
8. 2,220

CHAPTER 3

Review/Test

✓ CHECK VOCABULARY AND CONCEPTS

Choose the best term from the box.

greatest to least
compare
round

1. You can use $<$, $>$, or $=$ to __?__ numbers. (p. 42)
2. One way to estimate is to __?__ numbers. (p. 50)

Suppose you want to round 371 to the nearest hundred. (pp. 50–51)

3. Which hundreds is 371 between?
4. Which hundred is 371 closer to?

✓ CHECK SKILLS

Compare the numbers. Write $<$, $>$, or $=$ for each ●. (pp. 42–45)

5. 532 ● 523
6. 23,246 ● 32,325
7. 7,583 ● 7,583

Write the numbers in order from least to greatest. (pp. 46–47)

8. 143, 438, 92
9. 7,304; 7,890; 7,141
10. 23,256; 23,161; 23,470
11. Round 85 to the nearest ten. (pp. 50–51)
12. Round 824 to the nearest hundred. (pp. 50–51)
13. Round 3,721 to the nearest thousand and hundred. (pp. 52–53)

✓ CHECK PROBLEM SOLVING

USE DATA For 14–15, use the bar graph. (pp. 48–49)

14. On which night was the number of tickets sold greater than the number sold on Monday but less than the number sold on Wednesday?
15. On which night was the number of tickets sold less than the number sold on Friday but greater than the number sold on Wednesday?

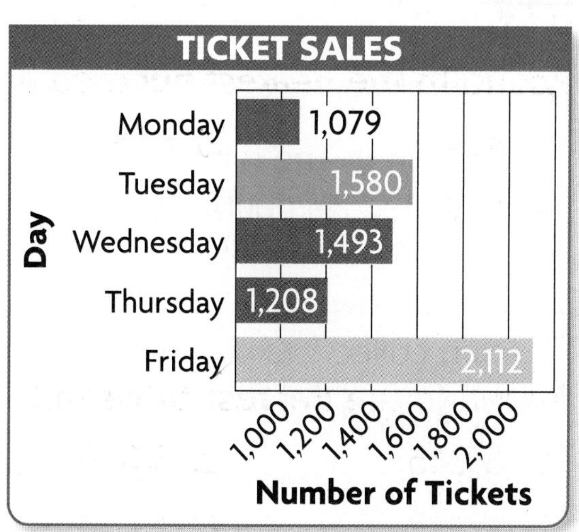

Standardized Test Prep

NUMBER SENSE, CONCEPTS, AND OPERATIONS

1. Springfield has three schools. The table shows how many students go to each school. Which list shows the number of students in order from **greatest** to **least**?

SPRINGFIELD SCHOOL STUDENTS	
School	**Number of Students**
Central	824
Eastgate	931
Westville	796

A $931 > 796 > 824$
B $796 > 824 > 931$
C $931 > 824 > 796$
D $824 > 796 > 931$

2. When Michael Jordan retired in 2003, he had scored 32,292 points. What is the value of the digit 9 in 32,292?

F 90
G 900
H 9,000
J 90,000

3. **Explain It** The recycling club collected 37 pounds of newspaper and 14 pounds of aluminum cans. About how many pounds did the club collect? Explain your estimate.

MEASUREMENT

4. Lilly wants to find how much water a bathtub holds. Which unit of measure should she use?

A gallon
B pound
C foot
D mile

5. Mrs. Lang wants to put a fence around her square flower garden. Each side of the garden is 4 feet long. How many feet of fencing does she need?

F 4 feet
G 8 feet
H 12 feet
J 16 feet

6. This is Ellie's cat.

About how much does Ellie's cat weigh?

A 900 pounds
B 90 pounds
C 9 pounds
D 9 ounces

7. **Explain It** Marco found a seashell on the beach. Explain which of these measurements best describes the length of the shell: 3 yards, 3 feet, or 3 inches.

ALGEBRAIC THINKING

TIP **Get the information you need.**
See item 8. You need to find the difference between 24 and 27, 27 and 30, and so on to solve this problem.

8. Jacob counts 24, 27, 30, 33, 36, 39. What is a rule for the pattern?

F Count by twos.
G Count by threes.
H Count by fives.
J Count by tens.

9. Anna baked 36 cookies in the morning. In the afternoon, she baked more cookies. When Anna finished, she had a total of 60 cookies. Which number sentence shows how many cookies Anna baked?

A $\blacksquare - 36 = 60$
B $36 + \blacksquare = 60$
C $60 + 36 = \blacksquare$
D $6 + \blacksquare = 36$

10. Explain It Describe a rule that could have been used to form the pattern shown below. Then use the same rule to make a similar pattern.

1, 8, 15, 22, 29

DATA ANALYSIS AND PROBABILITY

11. The bar graph below shows the favorite season of some third-grade students.

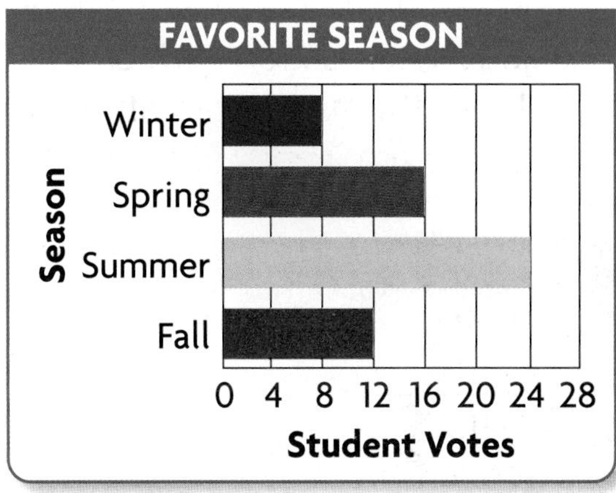

How many more students chose Summer than Fall?

F 4
G 8
H 12
J 14

12. Ethan made this table.

FAVORITE AFTER-SCHOOL ACTIVITY	
Activity	**Number of Students**
Bike Riding	25
In-line Skating	10
Playing Computer Games	15

How many students in all voted?

A 25
B 35
C 40
D 50

13. Explain It If Ethan made a pictograph using the above data, what key could he use? Explain.

IT'S IN THE BAG

Pocket Place Value

PROJECT Make and play a place-value game.

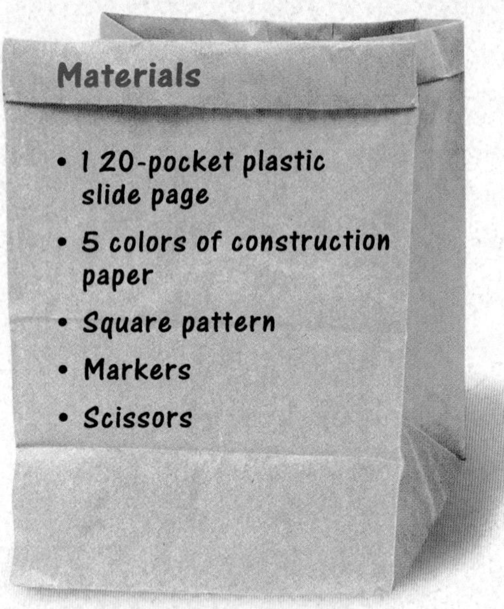

Materials

- 1 20-pocket plastic slide page
- 5 colors of construction paper
- Square pattern
- Markers
- Scissors

Directions

1. Use the square pattern. Cut ten $1\frac{1}{2}$-inch squares out of each piece of construction paper. *(Picture A)*

2. Choose one square of each color. Write *Ones, Tens, Hundreds, Thousands,* or *Ten Thousands.* Insert these place-value labels into the pockets in the top row of the slide page. Write a number 1 through 9 on each of the remaining colored squares. With a marker, write a comma between the hundreds and thousands columns in each row. *(Picture B)*

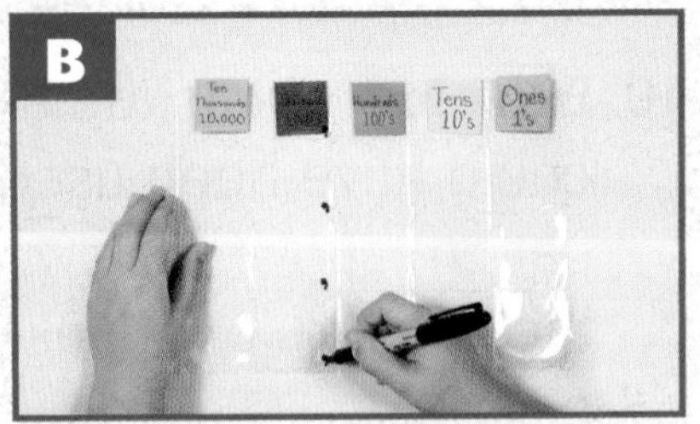

3. Work with a partner. The first student names a place value and a number. The partner finds the card for that number and slides it into the proper pocket. Players take turns naming place values and numbers and finding cards until all pockets are filled. One student reads the numbers aloud. *(Picture C)*

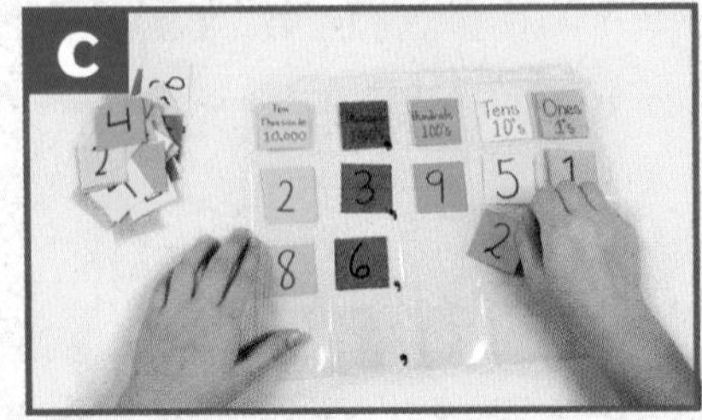

4. Now play the game without the place-value labels.

Challenge

Roman Numerals

The ancient Romans used only seven letters to name numbers. These Roman numerals are still used today. You may see them on clocks and buildings.

I	V	X	L	C	D	M
1	5	10	50	100	500	1,000

Place value is not used with Roman numerals. The values of the letters are added or subtracted to find the total value of the numeral.

Here are some rules for finding the value of Roman numerals.

When a letter is repeated, add the value of each letter.

$$\text{III} \rightarrow 1 + 1 + 1 = 3$$

When a letter with a lesser value follows a letter with a greater value, add the values of the letters.

$$\text{XVI} \rightarrow 10 + 5 + 1 = 16$$

When a letter with a greater value follows a letter with a lesser value, subtract the values of the letters.

$$\text{XL} \rightarrow 50 - 10 = 40$$

Talk About It

- Explain how to find the value of XXI.

Try It

Write the value of each Roman numeral.

1. VIII **2.** CX **3.** IX **4.** MMM

5. CD **6.** DCLXV **7.** XXXVII **8.** XLV

Study Guide and Review

VOCABULARY

Choose the best term from the box.

fact family
digits
pattern
inverse operations
benchmark numbers

1. Addition and subtraction are examples of _?_. (p. 2)
2. The symbols 0, 1, 2, 3, 4, 5, 6, 7, 8, and 9 are called _?_. (p. 22)
3. An ordered set of numbers or objects is a _?_. (p. 30)

STUDY AND SOLVE

Chapter 1

Make fact families.

9 + 5 = 14　　5 + 9 = 14
14 − 5 = 9　　14 − 9 = 5

Complete. (pp. 2–3)

4. $5 + 8 = 13$, so $13 - \blacksquare = 5$
5. $17 - 9 = 8$, so $\blacksquare + 9 = 17$

Add 2-digit numbers.

$$\begin{array}{r} {}^{1}\\ 27 \\ +34 \\ \hline 61 \end{array}$$

Add the ones. 7 + 4 = 11
Regroup 11 ones as 1 ten, 1 one. Add the tens.

Find the sum. (pp. 8–9)

6. $\begin{array}{r} 72 \\ +18 \\ \hline \end{array}$
7. $\begin{array}{r} 56 \\ +29 \\ \hline \end{array}$
8. $\begin{array}{r} 17 \\ 43 \\ +24 \\ \hline \end{array}$

Subtract 2-digit numbers.

$$\begin{array}{r} {}^{4\,13}\\ 53 \\ -26 \\ \hline 27 \end{array}$$

Since 6 > 3, regroup 53 as 4 tens 13 ones. Subtract the ones. Subtract the tens.

Find the difference. (pp. 10–11)

9. $\begin{array}{r} 63 \\ -\ 8 \\ \hline \end{array}$
10. $\begin{array}{r} 77 \\ -19 \\ \hline \end{array}$
11. $\begin{array}{r} 50 \\ -33 \\ \hline \end{array}$

Chapter 2

Identify odd and even numbers.

Even numbers have a 0, 2, 4, 6, or 8 in the ones place.
Odd numbers have a 1, 3, 5, 7, or 9 in the ones place.

Tell whether the number is *odd* or *even*. (pp. 20–21)

12. 9　　13. 23　　14. 40

Understand place value.

Ten Thousands	Thousands	Hundreds	Tens	Ones
4	2,	1	0	5

Standard form: 42,105
Expanded form:
40,000 + 2,000 + 100 + 5
Word form:
forty-two thousand, one hundred five

Write in standard form. (pp. 22–27, 32–33)

15. seven hundred twenty-eight

16. two hundred eighty

17. 10,000 + 2,000 + 500 + 20 + 2

18. 300,000 + 2,000 + 20 + 5

Write in expanded form. (pp. 22–27, 32–33)

19. 4,542 **20.** 571,061

Chapter 3

Compare and order numbers.

Write in order from greatest to least.
2,761; 1,793; 5,219

Compare the thousands.
5 > 2 > 1

5,219; 2,761; 1,793

Write <, >, or = for each ●. (pp. 42–45)

21. 739 ● 728 **22.** 461 ● 461

23. 3,125 ● 452 **24.** 1,203 ● 1,209

Write in order from greatest to least. (pp. 46–47)

25. 9,005; 5,009; 5,010

26. 27,423; 28,432; 29,417

Round numbers.

Round 4,483 to the nearest thousand.
4,483 is between 4,000 and 5,000.
It is closer to 4,000.
So, 4,483 rounded to the nearest thousand is 4,000.

Round to the nearest hundred. (pp. 50–51)

27. 184 **28.** 653 **29.** 247

Round to the nearest thousand. (pp. 52–53)

30. 3,609 **31.** 1,289

PROBLEM SOLVING PRACTICE

Solve. (pp. 12–13, 28–29)

32. Dan's mother cut out 23 coupons from the newspaper. She used 9 at the grocery store. How many does she have left?

33. Tamara modeled 368 with base-ten blocks. She used 3 hundreds and 18 ones. How many tens did she use?

PERFORMANCE ASSESSMENT

TASK A • TRIP TO THE BEACH

Jeremy and his family are driving from their home to the beach. The map shows the roads they can take and the distances in miles.

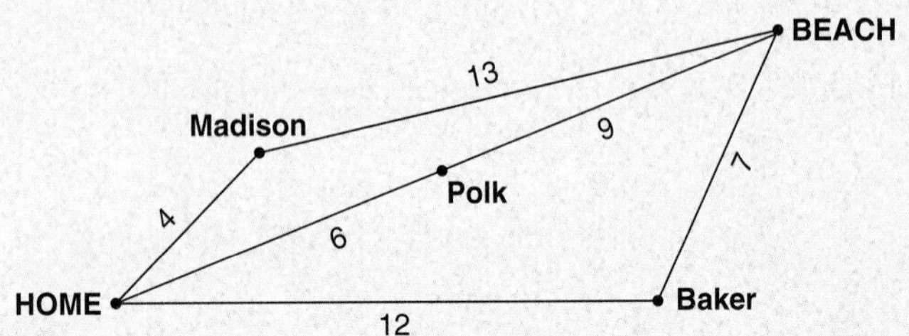

a. Write the name of one city they could drive through. Then find the total distance they will drive if they choose this road.

b. Which route is the longest? Which route is the shortest? Explain.

TASK B • MAKE A GOOD GUESS

Jar A has 250 jelly beans in it. Abe, Beth, Carla, and Devon guessed the number of jelly beans in Jar B. Beth guessed that there were 1,459. Abe, Carla, and Devon gave clues for their guesses.

Jar A

Jar B

a. Copy and complete the table. Use the clues to write possible numbers for the other three guesses.

JELLYBEAN GUESSES	
Abe	
Beth	1,459
Carla	
Devon	

Abe's clue: My guess is less than 1,500 but greater than Beth's guess.

Carla's clue: My guess is 100 less than Abe's guess.

Devon's clue: My guess rounded to the nearest hundred is 1,000.

b. Write the guesses in order from least to greatest.

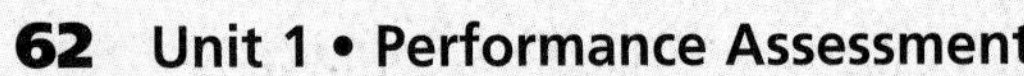

Number Patterns

Jung started with the number 8 and added 4 a total of 10 times. What patterns do you notice in the ones digits of the sums?

Start with 8. Add 4.

12	32
16	36
20	40
24	44
28	48

ones digits: 2, 6, 0, 4, 8, 2, 6, 0, 4, 8

All of the digits are even numbers. The digits 2, 6, 0, 4, and 8 repeat.

A calculator can help you explore number patterns. Start with 8 and add 5 at least 10 times. What patterns do you notice in the ones digits of the sums?

STEP 1

Enter the starting number, 8, and add 5.

ON/C 8 + 5 =

STEP 2

Press the equal key 10 times. Record each sum.

Start with 8. Add 5.

13	23
18	28

STEP 3

Look for a pattern.

Start with 8. Add 5.

13	23	33	43	53
18	28	38	48	58

The digits 3 and 8 repeat. They follow this pattern: odd, even.

Practice and Problem Solving

Use a calculator to find the number patterns.

1. Start with 7 and add 6 at least 10 times. What patterns do you notice in the ones digits of the sums?
2. **Write About It** Start with a number from 1–9. Choose a number from 1–9 to add at least 10 times. Record each sum, and describe the patterns you find in the ones digits.

GO ON-LINE **Multimedia Math Glossary** www.harcourtschool.com/mathglossary

Vocabulary Power Look up *digit* in the Multimedia Math Glossary. Choose a two-digit number. Add a number from 1–9 to it at least 10 times. Record each sum. Describe the pattern.

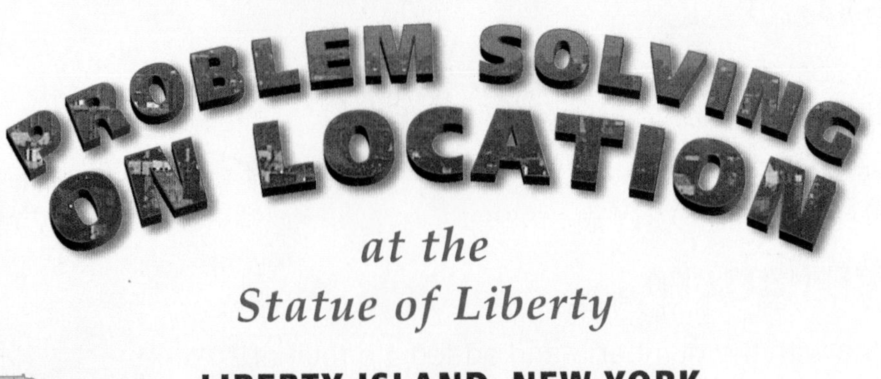

at the
Statue of Liberty

LIBERTY ISLAND, NEW YORK

People from all over the world visit the Statue of Liberty in New York City.

USE DATA For 1–5, use the table below.

1. The table lists the average number of visitors per day. What is this number rounded to the nearest thousand?
2. The Statue of Liberty is about 300 feet high. Is this number rounded to the nearest ten or to the nearest hundred? Explain.
3. Is the height from the heel to the top of the head an odd number or an even number?
4. Is the total weight of copper in the statue greater than or less than the total weight of steel in the statue?
5. **STRETCH YOUR THINKING** There are 12 inches in a foot. What is a reasonable estimate of the length of the tablet in feet? Explain.

Statue of Liberty Facts	
Average visitors per day	10,958 people
Total height	305 feet
Height from heel to top of head	111 feet
Length of right arm	42 feet
Length of tablet	23 feet, 7 inches
Total weight of copper	179,200 pounds
Total weight of steel	250,000 pounds

◀ **The Statue of Liberty was a gift of friendship from the people of France to the people of the United States. It was dedicated October 28, 1886.**

PARIS, FRANCE

A small version of the Statue of Liberty stands on a small island in the Seine River in Paris.

1. The Statue of Liberty in Paris is about 38 feet high. Round that number to the nearest ten.

2. The Statue of Liberty in Paris weighs about 28,000 pounds. If this weight has been rounded to the nearest thousand, could the actual weight be 28,500 pounds? Explain.

3. In the photograph, the Eiffel Tower is behind the small Statue of Liberty. The Eiffel Tower is the most famous landmark in Paris. Use these clues to find its height.
   - The height is between 1,000 feet and 1,070 feet.
   - The tens digit is greater than 5.
   - The ones digit is greater than 1 and less than 5.
   - The height is an odd number.

4. **REASONING** Two art students are touring Paris. They each buy a one-day museum pass for $14. Each student also buys a ticket to the Eiffel Tower for $11 and a boat ticket for $3. How much do the two students spend altogether?

▼ **The Statue of Liberty in Paris faces west toward New York, while the Statue of Liberty in New York faces east toward Paris.**

CHAPTER 4

Addition

FAST FACT • SOCIAL STUDIES **Dogs were first used as watchdogs, herding dogs, and hunting dogs. Now, more dogs are pets than workers. Some dogs are still trained to help disabled people.**

PROBLEM SOLVING **Look at the chart. How many dogs in all graduated in 2000 and 2001?**

NUMBER OF CANINE COMPANION GRADUATES

Year	1998	1999	2000	2001
Graduates	132	105	114	138

CHECK WHAT YOU KNOW

Use this page to help you review and remember important skills needed for Chapter 4.

ADDITION FACTS

Add.

1. $\begin{array}{r} 2 \\ +7 \\ \hline \end{array}$
2. $\begin{array}{r} 9 \\ +4 \\ \hline \end{array}$
3. $\begin{array}{r} 7 \\ +9 \\ \hline \end{array}$
4. $\begin{array}{r} 3 \\ +8 \\ \hline \end{array}$
5. $\begin{array}{r} 8 \\ +7 \\ \hline \end{array}$

COLUMN ADDITION

Find the sum.

6. $\begin{array}{r} 1 \\ 4 \\ +6 \\ \hline \end{array}$
7. $\begin{array}{r} 2 \\ 1 \\ +9 \\ \hline \end{array}$
8. $\begin{array}{r} 6 \\ 6 \\ +6 \\ \hline \end{array}$
9. $\begin{array}{r} 5 \\ 4 \\ +7 \\ \hline \end{array}$
10. $\begin{array}{r} 8 \\ 5 \\ +2 \\ \hline \end{array}$

2-DIGIT ADDITION

Add.

11. $\begin{array}{r} 21 \\ +48 \\ \hline \end{array}$
12. $\begin{array}{r} 43 \\ +35 \\ \hline \end{array}$
13. $\begin{array}{r} 14 \\ +79 \\ \hline \end{array}$
14. $\begin{array}{r} 53 \\ +18 \\ \hline \end{array}$
15. $\begin{array}{r} 15 \\ +45 \\ \hline \end{array}$

VOCABULARY POWER

REVIEW

sum [sum] *noun*

The word *sum* comes from the Latin word *summus*, which means "highest." When early Romans added columns of numbers, they wrote the answer at the top. What word for the top of a mountain comes from *summus*?

PREVIEW

estimate
front-end estimation
expression
not equal to ≠

www.harcourtschool.com/mathglossary

LESSON 1

Estimate Sums

Quick Review

1. 5 + 25
2. 30 + 20
3. 70 + 20
4. \$4 + \$6
5. 20 + 55

VOCABULARY

estimate

front-end estimation

Learn

MANATEE WINTER HOME Wildlife officers counted 329 manatees living in the warm waters of Florida's Gulf Coast. Along Florida's Atlantic Coast, officers counted 174 manatees. About how many manatees did the wildlife officers count in all?

To find *about* how many, you can **estimate**.

Example

One Way Use rounding. Round each number to the nearest hundred.

```
 329 →  300
+174 → +200
        500
```

Another Way Use **front-end estimation**. Add the front digit of each addend. Write zeros for the other digits.

```
 329 →  300
+174 → +100
        400
```

So, both 400 and 500 are reasonable estimates of how many manatees were counted.

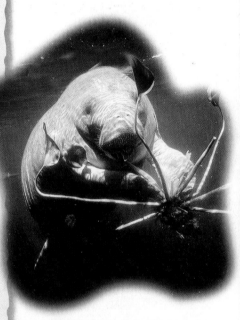

▲ A manatee spends 5 to 8 hours per day feeding on plants in the water and along the shoreline.

More Examples

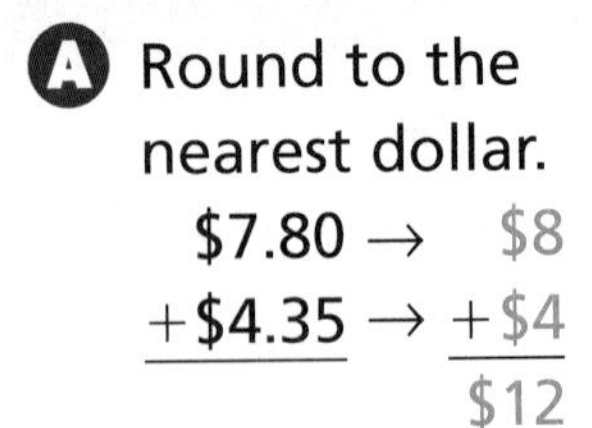

A Round to the nearest dollar.

```
 $7.80 →  $8
+$4.35 → +$4
         $12
```

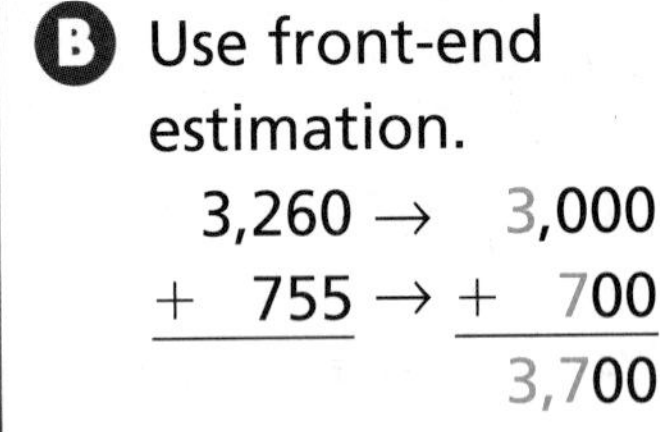

B Use front-end estimation.

```
 3,260 →  3,000
+  755 → +  700
          3,700
```

MATH IDEA When you do not need an exact answer, you can estimate by using rounding or front-end estimation.

- When you use front-end estimation, will your estimate be greater than or less than the actual sum? When you use rounding? Explain.

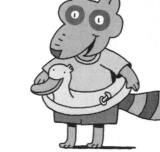

Check

1. **Explain** whether you should use front-end estimation to decide if you have enough money. You want to buy books that cost $4.69 and $3.98.

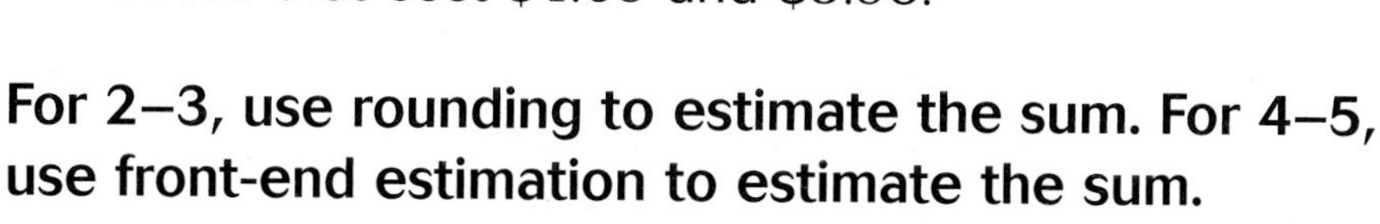

For 2–3, use rounding to estimate the sum. For 4–5, use front-end estimation to estimate the sum.

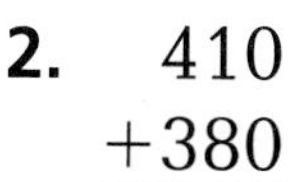

2. $\begin{array}{r} 410 \\ +380 \\ \hline \end{array}$ **3.** $\begin{array}{r} \$5.30 \\ +\$3.80 \\ \hline \end{array}$ **4.** $\begin{array}{r} 512 \\ +467 \\ \hline \end{array}$ **5.** $\begin{array}{r} 4{,}370 \\ +\ \ 980 \\ \hline \end{array}$

Practice and Problem Solving

Extra Practice, page 82, Set A

Use rounding to estimate the sum.

6. $\begin{array}{r} 206 \\ +668 \\ \hline \end{array}$ **7.** $\begin{array}{r} \$6.38 \\ +\$1.04 \\ \hline \end{array}$ **8.** $\begin{array}{r} 2{,}610 \\ +3{,}497 \\ \hline \end{array}$ **9.** $\begin{array}{r} \$19.49 \\ +\ \ \$4.67 \\ \hline \end{array}$

Use front-end estimation to estimate the sum.

10. $\begin{array}{r} 319 \\ +543 \\ \hline \end{array}$ **11.** $\begin{array}{r} 279 \\ +325 \\ \hline \end{array}$ **12.** $\begin{array}{r} 805 \\ +\ \ 79 \\ \hline \end{array}$ **13.** $\begin{array}{r} 6{,}278 \\ +7{,}913 \\ \hline \end{array}$

14. One young manatee weighs 175 pounds. Another weighs 258 pounds. Explain the method of estimation you would use to estimate their total weight.

15. Erica earned $2.90 on Monday. If she earns about the same amount on Tuesday and Wednesday, can she buy a $13.00 CD? Explain.

For 16–18, use the numbers at the right.

Choose two numbers whose sum is about:

16. 70. **17.** 500. **18.** 8,000.

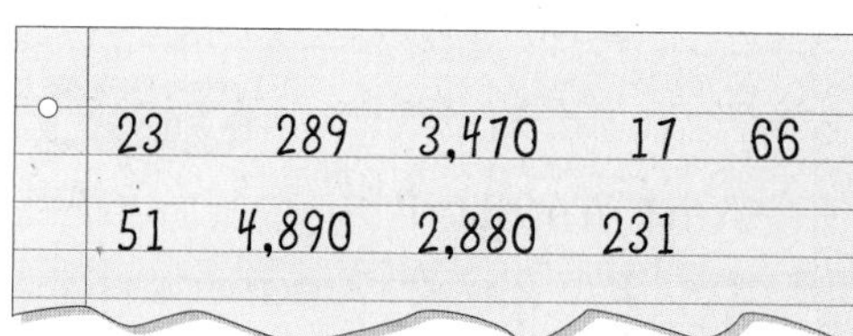

23 289 3,470 17 66
51 4,890 2,880 231

Mixed Review and Test Prep

Write $<$, $>$, or $=$ for each ●. (p. 42)

19. 27 ● 38 **20.** 723 ● 726

21. Write in order from least to greatest: 3,291; 3,245; 3,311. (p. 46)

22. Write 40,000 + 3,000 + 700 + 9 in standard form. (p. 32)

23. **TEST PREP** Which is sixty thousand, two hundred forty written in standard form? (p. 32)

A 60,024
B 60,204
C 60,240
D 62,040

LESSON 2

Addition with Regrouping

Quick Review

1. 12 + 10
2. 14 + 15
3. 41 + 39
4. 25 + 36
5. 21 + 57

MATERIALS
base-ten blocks

Explore

Make a model to add 134 and 279.

Activity

STEP 1

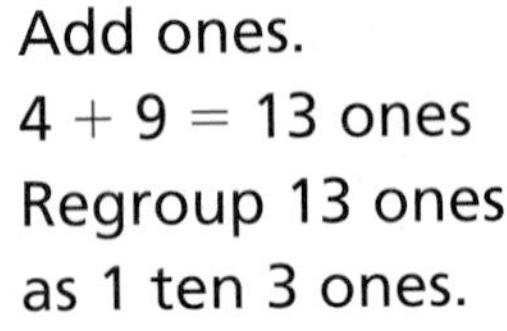

Add ones.
4 + 9 = 13 ones
Regroup 13 ones as 1 ten 3 ones.

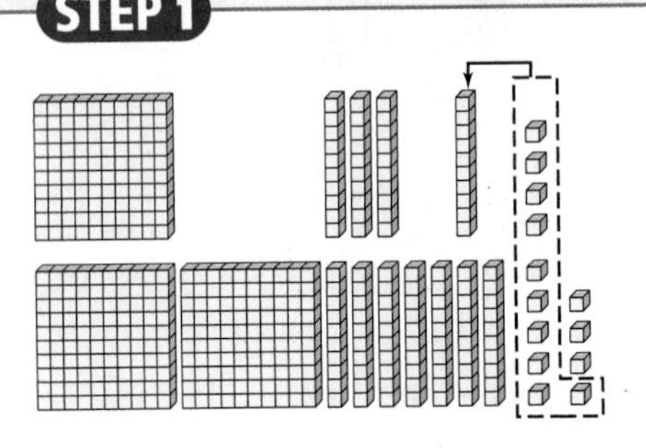

STEP 2

Add tens.
1 + 3 + 7 = 11 tens
Regroup 11 tens as 1 hundred 1 ten.

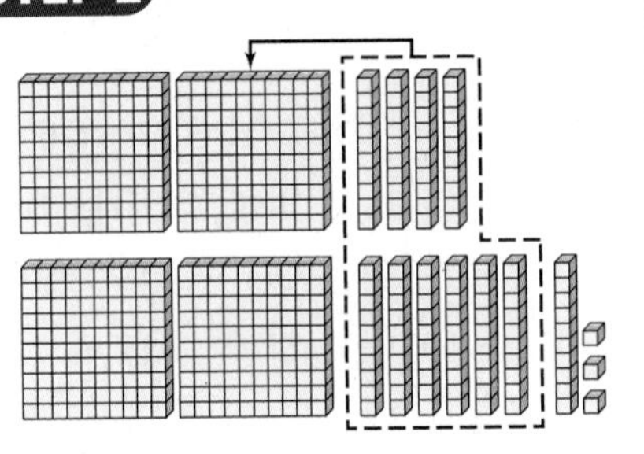

STEP 3

Add hundreds.
1 + 1 + 2 = 4 hundreds

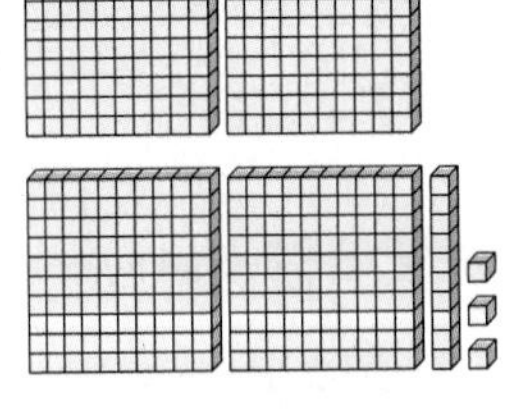

So, 134 + 279 = 413.

Technology Link
More Practice: Harcourt Mega Math Country Countdown, *Block Busters*, Levels V, W

We are adding 116 and 144. We now have 10 ones. What should we do next?

Try It

Use base-ten blocks. Draw a picture to show the sum.

a. 116 + 144 = ■ **b.** 269 + 358 = ■

Connect

Here is a way to record addition. To add 137 and 264, first line up hundreds, tens, and ones.

Example

STEP 1

Add the ones.
Regroup.
11 ones = 1 ten 1 one

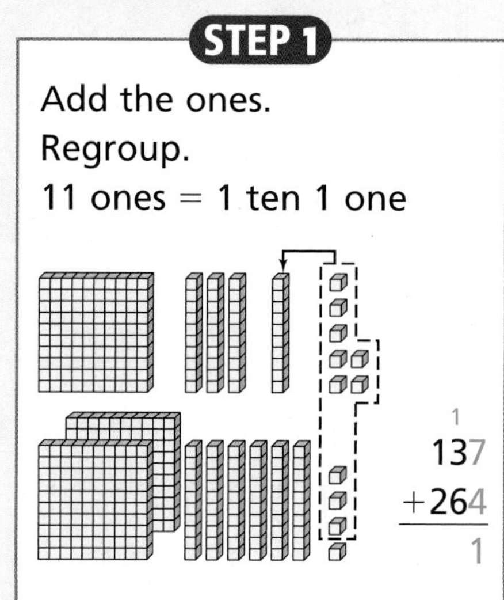

STEP 2

Add the tens.
Regroup.
10 tens = 1 hundred 0 tens

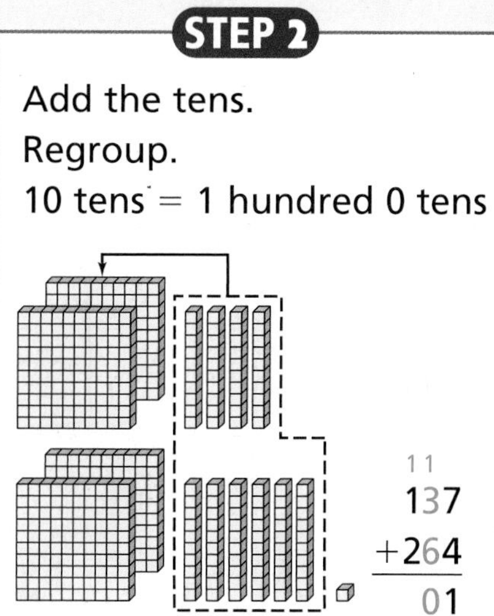

STEP 3

Add the hundreds.

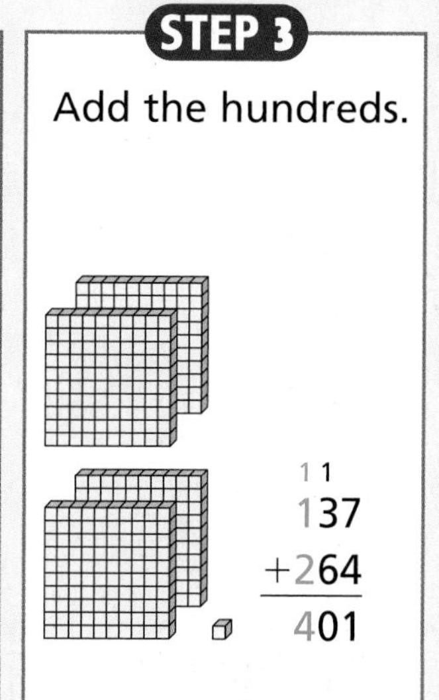

Practice and Problem Solving

Find each sum.

1. 134 + 217

2. 265 + 423

3. 368 + 416

4. 333 + 128

5. 295 + 382

6. 192 + 439

7. 493 + 256

8. 563 + 139

9. 612 + 308

10. 734 + 169

USE DATA For 11, use the map.

11. REASONING Theo drove from Pittsburgh to Allentown. David drove from Pittsburgh to Philadelphia. Who drove farther? How much farther?

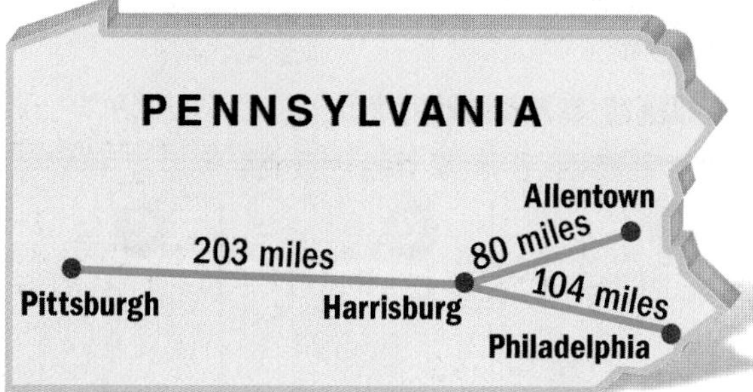

Mixed Review and Test Prep

Compare. Use <, >, or = for each ●. (p. 42)

12. 89 ● 78

13. 5,324 ● 5,342

14. 142 ● 412

15. 8 + 3 ● 20 − 7

16. TEST PREP Which group of numbers is in order from least to greatest? (p. 46)

A 394, 379, 380
B 521, 539, 540
C 427, 450, 431
D 201, 263, 229

LESSON 3

Add 3- and 4-Digit Numbers

Quick Review

1. 7 + ■ = 13
2. ■ + 9 = 18
3. 5 + 6
4. 8 + 7
5. 6 + 8

Learn

THOUSANDS OF BOOKS How many books did Grade 3 and Grade 4 read in all?

1,467 + 1,638 = ■

Estimate. 1,467 → 1,000; +1,638 → +2,000; 3,000

READ-A-THON RESULTS	
Grade 2	1,265 books
Grade 3	1,467 books
Grade 4	1,638 books

Example

STEP 1

Add the ones. Regroup. 15 ones = 1 ten 5 ones

```
     1
  1,467
 +1,638
      5
```

STEP 2

Add the tens. Regroup. 10 tens = 1 hundred 0 tens

```
    11
  1,467
 +1,638
     05
```

STEP 3

Add the hundreds. Regroup. 11 hundreds = 1 thousand 1 hundred

```
  1 11
  1,467
 +1,638
    105
```

STEP 4

Add the thousands.

```
  1 11
  1,467
 +1,638
  3,105
```

So, the two grades read 3,105 books in all. Since 3,105 is close to the estimate of 3,000, the answer is reasonable.

More Examples

A

```
   1  1
  4,325
 +  867
  5,192
```

B

```
    2
   591
   173
  +290
 1,054
```

C

```
dollar sign
 ↓11
  $24.83
 +$45.74
  $70.57
     ↑
decimal point
```

- Add money like whole numbers.
- Include a dollar sign, and use a decimal point to separate dollars and cents.

MATH IDEA Estimate to see if your answer is reasonable.

Check

1. **Explain** whether you would regroup to find how many books Grades 2 and 3 read in all.

Find the sum. Estimate to check.

2. $\begin{array}{r} 224 \\ +511 \\ \hline \end{array}$

3. $\begin{array}{r} \$9.07 \\ +\$1.25 \\ \hline \end{array}$

4. $\begin{array}{r} 1{,}298 \\ +1{,}872 \\ \hline \end{array}$

5. $\begin{array}{r} 214 \\ 468 \\ +\ 89 \\ \hline \end{array}$

Practice and Problem Solving

Extra Practice, page 82, Set B

Find the sum. Estimate to check.

6. $\begin{array}{r} 321 \\ +268 \\ \hline \end{array}$

7. $\begin{array}{r} 4{,}505 \\ +1{,}828 \\ \hline \end{array}$

8. $\begin{array}{r} 268 \\ 173 \\ +368 \\ \hline \end{array}$

9. $\begin{array}{r} 415 \\ 561 \\ +246 \\ \hline \end{array}$

10. $\begin{array}{r} 309 \\ 299 \\ +\ 66 \\ \hline \end{array}$

11. $\begin{array}{r} 2{,}984 \\ +\ 325 \\ \hline \end{array}$

12. $\begin{array}{r} \$7.44 \\ +\$5.02 \\ \hline \end{array}$

13. $\begin{array}{r} 629 \\ +\ 67 \\ \hline \end{array}$

14. $\begin{array}{r} \$31.42 \\ +\$48.61 \\ \hline \end{array}$

15. $\begin{array}{r} 152 \\ +339 \\ \hline \end{array}$

Copy and complete each table.

	Add 152.	
16.	174	■
17.	319	■
18.	457	■

	Add 306.	
19.	565	■
20.	798	■
21.	824	■

	Add 2,547.	
22.	1,149	■
23.	2,845	■
24.	5,854	■

25. **What's the Question?** Eva read to page 112 in her book. There are 67 more pages in the book. The answer is 179 pages.

26. Sharon added 458 and 83. Was her answer greater than or less than 500? Explain how you know.

27. **ALGEBRA** Write the missing addend. 230 + ■ + 40 = 282

28. **ALGEBRA** Write the missing addend. 1,475 + ■ + 95 = 1,745

Mixed Review and Test Prep

29. 19 + 24 = ■ (p. 8)

30. 30 + 62 = ■ (p. 8)

31. Predict the next number in the pattern. Explain. (p. 30)
86, 81, 76, 71, 66

32. What is the value of the blue digit in 34,241? (p. 32)

33. **TEST PREP** 50 − 27 = ■ (p. 10)

A 21 **B** 23 **C** 32 **D** 37

LESSON 4

Problem Solving Strategy
Predict and Test

Quick Review

1. 21 + 6
2. 45 + 15
3. 9 + 36
4. 72 + 8
5. 12 + 13

PROBLEM The third-grade classes bought 75 containers of food for the animal shelter. They had 15 more cans than bags of food. How many bags and cans did the classes buy?

UNDERSTAND

- What are you asked to find?
- What information will you use?
- Is there any information you will not use?

PLAN

- What strategy can you use to solve the problem?

You can *predict and test* to find the number of bags and cans the classes bought.

SOLVE

- How can you use the strategy to solve the problem?

Predict the number of bags the classes bought. Add 15 to that number for the number of cans. Then test to see if the sum is 75.

BAGS	CANS	TOTAL	NOTES
20	20+15=35	20+35=55	too low
50	50+15=65	50+65=115	too high
30	30+15=45	30+45=75	just right

So, the classes bought 30 bags and 45 cans of food.

CHECK

- How can you use the first two predictions to make a better prediction?

Problem Solving Practice

Use *predict and test* to solve.

1. **What if** the classes bought 120 containers and had 30 more cans than bags? How many bags and how many cans did they buy?

2. Pilar has 170 stamps in her collection. Her first book of stamps has 30 more stamps in it than her second book. How many stamps are in each book?

Strategies

- Draw a Diagram or Picture
- Make a Model or Act It Out
- Make an Organized List
- Find a Pattern
- Make a Table or Graph
- **Predict and Test**
- Work Backward
- Solve a Simpler Problem
- Write a Number Sentence
- Use Logical Reasoning

Problem Solving

Two numbers have a sum of 27. Their difference is 3. What are the two numbers?

3. Which is a reasonable prediction for one of the numbers?

   A 3 **C** 27
   B 10 **D** 30

4. What solution answers the question?

   F 3 and 27 **H** 10 and 17
   G 10 and 13 **J** 12 and 15

Mixed Strategy Practice

USE DATA For 5–6, use the table.

5. The number of pounds used in Week 2 was greater than in Week 1, but less than in Week 3. The number of pounds used in Week 2 is an odd number that does not end in 5. How many pounds were used in Week 2?

6. **Write a problem** about the dog food used at the shelter in which the difference is greater than 5.

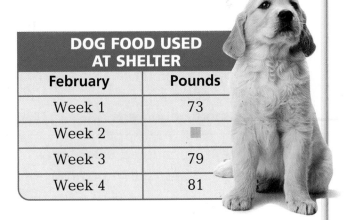

DOG FOOD USED AT SHELTER

February	Pounds
Week 1	73
Week 2	■
Week 3	79
Week 4	81

7. The sum of two numbers is 55. Their difference is 7. What are the numbers?

8. There are 4 students in line. Max is before Keiko but after Liz. Adam is fourth. Who is first?

LESSON 5

Choose a Method

Learn

You can find a sum by using paper and pencil, a calculator, or mental math.

PADDLE POWER Tom and Eli paddled from White Rock to Bear Corner to Raccoon Falls. How many yards did they paddle in all?

$$4{,}365 + 3{,}852 = \blacksquare$$

Estimate. $4{,}000 + 4{,}000 = 8{,}000$

Use Paper and Pencil The numbers are large. The problem involves regrouping. So, paper and pencil is a good choice.

STEP 1

Add the ones.

$$\begin{array}{r} 4{,}365 \\ +3{,}852 \\ \hline 7 \end{array}$$

STEP 2

Add the tens. Regroup. 11 tens = 1 hundred 1 ten

$$\begin{array}{r} \scriptstyle 1 \\ 4{,}365 \\ +3{,}852 \\ \hline 17 \end{array}$$

STEP 3

Add the hundreds. Regroup. 12 hundreds = 1 thousand 2 hundreds

$$\begin{array}{r} \scriptstyle 1\ 1 \\ 4{,}365 \\ +3{,}852 \\ \hline 217 \end{array}$$

STEP 4

Add the thousands.

$$\begin{array}{r} \scriptstyle 1\ 1 \\ 4{,}365 \\ +3{,}852 \\ \hline 8{,}217 \end{array}$$

So, Tom and Eli paddled 8,217 yards. Since 8,217 is close to the estimate of 8,000, the answer is reasonable.

Use a Calculator $4{,}365 + 3{,}852 + 3{,}978 = \blacksquare$

The numbers are large. The problem involves regrouping. So, a calculator is a good choice.

REASONING How can you estimate to check?

Quick Review

1. 350 + 40
2. 150 + 212
3. 560 + 161
4. 205 + 52
5. 90 + 215

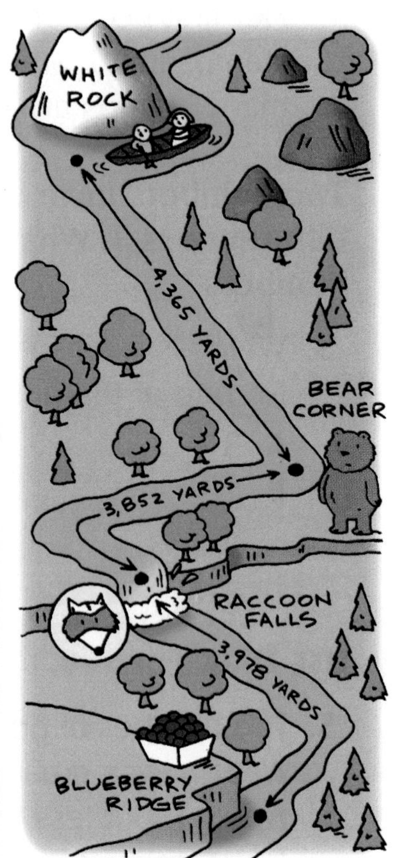

Use Mental Math

\$9.30 + \$5.60 = ■

There is no regrouping. You can add the dollar and cents amounts in your head. So, mental math is a good choice.

Think: Add the dollar amounts. \$9.00 + \$5.00 = \$14.00
Then add the cents. \$0.30 + \$0.60 = \$0.90
Find the sum. \$14.00 + \$0.90 = \$14.90

So, \$9.30 + \$5.60 = \$14.90.

Examples

A	**B**	**C**
$\begin{array}{r} {\scriptstyle 1\,1} \\ 373 \\ +497 \\ \hline 870 \end{array}$	$\begin{array}{r} {\scriptstyle 2\,1} \\ 2{,}094 \\ 167 \\ +5{,}041 \\ \hline 7{,}302 \end{array}$	$\begin{array}{r} \$5.10 \\ +\$2.20 \\ \hline \$7.30 \end{array}$

Technology Link
More Practice:
Harcourt Mega Math The Number Games, *Tiny's Think Tank,* Level B

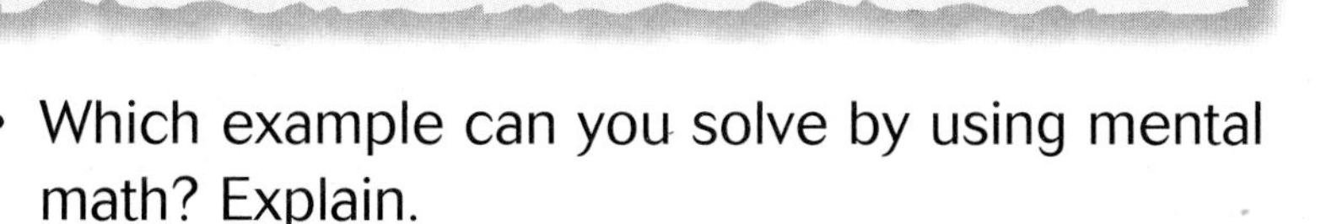

- Which example can you solve by using mental math? Explain.
- Which method would you choose to solve Example B? Explain.

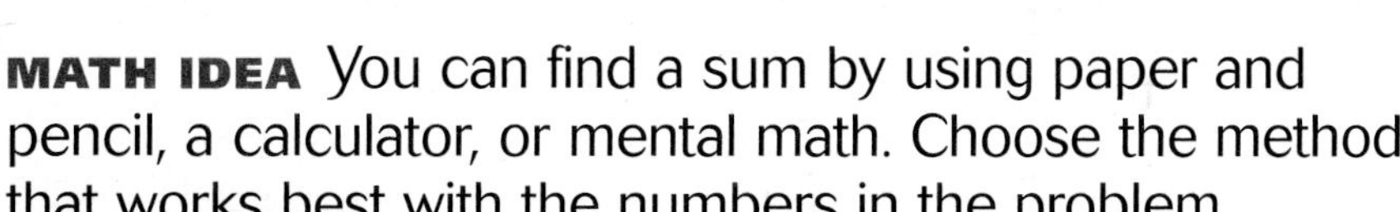

MATH IDEA You can find a sum by using paper and pencil, a calculator, or mental math. Choose the method that works best with the numbers in the problem.

Check

1. **Explain** how you can use mental math to add 747 and 242.

Find the sum. Tell what method you used.

2. $\begin{array}{r} 347 \\ +\ 91 \\ \hline \end{array}$ 3. $\begin{array}{r} 1{,}348 \\ +1{,}231 \\ \hline \end{array}$ 4. $\begin{array}{r} 919 \\ +489 \\ \hline \end{array}$ 5. $\begin{array}{r} 1{,}625 \\ +\ 350 \\ \hline \end{array}$ 6. $\begin{array}{r} \$5.80 \\ +\$5.25 \\ \hline \end{array}$

7. 1,032 + 5,198 = ■ 8. \$69.81 + \$23.11 = ■

9. 3,035 + 989 + 4,918 = ■ 10. 2,354 + 4,526 + 831 = ■

LESSON CONTINUES

Practice and Problem Solving

Extra Practice, page 82, Set C

Find the sum. Tell what method you used.

11. $709 + 226$ **12.** $\$2.78 + \$5.01$ **13.** $821 + 744$ **14.** $\$3.58 + \$2.65$

15. $259 + 74$ **16.** $458 + 221$ **17.** $\$7.35 + \$2.44$ **18.** $624 + 347$

19. $769 + 347$ **20.** $\$4.11 + \$3.48$ **21.** $641 + 989$ **22.** $329 + 110$

23. $5{,}492 + 1{,}205$ **24.** $1{,}895 + 1{,}700$ **25.** $9{,}294 + 2{,}104$ **26.** $2{,}164 + 6{,}235$

Find the sum. Explain your method.

27. 429 + 640 = ■ **28.** 565 + 424 = ■ **29.** \$14.40 + \$10.20 = ■

Use a calculator. Find the sum.

30. 1,647 + 897 + 3,467 = ■ **31.** \$12.79 + \$3.49 + \$6.98 = ■

32. NUMBER SENSE Write a number less than 3,425 + 8,630 but greater than 7,614 + 4,429.

33. ALGEBRA Write the missing addend. 4,020 + ■ = 4,222

34. ESTIMATION Allie estimates that 5,109 + 4,995 is about 1,000. Do you agree or disagree? Explain.

35. What's the Error? Sergio used paper and pencil to find this sum. Describe his error. Find the sum.

```
  1 11
 8,235
+  986
 9,211
```

36. USE DATA Use the price list. If Craig mows and rakes 2 lawns, has he earned more than \$20? Explain how you know.

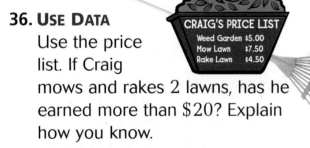

CRAIG'S PRICE LIST	
Weed Garden	\$5.00
Mow Lawn	\$7.50
Rake Lawn	\$4.50

37. Vocabulary Power The root of the word *calculator* is the Greek word *kalyx*, which means "pebble or small stone." Small stones were once counted to find sums. When do you use a calculator to find sums?

38. FAST FACT • SOCIAL STUDIES Volunteers raise Canine Companion puppies until they are about 18 months old. Use a calculator to find how many weeks this is.

39. Can you add two 3-digit numbers and get a sum greater than 2,000? Explain.

Mixed Review and Test Prep

40. $6 + 8 + 4 = ■$ (p. 6)

41. $24 + 36 + 19 = ■$ (p. 8)

42. $\$15.76 + \$22.19 + \$3.00 = ■$ (p. 72)

Choose <, >, or = for each ●. (p. 42)

43. $305 + 281$ ● 550

44. $416 + 966$ ● $1,600$

45. $223 + 100$ ● $50 + 50 + 223$

46. **TEST PREP** The sum of two numbers is 20. The difference of the numbers is 10. What are the numbers? (p. 74)

A 10, 10 C 12, 8
B 20, 10 D 15, 5

For 47, use the graph.

FAVORITE SEASONS

Summer	☼ ☼ ☼ ☼ ☼
Winter	☼ ☼ ☼
Spring	☼ ☼ ☼ ☼
Fall	☼ ☼

Key: Each ☼ = 2 votes.

47. **TEST PREP** How many students did NOT vote for summer?

F 12 G 18 H 20 J 24

Problem Solving Thinker's Corner

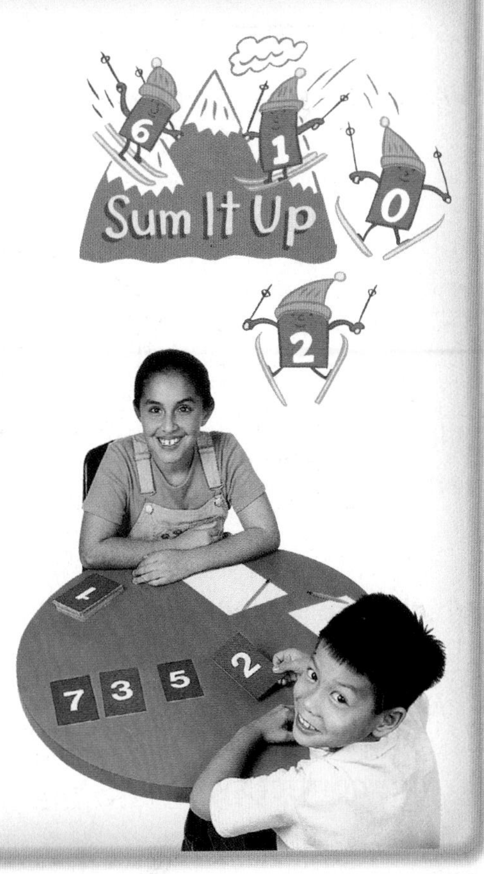

Try to make a greater sum than your partner's.

MATERIALS: index cards numbered 0–9

- Player 1 chooses 4 cards and uses the digits to write two different 4-digit addends. Each digit should be used twice. Player 1 replaces the cards.
- Player 2 repeats the first step.
- Both players find the sum. The player with the greater sum wins. Play this game several times. See if you can find a winning strategy.
- Repeat this game. Try to make the lesser sum.

1. When making the greater sum, where is the best place to put a 9?
2. When making the lesser sum, where is the best place to put a 9?

LESSON 6

Algebra: Expressions and Number Sentences

Quick Review

1. 14 + 14
2. 12 + 21
3. 42 + 25
4. 90 + 18
5. 25 + 49

VOCABULARY

expression
not equal to ≠

Learn

LUNCH LINE In the morning, visitors bought 34 packets of food for the animals in the petting zoo. In the afternoon, visitors bought 58 packets. How many food packets were bought in all?

You can write an expression for this problem. An **expression** is part of a number sentence. It combines numbers and operation signs. It does not have an equal sign.

$34 + 58$ is the expression that models the problem.

$34 + 58 = 92$ is a number sentence.

Visitors bought 92 food packets in all.

 **MATH IDEA** A number sentence can be true or false.

$4 + 3 = 7$ is true. $4 - 3 = 7$ is false.

Another way to show that $4 - 3$ does not equal 7 is to write $4 - 3 \neq 7$.

The ≠ is a symbol that means "**not equal to**."

Mike spent $12 for a cap and $18 for a shirt at the petting zoo. How much more did the shirt cost?

$18 ● $12 = $6

Which symbol will make the sentence *true*?

Try +. $18 + $12 = $6 False or $18 + $12 ≠ $6.
Try −. $18 − $12 = $6 **True**.

So, the correct symbol is −.

Check

For 1–2, write an expression. Then write a number sentence to solve.

1. Takeo had 273 cards. He gave away 35. How many cards does he have left?

2. Mia had 13 apples. She bought 7 more. How many does she have in all?

Write + or – to complete the number sentence.

3. $12 \bullet 2 = 10$ 4. $37 \bullet 11 \neq 40$ 5. $126 \bullet 79 = 47$ 6. $367 \bullet 43 = 410$

Practice and Problem Solving

Extra Practice, page 82, Set D

For 7–8, write an expression. Then write a number sentence to solve.

7. Gwen bought 12 red pencils, 2 blue pencils, and 22 yellow pencils. How many blue and red pencils did she buy?

8. Ned has 17 crayons. He has 15 pens. How many more crayons than pens does he have?

Write + or – to complete the number sentence.

9. $4 \bullet 3 = 1$
10. $28 \bullet 9 = 37$
11. $329 \bullet 87 = 222 + 20$
12. $559 \bullet 50 = 609$
13. $74 \bullet 47 = 17 + 10$
14. $444 \bullet 6 \neq 460 - 10$

Write the missing number.

15. $\blacksquare + 3 = 14$
16. $140 + 5 = \blacksquare$
17. $45 - \blacksquare = 25$
18. $309 - \blacksquare = 209$
19. $215 - \blacksquare = 120$
20. $\blacksquare - 125 = 318$

21. **Reasoning** Blair says, "$12 + 3 + 1 = 19 - 3$ is a true number sentence." Do you agree or disagree? Explain.

22. **Reasoning** Use the numbers 5, 9, and 14. Write two true number sentences—one using the equal sign and one using the not equal sign.

Mixed Review and Test Prep

Find each sum. (p. 8)

23.
```
  64
  91
 +26
```

24.
```
  15
  73
 +22
```

25.
```
  41
  66
 +19
```

26. Find $85 - 37$. (p. 10)

27. **TEST PREP** Benjy had 62 marbles. He gave 15 to Lisa, 14 to Lenny, and 9 to Jake. He kept the rest. Who has the most marbles? (pp. 8, 10)

A Lisa
B Lenny
C Benjy
D Jake

Extra Practice

Set A (pp. 68–69)

Use rounding to estimate the sum.

1. $611 + 323$
2. $248 + 174$
3. $\$5.63 + \$4.27$
4. $1,659 + 2,205$
5. $2,798 + 4,568$

Use front-end estimation to estimate the sum.

6. $645 + 594$
7. $584 + 248$
8. $560 + 439$
9. $2,375 + 4,082$
10. $6,757 + 4,446$

Set B (pp. 72–73)

Find the sum. Estimate to check.

1. $365 + 521$
2. $789 + 123$
3. $4,978 + 2,234$
4. $\$3.29 + \$5.75$
5. $368 + 919 + 453$

Set C (pp. 76–79)

Find the sum. Tell what method you used.

1. $310 + 470$
2. $\$8.40 + \$5.80$
3. $618 + 143$
4. $6,247 + 2,319$
5. $3,485 + 9,856$

6. Estimate to decide if the sum 1,874 + 3,205 is greater than 4,000. Explain your answer.

7. ALGEBRA Write the missing addend. 4,000 + ■ = 5,100

Set D (pp. 80–81)

Write + or – to complete the number sentence.

1. 8 ■ 15 = 23
2. 95 ■ 16 = 79
3. 517 ■ 483 = 1,000
4. 35 = 29 ■ 6
5. 42 ■ 9 = 51
6. 27 ■ 4 = 23

7. Shelby had \$18.50. She spent \$7.25 at the car wash. Write an expression that shows how much she spent.

Review/Test

✓ CHECK VOCABULARY AND CONCEPTS

Choose the best term from the box.

regroup estimate front-end estimation

1. To find *about* how many, you can ?. (p. 68)
2. When you estimate a sum by adding the front digit of each addend, you are using ?. (p. 68)

For 3, think of how to model 129 + 138. (pp. 70–71)

3. Do you need to regroup to find the sum 129 + 138? Explain.

✓ CHECK SKILLS

For 4–5, use rounding to estimate the sum. For 6–7, use front-end estimation to estimate the sum. (pp. 68–69)

4. $\begin{array}{r} 267 \\ +193 \\ \hline \end{array}$
5. $\begin{array}{r} \$5.92 \\ +\$3.25 \\ \hline \end{array}$
6. $\begin{array}{r} 420 \\ +589 \\ \hline \end{array}$
7. $\begin{array}{r} 6,528 \\ +1,347 \\ \hline \end{array}$

Find the sum. Estimate to check. (pp. 72–73, 76–79)

8. 419 + 451 = ■
9. 321 + 683 = ■
10. 127 + 315 + 299 = ■
11. $\begin{array}{r} \$6.33 \\ +\$2.98 \\ \hline \end{array}$
12. $\begin{array}{r} 5,436 \\ +7,695 \\ \hline \end{array}$
13. $\begin{array}{r} 4,782 \\ +3,917 \\ \hline \end{array}$
14. $\begin{array}{r} 3,764 \\ +8,109 \\ \hline \end{array}$

Write + or – to complete the number sentence. (pp. 80–81)

15. 58 ● 12 = 46
16. 42 ● 67 = 109
17. 845 ● 369 = 476
18. 92 = 165 ● 73

✓ CHECK PROBLEM SOLVING

19. Mr. Samuel has 150 pennies in two jars. There are 40 more pennies in one jar than in the other. How many pennies are in each jar? (pp. 74–75)
20. Two numbers have a sum of 47. Their difference is 5. What are the two numbers? (pp. 74–75)

Standardized Test Prep

NUMBER SENSE, CONCEPTS, AND OPERATIONS

Eliminate choices. See item 1. Look at the thousands place first. Eliminate any choices whose digits are greatest.

1. Ted wants to order these numbers from **least** to **greatest**.

   2,879; 3,798; 2,897

   What should he write?

   A 3,798; 2,897; 2,879
   B 2,897; 2,879; 3,798
   C 2,879; 2,897; 3,798
   D 2,879; 3,798; 2,897

2. Which number can be written as 400 + 10 + 3?

   F 431 **H** 314
   G 413 **J** 143

3. Which is fifty thousand three written in standard form?

   A 50,003 **C** 50,033
   B 53,000 **D** 50,300

4. **Explain It** The Oakdale Band has to sell 1,500 raffle tickets to buy new uniforms. Last week, band members sold 768 raffle tickets. They sold 622 tickets this week. Explain how you can estimate whether the band has sold enough tickets to buy the uniforms.

MEASUREMENT

5. What is another way to write the time?

   F six-thirty
   G 25 minutes after 6
   H half past 5
   J 5:25

6. What unit of measure would be most appropriate to determine the length of a crayon?

   A inch
   B cup
   C pound
   D gallon

7. What unit of measure would be most appropriate to determine the weight of a pencil?

   F meter **H** gram
   G liter **J** kilogram

8. **Explain It** A jar of coins contains 7 quarters, 11 dimes, and 18 nickels. About how much money is in the jar? Explain how you estimated the total.

ALGEBRAIC THINKING

9. Which are the next two figures in this pattern?

□□△□□△□□△□ ? ?

A □△

B △△

C □□

D △□

10. On Monday, Griffin's class sold 6 tickets for the fall festival. On Tuesday, the students sold 12 tickets. On Wednesday, 18 tickets were sold. If this pattern continues, how many tickets will be sold on Friday?

F 20
G 22
H 24
J 30

11. **Explain It** Laura wants to know how much it will cost to buy four tickets to the fall festival. Explain how she can find the cost.

FALL FESTIVAL TICKETS	
Number of Tickets	**Cost**
1	\$7.00
2	\$14.00
3	\$21.00
4	■

DATA ANALYSIS AND PROBABILITY

12. The table shows the number of books students in Kareem's book club have read.

NUMBER OF BOOKS READ	
Number of Books	**Number of Students**
6	𝍸 |
7	𝍸 ||||
8	𝍸 ||
9	|||

What is the range of the number of books read?

A 1 **C** 3
B 2 **D** 4

13. Use the table above. How many more students read 6 or 7 books than read 8 or 9 books?

F 1 **H** 6
G 5 **J** 7

14. **Explain It** The bar graph below shows the favorite winter sports of Tamara's classmates. How many more students voted for snowboarding than skiing? Explain how you found your answer.

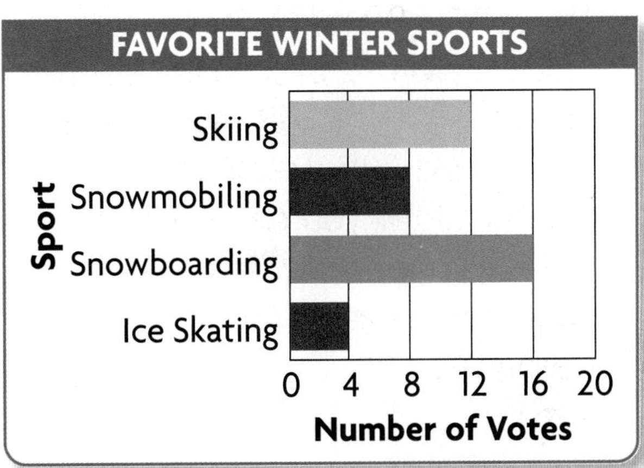

CHAPTER 5

Subtraction

FAST FACT • SOCIAL STUDIES The Appalachian Trail is over 2,100 miles long. It goes through 14 states from Maine to Georgia. It would take an experienced hiker about 180 days to travel from one end to the other.

PROBLEM SOLVING The table shows how many miles of the Trail are in each state. How many more miles are in Virginia than in Vermont?

APPALACHIAN TRAIL

State	Number of Miles
Maine	281
New Hampshire	161
Vermont	146
Massachusetts	90
Connecticut	52
New York	88
New Jersey	74
Pennsylvania	232
Maryland	41
West Virginia	2
Virginia	544
Tennessee	88
North Carolina	292
Georgia	75

CHECK WHAT YOU KNOW

Use this page to help you review and remember important skills needed for Chapter 5.

SUBTRACTION FACTS

1. $\begin{array}{r} 12 \\ -\ 9 \\ \hline \end{array}$ **2.** $\begin{array}{r} 15 \\ -\ 7 \\ \hline \end{array}$ **3.** $\begin{array}{r} 12 \\ -\ 8 \\ \hline \end{array}$ **4.** $\begin{array}{r} 14 \\ -\ 6 \\ \hline \end{array}$ **5.** $\begin{array}{r} 13 \\ -\ 5 \\ \hline \end{array}$

6. $\begin{array}{r} 13 \\ -\ 7 \\ \hline \end{array}$ **7.** $\begin{array}{r} 14 \\ -\ 9 \\ \hline \end{array}$ **8.** $\begin{array}{r} 12 \\ -\ 7 \\ \hline \end{array}$ **9.** $\begin{array}{r} 13 \\ -\ 4 \\ \hline \end{array}$ **10.** $\begin{array}{r} 16 \\ -\ 7 \\ \hline \end{array}$

11. $\begin{array}{r} 15 \\ -\ 6 \\ \hline \end{array}$ **12.** $\begin{array}{r} 18 \\ -\ 9 \\ \hline \end{array}$ **13.** $\begin{array}{r} 17 \\ -\ 8 \\ \hline \end{array}$ **14.** $\begin{array}{r} 16 \\ -\ 9 \\ \hline \end{array}$ **15.** $\begin{array}{r} 14 \\ -\ 7 \\ \hline \end{array}$

2-DIGIT SUBTRACTION

Subtract.

16. $\begin{array}{r} 56 \\ -\ 4 \\ \hline \end{array}$ **17.** $\begin{array}{r} 49 \\ -36 \\ \hline \end{array}$ **18.** $\begin{array}{r} 67 \\ -15 \\ \hline \end{array}$ **19.** $\begin{array}{r} 95 \\ -50 \\ \hline \end{array}$ **20.** $\begin{array}{r} 38 \\ -\ 9 \\ \hline \end{array}$

21. $\begin{array}{r} 33 \\ -18 \\ \hline \end{array}$ **22.** $\begin{array}{r} 90 \\ -48 \\ \hline \end{array}$ **23.** $\begin{array}{r} 98 \\ -17 \\ \hline \end{array}$ **24.** $\begin{array}{r} 57 \\ -27 \\ \hline \end{array}$ **25.** $\begin{array}{r} 25 \\ -19 \\ \hline \end{array}$

VOCABULARY POWER

REVIEW

subtract [səb•trakt′] *verb*

The word *subtract* begins with *sub*, which means "under" or "below." The second part of the word, *tract*, means "to pull" or "to carry away." What word beginning with the word part *tract* names a machine that is used to pull or to carry?

www.harcourtschool.com/mathglossary

LESSON 1

Estimate Differences

Quick Review

1. 50 − 30
2. 40 − 10
3. 35 − 10
4. 60 − 20
5. 50 − 40

Learn

TRACKING TURTLES Scientists counted the number of loggerhead sea turtle nests found on southwest Florida beaches in 2001. About how many more nests were counted on Charlotte County beaches than on Manatee County beaches?

LOGGERHEAD SEA TURTLE NESTS

County	Nests Found
Charlotte	775
Collier	954
Lee	660
Manatee	306

To find *about* how many more, you can estimate.

Example

One Way Use rounding. Round each number to the nearest hundred. Subtract.

$$\begin{array}{rcr} 775 & \rightarrow & 800 \\ -306 & \rightarrow & -300 \\ \hline & & 500 \end{array}$$

Another Way Use front-end estimation. Subtract, using the front digit of each number. Write zeros for the other digits.

$$\begin{array}{rcr} 775 & \rightarrow & 700 \\ -306 & \rightarrow & -300 \\ \hline & & 400 \end{array}$$

So, both 500 and 400 are reasonable estimates of how many more nests were counted.

More Examples

 Round to the nearest dollar.

$$\begin{array}{rcr} \$8.95 & \rightarrow & \$9 \\ -\$3.35 & \rightarrow & -\$3 \\ \hline & & \$6 \end{array}$$

B Use front-end estimation.

$$\begin{array}{rcr} 6{,}860 & \rightarrow & 6{,}000 \\ -4{,}655 & \rightarrow & -4{,}000 \\ \hline & & 2{,}000 \end{array}$$

Sometimes it makes sense to round to a different place. Try estimating 341 − 265 to the nearest hundred.

$$\begin{array}{rcr} 341 & \rightarrow & 300 \\ -265 & \rightarrow & -300 \\ \hline & & 0 \end{array}$$

Then round to the nearest ten to get a closer estimate.

$$\begin{array}{rcr} 341 & \rightarrow & 340 \\ -265 & \rightarrow & -270 \\ \hline & & 70 \end{array}$$

Check

1. **Explain** how you would estimate 201 − 181. Tell which method you chose and why.

For 2–4, use rounding to estimate the difference. For 5–6, use front-end estimation to estimate the difference.

2. $87 - 32$ **3.** $478 - 115$ **4.** $\$9.01 - \$2.60$ **5.** $813 - 491$ **6.** $5{,}020 - 1{,}750$

Practice and Problem Solving

Extra Practice, page 104, Set A

Use rounding to estimate the difference.

7. $42 - 19$ **8.** $613 - 371$ **9.** $\$7.08 - \$3.80$ **10.** $625 - 489$ **11.** $4{,}819 - 1{,}966$

Use front-end estimation to estimate the difference.

12. $84 - 23$ **13.** $880 - 114$ **14.** $322 - 199$ **15.** $\$5.17 - \$1.01$ **16.** $3{,}288 - 1{,}255$

Estimate the difference. Round to the place that makes sense.

17. $422 - 394$ **18.** $302 - 277$ **19.** $4{,}411 - 3{,}509$

20. Look at the table. How many loggerhead turtles weigh about the same as one leatherback turtle? Explain.

21. Write a problem using estimation and subtraction. Use the table at the right. Tell which method you would use to estimate the difference. Explain your choice.

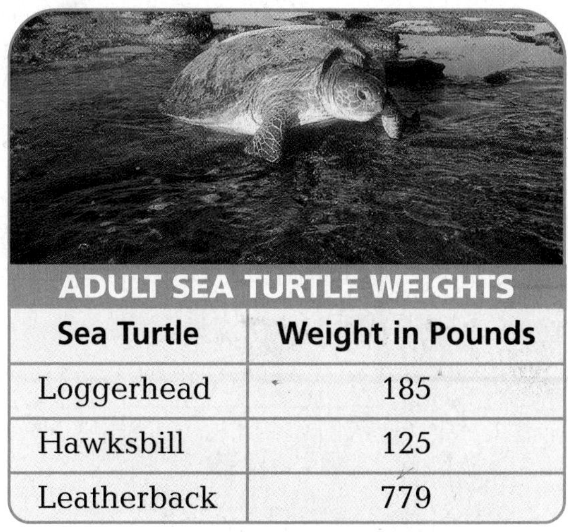

ADULT SEA TURTLE WEIGHTS

Sea Turtle	Weight in Pounds
Loggerhead	185
Hawksbill	125
Leatherback	779

Mixed Review and Test Prep

Write the value of the blue digit. (pp. 24, 32)

22. 2,051 **23.** 1,321

24. 37,820 **25.** 52,902

26. TEST PREP Amy had 34 shells. On Friday she found more and had a total of 45 shells. How many shells did she find on Friday? (p. 10)

A 9 **B** 11 **C** 55 **D** 79

LESSON 2

Subtraction with Regrouping

Quick Review

1. 30 − 20
2. 120 − 10
3. 62 − 32
4. 92 − 31
5. 35 − 15

MATERIALS
base-ten blocks

Explore

Use models to subtract 195 from 324.

$$\begin{array}{r} 324 \\ -195 \\ \hline \end{array}$$

Example 1

STEP 1

Show 324.

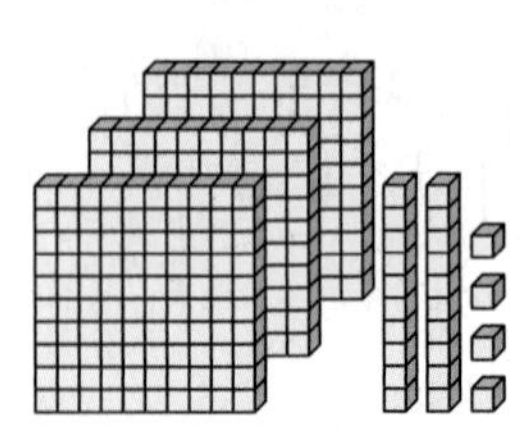

STEP 2

Try to subtract 5 ones. Since there are not enough ones, regroup 1 ten as 10 ones. Subtract 5 ones from 14 ones.

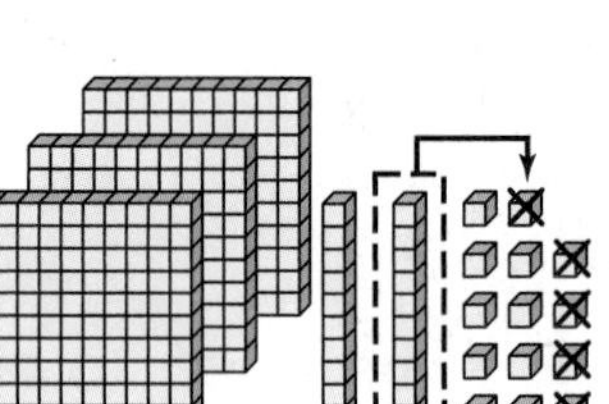

STEP 3

Try to subtract 9 tens. Since there are not enough tens, regroup 1 hundred as 10 tens. Subtract 9 tens from 11 tens.

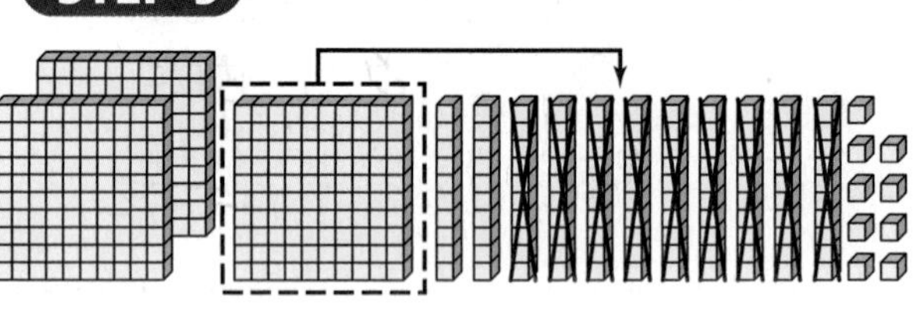

STEP 4

Subtract 1 hundred.

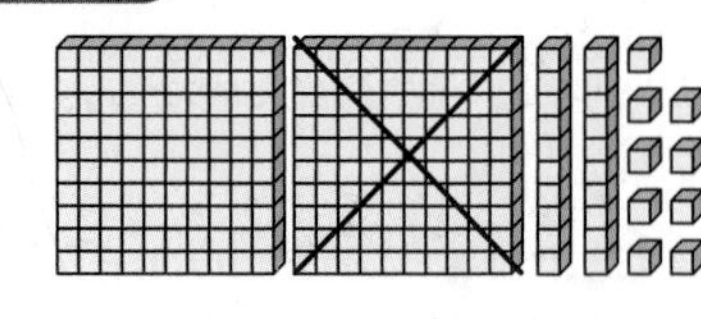

So, 324 − 195 = 129.

- **Explain** why you regroup 1 ten as 10 ones in Step 2.

Try It

Use base-ten blocks. Draw a picture to show the difference.

a. 181 − 93 = ■ **b.** 360 − 149 = ■

We are subtracting 93 from 181. We regrouped 8 tens 1 one as 7 tens 11 ones. What should we do next?

Connect

Here is a way to record subtraction. To subtract 126 from 215, first line up the hundreds, tens, and ones.

Technology Link

More Practice: Harcourt Mega Math Country Countdown, *Block Busters,* Levels Y and Z

Example 2

STEP 1

Subtract the ones. 6 > 5
Regroup.
1 ten 5 ones =
0 tens 15 ones

$$\begin{array}{r} \scriptstyle 0\ 15 \\ 2\ \not{1}\ \not{5} \\ -1\ 2\ 6 \\ \hline 9 \end{array}$$

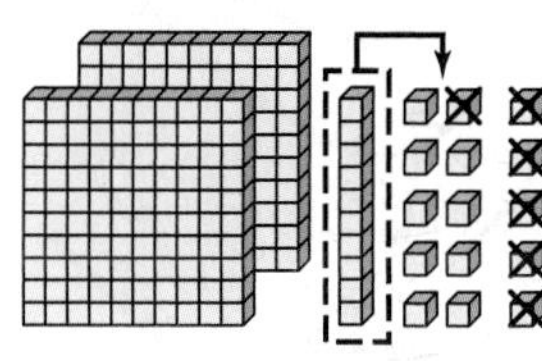

STEP 2

Subtract the tens. 2 > 0
Regroup.
2 hundreds 0 tens =
1 hundred 10 tens

$$\begin{array}{r} \scriptstyle 10 \\ \scriptstyle 1\ \not{0}\ 15 \\ \not{2}\ \not{1}\ \not{5} \\ -1\ 2\ 6 \\ \hline 8\ 9 \end{array}$$

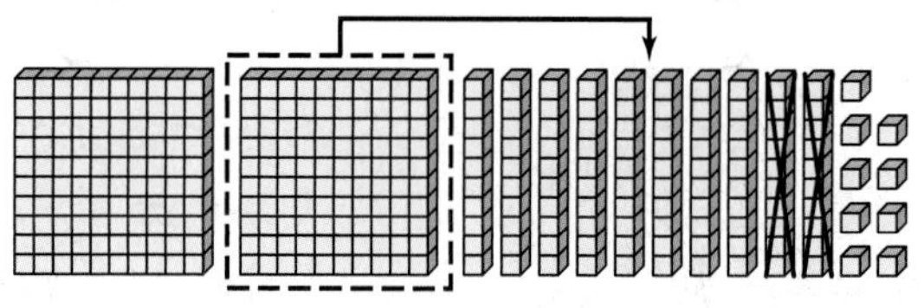

STEP 3

Subtract the hundreds.

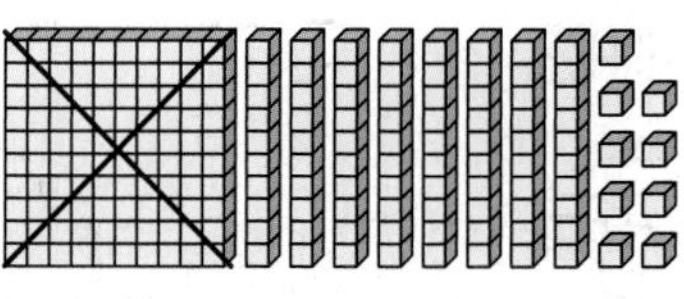

$$\begin{array}{r} \scriptstyle 10 \\ \scriptstyle 1\ \not{0}\ 15 \\ \not{2}\ \not{1}\ \not{5} \\ -1\ 2\ 6 \\ \hline 8\ 9 \end{array}$$

Practice and Problem Solving

Use base-ten blocks. Draw a picture to show the difference.

1. 94 − 28 = ■　　**2.** 212 − 123 = ■　　**3.** 437 − 243 = ■

4. 183 − 159 = ■　　**5.** 329 − 87 = ■　　**6.** 223 − 135 = ■

7. REASONING There are 32 more apples than oranges at a fruit stand. How many apples and oranges could there be?

Mixed Review and Test Prep

8. 14 − ■ = 9 (p. 4)　　**9.** 17 − ■ = 9 (p. 4)

10. ■ + 7 = 13 (p. 4)　　**11.** 8 + ■ = 15 (p. 4)

12. TEST PREP 3 + (8 + 12) (p. 6)

A 11　　**C** 23
B 20　　**D** 26

LESSON 3

Subtract Across Zeros

Quick Review

1. 12 − 5
2. 16 − 9
3. 11 − 7
4. 15 − 6
5. 15 − 8

Learn

TURTLE TALK After Hurricane Michelle, many green sea turtles that had escaped from the Cayman Turtle Farm were recaptured. One male weighed 300 pounds. One female weighed 226 pounds. How much more did the male weigh than the female?

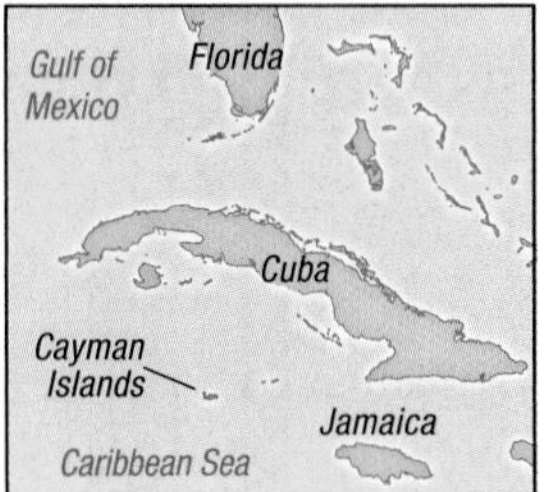

Subtract. 300 − 226 = ■

Estimate.

$$\begin{array}{r} 300 \\ -226 \\ \hline \end{array} \rightarrow \begin{array}{r} 300 \\ -200 \\ \hline 100 \end{array}$$

▲ About 15,000 turtles live at the Cayman Turtle Farm.

Example 1

STEP 1

6 > 0. Since there are 0 tens, regroup hundreds.
3 hundreds 0 tens = 2 hundreds 10 tens

$$\begin{array}{r} {\scriptstyle 2\ 10} \\ \not{3}\,\not{0}\,0 \\ -2\,2\,6 \\ \hline \end{array}$$

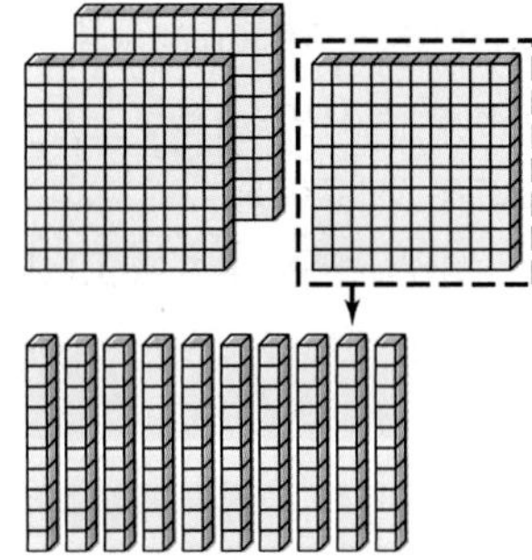

STEP 2

There are 0 ones, so regroup tens.
10 tens 0 ones = 9 tens 10 ones

$$\begin{array}{r} {\scriptstyle 9} \\ {\scriptstyle 2\ \not{10}\ 10} \\ \not{3}\,\not{0}\,\not{0} \\ -2\,2\,6 \\ \hline \end{array}$$

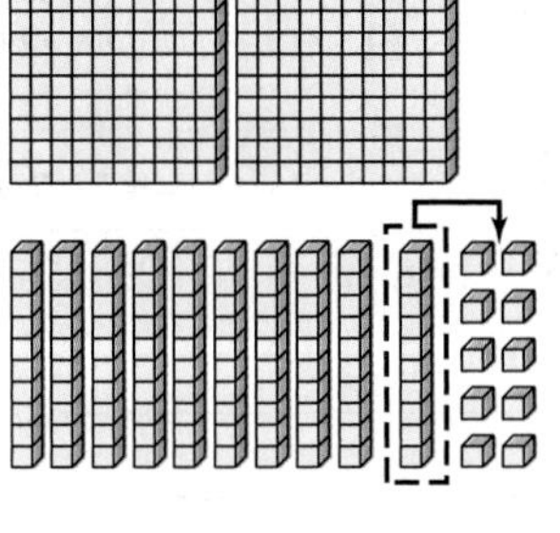

STEP 3

Subtract the ones.
Subtract the tens.
Subtract the hundreds.

$$\begin{array}{r} {\scriptstyle 9} \\ {\scriptstyle 2\ \not{10}\ 10} \\ \not{3}\,\not{0}\,\not{0} \\ -2\,2\,6 \\ \hline 74 \end{array}$$

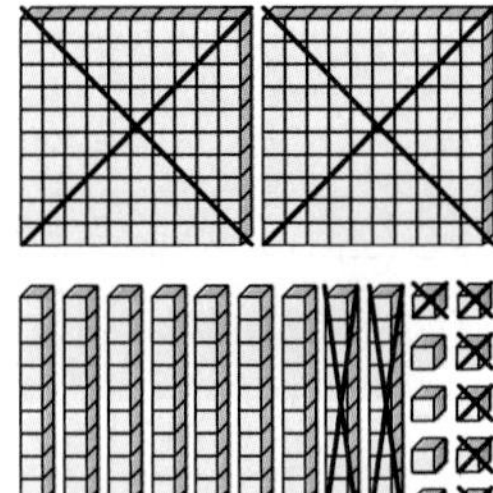

So, the male weighed 74 pounds more than the female. Since 74 is close to the estimate 100, the answer is reasonable.

More 3-Digit Subtraction

Another captured female green sea turtle weighed 332 pounds. Another captured male weighed 198 pounds. How much more did the female turtle weigh?

Subtract. $332 - 198 = \blacksquare$

Estimate.

$$\begin{array}{r} 332 \\ -198 \\ \hline \end{array} \rightarrow \begin{array}{r} 330 \\ -200 \\ \hline 130 \end{array}$$

Example 2

STEP 1

Subtract the ones.
8 > 2
Regroup.
3 tens 2 ones =
2 tens 12 ones

$$\begin{array}{r} {\scriptstyle 2\ 12} \\ 3\,\not3\,\not2 \\ -1\,9\,8 \\ \hline 4 \end{array}$$

STEP 2

Subtract the tens.
9 > 2
Regroup.
3 hundreds 2 tens =
2 hundreds 12 tens

$$\begin{array}{r} {\scriptstyle 12} \\ {\scriptstyle 2\ \ \not2\ 12} \\ \not3\,\not3\,\not2 \\ -1\,9\,8 \\ \hline 3\,4 \end{array}$$

STEP 3

Subtract the hundreds.

$$\begin{array}{r} {\scriptstyle 12} \\ {\scriptstyle 2\ \ \not2\ 12} \\ \not3\,\not3\,\not2 \\ -1\,9\,8 \\ \hline 1\,3\,4 \end{array}$$

So, the female weighed 134 pounds more than the male.
Since 134 is close to 130, the answer is reasonable.

More Examples

A

$$\begin{array}{r} {\scriptstyle 9} \\ {\scriptstyle 1\ \not10\ 14} \\ \not2\,\not0\,\not4 \\ -\ \ 8\,7 \\ \hline 1\,1\,7 \end{array}$$

B

$$\begin{array}{r} {\scriptstyle 9} \\ {\scriptstyle 7\ \not10\ 16} \\ \not8\,\not0\,\not6 \\ -6\,5\,9 \\ \hline 1\,4\,7 \end{array}$$

ADD TO CHECK ✓

$$\begin{array}{r} 147 \\ +659 \\ \hline 806 \end{array}$$

C

dollar sign ↓

$$\begin{array}{r} {\scriptstyle 9} \\ {\scriptstyle 4\ \not10\ 13} \\ \$\not5.\,\not0\,\not3 \\ -\$1.\,2\,4 \\ \hline \$3.\,7\,9 \end{array}$$

↑ decimal point

- Subtract money like whole numbers.
- Use a decimal point to separate the dollars and cents.

Check

1. **Explain** why 9 is written above the crossed-out 10 in Example B.

LESSON CONTINUES

Find the difference. Estimate to check.

2. $\begin{array}{r} 300 \\ -\ 84 \\ \hline \end{array}$
3. $\begin{array}{r} \$4.00 \\ -\$2.83 \\ \hline \end{array}$
4. $\begin{array}{r} 595 \\ -242 \\ \hline \end{array}$
5. $\begin{array}{r} 336 \\ -191 \\ \hline \end{array}$
6. $\begin{array}{r} 607 \\ -349 \\ \hline \end{array}$

Practice and Problem Solving

Extra Practice, page 104, Set B

Find the difference. Estimate to check.

7. $\begin{array}{r} 574 \\ -412 \\ \hline \end{array}$
8. $\begin{array}{r} 504 \\ -250 \\ \hline \end{array}$
9. $\begin{array}{r} 438 \\ -119 \\ \hline \end{array}$
10. $\begin{array}{r} 600 \\ -\ 68 \\ \hline \end{array}$
11. $\begin{array}{r} \$9.63 \\ -\$4.05 \\ \hline \end{array}$
12. $\begin{array}{r} 294 \\ -137 \\ \hline \end{array}$
13. $\begin{array}{r} 891 \\ -\ 86 \\ \hline \end{array}$
14. $\begin{array}{r} \$6.57 \\ -\$4.98 \\ \hline \end{array}$
15. $\begin{array}{r} 372 \\ -196 \\ \hline \end{array}$
16. $\begin{array}{r} 703 \\ -217 \\ \hline \end{array}$
17. $\begin{array}{r} 800 \\ -585 \\ \hline \end{array}$
18. $\begin{array}{r} 548 \\ -439 \\ \hline \end{array}$
19. $\begin{array}{r} \$7.00 \\ -\$2.11 \\ \hline \end{array}$
20. $\begin{array}{r} 805 \\ -\ 99 \\ \hline \end{array}$
21. $\begin{array}{r} \$9.06 \\ -\$4.08 \\ \hline \end{array}$
22. $\begin{array}{r} 354 \\ -\ 88 \\ \hline \end{array}$
23. $\begin{array}{r} 942 \\ -817 \\ \hline \end{array}$
24. $\begin{array}{r} 647 \\ -435 \\ \hline \end{array}$
25. $\begin{array}{r} 461 \\ -178 \\ \hline \end{array}$
26. $\begin{array}{r} 704 \\ -536 \\ \hline \end{array}$

Subtract. Use addition to check.

27. $900 - 312 = \blacksquare$
28. $308 - 149 = \blacksquare$
29. $604 - 485 = \blacksquare$
30. $401 - 173 = \blacksquare$
31. $304 - 255 = \blacksquare$
32. $300 - 92 = \blacksquare$

33. **ALGEBRA** Write the missing addend. $255 + \blacksquare = 305$

34. **What's the Error?** Michael wrote a subtraction problem like this. Describe his error. Find the difference.

$$\begin{array}{r} {\scriptstyle 16} \\ 2\not{6}1 \\ -170 \\ \hline 191 \end{array}$$

35. Sherrie is thinking of a number. It is 128 less than 509. What number is she thinking of?

36. **REASONING** Do you have to regroup to find $204 - 125$? Explain.

USE DATA For 37–38, use the graph.

37. How much do Tyson, Biggie, and Sparky weigh altogether?

38. If Tyson gained 75 pounds, how much more would he weigh than Sparky?

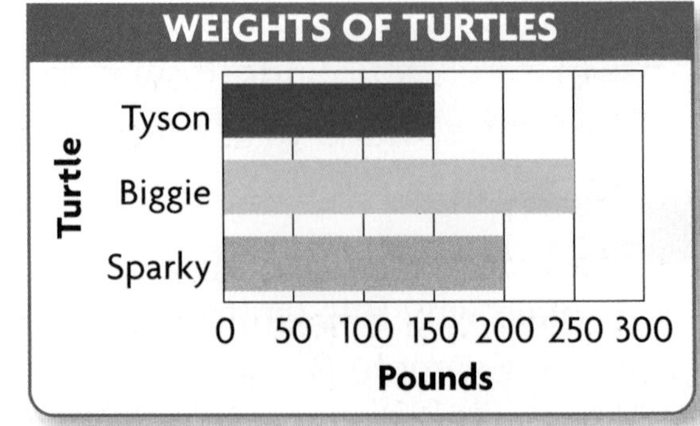

Mixed Review and Test Prep

Write <, >, or = for each ●. (p. 42)

39. 72 ● 27

40. 321 ● 213

41. (p. 10) $66 - 32$

42. (p. 72) $148 + 134$

43. (p. 72) $399 + 722$

44. TEST PREP Find 95 + 37. (p. 8)

- A 58
- B 122
- C 132
- D 300

45. Carlos found 112 green bottles, 115 soda cans, and 129 plastic cups. How many cups and cans did he find? (p. 72)

46. (p. 72) $182 + 28$

47. (p. 72) $325 + 149$

48. (p. 72) $456 + 344$

49. TEST PREP What is the value of the 8 in 185,413? (p. 32)

- F 800
- G 8,000
- H 80,000
- J 800,000

Problem Solving LINKUP . . . to Science

Turtles are the only reptiles with shells. A turtle can pull its head, legs, and tail into its shell. The female turtle digs a hole on land, lays her eggs, and covers them. The heat from the sun hatches the eggs.

1. There are about 250 kinds of turtles. About 60 kinds live in the United States and in Canada. About how many kinds don't live in the United States and Canada?

2. One of the largest green sea turtles ever measured weighed 871 pounds. If a green sea turtle weighs 395 pounds, how much heavier is the largest green sea turtle?

3. If a flatback sea turtle swam 752 miles in the spring and 374 miles in the summer, how much farther did the turtle swim in the spring?

4. If a leatherback sea turtle traveled 989 miles one year and 873 miles the next year, how far did it travel in the two years?

LESSON 

Subtract 3- and 4-Digit Numbers

Quick Review

Use rounding to estimate the difference.

1. 363 − 140 **2.** 515 − 272

3. 704 − 451 **4.** 281 − 165

5. 492 − 384

Learn

WALK OR RIDE? If you hiked the Appalachian National Scenic Trail, you would hike 2,167 miles. The driving distance from one end to the other along roads and highways is 1,377 miles. How many more miles is it to hike than to drive?

Subtract. 2,167 − 1,377 = ■

Estimate.

$$\begin{array}{r} 2{,}167 \\ -1{,}377 \\ \hline \end{array} \rightarrow \begin{array}{r} 2{,}000 \\ -1{,}000 \\ \hline 1{,}000 \end{array}$$

Example

STEP 1

Subtract the ones.

$$\begin{array}{r} 2{,}167 \\ -1{,}377 \\ \hline 0 \end{array}$$

STEP 2

Subtract the tens. Regroup.
1 hundred 6 tens =
0 hundreds 16 tens

$$\begin{array}{r} 0\ 16 \\ 2{,}\not{1}\not{6}7 \\ -1{,}377 \\ \hline 90 \end{array}$$

STEP 3

Subtract the hundreds. Regroup.
2 thousands 0 hundreds =
1 thousand 10 hundreds

$$\begin{array}{r} 10\ \ \\ 1\ \not{0}\ 16 \\ \not{2},\not{1}\not{6}7 \\ -1{,}377 \\ \hline 790 \end{array}$$

STEP 4

Subtract the thousands.

$$\begin{array}{r} 10\ \ \\ 1\ \not{0}\ 16 \\ \not{2},\not{1}\not{6}7 \\ -1{,}377 \\ \hline 790 \end{array}$$

So, it is 790 more miles to hike the Appalachian Trail than to drive. Since 790 is close to the estimate of 1,000, the answer is reasonable.

More Examples

A 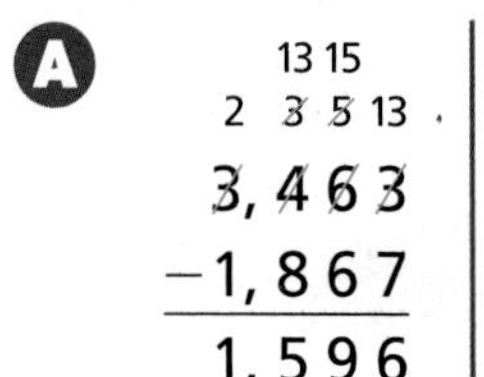

$$\begin{array}{r} 13\ 15\ \ \\ 2\ \not{3}\ \not{5}\ 13 \\ \not{3},\not{4}\not{6}\not{3} \\ -1{,}867 \\ \hline 1{,}596 \end{array}$$

B

$$\begin{array}{r} 9\ 11\ \ \\ 3\ 10\ \not{1}\ 17 \\ \not{4},\not{0}\not{2}\not{7} \\ -\quad 598 \\ \hline 3{,}429 \end{array}$$

C

$$\begin{array}{r} 11\ 10\ \ \\ 3\ \not{1}\ \not{0}\ 15 \\ \$\not{4}\not{2}.\not{1}\not{5} \\ -\$27.36 \\ \hline \$14.79 \end{array}$$

D

$$\begin{array}{r} 9\ \ 9\ \ \ \\ 4\ 10\ 10\ 10 \\ \not{5},\not{0}\not{0}\not{0} \\ -3{,}574 \\ \hline 1{,}426 \end{array}$$

Check

1. **Explain** how subtracting 4-digit numbers is like subtracting 3-digit numbers. How is it different?

Find the difference. Estimate to check.

2. $\begin{array}{r} 4{,}137 \\ -1{,}562 \\ \hline \end{array}$ 3. $\begin{array}{r} 2{,}421 \\ -\ \ 865 \\ \hline \end{array}$ 4. $\begin{array}{r} \$26.03 \\ -\$19.54 \\ \hline \end{array}$ 5. $\begin{array}{r} 734 \\ -588 \\ \hline \end{array}$ 6. $\begin{array}{r} 5{,}085 \\ -2{,}629 \\ \hline \end{array}$

Practice and Problem Solving

Extra Practice, page 104, Set C

Find the difference. Estimate to check.

7. $\begin{array}{r} 2{,}624 \\ -1{,}832 \\ \hline \end{array}$ 8. $\begin{array}{r} 8{,}716 \\ -5{,}940 \\ \hline \end{array}$ 9. $\begin{array}{r} 317 \\ -198 \\ \hline \end{array}$ 10. $\begin{array}{r} \$51.93 \\ -\$37.06 \\ \hline \end{array}$ 11. $\begin{array}{r} 6{,}102 \\ -\ \ 581 \\ \hline \end{array}$

12. $\begin{array}{r} 951 \\ -674 \\ \hline \end{array}$ 13. $\begin{array}{r} \$10.46 \\ -\$\ 8.58 \\ \hline \end{array}$ 14. $\begin{array}{r} 5{,}932 \\ -3{,}187 \\ \hline \end{array}$ 15. $\begin{array}{r} 3{,}005 \\ -1{,}643 \\ \hline \end{array}$ 16. $\begin{array}{r} \$32.98 \\ -\$18.59 \\ \hline \end{array}$

ALGEBRA Write <, >, or = for each ●.

17. 964 − 825 ● 1,029 − 893
18. 2,516 − 1,728 ● 1,964 − 1,139
19. 5,013 − 4,862 ● 785 − 634
20. 504 − 186 ● 3,380 − 3,061

21. **ESTIMATION** Estimate the difference between 1,836 and 1,754. Round each number to the place that makes sense.

22. The Appalachian Trail opened in 1937. Write a number sentence that shows how long the trail has been open.

23. **What's the Error?** Jada says that the difference between 4,152 and 3,861 is greater than the sum of 196 and 95. Explain her error and find the correct difference.

24. **FAST FACT** • SOCIAL STUDIES Mount Katahdin, in Maine, is 5,267 feet high. Springer Mountain, in Georgia, is 3,282 feet high. How much higher is Mount Katahdin?

Mixed Review and Test Prep

25. 843 + 197 = ■ (p. 72)

26. \$5.66 + \$4.05 = ■ (p. 72)

27. 2,037 + 1,856 = ■ (p. 72)

28. 3,209 + 5,087 = ■ (p. 72)

29. **TEST PREP** What is the value of the hundreds digit in 42,865? (p. 32)

A 200
B 600
C 800
D 8,000

LESSON 5

Choose a Method

Learn

Quick Review

1. 135 − 20
2. 500 − 50
3. 395 − 30
4. 671 − 421
5. 105 − 95

You can find a difference by using paper and pencil, a calculator, or mental math.

UP, UP AND AWAY A hot-air balloon rose to 1,025 feet above the ground. Then it rose to 1,920 feet above the ground. How much higher was it then?

Subtract. 1,920 − 1,025 = ■

Estimate. 2,000 − 1,000 = 1,000

Use Paper and Pencil The numbers are large. The problem involves regrouping. So, paper and pencil is a good choice.

STEP 1

Subtract the ones. 5 > 0
Regroup.
2 tens 0 ones =
1 ten 10 ones

```
      1 10
  1, 9 2 0
 −1, 0 2 5
 ---------
         5
```

STEP 2

Subtract the tens. 2 > 1
Regroup.
9 hundreds 1 ten =
8 hundreds 11 tens

```
       11
    8  1 10
  1, 9 2 0
 −1, 0 2 5
 ---------
       9 5
```

STEP 3

Subtract the hundreds.
Subtract the thousands.

```
       11
    8  1 10
  1, 9 2 0
 −1, 0 2 5
 ---------
     8 9 5
```

So, the hot-air balloon was 895 feet higher. Since 895 is close to 1,000, the answer is reasonable.

REASONING How can you add to check your answer?

Use a Calculator 3,894 − 2,596 = ■

The amounts are large. The problem involves regrouping. So, a calculator is a good choice.

REASONING How can you estimate to check your answer?

Use Mental Math

$\$6.80 - \$3.10 = \blacksquare$

There is no regrouping. You can subtract the dollar and cents amounts in your head. So, using mental math is a good choice.

Think: Subtract the dollar amounts. $6.00 − $3.00 = $3.00
Subtract the cents amounts. $0.80 − $0.10 = $0.70
The difference is $3.00 + $0.70, or $3.70.

Examples

A	**B**	**C**
$\begin{array}{r} {\scriptstyle 8\ 17} \\ 8\not{9}\not{7} \\ -\ 689 \\ \hline 208 \end{array}$	$\begin{array}{r} {\scriptstyle 11\ 12} \\ {\scriptstyle \not{1}\ \not{2}\ 16} \\ \not{1},2\not{3}\not{6} \\ -\ 847 \\ \hline 389 \end{array}$	$\begin{array}{r} 790 \\ -240 \\ \hline 550 \end{array}$

- Which problem can you solve using mental math? Explain.
- Which method would you use to solve Example A? Explain.

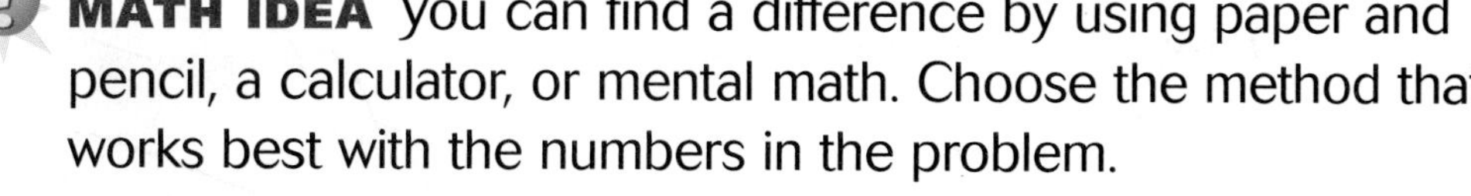

MATH IDEA You can find a difference by using paper and pencil, a calculator, or mental math. Choose the method that works best with the numbers in the problem.

Check

1. **Explain** how you can use mental math to subtract 656 from 987.

Find the difference. Tell what method you used.

2. $\begin{array}{r} 287 \\ -178 \\ \hline \end{array}$
3. $\begin{array}{r} \$7.98 \\ -\$3.56 \\ \hline \end{array}$
4. $\begin{array}{r} 127 \\ -\ 94 \\ \hline \end{array}$
5. $\begin{array}{r} 2,165 \\ -1,084 \\ \hline \end{array}$
6. $\begin{array}{r} \$35.98 \\ -\ \$15.46 \\ \hline \end{array}$

LESSON CONTINUES

Practice and Problem Solving

Extra Practice, page 104, Set D

Find the difference. Tell what method you used.

7. $\begin{array}{r} 365 \\ -104 \\ \hline \end{array}$
8. $\begin{array}{r} 884 \\ -282 \\ \hline \end{array}$
9. $\begin{array}{r} 951 \\ -148 \\ \hline \end{array}$
10. $\begin{array}{r} 821 \\ -631 \\ \hline \end{array}$
11. $\begin{array}{r} 930 \\ -821 \\ \hline \end{array}$
12. $\begin{array}{r} 211 \\ -120 \\ \hline \end{array}$
13. $\begin{array}{r} 545 \\ -438 \\ \hline \end{array}$
14. $\begin{array}{r} 900 \\ -642 \\ \hline \end{array}$
15. $\begin{array}{r} 760 \\ -479 \\ \hline \end{array}$
16. $\begin{array}{r} 397 \\ -254 \\ \hline \end{array}$
17. $\begin{array}{r} 5{,}000 \\ -1{,}294 \\ \hline \end{array}$
18. $\begin{array}{r} 7{,}116 \\ -2{,}005 \\ \hline \end{array}$
19. $\begin{array}{r} 4{,}690 \\ -3{,}282 \\ \hline \end{array}$
20. $\begin{array}{r} 3{,}050 \\ -1{,}422 \\ \hline \end{array}$
21. $\begin{array}{r} 2{,}860 \\ -\ \ 750 \\ \hline \end{array}$
22. $\begin{array}{r} 8{,}907 \\ -5{,}605 \\ \hline \end{array}$
23. $\begin{array}{r} 9{,}437 \\ -6{,}420 \\ \hline \end{array}$
24. $\begin{array}{r} 7{,}884 \\ -3{,}802 \\ \hline \end{array}$
25. $\begin{array}{r} 8{,}932 \\ -4{,}613 \\ \hline \end{array}$
26. $\begin{array}{r} 4{,}507 \\ -1{,}602 \\ \hline \end{array}$

Find the difference. Explain your method.

27. 8,000 − 5,000 = ■
28. 650 − 290 = ■
29. 5,850 − 4,420 = ■
30. 2,000 − 900 = ■

Use a calculator to solve.

31. 4,665 − ■ = 3,962
32. ■ − 978 = 396
33. ■ − 1,324 = 687

USE DATA For 34–37, use the table.

34. What is the difference between the lengths of the Ohio River and the Rio Grande?

35. The Ohio River is 998 miles shorter than which one of these rivers?

36. How much longer is the Mississippi River than the Ohio River?

37. **Write a problem** about the difference between river lengths. Exchange with a partner. Solve.

38. **Vocabulary Power** When you add the suffix *–or* to a word, it can mean "someone or something that does." How does adding this suffix change the meaning of the word *calculate?*

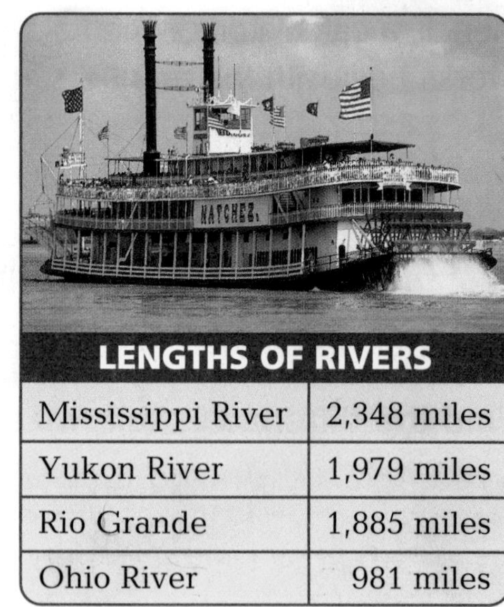

LENGTHS OF RIVERS

River	Length
Mississippi River	2,348 miles
Yukon River	1,979 miles
Rio Grande	1,885 miles
Ohio River	981 miles

39. Sheli's mother was born 25 years before 1987. How old was Sheli's mother in 2004?

40. Write a 3-digit number you could subtract from 274 without regrouping.

Mixed Review and Test Prep

Find each sum or difference. (pp. 8, 10)

41. $\begin{array}{r} 28 \\ +\ 7 \\ \hline \end{array}$

42. $\begin{array}{r} 45 \\ -\ 8 \\ \hline \end{array}$

43. $\begin{array}{r} 67 \\ -29 \\ \hline \end{array}$

44. $\begin{array}{r} 85 \\ -59 \\ \hline \end{array}$

Write the missing number. (p. 4)

45. 80 − ■ = 71

46. 45 + ■ = 52

47. ■ − 20 = 30

48. ■ − 25 = 40

Use the Grouping Property to find the sum. (p. 6)

49. 7 + 3 + 16

50. 21 + 8 + 9

51. **TEST PREP** Mrs. Jimenez baked 75 cookies and sold 58 of them at the bake sale. How many cookies were left? (p. 10)

A 17 B 23 C 27 D 133

52. **TEST PREP** Which number is between 3,478 and 4,309? (p. 46)

F 3,380
G 3,409
H 4,041
J 4,330

Problem Solving Thinker's Corner

SOLVE IT!

Find the sum or difference.

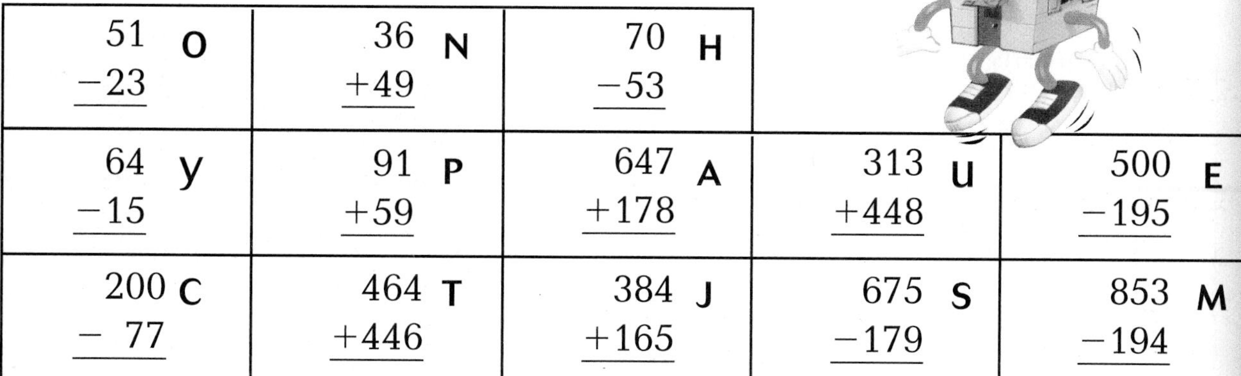

51 − 23 **O**	36 + 49 **N**	70 − 53 **H**		
64 − 15 **y**	91 + 59 **P**	647 + 178 **A**	313 + 448 **U**	500 − 195 **E**
200 − 77 **C**	464 + 446 **T**	384 + 165 **J**	675 − 179 **S**	853 − 194 **M**

To answer the riddle, match the letters from the sums and differences above to the numbers below.

Who can jump higher than a house? __ __ __ __ __ __.
825 85 49 28 85 305

__   __ __ __ __ __   __ __ __ ' __   __ __ __ __!
825   17 28 761 496 305   123 825 85 910   549 761 659 150

Problem Solving Skill
Estimate or Exact Answer

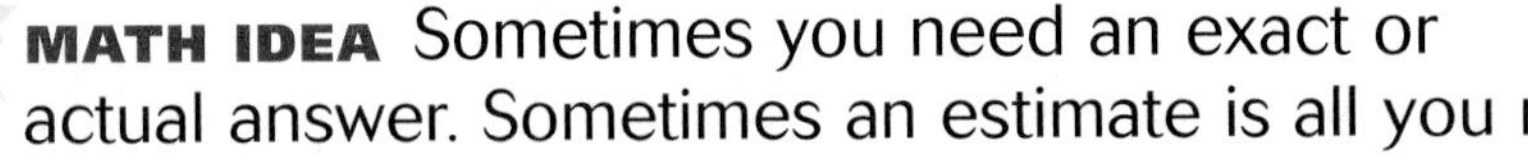

Quick Review

1. $(3 + 2) + 1 = \blacksquare$
2. $4 + (5 + 5) = \blacksquare$
3. $7 + (3 + 4) = \blacksquare$
4. $(12 + 8) + 5 = \blacksquare$
5. $32 + (6 + 14) = \blacksquare$

VIEW FROM THE TOP The table shows some of the highest points along the Appalachian Trail, which stretches from Maine to Georgia.

HIGH POINTS ALONG THE APPALACHIAN TRAIL

High Point	State	Height in Feet
Mount Katahdin	Maine	5,267
Mount Washington	New Hampshire	6,288
Mount Greylock	Massachusetts	3,491
Mount Rogers	Virginia	5,729
Clingmans Dome	Tennessee	6,643

MATH IDEA Sometimes you need an exact or actual answer. Sometimes an estimate is all you need.

Examples

A How many feet higher is Clingmans Dome than Mount Washington?

Since the problem asks *how many feet higher,* subtract to find the actual answer.

$$\begin{array}{r} 6{,}643 \\ -6{,}288 \\ \hline 355 \end{array}$$

So, Clingmans Dome is 355 feet higher than Mount Washington.

B Suppose an airplane is flying 2,390 feet above Mount Rogers. Estimate the height of the airplane.

Since the problem asks for an *estimate,* you can use rounding to find the height.

$$\begin{array}{rcr} 2{,}390 & \rightarrow & 2{,}000 \\ +5{,}729 & \rightarrow & +6{,}000 \\ \hline & & 8{,}000 \end{array}$$

So, the height of the airplane is about 8,000 feet.

Problem Solving Practice

Tell whether you need an exact answer or an estimate. Then solve.

1. Kayla's class went to a water park. Kayla took $35.00. She paid $24.95 for the ticket and $7.39 for a T-shirt. Does she have enough money to buy a bottle of juice that costs $2.50?

2. Records showed there were 783 students at the water park. There were 496 girls. About how many students were boys?

Eve has 439 stickers in her collection. Her sister Ellen has 674 stickers. How many stickers do the sisters have in all?

3. Which number sentence can you use to solve the problem?
   - **A** 439 + 439 = ▒
   - **B** 439 + 674 = ▒
   - **C** 674 − 439 = ▒
   - **D** 674 + 674 = ▒

4. How many stickers do Eve and Ellen have in all?
   - **F** 235
   - **G** 439
   - **H** 1,113
   - **J** 1,348

Mixed Applications

For 5-6, use the table.

5. **Write About It** Explain how you would compare the building heights, and put them in order from greatest to least.

6. How much taller is the Sears Tower than the John Hancock Center?

TALLEST BUILDINGS IN CHICAGO, ILLINOIS

Name	Height in Feet
Amoco Building	1,136
Sears Tower	1,454
John Hancock Center	1,127

7. I am a 2-digit number. My tens digit is two more than my ones digit. My ones digit is between 4 and 6. What number am I?

8. Wesley has 4 more hockey cards than baseball cards. If he has 28 cards in all, how many hockey cards does he have?

9. **What's the Question?** Last week Luann ran 50 miles and Patrick ran 15 miles. The answer is 35 miles.

10. **REASONING** Joel had 48 inches of rope. He cut 15 inches off each end of the rope. What is the length of the rope he has left?

Extra Practice

Set A (pp. 88–89)

Use rounding to estimate the difference.

1.	2.	3.	4.	5.
63 −49	547 −164	\$9.65 −\$5.48	595 −227	8,732 −4,759

Use front-end estimation to estimate the difference.

6.	7.	8.	9.	10.
795 −309	7,850 −2,187	8,026 −4,826	\$55.75 −\$47.46	2,521 −1,779

Set B (pp. 92–95)

Find the difference. Estimate to check.

1.	2.	3.	4.	5.
205 − 67	608 −409	500 −165	900 −198	402 −317

6. **ALGEBRA** The sum of 885 and another number is 901. What is the other number?

7. **MENTAL MATH** How might you use mental math to find 500 − 199?

Set C (pp. 96–97)

Find the difference. Estimate to check.

1.	2.	3.	4.	5.
475 −283	373 −197	6,032 − 748	3,744 −1,495	\$51.46 −\$33.28

Set D (pp. 98–101)

Find the difference. Tell what method you used.

1.	2.	3.	4.	5.
\$4.80 −\$2.30	8,135 −3,645	7,608 −5,810	4,005 −3,318	8,922 − 902

6. Lindsey paddled 4,033 feet in her canoe. Ronald paddled 2,077 feet in his. How much farther did Lindsey paddle than Ronald?

7. **REASONING** The library was built 6 years before the post office was built. The post office was built in 1971. How old was the library in 1988?

Review/Test

✓ CHECK VOCABULARY AND CONCEPTS

Choose the correct term from the box.

estimate
regroup

1. To find *about* how many more, you can ? . (p. 88)

Tell whether you need to regroup to find each difference. Explain. (pp. 90–91)

2. 342 − 214 = ■ **3.** 312 − 181 = ■ **4.** 162 − 51 = ■

✓ CHECK SKILLS

For 5–7, use rounding to estimate the difference. For 8–9, use front-end estimation to estimate the difference. (pp. 88–89)

5. 67 − 29

6. 967 − 283

7. 748 − 599

8. 4,175 − 1,832

9. 8,596 − 3,714

Find the difference. Estimate to check. (pp. 92–101)

10. 341 − 133 = ■ **11.** 837 − 247 = ■

12. $3.73 − $2.08 = ■ **13.** 645 − 347 = ■

14. 800 − 364

15. $4.02 − $2.56

16. 1,728 − 339

17. 2,073 − 1,895

18. $48.56 − $35.77

19. 4,250 − 2,872

20. 970 − 560

21. 8,029 − 6,047

22. 7,300 − 1,074

23. 5,789 − 898

✓ CHECK PROBLEM SOLVING

24. Abe wants each person at his party to have about 1 cup of punch. If he invites 18 children and 9 adults, about how many cups of punch should he make? (pp. 102–103)

25. Danielle wants to buy a favor for each child who attends her birthday party. She invited 16 girls and 15 boys. How many favors should she buy? (pp. 102-103)

Standardized Test Prep

NUMBER SENSE, CONCEPTS, AND OPERATIONS

1. Shelli picked 4 number cards and made this number. How many hundreds are there?

3 1 5 2

A 1
B 2
C 3
D 5

TIP **Eliminate choices.** See item 2. Look at the last two numbers in each answer choice. If the second number is greater than the third number, eliminate that choice.

2. Which group of numbers is ordered from **least** to **greatest**?

F 4,593; 3,549; 3,459
G 8,095; 9,058; 5,980
H 3,855; 5,853; 5,358
J 4,178; 7,418; 8,741

3. **Explain It** Rob has 538 trading cards. Seth has 252 trading cards. Rob says that he has about 300 more cards than Seth. Do you agree? Explain.

MEASUREMENT

4. The clock shows the time Dennis began to read. He read for one hour. At what time did Dennis stop reading?

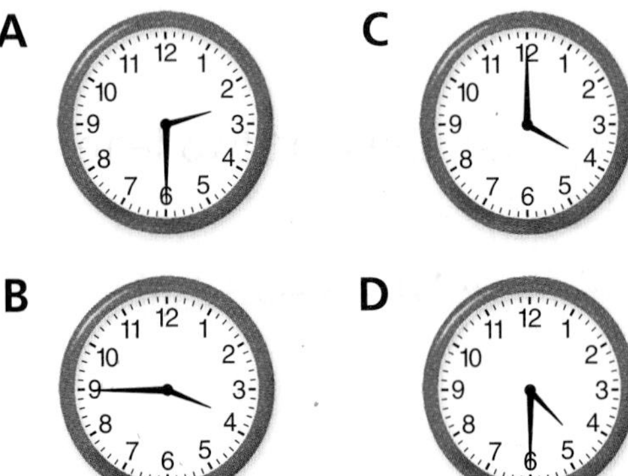

A

B

C

D

5. What is the length of Julia's hair clip to the nearest inch?

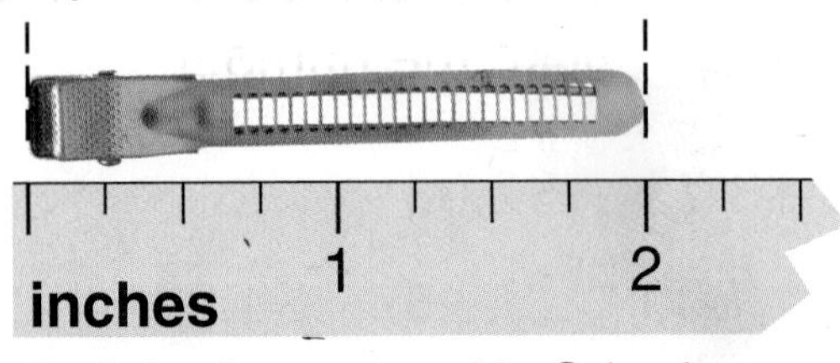

F 1 inch
G 2 inches
H 3 inches
J 4 inches

6. Which item weighs about one pound?

A football
B pen
C car
D eyeglasses

7. **Explain It** Skye has 20 inches of ribbon. She needs to cut 3 pieces of ribbon that are each 6 inches long to make bows. Should Skye estimate or measure with a ruler to cut each piece of ribbon? Explain.

ALGEBRAIC THINKING

8. Which figure is missing from this pattern?

F ▭

G □

H ○

J △

9. What are the next two letters in this pattern?

AAA AAB AAC AAD A

A E A
B A E
C E F
D F A

10. Which number can be used in the box to make the number sentence true?

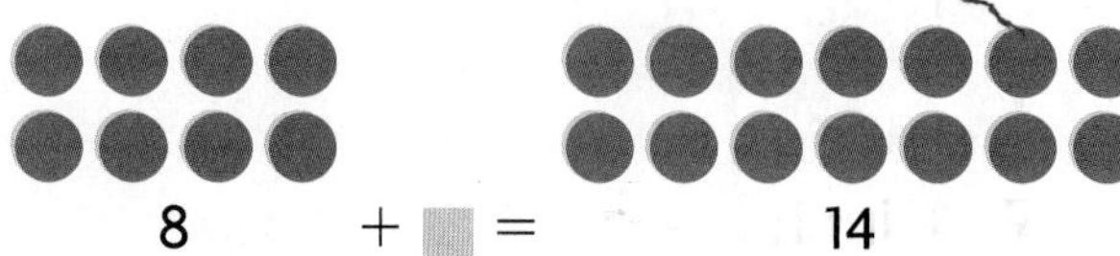

F 8
G 7
H 6
J 5

11. Explain It What are the next two numbers in Jonathan's pattern? Explain how you know.

1, 6, 11, 16, ____, ____

DATA ANALYSIS AND PROBABILITY

12. The pictograph shows the number of hours some animals sleep in one day.

NUMBER OF HOURS ANIMALS SLEEP

Python	🕒🕒🕒🕒🕒🕒🕒🕒🕒🕒
Lion	🕒🕒🕒🕒🕒🕒◐
Asian Elephant	🕒🕒
Giraffe	🕒

Key: Each 🕒 = 2 hours.

Which animal sleeps 13 hours each day?

A python
B lion
C Asian elephant
D giraffe

13. Guy writes the numbers 2, 4, 6, 8, and 10 on five cards. He puts the cards in a box. Without looking, he pulls a card from the box. Which of these statements is true?

F The number is even.
G The number is odd.
H The number is less than 2.
J The number is greater than 10.

14. Explain It Kerri put 3 red marbles and 3 blue marbles in a bag. Is Kerri **more** likely to draw a red marble or a blue marble from the bag? Explain your answer.

CHAPTER 6

Use Money

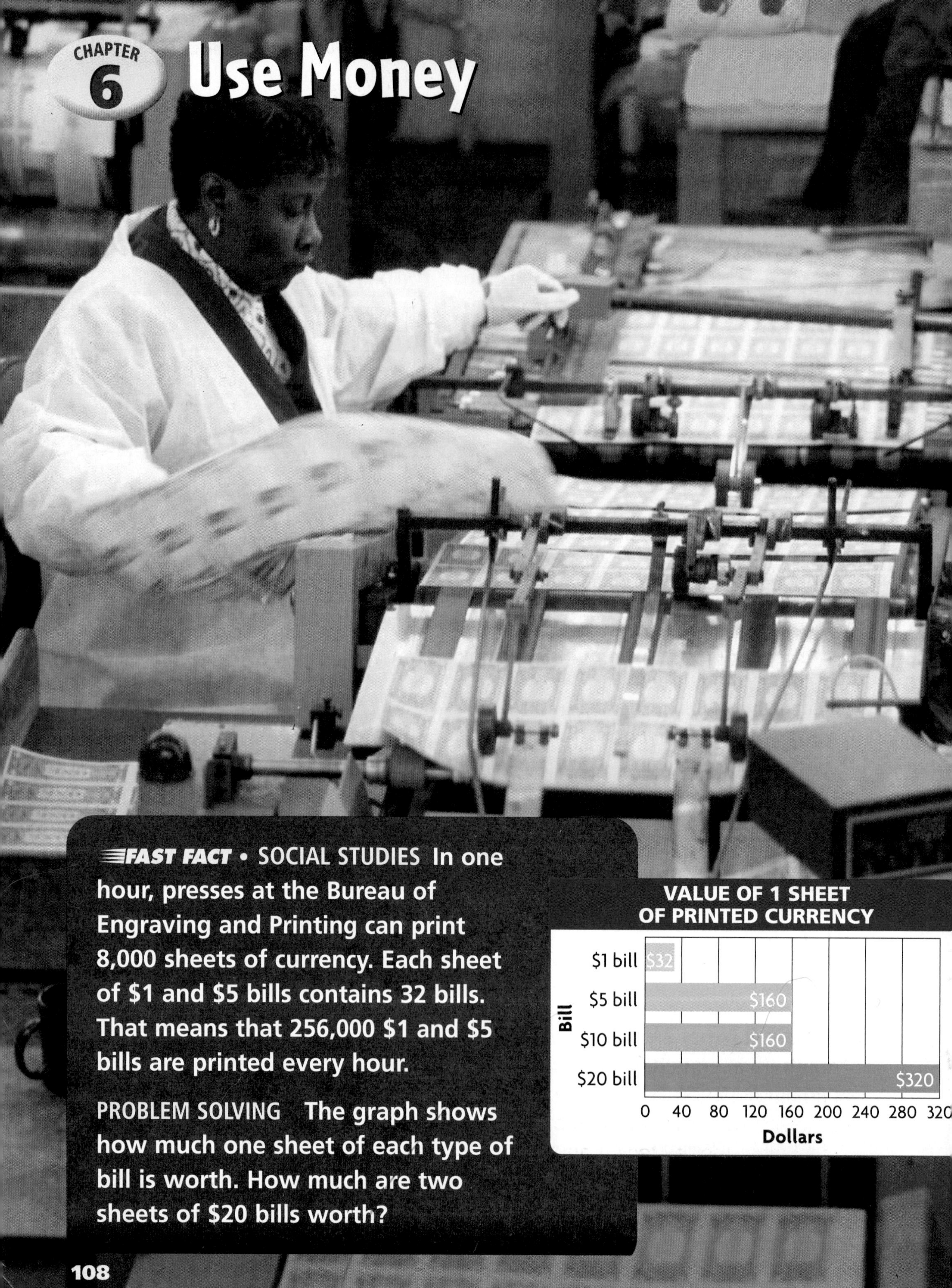

FAST FACT • SOCIAL STUDIES In one hour, presses at the Bureau of Engraving and Printing can print 8,000 sheets of currency. Each sheet of $1 and $5 bills contains 32 bills. That means that 256,000 $1 and $5 bills are printed every hour.

PROBLEM SOLVING The graph shows how much one sheet of each type of bill is worth. How much are two sheets of $20 bills worth?

CHECK WHAT YOU KNOW

Use this page to help you review and remember important skills needed for Chapter 6.

COUNT COINS

Count and write the amount.

1. 

2. 

3. 

4. 

SAME AMOUNTS

Show the amount of money in two ways. Draw and label each coin.

5. 

6. 

7. 

8. 

VOCABULARY POWER

REVIEW

dollar sign [dä′lər sīn] *noun*

The dollar sign was being used before the first United States dollar was printed in 1785. What other sign is used to show amounts of United States money less than $1?

PREVIEW

decimal point

equivalent

www.harcourtschool.com/mathglossary

LESSON 1

Count Bills and Coins

Quick Review

Add 5 to each number.

1. 15 **2.** 30 **3.** 55

4. 25 **5.** 95

VOCABULARY

decimal point

equivalent

Learn

EVERY CENT COUNTS Jolene has some coins. Andrew has some bills and coins. How much money does each person have?

Examples

Jolene's Money

A Start with the coin of greatest value. Count on to find the total.

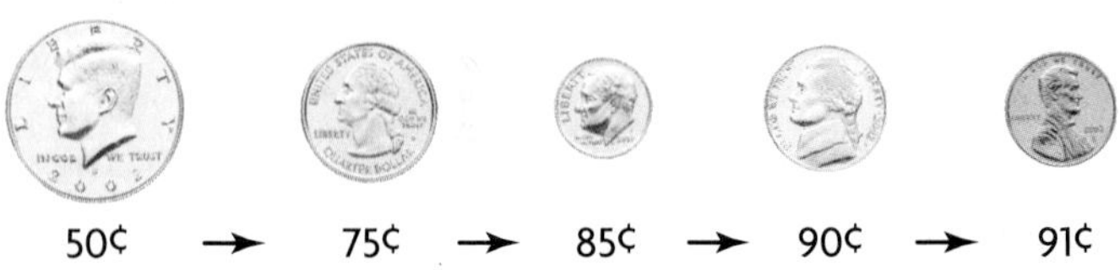

50¢ → 75¢ → 85¢ → 90¢ → 91¢

Read: 91 cents. Write: 91¢ or $0.91

dollar sign ↑ ↑ **decimal point**

So, Jolene has 91¢.

Remember

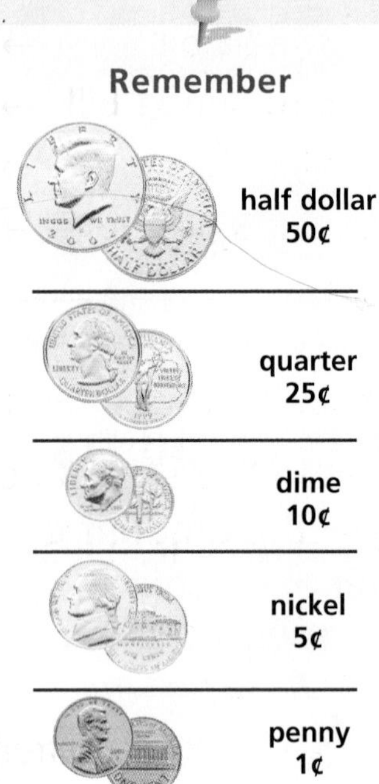

Andrew's Money

B Start with the bills. Then count on the coins.

$1.00 → $2.00 → $2.25 → $2.50 → $2.60 → $2.61 → $2.62

Read: 2 dollars and 62 cents. Write: $2.62

So, Andrew has $2.62.

- Would the total amount be the same if you counted the coins and bills in a different order? Explain.
- **What if** Jolene found 4 more pennies and another nickel? How much money would she then have in all?

Equivalent Sets

Sets of money that have the same value are **equivalent**. You can make two equivalent sets of money with a value of $6.13 by using different combinations of bills and coins.

One Way

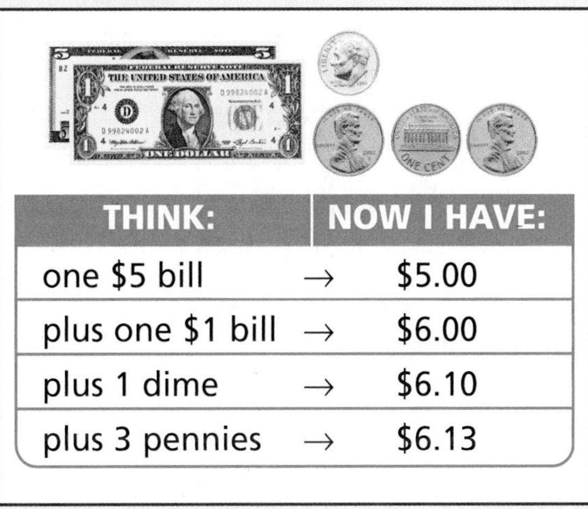

THINK:	NOW I HAVE:
one $5 bill →	$5.00
plus one $1 bill →	$6.00
plus 1 dime →	$6.10
plus 3 pennies →	$6.13

Another Way

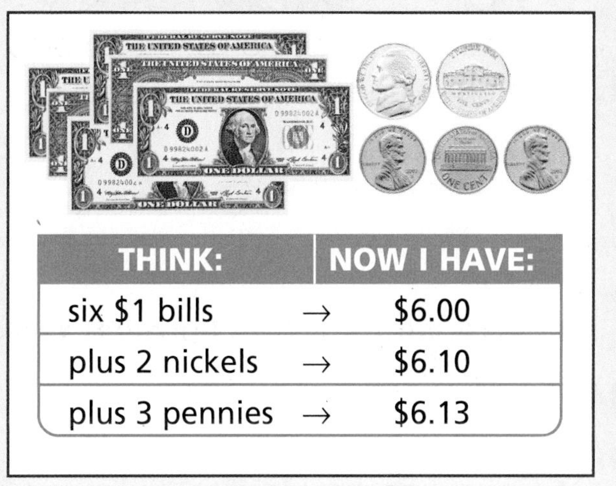

THINK:	NOW I HAVE:
six $1 bills →	$6.00
plus 2 nickels →	$6.10
plus 3 pennies →	$6.13

- Which set uses the fewest bills and coins?
- Name two sets of coins that are equivalent to one dollar.
- What are three ways to show 50¢?

Technology Link

More Practice: Harcourt Mega Math The Number Games, *Buggy Bargains,* Levels A, B

Check

1. **Explain** three different ways to make $2.26.

Write the amount.

2.  

3.  

4. 

5. 

Find two equivalent sets for each. List the coins and bills.

6. $0.35
7. $5.50
8. $2.46
9. $6.92

LESSON CONTINUES

Practice and Problem Solving

Extra Practice, page 122, Set A

Write the amount.

10. 

11. 

12. 

13. 

Find two equivalent sets for each. List the coins and bills.

14. $0.67
15. $5.03
16. $2.25
17. $3.75
18. $1.40
19. $2.15
20. $4.35
21. $8.04

Write the missing number.

22. 1 dime = ■ nickels
23. 5 pennies = ■ nickel
24. 2 quarters = ■ dimes
25. 1 quarter = ■ nickels
26. 1 half dollar = ■ quarters
27. 1 dollar = ■ quarters

For 28–31, list the fewest bills and coins you can use to make each amount.

28. $0.48
29. $1.79
30. $2.37
31. $8.86

32. Tom had $0.43 in his pocket. Three coins fell out of a hole in the pocket. Tom still has the coins shown at the right. What coins fell out of his pocket?

33. **Vocabulary Power** Colonial Americans used Spanish silver dollar coins. The dollar was cut into 8 bits called pieces of eight. If 2 bits equaled 25¢, what did 4 bits equal?

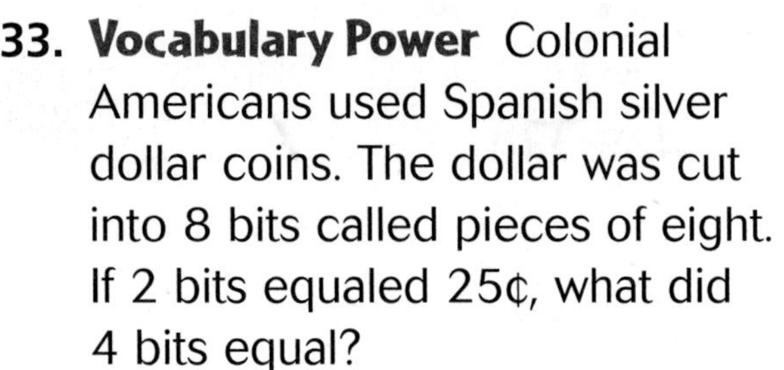

34. **REASONING** Fiona has 2 quarters and 1 nickel. Jake has an equivalent set using dimes and nickels. Jake has 8 coins. How many dimes and nickels does Jake have?

35. **FAST FACT • SOCIAL STUDIES** The United States Mint was established in 1792. How many years ago was this?

36. Abraham Lincoln's likeness was first used on the penny in 1909. This was 100 years after Lincoln's birth. In what year was Abraham Lincoln born?

Mixed Review and Test Prep

Round to the nearest hundred. (p. 50)

37. 87

38. 267

39. 142

40. 550

41. Which digit is in the thousands place of 5,723? (p. 24)

42. Estimate the sum 435 + 268. (p. 68)

43. TEST PREP Which number comes next in the pattern?
3, 7, 11, 15, 19, ■ (p. 30)

A 22 **C** 24

B 23 **D** 25

44. TEST PREP Which digit is in the ten thousands place of 62,950? (p. 32)

F 2 **G** 5 **H** 6 **J** 9

Problem Solving LINKUP . . . to Social Studies

NEW GOLDEN COIN In 2000 the golden dollar coin took the place of the Susan B. Anthony dollar coin. On the front of the golden coin is Sacagawea and her infant son. A Shoshone Indian, Sacagawea helped explorers Lewis and Clark on their expedition to the West.

Write the amount.

1.

2.

3.

4.

LESSON 2

Problem Solving Strategy
Make a Table

Quick Review

1. 2 quarters = ■ pennies
2. 10 dimes = ■ quarters
3. 4 nickels = ■ dimes
4. 1 quarter = ■ nickels
5. 10 pennies = ■ nickels

PROBLEM Patty has four $1 bills, 3 quarters, 5 dimes, 1 nickel, and 5 pennies. How many different equivalent sets of bills and coins can she use to pay for a magazine that costs $4.75?

UNDERSTAND

- What are you asked to find?
- What information will you use?

PLAN

- What strategy can you use?

You can *make a table* to find sets of bills and coins with a value of $4.75.

SOLVE

- How can you use the strategy to solve the problem?

Make a table to show equivalent sets of money.

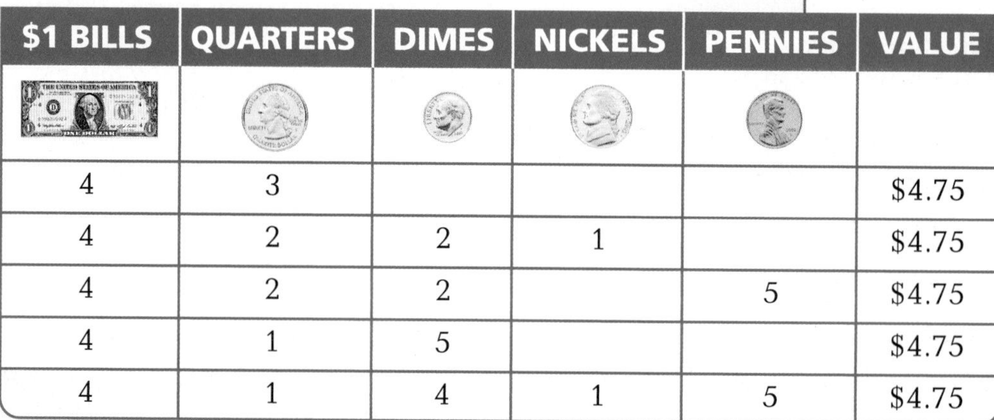

$1 BILLS	QUARTERS	DIMES	NICKELS	PENNIES	VALUE
4	3				$4.75
4	2	2	1		$4.75
4	2	2		5	$4.75
4	1	5			$4.75
4	1	4	1	5	$4.75

So, there are 5 equivalent sets.

CHECK

- How can you decide if your answer is correct?

Problem Solving Practice

Make a table to solve.

1. **What if** Patty's magazine costs $5.25? What equivalent sets of bills and coins can she use?
2. Tyler has one $1 bill, 5 quarters, 1 dime, and 2 nickels. What equivalent sets of bills and coins can he use to pay for a goldfish that costs $1.35?

Strategies

Draw a Diagram or Picture
Make a Model or Act It Out
Make an Organized List
Find a Pattern
Make a Table or Graph
Predict and Test
Work Backward
Solve a Simpler Problem
Write a Number Sentence
Use Logical Reasoning

Problem Solving

Kevin has 7 quarters, 4 dimes, and 1 nickel. He wants to buy a bookmark that costs $1.80.

3. Kevin wants to keep 1 quarter. Which set of coins should he use?
   - **A** 6 quarters, 2 dimes, 1 nickel
   - **B** 6 quarters, 3 dimes
   - **C** 7 quarters, 1 dime
   - **D** 6 quarters, 3 dimes, 1 nickel
4. If Kevin uses the fewest coins, which type of coin will he NOT use?
   - **F** quarters
   - **G** dimes
   - **H** nickels
   - **J** none of the above

Mixed Strategy Practice

USE DATA For 5–7, use the table.

5. Laura has one $5 bill, four $1 bills, 7 quarters, 2 dimes, 2 nickels, and 4 pennies. Using exact change, how many different ways can she pay for the flashlight?
6. Paco has only quarters and nickels in his pocket. What 9 coins would he use to buy the can opener, using exact change?
7. Fran, Geri, Harold, and Ivan each buy a different item. Use the clues to decide what each person buys.

   Fran pays with one $1 bill and 1 nickel. Ivan pays with one $5 bill. Geri pays with three $1 bills.

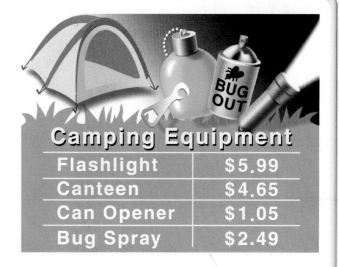

Camping Equipment

Item	Price
Flashlight	$5.99
Canteen	$4.65
Can Opener	$1.05
Bug Spray	$2.49

8. **Write About It** Betty has three $1 bills, 5 quarters, 7 dimes, and 2 nickels. Explain how Betty can trade some of her bills and coins for a $5 bill.

LESSON 3

Compare Money Amounts

Quick Review

Write $<$, $>$, or $=$ for each ●.

1. 463 ● 643
2. 510 ● 105
3. 874 ● 748
4. 296 ● 926
5. 713 ● 713

Learn

MONEY MATTERS Ming and Ben have the sets of bills and coins pictured below. Who has more money?

Count each amount and compare.

Ming has $\$5.75$.
Ben has $\$5.50$.

$\$5.75 > \$5.50$.
So, Ming has more money.

Ming's money

Ben's money

Examples Compare. Which amount is greater?

A

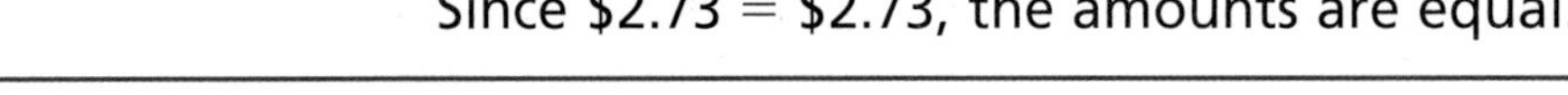

Since \$2.73 = \$2.73, the amounts are equal.

B

Since \$3.54 < \$4.12, then \$4.12 is the greater amount.

- **REASONING** Is a set of bills and coins always worth more than a set that has fewer bills and coins? Explain.

MATH IDEA To compare amounts of money, count each set and decide if one is greater than, less than, or equal to the other.

Check

1. **Explain** how you can use what you know about comparing whole numbers to compare amounts of money.

Use $<$ or $>$ to compare the amounts of money.

2. a. 

   b.   

Practice and Problem Solving

Extra Practice, page 122, Set B

Use $<$ or $>$ to compare the amounts of money.

3. a. 

   b. 

4. a. 

   b. 

5. a. 

   b. 

6. Setsuo sells lemonade for 25¢ a glass. He has 9 quarters, 6 dimes, and 3 nickels. How many glasses of lemonade did he sell? Draw a picture to explain.

7. **What's the Error?** Janice says that $4.87 is greater than $6.21 because 87 cents is greater than 21 cents. Describe her error. Explain which is greater.

Mixed Review and Test Prep

8. (p. 8) $\begin{array}{r} 21 \\ 98 \\ +45 \\ \hline \end{array}$

9. (p. 8) $\begin{array}{r} 18 \\ 24 \\ +42 \\ \hline \end{array}$

10. (p. 72) $\begin{array}{r} 256 \\ +148 \\ \hline \end{array}$

11. Describe and continue the pattern.
    13, 23, 33, 43, ■, ■, ■ (p. 30)

12. **TEST PREP** What is the value of the blue digit? 15,271 (p. 32)

    A 5 **B** 50 **C** 500 **D** 5,000

LESSON 4

Make Change

Quick Review

Add 10¢ to each amount.

1. 55¢ **2.** 70¢ **3.** 83¢
4. 29¢ **5.** 41¢

MATERIALS
play bills and coins

Explore

Jessica buys a kitty toy at Pal's Pet Store. She pays with a $5 bill. How much change will she get?

Activity

Start with $2.89, the cost of the kitty toy. Count on coins and bills to $5.00, the amount Jessica paid.

$2.90 → $3.00 → $4.00 → $5.00

Count the coins and bills she received to find the change.

1 penny, 1 dime, and two $1 bills equal $2.11.

PAL'S PET STORE

Item	Price
Dog Leash	$5.99
Dog Shampoo	$3.68
Kitty Toy	$2.89
Fish Food	$1.29
Chew Bone	$3.59
Bird Seed Bell	$2.63

So, Jessica will get $2.11 in change.

- Why do people start with the coin of least value when making change?

Try It

Each person pays with a $5 bill. Use play money to make change. Draw a picture to show the change each person will get.

a. Tony buys a bird seed bell.

b. Marian buys fish food. Show her change, using the fewest coins.

c. Emma buys a chew bone. Show at least two different ways to make change.

$2.64, $2.65, $2.75 . . .
What should I count next to make change?

Connect

MATH IDEA You can use the same steps to make change when paying with larger amounts of money.

Dog shampoo costs $3.68. Anton pays with a $10 bill. Show the change Anton will get.

Count on from the cost of the dog shampoo to the amount paid.

$3.69 → $3.70 → $3.75 → $4.00 → $5.00 → $10.00

Count the coins and bills. 2 pennies, 1 nickel, 1 quarter, one $1 bill, and one $5 bill equal $6.32.

So, Anton will get $6.32 in change.

Technology Link

More Practice:
Harcourt Mega Math The Number Games, *Buggy Bargains*, Level D

Practice and Problem Solving

Copy and complete the table. Use play money.

	COST OF ITEM	AMOUNT PAID	CHANGE IN COINS AND BILLS	TOTAL AMOUNT OF CHANGE
1.	$0.54	$1.00	■	■
2.	$3.23	$10.00	■	■
3.	$2.69	$5.00	■	■

4. **REASONING** Dana buys rocks for her fish tank for $0.65. She pays with a $1 bill. The clerk has run out of quarters. What is the least number of coins Dana can get? List the coins.

5. **What's the Question?** Evan bought a dog bowl for $2.85 and a chewbone for $3.59. He paid with a $10 bill. The answer is $3.56.

Mixed Review and Test Prep

6. 375 (p. 72) +499

7. 800 (p. 96) −274

8. 4,359 (p. 96) −2,276

9. What is one hundred more than 3,420? (p. 30)

10. **TEST PREP** What is the standard form of seven thousand, nine hundred twenty-three? (p. 24)

A 7,092 C 7,923
B 7,903 D 70,923

LESSON 5

Add and Subtract Money

Quick Review

1. 863 + 219
2. 673 − 482
3. 457 + 361
4. 1,073 − 845
5. 920 + 549

Learn

CHECK YOUR CHANGE Matthew bought a dog collar for $3.95 and a leash for $4.64. How much money did Matthew spend?

Example 1

Add. $3.95 + $4.64 = ■

STEP 1

Estimate the sum. Round to the nearest dollar.

$$\begin{array}{r} \$3.95 \\ +\$4.64 \\ \hline \end{array} \rightarrow \begin{array}{r} \$4.00 \\ +\$5.00 \\ \hline \$9.00 \end{array}$$

STEP 2

Add money like whole numbers.

$$\begin{array}{r} \$3.95 \\ +\$4.64 \\ \hline \end{array} \rightarrow \begin{array}{r} \overset{1}{3}95 \\ +464 \\ \hline 859 \end{array}$$

STEP 3

Write the sum in dollars and cents.

$$\begin{array}{r} \$3.95 \\ +\$4.64 \\ \hline \$8.59 \end{array}$$

So, Matthew spent $8.59. Since $8.59 is close to the estimate of $9.00, the answer is reasonable.

Julia bought a dog bed for $28.98. She paid for it with a $50 bill. How much change should she get?

Example 2

Subtract. $50.00 − $28.98 = ■

STEP 1

Estimate the difference. Round to the nearest ten dollars.

$$\begin{array}{r} \$50.00 \\ -\$28.98 \\ \hline \end{array} \rightarrow \begin{array}{r} \$50.00 \\ -\$30.00 \\ \hline \$20.00 \end{array}$$

STEP 2

Subtract money like whole numbers.

$$\begin{array}{r} \$50.00 \\ -\$28.98 \\ \hline \end{array} \rightarrow \begin{array}{r} \overset{4}{\cancel{5}},\overset{\overset{9}{10}}{\cancel{0}}\,\overset{\overset{9}{10}}{\cancel{0}}\,\overset{10}{\cancel{0}} \\ -2,8\,9\,8 \\ \hline 2,1\,0\,2 \end{array}$$

STEP 3

Write the difference in dollars and cents.

$$\begin{array}{r} \$50.00 \\ -\$28.98 \\ \hline \$21.02 \end{array}$$

So, Julia should get $21.02 in change. Since $21.02 is close to the estimate of $20.00, the answer is reasonable.

Check

1. **Explain** how you can check the subtraction to be sure Julia got the correct change.

Find the sum or difference. Estimate to check.

2. $\begin{array}{r} \$1.45 \\ +\$2.32 \\ \hline \end{array}$
3. $\begin{array}{r} \$5.00 \\ -\$1.19 \\ \hline \end{array}$
4. $\begin{array}{r} \$14.89 \\ +\$22.51 \\ \hline \end{array}$
5. $\begin{array}{r} \$31.45 \\ -\$19.76 \\ \hline \end{array}$

Practice and Problem Solving

Extra Practice, page 122, Set C

Find the sum or difference. Estimate to check.

6. $\begin{array}{r} \$2.63 \\ +\$1.74 \\ \hline \end{array}$
7. $\begin{array}{r} \$4.55 \\ +\$10.48 \\ \hline \end{array}$
8. $\begin{array}{r} \$4.64 \\ -\$1.80 \\ \hline \end{array}$
9. $\begin{array}{r} \$6.73 \\ -\$4.85 \\ \hline \end{array}$
10. $\begin{array}{r} \$50.00 \\ -\$23.46 \\ \hline \end{array}$
11. $\begin{array}{r} \$38.26 \\ +\$24.87 \\ \hline \end{array}$
12. $\begin{array}{r} \$47.69 \\ +\$34.54 \\ \hline \end{array}$
13. $\begin{array}{r} \$20.00 \\ -\$15.25 \\ \hline \end{array}$

14. $4.28 + $2.59 = ■
15. $6.72 − $3.94 = ■
16. $3.26 − $1.09 = ■

ALGEBRA Write <, >, or = for each ●.

17. $5.00 ● $3.94 + $1.06
18. $4.57 − $1.14 ● $5.71

USE DATA For 19–20, use Justin's money at the right.

19. A cat bed costs $8.59. Does Justin have enough money to buy it?

20. Does Justin have enough money to buy the cat bed and a cat collar that costs $2.99? Explain.

21. **Write a problem** using two money amounts greater than $5. Solve.

Mixed Review and Test Prep

Write <, >, or = for each ●. (p. 42)

22. 127 ● 171
23. 682 ● 659

24. Round 463 to the nearest hundred. (p. 50)

25. 723 − 581 = ■ (p. 90)

26. **TEST PREP** Which shows the numbers in order from least to greatest? (p. 46)

A 481, 419, 527
B 519, 531, 656
C 521, 518, 509
D 704, 698, 549

Extra Practice

Set A (pp. 110–113)

Write the amount.

1. 

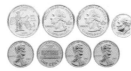

2. 

Find two equivalent sets for each. List the coins and bills.

3. $0.47
4. $4.38
5. $2.81
6. $6.76

Set B (pp. 116–117)

Use < or > to compare the amounts of money.

1. a. 

   b. 

2. Maria has 3 quarters, 3 dimes, and 1 nickel. She wants to buy a slice of pie for $1.10. Does she have enough money? Explain.

3. Ronnie has 1 quarter, 4 dimes, and 3 nickels. Lydia has 3 quarters. Who has more money? Explain.

Set C (pp. 120–121)

Find the sum or difference. Estimate to check.

1. $3.35 + $2.84
2. $8.45 − $4.56
3. $10.00 − $ 5.35
4. $25.47 + $32.98
5. $63.07 − $54.68

USE DATA For 6–7, use the table.

6. How much more does a pint of blueberries cost than an apple?

7. Ezra buys 2 plums and a pound of grapes and pays with a $5 bill. How much change does Ezra get?

FREIDA'S FRUIT STAND

Fruit	Price
Bananas	$0.65 each pound
Plums	$0.45 each
Grapes	$1.33 each pound
Apples	$0.24 each
Blueberries	$1.79 each pint

Review/Test

✓ CHECK VOCABULARY AND CONCEPTS

Choose the best term from the box.

decimal point
equivalent
change

1. Sets of money that have the same value are ___?___ . (p. 111)

Find two equivalent sets for each. List the coins and bills. (pp. 110–113)

2. $0.78 3. $3.65 4. $5.17 5. $8.42

Copy and complete the table. (pp. 118–119)

	COST OF ITEM	AMOUNT PAID	CHANGE IN COINS AND BILLS	AMOUNT OF CHANGE
6.	$4.62	$10.00	■	■
7.	$3.49	$5.00	■	■

✓ CHECK SKILLS

Use < or > to compare the amounts of money. (pp. 116–117)

8. a.  

b. 

Find the sum or difference. Estimate to check. (pp. 120–121)

9. $\$2.46 + \$3.37$

10. $\$6.39 - \$1.81$

11. $\$9.05 - \$2.88$

12. $\$60.00 - \$34.72$

13. $\$62.74 + \$27.46$

✓ CHECK PROBLEM SOLVING

Make a table to solve. (pp. 114–115)

14. Michelle has two $1 bills, 5 quarters, 3 dimes, and 4 nickels. How many different ways can she make $3.50?

15. Brian has one $5 bill, one $1 bill, 5 quarters, 3 dimes, and 3 nickels. How many different ways can he make $7.35?

Standardized Test Prep

NUMBER SENSE, CONCEPTS, AND OPERATIONS

1. The table shows the heights of volcanoes in the Three Sisters area of Oregon. Which is the height of the North Sister written in word form?

THREE SISTERS VOLCANOES, OREGON	
Volcano	**Height (in feet)**
North Sister	10,085
Middle Sister	10,047
South Sister	10,358

A ten thousand, eight hundred five
B ten thousand, eight hundred fifty
C ten thousand, eighty-five
D ten thousand, forty-seven

2. Justin buys dog treats for one dollar and eighty-nine cents. Which amount shows how much Justin spends?

F \$0.89
G \$1.00
H \$1.89
J \$1.98

3. **Explain It** Eva needs cat food that costs \$3.89. She wants to buy a cat toy for \$1.69. She has a \$5 bill. ESTIMATE to decide whether Eva has enough money for both items. Explain your estimate.

MEASUREMENT

4. Which tool would you use to find the weight of a seashell?

A 

B

C 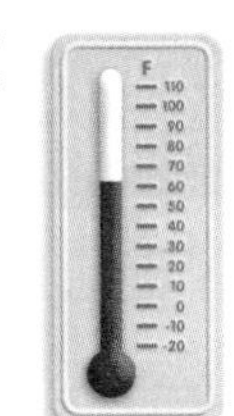

D 

5. Which unit of measure should Bart use to describe how much water a sink holds?

F inch
G meter
H milliliter
J gallon

6. **Explain It** Mike looks at this thermometer. He says that the temperature is about 50°F. Do you agree with Mike? Explain.

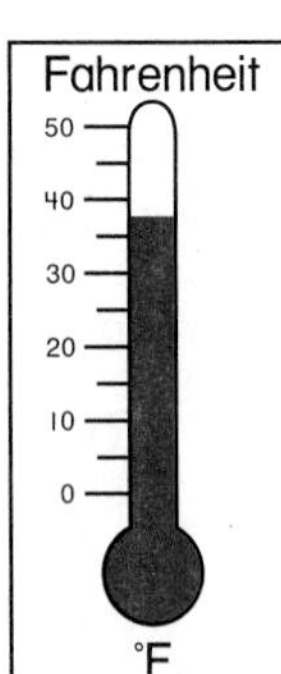

ALGEBRAIC THINKING

TIP **Get the information you need.** See item 7. Find the pattern in the figures. Each figure has 1 less side than the figure before it. Think what figure has 1 less than 6 sides.

7. Which is the next figure in this pattern?

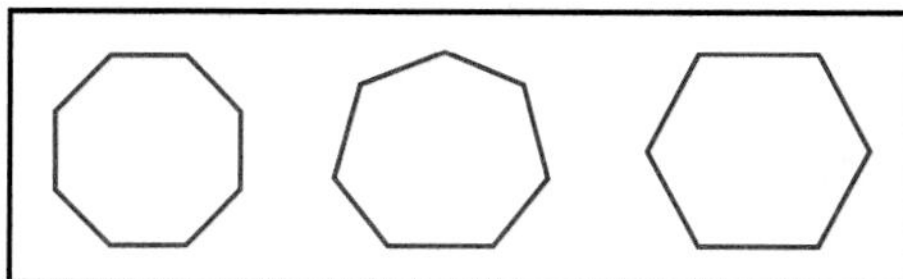

A 

C

B 

D 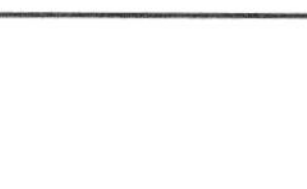

8. Which number sentence is true?

F $4 + 9 = 12$
G $16 + 4 = 19$
H $18 - 5 = 13$
J $20 - 11 = 8$

9. Explain It Chai wants to know how much it will cost to buy four tickets to the animal farm. Explain how he can find the total cost.

ANIMAL FARM TICKETS	
Number of Tickets	**Cost**
1	$4.00
2	$8.00
3	$12.00
4	■
5	$20.00

DATA ANALYSIS AND PROBABILITY

10. Terri asked four of her classmates how many library books they checked out. She made this bar graph of the data.

How many books did Clint check out?

A 2
B 3
C 4
D 6

11. Explain It Pat took a survey of the types of pets her classmates own. The table shows the data she collected. Pat wants to make a pictograph of the data. Explain what key she can use.

MY CLASSMATES' PETS	
Type of Pet	**Number**
Dogs	12
Birds	8
Cats	16
Fish	10

Understand Time

FAST FACT • SOCIAL STUDIES The Wrigley Building is in Chicago, Illinois. This clock on the Wrigley Building has an hour hand that is 6 feet 4 inches long, and a minute hand that is 9 feet 2 inches long.

PROBLEM SOLVING Boat tours on the Chicago River pass by the Wrigley Building. Find the end time for each tour.

BOAT TOURS

Start Time	Length of Tour
11:30 A.M.	1 hour 30 minutes
1:15 P.M.	1 hour 30 minutes
3:00 P.M.	1 hour 30 minutes
7:45 P.M.	2 hours

The Wrigley Building

CHECK WHAT YOU KNOW

Use this page to help you review and remember important skills needed for Chapter 7.

TELL TIME

Read and write the time.

1. 
2. 
3. 
4. 
5. 
6. 

CALENDAR

For 7–9, use the calendar.

November						
Sun	Mon	Tue	Wed	Thu	Fri	Sat
	1	2	3	4	5	6
7	8	9	10	11	12	13
14	15	16	17	18	19	20
21	22	23	24	25	26	27
28	29	30				

7. There are _?_ Fridays in November.
8. The second Monday in November is _?_.
9. The third Wednesday in November is _?_.

VOCABULARY POWER

REVIEW

minute [min′it] *noun*

Minute has meanings other than "small amount of time." When pronounced as [mī•n(y)o͞ot′], it is an adjective that means "very small." Can you think of other words that mean "very small"?

PREVIEW

half hour
quarter hour
A.M.
P.M.
noon
midnight
elapsed time
schedule
calendar
time line

GO ON-LINE www.harcourtschool.com/mathglossary

Tell Time

Quick Review

Add 5 to each number.

1. 25 **2.** 10

3. 15 **4.** 5

5. 30

VOCABULARY

half hour
quarter hour
clockwise
counterclockwise

Learn

WHAT TIME IS IT? The hands, numbers, and marks on a clock help you tell what time it is. In one minute, the minute hand moves from one mark to the next.

To find the number of minutes after the hour, count by fives and ones to where the minute hand is pointing.

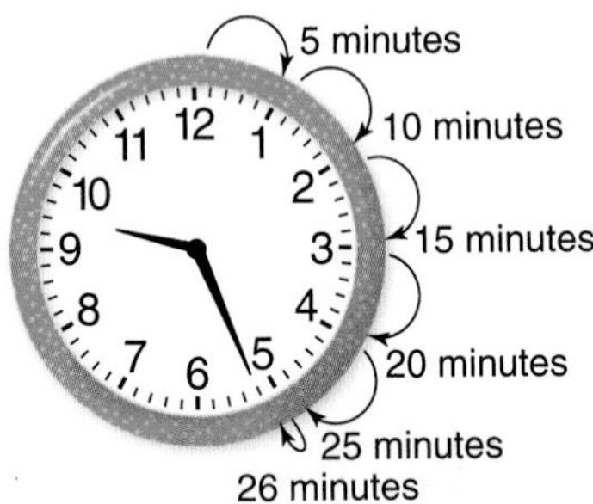

Read: nine twenty-six, or 26 minutes after nine

Write: 9:26

Remember

In five minutes, the minute hand moves from one number to the next.

When a clock shows 31 or more minutes *after* the hour, you can read the time as a number of minutes *before* the next hour.

Count back by fives and ones to where the minute hand is pointing.

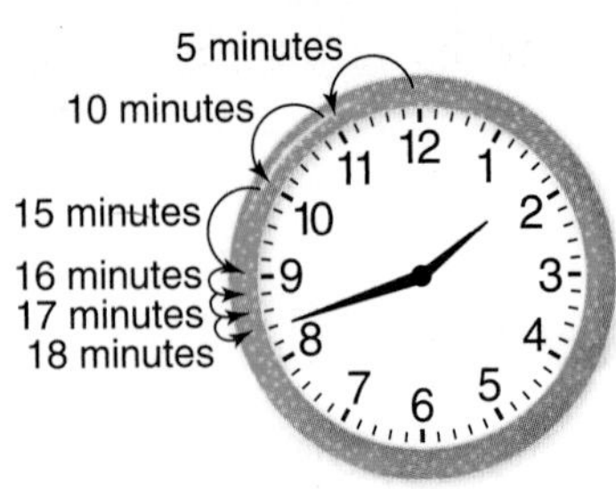

Read: 18 minutes before two

Write: 1:42

A digital clock uses numbers to show the hour and the number of minutes after the hour.

Read: seven fifty-two, or 8 minutes before eight

Write: 7:52

1:20

Read: one twenty, or 20 minutes after one

Write: 1:20

Half Hour and Quarter Hour

You can also tell time by parts of an hour. On the clocks below, you can see how one hour can be divided into 2 equal parts, or half hours, or into 4 equal parts, or quarter hours. A **half hour** has 30 minutes, and a **quarter hour** has 15 minutes.

Read: half past seven

Write: 7:30

Read: quarter past ten

Write: 10:15

Read: quarter to three

Write: 2:45

ESTIMATION Sometimes an estimate of the time is asked for. Look at where the minute hand is pointing to estimate the time to the nearest half hour.

Is the time closer to 8:00 or 8:30?

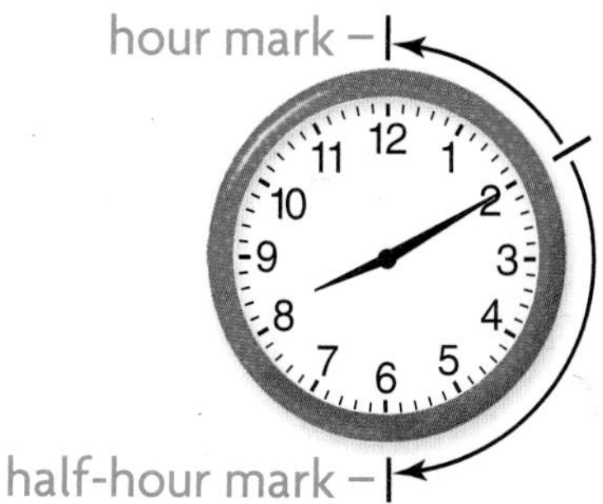

The minute hand is closer to the hour mark, so the estimated time is about 8:00.

Is the time closer to 3:30 or 4:00?

The minute hand is closer to the half hour mark, so the estimated time is about 3:30.

Check

1. **Explain** why 30 minutes is called a half hour.

Write each time. Then write two ways you can read each time.

2. 

3. 12:30

4. 

5. 

LESSON CONTINUES 

Practice and Problem Solving

Extra Practice, page 144, Set A

Write each time. Then write two ways you can read each time.

6. 

7. 

8. 

9. 

Write two ways you can read each time.

10. 

11. 

12. 

13. 

For 14–19, write the letter of the clock that matches each time.

a. 

b. 

c. 

d. 

14. 13 minutes before six
15. 10:28
16. twelve thirty-five
17. quarter past six
18. 5:47
19. 25 minutes before one

Estimate each time to the nearest half hour.

20. 

21. 

22. 

23. 

24. It takes Ann 28 minutes to walk to school. It takes Rob a half hour to walk to school. Who has the longer walk? Explain.

25. **REASONING** Look at the clock below. Is the time closer to 5:10 or 5:15? Explain.

26. **REASONING** Does it take about 1 minute or about 5 minutes to tie your shoe? to make your lunch?

27. Joni needs to leave at about 5:30. If the minute hand is on the 2, is it closer to 5:00 or 5:30?

28. Mr. Olsen bought 8 copies of the newspaper for his class. He spent $16. How much did each newspaper cost?

Mixed Review and Test Prep

Find each sum or difference. (pp. 72, 92)

29. 3,191 + 1,980

30. 2,744 + 2,309

31. 600 − 343

32. 5,163 + 3,572

33. 703 − 425

34. 800 − 326

35. TEST PREP What is the value of the 2 in 56,297? (p. 32)

A 2 **B** 20 **C** 200 **D** 2,000

36. TEST PREP Which number is 6,378 rounded to the nearest hundred? (p. 52)

F 7,000 **G** 6,400 **H** 6,380 **J** 6,000

Problem Solving Thinker's Corner

VISUAL THINKING You can describe the direction of turns by knowing how the hands of a clock move.

Think:
Turn to the right.

Think: Turn to the left.

The turns that the hands of a clock make are called **clockwise** turns.

Turns in the opposite direction are called **counterclockwise** turns.

Describe each turn. Write *clockwise* or *counterclockwise*.

1. 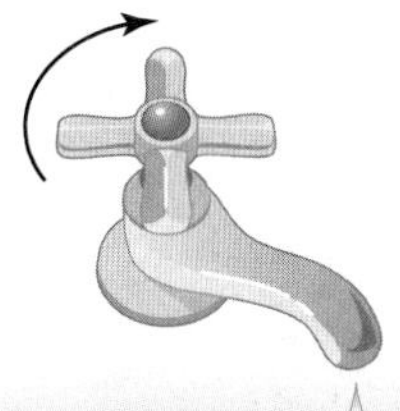

2. 

3. 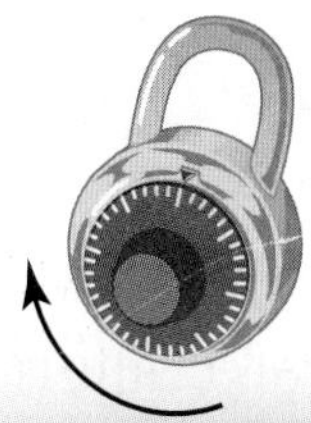

LESSON

2 A.M. and P.M.

Quick Review

Write one way to read each time.

1. 3:22 **2.** 12:34

3. 9:45 **4.** 5:10

5. 11:55

VOCABULARY

A.M. **noon**
P.M. **midnight**

Learn

IT'S ABOUT TIME Using A.M. and P.M. helps you know what time of the day or night it is. **A.M.** is used for the hours from 12 midnight to 12 noon. **P.M.** is used for the hours from 12 noon to 12 midnight.

12:00 in the day is **noon**.
12:00 at night is **midnight**.

Here are some ways to read and write times.

quarter to midnight
eleven forty-five P.M.
11:45 P.M.

quarter past seven
seven fifteen A.M.
7:15 A.M.

half past three
three thirty P.M.
3:30 P.M.

MATH IDEA The hours between midnight and noon are A.M. hours. The hours between noon and midnight are P.M. hours.

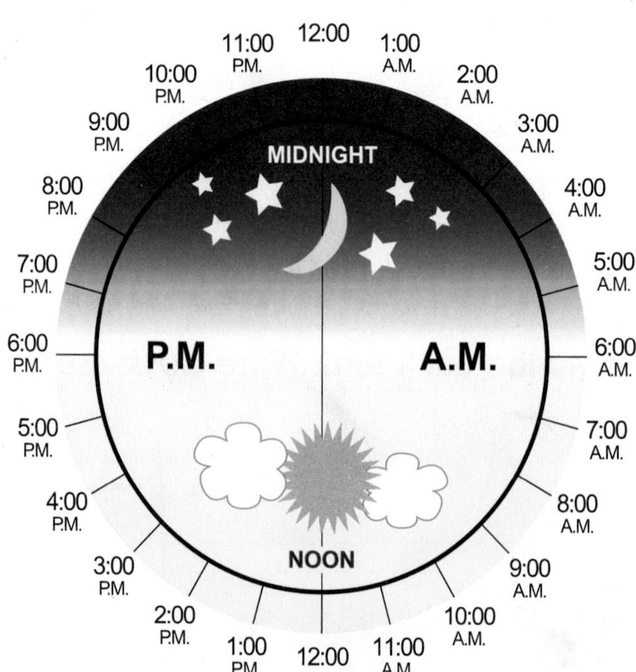

Check

1. **List** three things that you do in the A.M. hours.

2. **Name** something you do at 9:00 A.M. and something you do at 9:00 P.M. Explain how these times are different.

Write the time, using A.M. or P.M.

3. 

school starts

4. 

eat lunch

5. 

do homework

6. 

library closes

Practice and Problem Solving

Extra Practice, page 144, Set B

Write the time, using A.M. or P.M.

7. 

get ready for school

8. 

go to the store

9. 

recess

10. 

go to bed

Write two ways you can read each time. Then write the time, using A.M. or P.M.

11. 

play softball

12. 

moon shines

13. 

sun rises

14. 

eat dinner

15. **What's the Error?** Ty says that 11:45 A.M. is close to midnight. Explain his error. Then give a time that is close to midnight.

16. **REASONING** Are you awake during more A.M. or P.M. hours? Explain.

Mixed Review and Test Prep

Write + or − to make the number sentence complete. (p. 80)

17. 5 ● 3 = 2 **18.** 15 ● 9 = 24

19. 129 ● 5 = 134

20. 637 ● 42 = 595

21. **TEST PREP** Which set of coins is equivalent to $0.31? (p. 110)

A 1 dime, 3 pennies
B 1 quarter, 1 dime, 1 penny
C 1 quarter, 1 nickel, 1 penny
D 3 dimes, 1 nickel

LESSON 3

Elapsed Time

Quick Review

Skip-count by fives.

1. 5, 10, 15, ■
2. 15, 20, 25, ■
3. 30, 35, 40, ■
4. 10, 15, 20, ■
5. 40, 45, 50, ■

VOCABULARY

elapsed time

MATERIALS

clocks with movable hands

Explore

Abby and her father played basketball from 8:15 P.M. to 8:45 P.M. How long did they play basketball?

Activity

Move the minute hand on your clock to find the elapsed time.

30 minutes, 25 minutes, 20 minutes, 15 minutes, 10 minutes, 5 minutes

Start:
8:15

Count the minutes:
30 minutes

So, they played basketball for 30 minutes.

Technology Link

More Practice:
Harcourt Mega Math Country Countdown, ***Clock-a-Doodle-Doo,*** **Level K**

Elapsed time is the amount of time that passes from the start of an activity to the end of that activity.

- Find the elapsed time from 1:15 P.M. to 1:45 P.M.

Try It

Use a clock to find the elapsed time.

a. start: 9:15 A.M.
end: 10:00 A.M.

b. start: 3:45 P.M.
end: 5:45 P.M.

c. start: 10:00 A.M.
end: 11:15 A.M.

d. start: 11:45 A.M.
end: 1:15 P.M.

e. start: 5:10 P.M.
end: 9:20 P.M.

f. start: 11:30 P.M.
end: 12:30 A.M.

The start time was 9:15. The end time is 10:00. How much time has elapsed?

Connect

Soccer practice starts at 11:00 A.M. It lasts 2 hours 15 minutes. Use your clock to find the time that practice ends.

Start: 11:00

Count the hours.

Count the minutes.

So, practice ends at 1:15 P.M.

MATH IDEA If you know when an activity starts and how long it takes, you can find the time it ends.

Practice and Problem Solving

Use a clock to find the elapsed time.

1. start: 7:00 A.M.
   end: 10:00 A.M.
2. start: 5:15 P.M.
   end: 7:20 P.M.
3. start: 1:30 P.M.
   end: 2:15 P.M.

Use a clock to find the end time.

4. start: 4:15 P.M.
   elapsed time: 1 hour 15 minutes
5. start: 11:45 A.M.
   elapsed time: 65 minutes
6. **What's the Question?** The basketball game started at 11:30 A.M. It ended at 1:15 P.M. The answer is 1 hour 45 minutes.
7. **Write About It** Explain how you can use a clock to find the elapsed time from 10:30 A.M. to 1:15 P.M.

Mixed Review and Test Prep

Predict the next number in each pattern. Explain. (p. 30)

8. 3, 6, 9, 12, ■
9. 7, 14, 21, 28, ■
10. 4, 8, 12, 16, ■
11. Order 297, 179, and 253 from greatest to least. (p. 46)
12. **TEST PREP** Which is 100 less than 461? (p. 90)

    A 361 **B** 451 **C** 460 **D** 561

LESSON 4

Use a Schedule

Quick Review

1. 15 + 5 = ■
2. 15 + ■ = 25
3. ■ + 15 = 30
4. 15 + 30 = ■
5. 30 + ■ = 45

VOCABULARY
schedule

Learn

RIGHT ON TIME A **schedule** is a table that lists activities or events and the times they happen.

You can use what you know about elapsed time to finish Stacy's schedule.

STACY'S SCHEDULE		
Activity	Time	Elapsed Time
Eat snack	3:45 P.M.–4:05 P.M.	20 minutes
Do homework	4:05 P.M.–5:10 P.M.	■
Walk dog	5:10 P.M.–■	25 minutes

How long will Stacy do homework?

Think: Find the elapsed time.
4:05 P.M. to 5:05 P.M. 1 hour
5:05 P.M. to 5:10 P.M. 5 minutes

So, Stacy will do homework for 1 hour 5 minutes.

When will Stacy walk her dog?

Think: Find the end time.
Start: 5:10 P.M.
Count on 25 minutes to 5:35 P.M.

So, Stacy will walk her dog from 5:10 P.M. to 5:35 P.M.

MATH IDEA You can use a schedule to find elapsed times of events. If you know the elapsed times, you can find start or end times on a schedule.

Check

1. **Explain** why Stacy won't start walking her dog at 5:00 P.M.

USE DATA For 2–3, use Stacy's schedule above.

2. What time does Stacy finish her homework?
3. How long does it take Stacy to do her homework and walk the dog?

Practice and Problem Solving

Extra Practice, page 144, Set C

USE DATA **For 4–6, use the class schedule.**

MORNING CLASS SCHEDULE	
Activity	**Time**
Reading	8:30 A.M. – 9:15 A.M.
Math	9:15 A.M. – 10:15 A.M.
Recess	10:15 A.M. – 10:35 A.M.
Music	10:35 A.M. – 11:20 A.M.
Art	11:20 A.M. – 12:05 P.M.

4. Which activities last 45 minutes each?

5. Which activity is the longest?

6. **ESTIMATION** About how long are the reading and math activities altogether?

Copy and complete the schedule.

	THE SCIENCE CHANNEL SCHEDULE		
	Program	**Time**	**Elapsed Time**
7.	Animals Around Us	■ – 7:00 P.M.	1 hour
8.	Wonderful Space	7:00 P.M. – ■	25 minutes
9.	Weather in Your Town	7:25 P.M. – 7:30 P.M.	■
10.	Earthly Treasures	7:30 P.M. – ■	30 minutes

For 11–12, use the schedule you completed.

11. Find the time when *Wonderful Space* ends. Then estimate this time to the nearest half hour. Explain.

12. *Earthly Treasures* begins ■ hour and ■ minutes after *Animals Around Us* begins.

13. **REASONING** Sean needs at least 30 minutes to get ready for school. If he leaves for school at 8:05 A.M., what is the latest he can start getting ready?

14. **Write About It** Think about activities you do on a school day and how much time each takes. Make a schedule. Be sure to include start and end times.

Mixed Review and Test Prep

15. Kate has 5 quarters, 1 dime, and 2 nickels. Jim has one $1 bill and 1 half dollar. Who has more money? (p. 116)

16. (p. 8)
$$\begin{array}{r} 34 \\ 10 \\ +59 \\ \hline \end{array}$$

17. (p. 8)
$$\begin{array}{r} 19 \\ 25 \\ +17 \\ \hline \end{array}$$

18. Write 3,000 + 400 + 8 in standard form. (p. 24)

19. **TEST PREP** The difference between $4.35 and $1.67 is ■. (p. 120)

A $6.02 **C** $3.32

B $3.78 **D** $2.68

LESSON 5

Use a Calendar

Learn

DAYS AND DATES A **calendar** is a chart that shows the days, weeks, and months of a year. There are 12 months in one year.

Quick Review

What day of the week is

1. after Monday?
2. before Saturday?
3. after Wednesday?
4. before Tuesday?
5. after Thursday?

VOCABULARY

calendar

MATH IDEA You can use a calendar to find elapsed time in days, weeks, and months.

Examples

A The Book Fair begins on October 11. The last day will be October 15. How long will the Book Fair last?

Think: The dates of the fair are October 11, 12, 13, 14, and 15.
Count each day.

So, the Book Fair will last 5 days.

B Miss Hanson is painting a picture in the school lunchroom. She will paint from November 29 to December 15. For how long will she paint?

Think: Start: Monday, November 29.
Move down 2 weeks to December 13.
Then count on 2 days to December 15.

So, Miss Hanson will paint for 2 weeks and 2 days, or 16 days.

October

Sun	Mon	Tue	Wed	Thu	Fri	Sat
					1	2
3	4	5	6	7	8	9
10	11	12	13	14	15	16
17	18	19	20	21	22	23
24/31	25	26	27	28	29	30

November

Sun	Mon	Tue	Wed	Thu	Fri	Sat
	1	2	3	4	5	6
7	8	9	10	11	12	13
14	15	16	17	18	19	20
21	22	23	24	25	26	27
28	29	30				

December

Sun	Mon	Tue	Wed	Thu	Fri	Sat
			1	2	3	4
5	6	7	8	9	10	11
12	13	14	15	16	17	18
19	20	21	22	23	24	25
26	27	28	29	30	31	

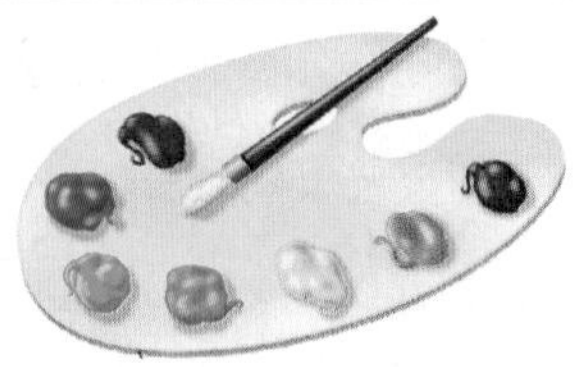

Units of Time

Short amounts of time are measured with a clock. Greater amounts of time are measured with a calendar. The table of measures shows how the different units of time are related.

TABLE OF MEASURES	
60 minutes = 1 hour	12 months = 1 year
24 hours = 1 day	365 days = 1 year
7 days = 1 week	

You can use these units of time to describe elapsed time in more than one way.

Examples

A The reading program at the library lasts for 3 weeks. For how many days does the program last?

Think: 7 days = 1 week
7 + 7 + 7 = 21

So, the program lasts for 21 days.

B Zack read a book for 1 hour 20 minutes. For how many minutes did he read?

Think: 60 minutes = 1 hour
60 + 20 = 80

So, Zack read for 80 minutes.

Check

Technology Link

More Practice: Harcourt Mega Math Country Countdown, *Clock-a-Doodle-Doo,* Level F

1. **Explain** how you know 3 weeks and 4 days is the same amount of time as 25 days.

For 2–3, use the calendars.

June						
Sun	Mon	Tue	Wed	Thu	Fri	Sat
		1	2	3	4	5
6	7	8	9	10	11	12
13	14	15	16	17	18	19
20	21	22	23	24	25	26
27	28	29	30			

July						
Sun	Mon	Tue	Wed	Thu	Fri	Sat
				1	2	3
4	5	6	7	8	9	10
11	12	13	14	15	16	17
18	19	20	21	22	23	24
25	26	27	28	29	30	31

August						
Sun	Mon	Tue	Wed	Thu	Fri	Sat
1	2	3	4	5	6	7
8	9	10	11	12	13	14
15	16	17	18	19	20	21
22	23	24	25	26	27	28
29	30	31				

2. The photo contest is on July 23. Today is June 21. How much time does Emily have to get her photos ready for the contest?

3. Brian's grandparents are visiting from July 17 to August 14. How many weeks is this? How many days?

LESSON CONTINUES 

Practice and Problem Solving

Extra Practice, page 144, Set D

For 4–7, use the calendars.

August						
Sun	Mon	Tue	Wed	Thu	Fri	Sat
1	2	3	4	5	6	7
8	9	10	11	12	13	14
15	16	17	18	19	20	21
22	23	24	25	26	27	28
29	30	31				

September						
Sun	Mon	Tue	Wed	Thu	Fri	Sat
			1	2	3	4
5	6	7	8	9	10	11
12	13	14	15	16	17	18
19	20	21	22	23	24	25
26	27	28	29	30		

October						
Sun	Mon	Tue	Wed	Thu	Fri	Sat
					1	2
3	4	5	6	7	8	9
10	11	12	13	14	15	16
17	18	19	20	21	22	23
24/31	25	26	27	28	29	30

4. Doug went on vacation from August 24 to September 14. How many weeks was his vacation?

5. Mr. Todd left for a 4-week trip on August 9. Did he return by August 31? Explain.

6. **ESTIMATION** Ms. Green's team practiced from September 13 to October 9. About how long did the team practice?

7. Chantel started her art project on October 1. She worked for 3 weeks and 4 days. When did she finish?

USE DATA For 8–10, use the calendars above and the pictograph.

8. "Raisins in the Sun" first hit number 1 on August 11. When did it lose its first-place spot?

9. Which song was number 1 for the longest time?

10. **REASONING** How many more days was "Dance and Sing" number 1 than "Music Time"?

TOP-OF-THE-CHART SONGS	
Dance and Sing	♪ ♪ ♪ ♪
Raisins in the Sun	♪ ♪
Music Time	♪ ♪ ♪

Key: Each ♪ = 1 week.

Find the missing numbers.

11. 2 weeks = ■ days
12. ■ hours = 1 day
13. 2 years = ■ months
14. 1 year = ■ months
15. 4 weeks = ■ days
16. ■ minutes = 2 hours

17. Carol had 32 pencils. She gave 3 pencils to a friend. Then she bought 5 more. How many pencils did she have then?

18. **Write a problem** about elapsed time, using minutes and hours. Explain how these units of time are related.

19. **Vocabulary Power** The word *quarter* can mean one of four equal parts. How does this meaning relate to *quarter hour*? What is another math meaning for *quarter*?

20. **FAST FACT** • SCIENCE Brown bears will hibernate for up to 7 months in a year. About how many months are they not hibernating in a year?

Mixed Review and Test Prep

Compare. Write <, >, or = for each ●. (p. 42)

21. 8,245 ● 8,262

22. 14,336 ● 15,109

23. 21,573 ● 21,565

Tell whether each number is *even* or *odd*. (p. 20)

24. 9 **25.** 30 **26.** 12

27. 63 **28.** 85 **29.** 90

30. **TEST PREP** Jay buys a book for \$4.70. He pays with a \$5 bill. Which coins can he get for change? (p. 118)

A 2 quarters **C** 4 nickels
B 3 dimes **D** 7 nickels

31. **TEST PREP** Ian has 127 marbles, and Carla has 215 marbles. How many more marbles does Carla have? (p. 90)

F 88 **G** 98 **H** 108 **J** 118

Problem Solving Thinker's Corner

VISUAL THINKING Use the knuckles on your fists to help you remember the number of days in each month.

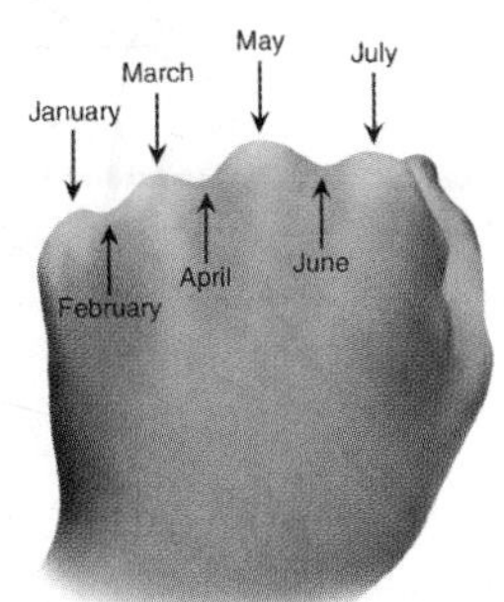

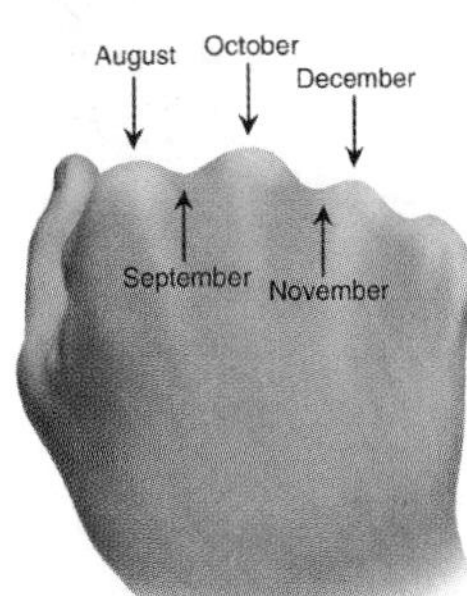

The months on the knuckles have 31 days. The months on the spaces have 30 days, except for February.

Write the number of days in each month.

1. September **2.** May **3.** June

LESSON 6

Problem Solving Skill
Sequence Events

UNDERSTAND PLAN SOLVE CHECK

Quick Review

Tell which number is greater.

1. 76 or 68
2. 52 or 60
3. 34 or 31
4. 245 or 243
5. 591 or 597

VOCABULARY
time line

OLD AND NEW Gina and Nick wanted to show the years that some toys were introduced. They made a time line.

A **time line** is a drawing that shows when and in what order events took place. It is read from left to right. The dates at the left happened first. The dates at the right happened later.

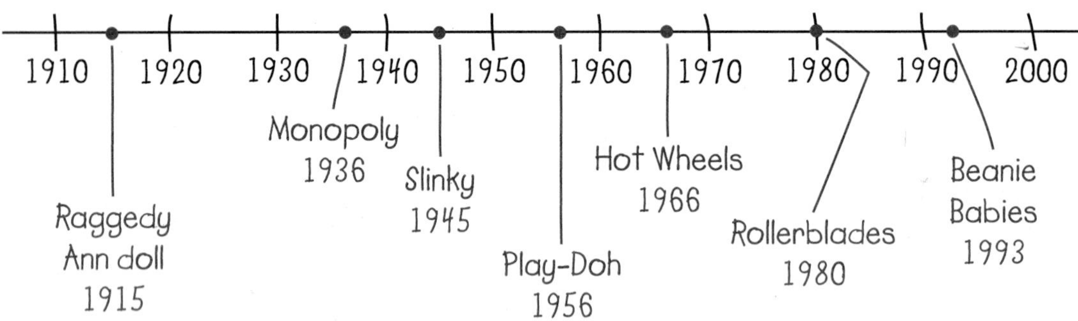

Use the time line to decide if Play-Doh was introduced before or after Hot Wheels.

Since Play-Doh is to the left of Hot Wheels, it was introduced before Hot Wheels.

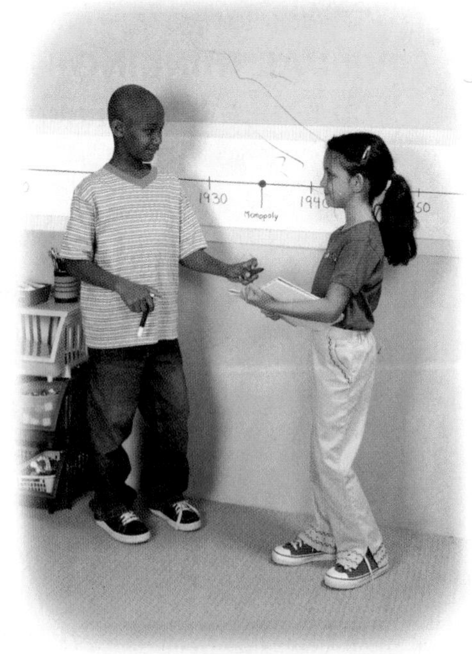

Talk About It

- **REASONING** Suppose you knew the years that Play-Doh and Hot Wheels were introduced, but they were not on the time line. How would you know which toy was introduced first?
- Tonka trucks were introduced in 1947. Describe where the point for Tonka trucks should be placed on the time line.

Problem Solving Practice

INTRODUCTION OF TOYS	
Toy	**Year**
Nerf ball	1969
Lincoln Logs	1916
Crayola crayons	1903
Mr. Potato Head	1952
Erector set	1913
Lego blocks	1949

Problem Solving

USE DATA For 1–2, use the table at the right.

1. Copy the time line below. Add a point to the time line for each toy listed. Label each point with the name of the toy.

1900 1910 1920 1930 1940 1950 1960 1970

2. Etch-A-Sketch was introduced in 1960. Between which two toys should it be on your time line?

For 3–4, use your time line.

3. Which toy was introduced after Lego blocks?
   A Crayola crayons
   B Mr. Potato Head
   C Erector set
   D Lincoln Logs

4. Which toy was introduced before Lincoln Logs?
   F Nerf ball
   G Mr. Potato Head
   H Lego blocks
   J Erector set

Mixed Applications

5. Mr. Brooks will need chairs for 8 adults and 14 children for a party. Should Mr. Brooks estimate to decide how many chairs to rent? Explain.

6. Ms. Tate leaves on May 15. She must reserve a room 10 days before she leaves and a flight 2 weeks before she leaves. Which should she do first?

7. The sum of two numbers is 72. Their difference is 24. What are the numbers?

8. **Write a problem** you can solve by using a time line. Trade problems with a partner and solve.

Extra Practice

Set A (pp. 128–131)

Write two ways you can read each time.

1. 

2. 

3. 

4. 

Set B (pp. 132–133)

Write the time, using A.M. or P.M.

1. 
recess

2. 
play at park

3. 
plant flowers

4. 1:49
go to library

Set C (pp. 136–137)

Copy and complete the schedule.

	MONDAY NIGHT ON CHANNEL 8		
	Program	**Time**	**Elapsed Time**
1.	Game Show	4:30 P.M. – 5:00 P.M.	■
2.	Evening News	5:00 P.M. – 5:45 P.M.	■
3.	Basketball Game	5:45 P.M. – ■	2 hours 15 minutes
4.	Mystery Theater	■ – 10:00 P.M.	2 hours

Set D (pp. 138–141)

Solve. Use the calendar.

1. What date is 3 weeks after July 9?
2. Enya went on a trip for 2 weeks and 3 days. She left on July 11. When did Enya return?

July						
Sun	Mon	Tue	Wed	Thu	Fri	Sat
				1	2	3
4	5	6	7	8	9	10
11	12	13	14	15	16	17
18	19	20	21	22	23	24
25	26	27	28	29	30	31

Review/Test

✓ CHECK VOCABULARY

Choose the best term from the box.

midnight
noon
schedule
elapsed time

1. 12:00 at night is ?. (p. 132)
2. The amount of time that passes from the start of an activity to the end of that activity is ?. (p. 134)
3. A ? is a table that lists activities or events and the times they happen. (p. 136)

✓ CHECK SKILLS

Write two ways you can read each time. Then write the time, using A.M. or P.M. (pp. 128–131, 132–133)

4. 
dance class

5. 
bedtime

6. 
eat lunch

7. 7:38
eat breakfast

8. Estimate the time shown in Exercise 5 to the nearest half hour. (p. 129)

USE DATA For 9–10, use the schedule. (pp. 136–137)

9. At what time does Bob start to read?
10. Which activity is the shortest?

BOB'S SATURDAY SCHEDULE	
Activity	**Time**
Breakfast	7:30 A.M. – 8:00 A.M.
Read book	8:00 A.M. – 8:45 A.M.
Play baseball	8:45 A.M.–10:15 A.M.

✓ CHECK PROBLEM SOLVING

For 11–12, use the time line. (pp. 142–143)

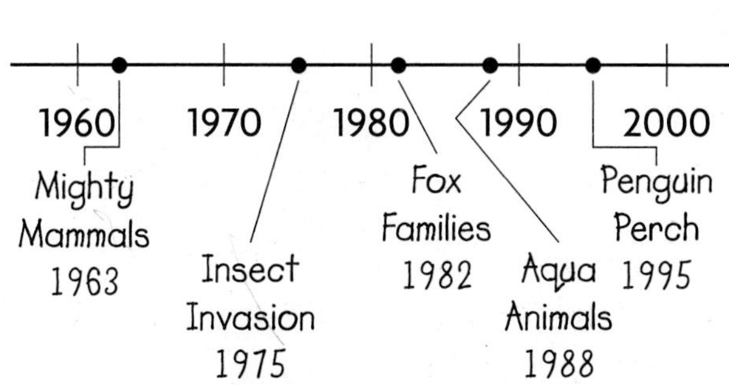

11. Which zoo exhibit opened at a later date than the Aqua Animals exhibit?
12. Which exhibits opened before the Fox Families exhibit?

Standardized Test Prep

NUMBER SENSE, CONCEPTS, AND OPERATIONS

1. Which expression has the same value as $55 + 23$?

A $98 - 20$
B $100 - 12$
C $87 - 10$
D $93 - 17$

2. Lorenzo has 4 quarters and 7 nickels. What is the total value of these coins?

F $0.47
G $1.25
H $1.35
J $1.70

3. Don paid $3.78 for markers. He gave the clerk a $5 bill. Which of the following is true?

A The change is greater than the cost of the markers.
B The cost of the markers is greater than the change.
C The sum of the change and the cost of the markers is less than $5.00.
D The sum of the change and the cost of the markers is greater than $5.00.

4. Explain It Gina wants to estimate the number of pennies in this jar.

Which benchmark should Gina use: 10, 100, or 1,000? Explain.

MEASUREMENT

5. How many inches are in 1 foot?

F 8 inches
G 10 inches
H 12 inches
J 14 inches

TIP **Understand the problem.** See item 6. The problem is asking for the unit that would be used to measure the weight of a bowling ball. Read each choice to find the unit that would be used to measure weight.

6. Will wants to measure the weight of a bowling ball. Which unit of measure should he use?

A inch
B foot
C gallon
D pound

7. Explain It What is the length of this piece of yarn measured to the nearest inch? Explain your answer.

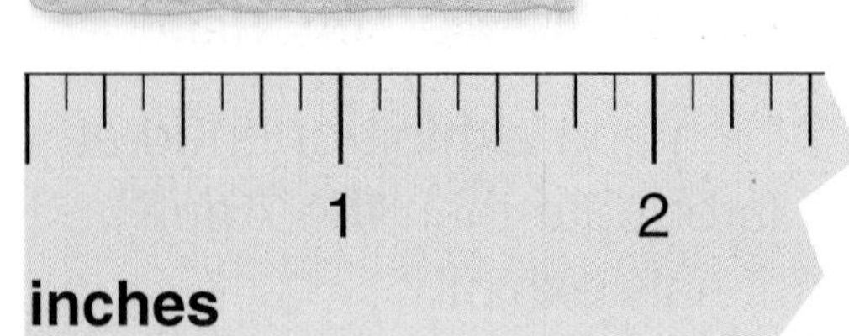

ALGEBRAIC THINKING

8. Which number will be next in this pattern?

5, 10, 15, 20, 25

F 20
G 26
H 28
J 30

9. Rebecca went to art class on June 1, June 5, June 9, and June 13.

If this pattern continues, what is the next date when Rebecca will go to art class?

A June 14
B June 15
C June 17
D June 19

10. Which number is the missing addend?

$9 + \blacksquare = 17$

F 9 **H** 7
G 8 **J** 6

11. Explain It Dan had 46 marbles. Russ gave Dan some more marbles. Then Dan had a total of 60 marbles. Write a number sentence to find how many marbles Russ gave to Dan. Explain how you chose the operation for your number sentence.

DATA ANALYSIS AND PROBABILITY

12. Paul surveyed the students in his class to find the favorite color. How many votes were there for red?

FAVORITE COLOR	
Color	**Number of Votes**
Red	卌 ||
Blue	卌 卌 |
Green	||||
Yellow	卌
Purple	|||

A 5
B 6
C 7
D 10

13. Look at the table above. How many more votes were there for blue than for yellow?

F 3
G 4
H 5
J 6

14. Explain It How many members are there in the drama club? Explain how you found your answer.

SCHOOL CLUBS	
Art Club	□ □ □
Drama Club	□ □ □ □
Singing Club	□ □ □

Key: Each □ = 4 members.

IT'S IN THE BAG

My Coin Keeper

PROJECT Make your own coin keeper, and practice making change.

Materials

- 35-mm film canister
- 1 eye screw
- 2 feet of cord
- 3 or 4 beads
- Play coins and bills
- Product cards with problems
- Label for canister
- Tape

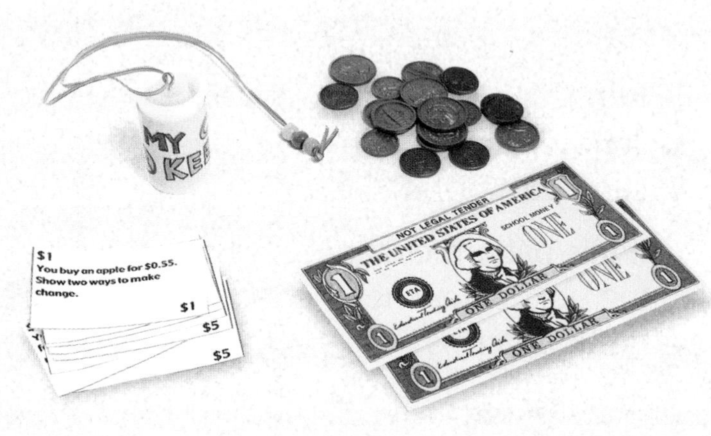

Directions

1. Push the eye screw into the lid of the canister (if this is difficult, poke a hole in the lid with a pen tip first). *(Picture A)*

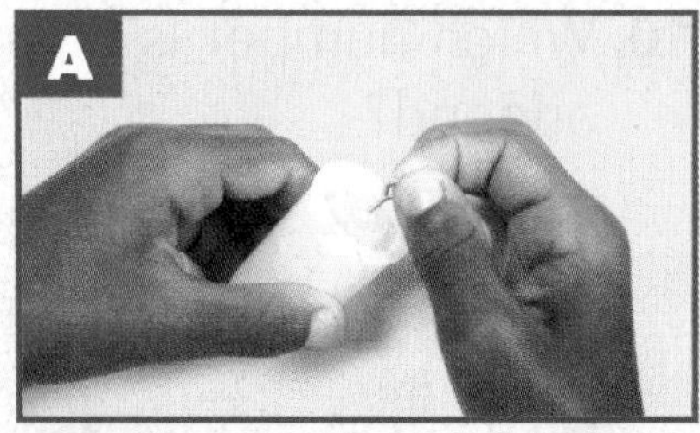

2. Lace one end of the cord through the eye screw, and then add 3 or 4 beads by pushing both ends of the cord through the beads. Tie a knot at the ends of the cord to make a loop. *(Picture B)*

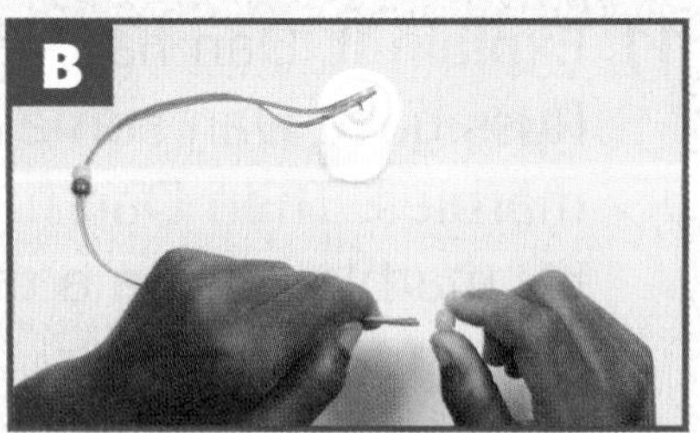

3. Write *My Coin Keeper* on the label, and tape it to the canister. Fill the canister with play coins and bills. *(Picture C)*

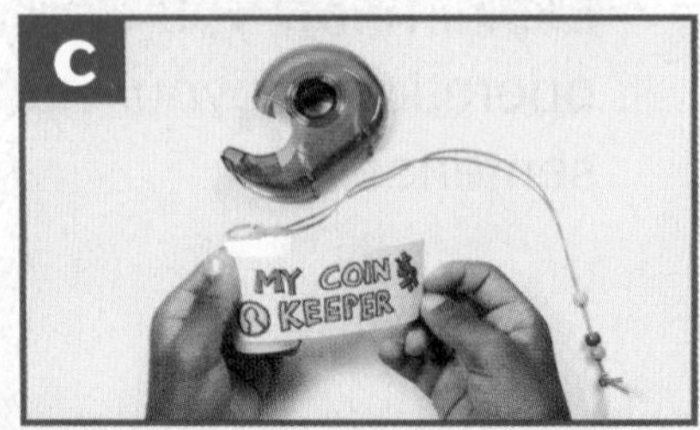

4. Work with a partner. Cut out and use the product cards to practice making change. Use the blank cards to write your own problems for the class to solve.

Challenge

Money Amounts to $100

Kari and her brother want to compare the amounts of money they saved. Kari saved $71.50, and her brother saved the amount shown below.

$50.00 → $70.00 → $75.00 → $75.10 → $75.15 → $75.16 → $75.17

So, Kari saved $71.50, and her brother saved $75.17. Who saved more?

$71.50 < $75.17, so Kari's brother saved more.

Talk About It

- How is comparing money amounts similar to comparing whole numbers? How is it different?

Try It

For 1–2, use the sets of money below.

a. 

b. 

1. What is the value of each set of money?
2. Which set of money has the lesser value?
3. Rodrigo has two $20 bills, one $10 bill, one $5 bill, one $1 bill, two quarters, one dime, and one nickel. Does he have enough money to buy a pair of gym shoes for $57.75? Explain.

Study Guide and Review

VOCABULARY

Choose the best term from the box.

1. A table that lists activities or events and the times they happen is called a __?__. (p. 136)
2. The hours from 12 midnight to 12 noon are __?__ hours. (p. 132)

calendar
schedule
A.M.
P.M.

STUDY AND SOLVE

Chapter 4

Add 3- and 4-digit numbers.

$$\begin{array}{r} \scriptstyle 1 \\ 437 \\ +155 \\ \hline 592 \end{array} \qquad \begin{array}{r} \scriptstyle 1\ 1 \\ 3{,}987 \\ +2{,}532 \\ \hline 6{,}519 \end{array}$$

Find the sum. Estimate to check. (pp. 72–73, 76–79)

3. $\begin{array}{r} 192 \\ +432 \\ \hline \end{array}$
4. $\begin{array}{r} 643 \\ +289 \\ \hline \end{array}$
5. $\begin{array}{r} 534 \\ +846 \\ \hline \end{array}$
6. $\begin{array}{r} 4{,}276 \\ +1{,}071 \\ \hline \end{array}$
7. $\begin{array}{r} 2{,}008 \\ +6{,}439 \\ \hline \end{array}$
8. $\begin{array}{r} 5{,}976 \\ +8{,}668 \\ \hline \end{array}$

Chapter 5

Subtract 3- and 4-digit numbers.

$$\begin{array}{r} \scriptstyle 8\,13 \\ 89\not{3} \\ -508 \\ \hline 385 \end{array} \qquad \begin{array}{r} \scriptstyle 9 \\ \scriptstyle 2\ \not{1}0\,10 \\ \not{3},\not{0}\not{0}0 \\ -1{,}650 \\ \hline 1{,}350 \end{array}$$

Subtract. (pp. 90–99)

9. $\begin{array}{r} 562 \\ -313 \\ \hline \end{array}$
10. $\begin{array}{r} 430 \\ -287 \\ \hline \end{array}$
11. $\begin{array}{r} 406 \\ -\ 89 \\ \hline \end{array}$
12. $\begin{array}{r} 6{,}314 \\ -2{,}509 \\ \hline \end{array}$
13. $\begin{array}{r} 2{,}000 \\ -1{,}734 \\ \hline \end{array}$
14. $\begin{array}{r} 3{,}508 \\ -2{,}779 \\ \hline \end{array}$

Chapter 6

Add or subtract money amounts.

Add or subtract money amounts like whole numbers. Then write the sum or difference in dollars and cents.

$$\begin{array}{r} \scriptstyle 1 \\ \$2.59 \\ +\$3.17 \\ \hline \$5.76 \end{array} \qquad \begin{array}{r} \scriptstyle 3\,12 \\ \$7.\not{4}\not{2} \\ -\$2.23 \\ \hline \$5.19 \end{array}$$

Find the sum or difference. Estimate to check. (pp. 120–121)

15. $\begin{array}{r} \$3.58 \\ +\$2.21 \\ \hline \end{array}$
16. $\begin{array}{r} \$2.46 \\ +\$6.54 \\ \hline \end{array}$
17. $\begin{array}{r} \$5.75 \\ -\$2.30 \\ \hline \end{array}$
18. $\begin{array}{r} \$50.00 \\ -\$\ 6.49 \\ \hline \end{array}$

Count on to make change.

A comb costs \$0.69. Nikki pays with a \$1 bill. How much change should she get?

\$0.69   

\$0.69 → \$0.70 → \$0.75 → \$1.00

1 penny, 1 nickel, and 1 quarter equal \$0.31. So, Nikki will get \$0.31.

Copy and complete the table. (pp. 118–119)

	COST OF ITEM	AMOUNT PAID	AMOUNT OF CHANGE
19.	\$1.25	\$2.00	■
20.	\$3.72	\$5.00	■
21.	\$6.34	\$10.00	■
22.	\$0.17	\$1.00	■

Chapter 7

Find elapsed time.

Jerry played basketball from 11:30 A.M. to 1:45 P.M. How long did Jerry play?

Think:
From 11:30 A.M. to 1:30 P.M. is 2 hours.
From 1:30 P.M. to 1:45 P.M. is 15 minutes.

So, Jerry played for 2 hours 15 minutes.

Copy and complete the schedule. (pp. 134–135)

	Activity	Time	Elapsed Time
23.	Reading	11:45 A.M.–12:30 P.M.	■
24.	Lunch	12:30 P.M.–1:00 P.M.	■
25.	Soccer	1:00 P.M.– ■	1 hour 30 minutes

PROBLEM SOLVING PRACTICE

Solve. (pp. 74–75, 102–103, 114–115)

26. Joyce bought 14 yellow apples and 17 red apples to bake holiday pies. How many apples did she buy in all?

27. Susan has 10 more goldfish than Gary. Together, they own 50 goldfish. How many goldfish does each have?

28. Ann has one \$1 bill, 8 dimes, and 7 nickels. What equivalent sets of bills and coins can she use to buy a notebook that costs \$1.35?

29. Jim has one \$5 bill, two \$1 bills, 5 quarters, 2 dimes, and 4 nickels. What equivalent sets of bills and coins can he use to make \$7.65?

PERFORMANCE ASSESSMENT

TASK A • MEETING A GOAL

The third-grade classes at Cliffside Elementary School are collecting toys to donate to the children's hospital. The chart shows how many toys have already been collected.

a. Explain how you can find out how the three classes have done so far with the toy collection. Show all your work.

b. What do the third graders need to do to reach their goal? Show all of your work.

TASK B • SAVING MONEY

Materials: bills and coins

Becka and Martin are saving money to buy a soccer ball.

a. Becka has saved $5.63. Use bills and coins to show $5.63 in different ways. Copy and complete the table.

b. Martin has saved more than $3.00 but less than Becka. Write an amount Martin could have saved.

c. How much could Becka and Martin have saved in all? Is this enough to buy a soccer ball that costs $12.00? Explain.

$1 bills	Quarters	Dimes	Nickels	Pennies
4				
4				
3				
3				

Add and Subtract Money

Riley had \$7.87. On Saturday he earned \$8.50 by mowing his neighbor's lawn. On Tuesday he spent \$9.52 on a book. How much money did Riley have on Sunday? on Wednesday?

You can use a calculator to add and subtract amounts of money.

Add to find how much money Riley had on Sunday.

7 . 8 7      + 8 . 5 0 = 16.37

So, Riley had \$16.37 on Sunday.

Subtract to find how much money Riley had left on Wednesday.

1 6 . 3 7 − 9 . 5 2 = 6.85

So, Riley had \$6.85 left on Wednesday.

Practice and Problem Solving

Use a calculator to find the sum or difference.

1. \$3.99 + \$2.09 = ■
2. \$9.27 − \$3.42 = ■
3. \$5.00 − \$0.63 = ■
4. \$16.45 + \$35.40 = ■
5. \$18.00 − \$4.06 = ■
6. \$8.57 + \$9.00 = ■
7. Josh wants to buy a CD that costs \$11.50. He has \$8.63. How much more money does Josh need to buy the CD?
8. **REASONING** Tanya has 3 quarters, 2 dimes, and 4 pennies. She spends \$0.53. How much money does Tanya have left?
9. Amber has \$3.45. Then she gets a birthday gift of \$12.00. How much money does Amber have in all?
10. **Write a problem** about adding or subtracting money. Use a calculator to solve.

GO ON-LINE **Multimedia Math Glossary** www.harcourtschool.com/mathglossary

Vocabulary Power Look up *decimal point* in the Multimedia Math Glossary. Write a money amount that uses a dollar sign and decimal point.

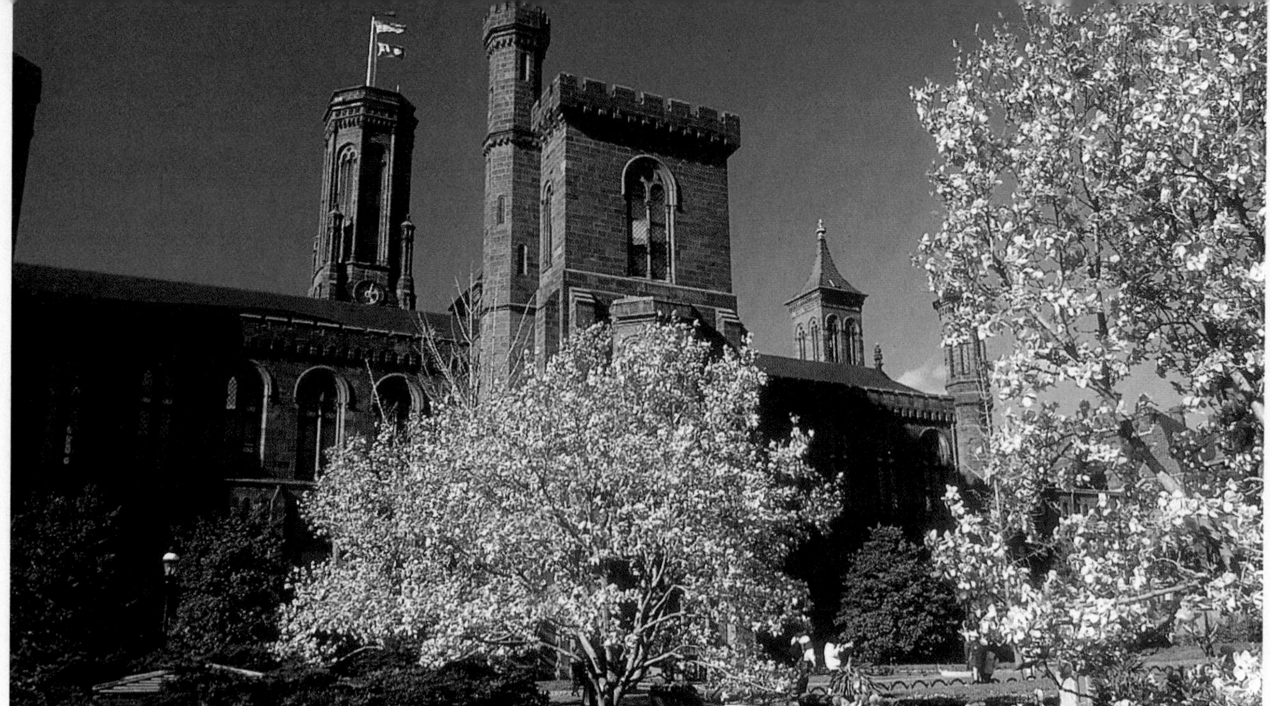

▲ The Castle is now the Smithsonian Information Center. You can find out about museum exhibits here.

in Washington, D.C.

SMITHSONIAN INSTITUTION

The Smithsonian Institution is the world's largest museum and art gallery complex. There are 16 museums and galleries, as well as the National Zoo.

IMAX at the Planetarium

Moviegoer	Price per Ticket
Adult	\$5.50
Youth/Senior	\$4.25
School Group	\$3.75

Times for *Cosmic Voyage*

Show 1	9:45 A.M.
Show 2	10:30 A.M.
Show 3	12:45 P.M.
Show 4	3:00 P.M.

USE DATA For 1–3, use the table and schedule.

1. You and your family get to the Castle at 9:00 A.M. You check the show times for *Cosmic Voyage*, and 20 minutes later you are in your seats. How much longer is it before the movie begins?

2. You buy 1 adult ticket and 1 youth ticket and pay with the exact amount. What is the least number of bills and coins you could use? List the bills and coins.

3. *Cosmic Voyage* lasts 45 minutes. How much time is there between the end of show 2 and the start of show 3?

4. **REASONING** Planetarium shows run every 40 minutes starting at 11:00 A.M. What is the last show you can go to and still meet your friends at 3:30 P.M?

THE NATIONAL GALLERY OF ART

The National Gallery of Art is just across the Mall from the Smithsonian. The Mall is a large grassy area surrounded by many museums and other national buildings.

A family of two adults and two children is planning a day trip to Washington, D.C. This chart shows what they want to do.

Event	Place	Time	Cost
Tour of the East Building Art Collection (45 minutes)	National Gallery of Art	11:30 A.M., 1:30 P.M., 3:30 P.M.	Free
IMAX film: *T-REX* (40 minutes)	Natural History Museum	10:20 A.M., 1:00 P.M., 2:00 P.M., 3:45 P.M., 5:45 P.M.	Adult: $7.50 Youth/Senior $6.00
Ebony Angels Double Dutch Team Performances	National Museum of American History	12:00 P.M.–4:00 P.M.	Free
Highlights Tour (45 minutes)	Air and Space Museum	10:15 A.M., 1:00 P.M.	Free

USE DATA For 1–2, use the information from the table.

1. Make a schedule for the family's visit.
   a. Show the events in the order the family will attend them. List the name and place of each event.
   b. Show the beginning and ending times for each event. Allow at least 1 hour to see the performance at the National Museum of American History.
   c. Allow at least 1 hour for the family to have lunch and at least 15 minutes between events.
2. Find the total cost for the events the family will attend.

I. M. Pei designed the East Building of the National Gallery of Art. ▼

CHAPTER 8

Understand Multiplication

FAST FACT • SOCIAL STUDIES Apples are grown in all 50 states. Millions of pounds of fruit are grown each year. Knowing how much different fruits weigh can help you decide how much fruit to buy.

PROBLEM SOLVING Use the pictograph. About how many plums should you buy to equal the weight of 1 apple?

WEIGHT OF FRUITS

Apple	🛍 🛍 🛍 🛍 🛍 🛍
Orange	🛍 🛍 🛍 🛍 🛍
Peach	🛍 🛍 🛍
Banana	🛍 🛍 🛍 🛍
Kiwi	🛍 🛍 🛍
Plum	🛍 🛍
Pear	🛍 🛍 🛍 🛍 🛍 🛍

Key: Each 🛍 = 1 ounce.

Apple orchard—Hope, Maine

CHECK WHAT YOU KNOW

Use this page to help you review and remember important skills needed for Chapter 8.

SKIP-COUNT

Skip-count to find the missing numbers.

1. 2, 4, 6, ■, ■, ■, 14, 16, ■, ■

2. 3, 6, ■, 12, ■, ■, 21

3. 5, 10, ■, ■, 25, ■, ■, ■, ■, 50

4. 10, 20, ■, ■, 50, ■, ■, ■, 90

EQUAL GROUPS

Write how many there are in all.

5.

3 groups of 3 = ■

6.

5 groups of 2 = ■

7.

3 groups of 4 = ■

Find how many in all. You may wish to draw a picture.

8. 2 groups of 6

9. 3 groups of 5

10. 4 groups of 2

VOCABULARY POWER

REVIEW

equal [ē′kwəl] *adjective*

When two things are *equal,* they have the same measure or amount. Name two amounts that are equal. Use an equal sign (=) to show that two amounts are equal.

PREVIEW

multiply

product

Commutative Property of Multiplication

factors

array

www.harcourtschool.com/mathglossary

LESSON 1

Algebra: Connect Addition and Multiplication

Quick Review

1. $3 + 3 + 3$
2. $5 + 5 + 5$
3. $2 + 2 + 2$
4. $2 + 2 + 2 + 2$
5. $4 + 4 + 4$

VOCABULARY
multiply

Learn

SLURP! There are 3 juice boxes in a package. If Cara buys 5 packages, how many juice boxes will she have?

You can add to find how many in all.

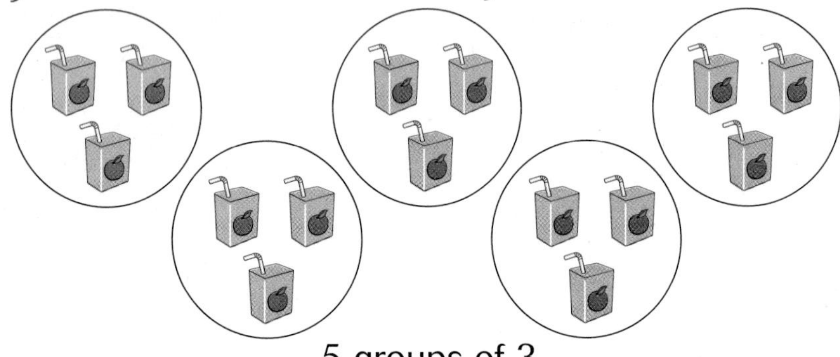

5 groups of 3

Write: $3 + 3 + 3 + 3 + 3 = 15$

Say: 5 threes equal 15.

You can multiply to find how many in all.

Write: $5 \times 3 = 15$

Say: 5 times 3 equals 15.

So, Cara will have 15 juice boxes.

Remember

You can use a number sentence to show addition.
$2 + 2 + 2 = 6$

MATH IDEA When you combine equal groups, you can **multiply** to find how many in all.

REASONING Can you use multiplication to find $2 + 3 + 2$? Why or why not?

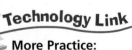

Technology Link
More Practice:
Harcourt Mega Math Country Countdown, *Counting Critters,* Level V

Check

1. **Explain** two ways to find the total if the juice boxes come in packages of 4, and Cara buys 3 packages.

Copy and complete.

2. 

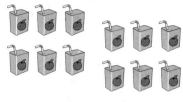

a. ■ groups of ■ = ■
b. ■ + ■ + ■ = ■
c. ■ × ■ = ■

3.   

a. ■ groups of ■ = ■
b. ■ + ■ + ■ + ■ = ■
c. ■ × ■ = ■

Practice and Problem Solving

Extra Practice, page 170, Set A

Copy and complete.

4. 

a. ■ groups of ■ = ■
b. ■ + ■ + ■ = ■
c. ■ × ■ = ■

5.   

a. ■ groups of ■ = ■
b. ■ + ■ = ■
c. ■ × ■ = ■

For 6–9, choose the letter of the number sentence that matches. Draw a picture that shows the multiplication sentence.

a. $6 \times 2 = 12$	**b.** $3 \times 8 = 24$	**c.** $3 \times 4 = 12$	**d.** $6 \times 4 = 24$

6. $4 + 4 + 4$

7. $2 + 2 + 2 + 2 + 2 + 2$

8. $8 + 8 + 8$

9. $4 + 4 + 4 + 4 + 4 + 4$

10. Can you write a multiplication sentence about this picture? Explain why or why not.

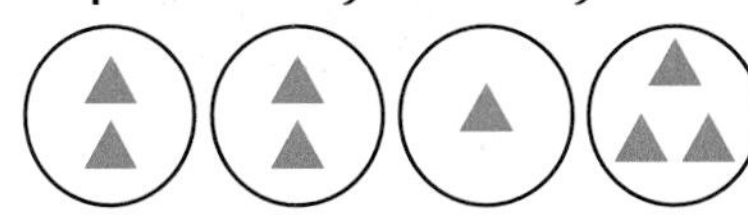

11. **Write a problem** that could be solved by using this multiplication sentence.

$$6 \times 2 = 12$$

Mixed Review and Test Prep

12. $437 - 229$ (p. 90)

13. $684 + 321$ (p. 70)

14. $9{,}239 + 1{,}605$ (p. 72)

15. $3{,}030 - 1{,}923$ (p. 96)

16. TEST PREP Which lists the *fewest* coins Caleb can use to make 78¢? (p. 110)

A 2 quarters, 5 nickels, 3 pennies
B 2 quarters, 2 dimes, 8 pennies
C 7 dimes, 8 pennies
D 3 quarters, 3 pennies

LESSON 2

Multiply with 2 and 5

Quick Review

How many are in all?

1. 1 group of 8
2. 3 groups of 2
3. 2 groups of 5
4. 4 groups of 2
5. 3 groups of 3

VOCABULARY

factors
product

Learn

SMART ROCKS The chips that run computers are made from a mineral found in rocks. Mrs. Frank asked 5 students to bring in 2 rocks each for a science project. How many rocks does she need?

Use counters.

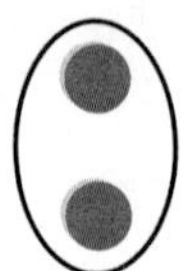 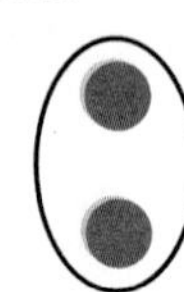 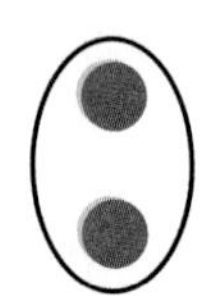 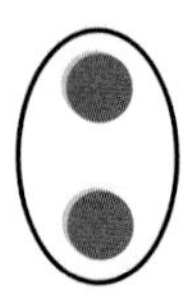 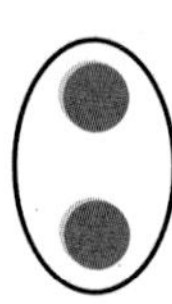

There are 5 groups, with 2 in each group.

Since each group has the same number, you can multiply to find how many in all.

$$\underset{\text{factor}}{5} \times \underset{\text{factor}}{2} = \underset{\text{product}}{10}$$

$$\begin{array}{r l} 2 & \leftarrow \text{factor} \\ \times 5 & \leftarrow \text{factor} \\ \hline 10 & \leftarrow \text{product} \end{array}$$

So, Mrs. Frank needs 10 rocks in all.

MATH IDEA The numbers that you multiply are **factors**. The answer is the **product**.

- Name the factors and product in $3 \times 2 = 6$.

Computer chip

Crystal

Check

1. Find the products 1×2 through 9×2. What do you notice about the products? Are they always even numbers or always odd numbers? Explain.

Find the product.

2. 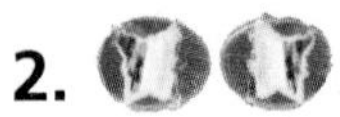 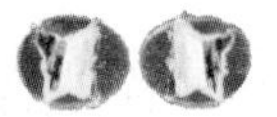 

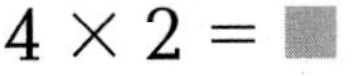

$4 \times 2 = ■$

3. 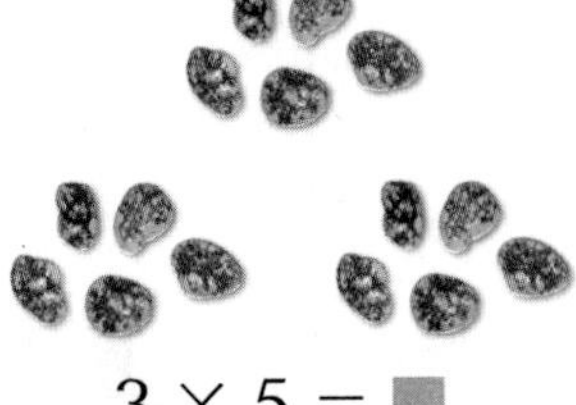

$3 \times 5 = ■$

4. $6 \times 2 = ■$

Practice and Problem Solving

Extra Practice, page 170, Set B

Find the product.

5. 

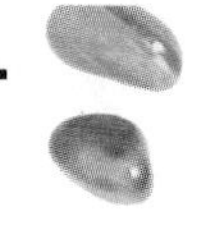  

$2 \times 2 = ■$

6.  

$5 \times 5 = ■$

7. 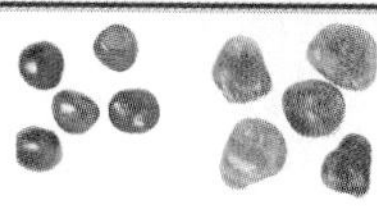 

$4 \times 5 = ■$

Copy and complete.

	×	1	2	3	4	5	6	7	8	9
8.	2	■	■	■	■	■	■	■	■	■
9.	5	■	■	■	■	■	■	■	■	■

Complete.

10. $8 \times 2 = ■$

11. $■ = 4 \times 5$

12. $6 \times 2 = ■$

13. $■ = 7 \times 5$

14. $■ = 9 \times 5$

15. $8 \times 5 = ■$

16. $■ = 7 \times 2$

17. $6 \times 5 = ■$

18. $\begin{array}{r} 2 \\ \times 8 \\ \hline \end{array}$

19. $\begin{array}{r} 5 \\ \times 8 \\ \hline \end{array}$

20. $\begin{array}{r} 2 \\ \times 9 \\ \hline \end{array}$

21. $\begin{array}{r} 5 \\ \times 9 \\ \hline \end{array}$

22. $3 + 3 = 2 \times ■$

23. $4 \times ■ = 4 + 4 + 4$

24. $2 \times 5 = ■ + 5$

25. Write a multiplication problem about the rocks below. Then solve.

26. **REASONING** Drew has 5 pairs of white socks and 2 pairs of black socks. How many more white socks than black socks does Drew have?

27. ***FAST FACT*** • SCIENCE Six Apollo space missions brought back 842 pounds of rocks, pebbles, sand, and dust from the surface of the moon. Write 842 in expanded form.

Mixed Review and Test Prep

28. 5 dimes = ■ quarters (p. 110)

29. 9 nickels = ■ pennies (p. 110)

30. Round 787 to the nearest ten. (p. 50)

31. $4.56 + $2.98 = ■ (p. 120)

32. **TEST PREP** Tony wrote this number pattern. Predict the next number. (p. 30)

869, 759, 649, 539, ___

A 549
B 459
C 449
D 429

LESSON 3

Arrays

Quick Review

Find how many in all.

1. 2 groups of 2
2. 3 groups of 3
3. 4 groups of 2
4. 5 groups of 5
5. 2 groups of 3

VOCABULARY

array

Commutative Property of Multiplication

MATERIALS

square tiles

Explore

An **array** shows objects in rows and columns.

Activity

Make an array to find how many are in 3 rows of 5.

STEP 1

Make an array with 3 rows and 5 columns.

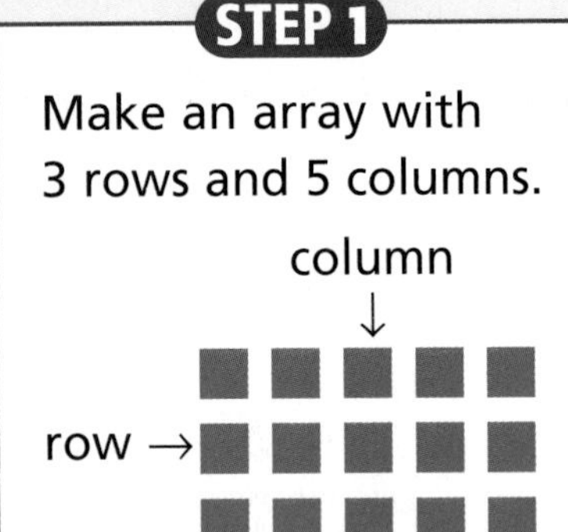

STEP 2

Count the tiles.

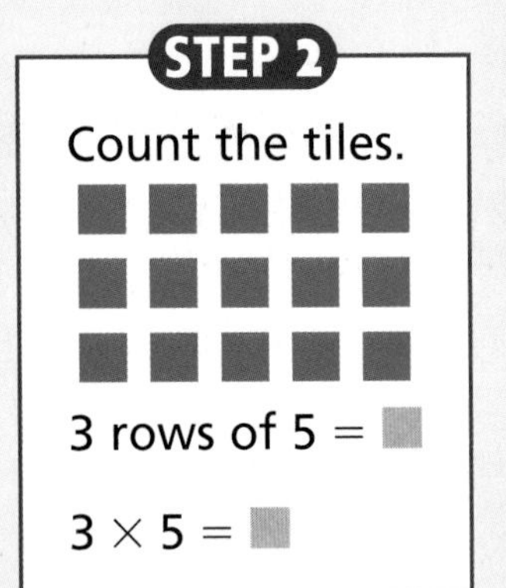

3 rows of 5 = ■

3 × 5 = ■

Technology Link

More Practice: Harcourt Mega Math Country Countdown, *Counting Critters*, Level W

- How many tiles are in the 3 rows of 5?
- What multiplication sentence can you write to find the number of tiles?
- Make an array with 3 rows of 3. What shape is formed by this array? What multiplication sentence can you write to find the number of tiles?

Try It

Copy and complete.

a.

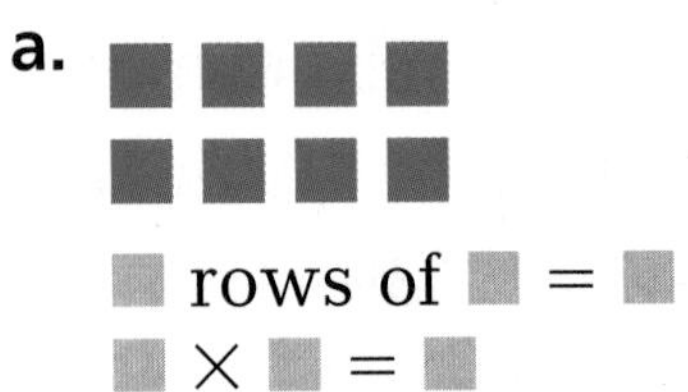

■ rows of ■ = ■

■ × ■ = ■

b.

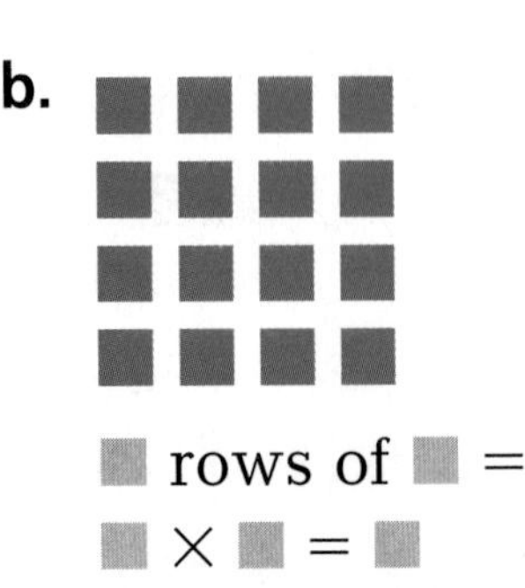

■ rows of ■ = ■

■ × ■ = ■

I have 2 rows of 4. How many are there in all?

Connect

The **Commutative Property of Multiplication**, or Order Property, states that two factors can be multiplied in any order. The product is the same.

Use arrays to show the Commutative Property of Multiplication.

Examples

A

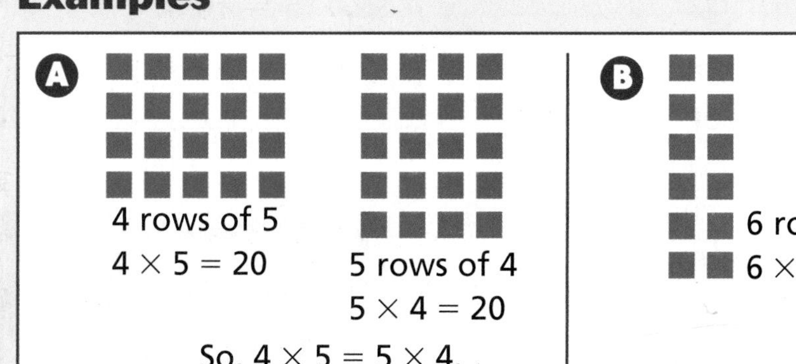

4 rows of 5

$4 \times 5 = 20$

5 rows of 4

$5 \times 4 = 20$

So, $4 \times 5 = 5 \times 4$.

B

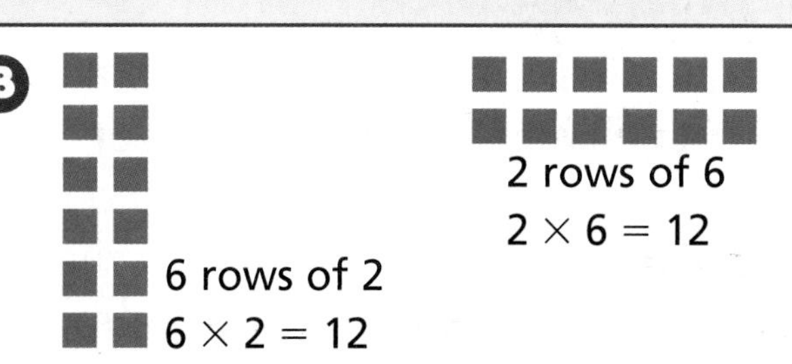

6 rows of 2

$6 \times 2 = 12$

2 rows of 6

$2 \times 6 = 12$

So, $6 \times 2 = 2 \times 6$.

Practice and Problem Solving

Copy and complete.

1. ■ rows of ■ = ■
   ■ × ■ = ■

2. ■ rows of ■ = ■
   ■ × ■ = ■

3. ■ rows of ■ = ■
   ■ × ■ = ■

Find the product. You may wish to draw an array.

4. $2 \times 5 =$ ■
5. $6 \times 4 =$ ■
6. $8 \times 3 =$ ■
7. $3 \times 5 =$ ■

8. **Write About It** Miguel needs a book cover that costs \$1.99 and a package of markers that costs \$2.79. He has \$5.00. Does he have enough money to buy both items?

9. **REASONING** The sum of Jarrod's age and Kayla's age is 21. Kayla is 5 years older than Jarrod. How old are Kayla and Jarrod?

Mixed Review and Test Prep

10. 24 + 46 + 93 (p. 8)

11. 446 − 267 (p. 90)

12. 34 − 15 (p. 10)

13. Write the value of the 7 in 67,409. (p. 32)

14. **TEST PREP** What is the total value of 3 dimes and 4 nickels? (p. 110)

 A 34¢
 B 50¢
 C 55¢
 D 70¢

LESSON 4

Multiply with 3

Quick Review

1. $2 + 2 = 2 \times ■$
2. $3 \times ■ = 5 + 5 + 5$
3. $2 \times 6 = 6 + ■$
4. $■ \times 5 = 10$
5. $2 \times 4 = ■$

Learn

PRACTICE, PRACTICE, PRACTICE

Pat practiced soccer 2 hours each day for 3 days. How many hours did he practice in all?

For 2 hours, move 2 spaces. For 3 days, make 3 jumps of 2 spaces.

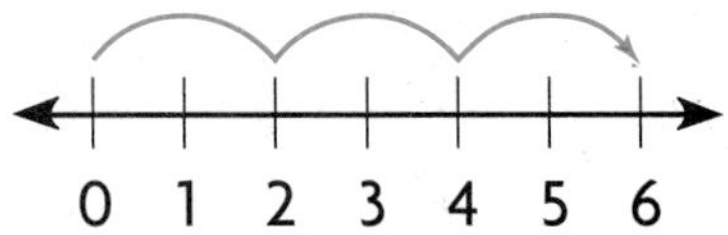

Multiply: $3 \times 2 = 6$

Val practiced soccer 3 hours each day for 2 days. How many hours did she practice in all?

For 3 hours, move 3 spaces. For 2 days, make 2 jumps of 3 spaces.

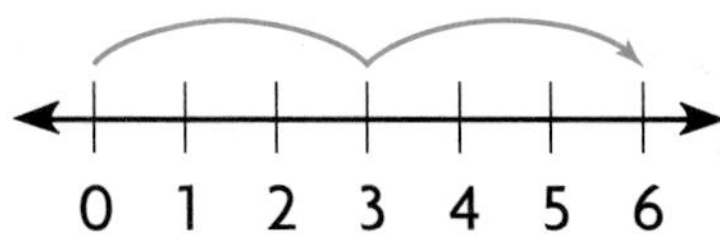

Multiply: $2 \times 3 = 6$

So, both Pat and Val practiced for 6 hours.

A number line can help you understand the Commutative Property of Multiplication.

One Way Use a number line.

Multiply. $3 \times 5 = 15$

0 1 2 3 4 5 6 7 8 9 10 11 12 13 14 15

Multiply. $5 \times 3 = 15$

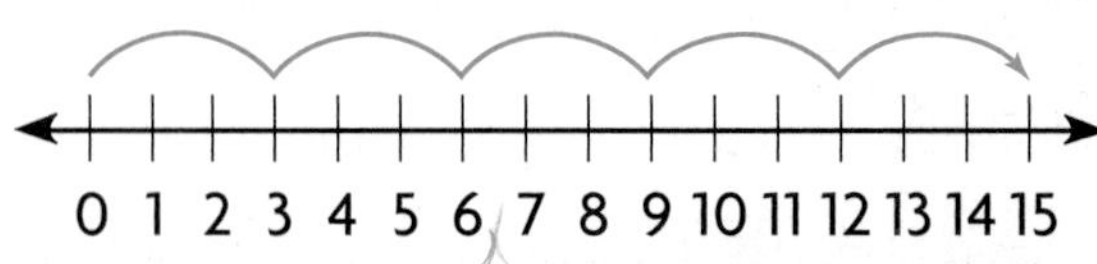

So, $3 \times 5 = 5 \times 3$.

- **REASONING** Use the factors 3 and 6 to explain the Commutative Property of Multiplication.

Multiplication Practice

What if Pat scored 4 goals in each of 3 games and Val scored 3 goals in each of 4 games? Which example shows Pat's goals? Val's goals? How many goals did each player score?

Another Way Draw a picture.

A   

$3 \times 4 = 12$

$4 \times 3 = 12$

Example A shows Pat's goals. Example B shows Val's goals.

Each player scored 12 goals.

- **What if** Val scored 8 goals in each of 3 games and Pat scored 3 goals in each of 8 games? How many goals did each player score?

Check

1. **Explain** how knowing the product 7×3 can help you find the product 3×7.

2. Is the product even or odd when you multiply 3 by an even number? by an odd number? Explain.

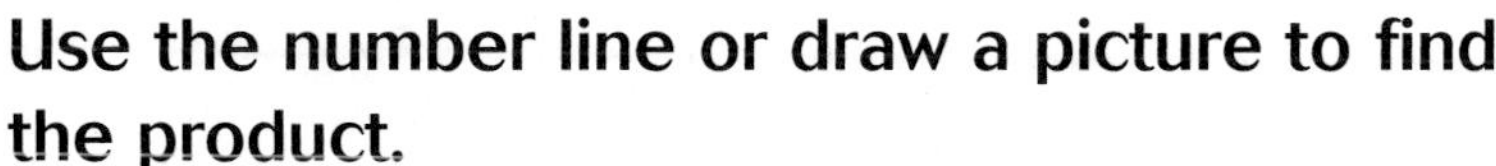

Use the number line or draw a picture to find the product.

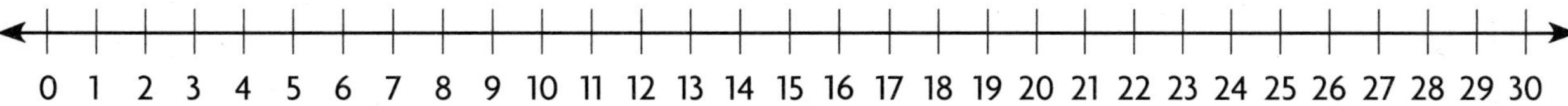

3. $4 \times 3 = ■$
4. $■ = 3 \times 4$
5. $7 \times 3 = ■$
6. $■ = 3 \times 7$
7. $■ = 6 \times 3$
8. $■ = 3 \times 6$
9. $3 \times 8 = ■$
10. $■ = 8 \times 3$
11. $\begin{array}{r} 5 \\ \times 3 \\ \hline \end{array}$
12. $\begin{array}{r} 3 \\ \times 5 \\ \hline \end{array}$
13. $\begin{array}{r} 3 \\ \times 9 \\ \hline \end{array}$
14. $\begin{array}{r} 9 \\ \times 3 \\ \hline \end{array}$

LESSON CONTINUES

Practice and Problem Solving

Extra Practice, page 170, Set C

Use the number line or draw a picture to find the product.

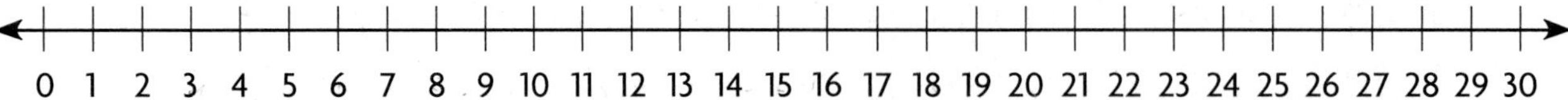

15. $3 \times 6 = \blacksquare$ **16.** $\blacksquare = 5 \times 5$ **17.** $3 \times 9 = \blacksquare$

18. $\blacksquare = 9 \times 3$ **19.** $\blacksquare = 9 \times 2$ **20.** $7 \times 3 = \blacksquare$

21. $\blacksquare = 4 \times 5$ **22.** $2 \times 8 = \blacksquare$ **23.** $7 \times 2 = \blacksquare$

24. $\begin{array}{r} 3 \\ \times 8 \\ \hline \end{array}$ **25.** $\begin{array}{r} 1 \\ \times 5 \\ \hline \end{array}$ **26.** $\begin{array}{r} 3 \\ \times 9 \\ \hline \end{array}$

Copy and complete.

27.

×	1	2	3	4	5	6	7	8	9
3	■	■	■	■	■	■	■	■	■

Write the missing factor.

28. $2 \times 3 = \blacksquare \times 2$ **29.** $3 \times \blacksquare = 7 \times 3$ **30.** $5 \times 3 = \blacksquare \times 5$

31. $6 \times 3 = \blacksquare \times 2$ **32.** $4 \times 3 = 6 \times \blacksquare$ **33.** $8 \times 3 = \blacksquare \times 8$

34. **What's the Error?** Sam played soccer for 2 hours a day, 3 days a week, for 4 weeks. Sam said he played soccer for a total of 6 hours during the month. What is Sam's error?

35. **REASONING** If you add 3 to an odd number, is the sum even or odd? If you multiply an odd number by 3, is the product even or odd? Explain.

USE DATA For 36–39, use the bar graph.

36. How many more goals did Matt's soccer team score in Game 4 than in Game 1?

37. How many goals did Matt's team score in the four games?

38. If Matt's team scores twice as many goals in Game 5 as in Game 3, how many goals will it score?

39. **Write a problem** using the bar graph.

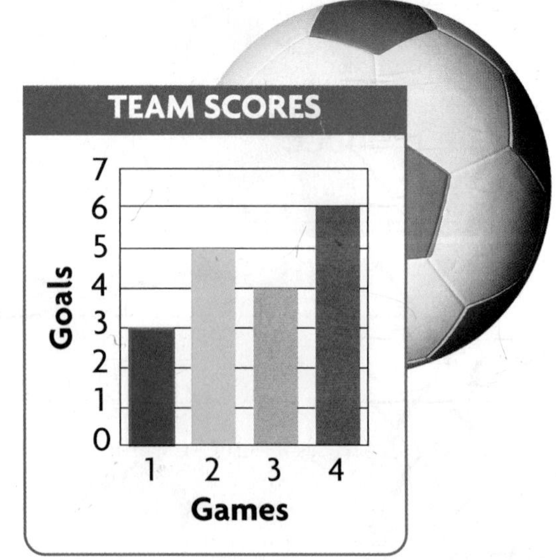

40. **Vocabulary Power** One number *times* another means that you multiply. Write a multiplication sentence. Circle the "times" sign, ×. Then draw a picture to show your sentence.

41. Matt needs 25 tennis balls. There are 5 balls in 1 package. If he buys 4 packages, will he have enough tennis balls? Draw a picture to show your answer.

Mixed Review and Test Prep

Write *A.M.* or *P.M.* for each. (p. 132)

42. see the sun: 10:00 ?

43. eat lunch: 11:45 ?

44. play at the park: 4:30 ?

Find the product. (p. 160)

45. $6 \times 2 = \blacksquare$

46. $8 \times 2 = \blacksquare$

47. $4 \times 5 = \blacksquare$

48. $6 \times 5 = \blacksquare$

49. **TEST PREP** $35 + 14 + 26$ (p. 8)

A 65 **B** 75 **C** 76 **D** 85

50. **TEST PREP** Lucy wants to buy a book that costs $1.65. Which set of bills and coins makes exactly $1.65? (p. 110)

F $1 bill, 2 quarters, 2 dimes
G $1 bill, 3 quarters, 3 dimes
H $1 bill, 2 quarters, 3 nickels
J $1 bill, 1 quarter, 3 dimes

Problem Solving Thinker's Corner

SOLVE THE RIDDLE! Find the product. To answer the riddle, match the letters to the products below.

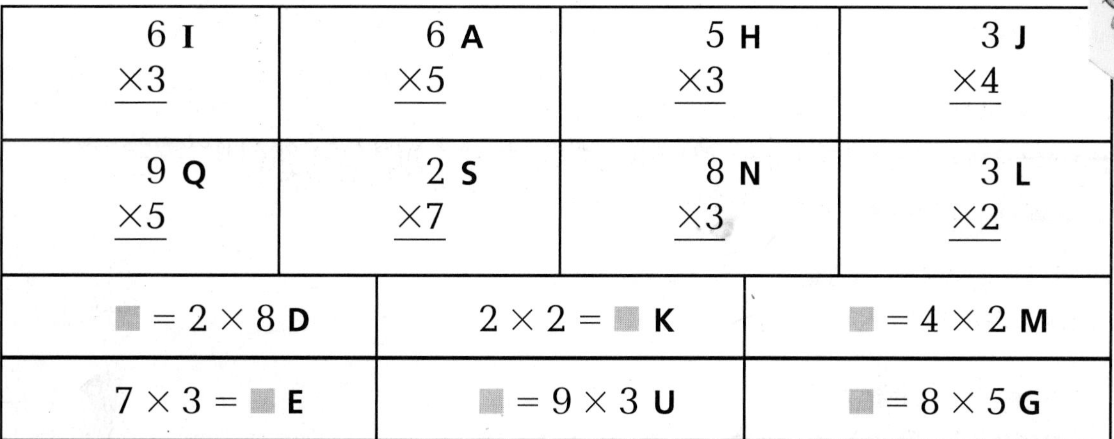

6×3 **I**	6×5 **A**	5×3 **H**	3×4 **J**
9×5 **Q**	2×7 **S**	8×3 **N**	3×2 **L**

$\blacksquare = 2 \times 8$ **D**	$2 \times 2 = \blacksquare$ **K**	$\blacksquare = 4 \times 2$ **M**
$7 \times 3 = \blacksquare$ **E**	$\blacksquare = 9 \times 3$ **U**	$\blacksquare = 8 \times 5$ **G**

What is a mouse's favorite game?

?	?	?	?		?	?	?		?	?	?	?	?	?
15	18	16	21		30	24	16		14	45	27	21	30	4

LESSON 5

Problem Solving Skill
Too Much/Too Little Information

Quick Review

1. 3×5
2. 4×3
3. 3×3
4. 9×3
5. 3×6

UNDERSTAND PLAN SOLVE CHECK

FIND THE FACTS Three students walked 6 blocks to the craft store. Each one bought 5 pieces of poster board to make posters for the school book fair. They stayed at the store for 45 minutes. How many pieces of poster board did the students buy in all?

Example

STEP 1

Find what the problem asks.

- How many pieces of poster board did the students buy in all?

STEP 2

Find what facts are needed to solve the problem.

- the number of students
- the number of pieces of poster board each one buys

STEP 3

Look for extra information.

- how far they walked
- how long they were at the store

Do you need this information to solve the problem?

STEP 4

Solve the problem.

- multiply

  3 students $\times$ 5 pieces $=$ 15 pieces

So, the students bought 15 pieces of poster board in all.

Talk About It

- Is there too much or too little information in the problem above?
- Three students went to a restaurant. They each bought a sandwich. How much did they spend in all? Does this problem have too much, too little, or the right amount of information? What information is missing from the problem?

Problem Solving Practice

USE DATA For 1–4, use the table. Write *a*, *b*, or *c* to tell whether the problem has

a. too much information. **b.** too little information. **c.** the right amount of information.

Solve those with too much or the right amount of information. Tell what is missing for those with too little information.

SCHOOL SUPPLIES	
Pack of Paper	$1
Backpack	$9
Pack of Pencils	$3
Lunch Box	$4

1. Felix wants to buy a backpack and a box of crayons. How much will he spend?

2. Marisa bought 2 packs of pencils. She was second in line to pay for her supplies. How much did Marisa spend?

3. Sam bought 2 backpacks and a lunch box. He received $3 change. How much money had he given the clerk?

4. Sally had $15. She bought 5 packs of paper and a lunch box. How much did she spend?

Mixed Applications

USE DATA For 5–6, use the table above.

You have $15 to spend on school supplies.

5. Which items can you buy?

A a backpack, 3 packs of pencils
B a backpack, a pack of pencils, a lunch box
C a lunch box, 2 packs of paper, a backpack
D 4 packs of pencils, a backpack

6. How much more money do you need if you choose to buy 2 packs of pencils, a lunch box, and a backpack?

F $1 **H** $3
G $2 **J** $4

7. Joe bought two tapes at the music store. They cost $7.28 and $7.71. How much change did he receive from $20.00?

8. **What's the Question?** There are 4 people in the Tamura family. Movie tickets cost $6 each. The answer is $24.

Extra Practice

Set A (pp. 158–159)

Copy and complete.

1. 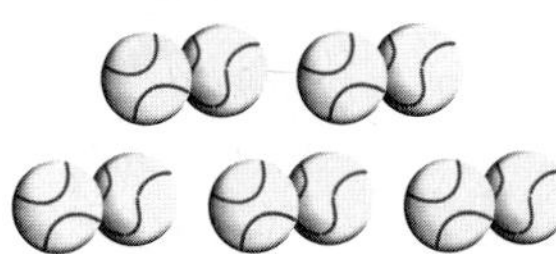

   a. ■ groups of ■ = ■

   b. ■ + ■ + ■ + ■ + ■ = ■

   c. ■ × ■ = ■

2. 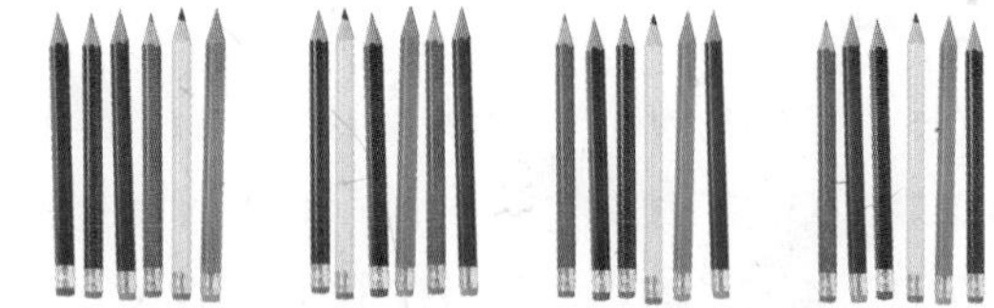

   a. ■ groups of ■ = ■

   b. ■ + ■ + ■ + ■ = ■

   c. ■ × ■ = ■

For 3–8, find how many in all.

3. 5 groups of 3
4. 4 + 4 + 4 + 4
5. 7 + 7 + 7
6. 5 × 4
7. 4 groups of 5
8. 5 × 5
9. Ana bought 6 packages of 5 cards each. How many cards did she buy?

Set B (pp. 160–161)

Find the product.

1. 7 × 2 = ■
2. 5 × 2 = ■
3. 7 × 5 = ■
4. 8 × 2 = ■
5. 4 × 5 = ■
6. 9 × 5 = ■
7. ■ = 6 × 5
8. ■ = 2 × 2
9. ■ = 5 × 5
10. Keith bought 5 packages of 3 toy cars each. David has 16 toy cars. Who has more cars? How do you know?

Set C (pp. 164–167)

Find the product.

1. 7 × 3 = ■
2. 5 × 3 = ■
3. ■ = 3 × 9
4. $\begin{array}{r} 6 \\ \times 3 \\ \hline \end{array}$
5. $\begin{array}{r} 5 \\ \times 6 \\ \hline \end{array}$
6. $\begin{array}{r} 3 \\ \times 8 \\ \hline \end{array}$
7. $\begin{array}{r} 3 \\ \times 9 \\ \hline \end{array}$
8. $\begin{array}{r} 5 \\ \times 9 \\ \hline \end{array}$

Find the missing factor.

9. 4 × 3 = ■ × 4
10. 5 × ■ = 9 × 5
11. ■ × 8 = 8 × 3

Review/Test

✓ CHECK VOCABULARY AND CONCEPTS

Choose the best term from the box.

array
factors
multiply
product

1. When groups have the same number, you can __?__ to find how many in all. (p. 158)
2. The numbers you multiply are __?__. (p. 160)
3. The answer to a multiplication problem is the __?__. (p. 160)

Find the product. You may wish to draw an array. (pp. 162–166)

4. $4 \times 5 = \blacksquare$
5. $3 \times 2 = \blacksquare$
6. $3 \times 6 = \blacksquare$
7. $7 \times 3 = \blacksquare$

✓ CHECK SKILLS

For 8–9, choose the letter of the number sentence that matches. (pp. 158–159)

8. $3 + 3 + 3 + 3$
9. $4 + 4 + 4 + 4 + 4$

a. $5 \times 4 = 20$
b. $6 \times 2 = 12$
c. $4 \times 3 = 12$

Find the product. (pp. 160–167)

10. $3 \times 8 = \blacksquare$
11. $3 \times 7 = \blacksquare$
12. $\blacksquare = 5 \times 6$
13. $4 \times 2 = \blacksquare$
14. 3×9
15. 6×3
16. 8×5
17. 7×5
18. 5×9

✓ CHECK PROBLEM SOLVING

Write *a*, *b*, or *c* to tell whether the problem has

a. too much information.
b. too little information.
c. the right amount of information.

Solve those with too much or the right amount of information. Tell what is missing for those with too little information. (pp. 168–169)

19. Pete practices 3 hours a day, Monday through Friday. How many hours does he practice each week?

20. Ramiro worked on his science project 3 hours longer than Sue. How much time did each of them spend on the project?

Standardized Test Prep

NUMBER SENSE, CONCEPTS, AND OPERATIONS

1. Dixie has 78 beads. She makes a bracelet with 23 of the beads. How many beads are left?

A 65
B 55
C 50
D 44

2. Sanjay has 7 packs of trading cards. There are 5 cards in each pack. Which of the following could he use to find the total number of cards?

F $7 + 5 = \blacksquare$
G $7 - 5 = \blacksquare$
H $7 \times 5 = \blacksquare$
J $5 + \blacksquare = 7$

3. Tony has 4 pairs of sneakers in his closet. How many sneakers does he have in all?

A 4
B 6
C 8
D 10

4. Explain It At Sunrise Elementary School there are 126 third graders and 152 fourth graders. About how many more fourth graders are there than third graders? Explain how you know.

MEASUREMENT

TIP **Check your work.** See item 5. Check your work by adding one hour to your answer. The sum should be the time shown on the clock.

5. Rhonda has been at the library for one hour. This clock shows the time it is now. At what time did Rhonda arrive at the library?

F 12:15 **H** 1:45
G 1:00 **J** 2:15

6. Ben put these coins in a bank. How much money did Ben put in the bank?

A \$1.25 **C** \$2.25
B \$1.80 **D** \$3.00

7. Explain It Megan said the length of a dollar bill is about 6 feet. Explain her error.

ALGEBRAIC THINKING

8. Carl wrote this number sentence about the picture below. Which number does ■ stand for?

$3 \times ■ = 15$

F 3
G 5
H 7
J 12

9. Together Karen and Shelly have 31 postcards. Karen has 17 postcards. How many postcards does Shelly have?

$17 + ■ = 31$

A 4
B 6
C 12
D 14

10. Which number makes this equation true?

$■ \times 5 = 40$

F 4
G 5
H 6
J 8

11. Explain It Tom wrote this pattern.

4, 8, 12, ■, 20

What number is missing? Explain how you know.

DATA ANALYSIS AND PROBABILITY

12. Which statement is true about this spinner?

A It is certain that the pointer will land on an even number.
B It is certain that the pointer will land on a number greater than 3.
C It is certain that the pointer will land on a number less than 2.
D It is certain that the pointer will land on an odd number.

13. Mike asks six classmates how many hats they own. The table shows their answers. What is the range of these data?

HATS OWNED	
Roger	5
Heather	7
Bill	4
Nancy	3
Lisa	4
David	6

F 3
G 4
H 5
J 6

14. Explain It Mike said that the boys have more hats than the girls. Is he correct? Use Mike's survey above to explain your answer.

CHAPTER 9

Multiplication Facts Through 5

Mantis is a stand-up roller coaster in Sandusky, Ohio. Each train has eight rows of four riders.

FAST FACT • SOCIAL STUDIES There are more than 600 roller coasters in North America today. Some can reach speeds greater than 70 miles per hour!

PROBLEM SOLVING Compare the number of riders on the roller coasters in the pictograph with the coaster in the photo. Which roller coasters have the same number of riders per train as the Mantis?

ROLLER COASTER RIDERS PER TRAIN

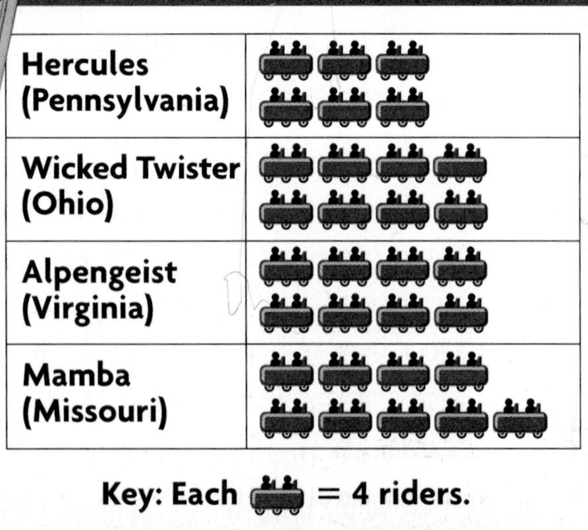

Hercules (Pennsylvania)	
Wicked Twister (Ohio)	
Alpengeist (Virginia)	
Mamba (Missouri)	

Key: Each = 4 riders.

CHECK WHAT YOU KNOW

Use this page to help you review and remember important skills needed for Chapter 9.

MODEL MULTIPLICATION

Copy and complete.

1. $6 \times 2 = \blacksquare$

2. $3 \times 4 = \blacksquare$

3. $5 \times 3 = \blacksquare$

4. $4 \times 2 = \blacksquare$

COMMUTATIVE PROPERTY OF MULTIPLICATION

Complete.

5. $4 \times 5 = \blacksquare \times 4$
6. $3 \times 6 = \blacksquare \times 3$
7. $2 \times 7 = \blacksquare \times 2$
8. $5 \times 8 = \blacksquare \times 5$
9. $4 \times 7 = \blacksquare \times 4$
10. $3 \times 9 = \blacksquare \times 3$

VOCABULARY POWER

REVIEW

factor [fak′tər] *noun*

A factory is a place where parts are put together to make something. A *factor* is one of the numbers that is put together to make a product. How are the meanings of *factory* and *factor* alike? What are the factors in $4 \times 6 = 24$?

PREVIEW

multiple

www.harcourtschool.com/mathglossary

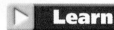

LESSON

Multiply with 1 and 0

Quick Review

1. $2 \times 5 = ■$
2. $3 \times 4 = 4 + 4 + ■$
3. $6 \times 2 = ■$
4. $5 + 5 + 5 = ■ \times 5$
5. $3 \times 2 = ■$

Learn

ALL OR NOTHING Tina saw 5 cars. One clown sat in each car. How many clowns were there in all?

Example

STEP 1

Count the cars.

STEP 2

Count the clowns in the cars.

STEP 3

Write the multiplication sentence.

5	×	1	=	5
↑		↑		↑
number of groups		number in each group		number in all

So, there were 5 clowns in all.

Suppose Tina saw 3 cars with 0 clowns in each car. How many clowns were there in all?

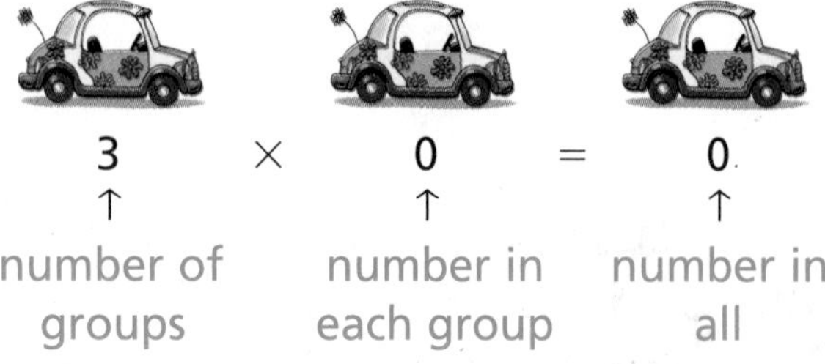

3	×	0	=	0
↑		↑		↑
number of groups		number in each group		number in all

So, there were 0 clowns in all.

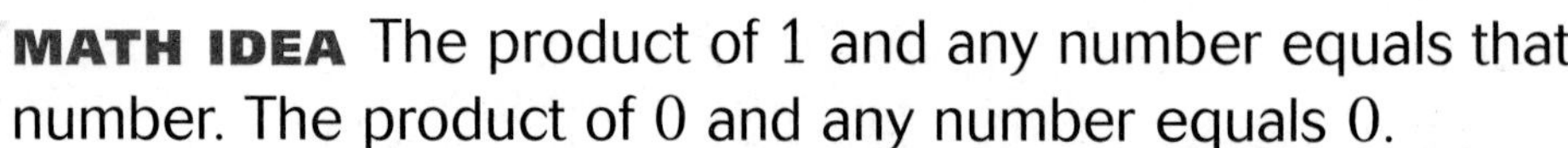

MATH IDEA The product of 1 and any number equals that number. The product of 0 and any number equals 0.

REASONING What is 498×1? 498×0? How do you know?

Check

1. **Explain** what happens when you multiply by 1. What happens when you multiply by 0?

Find the product.

2. $4 \times 1 = ■$ 3. $5 \times 0 = ■$ 4. $1 \times 3 = ■$

Practice and Problem Solving

Extra Practice, page 188, Set A

Find the product.

5. $2 \times 1 = ■$ 6. $4 \times 0 = ■$ 7. $0 \times 5 = ■$ 8. $■ = 9 \times 1$

9. $■ \times 6 = ■$ 10. $■ = 0 \times 9$ 11. $7 \times 1 = ■$ 12. $2 \times 4 = ■$

13. $■ = 0 \times 7$ 14. $3 \times 3 = ■$ 15. $■ = 1 \times 8$ 16. $0 \times 0 = ■$

17. $\begin{array}{r} 9 \\ \times 0 \\ \hline \end{array}$ 18. $\begin{array}{r} 1 \\ \times 3 \\ \hline \end{array}$ 19. $\begin{array}{r} 5 \\ \times 4 \\ \hline \end{array}$ 20. $\begin{array}{r} 8 \\ \times 5 \\ \hline \end{array}$

21. Multiply 4 by 1.

22. Find the product of 0 and 8.

Complete.

23. $■ = 9 \times 5$ 24. $3 + 9 = 3 \times ■$ 25. $3 \times 6 = ■ \times 9$

26. $8 + 7 = ■ \times 5$ 27. $0 \times 8 = ■ \times 9$ 28. $9 \times ■ = 3 \times 3$

29. **REASONING** Ann is younger than Rick. Rick is older than Tracy. Tracy is older than Ann. Who is the oldest?

30. **Write About It** Which is less, the product of your age and 1 or the product of your age and 0? Explain.

31. **Vocabulary Power** The word *zero* comes from an old Arabic word that means "empty." Explain what it means for a group to have zero items.

Mixed Review and Test Prep

Find the value of the blue digit. (p. 32)

32. 92,348 33. 38,965

34. Find the sum of 652 and 738. (p. 72)

35. Put the numbers in order from least to greatest. 4,543; 2,960; 3,534; 4,243 (p. 46)

36. **TEST PREP** Carol bought a pencil for $0.32. She paid with a $1 bill. How much change did she get? (p. 118)

A $0.32 C $0.78
B $0.68 D $1.32

LESSON

2 Multiply with 4 on a Multiplication Table

Quick Review

1. 0×3
2. 4×2
3. 1×9
4. 8×1
5. 2×5

VOCABULARY

multiple

Learn

TWISTS AND TURNS There are 6 cars in the Twister ride at the amusement park. Each car holds 4 people. How many people does the Twister ride hold?

$$6 \times 4 = ■$$

- How could you use an array to find 6×4?

You can use a multiplication table to find the product. The product is found where row 6 and column 4 meet.

Multiplication Table

column ↓ (4); row → (6)

×	0	1	2	3	4	5	6	7	8	9
0	0	0	0	0	0	0	0	0	0	0
1	0	1	2	3	4	5	6	7	8	9
2	0	2	4	6	8	10	12	14	16	18
3	0	3	6	9	12	15	18	21	24	27
4	0	4	8	12	16	20	24	28	32	36
5	0	5	10	15	20	25	30	35	40	45
6	0	6	12	18	24	30	36	42	48	54
7	0	7	14	21	28	35	42	49	56	63
8	0	8	16	24	32	40	48	56	64	72
9	0	9	18	27	36	45	54	63	72	81

$$\underset{\text{factor}}{6} \times \underset{\text{factor}}{4} = \underset{\text{product}}{24}$$

$$\begin{array}{rl} 4 & \leftarrow \text{factor} \\ \times 6 & \leftarrow \text{factor} \\ \hline 24 & \leftarrow \text{product} \end{array}$$

So, the Twister ride holds 24 people.

MATH IDEA A **multiple** of 4 is any product that has 4 as a factor. 4, 8, 12, 16, and so on are all multiples of 4.

REASONING How can you use the multiplication table to find other multiples of 4?

- Name the multiples of 3 in the multiplication table.
- Are the multiples of 5 all even numbers? Explain.

Check

1. **Explain** how you can use the multiplication table to find 5×8.

Find the product.

2. $2 \times 4 = ■$
3. $9 \times 4 = ■$
4. $■ = 4 \times 5$
5. $4 \times 3 = ■$

Practice and Problem Solving

Extra Practice, page 188, Set B

Find the product.

6. $4 \times 2 = \blacksquare$ 7. $9 \times 0 = \blacksquare$ 8. $4 \times 5 = \blacksquare$

9. $\blacksquare = 5 \times 8$ 10. $4 \times 4 = \blacksquare$ 11. $1 \times 9 = \blacksquare$

12. $\blacksquare = 4 \times 7$ 13. $3 \times 0 = \blacksquare$ 14. $\blacksquare = 8 \times 4$

15. 2×3 16. 5×1 17. 4×6 18. 0×4 19. 7×4 20. 5×5

21. 3×6 22. 4×9 23. 8×2 24. 7×5 25. 4×8 26. 9×4

Copy and complete.

27.

×	0	1	2	3	4	5	6	7	8	9
4	■	■	■	■	■	■	■	■	■	■

28. $9 \times 0 = \blacksquare \times 4$ 29. $2 \times 9 = \blacksquare \times 3$ 30. $4 \times 4 = \blacksquare \times 2$

31. Name some multiples of 2. Explain.

32. Find the product of 4 and 9.

33. Find the product of 7 and 0.

34. Is 12 a multiple of 6? Explain.

35. Each ride costs 4 tickets. If Tonya went on 7 different rides, how many tickets did she use? Draw a picture to show your answer.

36. **FAST FACT** • **SOCIAL STUDIES** There are 520 steel roller coasters and 124 wooden roller coasters in North America. How many more steel than wooden ones are there?

37. Ahmed has 3 packs of 8 baseball cards and 11 extra cards. How many cards does he have in all?

38. Since $9 \times 4 = 36$ and $10 \times 4 = 40$, what is 11×4? How do you know?

Mixed Review and Test Prep

39. Ida has one $1 bill, 4 quarters, 2 dimes, and 1 nickel. How much money does she have? (p. 110)

40. $\$4.89 + \$7.77$ (p. 120)

41. $\$9.42 - \$5.54$ (p. 120)

42. Round 547 to the nearest ten. (p. 50)

43. **TEST PREP** Which shows the numbers in order from least to greatest? (p. 46)

A 468, 486, 648
B 468, 648, 486
C 486, 468, 648
D 648, 486, 468

LESSON 3

Problem Solving Strategy
Find a Pattern

Quick Review

1. 3 × ■ = 6
2. 3 + ■ = 9
3. ■ × 2 = 12
4. 12 + ■ = 15
5. 14 + ■ = 18

PROBLEM Emily is playing a number pattern game. She says the numbers 3, 5, 8, 10, 13, 15, 18, 20, and 23. What is a rule for her pattern? What are the next four numbers she will say?

UNDERSTAND

- What are you asked to find?
- What information will you use?
- Is there information you will not use? If so, what?

PLAN

- What strategy can you use to solve the problem?
  You can *find a pattern.*

SOLVE

- How can you use the strategy to solve the problem?
  Use a number line to find the pattern. Then write a rule and the next four numbers.

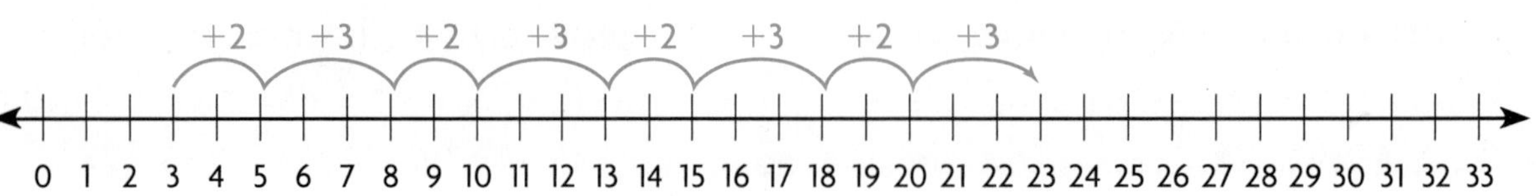

So, a rule is *add 2 and then add 3*. The next four numbers in Emily's pattern will be 25, 28, 30, and 33.

CHECK

- How do you know if your answer is correct?

Problem Solving Practice

Use *find a pattern* to solve.

1. **What if** the first number in Emily's pattern is 3 and the rule is *multiply by 2 and then subtract 2*? What are the first five numbers in her pattern?

2. Albert's pattern is 3, 6, 9, and 12. What is a rule for his pattern? What are the next four numbers?

Strategies

- Draw a Diagram or Picture
- Make a Model or Act It Out
- Make an Organized List
- **Find a Pattern**
- Make a Table or Graph
- Predict and Test
- Work Backward
- Solve a Simpler Problem
- Write a Number Sentence
- Use Logical Reasoning

Problem Solving

Karen is thinking of a number pattern. The first four numbers are 4, 8, 12, and 16.

3. What are the next three numbers in Karen's pattern?

   A 16, 20, 24 **C** 18, 20, 22

   B 17, 19, 21 **D** 20, 24, 28

4. Which number doesn't fit in Karen's pattern?

   F 20 **H** 32

   G 28 **J** 35

Mixed Strategy Practice

5. Bo bicycled 4 miles a day last week. He did not bicycle on Saturday or Sunday. How far did he bicycle last week?

6. **What's the Error?** Look at this pattern. Which number doesn't fit this pattern? Explain.
   11, 21, 31, 41, 51, 60, 71

7. **Reasoning** Use the digits 0–9 to write the greatest possible 4-digit number using 4 different digits. Write the least possible 4-digit number using 4 different digits.

8. If this is the time now, what time will it be in 2 hours 35 minutes?

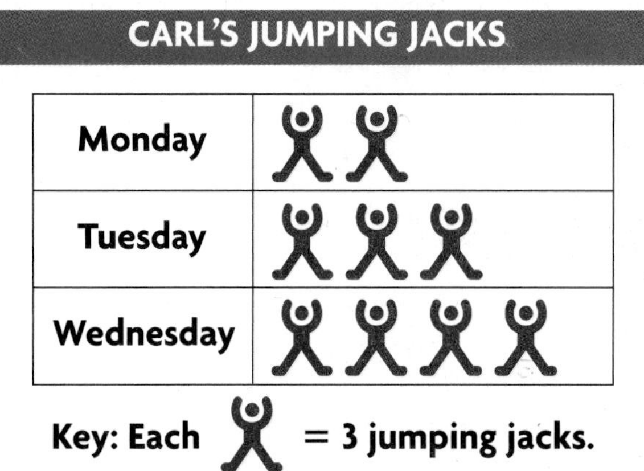

9. **Use Data** If Carl continues the pattern above, how many jumping jacks will he do on Saturday?

10. **Write a problem** about a number pattern. Tell how you would explain to a second grader how to find the next number in your pattern.

LESSON 4

Practice Multiplication

Quick Review

1. 3 × ▒ = 12
2. 2 × 6 = ▒
3. 0 × 8 = ▒
4. 4 × 5 = ▒
5. 9 × ▒ = 9

Learn

FACTS IN FLIGHT At the airport, Nicole saw 6 jets waiting to take off. Each jet had 3 engines. How many engines were there in all?

$$6 \times 3 = ▒$$

There are many ways to find a product.

A. You can make equal groups or arrays.

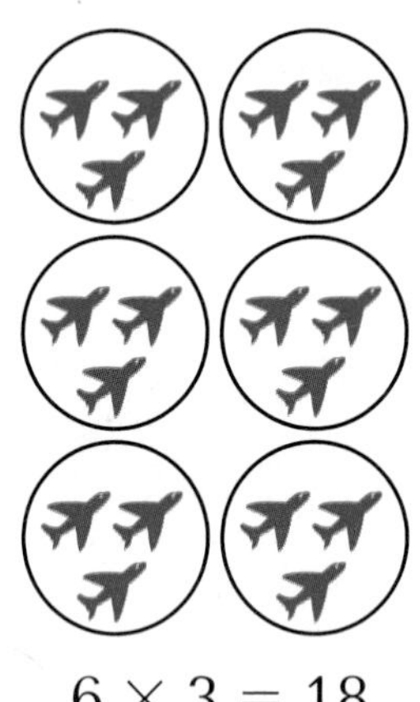

$6 \times 3 = 18$

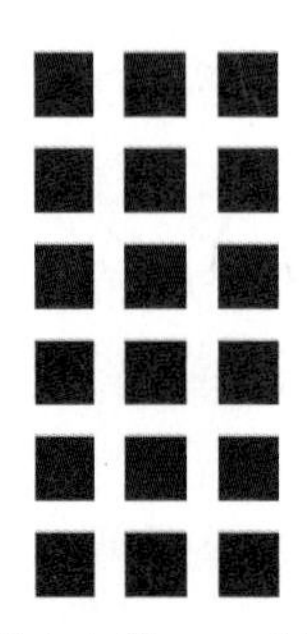

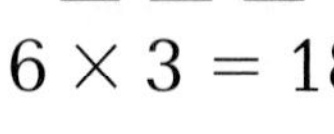

$6 \times 3 = 18$

B. You can skip-count on a number line.

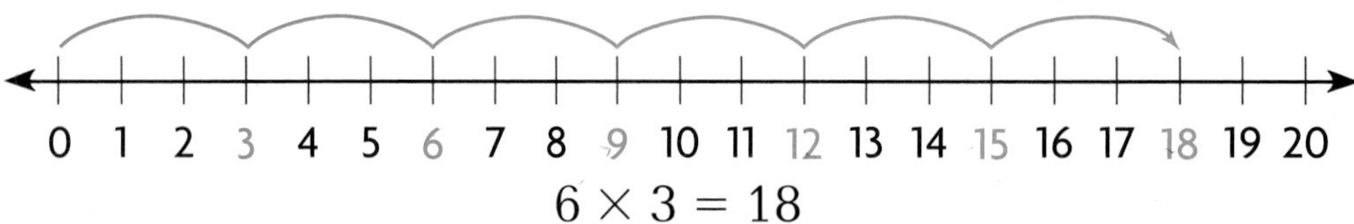

$6 \times 3 = 18$

C. You can double a fact that you already know.

Think: $3 \times 3 = 9$ and $9 + 9 = 18$, so $6 \times 3 = 18$.

Technology Link

More Practice: Harcourt Mega Math The Number Games, *Up, Up, and Array,* Level A

D. You can use the Commutative Property of Multiplication.

Think: $3 \times 6 = 6 \times 3 = 18$.

Another Way to Find a Product

E. You can use a multiplication table.

×	0	1	2	3	4	5	6	7	8	9
0	0	0	0	0	0	0	0	0	0	0
1	0	1	2	3	4	5	6	7	8	9
2	0	2	4	6	8	10	12	14	16	18
3	0	3	6	9	12	15	18	21	24	27
4	0	4	8	12	16	20	24	28	32	36
5	0	5	10	15	20	25	30	35	40	45
6	0	6	12	18	24	30	36	42	48	54
7	0	7	14	21	28	35	42	49	56	63
8	0	8	16	24	32	40	48	56	64	72
9	0	9	18	27	36	45	54	63	72	81

(column ↓ points to column 3; row → points to row 6)

Think: The product is found where row 6 and column 3 meet.

$$6 \times 3 = 18$$

So, there are 18 engines in all.

MATH IDEA You can use equal groups, arrays, skip-counting, doubles, the Commutative Property of Multiplication, or a multiplication table to help you find products or multiples.

- Are the multiples of 6 always even numbers? Explain why or why not.

Check

1. **Explain** two ways to find 4×8.

Write a multiplication sentence for each.

2. 

3.  

4. 

Find the product.

5. $2 \times 6 = ■$

6. $5 \times 3 = ■$

7. $■ = 1 \times 7$

8. $■ = 7 \times 3$

LESSON CONTINUES

Practice and Problem Solving

Extra Practice, page 188, Set C

Find the product.

9. $7 \times 4 = \blacksquare$ **10.** $2 \times 8 = \blacksquare$ **11.** $7 \times 5 = \blacksquare$ **12.** $4 \times 2 = \blacksquare$

13. $\blacksquare = 5 \times 4$ **14.** $9 \times 4 = \blacksquare$ **15.** $\blacksquare = 2 \times 5$ **16.** $9 \times 1 = \blacksquare$

17. $\blacksquare = 1 \times 9$ **18.** $6 \times 2 = \blacksquare$ **19.** $5 \times 6 = \blacksquare$ **20.** $\blacksquare = 8 \times 4$

21. $5 \times 1 = \blacksquare$ **22.** $3 \times 0 = \blacksquare$ **23.** $2 \times 9 = \blacksquare$ **24.** $6 \times 5 = \blacksquare$

25. $2 \times 4 = \blacksquare$ **26.** $\blacksquare = 3 \times 7$ **27.** $8 \times 5 = \blacksquare$ **28.** $\blacksquare = 9 \times 3$

29. $\begin{array}{r} 9 \\ \times 3 \\ \hline \end{array}$ **30.** $\begin{array}{r} 0 \\ \times 6 \\ \hline \end{array}$ **31.** $\begin{array}{r} 5 \\ \times 7 \\ \hline \end{array}$ **32.** $\begin{array}{r} 8 \\ \times 3 \\ \hline \end{array}$ **33.** $\begin{array}{r} 4 \\ \times 9 \\ \hline \end{array}$ **34.** $\begin{array}{r} 4 \\ \times 4 \\ \hline \end{array}$

Copy and complete.

35.

×	2	4	7	8	9
2	■	■	■	■	■

36.

×	3	5	7	8	9
3	■	■	■	■	■

37.

×	2	7	5	3	8
4	■	■	■	■	■

38.

×	1	6	9	7	8
5	■	■	■	■	■

Compare. Write <, >, or = for each ●.

39. 3×2 ● 4×1 **40.** 7×4 ● 4×8 **41.** 5×8 ● $35 + 6$

42. 4×6 ● 8×3 **43.** 3×6 ● 5×4 **44.** 7×5 ● 8×3

45. REASONING Jenny baked some cookies. She put 4 chocolate chips and 2 pecans on each cookie. If she used 24 chocolate chips in all, how many pecans did she use?

46. Pedro and Jon have 20 toy cars altogether. If Jon buys another toy car, he will have twice as many toy cars as Pedro. How many toy cars does Pedro have?

47. **? What's the Error?** To find the product 5×6, Ellen made this array. What did Ellen do wrong?

48. REASONING Look at this number pattern. What is a rule? What are the missing numbers?

8, 11, 14, ■, ■, ■, 26

49. Three vans are going to the airport. There are 9 people in each van. How many people are going to the airport?

50. Marie has 4 loose stamps and 5 sheets of 8 stamps each. How many stamps does she have in all?

Mixed Review and Test Prep

51. How many minutes are between 12:25 P.M. and 12:30 P.M.? (p. 134)

52. $\begin{array}{r} 3{,}509 \\ +4{,}737 \\ \hline \end{array}$ (p. 72)

53. $\begin{array}{r} 7{,}324 \\ -2{,}195 \\ \hline \end{array}$ (p. 96)

54. What time will it be in 1 hour 45 minutes? (p. 134)

55. $17 + 88 + 71 = \blacksquare$ (p. 8)

56. $\blacksquare + 14 = 23$ (p. 8)

57. $51 - \blacksquare = 39$ (p. 10)

58. $872 + 208 = \blacksquare$ (p. 72)

59. **TEST PREP** Which shows the numbers in order from greatest to least? (p. 46)

A 998, 989, 999
B 989, 998, 999
C 999, 989, 998
D 999, 998, 989

60. **TEST PREP** Leo bought a comic book for $2.59. He paid with a $5 bill. How much change did he get back? (p. 120)

F $2.41 **H** $3.41
G $2.51 **J** $3.51

Problem Solving Thinker's Corner

FINDING MULTIPLES

You can use a hundred chart to show multiples.

MATERIALS: hundred chart, crayons

a. Start at 2. Shade all of the multiples of 2 with a yellow crayon.

b. Start at 3. Shade all of the multiples of 3 with a blue crayon.

c. What numbers are now shaded both yellow and blue (green)?

d. Look at the green numbers. These numbers are multiples of which number?

1	2	3	4	5	6	7	8	9	10
11	12	13	14	15	16	17	18	19	20
21	22	23	24	25	26	27	28	29	30
31	32	33	34	35	36	37	38	39	40
41	42	43	44	45	46	47	48	49	50
51	52	53	54	55	56	57	58	59	60
61	62	63	64	65	66	67	68	69	70
71	72	73	74	75	76	77	78	79	80
81	82	83	84	85	86	87	88	89	90
91	92	93	94	95	96	97	98	99	100

LESSON

5 Algebra: Missing Factors

Quick Review

1. 4×6
2. 2×7
3. 3×0
4. 6×1
5. 3×6

Learn

BLUE RIBBON BAKING Mike's muffins won first prize at the county fair. Each plate held 5 muffins. He made 35 muffins. How many plates did he use?

$\blacksquare \times 5 = 35$ How can you find the missing factor?

One Way Use square tiles.

Make an array with 35 tiles.
Use 5 tiles in a row.
Count how many rows of 5 tiles.
There are 7 rows of 5 tiles.
The missing factor is 7.

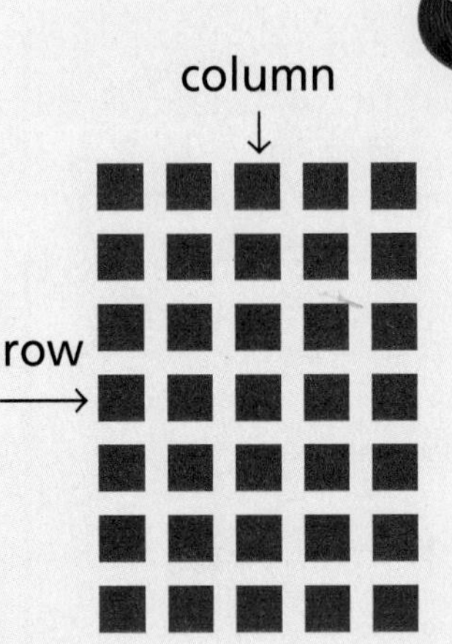

$\blacksquare$	×	5	=	35
7	×	5	=	35
↑		↑		↑
factor		factor		product
rows		*columns*		*total number of tiles*

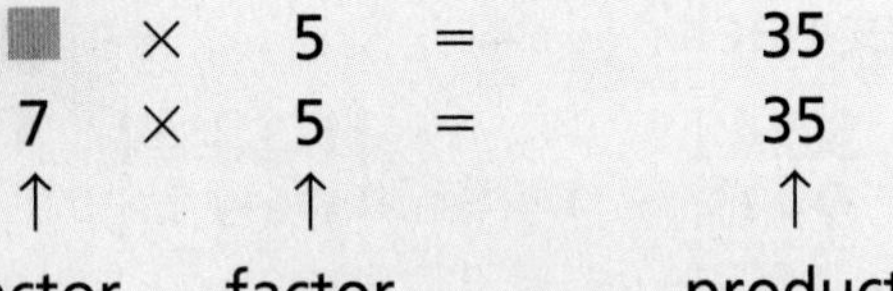

Another Way Use a multiplication table.

Start at the column for 5.
Look down to the product, 35.
Look left across the row from 35.
The missing factor is 7.

$\blacksquare$	×	5	=	35
7	×	5	=	35
↑		↑		↑
factor		factor		product
row		*column*		*row 7 column 5*

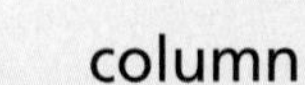

column ↓, row →

×	0	1	2	3	4	5	6	7	8	9
0	0	0	0	0	0	0	0	0	0	0
1	0	1	2	3	4	5	6	7	8	9
2	0	2	4	6	8	10	12	14	16	18
3	0	3	6	9	12	15	18	21	24	27
4	0	4	8	12	16	20	24	28	32	36
5	0	5	10	15	20	25	30	35	40	45
6	0	6	12	18	24	30	36	42	48	54
7	0	7	14	21	28	35	42	49	56	63
8	0	8	16	24	32	40	48	56	64	72
9	0	9	18	27	36	45	54	63	72	81

So, Mike used 7 plates.

MATH IDEA When you know the product and one factor, square tiles or a multiplication table can help you find the missing factor.

REASONING How can you use square tiles or a multiplication table to find factors for 24?

Check

1. **Explain** how to use the table to find the missing factor in $\blacksquare \times 6 = 18$.

Find the missing factor.

2. $\blacksquare \times 2 = 8$ **3.** $3 \times \blacksquare = 9$ **4.** $5 \times \blacksquare = 20$

Practice and Problem Solving

Extra Practice, page 188, Set D

Find the missing factor.

5. $\blacksquare \times 4 = 12$ **6.** $\blacksquare \times 3 = 21$ **7.** $5 \times \blacksquare = 0$ **8.** $2 \times \blacksquare = 12$

9. $1 \times \blacksquare = 9$ **10.** $8 \times \blacksquare = 24$ **11.** $\blacksquare \times 6 = 30$ **12.** $\blacksquare \times 4 = 32$

13. $\blacksquare \times 2 = 18$ **14.** $4 \times \blacksquare = 16$ **15.** $5 \times \blacksquare = 15$ **16.** $\blacksquare \times 6 = 24$

17. $\blacksquare \times 4 = 36$ **18.** $\blacksquare \times 3 = 27$ **19.** $6 \times \blacksquare = 18$ **20.** $8 \times \blacksquare = 40$

21. $4 \times 6 = \blacksquare \times 3$ **22.** $9 \times \blacksquare = 50 - 5$ **23.** $7 \times \blacksquare = 32 - 4$

24. The product of 4 and another factor is 28. What is the other factor?

25. If you multiply 9 by a number, the product is 27. What is the number?

26. There are 2 chairs at each table. If there are 14 chairs, how many tables are there? Write a multiplication sentence to solve.

27. There are 4 oatmeal cookies and 3 sugar cookies on each plate. How many cookies are on 5 plates?

28. **Write About It** How can you use a multiplication table to find the multiples of 6?

29. **? What's the Question?** Pies are on sale for \$3 each. Carly spent \$12 on pies. The answer is 4 pies.

Mixed Review and Test Prep

30. Tony has two \$1 bills and 1 dime. Benita has one \$1 bill and 4 quarters. Who has the greater amount of money? (p. 116)

31. $400 - 137$ (p. 92)

32. $453 + 487$ (p. 70)

33. Write $<$, $>$, or $=$. (p. 42)

5,450 ● 5,405

34. **TEST PREP** Which number means $10{,}000 + 1{,}000 + 10 + 1$? (p. 32)

A 10,111 **C** 11,101
B 11,011 **D** 11,110

Extra Practice

Set A (pp. 176–177)

Find the product.

1. $0 \times 5 = ■$ **2.** $3 \times 7 = ■$ **3.** $1 \times 7 = ■$ **4.** $4 \times 3 = ■$

5. $■ = 6 \times 3$ **6.** $■ = 8 \times 5$ **7.** $■ = 0 \times 9$ **8.** $■ = 1 \times 1$

9. Is the product of 3 and 0 *greater than, less than,* or *equal to* the product of 0 and 6? Explain.

Set B (pp. 178–179)

Find the product.

1. $\begin{array}{r} 8 \\ \times 4 \\ \hline \end{array}$ **2.** $\begin{array}{r} 4 \\ \times 0 \\ \hline \end{array}$ **3.** $\begin{array}{r} 4 \\ \times 6 \\ \hline \end{array}$ **4.** $\begin{array}{r} 4 \\ \times 4 \\ \hline \end{array}$ **5.** $\begin{array}{r} 4 \\ \times 9 \\ \hline \end{array}$

6. $3 \times 4 = ■$ **7.** $■ = 2 \times 4$ **8.** $■ = 4 \times 7$ **9.** $5 \times 4 = ■$

10. Mario has 4 packs of 8 stickers. He also has 19 loose stickers. How many stickers does he have in all?

Set C (pp. 182–185)

Find the product.

1. $4 \times 6 = ■$ **2.** $5 \times 3 = ■$ **3.** $8 \times 0 = ■$ **4.** $9 \times 5 = ■$

5. $5 \times 8 = ■$ **6.** $3 \times 6 = ■$ **7.** $7 \times 4 = ■$ **8.** $3 \times 9 = ■$

9. $8 \times 2 = ■$ **10.** $3 \times 7 = ■$ **11.** $6 \times 5 = ■$ **12.** $4 \times 8 = ■$

13. A movie is shown 5 times each day. How many times is that movie shown in one week?

Set D (pp. 186–187)

Find the missing factor.

1. $■ \times 9 = 18$ **2.** $5 \times ■ = 20$ **3.** $■ \times 1 = 8$ **4.** $■ \times 9 = 9$

5. $2 \times ■ = 14$ **6.** $4 \times ■ = 16$ **7.** $3 \times ■ = 21$ **8.** $■ \times 8 = 32$

9. Jill has 9 baskets with an equal number of eggs in each. If she has 36 eggs in all, how many are in each basket?

Review/Test

✓ CHECK VOCABULARY

Choose the best term from the box.

array
zero
multiple
one
factor

1. The product of _?_ and any number equals that number. (p. 176)
2. The product of _?_ and any number equals zero. (p. 176)
3. A _?_ of 5 is any product that has 5 as a factor, such as 5, 10, 15, and so on. (p. 178)

✓ CHECK SKILLS

Find the product. (pp. 176–177)

4. $5 \times 1 = ■$
5. $0 \times 6 = ■$
6. $■ = 1 \times 8$
7. $■ = 9 \times 0$

Find the product. (pp. 178–179)

8. $■ = 4 \times 3$
9. $2 \times 4 = ■$
10. $5 \times 4 = ■$
11. $■ = 8 \times 4$
12. $4 \times 9 = ■$
13. $4 \times 4 = ■$
14. $■ = 6 \times 4$
15. $4 \times 0 = ■$

Find the missing factor. (pp. 186–187)

16. $2 \times ■ = 8$
17. $■ \times 5 = 30$
18. $1 \times ■ = 9$
19. $■ \times 6 = 18$
20. $■ \times 1 = 9$
21. $4 \times ■ = 32$
22. $■ \times 3 = 18$
23. $7 \times ■ = 0$

✓ CHECK PROBLEM SOLVING

Solve. (pp. 180–181)

24. The first four numbers in the pattern are 4, 8, 12, 16. What is a rule? What are the next three numbers?

25. Lin saw this number pattern: 10, 13, 16, 19, 22, 25, and 28. What is a rule? What are the next three numbers?

Standardized Test Prep

NUMBER SENSE, CONCEPTS, AND OPERATIONS

TIP **Understand the problem.** See item 1. The shaded box stands for the *same* number in all of the fact family sentences. Replace the shaded box with each answer choice to find which number makes all of the sentences true.

1. What number completes this fact family?

   $\blacksquare + 5 = 8$ $5 + \blacksquare = 8$

   $8 - 5 = \blacksquare$ $8 - \blacksquare = 5$

   A 0
   B 3
   C 5
   D 8

2. What multiplication sentence does the array show?

   F $5 \times 5 = 25$
   G $2 \times 5 = 10$
   H $4 \times 5 = 20$
   J $4 \times 4 = 16$

3. **Explain It** There are 157 third-grade students. Tana wants to give each student an ice pop at the third-grade picnic. She estimates she will need 5 boxes of pops. Each box holds 30 pops. Explain whether you agree with Tana's estimate.

MEASUREMENT

4. The clock shows when Mark finished a science project. He had been working on it for two hours. At what time did Mark start his science project?

   A 3:15
   B 2:30
   C 1:15
   D 11:15

5. If October 21 falls on a Monday, what day does October 29 fall on?

   F Monday
   G Tuesday
   H Sunday
   J Thursday

6. Jill measured the height of her school desk. She wrote 1 as her answer. What unit of measure should Jill use to label her answer?

   A cup
   B pound
   C yard
   D gallon

7. **Explain It** It takes 25 minutes to bake 1 batch of brownies in Jack's oven. Jack estimates that he could bake 4 batches of brownies in 1 hour. Do you agree with his estimate? Explain why or why not.

ALGEBRAIC THINKING

8. What is the missing number in this pattern?

4, 8, 12, 16, ■, 24

F 4
G 18
H 20
J 22

9. Which rule was used to find the numbers in column B?

A	B
6	18
7	21
8	24
9	27

A Add 6 to the number in column A.
B Multiply the number in column A by 4.
C Subtract 2 from the number in column A.
D Multiply the number in column A by 3.

10. Explain It Jan is making a bracelet. She strings the beads according to this pattern.

Describe the next three beads that Jan will use. Explain how you found your answer.

DATA ANALYSIS AND PROBABILITY

11. The graph shows the number of cans collected at Bryce Elementary School. How many more cans did Grade 3 students collect than Grade 5 students?

F 52
G 22
H 18
J 12

12. Which shows the grades shown in the graph above in order from the **least** number of cans collected to the **greatest** number?

A grade 2, grade 3, grade 5, grade 4
B grade 5, grade 2, grade 4, grade 3
C grade 3, grade 4, grade 2, grade 5
D grade 5, grade 4, grade 3, grade 2

13. Explain It Gail also made a pictograph of the data above. Explain why Gail's pictograph has twice as many symbols as the graph above.

CHAPTER 10

Multiplication Facts and Strategies

FAST FACT • MUSIC

A marching band plays music and moves in formation. Marching bands are popular at parades and football games. Many bands compete in state and national marching band contests.

PROBLEM SOLVING Look at the pictograph. Draw an array that each band could use as a formation for its brass players.

MARYLAND MARCHING BANDS

High School	Brass Players
Loch Raven	🎺 🎺 🎺
Patapsco	🎺 🎺 🎺 🎺 🎺 🎺 🎺 🎺
Severna Park	🎺 🎺 🎺 🎺 🎺 🎺 🎺

Key: Each 🎺 = 4 Brass Players.

CHECK WHAT YOU KNOW

Use this page to help you review and remember important skills needed for Chapter 10.

ARRAYS

Find the product.

1. $2 \times 4 = ■$
2. $3 \times 6 = ■$
3. $4 \times 5 = ■$
4. $5 \times 6 = ■$
5. $4 \times 4 = ■$
6. $3 \times 7 = ■$

MULTIPLICATION FACTS THROUGH 5

Find the product.

7. $7 \times 3 = ■$
8. $5 \times 5 = ■$
9. $■ = 7 \times 4$
10. $1 \times 2 = ■$
11. $4 \times 1 = ■$
12. $6 \times 3 = ■$
13. $9 \times 5 = ■$
14. $■ = 6 \times 1$
15. 6×4
16. 4×2
17. 2×3
18. 8×4
19. 3×1

VOCABULARY POWER

REVIEW

array [ə•rā′] *noun*

An array is an orderly arrangement of objects, pictures, or numbers in rows and columns. Why can you use an array to show 4×6 but not $4 + 6$?

www.harcourtschool.com/mathglossary

LESSON

Multiply with 6

Quick Review

1. 5 × 3 = ■
2. 5 × ■ = 25
3. 5 × 9 = ■
4. ■ × 5 = 30
5. 40 = 5 × ■

Learn

MARCHING MULTIPLES The school band has 6 rows, with 6 students in each row. How many students are in the band?

Example

Find 6 × 6 = ■.

One Way Break apart an array to find the product.

STEP 1

Make an array that shows 6 rows of 6.

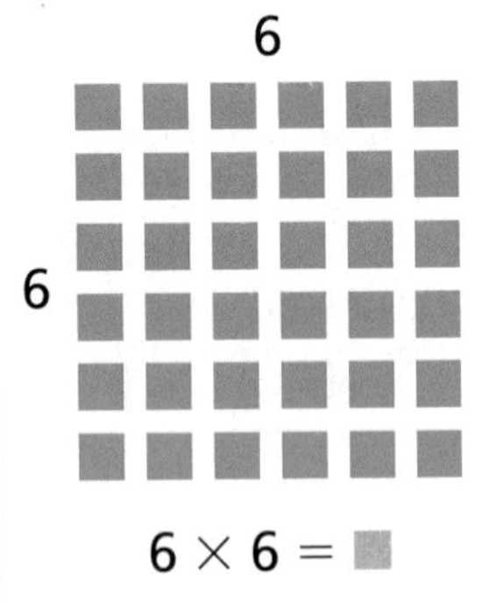

6 × 6 = ■

STEP 2

Break the array into two smaller arrays.

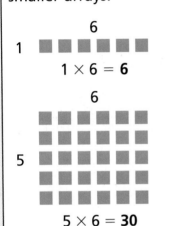

1 × 6 = **6**

5 × 6 = **30**

STEP 3

Add the products of the two arrays.

$$\begin{array}{r} 6 \\ +30 \\ \hline 36 \end{array}$$

6 × 6 = 36

So, there are 36 students in the band.

- What are two other ways to break apart the 6 × 6 array?

Another Way When one factor is an even number, you can use doubles. The product of each 6's fact is double the product of each 3's fact.

To find 6 × 6

- First find the 3's fact.
  Think: 6 × 3 = 18
- Double the product.
  18 + 18 = 36
- So, 6 × 6 = 36.

3's facts	6's facts
0 × 3 = 0	0 × 6 = 0
1 × 3 = 3	1 × 6 = 6
2 × 3 = 6	2 × 6 = 12
3 × 3 = 9	3 × 6 = 18
4 × 3 = 12	4 × 6 = 24
5 × 3 = 15	5 × 6 = 30
6 × 3 = 18	6 × 6 = ■
7 × 3 = 21	7 × 6 = 42
8 × 3 = 24	8 × 6 = 48
9 × 3 = 27	9 × 6 = 54

Check

1. Explain how you can use 8×3 to find 8×6.

Find each product.

2. $7 \times 6 =$ ■
3. $4 \times 6 =$ ■
4. $5 \times 6 =$ ■

Practice and Problem Solving

Extra Practice, page 206, Set A

Find each product.

5. $3 \times 6 =$ ■
6. $6 \times 5 =$ ■
7. $5 \times 9 =$ ■
8. ■ $= 8 \times 6$
9. $4 \times 7 =$ ■
10. ■ $= 3 \times 4$
11. $4 \times 9 =$ ■
12. $6 \times 0 =$ ■
13. ■ $= 2 \times 9$
14. ■ $= 8 \times 4$
15. $3 \times 5 =$ ■
16. $9 \times 6 =$ ■
17. 5×7
18. 6×7
19. 8×3
20. 6×1
21. 5×8
22. 6×6

Copy and complete each table.

	Multiply by 3.	
23.	4	■
24.	6	■
25.	9	■

	Multiply by 5.	
26.	6	■
27.	3	■
28.	8	■

	Multiply by 6.	
29.	4	■
30.	7	■
31.	9	■

Complete.

32. ■ $\times 4 = 12$
33. ■ $\times 6 = 42$
34. $48 = 8 \times$ ■
35. ■ $\times 4 = 4 \times 3$
36. $3 \times 6 =$ ■ $\times 2$
37. ■ $\times 6 = 40 + 8$

38. **FAST FACT** • MUSIC A guitar has 6 strings. A banjo has 5 strings. How many strings are on 4 guitars and 2 banjos?

39. **Write About It** Draw arrays to show that 6×4 is the same as 1×4 plus 5×4.

Mixed Review and Test Prep

40. $327 - 82$ (p. 90)
41. $600 - 346$ (p. 92)

Write the value of the blue digit. (p. 32)

42. 57,899
43. 98,365

44. **TEST PREP** Find the sum of 452 and 678. (p. 72)

A 226
B 1,030
C 1,120
D 1,130

LESSON

Multiply with 8

Learn

BAKE-OFF Mr. Lee baked 6 peach pies for the state fair. He used 8 peaches in each pie. How many peaches did he use in all?

Quick Review

1. 30 = ■ × 6
2. 2 × 6 = ■
3. 6 × 3 = ■
4. 6 × ■ = 42
5. 7 × 6 = ■

Example

Find 6 × 8 = ■.

One Way Break apart an array to find the product.

STEP 1

Make an array that shows 6 rows of 8.

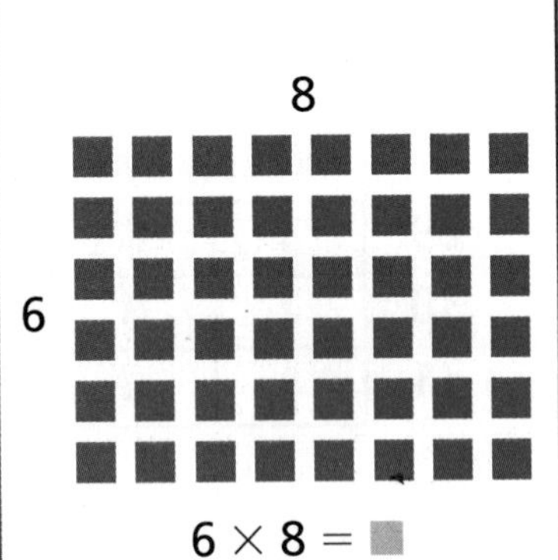

6 × 8 = ■

STEP 2

Break the array into two smaller arrays.

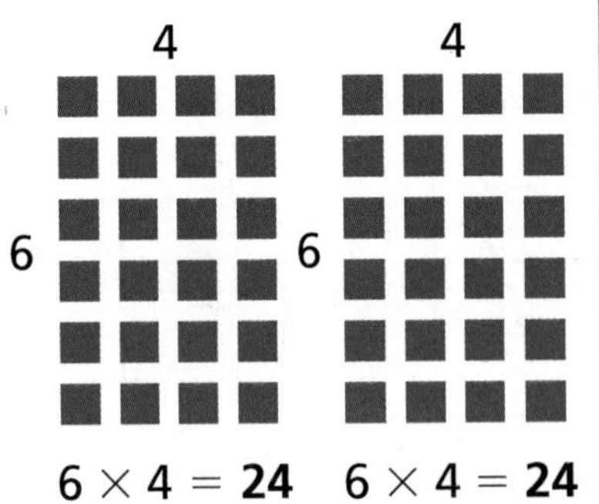

6 × 4 = **24** 6 × 4 = **24**

STEP 3

Add the products of the two arrays.

$$\begin{array}{r} 24 \\ +24 \\ \hline 48 \end{array}$$

6 × 8 = 48

So, Mr. Lee used 48 peaches in all.

- What are two other ways to break apart the 6 × 8 array?

Another Way When one factor is an even number, you can use doubles. The product of each 8's fact is double the product of each 4's fact.

To find 6 × 8

- First find the 4's fact.
  Think: 6 × 4 = 24
- Double the product.
  24 + 24 = 48
- So, 6 × 8 = 48.

4's facts	8's facts
0 × 4 = 0	0 × 8 = 0
1 × 4 = 4	1 × 8 = 8
2 × 4 = 8	2 × 8 = 16
3 × 4 = 12	3 × 8 = 24
4 × 4 = 16	4 × 8 = 32
5 × 4 = 20	5 × 8 = 40
6 × 4 = 24	6 × 8 = ■
7 × 4 = 28	7 × 8 = 56
8 × 4 = 32	8 × 8 = 64
9 × 4 = 36	9 × 8 = 72

Check

1. **Explain** how you can use $4 \times 5 = 20$ to find 8×5.

Find each product.

2. $4 \times 8 = ■$
3. $7 \times 8 = ■$
4. $6 \times 8 = ■$
5. $8 \times 8 = ■$

Practice and Problem Solving

Extra Practice, page 206, Set B

Find each product.

6. $5 \times 4 = ■$
7. $8 \times 3 = ■$
8. $9 \times 8 = ■$
9. $7 \times 4 = ■$
10. $8 \times 6 = ■$
11. $3 \times 4 = ■$
12. $7 \times 5 = ■$
13. $8 \times 8 = ■$
14. $2 \times 9 = ■$
15. $7 \times 8 = ■$
16. $5 \times 9 = ■$
17. $6 \times 6 = ■$
18. 4×8
19. 6×7
20. 9×6
21. 4×9
22. 3×7
23. 6×8

Copy and complete each table.

	Multiply by 4.	
24.	5	■
25.	6	■
26.	8	■

	Multiply by 6.	
27.	7	■
28.	9	■
29.	8	■

	Multiply by 8.	
30.	9	■
31.	6	■
32.	8	■

Compare. Write <, >, or = for each ●.

33. 2×3 ● 2×4
34. 5×8 ● 8×5
35. 5×5 ● 4×6

36. **ALGEBRA** Hal has 7 bags of 8 green apples and 1 bag of red apples. He has 60 apples in all. How many red apples does he have?

37. **What's the Error?** Robin says, "I can find 8×6 by thinking of $3 \times 6 = 18$ and doubling it."

Mixed Review and Test Prep

38. $172 + 781$ (p. 72)
39. $399 + 421$ (p. 72)
40. $2{,}523 + 1{,}607$ (p. 76)
41. $3{,}627 + 4{,}482$ (p. 76)

42. **TEST PREP** What is another way to show $2 + 2 + 2 + 2$? (p. 158)

A 2×2 B 4×2 C 2×8 D 8×4

LESSON 3

Problem Solving Skill
Use a Pictograph

Quick Review

1. $6 \times 4 = \blacksquare$
2. $\blacksquare = 9 \times 2$
3. $7 \times 2 = \blacksquare$
4. $8 \times 4 = \blacksquare$
5. $7 \times \blacksquare = 28$

OUTER PLANETS Madison read in her science book that the five planets farthest from the sun are called the outer planets. How many named moons does Saturn have?

OUTER PLANETS: NUMBER OF NAMED MOONS

Jupiter	● ● ● ● ● ● ● ●
Saturn	● ● ● ● ● ● ● ● ●
Uranus	● ● ● ● ● ● ● ● ● ●
Neptune	● ● ● ●
Pluto	◐

Key: Each ● = 2 moons.

Look at the pictograph. Saturn has 9 symbols.

You can use multiplication to find the number of named moons Saturn has.

9	×	2	=	18
factor		factor		product
number of symbols		each symbol stands for 2 moons		number of Saturn's named moons

Talk About It

- The number of moons Pluto has is shown with $\frac{1}{2}$ of a symbol. How many named moons does Pluto have?
- How would you find the number of named moons Jupiter has?
- If Neptune had 11 named moons, how many symbols would be needed in all?

REASONING Why do you think a key of 2 was used on this pictograph?

Problem Solving Practice

USE DATA For 1–3, use the pictograph.

PLANETS: LENGTH OF DAY	
Jupiter	☼ ☼ ☼ ☼ ☼
Saturn	☼ ☼ ☼ ☼ ☼
Uranus	☼ ☼ ☼ ☼ ☼ ☼ ☼ ☼ ◐
Neptune	☼ ☼ ☼ ☼ ☼ ☼ ☼ ☼ ☼ ◐

Key: Each ☼ = 2 Earth hours.

1. Explain how to use this pictograph to find which of these planets has the longest day. How many Earth hours long is it?
2. How many Earth hours are in a day on Uranus?
3. How much longer is a day on Neptune than a day on Jupiter?

USE DATA For 4–5, use the pictograph.

NEW SCIENCE BOOKS IN THE LIBRARY	
Solar System	📖 📖 📖 📖 📖 📖
Plants	📖 📖 📖 📖 ◧
Mammals	📖 📖 📖 📖 📖 📖 📖
Reptiles	📖 📖 📖

Key: Each 📖 = 4 books.

4. How many new science books are in the library?
   - **A** 81
   - **B** 41
   - **C** 82
   - **D** 72
5. Which three numbers represented on the pictograph are multiples of 4?
   - **F** 12, 18, 24
   - **G** 12, 24, 28
   - **H** 18, 24, 28
   - **J** 12, 18, 28

Mixed Applications

USE DATA For 6–9, use the table.

SCIENCE CENTER	
Activity	**Tickets**
Admission	5
Space exhibits	3
Dinosaur exhibits	4
Animal exhibits	2

6. How many tickets do Brandon and his 3 friends need in all for admission to the Science Center?
7. Brandon and his 3 friends used 28 tickets. They used 4 more tickets for dinosaur exhibits than for space exhibits. How many tickets did they use for each?
8. Abigail's father gave her 14 tickets. She used tickets for admission and the space exhibits. How many tickets did she have left?
9. **Write a problem** about tickets used at the Science Center in which the product is greater than 15 and is a multiple of 3.

LESSON 4

Multiply with 7

Quick Review

1. $8 \times 5 = \blacksquare$
2. $6 \times 4 = \blacksquare$
3. $3 \times 8 = \blacksquare$
4. $2 \times 6 = \blacksquare$
5. $5 \times 6 = \blacksquare$

Learn

PARADE! PARADE! Students built a float for a parade. They worked on the float for 8 weeks. How many days did they work on the float?

Example

Find $8 \times 7 = \blacksquare$.

Break apart an array to find the product.

STEP 1

Make an array that shows 8 rows of 7.

$8 \times 7 = \blacksquare$

STEP 2

Break the array into two smaller arrays.

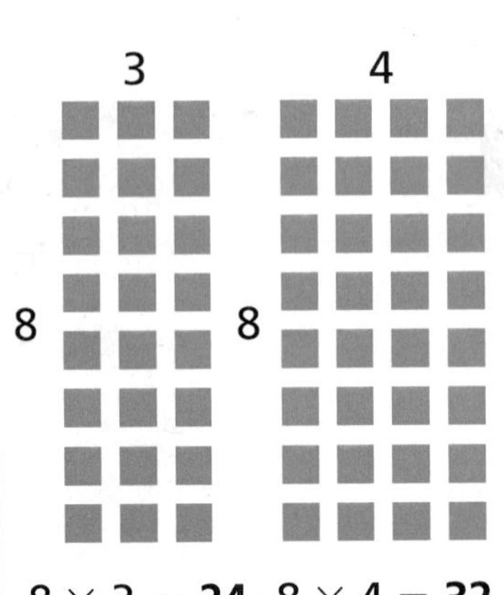

$8 \times 3 =$ **24** $8 \times 4 =$ **32**

STEP 3

Add the products of the two arrays.

$$\begin{array}{r} 24 \\ +32 \\ \hline 56 \end{array}$$

$8 \times 7 = 56$

So, the students worked on the float for 56 days.

- What are two other ways to break apart the 8×7 array?

Check

1. **Explain** how you could break apart 7×5 into two arrays to help you find the product.

Technology Link

More Practice: Harcourt Mega Math The Number Games, *Up, Up, and Array,* Level B

Find each product.

2. $4 \times 7 = \blacksquare$
3. $0 \times 7 = \blacksquare$
4. $8 \times 7 = \blacksquare$
5. $6 \times 7 = \blacksquare$

Practice and Problem Solving

Extra Practice, page 206, Set C

Find each product.

6. $2 \times 7 = ■$
7. $2 \times 9 = ■$
8. $3 \times 7 = ■$
9. $6 \times 6 = ■$
10. $7 \times 6 = ■$
11. $■ = 6 \times 9$
12. $■ = 5 \times 9$
13. $7 \times 7 = ■$
14. $4 \times 7 = ■$
15. $3 \times 6 = ■$
16. $■ = 4 \times 9$
17. $■ = 5 \times 5$
18. 1×7
19. 7×9
20. 6×8
21. 8×8
22. 4×5
23. 8×7

Copy and complete each table.

	Multiply by 6.	
24.	4	■
25.	6	■
26.	9	■

	Multiply by 7.	
27.	6	■
28.	5	■
29.	8	■

	Multiply by 8.	
30.	6	■
31.	7	■
32.	9	■

Complete.

33. $7 \times 6 = ■ + 21$
34. $■ \times 4 = 30 - 2$
35. $8 + 6 = 7 \times ■$

36. **REASONING** How can you tell without multiplying that 7×9 is less than 9×8?

37. **What's the Question?** Joanna has 9 boxes of pears. She has 72 pears in all. The answer is 8 pears.

38. Shayla was on vacation for 7 weeks. She spent 3 weeks at band camp and the rest of the time at home. How many days did she spend at home?

39. Break apart the array. Then write the multiplication fact.

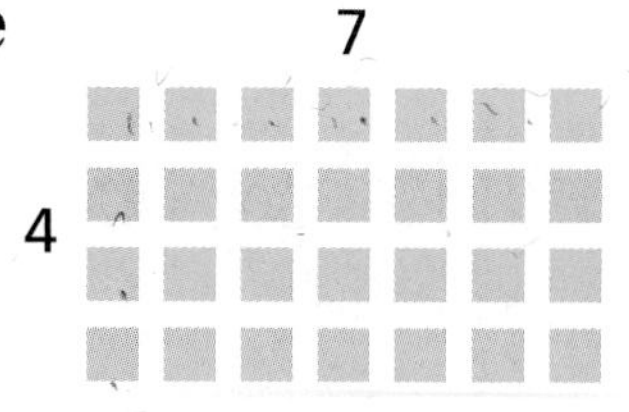

40. **ALGEBRA** Find a one-digit number to make this number sentence true. $■ \times 7 + 10 > 67 - 9$

Mixed Review and Test Prep

41. $3{,}458 + 1{,}679$ (p. 72)
42. $2{,}008 + 1{,}256$ (p. 72)
43. $2{,}814 - 1{,}680$ (p. 96)
44. $8{,}093 - 5{,}934$ (p. 96)

45. **TEST PREP** Subtract 49 from 201. (p. 90)

A 152 **B** 162 **C** 250 **D** 252

LESSON 5

Algebra: Practice the Facts

Quick Review

1. $6 \times 3 = \blacksquare$
2. $5 \times 4 = \blacksquare$
3. $2 \times 8 = \blacksquare$
4. $4 \times 9 = \blacksquare$
5. $7 \times 8 = \blacksquare$

Learn

SPLASH! Each instructor teaches a group of 6 children. If there are 7 instructors, how many children are taking swimming lessons?

$$7 \times 6 = \blacksquare$$

You have learned many ways to find 7×6.

A. Break an array into known facts.

6

2

$2 \times 6 =$ **12**

6

5

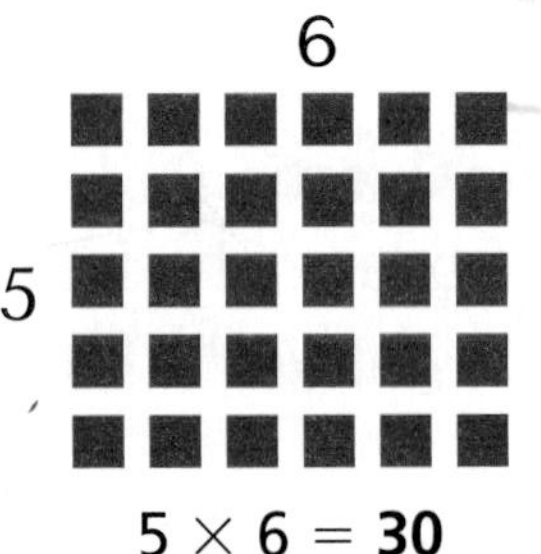

$5 \times 6 =$ **30**

$12 + 30 = 42$, so $7 \times 6 = 42$.

B. Use a multiplication table.

×	0	1	2	3	4	5	6	7	8	9
0	0	0	0	0	0	0	0	0	0	0
1	0	1	2	3	4	5	6	7	8	9
2	0	2	4	6	8	10	12	14	16	18
3	0	3	6	9	12	15	18	21	24	27
4	0	4	8	12	16	20	24	28	32	36
5	0	5	10	15	20	25	30	35	40	45
6	0	6	12	18	24	30	36	42	48	54
7	0	7	14	21	28	35	42	49	56	63
8	0	8	16	24	32	40	48	56	64	72
9	0	9	18	27	36	45	54	63	72	81

$7 \times 6 = 42$

C. Use the Commutative Property of Multiplication.

Try changing the order of the factors:

Think: If $6 \times 7 = 42$, then $7 \times 6 = 42$.

D. When one of the factors is an even number, you can use doubles.

To find a 6's fact, you can double a 3's fact.

- First find the 3's fact.
  Think: $7 \times 3 = 21$
- Double the product. $21 + 21 = 42$
  $7 \times 6 = 42$

So, 42 children are taking lessons.

Ways to Find a Product

What if there are 8 instructors with 5 swimmers each? How many children are taking lessons?

$$8 \times 5 = \blacksquare$$

David and Niam use different ways to find 8×5.

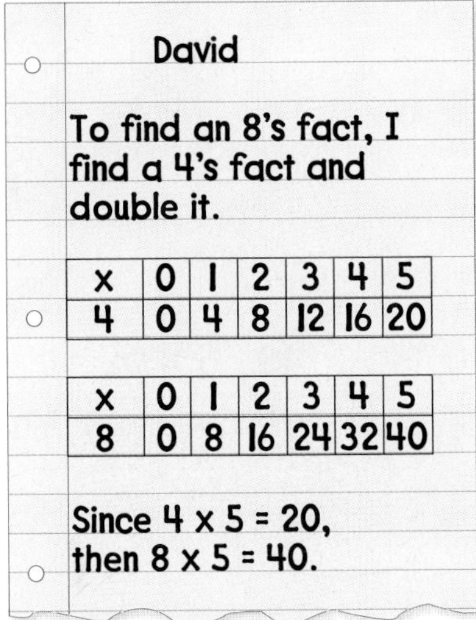

David

To find an 8's fact, I find a 4's fact and double it.

x	0	1	2	3	4	5
4	0	4	8	12	16	20

x	0	1	2	3	4	5
8	0	8	16	24	32	40

Since 4 x 5 = 20, then 8 x 5 = 40.

Niam

I can use the Order Property of Multiplication.

I know that 8 x 5 is the same as 5 x 8.

5 x 8 = 8 x 5 = 40

- What is another way that David or Niam could find 8×5?

REASONING As you multiply two factors, when is the product *less than* the greater factor? *equal to* the greater factor? *greater than* either of the factors? Explain.

Check

1. **Explain** how you could use $9 \times 5 = 45$ to find 8×5.
2. **Describe** how you could use doubles to find 6×9.

Find each product.

3. $4 \times 5 = \blacksquare$
4. $3 \times 7 = \blacksquare$
5. $6 \times 4 = \blacksquare$
6. $7 \times 6 = \blacksquare$
7. $2 \times 5 = \blacksquare$
8. $6 \times 6 = \blacksquare$
9. $\blacksquare = 4 \times 3$
10. $2 \times 2 = \blacksquare$
11. $1 \times 8 = \blacksquare$
12. $\blacksquare = 5 \times 3$
13. $9 \times 2 = \blacksquare$
14. $5 \times 5 = \blacksquare$
15. $\begin{array}{r} 5 \\ \times 9 \\ \hline \end{array}$
16. $\begin{array}{r} 6 \\ \times 3 \\ \hline \end{array}$
17. $\begin{array}{r} 7 \\ \times 7 \\ \hline \end{array}$
18. $\begin{array}{r} 4 \\ \times 8 \\ \hline \end{array}$
19. $\begin{array}{r} 0 \\ \times 4 \\ \hline \end{array}$
20. $\begin{array}{r} 3 \\ \times 3 \\ \hline \end{array}$

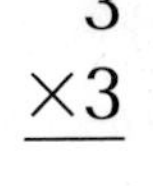

Practice and Problem Solving

Extra Practice, page 206, Set D

Find each product.

21. $8 \times 5 = \blacksquare$
22. $0 \times 6 = \blacksquare$
23. $9 \times 3 = \blacksquare$
24. $5 \times 6 = \blacksquare$
25. $9 \times 8 = \blacksquare$
26. $8 \times 3 = \blacksquare$
27. $\blacksquare = 1 \times 8$
28. $8 \times 8 = \blacksquare$
29. $6 \times 8 = \blacksquare$
30. $\blacksquare = 4 \times 9$
31. $\blacksquare = 2 \times 8$
32. $8 \times 7 = \blacksquare$
33. 2×6
34. 6×7
35. 8×9
36. 5×7
37. 5×1
38. 4×4
39. 2×9
40. 0×3
41. 2×4
42. 4×7
43. 9×6
44. 7×9

Find each missing factor.

45. $\blacksquare \times 4 = 20$
46. $8 \times \blacksquare = 56$
47. $\blacksquare \times 6 = 0$
48. $6 \times \blacksquare = 42$
49. $8 \times \blacksquare = 24$
50. $\blacksquare \times 5 = 40$
51. $4 \times \blacksquare = 16$
52. $3 \times \blacksquare = 12$

Write $<$, $>$, or $=$ for each $\bullet$.

53. $3 \times 2 \bullet 6$
54. $4 \times 2 \bullet 5 + 2$
55. $6 \times 3 \bullet 7 \times 2$
56. $4 \times 9 \bullet 6 \times 6$
57. $3 \times 4 \bullet 18$
58. $5 \times 9 \bullet 6 \times 8$
59. $7 \times 4 \bullet 30 - 4$
60. $3 \times 8 \bullet 6 \times 4$
61. $5 \times 7 \bullet 6 \times 6$
62. $8 + 9 \bullet 8 \times 9$
63. $7 \times 7 \bullet 50$
64. $9 \times 3 \bullet 9 + 9$

65. **Vocabulary Power** The word *double* means "twice as many." A double scoop is two scoops of ice cream. What number is the double of 8?

66. **ALGEBRA** Write *true* or *false* for each.
    a. $1 \times 8 = 9$
    b. $0 \times 7 = 0$
    c. $0 \times 0 = 0$
    d. $1 \times 9 = 1$

USE DATA For 67–68, use the table.

BAKE SALE
Cake - $3
Brownie - $1
Cupcake - $0.50
Loaf of Bread - $2

67. Sara buys 4 cakes and 1 loaf of bread at the bake sale. How much does she pay?

68. Greg buys 2 cakes and one cupcake. How much change does he get from a $10 bill?

69. **REASONING** List as many factors as you can for each of the following numbers: 12, 18, and 24.

70. Mr. Wu taught 3 lessons each day for 6 days. Then he taught 2 lessons each day for 3 days. How many lessons did he teach?

71. Ed arranged 5 rows of 6 pennies each. He had one more coin in his pocket. If he had a total of $0.35, what coin was in his pocket?

Mixed Review and Test Prep

Choose <, >, or = for each ●. (p. 42)

72. 67 ● 76
73. 254 ● 257
74. 1,007 ● 985
75. 4,902 ● 4,092

Write + or − to make each sentence true. (p. 80)

76. 39 ● 14 = 25
77. 47 ● 7 = 54

Write the missing addend. (p. 80)

78. 350 + ■ = 402

79. ■ + 120 = 135

80. **TEST PREP** Tameo bought some tape for $1.39 and a sheet of stickers for $1.53. How much did he spend? (p. 120)

- **A** $0.14
- **B** $1.81
- **C** $2.92
- **D** $3.51

Problem Solving Thinker's Corner

MULTIPLICATION CONCENTRATION
MATERIALS: 40 index cards
PLAYERS: 2

Using index cards, record all of the multiplication facts for 7's and 8's. Write a fact on one card and the product on another card.

Shuffle cards and place cards in 5 rows with numbers face down.

a. Player One turns over two cards and tries to match a multiplication sentence and a product.

b. If there is a match, Player One keeps the two cards. If there is no match, the cards are turned face down again.

c. Players take turns turning over cards. When all of the pairs have been matched, the player with the greater number of cards wins.

Extra Practice

Set A (pp. 194–195)

Find each product.

1. $5 \times 6 = \blacksquare$ **2.** $6 \times 2 = \blacksquare$ **3.** $0 \times 6 = \blacksquare$ **4.** $6 \times 7 = \blacksquare$

5. $6 \times 4 = \blacksquare$ **6.** $6 \times 3 = \blacksquare$ **7.** $\blacksquare = 8 \times 6$ **8.** $4 \times 7 = \blacksquare$

9. $8 \times 2 = \blacksquare$ **10.** $\blacksquare = 6 \times 6$ **11.** $6 \times 1 = \blacksquare$ **12.** $6 \times 9 = \blacksquare$

Complete.

13. $\blacksquare \times 4 = 16$ **14.** $\blacksquare \times 5 = 35$ **15.** $2 \times \blacksquare = 8$ **16.** $8 \times \blacksquare = 24$

Set B (pp. 196–197)

Find each product.

1. $7 \times 8 = \blacksquare$ **2.** $8 \times 0 = \blacksquare$ **3.** $8 \times 3 = \blacksquare$ **4.** $6 \times 8 = \blacksquare$

5. $\blacksquare = 8 \times 4$ **6.** $\blacksquare = 2 \times 5$ **7.** $8 \times 1 = \blacksquare$ **8.** $8 \times 8 = \blacksquare$

9. $8 \times 2 = \blacksquare$ **10.** $5 \times 8 = \blacksquare$ **11.** $2 \times 2 = \blacksquare$ **12.** $8 \times 9 = \blacksquare$

13. Dolores has 8 bags of 4 apples. Ruth has 3 bags of 8 apples. How many more apples does Dolores have?

Set C (pp. 200–201)

Find each product.

1. $1 \times 7 = \blacksquare$ **2.** $\blacksquare = 7 \times 5$ **3.** $6 \times 7 = \blacksquare$ **4.** $3 \times 7 = \blacksquare$

5. $2 \times 7 = \blacksquare$ **6.** $3 \times 3 = \blacksquare$ **7.** $7 \times 7 = \blacksquare$ **8.** $4 \times 7 = \blacksquare$

9. $8 \times 1 = \blacksquare$ **10.** $0 \times 7 = \blacksquare$ **11.** $\blacksquare = 7 \times 8$ **12.** $9 \times 7 = \blacksquare$

13. Alex has 8 bags of rocks. Each bag has 7 rocks. Vera takes 3 bags. How many rocks does Alex have left?

Set D (pp. 202–205)

Find each product.

1. $8 \times 7 = \blacksquare$ **2.** $6 \times 7 = \blacksquare$ **3.** $\blacksquare = 6 \times 4$ **4.** $7 \times 3 = \blacksquare$

5. $9 \times 8 = \blacksquare$ **6.** $8 \times 6 = \blacksquare$ **7.** $7 \times 7 = \blacksquare$ **8.** $3 \times 5 = \blacksquare$

9. $9 \times 7 = \blacksquare$ **10.** $\blacksquare = 6 \times 5$ **11.** $8 \times 8 = \blacksquare$ **12.** $9 \times 6 = \blacksquare$

13. List the factors for 16.

Review/Test

✓ CHECK CONCEPTS

Name a way to break apart each array. Then write the product. (pp. 194–195, 200–201)

1. 
6 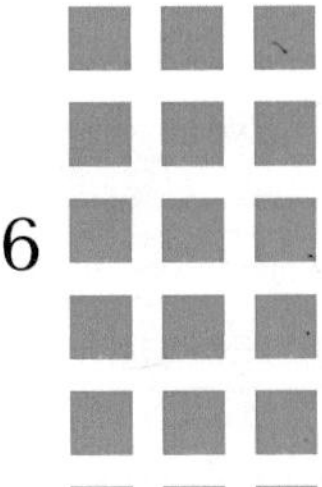

2.  
7 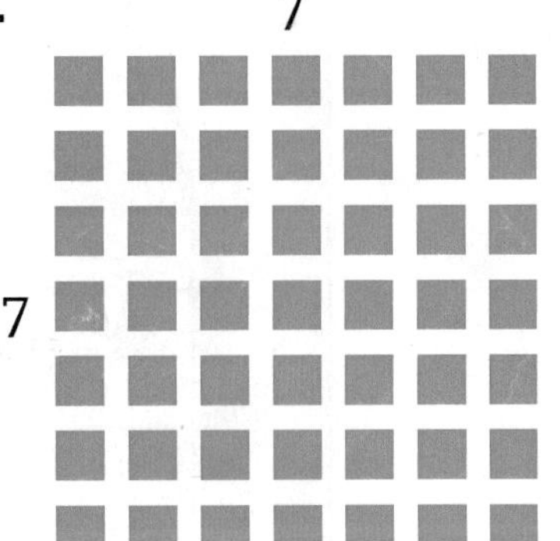

3. 
6 

✓ CHECK SKILLS

Find each product. (pp. 194–195, 196–197, 200–201)

4. $6 \times 7 = \blacksquare$ **5.** $\blacksquare = 8 \times 7$ **6.** $4 \times 6 = \blacksquare$ **7.** $9 \times 7 = \blacksquare$

8. $\blacksquare = 5 \times 8$ **9.** $6 \times 0 = \blacksquare$ **10.** $3 \times 8 = \blacksquare$ **11.** $5 \times 7 = \blacksquare$

12. $6 \times 6 = \blacksquare$ **13.** $8 \times 9 = \blacksquare$ **14.** $8 \times 6 = \blacksquare$ **15.** $6 \times 9 = \blacksquare$

16. $\begin{array}{r} 8 \\ \times 8 \\ \hline \end{array}$ **17.** $\begin{array}{r} 8 \\ \times 4 \\ \hline \end{array}$ **18.** $\begin{array}{r} 2 \\ \times 7 \\ \hline \end{array}$ **19.** $\begin{array}{r} 7 \\ \times 3 \\ \hline \end{array}$ **20.** $\begin{array}{r} 6 \\ \times 2 \\ \hline \end{array}$ **21.** $\begin{array}{r} 7 \\ \times 4 \\ \hline \end{array}$

✓ CHECK PROBLEM SOLVING

Solve. (pp. 198–199)

For 22–25, use the pictograph.

22. How many more students voted for summer than for winter?

23. Which season received the most votes?

24. How many more students voted for summer and winter than voted for spring and fall?

25. How many students voted in all?

FAVORITE SEASONS

Spring	🍂 🍂 🍂 🍂
Summer	🍂 🍂 🍂 🍂 🍂 🍂 🍂 🍂
Fall	🍂 🍂
Winter	🍂 🍂 🍂 🍂 🍂 🍂

Key: Each 🍂 = 2 student votes.

Standardized Test Prep

NUMBER SENSE, CONCEPTS, AND OPERATIONS

1. Desi bought 7 boxes of crayons. There are 8 crayons in each box. How many crayons did Desi buy?

A 15 **C** 32
B 28 **D** 56

2. Which of the following should Mindy choose to complete the equation?

$6 \times 4 = \blacksquare$

F $6 + 2 + 2$
G 4×6
H $3 + 3 + 4$
J 3×2

3. What multiplication fact does the array show?

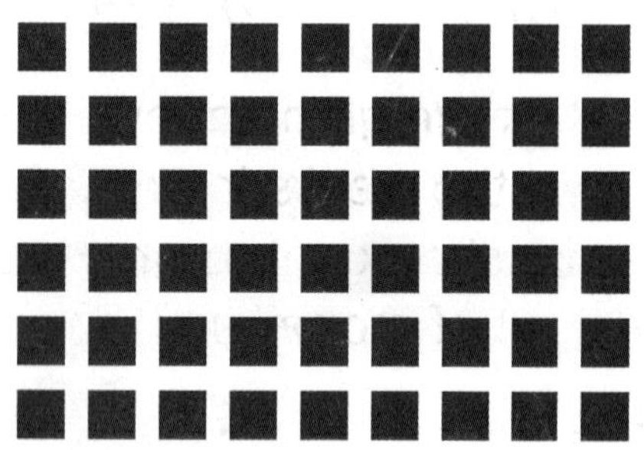

A $6 \times 9 = 54$
B $6 \times 6 = 36$
C $5 \times 9 = 45$
D $6 \times 8 = 48$

4. Explain It Akiko has read 28 pages of a book that has 96 pages. ESTIMATE the number of pages Akiko needs to read to finish the book. Explain how you estimated.

MEASUREMENT

5. The schedule below shows Steve's day at school. Where is Steve at 10:30?

STEVE'S SCHEDULE

Time	Class
8:15–8:30	Homeroom
8:35–9:25	Math
9:30–10:20	Social studies
10:25–11:15	Science
11:20–12:10	Reading
12:15–12:45	Lunch

F reading **H** science
G lunch **J** math

TIP **Understand the problem.** See item 6. Find the difference between the time that the lunch period starts and the time it ends.

6. Look at Steve's schedule above. How long is Steve's lunch period?

A 50 minutes
B 45 minutes
C 30 minutes
D 15 minutes

7. Explain It Lucy cooked a turkey from 2:15 P.M. to 6:20 P.M. About how many hours did the turkey cook? Explain how you found your answer.

ALGEBRAIC THINKING

8. This week, Marian jogged on Tuesday, Thursday, and Saturday. If she continues this pattern, on which day will Marian jog next?

   F Sunday
   G Monday
   H Wednesday
   J Friday

9. Jon made this number pattern. What is the missing number in his pattern?

   115, 125, 135, ■, 155, 165

   A 130
   B 145
   C 185
   D 205

10. The table shows Carly's pattern.

CARLY'S PATTERN TABLE	
1	7
3	21
5	35
7	■
9	63

Which number should replace the ■ in the table?

   F 42
   G 45
   H 47
   J 49

11. **Explain It** What rule did Carly use to make the table above? Explain how you found your answer.

DATA ANALYSIS AND PROBABILITY

12. Leo made the graph below to show how much money he saved. How much more money did Leo save during Week 3 than he saved in Week 1?

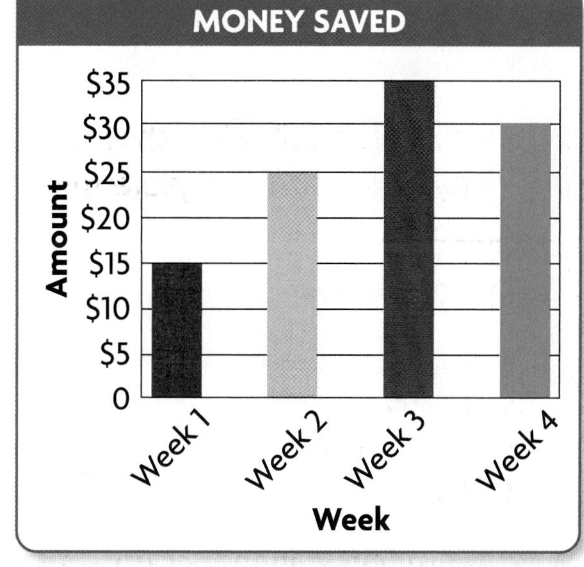

   A $5
   B $10
   C $20
   D $35

13. Look at the graph above. Which shows the weeks in order from the **least** amount to **greatest** amount of money saved?

   F 4, 2, 3, 1
   G 3, 2, 4, 1
   H 1, 2, 4, 3
   J 2, 4, 1, 3

14. **Explain It** Todd put marbles in this bag. Which two colors is Todd equally likely to pull? Explain how you know.

CHAPTER 11

Multiplication Facts and Patterns

FAST FACT • SOCIAL STUDIES **Dogsled teams were used to deliver mail in places such as Michigan, Minnesota, Wisconsin, and Alaska. Large teams of dogs could pull 400 to 500 pounds of mail.**

PROBLEM SOLVING **A full-grown Samoyed sled dog weighs about 50 pounds. A team of 10 Samoyeds weighs about 500 pounds. What would 10 newborn Samoyed puppies weigh?**

WEIGHT OF A NEWBORN PUPPY

Siberian Husky	🐶🐶🐶🐶🐶🐶
Alaskan Malamute	🐶🐶🐶🐶🐶🐶🐶🐶
American Eskimo	🐶🐶🐶🐶🐶
Samoyed	🐶🐶🐶🐶🐶

Key: Each 🐶 = 2 ounces.

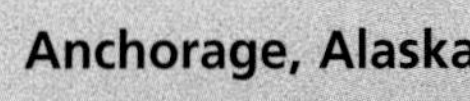

Anchorage, Alaska

CHECK WHAT YOU KNOW

Use this page to help you review and remember important skills needed for Chapter 11.

SKIP-COUNT BY TENS

Continue the pattern.

1. 10, 20, 30, 40, ■, ■
2. 30, 40, 50, 60, 70, ■, ■

Skip-count by tens to find the missing numbers.

3. 3, 13, 23, ■, ■, 53, ■, ■, 83, ■
4. 7, 17, 27, ■, ■, 57, ■, 77, ■, ■
5. 5, 15, 25, ■, ■, 55, ■, ■, ■
6. 64, 54, 44, ■, ■, ■, ■

FIND MISSING FACTORS

Find the missing factor.

7. ■ × 4 = 32
8. 5 × ■ = 35
9. ■ × 6 = 36
10. 2 × ■ = 18
11. 7 × ■ = 28
12. ■ × 8 = 16
13. 5 × ■ = 45
14. ■ × 4 = 36
15. ■ × 4 = 24
16. 6 × ■ = 54
17. 3 × ■ = 24
18. ■ × 8 = 64
19. 5 × ■ = 40
20. 9 × ■ = 9
21. ■ × 4 = 0
22. 7 × ■ = 56

VOCABULARY POWER

REVIEW

product [prä′dəkt] *noun*

A product in mathematics is the answer to a multiplication problem. Tell another meaning for *product* that you find in your social studies book.

PREVIEW

Associative Property
Identity Property
Zero Property
Distributive Property
multistep problem

www.harcourtschool.com/mathglossary

LESSON 1

Multiply with 9 and 10

Quick Review

1. $4 \times 8 = ■$
2. $7 \times 5 = ■$
3. $8 \times 0 = ■$
4. $3 \times 6 = ■$
5. $6 \times 7 = ■$

Learn

TIMBER! Beavers cut down trees with their large front teeth. If 5 beavers each cut down 10 trees, how many trees did they cut down in all?

$$5 \times 10 = ■$$

One Way You can skip-count by tens 5 times.

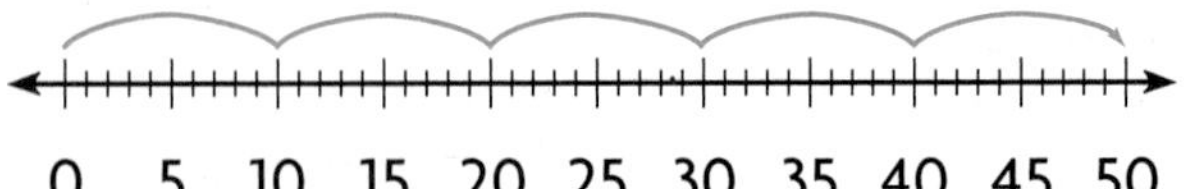

Think: 10, 20, 30, 40, 50

So, $5 \times 10 = 50$.

Another Way Use a pattern to multiply by 10.

The product of 1 and any number equals that number.

$0 \times 1 = 0$
$1 \times 1 = 1$
$2 \times 1 = 2$
$3 \times 1 = 3$
$4 \times 1 = 4$
$5 \times 1 = 5$
$6 \times 1 = 6$
$7 \times 1 = 7$
$8 \times 1 = 8$
$9 \times 1 = 9$
$10 \times 1 = 10$

The product of 10 and any factor equals the other factor followed by a zero.

$0 \times 10 = 0$
$1 \times 10 = 10$
$2 \times 10 = 20$
$3 \times 10 = 30$
$4 \times 10 = 40$
$5 \times 10 = ■$
$6 \times 10 = 60$
$7 \times 10 = 70$
$8 \times 10 = 80$
$9 \times 10 = 90$
$10 \times 10 = 100$

So, $5 \times 10 = 50$. The beavers cut down 50 trees in all.

REASONING

- How can you use skip-counting to find 6×10?

▲ When beavers cut down trees, they eat the bark and use the branches to build homes in the water.

×	0	1	2	3	4	5	6	7	8	9	10
0	0	0	0	0	0	0	0	0	0	0	0
1	0	1	2	3	4	5	6	7	8	9	10
2	0	2	4	6	8	10	12	14	16	18	20
3	0	3	6	9	12	15	18	21	24	27	30
4	0	4	8	12	16	20	24	28	32	36	40
5	0	5	10	15	20	25	30	35	40	45	50
6	0	6	12	18	24	30	36	42	48	54	60
7	0	7	14	21	28	35	42	49	56	63	70
8	0	8	16	24	32	40	48	56	64	72	80
9	0	9	18	27	36	45	54	63	72	81	90
10	0	10	20	30	40	50	60	70	80	90	100

Multiply with 9

Lynn's class made 7 animal posters. The students drew 9 animals on each poster. How many animals did they draw in all?

$$7 \times 9 = ■$$

Lynn and Jeff use different ways to find 7×9.

Lynn

I'll think of the 10's fact first.

7 x 10 = 70

Next, I'll subtract the first factor, 7.

70 - 7 = 63

Since 70 - 7 = 63, 7 x 9 = 63.

Jeff

I'll use a pattern in the products of the 9's facts.

7 x 9 = ■

- The tens digit will be 1 less than the factor 7.
- The sum of the digits in the product will be 9.

So, 7 x 9 = 63.

$0 \times 9 = 0$
$1 \times 9 = 9$
$2 \times 9 = 18$
$3 \times 9 = 27$
$4 \times 9 = 36$
$5 \times 9 = 45$
$6 \times 9 = 54$
$7 \times 9 = ■$
$8 \times 9 = 72$
$9 \times 9 = 81$

So, Lynn's class drew 63 animals.

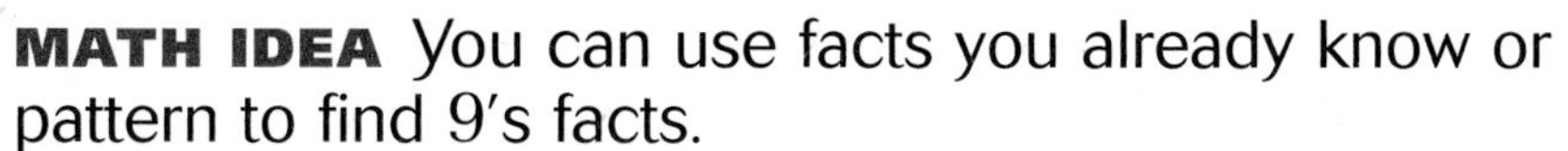

MATH IDEA You can use facts you already know or a pattern to find 9's facts.

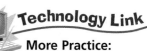

Technology Link

More Practice: Harcourt Mega Math The Number Games, *Up, Up, and Array,* Level C

Check

1. **Explain** how to use a 10's fact to find 3×9.
2. **Explain** how to use a pattern to find 6×9.

Find the product.

3. $3 \times 10 = ■$	**4.** $10 \times 6 = ■$	**5.** $■ = 7 \times 9$	**6.** $1 \times 9 = ■$
7. $8 \times 9 = ■$	**8.** $■ = 9 \times 2$	**9.** $4 \times 10 = ■$	**10.** $2 \times 10 = ■$

Find the missing factor.

11. $■ \times 7 = 63$	**12.** $5 \times ■ = 30$	**13.** $10 \times ■ = 60$	**14.** $■ \times 6 = 48$
15. $■ \times 9 = 90$	**16.** $6 \times ■ = 24$	**17.** $■ \times 8 = 64$	**18.** $9 \times ■ = 45$

LESSON CONTINUES

Practice and Problem Solving

Extra Practice, page 224, Set A

Find the product.

19. ■ $= 10 \times 4$ **20.** $4 \times 8 =$ ■ **21.** $9 \times 8 =$ ■ **22.** ■ $= 8 \times 6$

23. $9 \times 9 =$ ■ **24.** ■ $= 7 \times 10$ **25.** $10 \times 10 =$ ■ **26.** $2 \times 8 =$ ■

27. $\begin{array}{r} 10 \\ \times\ 8 \\ \hline \end{array}$ **28.** $\begin{array}{r} 9 \\ \times 4 \\ \hline \end{array}$ **29.** $\begin{array}{r} 5 \\ \times 10 \\ \hline \end{array}$ **30.** $\begin{array}{r} 8 \\ \times 8 \\ \hline \end{array}$ **31.** $\begin{array}{r} 9 \\ \times 3 \\ \hline \end{array}$ **32.** $\begin{array}{r} 7 \\ \times 8 \\ \hline \end{array}$

33. $\begin{array}{r} 4 \\ \times 3 \\ \hline \end{array}$ **34.** $\begin{array}{r} 10 \\ \times\ 1 \\ \hline \end{array}$ **35.** $\begin{array}{r} 8 \\ \times 3 \\ \hline \end{array}$ **36.** $\begin{array}{r} 6 \\ \times 9 \\ \hline \end{array}$ **37.** $\begin{array}{r} 9 \\ \times 7 \\ \hline \end{array}$ **38.** $\begin{array}{r} 10 \\ \times\ 6 \\ \hline \end{array}$

Find the missing factor.

39. ■ $\times 6 = 0$ **40.** $10 \times$ ■ $= 20$ **41.** ■ $\times 7 = 28$

42. $5 \times$ ■ $= 4 \times 10$ **43.** ■ $\times 2 = 12 + 8$ **44.** $6 \times 6 =$ ■ $\times 4$

Copy and complete each table.

	Multiply by 10.	
45.	6	■
46.	8	■

	Multiply by 8.	
47.	5	■
48.	7	■

	Multiply by 9.	
49.	8	■
50.	9	■

Compare. Write <, >, or = for each ●.

51. 10×6 ● $75 - 15$ **52.** 9×9 ● 10×8 **53.** 7×9 ● 10×7

54. 8×9 ● 9×8 **55.** $16 + 40$ ● 9×6 **56.** 10×10 ● $50 + 50$

57. ***FAST FACT*** • **SOCIAL STUDIES** The beaver was adopted as the New York state animal in 1975. How many years ago was that?

58. Malcolm cut 3 pies into 10 pieces each and 2 pies into 8 pieces each. How many pieces of pie did he have in all?

59. **? What's the Error?** Describe Mike's error. Then solve the problem correctly.

Mike

9 x 4 = ■

Think: 10 x 4 = 40
40 − 9 = 31
So, 9 x 4 = 31.

60. Emiko had 4 sheets with 10 animal stickers on each. After she gave some stickers away, she had 37 left. How many stickers did she give away?

Mixed Review and Test Prep

Order each group of numbers from least to greatest. (p. 46)

61. 243, 536, 144

62. 1,390; 1,039; 1,930

63. 16,321; 16,967; 15,644

Find the sum. (p. 72)

64. 1,568 + 3,215 = ■

65. 2,513 + 874 = ■

66. TEST PREP Meg went to the store at 11:15 A.M. She got home 2 hours later. At what time did she get home? (pp. 132, 134)

A 9:15 A.M. **C** 1:15 P.M.
B 12:15 P.M. **D** 2:15 P.M.

67. TEST PREP Jesse has 3 rows of 9 stamps. Lou has 2 rows of 6 stamps. How many stamps do they have in all? (p. 202)

F 27 **G** 39 **H** 56 **J** 60

Problem Solving LINKUP . . . to Reading

STRATEGY • CLASSIFY AND CATEGORIZE
When you *classify* information, you group similar information. When you *categorize,* you name the groups that you have classified.

MATERIALS: hundred charts, colored pencils

Shade the multiples of 2, 3, 4, 5, 6, and 7 on your charts.

1	2	3	4	5	6	7	8	9	10
11	12	13	14	15	16	17	18	19	20
21	22	23	24	25	26	27	28	29	30
31	32	33	34	35	36	37	38	39	40
41	42	43	44	45	46	47	48	49	50
51	52	53	54	55	56	57	58	59	60
61	62	63	64	65	66	67	68	69	70
71	72	73	74	75	76	77	78	79	80
81	82	83	84	85	86	87	88	89	90
91	92	93	94	95	96	97	98	99	100

For 1–6, use your hundred charts. Tell if the statement is *true* or *false*. If the statement is false, tell why.

1. Even numbers have even multiples.

2. Odd numbers have odd and even multiples.

3. The product of any number and an odd number is an odd number.

4. The product of any number and an even number is an even number.

5. The product of any number and 6 can be even or odd.

6. The product of 9 and 6 is an even number.

LESSON 2

Algebra: Find a Rule

Quick Review

1. $5 \times 4 = \blacksquare$
2. $7 \times 5 = \blacksquare$
3. $6 \times 8 = \blacksquare$
4. $7 \times 2 = \blacksquare$
5. $8 \times 6 = \blacksquare$

Learn

CLIP CLOP Horses wear a horseshoe on each of their 4 hooves. How many horseshoes are needed for 6 horses?

Think: 1 horse needs 4 horseshoes.
2 horses need 8 horseshoes.
3 horses need 12 horseshoes, and so on.

Look for a pattern. Write a rule.

Horses	1	2	3	4	5	6
Horseshoes	4	8	12	16	20	■

Pattern: The number of horseshoes equals the number of horses times 4.

Rule: Multiply the number of horses by 4.

Since $6 \times 4 = 24$, then 24 horseshoes are needed for 6 horses.

MATH IDEA You can write a rule to describe a number pattern in a table.

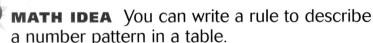

Example

Write a rule to find the cost of the bread.

Loaves of bread	1	2	4	5	7	9
Cost	\$3	\$6	\$12	\$15	\$21	\$27

Rule: Multiply the number of loaves of bread by \$3.

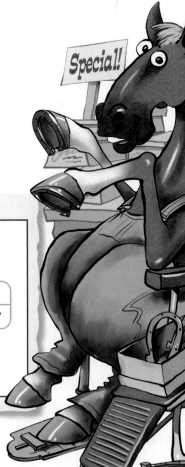

- How can you use the rule to find the cost of 3 loaves of bread?

Technology Link

More Practice: Harcourt Mega Math Ice Station Exploration, *Arctic Algebra*, Level D

Check

1. **Explain** how you could use a rule to find the number of horseshoes on 8 horses.

2. Write a rule for the table. Then copy and complete the table.

Nickels	1	2	3	4	5	6	7	8	9	10
Pennies	5	10	15	■	■	■	■	■	■	■

Practice and Problem Solving

Extra Practice, page 224, Set B

Write a rule for each table. Then copy and complete the table.

3.

Spiders	1	2	3	4	5	6
Legs	8	16	24	■	■	■

4.

Toy cars	1	2	3	4	5	6
Cost	$2	$4	$6	■	■	■

5.

Tables	3	4	5	7	8	9
Legs	12	16	20	■	■	■

6.

Guitars	2	3	5	6	7	8
Strings	12	18	30	■	■	■

For 7–8, use the table below.

Dimes	1	2	3	4	5	6	7	8	9	10
Nickels	2	4	6	■	■	■	■	■	■	■

7. Write a rule to find the number of nickels. Copy and complete the table.

8. **REASONING** How many dimes can you trade for 18 nickels? How many nickels can you trade for 8 dimes?

9. **REASONING** Yogurt comes in packages of 6 cups. How many packages are needed to serve 23 students each a cup of yogurt?

10. Each pudding pack costs $4. How much do 5 packs cost? Make a table and write a rule to find your answer.

Mixed Review and Test Prep

For 11–14, find the elapsed time. (p. 134)

11. 8:00 A.M. to 3:00 P.M.

12. 11:30 A.M. to 1:05 P.M.

13. 3:00 A.M. to 5:45 A.M.

14. 11:00 A.M. to midnight

15. **TEST PREP** Nieta had 314 stickers. She gave 54 away and collected 32 more. How many does she have now? (p. 96)

A 400 C 260
B 292 D 228

LESSON 3

Algebra: Multiply with 3 Factors

Quick Review

1. $2 \times 2 = \blacksquare$
2. $4 \times 7 = \blacksquare$
3. $3 \times 2 = \blacksquare$
4. $6 \times 5 = \blacksquare$
5. $9 \times 4 = \blacksquare$

VOCABULARY

Associative Property of Multiplication

Learn

PRACTICE, PRACTICE . . . Julia has been taking horseback riding lessons for 3 months. At each lesson she rides for 2 hours. If she has 4 lessons each month, for how many hours has she ridden?

$$3 \times 2 \times 4 = \blacksquare$$

MATH IDEA The **Associative Property of Multiplication**, or Grouping Property, states that when the grouping of factors is changed, the product remains the same.

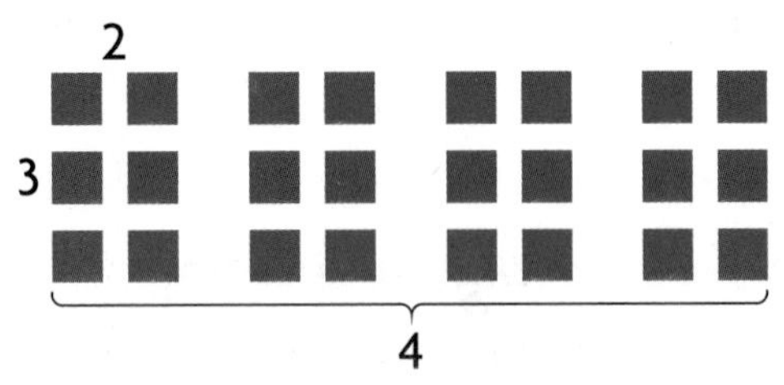

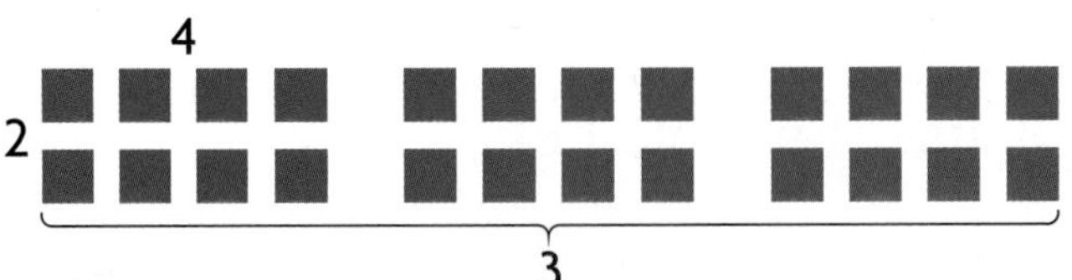

$(3 \times 2) \times 4 = \blacksquare$
↓
$6 \times 4 = 24$

$3 \times (2 \times 4) = \blacksquare$
↓
$3 \times 8 = 24$

Multiply the numbers in parentheses ( ) first.

So, Julia has ridden for 24 hours.

Check

1. **Tell** which numbers you would multiply first to find $7 \times 2 \times 3$ mentally.

Find each product.

2. $(2 \times 4) \times 1 = \blacksquare$
3. $2 \times (1 \times 3) = \blacksquare$
4. $2 \times (4 \times 2) = \blacksquare$
5. $(3 \times 3) \times 2 = \blacksquare$

Practice and Problem Solving

Extra Practice, page 224, Set C

Find each product.

6. $(4 \times 2) \times 5 = ■$ **7.** $(3 \times 3) \times 6 = ■$ **8.** $8 \times (2 \times 2) = ■$

9. $(6 \times 1) \times 2 = ■$ **10.** $■ = 5 \times (7 \times 1)$ **11.** $■ = 3 \times (3 \times 3)$

12. $■ = (2 \times 3) \times 5$ **13.** $■ = (5 \times 2) \times 7$ **14.** $(4 \times 2) \times 4 = ■$

Use parentheses. Find the product.

15. $6 \times 1 \times 8 = ■$ **16.** $9 \times 2 \times 1 = ■$ **17.** $■ = 7 \times 4 \times 2$

18. $■ = 9 \times 8 \times 0$ **19.** $6 \times 5 \times 2 = ■$ **20.** $4 \times 2 \times 9 = ■$

Find the missing factor.

21. $(1 \times ■) \times 8 = 64$ **22.** $(2 \times 4) \times ■ = 24$ **23.** $42 = 7 \times (■ \times 2)$

24. $2 \times 4 \times ■ = 8$ **25.** $2 \times 4 \times ■ = 40$ **26.** $14 = ■ \times 2 \times 7$

27. Jed has three $1 bills, 5 quarters, and 2 nickels. How much money does he have?

28. **REASONING** Explain why 18×2 is the same as $9 \times (2 \times 2)$.

29. Ross made 2 cakes for each of 3 friends. In each cake he used 3 apples. How many apples did he use?

30. **ALGEBRA** Darla had 2 singing lessons a month for 2 months. She learned the same number of songs at each lesson. She learned 12 songs in all. How many songs did she learn at each lesson?

31. **Vocabulary Power** One meaning for the word *property* is "any of the special features that belong to something." Use the numbers 2, 3, and 4 to explain the Associative Property of Multiplication.

Mixed Review and Test Prep

Choose <, >, or = for each ●. (p. 194)

32. 6×8 ● $50 - 2$

33. 7×6 ● 8×5

34. 9×6 ● 6×9

35. 4×6 ● $18 + 6$

36. **TEST PREP** Irene bought 100 apples. She made 7 pies. Each pie had 8 apples in it. How many apples were left over? (p. 196)

A 56 **B** 44 **C** 34 **D** 16

LESSON 4

Algebra: Multiplication Properties

Quick Review

1. 6×3
2. 9×1
3. 2×8
4. 4×4
5. 3×5

Vocabulary

Identity Property
Zero Property
Distributive Property

Learn

You can use multiplication properties to help you find products.

Identity Property The product of 1 and any number equals that number.

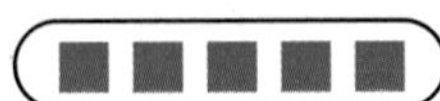

$1 \times 5 = 5$

Zero Property The product of 0 and any number equals 0.

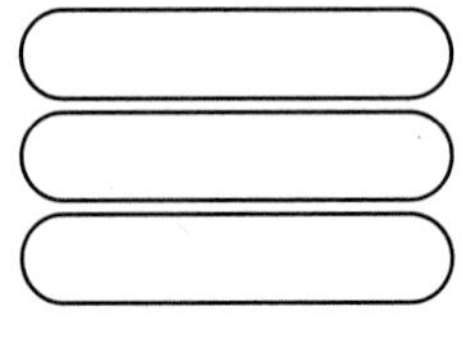

$3 \times 0 = 0$

Commutative Property You can multiply two factors in any order and get the same product.

$2 \times 4 = 8$ $4 \times 2 = 8$

Associative Property You can group factors in different ways and get the same product.

$(2 \times 3) \times 3 = \blacksquare$
$6 \times 3 = 18$

$2 \times (3 \times 3) = \blacksquare$
$2 \times 9 = 18$

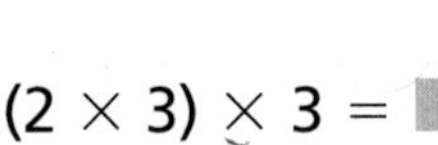

Distributive Property You can think of one factor as the sum of two addends. Then multiply each addend by the other factor and add the products.

Find 5×7.

Think: $5 \times 7 = 5 \times (3 + 4)$
$= (5 \times 3) + (5 \times 4)$
$= \quad 15 \quad + \quad 20$

So, $5 \times 7 = 35$.

Make an array.

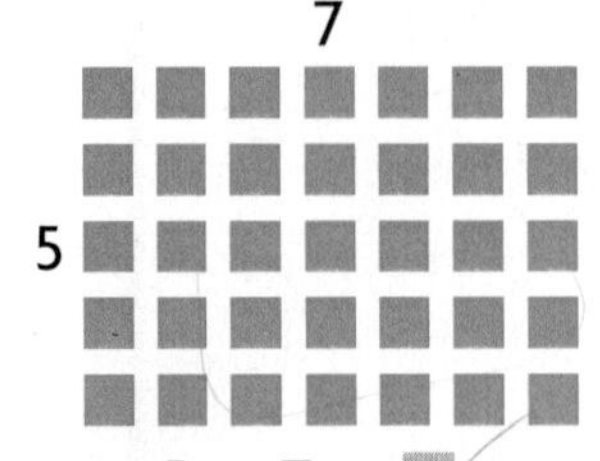

$5 \times 7 = \blacksquare$

Break the array into two smaller arrays.

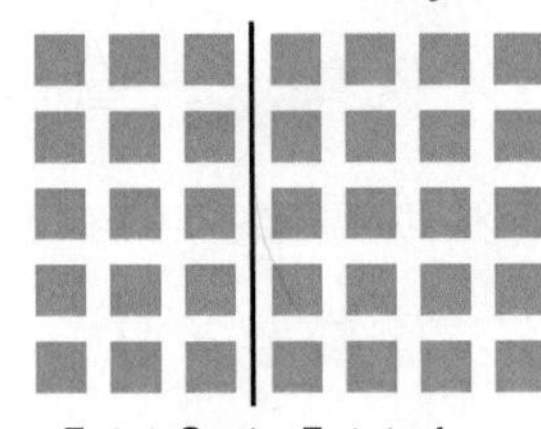

$5 \times 3 + 5 \times 4$

Check

1. **Explain** how the Commutative Property helps you find 8×5 when you know that $5 \times 8 = 40$.

Find the product. Tell which property you used to help you.

2. 9×0	**3.** 1×7	**4.** 3×8	**5.** 6×9
6. 6×1	**7.** 7×8	**8.** 0×5	**9.** 7×7
10. $(2 \times 3) \times 5$	**11.** $(4 \times 4) \times 2$	**12.** $3 \times (2 \times 7)$	**13.** $2 \times (3 \times 8)$

Practice and Problem Solving

Extra Practice, page 224, Set D

Find the product. Tell which property you used to help you.

14. 0×6	**15.** 9×4	**16.** 8×1	**17.** 8×9
18. 5×9	**19.** 6×6	**20.** 7×4	**21.** 8×8
22. $(4 \times 2) \times 3$	**23.** $2 \times (4 \times 5)$	**24.** $5 \times (2 \times 3)$	**25.** $(3 \times 3) \times 9$

Write the missing number for each ■.

26. $6 \times 7 = ■ \times 6$	**27.** $2 \times (3 \times 5) = (■ \times 3) \times 5$	**28.** $5 \times ■ = 1 \times 5$
29. $9 \times 5 = ■ \times 9$	**30.** $3 \times 5 = (3 \times ■) + (3 \times 2)$	**31.** $■ \times 7 = 7 \times 4$

32. **Write About It** Explain how you can use the Distributive Property to find 7×8. Draw an array to show your answer.

33. **REASONING** On Tuesday Kim bought 4 shirts for \$8 each. On Friday she bought more of the same shirts. In the two days, she spent \$48. How many shirts did she buy on Friday? Explain.

Mixed Review and Test Prep

34. $583 + 258$ (p. 72)

35. $1{,}964 + 3{,}057$ (p. 72)

36. $826 - 419$ (p. 96)

37. $2{,}038 - 1{,}245$ (p. 96)

38. **TEST PREP** Gordon leaves his house at 7:55 A.M. School starts at 8:15 A.M. How much time does Gordon have to get to school? (p. 134)

A 15 min
B 20 min
C 25 min
D 30 min

LESSON 5

Problem Solving Skill
Multistep Problems

UNDERSTAND PLAN SOLVE CHECK

KNOW THE SCORE Jeff's team scored 6 points for a touchdown but missed the extra point. Then they scored 3 points for each of 4 field goals. How many points did they score in all?

To find how many points in all, you must solve a **multistep problem**, or a problem with more than one step.

Quick Review

1. $(2 \times 3) \times 4 = \square$
2. $(5 \times 1) \times 7 = \square$
3. $4 + 16 + 5 = \square$
4. $7 + 8 + 2 = \square$
5. $3 \times (4 \times 2) = \square$

VOCABULARY

multistep problem

Example

STEP 1

Find how many points were scored by touchdowns.

1 touchdown was scored. Each touchdown = 6 points.

$1 \times 6 = 6$ 6 points were scored in touchdowns.

STEP 2

Find how many points were scored by field goals.

4 field goals were scored. Each field goal = 3 points.

$4 \times 3 = 12$ 12 points were scored in field goals.

STEP 3

Find how many points were scored in all.

Add the points scored by touchdowns and field goals.

$6 + 12 = 18$ So, 18 points were scored in all.

Talk About It

- Does it matter if you find the points scored in touchdowns first or the points scored in field goals first? Explain.

Problem Solving Practice

Problem Solving

Solve.

1. To raise money for the school, Lucia sold 9 boxes of cards. Ginger sold 7 boxes. Each box cost \$3. How much money did they raise in all?

2. The Wilsons drove 598 miles in 3 days. They drove 230 miles the first day and 175 miles the second day. How far did they go the third day?

Kelsey bought 3 boxes of tacos. Each box had 6 tacos. Then she gave 4 tacos away.

3. Which shows the first step you take to find how many tacos Kelsey had left?

   A $3 + 6 = 9$
   B $6 - 3 = 3$
   C $3 \times 6 = 18$
   D $3 \times 4 = 12$

4. How many tacos did Kelsey have left?

   F 12
   G 14
   H 18
   J 22

Mixed Applications

USE DATA For 5–7, use the pictograph.

5. How many students did NOT vote for hot dogs?

6. How many students voted in all?

7. **Write a problem** about the graph. Exchange with a partner and solve.

8. **What's the Question?** Rob spent \$30 for 4 tickets. He bought 3 children's tickets for \$7 each and 1 adult ticket. The answer is \$9.

FAVORITE HOT LUNCHES

Tacos	🍕 🍕 🍕
Hot Dogs	🍕 🍕 🍕 🍕
Hamburgers	🍕 🍕
Pizza	🍕 🍕 🍕

Key: Each 🍕 = 5 votes.

Extra Practice

Set A (pp. 212–215)

Find the product.

1. 9 × 7 = ■ 2. 6 × 9 = ■ 3. 6 × 10 = ■ 4. 10 × 3 = ■

5. 3 × 9 = ■ 6. 8 × 9 = ■ 7. 10 × 7 = ■ 8. 9 × 5 = ■

Find the missing factor.

9. ■ × 9 = 36 10. 90 = 9 × ■ 11. 7 × ■ = 56 12. 21 = ■ × 7

Set B (pp. 216–217)

Write a rule for each table. Then copy and complete the table.

1.

Packs	1	2	3	4	5	6
Cards	4	8	12	■	■	■

2.

Bags	1	2	3	4	5	6
Oranges	6	12	18	■	■	■

3.

Cans	1	2	3	4	5	6
Tennis Balls	3	6	9	■	■	■

4.

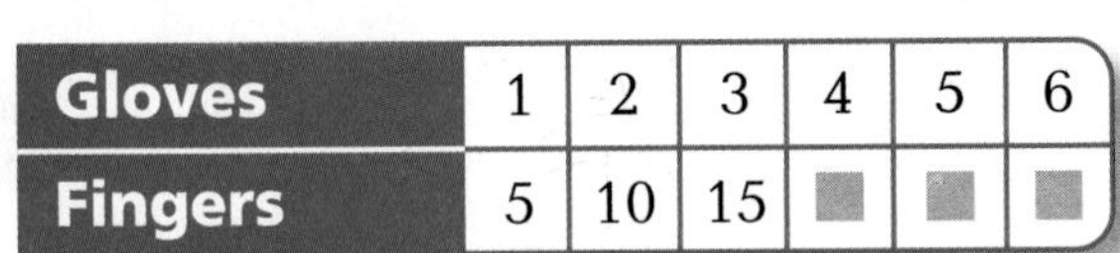

Gloves	1	2	3	4	5	6
Fingers	5	10	15	■	■	■

Set C (pp. 218–219)

Find each product.

1. (4 × 1) × 3 = ■ 2. (3 × 2) × 3 = ■ 3. (5 × 1) × 5 = ■

4. 4 × (2 × 2) = ■ 5. 10 × (3 × 3) = ■ 6. (6 × 1) × 7 = ■

Find the missing factor.

7. (4 × ■) × 1 = 16 8. 5 × (2 × ■) = 20 9. ■ × (7 × 1) = 49

Set D (pp. 220–221)

Find the product. Tell which property you used to help you.

1. 0 × 7 2. 9 × 2 3. 1 × 8 4. 3 × 8

5. 5 × 9 6. 5 × 0 7. 4 × 8 8. 9 × 9

9. (6 × 2) × 2 10. (4 × 5) × 2 11. 2 × (3 × 5) 12. (3 × 8) × 3

Review/Test

✓ CHECK VOCABULARY AND CONCEPTS

Choose the best term from the box.

factor
Associative Property
multistep problem

1. A problem with more than one step is a _?_. (p. 222)
2. The _?_ of Multiplication states that when the grouping of factors is changed, the product remains the same. (p. 218)

✓ CHECK SKILLS

Find the product. (pp. 212–215)

3. $9 \times 7 = \blacksquare$
4. $\blacksquare = 9 \times 4$
5. $6 \times 9 = \blacksquare$
6. $8 \times 9 = \blacksquare$
7. $10 \times 5 = \blacksquare$
8. $3 \times 10 = \blacksquare$
9. $\blacksquare = 9 \times 9$
10. $10 \times 7 = \blacksquare$

Write a rule for the table. Then copy and complete the table. (pp. 216–217)

11.

Insects	1	2	3	4	5	6	7
Legs	6	12	18	■	■	■	■

Find each product. (pp. 218–219)

12. $(3 \times 1) \times 6 = \blacksquare$
13. $\blacksquare = 5 \times (2 \times 2)$
14. $(3 \times 3) \times 9 = \blacksquare$
15. $4 \times (2 \times 5) = \blacksquare$
16. $\blacksquare = (2 \times 4) \times 8$
17. $9 \times (4 \times 1) = \blacksquare$

Find the product. Tell which property you used to help you. (pp. 220–221)

18. 1×6
19. 2×9
20. 8×0
21. 7×8
22. 4×6
23. 5×9

✓ CHECK PROBLEM SOLVING

Solve. (pp. 222–223)

24. In March, Mr. Holly's class raised \$176. In April, the students raised \$209. How much do they still need in order to raise \$500?
25. Joe bought 5 guppies for \$3 each and 8 goldfish for \$2 each. How much did he spend?

Standardized Test Prep

NUMBER SENSE, CONCEPTS, AND OPERATIONS

1. Mrs. Walsh bought 6 bags of oranges. Each bag contains 10 oranges. How many oranges did she buy?

   A 4
   B 16
   C 30
   D 60

2. Which multiplication fact does the array show?

   F $2 \times 9 = 18$
   G $4 \times 9 = 36$
   H $8 \times 3 = 24$
   J $4 \times 5 = 20$

3. Which number should Karen write to make the equation true?

   $(8 \times \blacksquare) \times 1 = 72$

   A 4
   B 7
   C 8
   D 9

4. **Explain It** Abby has 218 beads. Sasha has 53 beads. Abby says she has about 150 more beads than Sasha. Tell how Abby estimated the difference.

MEASUREMENT

5. The clock shows the time Milla woke up this morning. At what time did Milla wake up?

   F 7:25 A.M.
   G 5:35 A.M.
   H 7:35 P.M.
   J 5:35 P.M.

6. These coins are in Jana's purse.

   How much money is in Jana's purse?

   A \$4.41
   B \$2.41
   C \$1.41
   D \$1.31

7. **Explain It** Lance bought a pen for \$1.89 and a notebook for \$1.09. He gave the clerk a \$5 bill. About how much change did Lance receive? Explain how you found your answer.

GEOMETRY AND SPATIAL SENSE

TIP **Eliminate choices.** See item 8. Look for figures that have the same shape as Tomás's figure. Then find the figure that is the same size as Tomás's figure.

8. Tomás drew this figure. Which figure below is congruent?

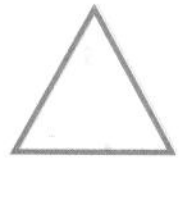

F 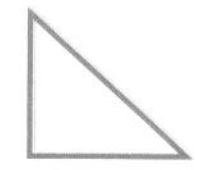

H 

G 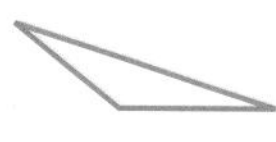

J

9. Forrest measured a window in the classroom. It was 2 feet wide and 3 feet tall. What is the perimeter of the window?

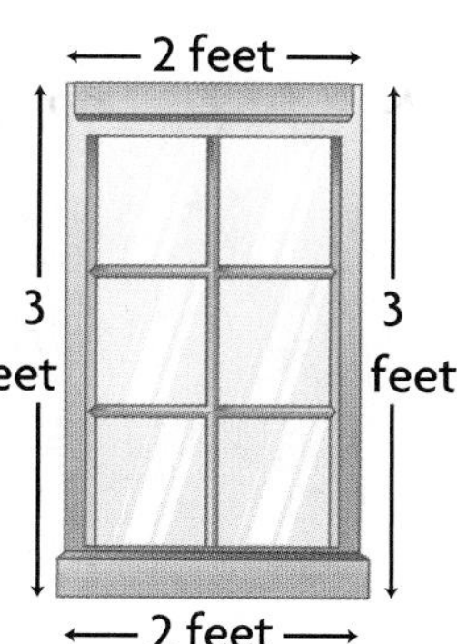

A 1 foot
B 5 feet
C 6 feet
D 10 feet

10. **Explain It** Marla made this quilt. She wants to put a ribbon border around the outside. How many feet of ribbon will she need? Explain how you found your answer.

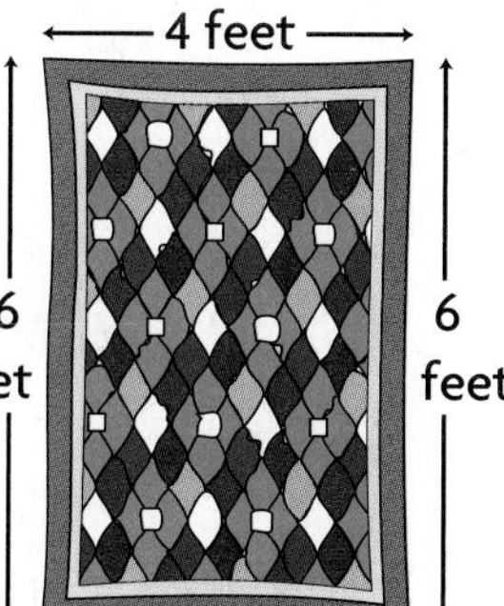

DATA ANALYSIS AND PROBABILITY

11. The pictograph shows the number of books read by 4 students. How many more books did Emma read than Jack?

F 4
G 3
H 2
J 1

12. Look at the pictograph above. Which students together read the same number of books as Gary?

A Fran and Jack
B Jack and Emma
C Emma and Fran
D Fran, Jack, and Emma

13. **Explain It** Tell how you could use the symbols on the pictograph above to order the students from the one who read the fewest books to the one who read the most.

IT'S IN THE BAG

Multiplication Rocks

PROJECT Use rocks to practice the multiplication facts.

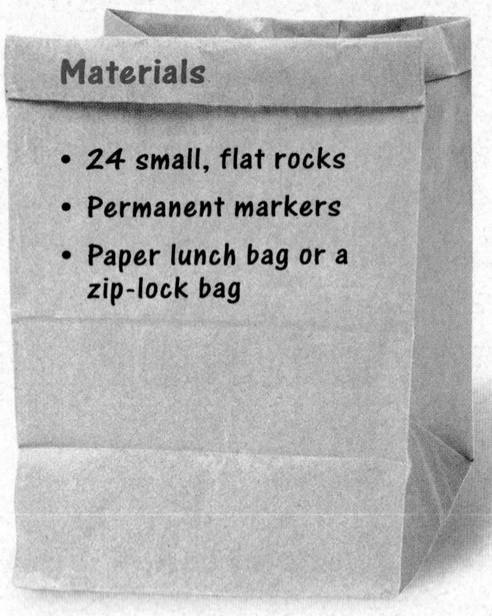

Materials

- 24 small, flat rocks
- Permanent markers
- Paper lunch bag or a zip-lock bag

Directions

1. Collect a variety of small, flat rocks.
2. Write a number from 0–10 on each rock. Make two sets of 0–10 rocks. *(Picture A)*
3. Write a × sign on one of the rocks.
4. Write an = sign on one of the rocks. *(Picture B)*
5. Label and decorate the bag.
6. Choose one rock from the bag and place it to the left of the × sign. Choose a second rock from the bag and place it to the right of the × sign. Place the = sign.
7. Then find the rocks in the bag to show the product. *(Picture C)*

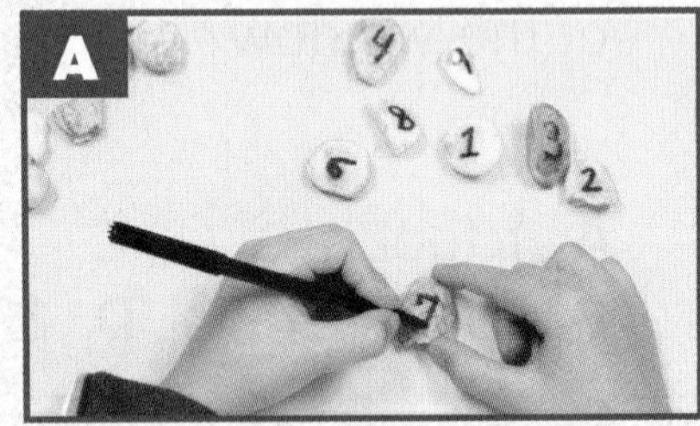
A

B

C

Challenge

Multiply with 11 and 12

There are 11 players on a soccer team. In a soccer game, there are two teams on the field. How many players are on the field?

$2 \times 11 = ■$

You can use a multiplication table to find the product.

The product is found where the row for 2 and the column for 11 meet.

So, there are 22 players on the field.

×	0	1	2	3	4	5	6	7	8	9	10	11	12
0	0	0	0	0	0	0	0	0	0	0	0	0	0
1	0	1	2	3	4	5	6	7	8	9	10	11	12
2	0	2	4	6	8	10	12	14	16	18	20	22	24
3	0	3	6	9	12	15	18	21	24	27	30	33	36
4	0	4	8	12	16	20	24	28	32	36	40	44	48
5	0	5	10	15	20	25	30	35	40	45	50	55	60
6	0	6	12	18	24	30	36	42	48	54	60	66	72
7	0	7	14	21	28	35	42	49	56	63	70	77	84
8	0	8	16	24	32	40	48	56	64	72	80	88	96
9	0	9	18	27	36	45	54	63	72	81	90	99	108
10	0	10	20	30	40	50	60	70	80	90	100	110	120
11	0	11	22	33	44	55	66	77	88	99	110	121	132
12	0	12	24	36	48	60	72	84	96	108	120	132	144

Talk About It

- Explain how to use a multiplication table to find 6×12.
- What patterns do you notice in the column for 12 of the multiplication table?

Try It

Use the multiplication table to solve.

1. $3 \times 11 = ■$ **2.** $■ = 7 \times 11$ **3.** $■ = 4 \times 12$

4. $8 \times 11 = ■$ **5.** $■ = 6 \times 11$ **6.** $5 \times 12 = ■$

7. $1 \times 12 = ■$ **8.** $■ = 2 \times 12$ **9.** $9 \times 12 = ■$

10. 12×7 **11.** 11×9 **12.** 11×5 **13.** 12×3 **14.** 12×8

Study Guide and Review

VOCABULARY

Choose the best term from the box.

factors
Associative Property of Multiplication
Commutative Property of Multiplication

1. The _?_ means that two factors can be multiplied in any order. The product is the same. (p. 163)
2. The _?_ means that when the grouping of factors is changed, the product remains the same. (p. 218)

STUDY AND SOLVE

Chapter 8

Use the Commutative Property of Multiplication.

Factors can be multiplied in any order. The product is the same.

$3 \times 4 = 12$

$4 \times 3 = 12$

Find the product. (pp. 162–167)

3. $2 \times 3 = \blacksquare$ $\quad 3 \times 2 = \blacksquare$
4. $3 \times 7 = \blacksquare$ $\quad 7 \times 3 = \blacksquare$
5. $4 \times 5 = \blacksquare$ $\quad 5 \times 4 = \blacksquare$
6. $3 \times 5 = \blacksquare$ $\quad 5 \times 3 = \blacksquare$
7. $2 \times 7 = \blacksquare$ $\quad 7 \times 2 = \blacksquare$

Chapter 9

Find missing factors.

$\blacksquare \times 7 = 28$

The multiplication table on page 229 can help you. Look down the column for 7 to the product 28. Look left across the row from 28. The factor in that row is 4.

So, $4 \times 7 = 28$.

Find the missing factor. (pp. 186–187)

8. $\blacksquare \times 8 = 16$
9. $5 \times \blacksquare = 30$
10. $9 \times \blacksquare = 45$
11. $3 \times \blacksquare = 3$
12. $4 \times \blacksquare = 0$
13. $\blacksquare \times 3 = 15$
14. $\blacksquare \times 6 = 18$
15. $4 \times \blacksquare = 36$

Chapter 10

Write multiplication facts with factors 6, 7, and 8.

You can double products of facts you already know to help you find products you don't know.

$6 \times 8 = ■$
Think: $6 \times 4 = 24$
$24 + 24 = 48$, so $6 \times 8 = 48$.

Use the Commutative Property of Multiplication.
$5 \times 7 = ■$
$7 \times 5 = 35$, so $5 \times 7 = 35$.

Find the product. (pp. 194–197, 200–201)

16. $6 \times 8 = ■$
17. $7 \times 6 = ■$
18. $8 \times 4 = ■$
19. $6 \times 6 = ■$
20. $6 \times 3 = ■$
21. $4 \times 8 = ■$
22. $8 \times 7 = ■$
23. $8 \times 8 = ■$
24. $7 \times 9 = ■$
25. $7 \times 7 = ■$
26. $8 \times 5 = ■$
27. $7 \times 4 = ■$

Chapter 11

Find a rule for the pattern.

Write a rule for the pattern in the table.

Cars	1	2	3	4	5	6	7	8	9	10
Tires	4	8	12	16	20	■	■	■	■	■

Think: The number of tires is 4 times the number of cars.
Rule: Multiply by 4.

For 28–29, use the table below.

(pp. 216–217)

Spiders	1	2	4	5	6	8
Legs	8	16	32	40	■	■

28. Write a rule for the table.
29. Use the rule from Exercise 28 to complete the table.

PROBLEM SOLVING PRACTICE

Solve. (pp. 168–169, 222–223)

30. Pencils are in packages of 4. Erasers are in packages of 7. Marian bought 16 pencils. How many packages of pencils did she buy? Is there too much or too little information? Explain.

31. A box of cookies costs $3. A bag of nuts costs $2. Aimee bought 4 boxes of cookies and 7 bags of nuts for her friends. How much did she spend?

PERFORMANCE ASSESSMENT

TASK A • CLASS PLAY

Materials: square tiles

You need to set up 24 chairs for people to watch the class play. You must put the chairs into rows with an equal number of chairs in each row.

a. Use square tiles to represent the chairs. Make arrays to show two possible ways to set up the chairs. Draw a picture of each array.

b. Write a multiplication sentence for each array.

c. Are the two multiplication sentences you wrote examples of the Order Property of Multiplication? Why or why not?

TASK B • A NEW GAME

You and a friend invent a new game using 2 spinners. You spin the pointer on each spinner. Use the numbers the pointers land on as factors to write a multiplication sentence. If a pointer lands on a shaded section, you can choose any number on that spinner as the factor. The winner of the round is the player with the greater product.

a. Your friend spins a 4 and a 5. You spin a 3 and a shaded section. Which numbers could you choose to make yourself the winner?

b. Write three multiplication sentences for factors you can spin on the spinners that give a product less than 20.

c. Suppose you want to change the game so that you can spin factors with products more than 100. What numbers would you put on the spinners?

The Learning Site • Multiplication Mystery

If you know your multiplication facts, it is easy to count groups of coins and other objects.

You can practice your multiplication facts at the Harcourt School Learning Site.

- Go to The Learning Site. **www.harcourtschool.com**
- Click on *Multiplication Mystery.*
- Drag the products into the multiplication table to uncover the picture.
- What picture did you uncover?

Multiplication Mystery

9

This tile is a product of two factors. Drag it to a square where the missing factors meet.

Practice and Problem Solving

Find the product.

1. $2 \times 10 = ■$ **2.** $3 \times 5 = ■$ **3.** $4 \times 2 = ■$ **4.** $6 \times 2 = ■$

5. $7 \times 4 = ■$ **6.** $5 \times 5 = ■$ **7.** $2 \times 7 = ■$ **8.** $3 \times 9 = ■$

Find the missing factor.

9. $4 \times ■ = 12$ **10.** $■ \times 8 = 40$ **11.** $■ \times 5 = 35$ **12.** $10 \times ■ = 90$

13. $7 \times ■ = 42$ **14.** $■ \times 7 = 63$ **15.** $8 \times ■ = 56$ **16.** $■ \times 3 = 24$

17. **Write a problem** involving two multiplication facts.

18. **STRETCH YOUR THINKING** Joanne has 88 stickers. She has 7 sheets of 8 animal stickers. How many sheets of 8 stickers without animals does she have?

GO ON-LINE **Multimedia Math Glossary** **www.harcourtschool.com/mathglossary**

Vocabulary Power Look up *Commutative Property of Multiplication* in the Multimedia Math Glossary. Write a problem that uses the examples shown in the glossary, and use counters to model it.

▲ Each year some people hike the whole length of the Appalachian Trail.

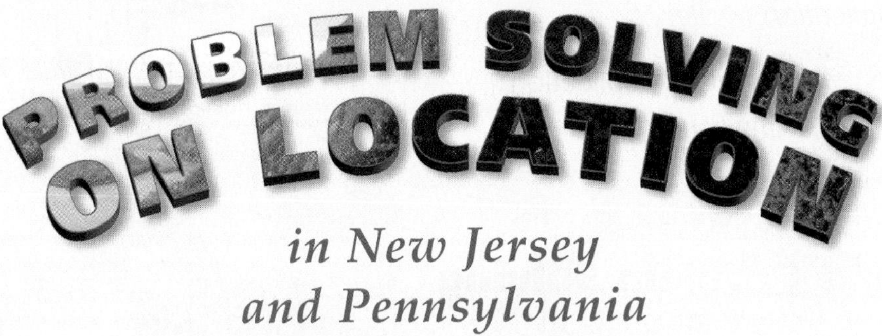

in New Jersey and Pennsylvania

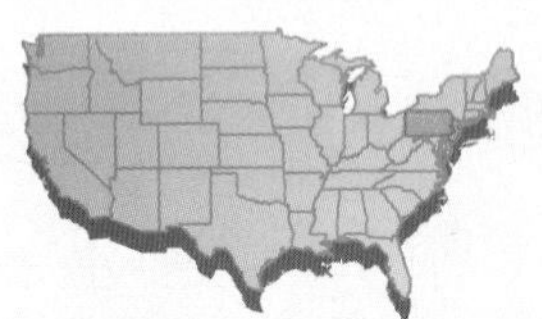

THE APPALACHIAN TRAIL

Each fall many people hike the Appalachian Trail. This is a pretty time of the year because of the fall colors of the trees.

USE DATA For 1–2, use the information on the map.

Suppose you and your family are planning a hike on the Appalachian Trail. The map at the right shows the area you have chosen for your hike. Estimated distances are shown for each trail.

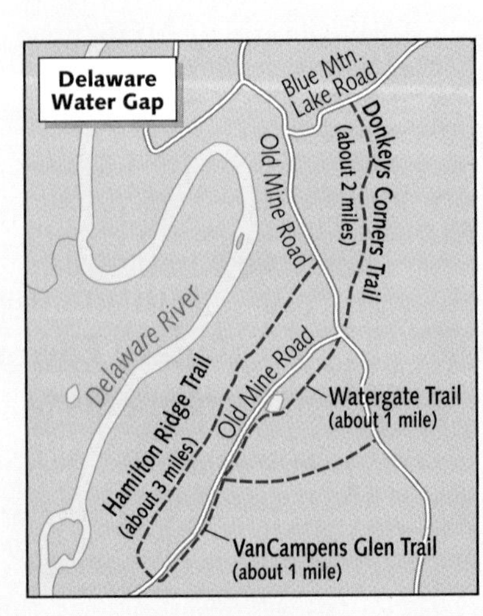

1. If you can hike 2 miles in 1 hour, how far can you hike in 2 hours? in 3 hours?
2. Use the information on the map and your answers to Exercise 1. Plan a hike that will take at least 3 hours.
   - Make a chart to show your route.
   - List each trail you will hike, and show its length.
   - Find the total length of your hike.
   - Find the total time for your hike.

THE DELAWARE WATER GAP

Visitors to the Delaware Water Gap can enjoy hiking, boating, camping, fishing, and watching wildlife.

This table shows distances between points on the Delaware River. The miles listed for each point show its distance from the Depew Access. For example, the distance from Depew to Smithfield Beach is 4 miles. The distance from Poxono to Kittatinny is 8 miles.

▲ Hikers will see many beautiful sights.

BOAT ACCESS POINTS (miles from Depew Access, NJ)				
Depew Access, NJ	**Poxono Access, NJ**	**Smithfield Beach Access, PA**	**Worthington Access, NJ**	**Kittatinny Access, NJ**
Mile 0	Mile 2	Mile 4	Mile 6	Mile 10

USE DATA For 1–3, use the table.

1. A family canoes down the Delaware River. They travel 2 miles of the river each hour. They start at Depew and travel 3 hours. Where do they stop?
2. A river guide tells campers that they will reach their campsite in 5 hours. They start at Depew, paddling 2 miles each hour. Where will they end up?
3. A fishing boat slowly travels down the river from Poxono. It covers 4 miles in 1 hour. Where will it be in 2 hours?
4. Campsites along a trail are about 7 miles apart. A hiker has passed 6 campsites. Draw an array to show how far the hiker walked.
5. **REASONING** A company rents different kinds of boats. Canoes hold 3 people each, while kayaks hold 2 people, and rafts hold 6 people. One day there are 50 people out in rental boats. Each boat is full. What is a possible group of boats rented this day?

▲ Deer, raccoons, turkey vultures, beavers, and even bears call the Delaware Water Gap home.

CHAPTER 12

Understand Division

FAST FACT • SOCIAL STUDIES North Carolina has more than 150 white-water rapids. In the sport of white-water rafting, people use paddles to move boats along rivers through shallow, fast-moving water called rapids.

PROBLEM SOLVING The graph shows different kinds of white-water boats and the number of people each can hold. If 24 friends want to go white-water rafting together, how many big rafts will they need? Explain.

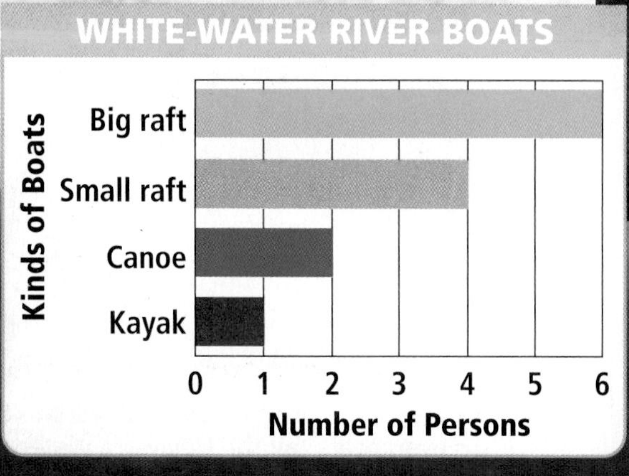

WHITE-WATER RIVER BOATS

Kinds of Boats

Big raft

Small raft

Canoe

Kayak

0 1 2 3 4 5 6

Number of Persons

CHECK WHAT YOU KNOW

Use this page to help you review and remember important skills needed for Chapter 12.

MULTIPLICATION FACTS THROUGH 10

Find the product.

1. $6 \times 7 = ■$
2. $3 \times 8 = ■$
3. $■ = 8 \times 9$
4. $9 \times 0 = ■$
5. $5 \times 7 = ■$
6. $■ = 10 \times 4$
7. $4 \times 4 = ■$
8. $2 \times 4 = ■$
9. $■ = 9 \times 9$
10. $■ = 6 \times 8$
11. $8 \times 7 = ■$
12. $4 \times 3 = ■$

MAKE EQUAL GROUPS

Complete.

13. 

■ groups
■ in each group

14. 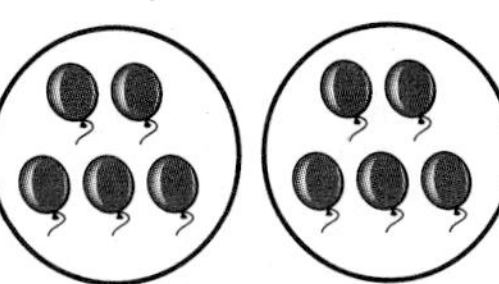
■ groups
■ in each group

15.   
■ groups
■ in each group

16. 

■ groups
■ in each group

17. 
■ groups
■ in each group

18. 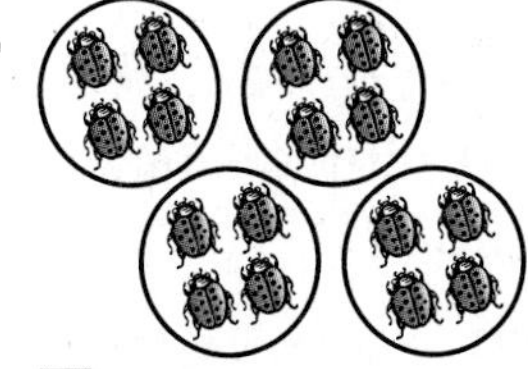
■ groups
■ in each group

VOCABULARY POWER

REVIEW

group [gro͞op] *noun*

Group means "a number of persons or things that are collected." Suppose you have 20 marbles. How many groups of 5 marbles do you have?

PREVIEW

divide
dividend
divisor
quotient
inverse operations
variable
fact family

www.harcourtschool.com/mathglossary

LESSON 1

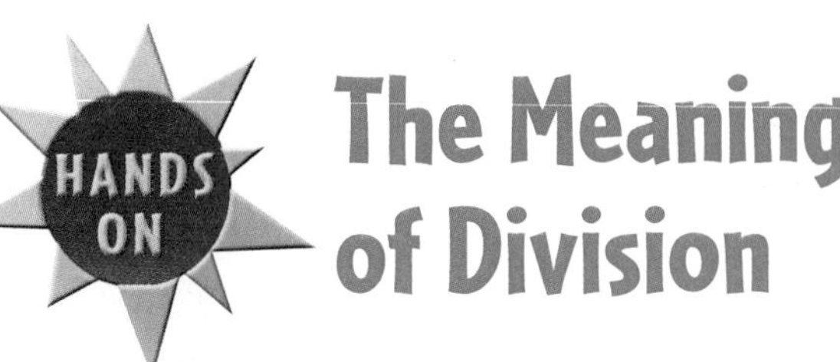

Quick Review

1. 6×4
2. 3×5
3. 2×6
4. 7×3
5. 4×3

VOCABULARY
divide

MATERIALS
counters

When you multiply, you put equal groups together. When you **divide**, you separate into equal groups.

Activity 1 Divide 14 counters into 2 equal groups. How many counters are in each group?

STEP 1

Use 14 counters.

STEP 2

Show 2 groups. Place a counter in each group

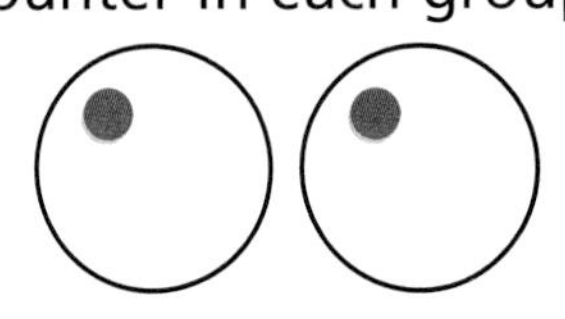

STEP 3

Continue until all counters are used.

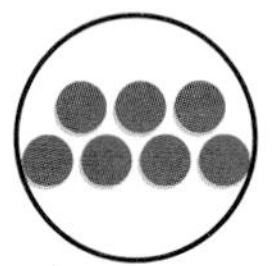
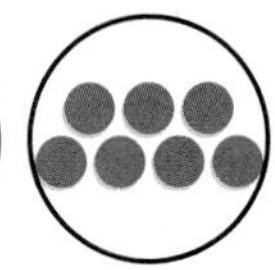

So, there are 7 counters in each of 2 groups.

Activity 2 Divide 14 counters into groups of 2. How many groups of 2 counters can you make?

STEP 1

Use 14 counters.

STEP 2

Make groups of 2.

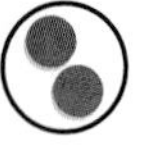

STEP 3

Continue making groups of 2 until all counters are used.

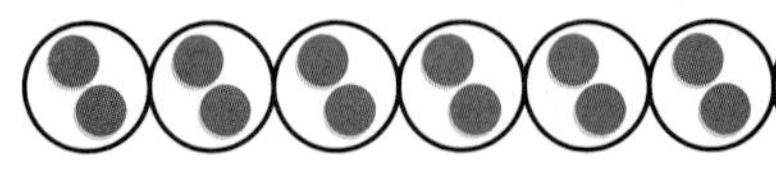

So, there are 7 groups of 2 counters.

Try It

Use counters to make equal groups. Draw a picture to show how you divided.

a. Divide 15 counters into 5 equal groups. How many are in each group?

b. Divide 15 counters into groups of 5. How many groups of 5 counters can you make?

We are putting 15 counters in 5 equal groups. How many should be in each group?

Connect

MATH IDEA You can divide to find how many items are in each group or how many equal groups there are.

Four friends share 20 marbles equally. How many marbles will each person get?

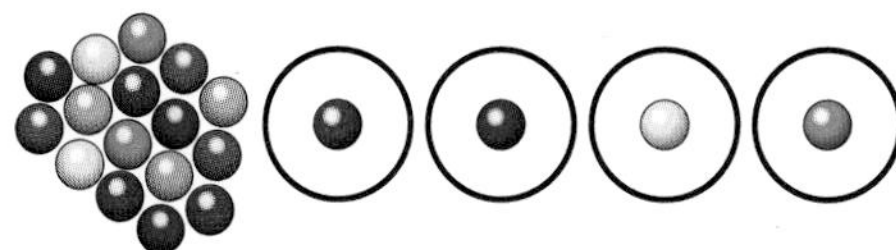

Put one marble in each group until all marbles are used.

Each person will get 5 marbles.

Each person wants 4 marbles. How many people can share 20 marbles?

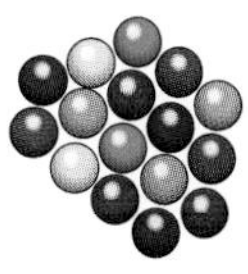

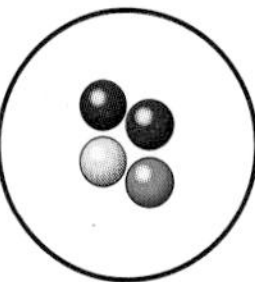

Make equal groups of 4 marbles until all marbles are used.

Five people can share 20 marbles.

Practice and Problem Solving

Copy and complete the table. Use counters to help.

	COUNTERS	NUMBER OF EQUAL GROUPS	NUMBER IN EACH GROUP
1.	15	5	■
2.	21	■	3
3.	24	3	■
4.	28	■	7

For 5–8, use counters and draw a picture.

5. Five friends share 30 stickers equally. How many will each person get?

6. Elijah has 18 books that he wants to put into equal groups. List three different ways that he could do this.

7. REASONING Three friends share some grapes equally. If each gets 9 grapes, how many grapes are there altogether?

8. **Write About It** Explain how to divide 32 counters into 4 equal groups.

Mixed Review and Test Prep

9. $463 + 297$ (p. 72)

10. $805 - 176$ (p. 96)

11. 2×9 (p. 160)

12. 3×8 (p. 164)

13. TEST PREP The sixth graders charged $4 to wash each car. How much money did they make for washing 8 cars? (p. 178)

A $2 **B** $4 **C** $12 **D** $32

LESSON 2

Subtraction and Division

Learn

GET IN THE GAME Ana has 12 game pieces for a game. Each player gets 4 pieces. How many people can play?

12	÷	4	=	■
↑		↑		↑
number of pieces		number for each player		number of players

Quick Review

How many are there in all?

1. 2 groups of 3
2. 4 groups of 4
3. 5 groups of 2
4. 3 groups of 9
5. 1 group of 8

One Way Use a number line. Start at 12. Count back by 4s until you reach 0. Count the number of times you subtract 4.

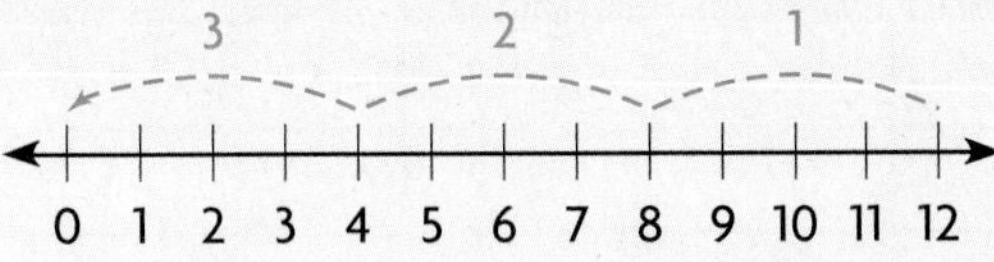

You subtract 4 three times.

Another Way Start with 12. Take away groups of 4 until you reach 0. Count the number of times you subtract 4.

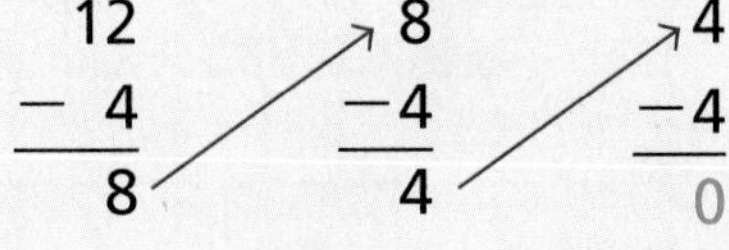

Number of times you subtract 4: **1** **2** **3**

Since you subtract 4 from 12 three times, there are 3 groups of 4 in 12.

So, 3 people can play.

Write: $12 \div 4 = 3$ or $4\overline{)12}$ with quotient 3

Read: Twelve divided by four equals three.

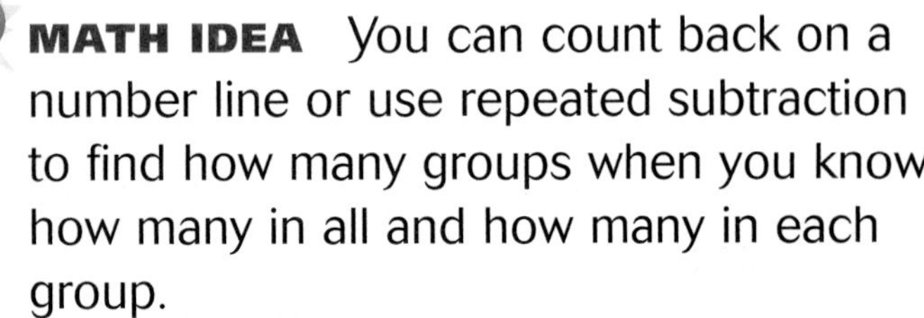

MATH IDEA You can count back on a number line or use repeated subtraction to find how many groups when you know how many in all and how many in each group.

- **Discuss** how to count back to find $15 \div 5$.

Check

1. **Explain** how to use repeated subtraction to prove that $18 \div 6 = 3$.

Write the division sentence for each.

2.  (number line 0 1 2 3 4 5 6 7 8 9 10 11 12)

3. $\begin{array}{r} 8 \\ -2 \\ \hline 6 \end{array}$ $\begin{array}{r} 6 \\ -2 \\ \hline 4 \end{array}$ $\begin{array}{r} 4 \\ -2 \\ \hline 2 \end{array}$ $\begin{array}{r} 2 \\ -2 \\ \hline 0 \end{array}$

Practice and Problem Solving

Extra Practice, page 252, Set A

Write a division sentence for each.

4. 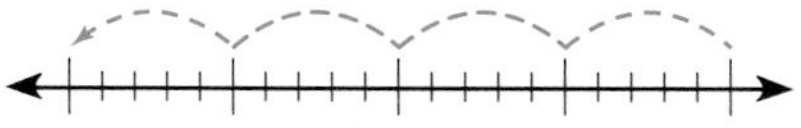 (number line 0 5 10 15 20)

5. $\begin{array}{r} 24 \\ -\ 8 \\ \hline 16 \end{array}$ $\begin{array}{r} 16 \\ -\ 8 \\ \hline 8 \end{array}$ $\begin{array}{r} 8 \\ -8 \\ \hline 0 \end{array}$

Use a number line or subtraction to solve.

6. $15 \div 3 = ■$
7. $21 \div 7 = ■$
8. $30 \div 5 = ■$
9. $36 \div 6 = ■$
10. $2\overline{)10}$
11. $8\overline{)16}$
12. $7\overline{)35}$
13. $5\overline{)25}$

ALGEBRA Complete. Write +, −, ×, or ÷ for each ●.

14. $20 - 5 = 5$ ● 3
15. $24 \div 6 = 18$ ● 14
16. 32 ● $8 = 4 \times 10$
17. 8 ● $2 = 2 + 2$

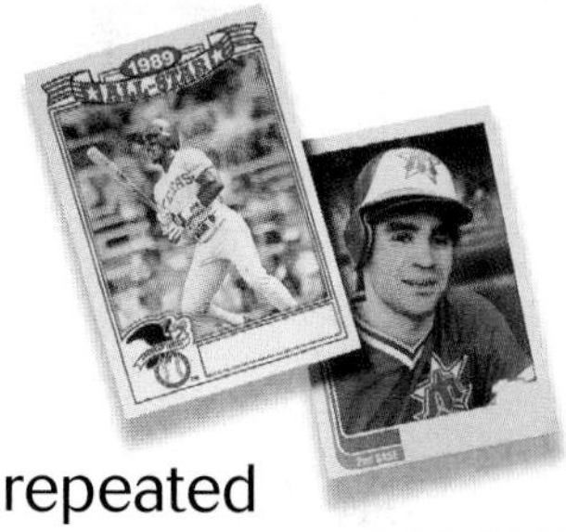

18. Scott buys 22 baseball cards. He keeps 10 cards and divides the rest equally between 2 friends. How many cards will each friend get?

19. **REASONING** Nora says that $8 \div 4 = 0$ because $8 - 4 = 4$ and $4 - 4 = 0$. Is Nora correct? Explain.

20. Explain how to use repeated subtraction to find $100 \div 10$.

Mixed Review and Test Prep

21. $\begin{array}{r} 3 \\ \times 6 \\ \hline \end{array}$ (p. 164)

22. $\begin{array}{r} 4 \\ \times 7 \\ \hline \end{array}$ (p. 178)

23. $\begin{array}{r} \$3.57 \\ +\$7.94 \\ \hline \end{array}$ (p. 120)

24. $\begin{array}{r} \$9.26 \\ -\$5.83 \\ \hline \end{array}$ (p. 120)

25. **TEST PREP** Felipe buys a notebook for \$1.39. He pays with a \$5 bill. How much change should he get? (p. 118)

A \$3.61
B \$3.71
C \$4.61
D \$6.39

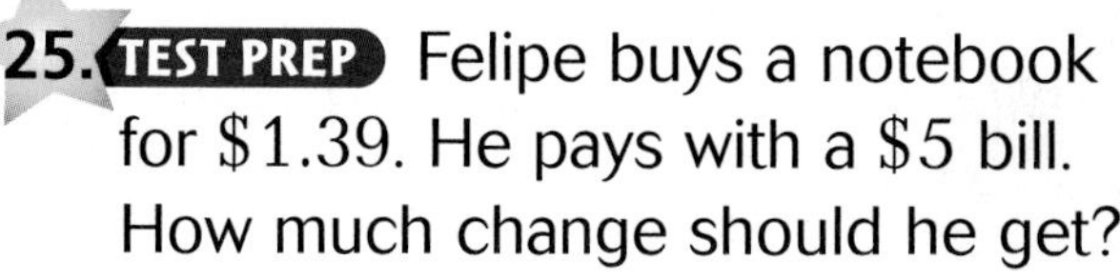

LESSON 3

Algebra: Multiplication and Division

Quick Review

1. 2×7
2. 4×2
3. 2×9
4. 6×3
5. 3×8

VOCABULARY

dividend divisor
quotient
inverse operations
variable

Learn

STICK WITH STAMPS Use what you know about arrays and multiplication to understand division.

Mark is putting stamps into his stamp album. Each page holds 18 stamps in 3 equal rows. How many stamps are in each row?

$18 \div 3 = \blacksquare$

18 ↑ number of stamps; 3 ↑ number of rows; ■ ↑ number in each row

Show an array with 18 in 3 equal rows. Find how many are in each row.

Since $3 \times 6 = 18$, then $18 \div 3 = 6$.

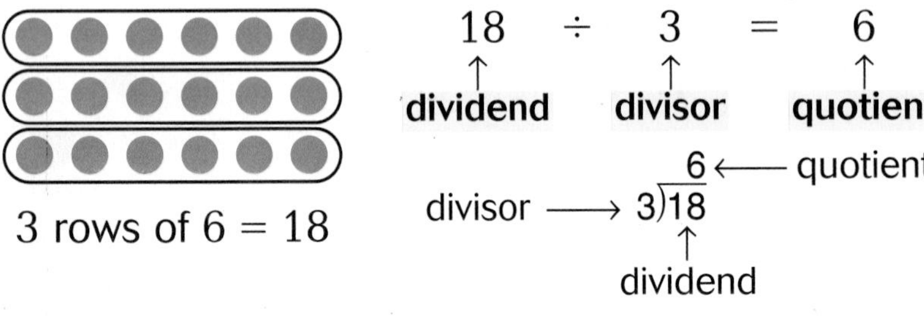

3 rows of 6 = 18

$18 \div 3 = 6$

18 ↑ **dividend**; 3 ↑ **divisor**; 6 ↑ **quotient**

$$3\overline{)18}$$

6 ⟵ quotient; divisor ⟶ 3; 18 ↑ dividend

So, there are 6 stamps in each row.

MATH IDEA Multiplication and division are opposite or **inverse operations**.

Technology Link

More Practice:
Harcourt Mega Math
Ice Station Exploration,
Arctic Algebra, Level E

Examples

A

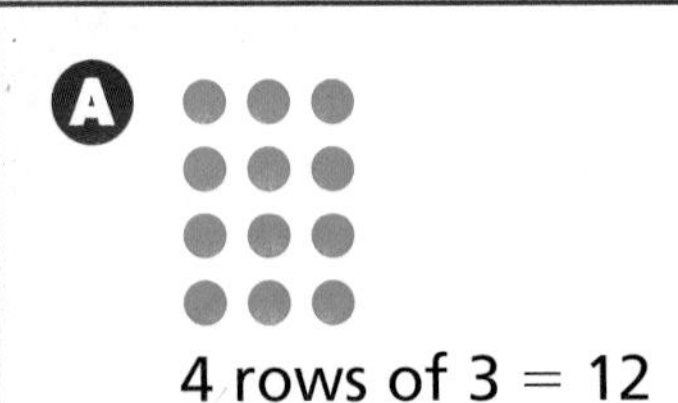

4 rows of 3 = 12
$12 \div 4 = 3$

B

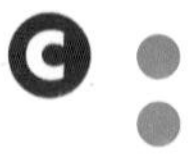

2 rows of 7 = 14
$14 \div 2 = 7$

C

3 rows of 5 = 15
$15 \div 3 = 5$

Use Variables

A **variable** is something that stands for an unknown number. A box, ■, can be a variable.

$16 \div 2 = ■$

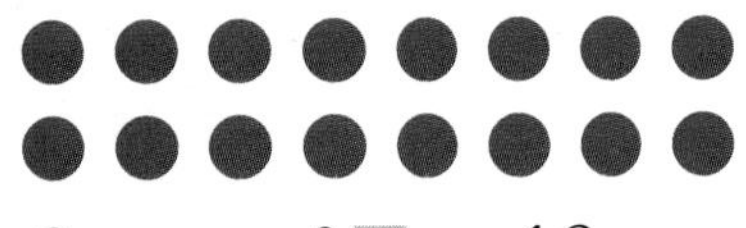

Think: $2 \times ■ = 16$
$2 \times 8 = 16$

2 rows of ■ = 16

So, $16 \div 2 = 8$.

A letter can also be a variable.

$24 \div 4 = a$

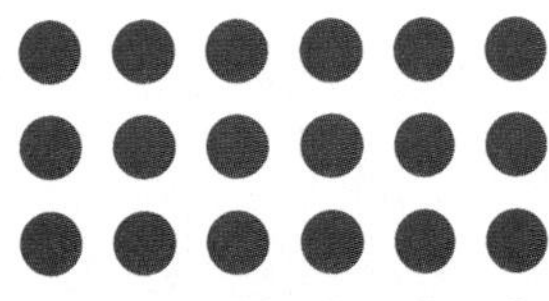

Think: $4 \times a = 24$
$4 \times 6 = 24$

4 rows of a = 24

So, $24 \div 4 = 6$.

Examples

A $12 \div 2 = b$

Think: $2 \times b = 12$
$2 \times 6 = 12$, so, $b = 6$.

So, $12 \div 2 = 6$.

B $15 \div 5 = c$

Think: $5 \times c = 15$
$5 \times 3 = 15$, so, $c = 3$.

So, $15 \div 5 = 3$.

MATH IDEA You can use a variable to stand for an unknown number.

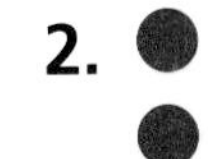

Check

1. **Explain** how to use this array to multiply and divide.

Copy and complete.

2.

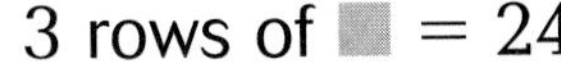

3 rows of ■ = 24

$24 \div 3 = ■$

3.

2 rows of ■ = 18

$18 \div 2 = ■$

4.

3 rows of ■ = 18

$18 \div 3 = ■$

Find the number that the variable stands for.

5. $12 \div 3 = r$
$r =$?

6. $16 \div 4 = s$
$s =$?

7. $20 \div 4 = t$
$t =$?

LESSON CONTINUES

Practice and Problem Solving

Extra Practice, page 252, Set B

Copy and complete.

8. 3 rows of ■ = 21
   $21 \div 3 =$ ■

9. 5 rows of ■ = 30
   $30 \div 5 =$ ■

10. 5 rows of ■ = 40
   $40 \div 5 =$ ■

Complete each number sentence. Draw an array to help.

11. $3 \times$ ■ $= 18$ $\quad 18 \div 3 =$ ■

12. $5 \times$ ■ $= 25$ $\quad 25 \div 5 =$ ■

13. $6 \times$ ■ $= 24$ $\quad 24 \div 6 =$ ■

14. $3 \times$ ■ $= 24$ $\quad 24 \div 3 =$ ■

Find the number that the variable stands for.

15. $12 \div 2 = a$
   $a =$?

16. $15 \div 3 = b$
   $b =$?

17. $18 \div 6 = c$
   $c =$?

18. $14 \div 7 = p$
   $p =$?

19. $25 \div 5 = q$
   $q =$?

20. $24 \div 8 = r$
   $r =$?

21. $5 \times a = 20$
   $a =$?

22. $6 \times b = 18$
   $b =$?

23. $3 \times c = 21$
   $c =$?

24. $p \times 4 = 16$
   $p =$?

25. $q \times 5 = 10$
   $q =$?

26. $r \times 7 = 14$
   $r =$?

ALGEBRA Complete.

27. $4 \times 2 = 24 \div a$
   $a =$?

28. $b \times 3 = 30 \div 5$
   $b =$?

29. $4 \times 1 = c \div 4$
   $c =$?

30. Tory arranged 28 stamps so that 7 were in each row. How many rows did she make?

31. **What's the Question?** Christy puts 36 pennies into 4 equal piles. The answer is 9 pennies.

32. **Vocabulary Power** One definition of *array* is "a number of objects arranged in rows and columns." Tell the number of rows and columns shown in the array in Exercise 10.

33. **REASONING** Mark bakes 14 muffins. He eats 2 muffins and divides the rest equally among 6 friends. What division sentence shows how many muffins each friend gets?

34. **FAST FACT** • SCIENCE Frogs lay many eggs which hatch into tadpoles. In about 12 to 16 weeks, the tadpoles become frogs. About how many months does it take for a tadpole to become a frog?

35. Colin has 24 toy cars. He puts an equal number of cars into each of 3 boxes. How many cars will be in 2 of the boxes?

Mixed Review and Test Prep

Write + or − for each ●. (p. 240)

36. 20 ● $5 = 5 \times 3$

37. $24 \div 3 = 6$ ● 2

38. $4 \times 9 = 38$ ● 2

39. 7 ● $2 = 36 \div 4$

Find each missing factor. (p. 186)

40. ■ $\times 5 = 40$

41. $8 \times$ ■ $= 56$

42. $4 \times$ ■ $= 32$

43. ■ $\times 6 = 0$

44. **TEST PREP** Zach puts 1 ice cube in each of 7 cups. How many ice cubes are there in all? (p. 176)

A 1 **B** 6 **C** 7 **D** 8

45. **TEST PREP** Predict which numbers continue this pattern. (p. 180)

14, 21, 28, 35

F 40, 47, 54
G 42, 49, 56
H 32, 39, 46
J 42, 50, 59

Problem Solving Thinker's Corner

THE HOBBY STORE

VISUAL THINKING Mr. Burns wrote number sentences to help him remember how to place the shells in the display cases at the Hobby Store.

For 1–3, draw a picture to show how the shells will be displayed.

1. $5 \times 8 = 40$
$40 \div 5 = 8$

2. $4 \times 7 = 28$
$28 \div 4 = 7$

3. $4 \times 9 = 36$
$36 \div 4 = 9$

4. Write a problem using division to find how many equal groups. Write a number sentence to solve.

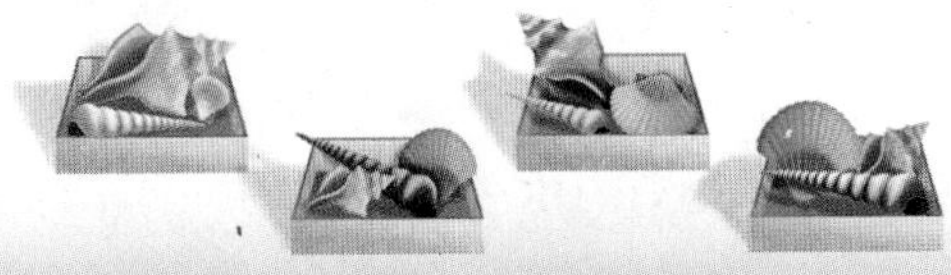

5. Mr. Burns has 16 new shells. He wants to put them into 8 equal groups. Write a problem using division to find how many shells are in each group. Write a number sentence to solve.

LESSON 4

Algebra: Fact Families

Quick Review

1. $3 \times \blacksquare = 18$
2. $\blacksquare \times 6 = 18$
3. $18 \div 6 = \blacksquare$
4. $5 \times \blacksquare = 25$
5. $25 \div 5 = \blacksquare$

VOCABULARY
fact family

Learn

FUN FACTS A set of related multiplication and division number sentences is called a **fact family**.

Fact Family for 3, 5, and 15

factor		factor		product	dividend		divisor		quotient
3	×	5	=	15	15	÷	5	=	3
5	×	3	=	15	15	÷	3	=	5

HANDS ON

Activity

Materials: square pieces of paper, scissors

Use this triangle fact card to think of the fact family for 3, 5, and 15.

Make a set of triangle fact cards. Use them to write fact families.

Product
15

Factor 3
5 Factor

A Fold each paper in half three times. Open up the paper and cut along the folds to make triangle cards.

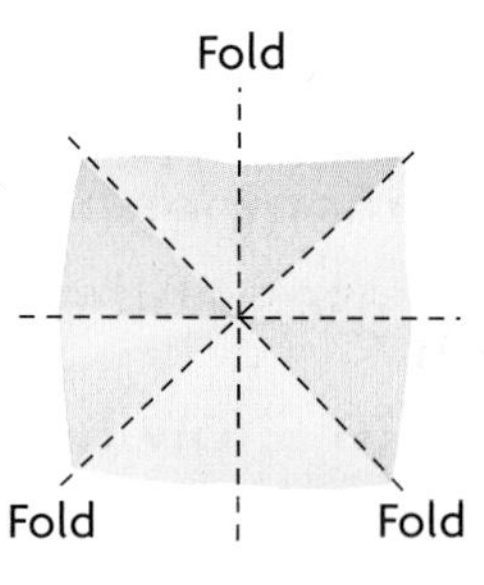

B Make triangle fact cards for each of these products: 12, 15, 18, 20, 24, 25, and 30.

C Write fact families for at least 3 triangle fact cards.

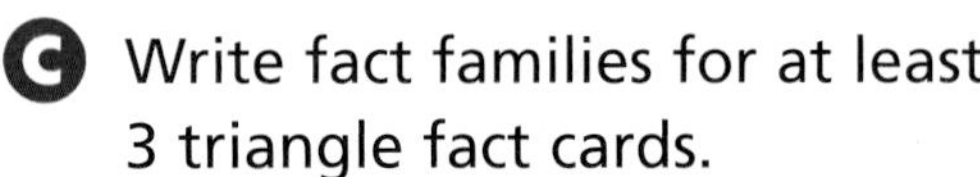

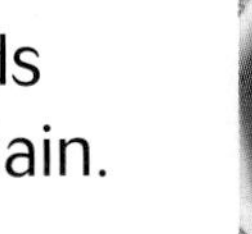

- **REASONING** How many triangle fact cards can you make for the product 12? Explain.

Using a Multiplication Table

MATH IDEA Use related multiplication facts to find quotients or missing divisors in division sentences.

Examples

A Find the quotient.
12 ÷ 3 = ■

Think: 3 × ■ = 12

Find the row for the factor 3. Look across to find the product 12.
Look up to find the missing factor, 4.
3 × 4 = 12

So, 12 ÷ 3 = 4.

B Find the missing divisor.
30 ÷ ■ = 5

Think: ■ × 5 = 30

Find the factor 5 in the top row. Look down to find the product 30. Look left to find the missing factor, 6.
6 × 5 = 30

So, 30 ÷ 6 = 5.

Remember

3	×	4	=	12
↑		↑		↑
factor		factor		product

×	0	1	2	3	4	5	6
0	0	0	0	0	0	0	0
1	0	1	2	3	4	5	6
2	0	2	4	6	8	10	12
3	0	3	6	9	12	15	18
4	0	4	8	12	16	20	24
5	0	5	10	15	20	25	30
6	0	6	12	18	24	30	36

- **REASONING** How can you use multiplication to check 20 ÷ 5 = 4?

Technology Link

More Practice:
Harcourt Mega Math
Ice Station Exploration, *Arctic Algebra*, Level E

Check

1. **Explain** how you can use a multiplication table to show how 5 × 2 = 10 and 10 ÷ 2 = 5 are related.

Write the missing number for each triangle fact card.

2. 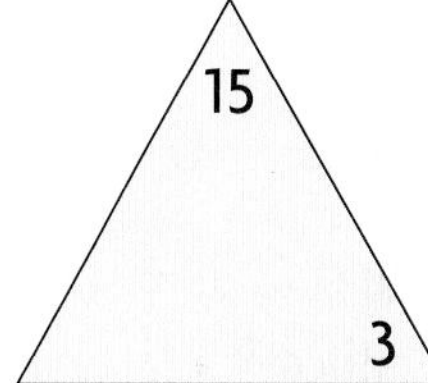

3. 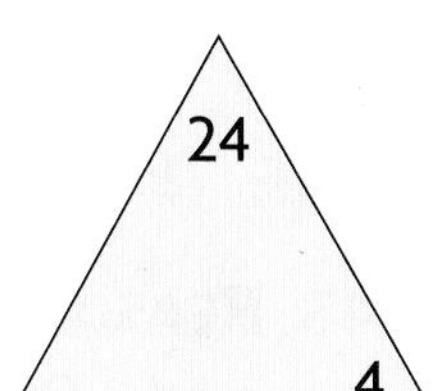

4. 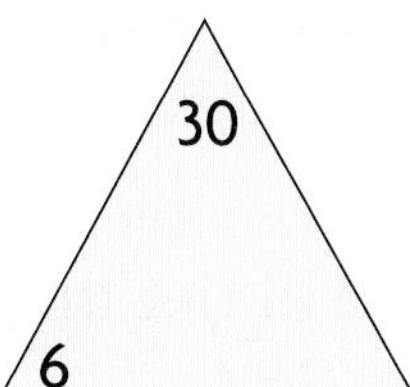

5. 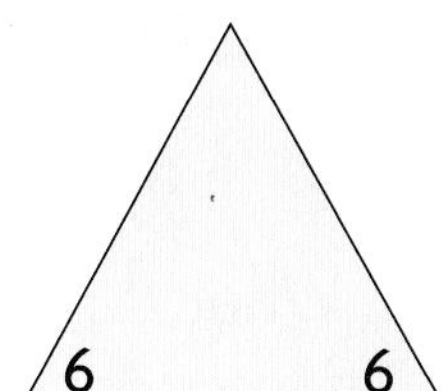

Write the fact family.

6. 3, 6, 18
7. 4, 4, 16
8. 4, 5, 20
9. 3, 7, 21

LESSON CONTINUES

Practice and Problem Solving

Extra Practice, page 252, Set C

Write the missing number for each triangle fact card.

10. 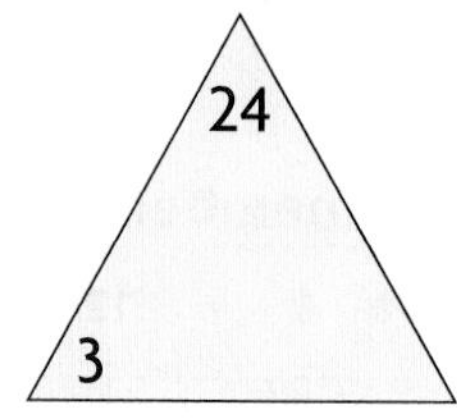

11. 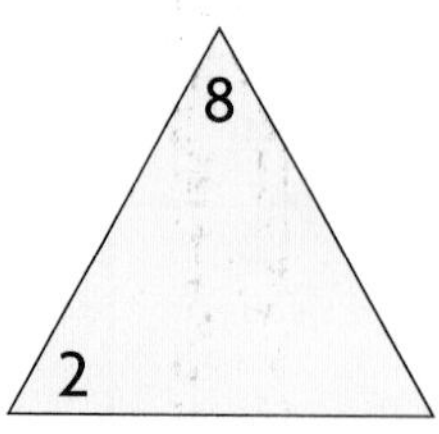

12. 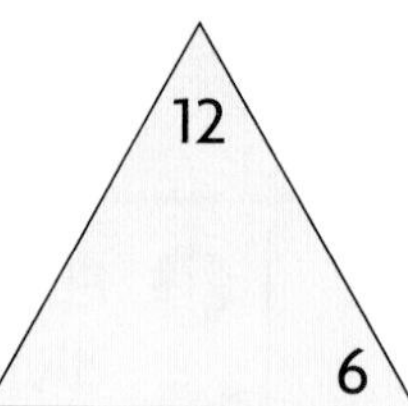

13. 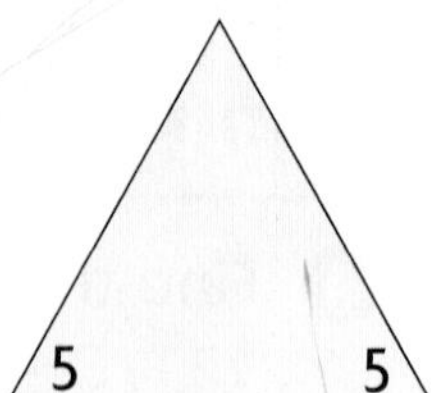

Write the fact family.

14. 5, 6, 30
15. 2, 8, 16
16. 4, 7, 28
17. 5, 5, 25

Find the quotient or product.

18. $3 \times 6 = \blacksquare$
19. $6 \times 3 = \blacksquare$
20. $18 \div 3 = \blacksquare$
21. $18 \div 6 = \blacksquare$
22. $4 \times 9 = \blacksquare$
23. $9 \times 4 = \blacksquare$
24. $36 \div 4 = \blacksquare$
25. $36 \div 9 = \blacksquare$
26. $8 \times 5 = \blacksquare$
27. $5 \times 8 = \blacksquare$
28. $40 \div 8 = \blacksquare$
29. $40 \div 5 = \blacksquare$

Write the other three sentences in the fact family.

30. $3 \times 7 = 21$
31. $1 \times 5 = 5$
32. $4 \times 3 = 12$
33. $5 \times 3 = 15$
34. $6 \times 4 = 24$
35. $9 \times 2 = 18$

Find the quotient or the missing divisor.

36. $8 \div 4 = \blacksquare$
37. $16 \div 2 = \blacksquare$
38. $7 = 21 \div \blacksquare$
39. $2 = 12 \div \blacksquare$
40. $24 \div 8 = \blacksquare$
41. $10 \div \blacksquare = 2$
42. $30 \div \blacksquare = 6$
43. $28 \div 4 = \blacksquare$

ALGEBRA Complete.

44. $\blacksquare \div 5 = 6 + 3$
45. $6 \times \blacksquare = 54 \div 9$
46. $42 - 6 = \blacksquare \times 9$

47. What do you notice about the fact family for 6, 6, and 36?

48. **REASONING** How are $20 \div 5 = 4$ and $20 \div 4 = 5$ alike? How are they different?

49. Geri made 20 bookmarks. She kept 2 and then put an equal number in each of 3 gift boxes. How many bookmarks are in each box?

50. **REASONING** Kendra says, "There are 3 teaspoons in 1 tablespoon, so there are 15 teaspoons in 5 tablespoons." Do you agree or disagree? Explain.

51. Mr. Tapia has a water bowl and a food bowl for each cat and dog in his pet store. He has 5 dogs and 4 cats. How many bowls does he have?

52. **? What's the Error?** John says that since $4 + 4 = 8$, then $8 \div 4 = 4$. Describe his error and give the correct quotient.

Mixed Review and Test Prep

Find the sum or difference. (p. 120)

53. $\begin{array}{r} \$4.57 \\ +\$0.82 \\ \hline \end{array}$

54. $\begin{array}{r} \$3.19 \\ -\$1.35 \\ \hline \end{array}$

Complete. Write +, −, ×, or ÷ for each ●. (p. 240)

55. $14 \bullet 7 = 7$

56. $9 \bullet 5 = 45$

57. $28 \bullet 4 = 7$

58. $9 \bullet 9 = 18$

59. **TEST PREP** Denise spent 3 hours at math camp each day for 1 week. How many hours did she spend at math camp? (p. 164)

A 3 hours
B 4 hours
C 14 hours
D 21 hours

60. **TEST PREP** Mr. Li picked up Frank from soccer practice 20 minutes before 5:00. What time was it? (p. 128)

F 4:20
G 4:40
H 5:20
J 5:40

Problem Solving Thinker's Corner

MATERIALS: triangle fact cards, paper

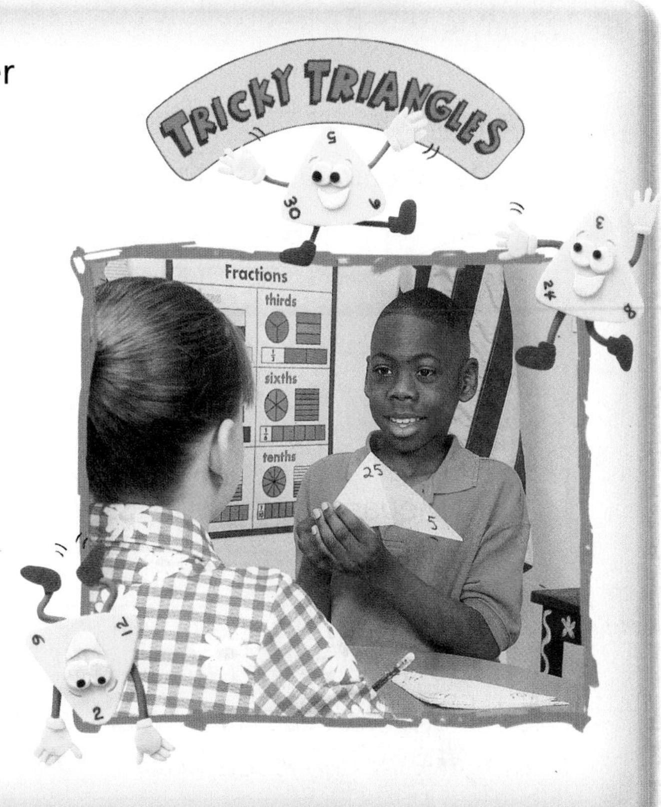

Players: 2

a. One player chooses a triangle fact card and holds it so that one number is hidden.

b. The other player names the hidden number and writes the fact family.

c. Players take turns until all cards are used. The player with the most correct number sentences wins.

1. How can you make sure your fact families are complete?

2. What card did you hope to choose for your opponent? Explain.

LESSON 5

Problem Solving Strategy
Write a Number Sentence

Quick Review

1. $8 \times 4 = ■$
2. $30 = 6 \times ■$
3. $10 \times 5 = ■$
4. $18 = ■ \times 6$
5. $27 = 9 \times ■$

PROBLEM Megan puts 36 animal trading cards in her binder. She puts 9 cards on each page. How many pages will Megan need for her cards?

UNDERSTAND

- What are you asked to find?
- What information will you use?
- Is there information you will not use? If so, what?

PLAN

- What strategy can you use?

Write a number sentence to find the number of pages Megan will need.

SOLVE

- How can you use the strategy to solve the problem?

Write a number sentence and solve.

36	÷	9	=	4
↑		↑		↑
number of trading cards		number on each page		number of pages

So, Megan needs 4 pages for her cards.

CHECK

- How can you decide if your answer is correct?
- What other strategy could you use?

Problem Solving Practice

Strategies

- Draw a Diagram or Picture
- Make a Model or Act It Out
- Make an Organized List
- Find a Pattern
- Make a Table or Graph
- Predict and Test
- Work Backward
- Solve a Simpler Problem
- **Write a Number Sentence**
- Use Logical Reasoning

Problem Solving

Write a number sentence to solve.

1. **What if** Megan buys 27 trading cards to add to her collection? How many pages will she need for the new cards?
2. Rosita has 28 cards. She wants to keep 4 cards and divide the rest equally among 4 friends. How many cards will each friend get?

Jorge has 45 trading cards in his collection. His binder holds 10 pages. Each page holds 9 trading cards.

3. How many pages will Jorge use for the cards he has?
   A 5
   B 10
   C 45
   D 90
4. Which number sentence shows how to find how many trading cards fit in Jorge's binder?
   F $45 + 10 = 55$ **H** $10 + 9 = 19$
   G $9 \times 10 = 90$ **J** $45 \div 9 = 5$

Mixed Strategy Practice

USE DATA For 5–8, use the graph.

5. Sebastian collects coins. How many coins in all are in Sebastian's coin collection?
6. Tim has 4 times as many quarters in his collection as Sebastian has. How many quarters are in Tim's collection?
7. Sebastian added some half dollars to his collection. There are 5 more pennies than half dollars in his collection. How many half dollars did Sebastian add to his collection?

SEBASTIAN'S COIN COLLECTION

pennies	
nickels	
dimes	
quarters	

Key: Each  **= 5 coins.**

8. **Write a problem** using the data in the pictograph.

Extra Practice

Set A (pp. 240–241)

Write a division sentence for each.

1. 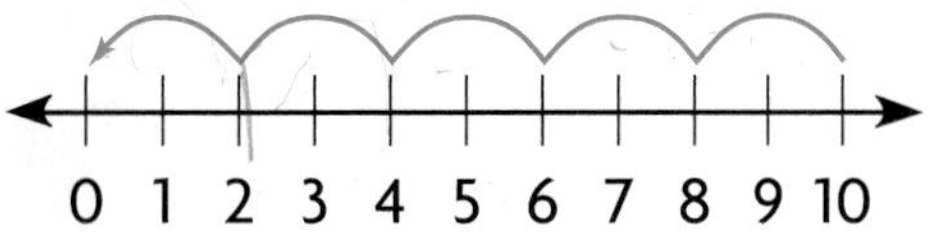

2. $$\begin{array}{r} 36 \\ -\ 9 \\ \hline 27 \end{array} \quad \begin{array}{r} 27 \\ -\ 9 \\ \hline 18 \end{array} \quad \begin{array}{r} 18 \\ -\ 9 \\ \hline 9 \end{array} \quad \begin{array}{r} 9 \\ -9 \\ \hline 0 \end{array}$$

Use a number line or subtraction to solve.

3. $15 \div 5 =$ ■ 4. $18 \div 3 =$ ■ 5. $12 \div 4 =$ ■ 6. $16 \div 4 =$ ■

7. $7\overline{)14}$ 8. $5\overline{)20}$ 9. $3\overline{)24}$ 10. $8\overline{)40}$

Set B (pp. 242–245)

Complete each number sentence. Draw an array to help.

1. $4 \times$ ■ $= 8$ $8 \div 4 =$ ■
2. $6 \times$ ■ $= 30$ $30 \div 6 =$ ■
3. $8 \times$ ■ $= 32$ $32 \div 8 =$ ■
4. $4 \times$ ■ $= 12$ $12 \div 4 =$ ■
5. What division sentence could you write for an array that shows $5 \times 8 = 40$?
6. How can you use $5 + 5 + 5 + 5 = 20$ to help you find $20 \div 5$?

Find the number that the variable stands for.

7. $2 \times a = 12$
 $a =$ __?__
8. $b \times 4 = 36$
 $b =$ __?__
9. $20 \div 4 = c$
 $c =$ __?__

Set C (pp. 246–249)

Write the fact family.

1. 2, 3, 6 2. 3, 7, 21 3. 3, 9, 27 4. 3, 6, 18

5. 4, 6, 24 6. 4, 8, 32 7. 5, 5, 25 8. 3, 8, 24

Find the quotient or the missing divisor.

9. $6 \div$ ■ $= 3$ 10. $18 \div 6 =$ ■ 11. ■ $= 12 \div 3$ 12. $20 \div$ ■ $= 4$

13. $30 \div 6 =$ ■ 14. $3 = 15 \div$ ■ 15. $9 \div$ ■ $= 3$ 16. $16 \div 4 =$ ■

17. Jerome made 30 cookies. He ate 3 and divided the rest equally among 3 friends. How many cookies did each friend get?

Review/Test

CHECK VOCABULARY AND CONCEPTS

Choose the best term from the box.

variable
divide
divisor
quotient
inverse operations

1. Multiplication and division are opposite operations, or __?__. (p. 242)
2. In $18 \div 6 = 3$, the number 3 is called the __?__. (p. 242)
3. When you separate into equal groups, you __?__. (p. 238)
4. A letter that is used to stand for an unknown number is called a __?__. (p. 243)

Use a number line or subtraction to solve. (pp. 240–241)

5. $10 \div 5 = \blacksquare$
6. $27 \div 9 = \blacksquare$
7. $4\overline{)20}$
8. $8\overline{)32}$

CHECK SKILLS

Complete each number sentence.
Draw an array to help. (pp. 242–245)

9. $2 \times \blacksquare = 6$ $\quad 6 \div 2 = \blacksquare$
10. $3 \times \blacksquare = 15$ $\quad 15 \div 3 = \blacksquare$
11. $4 \times \blacksquare = 4$ $\quad 4 \div 4 = \blacksquare$
12. $5 \times \blacksquare = 30$ $\quad 30 \div 5 = \blacksquare$

Find the number that the variable stands for. (pp. 242–245)

13. $14 \div 2 = a$
    $a =$ __?__
14. $b \times 5 = 20$
    $b =$ __?__
15. $18 \div 9 = c$
    $c =$ __?__

Write the fact family. (pp. 246–249)

16. 4, 5, 20
17. 2, 7, 14
18. 4, 9, 36

CHECK PROBLEM SOLVING

Write a number sentence to solve. (pp. 250–251)

19. Ms. Kraft has 20 pencils to divide equally among 5 groups of students. How many pencils does each group get?
20. Fernando has 24 rocks in his collection. If a box holds 6 rocks, how many boxes will Fernando need for his collection?

Standardized Test Prep

NUMBER SENSE, CONCEPTS, AND OPERATIONS

1. Scott had 20 juice boxes. He gave 4 juice boxes to each friend. How many friends received juice boxes?

A 2
B 4
C 5
D 8

2. Jon bought 9 packs of trading cards. There were 8 cards in each pack. How many cards did Jon buy?

F 17
G 64
H 72
J 81

3. Which subtraction fact belongs to the same fact family as these addition facts?

$3 + 8 = 11 \qquad 8 + 3 = 11$

A $11 - 2 = 9$
B $11 - 4 = 7$
C $11 - 6 = 5$
D $11 - 8 = 3$

4. Explain It Which pair of numbers has a difference of about 500? Explain how you know.

a. 647 and 374
b. 659 and 188

MEASUREMENT

5. Holly signed up for flute lessons on April 7. Her first lesson was 2 weeks later. On which date was her first lesson?

April						
Sun	Mon	Tue	Wed	Thu	Fri	Sat
				1	2	3
4	5	6	7	8	9	10
11	12	13	14	15	16	17
18	19	20	21	22	23	24
25	26	27	28	29	30	

F April 7
G April 9
H April 16
J April 21

6. Where is Erica at 11:10?

ERICA'S CAMP SCHEDULE	
Time	**Activity**
7:30	Breakfast
8:45	Nature hike
10:00	Horseshoes
10:45	Swim lessons
12:00	Lunch
1:00	Bugs and plants

A Swim lessons
B Lunch
C Nature hike
D Horseshoes

7. Explain It Brad has two \$1 bills, 6 quarters, 4 dimes, and 5 nickels. How much money does he have in all? Tell how you found your answer.

ALGEBRAIC THINKING

8. Pam read 8 pages of a book on Monday, 16 pages on Tuesday, and 24 pages on Wednesday. If this pattern continues, how many pages will Pam read on Friday?

   F 8
   G 32
   H 34
   J 40

9. What rule was used to make this table?

Starfish	1	2	3	4
Arms	5	10	15	20

   A Multiply by 6.
   B Add 4.
   C Multiply by 5.
   D Divide by 4.

TIP **Understand the problem.** See item 10. Use the rule with an odd number and an even number. See if the product is always an even number. Remember to think about the first number in the pattern.

10. **Explain It** Julie wants to make a pattern that uses only even numbers. She uses the rule *multiply by 10*. Will Julie's rule form a pattern of even numbers? Explain why or why not.

DATA ANALYSIS AND PROBABILITY

11. Tim's class took a survey and made this bar graph. What is the mode of these data?

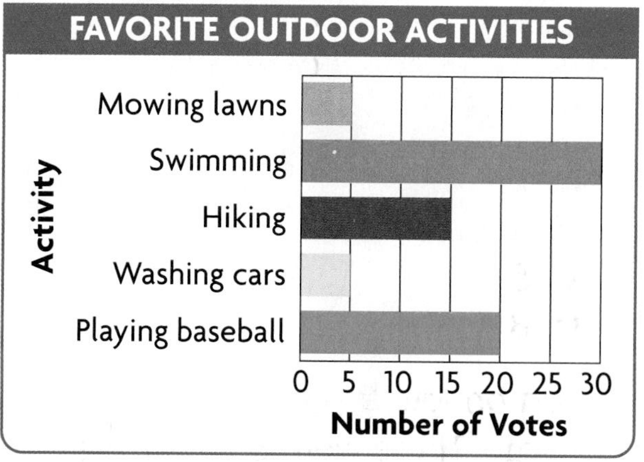

   F 30
   G 20
   H 15
   J 5

12. **Explain It** Geri's class took a survey to find out their favorite ice cream flavors. They made the bar graph below to show the results. How many students answered the survey? Explain how you found your answer.

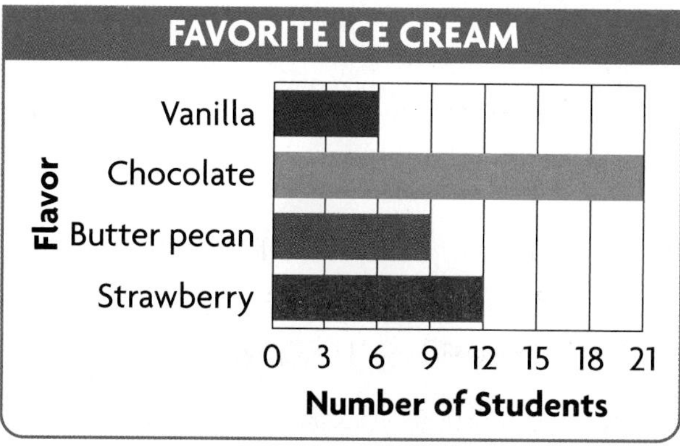

CHAPTER 13 Division Facts Through 5

FAST FACT • SCIENCE A pelican is a large seabird. Under its long bill, a pelican has a pouch for catching and storing food. Some kinds of pelicans fly over the water and dive for fish.

PROBLEM SOLVING The pictograph shows the number of fish that some pelicans caught by diving. Suppose each pelican caught 4 fish on each dive. How many dives did it take for each pelican to catch the fish shown in the pictograph?

FISH CAUGHT

Pelican 1	🐟 🐟 🐟 🐟 🐟 🐟
Pelican 2	🐟 🐟 🐟 🐟 🐟 🐟 🐟 🐟
Pelican 3	🐟 🐟 🐟 🐟

Key: Each 🐟 = 2 fish.

CHECK WHAT YOU KNOW

Use this page to help you review and remember important skills needed for Chapter 13.

✓ MULTIPLICATION FACTS THROUGH 5

Find each product.

1. $6 \times 3 = ■$ **2.** $3 \times 5 = ■$ **3.** $■ = 9 \times 2$ **4.** $7 \times 4 = ■$

5. $■ = 1 \times 7$ **6.** $■ = 3 \times 1$ **7.** $5 \times 8 = ■$ **8.** $3 \times 9 = ■$

9. $1 \times 1 = ■$ **10.** $6 \times 5 = ■$ **11.** $4 \times 6 = ■$ **12.** $■ = 2 \times 8$

✓ MODEL DIVISION

Copy and complete.

13.

3 rows of ■ = 18

$18 \div 3 = ■$

14. 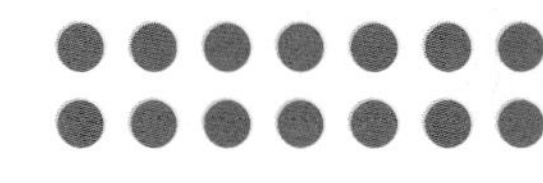

2 rows of ■ = 14

$14 \div 2 = ■$

15. 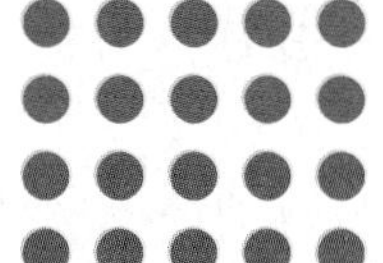

4 rows of ■ = 20

$20 \div 4 = ■$

✓ FACT FAMILIES

Write the fact family.

16. 3, 7, 21 **17.** 2, 4, 8 **18.** 5, 3, 15 **19.** 4, 4, 16

VOCABULARY POWER

REVIEW

divide [di•vīd′] *verb*

When you *multiply*, you use *multiplication*. When you *divide*, what operation do you use? Use *multiply* and *divide* in a sentence.

PREVIEW

equation

www.harcourtschool.com/mathglossary

LESSON 1

Divide by 2 and 5

Quick Review

1. $2 \times \square = 10$
2. $4 \times \square = 8$
3. $5 \times \square = 20$
4. $\square \times 5 = 35$
5. $\square \times 2 = 18$

Learn

CRAFTY MATH Mrs. Jackson knit 12 hats. She put an equal number of hats on each of 2 shelves in the craft shop. How many hats are on each shelf?

$12 \div 2 = \square$

Use a related multiplication fact to find the quotient.

Think: $2 \times \square = 12$

$2 \times 6 = 12$

$12 \div 2 = 6$, or $2\overline{)12}$ with quotient 6

So, there are 6 hats on each shelf.

Remember

16	÷	2	=	8
↑		↑		↑
dividend		divisor		quotient

What if Mrs. Jackson knits 15 hats and puts an equal number of hats on each of 5 shelves? How many hats are on each shelf?

$15 \div 5 = \square$

Use the multiplication table to find the quotient.

×	0	1	2	3	4	5
0	0	0	0	0	0	0
1	0	1	2	3	4	5
2	0	2	4	6	8	10
3	0	3	6	9	12	15
4	0	4	8	12	16	20
5	0	5	10	15	20	25
6	0	6	12	18	24	30

Think: $5 \times \square = 15$ $\quad 5 \times 3 = 15$

$15 \div 5 = 3$, or $5\overline{)15}$ with quotient 3

So, there are 3 hats on each shelf.

MATH IDEA You can find missing factors in related multiplication facts to help you divide.

- How can you use $3 \times 2 = 6$ to help you find $6 \div 2$?

Check

1. **Explain** how you can use multiplication to check $20 \div 5 = 4$.

Copy and complete each table.

2.

÷	2	4	6	8
2	■	■	■	■

3.

÷	10	15	20	25
5	■	■	■	■

Practice and Problem Solving

Extra Practice, page 268, Set A

Copy and complete each table.

4.

÷	10	12	14	16
2	■	■	■	■

5.

÷	30	35	40	45
5	■	■	■	■

Find each missing factor and quotient.

6. $2 \times ■ = 4$ $4 \div 2 = ■$

7. $5 \times ■ = 20$ $20 \div 5 = ■$

8. $5 \times ■ = 35$ $35 \div 5 = ■$

9. $2 \times ■ = 16$ $16 \div 2 = ■$

Find each quotient.

10. $6 \div 2 = ■$

11. $10 \div 2 = ■$

12. $■ = 10 \div 5$

13. $5 \div 5 = ■$

14. $25 \div 5 = ■$

15. $■ = 14 \div 2$

16. $40 \div 5 = ■$

17. $20 \div 2 = ■$

18. $2\overline{)2}$

19. $5\overline{)15}$

20. $5\overline{)35}$

21. $2\overline{)16}$

ALGEBRA Complete.

22. $10 \div 2 = ■ \times 1$

23. $40 \div 5 = 4 \times ■$

24. $■ \div 2 = 3 + 4$

25. **REASONING** What do you notice about the numbers that can be evenly divided by 2?

26. Mrs. Jackson sells hats for $5. She has $15. How many more hats must she sell to have $35 in all?

27. **What's the Error?** Philip used the multiplication fact $2 \times 8 = 16$ to find $8 \div 2 = ■$. Describe his error. What is the correct quotient?

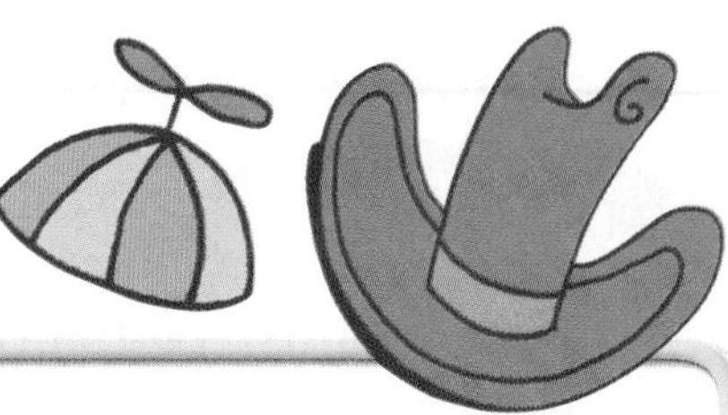

Mixed Review and Test Prep

28. $\begin{array}{r} 7 \\ \times 8 \\ \hline \end{array}$ (p. 200)

29. $\begin{array}{r} 8 \\ \times 6 \\ \hline \end{array}$ (p. 196)

30. $76 + 67 + 22 = ■$ (p. 8)

31. $3 \times 2 \times ■ = 48$ (p. 218)

32. **TEST PREP** James made an array with 3 rows of 9 tiles. Choose the number sentence that shows how many tiles are in the array. (p. 212)

A $9 - 3 = 6$

B $3 + 9 = 12$

C $9 \div 3 = 3$

D $3 \times 9 = 27$

LESSON

2 Divide by 3 and 4

Quick Review

1. ■ × 3 = 18
2. 4 × ■ = 12
3. ■ × 4 = 16
4. 4 × ■ = 32
5. 3 × ■ = 21

Learn

PADDLE POWER The Traveler Scouts want to rent canoes. There are 24 people in the group. A canoe can hold 3 people. How many canoes should the group rent?

$24 \div 3 = ■$

Use the multiplication table to find a related multiplication fact.

×	0	1	2	3	4	5	6	7	8	9
0	0	0	0	0	0	0	0	0	0	0
1	0	1	2	3	4	5	6	7	8	9
2	0	2	4	6	8	10	12	14	16	18
3	0	3	6	9	12	15	18	21	24	27
4	0	4	8	12	16	20	24	28	32	36
5	0	5	10	15	20	25	30	35	40	45

Think: $3 \times ■ = 24$
$3 \times 8 = 24$ $\qquad 24 \div 3 = 8$, or $3\overline{)24}$ with quotient 8

So, the group should rent 8 canoes.

What if the group wants to rent rowboats instead? If each rowboat holds 4 people, how many rowboats should they rent?

$24 \div 4 = ■$

Think: $4 \times ■ = 24$
$4 \times 6 = 24$ $\qquad 24 \div 4 = 6$, or $4\overline{)24}$ with quotient 6

So, the group should rent 6 rowboats.

- **REASONING** How can you use $21 \div 3 = 7$ to find $24 \div 3$?

Check

1. **Explain** how you can use multiplication to find $12 \div 4$.

Write the multiplication fact you can use to find the quotient. Then write the quotient.

2. $12 \div 3 = ■$
3. $8 \div 4 = ■$
4. $15 \div 3 = ■$
5. $28 \div 4 = ■$

Practice and Problem Solving

Extra Practice, page 268, Set B

Technology Link
More Practice: Harcourt Mega Math The Number Games, *Up, Up, and Array*, Level E

Write the multiplication fact you can use to find the quotient. Then write the quotient.

6. $27 \div 3 = ■$ **7.** $■ = 4 \div 4$ **8.** $30 \div 3 = ■$

9. $16 \div 4 = ■$ **10.** $18 \div 3 = ■$ **11.** $■ = 20 \div 4$

Copy and complete each table.

12.

÷	9	12	15	18
3	■	■	■	■

13.

÷	16	20	24	28
4	■	■	■	■

Find each quotient.

14. $12 \div 4 = ■$ **15.** $■ = 6 \div 3$ **16.** $■ = 14 \div 2$ **17.** $12 \div 2 = ■$

18. $15 \div 3 = ■$ **19.** $25 \div 5 = ■$ **20.** $24 \div 4 = ■$ **21.** $■ = 40 \div 4$

22. $■ = 18 \div 2$ **23.** $32 \div 4 = ■$ **24.** $■ = 9 \div 3$ **25.** $30 \div 5 = ■$

26. $3\overline{)3}$ **27.** $3\overline{)18}$ **28.** $4\overline{)36}$ **29.** $5\overline{)20}$

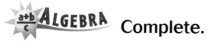

ALGEBRA Complete.

30. $20 \div 4 = 8 - ■$ **31.** $24 \div 3 = ■ \times 2$ **32.** $36 \div ■ = 18 \div 2$

33. Yusef collected 38 pinecones. He kept 11 pinecones for himself and divided the rest equally among 3 friends. How many pinecones did each friend get?

34. The scouts saw squirrels and birds. If there were 4 animals and 12 legs, how many squirrels and birds were there? Draw a picture to show your answer.

35. **REASONING** Two numbers have a product of 16 and a quotient of 4. What are they?

36. **Write About It** Explain how to solve $32 \div 4$ in 2 different ways.

Mixed Review and Test Prep

37. 3×5 (p. 164)

38. 5×7 (p. 160)

39. 4×7 (p. 178)

40. 9×8 (p. 212)

41. **TEST PREP** Paula had \$1.36. Her aunt gave her \$5.25 for her birthday. How much money does Paula have now? (p. 120)

A \$3.89 **C** \$6.51
B \$5.61 **D** \$6.61

LESSON 3

Divide with 1 and 0

Quick Review

1. $8 \times \square = 8$
2. $3 \times 0 = \square$
3. $\square \times 1 = 4$
4. $0 \times 10 = \square$
5. $1 \times \square = 7$

Learn

MOO . . . VE OVER Here are some rules for dividing with 1 and 0.

RULE A

Any number divided by 1 equals that number.

3	÷	1	=	3
↑		↑		↑
number of cows		number of stalls		number in each stall

If there is only 1 stall, then all of the cows must be in that stall.

RULE B

Any number (except 0) divided by itself equals 1.

3	÷	3	=	1
↑		↑		↑
number of cows		number of stalls		number in each stall

If there are the same number of cows and stalls, then one cow goes in each stall.

RULE C

Zero divided by any number (except 0) equals 0.

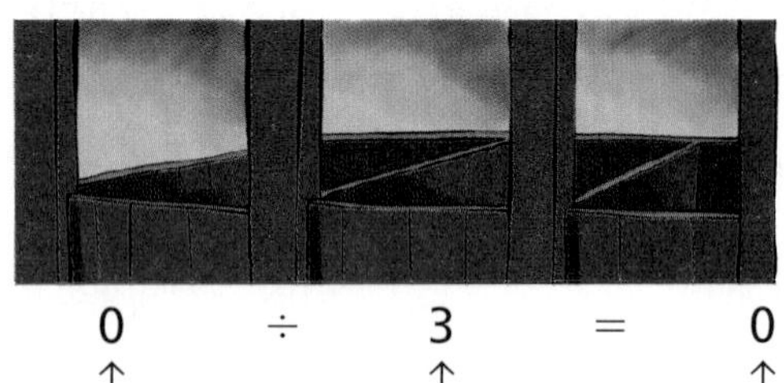

0	÷	3	=	0
↑		↑		↑
number of cows		number of stalls		number in each stall

If there are no cows, then no matter how many stalls you have, there won't be any cows in the stalls.

RULE D

You cannot divide by 0.

If there are no stalls, then you aren't separating cows into equal groups. So, using division doesn't make sense.

- **REASONING** How can you use multiplication to show that $3 \div 0 = \square$ doesn't make sense?

Check

1. **Explain** how you can use multiplication to check $0 \div 9 = 0$.

Find each quotient.

2. $3 \div 3 = ■$	**3.** $■ = 5 \div 1$	**4.** $0 \div 2 = ■$	**5.** $■ = 6 \div 6$
6. $7 \div 1 = ■$	**7.** $0 \div 6 = ■$	**8.** $■ = 4 \div 4$	**9.** $10 \div 1 = ■$

Practice and Problem Solving

Extra Practice, page 268, Set C

Find each quotient.

10. $2 \div 1 = ■$	**11.** $8 \div 8 = ■$	**12.** $■ = 6 \div 3$	**13.** $1 \div 1 = ■$	
14. $20 \div 5 = ■$	**15.** $■ = 0 \div 4$	**16.** $■ = 5 \div 5$	**17.** $10 \div 2 = ■$	
18. $3 \div 1 = ■$	**19.** $21 \div 3 = ■$	**20.** $32 \div 4 = ■$	**21.** $■ = 0 \div 7$	
22. $■ = 0 \div 8$	**23.** $18 \div 2 = ■$	**24.** $■ = 9 \div 1$	**25.** $24 \div 4 = ■$	
26. Divide 2 by 2.	**27.** Divide 4 by 1.	**28.** Divide 0 by 3.	**29.** Divide 14 by 2.	
30. $5\overline{)35}$	**31.** $9\overline{)9}$	**32.** $2\overline{)16}$	**33.** $5\overline{)0}$	**34.** $2\overline{)14}$
35. $3\overline{)18}$	**36.** $1\overline{)8}$	**37.** $4\overline{)36}$	**38.** $7\overline{)7}$	**39.** $1\overline{)0}$

ALGEBRA Compare. Write $<$, $>$, or $=$ for each ●.

40. $4 \div 1$ ● $4 \div 4$ **41.** $0 \div 9$ ● $9 \div 1$ **42.** $6 + 4$ ● $5 \div 1$

43. A farmer has 6 bales of hay. He feeds 2 bales to his cows. He divides the rest equally among 4 stalls. How many bales are in each stall?

44. REASONING Chelsea says, "Ask me to divide any number by 1, and I'll give you the quotient." What is her strategy?

45. Use what you know about 0 and 1 to find each quotient.
a. $398 \div 398 = ■$ **b.** $971 \div 1 = ■$ **c.** $0 \div 426 = ■$

Mixed Review and Test Prep

46. 0×4 (p. 176)

47. 5×1 (p. 176)

48. $387 + 132 + 155 = ■$ (p. 72)

49. $\$10.00 - \$5.69 = ■$ (p. 120)

50. TEST PREP Akiko bought 3 sandwiches. Each sandwich cost \$4. How much did she spend for the sandwiches? (p. 178)

A \$4 **B** \$7 **C** \$12 **D** \$15

LESSON 4

Algebra: Expressions and Equations

Quick Review

1. $20 \div 4 = \blacksquare$
2. $0 \div 7 = \blacksquare$
3. $10 \div 10 = \blacksquare$
4. $36 \div 4 = \blacksquare$
5. $16 \div 2 = \blacksquare$

VOCABULARY

equation

Learn

HAPPY CAMPERS The 21 campers were divided into 3 equal groups. How many campers are in each group?

Write an expression to show how many campers are in each group.

21 campers	divided into	3 groups
↓	↓	↓
21	÷	3

You can use the expression to write an equation. An **equation** is a number sentence. It uses an equal sign to show that two amounts are equal. Use the equation to solve the problem.

21 campers	divided into	3 groups	is equal to	7 campers in each group.
↓	↓	↓	↓	↓
21	÷	3	=	7

So, there are 7 campers in each group.

Remember

An *expression* is part of a number sentence.

Examples:

$3 + 4$ 4×2

$25 - 12$ $12 \div 6$

Mr. Gonzales is lining up 4 rows of 5 campers for relay races. There are 20 campers lined up.

$$4 \bullet 5 = 20$$

Which symbol will complete the equation?

Try + $4 + 5 \neq 20$

Try − $4 - 5 \neq 20$

Try ÷ $4 \div 5 \neq 20$

Try × $4 \times 5 = 20$

So, the correct symbol is ×.

Check

1. Write an expression to describe the relay race problem above.

Write an expression to describe each problem.

2. Nine campers each ate 7 carrot sticks. How many carrot sticks did the campers eat in all?

3. Jo had 9 carrot sticks. She ate 7 of them. How many carrot sticks does she have left?

Write $+$, $-$, $\times$, or $\div$ to complete the equation.

4. $9 = 18$ ● 9

5. $6 \times 6 = 4$ ● 9

6. 72 ● $8 = 3 \times 3$

Practice and Problem Solving

Extra Practice, page 268, Set D

Write an expression to describe each problem.

7. On the nature hike, Beth picked up two pinecones. There were 48 seeds in one and 55 seeds in the other. How many seeds were in the two pinecones in all?

8. ***FAST FACT*** • SCIENCE About 65 species of pine trees grow in North America. Thirty-six of them grow in the United States. How many do not grow in the United States?

Write an equation to solve.

9. Matt and 7 other campers made bird feeders from pinecones and peanut butter. They shared 40 pinecones equally. How many pinecones did each camper use?

10. **Vocabulary Power** A *symbol* can be used to show something easily and quickly. A stop sign is a symbol that tells drivers to stop. Name other symbols that you see every day.

Write $+$, $-$, $\times$, or $\div$ to complete the equation.

11. 13 ● $7 = 2 \times 3$

12. $12 + 5 = 9$ ● 8

13. $6 \times 4 = 8$ ● 3

14. **Write a problem** for each expression.

a. $35 \div 5$

b. 7×3

c. $15 - 3$

Mixed Review and Test Prep

15. $125 + 291$ (p. 70)

16. $3{,}538 + 1{,}896$ (p. 72)

17. $345 - 77$ (p. 90)

18. $622 - 404$ (p. 90)

19. **TEST PREP** There were 8 people on the bus. When the bus got to the mall, there were 36 people on it. Which of the following could be used to find how many more people got on the bus? (p. 80)

A $36 + 8$

B $36 - 8$

C 36×8

D $36 \div 8$

LESSON 5

Problem Solving Skill
Choose the Operation

UNDERSTAND → PLAN → SOLVE → CHECK

Quick Review

Choose +, −, ×, or ÷ for each ●.

1. 18 ● 5 = 13
2. 16 ● 8 = 2
3. 3 ● 2 = 6
4. 4 ● 4 = 16
5. 15 − 7 = 4 ● 4

NATURE WALK On a hike, the campers saw 6 chipmunks, 4 deer, and 8 butterflies. They also saw 3 turtles on each of 4 large rocks. How many turtles did they see in all?

This chart can help you decide when to use each operation.

ADD	• Join groups of different sizes.
SUBTRACT	• Take away. • Compare amounts.
MULTIPLY	• Join equal groups.
DIVIDE	• Separate into equal groups. • Find the number in each group.

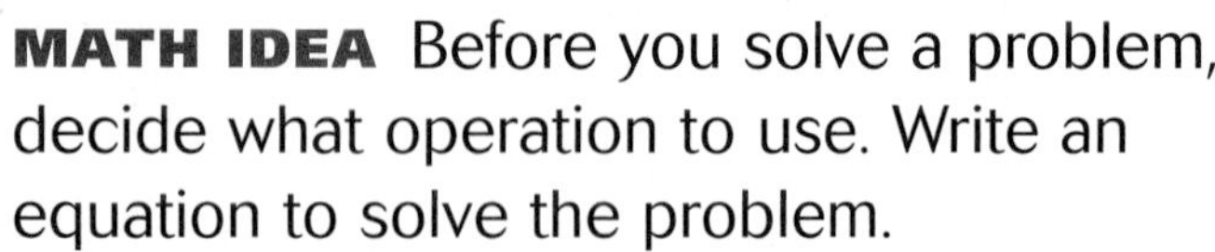

MATH IDEA Before you solve a problem, decide what operation to use. Write an equation to solve the problem.

Since you are joining equal groups, multiply.

4	×	3	=	12
↓		↓		↓
number of rocks		number of turtles on each rock		total number of turtles

So, they saw 12 turtles in all.

- **REASONING** When would you use division to solve a problem?
- Write an equation to find how many animals they saw in all.

Problem Solving Practice

Choose the operation. Write an equation. Then solve.

1. David collected 8 acorns and 16 wildflowers. He put the same number of wildflowers in each of 8 vases. How many wildflowers were in each vase?
2. The camp counselor put 4 pears, 5 apples, and 7 bananas in a basket. If 3 pieces of fruit were eaten, how many pieces of fruit were left?
3. Beth has a scrapbook. Each page can hold 8 small postcards or 6 large postcards. How many small postcards fit on 4 pages?
4. Shawn took 8 photos of birds, 9 photos of wildflowers, and 15 photos of campers. How many photos did he take?

Thirty students went on a camp cookout. Six students sat at each picnic table. How many tables did they fill?

5. Which number sentence can you use to solve the problem?
   - **A** $30 + 6 = \blacksquare$
   - **B** $30 - 6 = \blacksquare$
   - **C** $30 \div 6 = \blacksquare$
   - **D** $30 \times 6 = \blacksquare$
6. What is the answer to the question?
   - **F** 24 students
   - **G** 5 tables
   - **H** 5 students
   - **J** 1 table

Mixed Applications

USE DATA For 7–9, use the graph.

7. Gina took 5 packs of soda to the cookout. Were there enough bottles of soda for 28 people? Explain.
8. Khar bought 3 packs of water. He gave 4 bottles to friends. How many bottles of water did he have left?
9. **What's the Question?** The answer is 30 bottles of juice.

Extra Practice

Set A (pp. 258–259)

Find each missing factor and quotient.

1. $2 \times ■ = 10$ $10 \div 2 = ■$ **2.** $5 \times ■ = 30$ $30 \div 5 = ■$

Find each quotient.

3. $15 \div 5 = ■$ **4.** $■ = 16 \div 2$ **5.** $■ = 45 \div 5$ **6.** $10 \div 5 = ■$

7. $2\overline{)2}$ **8.** $5\overline{)20}$ **9.** $2\overline{)18}$ **10.** $5\overline{)25}$ **11.** $2\overline{)12}$

12. Divide 20 by 2. **13.** Divide 35 by 5. **14.** Divide 6 by 2.

Set B (pp. 260–261)

Write the multiplication fact you can use to find the quotient. Then write the quotient.

1. $18 \div 3 = ■$ **2.** $32 \div 4 = ■$ **3.** $9 \div 3 = ■$

Find each quotient.

4. $28 \div 4 = ■$ **5.** $12 \div 3 = ■$ **6.** $■ = 27 \div 3$ **7.** $■ = 8 \div 4$

8. $4\overline{)16}$ **9.** $3\overline{)15}$ **10.** $4\overline{)24}$ **11.** $3\overline{)21}$ **12.** $4\overline{)12}$

13. Divide 30 by 3. **14.** Divide 20 by 4. **15.** Divide 36 by 4.

Set C (pp. 262–263)

Find each quotient.

1. $0 \div 4 = ■$ **2.** $■ = 3 \div 3$ **3.** $■ = 8 \div 1$ **4.** $10 \div 10 = ■$

5. $7\overline{)7}$ **6.** $8\overline{)0}$ **7.** $1\overline{)4}$ **8.** $3\overline{)0}$ **9.** $9\overline{)9}$

Set D (pp. 264–265)

Write an expression to describe each problem.

1. Four friends share 28 stickers equally. How many stickers does each friend get?

2. Melinda had \$15. She buys slippers for \$8. How much money does she have now?

Write +, −, ×, or ÷ to complete the equation.

3. $6 \times 3 = 12 ■ 6$ **4.** $5 \times 7 = 38 ■ 3$ **5.** $24 \div 3 = 4 ■ 2$

Review/Test

CHECK VOCABULARY

Choose the best term from the box.

equation
divided
multiplied
zero

1. You cannot divide by __?__. (p. 262)
2. Any number (except 0) __?__ by itself equals 1. (p. 262)
3. A number sentence like $12 \div 2 = 6$ or $3 \times 5 = 15$ is called an __?__. (p. 264)

CHECK SKILLS

Find each quotient. (pp. 258–263)

4. $16 \div 4 = \blacksquare$
5. $\blacksquare = 21 \div 3$
6. $6 \div 1 = \blacksquare$
7. $\blacksquare = 25 \div 5$
8. $8 \div 2 = \blacksquare$
9. $0 \div 5 = \blacksquare$
10. $\blacksquare = 9 \div 3$
11. $\blacksquare = 8 \div 1$
12. $4\overline{)32}$
13. $1\overline{)10}$
14. $2\overline{)18}$
15. $3\overline{)0}$
16. $5\overline{)15}$
17. $2\overline{)14}$
18. $3\overline{)15}$
19. $5\overline{)0}$
20. $4\overline{)24}$
21. $5\overline{)40}$

Write an expression to describe each problem. (pp. 264–265)

22. Lila made 18 muffins. She put 3 muffins in each bag. How many bags did Lila fill?
23. Kyle had 32 shells. He gave 8 to his friend. How many shells does Kyle have now?

CHECK PROBLEM SOLVING

Choose the operation. Write an equation. Then solve. (pp. 266–267)

24. Chiang has 24 trading cards. She puts the cards into piles of 6. How many piles does she make?
25. Casey has 5 packs of stickers. Each pack has 8 stickers. How many stickers does he have?

Standardized Test Prep

NUMBER SENSE, CONCEPTS, AND OPERATIONS

1. Joe wrote these multiplication facts.

$4 \times 6 = 24$ $\quad$ $6 \times 4 = 24$

Which division fact belongs to the same fact family as these multiplication facts?

A $24 \div 2 = 12$
B $24 \div 3 = 8$
C $24 \div 8 = 3$
D $24 \div 6 = 4$

2. Which division fact does the picture show?

3 rows of 7 = 21

F $24 \div 3 = 8$
G $21 \div 3 = 7$
H $12 \div 3 = 4$
J $12 \div 6 = 2$

3. Ella bakes 18 muffins. She puts 3 muffins in each bag. How many bags does Ella use?

A 9 $\quad$ **C** 4
B 6 $\quad$ **D** 3

4. **Explain It** Colin has 24 toy cars in each of 3 boxes. ESTIMATE the number of toy cars Colin has in all. Explain your estimate.

ALGEBRAIC THINKING

5. Which numbers complete the table?

×	4	5	■	■	■
5	20	25	30	35	40

F 4, 5, 6 $\quad$ **H** 6, 7, 8
G 5, 6, 7 $\quad$ **J** 7, 8, 9

TIP **Understand the problem.** See Item 6. An equation is a number sentence which states that two amounts are equal. So, the answer will have the same product as 4×6.

6. Which of the following could Rex write to make the equation true?

$4 \times 6 = \blacksquare$

A 10×2 $\quad$ **C** 2×5
B 8×3 $\quad$ **D** 3×9

7. Jay bought 6 bags of marbles. Each bag holds 8 marbles. Which number sentence can be used to find the total number of marbles Jay bought?

F $8 - 6 = \blacksquare$ $\quad$ **H** $6 \times 8 = \blacksquare$
G $8 + 6 = \blacksquare$ $\quad$ **J** $6 + \blacksquare = 8$

8. **Explain It** Katie wants to write a word problem that can be solved with this division sentence.

$18 \div 3 = \blacksquare$

Write a word problem that Katie could use.

DATA ANALYSIS AND PROBABILITY

9. The pictograph shows the goals scored last year by 5 members of the Westview soccer team. What information does the key tell you?

GOALS SCORED

Dave	⚽⚽⚽
Gina	⚽⚽
Kyle	⚽⚽⚽⚽
Melanie	⚽⚽⚽⚽⚽⚽
Zack	⚽⚽⚽

Key: Each ⚽ = 3 goals.

A how many goals Gina scored
B how many players are on a soccer team
C the total number of goals scored by the team
D what each soccer ball stands for

10. Look at the pictograph above. Which players scored an equal number of goals?

F Gina and Kyle
G Dave and Zack
H Kyle and Melanie
J Dave and Gina

11. Explain It Tell how you can use the pictograph above to order the players from **least** to **greatest** number of goals scored. Then order the players.

GEOMETRY AND SPATIAL SENSE

12. Which figure shows a line of symmetry?

A 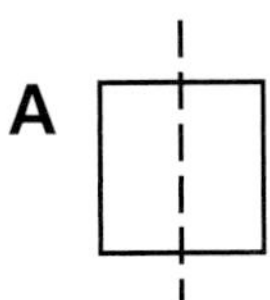

C 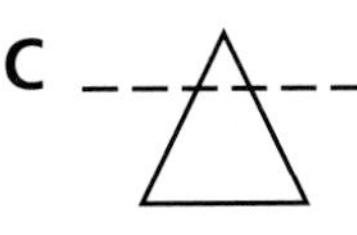

B 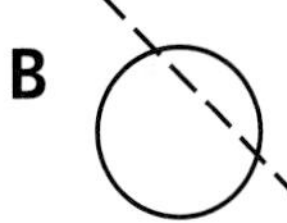

D 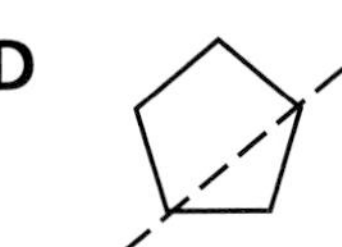

13. Pete flips this figure.

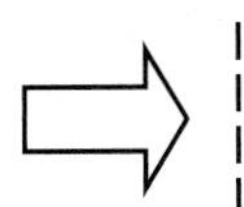

What figure is formed?

F 

G 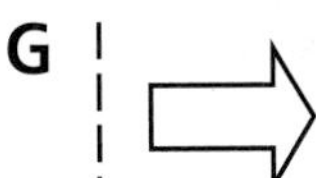

H 

J 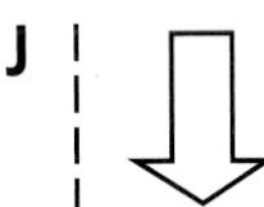

14. Explain It Jean traced the top of this solid figure on a sheet of paper. What figure appeared on her paper? Explain how you found your answer.

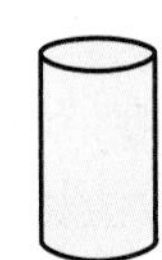

Division Facts Through 10

PEPPERONI PIZZA	
Restaurant	Pieces of Pepperoni
Mario's Pizza	32
Broadway Pizza	56
Mamma Mia's	40
Lorenzo's Pizza	48

FAST FACT • SOCIAL STUDIES The first pizzeria in the United States was opened in 1905 in New York City. America's favorite pizza topping is pepperoni.

PROBLEM SOLVING Suppose each pizza in the table is cut into 8 slices and the pieces of pepperoni are divided equally among the 8 slices. How many pieces of pepperoni are on 1 slice of pizza from each restaurant?

CHECK WHAT YOU KNOW

Use this page to help you review and remember important skills needed for Chapter 14.

COMMUTATIVE PROPERTY OF MULTIPLICATION

Use the Commutative Property of Multiplication to help you find each product.

1. $7 \times 8 = \blacksquare$ $8 \times 7 = \blacksquare$
2. $6 \times 8 = \blacksquare$ $8 \times 6 = \blacksquare$
3. $7 \times 9 = \blacksquare$ $9 \times 7 = \blacksquare$
4. $6 \times 10 = \blacksquare$ $10 \times 6 = \blacksquare$

DIVISION FACTS THROUGH 5

Find each quotient.

5. $35 \div 5 = \blacksquare$
6. $8 \div 2 = \blacksquare$
7. $20 \div 4 = \blacksquare$
8. $0 \div 5 = \blacksquare$
9. $\blacksquare = 18 \div 3$
10. $12 \div 4 = \blacksquare$
11. $\blacksquare = 9 \div 1$
12. $16 \div 2 = \blacksquare$

MISSING FACTORS

Find the missing factor.

13. $3 \times \blacksquare = 27$
14. $25 = \blacksquare \times 5$
15. $\blacksquare \times 6 = 12$
16. $45 = 9 \times \blacksquare$
17. $6 \times \blacksquare = 48$
18. $\blacksquare \times 8 = 32$
19. $35 = 5 \times \blacksquare$
20. $20 = \blacksquare \times 4$

VOCABULARY POWER

REVIEW

quotient [kwō′shənt] *noun*

The word *quotient* comes from the Latin root *quot*, which means "how many." Write a word problem that could be solved by finding a quotient. Use the words *how many* in your problem.

www.harcourtschool.com/mathglossary

LESSON 1

Divide by 6, 7, and 8

Quick Review

1. $6 \times 3 = \blacksquare$
2. $6 \times 7 = \blacksquare$
3. $7 \times 4 = \blacksquare$
4. $7 \times 8 = \blacksquare$
5. $8 \times 4 = \blacksquare$

Learn

IT'S IN THE BAG The Bagel Stop sells bagels in bags of 6. Ramona has 24 fresh bagels to put in bags. How many bags does she need?

$24 \div 6 = \blacksquare$

Use a related multiplication fact to find the quotient.

Think: $6 \times \blacksquare = 24$
$6 \times 4 = 24$

$24 \div 6 = 4$, or $6\overline{)24}$ with quotient 4

So, Ramona needs 4 bags.

Examples

A $63 \div 7 = \blacksquare$
Think: $7 \times \blacksquare = 63$
$7 \times 9 = 63$

$63 \div 7 = 9$, or $7\overline{)63}$ with quotient 9

B $56 \div 8 = \blacksquare$
Think: $8 \times \blacksquare = 56$
$8 \times 7 = 56$

$56 \div 8 = 7$, or $8\overline{)56}$ with quotient 7

MATH IDEA Think of related multiplication facts to help you divide.

- What multiplication fact can you use to find $42 \div 7$? What is the quotient?

Technology Link

More Practice: Harcourt Mega Math The Number Games, *Up Up and Array,* Level F.

Equal Groups

Remember, you can also use equal groups and arrays to help you find a quotient.

Here are two different ways to find 28 ÷ 7.

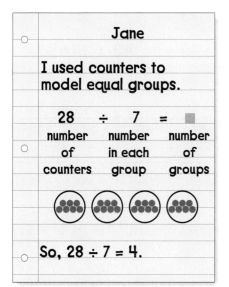

Jane

I used counters to model equal groups.

28	÷	7	=	■
number of counters		number in each group		number of groups

So, 28 ÷ 7 = 4.

Kevin

I modeled the problem with an array.

28	÷	7	=	■
number in array		number in each row		number of rows

So, 28 ÷ 7 = 4.

- **REASONING** You have used equal groups and arrays to help you find products. Why can you also use them to help you find quotients?

Check

1. **Explain** how you would use a related multiplication fact to find 18 ÷ 6.

Find the missing factor and quotient.

2. 8 × ■ = 16 16 ÷ 8 = ■
3. 7 × ■ = 35 35 ÷ 7 = ■
4. 6 × ■ = 36 36 ÷ 6 = ■
5. 6 × ■ = 30 30 ÷ 6 = ■

Copy and complete each table.

6.

÷	14	21	28	35
7	■	■	■	■

7.

÷	6	12	18	24
6	■	■	■	■

Find the quotient.

8. 21 ÷ 7 = ■
9. 42 ÷ 6 = ■
10. ■ = 56 ÷ 7
11. 32 ÷ 8 = ■
12. $8\overline{)40}$
13. $7\overline{)42}$
14. $8\overline{)24}$
15. $6\overline{)24}$

LESSON CONTINUES

Practice and Problem Solving

Extra Practice, page 288, Set A

Find the missing factor and quotient.

16. $7 \times ■ = 14$ $14 \div 7 = ■$

17. $6 \times ■ = 60$ $60 \div 6 = ■$

18. $6 \times ■ = 48$ $48 \div 6 = ■$

19. $8 \times ■ = 72$ $72 \div 8 = ■$

20. $7 \times ■ = 42$ $42 \div 7 = ■$

21. $8 \times ■ = 40$ $40 \div 8 = ■$

Copy and complete each table.

22.

÷	42	63	56	49
7	■	■	■	■

23.

÷	56	40	48	32
8	■	■	■	■

Find the quotient.

24. $36 \div 6 = ■$

25. $80 \div 8 = ■$

26. $■ = 0 \div 7$

27. $8 \div 1 = ■$

28. $■ = 15 \div 3$

29. $■ = 18 \div 6$

30. $45 \div 5 = ■$

31. $24 \div 8 = ■$

32. $8\overline{)64}$

33. $2\overline{)14}$

34. $7\overline{)28}$

35. $6\overline{)0}$

36. $5\overline{)10}$

37. $7\overline{)7}$

38. $8\overline{)0}$

39. $3\overline{)30}$

40. Divide 42 by 6.

41. Divide 8 by 8.

42. Divide 35 by 5.

Write a division sentence for each.

43.

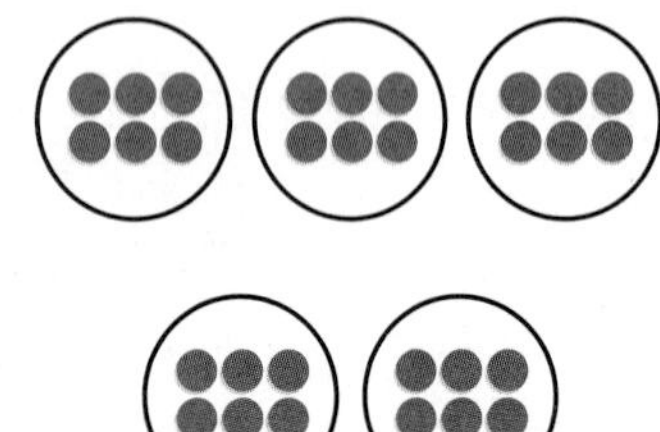

44.

ALGEBRA Complete.

45. $3 + ■ = 49 \div 7$

46. $8 \times 5 = ■ \times 10$

47. $■ - 4 = 24 \div 6$

48. $■ \times 4 = 8 \times 3$

49. $6 \div 6 = 0 + ■$

50. $5 + 3 = 16 \div ■$

51. REASONING Is the quotient $24 \div 6$ greater than or less than the quotient $24 \div 4$? How do you know?

52. What's the Question? Hikara bought 35 fruit chews. Fruit chews come in packs of 5. The answer is 7 packs.

53. ***FAST FACT*** • SOCIAL STUDIES
The bagel is the only bread product that is boiled before it is baked. A baker made 48 bagels and placed an equal number in each of 6 bags. How many bagels are in 2 bags?

54. Asha had 24 pictures of her friends. She put 8 pictures on each page in a photo album. Her album has 20 pages. How many album pages do not have pictures?

Mixed Review and Test Prep

Write the time. (p. 128)

55.

56.

Find the missing factor. (p. 186)

57. $3 \times \blacksquare = 24$

58. $4 \times \blacksquare = 28$

59. $\blacksquare \times 8 = 72$

60. $\blacksquare \times 1 = 8$

61. **TEST PREP** Luther read 54 pages of his book on Saturday. He read 39 pages on Sunday. How many pages did he read in all? (p. 8)

A 15 **B** 83 **C** 93 **D** 94

62. **TEST PREP** Patricia collected 205 stickers. She gave 28 stickers to her sister. How many stickers does Patricia have left? (p. 92)

F 177 **G** 187 **H** 233 **J** 277

Problem Solving LINKUP . . . to Reading

STRATEGY • CHOOSE IMPORTANT INFORMATION

Some word problems have more information than you need. Before you solve a problem, find the facts you need to solve the problem.

Mrs. Taylor baked 8 batches of muffins. She had a total of 48 muffins. She also baked 2 cakes. How many muffins were in each batch?

Facts You Need: baked 8 batches of muffins, total of 48 muffins

Fact You Don't Need: baked 2 cakes

$$48 \div 8 = 6$$

So, there were 6 muffins in each batch.

Write the important facts. Solve the problem.

1. Bonnie made 4 batches of cookies and 3 pies in the morning. She made 3 batches of cookies in the afternoon. She made 63 cookies in all. How many cookies were in each batch?

LESSON **2**

Divide by 9 and 10

Quick Review

1. $9 \times 3 = ■$
2. $9 \times 5 = ■$
3. $10 \times 4 = ■$
4. $8 \times 10 = ■$
5. $9 \times 10 = ■$

Learn

PLENTY OF PINS Katie collects different kinds of pins. She has boxes that hold 9 or 10 pins. Help Katie organize her collection.

Examples

A Katie puts her 45 state flag pins in boxes that hold 9 pins each. How many boxes does she need?

$45 \div 9 = ■$

Think: $9 \times ■ = 45$

$9 \times 5 = 45$

$45 \div 9 = 5$, or $9\overline{)45}$ with quotient 5

So, Katie needs 5 boxes for her state flag pins.

B Katie puts her 60 flower pins in boxes that hold 10 pins each. How many boxes does she need?

$60 \div 10 = ■$

Think: $10 \times ■ = 60$

$10 \times 6 = 60$

$60 \div 10 = 6$, or $10\overline{)60}$ with quotient 6

So, Katie needs 6 boxes for her flower pins.

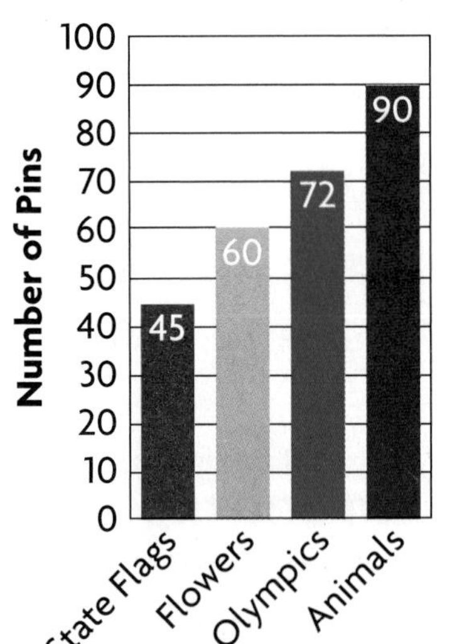

Check

1. **Explain** how to use a related multiplication fact to find $36 \div 9$. What is the quotient?

Copy and complete each table.

2.

÷	9	18	27	36
9	■	■	■	■

3.

÷	20	30	40	50
10	■	■	■	■

Practice and Problem Solving

Extra Practice, page 288, Set B

Copy and complete each table.

4.

÷	54	72	63	81
9	■	■	■	■

5.

÷	70	90	80	100
10	■	■	■	■

Find the quotient.

6. $45 \div 9 = \blacksquare$
7. $\blacksquare = 10 \div 10$
8. $\blacksquare = 0 \div 9$
9. $60 \div 10 = \blacksquare$
10. $9 \div 1 = \blacksquare$
11. $12 \div 6 = \blacksquare$
12. $18 \div 3 = \blacksquare$
13. $\blacksquare = 36 \div 9$
14. $\blacksquare = 50 \div 10$
15. $14 \div 2 = \blacksquare$
16. $\blacksquare = 12 \div 4$
17. $40 \div 5 = \blacksquare$
18. $10\overline{)0}$
19. $6\overline{)42}$
20. $9\overline{)90}$
21. $9\overline{)63}$
22. $8\overline{)64}$
23. $5\overline{)25}$
24. $7\overline{)28}$
25. $3\overline{)24}$
26. Divide 72 by 8.
27. Divide 42 by 7.
28. Divide 70 by 10.

ALGEBRA Write +, −, ×, or ÷ for each ●.

29. $10 \bullet 10 = 2 - 1$
30. $8 \times 3 = 20 \bullet 4$
31. $12 \bullet 7 = 50 \div 10$
32. $3 \times 6 = 2 \bullet 9$
33. $81 \bullet 9 = 3 \times 3$
34. $6 \times 7 = 35 \bullet 7$

35. **REASONING** Ken has 89 patches in his collection. He puts 8 patches on his vest and puts the rest in boxes of 9 patches each. How many boxes does Ken need?

36. **REASONING** Boxes for 9 pins cost $4 each. Boxes for 10 pins cost $5 each. Janine has 90 pins. If she wants to spend the least amount of money, what type of boxes should she buy?

37. **Vocabulary Power** The words *division, dividend,* and *divisor* come from a Latin word that means "to take apart." How is division like taking something apart?

38. **Write About It** Make a table showing the 9's division facts. Describe any patterns you see in your table.

Mixed Review and Test Prep

39. $8 \times 7 = \blacksquare$ (p. 200)
40. $\blacksquare = 6 \times 9$ (p. 212)
41. $24 \div 3 = \blacksquare$ (p. 260)
42. $28 \div 4 = \blacksquare$ (p. 260)

43. **TEST PREP** Which expression has the same product as $2 \times 3 \times 9$? (p. 218)

A $2 \times 2 \times 8$
B $5 \times 9 \times 1$
C $3 \times 3 \times 7$
D $9 \times 6 \times 1$

LESSON 3

Practice Division Facts

Quick Review

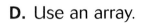

1. 7 × ■ = 56
2. ■ × 3 = 27
3. 6 × ■ = 30
4. ■ × 4 = 16
5. 5 × ■ = 40

Learn

BOXED CARS Bobby has 36 toy cars that he wants to put in display boxes. Each display box holds 9 cars. How many display boxes will Bobby need?

$36 \div 9 = ■$

There are many ways to find the quotient.

A. Use counters.

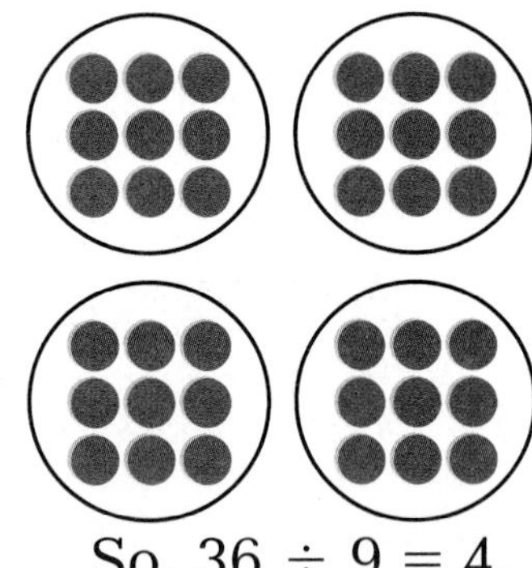

So, $36 \div 9 = 4$.

B. Use repeated subtraction.

36 − 9 = 27	27 − 9 = 18	18 − 9 = 9	9 − 9 = 0
Number of times you subtract 9: 1	2	3	4

So, $36 \div 9 = 4$.

C. Use fact families.

Fact Family for 4, 9, and 36

factor		factor		product	dividend		divisor		quotient
4	×	9	=	36	36	÷	9	=	4
9	×	4	=	36	36	÷	4	=	9

So, $36 \div 9 = 4$.

D. Use an array.

Make an array with 36 tiles.
Count the rows of 9 tiles each.
There are 4 rows of 9 tiles.

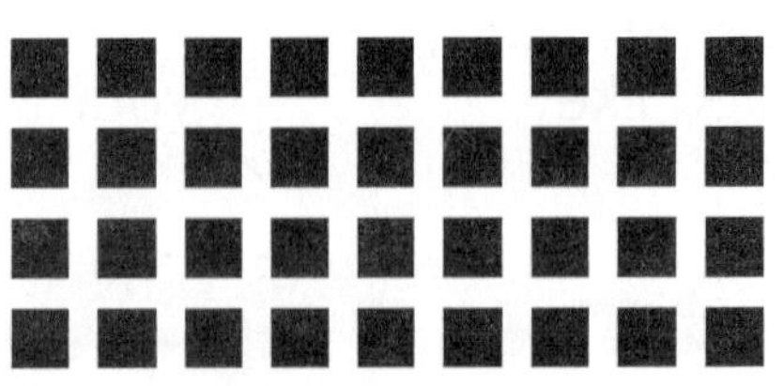

Since $4 \times 9 = 36$, then $36 \div 9 = 4$.

Find Missing Factors

E. Use a multiplication table.

Think: ■ × 9 = 36

- Find the given factor 9 in the top row.
- Look down the column to find the product, 36.
- Look left across the row to find the missing factor, 4.

$4 \times 9 = 36 \quad 36 \div 9 = 4$

So, Bobby needs 4 display boxes.

×	0	1	2	3	4	5	6	7	8	9	10
0	0	0	0	0	0	0	0	0	0	0	0
1	0	1	2	3	4	5	6	7	8	9	10
2	0	2	4	6	8	10	12	14	16	18	20
3	0	3	6	9	12	15	18	21	24	27	30
4	0	4	8	12	16	20	24	28	32	36	40
5	0	5	10	15	20	25	30	35	40	45	50
6	0	6	12	18	24	30	36	42	48	54	60
7	0	7	14	21	28	35	42	49	56	63	70
8	0	8	16	24	32	40	48	56	64	72	80
9	0	9	18	27	36	45	54	63	72	81	90
10	0	10	20	30	40	50	60	70	80	90	100

MATH IDEA Use equal groups, repeated subtraction, fact families, arrays, and multiplication tables to help you find quotients.

Technology Link

More Practice: Harcourt Mega Math Ice Station Exploration, *Arctic Algebra*, Level F

Check

1. **Explain** how to find $56 \div 8$ in two different ways.

Write a division sentence for each.

2. 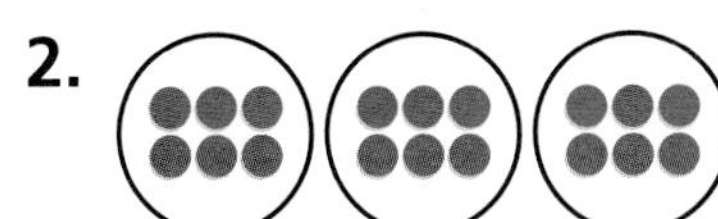

3. 

4. $\begin{array}{r} 21 \\ -\ 7 \\ \hline 14 \end{array} \rightarrow \begin{array}{r} 14 \\ -\ 7 \\ \hline 7 \end{array} \rightarrow \begin{array}{r} 7 \\ -7 \\ \hline 0 \end{array}$

Find the missing factor and quotient.

5. $3 \times$ ■ $= 15 \quad 15 \div 3 =$ ■

6. $8 \times$ ■ $= 32 \quad 32 \div 8 =$ ■

7. $4 \times$ ■ $= 40 \quad 40 \div 4 =$ ■

8. $7 \times$ ■ $= 56 \quad 56 \div 7 =$ ■

Find the quotient.

9. $10 \div 2 =$ ■

10. $18 \div 9 =$ ■

11. ■ $= 49 \div 7$

12. $80 \div 10 =$ ■

13. $6\overline{)0}$

14. $9\overline{)9}$

15. $8\overline{)40}$

16. $5\overline{)20}$

LESSON CONTINUES

Practice and Problem Solving

Extra Practice, page 288, Set C

Write a division sentence for each.

17. 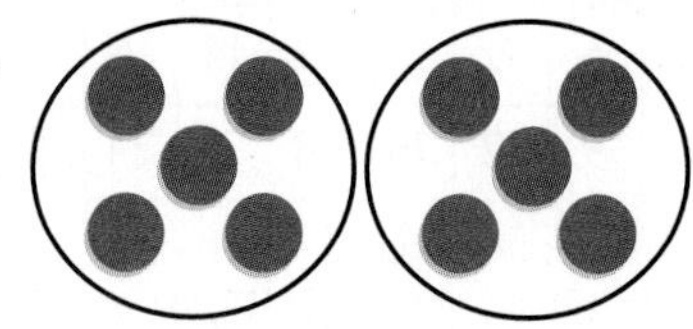

18. 

19.

$$\begin{array}{r} 27 \\ -\ 9 \\ \hline 18 \end{array} \rightarrow \begin{array}{r} 18 \\ -\ 9 \\ \hline 9 \end{array} \rightarrow \begin{array}{r} 9 \\ -9 \\ \hline 0 \end{array}$$

Find the missing factor and quotient.

20. $10 \times ■ = 90$ $90 \div 10 = ■$ **21.** $7 \times ■ = 35$ $35 \div 7 = ■$

22. $4 \times ■ = 16$ $16 \div 4 = ■$ **23.** $9 \times ■ = 63$ $63 \div 9 = ■$

Find the quotient.

24. $10 \div 1 = ■$ **25.** $■ = 35 \div 5$ **26.** $50 \div 10 = ■$ **27.** $■ = 16 \div 2$

28. $■ = 81 \div 9$ **29.** $■ = 20 \div 10$ **30.** $60 \div 6 = ■$ **31.** $24 \div 3 = ■$

32. $9\overline{)54}$ **33.** $7\overline{)28}$ **34.** $8\overline{)72}$ **35.** $10\overline{)100}$

36. $8\overline{)24}$ **37.** $2\overline{)0}$ **38.** $4\overline{)4}$ **39.** $3\overline{)21}$

40. Divide 63 by 7. **41.** Divide 30 by 5. **42.** Divide 0 by 9.

Choose the letter of the division sentence that matches each.

a. $42 \div 6 = 7$ **b.** $32 \div 8 = 4$ **c.** $56 \div 7 = 8$ **d.** $24 \div 8 = 3$

43. 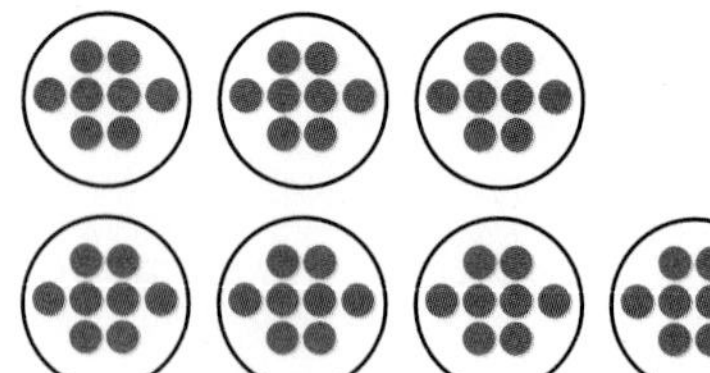

44. 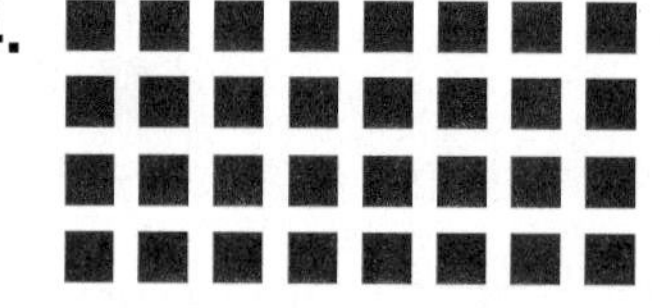

Compare. Write <, >, or = for each ●.

45. 9×6 ● 9×5 **46.** $24 \div 6$ ● $16 \div 4$ **47.** $4 + 4$ ● $72 \div 8$

48. 8×5 ● 10×4 **49.** $23 - 18$ ● $45 \div 5$ **50.** 3×3 ● $70 \div 10$

51. REASONING Roberta has some boxes that hold 8 cars in each. Could the full boxes hold 20 cars in all? Explain.

52. **Write a problem** about Jonah buying several toy cars that cost $3 each. Use division in your problem.

53. Chi has 2 sheets of stickers. Each sheet has 9 rows of 7 stickers. If Chi uses 2 rows of stickers, how many stickers will Chi have left?

54. Carla put 24 toy animals in 4 boxes. Each box has the same number of animals. How many animals are in 3 boxes?

Mixed Review and Test Prep

55. (p. 8)

$$\begin{array}{r} 35 \\ 22 \\ +15 \\ \hline \end{array}$$

56. (p. 72)

$$\begin{array}{r} 137 \\ 353 \\ +229 \\ \hline \end{array}$$

Compare. Write <, >, or = for each ●. (p. 42)

57. 458 ● 584

58. 1,602 ● 1,062

59. 3,459 ● 3,459

60. 15,891 ● 15,981

61. **TEST PREP** Maria buys pencils for \$1.39, a notebook for \$1.79, and a marker for \$0.85. If she pays with a \$5 bill, how much change will she get? (p. 118)

A \$4.03 **C** \$1.82
B \$1.97 **D** \$0.97

62. **TEST PREP** Find the number that the letter *r* stands for. (p. 243)

$$28 \div 7 = r$$

F 3 **G** 4 **H** 6 **J** 7

Problem Solving Thinker's Corner

MAKE A PREDICTION **Using what you know about multiplication and division, make a prediction to complete each statement. Choose from the terms below.**

greater than less than equal to

1. The quotient will be __?__ the dividend in the division problems below.
2. The product will be __?__ each factor in the multiplication problems below.

Check your predictions by completing the number sentences below. Use each number in the box only once.

48	6	4
30	63	8
9	5	36

3. ■ ÷ 6 = ■
4. 9 × ■ = ■
5. ■ ÷ 7 = ■
6. ■ × ■ = ■

LESSON 4

Algebra: Find the Cost

Quick Review

1. $2 \times 9 = ■$
2. $4 \times 4 = ■$
3. $6 \times 2 = ■$
4. $3 \times 5 = ■$
5. $10 \times 2 = ■$

Learn

WHAT'S FOR LUNCH? Mrs. Hugo buys 3 pizzas for her family. How much does Mrs. Hugo spend?

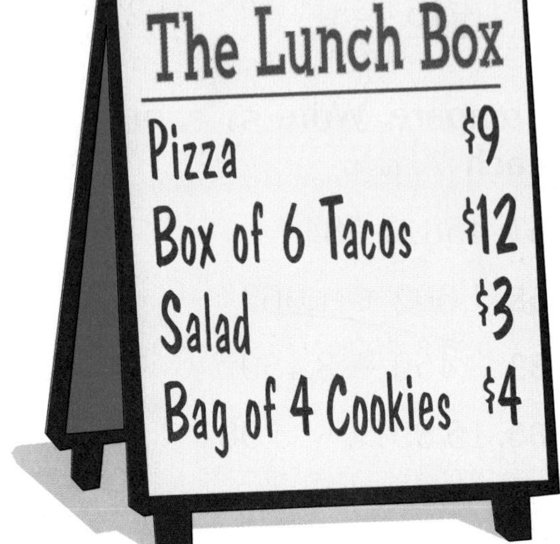

The Lunch Box
Pizza $9
Box of 6 Tacos $12
Salad $3
Bag of 4 Cookies $4

To find the total amount spent, multiply the number of pizzas by the cost of one pizza.

3	×	\$9	=	\$27
↑		↑		↑
number of pizzas		cost of one		total spent

So, Mrs. Hugo spends \$27 for 3 pizzas.

Nicolas buys a box of 6 tacos. How much does each taco cost?

To find the cost of one taco, divide the total amount spent by the number of tacos bought.

\$12	÷	6	=	\$2
↑		↑		↑
total spent		number of tacos		cost of one

So, each taco costs \$2.

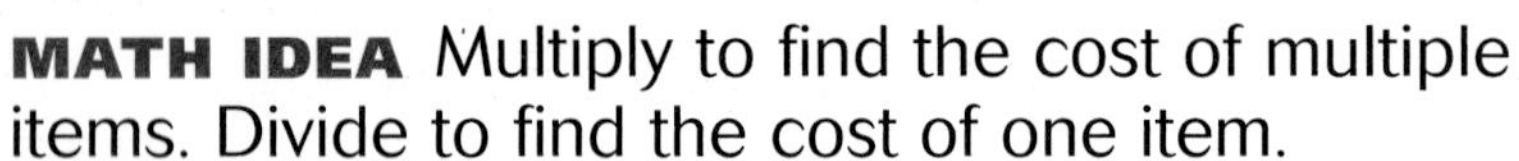

MATH IDEA Multiply to find the cost of multiple items. Divide to find the cost of one item.

Check

1. **Explain** how you can find the cost of one cookie.

For 2–3, write a number sentence. Then solve.

2. Alan bought 4 salads. Each salad cost \$3. How much did Alan spend?
3. Kim spent \$12 on bags of cookies. How many cookies did she buy?

Practice and Problem Solving

Extra Practice, page 288, Set D

For 4–5, write a number sentence. Then solve.

4. Sherry bought 4 hot dogs. Each hot dog cost \$4. How much did Sherry spend?

5. Mr. Hess spends \$18 for an order of 6 sandwiches. How much does each sandwich cost?

USE DATA For 6–16, use the price list at the right to find the cost of each number of items.

6. 4 videos **7.** 6 CDs **8.** 8 CDs

9. 7 books **10.** 2 CDs **11.** 5 videos

12. 3 books **13.** 9 CDs **14.** 5 books

15. 2 videos and 6 books

16. 4 books and 5 CDs

Read-n-Rock

PRICE LIST	
Books	\$4 each
CDs	\$7 each
Videos	\$9 each

Find the cost of one of each item.

17. 9 markers cost \$27. **18.** 6 notepads cost \$18. **19.** 3 stamps cost \$15.

20. 5 baseballs cost \$30. **21.** 8 pencils cost \$8. **22.** 4 games cost \$32.

23. 7 toy cars cost \$28. **24.** 10 pens cost \$20. **25.** 2 T-shirts cost \$12.

26. REASONING Ako has \$20. She wants to buy rubber stamps that cost \$6 each. How many rubber stamps can she buy? Explain.

27. Heidi buys 3 puzzle books for \$24. She gives the clerk \$30. How much does each book cost? How much change does she get?

Mixed Review and Test Prep

Continue each pattern. (p. 180)

28. 4, 9, 14, 19, ■, ■

29. 44, 40, 36, 32, ■, ■

30. (p. 96)

$$\begin{array}{r} 2{,}391 \\ -1{,}236 \\ \hline \end{array}$$

31. (p. 76)

$$\begin{array}{r} 3{,}529 \\ +9{,}382 \\ \hline \end{array}$$

32. TEST PREP Latasha makes 2 sandwiches for each of her 4 friends. She puts 2 slices of ham in each sandwich. How many slices of ham does she use? (p. 218)

A 2
B 4
C 8
D 16

LESSON 5

Problem Solving Strategy
Work Backward

PROBLEM Mike baked 3 batches of popovers. The extra batter made 4 more popovers. He made 31 popovers in all. How many popovers does the tin hold?

Quick Review

1. $18 \div 3 = ■$
2. $12 \div 4 = ■$
3. $24 \div 6 = ■$
4. $20 \div 2 = ■$
5. $10 \div 5 = ■$

UNDERSTAND

- What are you asked to find?
- What information will you use?

PLAN

- What strategy can you use to solve the problem?

You can *work backward* to find how many popovers the tin holds.

SOLVE

- How can you use the strategy to solve the problem?

Begin with the total number of popovers. Subtract the number of extra popovers from the total.

31	−	4	=	27
↑		↑		↑
total popovers		extra popovers		popovers in 3 batches

Divide to find the number of popovers in each batch.

27	÷	3	=	9
↑		↑		↑
popovers in 3 batches		number of batches		number in each batch

So, Mike's tin holds 9 popovers.

CHECK

- Look back. Does your answer make sense?

Problem Solving Practice

Work backward to solve.

1. What if Mike used a different tin to bake 4 batches of popovers? Then he used the extra batter to make 3 more popovers. He made 27 popovers in all. How many popovers does this tin hold?

2. Mr. Jones spent $30 at the sports shop. He bought a mitt for $10 and 4 baseballs. How much did each baseball cost?

Strategies

- Draw a Diagram or Picture
- Make a Model or Act It Out
- Make an Organized List
- Find a Pattern
- Make a Table or Graph
- Predict and Test
- **Work Backward**
- Solve a Simpler Problem
- Write a Number Sentence
- Use Logical Reasoning

Problem Solving

Mr. Lo bought 2 books that cost the same amount. He gave the cashier $20 and received $6 in change. How much money did each book cost?

3. Which number sentence shows how to find the total cost of the 2 books?

   A $\$20 + \$6 = \$26$
   B $2 \times \$6 = \$12$
   C $\$20 - \$6 = \$14$
   D $\$20 \div 2 = \$10$

4. How much money did each book cost?

   F $6
   G $7
   H $10
   J $14

Mixed Strategy Practice

USE DATA For 5–7, use the price list.

5. Zach pays for an apple pie and a bag of cookies with a $10 bill. He gets his change in quarters and dimes. There are 13 coins in all. How many of each coin does Zach get?

6. **? What's the Error?** Lara says a lemon tart and 2 boxes of muffins cost $11.65. Describe Lara's error and give the correct cost of the items.

Bake Sale Price List	
Bag of 3 Cookies	$0.75
Box of 6 Muffins	$3.45
Apple Pie	$6.75
Lemon Tart	$8.20

7. Tim has 3 quarters, 2 dimes, 2 nickels, and 5 pennies. List all the ways he can pay for a bag of cookies.

Extra Practice

Set A (pp. 274–277)

Find the missing factor and quotient.

1. $8 \times ■ = 32$ $32 \div 8 = ■$
2. $7 \times ■ = 35$ $35 \div 7 = ■$

Find the quotient.

3. $42 \div 6 = ■$
4. $■ = 24 \div 4$
5. $64 \div 8 = ■$
6. $■ = 21 \div 7$
7. $7\overline{)49}$
8. $2\overline{)2}$
9. $6\overline{)36}$
10. $5\overline{)40}$
11. $8\overline{)48}$
12. Divide 63 by 7.
13. Divide 80 by 8.
14. Divide 15 by 3.

Set B (pp. 278–279)

Find the quotient.

1. $■ = 36 \div 9$
2. $20 \div 10 = ■$
3. $■ = 20 \div 5$
4. $54 \div 6 = ■$
5. $3\overline{)12}$
6. $10\overline{)70}$
7. $9\overline{)72}$
8. $4\overline{)16}$
9. $9\overline{)27}$
10. Divide 56 by 8.
11. Divide 60 by 6.
12. Divide 100 by 10.

Set C (pp. 280–283)

Find the quotient.

1. $6 \div 6 = ■$
2. $■ = 7 \div 1$
3. $■ = 0 \div 5$
4. $28 \div 7 = ■$
5. $9\overline{)81}$
6. $3\overline{)18}$
7. $6\overline{)24}$
8. $2\overline{)20}$
9. $7\overline{)0}$
10. Divide 32 by 4.
11. Divide 40 by 10.
12. Divide 16 by 8.

Set D (pp. 284–285)

PRICE LIST	
Mugs	$4
Aprons	$8

USE DATA For 1–4, use the price list at the right to find the cost of each number of items.

1. 3 aprons
2. 5 mugs
3. 6 aprons
4. 8 mugs

Find the cost of one of each item.

5. 2 pizzas cost $14.
6. 4 tapes cost $32.
7. 5 books cost $25.
8. 6 pens cost $12.
9. 7 balls cost $21.
10. 3 shirts cost $27.

Review/Test

✓ CHECK CONCEPTS

Write a division sentence for each. (pp. 280–283)

1. 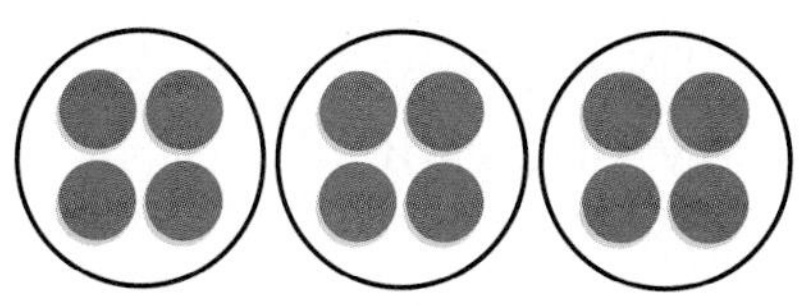

2. 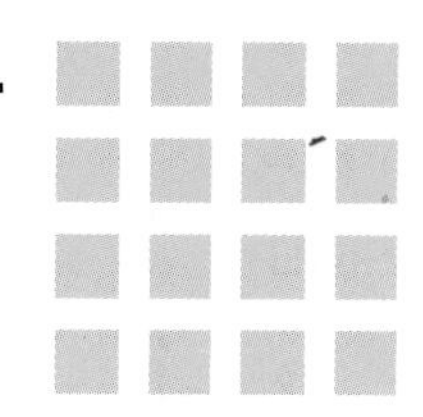

3.

$$\begin{array}{r} 24 \\ -\ 8 \\ \hline 16 \end{array} \quad \begin{array}{r} 16 \\ -\ 8 \\ \hline 8 \end{array} \quad \begin{array}{r} 8 \\ -8 \\ \hline 0 \end{array}$$

✓ CHECK SKILLS

Find the missing factor and quotient. (pp. 274–277)

4. $8 \times ■ = 40$ $40 \div 8 = ■$

5. $6 \times ■ = 42$ $42 \div 6 = ■$

6. $7 \times ■ = 56$ $56 \div 7 = ■$

7. $8 \times ■ = 32$ $32 \div 8 = ■$

Find the quotient. (pp. 274–283)

8. $14 \div 7 = ■$

9. $■ = 30 \div 5$

10. $40 \div 4 = ■$

11. $■ = 63 \div 9$

12. $8\overline{)24}$

13. $10\overline{)90}$

14. $2\overline{)14}$

15. $9\overline{)18}$

16. $3\overline{)27}$

For 17–20, use the price list at the right to find the cost of each number of items. (pp. 284–285)

17. 4 balloons

18. 7 noisemakers

19. 3 noisemakers

20. 9 balloons

PARTY SUPPLIES PRICE LIST	
Balloons	$3 each
Noisemakers	$2 each

Find the cost of one of each item. (pp. 284–285)

21. 5 notebooks cost $10.

22. 6 markers cost $18.

23. 5 caps cost $35.

✓ CHECK PROBLEM SOLVING

Work backward to solve. (pp. 286–287)

24. Nikki used a tin to make 3 batches of popovers. Then she made 2 extra popovers. She made 26 popovers in all. How many popovers does the tin hold?

25. Roger earned $35. He made $15 from a paper route. He also walked 4 dogs after school. How much did Roger charge to walk each dog?

Standardized Test Prep

NUMBER SENSE, CONCEPTS, AND OPERATIONS

1. Which of the following multiplication facts belongs to the same fact family as these division facts?

$56 \div 8 = 7$ $\quad$ $56 \div 7 = 8$

A $8 \times 8 = 64$
B $7 \times 8 = 56$
C $7 \times 7 = 49$
D $5 \times 6 = 30$

2. Ramona baked 36 muffins. She put 9 muffins in each bag. How many bags did Ramona use?

F 24 **H** 9
G 18 **J** 4

3. Which of the following number sentences does the drawing show?

A $10 \div 2 = 5$
B $80 \div 10 = 8$
C $40 \div 5 = 8$
D $50 \div 5 = 10$

4. Explain It Barb scored 211 points in a video game. Kelsey scored 58 fewer points than Barb. ESTIMATE the number of points Kelsey scored. Tell how you found your answer.

GEOMETRY AND SPATIAL SENSE

5. How many lines of symmetry does the figure have?

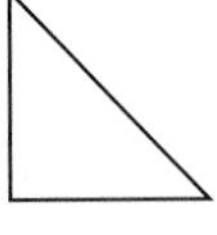

F 0 **G** 1 **H** 2 **J** 3

6. Which pair of figures appears to be congruent?

A  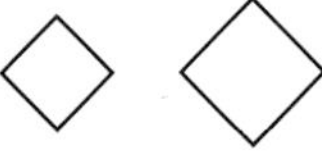

B  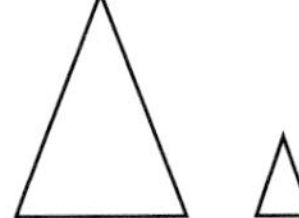

C  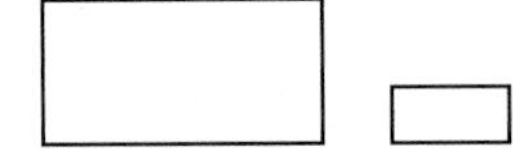

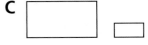

D 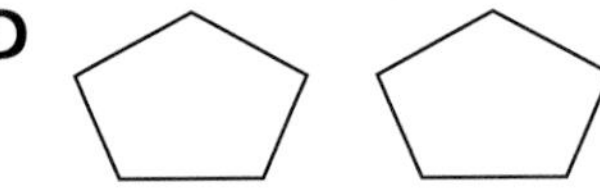

TIP **Eliminate choices.** See item 7. The answer is a 5-sided figure. So, you can eliminate any choice that does not have 5 sides.

7. Helen drew a polygon with 5 equal sides. Which shape did she draw?

F pentagon **H** triangle
G square **J** circle

8. Explain It Tony traced the faces of a solid figure. He counted 6 squares. What solid figure did Tony trace? Explain how you found your answer.

ALGEBRAIC THINKING

9. What is the next number in this pattern?

90, 81, 72, 63, ■

A 64 **C** 54
B 59 **D** 51

10. Which group contains only numbers that are multiples of 6?

F 3, 6, 20
G 15, 30, 45
H 12, 18, 30
J 16, 33, 36

11. Kevin bought 8 pies at the farmer's market. He paid a total of \$48 for the pies. Which of the following could be used to find the cost of each pie?

A $48 \div 8 = ■$
B $48 \div 6 = ■$
C $■ - 8 = 48$
D $48 - ■ = 8$

12. Explain It Lee made this division table. Find a rule for his pattern. What is the missing number? Explain how you found your answer.

LEE'S DIVISION TABLE	
56	8
49	7
42	6
35	5
28	■

DATA ANALYSIS AND PROBABILITY

13. What is the probability of pulling a green tile?

F impossible **H** certain
G unlikely **J** likely

14. Jada made a bar graph to show the sales at her snow cone stand. How many more snow cones did Jada sell on Monday than on Wednesday?

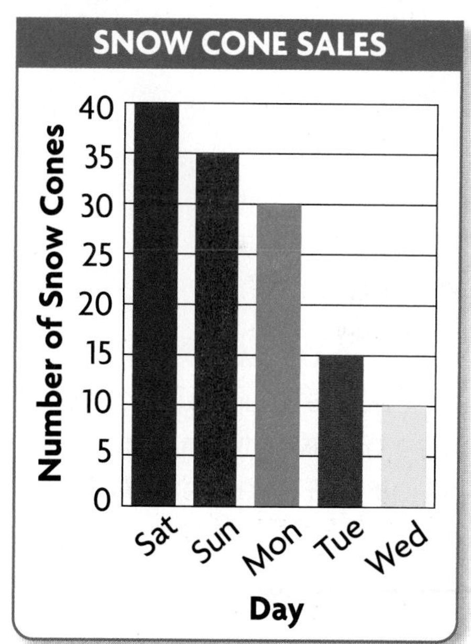

A 5 **C** 20
B 10 **D** 30

15. Explain It After looking at the bar graph above, Jada said that people bought more snow cones on Saturday and Sunday than on weekdays. Do you agree with her? Explain why or why not.

IT'S IN THE BAG

Candy Bar Division

PROJECT Make a "candy bar" booklet for practicing division facts.

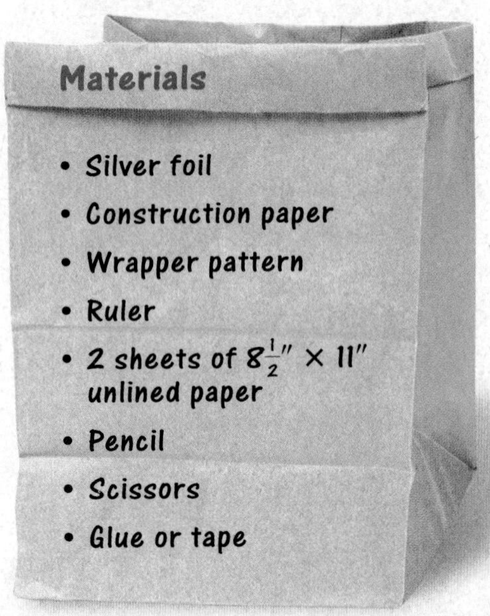

Materials

- Silver foil
- Construction paper
- Wrapper pattern
- Ruler
- 2 sheets of $8\frac{1}{2}'' \times 11''$ unlined paper
- Pencil
- Scissors
- Glue or tape

Directions

1. Using the construction paper and the pattern make and decorate a large "candy bar" wrapper. Glue a piece of silver foil inside each end of the wrapper to look like a real candy bar. Name the candy bar.

2. Measure the width of the wrapper. *(Picture A)* Draw a line slightly shorter than that width on unlined paper. Fold the paper accordion style (back and forth) so that the folded paper will fit into the wrapper.

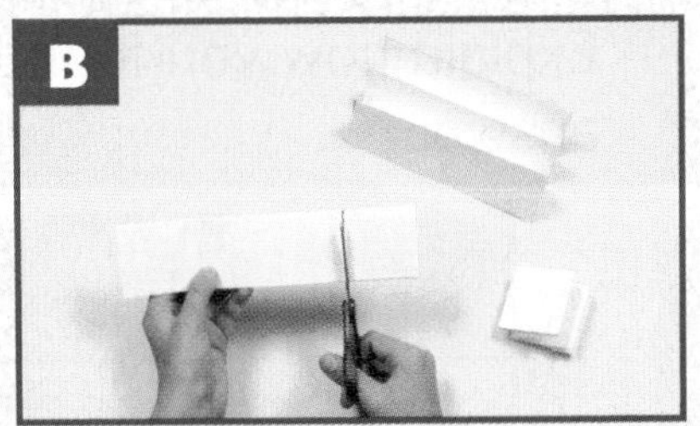

3. Cut the folded paper about 1 inch longer than the length of the candy bar wrapper. Repeat with the second sheet of paper and glue or tape the two folded sheets together. *(Picture B)*

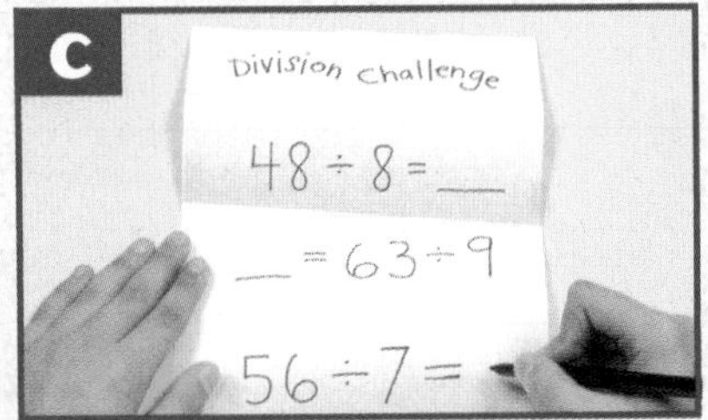

4. Write a different division problem on each space of the folded paper. *(Picture C)*

5. Fold up the paper and then solve the problems in the candy bar booklet.

Challenge

Divide by 11 and 12

Mr. Samson gathered 132 eggs. He wants to put them into egg cartons that hold 12 eggs each. How many egg cartons does Mr. Samson need?

132	÷	12	=	■
↑		↑		↑
number of eggs		number in each carton		number of cartons

×	0	1	2	3	4	5	6	7	8	9	10	11	12
0	0	0	0	0	0	0	0	0	0	0	0	0	0
1	0	1	2	3	4	5	6	7	8	9	10	11	12
2	0	2	4	6	8	10	12	14	16	18	20	22	24
3	0	3	6	9	12	15	18	21	24	27	30	33	36
4	0	4	8	12	16	20	24	28	32	36	40	44	48
5	0	5	10	15	20	25	30	35	40	45	50	55	60
6	0	6	12	18	24	30	36	42	48	54	60	66	72
7	0	7	14	21	28	35	42	49	56	63	70	77	84
8	0	8	16	24	32	40	48	56	64	72	80	88	96
9	0	9	18	27	36	45	54	63	72	81	90	99	108
10	0	10	20	30	40	50	60	70	80	90	100	110	120
11	0	11	22	33	44	55	66	77	88	99	110	121	132
12	0	12	24	36	48	60	72	84	96	108	120	132	144

Use a multiplication table to find the quotient.

Think: $12 \times$ ■ $= 132$

Find the factor 12 in the top row. Look down the column to find the product, 132. Look left along the row to find the missing factor, 11.

$12 \times 11 = 132$

$132 \div 12 = 11$

So, Mr. Samson needs 11 egg cartons.

Talk About It

- Explain how to use repeated subtraction to find $48 \div 12$.
- What patterns do you notice in the column for 11 on the multiplication table?

Try It

Use the multiplication table to solve.

1. $99 \div 11 =$ ■ **2.** ■ $= 108 \div 12$ **3.** $110 \div 11 =$ ■ **4.** ■ $= 84 \div 12$

5. $72 \div 12 =$ ■ **6.** $66 \div 11 =$ ■ **7.** ■ $= 144 \div 12$ **8.** $0 \div 11 =$ ■

9. $12\overline{)120}$ **10.** $11\overline{)121}$ **11.** $11\overline{)77}$ **12.** $12\overline{)36}$

UNIT 4

Study Guide and Review

VOCABULARY

Choose the best term from the box.

1. A set of related multiplication and division sentences is a ___?___. (p. 246)
2. Any number divided by ___?___ is that number. (p. 262)

one
fact family
quotient
zero

STUDY AND SOLVE

Chapter 12

Use repeated subtraction to divide.

$28 \div 7 = ■$

$28 - 7 = 21$, $21 - 7 = 14$, $14 - 7 = 7$, $7 - 7 = 0$

You subtracted 7 from 28 four times.
So, $28 \div 7 = 4$.

Write the division sentence shown by the repeated subtraction. (pp. 240–241)

3. $15 - 5 = 10$, $10 - 5 = 5$, $5 - 5 = 0$

4. $32 - 8 = 24$, $24 - 8 = 16$, $16 - 8 = 8$, $8 - 8 = 0$

Use arrays to divide.

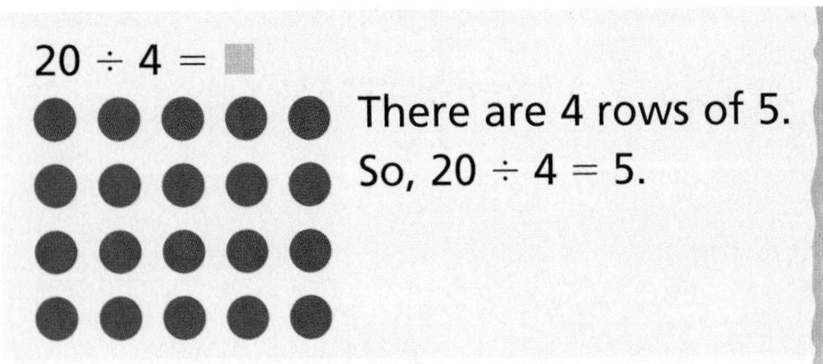

$20 \div 4 = ■$

There are 4 rows of 5.
So, $20 \div 4 = 5$.

Use the array to find the quotient. (pp. 242–245)

5. 2 rows of ■ = 8
$8 \div 2 = ■$

6. 3 rows of ■ = 9
$9 \div 3 = ■$

Write fact families.

This is the fact family for 3, 4, and 12.

$3 \times 4 = 12$ $12 \div 4 = 3$
$4 \times 3 = 12$ $12 \div 3 = 4$

Write the fact family for each set of numbers. (pp. 246–249)

7. 3, 9, 27
8. 6, 7, 42
9. 5, 8, 40
10. 4, 9, 36

Chapter 13

Use related multiplication facts to find quotients.

$45 \div 5 = \blacksquare$
Think: $5 \times \blacksquare = 45$
$5 \times 9 = 45$
So, $45 \div 5 = 9$, or $5\overline{)45}$ with quotient 9.

Find each quotient. (pp. 258–263)

11. $18 \div 3 = \blacksquare$

12. $30 \div 5 = \blacksquare$

13. $20 \div 4 = \blacksquare$

14. $16 \div 2 = \blacksquare$

15. $40 \div 5 = \blacksquare$

16. $24 \div 4 = \blacksquare$

17. $4\overline{)32}$

18. $3\overline{)9}$

19. $2\overline{)10}$

Chapter 14

Multiply to find the cost of multiple items.

Pens cost \$4 each. Find the cost of 7 pens.
$7 \times \$4 = \$28$
So, 7 pens cost \$28.

Beach balls cost \$3 each. Find the cost of each number of items. (pp. 284–285)

20. 6 beach balls

21. 2 beach balls

22. 5 beach balls

Divide to find the cost of one item.

8 erasers cost \$16.
$\$16 \div 8 = \$2$
So, each eraser costs \$2.

Find the cost of one of each item. (pp. 284–285)

23. 9 tennis balls cost \$18.

24. 7 baskets cost \$42.

25. 10 notepads cost \$10.

PROBLEM SOLVING PRACTICE

Solve. (pp. 250–251, 266–267, 286–287)

26. Marcie bought 5 packs of juice. There are 3 juice boxes in each pack. How many juice boxes did Marcie buy? Write a number sentence and solve.

27. Noah spent 15 minutes eating lunch and then played kickball for 25 minutes. Now it is 12:45 P.M. At what time did Noah start eating lunch?

28. Janet had \$7.35 and spent \$2.50 on a snack. How much money does Janet have left?

PERFORMANCE ASSESSMENT

TASK A • DAISY GARDEN

Materials: counters

Blair has 30 daisy plants. She wants to plant them in her garden so that each row has the same number of plants.

a. Use counters to make a model. Show one way Blair could place the plants in her garden. Draw a picture of your model.

b. Write the multiplication and division sentences that belong to the fact family for the model you drew.

c. How does the model you drew show that multiplication and division are related?

TASK B • AT THE BALL PARK

Kade and Lydia are going to a baseball game. There are special bargains at the ball park if you buy more than one of the same item. Kade and Lydia will buy items with friends who want the same thing. Each friend will get one item and will pay an equal part.

Kade has $3 and Lydia has $4.

a. What is one item Kade could buy?

b. Lydia wants to buy a different item. Which item could she buy? Write a division sentence to show how much Lydia's item will cost.

c. If Kade and Lydia combine their money, can they pay for one baseball to share? Explain.

Calculator • Find the Unit Cost

Joanne sees a sign that says, "Kites—4 for $15!" How much would Joanne pay for 1 kite?

The unit cost will tell you. The **unit cost** is the cost of one item when several items are sold for a single price.

Find the unit cost. Use a calculator.

STEP 1

Enter the total cost.

ON/C 1 5

STEP 2

Divide by the number of items.

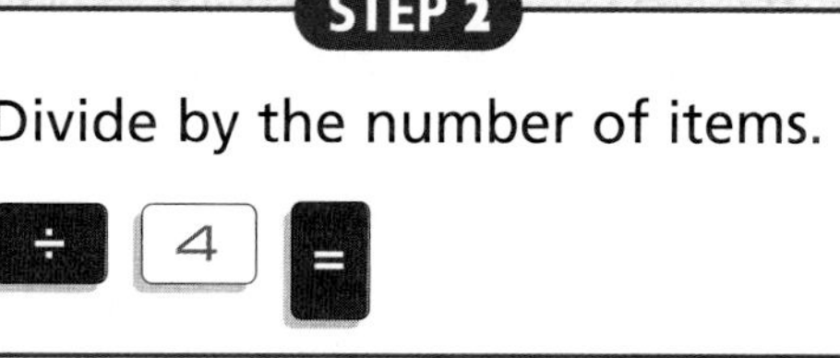

STEP 3

The quotient is the unit cost.

3.75

So, Joanne would pay $3.75 for 1 kite.

Practice and Problem Solving

Use a calculator to find each unit cost.

1. 4 for $18

2. 2 for $7

3. 8 for $18

4. 2 for $24

5. 5 for $35

6. 6 for $39

7. 3 for $27

8. 4 for $27

9. 4 for $11

Use a calculator to solve.

10. A hobby shop sells 6 puzzles for $12. How much will 2 puzzles cost? Explain.

11. **STRETCH YOUR THINKING** Ricardo bought 5 toy cars for $8.45. How much did each toy car cost?

GO ON-LINE **Multimedia Math Glossary** www.harcourtschool.com/mathglossary

Vocabulary Power Look up *dividend*, *divisor*, and *quotient* in the Multimedia Math Glossary. Write a riddle that someone could use to help remember these terms.

▲ Many theaters, like the Auditorium Theatre, have two balconies.

in Chicago, Illinois

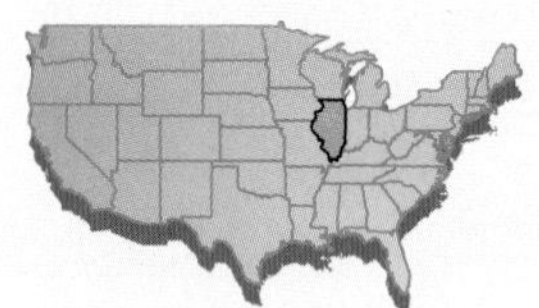

THE AUDITORIUM THEATRE

Many ballet companies and other dance companies perform at the Auditorium Theatre in Chicago.

USE DATA For 1–4, use the diagram.

Center Orchestra Section

				STAGE				
Row A	□	□	□	□	□	□	□	□
Row B	□	□	□	□	□	□	□	□
Row C	□	□	□	□	□	□	□	□
Row D	□	□	□	□	□	□	□	□

1. The diagram to the right shows 32 seats. Write a number sentence to show how to find the number of seats in each row.
2. If your class went to the Auditorium Theatre, would it fill more than 3 rows, less than 3 rows, or exactly 3 rows? Explain.
3. Each row in the center orchestra section of the Auditorium Theatre has the same number of seats. How many rows are needed for 40 people? Explain.
4. How many rows are needed in the center orchestra section for 72 people? Draw an array and write a number sentence to show your answer.

THE SHUBERT THEATRE

The Shubert Theatre is another theater in Chicago where you can see live performances.

USE DATA For 1–4, use the diagram.

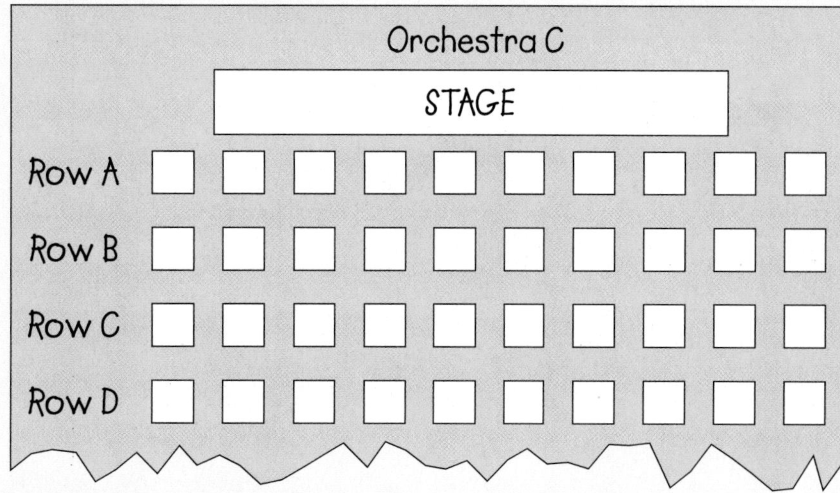

1. The section called Orchestra C is in the center of the first floor. Suppose 50 students want to sit in this section. How many rows of seats will they need? Explain.
2. A group buys 80 seats together in Orchestra C. How many full rows is that? The first row the students sit in is Row C. Then they continue to fill in the rows behind Row C. What is the letter of the last row that they fill in?
3. Suppose a group fills the seats in Rows A, B, C, and D. Write the fact family for this array of seats.
4. **STRETCH YOUR THINKING** A teacher orders 24 seats in Orchestra C for a field trip. She wants the same number of students to sit in each row. List 3 different ways that they could do this.

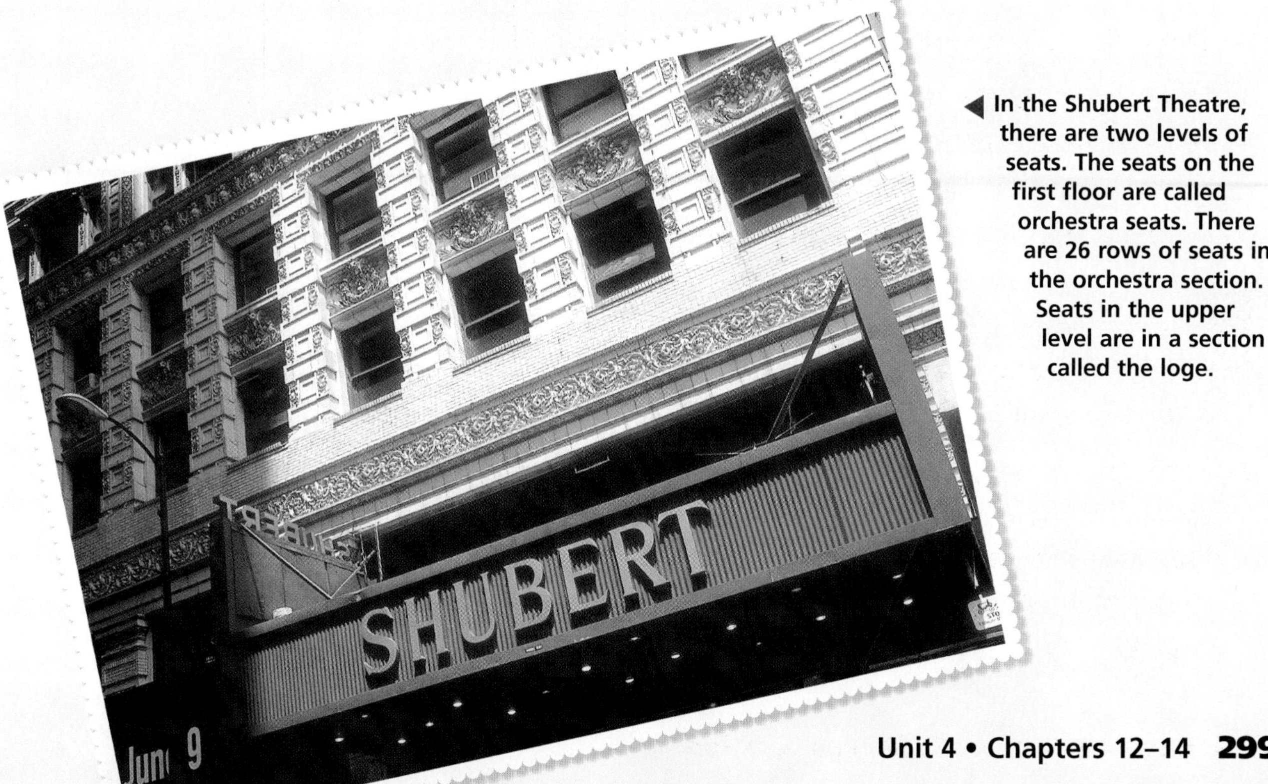

◀ **In the Shubert Theatre, there are two levels of seats. The seats on the first floor are called orchestra seats. There are 26 rows of seats in the orchestra section. Seats in the upper level are in a section called the loge.**

CHAPTER 15 Collect and Record Data

Sue Hendrickson

◀ Sue is the largest, most complete Tyrannosaurus rex fossil skeleton ever found.

FAST FACT • SCIENCE Dinosaurs lived on Earth many years ago. This Tyrannosaurus rex skeleton, named Sue, was found in South Dakota in 1990 by Sue Hendrickson. It is 41 feet long.

PROBLEM SOLVING Use the chart. Make a table that lists the dinosaurs in order from smallest to largest.

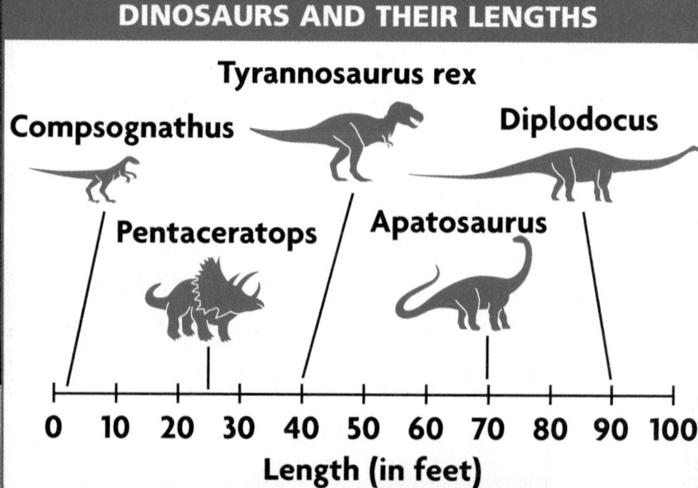

CHECK WHAT YOU KNOW

Use this page to help you review and remember important skills needed for Chapter 15.

COLUMN ADDITION

Find the sum.

1. $\begin{array}{r} 8 \\ 3 \\ 4 \\ +7 \\ \hline \end{array}$

2. $\begin{array}{r} 9 \\ 3 \\ 1 \\ +6 \\ \hline \end{array}$

3. $\begin{array}{r} 8 \\ 6 \\ 4 \\ +2 \\ \hline \end{array}$

4. $\begin{array}{r} 5 \\ 4 \\ 7 \\ +3 \\ \hline \end{array}$

5. $\begin{array}{r} 9 \\ 5 \\ 9 \\ +3 \\ \hline \end{array}$

READ A TABLE

For 6–9, use the information in this table.

6. What is the title of the table?
7. How many students like snowy weather best?
8. What kind of weather had the fewest votes?
9. How many students were asked?

OUR FAVORITE WEATHER

Type	Students
Sunny	7
Rainy	4
Snowy	8
Cloudy	3

VOCABULARY POWER

REVIEW

table [tā′bəl] *noun*

Table comes from the French word for *tablet,* which means "a slab of metal, stone, or wood used for writing." In mathematics, the meaning of *table* is "an arrangement of data in rows and columns." What is another meaning of *table*?

PREVIEW

data
tally table
frequency table
survey
results
classify
line plot
mode
range
circle graph
mean
median

GO ON-LINE www.harcourtschool.com/mathglossary

LESSON 1

Collect Data

Quick Review

Write numbers for the tally marks.

1. |||
2. ||
3. 𝍸
4. 𝍸 𝍸 |
5. 𝍸 ||

VOCABULARY

data **tally table** **frequency table**

MATERIALS

pencils, paper

Explore

Information collected about people or things is called **data**.

The students in Kelly's class voted for their favorite dinosaurs and made tables to show the results.

A **tally table** uses tally marks to record data.

A **frequency table** uses numbers to record data.

FAVORITE DINOSAUR

Name	Tally
Apatosaurus	𝍸 |
Brachiosaurus	𝍸 ||
Tyrannosaurus	𝍸 𝍸 ||
Stegosaurus	|||

FAVORITE DINOSAUR

Name	Number
Apatosaurus	6
Brachiosaurus	7
Tyrannosaurus	12
Stegosaurus	3

Collect data about your classmates' favorite dinosaurs. Organize the data in a tally table.

Activity 1

STEP 1

Write the title and headings. List four answer choices.

STEP 2

Ask classmates *What's your favorite dinosaur*? Make a tally mark for each answer.

Favorite Dinosaur

Name	Tally

- Why is a tally table good for recording data?

Try It

Decide on a question to ask your classmates.

a. Write four answer choices in a tally table.

b. Ask your classmates the question. Complete the tally table.

Connect

Use the data you organized in the tally table on page 302 to make a frequency table.

Activity 2

STEP 1

Write the title and headings. List the four answer choices.

STEP 2

Count the number of tally marks in each row. Write each number in the frequency table.

Favorite Dinosaur

Name	Number

- Why is a frequency table a good way to show data?

Practice and Problem Solving

1. Make a tally table about three after-school activities. Ask your classmates which activity they like best. For each answer, make a tally mark beside the activity.

2. Use the data from your tally table to make a frequency table. Which activity was chosen by the greatest number of classmates? the least number?

3. Which table is better for reading results? Which table is better for collecting data?

4. How many more students chose oranges and apples than chose bananas?

5. **Write a problem** using the information in the Favorite Fruit tally table.

FAVORITE FRUIT	
Name	**Tally**
Grapes	卌 卌 卌 I
Oranges	IIII
Apples	卌
Bananas	卌 III

Mixed Review and Test Prep

6. $2 \times 10 = \blacksquare$ (p. 212)

7. $7 \times 10 = \blacksquare$ (p. 212)

8. Which number is greater: 4,545 or 4,454? (p. 42)

9. Round 3,495 to the nearest thousand. (p. 52)

10. **TEST PREP** Ebony buys a sandwich for \$3.49. She has a coupon for \$0.50 off. She pays with a \$5 bill. How much change will she receive? (p. 118)

A \$1.01 **C** \$2.01
B \$1.51 **D** \$3.99

LESSON 2

Use Data from a Survey

Quick Review

1. 17 + 21 + 12
2. 13 + 9 + 6
3. 24 + 5 + 7
4. 8 + 14 + 7
5. 19 + 13 + 21 + 5

VOCABULARY

survey
results

Learn

SURVEY SAYS . . . A **survey** is a method of gathering information or data. The answers from a survey are called the **results** of the survey.

Jillian and Ted took a survey to find their classmates' favorite snacks. The tally table shows the choices and votes of their classmates.

What are the favorite snacks of their classmates?

Since cookies got the greatest number of votes, 12, cookies are the favorite snack.

FAVORITE SNACK	
Snack	**Tally**
Popcorn	||||
Cookies	𝍸 𝍸 ||
Granola bars	𝍸
Apples	𝍸 ||
Pretzels	||

Check

1. **Explain** how you can find the number of students who answered Jillian and Ted's survey.
2. List the snacks at the right in order from the most votes to the fewest votes.

For 3–4, use the tally table below.

DO YOU HAVE AN OLDER BROTHER OR SISTER?	
Answer	**Tally**
Yes	𝍸 𝍸 ||
No	𝍸 𝍸 𝍸 ||

3. How many people were surveyed?
4. Write a statement that describes the survey results.

Practice and Problem Solving

Extra Practice, page 316, Set A

For 5–8, use the tally table.

FAVORITE SCHOOL SUBJECT	
Subject	**Tally**
Math	卌 卌 |||
Science	卌 ||||
Reading	卌 卌 卌
Social Studies	卌 |
Art	卌 ||

5. List the subjects in order from the most votes to the fewest votes.

6. How many students answered the survey?

7. How many more students chose math than chose social studies?

8. How many fewer students chose art than chose reading?

For 9–12, use the frequency table.

FAVORITE SPORT	
Sport	**Number**
Basketball	26
Football	15
Baseball	17
Hockey	21
Swimming	30

9. How many more students chose basketball than chose baseball?

10. Which sport did the greatest number of students choose?

11. How many students answered this survey?

12. **What if** 5 more students chose basketball? How would that change the results of the survey?

13. **? What's the Error?** Lily wrote the following number sentence: $24 \times 0 = 24$. What's her error?

14. **Write About It** Think of a survey question. Write four possible answers. Survey your classmates. Make a tally table and a frequency table to record your classmates' choices. Explain the results.

15. Jamie has 48 stickers. They are arranged on 6 sheets so that each sheet has the same number of stickers. How many stickers do 3 sheets contain?

Mixed Review and Test Prep

16. (p. 72) $\begin{array}{r} 134 \\ +159 \\ \hline \end{array}$

17. (p. 92) $\begin{array}{r} 902 \\ -453 \\ \hline \end{array}$

18. (p. 72) $\begin{array}{r} 166 \\ +384 \\ \hline \end{array}$

19. Three friends shared 27 baseball cards equally. How many cards did each friend receive? (p. 260)

20. **TEST PREP** Toshio had 4 packages of 6 bagels. He gave one package away. How many bagels in all does he have now? (p. 164)

A 10 **B** 18 **C** 24 **D** 28

LESSON 3

Classify Data

Quick Review

Quick Review

1. 6 + 2 + 3
2. 5 + 7 + 6
3. 9 + 1 + 4
4. 3 + 8 + 5
5. 13 + 4 + 8

VOCABULARY

classify

Learn

MARBLES IN MOTION You can group, or **classify**, data in many different ways, such as by size, color, or shape.

Ms. Vernon gave each pair of students in her class a bag of marbles. She asked students to think about ways that they could group the marbles.

Luis and Joey made a table to show what they did.

Bag of Marbles

	Small	Medium	Large
Blue	2	2	5
Red	3	1	5
Multicolor	3	3	2

- How did Luis and Joey classify their data?

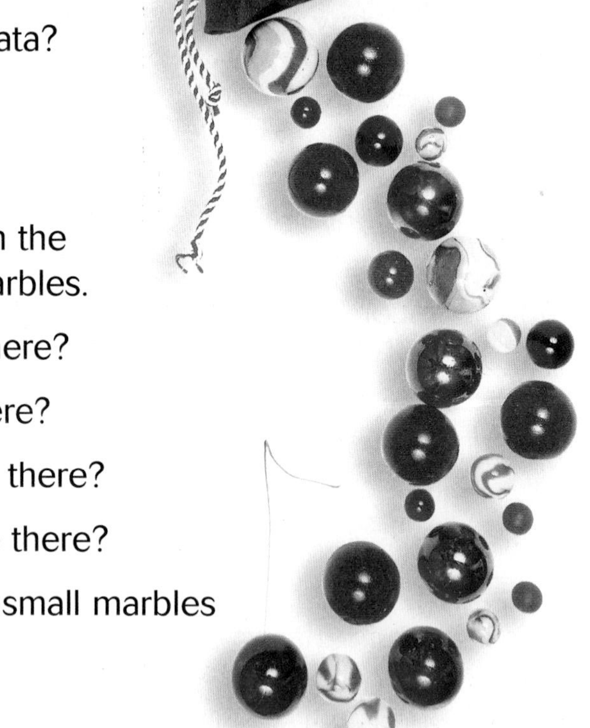

Check

1. **Explain** 3 things that the groupings in the table helped you know about the marbles.
2. How many small blue marbles are there?
3. How many large red marbles are there?
4. How many multicolored marbles are there?
5. How many medium-size marbles are there?
6. How many more large marbles than small marbles are there?

Practice and Problem Solving

Extra Practice, page 316, Set B

For 7–10, use the table.

COLOR OF SHIRTS IN OUR CLASS				
	Green	**Blue**	**Red**	**Yellow**
Girls	1	6	2	5
Boys	3	4	4	0

7. How many girls are wearing red shirts?

8. How many students are wearing blue shirts?

9. How many more students' shirts are red than are green?

10. How many students are in the class?

For 11–13, use the table.

PICTURES IN THE ART SHOW				
	Chalk	Crayon	Paint	Pencil
People	3	5	8	1
Animals	4	5	4	3
Plants	6	2	9	5

11. How many pictures are in the art show in all?

12. What is the subject of the greatest number of pictures in the art show: people, animals, or plants?

13. There are 12 possible categories of pictures in the art show. Which one was represented the least?

14. REASONING Look at the figures below. Make a table to classify, or group, them. Explain how you grouped the figures.

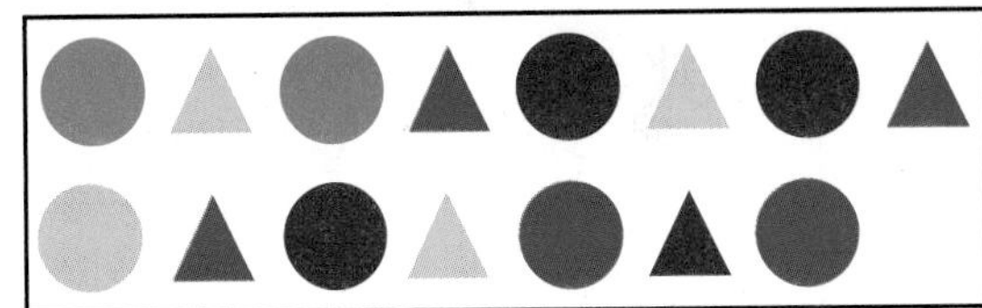

15. *FAST FACT* • SOCIAL STUDIES The first machine to make marbles was invented in about 1905 in Akron, Ohio. How many years ago was this?

16. There are 11 girls and 8 boys in a music club. Of the girls, 6 are dancers and the rest are singers. Of the boys, 3 are dancers and the rest are singers. Make a table to classify, or group, the students.

Mixed Review and Test Prep

17. $700 - 238 = \blacksquare$ (p. 92)

18. $306 - 67 = \blacksquare$ (p. 92)

19. $5 \times 2 \times 5 = \blacksquare$ (p. 218)

20. If 4 tapes cost $32, how much does 1 tape cost? (p. 284)

21. TEST PREP Caroline left her house at 7:15 A.M. She arrived at school 20 minutes later. At what time did she arrive at school? (p. 134)

A 6:55 A.M.
B 7:20 A.M.
C 7:30 A.M.
D 7:35 A.M.

LESSON 4

Problem Solving Strategy
Make a Table

Quick Review

1. 6 + 4
2. 3 + 5
3. 8 + 7
4. 9 + 6
5. 6 + 7

PROBLEM Leo and Sally used the two spinners shown at the right. They spun the pointers and recorded the sum of the two numbers. They spun 20 times. Their results were 2, 4, 6, 5, 4, 5, 4, 4, 2, 4, 4, 3, 4, 5, 6, 4, 6, 4, 3, and 4. Which sum occurred most often?

3 + 1 = 4

UNDERSTAND

- What are you asked to find?
- What information will you use?

PLAN

- What strategy can you use to solve the problem?

You can *make a table* to organize the data.

SOLVE

- What should you put in the table?

Leo and Sally recorded the sums of the two numbers. So, label one column *Sums*. In this column, list all the sums that are possible. Label another column *Number of Spins*. Use a tally mark to record each spin.

SPINNER SUM	
Sums	**Number of Spins**
2	||
3	||
4	𝍸 𝍸
5	|||
6	|||

So, the sum 4 occurred most often.

CHECK

- What other strategy could you use to solve the problem?

Problem Solving Practice

Strategies

- Draw a Diagram or Picture
- Make a Model or Act It Out
- Make an Organized List
- Find a Pattern
- ▶ **Make a Table or Graph**
- Predict and Test
- Work Backward
- Solve a Simpler Problem
- Write a Number Sentence
- Use Logical Reasoning

Problem Solving

Solve.

1. **What if** Leo and Sally spin the pointers 25 times and record the sums in a table? How many tallies should there be?

2. Marta and Dan rolled two number cubes 15 times and recorded the sums. Their results were 9, 9, 5, 6, 9, 3, 7, 7, 3, 5, 12, 12, 10, 8, and 5. Make a table and find the sum rolled most often.

Roll two number cubes, numbered 1–6, twenty times to find out what difference you will roll most often.

3. What are all the differences you will list in your table?
   A 0, 2, 4, 6
   B 0, 1, 2, 3, 4, 5, 6
   C 0, 1, 2, 3, 4, 5
   D 1, 2, 3, 4, 5, 6

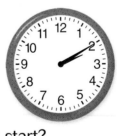

4. What should the total number of tallies be in your table for this experiment?
   F 10
   G 15
   H 20
   J 25

Mixed Strategy Practice

5. **REASONING** Louise is older than Jim and Marsha. Marsha is younger than Jim. Al is the youngest of the group. What is the order of the group from youngest to oldest?

6. The clock shows the time when the game ended. If the game lasted 2 hours and 15 minutes, when did it start?

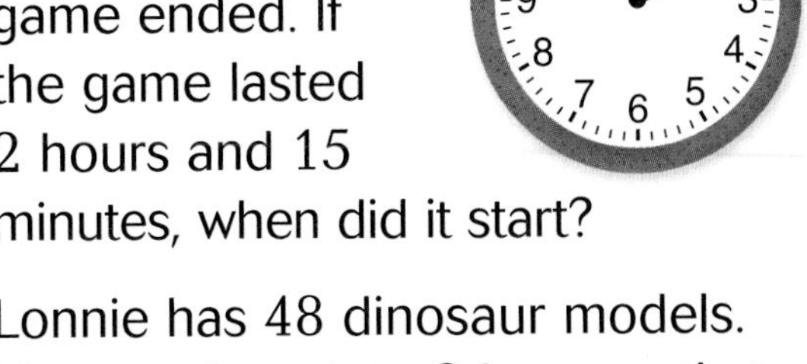

7. In the library, there are 3 shelves with 9 new books on each shelf. How many new books are on the shelves?

8. Lonnie has 48 dinosaur models. He puts them into 8 bags so that there are the same number in each bag. How many models do 2 bags contain?

9. **What's the Question?** Sylvia spent $7 at the movies. She still had $8 when she got home. The answer is $15.

LESSON

5 Line Plots

Learn

LOTS OF PLOTS All 24 third-grade students were measured to find their heights in inches.

HEIGHTS OF THIRD GRADERS	
Height in Inches	**Number of Students**
49	|
50	|||
51	||
52	𝍸 |
53	𝍸 ||
54	||||
55	|

Quick Review

1. 27 − 12
2. 36 − 18
3. 98 − 35
4. 74 − 47
5. 56 − 39

VOCABULARY

line plot
mode
range
circle graph

You can make a **line plot** to record each piece of data on a number line.

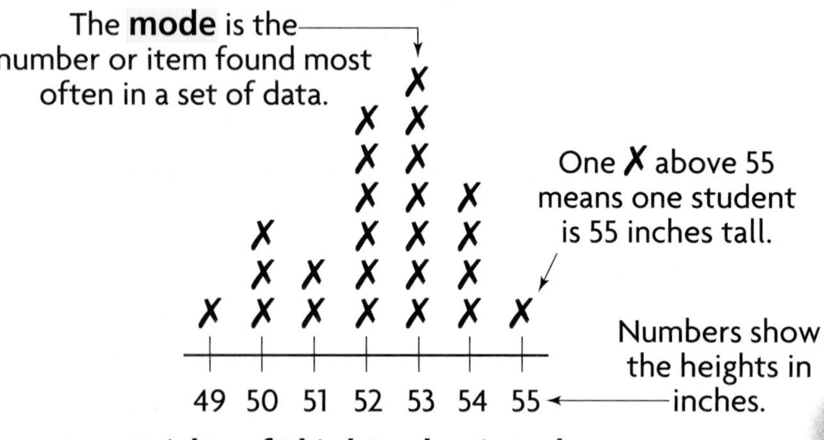

The mode is the number or item found most often in a set of data.
One X above 55 means one student is 55 inches tall.
Numbers show the heights in inches.
49 50 51 52 53 54 55

Heights of Third Graders in Inches

5 feet
1 foot

The **range** is the difference between the greatest number and the least number.

greatest number
least number
range
55 − 49 = 6

- What are the range and mode for this data?
- How many students are 50 inches tall?

Make a Line Plot

Debbie took a survey in her third-grade class to find out how many peanut butter and jelly sandwiches the students ate last week.

She put the survey data in a tally table.

PEANUT BUTTER AND JELLY SANDWICHES	
Number of Sandwiches	Tallies
0	|
1	~~||||~~
2	|||
3	~~||||~~ |
4	||||
5	||

Activity

Materials: number line

Make a line plot of the data in the table.

STEP 1

Write a title for the line plot. Label the numbers from 0 to 5.

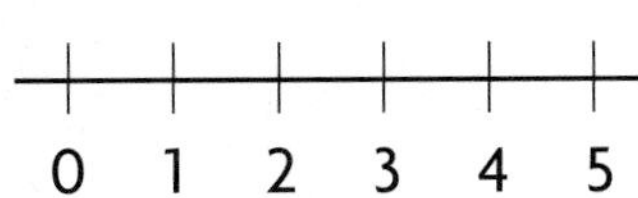

Peanut Butter and Jelly Sandwiches Eaten Last Week

STEP 2

Draw ✗'s above the number line to show how many students ate each number of sandwiches.

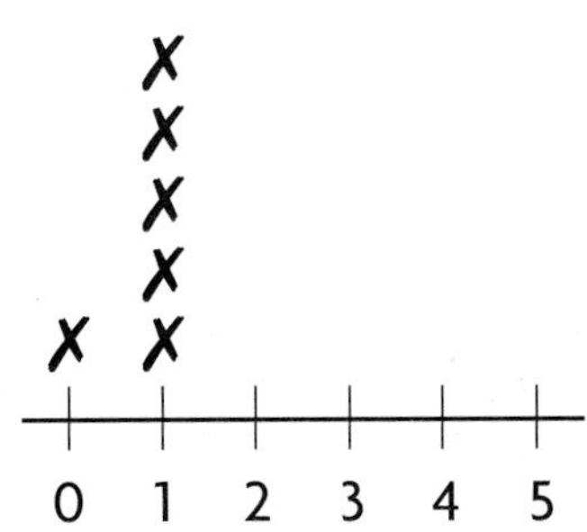

Peanut Butter and Jelly Sandwiches Eaten Last Week

- How are the tally table and the line plot alike? How are they different?

Technology Link

More Practice: Harcourt Mega Math The Number Games, *Arachna-Graph,* Level E

Check

1. **Explain** how to find the mode for the data above.

For 2–3, use your line plot.

2. How many students ate exactly 3 peanut butter and jelly sandwiches last week?

3. How many more students ate 1 or 2 sandwiches than ate 4 or 5 sandwiches?

LESSON CONTINUES

Practice and Problem Solving

Extra Practice, page 316, Set C

For 4–6, use the line plot at the right.

4. The **X**'s on the line plot stand for the band members. What do the numbers stand for?

5. What is the greatest number of hours any student practiced? What is the least number? What is the range for this set of data?

6. Did more band members practice for *less than* 5 hours or for *more than* 5 hours? Explain.

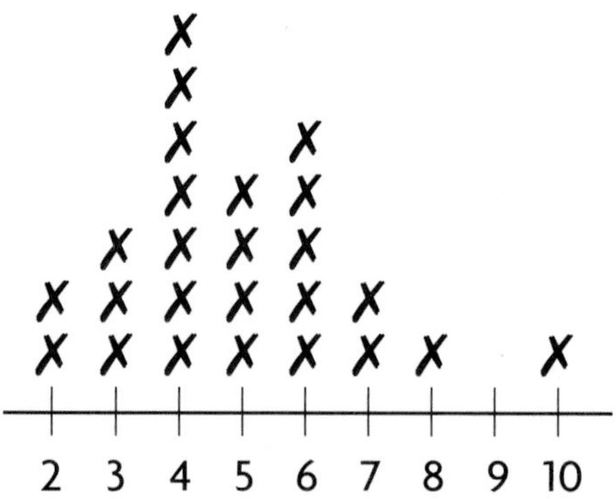

Hours Band Members Practiced

7. **Vocabulary Power** To remember the meaning of *mode*, think of the word *most*. In this set of numbers, what is the mode? 9, 2, 8, 9, 7, 3, 9, 5, 6, 9

For 8–11, use the line plot below.

Mrs. Brown's class recorded the high temperature each day for 3 weeks.

8. What high temperature occurred most often in the 3 weeks? On how many days?

9. On how many days was the high temperature below 70 degrees?

10. What was the range of high temperatures?

11. Predict what you think the high temperature will be the fourth week. Explain.

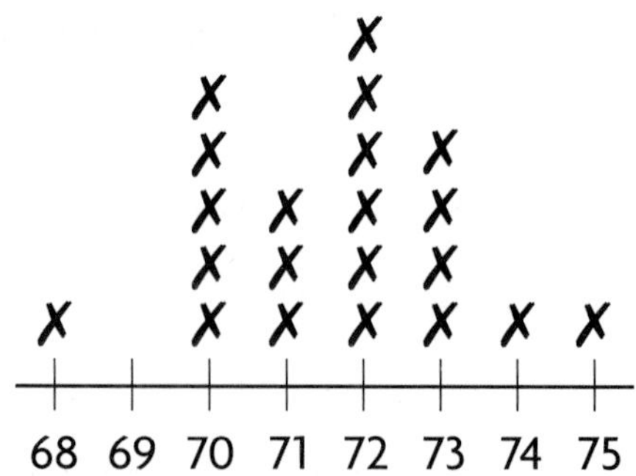

High Temperatures Each Day (in Degrees)

12. Take a survey to find out how many pets each student in your class has. Show the results in a tally table and a line plot.

13. **Write About It** Explain how you decided which numbers to use in your line plot in Problem 12.

Mixed Review and Test Prep

Find each product. (p. 202)

14. $4 \times 7 = \blacksquare$ **15.** $3 \times 8 = \blacksquare$

16. $6 \times 6 = \blacksquare$ **17.** $7 \times 8 = \blacksquare$

Find each quotient. (p. 280)

18. $35 \div 7 = \blacksquare$ **19.** $27 \div 9 = \blacksquare$

20. $48 \div 8 = \blacksquare$ **21.** $49 \div 7 = \blacksquare$

22. **TEST PREP** What multiplication fact could you use to solve $8 \div 2$? (p. 242)

A $2 \times 2 = 4$ **C** $8 \times 2 = 16$
B $2 \times 4 = 8$ **D** $4 \times 8 = 32$

23. **TEST PREP** Sonya bought juice for \$1.09 and a sandwich for \$3.45. She paid the cashier with a \$10 bill. How much change should she receive? (p. 120)

F \$5.46 **H** \$6.46
G \$5.56 **J** \$6.56

Problem Solving LINKUP . . . to Reading

STRATEGY • USE GRAPHIC AIDS Graphic aids organize information so that it can be compared and analyzed. When you use a graphic aid, you "read" a picture rather than just words.

Brandi took a survey to find her classmates' favorite pets. She made a line plot and a circle graph of the data.

A **circle graph** shows data as parts of a whole circle.

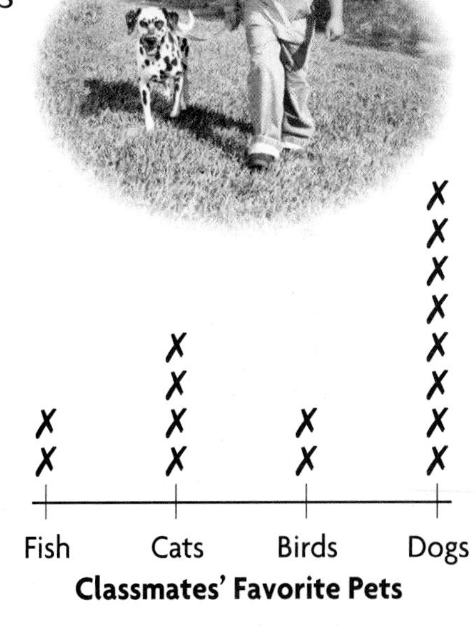

Classmates' Favorite Pets

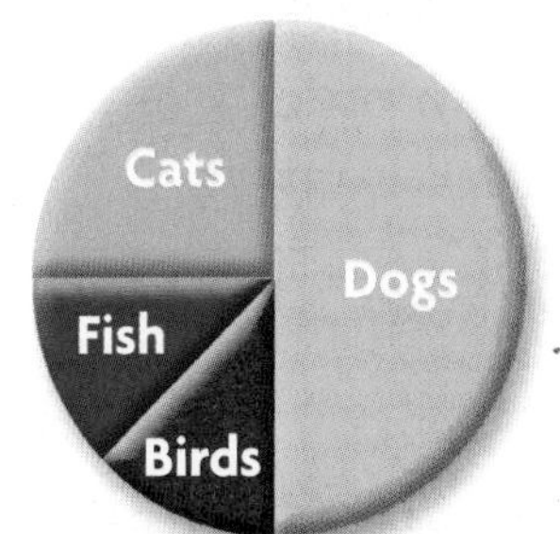

Classmates' Favorite Pets

1. How many classmates did Brandi survey?
2. What is the mode of the data?
3. Which pet received half of the votes?
4. Which two pets received the same number of votes?
5. **Write About It** Tell whether you think the circle graph or the line plot is easier to read. Explain the reason for your choice.

LESSON 6

Mean and Median

Quick Review

1. $32 \div 4$ **2.** $54 \div 6$

3. $28 \div 7$ **4.** $25 \div 5$

5. $48 \div 8$

VOCABULARY

mean **median**

Explore

BIRD COUNT Cari recorded in a tally table the number of robins she saw on her way to school. Find the mean and median of this data.

The **mean** is the average of a set of data. The **median** is the middle number in an ordered set of data.

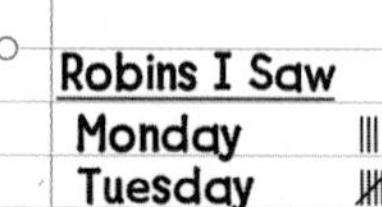

Robins I Saw	
Monday	|||
Tuesday	卌 |||
Wednesday		
Thursday	卌	
Friday	||

Activity 1 Find the mean.

One Way Use connecting cubes.

STEP 1

Model the number of robins counted each day.

STEP 2

Rearrange the cubes so each stack has the same number of cubes.

The mean is the number of cubes in each stack. So, the mean is 4 robins.

Another Way Use addition and division.

STEP 1

Add the numbers for each day.
$3 + 8 + 1 + 6 + 2 = 20$

STEP 2

Divide the sum by the number of addends.
$20 \div 5 = 4$ So, the mean is 4 robins.

Activity 2 Find the median.

STEP 1

Model the number of robins counted each day. Arrange the stacks in order from least to greatest.

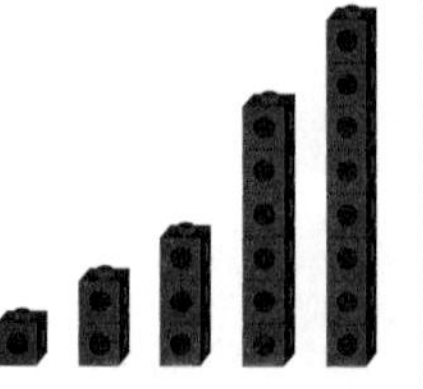

STEP 2

Count the number of cubes in the middle stack. So, the median is 3 robins.

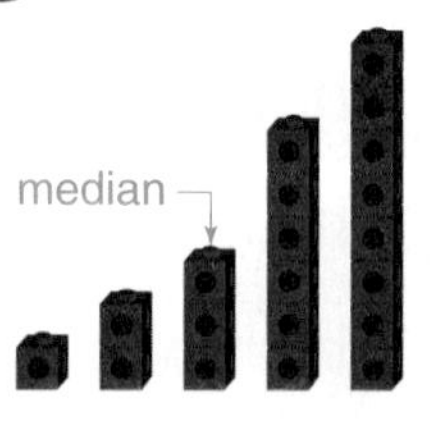

Try It

Find the mean and median.

a. 4, 9, 8 **b.** 5, 7, 6, 3, 9

Connect

If a set of data uses numbers, you can find the median of the data without using connecting cubes.

In the spring, Travis and his friends saw 7 robins' nests with eggs and used a picture to show their data. What is the median?

Record the number of eggs that are in each nest. List the data in order from least to greatest. Then find the middle number.

3, 3, 3, 4, 4, 5, 6

So, the median of the set of data is 4 eggs.

- What are the mode and the range of this set of data?
- What is the mean of this set of data? Use connecting cubes to help.

Technology Link

More Practice: Harcourt Mega Math The Number Games, *Arachna-Graph,* Level F

Practice and Problem Solving

Find the mean and the median.

1. 7, 2, 6

2. 5, 8, 5

3. 5, 8, 9, 6, 7

4. 1, 5, 3, 2, 4

5. 1, 4, 0, 3, 1, 2, 3

6. 2, 6, 5, 3, 1, 7, 4

7. **REASONING** Teri says using connecting cubes to find the mean of a set of data is like dividing. Do you agree or disagree? Explain.

8. **Write About It** Choose your favorite fruit. Record in a tally table the number of times you eat the fruit each day for one week. Then find the range, mode, and median of the data.

Mixed Review and Test Prep

Find the product. (pp. 178, 194)

9. $\begin{array}{r} 8 \\ \times 4 \\ \hline \end{array}$

10. $\begin{array}{r} 7 \\ \times 6 \\ \hline \end{array}$

Find the quotient. (pp. 258, 278)

11. $5\overline{)35}$

12. $9\overline{)54}$

13. **TEST PREP** Jonathan bought a pencil for $0.89 and a notepad for $1.35. He paid with a $5 bill. How much change did Jonathan receive? (p. 118)

A $2.24 **C** $2.76
B $2.66 **D** $3.76

Extra Practice

Set A (pp. 304–305)

For 1–3, use the tally table.

FAVORITE HOBBY	
Hobby	**Tally**
Collecting stamps	||||
Collecting sports cards	𝍸 𝍸
Collecting coins	||
Reading	𝍸 |||

1. How many people answered the survey?
2. What is the most popular hobby?
3. How many fewer people chose collecting coins than chose reading?

For 4–6, use the frequency table.

4. How many people answered the survey?
5. Did more people choose peas or carrots?
6. How many more people chose corn than chose beans?

FAVORITE VEGETABLE	
Type	**Number**
Carrots	6
Peas	6
Beans	3
Corn	12

Set B (pp. 306–307)

For 1–3, use the table.

FAVORITE BREAKFAST FOOD				
	Bacon and Eggs	**French Toast**	**Cereal**	**Muffins**
Boys	9	6	4	1
Girls	4	8	5	3

1. How many girls were surveyed?
2. How many boys liked French toast the best?
3. How many students chose bacon and eggs?

Set C (pp. 310–313)

For 1–2, use the line plot.

1. What are the range and the mode of the data? Explain.
2. How many students were surveyed?

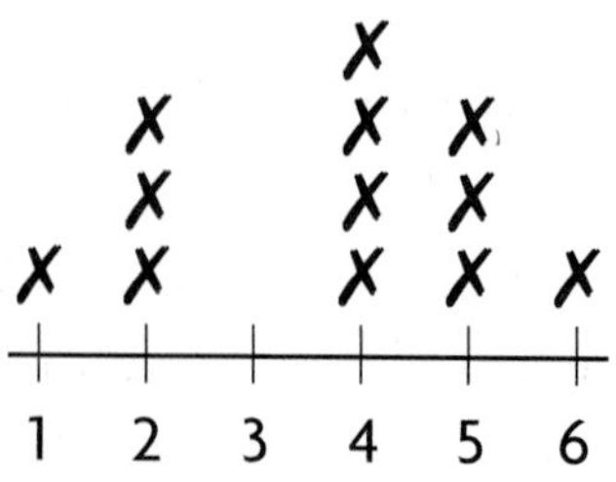

Number of Chores Students Did Last Week

Review/Test

CHECK VOCABULARY

Choose the best term from the box.

data
survey
tally table
frequency table
median
mode

1. A method of gathering information is a ___?___. (p. 304)
2. Information collected about people or things is called ___?___. (p. 302)
3. A table that uses numbers to record data is a ___?___. (p. 302)
4. The number or item found most often in a set of data is the ___?___. (p. 310)

CHECK SKILLS

For 5–6, use the tally table. (pp. 304–305)

5. List the instruments in order from the most votes to the fewest votes.
6. How many people answered the survey?

FAVORITE MUSICAL INSTRUMENT

Musical Instrument	Tally
Guitar	卌 卌 卌
Flute	卌 ||||
Drums	卌 卌 卌 |||
Piano	卌 卌 |||

For 7–8, use the frequency table. (pp. 306–307)

7. How many students have brown eyes?
8. How many girls were surveyed?

EYE COLOR OF STUDENTS

	Blue	Brown	Green
Girls	4	8	1
Boys	5	7	2

CHECK PROBLEM SOLVING

Solve. (pp. 308–309)

9. There are 12 fourth graders and 13 fifth graders in the Science Club. Five of the fourth graders and 9 of the fifth graders are girls. Make a table to group the students in the Science Club.

10. Sancho rolled two number cubes 10 times and recorded the sums. His results were 7, 6, 11, 2, 8, 9, 6, 8, 11, and 8. Make a table and find the sum rolled most often.

Standardized Test Prep

NUMBER SENSE, CONCEPTS, AND OPERATIONS

1. Lisa has 21 stuffed animals. She wants to put an equal number on each of 3 shelves in her room. How many animals will she put on each shelf?

A 24
B 18
C 14
D 7

TIP **Check your work.** See item 2. Draw a picture to check your work. Be sure to draw 8 stickers on each of 6 packages.

2. Crystal has 6 packages of stickers. Each package has 8 stickers. How many stickers does she have?

F 42
G 46
H 48
J 54

3. **Explain It** This jar has 50 jellybeans in it. Which jar below has about 200 jellybeans in it? Explain your thinking.

A

B

MEASUREMENT

4. Colin leaves for a trip on May 3. He will be gone for 2 weeks. What date will Colin return from his trip?

May						
Sun	Mon	Tue	Wed	Thu	Fri	Sat
						1
2	3	4	5	6	7	8
9	10	11	12	13	14	15
16	17	18	19	20	21	22
23	24	25	26	27	28	29
30	31					

A May 5
B May 10
C May 17
D May 24

5. **Explain It** Arthur made this schedule for his class field day. ESTIMATE how many hours Arthur's class will spend playing softball. Explain how you estimated the elapsed time.

FIELD DAY SCHEDULE	
Activity	**Time**
Relay Races	9:00 A.M. to 10:15 A.M.
Scavenger Hunt	10:30 A.M. to 11:45 A.M.
Lunch	Noon to 12:45 P.M.
Softball Game	12:50 P.M. to 4:00 P.M.
Team Awards	4:10 P.M. to 4:45 P.M.

GEOMETRY AND SPATIAL SENSE

6. Marta flips this letter. What will the letter look like after the flip?

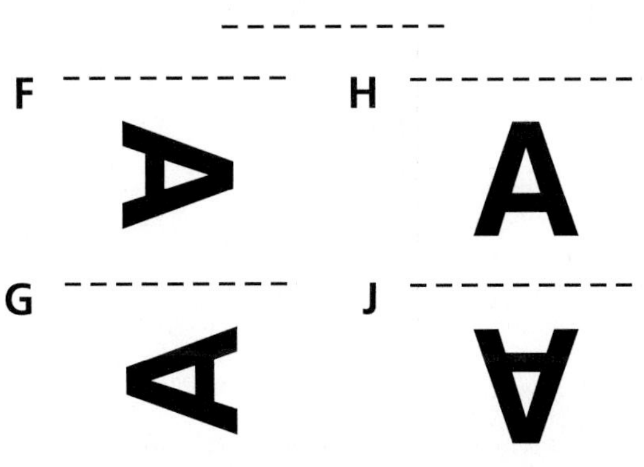

7. Davis traced the face of a solid figure. He drew a square. Which solid figure did Davis trace?

A cube
B cone
C cylinder
D sphere

8. Which dashed line shows a line of symmetry?

F 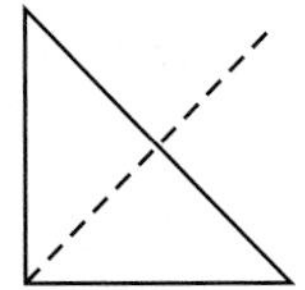

H 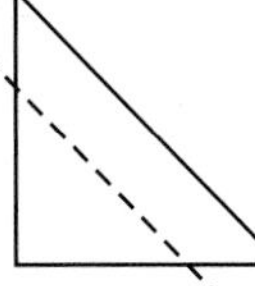

G 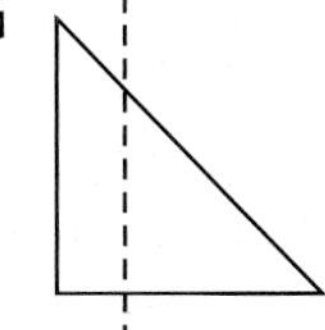

J 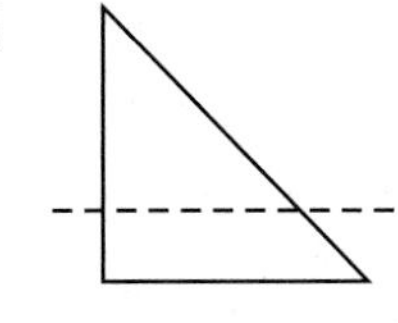

9. Explain It Draw a polygon with three sides. Then draw a polygon with twice as many sides as the first figure. Name the polygons you drew.

DATA ANALYSIS AND PROBABILITY

10. Carla surveyed her classmates to find their favorite breakfast foods. The tally table below shows the results of Carla's survey.

FAVORITE BREAKFAST FOODS	
Type of Food	**Tally**
Cereal	𝍸 𝍸 |||
Eggs	𝍸 ||
Oatmeal	|||
Pancakes	𝍸 𝍸 |

Which types of food each received at least 10 votes?

A pancakes and eggs
B eggs and oatmeal
C cereal and pancakes
D cereal and eggs

11. Which color is the pointer of the spinner **more likely** to land on?

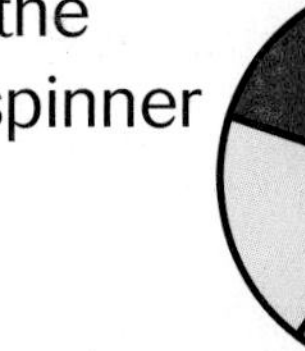

F red
G blue
H green
J yellow

12. Explain It Look at the line plot. Tell how to find the range and the mode.

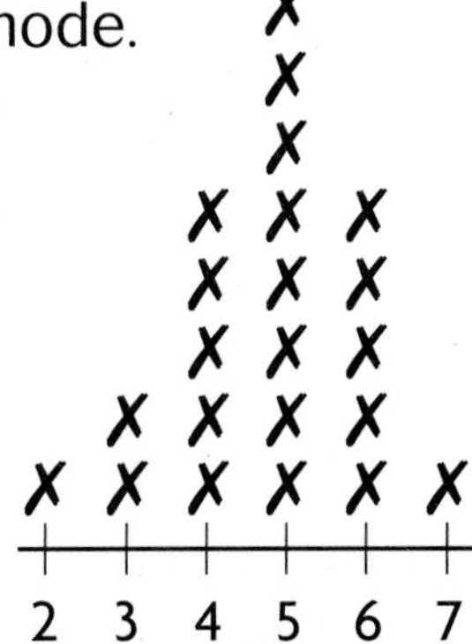

CHAPTER 16 Analyze and Graph Data

FAST FACT • SCIENCE There are about 1,000 giant pandas in the world today. Giant pandas can be 5 feet tall and can weigh more than 300 pounds!

PROBLEM SOLVING Look at the pictograph and make a bar graph of the data.

SMITHSONIAN NATIONAL ZOOLOGICAL PARK	
Giant panda	🐾
Asian elephant	🐾🐾
Gorilla	🐾🐾🐾🐾◖
Leopard gecko	🐾🐾🐾🐾🐾
Green tree python	🐾🐾🐾🐾🐾🐾🐾🐾🐾🐾🐾
Brown pelican	🐾🐾🐾◖

Key: Each 🐾 = 2 animals.

Giant panda eating bamboo

CHECK WHAT YOU KNOW

Use this page to help you review and remember important skills needed for Chapter 16.

USE A TALLY TABLE

For 1–3, use the tally table.

HOW DO YOU GET TO SCHOOL?	
Car	𝍸 ||||
Walk	𝍸 𝍸 𝍸
Bus	𝍸 𝍸 ||
Bike	𝍸 𝍸 |

1. How many children ride in a car to school?
2. How many children ride their bikes?
3. How many children answered the question?

SKIP-COUNT

Find the missing numbers in the pattern.

4. 2, 4, 6, 8, 10, ■, ■, ■
5. 4, 8, 12, 16, 20, ■, ■, ■
6. 45, 40, 35, 30, ■, ■, ■
7. 3, 6, 9, 12, 15, ■, ■, ■

USE SYMBOLS

Use the value of the symbol to find the missing number.

8. If $\Delta = 2$, then

   $\Delta + \Delta + \Delta =$ ■.

9. If $\square = 3$, then

   $\square + \square + \square + \square =$ ■.

10. If ❀ = 4, then

    ❀ + ❀ + ❀ + ❀ + ❀ + ❀ = ■.

11. If ♥ = 5, then

    ♥ + ♥ + ♥ + ♥ + ♥ + ♥ + ♥ = ■.

VOCABULARY POWER

REVIEW

graph [graf] *noun*

Graph comes from the Greek word *graphein*, which means "to write." In a pictograph, what are you writing or drawing to show the data?

PREVIEW

bar graph
scale
horizontal bar graph
vertical bar graph
grid
ordered pair
line graph
trends

www.harcourtschool.com/mathglossary

LESSON 1

Problem Solving Strategy
Make a Graph

PROBLEM The soccer team sold boxes of greeting cards to raise money. Rafael sold 14 boxes, Joselyn sold 7, Phil sold 24, Ken sold 12, and Felicia sold 10. What is one way the sales could be shown in a graph?

Quick Review

1. 4 + 4 + 4 = ■
2. 3 + 3 + 3 + 3 = ■
3. 2 + 2 + 2 + 2 = ■
4. 5 + 5 + 5 = ■
5. 2 + 2 + 2 = ■

UNDERSTAND

- What are you asked to do?

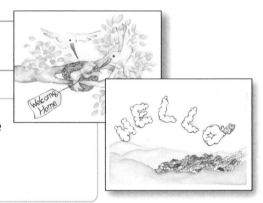

PLAN

- What strategy can you use to solve the problem?

  You can *make a pictograph*.

SOLVE

- How can you show the data in a pictograph?
  a. Choose a **title** that tells about the graph.
  b. Write a **label** for each row.
  c. Look at the numbers. Choose a **key** to tell how many each picture stands for.
  d. Decide how many **pictures** should be placed next to each person's name.

BOXES OF GREETING CARDS SOLD

Rafael	✉✉✉✉✉✉✉
Joselyn	✉✉✉½
Phil	✉✉✉✉✉✉✉✉✉✉✉✉
Ken	✉✉✉✉✉✉
Felicia	✉✉✉✉✉

Key: Each ✉ = 2 boxes.

CHECK

- How can you know if the total number of pictures in your graph is correct?
- Why was a key of 2 used?

Problem Solving Practice

1. **What if** Derek sold 30 boxes of cards, Andy sold 25 boxes, and Kay sold 15 boxes? Make a pictograph to show the information.

2. Barry sold 11 boxes of cards. Using a key of 2, explain how you would show his sales in a pictograph.

Strategies

Draw a Diagram or Picture
Make a Model or Act It Out
Make an Organized List
Find a Pattern
Make a Table or Graph
Predict and Test
Work Backward
Solve a Simpler Problem
Write a Number Sentence
Use Logical Reasoning

Problem Solving

Torrie and Jeremy made pictographs using the data in the table.

3. Torrie used a key of 3. How many symbols should she draw to show the votes for soccer?

   A 2　　**C** 5
   B 3　　**D** 6

4. What key did Jeremy use if he drew $7\frac{1}{2}$ symbols to show the votes for football?

   F key of 1　　**H** key of 3
   G key of 2　　**J** key of 4

FAVORITE SPORTS

Sport	Number of Votes
Soccer	18
Softball	12
Basketball	21
Football	15

Mixed Strategy Practice

5. It was 12:05 P.M. when Liza and Nick began eating lunch. Nick finished in 15 minutes. Liza finished 8 minutes later than Nick. At what time did Liza finish lunch?

6. **FAST FACT** • SCIENCE Panda cubs are born weighing about one-fourth of a pound. There are 16 ounces in one pound. About how many ounces does a newborn panda weigh? Think: 16 ÷ 4 = ?

7. Lloyd spent $3.59, $4.50, and $9.75 for games. He gave the clerk $20.00. How much change should he receive?

8. **REASONING** If December 1 is on a Wednesday, on which day of the week is December 15?

9. Sydney's team scored 89 points, 96 points, 98 points, and 107 points. How many points did the team score in all?

10. **What's the Question?** Marty bought 2 packs of trading cards. He gave the clerk $10. His change was $4. The answer is $3.

LESSON

Bar Graphs

Quick Review

1. 4 × 10 = ■ 2. 7 × 7 = ■
3. 8 × 3 = ■ 4. ■ × 6 = 36
5. 9 × ■ = 81

VOCABULARY

bar graph
scale
horizontal bar graph
vertical bar graph

Learn

SLEEPY ANIMALS A **bar graph** uses bars to show data. A **scale** of numbers helps you read the number each bar shows.

These bar graphs show the same data.

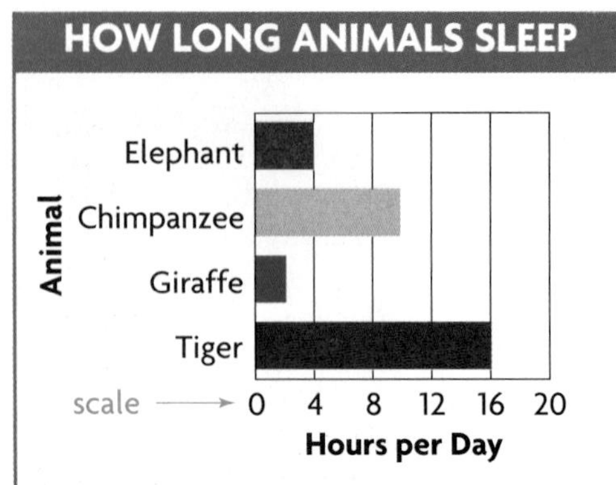

In a **horizontal bar graph**, the bars go across from left to right.

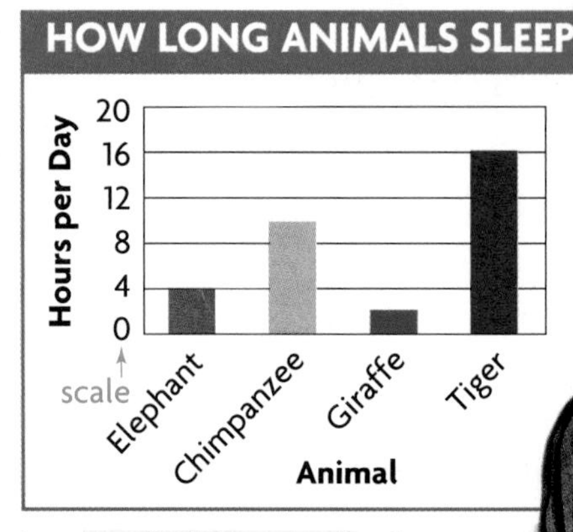

In a **vertical bar graph**, the bars go up from the bottom.

- What scale is used in the bar graphs? Why is this a good scale?
- How do you read the bar for the chimpanzee, which ends halfway between two lines?

Examples

A

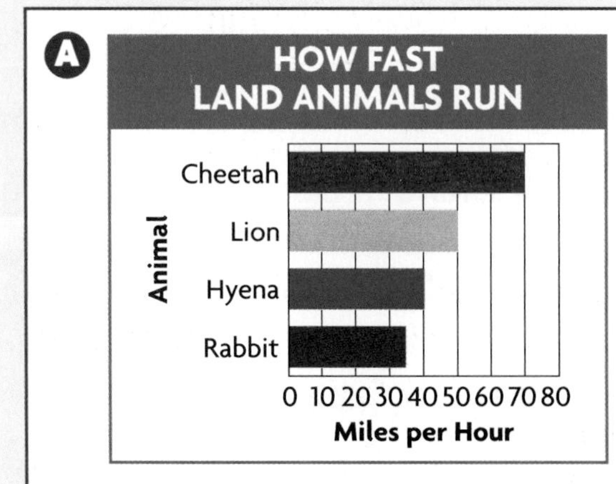

B

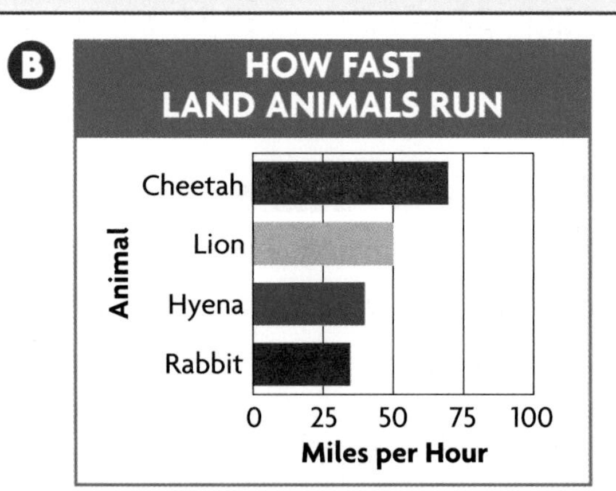

- How are these graphs alike? How are they different?

Check

Technology Link
More Practice:
Harcourt Mega Math
The Number Games,
ArachnaGraph, Level B

1. **Explain** how you would use the graph in Example A to tell how fast a rabbit runs.

For 2–3, use the bar graphs in Examples A and B.

2. How fast can a lion run?
3. How fast can a cheetah run?

Practice and Problem Solving

Extra Practice, page 332, Set A

For 4–6, use the Length of Sea Animals bar graph.

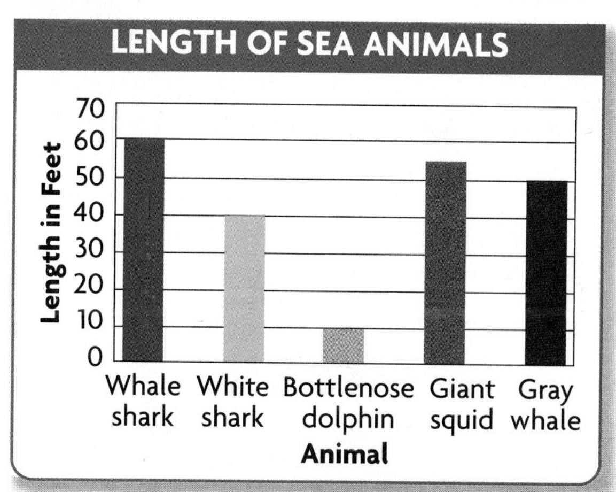

4. Is this a vertical or horizontal bar graph?
5. How long is a giant squid?
6. How much longer is a gray whale than a bottlenose dolphin?

For 7–8, use the Favorite Wild Animals bar graph.

7. Which animal received the most votes?
8. Were there more votes in all for crocodile and lion, or for giraffe and elephant? Explain.
9. **Vocabulary Power** The word *scale* has more than one meaning. What meaning is found in your math book? What is another meaning for *scale*?

Mixed Review and Test Prep

10. $6 \div 2 = ■$ (p. 258)
11. $14 \div 2 = ■$ (p. 258)
12. $30{,}000 + 1{,}000 + 300 + 5 = ■$ (p. 32)
13. Find the product of 7 and 8. (p. 200)
14. **TEST PREP** Meg put 24 counters in 4 equal piles. How many counters are in each pile? (p. 260)

A 4 **C** 7
B 6 **D** 20

LESSON 3

Make Bar Graphs

Quick Review

1. 3×2 **2.** 4×5 **3.** 6×3

4. 8×10 **5.** 7×4

MATERIALS
bar graph pattern, crayons

Explore

You can make a bar graph to show the number of each type of animal at the Oglebay Zoo in West Virginia. Use the data in the table to make a horizontal bar graph.

Oglebay Zoo
Wheeling
WEST VIRGINIA

OGLEBAY ZOO	
Animal	**Number**
Snakes	6
Goats	10
Owls	4
Turtles	3

Activity

STEP 1

Write a title and labels. Decide on the best scale to use, and write the numbers.

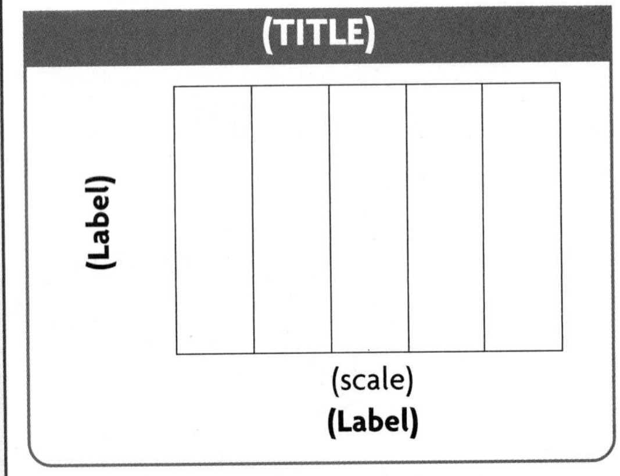

STEP 2

Complete the bar graph. Make the length of each bar equal to the number of each type of animal.

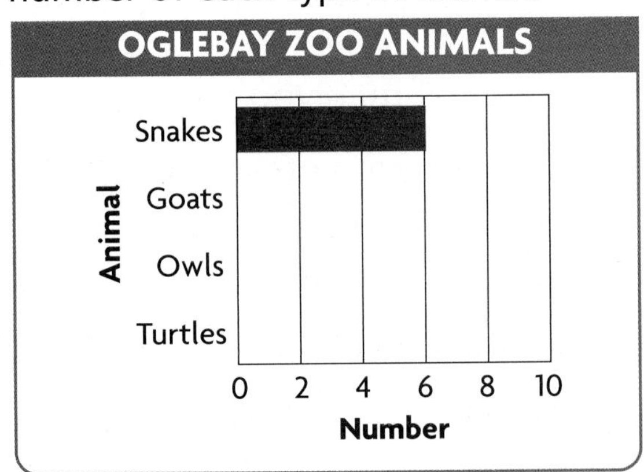

- Name the parts of a bar graph.
- Explain where you would draw the bar for turtles.

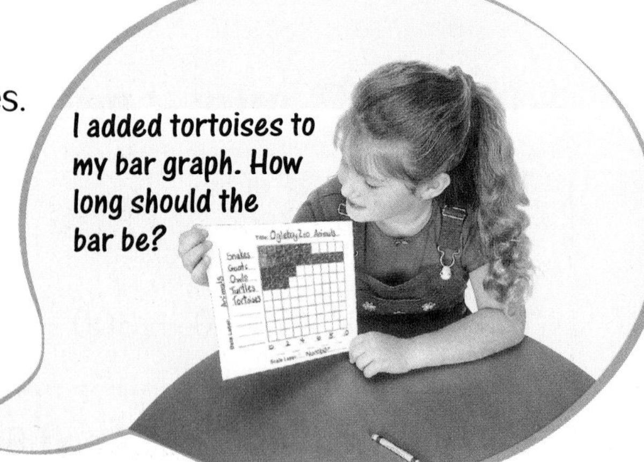

I added tortoises to my bar graph. How long should the bar be?

Try It

Use your bar graph.

a. There are 5 tortoises at the Oglebay Zoo. Make a bar for the tortoises.

b. There are 6 deer at the Oglebay Zoo. Make a bar for the deer.

Connect

You can make a bar graph of data you collect from a survey.

- Take a survey in your classroom. Decide on a question. Give your classmates four possible choices. Record the choices in a table. Make a bar graph of the data in the table.
- How many classmates answered your survey?
- What scale did you use?
- What is the title of your graph?
- What did you find from your survey?

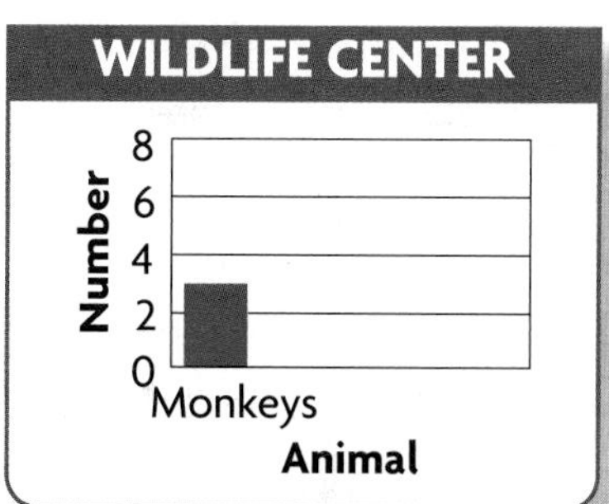

Practice and Problem Solving

1. Copy and complete the Wildlife Center bar graph. Use the data in the table at the right.
2. Why is 2 a good scale to use?

WILDLIFE CENTER	
Animal	**Number**
Monkeys	3
Zebras	8
Polar bears	2

WILDLIFE CENTER

Number: 0, 2, 4, 6, 8

Monkeys

Animal

For 3–5, use the Favorite Pets table.

3. Make a bar graph. Why is 5 a good scale to use?
4. For which pet is the bar the longest?
5. Are there more birds and cats, or more dogs and fish? Explain.

FAVORITE PETS	
Animal	**Number**
Birds	30
Fish	15
Dogs	50
Cats	40

Mixed Review and Test Prep

Write <, >, or = for each ●. (p. 202)

6. 10×3 ● 6×5
7. 5×8 ● 7×6
8. 6×6 ● 5×7
9. 4×9 ● 9×5

10. **TEST PREP** What is the elapsed time from 10:45 A.M. to 1:15 P.M.? (p. 134)

A 2 hr 5 min
B 2 hr 20 min
C 2 hr 30 min
D 2 hr 45 min

LESSON 4

Algebra: Ordered Pairs

Quick Review

1. $28 \div 4 = \blacksquare$
2. $56 \div \blacksquare = 7$
3. $35 \div 5 = \blacksquare$
4. $45 \div 5 = \blacksquare$
5. $30 \div 3 = \blacksquare$

VOCABULARY

grid

ordered pair

Learn

GET TO THE POINT Jack is using a map to help him find different animal areas at the zoo. He wants to see the elephants first. How can this map help Jack find the elephants?

The horizontal and vertical lines on the map make a **grid**.

ZOO GRID

N

W E

S

0 1 2 3 4 5 6 7

Start at 0. Move 2 spaces to the right. Then move 3 spaces up. The elephants are located at (2,3).

(2,3)

The first number tells how many spaces to move to the right.

The second number tells how many spaces to move up.

MATH IDEA An **ordered pair** of numbers within parentheses, like (2,3), names a point on a grid.

Example

Which animal is found at (5,4) on the grid?

Start at 0.

Move 5 spaces to the right.

Then move 4 spaces up.

So, the monkey is found at (5,4).

- Suppose a butterfly is at (6,5). Tell how you locate that point on the grid.

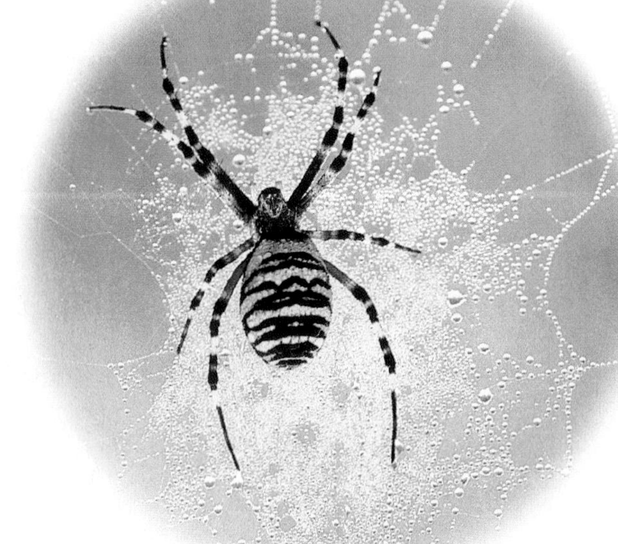

Wasp spider ▲

Check

1. **Explain** how you would locate (11,12) on a grid.
2. Does (4,3) show the same point on a grid as (3,4)? Explain.

For 3–5, use the zoo grid on page 328. Write the ordered pair for each animal.

3. tiger
4. bear
5. giraffe

▲ Emerald tree boa

Practice and Problem Solving

Extra Practice, page 332, Set B

For 6–11 and 18, use the zoo grid on page 328. Write the ordered pair for each animal.

6. bird
7. snake
8. zebra
9. mouse
10. deer
11. alligator

For 12–17, copy the grid. Locate each ordered pair. Draw a point. Label it with the letter.

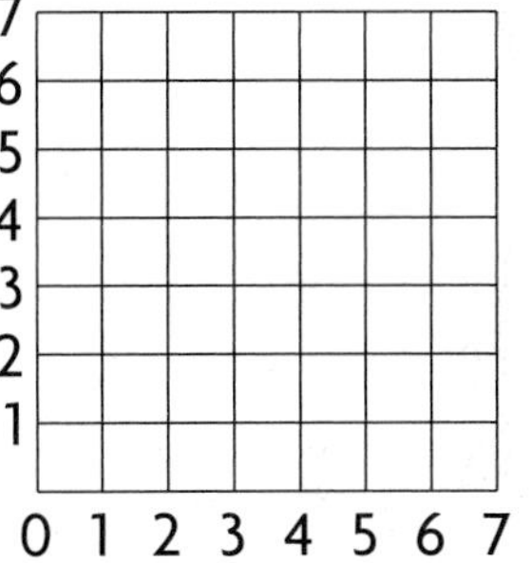

12. (6,3) **A**
13. (1,3) **B**
14. (4,4) **C**
15. (2,6) **D**
16. (7,1) **E**
17. (3,2) **F**

18. **REASONING** Rachel saw the zebra at (2,1) on the zoo grid. Mary saw the elephant at (2,3). What ordered pair names the point between the zebra and the elephant?

19. **? What's the Error?** Jerry said, "To find the point (2,3), start at 0, move 2 spaces up and 3 spaces to the right." What error did Jerry make?

20. Walt has 45 pennies. Arthur has 11 nickels. Which boy has more money? How much more does he have?

Mixed Review and Test Prep

21. $5 \times 9 = \blacksquare$ (p. 160)
22. $7 \times 6 = \blacksquare$ (p. 200)
23. $6 \times 8 = \blacksquare$ (p. 194)
24. $4 \times 7 = \blacksquare$ (p. 178)

25. **TEST PREP** Find the difference between 567 and 288. (p. 96)
    - **A** 279
    - **B** 289
    - **C** 379
    - **D** 855

LESSON 5

Line Graphs

Quick Review

1. $5 \times ■ = 0$
2. $■ \times 9 = 63$
3. $30 = ■ \times 6$
4. $9 \times 4 = ■$
5. $7 \times ■ = 7$

VOCABULARY
line graph
trends

Learn

LINE UP A **line graph** uses a line to show how data change over time. What was the normal, or average, temperature in Des Moines, Iowa, in March?

A line graph is like a grid.

a. From 0, find the vertical line for March. Move up to the point.

b. Follow the horizontal line left to the scale.

c. The point for March is at 40 degrees.

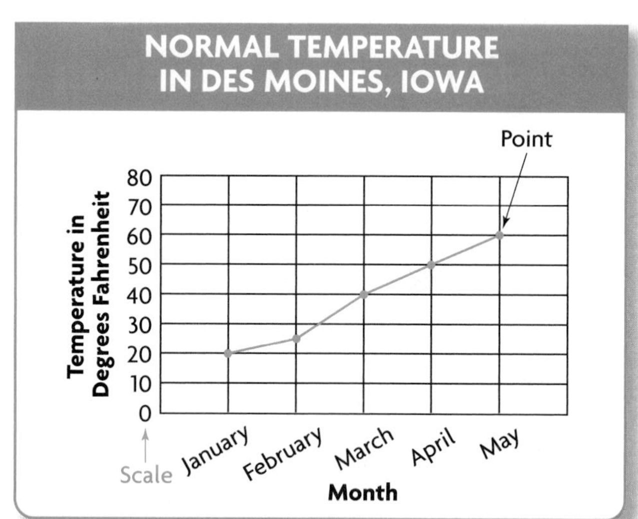

So, the normal temperature in Des Moines in March is 40 degrees.

In a line graph, you can see **trends**, or areas where data increase, decrease, or stay the same over time.

- Describe a trend you see in the line graph.

Technology Link
More Practice: Harcourt Mega Math The Number Games, *ArachnaGraph*, Level I

Check

1. **Explain** how the line graph would look if the normal temperature in Des Moines was getting colder each month.

For 2–3, use the line graph above.

2. What is the normal temperature in January?
3. In what month is the normal temperature 60 degrees?

Practice and Problem Solving

Extra Practice, page 332, Set C

For 4–7, use the Alaska line graph.

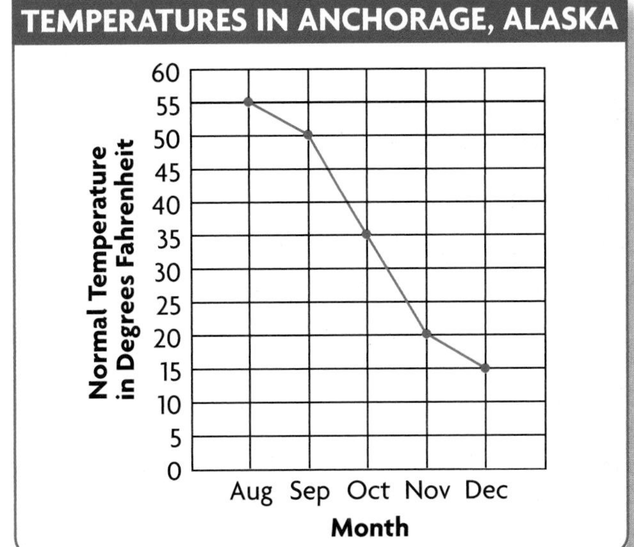

4. What is the normal temperature in December?
5. In what month is the normal temperature 50 degrees?
6. How many degrees higher is the normal temperature in August than in November?
7. Describe a trend you see in the line graph.

For 8–10, use the Pencils line graph.

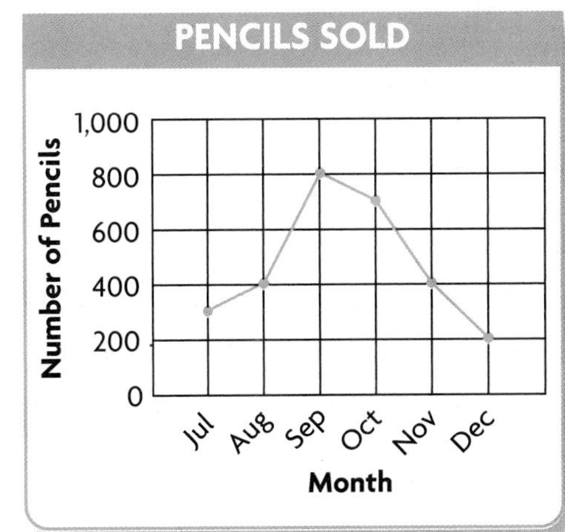

8. In what month were the most pencils sold? the fewest?
9. In which months were more than 400 pencils sold?
10. In which two months were the same number of pencils sold? How many pencils?
11. **Write About It** Why do you think more pencils are sold in September?

12. Sachio decorated 17 cookies and Linda decorated 12 cookies. They gave 20 cookies to their neighbors. How many cookies are left?

13. The total cost of a watch and a calculator is $50. The watch costs $20 more than the calculator. Find the cost of the calculator.

Mixed Review and Test Prep

Find the quotient.

14. $3\overline{)12}$ (p. 260)
15. $4\overline{)24}$ (p. 260)
16. $5\overline{)15}$ (p. 258)
17. $2\overline{)18}$ (p. 258)

18. **TEST PREP** In a multiplication sentence, the product is 56. One factor is 8. What is the other factor? (p. 186)

A 6 B 7 C 8 D 9

Extra Practice

Set A (pp. 324–325)

For 1–5, use the bar graph.

1. What scale is used?
2. How many moths are there?
3. What is the total number of Dr. Cooper's insects?
4. How many more butterflies are there than beetles?
5. How many fewer bees than moths are there?

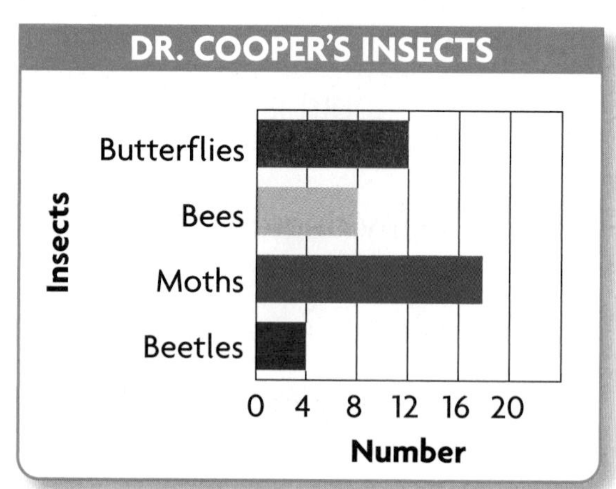

Set B (pp. 328–329)

For 1–10, copy the grid. Locate each ordered pair. Draw a point. Label it with the letter.

1. (3,1) A
2. (6,3) B
3. (5,2) C
4. (1,3) D
5. (4,4) E
6. (2,4) F
7. (7,4) G
8. (6,5) H
9. (8,3) I
10. (5,6) J

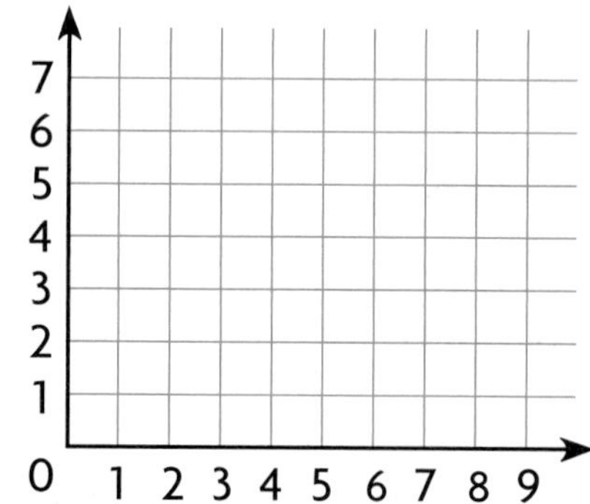

Set C (pp. 330–331)

For 1–3, use the line graph.

1. In what month did Anita's Inn have the most guests? In what month were there the fewest guests?
2. How many guests stayed at Anita's Inn from January through June?
3. What trend do you see in the number of guests from February to April?

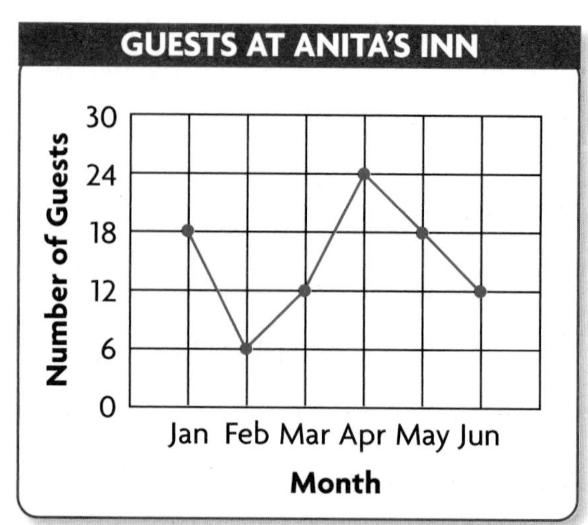

Review/Test

CHECK VOCABULARY AND CONCEPTS

For 1–3, choose the best term from the box.

bar graph line graph grid trends

1. A graph that uses bars to show data is a __?__. (p. 324)
2. The horizontal and vertical lines on a map make a __?__. (p. 328)
3. A graph that shows change over time is a __?__. (p. 330)
4. How would you find (4,5) on a grid? (p. 328)

For 5–7, choose the letter that names each. (pp. 322–325; 330–331)

A. bar graph **B.** pictograph **C.** line plot **D.** line graph

5.

STUDENTS' PETS

Dog
Cat
Fish
Bird

Key: Each = 2 pets.

6.

FAVORITE SPORT

Baseball
Soccer
Basketball
Football

Sport

0 2 4 6 8 10

Number of Students

7.

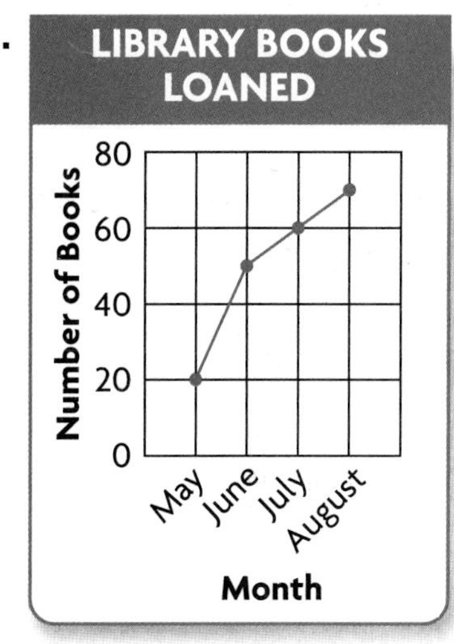

CHECK SKILLS

For 8–9, use the bar graph above. (pp. 324–325)

8. What scale is used on this graph?
9. How many students chose soccer?

For 10–11, use the line graph above. (pp. 330–331)

10. In what month were the fewest books loaned?
11. How many books were loaned from June through August?

CHECK PROBLEM SOLVING

For 12–15, use the pictograph above. (pp. 322–323)

12. What key is used on this graph?
13. How many pets does a ◖ equal?
14. How many more dogs than cats do the students have?
15. How many pets do the students have in all?

Standardized Test Prep

NUMBER SENSE, CONCEPTS, AND OPERATIONS

1. Maura buys a pen for $1.89 and a card for $1.99. She pays with a $5 bill. How much change does she receive?

A $3.88 **C** $1.22
B $2.12 **D** $1.12

2. Connie separates 24 marbles into 4 equal groups. Which shows Connie's groups?

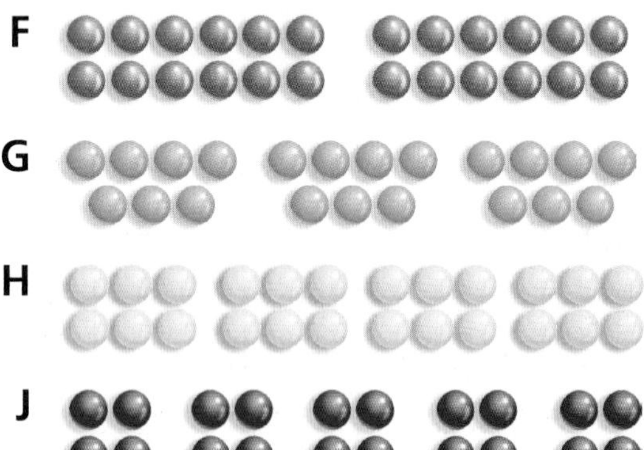

3. A group of students will travel to the aquarium in 3 vans. Each van holds 9 students. How many students can be taken to the aquarium?

A 12 **C** 27
B 18 **D** 36

4. **Explain It** Taro collected 378 stamps. He has 119 stamps from the United States. About how many stamps in Taro's collection are NOT from the United States? Explain your answer.

MEASUREMENT

5. Jake has a trumpet lesson at 1:15 P.M. The lesson lasts 1 hour. At what time will Jake be finished with his lesson?

F 12:15 P.M.
G 1:30 P.M.
H 1:45 P.M.
J 2:15 P.M.

6. The clock shows the time when soccer practice ends. At what time does practice end?

A 6:30
B 6:25
C 5:30
D 5:15

7. **Explain It** The table shows the bills and coins in Cory's bank. Estimate to the nearest dollar how much money Cory has. Explain your estimate.

CORY'S BILLS AND COINS	
Type	**Number**
$1 Bills	2
Half dollars	3
Quarters	5
Dimes	0
Nickels	3
Pennies	0

ALGEBRAIC THINKING

8. Emily wrote this number pattern. What number is missing?

8, 16, 24, ■, 40

F 28 **H** 32
G 30 **J** 36

9. There are 4 chairs at each table in the diner. If there are 32 chairs, what number sentence can you use to find the number of tables?

A $4 + 8 = 12$ **C** $32 + 4 = 36$
B $32 - 4 = 28$ **D** $32 \div 4 = 8$

TIP **Eliminate choices.** See item 10. Since the difference between the numbers is 7, you can eliminate answer choices where the difference is greater than or less than 7.

10. The first four houses on Joan's block are numbered 11, 18, 25, and 32. What are the numbers on the next two houses?

F 46 and 53 **H** 41 and 45
G 43 and 54 **J** 39 and 46

11. Explain It Mandy jogged on Sunday, Tuesday, Thursday, and Saturday. Predict what day Mandy will jog next. Explain your answer.

April						
Sun	Mon	Tue	Wed	Thu	Fri	Sat
	1	2	3	4	5	6
7	8	9	10	11	12	13
14	15	16	17	18	19	20
21	22	23	24	25	26	27
28	29	30				

DATA ANALYSIS AND PROBABILITY

12. Brad made this bar graph of his friends' favorite rides.

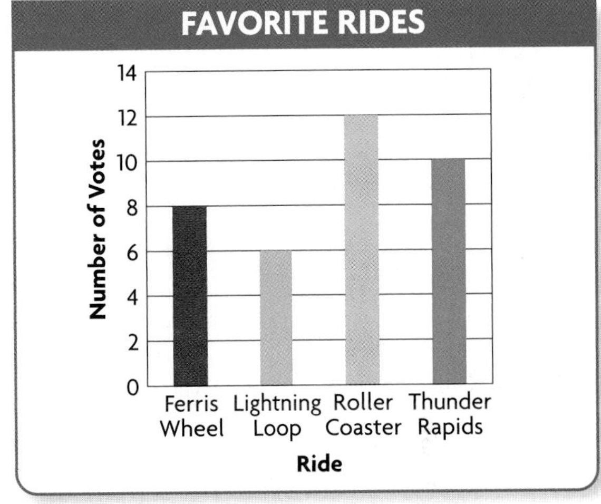

What scale did Brad use?

A scale of 8 **C** scale of 4
B scale of 6 **D** scale of 2

13. Explain It The line graph shows the number of loggerhead turtle nests counted on the dates shown.

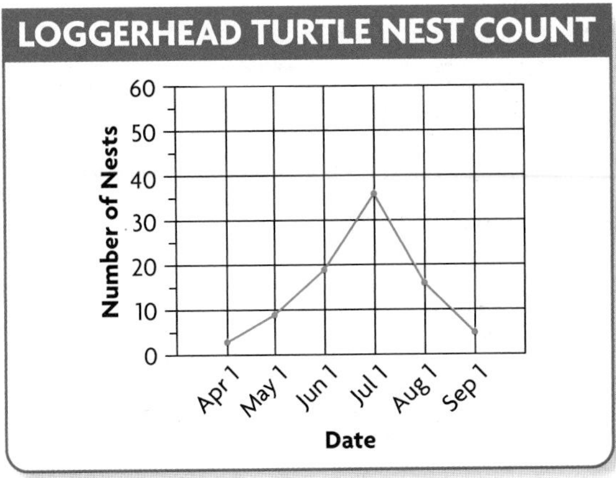

What do you notice about the number of nests counted between April 1 and September 1? On what date would you expect to find the **most** nests next year? Explain.

17 Customary Units

FAST FACT • SCIENCE The Saturn V rocket that took astronauts to the moon was made at the Marshall Space Flight Center in Huntsville, Alabama. This rocket had more than 3 million parts!

PROBLEM SOLVING Look at the graph. How much greater was the length of the Saturn V rocket than the length of the space shuttle?

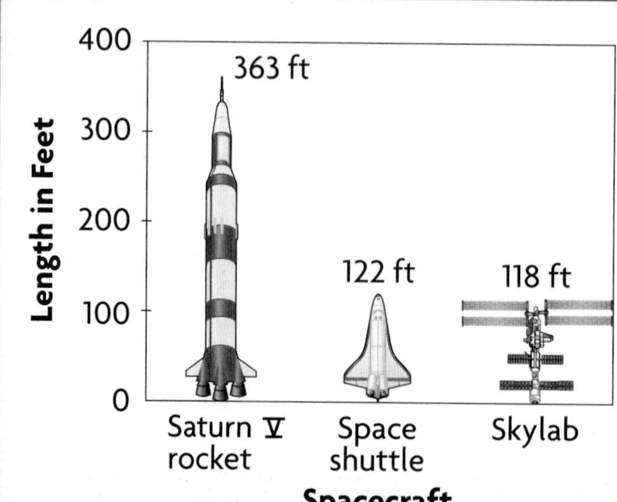

CHECK WHAT YOU KNOW

Use this page to help you review and remember important skills needed for Chapter 17.

MEASURE TO THE NEAREST INCH

Write the length to the nearest inch.

1. 

2. 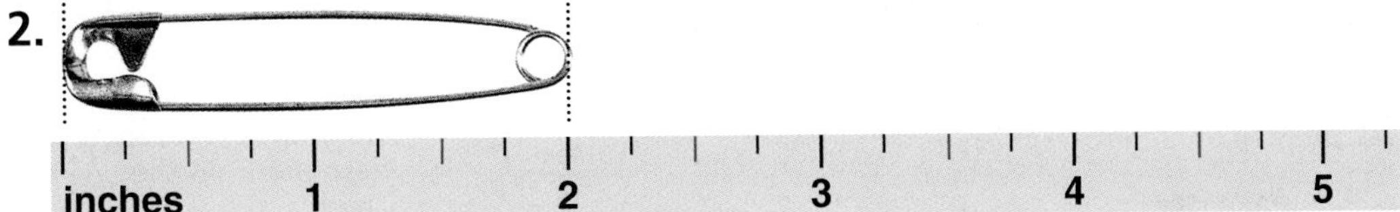

FIND A RULE

Write a rule for the table. Then copy and complete the table.

3.

gloves	1	2	3	4	5	6
fingers	5	10	15	■	■	■

4.

rings	1	2	3	4	5	6
cost	\$3	\$6	\$9	■	■	■

5.

butterflies	1	5	3	4	7	9
wings	2	10	6	■	■	■

6.

packs	3	2	7	5	1	8
crackers	21	14	49	■	■	■

VOCABULARY POWER

REVIEW

inch [inch] *noun*

When used as a noun, an *inch* is a customary unit used to measure length. When used as a verb, *inch* means "to move by small amounts" or "to move slowly." Write one sentence using *inch* as a noun and one sentence using *inch* as a verb.

PREVIEW

foot (ft)
yard (yd)
mile (mi)
capacity
cup (c)
pint (pt)
quart (qt)
gallon (gal)
ounce (oz)
pound (lb)

www.harcourtschool.com/mathglossary

Length

Quick Review

1. $7 \times ■ = 42$
2. $■ \times 5 = 45$
3. $■ \times 8 = 32$
4. $6 \times ■ = 48$
5. $9 \times ■ = 63$

Learn

HOW LONG? An estimate is an answer that is close to the actual answer. You can estimate length by using an item close to 1 inch, like a small paper clip or your knuckle.

Activity

MATERIALS: small paper clips, ruler

STEP 1

Copy the table.

LENGTHS OF RIBBONS		
Color	**Estimate**	**Measure**
green	about 1 inch	1 inch
blue		
yellow		
orange		
red		

STEP 2

Use paper clips to estimate the length of the blue ribbon. Record your estimate in your table.

STEP 3

Use a ruler. Measure the length of the blue ribbon to the nearest inch. Record your measurement in your table.

STEP 4

Repeat Steps 2 and 3 for the yellow, orange, and red ribbons.

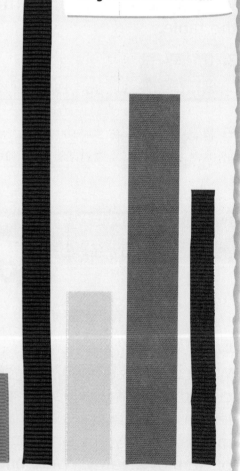

Remember

To use a ruler:

- line up one end of the object with the zero mark on the ruler.
- find the inch mark closest to the object's other end.

The ribbon is 2 inches long to the nearest inch.

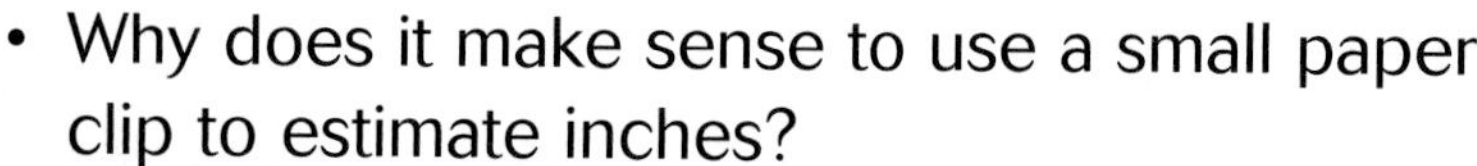

- Why does it make sense to use a small paper clip to estimate inches?

Measuring to the Nearest Half Inch

You can also measure to the nearest half inch.

Example

What is the length of this crayon to the nearest half inch?

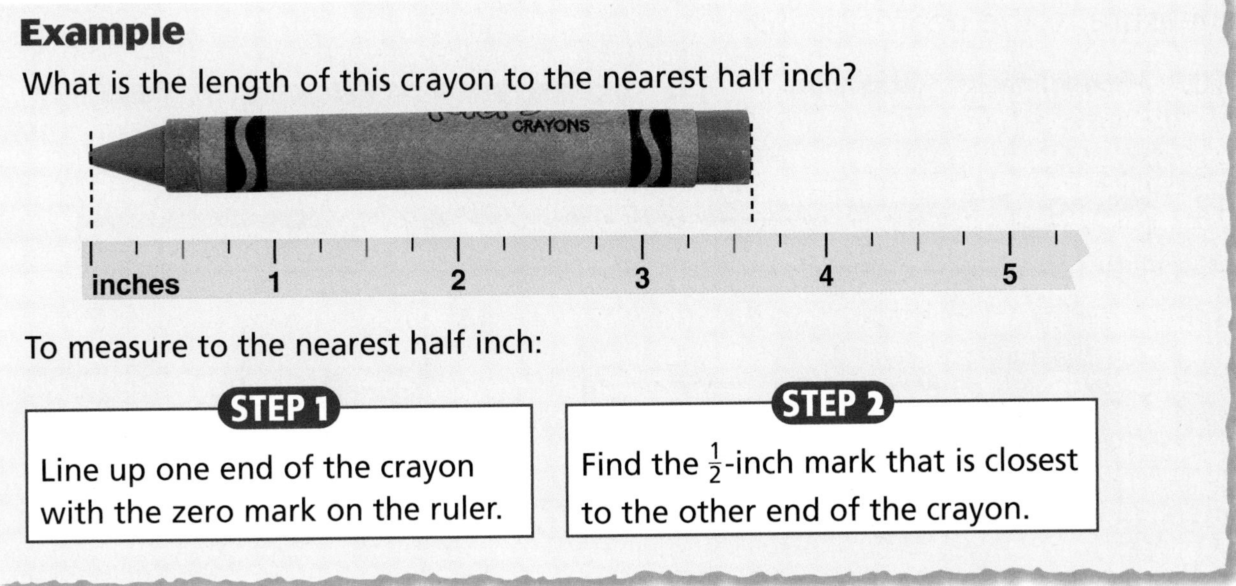

To measure to the nearest half inch:

STEP 1

Line up one end of the crayon with the zero mark on the ruler.

STEP 2

Find the $\frac{1}{2}$-inch mark that is closest to the other end of the crayon.

So, the length of the crayon to the nearest half inch is $3\frac{1}{2}$ inches.

1. **Describe** where you find $\frac{1}{2}$-inch marks on a ruler.

Estimate the length in inches. Then use a ruler to measure to the nearest inch.

Measure the length to the nearest half inch.

LESSON CONTINUES

Practice and Problem Solving

Extra Practice, page 352, Set A

Estimate the length in inches. Then use a ruler to measure to the nearest inch.

10.

11.

12.

13.

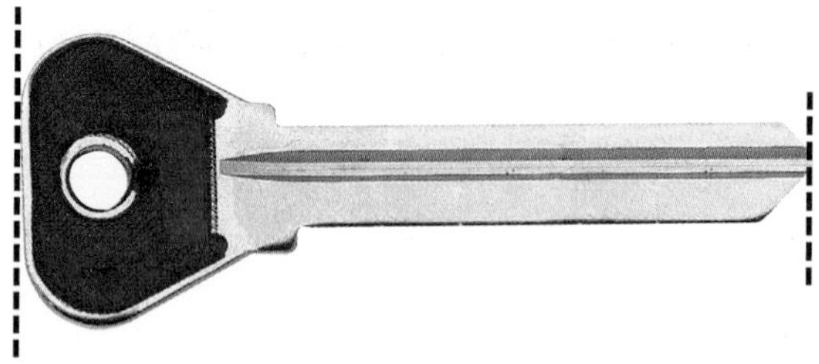

14.

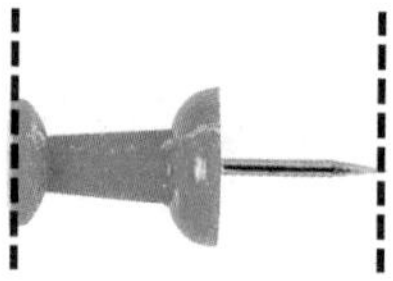

Measure the length to the nearest half inch.

15.

16.

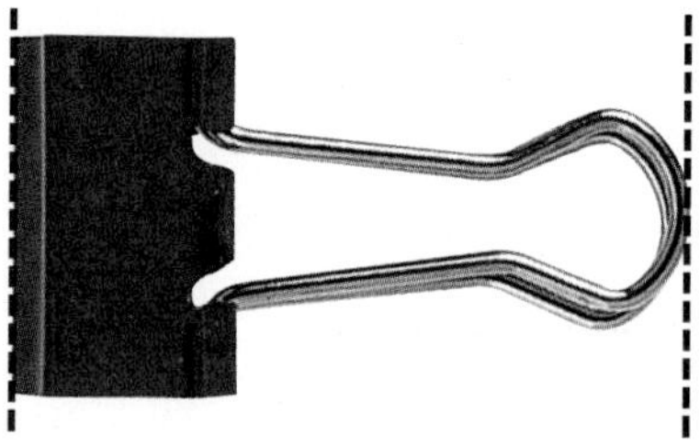

17.

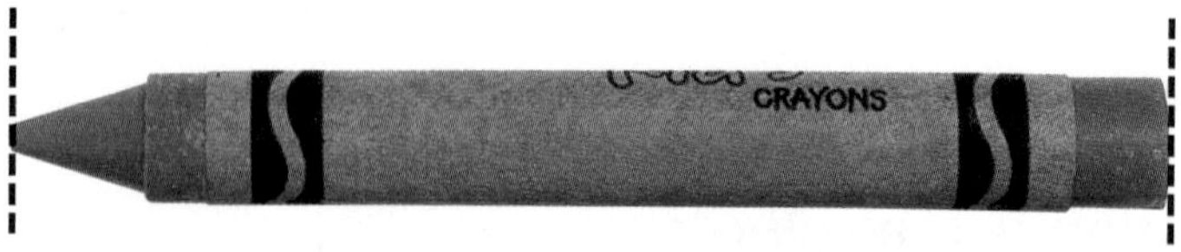

CRAYONS

18.

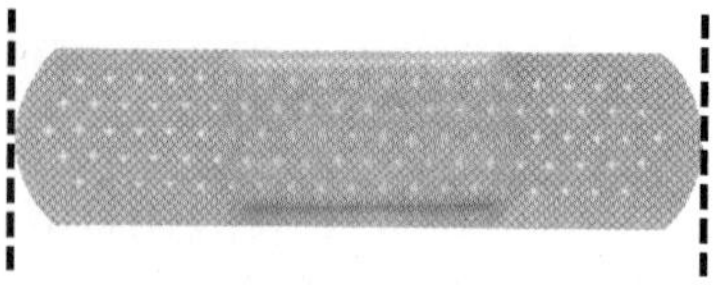

19.

MARKER

Use a ruler. Draw a line for each length.

20. 1 inch

21. $2\frac{1}{2}$ inches

22. 4 inches

23. $5\frac{1}{2}$ inches

24. ***FAST FACT*** • SCIENCE The ruby-throated hummingbird is about 4 inches long. The brown pelican is about 40 inches long. The pelican is about how many times as long as the hummingbird?

25. Vocabulary Power The word *rule* comes from the Latin word *regula*, which means "straight stick." What math word is related to *rule* and could be described as a straight stick?

26. Measure the classroom door from side to side to the nearest inch. Then measure a door at home in the same way. Which door has the greater measure?

27. Joyce used 72 beads to make 9 necklaces with an equal number of beads on each. How many beads were on 2 necklaces?

28. A brush measures $6\frac{1}{2}$ inches. Between which two inch marks does the end of the brush lie? Explain.

29. Find two different-sized books. Measure the length of each cover to the nearest half inch. Use < or > to compare the measurements.

30. Suppose you need at least 5 inches of yarn for an art project. Is this blue piece of yarn long enough? Explain.

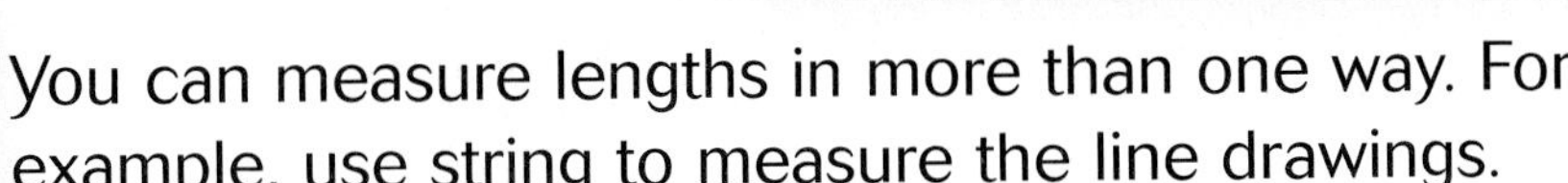

Mixed Review and Test Prep

31. Write the following numbers in order from greatest to least. (p. 46)
579, 572, 597

32. TEST PREP Noah had 8 rows of 6 toy cars. He gave 5 cars to his brother. How many cars does Noah have left? (p. 222)
A 58 B 53 C 43 D 19

33. $3 \times 1 \times 4 = \blacksquare$ (p. 218)

34. $5 \times 2 \times 4 = \blacksquare$ (p. 218)

35. TEST PREP The movie begins at 11:15 A.M. It is 2 hours and 10 minutes long. At what time will it end? (p. 134)
F 11:25 A.M. H 1:15 P.M.
G 12:25 P.M. J 1:25 P.M.

Problem Solving Thinker's Corner

You can measure lengths in more than one way. For example, use string to measure the line drawings.

MATERIALS: 2 pieces of string, each 1 ft long
2 different-colored markers

a. Start with one end of string on one end of line drawing A. Cover the line drawing with the string.

b. Make a mark on the string for the end of the line drawing.

c. Repeat for line drawing B.

1. Which line drawing has the greater length?

2. Measure the lengths marked on the pieces of string. Record the measurements.

LESSON

Inch, Foot, Yard, and Mile

Learn

CHOOSING UNITS You know that an inch (in.) is used to measure length and distance. Other customary units used to measure length and distance are the **foot (ft)**, **yard (yd)**, and **mile (mi)**.

Quick Review

1. 41 + 52
2. 38 + 39
3. 12 + 34
4. 27 + 63
5. 12 + 12 + 12

VOCABULARY
foot (ft)
yard (yd)
mile (mi)

Examples

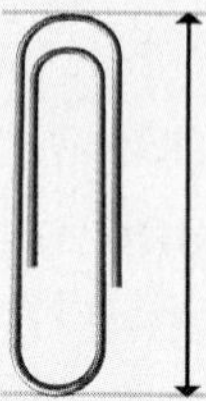

A paper clip is about 1 inch long.

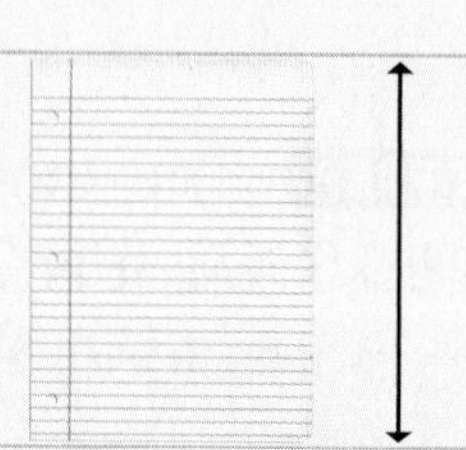

A sheet of notebook paper is about 1 foot long.

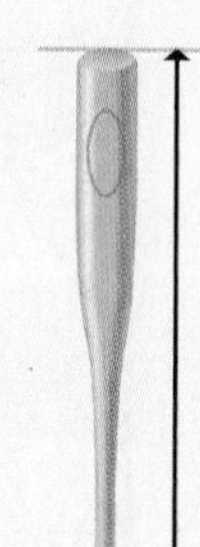

A baseball bat is about 1 yard long.

You can walk 1 mile in about 20 minutes.

TABLE OF MEASURES
1 foot = 12 inches
1 yard = 3 feet = 36 inches
1 mile = 5,280 feet

- Explain which unit you would use to measure the length of your hand.

Check

1. **Build** a 1-foot "ruler" using 1-inch square tiles. Use it to measure one side of a sheet of paper.

Choose the unit you would use to measure each. Write *inch, foot, yard,* or *mile*.

2. the length of a pencil
3. the length of a car
4. the length of a parking lot
5. the distance a train goes in 30 minutes

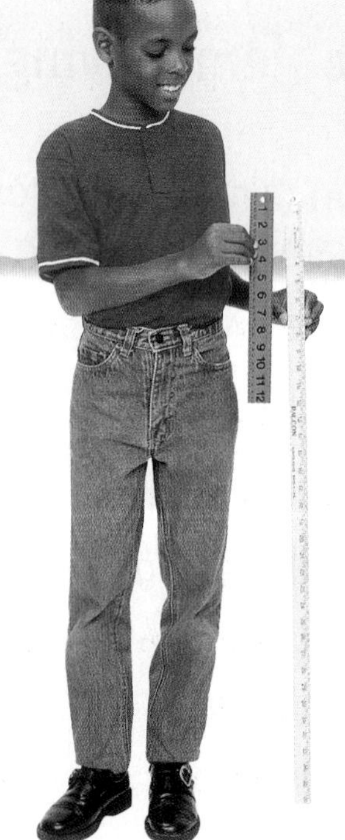

A yardstick is 3 times as long as a 1-foot ruler.

Practice and Problem Solving

Extra Practice, page 352, Set B

Choose the unit you would use to measure each. Write *inch, foot, yard*, or *mile*.

6. the height of a refrigerator
7. the length of your shoe
8. the length of the cafeteria
9. the distance between two cities

Choose the best unit of measure. Write *inches, foot* or *feet, yards*, or *miles*.

10. Sal rides the bus 3 _?_ to school.
11. A football is about 1 _?_ long.
12. The distance between the floor and the doorknob is about 3 _?_ .
13. Sarah's math book is 11 _?_ long.
14. Cut a sheet of 1-inch grid paper into 6-inch strips. Use the strips and tape to make a 1-foot strip and a 1-yard strip. How many strips were needed for each?
15. Mitchell got 5 stickers from each of 6 friends. He bought 13 more stickers. How many stickers does Mitchell have in all?

16. Angie thinks this grasshopper is about 4 inches long. Do you agree with her estimate? Measure to check and record the length.
17. **Write About It** Estimate the distance from your desk to the classroom door in feet and in yards. Then measure the distance. Record your estimates and the actual measurement.

Mixed Review and Test Prep

For 18–21, use the graph. (p. 324)

18. How many votes are for red?
19. Which color has the most votes?
20. What is the total number of votes?
21. What kind of graph is this?

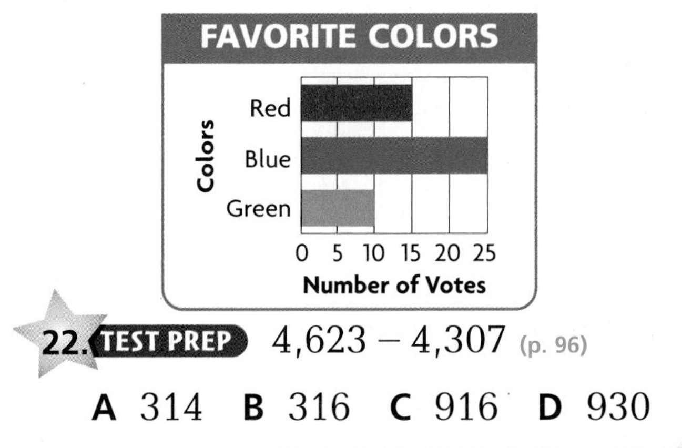

22. **TEST PREP** 4,623 − 4,307 (p. 96)

A 314 **B** 316 **C** 916 **D** 930

LESSON 3

Capacity

Quick Review

1. $2\overline{)8}$
2. $4\overline{)16}$
3. $4\overline{)8}$
4. $4\overline{)32}$
5. $2\overline{)16}$

VOCABULARY
capacity
cup (c)
pint (pt)
quart (qt)
gallon (gal)

MATERIALS
cup, pint, quart, and gallon containers; water, rice, or beans

Explore

Capacity is the amount a container can hold. **Cup (c)**, **pint (pt)**, **quart (qt)**, and **gallon (gal)** are customary units for measuring capacity.

cup (c)

pint (pt)

quart (qt)

gallon (gal)

Activity

Copy the table to help find how many cups are in a pint, a quart, and a gallon.

NUMBER OF CUPS		
	Estimate	Measure
Cups in a pint?		
Cups in a quart?		
Cups in a gallon?		

STEP 1
Estimate the number of cups it will take to fill the pint container. Record your estimate.

STEP 2
Fill a cup and pour it into the pint container. Repeat until the pint container is full.

STEP 3
Record the actual number of cups it took to fill the pint container.

STEP 4
Repeat Steps 1–3 for the quart and the gallon containers.

We are using pints to fill a quart. How many pints will it take?
ONE PINT
ONE QUART

Try It

a. How many pints does it take to fill a quart?

b. How many pints does it take to fill a gallon?

Connect

How are cups, pints, quarts, and gallons related?

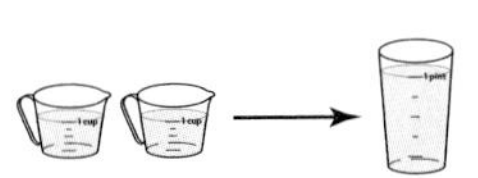

2 cups in 1 pint

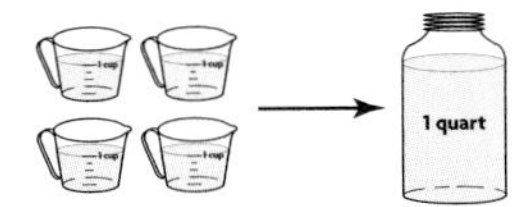

4 cups in 1 quart

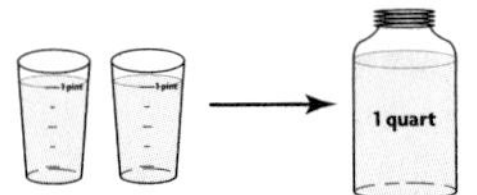

2 pints in 1 quart

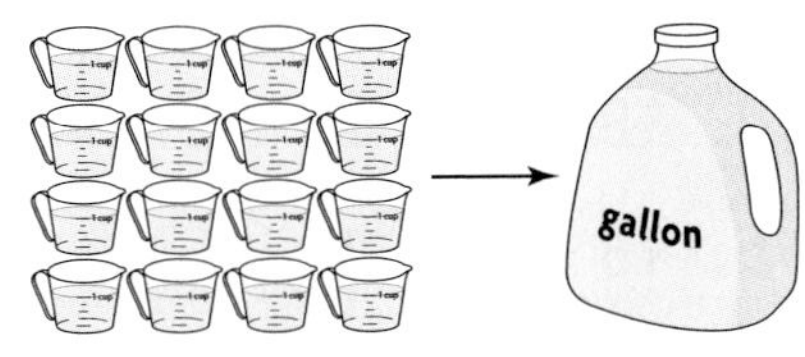

16 cups in 1 gallon

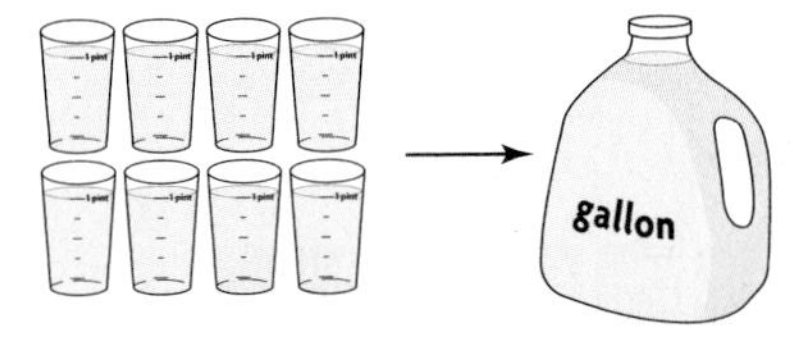

8 pints in 1 gallon

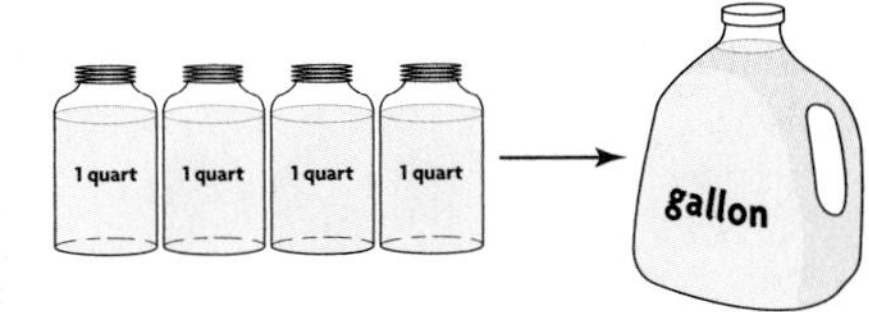

4 quarts in 1 gallon

Practice and Problem Solving

Choose the better estimate.

1. 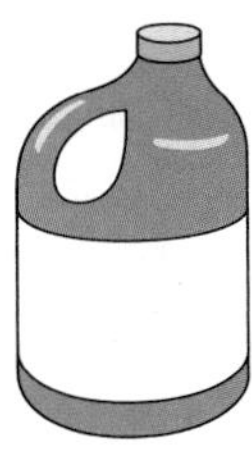

1 cup or
1 gallon?

2. 

3 cups or
3 quarts?

3. 

2 cups or
2 quarts?

4.

30 pints or
30 gallons?

Compare. Write <, >, or = for each ●.

5. 1 cup ● 3 pints **6.** 1 gallon ● 3 quarts **7.** 4 pints ● 1 quart

8. Alan had 6 boxes of cookies. Each box had 8 cookies. He sold 2 boxes. How many cookies does he have left?

9. Write these units of capacity in order from least to greatest: *pint, cup, gallon, quart.*

Mixed Review and Test Prep

Multiply. (p. 194)

10. $6 \times 5 = \blacksquare$ **11.** $6 \times 9 = \blacksquare$

Divide. (p. 274)

12. $56 \div 7 = \blacksquare$ **13.** $49 \div 7 = \blacksquare$

14. **TEST PREP** Donato gave away 23 marbles. He bought 16 more. Then he had 361 marbles. How many marbles did he have to begin with? (p. 222)

A 368 **B** 345 **C** 322 **D** 300

LESSON 4

Weight

Explore

An **ounce (oz)** and a **pound (lb)** are customary units for measuring weight.

9 pennies weigh about 1 ounce.

144 pennies weigh about 1 pound.

You can estimate and then weigh objects to decide if they weigh about 1 ounce or about 1 pound.

Quick Review

Compare. Use <, >, or = for each ●.

1. 16 ÷ 8 ● 2 × 2
2. 10 ● 24 ÷ 3
3. 81 ÷ 9 ● 9
4. 18 ÷ 3 ● 10 ÷ 2
5. 13 ● 3 × 4

VOCABULARY
ounce (oz) **pound (lb)**

MATERIALS
simple balance, pennies, scale

Activity

STEP 1
Place 9 pennies on one side of a balance to show 1 ounce. Find two objects that you think weigh about 1 ounce each. Weigh them to check.

STEP 2
Record what your objects are and whether they weigh more than, less than, or the same as 1 ounce.

STEP 3
Place 144 pennies on one side of the balance to show 1 pound. Find two objects that you think weigh about 1 pound each. Weigh them to check.

STEP 4
Record what your objects are and whether they weigh more than, less than, or the same as 1 pound.

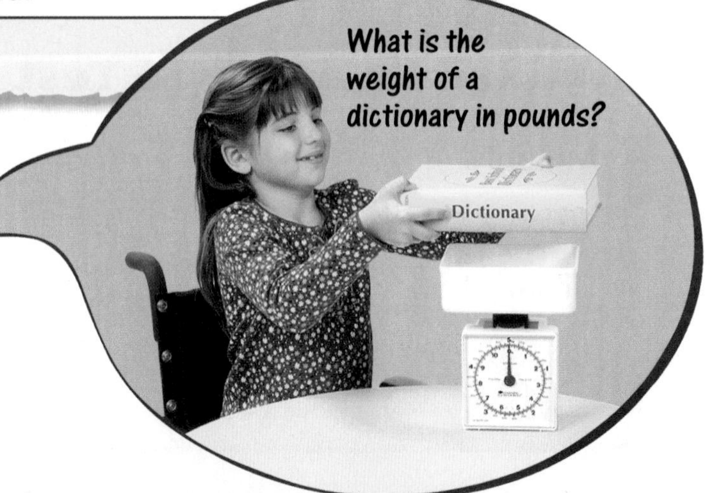

What is the weight of a dictionary in pounds?
Dictionary

Try It

Estimate the weight of each object in pounds. Then use a scale to measure to the nearest pound.

a. dictionary **b.** shoe
c. bottle of water **d.** stapler

Connect

How are pounds and ounces related?

 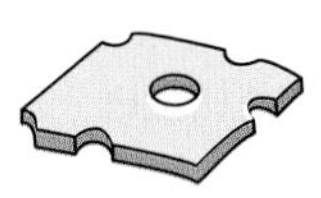 

These things each weigh about 1 ounce.

A loaf of bread weighs about 1 pound.

16 ounces = 1 pound

Practice and Problem Solving

Choose the unit you would use to weigh each. Write *ounce* or *pound*.

1. 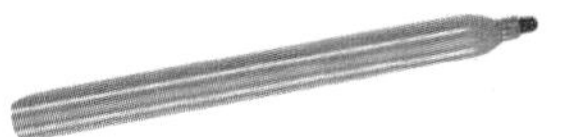

2. 

3. 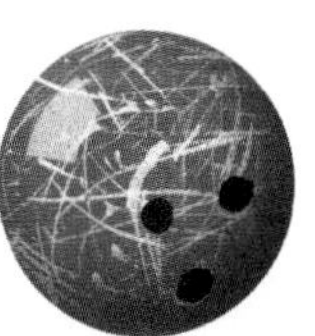

4. 

Choose the better estimate.

5. 
1 ounce or 1 pound?

6. 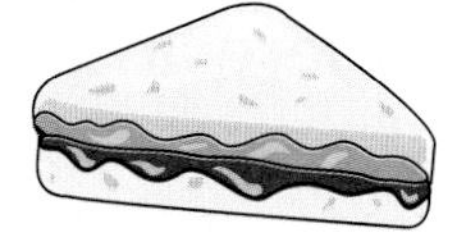
3 ounces or 3 pounds?

7. 

2 ounces or 2 pounds?

8. 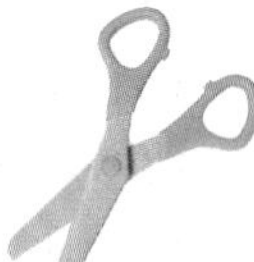
2 ounces or 2 pounds?

Choose the better unit of measure. Write *ounces* or *pounds*.

9. A chair weighs about 12 _?_.

10. A plate weighs about 12 _?_.

11. **REASONING** Bill has 24 cookies divided equally into 6 bags. How many cookies are in 3 bags?

12. **Write a problem** about items from your home. Use pounds and ounces in your problem.

Mixed Review and Test Prep

13. $1 \times 5 \times 7 = \blacksquare$ (p. 218)

14. $3 \times 2 \times 8 = \blacksquare$ (p. 218)

15. $2 \times 3 \times 3 = \blacksquare$ (p. 218)

16. $12 + 16 + 8 = \blacksquare$ (p. 8)

17. **TEST PREP** Find the difference. (p. 92)

$$\begin{array}{r} 500 \\ -362 \\ \hline \end{array}$$

A 132 **B** 138 **C** 148 **D** 238

LESSON 5

Ways to Change Units

Quick Review

Choose the smaller unit of measure in each.

1. pound, ounce
2. cup, pint
3. quart, cup
4. yard, foot
5. pint, quart

Learn

CHANGE IT The students in Mrs. Lopez's class need 32 cups of juice for a picnic. How many quarts of juice should they buy?

To change cups into quarts, they must know how these units are related.

- A quart is larger than a cup.
- 4 cups = 1 quart

cup (c)

quart (qt)

Remember

Table of Measures

Length
12 inches = 1 foot
3 feet = 1 yard

Capacity
2 cups = 1 pint
4 cups = 1 quart
2 pints = 1 quart
8 pints = 1 gallon
4 quarts = 1 gallon

Weight
16 ounces = 1 pound

Jake and Theresa used different ways to change cups into quarts.

Jake
I'll draw 32 cups. I'll circle groups of 4 to show quarts.

There are 8 groups of 4 cups. So, 32 cups equals 8 quarts.

Theresa
I'll make a table.

Quarts	1	2	3	4	5	6	7	8
Cups	4	8	12	16	20	24	28	32

The table shows that 8 quarts equals 32 cups.

So, they should buy 8 quarts of juice.

MATH IDEA To change one unit into another, first decide how the units are related.

- Explain why Jake circled groups of 4 cups.

Technology Link

More Practice: Harcourt Mega Math The Number Games, *Tiny's Think Tank*, Level M

Check

1. Write how many pints are in 2 gallons. Use the Table of Measures to help.

Copy and complete. Use the Table of Measures to help.

2. Change gallons to pints.
larger unit: ?

1 gallon = ■ pints

3. Change feet to inches.
larger unit: ?

1 foot = ■ inches

Practice and Problem Solving

Extra Practice, page 352, Set C

Copy and complete. Use the Table of Measures to help.

4. Change yards to feet.
larger unit: ?

1 yard = ■ feet

5. Change quarts to gallons.
larger unit: ?

■ quarts = 1 gallon

Change the units. Use the Table of Measures to help.

6. ■ cups = 1 pint

12 cups = ■ pints

7. ■ inches = 1 foot

feet	1	2
inches	12	■

■ inches = 2 feet

Compare. Write <, >, or = for each ●.

8. 6 cups ● 2 quarts

9. 1 yard ● 36 inches

10. 20 ounces ● 1 pound

11. Neil bought 2 sandwiches. He paid with a $10 bill. He received $4 in change. How much did each sandwich cost?

12. Callie has 23 inches of yarn. Is this more than or less than 2 feet? Explain.

13. **What's the Error?** Dylan said that 24 pints equal 6 gallons. Describe his error. Draw a model to show your answer.

Mixed Review and Test Prep

Multiply. (p. 212)

14. $9 \times 4 =$ ■

15. $9 \times 7 =$ ■

Divide. (p. 260)

16. $12 \div 4 =$ ■

17. $28 \div 4 =$ ■

18. **TEST PREP** Yolanda had $2.19. She lost a quarter. She wants to buy a book for $2.15. How much more does she need? (p. 120)

A $0.24
B $0.21
C $0.11
D $0.04

LESSON 6

Problem Solving Skill
Estimate or Measure

Quick Review
1. ■ inches = 1 foot
2. ■ cups = 1 pint
3. ■ ounces = 1 pound
4. 6 feet = ■ yards
5. 1 gallon = ■ quarts

UNDERSTAND › PLAN › SOLVE › CHECK

HOW MUCH? Ethan's job is to water 4 plants in the classroom. Each plant needs about 1 cup of water. He has a 1-quart pitcher to use. Should Ethan estimate or measure the amount of water for each plant?

Each plant needs *about* 1 cup of water, so Ethan can use an estimate. There are 4 cups in 1 quart, so he can look at the pitcher and decide about how much to pour for 1 plant. He can use this as a benchmark.

What if Ethan's job is to mix water with the paint powder?

PAINT POWDER
Directions:
1. Pour one cup of water into the jar.
2. Stir for one minute.

Ethan needs to measure 1 cup of water to add to the jar. He should use a measuring cup because he needs a measured amount to mix the paint correctly.

Talk About It

- Why is an estimate close enough to use for watering the plants?
- Why would Ethan need to measure the amount of water to mix with the paint powder?

Problem Solving Practice

USE DATA For 1–2, use the table. Tell if you need to measure or if an estimate will do.

SUPPLIES	
Item	**Size**
Ribbon	20 ft roll
Ribbon	30 ft roll
Dried Beans	6 oz package
Dried Beans	1 lb package

1. Each student in Mrs. Garcia's class needs a 10-inch piece of ribbon for an art project. There are 20 students in the class. Which roll of ribbon should she buy? Explain.

2. Coach Davis is making 8 bean bags. He needs 4 ounces of dried beans for each bean bag. What packages should he buy? Explain.

Mr. Weston is buying soda water for a science activity. It is sold in 1-quart bottles. There are 6 groups of students in his class.

3. Each group needs 1 pint of soda water. How many bottles should Mr. Weston buy?

   A 1 **C** 3
   B 2 **D** 4

4. Which tool should Mr. Weston use to measure the soda water for each group?

   F balance **H** ruler
   G measuring cup **J** thermometer

Mixed Applications

USE DATA For 5–7, use the graph.

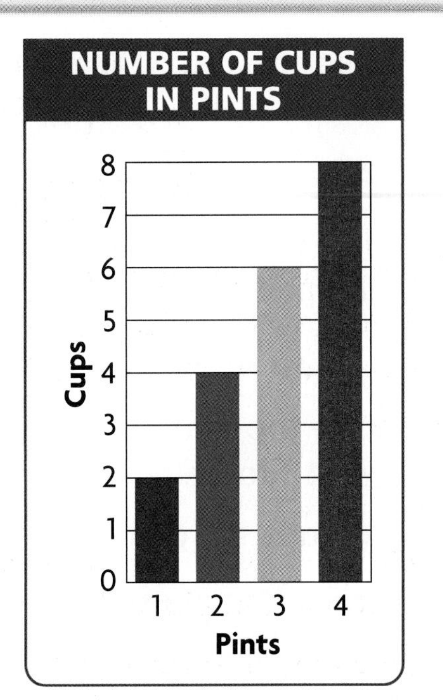

5. **What's the Question?** The answer is 4 cups.

6. Stacy mixed 3 cups of orange juice, 2 cups of pineapple juice, and 3 cups of cranberry juice. How many *pints* of fruit juice did she mix in all?

7. **REASONING** There are 2 pints in 1 quart. How many *cups* are there in *3 quarts*?

8. **Write About It** Give an example of when you would need to measure and an example of when an estimate would do.

Extra Practice

Set A (pp. 338–341)

Measure the length to the nearest inch.

1.

2.

Measure the length to the nearest half inch.

3.

4.

5.

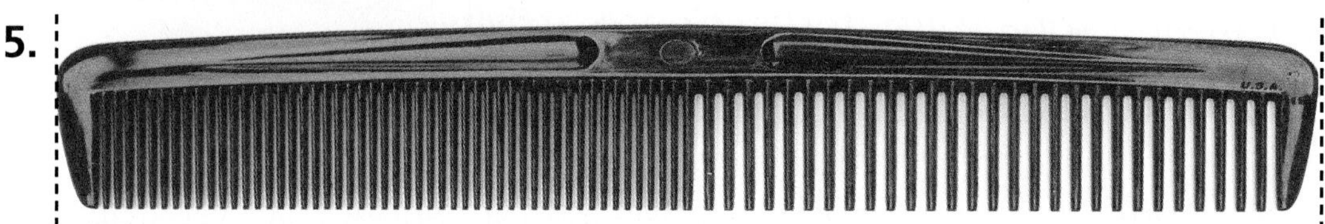

Set B (pp. 342–343)

Choose the unit you would use to measure each.
Write *inch, foot, yard,* or *mile*.

1. the height of a 2-story house
2. the distance between 2 towns
3. the length of a hockey stick
4. the length of your thumb

Choose the best unit of measure.
Write *inches, feet, yards,* or *miles*.

5. A pen is about 6 ? long.
6. A car is about 4 ? long.
7. The distance from the school to the park is about 2 ? .
8. The height of a chair is about 3 ? .

Set C (pp. 348–349)

Change the units. Use the Table of Measures on page 348 to help.

1. ■ cups = 1 quart

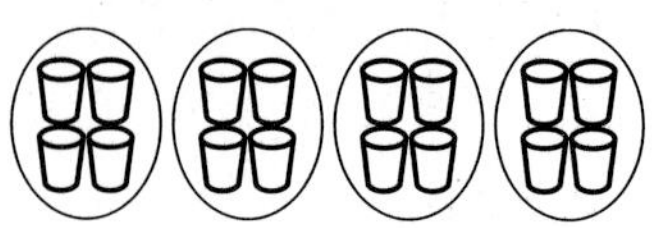

16 cups = ■ quarts

2. ■ feet = 1 yard

feet	3	6		
yards	1	2	3	4

■ feet = 4 yards

Review/Test

✓ CHECK CONCEPTS

Choose the better estimate. (pp. 346–347)

1. 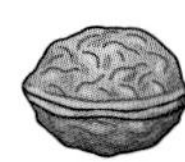

   1 ounce or
   1 pound?

2. 

   2 ounces or
   2 pounds?

3. 

   30 ounces or
   30 pounds?

Choose the better estimate. (pp. 344–345)

4. 

   1 cup or
   1 quart?

5. 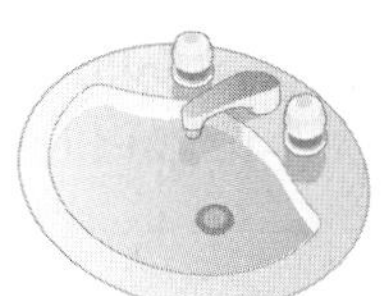

   5 quarts or
   5 gallons?

6. 

   1 cup or
   1 quart?

7. 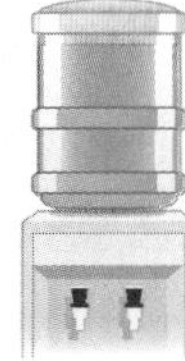

   4 pints or
   4 gallons?

✓ CHECK SKILLS

Measure the length to the nearest inch. (pp. 338–341)

8.

9. 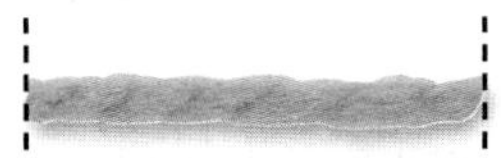

Choose the unit you would use to measure each.
Write *inch, foot, yard,* or *mile*. (pp. 342–343)

10. the length of a marker
11. the height of a wall
12. the distance a bus goes in 15 minutes
13. the distance between the classroom and the playground

✓ CHECK PROBLEM SOLVING (pp. 350–351)

14. Gail needs a piece of string to tie flowers together. Can she estimate the length of string or does she need to measure? Explain.
15. Joe needs 2 cups of flour for a cookie recipe. Should he estimate or measure the amount of flour? Explain.

Standardized Test Prep

NUMBER SENSE, CONCEPTS, AND OPERATIONS

1. Lynn sold 8 bracelets at a craft fair. She charged $3 for each bracelet. Which operation should you use to find how much money she made at the fair?

   A addition
   B subtraction
   C multiplication
   D division

2. Which division fact belongs to the same fact family as these multiplication facts?

   $6 \times 4 = 24 \qquad 4 \times 6 = 24$

   F $24 \div 8 = 3$
   G $24 \div 6 = 4$
   H $24 \div 3 = 8$
   J $24 \div 1 = 24$

3. Tara has 56 trading cards. She can put 8 cards on each page of her collection binder. Which of the following can be used to find the number of pages she needs for all of her cards?

   A $56 - 8 = 48$ **C** $56 \div 8 = 7$
   B $56 + 8 = 64$ **D** $54 \div 9 = 6$

4. **Explain It** Dylan says the difference between 5,609 and 1,198 is about 3,000. Do you agree or disagree with Dylan's estimate? Explain.

MEASUREMENT

5. Which units of measure would be the most appropriate to determine the length of a football field?

   F inches **H** yards
   G feet **J** miles

TIP **Understand the problem.** See item 6. Each sports bottle holds one pint. You need to find how many pints are in one gallon. Then multiply that number by 2 to find the number of pints in 2 gallons.

6. Coach Walton is filling sports bottles that each hold 1 pint. He has a water cooler with 2 gallons of water in it. How many bottles can he fill?

   1 quart = 2 pints
   1 gallon = 4 quarts

   A 8 **C** 12
   B 10 **D** 16

7. Which would be **best** to measure the weight of a loaf of bread?

   F inch **H** ounce
   G quart **J** pound

8. **Explain It** Gail's cookie recipe calls for $1\frac{1}{2}$ cups of flour. She has 2 cups of flour. Should she estimate or measure the amount of flour that she will use? Explain.

ALGEBRAIC THINKING

9. How many quarts are in 2 gallons?

Gallons	1	2	3	4
Quarts	4	■	12	16

A 5 quarts
B 6 quarts
C 8 quarts
D 10 quarts

10. Kendra wrote this number pattern:

40, 36, 32, 28

Which is a rule for her pattern?

F Divide by 3.
G Add 3.
H Multiply by 4.
J Subtract 4.

11. Which equation is true?

A $36 - 8 = 28$
B $18 - 5 = 12$
C $15 + 7 = 23$
D $13 + 9 = 21$

12. Explain It Angie thought of a number pattern and made this table. Explain how to find a rule for the table. Then use that rule to find the missing numbers.

In	2	4	6	8	10
Out	16	■	■	64	80

DATA ANALYSIS AND PROBABILITY

13. The line plot shows the high temperature in Pat's town for each day in April. What is the mode of this data?

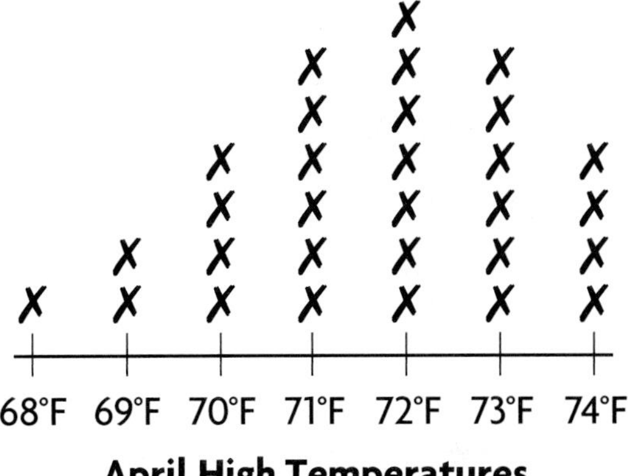

F 68°F
G 70°F
H 71°F
J 72°F

14. What are all of the possible outcomes for this spinner?

A blue, green, yellow
B blue, red, yellow, blue
C yellow, blue, green
D red, yellow

15. Explain It Jared asked his classmates to name their favorite foods. These are the results.

FOOD	NUMBER OF VOTES
Pizza	𝍸 𝍸 |
Corn Dogs	||
Hamburgers	𝍸 |

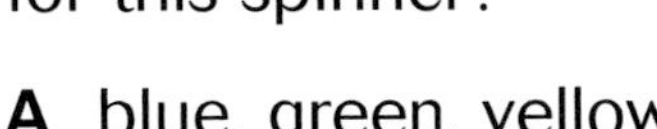

Jared says that pizza should be ordered for the class party. Do you agree or disagree? Explain.

CHAPTER 18

Metric Units and Temperature

FAST FACT • SCIENCE
If the temperature is 32°F or below, water freezes. When it is this cold, rain can become snow. Temperatures are an important part of predicting the weather.

PROBLEM SOLVING The table shows average, or normal, temperatures in February for six cities. Name the cities where snow might be predicted in February.

FEBRUARY TEMPERATURES

City	Temperature	
	Low	High
Boise, ID	28°F	44°F
Tulsa, OK	29°F	51°F
Birmingham, AL	35°F	57°F
Richmond, VA	28°F	49°F
Tampa, FL	52°F	71°F
Grand Rapids, MI	16°F	32°F

Boulder Mountains in Idaho

Relating Units

Use the Table of Measures to find out how the metric units are related.

TABLE OF MEASURES
10 centimeters = 1 decimeter
100 centimeters = 1 meter
1,000 meters = 1 kilometer

Activity

MATERIALS: centimeter grid paper, crayons, tape

STEP 1

Use the Table of Measures to decide how many decimeters are in one meter.

STEP 2

Cut enough decimeter strips out of grid paper to make a 1-meter strip. Color each decimeter strip a different color.

STEP 3

Tape the decimeter strips together so that the edges do not overlap.

STEP 4

Estimate the length of your classroom. Then use your meter strip to find the actual measure.

- How did you decide how many decimeter strips were needed to make a meter strip?

Check

1. **Explain** how to find the length in centimeters of objects that do not line up exactly with a centimeter mark.

Estimate the length in centimeters. Then use a ruler to measure to the nearest centimeter.

2.

3.

4.

5.

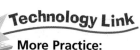

Technology Link

More Practice: Harcourt Mega Math Ice Station Exploration, *Linear Lab*, Levels H and I

Choose the unit you would use to measure each. Write *cm, m,* or *km*.

6. the length of a crayon
7. the length of a chalkboard
8. the length of a carrot
9. the length of a playground
10. the length of a highway
11. the length of a butterfly

LESSON CONTINUES

Practice and Problem Solving

Extra Practice, page 370, Set A

Estimate the length in centimeters. Then use a ruler to measure to the nearest centimeter.

12.

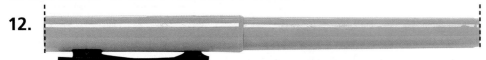

13. 

14. 

15. 

Choose the unit you would use to measure each. Write *cm, m,* or *km*.

16. the distance you can ride a bike in 30 minutes

17. the distance from your classroom to the playground

18. the length of a pencil

19. the length of your classroom

Choose the better estimate.

20. Ali walked 4 __?__ in one hour.
A kilometers **B** decimeters

21. Carole's ponytail is 1 __?__ long.
A decimeter **B** kilometer

22. The wall is 3 __?__ high.
A centimeters **B** meters

23. The paper clip is 3 __?__ long.
A decimeters **B** centimeters

Compare. Write $<$ or $>$ for each ●. Use the Table of Measures on page 359 to help.

24. 5 cm ● 1 dm

25. 1 m ● 50 cm

26. 1 dm ● 10 m

Use a ruler. Draw a line for each length.

27. 2 centimeters

28. 1 decimeter

29. 14 centimeters

30. **Write About It** Choose 3 objects inside your classroom and 3 outside. Estimate and measure the lengths. Record the results. Tell what tool you used to measure each.

31. ***FAST FACT*** **• GEOGRAPHY** Snake River Canyon in Idaho has a maximum depth of 2,400 meters. Write this number in word form and expanded form.

32. **REASONING** Chad says 23 centimeters is the same as 2 decimeters plus 3 centimeters. Do you agree? Explain.

33. Adam was second in line. Susan stood behind Adam and in front of Jean. Tim was first in line. Who was fourth in line?

34. **What's the Error?** Nick said that the line below measures about 2 cm. Describe his error. Give the correct measure.

35. Sarah drew this poster for her science project. What is the length of the bottom edge of her poster in decimeters? Explain.

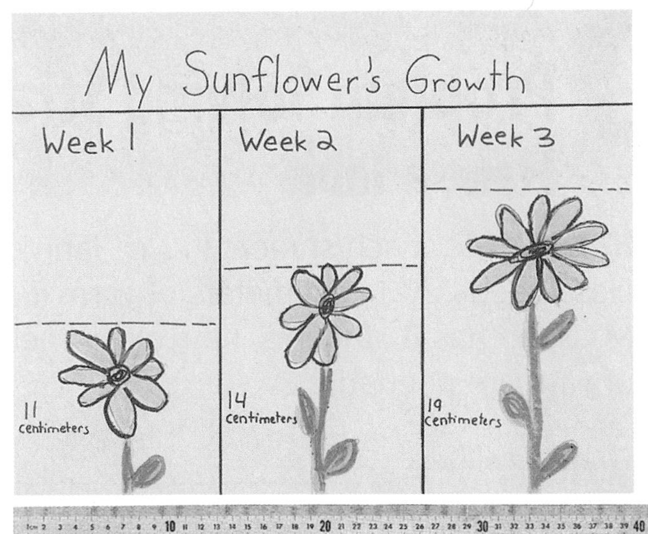

Mixed Review and Test Prep

Find the product. (p. 212)

36. $9 \times 6 = \blacksquare$ **37.** $4 \times 9 = \blacksquare$

38. $7 \times 9 = \blacksquare$ **39.** $10 \times 9 = \blacksquare$

40. TEST PREP What is 3,217 rounded to the nearest ten? (p. 52)

A 3,200 **C** 3,220

B 3,210 **D** 3,300

Find the quotient. (p. 260)

41. $18 \div 3 = \blacksquare$ **42.** $24 \div 4 = \blacksquare$

43. $32 \div 4 = \blacksquare$ **44.** $27 \div 3 = \blacksquare$

45. TEST PREP How many feet are equal to 4 yards? (p. 342)

F 16 **H** 8

G 12 **J** 4

Problem Solving Thinker's Corner

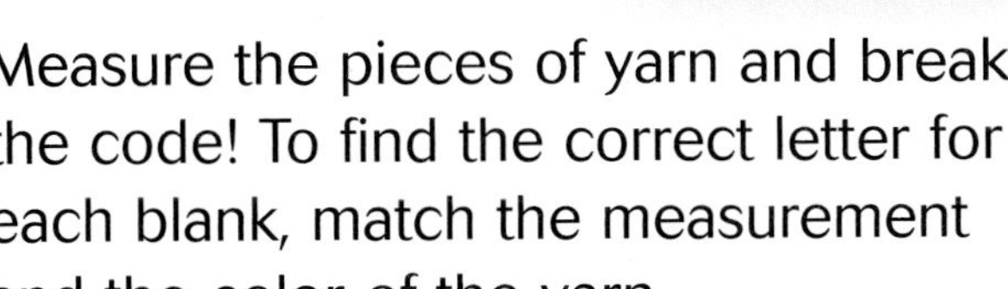

Measure the pieces of yarn and break the code! To find the correct letter for each blank, match the measurement and the color of the yarn.

S
E
C

What did the mother bird call the baby bird?

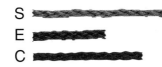

?	?	?	?	?	?	?	?	?	?
3 cm	5 cm	2 cm	2 cm	4 cm	5 cm	2 cm	1 cm	1 cm	3 cm

LESSON 2

Problem Solving Strategy
Make a Table

PROBLEM Each student in Ms. Tahn's art class needs 200 centimeters of yarn. If Ms. Tahn has 8 students, how many meters of yarn are needed?

Quick Review

1. 10×2
2. $200 + 200$
3. $100 + 100$
4. $400 + 400$
5. $1,000 + 1,000$

UNDERSTAND

- What are you asked to find?
- What information will you use?
- Is there any information you will not use? If so, what?

PLAN

- What strategy can you use to solve the problem?

You can *make a table* to show how to change centimeters into meters.

SOLVE

- How can you use the strategy to solve the problem?

Think: 100 cm = 1 m

Students	1	2	3	4	5	6	7	8
Centimeters	200	400	600	800	1,000	1,200	1,400	1,600
Meters	2	4	6	8	10	12	14	16

The 8 students need 1,600 centimeters of yarn.

1,600 centimeters = 16 meters

So, 16 meters of yarn are needed.

CHECK

- How can you decide if your answer is correct?

Problem Solving Practice

Use *make a table* to solve.

1. **What if** Ms. Tahn had 10 students? Use the table on page 362 to help decide how many meters of yarn are needed.
2. Patty needs 150 centimeters of green yarn and 350 centimeters of white yarn. How many meters of yarn does she need in all?

Strategies

- Draw a Diagram or Picture
- Make a Model or Act It Out
- Make an Organized List
- Find a Pattern
- **Make a Table or Graph**
- Predict and Test
- Work Backward
- Solve a Simpler Problem
- Write a Number Sentence
- Use Logical Reasoning

Problem Solving

Barb jogged 3,000 meters. How many kilometers did she jog? (HINT: 1 km = 1,000 m)

3. Which table helps solve the problem?

A

Kilometers	1	2	3
Meters	1,000	2,000	3,000

B

Centimeters	100	200	300
Meters	1	2	3

C

Meters	1	2	3
Decimeters	10	20	30

D

Decimeters	1	2	3
Centimeters	10	20	30

4. Which answers the question?

   F 3,000 km **H** 30 km
   G 300 km **J** 3 km

Mixed Strategy Practice

USE DATA For 5–6, use the table.

5. Compare the heights of the mountain peaks. List them in order from the least to the greatest heights.
6. Which two mountain peaks have a difference in height of 178 meters?
7. **Write a problem** that uses kilometers, meters, decimeters, or centimeters.

IDAHO MOUNTAIN PEAKS	
Peak	**Height**
Hyndman Peak	3,681 meters
Borah Peak	3,859 meters
Twin Peaks	3,152 meters

8. Reece had some walnuts. He ate 3 walnuts. Then he gave 4 friends 5 walnuts each. He had 1 walnut left. How many walnuts did he start with?

LESSON 3

Capacity

Quick Review

1. 300 + 400
2. 800 + 100
3. 2,000 + 2,000
4. 250 + 250
5. 900 + 200

VOCABULARY
milliliter (mL)
liter (L)

MATERIALS
plastic glass that holds about 250 mL, liter container, large plastic pitcher, water

Explore

Capacity can be measured by using metric units such as the **milliliter (mL)** and **liter (L)**.

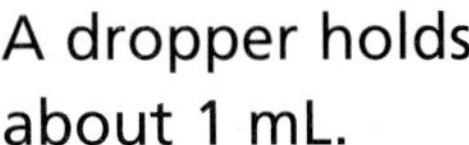

A dropper holds about 1 mL.

A glass holds about 250 mL.

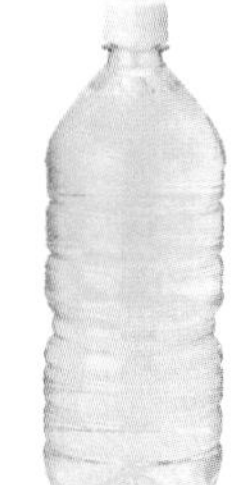

A water bottle holds about 1 L.

Activity

Copy the table to help find the capacity of different containers.

FINDING CAPACITY		
How many:	Estimate	Measure
milliliters in a liter?		
liters in the pitcher?		

STEP 1
Estimate the number of milliliters that are in 1 liter. Estimate the number of liters that will fill the pitcher.

STEP 2
Use the plastic water glass. Pour 250 mL of water into the liter container.

STEP 3
Repeat until the liter container is full. Record how many milliliters you poured.

STEP 4
Pour 1 liter of water at a time into the pitcher. Repeat until the pitcher is full. Record the number of liters.

Try It

a. How many milliliters did it take to fill the liter container?

b. How many liters did you pour into the pitcher?

Connect

How are liters and milliliters related?

1,000 milliliters = 1 liter

Liters	1	2	3	4
Milliliters	1,000	2,000	3,000	4,000

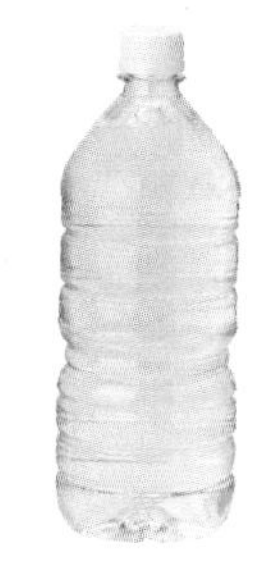

1,000 mL, or 1 L

Practice and Problem Solving

Choose the better estimate.

1. 

3 mL or 3 L?

2. 

400 mL or 400 L?

3. 

2 mL or 2 L?

4. 

200 mL or 200 L?

Choose the unit you would use to measure the capacity of each. Write *mL* or *L*.

5. 

6. 

7. 

8. 

9. REASONING Rashad wants to measure the capacity of a bucket. Should he use a soup can or a spoon? Explain.

10. **What's the Question?** Jamal had some stamps. He gave away 2 stamps and then arranged the rest in 4 rows of 3. The answer is 14 stamps.

Mixed Review and Test Prep

Compare. Use <, >, or = for each ●.

11. 4×8 ● 36 (p. 178)

12. $56 \div 7$ ● 7 (p. 274)

13. 3×7 ● 7×3 (p. 164)

14. $18 \div 2$ ● $27 \div 3$ (p. 280)

15. TEST PREP Jackie put 8 beads on each of 4 bracelets, and 20 beads on a necklace. How many beads did she use in all? (p. 222)

A 12 **C** 40
B 32 **D** 52

LESSON 4

Mass

Quick Review

1. 10 + 40 = ■
2. 65 + 10 = ■
3. 1,000 + 7,000 = ■
4. 200 + 600 = ■
5. 6,000 + 5,000 = ■

VOCABULARY
gram (g)
kilogram (kg)
mass

MATERIALS
classroom objects, small paper clips, simple balance, book with a mass of about 1 kilogram

Explore

The **gram (g)** and the **kilogram (kg)** are metric units for measuring **mass**, or the amount of matter in an object.

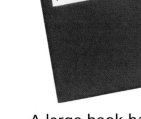

A paper clip has a mass of about 1 gram.

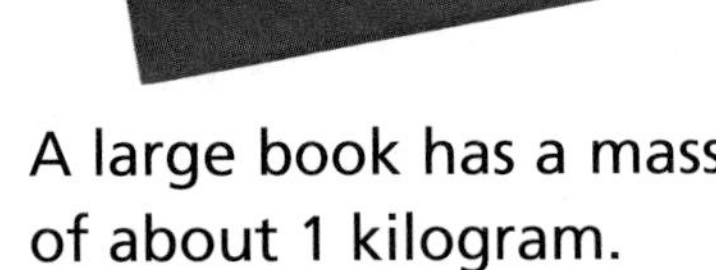

A large book has a mass of about 1 kilogram.

Activity

Find the mass of objects in your classroom.

STEP 1

Place 10 paper clips on one side of the simple balance to show 10 g.

STEP 2

Find an object that you think might equal 10 g. Use the balance to check.

STEP 3

Repeat Steps 1 and 2 for 25 g and 1 kg. Use the book to show 1 kg.

A nickel has a mass of about 5 grams. What things in your classroom have a mass of about 5 grams?

Try It

Name an object that has a mass of each amount.

a. 5 grams **b.** 2 kilograms

Connect

This cat has a mass of 5 kg. How many grams is that?

1,000 grams = 1 kilogram

Kilograms	1	2	3	4	5
Grams	1,000	2,000	3,000	4,000	5,000

So, the cat has a mass of 5,000 g.

Practice and Problem Solving

Choose the better estimate.

1. 

200 g or 200 kg?

2. 

18 g or 18 kg?

3. 

9 g or 9 kg?

Choose the tool and unit to measure each.

4. length of a pencil

5. mass of a grape

6. capacity of a bucket

7. capacity of a tea kettle

8. mass of a flower

9. length of a stamp

Tools	Units	
ruler	cm	g
liter container	kg	mL
simple balance	L	m

10. Sue had 3 red pens and 9 blue pens. She put the same number of pens into 2 cups. How many pens were in each cup?

11. **Write About It** Do objects of about the same size always have about the same mass? Give an example.

Mixed Review and Test Prep

For 12–15, subtract. (pp. 92, 96)

12. 441 − 78 **13.** 703 − 264

14. 157 − 139 **15.** 500 − 167

16. **TEST PREP** Lino had 15 photos. He put an equal number of photos on each of 3 album pages. How many photos are on each page? (p. 260)

A 45 **B** 12 **C** 5 **D** 3

LESSON 5

Fahrenheit and Celsius

Quick Review

1. 34 − 3
2. 58 + 4
3. 41 + 5
4. 65 − 7
5. 82 − 6

VOCABULARY

degrees Fahrenheit (°F)
degrees Celsius (°C)

MATERIALS

Celsius and Fahrenheit thermometers

Explore

Degrees Fahrenheit (°F) are customary units of temperature, and **degrees Celsius (°C)** are metric units of temperature.

Activity

STEP 1

Estimate the temperature outside the classroom in degrees Celsius and in degrees Fahrenheit. Record your estimates.

STEP 2

Measure the temperature outside the classroom using thermometers. Record the differences between your estimates and the actual measurements.

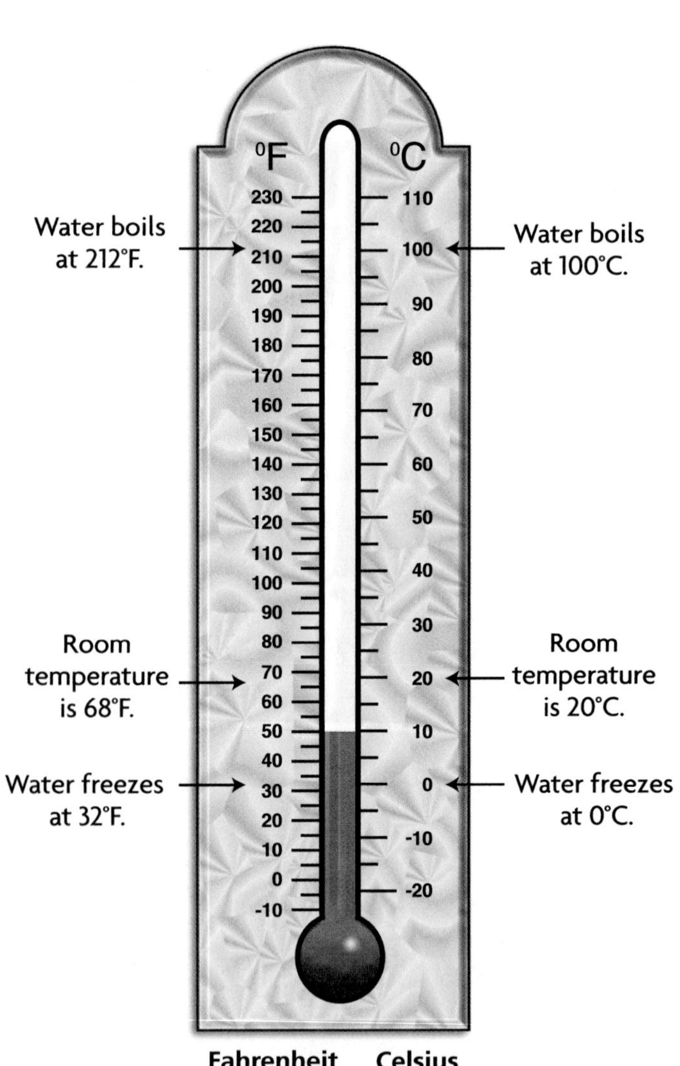

Try It

What is the temperature now?

a. The temperature was 71°F. It dropped 20°F.

b. The temperature was 25°C. It dropped 3°C.

c. The temperature was 58°F. It went up 15°F.

d. The temperature was 17°C. It went up 4°C.

Connect

On a thermometer, use the scale along each side like a number line. Then look at the top of the red bar. The thermometer on page 368 shows that the temperature is

50°F **Read:** fifty degrees Fahrenheit
10°C **Read:** ten degrees Celsius

Practice and Problem Solving

Write each temperature in °F.

1. 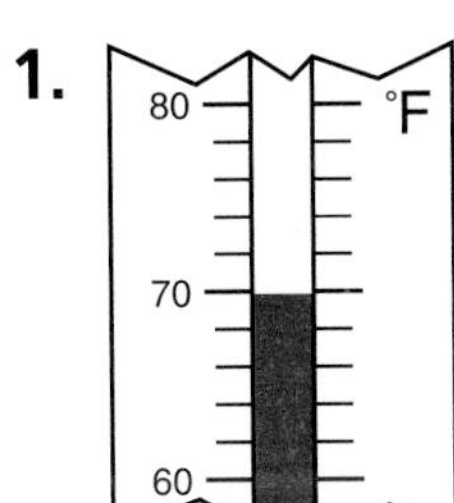

2. 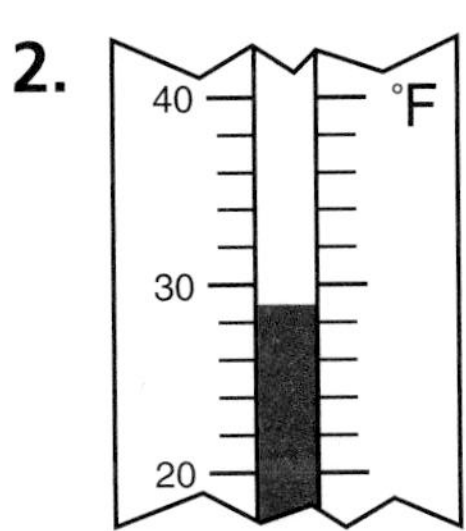

Write each temperature in °C.

3. 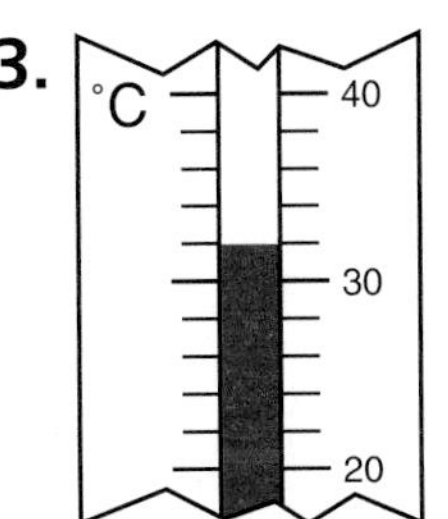

4. 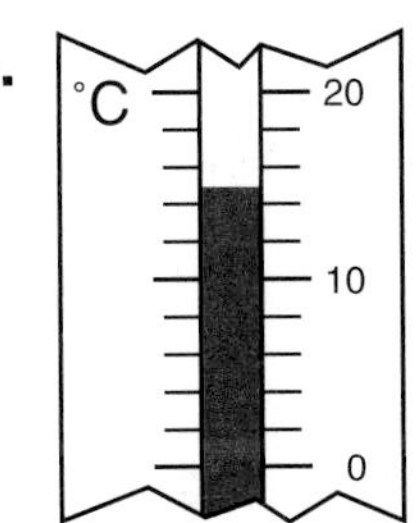

5. Look at the thermometer in Exercise 2. Is the temperature closer to 25°F or 30°F?

6. Look at the thermometer in Exercise 3. Is the temperature closer to 30°C or 35°C?

Choose the better estimate.

7. 

25°F or 95°F?

8. 

56°F or 98°F?

9. 

8°C or 25°C?

10. 

0°C or 22°C?

11. Vocabulary Power *Kilo-* means "one thousand" when used at the beginning of a word. What do you think *kiloliter* means?

12. Sheli has 2 shelves with 10 books on each shelf. She has 4 books on her desk. How many books does she have in all?

Mixed Review and Test Prep

Find the number that the variable stands for. (p. 242)

13. $8 \times a = 72$ **14.** $9 \times b = 81$

15. $c \times 9 = 36$ **16.** $9 \times d = 54$

17. TEST PREP Tom put 42 dimes into 6 equal piles. How many dimes were in 2 piles? (p. 222)

A 14
B 10
C 8
D 6

Extra Practice

Set A (pp. 358–361)

Estimate the length in centimeters. Then use a ruler to measure to the nearest centimeter.

1. 

2. 

3. 

4. 

5. 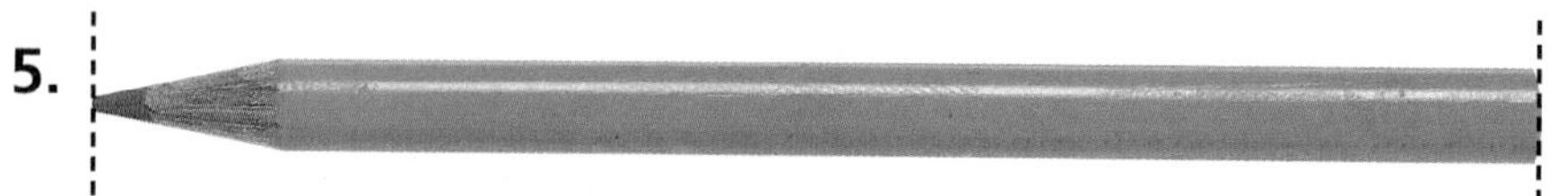

Choose the unit you would use to measure each. Write *cm, m,* or *km*.

6. the length of a marker
7. the height of a two-story building
8. the distance you can kick a ball
9. the distance you can walk in half an hour

Choose the better estimate.

10. Jana's math book is almost 3 __?__ long.

    A meters
    B decimeters

11. Ed walked 1 __?__ to get to Jeff's house.

    A kilometer
    B centimeter

12. The tree is about 6 __?__ high.

    A kilometers
    B meters

13. The ant is 1 __?__ long.

    A decimeter
    B centimeter

Solve.

14. Mathias has a piece of yarn that measures 13 centimeters. Is that more or less than 2 decimeters? Explain.
15. Alice had a ribbon 1 meter long. She cut 12 centimeters off of the ribbon. How many centimeters long is the ribbon now?

Review/Test

✓ CHECK VOCABULARY AND CONCEPTS

Choose the best term from the box.

degrees Celsius
degrees Fahrenheit
gram
liter
meter

1. Capacity can be measured by using metric units such as the __?__. (p. 364)
2. A metric unit for measuring mass is the __?__. (p. 366)
3. Customary units of temperature are __?__. (p. 368)
4. Metric units of temperature are __?__. (p. 368)

Choose the better estimate. (pp. 364–365, 366–367, 368–369)

5. 

2 mL or 2 L?

6. 

2 g or 2 kg?

7. 

30°F or 60°F?

✓ CHECK SKILLS

Estimate the length in centimeters. Then use a ruler to measure to the nearest centimeter. (pp. 358–361)

8. ⊢————⊣

9. 

Choose the unit you would use to measure each. Write *cm, m,* or *km*. (pp. 358–361)

10. the length of a pencil
11. the distance to the moon
12. the length of a bee
13. the distance you run in 10 seconds

✓ CHECK PROBLEM SOLVING

Use *make a table* to solve. (pp. 362–363)

14. Ashley has 5 meters of yarn. How many centimeters of yarn does she have?
15. Ray had 3 meters of string. Then he bought 400 centimeters more. How many meters does he have in all?

Standardized Test Prep

NUMBER SENSE, CONCEPTS, AND OPERATIONS

1. Elizabeth has 6 blue T-shirts, 8 red T-shirts, and 4 white T-shirts. How many T-shirts does she have altogether?

   A 18 **C** 14
   B 16 **D** 10

2. Bob put $15.00 into a bank. He added $8.00 to the bank each week for 3 weeks. How much money is in his bank now?

   F $23.00 **H** $39.00
   G $31.00 **J** $47.00

3. Terry bought 4 packs of markers. Each pack had 8 markers. Jim bought twice as many packs as Terry. Which expression shows how many markers Jim bought?

   A $(4 + 8) + 2$ **C** $(4 \times 8) \times 2$
   B $(8 - 2) + 4$ **D** $(4 \times 4) \times 8$

4. **Explain It** The table shows the number of students in each grade at Main Street School. ESTIMATE how many students are in the third and fourth grades. Tell how you estimated.

MAIN STREET SCHOOL	
Grade	**Number of Students**
Third	419
Fourth	487
Fifth	425

MEASUREMENT

5. Which is the best unit to use to measure the length of a house?

   F centimeter
   G decimeter
   H meter
   J kilometer

6. Which of these objects has a mass of about 5 kilograms?

   A stamp
   B dog
   C banana
   D car

7. Marlee looks at the outdoor thermometer.

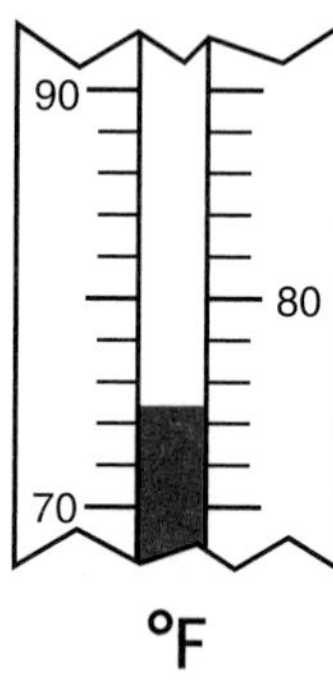

   Which is the temperature outside?

   F 85°F **H** 79°F
   G 80°F **J** 75°F

8. **Explain It** Alicia estimates that the weight of her puppy is about 3 ounces. Do you think her estimate is correct? Explain why or why not.

GEOMETRY AND SPATIAL SENSE

9. Which figure is a rectangle?

A
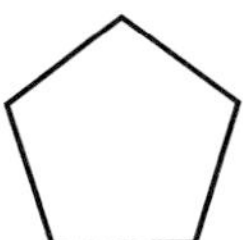

B
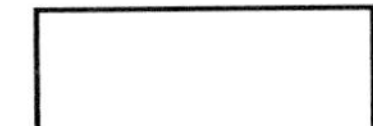

C
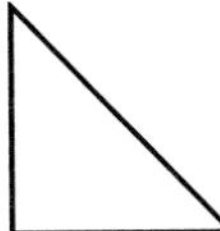

D

10. Marco saw a solid figure that had 6 faces. All of the faces were squares. Which solid figure did he see?

F cylinder
G cube
H cone
J sphere

11. **Explain It** Jenny drew the two shapes below.

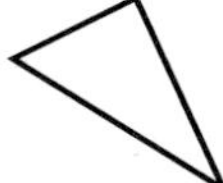

What are the shapes that she drew? Describe each shape by telling how many sides and angles it has.

ALGEBRAIC THINKING

TIP **Understand the problem.** See item 12. To find the pattern in the numbers on the lockers, see how the numbers change. Then find the missing number in the pattern.

12. The picture below shows the numbers on some lockers. What is the number for the open locker?

A 10
B 11
C 12
D 14

13. Which rule could be used to complete the table?

Decimeters	1	2	3	4
Centimeters	10	20	30	■

F Add 100.
G Subtract 100.
H Multiply by 10.
J Multiply by 100.

14. **Explain It** Write a story problem using the number sentence $12 \div 4 = 3$. Draw a picture to show what happens in your story.

IT'S IN THE BAG

Stamp-O-Graph Math

PROJECT Make stamps, and use them to make a graph or locate points on a grid.

Materials

- Spools of all sizes
- Empty water bottle lids
- Film canisters
- Precut foam shapes
- Colored ink pads or markers
- Grid paper
- Construction paper
- Scissors and glue
- Data

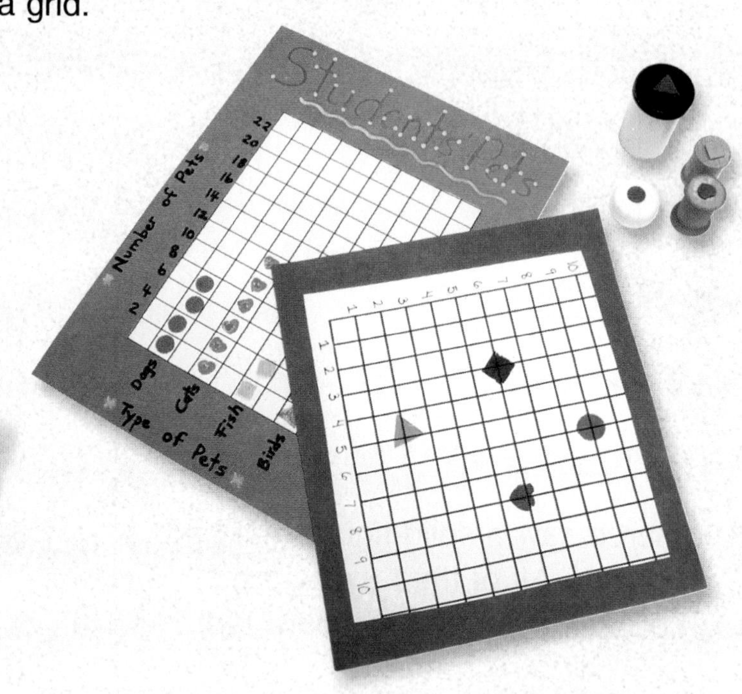

Directions

1. Glue a piece of grid paper to construction paper to make a bar graph. Write a title and labels to match your data. Add a scale of numbers. *(Picture A)*
2. To make the stamps, glue the foam shapes onto the ends of spools, water bottle lids, or film canisters. Color the stamps with markers, or use rubber-stamp ink. *(Picture B)*
3. Use your data and the stamps to complete the bar graph. *(Picture C)*
4. Use another piece of grid paper and construction paper to make a grid for ordered pairs. Take turns with a partner locating points on the grid. Use a stamp to mark the position of each point.

A

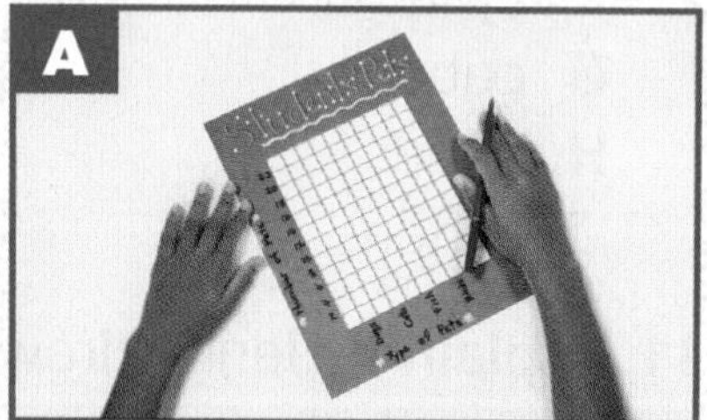

B

C

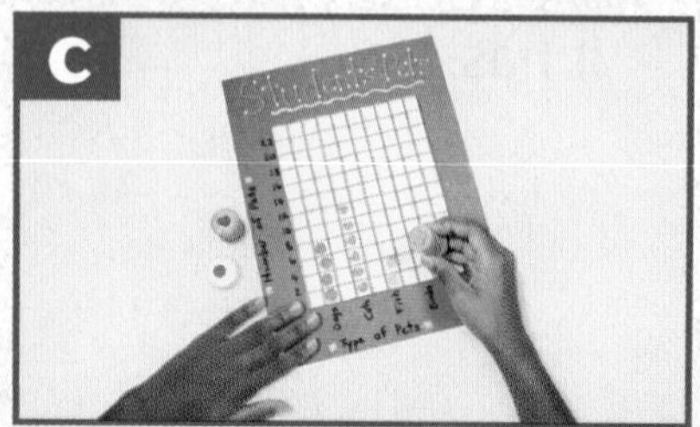

Challenge

Read a Circle Graph

A **circle graph** shows data as parts of a whole circle.

The students at Tony's school were surveyed to find out what activities they could do to help raise money for a new school library. Tony made a circle graph to show the results of the survey. Which activity was the most popular?

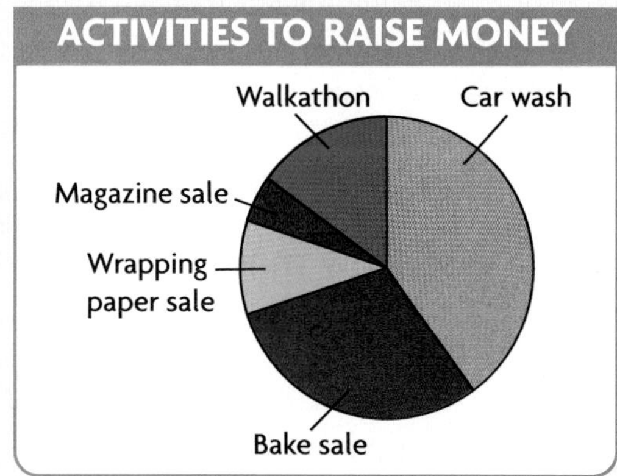

The section for the car wash is larger than any other section. So, the car wash was the most popular activity.

Talk About It

- What activity did the fewest students choose?
- Do fewer students want to have a walkathon or sell wrapping paper? Explain.

Try It

For 1–4, use the circle graph at the right.

1. What does the graph show?
2. Which sport was named by the fewest students?
3. What part of the class named baseball?
4. Suppose another class was surveyed. Which sport do you think would be the most popular? Explain.

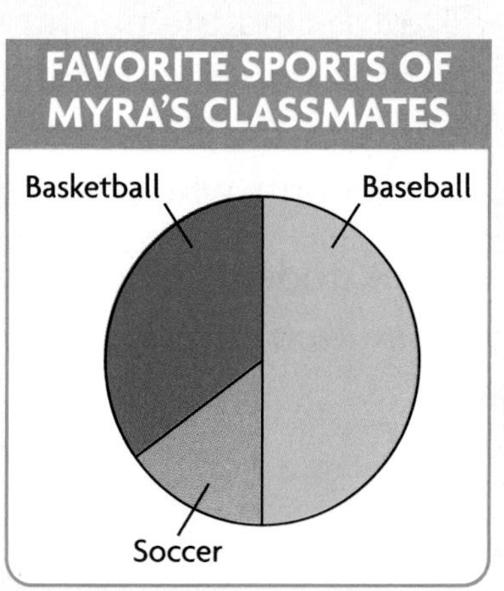

Study Guide and Review

VOCABULARY

Choose the best term from the box.

data
survey
bar graph
line graph

1. Information collected about people or things is called ? . (p. 302)
2. A graph that uses a line to show how data change over time is a ? . (p. 330)

STUDY AND SOLVE

Chapter 15

Classify data.

FAVORITE JUICE			
	Apple	Orange	Grape
Boys	6	8	3
Girls	5	4	6

How many boys voted in all?
Think: Find the sum. $6 + 8 + 3 = 17$
So, 17 boys voted in all.

For 3–5, use the table. (pp. 306–307)

3. How many more boys than girls voted?
4. What is the most popular juice among the girls?
5. What is the most popular juice overall? Explain.

Chapter 16

Read a bar graph.

How many students play soccer?

Step 1: Find the bar for soccer.
Step 2: Compare the height of the bar with the scale to find the number of students who play soccer.

So, 8 students play soccer.

For 6–7, use the bar graph. (pp. 324–325)

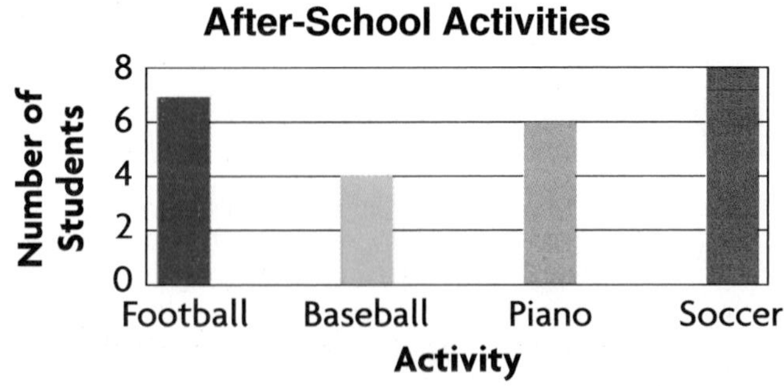

6. How many more students play soccer than play baseball?
7. How many students play football?

Chapter 17

Change units.

There are 16 quarts of juice on the store shelf. How many gallons of juice is this?
Remember: 4 quarts = 1 gallon

Quarts	4	8	12	16
Gallons	1	2	3	4

So, there are 4 gallons of juice.

Change the units. (pp. 348–349)

Pints	1	2	3	4	5
Cups	2	4	6	8	10

8. 3 pints = ■ cups

9. ■ pints = 10 cups

10. ■ cups = 4 pints

Chapter 18

Estimate length and distance.

Choose the better estimate.

5 cm or 5 dm? ⟶ 5 cm

Choose the better estimate.

(pp. 358–361)

11. Your thumb: 5 dm or 5 cm?

12. A lamp post: 3 dm or 3 m?

13. A pen: 15 cm or 15 dm?

PROBLEM SOLVING PRACTICE

Solve. (pp. 308–309, 322–323, 350–351, 362–363)

14. Mr. Lind surveyed his customers to find out what to add to the menu. There were 20 votes for chili, 15 votes for ice cream, and 10 votes for pizza. Make a pictograph that shows the results of the survey.

15. Chris and Jill rolled 2 number cubes 15 times and recorded the sums. Their results were 6, 9, 5, 7, 7, 8, 7, 12, 3, 8, 2, 6, 4, 7, and 6. Make a table to find the sum rolled most often.

16. Andre needs 2 cups of flour for a muffin recipe. Should he estimate or measure the amount of flour? Explain.

17. Philip made 4 gallons of iced tea. How many cups did he make? (HINT: 16 cups = 1 gallon)

PERFORMANCE ASSESSMENT

TASK A • OUTDOOR FUN

You decide to write a report about your classmates' favorite outdoor game.

a. Take a survey to find your classmates' favorite outdoor game. Copy the tally table and the frequency table, and record their choices on both tables.

b. Decide which type of graph would be best to display the data. Then make the graph.

c. Write a question your classmates could answer by looking at your graph.

OUTDOOR GAMES	
Name	Tally

OUTDOOR GAMES	
Name	Number

TASK B • YARN DOLLS

Materials: ruler

Natalie is making yarn dolls. These pictures show the lengths of some of the pieces of yarn Natalie needs.

1.

2.

3.

a. Copy and complete the table. Estimate the length of each piece of yarn to the nearest inch. Use a ruler to measure each piece of yarn to the nearest half inch.

b. Compare each estimate to the measured length. Write *greater than, less than,* or *equal to.*

YARN MEASUREMENT	
Estimate	Actual
1.	
2.	
3.	

Enter Data on a Spreadsheet

Four friends recorded the number of miles they walked.

Lauren		Clark		Raul		Tina	
Week 1	7 mi	Week 1	6 mi	Week 1	9 mi	Week 1	5 mi
Week 2	10 mi	Week 2	8 mi	Week 2	10 mi	Week 2	8 mi
Week 3	12 mi	Week 3	9 mi	Week 3	12 mi	Week 3	10 mi

You can organize the data in a spreadsheet.

- Type the labels *Name, Week 1, Week 2,* and *Week 3.*
- Use the Tab or the arrow keys to enter each name and the number of miles each person walked.
- Use the spreadsheet to find who walked the greatest number of miles in Week 3.

	A	B	C	D
1	Name	Week 1	Week 2	Week 3
2	Lauren	7	10	12
3	Clark	6	8	9
4	Raul	9	10	12
5	Tina	5	8	10

Practice and Problem Solving

1. Three friends recorded the number of pages they read each day for four days. Jake read 23, 25, 38, and 17 pages. Val read 14, 31, 29, and 22 pages. Emily read 25, 36, 21, and 10 pages. Enter the data on a spreadsheet.
2. George read 36, 22, 11, and 14 pages in four days. Add this data to the spreadsheet.
3. **Write a problem** Use the data on your spreadsheet to write a problem. Exchange problems with a classmate and solve.

GO ON-LINE **Multimedia Math Glossary** **www.harcourtschool.com/mathglossary**

Vocabulary Power Look up *mean* and *median* in the Multimedia Math Glossary. Are the mean and the median of a data set ever the same number? Explain.

▲ The highest point on the Ice Age Trail is on Lookout Mountain.

▲ The trail curves across 31 counties in the state of Wisconsin.

ICE AGE NATIONAL SCENIC TRAIL

On the Ice Age National Scenic Trail, people can take the same path that a glacier once took. The Wisconsin Glacier, a large sheet of ice, moved through Wisconsin over 10,000 years ago.

For 1–3, use the photographs. Choose the unit of measure. Write *inches, feet, yards, miles,* or *pounds*.

1. The Ice Age Trail is about 1,000 __?__ long.
2. A snowshoe hare weighs about 3 __?__.
3. Lookout Mountain is 1,920 __?__ high.
4. **REASONING** Ask your classmates which of the activities below they would choose to do at Ice Age Park in the winter. Copy and complete the tally table. Then make a frequency table.

Favorite Activity at Ice Age Park and Trail

Activity	Tally
Hiking	
Cross-Country Skiing	
Snowshoeing	
Horseback Riding	

In the winter, the snowshoe hare's coat changes from brown to white. This helps protect the hare from predators. ▶

HORICON MARSH STATE WILDLIFE AREA

Year after year, groups of birds migrate through the Horicon Marsh State Wildlife Area. The same kinds of birds come to the wildlife area at about the same time every year.

▲ In the spring, visitors may see up to 100 different kinds of birds on a single day.

Solve.

Becca visited the wildlife area in April. She made a tally table to show how many birds she saw.

USE DATA For 1–2, use the tally table.

Birds I Saw	
Birds	**Tally**
Red-Winged Blackbird	𝍸 |||
Canada Goose	|||
Sandhill Crane	𝍸 𝍸
Swamp Sparrow	𝍸	

1. How many birds did Becca see in all?
2. How many more red-winged blackbirds did Becca see than Canada Geese?
3. Use the data in the table to make a bar graph.
4. How is the bar graph similar to the tally table? How is it different?
5. **Write a problem** using the information in your bar graph. Exchange problems with a classmate. Tell how you solved the problem.

CHAPTER 19

Geometric Figures

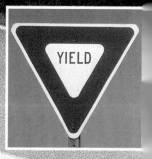

FAST FACT • SOCIAL STUDIES **Different shapes are used for different traffic signs. The stop sign is the only sign in the shape of an octagon. Signs for school zones are in the shape of a pentagon. Yield signs are triangles.**

PROBLEM SOLVING **Make a list of the traffic signs you see on your way to school. Tell what geometric shapes are used for the signs.**

Rockland County, New York

CHECK WHAT YOU KNOW

Use this page to help you review and remember important skills needed for Chapter 19.

IDENTIFY PLANE FIGURES

Choose the best term from the box.

circle
rectangle
square
triangle

1.

2.

3.

4. 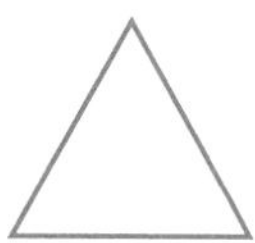

5. 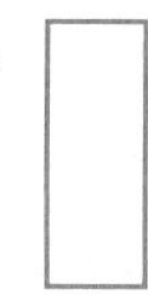

6. 

SIDES AND VERTICES

Tell the number of sides and vertices in each figure.

7. 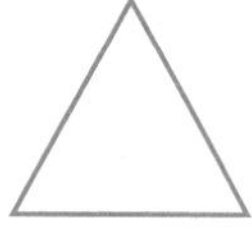

8. 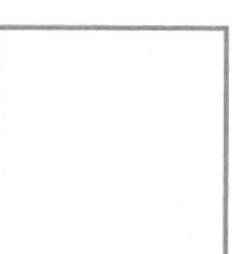

9. 

10. 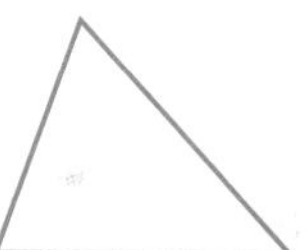

11. 

12. 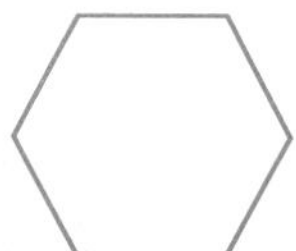

13. 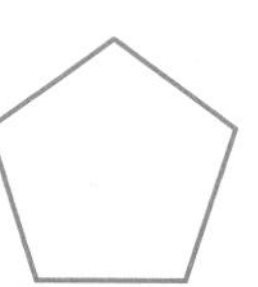

14. 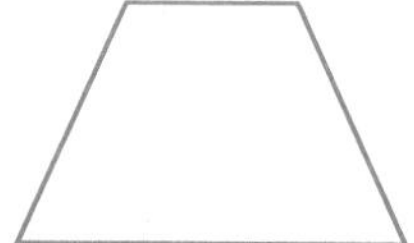

VOCABULARY POWER

REVIEW

triangle [trī′ang′gəl] *noun*

Tri- at the beginning of *triangle* means "three." List some other words that begin with *tri-*, and tell how *three* is part of their meanings.

PREVIEW

point
line segment
right angle
acute angle
obtuse angle
intersecting lines
polygon
quadrilateral

www.harcourtschool.com/mathglossary

LESSON

Line Segments and Angles

Learn

POINT TO POINT Victor drew this plane figure by connecting points on grid paper. The sides of his figure are line segments. The terms below can help you describe figures in geometry.

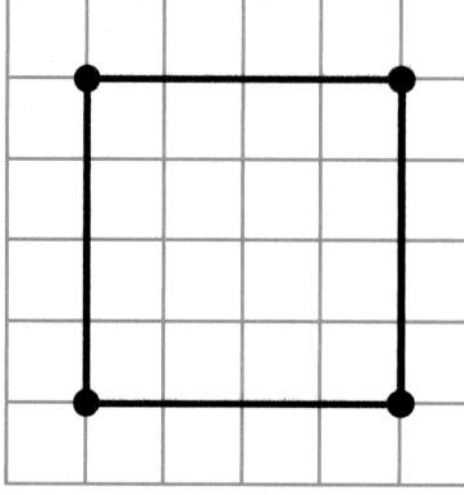

Quick Review

Write the number of sides each figure has.

1. 2. 3.

4. 5.

VOCABULARY

line
point
line segment
ray
angle
right angle
degree (°)
acute angle
obtuse angle

A **line** is straight. It continues in both directions. It does not end.	
A **point** is an exact position or location.	point
A **line segment** is straight. It is part of a line, and it has two endpoints.	
A **ray** is part of a line. It has one endpoint. It is straight and continues in one direction.	
An **angle** is formed by two rays or line segments that share an endpoint.	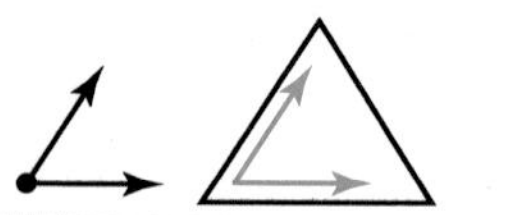

- How many line segments did Victor draw?
- **REASONING** How are lines and line segments alike? How are they different?

Look at the angles in the plane figure that Victor drew. These four angles are right angles. A **right angle** is a special angle that forms a square corner. Use the corner of a sheet of paper to tell whether an angle is a right angle.

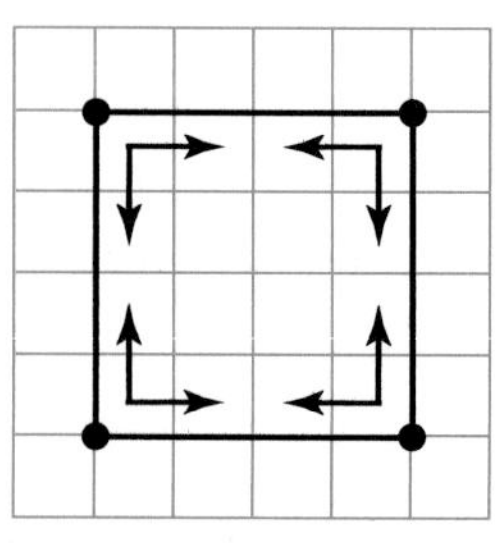

Naming Angles

The unit used to measure an angle is a **degree (°)**. A right angle measures 90°. It can be shown as $\frac{1}{4}$ of a turn around a circle.

right angle

You can name angles by the size of the opening between the rays.

The measure of some angles is less than a right angle. These are **acute angles**.

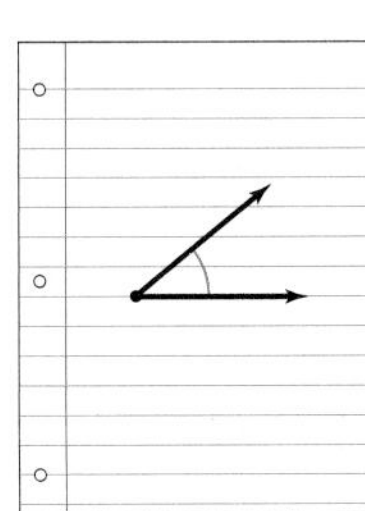

The measure of some angles is greater than a right angle. These are **obtuse angles**.

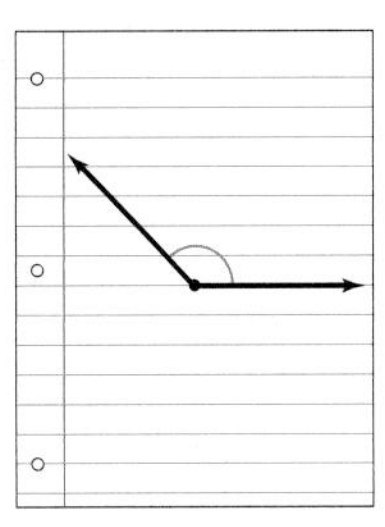
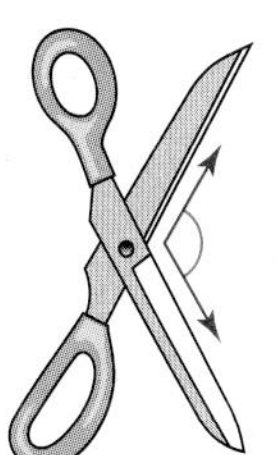

- **REASONING** The angle shown at the right is made up of two $\frac{1}{4}$ turns around the circle. Use what you know about right angles to find the degree measure of this angle.

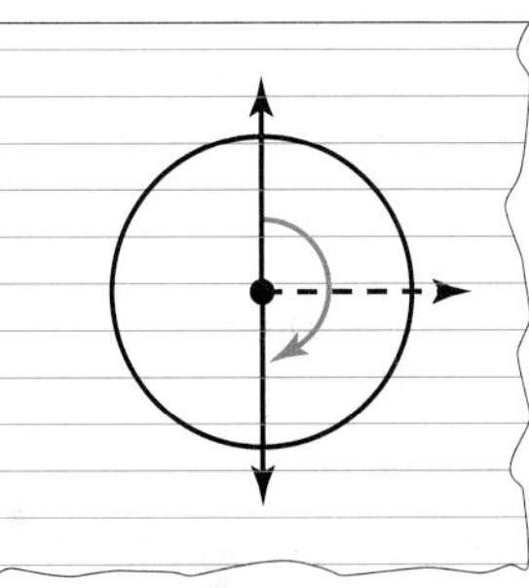

MATH IDEA You can identify angles in plane figures. You can tell if an angle is a right angle, an acute angle, or an obtuse angle.

Check

1. **Draw** a triangle on grid paper like the one shown at the right. What kinds of angles does this triangle have?

Name each figure.

2. 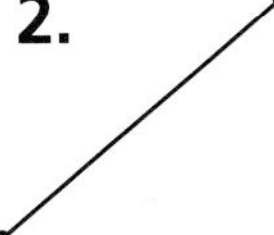

3. 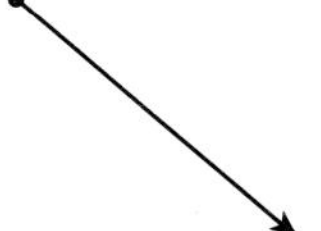

4. 

5. •

LESSON CONTINUES

Practice and Problem Solving

Extra Practice, page 402, Set A

Name each figure.

6. 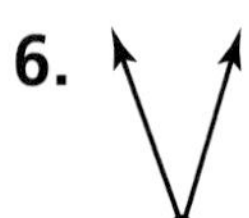

7. 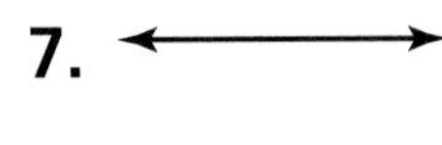

8. 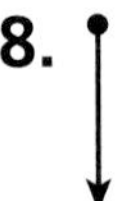

9. 

Use a corner of a sheet of paper to tell whether each angle is a *right angle*, an *acute angle*, or an *obtuse angle*.

10. 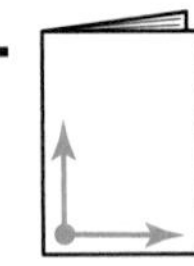

11. 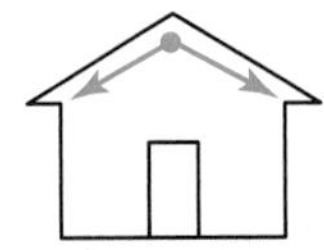

12. 

13. 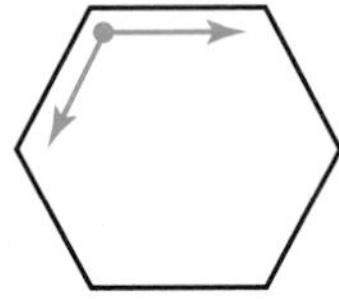

Draw and label each figure. You may wish to use a ruler or straightedge.

14. line segment **15.** ray **16.** line **17.** acute angle

Copy and complete the table.

	Figure	Number of Line Segments	Number of Angles	Number of Right Angles
18.		■	■	■
19.		■	■	■
20.		■	■	■
21.		■	■	■
22.		■	■	■
23.		■	■	■

24. Blanca bought 3 packs of stickers. Each pack has 10 stickers. If she gives 4 stickers to a friend, how many will she have left?

25. **Write About It** Use a ruler or a straightedge to draw a triangle and a right angle. Describe the parts of each figure.

26. **FAST FACT** • SCIENCE Geese fly in a "V" formation to save energy so that they can fly farther. What kind of angle describes this formation?

27. List at least 3 objects in the room that contain right angles. How can you be sure the angles are right angles?

Mixed Review and Test Prep

Find each quotient. (p. 280)

28. $16 \div 2 = \blacksquare$

29. $36 \div 4 = \blacksquare$

30. $25 \div 5 = \blacksquare$

31. $21 \div 3 = \blacksquare$

Find each product. (p. 164)

32. 3×3

33. 3×7

34. 5×3

35. 3×6

36. 4×3

37. 9×3

38. **TEST PREP** What is the value of the blue digit in 3,495? (p. 24)

A 4,000
B 400
C 40
D 4

39. **TEST PREP** Will bought a magazine for $2.79 and 3 pieces of candy for 9¢ each. How much money did he spend? (p. 120)

F $2.88
G $2.96
H $3.06
J $5.49

Problem Solving

CLOCKS AND ANGLES Use what you learned in this lesson to describe the angles made by the hands of a clock.

Write whether each angle is a *right angle,* an *acute angle,* or an *obtuse angle.*

1. 
7:45

2. 
11:15

3. 
9:00

4. 
3:30

5. **REASONING** The hour hand is between the 3 and 4. The minute hand is pointing to the 5. What time is it? Describe the angle made by the hands.

6. Joy left for school at 7:50 A.M. It took her 15 minutes to walk to school. What time is it? Describe the angle made by the hands.

LESSON

2 Types of Lines

Learn

GET IN LINE Here are some ways to describe the relationships between lines.

Lines that cross are **intersecting lines**. Intersecting lines form angles.

Intersecting lines that cross to form right angles are **perpendicular lines**.

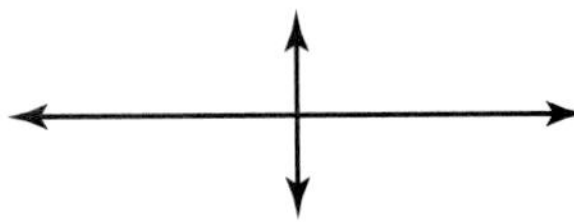

Lines that never cross are **parallel lines**. Since parallel lines never cross, they do not form angles. They are always the same distance apart.

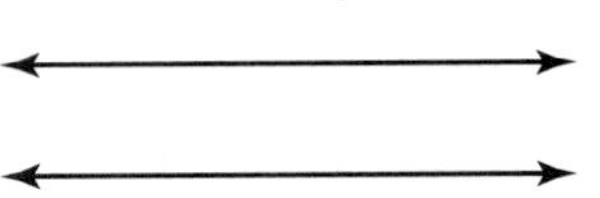

Quick Review

Write *right angle*, *obtuse angle*, or *acute angle*.

1.

2. 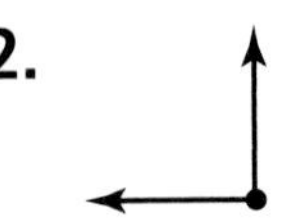

3.

4. 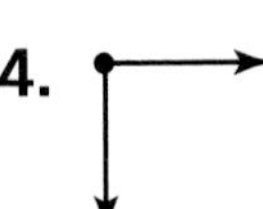

5.

VOCABULARY
intersecting lines
perpendicular lines
parallel lines

You may see models of intersecting, perpendicular, and parallel lines in the world around you.

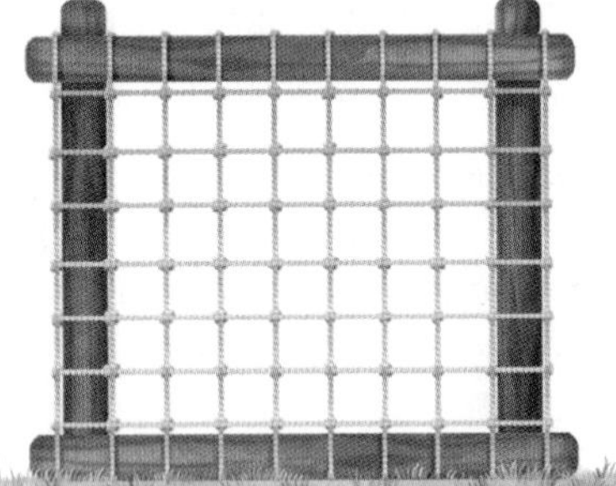

- Are the angles in the climbing net right angles? How can you check?
- **REASONING** Are intersecting lines always perpendicular lines? Explain.

Check

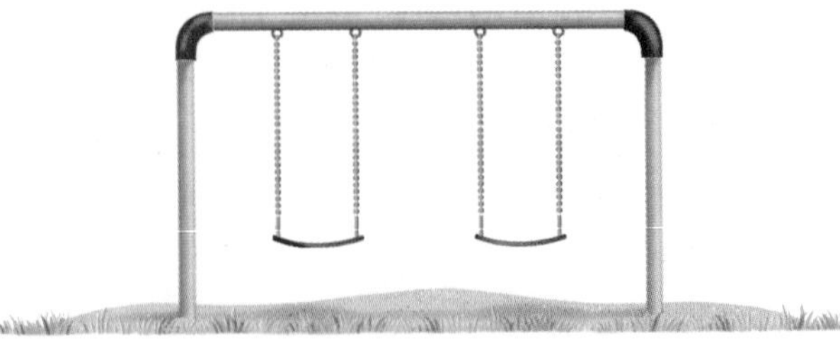

1. **Explain** how to tell whether the swing chains are intersecting or parallel.

Describe the lines. Write *parallel* or *intersecting*.

2. 

3.

4. 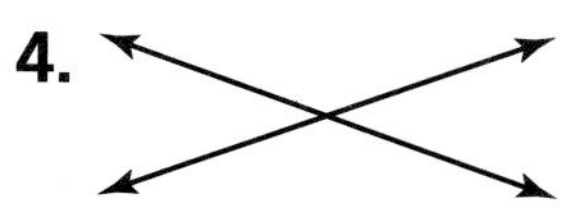

Practice and Problem Solving

Extra Practice, page 402, Set B

Describe the lines. Write *parallel* or *intersecting*.

5. 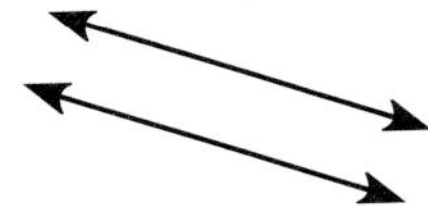

6. 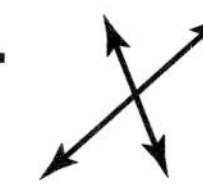

7. 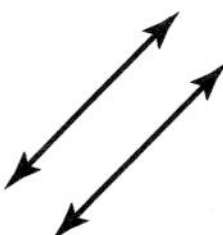

Describe the intersecting lines. Write *perpendicular* or *not perpendicular*.

8. 

9. 

10. 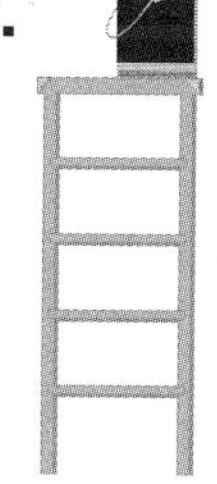

USE DATA For 11–13, use the map at the right.

11. Which street is parallel to Oak Street?

12. Is Oak Street perpendicular to Pine Street or Maple Street? Explain.

13. **? What's the Question?** The answer is obtuse angle.

14. REASONING Use what you know about line relationships to describe the sides of a rectangle.

15. **Write About It** Draw and label sets of intersecting, parallel, and perpendicular lines. Use a ruler to help. Describe the angles in each of your drawings.

Mixed Review and Test Prep

Find the quotient. (p. 280)

16. $8\overline{)40}$ **17.** $7\overline{)49}$

18. $9\overline{)72}$ **19.** $10\overline{)30}$

20. TEST PREP Talia is paid $5 to baby-sit for 1 hour. How much will she earn in 4 hours? (p. 160)

A $9 **B** $20 **C** $25 **D** $30

LESSON

3 Plane Figures

Learn

SHAPE UP! A closed figure begins and ends at the same point. An open figure has ends that do not meet. A **polygon** is a closed plane figure with straight sides that are line segments. A circle is an example of a plane figure that has no straight sides.

polygons

A 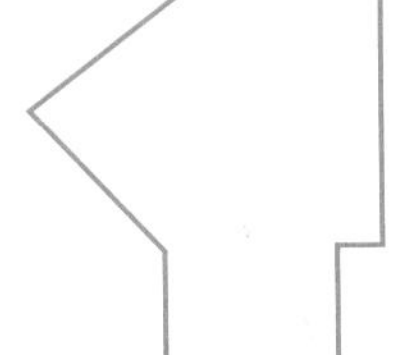

B 

not polygons

C 

D 

Quick Review

Write the number of sides each figure has.

1. ▽ 2. □

3. ▯ 4. ◇ 5. ◺

VOCABULARY

polygon
quadrilateral
pentagon
hexagon
octagon

MATH IDEA You can name and sort polygons by the number of *sides* or *angles* they have.

Examples of Polygons

triangles	quadrilaterals	pentagons	hexagons	octagons
3 sides 3 angles	4 sides 4 angles	5 sides 5 angles	6 sides 6 angles	8 sides 8 angles

• What do you notice about the number of sides and the number of angles in polygons?

Check

1. Explain why a circle is *not* a polygon.

Tell if each figure is a polygon. Write *yes* or *no*.

2. 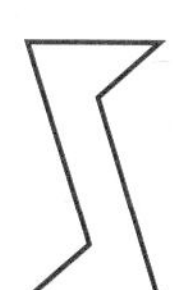
3. 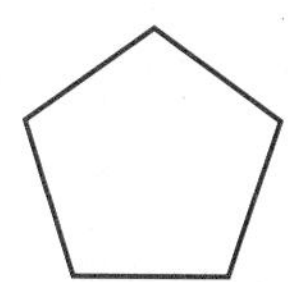
4. 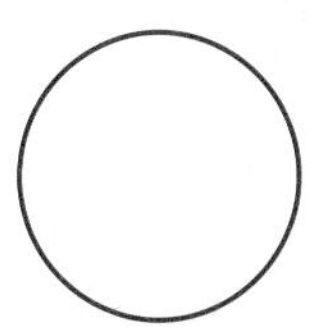
5. 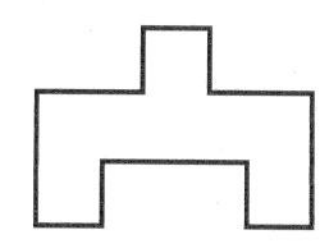
6. 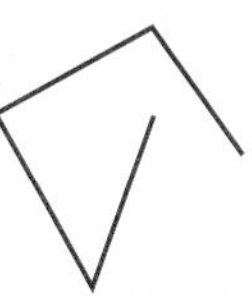

Practice and Problem Solving

Extra Practice, page 402, Set C

Tell if each figure is a polygon. Write *yes* or *no*.

7. 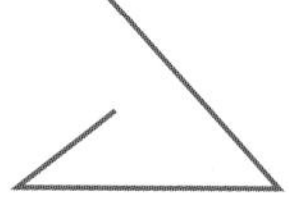
8. 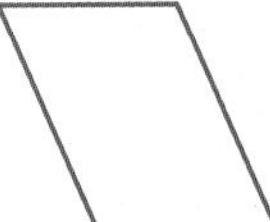
9. 
10. 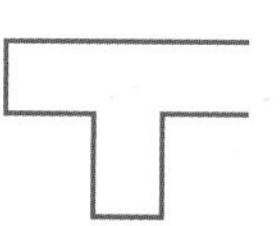
11. 

Write the number of sides and angles each polygon has. Then name the polygon.

12. 

13. 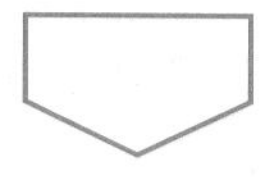
14. 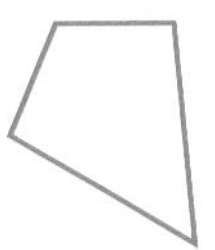
15. 

16. 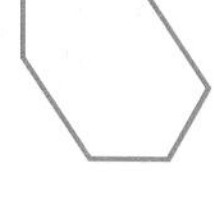

For 17–19, write the letters of the figures that answer the questions.

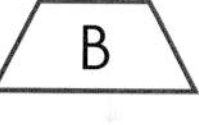

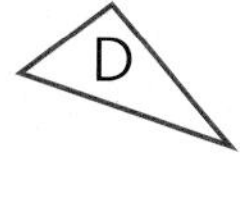

17. Which are polygons?
18. Which is a quadrilateral?
19. Which figures have some angles that are acute angles?
20. Mr. Gomez delivered 3 cases of pasta to each of 3 stores. Each case had 8 boxes. How many boxes of pasta did he deliver?
21. **Write About It** Draw polygons with 3, 4, 5, 6, and 8 sides. Then label each polygon.

Mixed Review and Test Prep

22. $\begin{array}{r} 466 \\ +527 \\ \hline \end{array}$ (p. 72)

23. $\begin{array}{r} 684 \\ +359 \\ \hline \end{array}$ (p. 72)

24. $\begin{array}{r} 700 \\ -293 \\ \hline \end{array}$ (p. 92)

25. $\begin{array}{r} 900 \\ -564 \\ \hline \end{array}$ (p. 92)

26. **TEST PREP** Dawson got to the soccer field at 3:35 P.M. The game started 40 minutes later. What time did the game start? (p. 134)

A 3:55 P.M. **C** 4:15 A.M.
B 4:00 P.M. **D** 4:15 P.M.

Triangles

Learn

TIME FOR TRIANGLES Beverly and Armando sorted these triangles in different ways.

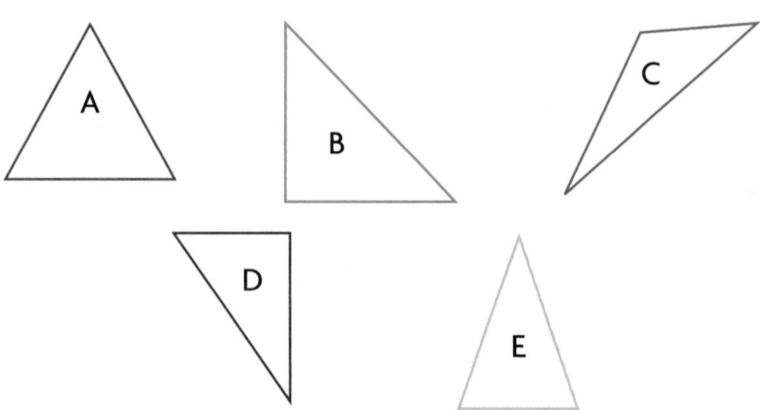

Quick Review

Write if each angle is a *right angle, obtuse angle*, or *acute angle*.

1. 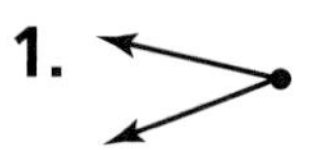
2. 
3. 
4.
5.

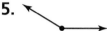

VOCABULARY

equilateral triangle
isosceles triangle
scalene triangle
right triangle
obtuse triangle
acute triangle

This is how Beverly sorted the triangles.

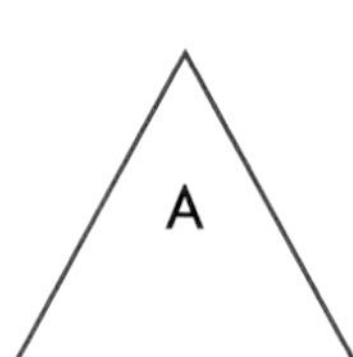

All sides are equal.

Two sides are equal.

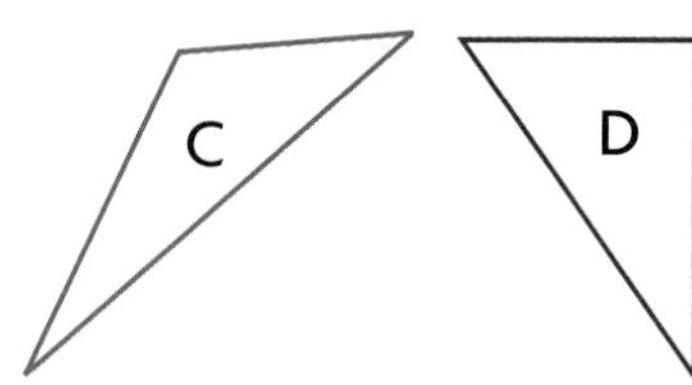

No sides are equal.

This is how Armando sorted the triangles.

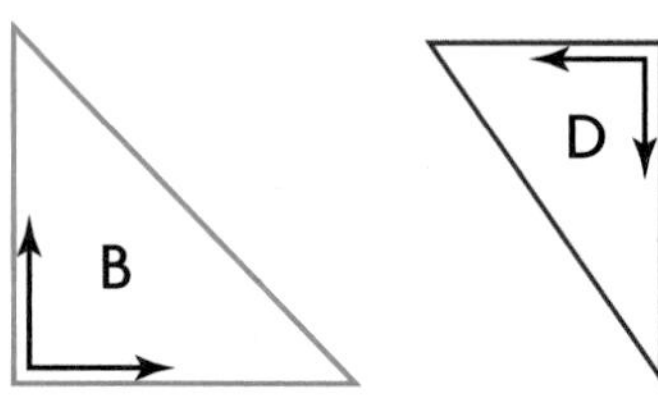

One angle is a right angle.

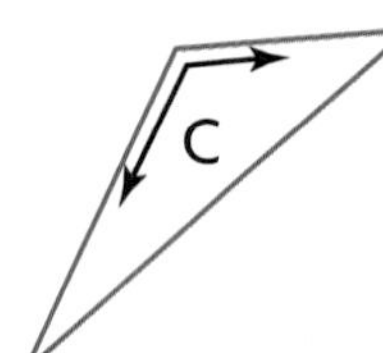

One angle is an obtuse angle.

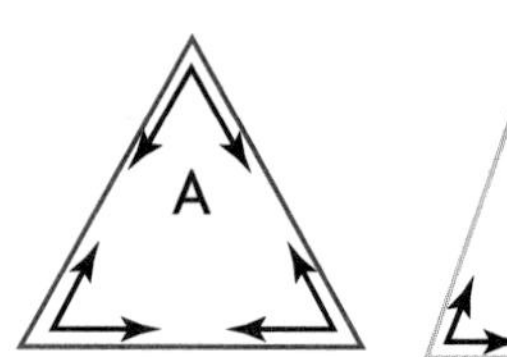

All angles are acute angles.

- How did Beverly sort the triangles? How did Armando sort the triangles?
- How can you check if an angle is an obtuse angle or an acute angle?

Name Triangles

You can name triangles by their equal sides.

equilateral triangle

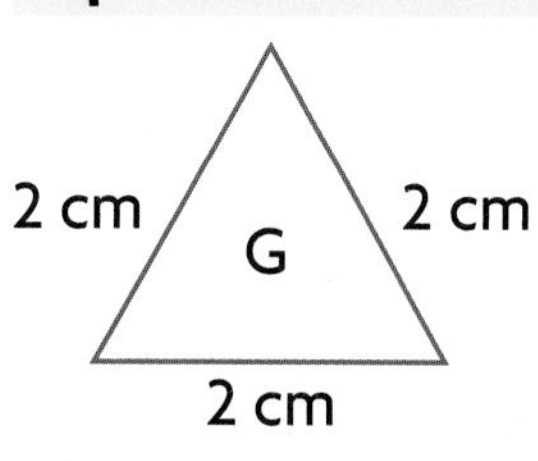

3 equal sides

isosceles triangle

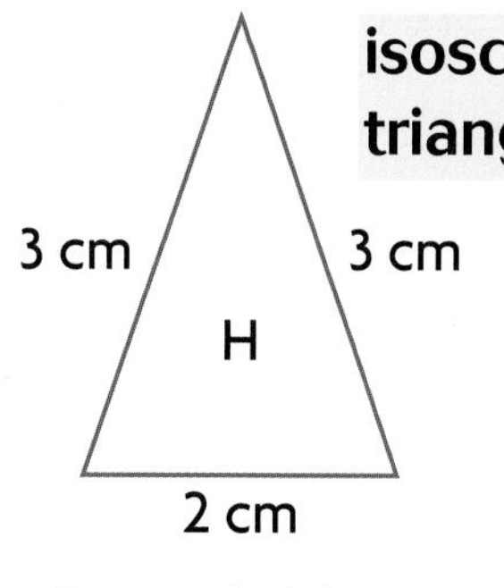

2 equal sides

scalene triangle

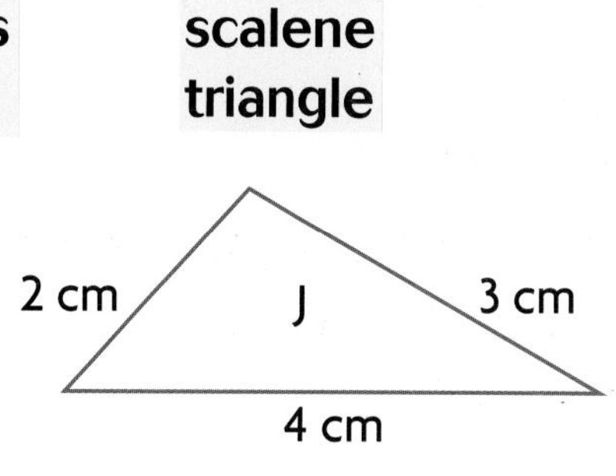

0 equal sides

You can name triangles by their angles.

right triangle

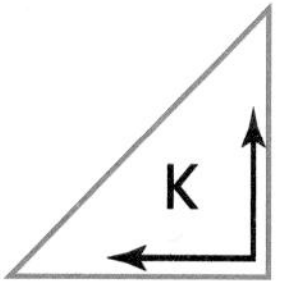

1 right angle

obtuse triangle

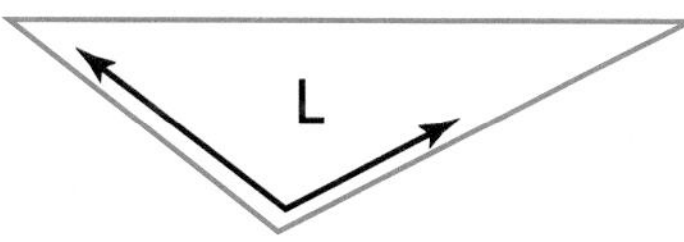

1 obtuse angle

acute triangle

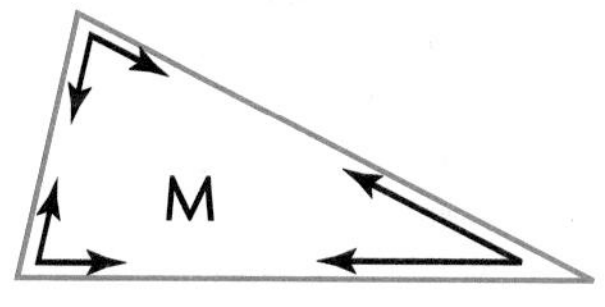

3 acute angles

- How are triangles J and M alike? How are they different?

MATH IDEA You can name and sort triangles by their sides or their angles.

Check

1. **Describe** triangle N by its sides. Then describe it by its angles.

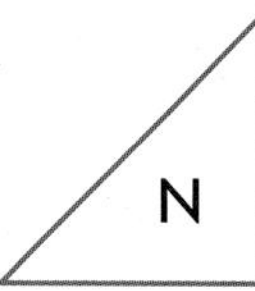

For 2–5, use the triangles at the right. Write *O, P, Q,* or *R*.

2. Which triangles have 0 equal sides?
3. Which triangle is an equilateral triangle?
4. Which triangles have 3 acute angles?
5. Which triangle is obtuse?

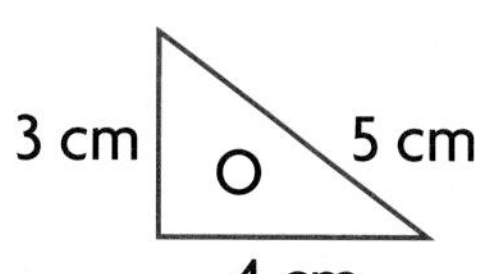

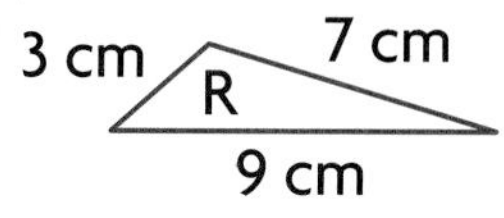

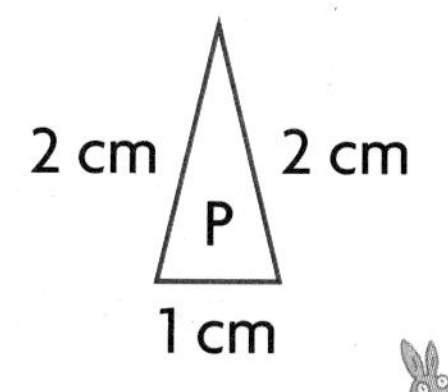

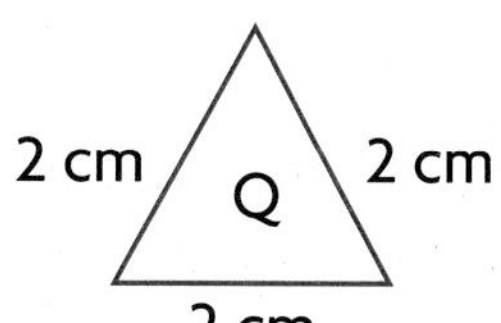

LESSON CONTINUES

Practice and Problem Solving

Extra Practice, page 402, Set D

For 6–8, use the triangles at the right. Write *A, B,* or *C*.

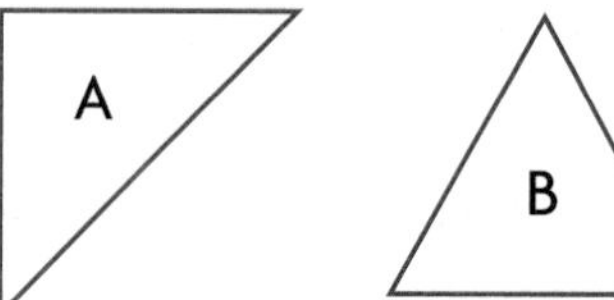

6. Which triangle is scalene?
7. Which triangles have at least 2 equal sides?
8. Which triangle has 1 obtuse angle? Which triangle has 3 acute angles?

Write one letter from each box to describe each triangle.

a. equilateral triangle	**d.** right triangle
b. isosceles triangle	**e.** obtuse triangle
c. scalene triangle	**f.** acute triangle

9. 2 cm 2 cm 2 cm

10.

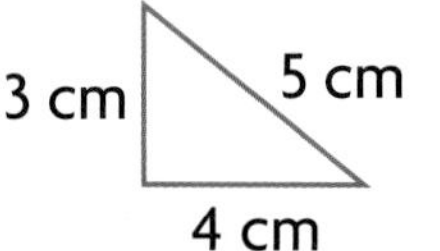

11.

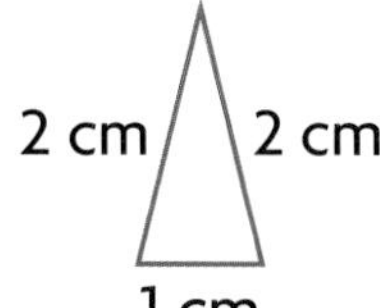

12. 3 cm 2 cm 4 cm

Name each triangle. Write *equilateral, isosceles,* or *scalene.*

13.

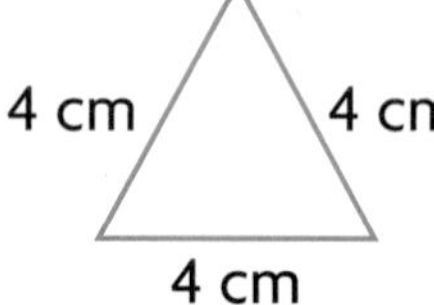

14. 4 cm 6 cm 8 cm

15. 2 cm 2 cm 3 cm

Name each triangle. Write *right, obtuse,* or *acute.*

16.

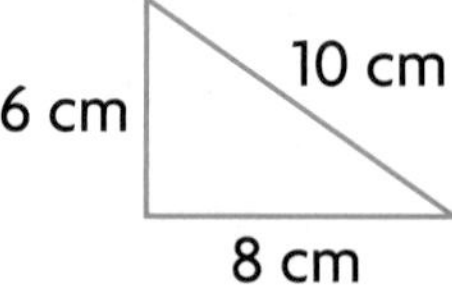

17.

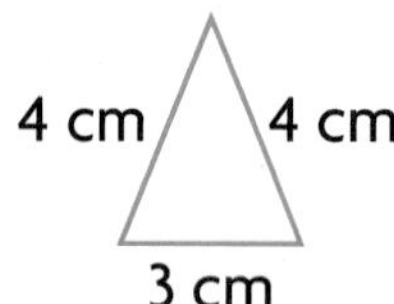

18.

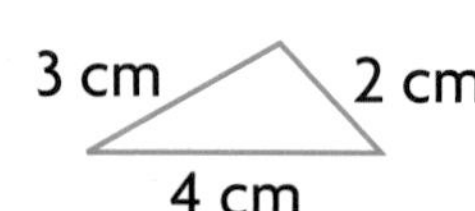

USE DATA For 19–20, use the diagram at the right.

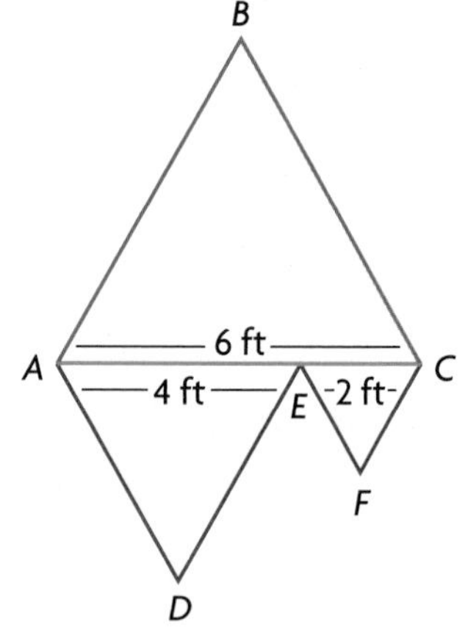

19. Mrs. Liu has a garden with paths that are equilateral triangles. The shortest path from *A* to *C* is the green path. Which path is longer: the blue path or the red path? Explain.

20. **What's the Question?** The answer is 4 feet longer.

21. **Vocabulary Power** The word *parallel* comes from a Greek word, *parallelos*, which means "beside each other." How does this help explain the meaning of *parallel lines*?

22. Draw a triangle with 2 equal sides and one right angle. You may use grid paper to help. Name the triangle.

Mixed Review and Test Prep

23. 6×8 (p. 194)

24. 9×7 (p. 200)

25. 3×9 (p. 164)

26. $5\overline{)35}$ (p. 258)

27. $8\overline{)48}$ (p. 274)

28. $7\overline{)49}$ (p. 274)

For 29–30, use the bar graph. (p. 324)

29. **TEST PREP** How many more people went to the Summer Concert and Storytelling Festival altogether than to the Heritage Parade?

A 20   C 110
B 70   D 130

30. **TEST PREP** About 40 more people are expected to attend the Summer Concert next year. Choose the best number of seats to set up for the concert.

F 50   H 120
G 80   J 130

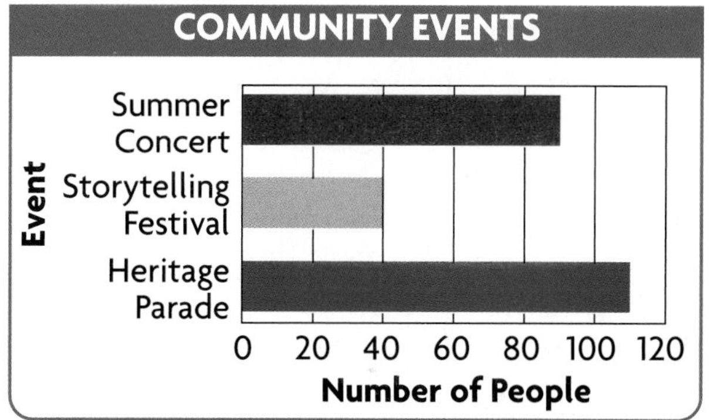

Problem Solving LINKUP ... to Art

Many artists use triangles in their works. The Native American blanket at the right uses different kinds of triangles. Find and name as many triangles on the blanket as you can.

MATERIALS: grid paper, pencil, crayons

1. Draw and color a blanket design on grid paper. Use different kinds of triangles in your design.
2. Trade designs with a classmate and describe the triangles you see.

LESSON 5

Quadrilaterals

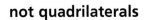

Learn

LIMIT OF FOUR Polygons with 4 sides and 4 angles are quadrilaterals.

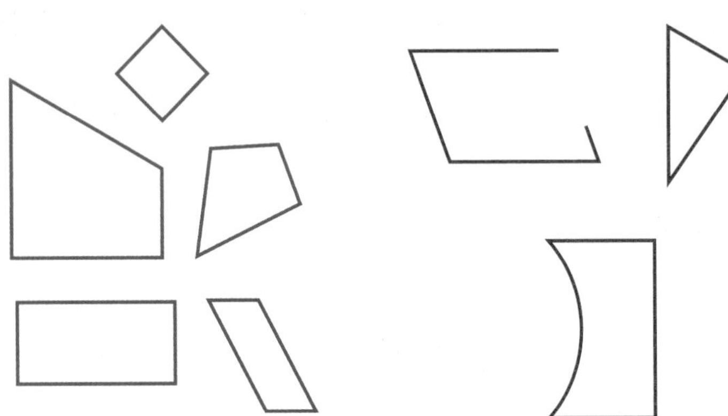

A **trapezoid** is a special kind of quadrilateral. Trapezoids always have one pair of parallel sides, but the sizes of the angles are not always the same.

Quick Review

Describe the lines. Write *parallel* or *intersecting.*

1.
2.
3.
4.
5.

VOCABULARY

trapezoid
parallelogram
rhombus

Technology Link

More Practice:
Harcourt Mega Math
Ice Station Exploration,
Polar Planes,
Level G

Examples of Trapezoids

A

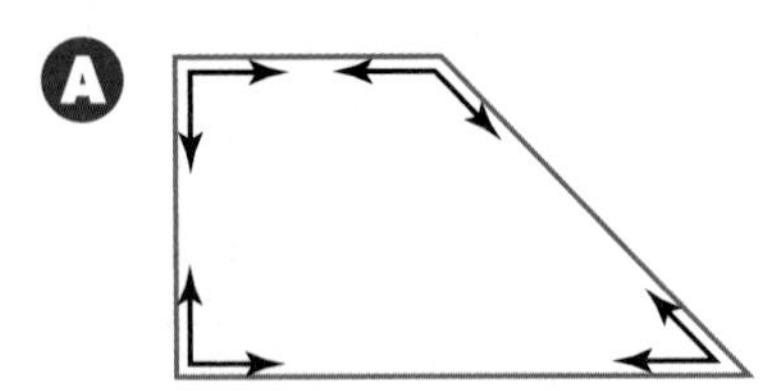

2 right angles
1 acute angle
1 obtuse angle
1 pair of parallel sides

B

2 acute angles
2 obtuse angles
1 pair of parallel sides

- How can you check if two sides of a quadrilateral are parallel?

Other Names for Quadrilaterals

Here are some quadrilaterals with pairs of parallel sides and pairs of equal sides.

parallelograms

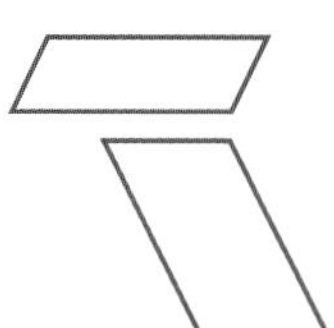

2 pairs of parallel sides
2 pairs of equal sides

rhombuses

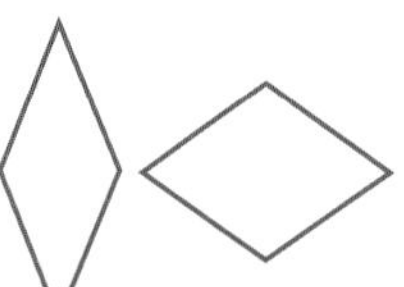

2 pairs of parallel sides
4 equal sides

rectangles

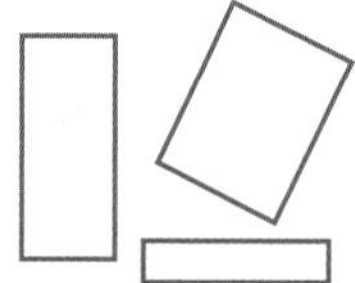

2 pairs of parallel sides
2 pairs of equal sides
4 right angles

squares

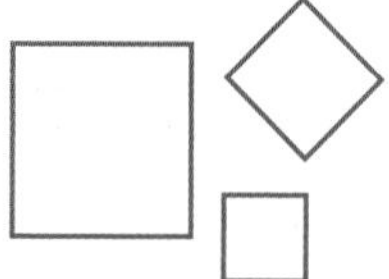

2 pairs of parallel sides
4 equal sides
4 right angles

- Why is a square a rectangle? Why is a square a parallelogram?

MATH IDEA You can name and sort quadrilaterals by looking at their sides and angles.

Check

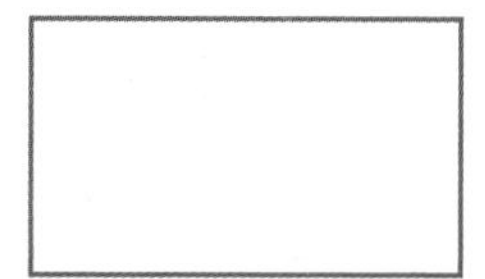

1. **Describe** the sides and angles of this quadrilateral. What is another name for it?

For 2–4, use the quadrilaterals at the right.

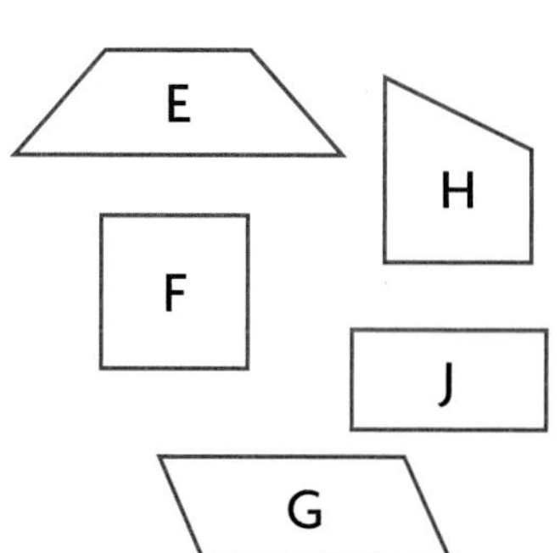

2. Which quadrilaterals have 2 pairs of parallel sides?
3. Which quadrilaterals have 2 or more right angles?
4. How are quadrilateral E and quadrilateral G alike? How are they different?

Write as many names for each quadrilateral as you can.

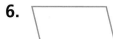

5. 
6. 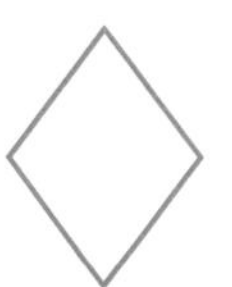
7. 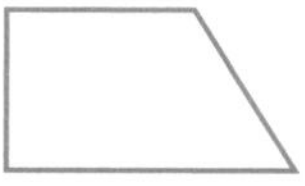
8. 
9.
10. 

LESSON CONTINUES

Practice and Problem Solving

Extra Practice, page 402, Set E

For 11–13, use the quadrilaterals at the right. Write *A, B, C, D,* and *E*.

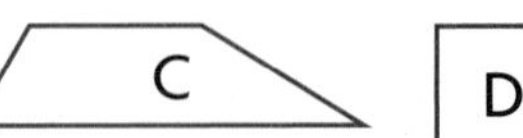

11. Which quadrilaterals have 2 pairs of equal sides?

12. Which quadrilaterals have no right angles?

13. How are quadrilateral A and quadrilateral D alike? How are they different?

For 14–19, write as many names for each quadrilateral as you can.

14. 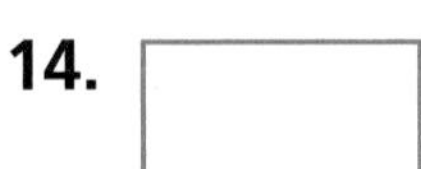

15.

16. 

17.

18. 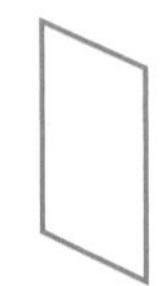

19. 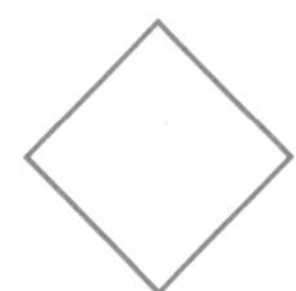

For 20–23, write *all* the letters that describe each quadrilateral.

20. 

21. 

22. 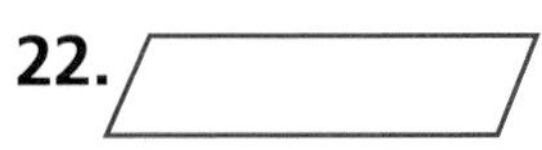

23. 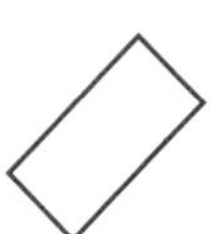

a. It has 4 equal sides.
b. It has 2 pairs of parallel sides.
c. It has 4 right angles.
d. It has 2 pairs of equal sides.

24. Reasoning How is figure G like the figures to its right?

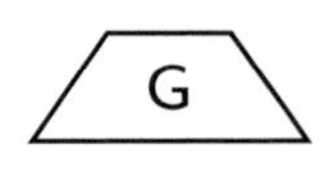

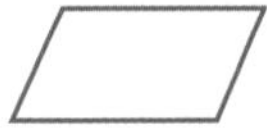

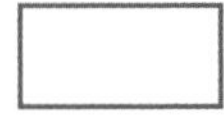

25. I have 4 equal sides and 4 right angles. What am I?

26. I have 5 sides and 5 angles. What am I?

27. **? What's the Error?** Colin said that a square is not a quadrilateral. Explain his error.

28. **Write About It** Draw and label 4 different quadrilaterals on grid paper. Explain how each is different from the others.

29. Akemi sees a tile with 4 right angles. She says it must be a square. Do you agree or disagree? Explain.

30. Dante drew a quadrilateral with 4 right angles and 2 pairs of parallel sides. What could he have drawn?

Mixed Review and Test Prep

Which number is greater? (p. 42)

31. 9,362 or 9,529

32. 35,108 or 35,018

Which number is less? (p. 42)

33. 2,814 or 2,148

34. 8,730 or 998

35. Round 6,398 to the nearest thousand. (p. 52)

36. Maurice will meet his mother in 30 minutes. What time will it be? (p. 134)

For 37–38, use the grid. (p. 328)

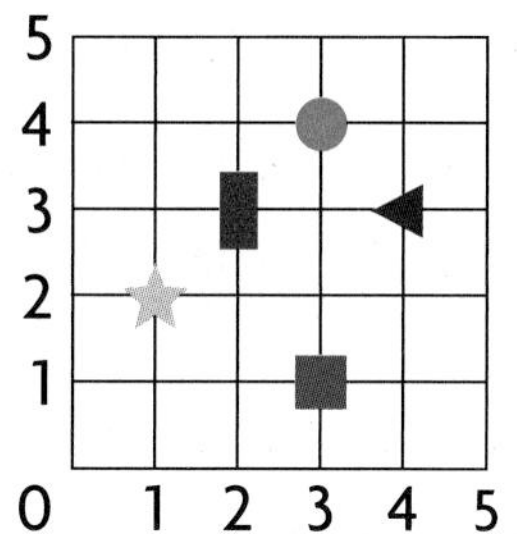

37. **TEST PREP** Which is the ordered pair for the triangle?

A (1,2) **B** (2,3) **C** (3,4) **D** (4,3)

38. **TEST PREP** Which shape is found at (3,4) on the grid?

F square
G circle
H rectangle
J triangle

Problem Solving LINKUP . . . to Reading

STRATEGY • USE GRAPHIC AIDS Graphic aids, such as charts, diagrams, and maps, display information. Drawings and diagrams can be used to show how to build things, such as houses and bridges.

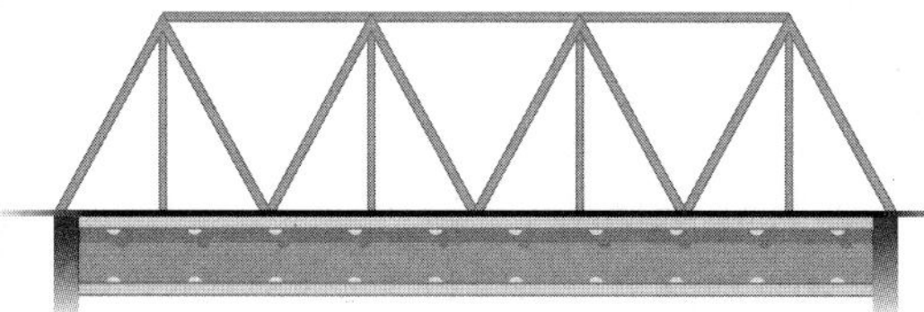

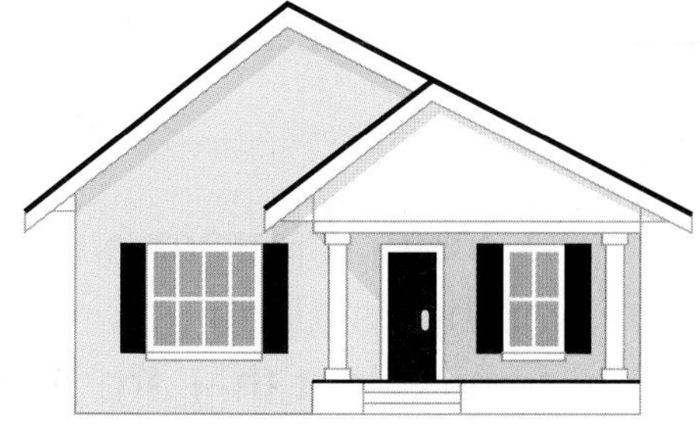

1. Look at the drawing of the bridge. What kinds of angles do you see? What plane figures were used in the drawing?

2. Look at the drawing of the house. What kind of angle was used for the roof? What other angles do you see in the drawing?

LESSON 6

Problem Solving Strategy
Draw a Diagram

PROBLEM Mr. Carter drew some plane figures on a chalkboard. He asked his students to show how the figures were alike, and how they were different.

Quick Review

Tell how many sides each figure has.

1. △ 2. ⬠

3. ▭ 4. □

5. ⬡

VOCABULARY

Venn diagram

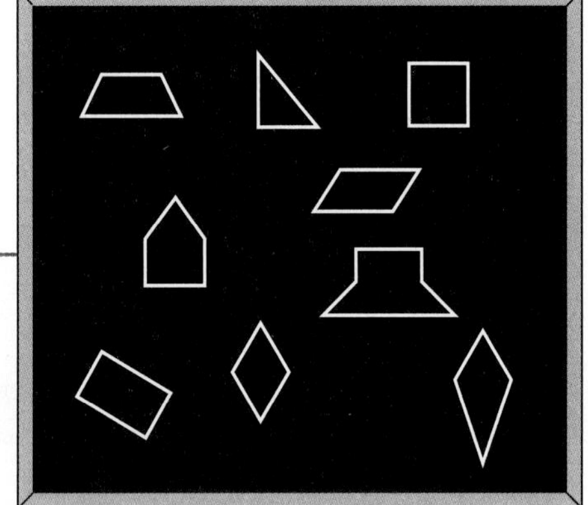

UNDERSTAND

- What are you asked to find?
- What information will you use?

PLAN

- What strategy can you use?

You can *draw a diagram*.

SOLVE

- How can you show how the figures are alike and how they are different?

You can *draw a Venn diagram*.

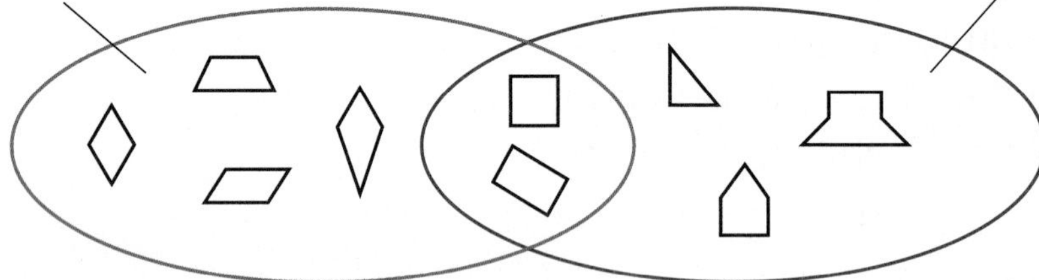

A **Venn diagram** shows relationships among sets of things. Each set in the diagram above has plane figures in it that are described by its label. The figures inside the area where the sets overlap are described by both labels.

CHECK

- What other strategy could you use?

Problem Solving Practice

1. **What if** the plane figure shown below was one of the figures on the chalkboard? Describe where it would be in the Venn diagram on page 400.

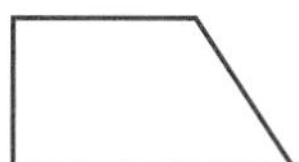

2. Some Venn diagrams have sets that do not overlap. Explain why the sets in the diagram below do not overlap.

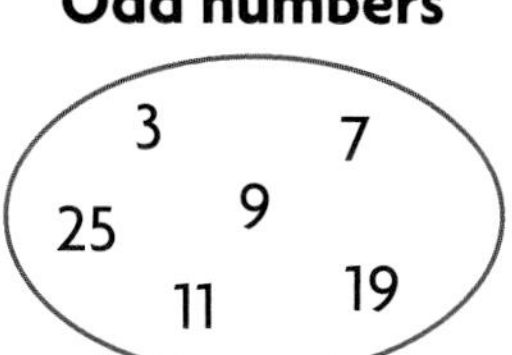

Strategies

- **Draw a Diagram or Picture**
- Make a Model or Act It Out
- Make an Organized List
- Find a Pattern
- Make a Table or Graph
- Predict and Test
- Work Backward
- Solve a Simpler Problem
- Write a Number Sentence
- Use Logical Reasoning

Problem Solving

Marisa used the labels *multiples of 4* and *multiples of 6* for the sets in her Venn diagram.

3. Which number could be in the area where the sets overlap?

   A 36   **C** 28
   B 32   **D** 26

4. Which number would *not* be in the area where the sets overlap?

   F 12   **H** 30
   G 24   **J** 36

Mixed Strategy Practice

USE DATA For 5–7, use the bar graph.

5. Ms. Colmery's class filled 5 rows and 2 extra chairs in the museum auditorium. How many chairs were in each row?

6. **REASONING** Describe at least two ways chairs can be arranged in equal rows for Mr. Leong's class.

7. How many students visited the museum in all? Write a number sentence and solve.

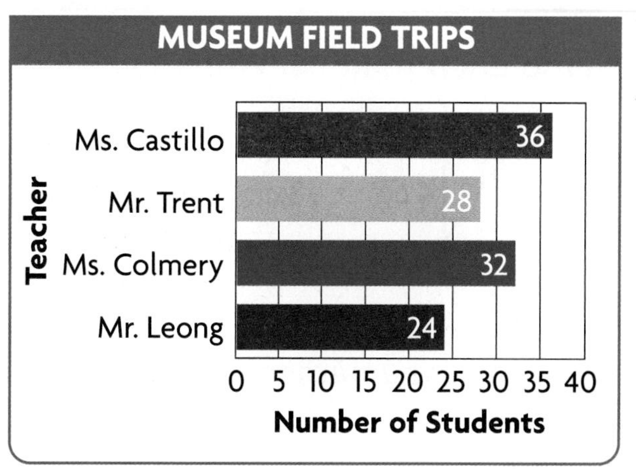

Extra Practice

Set A (pp. 384–387)

Name each figure.

1. •
2. 
3.
4. ⟷

Write whether each angle is a *right angle,* an *acute angle,* or an *obtuse angle.*

5. 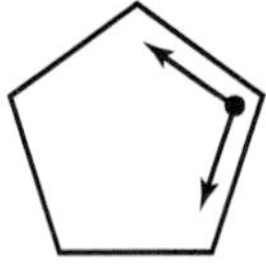
6. 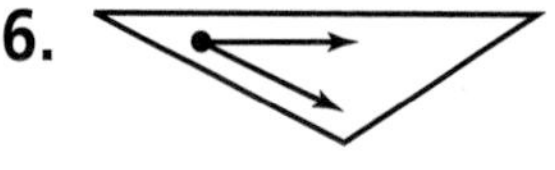
7. 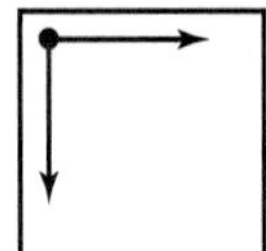

Set B (pp. 388–389)

Describe the lines. Write *parallel* or *intersecting*. Tell whether the intersecting lines are *perpendicular* or *not perpendicular*.

1. 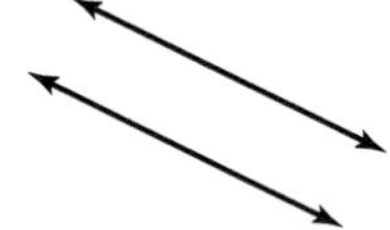
2. 
3. 
4. 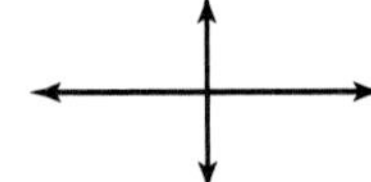

Set C (pp. 390–391)

Write the number of sides and angles each polygon has. Then name the polygon.

1. 
2. 
3. 
4. 
5. 

Set D (pp. 392–395)

Name each triangle. Write *equilateral, isosceles,* or *scalene.*

1. 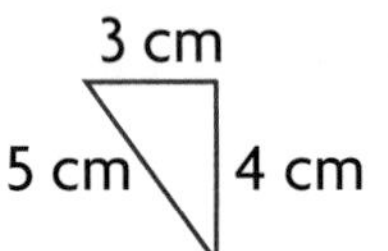

2. 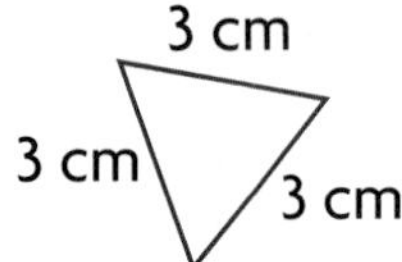

3. 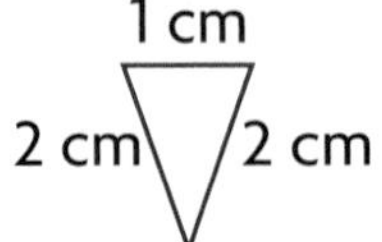

4. 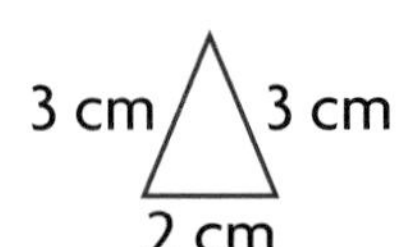

5. 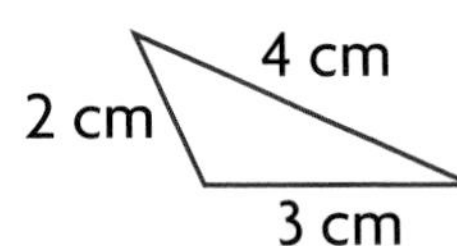

Set E (pp. 396–399)

Write as many names for each quadrilateral as you can.

1. 
2. 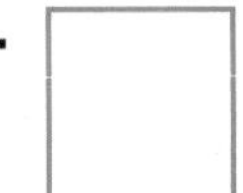
3. 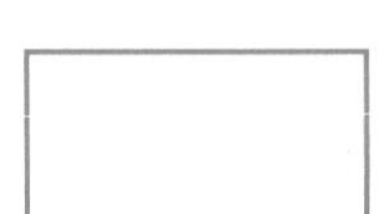
4. 
5. 

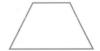

Review/Test

✓ CHECK VOCABULARY

Choose the best term from the box.

equilateral
line segment
perpendicular
angle
parallel

1. An _?_ is formed by two rays with the same endpoint. (p. 384)
2. Intersecting lines that cross to form right angles are _?_ lines. (p. 388)
3. A triangle with 3 equal sides is _?_. (p. 393)

✓ CHECK SKILLS

Write whether each angle is a *right angle*, an *acute angle*, or an *obtuse angle*. (pp. 384–387)

4. 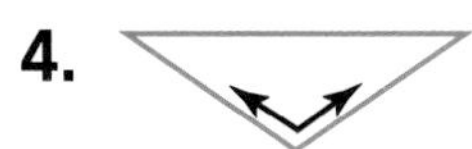
5. 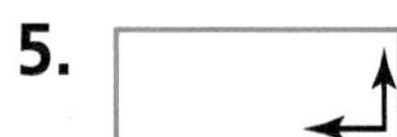
6. 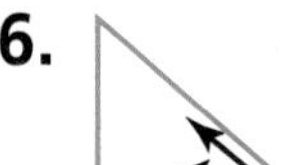
7. 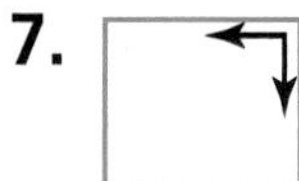

Write the number of sides and angles each polygon has. Then name the polygon. (pp. 390–391)

8. 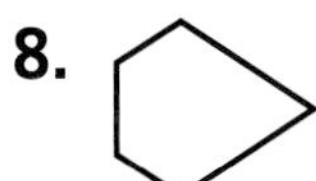
9.
10.
11.

Name each triangle. Write *equilateral, isosceles,* or *scalene*. (pp. 392–395)

12. 3 cm, 3 cm, 2 cm
13. 3 cm, 3 cm, 3 cm
14. 3 cm, 4 cm, 2 cm
15. 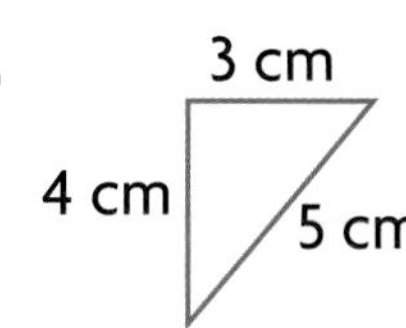

Write as many names for each quadrilateral as you can. (pp. 396–399)

16.
17. 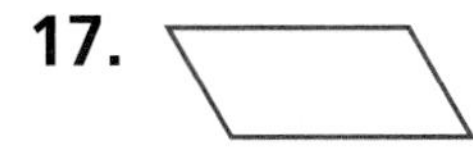
18. 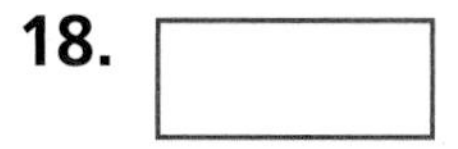
19. 

✓ CHECK PROBLEM SOLVING

20. Describe where the figure below should be in the Venn diagram. Explain. (pp. 400–401)

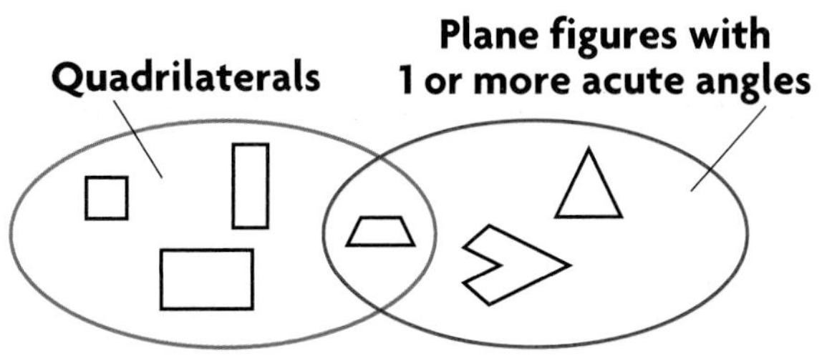

Standardized Test Prep

NUMBER SENSE, CONCEPTS, AND OPERATIONS

TIP **Check your work.** See item 1. Multiply the number of cookies in each bag by the number of bags you think Barry used. Your answer should equal the number of cookies Barry made.

1. Barry made 36 cookies for a bake sale. He put 4 cookies in each bag. How many bags did he use?

A 6
B 8
C 9
D 12

2. Mr. Dixon planted 8 rows of tomato plants in his garden. There are 6 plants in each row. How many tomato plants are in Mr. Dixon's garden?

F 14
G 16
H 24
J 48

3. Which division sentence belongs to the same fact family as these multiplication sentences?

$6 \times 4 = 24$ $4 \times 6 = 24$

A $24 \div 4 = 6$
B $24 \div 3 = 8$
C $24 \div 8 = 3$
D $24 \div 1 = 24$

4. Explain It Ben has 1,109 stamps. Ali has 1,372 stamps. Explain how to ESTIMATE about how many more stamps Ali has than Ben.

ALGEBRAIC THINKING

5. Which number sentence is shown by the stars below?

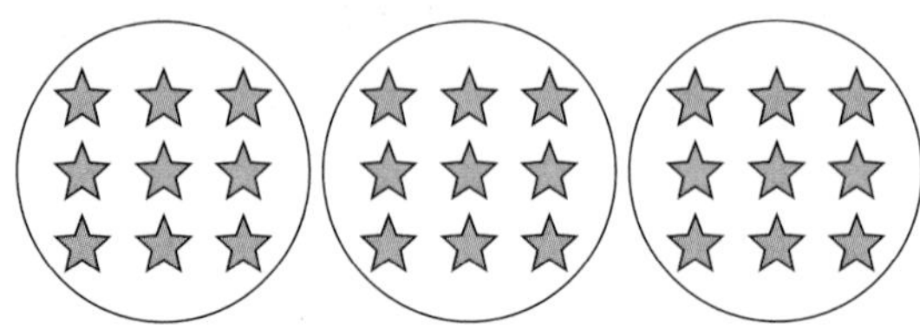

F $12 \div 3 = 4$
G $3 + 9 = 12$
H $27 \div 3 = 9$
J $9 - 3 = 6$

6. Pat wrote this expression.

$40 \div 5$

Which of the following has the same value as Pat's expression?

A 4×5
B $10 - 2$
C $15 - 6$
D 5×2

7. Explain It Tyler collected 36 trading cards. He stacked the cards in 6 equal piles. How many cards were in each pile?

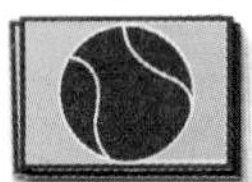

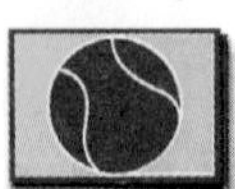

Write a number sentence to solve the problem. Tell how you decided what operation to use.

DATA ANALYSIS AND PROBABILITY

8. The line plot below shows the number of books read by a third-grade class during the summer. Each *X* on the line plot stands for 1 student. How many students read more than 8 books?

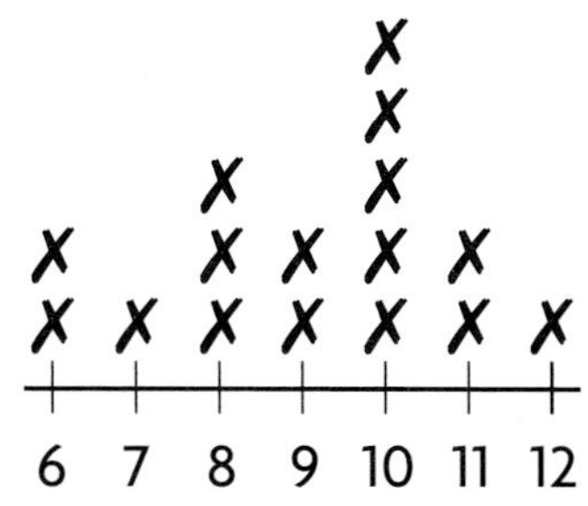

F 3 H 8
G 6 J 10

9. Look at the line plot above. How many students read fewer than 10 books?

A 6 C 10
B 8 D 12

10. **Explain It** Nicole made this bar graph to show the number of coins in her collection. Describe the data in the bar graph.

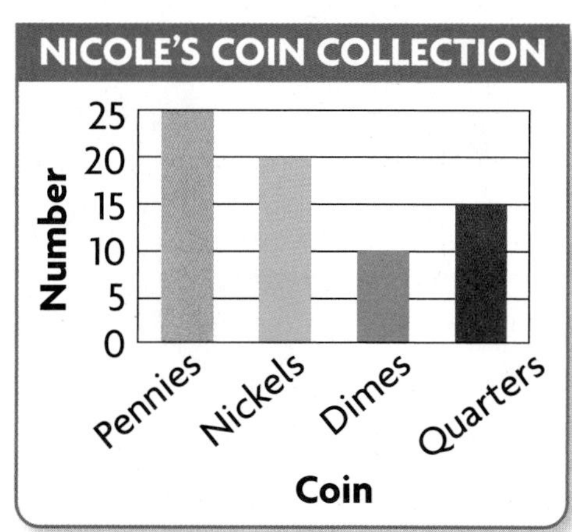

GEOMETRY AND SPATIAL SENSE

11. A garden is in the shape of a rhombus. Which figure below shows the shape of the garden?

F H 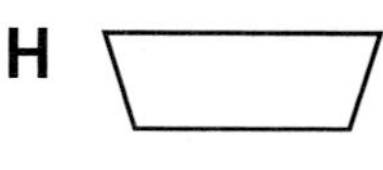

G J 

12. Jessica is making a design with this triangle.

What kind of triangle is she using?

A obtuse C right
B acute D equilateral

13. George wants to draw a pentagon. How many sides does he need to draw?

F 4 H 6
G 5 J 8

14. **Explain It** Carla wants to put a ribbon border around this picture.

7 inches

5 inches  5 inches

7 inches

How much ribbon will she need? How do you know?

CHAPTER 20

Congruence and Symmetry

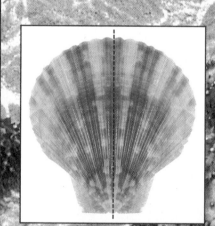

FAST FACT • SCIENCE Many starfish have five arms, but some kinds have many more. These arms move, so you will see symmetry on a starfish some of the time. Symmetry can also be seen in other animals and objects.

PROBLEM SOLVING **Is the dashed line on the shell a line of symmetry? How do you know?**

CHECK WHAT YOU KNOW

Use this page to help you review and remember important skills needed for Chapter 20.

SAME SIZE, SAME SHAPE

Tell whether the figures are the same size and shape. Write *yes* or *no*.

1.

2.

3.

4.

5.

6.

7.

8.

9.

VOCABULARY POWER

REVIEW

half [haf] *noun*

The word *half* is sometimes used as part of a word or part of a phrase. Write a sentence using one of the following:

half dollar, half hour, half-moon, half note, halftime

PREVIEW

congruent
symmetry
line of symmetry
similar
slide
flip
turn

www.harcourtschool.com/mathglossary

LESSON 1

Congruent Figures

Quick Review

Write the number of sides and angles each polygon has.

1. (triangle) 2. (rectangle)
3. (hexagon) 4. (square)
5. (pentagon)

VOCABULARY
congruent

MATERIALS
pattern blocks, triangle dot paper, crayons

Explore

ARE THEY THE SAME? **Congruent** figures have the same *size* and *shape*. Figures can be in different positions and still be congruent.

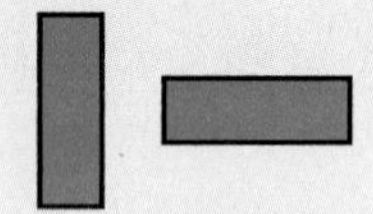

These pairs of figures are congruent.

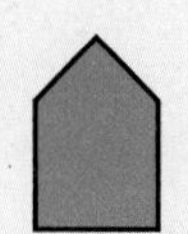

These pairs of figures are not congruent.

Technology Link
More Practice:
Harcourt Mega Math
Ice Station Exploration,
Polar Planes,
Level H

Use pattern blocks to find and build congruent figures.

- Sort a group of pattern blocks. Look for blocks that are the same size and shape. Put congruent pieces together.
- Use only small green triangles to make a figure that is congruent to the yellow hexagon. On triangle dot paper, draw the figure you made.
- Use any pattern blocks to make a different figure that is congruent to the yellow hexagon. Draw the figure you made.

How many green triangles do I use to make a figure that is congruent to the yellow hexagon?

Talk About It

- How do you know that the figures you made are congruent?

Connect

You can tell if two figures are congruent by tracing one figure and placing it over the second figure. If one figure covers the other exactly, they are congruent.

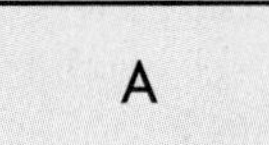

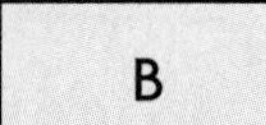

C

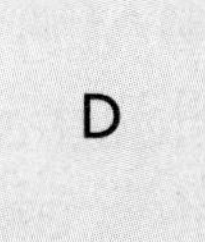

Trace and cut out rectangle A. Place it over rectangle B. Are rectangles A and B congruent?

Trace and cut out square C. Place it over square D. Are squares C and D congruent?

Practice and Problem Solving

Trace and cut out each pair of figures. Tell if the figures are congruent. Write *yes* or *no*.

1. 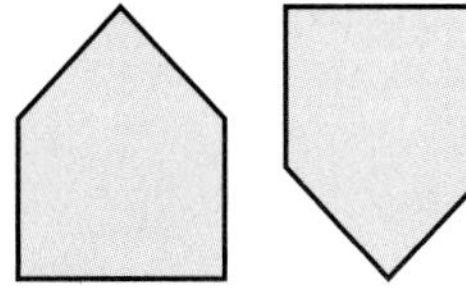

2. 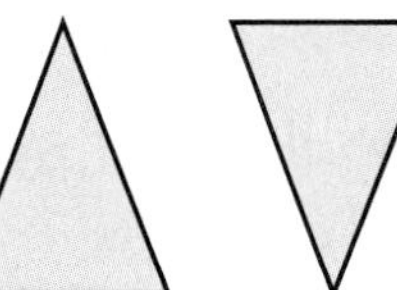

3.  

4. REASONING Joe says that the two figures below are congruent. Do you agree? Explain.

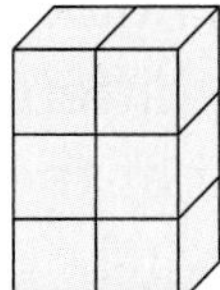 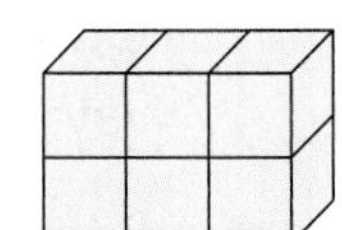

5. **Write About It** Copy this figure on grid paper. Draw a congruent figure. Then explain how you know the figures are congruent.

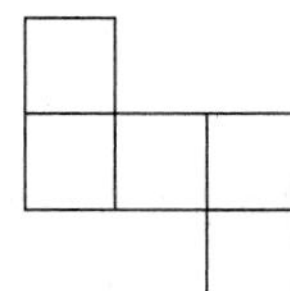

Mixed Review and Test Prep

6. $328 + 846$ (p. 72)

7. $574 + 659$ (p. 72)

8. $728 - 485$ (p. 96)

9. $932 - 267$ (p. 96)

10. **TEST PREP** Karson's play began at 6:25 P.M. It lasted 50 minutes. At what time did the play end? (p. 134)

A 5:35 P.M.
B 6:50 P.M.
C 7:15 P.M.
D 7:50 P.M.

LESSON 2

Symmetry

Quick Review

Does each figure appear to be congruent to the figure at the right?

1. 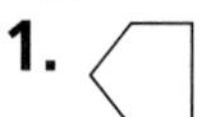
2.
3.
4.
5.

VOCABULARY

symmetry line of symmetry

Learn

HALF AND HALF A figure has **symmetry** if it can be folded along a line so that the two parts match exactly. The line is called a **line of symmetry**.

MATH IDEA Some figures have one or more lines of symmetry. Some figures have no lines of symmetry.

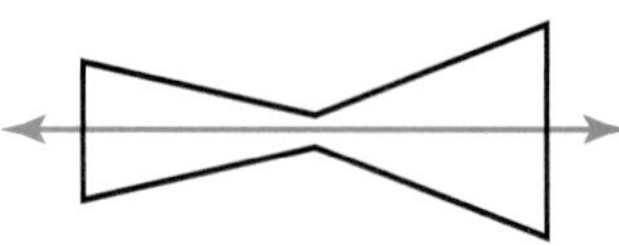

1 line of symmetry

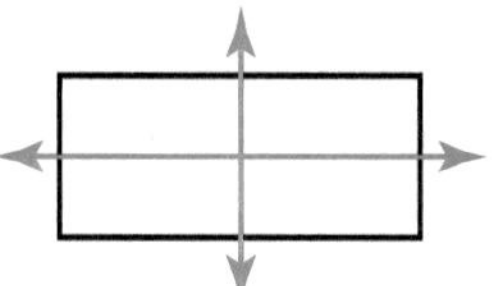

2 lines of symmetry

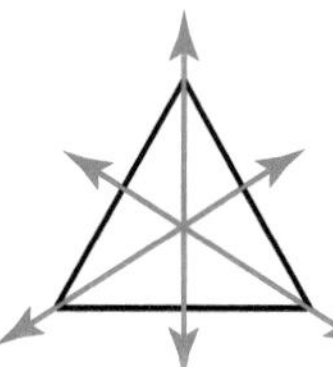

3 lines of symmetry

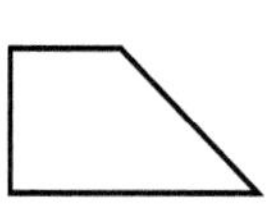

0 lines of symmetry

You can trace and fold a figure to find lines of symmetry.

Activity

MATERIALS: pattern blocks, paper, scissors

STEP 1

Trace a blue rhombus on a sheet of paper. Cut out the figure.

STEP 2

Fold the figure in half so that the two halves match. Draw a line along the fold.

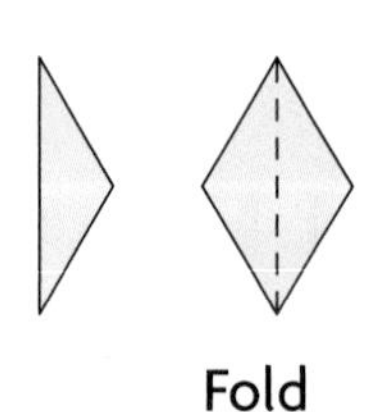

STEP 3

Fold the figure in half in a different way so that the two halves match. Draw a line along this fold.

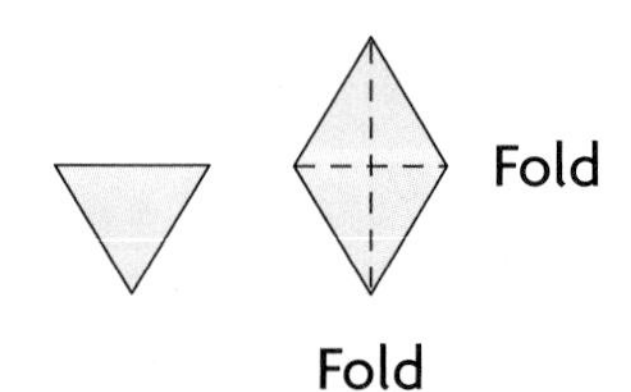

- How many lines of symmetry does the figure have?
- Repeat the activity with an orange square and a red trapezoid. How many lines of symmetry does each figure have?

Check

1. **Explain** how you know the blue line in the figure at the right is a line of symmetry.

Tell if the blue line is a line of symmetry. Write *yes* or *no*.

2. 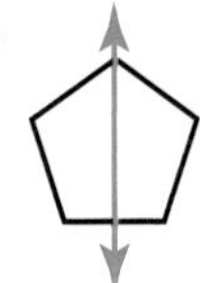

3. 

4. 

Practice and Problem Solving

Extra Practice, page 418, Set A

Tell if the blue line is a line of symmetry. Write *yes* or *no*.

5. 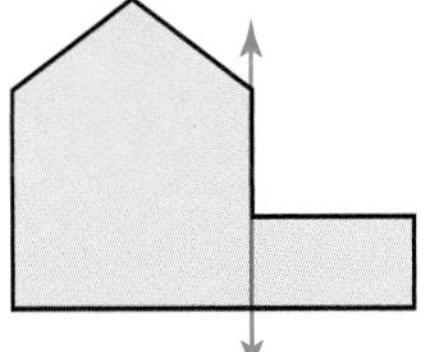

6. 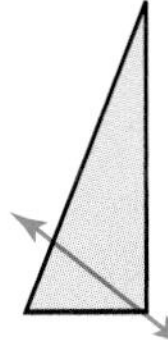

7. 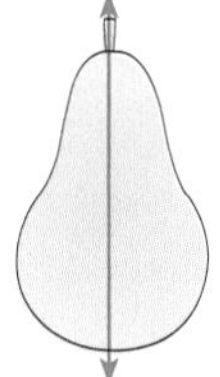

Trace each figure. Then draw the line or lines of symmetry.

8. 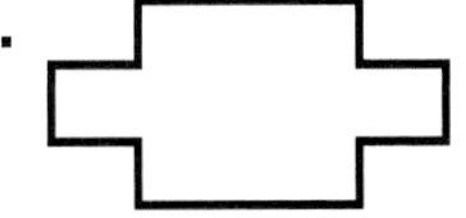

9. 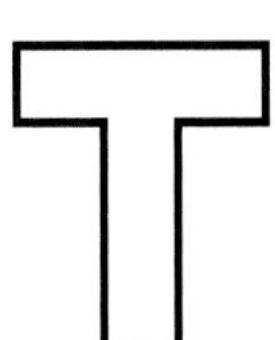

10. 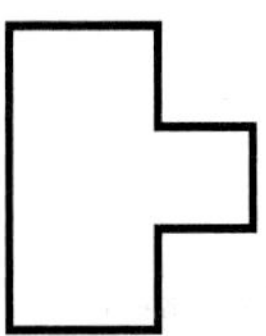

11. Jody says that a circle has too many lines of symmetry to count. Do you agree or disagree? Explain.

12. **Write a problem** about a figure that has no lines of symmetry. Draw the figure on grid paper.

13. **Vocabulary Power** The word *figure* comes from a Latin word, *figura*, which means "to form or shape." List four geometric figures and draw a picture of each.

14. ***FAST FACT*** • SCIENCE In 1959, John Pennekamp Coral Reef State Park in Florida became the first undersea park in the United States. How many years ago was this?

Mixed Review and Test Prep

Find the product. (p. 218)

15. $(4 \times 2) \times 5$ 16. $7 \times (3 \times 0)$

Write + or − to make the number sentence true. (p. 80)

17. 32 ● 26 = 6 18. 48 ● 24 = 72

19. **TEST PREP** Larry bought a book for $6.75. He paid with a $10 bill. How much change did he get? (p. 120)

A $2.25 C $6.75
B $3.25 D $16.75

LESSON 3

Similar Figures

Learn

SIZE WISE Figures that have the same shape but may have different sizes are called **similar** figures.

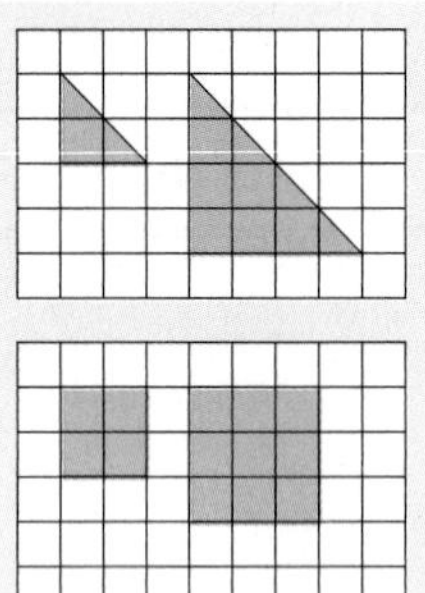

These pairs of figures are similar.

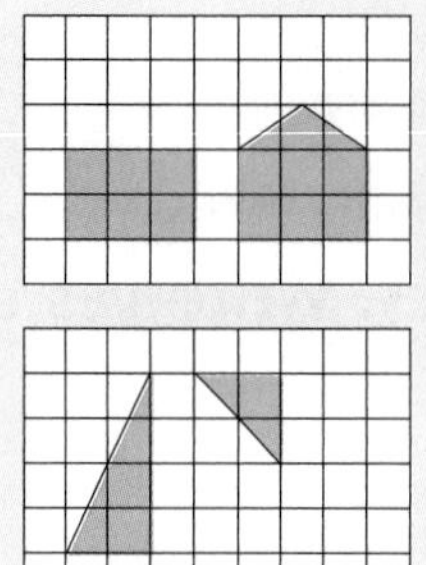

These pairs of figures are not similar.

When you enlarge or reduce the size of a figure, the figure you make is similar to the first one.

Quick Review

Tell if the blue line is a line of symmetry. Write *yes* or *no*.

1.
2.
3.
4.
5.

VOCABULARY
similar

MATERIALS
1-inch grid paper, 1-centimeter grid paper

Activity

- Copy the figure at the right on 1-inch grid paper. Copy one square at a time.

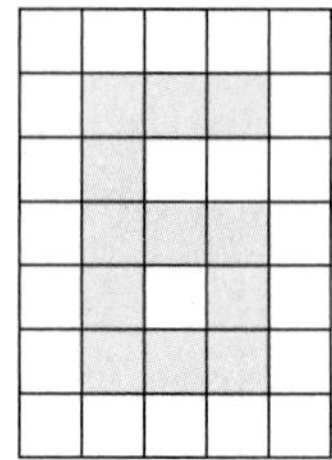

- Is the figure you drew similar to the figure at the right? Is it congruent? Explain how you know.
- Draw a figure on 1-centimeter grid paper. Copy the figure you drew, one square at a time, on 1-inch grid paper.
- Compare the two figures you drew. Tell what you know about the figures.

MATH IDEA Figures that are the same shape are similar, no matter what size they are or what position they are in.

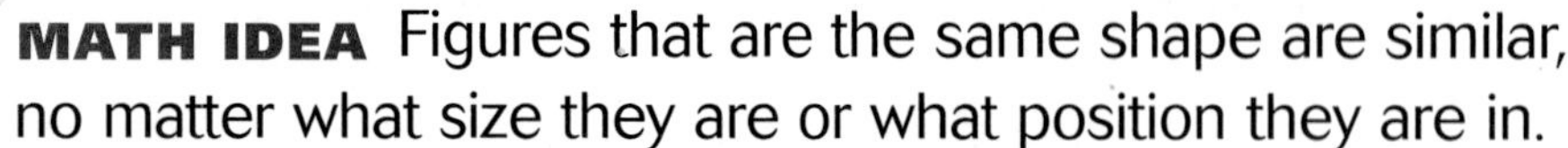

Check

1. **Explain** whether or not these two figures are both similar and congruent.

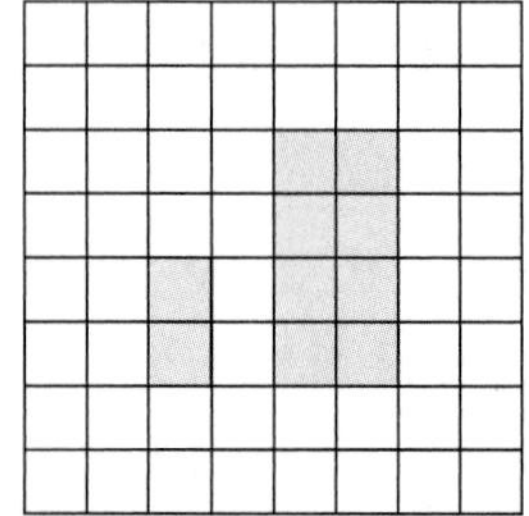

Tell if the figures appear to be similar. Write *yes* or *no*.

2. 

3. 

4.

Practice and Problem Solving

Extra Practice, page 418, Set B

Tell if the figures appear to be similar. Write *yes* or *no*.

5.

6. 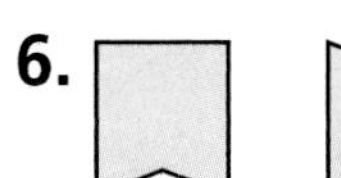

7. 

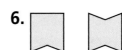

Draw a similar figure for each. Use 1-inch grid paper.

8. 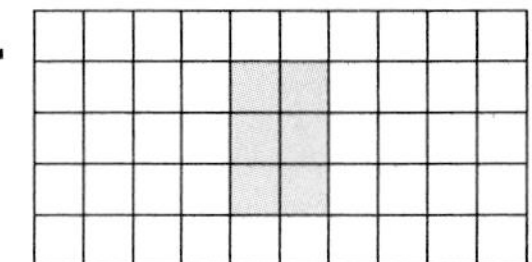

9. 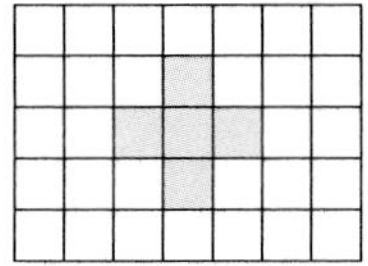

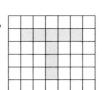

10. 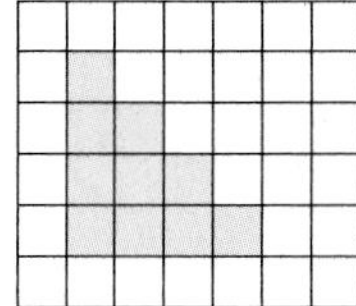

Draw a similar figure for each. Use 1-centimeter grid paper.

11. 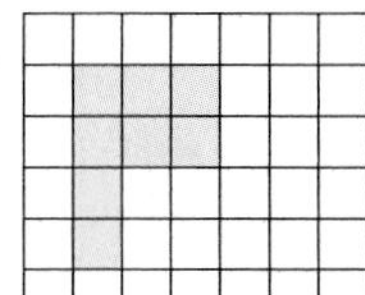

12. 

13. 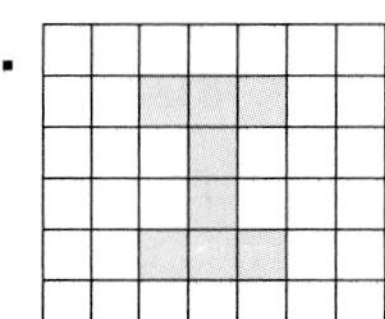

14. **REASONING** Do figures have to be in the same position for them to be similar? Explain.

15. **REASONING** Are all rectangles similar? Draw pictures to explain.

16. **Write About It** Draw a design on 1-inch grid paper. Have a classmate draw the design on 1-centimeter grid paper. Are the designs similar? How can you tell?

Mixed Review and Test Prep

17. $4 \times 6 = \blacksquare$ (p. 178)

18. $8 \times 10 = \blacksquare$ (p. 212)

19. $28 \div 7 = \blacksquare$ (p. 274)

20. $32 \div 4 = \blacksquare$ (p. 260)

21. **TEST PREP** Choose a rule for the table. (p. 216)

bicycles	1	2	3	4
wheels	2	4	6	8

A Multiply bicycles by 2.
B Multiply wheels by 2.
C Add 2 to bicycles.
D Subtract 2 from wheels.

Slides, Flips, and Turns

Quick Review

Does each figure appear to be congruent to the figure at the right?

1.
2.
3.
4.
5.

VOCABULARY
slide flip turn

MATERIALS
pattern blocks, paper

Explore

A plane figure can be moved in different ways.

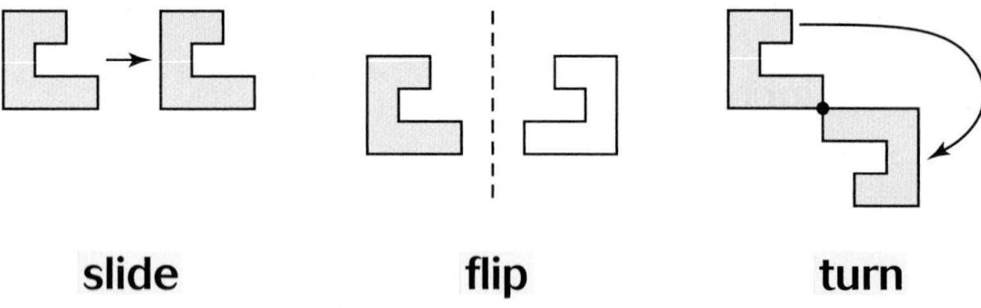

slide flip turn

Activity

Use a red trapezoid. Show different ways to move the block.

STEP 1

Trace the block on your paper.

STEP 2

Slide the block and trace it. Label the drawing "slide."

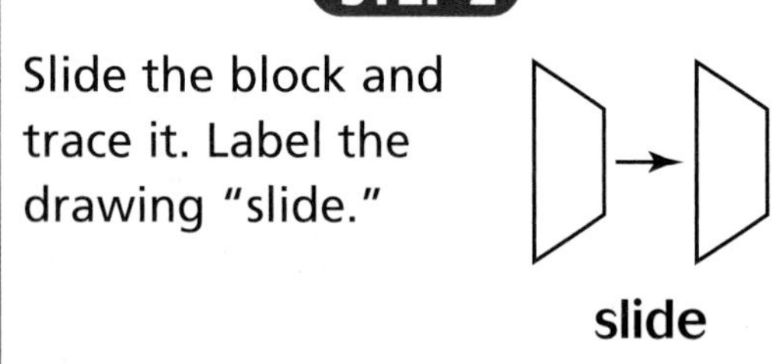

STEP 3

Flip the block and trace it. Label the drawing "flip."

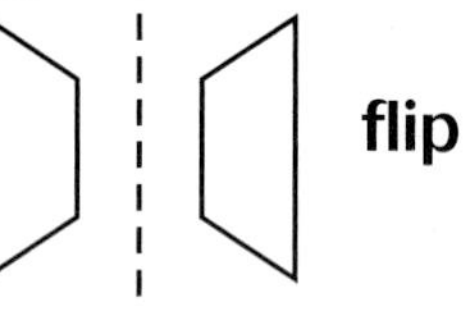

STEP 4

Turn the block 180° and trace it. Label the drawing "turn."

turn

- Use a different pattern block. Repeat the steps above.

Talk About It

- Describe your drawings. Does a slide ever look like a flip?
- **REASONING** Does the size or shape of the block change when you slide, flip, or turn it? Explain.

More Practice:
Harcourt Mega Math
Ice Station Exploration,
Polar Planes, Level M

Connect

Think about how you use slides, flips, and turns to describe motions of real-life objects.

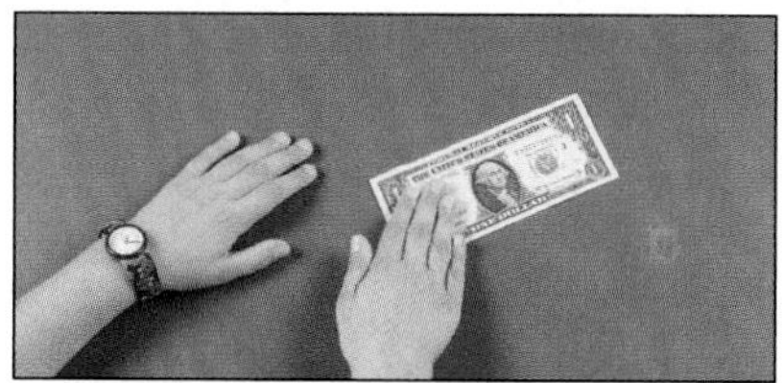

You can slide a dollar bill across a counter.

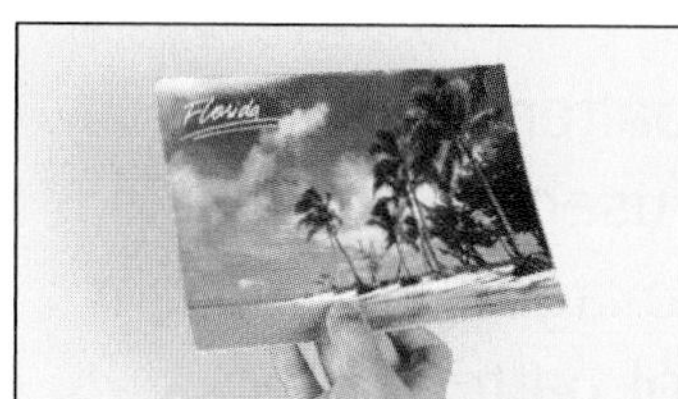

You can flip a postcard.

You can turn a puzzle piece.

MATH IDEA You can describe a motion used to move a plane figure as a slide, a flip, or a turn.

Practice and Problem Solving

Tell what kind of motion was used to move each plane figure. Write *slide, flip,* or *turn*.

1. 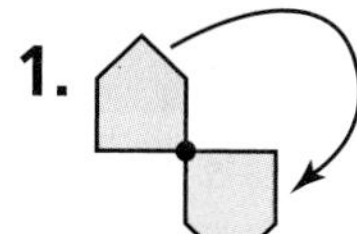

2. 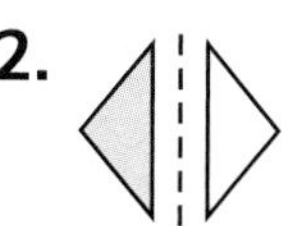

3. 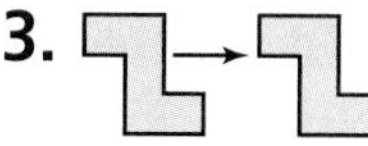

4. 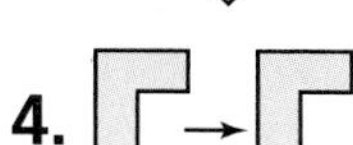

5. 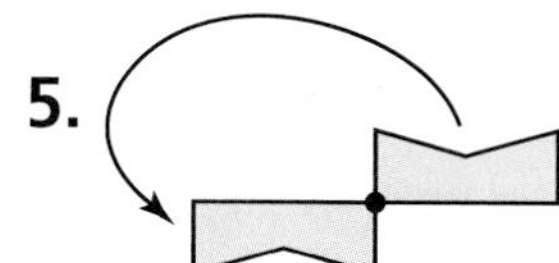

6. 

7. Which figure shows what Figure A would look like after a flip? Write *X*, *Y*, or *Z*.

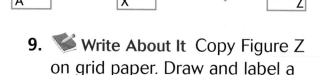

8. **REASONING** Draw a picture to predict the result of turning Figure A. What do you notice?

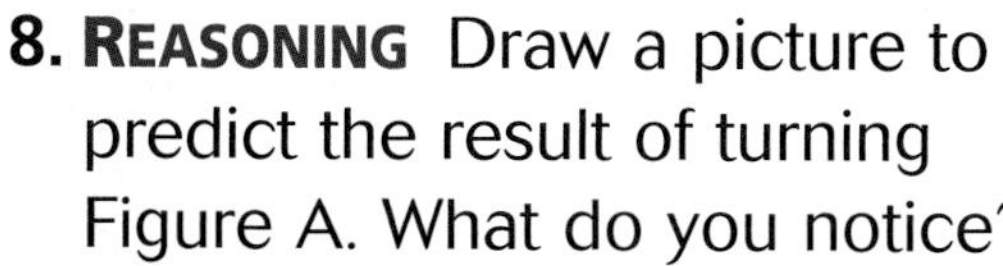

9. **Write About It** Copy Figure Z on grid paper. Draw and label a slide, flip, and turn of the figure.

Mixed Review and Test Prep

10. $9 \times 3 = ■$ (p. 164)

11. $6 \times 5 = ■$ (p. 160)

Write a rule for each pattern and predict the next three numbers. (p. 30)

12. 67, 63, 59, 55, ■, ■, ■

13. 28, 36, 44, 52, ■, ■, ■

14. **TEST PREP** The library ordered six copies of a book for $54. How much did each book cost? (p. 284)

A $6 **C** $8

B $7 **D** $9

LESSON 5

Problem Solving Strategy
Make a Model

Quick Review

Does each figure appear to be congruent to △ the figure at the right?

1. △
2. △
3. ◺
4. ◿
5. ▽

PROBLEM Tina combined pattern blocks to make one large polygon. She used 3 trapezoids and 7 triangles to make the hexagon at the right. What is another combination of pattern blocks that can be used to make a hexagon that is congruent to this one?

Tina's hexagon

UNDERSTAND

- What are you asked to find?
- What information will you use?

PLAN

- What strategy can you use to solve the problem?

  You can *make a model.*

SOLVE

- How can you use the strategy to solve the problem?

  Make a model of Tina's hexagon. Then use some different blocks to make a hexagon that is congruent to Tina's hexagon. The hexagon shown at the right is congruent to Tina's hexagon.

  So, 1 hexagon, 1 rhombus, 1 trapezoid, and 5 triangles can be used to make the same shape.

CHECK

- How can you check your answer?
- Are there any other possible models? Make a model to explain.

Problem Solving Practice

Make a model to solve.

1. **What if** Tina used pattern blocks to make the rhombus shown at the right? What is another combination of pattern blocks that can be used to make a rhombus that is congruent to this one?

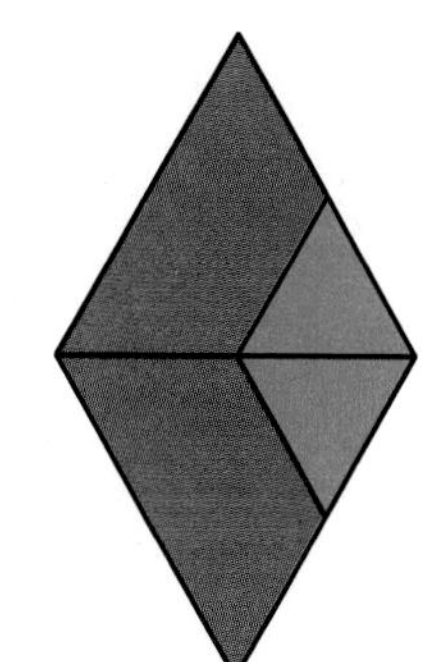

2. Use a different combination of pattern blocks to make another congruent rhombus.

Strategies

- Draw a Diagram or Picture
- **Make a Model or Act It Out**
- Make an Organized List
- Find a Pattern
- Make a Table or Graph
- Predict and Test
- Work Backward
- Solve a Simpler Problem
- Write a Number Sentence
- Use Logical Reasoning

Problem Solving

For 3–4, use pattern blocks to solve.

3. How many green triangles are needed to make a figure that is congruent to a red trapezoid?

   A 2 **C** 4
   B 3 **D** 5

4. How many red trapezoids are needed to make a figure that is congruent to a yellow hexagon?

   F 2 **H** 4
   G 3 **J** 5

Mixed Strategy Practice

USE DATA For 5–6, use the line plot at the right.

5. Each X on the line plot stands for one student. How many students saw more than 4 movies last year?

6. What is the range for this set of data? What is the mode?

7. There were 438 people on a train. At the station, 113 people got off and 256 people got on. How many people are on the train now?

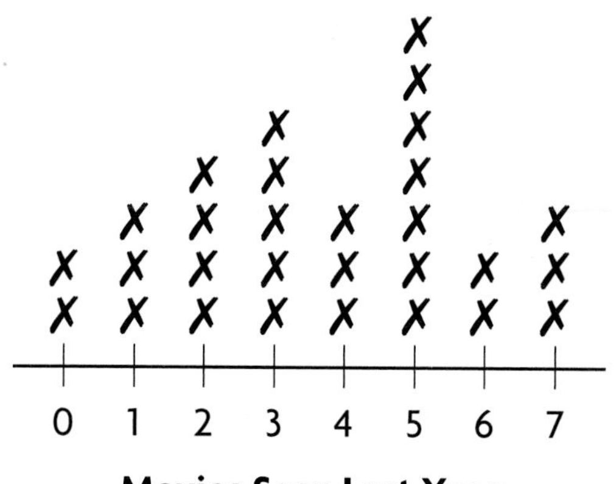

8. Mimi bought a sandwich for $2.75 and a carton of milk for $1.25. She paid with a $5 bill. How much change should she get?

Extra Practice

Set A (pp. 410–411)

Tell if the blue line is a line of symmetry. Write *yes* or *no*.

1. 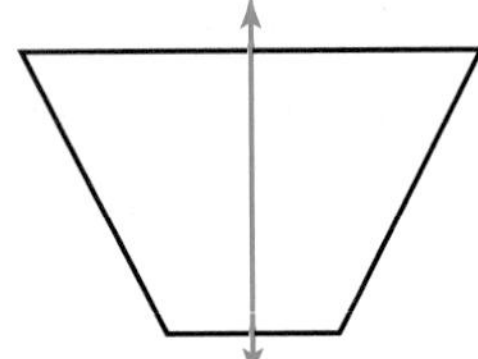

2. 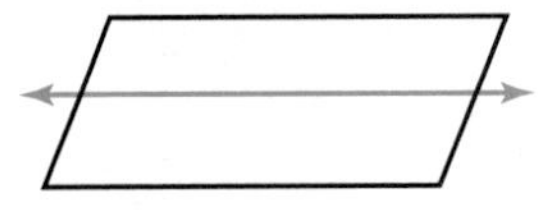

3. 

Trace each figure. Then draw the line or lines of symmetry.

4. 

5. 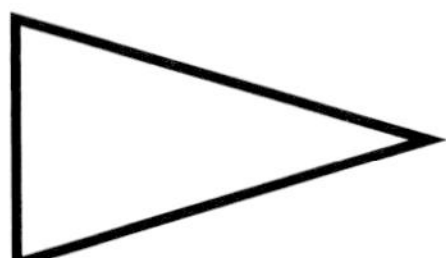

6. 

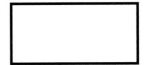

7. Look at the letters in the word MATH. Which letters have one line of symmetry? Do any of the letters have more than one line of symmetry? Explain.

8. On grid paper, draw a figure that has only one line of symmetry. Be sure to draw the line of symmetry on the figure.

Set B (pp. 412–413)

Tell if the figures appear to be similar. Write *yes* or *no*.

1. 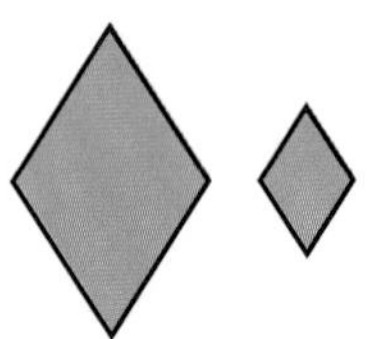

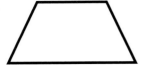

2. 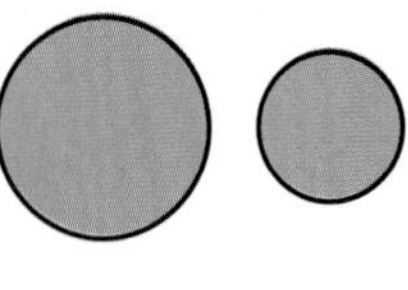

3. 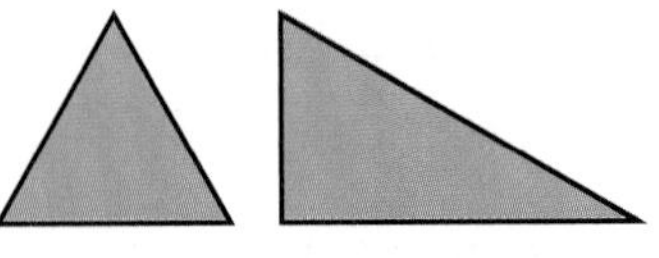

4. 

5. 

6. 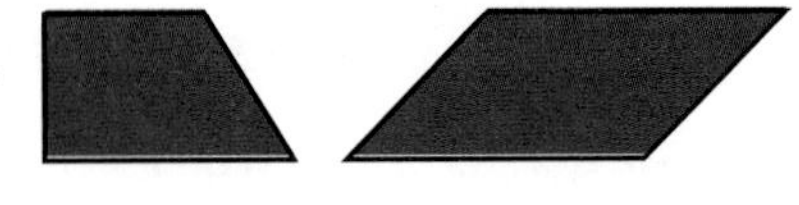

7. Patty says that all squares are similar. Do you agree or disagree? Draw pictures to explain.

Review/Test

✓ CHECK VOCABULARY AND CONCEPTS

Complete. Choose the best term from the box.

symmetry similar congruent

1. Figures that are the same size and shape are __?__. (p. 408)
2. A figure has __?__ if it can be folded along a line so that the two parts match exactly. (p. 410)

Tell what kind of motion was used to move each plane figure. Write *slide, flip,* or *turn*. (pp. 414–415)

3. 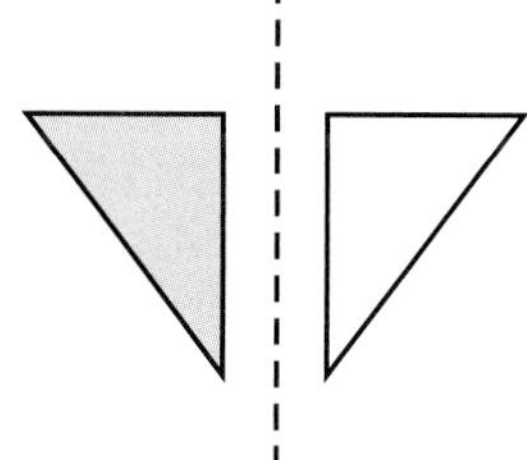

4. 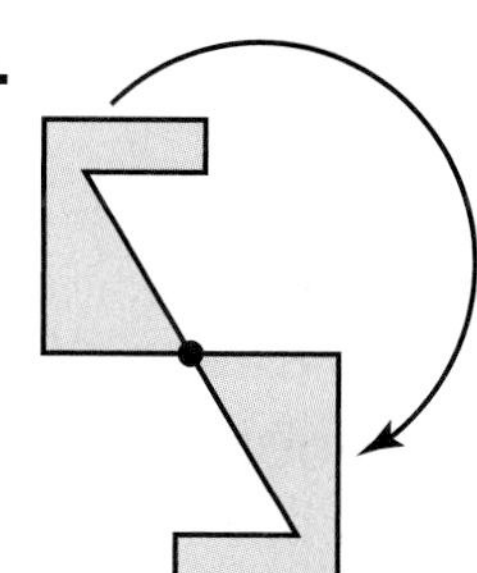

5. 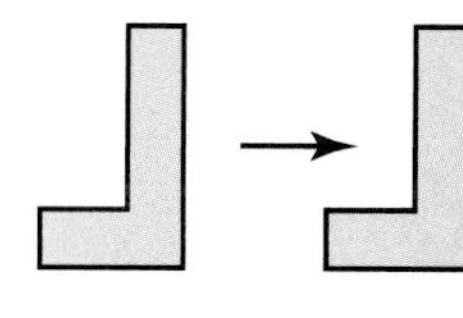

✓ CHECK SKILLS

Tell if the blue line is a line of symmetry. Write *yes* or *no*. (pp. 410–411)

6. 

7. 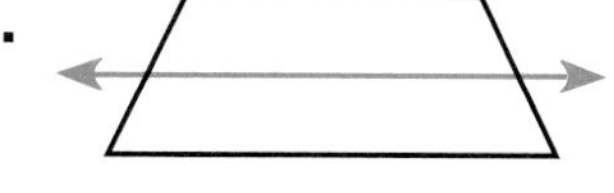

Tell if the figures appear to be similar. Write *yes* or *no*. (pp. 412–413)

8. 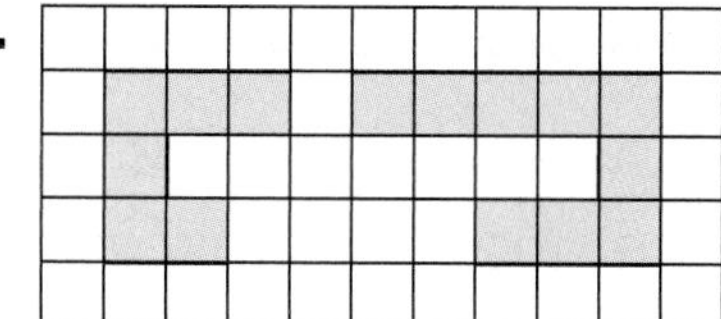

9. 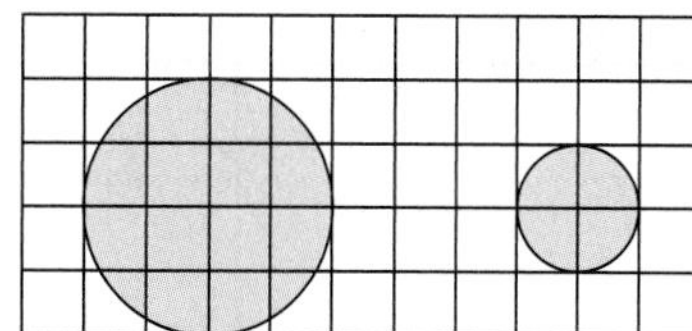

✓ CHECK PROBLEM SOLVING

Solve. (pp. 416–417)

10. Make a model of this hexagon using pattern blocks. What is another combination of pattern blocks that can be used to make a hexagon that is congruent to this one?

Standardized Test Prep

NUMBER SENSE, CONCEPTS, AND OPERATIONS

1. Russ has 64 marbles. Tanika has 52 marbles. Anthony has 13 more marbles than Tanika. How many marbles do the three friends have in all?

A 193
B 181
C 142
D 129

2. Which division sentence belongs to the same fact family as these multiplication sentences?

$5 \times 4 = 20 \qquad 4 \times 5 = 20$

F $20 \div 1 = 20$
G $20 \div 2 = 10$
H $20 \div 5 = 4$
J $20 \div 10 = 2$

3. Which is the missing product in the table?

×	3	4	5	6	7
9	27	36	■	54	63

A 39
B 45
C 48
D 49

4. **Explain It** Tyler read 528 pages over the summer. Liz read 708 pages. About how many more pages did Liz read than Tyler? Explain how you estimated.

GEOMETRY AND SPATIAL SENSE

5. How many lines of symmetry does the figure below have?

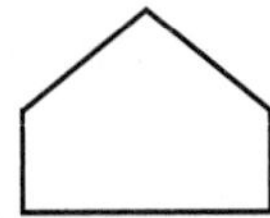

F 1
G 2
H 3
J 5

6. Which solid figure does a globe look like?

A cube
B cone
C cylinder
D sphere

7. **Explain It** What figure is found at (3,2) on the grid? Tell how you found the answer.

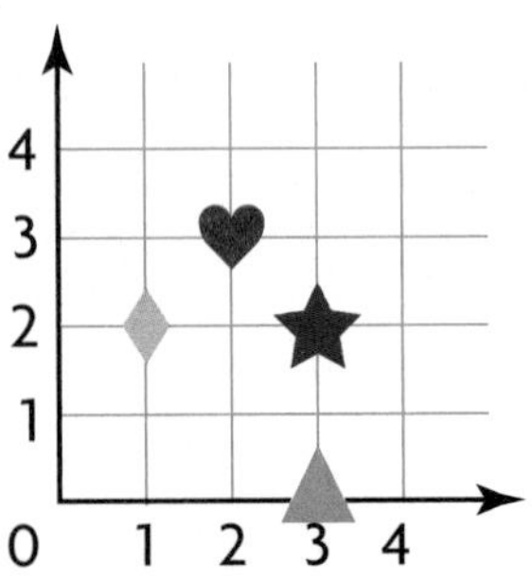

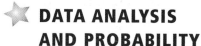

ALGEBRAIC THINKING

8. Chris made a table of the money he earns working at the store. How much money does he earn if he works 7 hours?

MONEY CHRIS EARNS	
Hours Worked	Amount Earned
4	\$20
5	\$25
6	\$30
7	■

F \$12
G \$32
H \$35
J \$40

TIP **Eliminate choices.** See item 9. Substitute each answer choice in both equations. Eliminate answer choices that make one or both of the equations NOT true.

9. Which number makes both equations true?

$5 + ■ = 6$ $\quad\quad$ $5 \times ■ = 5$

A 0 **C** 5
B 1 **D** 6

10. **Explain It** Describe the pattern of shapes below. Then name the next shape in this pattern.

DATA ANALYSIS AND PROBABILITY

11. The table shows the test scores for eight students. What is the mode of the data?

TEST SCORES	
Student	Score
Amy	94
Ben	96
Ellie	98
Chad	95
Tanya	96
Danny	97
Jung	92
Laney	96

F 93
G 94
H 95
J 96

12. **Explain It** Pedro asked his classmates about their pets. He found out that his classmates had 12 dogs, 9 cats, and 6 fish in all. Describe what Pedro should draw in his pictograph to show this data.

PETS	
Dogs	
Cats	
Fish	

Key: ☺ = 3 animals.

CHAPTER 21 Solid and Plane Figures

FAST FACT • SOCIAL STUDIES From 1699 to 1780, Williamsburg was the capital of the colony of Virginia. Many of the original buildings there have been restored to look as they did hundreds of years ago.

PROBLEM SOLVING Look at the historic capitol building. What plane figures do the windows form? What solid figures do you see?

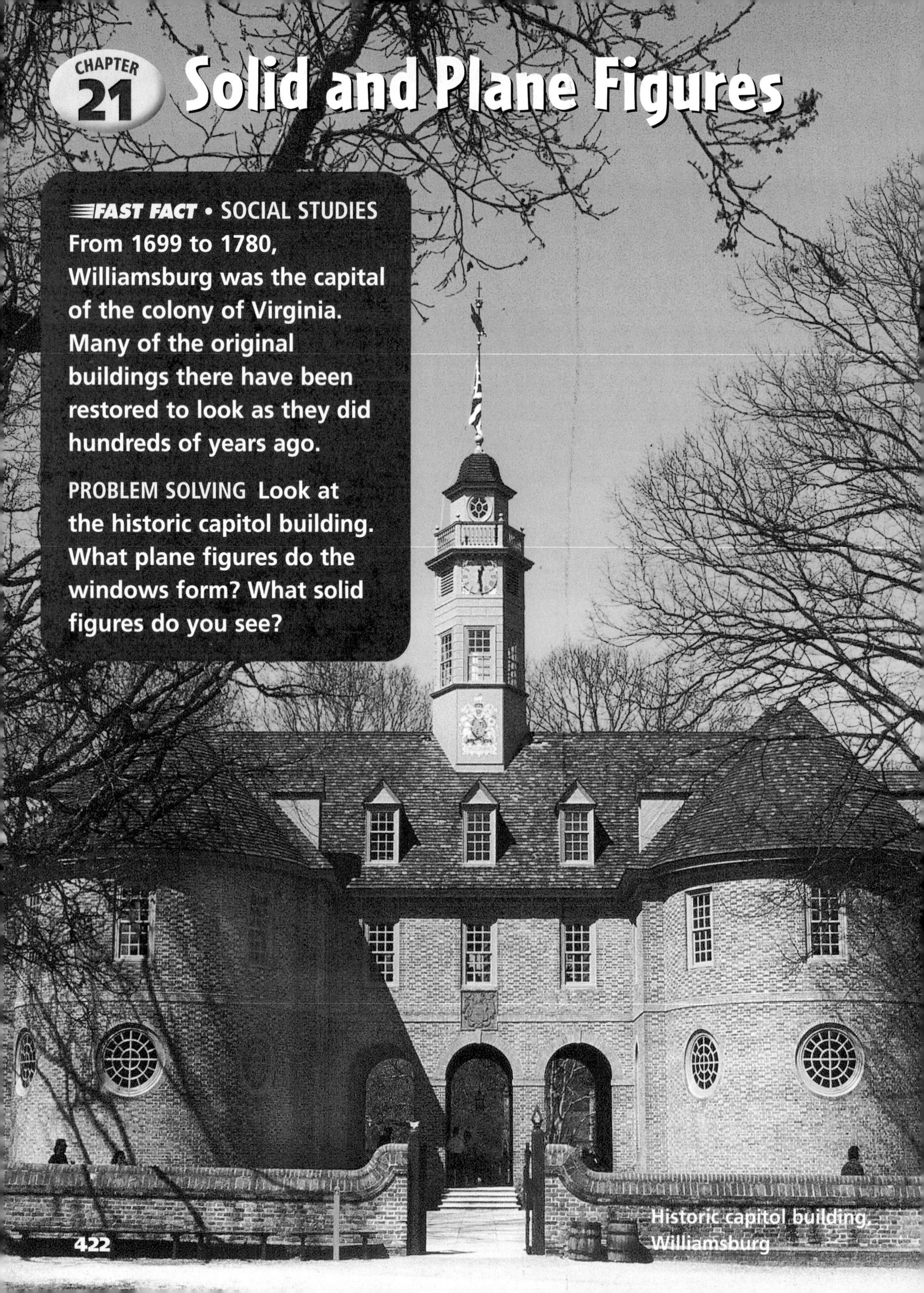

Historic capitol building, Williamsburg

CHECK WHAT YOU KNOW

Use this page to help you review and remember important skills needed for Chapter 21.

IDENTIFY SOLID FIGURES

Choose the best term from the box.

cone
cube
cylinder
pyramid
rectangular prism
sphere

1. 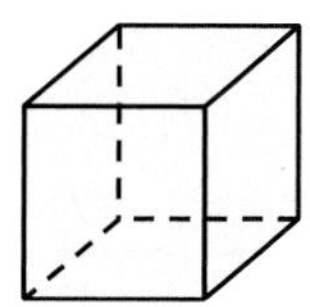
2. 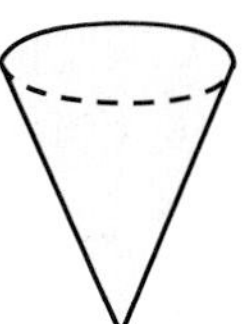
3. 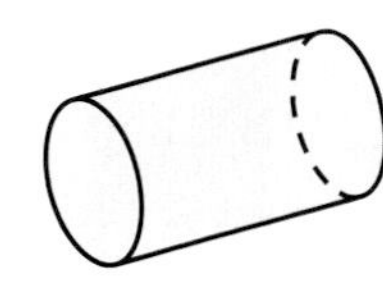
4. 
5. 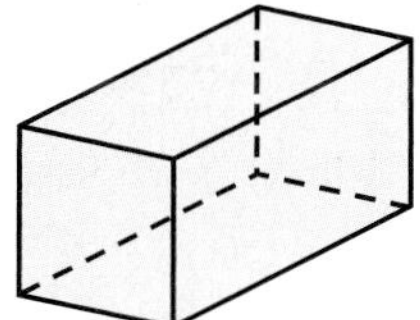
6. 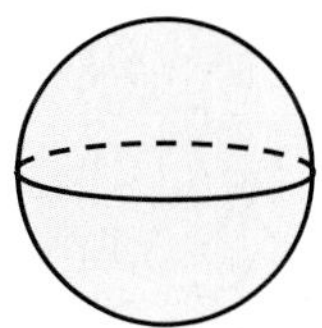
7. 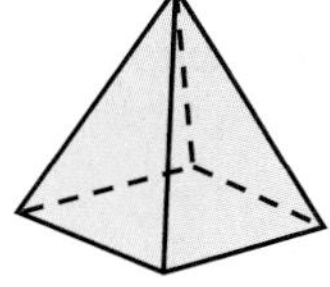
8. 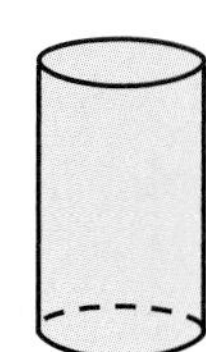
9. 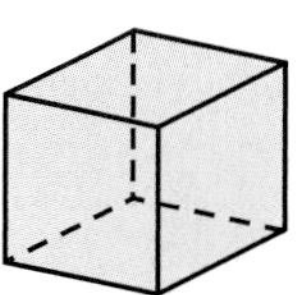

VOCABULARY POWER

REVIEW

quadrilateral [kwä•drə•lat′ər•əl] *noun*

A quadrilateral is a polygon that has four sides. Look in a dictionary for *quadruple*. Is *four* part of its definition? Explain.

PREVIEW

face

edge

vertex

tessellate

tessellation

www.harcourtschool.com/mathglossary

LESSON 1

Solid Figures

Learn

FIGURE IT OUT Use names of solid figures to describe objects around you.

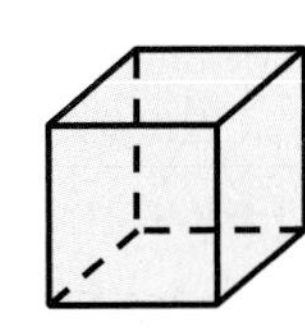

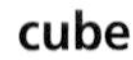

cube

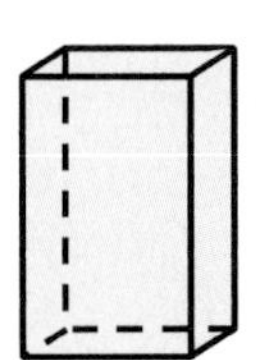

rectangular prism

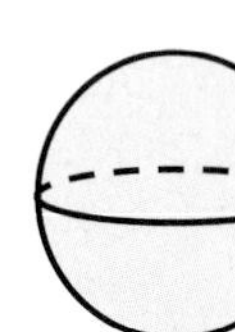

sphere

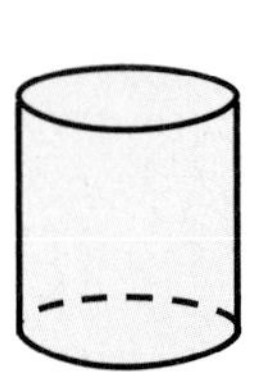

cylinder

square pyramid

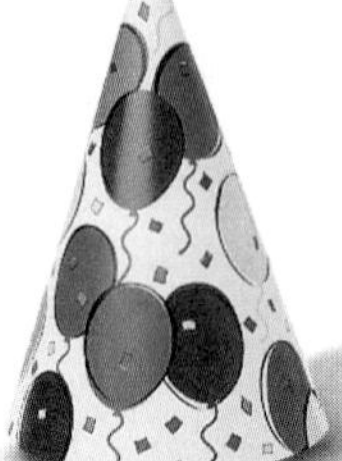

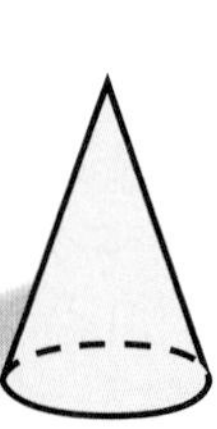

cone

A **face** is a flat surface of a solid figure.

An **edge** is the line segment formed where two faces meet.

A **vertex** is a point where three or more edges meet. Two or more are called vertices.

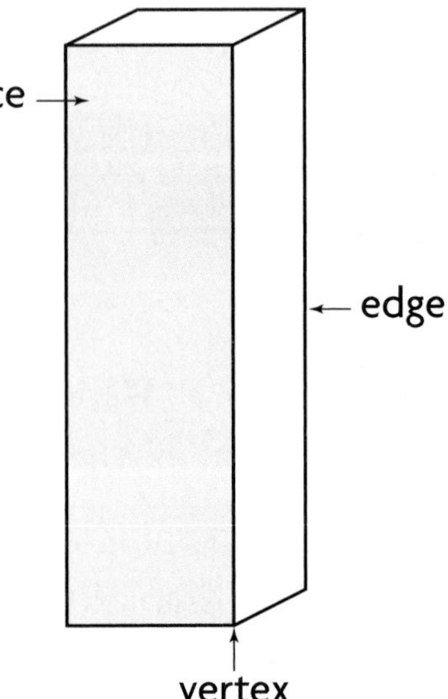

A rectangular prism has 6 faces, 12 edges, and 8 vertices.

- How many edges does a cube have?
- **REASONING** Which solid figures will roll? Explain how you know.

Quick Review

Name each plane figure.

1. 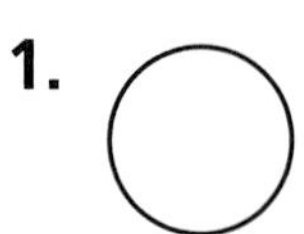
2. 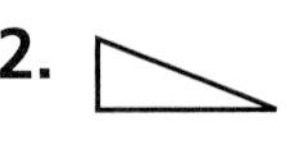
3. 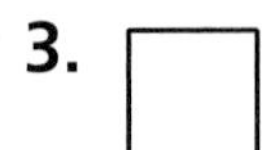
4. 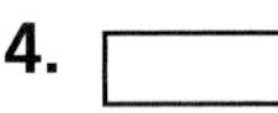
5. 

VOCABULARY

face edge vertex

Technology Link

More Practice:
Harcourt Mega Math
Ice Station Exploration,
Frozen Solids,
Levels A, C, D, E, and F

Tracing Faces

Use names of plane figures to describe the faces of solid figures.

Activity

MATERIALS: solid figures (square pyramid, rectangular prism, cube), paper, crayons

Trace the faces of several solid figures. Then name the faces that make up each solid figure.

STEP 1

On a large sheet of paper, make a chart like the one below. Trace the faces of each solid figure.

Name of Figure	Faces	Names and Number of Faces
Square pyramid	□ △ △ △ △	

STEP 2

Record the names and number of faces for each solid figure.

Name of Figure	Faces	Names and Number of Faces
Square pyramid	□ △ △ △ △	1 square 4 triangles

- **REASONING** Use the words *all, some,* or *none* to describe the faces of the solid figures you traced.

MATH IDEA Some solid figures have faces, edges, and vertices. Faces of solid figures are plane figures such as squares, rectangles, and triangles.

Check

1. Describe the faces of a cube.

Name the solid figure that each object looks like.

2. 

3. 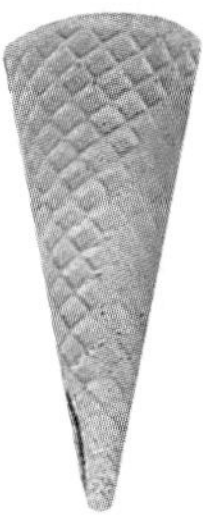

4. 

5. 

LESSON CONTINUES

Practice and Problem Solving

Extra Practice, page 438, Set A

Name the solid figure that each object looks like.

6. 

7. 

8. 

9. 

Which solid figure has the faces shown? Write *a, b,* or *c.*

10. 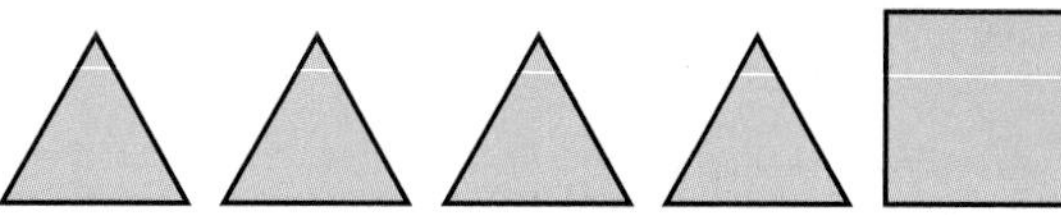

11. 

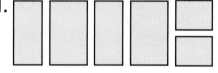

12. 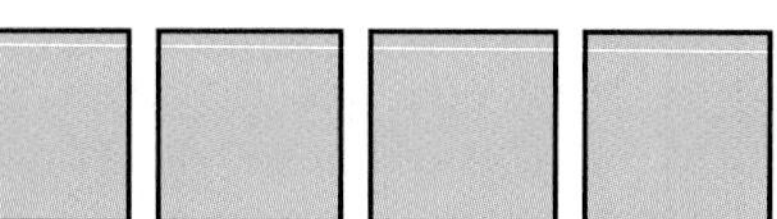

a. rectangular prism
b. square pyramid
c. cube

Copy and complete the table.

	FIGURE	FACES	EDGES	VERTICES
13.	Rectangular prism	■	■	■
14.	Cube	■	■	■
15.	Square pyramid	■	■	■

16. **REASONING** An analogy is a comparison of similar features of objects. For example, *day* is to *light* as *night* is to *darkness*. Complete each analogy.

    a. A cereal *box* is to a *rectangular prism* as a *ball* is to a ___?___.

    b. A *square* is to a *cube* as a *rectangle* is to a ___?___.

17. **Write About It** List objects you might find at a grocery store that look like each of the following solid figures. Think of at least two objects for each figure.

    a. sphere

    b. rectangular prism

    c. cylinder

18. Josh painted a box shaped like a rectangular prism. Each face was a different color. How many colors did Josh use?

19. Cindy has 19 large shells and 17 small shells. How many groups of 4 shells can she make?

20. **Write a problem** about a solid figure. Give clues about the figure. Exchange with a classmate and decide what the figure is.

Mixed Review and Test Prep

21. $7 \times 4 = ■$ (p. 178)

22. $8 \times 0 = ■$ (p. 176)

23. $3 \times ■ = 15$ (p. 186)

24. $4 \times ■ = 8$ (p. 186)

Find each sum or difference. (p. 120)

25. $\$10.48 + \$6.97$

26. $\$8.36 + \$4.52$

27. $\$9.41 - \$3.73$

28. $\$10.00 - \$1.25$

29. **TEST PREP** How much is one \$5 bill, 8 quarters, 2 dimes, 2 nickels, and 1 penny? (p. 110)

A \$8.31 **C** \$8.06
B \$8.26 **D** \$7.31

30. **TEST PREP** Wendy says, "The movie starts at ten minutes after six." At what time does the movie start? (p. 128)

F 5:50 **H** 6:10
G 6:01 **J** 10:06

Problem Solving Thinker's Corner

VISUAL THINKING You can use connecting cubes or other blocks to model solid figures.

For 1–4, build and name the figure.

1. 

2. 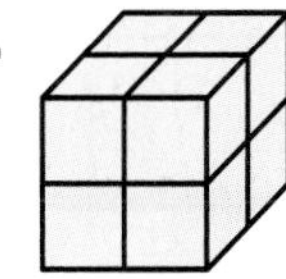

3. 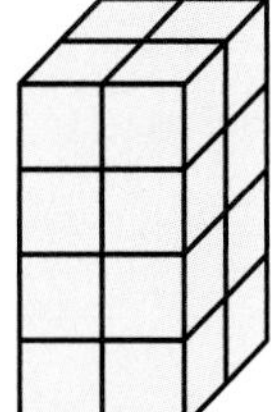

4. 

5. Use 27 blocks to build a cube. Then use the same number of blocks to build a rectangular prism.

LESSON

2 Combine Solid Figures

Quick Review

Name each solid figure.

1. 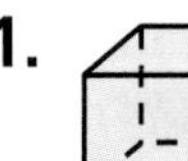
2.  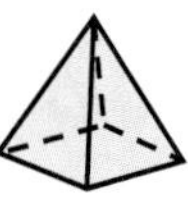
3.  
4. 
5. 

Learn

PUT IT ALL TOGETHER Some objects are made up of two or more solid figures put together. Look at the house on the right. What solid figures make up the shape of the house?

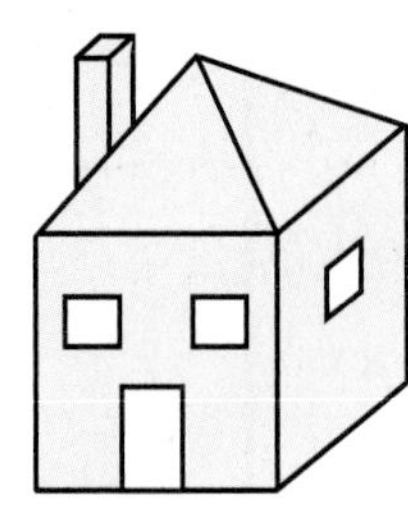

Look at each part of the house separately. Think about the solid figures you know.

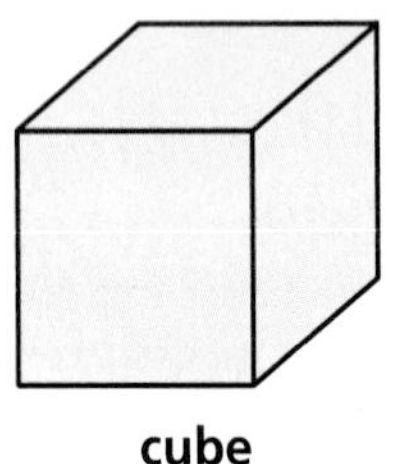

cube

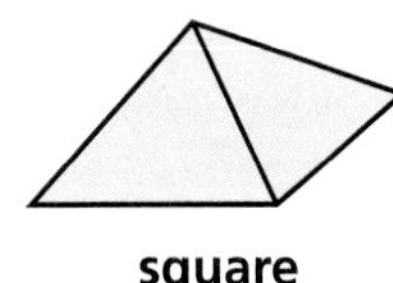

square pyramid

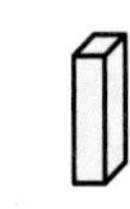

rectangular prism

So, the house is made up of a cube, a square pyramid, and a rectangular prism.

▲ **Craigievar Castle, near Alford, Scotland**

MATH IDEA Solid figures can be combined to make different solid objects.

Examples

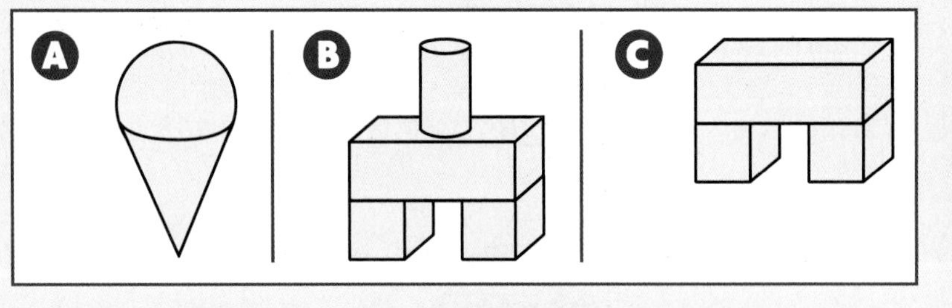

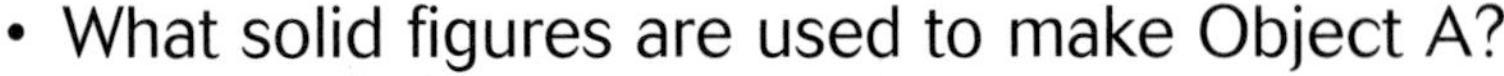

- What solid figures are used to make Object A?
- What solid figures are used to make Object B?

Check

1. **Explain** how you can make Object B look like Object C.

Name the solid figures used to make each object.

2. 

3. 

4. 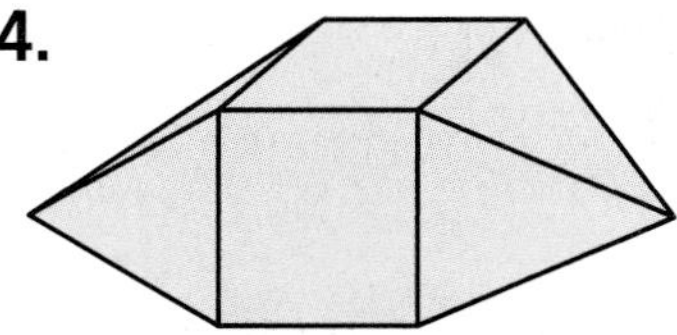

Practice and Problem Solving

Extra Practice, page 438, Set B

Name the solid figures used to make each object.

5. 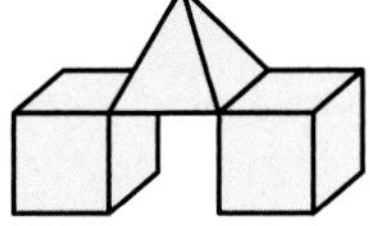

6. 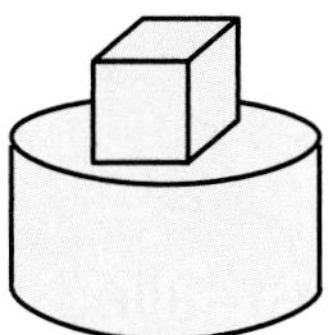

7. 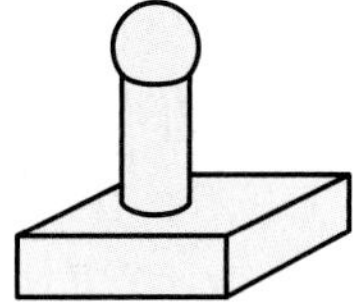

Each pair of objects should be the same. Name the solid figure that is missing.

8. 

9. 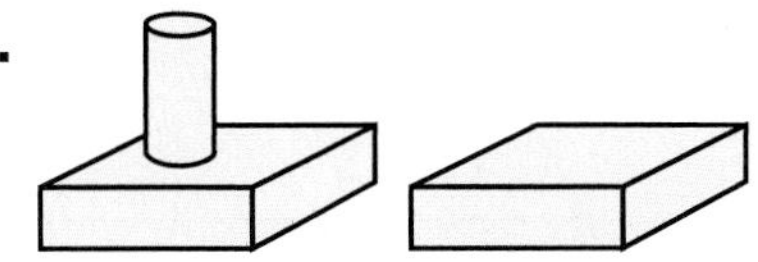

10. 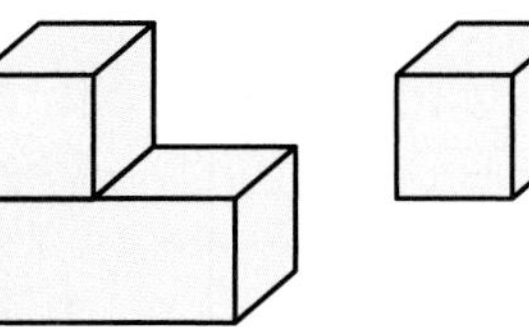

11. 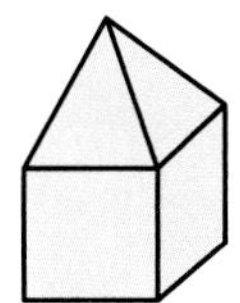 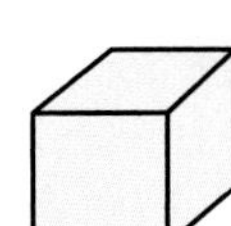

12. 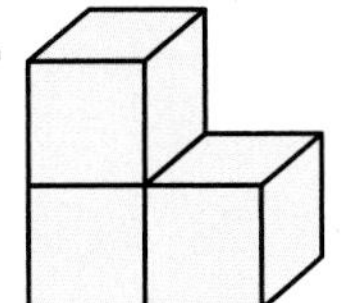

13. 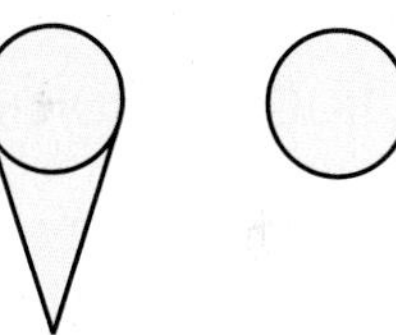

14. Gwen had three $1 bills and 4 dimes. She paid $0.75 for a pen and $1.20 for a snack. How much money does she have left?

15. **Vocabulary Power** The word *polygon* comes from a Greek word that means "many angles." Draw a polygon. How many angles does it have?

Mixed Review and Test Prep

16. Round 765 to the nearest hundred. (p. 50)

17. Round 1,080 to the nearest thousand. (p. 52)

18. $\begin{array}{r} 343 \\ +239 \\ \hline \end{array}$ (p. 72)

19. $\begin{array}{r} 751 \\ -390 \\ \hline \end{array}$ (p. 96)

20. **TEST PREP** Four friends shared 32 crackers equally. How many crackers did each friend get? (p. 260)

A 4
B 7
C 8
D 28

LESSON 3

Tessellations

Quick Review

Name each figure.

1. 2.

3. 4. 5.

VOCABULARY

tessellate

tessellation

Learn

TWIST AND TURN M. C. Escher, a Dutch artist, created many works of art by combining figures in a special way.

When plane figures combine to cover a surface without overlapping or leaving any space between them, those figures **tessellate**. The repeating pattern formed by the figures is called a **tessellation**.

These figures tessellate.

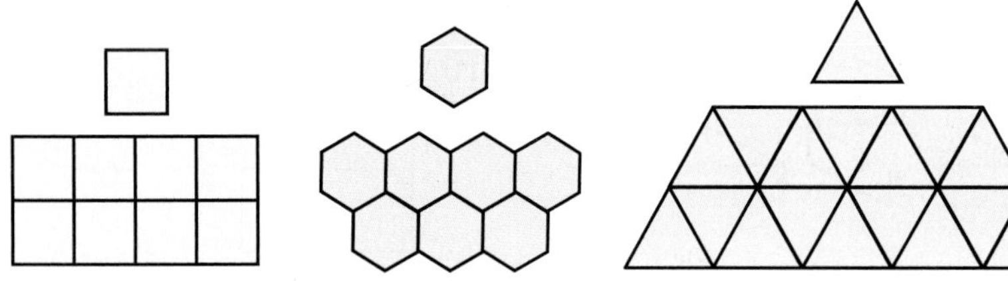

These figures do not tessellate.

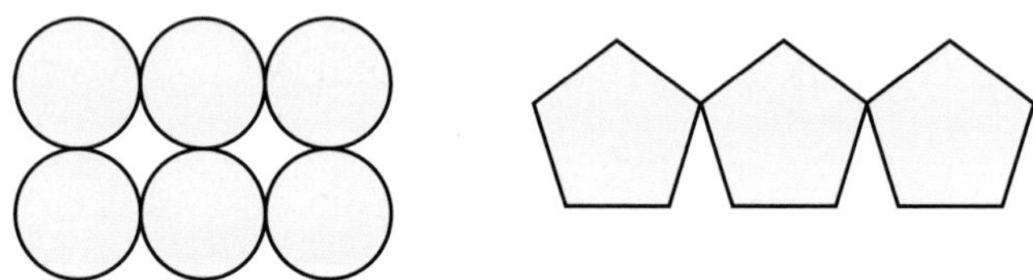

- Describe the figure in the art by M. C. Escher. Does the figure tessellate? How do you know?

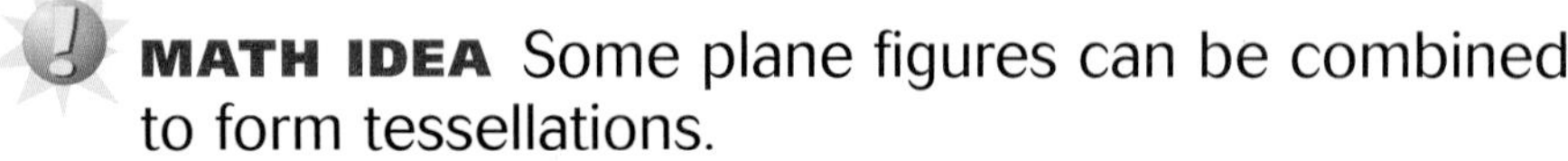

MATH IDEA Some plane figures can be combined to form tessellations.

▲ *Symmetry Drawing E21* **by M. C. Escher.**

Check

1. **Explain** how you know that circles do not tessellate.

Tell if each figure will tessellate. Write *yes* or *no*.

2. 

3. 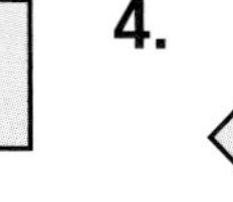

4.

5. 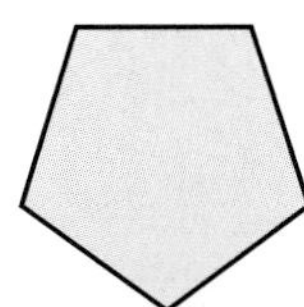

Practice and Problem Solving

Extra Practice, page 438, Set C

Tell if each figure will tessellate. Write *yes* or *no*.

6. 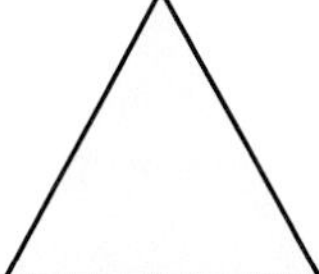

7. 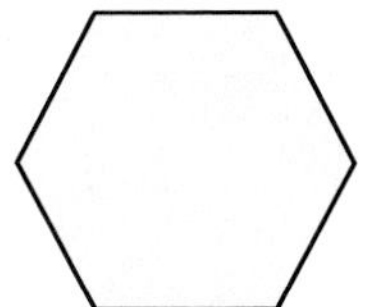

8. 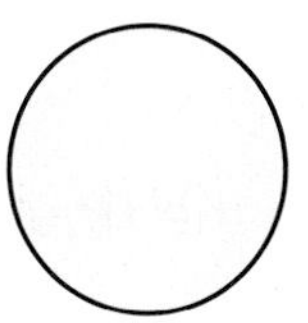

9. 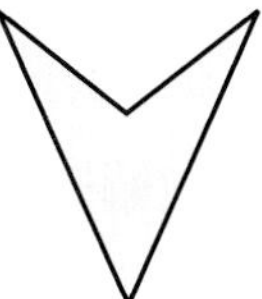

Trace and cut out each figure. Use each figure to make a tessellation. You may color your design.

10. 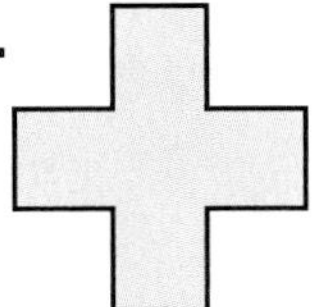

11. 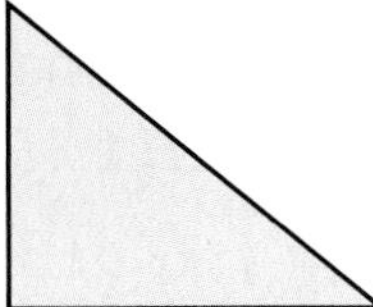

12. 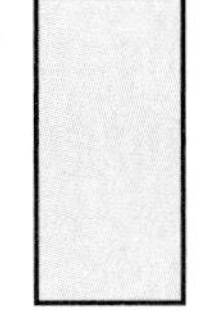

13. Is this a tessellation? Explain why or why not.

14. **Write About It** Explain how you know that this figure will not tessellate.

15. Pilar wants to buy 6 pencils. Store A sells 6 pencils for $0.49. Store B's price is $0.09 each. Where should Pilar buy her pencils in order to spend the least amount of money? Explain.

Mixed Review and Test Prep

For 16–19, find each sum. (p. 8)

16. $\begin{array}{r} 43 \\ 11 \\ +27 \\ \hline \end{array}$

17. $\begin{array}{r} 32 \\ 28 \\ +16 \\ \hline \end{array}$

18. $\begin{array}{r} 15 \\ 59 \\ +15 \\ \hline \end{array}$

19. $27 + 24 + 38 = \blacksquare$

20. **TEST PREP** What is this number in standard form? (p. 32)

$30{,}000 + 500 + 2$

A 352
B 3,502
C 30,502
D 35,002

LESSON 4

Draw Figures

Quick Review

Write the number of sides each figure has.

1.

2. 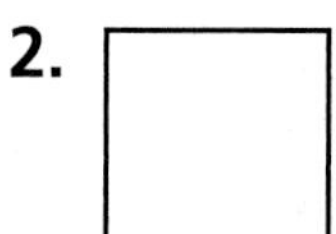

3. 

4. 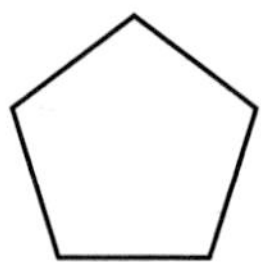

5. 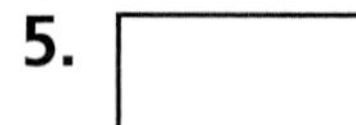

Learn

DRAW IT You can draw polygons using line segments. Since a polygon is a closed figure, it will begin and end at the same point.

Activity 1 Draw plane figures.

MATERIALS: polygon worksheet, pencil, ruler

STEP 1

On your worksheet, use a ruler to draw line segments from *A* to *B*, from *B* to *C*, and from *C* to *A*.

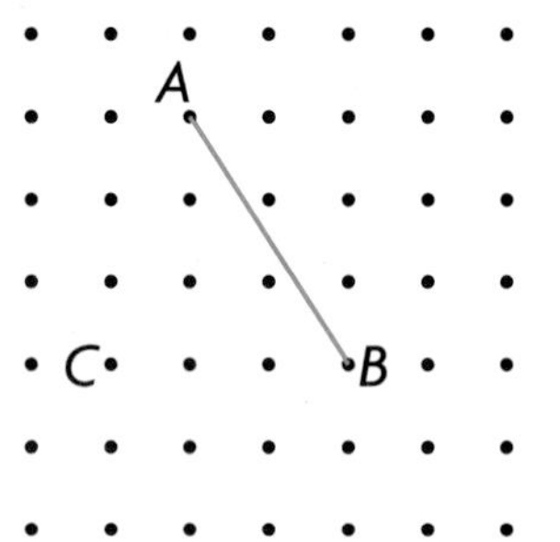

STEP 2

Use a ruler to draw line segments from *D* to *E*, *E* to *F*, *F* to *G*, *G* to *H*, *H* to *I*, and *I* to *D*.

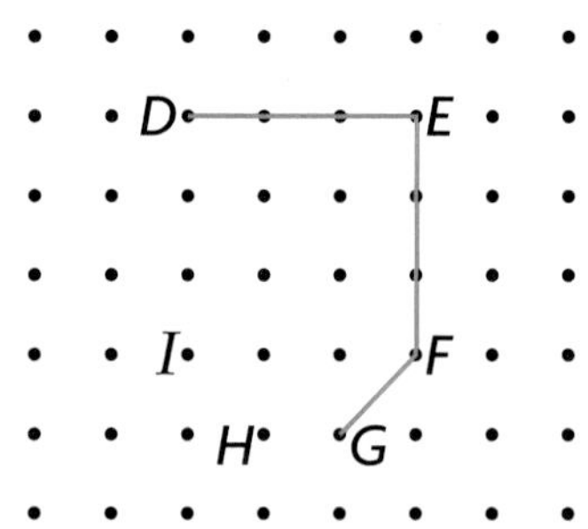

STEP 3

Use a ruler to draw line segments from *J* to *K*, *K* to *L*, *L* to *M*, and *M* to *J*.

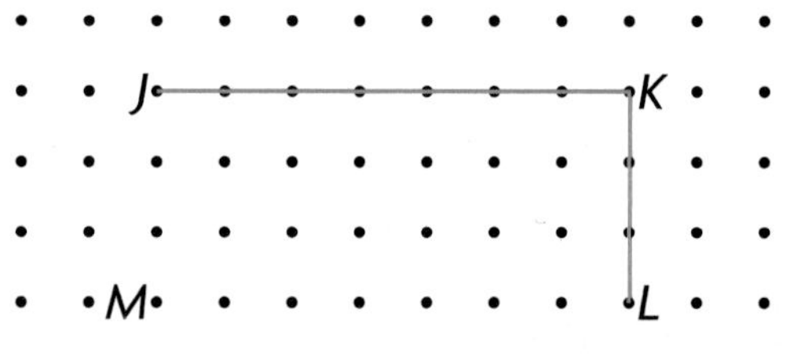

- What polygons did you draw? How many sides and angles does each polygon have?
- Describe the angles in each polygon that you drew.
- **REASONING** Can a line segment be drawn on a rectangle to form 2 congruent triangles? to form 2 congruent rectangles? Draw pictures on dot paper to explain.

Draw a Solid Figure

The faces of solid figures are polygons. Look to see where these faces meet to find edges and vertices.

Activity 2

MATERIALS: dot paper, pencil, ruler

STEP 1

Use a ruler to draw a square. Make each line segment 4 units long.

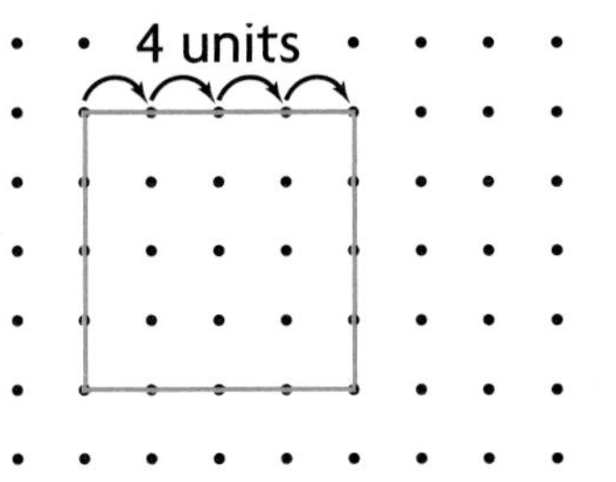

STEP 2

Draw slanted line segments from 3 of the corners, as shown.

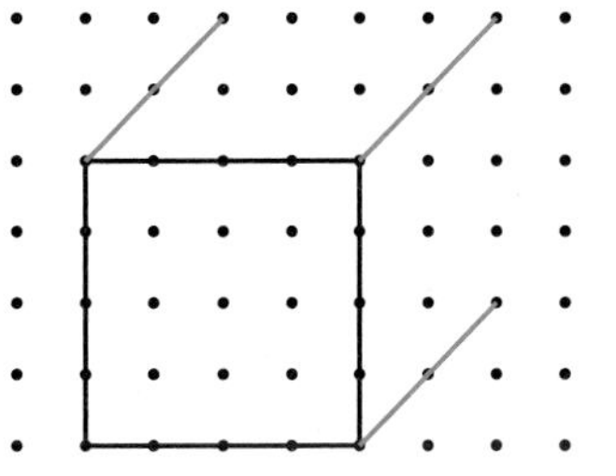

STEP 3

Draw line segments to connect the endpoints of the slanted line segments, as shown.

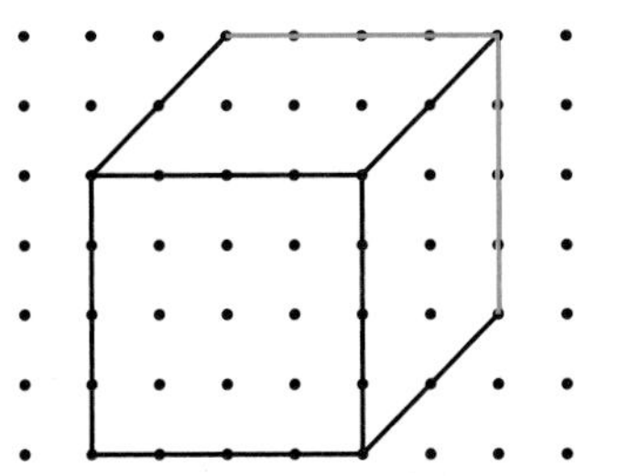

STEP 4

Draw dashed line segments to show the faces that cannot be seen.

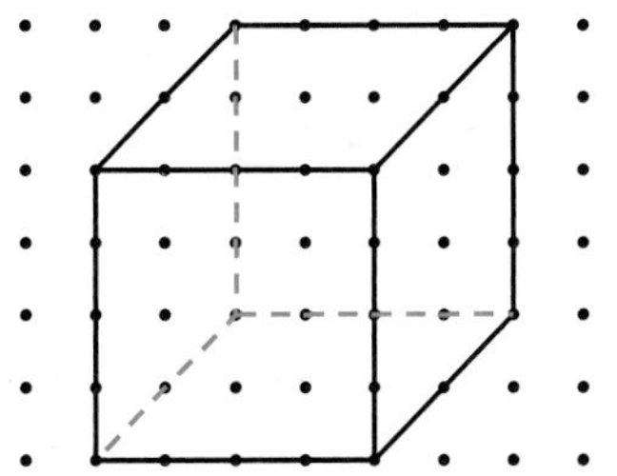

- How many faces does a cube have? How many edges and vertices does a cube have?

1. **Explain** what a vertex is. Compare the number of vertices of a cube and a square pyramid.

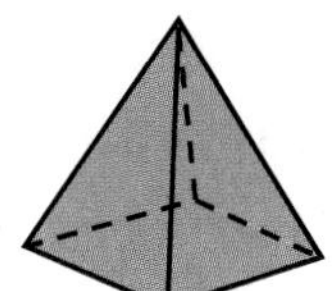

For 2–4, draw each figure on dot paper. Then, write the number of line segments needed to draw each figure.

2. pentagon
3. rectangle
4. hexagon

LESSON CONTINUES

Practice and Problem Solving

Extra Practice, page 438, Set D

For 5–7, draw each figure on dot paper. Then, write the number of line segments needed to draw each figure.

5. parallelogram **6.** octagon **7.** triangle

For 8, copy the solid figure on dot paper. Name the figure.

8.

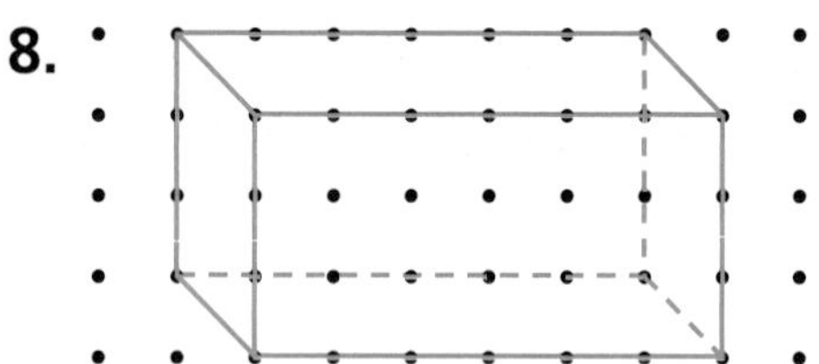

For 9–14, copy each figure on dot paper. Draw the missing line segments so that the figure matches its label.

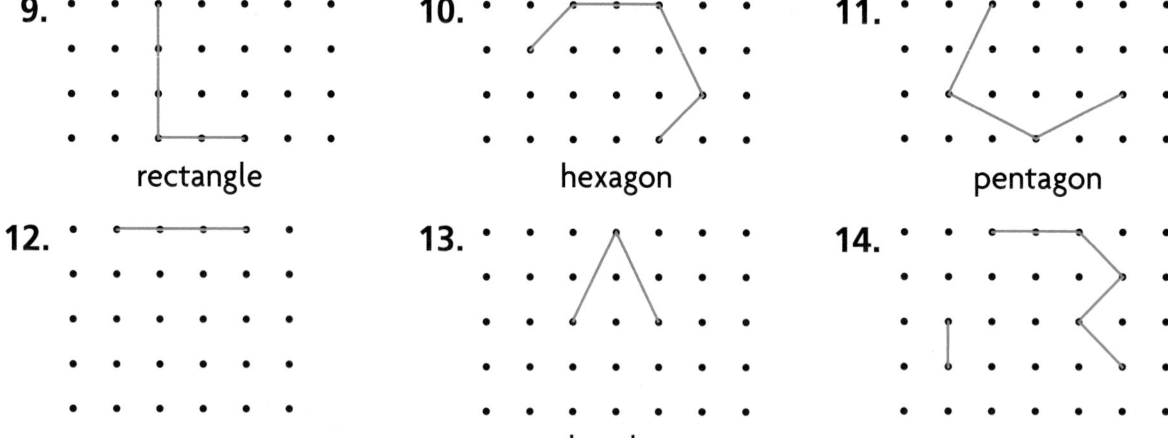

15. **FAST FACT • SOCIAL STUDIES** The Olympic flag was first used at the 1920 Summer Olympics. There were 2,669 athletes taking part. At the 1992 Summer Olympics, there were 9,367 athletes. Which Olympics had more athletes? How many more?

16. Trace the figure shown at the right. Cut out the figure along the solid lines. Then fold along the 4 dotted lines. Tape the edges of the figure together. What solid figure do you have?

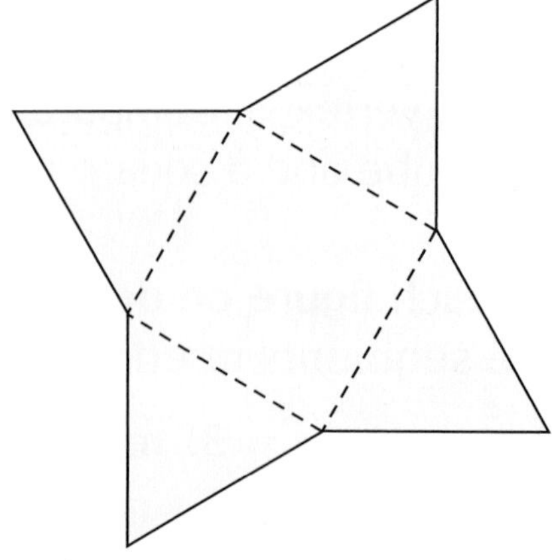

17. Rex drew 2 quadrilaterals and 2 hexagons. Ali drew an octagon, 2 pentagons, and a triangle. Who drew more angles? Explain.

18. **? What's the Error?** The lengths of the sides of a triangle are 3 inches, 3 inches, and 2 inches. Justin said it is an equilateral triangle. Describe his error.

Mixed Review and Test Prep

Find each quotient. (p. 260)

19. $18 \div 3$ **20.** $20 \div 4$

21. $28 \div 4$ **22.** $27 \div 3$

Write each number in expanded form. (pp. 24, 32)

23. 30,251 **24.** 8,680

25. 7,443 **26.** 12,097

27. TEST PREP Which unit would be used to measure the weight of a marble? (p. 346)

A ounce **C** inch
B pint **D** quart

28. TEST PREP Find the product. $4 \times 2 \times 7$ (p. 218)

F 28 **G** 42 **H** 56 **J** 63

Problem Solving LINKUP . . . to Social Studies

The 5 circles on the Olympic flag represent the 5 regions of the world that join together for the Olympic Games. A circle is a plane figure made of points that are the same distance from a center point.

Follow the directions to draw a circle.

MATERIALS: paper clip, 2 pencils, ruler

1. Draw a point. Draw a circle by placing the pencils in the ends of the paper clip. The pencil on the point should not move.

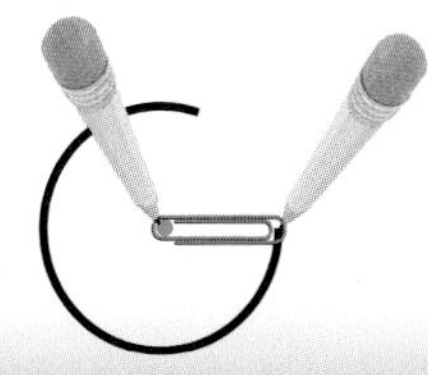

2. Place three points on top of the circle that you drew. Measure the distance from the center point to each of the points on the circle. Are they the same distance from the center?

LESSON 5

Problem Solving Skill
Identify Relationships

UNDERSTAND › PLAN › SOLVE › CHECK

DIFFERENT VIEWS Mrs. Pine is teaching her students about solid figures. The students looked at the different views of solid figures. Which solid figures could this be?

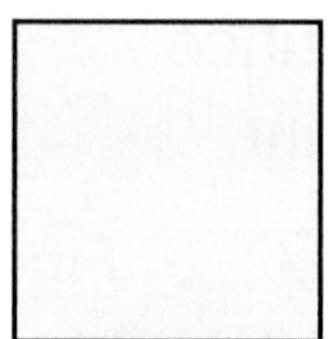

top view

All of the faces of a cube are squares. So, this could be a cube.

Some rectangular prisms have two faces that are squares. So, this could be a rectangular prism.

Which solid figures could this be?

bottom view

The bottom of a cone is a circle. So, this could be a cone.

The bottom of a cylinder is a circle. So, this could be a cylinder.

The view of a sphere from *any* direction looks like a circle. So, this could be a sphere.

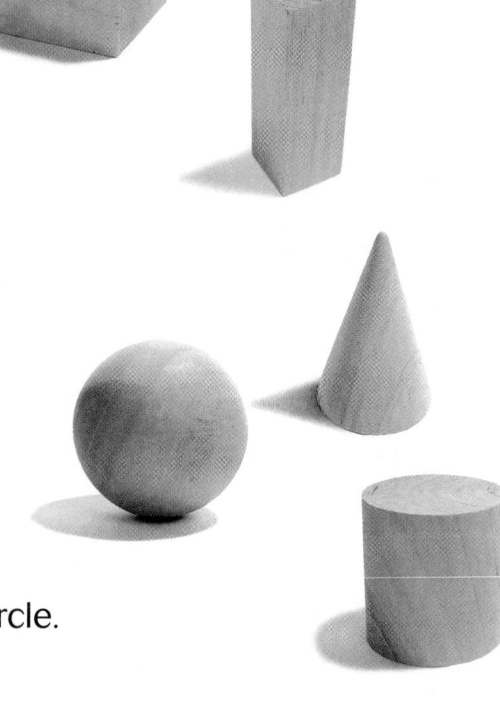

Quick Review

Name each solid figure.

1. 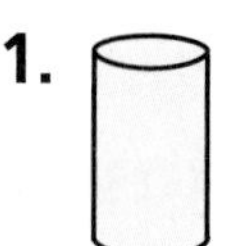

2.  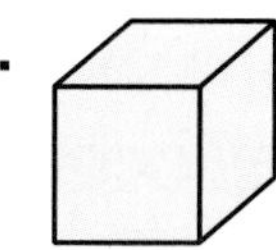

3. 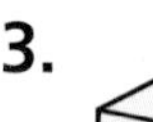 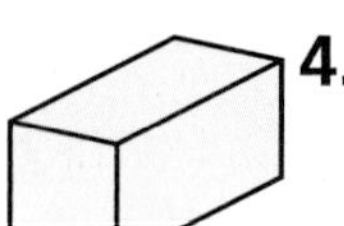

4. 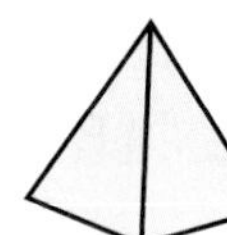

5.  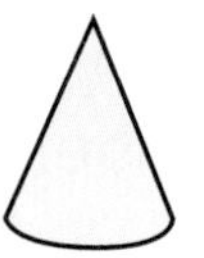

Talk About It

- The figure at the right is the top view of a cone. Explain what you see when you look at the top of a cone.

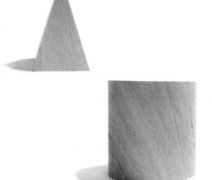

Problem Solving Practice

1. **What if** Mrs. Pine's class looked at the side view of a square pyramid? What plane figure could be used to describe the shape that the students would see?

2. Look at the cylinder. Even though the side of the cylinder is a curved surface, a plane figure can be used to describe the side view. Name this plane figure.

For 3–4, use the figures below.

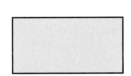

Figure Q

Figure R

Figure S

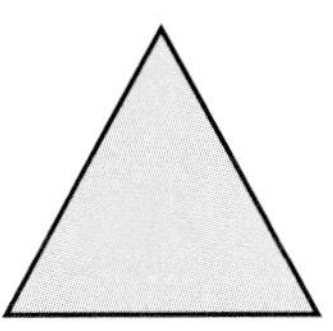
Figure T

3. Which figure is the top view of a cylinder?

   A Figure Q **C** Figure S
   B Figure R **D** Figure T

4. Which figure is the bottom view of a square pyramid?

   F Figure Q **H** Figure S
   G Figure R **J** Figure T

Mixed Applications

USE DATA For 5–8, use the bar graph.

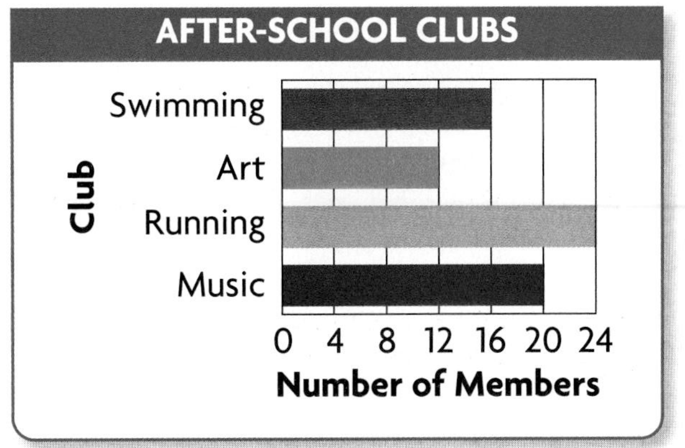

5. How many more members are in the Music Club than in the Swimming Club?

6. How many members are in the four clubs altogether?

7. List the clubs in order from the greatest number of members to the least number of members.

8. **Write a problem** using the data in the bar graph. Explain how to find the answer.

9. **What's the Question?** The answer is 5 faces, 8 edges, and 5 vertices.

Extra Practice

Set A (pp. 424–427)

Name the solid figure that each object looks like.

1. 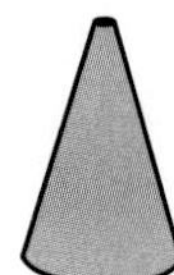
2. 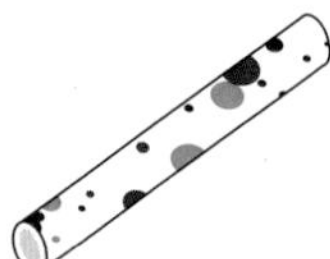
3. 
4. 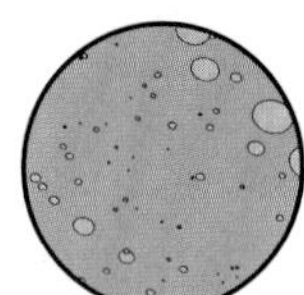

Set B (pp. 428–429)

Name the solid figures used to make each object.

1. 
2. 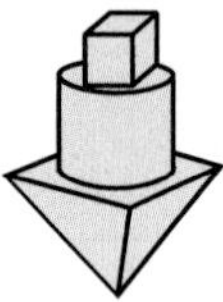
3. 

Set C (pp. 430–431)

Tell if each figure will tessellate. Write *yes* or *no*.

1. 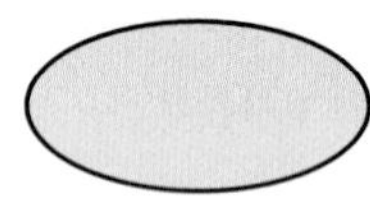
2. 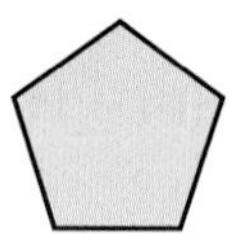
3. 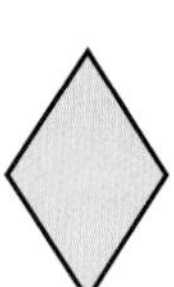
4. 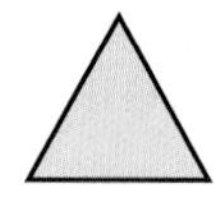
5. Use grid paper and pattern blocks to make a design. Repeat your design to make a tessellation.

Set D (pp. 432–435)

For 1–3, draw each figure on dot paper. Then, write the number of line segments needed to draw each figure.

1. rhombus
2. hexagon 
3. quadrilateral

For 4–6, copy each figure on dot paper. Draw the missing line segments so that the figure matches its label.

4. 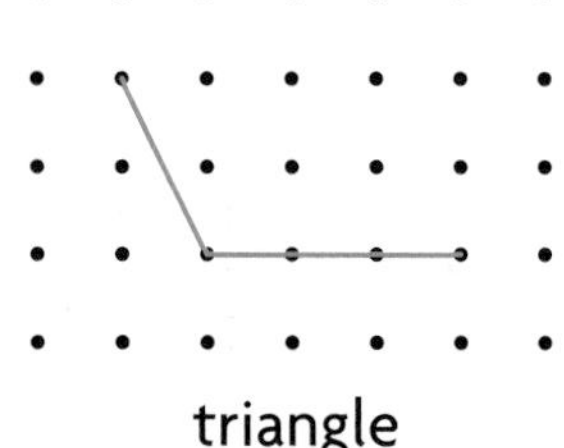
triangle
5. 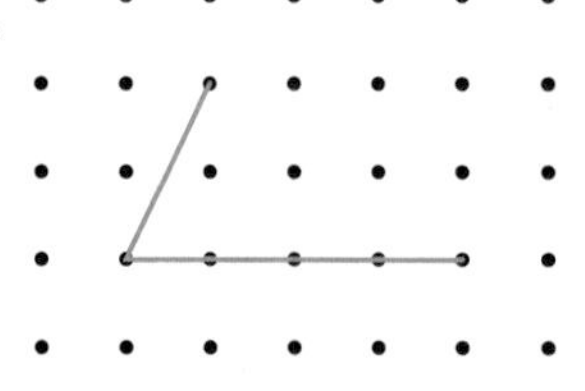
trapezoid
6. 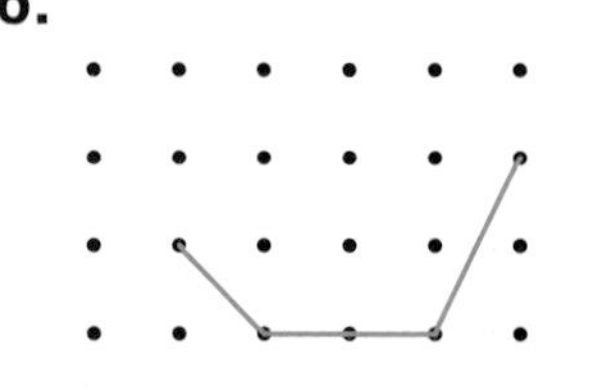
pentagon

Review/Test

✓ CHECK VOCABULARY AND CONCEPTS

For 1–2, choose the best term from the box.

tessellation
face
edge

1. A flat surface of a solid figure is a _?_. (p. 424)
2. The line segment formed where two faces meet is called an _?_. (p. 424)
3. A solid figure has 6 square faces. What is it? (pp. 424–427)
4. A solid figure has 6 rectangular faces. What is it? (pp. 424–427)

✓ CHECK SKILLS

For 5–6, name the solid figures used to make each object. (pp. 428–429)

5. 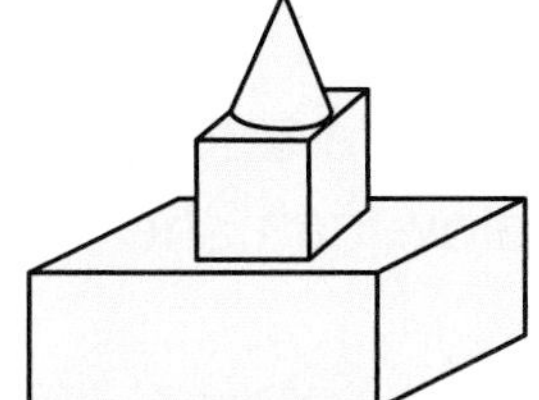

6. 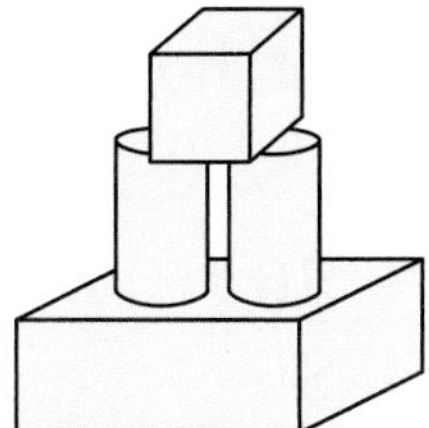

Tell if each figure will tessellate. Write *yes* or *no*. (pp. 430–431)

7. 

8. 

9. 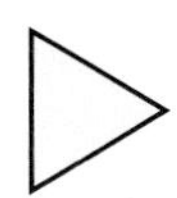

10. 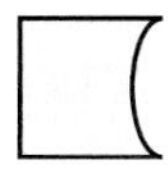

For 11–13, copy each figure on dot paper. Draw the missing line segments so that the figure matches its label. (pp. 432–435)

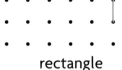

11. rectangle

12. 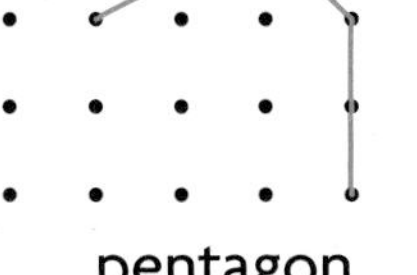
pentagon

13. 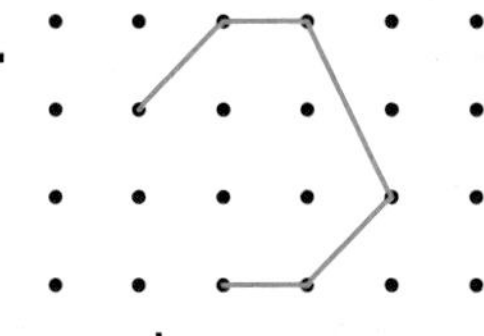
hexagon

✓ CHECK PROBLEM SOLVING

For 14–15, use the figures at the right. (pp. 436–437)

14. Which figure is the bottom view of a cone?
15. Which figure is the side view of a cube?

Figure A

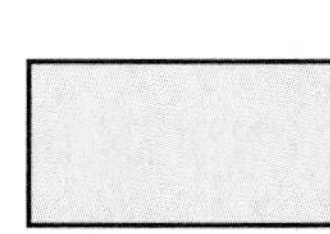
Figure B

Figure C

Standardized Test Prep

NUMBER SENSE, CONCEPTS, AND OPERATIONS

1. Marci planted 8 seeds in each of 4 rows in her garden. Which number sentence shows how many seeds she planted in all?

A $4 + 8 = 12$ **C** $8 \div 4 = 2$
B $4 \times 8 = 32$ **D** $8 - 4 = 4$

2. Toshi and 6 teammates want to buy a shirt for their coach. The shirt costs $42. If each player pays the same amount, how much will Toshi pay?

F $8 **H** $6
G $7 **J** $5

3. Which division sentence belongs to the same fact family as these multiplication facts?

$3 \times 9 = 27$ $9 \times 3 = 27$

A $9 \div 3 = 3$
B $9 \div 9 = 1$
C $27 \div 9 = 3$
D $27 \div 1 = 27$

TIP **Understand the problem.** See item 4. The word *about* tells you that you need an estimate rather than an exact answer.

4. Explain It A school band uses 129 instruments. There are 57 wind instruments. About how many instruments are NOT wind instruments? Explain your answer.

GEOMETRY AND SPATIAL SENSE

5. Victor made a model of a solid figure that has 4 faces that are triangles and 1 face that is a square. Which solid figure could he have made?

F cube
G cylinder
H rectangular prism
J square pyramid

6. Pilar wants to make a tessellation. Which figure below can she use?

A 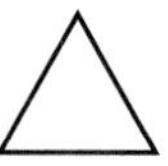

B 

C 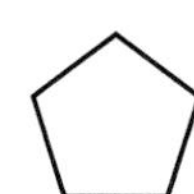

D 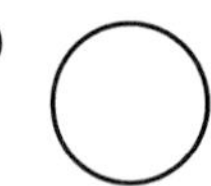

7. Explain It Gwen pressed the bottom of a solid figure into clay. It left the outline of a circle. Can you tell for certain which solid figure Gwen used? Explain why or why not.

ALGEBRAIC THINKING

8. Henry wrote the pattern below.

8, 13, 18, 23, 28

Which statement is the **best** description of how the numbers in the pattern are related?

F Each number is two times the number before it.
G Each number is 5 less than the number before it.
H Each number is 6 more than the number before it.
J Each number is 5 more than the number before it.

9. Which figure comes next in this pattern?

A

B

C

D

10. Explain It Mrs. Turner waters her plants once every three days. This week, she watered the plants on Tuesday and Friday. What are the next two days when she will water her plants? Explain how you found your answer.

DATA ANALYSIS AND PROBABILITY

11. The table shows the number of books the students read. How many more books did the girls read than the boys?

BOOKS READ BY OUR CLASS		
	Fiction	Nonfiction
Girls	29	34
Boys	24	37

F 1
G 2
H 3
J 4

12. Explain It Mr. Clark made a bar graph to show the amount of bird seed that he sold in the beginning of the summer.

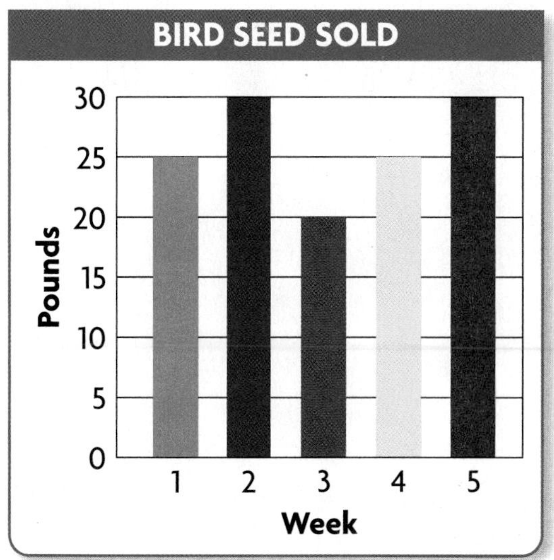

If Mr. Clark made a pictograph of this data, how many pounds should each symbol stand for? Explain your answer, and tell how many symbols would be used for each week.

CHAPTER 22 Perimeter, Area, and Volume

FAST FACT • SOCIAL STUDIES **People have grown flowers for thousands of years. In the 1600s, tulips in Holland were so valuable that the bulbs were used as money!**

PROBLEM SOLVING **Look below at the diagram of a garden. How can you find how many feet of fencing you would need to go around this garden?**

CHECK WHAT YOU KNOW

Use this page to help you review and remember important skills needed for Chapter 22.

COLUMN ADDITION

Find each sum.

1. $\begin{array}{r} 3 \\ 7 \\ +5 \\ \hline \end{array}$ **2.** $\begin{array}{r} 2 \\ 4 \\ +8 \\ \hline \end{array}$ **3.** $\begin{array}{r} 1 \\ 3 \\ +9 \\ \hline \end{array}$ **4.** $\begin{array}{r} 6 \\ 2 \\ +9 \\ \hline \end{array}$

5. $\begin{array}{r} 6 \\ 7 \\ +3 \\ \hline \end{array}$ **6.** $\begin{array}{r} 4 \\ 9 \\ +3 \\ \hline \end{array}$ **7.** $\begin{array}{r} 5 \\ 5 \\ +7 \\ \hline \end{array}$ **8.** $\begin{array}{r} 9 \\ 8 \\ +1 \\ \hline \end{array}$

9. $4 + 3 + 3 + 5$ **10.** $8 + 3 + 2 + 9$ **11.** $5 + 6 + 2 + 5$ **12.** $9 + 2 + 9$

MULTIPLICATION FACTS

Find each product.

13. $7 \times 4 = \blacksquare$ **14.** $3 \times 6 = \blacksquare$ **15.** $2 \times 5 = \blacksquare$

16. $4 \times 9 = \blacksquare$ **17.** $7 \times 2 = \blacksquare$ **18.** $6 \times 6 = \blacksquare$

19. $9 \times 8 = \blacksquare$ **20.** $10 \times 3 = \blacksquare$ **21.** $4 \times 5 = \blacksquare$

VOCABULARY POWER

REVIEW

square [skwâr] *noun*

A square is a quadrilateral that has 4 right angles and 4 equal sides. On grid paper, draw 2 squares that are different sizes. Include labels showing the lengths of the sides.

PREVIEW

perimeter
volume
square unit
cubic unit
area

www.harcourtschool.com/mathglossary

LESSON 1

Perimeter

Quick Review

1. 2 + 3 + 3 = ■
2. 5 + 6 + 7 = ■
3. 7 + 3 + 6 = ■
4. 4 + 2 + 9 = ■
5. 10 + 4 + 4 + 2 = ■

VOCABULARY

perimeter

Learn

AROUND AND AROUND The distance around a figure is called its **perimeter**.

You can estimate the perimeter of your math book.

Activity

MATERIALS: toothpicks, paper clips

PERIMETER OF MY MATH BOOK		
	Estimate	Measurement
Number of paper clips		
Number of toothpicks		

STEP 1

Copy the table. Estimate the perimeter of your math book in paper clips and in toothpicks. Record your estimates.

STEP 2

Use paper clips. Record how many paper clips it takes to go around all the edges of your math book.

STEP 3

Use toothpicks. Record how many toothpicks it takes to go around all the edges of your math book.

- How does your estimate compare with your actual measurement?
- Did it take more paper clips or more toothpicks to measure the perimeter of your math book? Explain.
- **REASONING** Would it be better to measure the perimeter of your math book with paper clips or with your shoe? Explain.

Other Ways to Find Perimeter

You can count the units to find the perimeter.

Examples Count the units to find the perimeter.

A

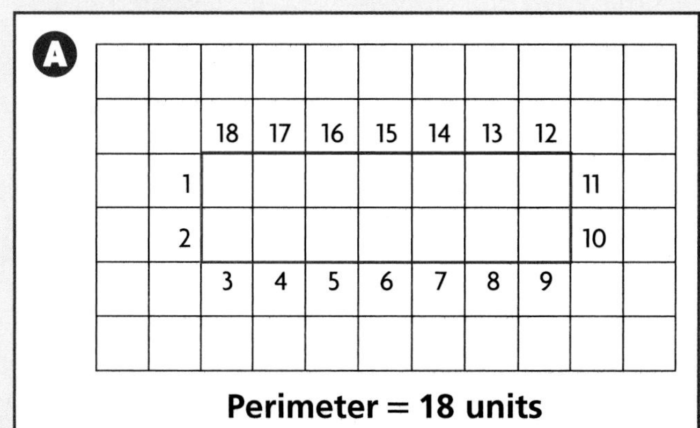

Perimeter = 18 units

B

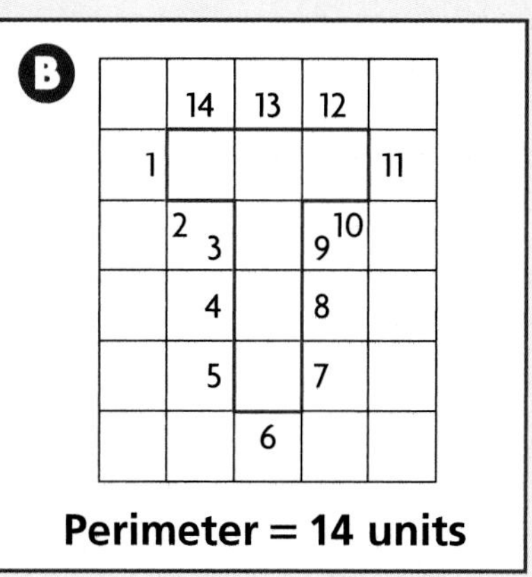

Perimeter = 14 units

You can add the lengths of the sides to find the perimeter.

More Examples Find the perimeter.

C

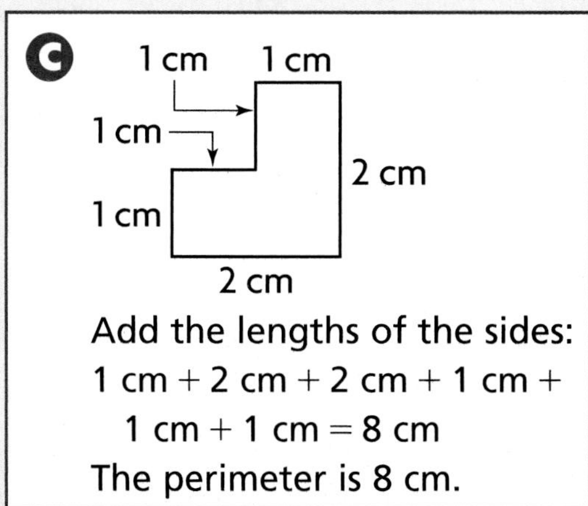

Add the lengths of the sides:
1 cm + 2 cm + 2 cm + 1 cm + 1 cm + 1 cm = 8 cm
The perimeter is 8 cm.

D

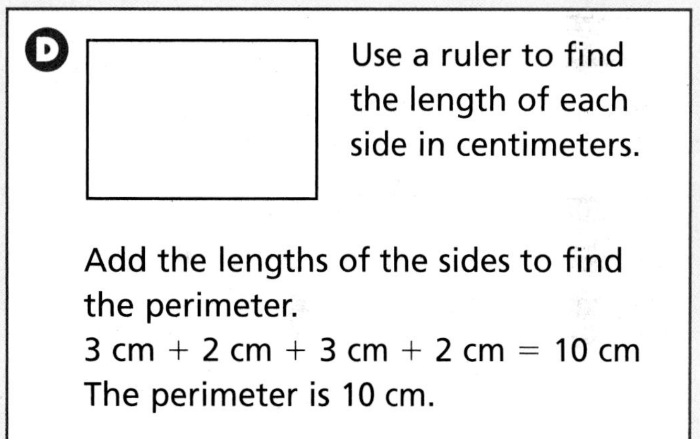

Use a ruler to find the length of each side in centimeters.

Add the lengths of the sides to find the perimeter.
3 cm + 2 cm + 3 cm + 2 cm = 10 cm
The perimeter is 10 cm.

- **REASONING** Explain how to find the perimeter of a square if the length of one side is 5 inches.

Check

1. **Explain** how you could measure only 2 sides to find the perimeter in Example D.

Find the perimeter.

2. 

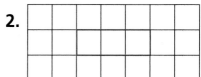

3. 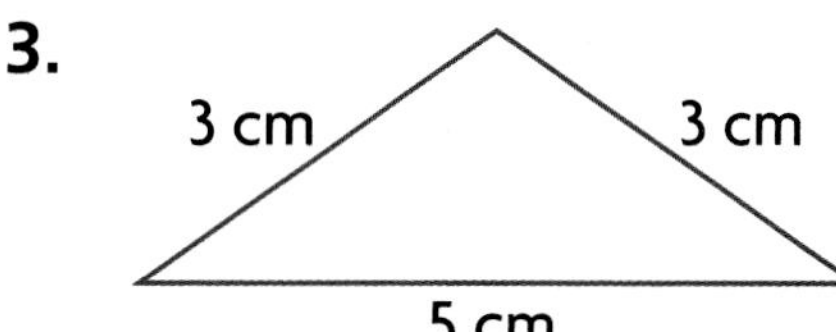

LESSON CONTINUES

Practice and Problem Solving

Extra Practice, page 456, Set A

Find the perimeter.

4. 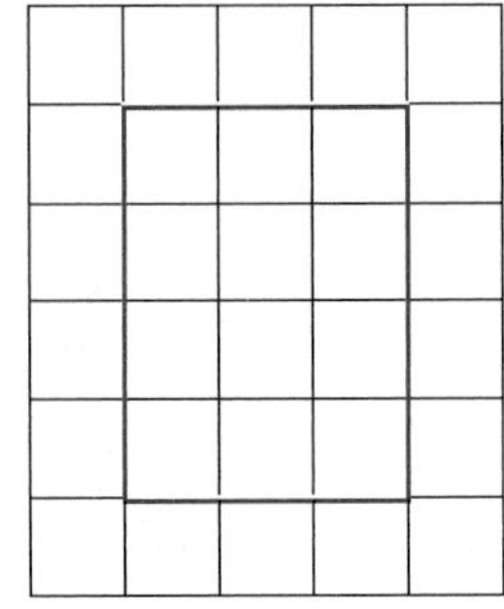

5. 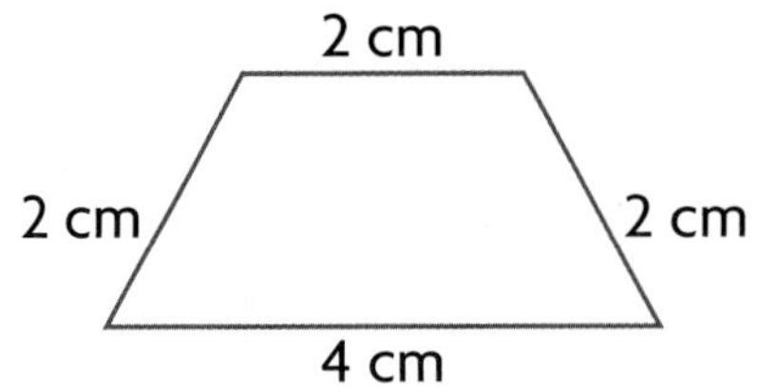

6. 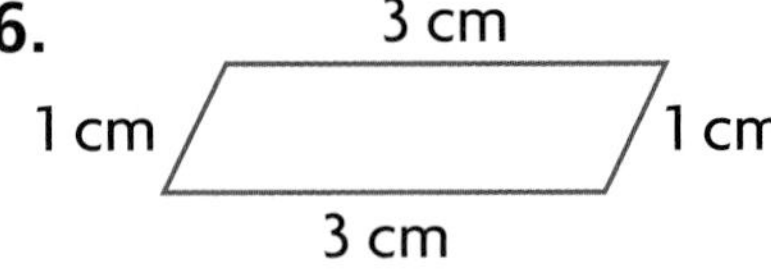

7. 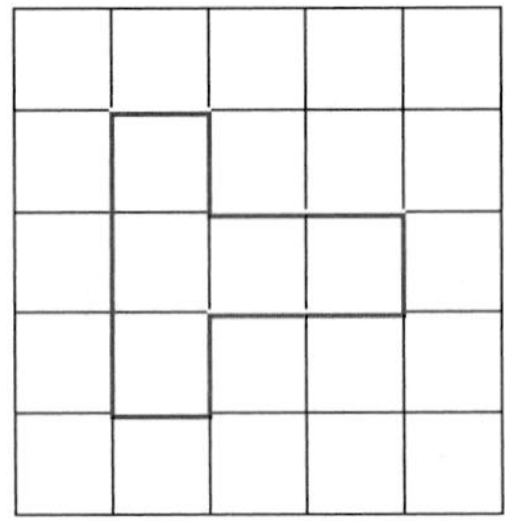

8. 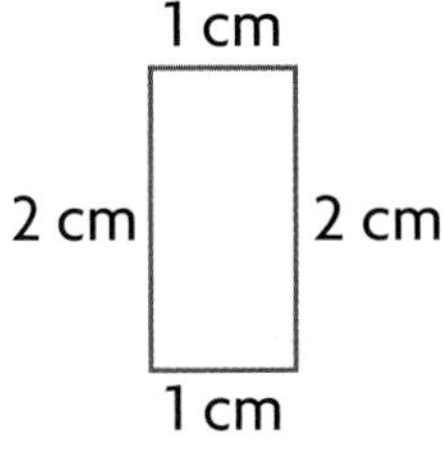

9. 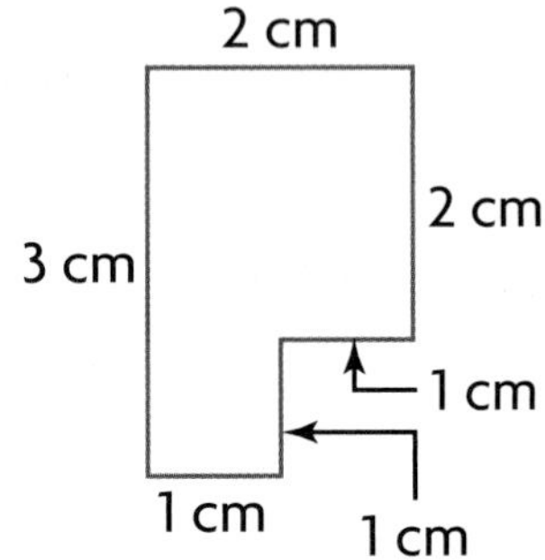

Estimate the perimeter in centimeters. Then use your centimeter ruler to find the perimeter.

10.

11. 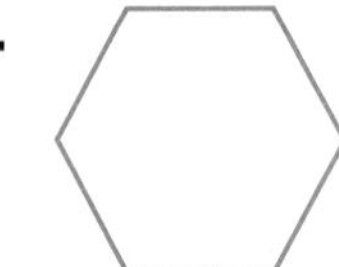

12. USE DATA The drawing at the right shows the size of Mrs. Gibson's vegetable garden. She wants to put a fence around her garden. Use the scale to find how many yards of fencing she will need.

Mrs. Gibson's Garden

Scale: ⊢⊣ = 1 yard

13. ALGEBRA This triangle has a perimeter of 8 cm. How long is Side C?

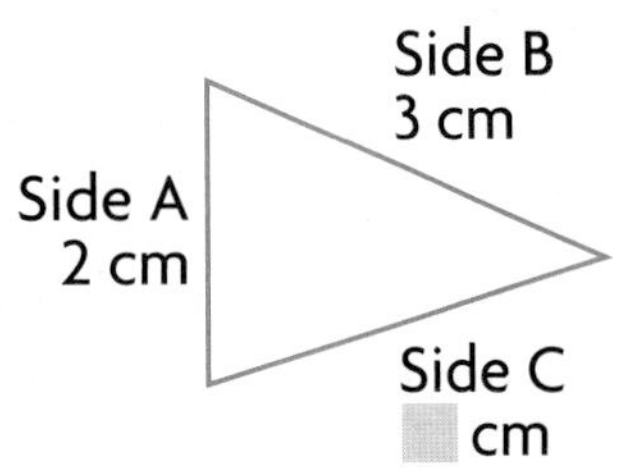

14. **Write About It** Choose an object. Explain how to estimate and measure its perimeter. Then use a ruler to measure its perimeter in inches.

15. Use grid paper. Draw a rectangle with a perimeter of 12 units.

16. Jana's beach towel is 5 feet long and 3 feet wide. What is its perimeter?

Mixed Review and Test Prep

USE DATA For 17–21, use the graph. (p. 324)

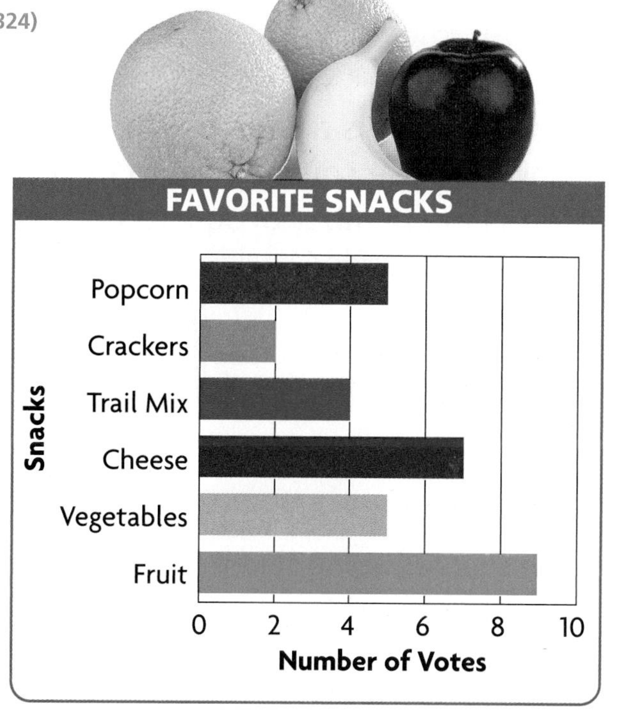

17. How many students voted for cheese?

18. How many more students voted for cheese than for vegetables?

19. How many students voted for crackers and trail mix in all?

20. **TEST PREP** How many students did NOT vote for popcorn?

A 21 **B** 24 **C** 27 **D** 31

21. **TEST PREP** How many students voted in all?

F 12 **G** 32 **H** 40 **J** 50

Problem Solving LINKUP ... to Social Studies

In 1806, Thomas Jefferson built a house in the Blue Ridge Mountains of Virginia. In the center of the house, Jefferson built a special room that is a perfect cube. This room is 20 feet long, 20 feet wide, and 20 feet tall. Jefferson's granddaughter would draw in this room because a large window called a skylight was in the ceiling.

1. The floor of the center room is a square with each side measuring 20 feet. What is the perimeter of this floor?

2. Around the house, Jefferson built a circular road that measured 540 yards. Write an expression to find how many feet this is. Find the value of the expression.

LESSON 2

Area

Quick Review

1. $5 \times 8 = \blacksquare$
2. $7 \times 6 = \blacksquare$
3. $3 \times 3 = \blacksquare$
4. $2 \times 8 = \blacksquare$
5. $6 \times 4 = \blacksquare$

VOCABULARY
square unit
area

MATERIALS
square tiles
grid paper

Explore

A **square unit** is a square with a side length of 1 unit. You use square units to measure area. **Area** is the number of square units needed to cover a flat surface.

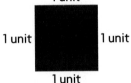

1 square unit: 

Activity

Use square tiles to find the area of your math book cover.

STEP 1

Estimate how many squares will cover your math book. Then place square tiles in rows on the front of your math book. Cover the whole surface.

STEP 2

Use grid paper. Draw a picture to show how you covered the math book.

STEP 3

Count and record the number of square tiles you used. This number is the book cover's area in square units.

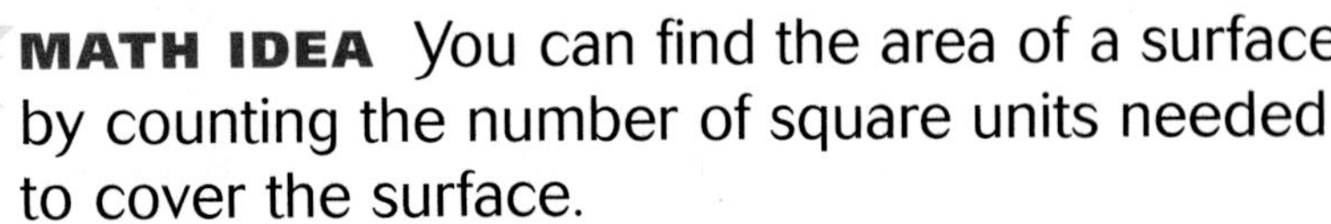

MATH IDEA You can find the area of a surface by counting the number of square units needed to cover the surface.

- Look at the picture you made. How could you use multiplication to find the area?

Try It

Use square tiles to find the area of each.

a. an index card **b.** a sheet of paper

How many rows of tiles do I need to cover an index card?

Connect

To find the area of a rectangle, multiply the number of rows times the number in each row.

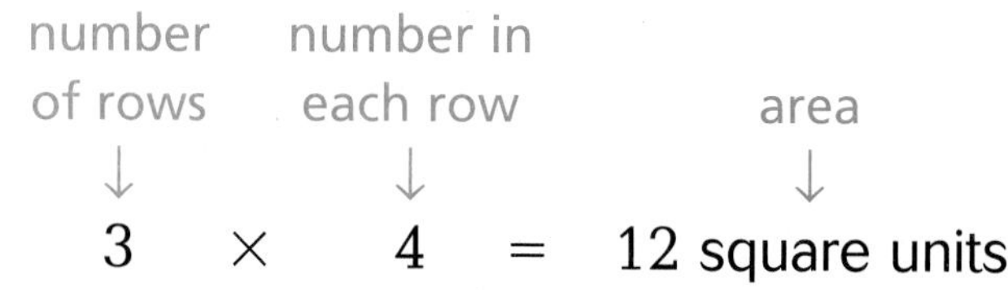

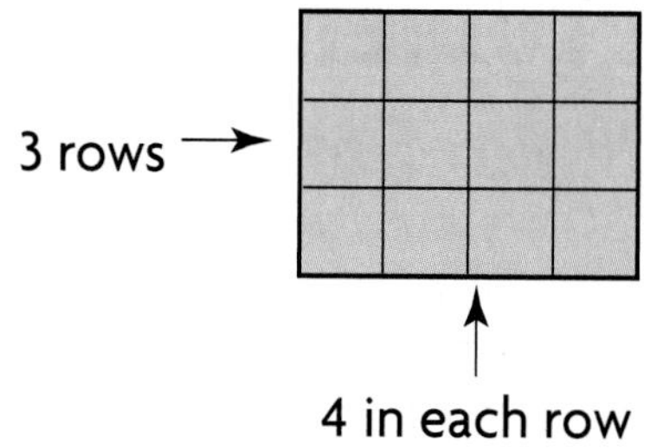

Practice and Problem Solving

Find the area of each figure. Write the area in square units.

1. 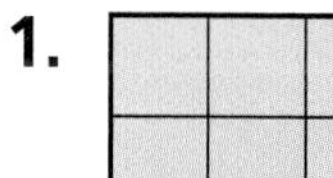 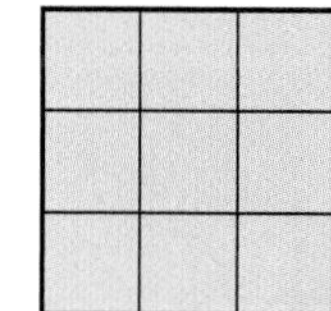

2. 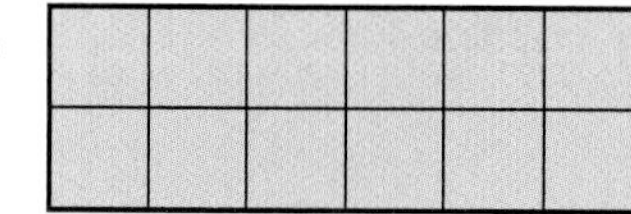

3. 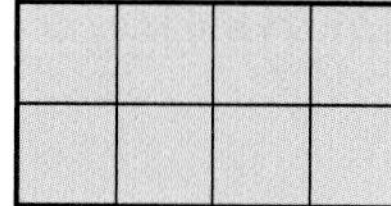

4. 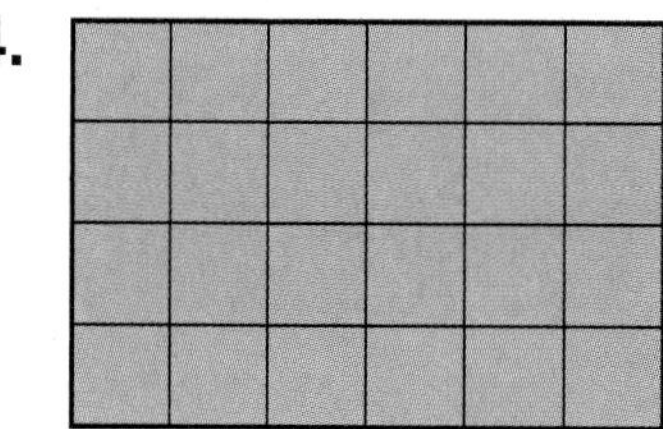

5. 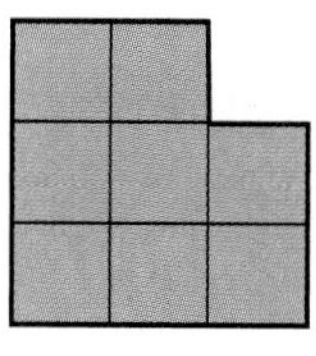

6. 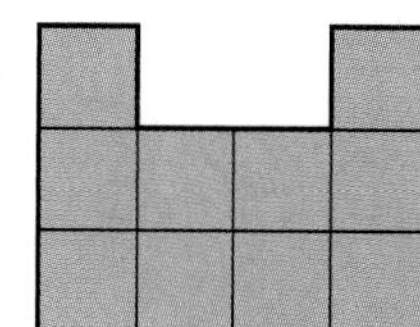

7. REASONING For which of the figures in Exercises 1–6 could you use multiplication to find the area? Explain.

8. **What's the Question?** Rachel's blanket is 6 feet wide and 4 feet long. The answer is 24 square feet.

9. Copy the figure at the right on grid paper. Show the perimeter in red, and show the area in blue. Record the perimeter and area of the figure.

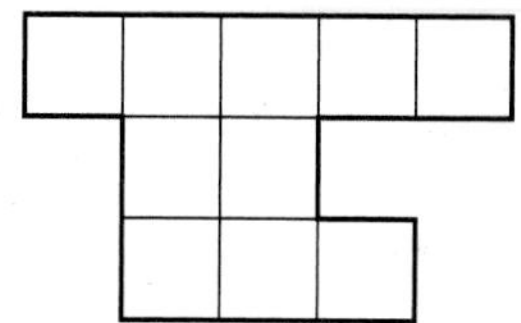

Mixed Review and Test Prep

Find each missing addend. (p. 4)

10. 5 + ■ = 12 **11.** 6 + ■ = 14

12. ■ + 9 = 15 **13.** ■ + 4 = 11

14. TEST PREP Erma had 45 beads. She put 9 beads on each key chain. How many key chains did she make? (p. 278)

A 10 **B** 9 **C** 5 **D** 3

LESSON 3

Problem Solving Skill
Make Generalizations

UNDERSTAND | PLAN | SOLVE | CHECK

Quick Review

1. $4 + 2 + 4 + 2 = \blacksquare$
2. $8 + 3 + 8 + 3 = \blacksquare$
3. $3 \times 4 = \blacksquare$
4. $7 \times 3 = \blacksquare$
5. $8 \times 4 = \blacksquare$

DON'T FENCE ME IN Maura plans to plant a flower garden and put a fence around it. She has 12 feet of fencing to make a square or rectangular garden. If she wants to have the greatest area possible, should her fence be a square or a rectangle?

Maura draws a picture to show all the square and rectangular gardens she can make.

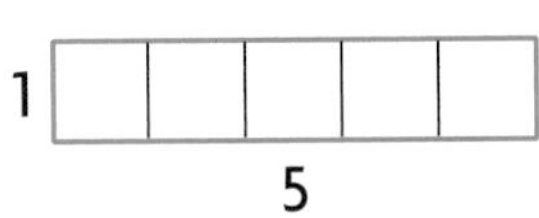

Perimeter:
$1 + 5 + 1 + 5 = 12$ feet

Area:
$1 \times 5 = 5$ square feet

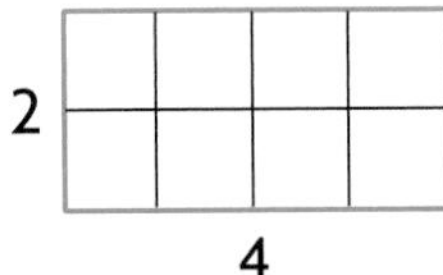

Perimeter:
$2 + 4 + 2 + 4 = 12$ feet

Area:
$2 \times 4 = 8$ square feet

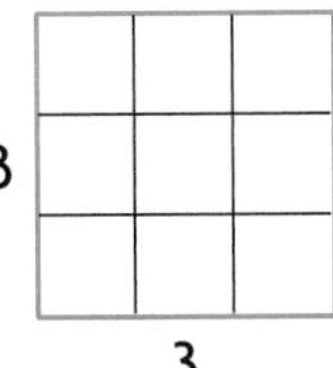

Perimeter:
$3 + 3 + 3 + 3 = 12$ feet

Area:
$3 \times 3 = 9$ square feet

Order the areas: $5 < 8 < 9$

9 square feet is the greatest area.

So, Maura's fence should be a square.

Talk About It

- **Describe** how the area changes when rectangles with the same perimeter change from long and thin to square.
- **What if** Maura had 20 feet of fencing? To have the greatest area, should her fence be a square or a rectangle?

Problem Solving Practice

1. **What if** Maura had 8 feet of fencing to make a rectangle or square with the greatest possible area? How long should it be? How wide should it be?

2. Kyle used 16 feet of fencing to make a square play yard for his rabbit. What was the length of each side? What was the area of the play yard?

Jane drew some figures on grid paper.

3. Which figure has a perimeter of 16 units?

A

B
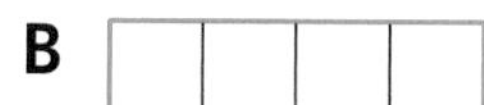

C
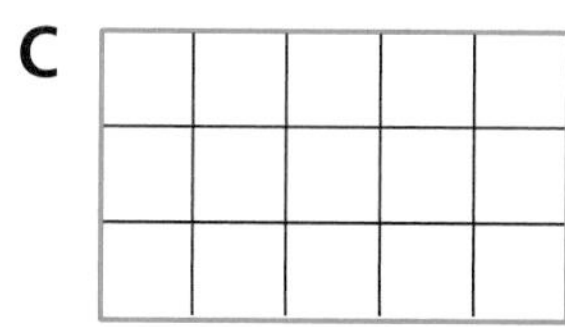

D

4. Which figure has an area of 15 square units?

F

G
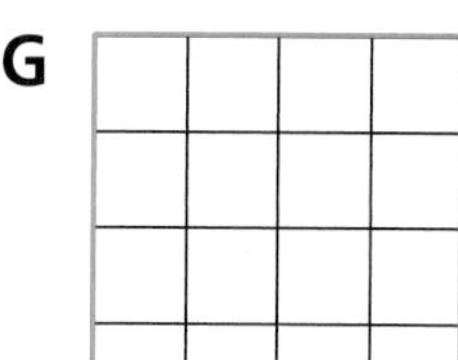

H
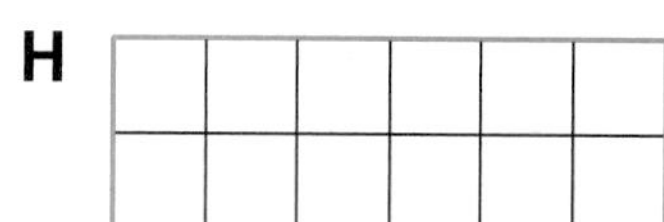

J
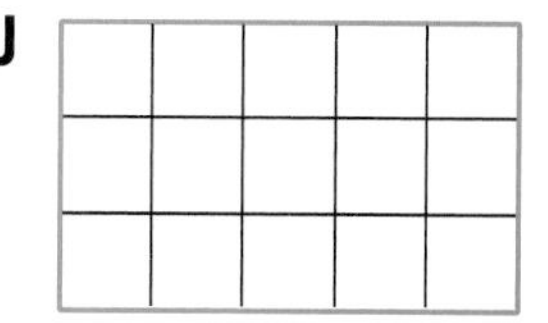

Mixed Applications

5. Abe bought 3 muffins for $1 each and 2 cartons of milk for $0.50 each. How much did he spend in all?

6. Ted eats 1 sandwich and drinks 2 glasses of milk each day. How many glasses of milk does he drink in one week?

7. **REASONING** I am a 2-digit number less than 20. I can be divided evenly into groups of 4. I cannot be divided evenly into groups of 3. What number am I?

8. **Write a problem** about the perimeter and area of a rectangle. Use square tiles to make the rectangle. Then draw a picture of your rectangle.

LESSON 4

Volume

Learn

FILL IT UP **Volume** is the amount of space a solid figure takes up.

A **cubic unit** is used to measure volume. A cubic unit is a cube with a side length of 1 unit. You can use connecting cubes to show cubic units.

1 cubic unit

Quick Review

1. $1 \times 4 \times 2 = \blacksquare$
2. $2 \times 3 \times 2 = \blacksquare$
3. $5 \times 1 \times 2 = \blacksquare$
4. $3 \times 2 \times 8 = \blacksquare$
5. $4 \times 2 \times 3 = \blacksquare$

VOCABULARY
volume
cubic unit

HANDS ON

Activity

Use connecting cubes to find the volume of a box.

MATERIALS: connecting cubes, small box

STEP 1

Estimate how many cubes it will take to fill the box. Record your estimate.

STEP 2

Count the cubes you use. Place the cubes in rows along the bottom of the box. Then continue to make layers of cubes until the box is full.

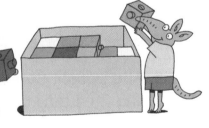

STEP 3

Record how many cubes it took to fill the box. This is the volume of the box in cubic units.

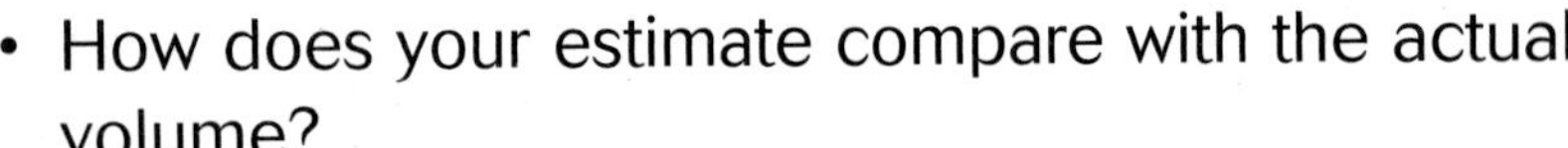

- How does your estimate compare with the actual volume?

MATH IDEA To measure the volume of a solid, find the number of cubic units needed to fill the solid.

Technology Link

More Practice:
Harcourt Mega Math
Ice Station Exploration,
Frozen Solids, Level J

Find the Volume

When you cannot count each cube, you can think about layers to find the volume.

Example

Find the volume of each solid.

Since you cannot see each cube, look at the top layer of cubes. For a rectangular prism,

number of layers × number of cubes in each layer = volume.

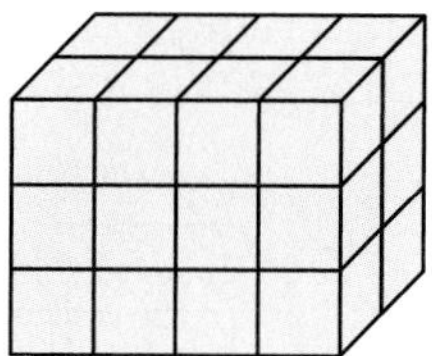

3 layers × 8 cubes per layer = 24 cubic units

So, the volume is 24 cubic units.

2 layers × 6 cubes per layer = 12 cubic units

So, the volume is 12 cubic units.

Check

1. **Explain** how you would find the volume of a box that has 4 layers and each layer is 3 cubes long and 2 cubes wide.

Use cubes to make each solid. Then write the volume in cubic units.

2. 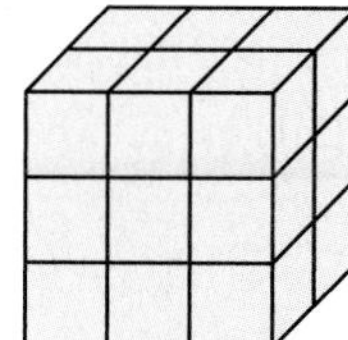

3. 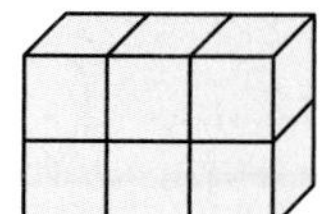

4. 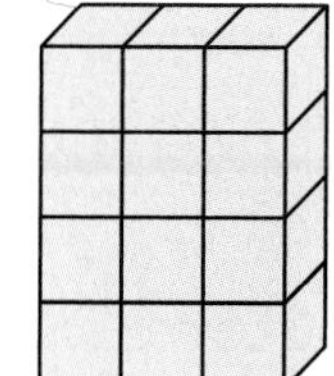

5. 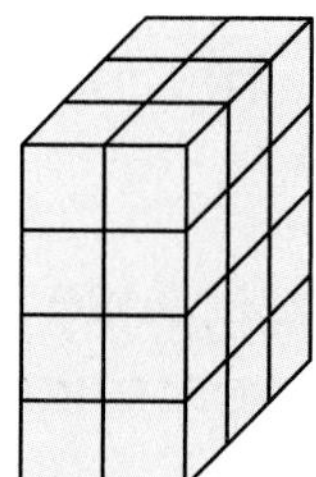

6. 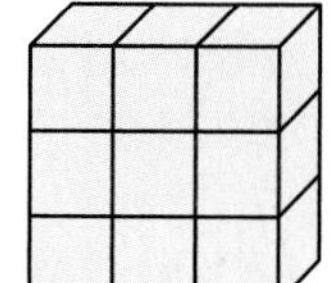

7. 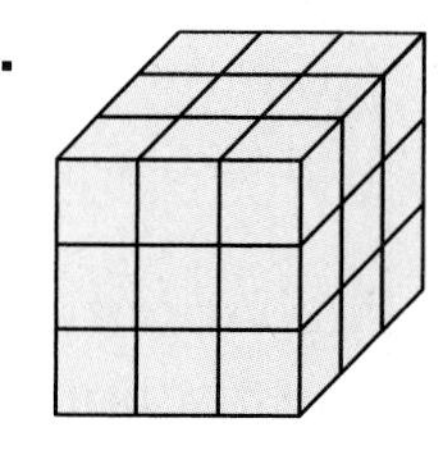

LESSON CONTINUES

Practice and Problem Solving

Extra Practice, page 456, Set B

Use cubes to make each solid. Then write the volume in cubic units.

8. 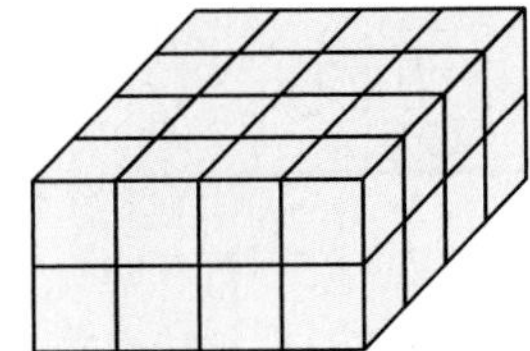

9. 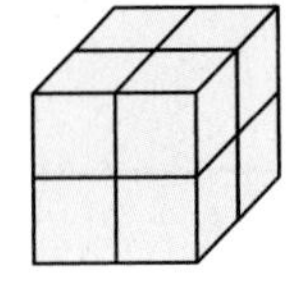

10. 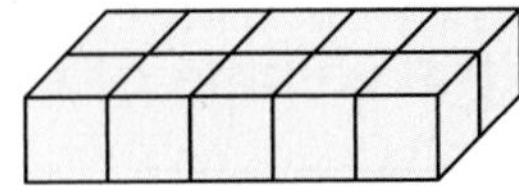

Find the volume of each solid. Write the volume in cubic units.

11. 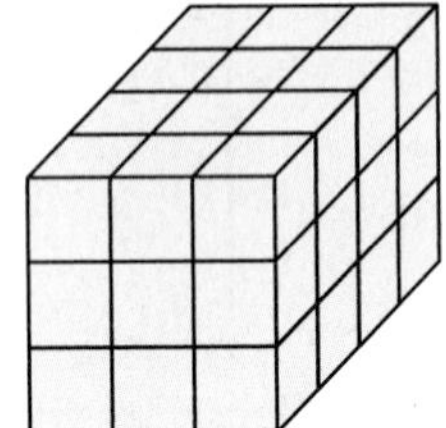

12. 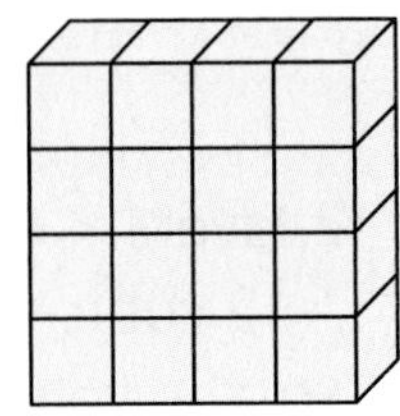

13. 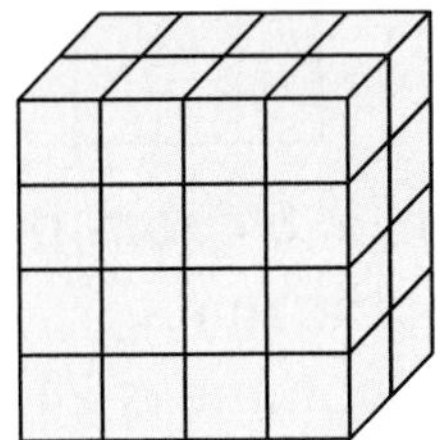

14. **Vocabulary Power** The word *perimeter* comes from the Greek words *peri*, which means "around," and *metron*, which means "measure." Describe how to find the perimeter of a poster.

15. **What's the Error?** Justin found the volume of this solid. He said the volume was 16 cubic units. Describe his error. Give the correct volume.

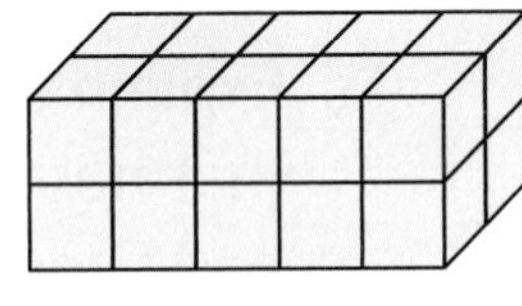

16. Sam's box is 2 cubes long, 2 cubes wide, and 3 cubes high. What is the volume of his box?

17. Todd's box is 4 cubes long and 4 cubes wide. It has a volume of 32 cubic units. What is the height of the box?

18. **ALGEBRA** Each layer of Andrew's prism is 6 cubic units. Its volume is 12 cubic units. How many layers are in the prism? You may use cubes to help.

19. **FAST FACT** • ART The St. Louis Gateway Arch is 630 feet high. It is 325 feet taller than the Statue of Liberty. What is the height of the Statue of Liberty?

20. **Write About It** How is finding the area of a figure different from finding the volume of a solid?

21. Look at the figure in Exercise 13. Write a multiplication sentence to find the volume of the figure.

Mixed Review and Test Prep

Find each sum. (p. 8)

22. $45 + 12 + 5 = \blacksquare$

23. $35 + 15 + 20 = \blacksquare$

24. $10 + 28 + 15 = \blacksquare$

25. $7 + 46 + 10 = \blacksquare$

26. $13 + 22 + 14 = \blacksquare$

27. $20 + 34 + 2 = \blacksquare$

28. $9 + 26 + 11 = \blacksquare$

29. **TEST PREP** Jane had 205 stickers. She gave 28 stickers to her sister. How many stickers does Jane have left? (p. 92)

A 175 **C** 180
B 177 **D** 182

30. **TEST PREP** Which is NOT true? (p. 176)

F $0 \times 4 = 0$ **H** $1 \times 3 = 3$
G $1 \times 0 = 1$ **J** $7 \times 1 = 7$

Problem Solving LINKUP . . . to Reading

STRATEGY • ANALYZE INFORMATION To solve some problems, you need to *analyze*, or look carefully at, each part.

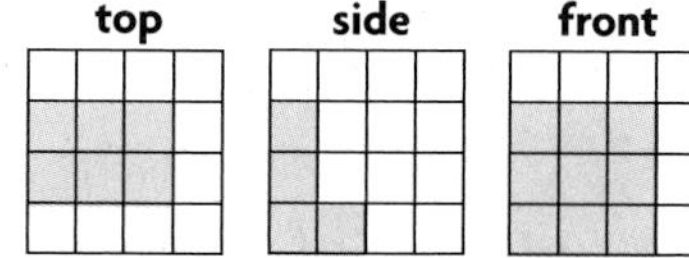

Analyze these drawings to identify the solid figure. Notice that the drawings of the top, side, and front views are plane shapes, not solid figures.

So, the solid figure looks like this.

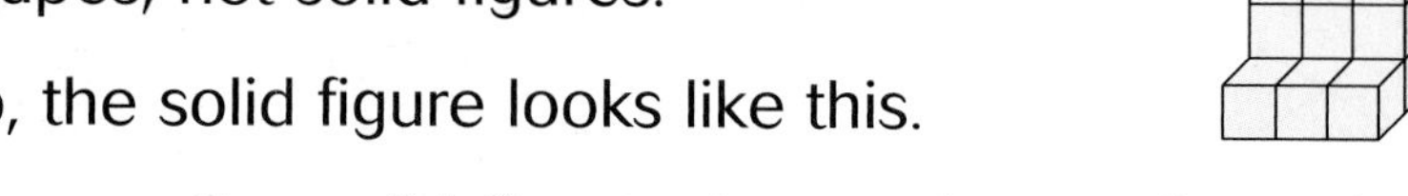

Choose the solid figure that each set of drawings shows.

1.

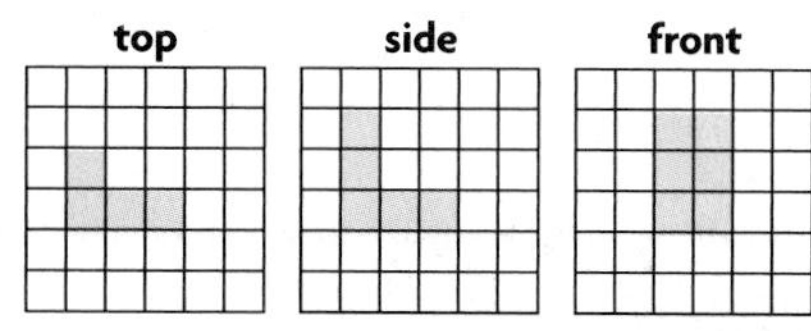

2.

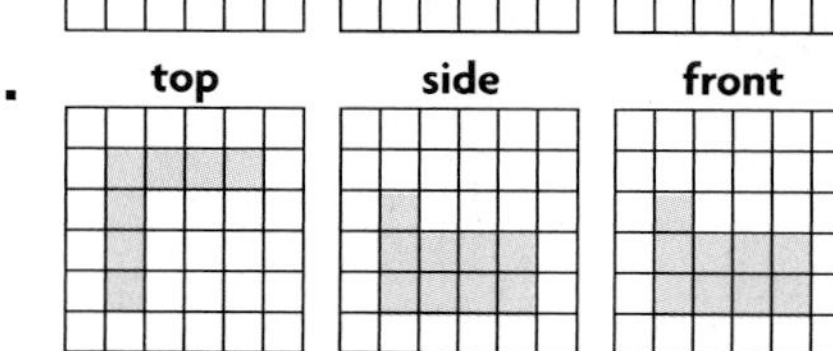

3.

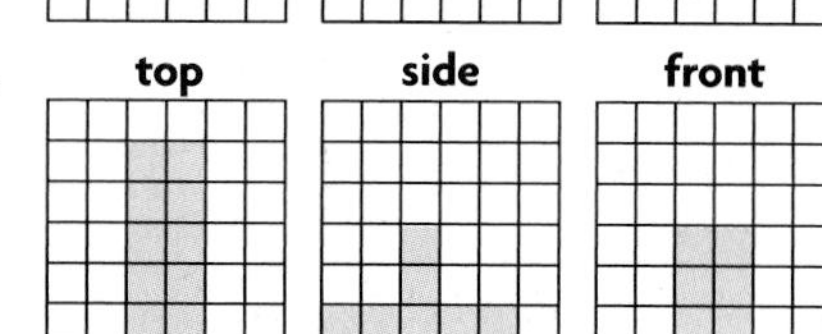

a.

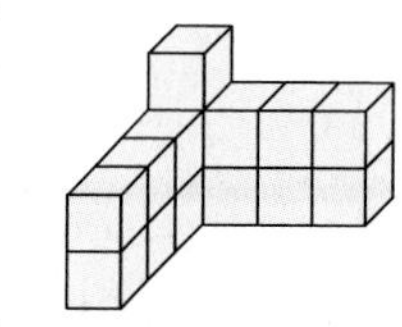

b.

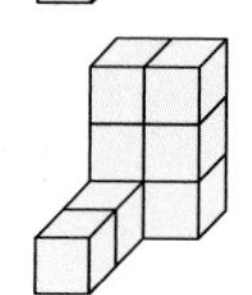

c.

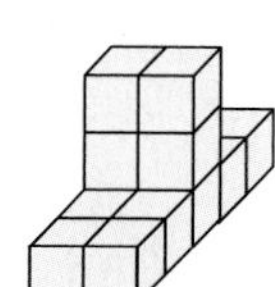

4. Build a figure with connecting cubes. Then use grid paper and draw its top, side, and front views.

Extra Practice

Set A (pp. 444–447)

Find the perimeter.

1. 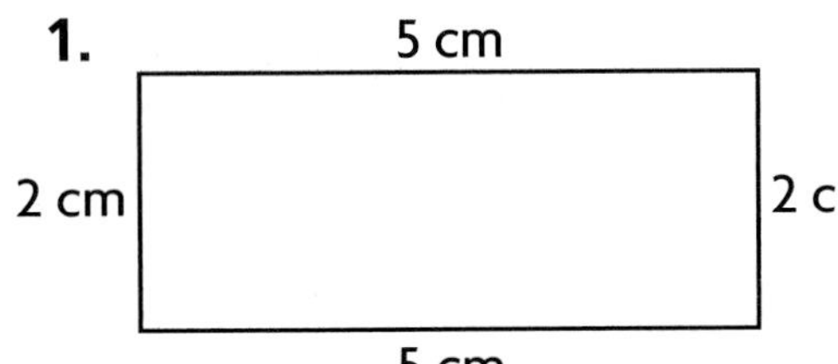

2. 3 cm, 2 cm, 2 cm

3. 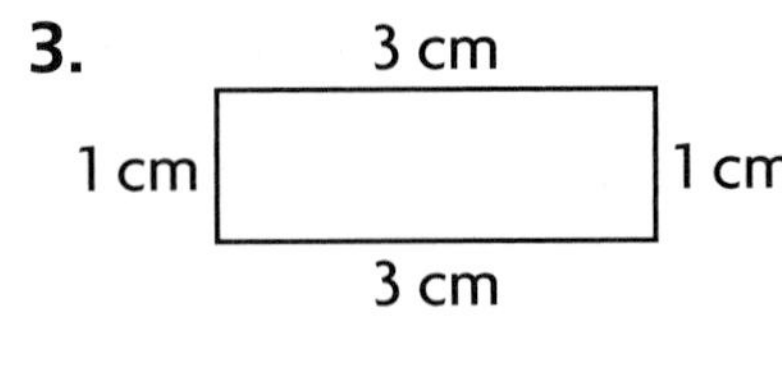

Estimate the perimeter in centimeters. Then use your centimeter ruler to find the perimeter.

4. 

5.  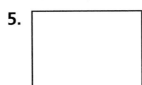

6. 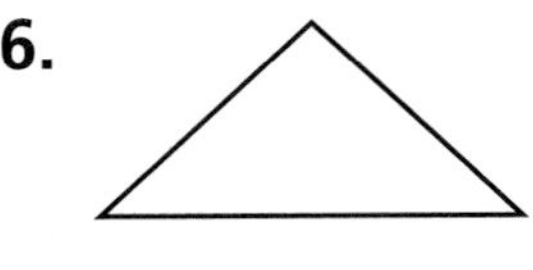

Set B (pp. 452–455)

Find the volume of each solid. Write the volume in cubic units.

1.

2. 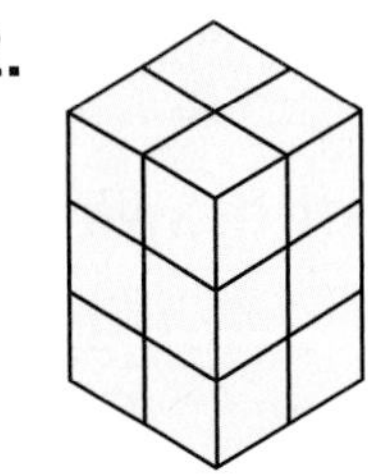

3. 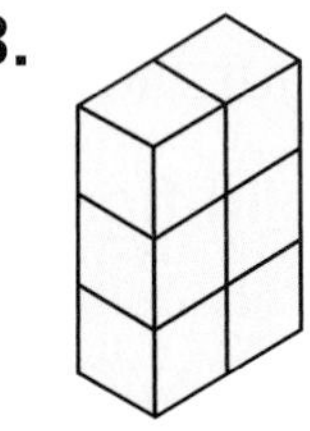

4.

5. 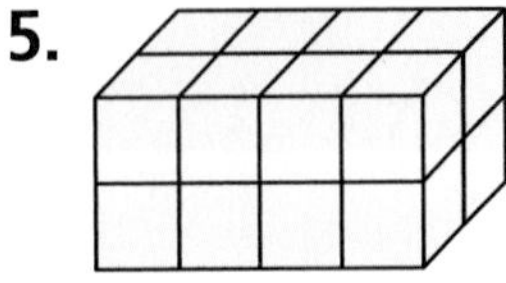

6. 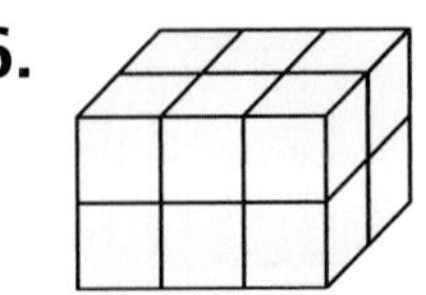

7.

8. 

9. 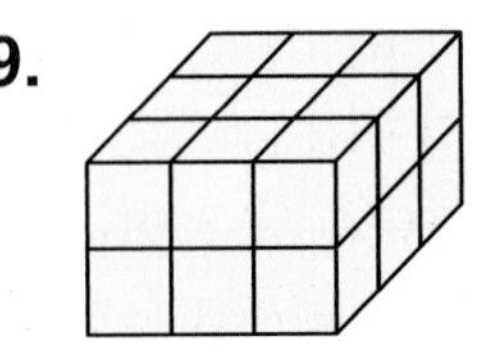

Review/Test

✓ CHECK VOCABULARY AND CONCEPTS

Choose the best term from the box.

area
cubic units
perimeter

1. To measure volume, you use ___?___. (p. 452)
2. The distance around a figure is called its ___?___. (p. 444)

Find the perimeter of each figure. (pp. 444–447)

3.

4.

5. 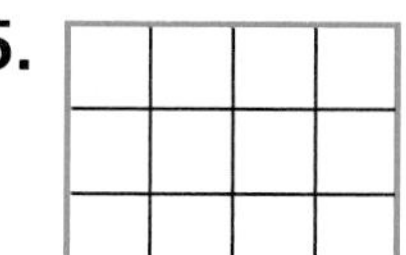

Write the area in square units. (pp. 448–449)

6. 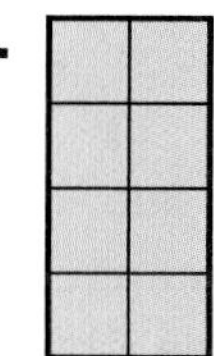

7. 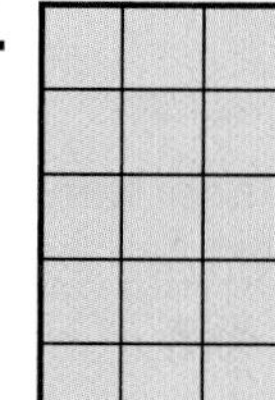

✓ CHECK SKILLS

Find the perimeter. (pp. 444–447)

8. 1 cm 1 cm 1 cm

9. 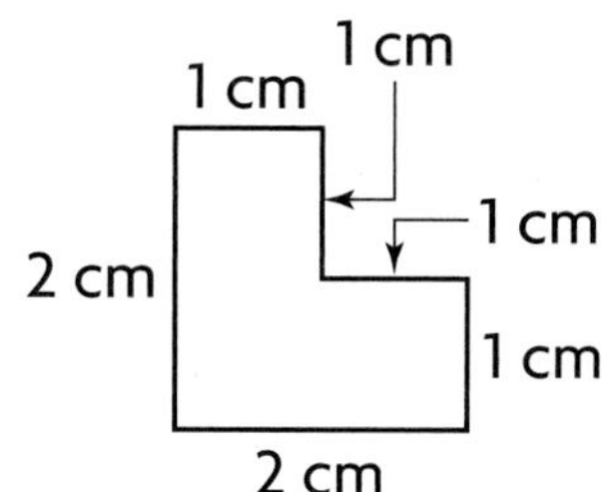

10. 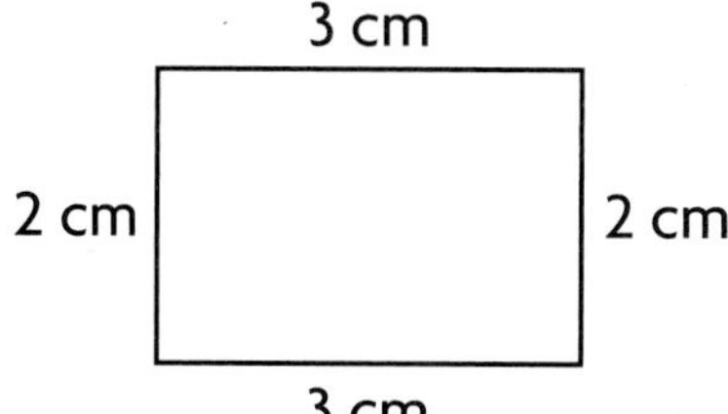

Write the volume in cubic units. (pp. 452–455)

11. 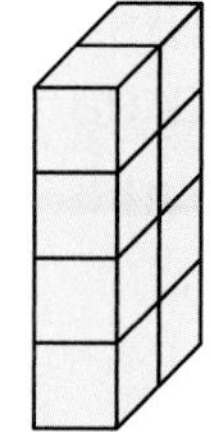

12. 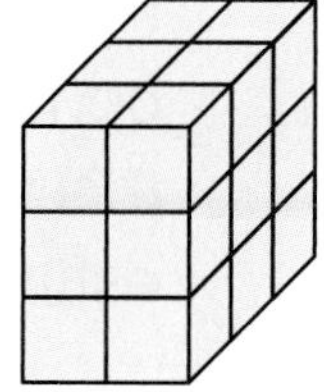

13. 

✓ CHECK PROBLEM SOLVING

Solve. (pp. 450–451)

14. Pedro has 20 inches of string. He wants to make a rectangle or square with the greatest possible area. How wide should it be? How long should it be?

15. Nora has 16 inches of ribbon. She wants to make a rectangle or square with the greatest possible area. How long should it be? How wide should it be?

Standardized Test Prep

NUMBER SENSE, CONCEPTS, AND OPERATIONS

1. What is the value of the digit 5 in 35,468?

   A 50
   B 500
   C 5,000
   D 50,000

TIP **Understand the problem.** See item 2. You are asked to find the number of boxes sold *in all*. You must decide which operation to use to find the answer.

2. The table shows how many boxes of cookies Austin, Taylor, and Caroline sold.

COOKIES SOLD	
Name	Number of Boxes
Austin	68
Taylor	56
Caroline	60

   How many boxes of cookies did they sell in all?

   F 174
   G 184
   H 190
   J 204

3. **Explain It** In October, 6 classes went on a field trip. There were 18 students in each class. About how many students went on the trip? Tell how you estimated.

MEASUREMENT

4. Maura drew this figure. The lengths of the sides are measured in centimeters (cm).

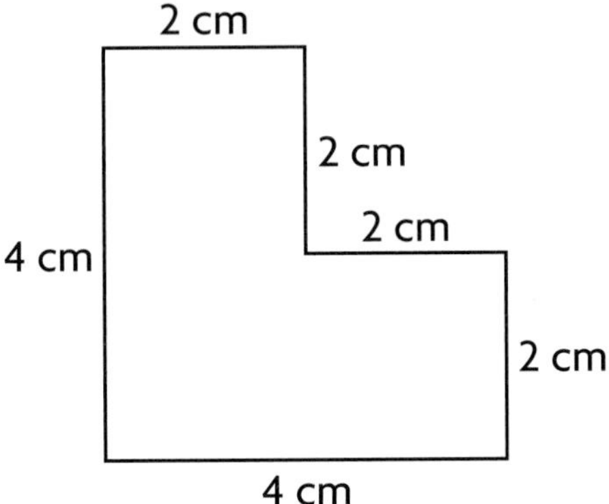

   Which is the perimeter of the figure?

   A 12 centimeters
   B 16 centimeters
   C 18 centimeters
   D 20 centimeters

5. **Explain It** Each small square of the figure below is one square centimeter. Estimate the area of this figure. Explain how you estimated.

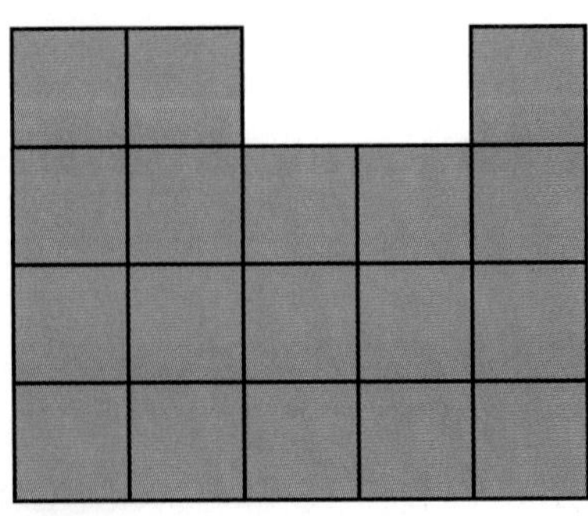

GEOMETRY AND SPATIAL SENSE

6. Tonya drew this figure.

Which figure is similar to the one that Tonya drew?

F   **H**

G   **J**

7. Mrs. Conner put this poster on a wall of her classroom.

YOU ARE
IN A
READING
ZONE

Which polygon describes the shape of the poster?

A triangle
B pentagon
C octagon
D hexagon

8. Explain It Greta said that these lines are parallel. Tom said that they are perpendicular.

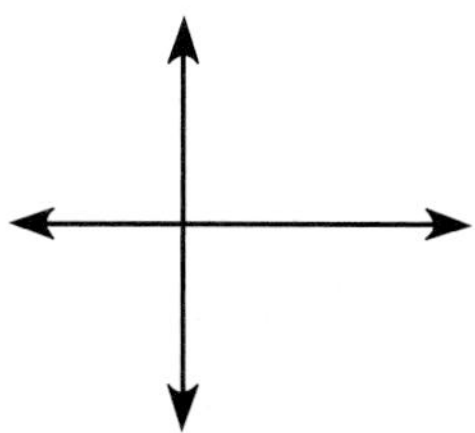

Do you agree with Greta or with Tom? Explain why.

ALGEBRAIC THINKING

9. The table below shows the number of note cards in boxes. Which number is missing in the table?

Boxes	1	2	3	4
Cards	12	24	■	48

F 28
G 30
H 32
J 36

10. Robin wrote this number pattern.

24, 21, 18, 15, 12

Which is a rule that she could have used to make the pattern?

A Add 4.
B Subtract 3.
C Multiply by 2.
D Divide by 3.

11. Explain It Michael had 136 coins. He gave some coins to his brother. Now Michael has 119 coins.

Write an equation to find how many coins Michael gave to his brother. Then describe the steps you followed to write your equation.

IT'S IN THE BAG

Pocketful of Polygons

PROJECT Make polygons and describe them.

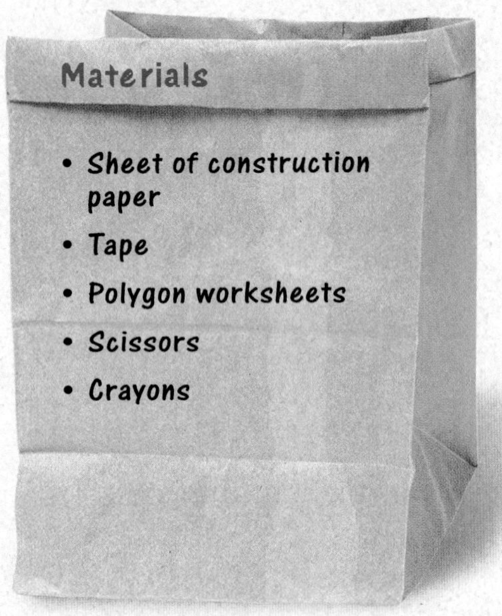

Directions

1. Fold the sheet of construction paper in half. Tape the left and right sides closed, leaving the top of the pocket open. *(Picture A)* Decorate the front of your pocket.
2. On the worksheets, complete the sentences to describe each polygon. *(Picture B)*
3. Use crayons to color your polygons. Then cut out the polygons. *(Picture C)*
4. Share your descriptions with classmates. Store your polygons in the pocket that you made.

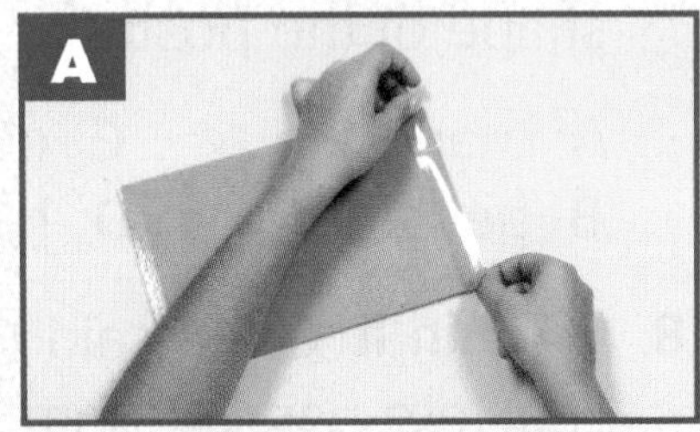

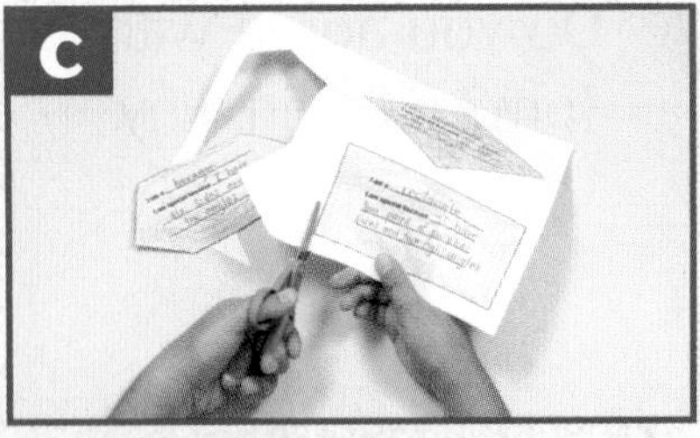

Challenge

Measure with Degrees

You can use a circle to measure angles in degrees.

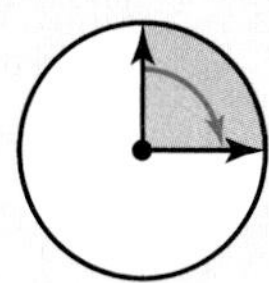

A $\frac{1}{4}$ turn around a circle measures $90°$.

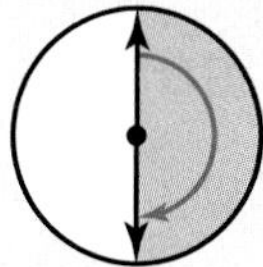

A $\frac{1}{2}$ turn measures $180°$.

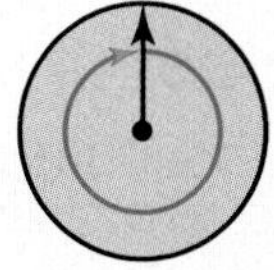

A full turn measures $360°$.

Activity

MATERIALS: circle pattern, pencil, tracing paper

Measure the angle at the right.

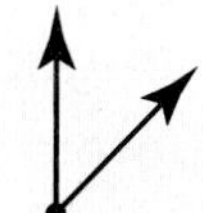

STEP 1

Trace the circle pattern onto tracing paper. Fold it in half 3 times. Open up the circle and mark the center.

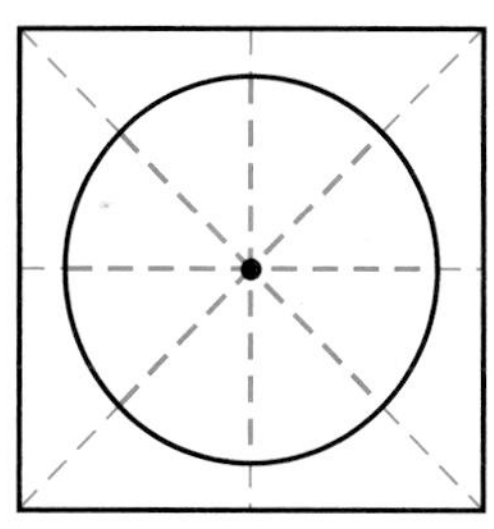

STEP 2

Label each fold with the measures shown.

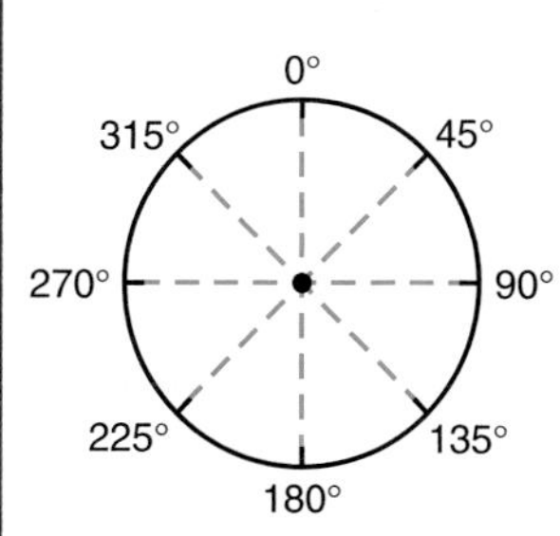

STEP 3

Place the center of the circle on the vertex of the angle. Line up one ray with the 0° mark. Read the measure at the other ray.

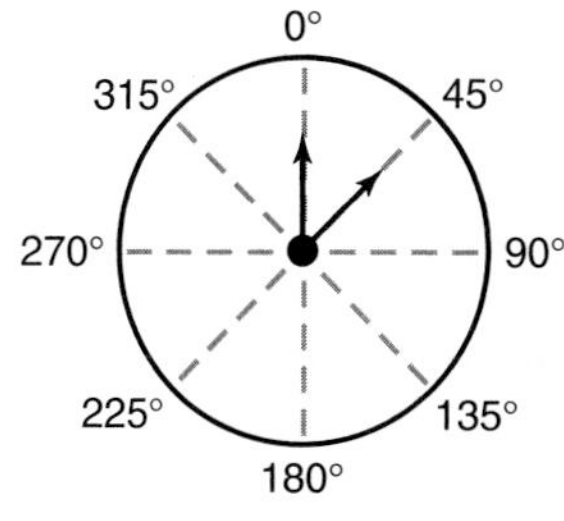

So, the angle measures $45°$.

Try It

Use your circle to measure each angle.

1.

2.

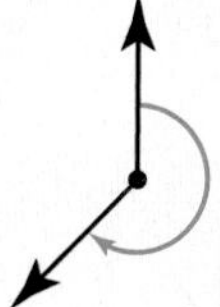

3.

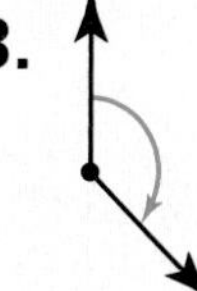

4.

Study Guide and Review

VOCABULARY

Choose the best term from the box.

face
polygon
vertex

1. A closed plane figure with straight sides is a ___?___. (p. 390)
2. A corner of a solid figure where three or more edges meet is called a ___?___. (p. 424)

STUDY AND SOLVE

Chapter 19

Classify angles.

This angle is a **right angle.** It forms a square corner.

This angle is an **acute angle.**

This angle is an **obtuse angle.**

Write whether the angle is a *right angle,* an *obtuse angle,* or an *acute angle.* (pp. 384–387)

3. 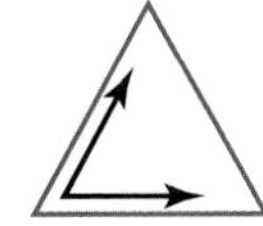

4. 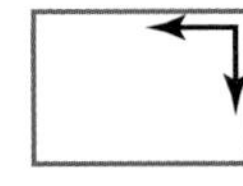

5. 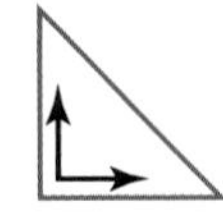

6. 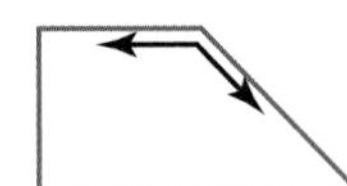

Classify polygons.

Which figure is a pentagon?

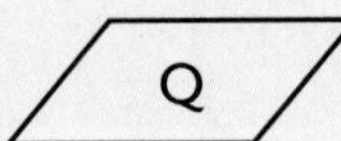

R

Figure R is a pentagon. It has 5 sides.

For 7–8, use the figures. (pp. 390–391)

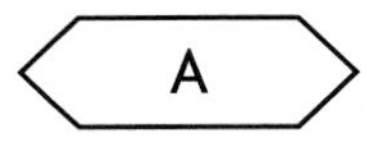

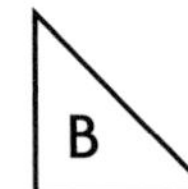

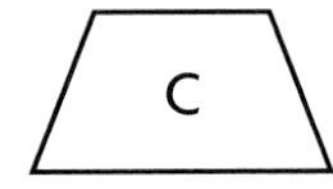

7. Which is a quadrilateral?
8. Which is a hexagon?

Chapter 20

Identify lines of symmetry.

When a figure is folded along a line of symmetry, the two parts match exactly.

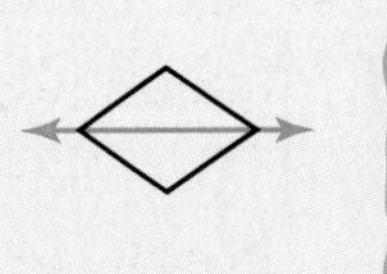

For 9–10, tell if the blue line is a line of symmetry. Write *yes* or *no*.

(pp. 410–411)

9. 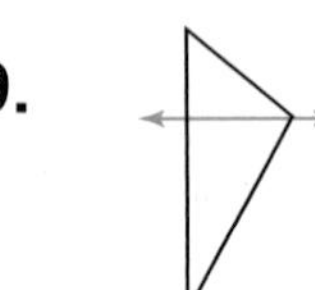

10. 

Chapter 21

Describe solid figures.

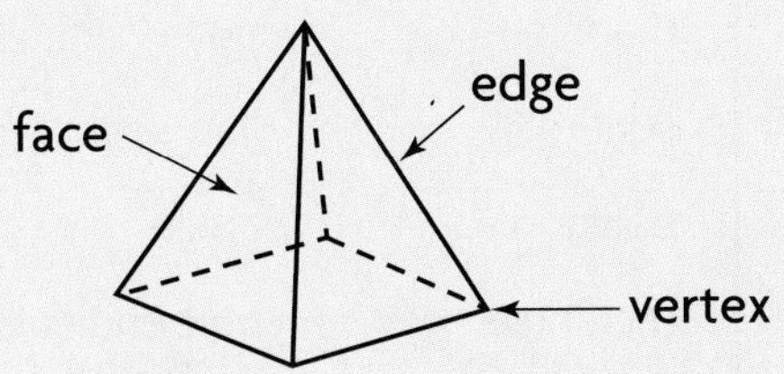

This square pyramid has 5 faces, 8 edges, and 5 vertices. One face is a square, and the other four faces are triangles.

For 11–13, use the figure. (pp. 424–427)

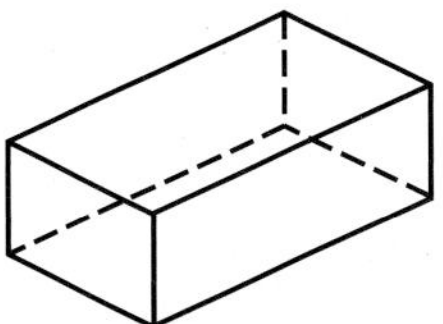

11. How many faces, edges, and vertices does the figure have?

12. What shape are the faces of this figure?

13. What is this figure called?

Chapter 22

Find perimeter and area.

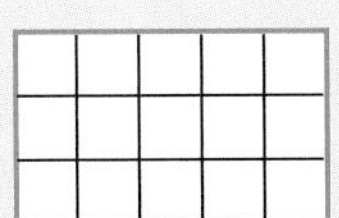

Add the lengths of the sides to find the perimeter.

$3 + 5 + 3 + 5 = 16$

So, the perimeter is 16 units.

Multiply the number of rows times the number in each row to find the area.

$3 \times 5 = 15$

So, the area is 15 square units.

Find the perimeter. (pp. 444–447)

14.

3 cm

1 cm 1 cm

3 cm

Write the area in square units. (pp. 448–449)

15.

16.

PROBLEM SOLVING PRACTICE

Solve. (pp. 416–417, 450–451)

17. Use pattern blocks to make a quadrilateral. Then use a different combination of pattern blocks to make a figure that is congruent to your quadrilateral.

18. Jed makes a rectangle with the greatest possible area using 16 inches of string. What are the length and width of his rectangle?

PERFORMANCE ASSESSMENT

TASK A • ART CLASS

Matthew is learning how to draw these solid figures in art class.

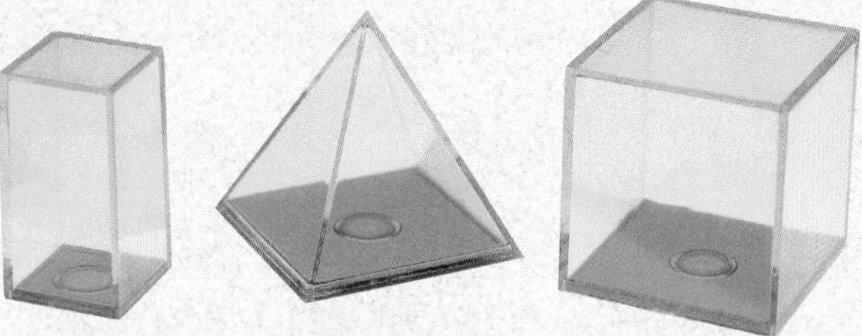

triangle	point
square	line segment
polygon	angle
rectangle	perpendicular
quadrilateral	right angle
parallelogram	parallel

a. Choose one of the solid figures. Tell how many faces, edges, and vertices it has.

b. Draw each plane figure that is a face of the solid figure you chose. Label each plane figure with its name.

c. Write at least three sentences to describe one of the faces. Use as many of the terms from the box at the top of the page as you can.

TASK B • MATH T-SHIRTS

Materials: pattern blocks, ruler

The math club members want to design special T-shirts to wear on meeting days. These are the rules for the design.

Design Rules

1. The design must be made of pattern-block shapes.
2. The design must be in the shape of a triangle.
3. One side of the triangle must be at least 6 inches long.
4. Congruent shapes must be the same color.

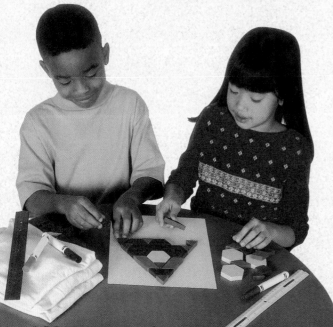

a. Follow all the design rules listed in the box. First, use pattern blocks to make a design for the T-shirt. Then, draw your design.

b. Explain whether your design has any lines of symmetry.

c. Explain how you would enlarge the design for a poster.

Symmetry

Computers can help you draw geometric figures. Use drawing tools on a computer to draw a square. Draw one line of symmetry on the square.

STEP 1

Open a computer application that has drawing tools. Choose the tool to make a square.

STEP 2

Go to the place on the screen where you want to draw the figure. Use the tool to draw a square.

STEP 3

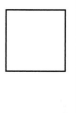

Choose the line tool. Use the tool to draw a line of symmetry on the square.

Practice and Problem Solving

Use computer drawing tools to draw each figure.

1. square **2.** rectangle **3.** triangle **4.** circle

5. Draw a rectangle. Draw two lines of symmetry on the rectangle.

6. Draw a circle. Draw two lines of symmetry on the circle.

7. **STRETCH YOUR THINKING** Make a figure by combining at least two different geometric figures.

GO ON-LINE **Multimedia Math Glossary** www.harcourtschool.com/mathglossary

Vocabulary Power Look up *congruent figures* in the Multimedia Math Glossary. Draw two figures that are congruent. Then draw the line or lines of symmetry on each.

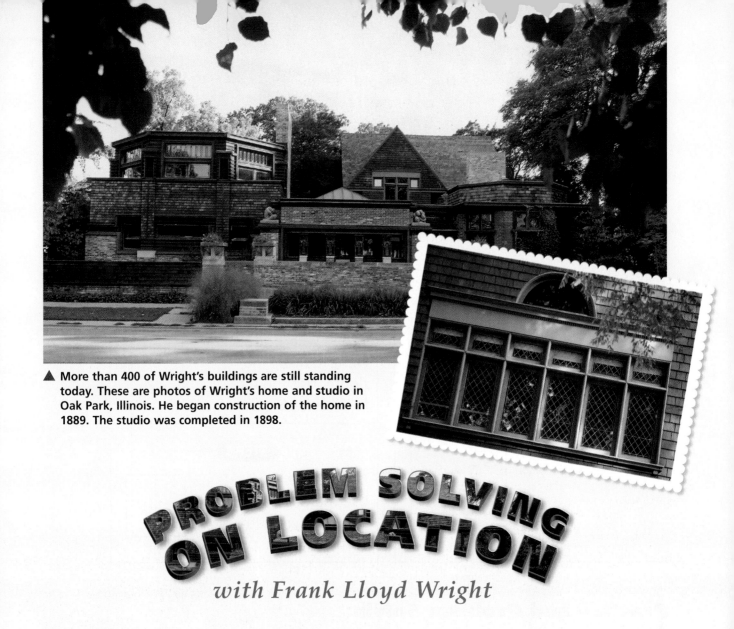

▲ More than 400 of Wright's buildings are still standing today. These are photos of Wright's home and studio in Oak Park, Illinois. He began construction of the home in 1889. The studio was completed in 1898.

PROBLEM SOLVING ON LOCATION

with Frank Lloyd Wright

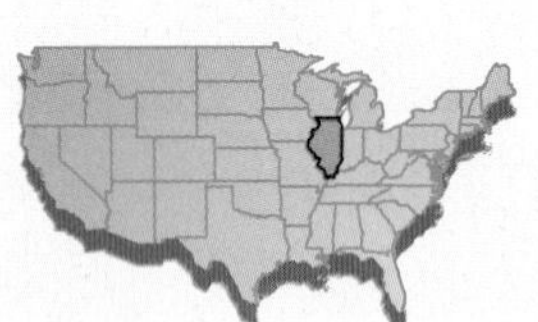

IN OAK PARK, ILLINOIS

Frank Lloyd Wright lived from 1867 to 1959. During his lifetime he designed and built more than 500 homes, museums, and office buildings.

1. Look at the different views of the house. Find a polygon that has a line of symmetry. Draw the polygon and show a line of symmetry.

2. Describe a pair of congruent figures in one of the photos. Tell how you know the figures are congruent.

3. Look for an example of a right angle, an acute angle, and an obtuse angle. Trace the angles from the photos and label each angle.

4. Look at the photos and find one example of parallel lines and one example of intersecting lines. Draw the lines.

IN MILL RUN, PENNSYLVANIA

Frank Lloyd Wright was an architect perhaps best known for houses he designed. Fallingwater is the weekend retreat he built for the Edgar J. Kaufmann family in 1936. It is now open for public tours from mid-March through November.

For 1–3, use the picture.

1. Name a solid figure in the photo. Describe where you see this figure in the photo.
2. How many faces, vertices, and edges does the solid figure that you named in Exercise 1 have?
3. Write three sentences to describe plane figures in the photo. Use as many of the words from the box below as you can.

triangle	parallelogram	line segment	right angle	square
polygon	quadrilateral	rectangle	circle	intersecting

▼ **Frank Lloyd Wright designed houses and buildings that seemed to be part of the landscape. In Fallingwater, the stream flows parallel to the house and partially under the house. The horizontal levels appear to be floating amid the rock ledges.**

Algebra: Patterns

FAST FACT • ART Patterns can be seen in many Native American works of art such as baskets, jewelry, blankets, and pottery. The Pima baskets shown here are woven to be watertight.

PROBLEM SOLVING Look closely at the Navajo serape (shawl) pictured below. Describe the different patterns that you see.

Pima baskets were used for storing food, holding water, and sometimes used as drums.

CHECK WHAT YOU KNOW

Use this page to help you review and remember important skills needed for Chapter 23.

ORDINAL NUMBERS

For 1–4, use the list of names.

Kelly
Tom
Sally
Susan
Timothy
Julie
Juan
Matt

1. Kelly is first on the list. Who is seventh?
2. In which position is Julie on the list?
3. Who is fifth on the list?
4. In which position is Tom on the list?

USE A RULE

Copy and complete the table.

5.

Dimes	1	2	3	4	5
Nickels	2	4	6	■	■

Rule: Multiply the number of dimes by 2.

6.

Bags	1	2	3	4	5
Marbles	10	20	■	40	■

Rule: Multiply the number of bags by 10.

7.

Baskets	1	2	3	4	5
Oranges	8	16	■	32	■

Rule: Multiply the number of baskets by 8.

8.

Cars	1	2	3	4	5
Tires	4	■	12	16	■

Rule: Multiply the number of cars by 4.

VOCABULARY POWER

REVIEW

pattern [pat′ərn] *noun*

A pattern is an ordered set of numbers or objects. Find one example of a pattern and describe the order seen in that pattern.

PREVIEW

pattern unit

www.harcourtschool.com/mathglossary

LESSON 1

Geometric Patterns

Quick Review

Name each polygon.

1.

2.

3.

4.

5.

VOCABULARY

pattern unit

Learn

LOOK CLOSELY Some patterns are made with figures that repeat. The part of a pattern that repeats is called the **pattern unit**.

Ben used pattern blocks to make this pattern. What is the pattern unit?

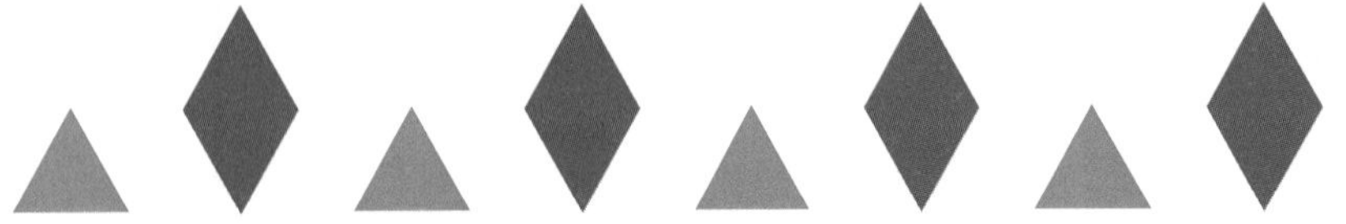

The pattern unit is *green triangle, blue rhombus*.

Carla used tiles and counters to make a pattern. Look for the pattern unit. What will the next two shapes in her pattern be?

The pattern unit is *red circle, green square, yellow circle*. The next two shapes will be a red circle and a green square.

Look at Dee's pattern below. Look for the pattern unit. What shape is missing?

The pattern unit is *blue square, red square, green triangle*. The missing shape is a red square.

- **REASONING** Look closely at the picture of the kingsnake. Do you see a pattern unit? Describe the pattern that you see.

Translating Patterns

The same pattern can be shown using different objects or symbols.

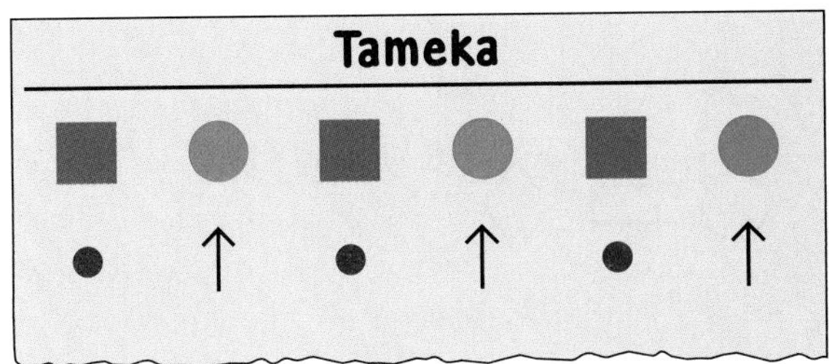

Tameka's pattern is shown using squares and circles and again using dots and arrows.

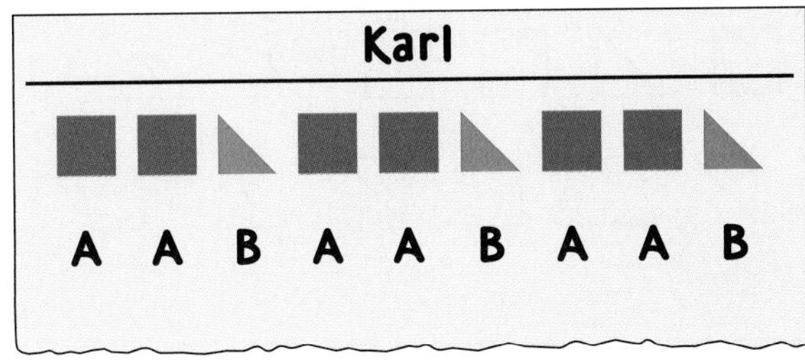

Karl's pattern is shown using squares and triangles and again using the letters A and B.

- **REASONING** How are Tameka's two patterns the same? How are Karl's two patterns the same?

Check

1. **Explain** how you could use rectangles and circles to show the following pattern.

   A B B A B B A B B

Name the pattern unit for each.

2. ○ △ ○ △ ○ △ ○ △

3. ▽ ▯ ⬠ ▽ ▯ ⬠ ▽ ▯ ⬠ ▽ ▯ ⬠

Draw the next two shapes in each pattern.

4. ◺ ◺ □ ◺ ◺ □ ◺ ◺ □ ◺ ◺ □ ? ?

5. □ ○ ▯ □ ○ ▯ □ ○ ▯ □ ○ ▯ ? ?

LESSON CONTINUES

Practice and Problem Solving

Extra Practice, page 482, Set A

Name the pattern unit for each.

6.
7.

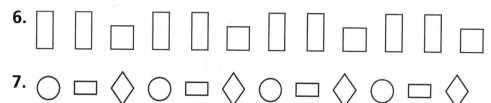

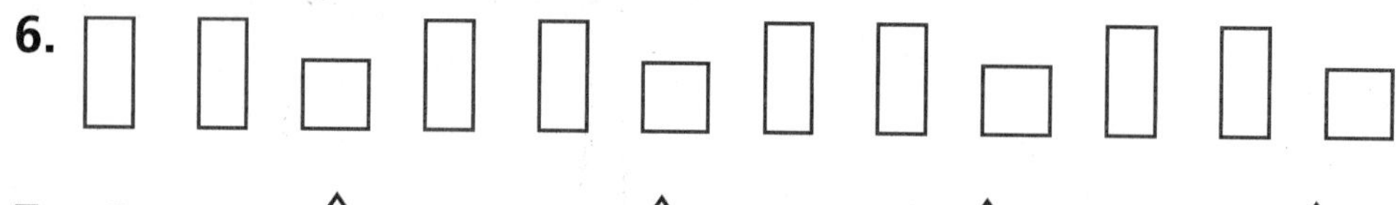

Draw the next two shapes in each pattern.

8. ? ?
9. ? ?

Copy each pattern on dot paper. Find the pattern unit. Then draw the next two figures in each pattern.

10.

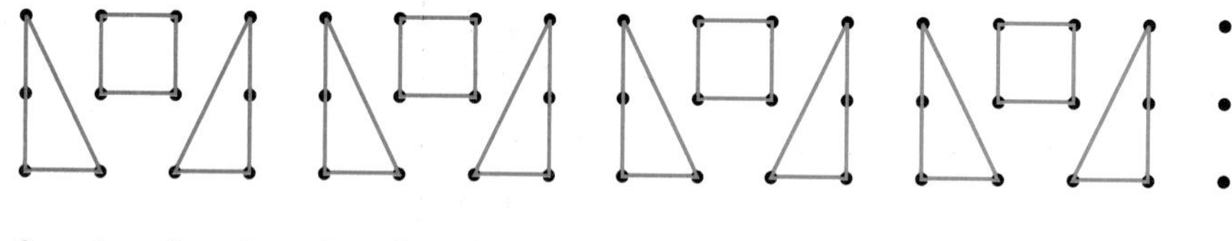

11.

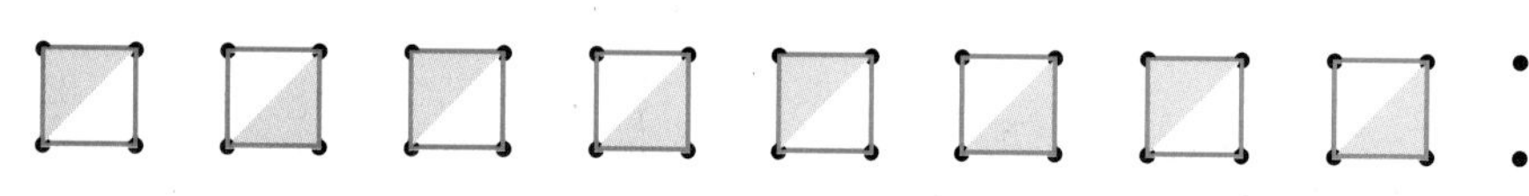

12. Jack drew the pattern below. Show his pattern another way using the letters A and B.

13. **Vocabulary Power** When something *repeats*, it happens again. Explain how this applies to the patterns in this lesson.

14. **REASONING** Mr. Griffin is teaching a sound pattern to his class. The pattern unit is *clap*, *clap*, *snap*. What will the eleventh sound be? Explain.

15. **Write a problem** in which a pattern has a missing part. Explain how you know what is missing in the pattern.

16. Four students are working on art projects. There are 3 bags of markers with 8 markers in each bag. Can they share all of the markers equally? Explain.

17. Kelly had a $5 bill, two $1 bills, and three quarters. She bought a snack for $1.35 and a book for $4.55. How much money did Kelly have left?

Mixed Review and Test Prep

Write each number in expanded form. (p. 32)

18. 54,389 **19.** 72,186

20. 237,524 **21.** 62,309

22. 921,630 **23.** 26,375

Find the missing factor. (p. 186)

24. $5 \times ■ = 25$

25. $4 \times ■ = 32$

26. TEST PREP How many meters are in two kilometers? (p. 358)

A 20 **C** 2,000
B 200 **D** 20,000

27. TEST PREP Find the product.

$4 \times 2 \times 7 = ■$ (p. 218)

F 56 **H** 42
G 49 **J** 36

Problem Solving Thinker's Corner

VISUAL THINKING

MATERIALS: connecting cubes, grid paper, crayons

Patterns can be made by turning figures. The pattern below is of a figure moving clockwise in 180° turns.

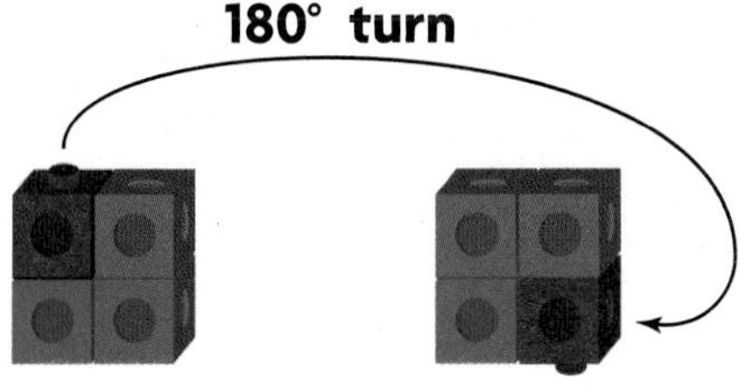

1. Make a figure using three colors of connecting cubes. On grid paper, draw a pattern in which the figure moves clockwise in 180° turns.

2. Use the figure you made in Exercise 1. On grid paper, draw a pattern in which the figure moves clockwise in 90° turns.

LESSON 2

Visual Patterns

Learn

DESCRIBE IT! A rule can be used to describe a pattern. Look at this pattern made with cubes. How are the figures related?

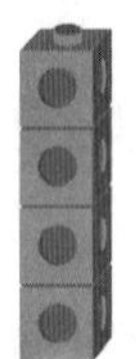

The number of cubes increases by 1 from one figure to the next. *Add 1 cube to the stack* is a rule that describes the pattern.

- What will the next two figures be?

Look at the pattern on grid paper. What rule describes this pattern?

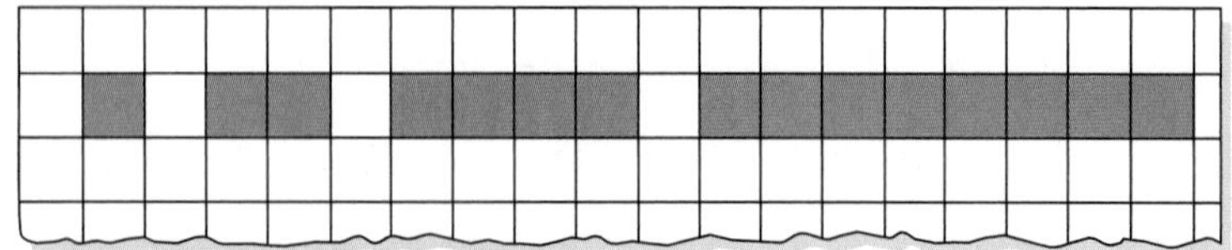

Look at the figures:

1st figure—1 square
2nd figure—2 squares
3rd figure—4 squares
4th figure—8 squares

Each figure has twice as many squares as the figure before it. So, a rule for this pattern is *multiply the number of squares in a row by 2.*

Quick Review

Skip-count to complete.

1. 2, 4, 6, 8, ■
2. 1, 3, 5, 7, 9, ■
3. 4, 8, 12, 16, ■
4. 3, 6, 9, 12, ■
5. 5, 10, 15, 20, ■

Check

1. **Explain** how to find a rule for the dot pattern.

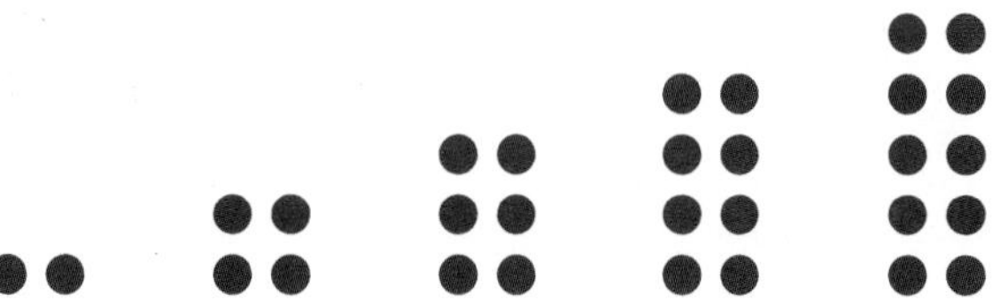

Write a rule for each pattern.

2. 

3. 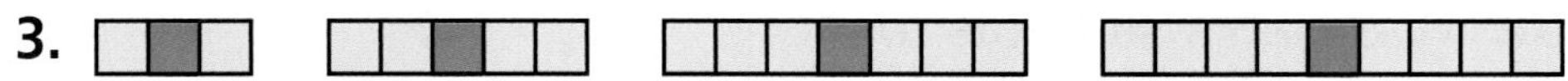

Practice and Problem Solving

Extra Practice, page 482, Set B

Write a rule for each pattern.

4. 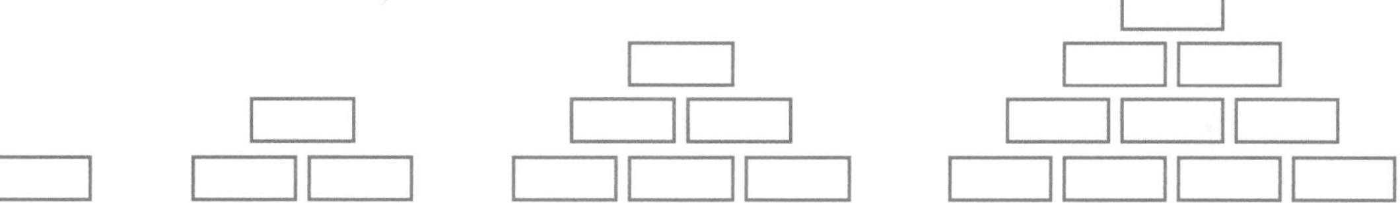

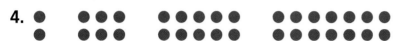

5.

For 6–7, use the tile pattern below.

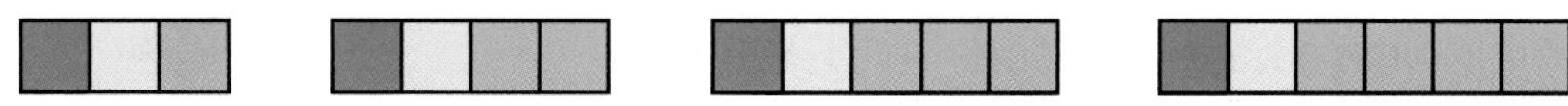

6. What is a rule for the pattern?

7. Describe the next figure in the pattern.

8. **What's the Question?** Ellen has 250 centimeters of red yarn, 510 centimeters of purple yarn, and 120 centimeters of white yarn. The answer is 390 centimeters.

9. **Write About It** Patterns are found in many places. Describe one pattern that you see at school, and one pattern that you see at home.

Mixed Review and Test Prep

Find each sum. (p. 72)

10. $\begin{array}{r} 256 \\ +188 \\ \hline \end{array}$

11. $\begin{array}{r} 349 \\ +207 \\ \hline \end{array}$

12. $\begin{array}{r} 472 \\ +135 \\ \hline \end{array}$

13. $\begin{array}{r} 508 \\ +364 \\ \hline \end{array}$

14. **TEST PREP** Jake worked on the computer from 11:25 A.M. to 12:10 P.M. How long did he work on the computer? (p. 134)

A 50 minutes
B 45 minutes
C 40 minutes
D 35 minutes

LESSON 3

Number Patterns

Learn

NAME THE CHANGE Miss Hart's students made number patterns. How did the numbers change in Derek's pattern? What rule did he use?

Derek
7, 11, 15, 19, 23, 27

7 11 15 19 23 27

+4 +4 +4 +4 +4

The numbers increased by 4. So, Derek used the rule *add 4*.

- Predict the next three numbers in Derek's pattern.

The rule for Nina's pattern is *subtract 3*. What number is missing?

Nina
52, 49, 46, 43, 40, ■, 34

Use the rule to find the missing number.

Since $40 - 3 = 37$, the missing number is 37.

Quick Review

Skip-count by fives to complete.

1. 3, 8, 13, ■, ■
2. 15, 20, 25, ■, ■
3. 12, 17, 22, ■, ■
4. 21, 26, 31, ■, ■
5. 44, 49, 54, ■, ■

Technology Link

More Practice: Harcourt Mega Math The Number Games, *Tiny's Think Tank,* Level K

Check

1. **Explain** the number pattern on the doors below.

Write a rule for each pattern.

2. 16, 21, 26, 31, 36, 41

3. 52, 50, 48, 46, 44, 42

4. 123, 113, 103, 93, 83, 73

5. 18, 26, 34, 42, 50, 58

Practice and Problem Solving

Extra Practice, page 482, Set C

Write a rule for each pattern.

6. 255, 270, 285, 300, 315, 330

7. 33, 36, 39, 42, 45, 48

8. 54, 63, 72, 81, 90, 99

9. 74, 71, 68, 65, 62, 59

Write a rule for each pattern. Then find the missing numbers.

10. 24, 28, 32, 36, 40, ■, 48, 52, ■, ■

11. 105, 102, 99, 96, ■, ■, 87, 84, 81, ■

12. 937, 917, 897, 877, ■, ■, 817, ■

13. 336, 348, 360, 372, 384, ■, 408, ■, ■

14. There are 2 stacks of boxes with 5 boxes in each stack. If there are 10 books in each box, how many books are there in all?

15. **Write a problem** about a number pattern. Exchange problems with a classmate and solve.

16. **What's the Error?** Tom wrote this pattern:

8, 25, 42, 59, 75

He said the rule was *add 17*. Describe his error.

17. **FAST FACT** • SOCIAL STUDIES Games like checkers are played around the world. The pattern on a United States checkerboard has 8 rows of 8 equal-sized squares. How many of these squares are there in all?

Mixed Review and Test Prep

Complete. (pp. 342, 358)

18. 1 foot = ■ inches

19. 1 yard = ■ feet

20. ■ decimeters = 1 meter

21. ■ centimeters = 1 meter

22. **TEST PREP** Alesha has a journal with 200 pages in it. Forty-three pages are blank. How many pages have been written on? (p. 92)

A 167
B 157
C 143
D 67

LESSON 4

Make Patterns

Quick Review

Find each sum.

1. 54 + 5

2. 19 + 3

3. 142 + 4

4. 37 + 10

5. 230 + 8

MATERIALS
pattern blocks, paper, crayons, index cards

Explore

You can make patterns using a repeating pattern unit or a rule.

Activity 1

STEP 1

Use pattern blocks of your choice to make a pattern unit.

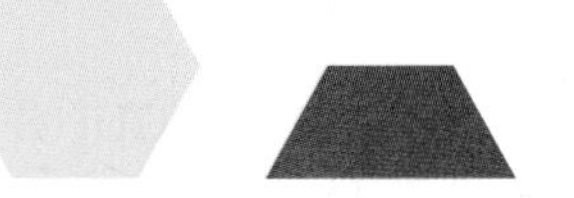

STEP 2

Repeat the pattern unit two times. Trace each figure and color the figures to match your block pattern.

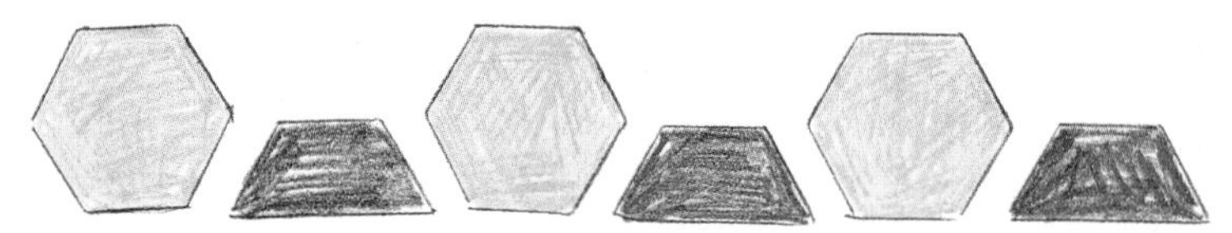

- What will the fifteenth figure in your pattern be?

Activity 2

STEP 1

Choose a 2-digit number to use as the first number in your pattern. Write a rule for your pattern using addition.

STEP 2

Write the first five numbers in your pattern. Make a card for each number.

12

Try It

a. Make another block pattern using the steps in Activity 1.

b. Exchange your number cards from Activity 2 with a classmate. Write a rule to describe your classmate's pattern. Make a number card for the sixth number in the pattern.

How many blocks should I use in my pattern unit?

Connect

You can also use a calculator to make number patterns. The pattern below starts with 24, and the rule is *add 3*.

Press these keys to find the second number in the pattern.

By pressing = over and over, you can continue the pattern.

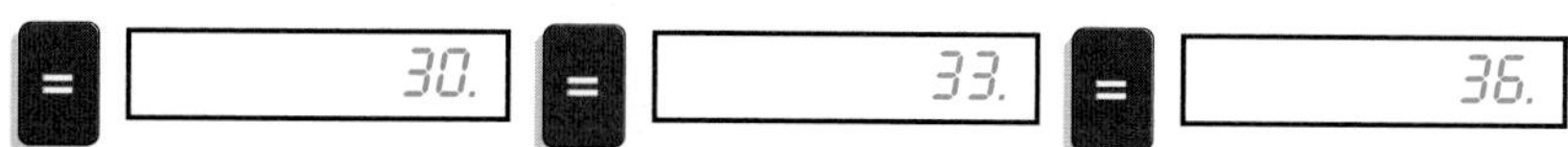

The first five numbers in the pattern are 24, 27, 30, 33, and 36.

Practice and Problem Solving

For 1–2, use pattern blocks.

1. Make a pattern unit with three shapes. Repeat the pattern unit two times. Draw your pattern.

2. Make a pattern unit with four shapes. Repeat the pattern unit two times. Draw your pattern.

For 3–4, you may wish to use a calculator.

3. Think of a 2-digit number. Write a rule for a pattern so that a 2-digit number is added to find the next number. Write the first four numbers in the pattern.

4. Think of a 3-digit number. Write a rule for a pattern so that a 1-digit number is subtracted to find the the next number. Write the first four numbers in the pattern.

5. **REASONING** I am a 3-digit number. My tens digit is two times as great as my hundreds digit. My ones digit is two times as great as my tens digit. One of my digits is odd. What number am I?

6. Dale is building this fence with short and tall posts. If he continues the pattern, what will the next two posts be?

Mixed Review and Test Prep

Find each quotient. (p. 274)

7. $49 \div 7$ **8.** $32 \div 8$

9. $36 \div 6$ **10.** $56 \div 7$

11. **TEST PREP** How many sides does a parallelogram have? (p. 396)

A 4 **B** 5 **C** 6 **D** 7

LESSON 5

Problem Solving Strategy
Find a Pattern

Quick Review

1. 245 + ■ = 253
2. 1,862 + ■ = 1,897
3. 409 + ■ = 422
4. 3,247 + ■ = 3,254
5. 716 + ■ = 727

PROBLEM Mr. Jenson needs to deliver a computer to 2364 Sunshine Circle. He cannot see all of the house numbers. To which house should Mr. Jenson deliver the computer? Use the map to help.

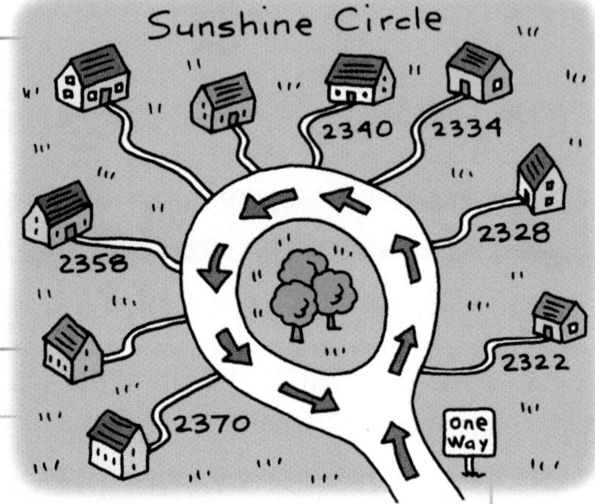

UNDERSTAND

- What are you asked to find?
- What information will you use?
- Is there any information you will not use?

PLAN

- What strategy can you use to solve the problem?

You can *find a pattern*.

SOLVE

- How can you use the pattern to solve the problem?

Find the rule for the order of the house numbers. Then use the rule to find the missing house numbers.

2322 2328 2334 2340 ■ ■ 2358 ■ 2370
+6 +6 +6

The house numbers increase by 6. The missing house numbers are 2346, 2352, and 2364. The eighth house is numbered 2364. So, Mr. Jenson should deliver the computer to the eighth house on Sunshine Circle.

CHECK

- Look back. How can you check your answer?

Problem Solving Practice

Use *find a pattern* to solve.

1. What if the numbers below were the house numbers that Mr. Jenson saw on Sunshine Circle? Which house would be numbered 2364? What rule describes the pattern?

   2344, 2348, 2352, 2356, ■, ■, 2368, ■, 2376

2. Miss Kane gave her students this pattern. What numbers are missing?

   582, 587, 592, 597, ■, 607, ■

Strategies

- Draw a Diagram or Picture
- Make a Model or Act It Out
- Make an Organized List
- **Find a Pattern**
- Make a Table or Graph
- Predict and Test
- Work Backward
- Solve a Simpler Problem
- Write a Number Sentence
- Use Logical Reasoning

Lisa wrote the following pattern.

142, 139, 136, 133, ■, 127, ■

3. Which is a rule for Lisa's pattern?

   A Add 4.
   B Subtract 3.
   C Add 2.
   D Subtract 4.

4. What numbers are missing in Lisa's pattern?

   F 136, 132
   G 132, 125
   H 130, 124
   J 131, 124

Mixed Strategy Practice

USE DATA For 5–8, use the price list.

THE PUZZLE SHOP	
Puzzle Size	**Price**
Small	$3.00
Medium	$5.25
Large	$6.75
Extra Large	$8.50

5. Mrs. Davis bought two puzzles. She gave the clerk a $20 bill. Her change was $6.25. What puzzles did she buy?

6. José bought 2 large puzzles and 1 medium puzzle. Luke bought 2 medium puzzles and 1 extra large puzzle. Who spent more? Explain.

7. Karen has $9.00 to spend. She wants to buy two puzzles. Which two puzzles could she buy?

8. Vern has a $5 bill and 3 dimes. How much more money does he need to buy a large puzzle?

Extra Practice

Set A (pp. 470–473)

Name the pattern unit for each.

1.

2.

Draw the next two shapes in each pattern.

3. ? ?

4. ? ?

Set B (pp. 474–475)

Write a rule for each pattern.

1.

2.

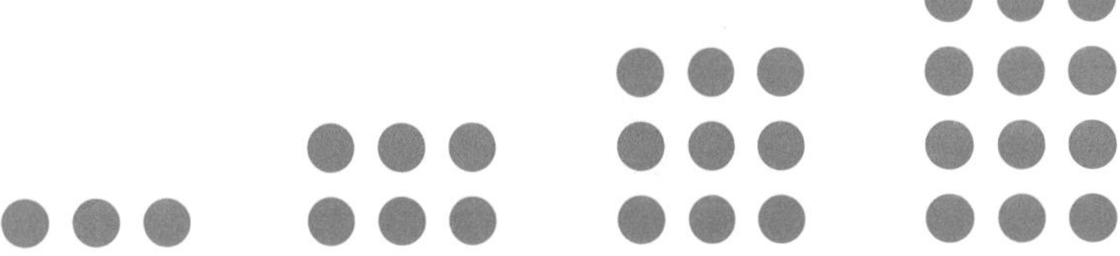

Set C (pp. 476–477)

Write a rule for each pattern.

1. 12, 15, 18, 21, 24, 27
2. 49, 47, 45, 43, 41, 39
3. 235, 241, 247, 253, 259, 265
4. 98, 108, 118, 128, 138, 148

Write a rule for each pattern. Then find the missing numbers.

5. 305, 302, 299, 296, ■, 290, ■, ■
6. 719, 723, 727, 731, ■, ■, 743, ■
7. 89, 98, 107, 116, ■, 134, ■, ■

CHAPTER 23

Review/Test

✓ CHECK VOCABULARY

Choose the best term from the box.

pattern unit
dividend

1. The part of a pattern that repeats is called the __?__ . (p. 470)

✓ CHECK SKILLS

Draw the next two shapes in each pattern. (pp. 470–473)

2. □ ◺ □ ◺ □ ◺ □ ◺ __?__ __?__

3. □ □ ○ □ □ ○ □ □ ○ □ □ ○ __?__ __?__

Write a rule for each pattern. (pp. 474–475)

4. ●

5. ☆ ☆☆☆ ☆☆☆☆☆ ☆☆☆☆☆☆☆

Write a rule for each pattern. (pp. 476–477)

6. 49, 51, 53, 55, 57, 59
7. 99, 90, 81, 72, 63, 54
8. 88, 98, 108, 118, 128, 138
9. 340, 325, 310, 295, 280, 265

✓ CHECK PROBLEM SOLVING

Solve. (pp. 480–481)

10. The number is missing from the fifth mailbox. Find a rule for the pattern. What is the missing number?

Standardized Test Prep

NUMBER SENSE, CONCEPTS, AND OPERATIONS

1. Mr. Lee buys 8 packs of pens. Each pack holds 4 pens. How many pens does he buy?

A 12 **C** 32
B 24 **D** 36

2. Which of the following has the same value as 9×6?

F $(5 + 6) \times (4 + 6)$
G $(5 \times 6) + (4 \times 6)$
H $(5 \times 6) \times (4 \times 6)$
J $(9 \times 9) + (6 \times 6)$

TIP **Look for important words.** See item 3. The word *most* tells you to compare. Find the total number of pages for each book. Then compare these totals to find the greatest number.

3. Ken's book has 367 pages. Al's book has 411 pages. Ed's book has 65 more pages than Ken's book. Tom's book has 15 more pages than Al's book. Whose book has the **most** pages?

A Ken's book **C** Ed's book
B Al's book **D** Tom's book

4. Explain It The swim team has 9 swimmers. The coach has 36 badges. Will the coach be able to give 6 badges to each swimmer? Explain.

ALGEBRAIC THINKING

5. Which rule was used to complete the table?

Quarters	1	2	3	4	5
Nickels	5	10	15	20	25

F Multiply the number of quarters by 5.
G Multiply the number of quarters by 10.
H Multiply the number of nickels by 5.
J Multiply the number of nickels by 10.

6. What are the next two shapes in this pattern?

A ★■ **C** ■■
B ■★ **D** ★★

7. Blanca spent \$24 on plants. Each plant cost \$3. Which equation could be used to find the number of plants that she bought?

F $\blacksquare - 3 = 24$
G $24 - 3 = \blacksquare$
H $24 \div 3 = \blacksquare$
J $\blacksquare + 3 = 24$

8. Explain It Dan is six years older than Darla. Dan is 25 years old. Write an equation to find Darla's age. Explain what you did.

DATA ANALYSIS AND PROBABILITY

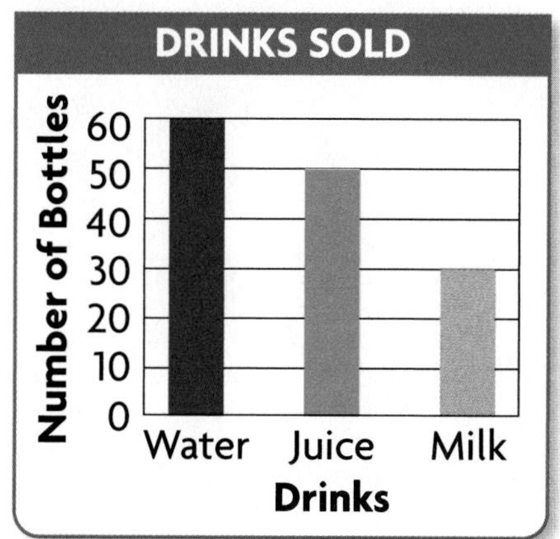

9. The bar graph shows the number of drinks sold in one hour at the zoo. How many more bottles of water than bottles of juice were sold?

A 10
B 20
C 30
D 60

10. Look at the bar graph above. How many bottles of drinks were sold in all?

F 125
G 130
H 140
J 150

11. **Explain It** This table shows the results of Lisa's survey.

FAVORITE ZOO ANIMAL	
Animal	**Tallies**
Giraffe	卌
Tiger	卌 卌 ǁ
Elephant	ǁǁ

Describe what Lisa found out.

GEOMETRY AND SPATIAL SENSE

12. Which pair of lines is parallel?

A
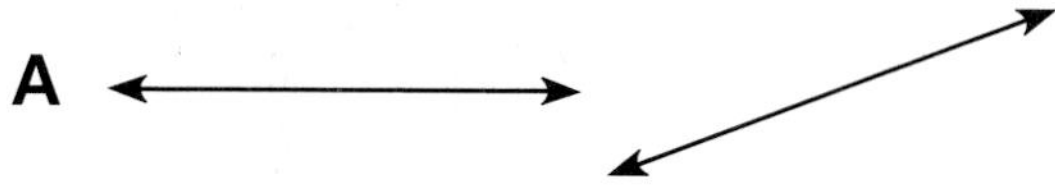

B
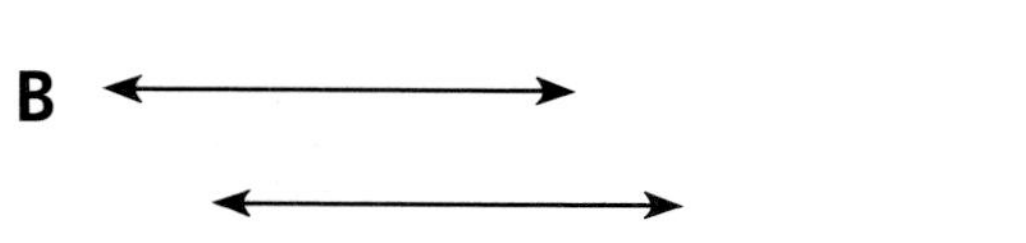

C

D
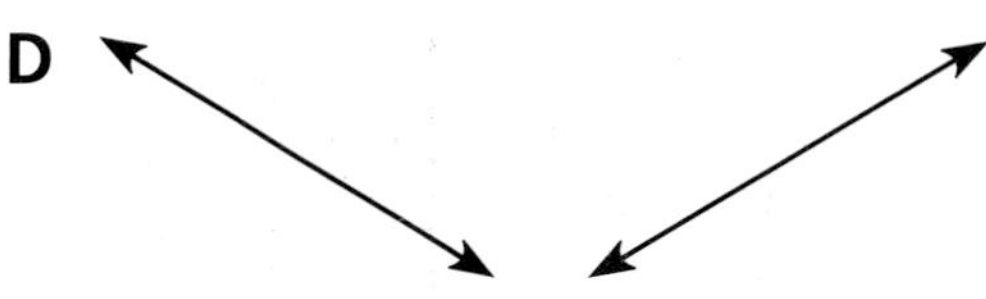

13. Kendra drew this polygon.

Which polygon did she draw?

F octagon
G quadrilateral
H hexagon
J pentagon

14. **Explain It** Travis said that the perimeter of a square is always four times the length of one side. Do you agree? Explain why or why not.

CHAPTER 24 Probability

FAST FACT • SCIENCE **Female alligators build nests in wet areas such as swamps. When baby alligators hatch, they are from 9 to 11 inches long. Adult female alligators rarely reach 9 feet in length, but adult males can reach 12 feet in length.**

PROBLEM SOLVING **Rain is important in alligators' habitats. Use the line graph. In which months is the rainfall greater than 6 inches?**

NORMAL MONTHLY RAINFALL IN NEW ORLEANS, LOUISIANA (in inches)

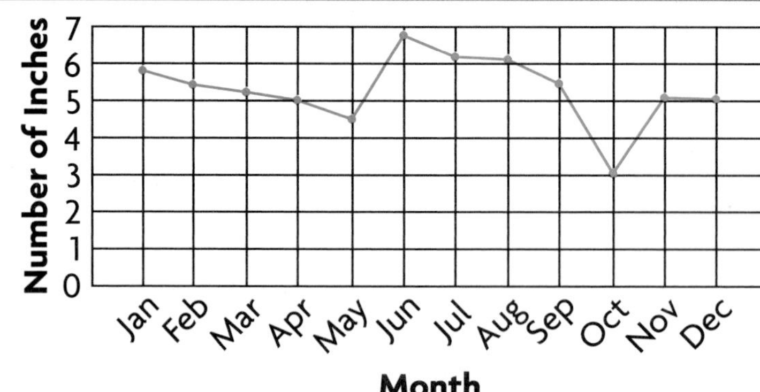

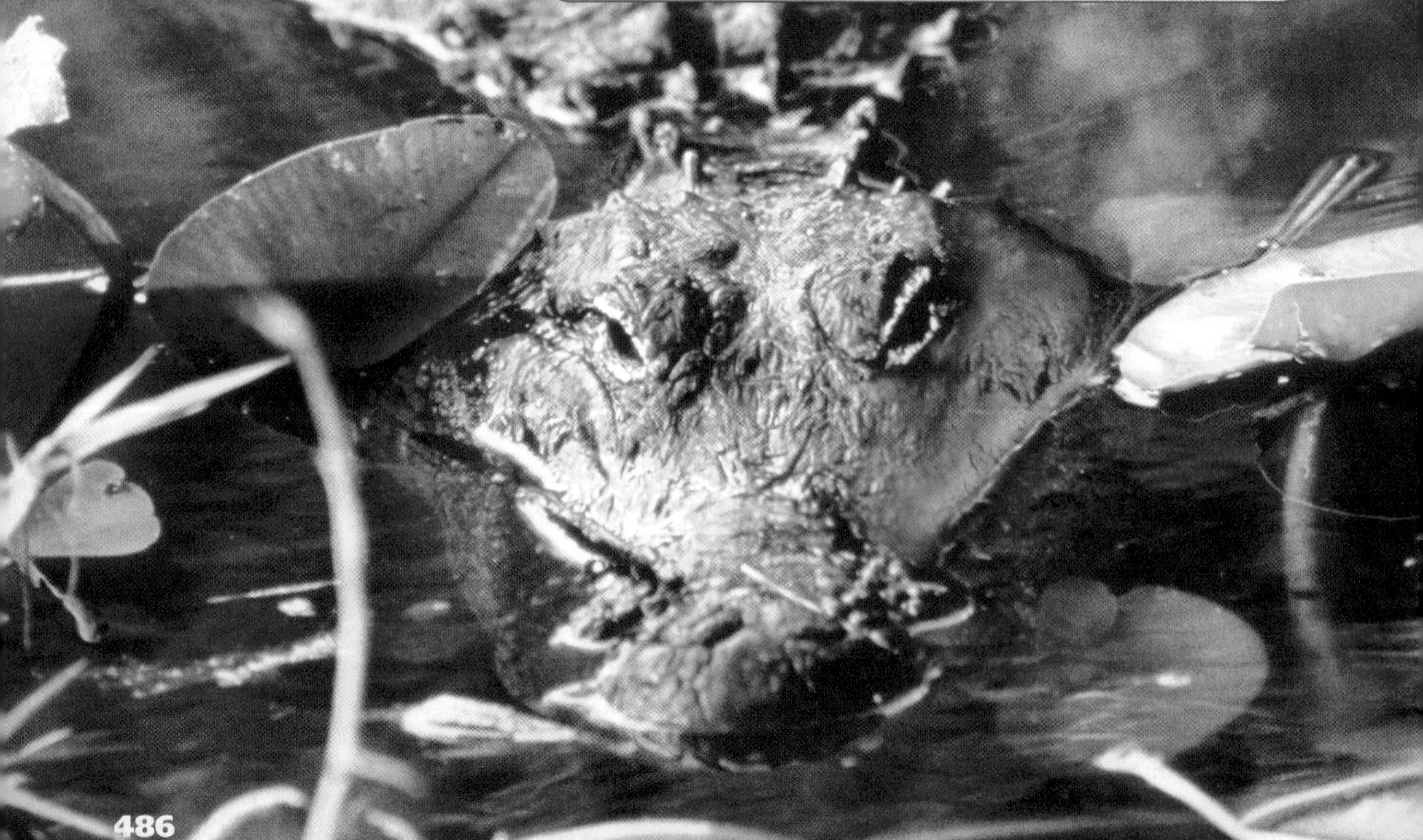

CHECK WHAT YOU KNOW

Use this page to help you review and remember important skills needed for Chapter 24.

COMPARE PARTS OF A WHOLE

For 1–4, write the color shown by the largest part of each spinner.

1. 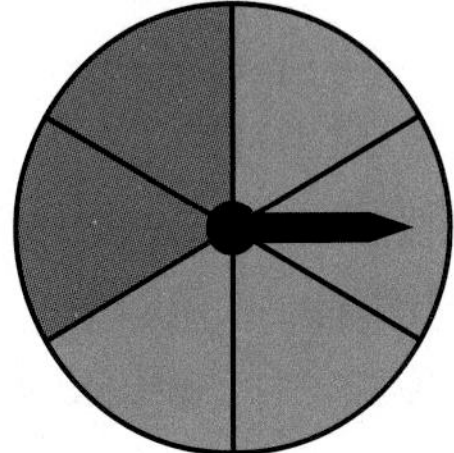

2. 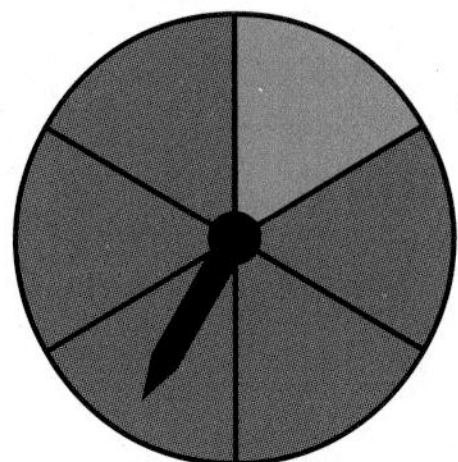

3. 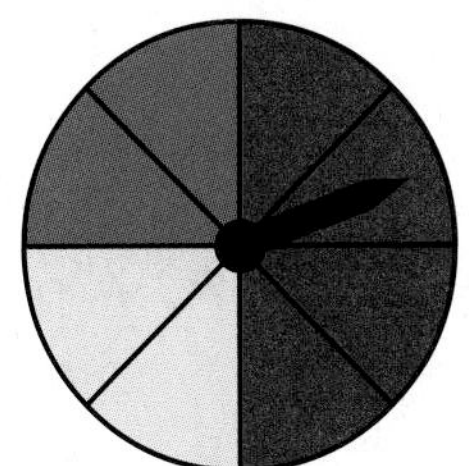

4. 

USE A TALLY TABLE

For 5–9, use the tally table.

5. What color was landed on the most times?

6. What color was landed on the fewest times?

7. How many more times was purple landed on than blue?

8. How many fewer times was red landed on than green?

9. How many times was the spinner used in all?

SPINNER RESULTS

Color	Tallies
yellow	||
green	||||
red	||
blue	|
purple	~~||||~~ |

VOCABULARY POWER

REVIEW

tally [ta′ lē] *noun*

Tally comes from the name of a stick on which cuts were made to keep a count or a score. Why do you think that tally marks are grouped in fives?

PREVIEW

event, likely, equally likely, probability, unlikely, predict, certain, outcome, tree diagram, impossible

www.harcourtschool.com/mathglossary

LESSON

Probability

Quick Review

Complete. Use <, >, or = for each ●.

1. 5 + 23 ● 28
2. 54 ● 95 − 40
3. 436 − 25 ● 409
4. 87 + 6 ● 95
5. 32 ÷ 4 ● 64 ÷ 8

VOCABULARY

event **probability** **certain** **impossible** **likely** **unlikely**

Learn

YES, NO, MAYBE An **event** is something that happens. **Probability** is the chance that an event will happen. An event is **certain** if it will always happen. An event is **impossible** if it will never happen.

CERTAIN

A. You will get wet if you jump into a swimming pool full of water.
B. Ice cubes will feel cold.

IMPOSSIBLE

A. A rock will turn into a piece of cheese.
B. A mouse will talk to you today.

- Name some events that are certain. Name some events that are impossible.

An event is **likely** to happen if it has a good chance of happening. An event is **unlikely** if it does not have a good chance of happening. Look at the spinner.

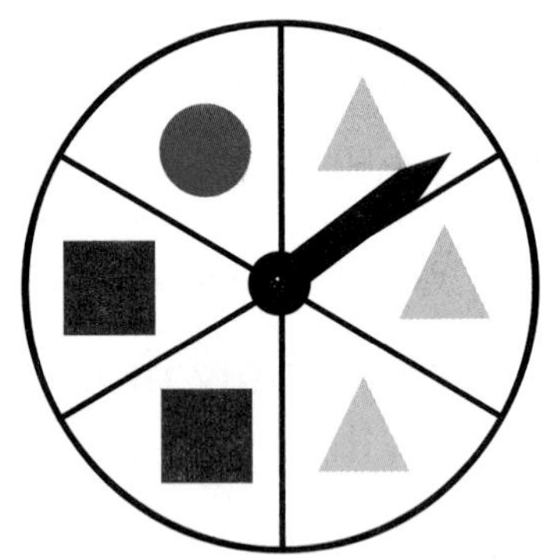

LIKELY

You will spin a yellow triangle.

UNLIKELY

You will spin a blue circle.

REASONING What is the difference between *certain* and *likely*? What is the difference between *impossible* and *unlikely*?

Check

1. **Explain** if it is certain or impossible that you will pull a yellow marble from this bag.
2. Is it certain or likely that you will pull a red, blue, or green marble from this bag? Explain.
3. Which color marble is most likely to be pulled?
4. Which color marble is most unlikely to be pulled?

Practice and Problem Solving

Extra Practice, page 502, Set A

Tell whether each event is *certain* or *impossible*.

5. If you add any two 1-digit numbers, the sum will be 19.

6. A box contains only 100 pennies. You choose a coin from the box. It is a penny.

For 7–8, look at the spinner.

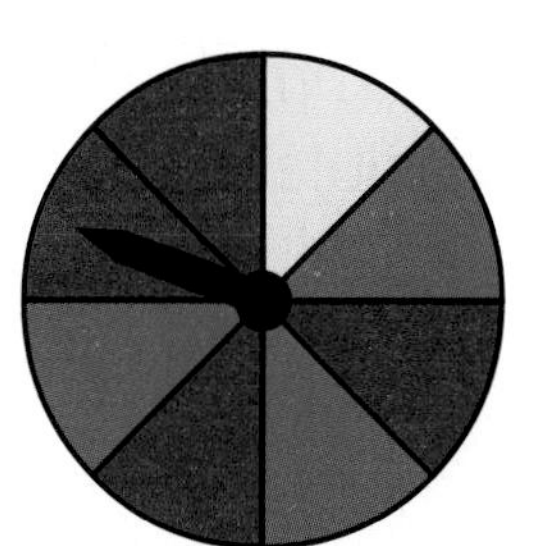

7. Name the color you are most likely to spin.

8. Name the color you are most unlikely to spin.

Technology Link

More Practice: Harcourt Mega Math Fraction Action, *Last Chance Canyon,* Levels A and B

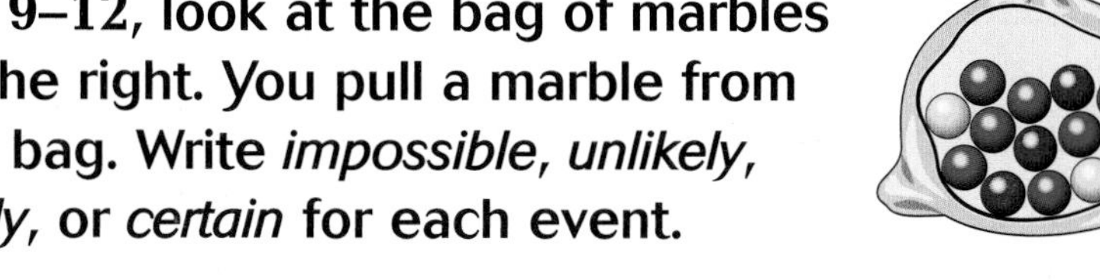

For 9–12, look at the bag of marbles at the right. You pull a marble from the bag. Write *impossible, unlikely, likely,* or *certain* for each event.

9. You pull a marble.

10. You pull a yellow marble.

11. You pull a black marble.

12. You pull a blue marble.

13. Kaitlin rolled two cubes, each numbered 1 through 6. If she adds the numbers, is it certain or impossible that she will get a sum less than 2?

14. **REASONING** Elena rolled a cube numbered 1 through 6. She rolled the cube 4 times and added the numbers. Their sum was 18. Two of the numbers she rolled were sixes. What numbers could Elena have rolled?

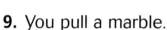

Mixed Review and Test Prep

15. $\begin{array}{r} 246 \\ +323 \\ \hline \end{array}$ (p. 72)

16. $\begin{array}{r} 700 \\ -515 \\ \hline \end{array}$ (p. 92)

17. $\begin{array}{r} 4,819 \\ +5,073 \\ \hline \end{array}$ (p. 72)

18. $\begin{array}{r} 6,342 \\ -5,107 \\ \hline \end{array}$ (p. 96)

19. **TEST PREP** Vera's math class begins at 11:30 A.M. and lasts for 1 hour 15 minutes. At what time is the class over? (p. 134)

A 11:45 A.M.
B 12:00 P.M.
C 12:30 P.M.
D 12:45 P.M.

LESSON 2

Outcomes

Quick Review

1. 5×6
2. 3×9
3. $56 = 8 \times$ ■
4. $4 \times$ ■ $= 16$
5. 7×8

VOCABULARY

outcome
equally likely
predict

MATERIALS

coins

Explore

Tossing a coin several times is an example of an experiment. An **outcome** is a possible result in an experiment.

Two outcomes are **equally likely** if they have the same chance of happening.

Activity

Record the outcomes of tossing a coin.

STEP 1

Look at a coin. Decide on the possible outcomes.

heads tails

The possible outcomes are heads and tails.

STEP 2

Toss the coin 20 times. Record the results in a tally table.

COIN TOSS	
Outcome	**Tallies**
Heads	
Tails	

- What did you notice about your results?

Since they have an equal chance of happening, the outcomes *heads* and *tails* are equally likely.

When you do an experiment, you can **predict**, or tell what you think will happen.

Try It

a. **What if** you tossed the coin 50 times? Predict how many times you would expect to toss heads.

b. Now toss 2 coins. What are the possible outcomes? Toss the coins 25 times. Record the results.

We are tossing a coin 50 times. How many times do you think the coin will show heads?

Connect

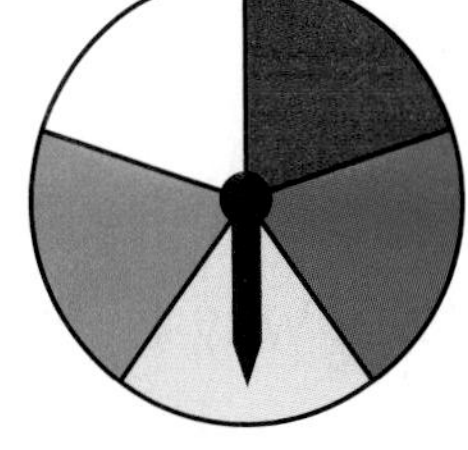

Look at this spinner. There are 5 possible outcomes. The pointer can land on red, blue, yellow, green or white.

Each space on the spinner is the same size, so the outcomes are *equally likely* that you will spin any color.

The chance is *1 out of 5* that you will spin any color.

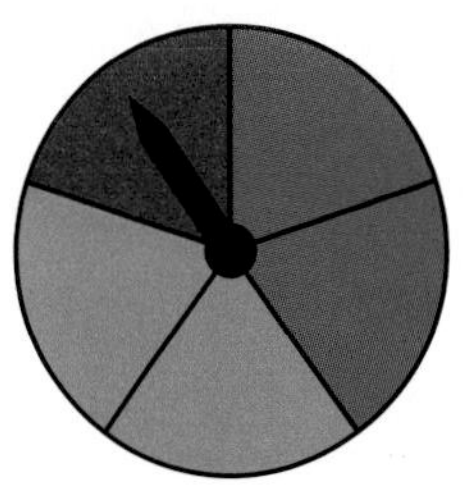

- What are the possible outcomes for this spinner? Which outcomes are equally likely? Explain.
- What is the chance that you will spin blue? that you will spin green? that you will spin red?

Practice and Problem Solving

For 1–3, list the possible outcomes of each experiment.

1. rolling a cube numbered 1–6

2. pulling blocks from this bag

3. using this spinner

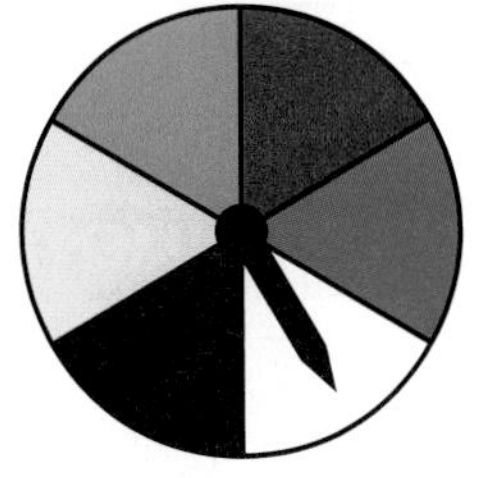

4. I am a 4-digit number. The sum of my digits is 17. My hundreds digit is 2. My thousands and ones digits are the product of 2×3. What number am I?

5. Maggie used the spinner at the right. The pointer landed 6 times on red, 3 times on blue, and 1 time on yellow. Predict the color it will land on next. What is the chance that she will spin yellow?

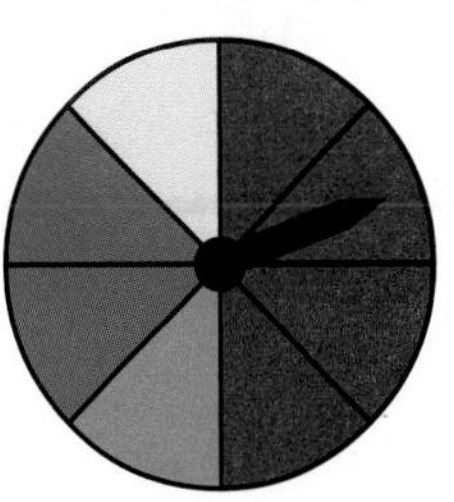

Mixed Review and Test Prep

6. 9×3 (p. 164)

7. 5×6 (p. 160)

8. $8 \times ■ = 64$ (p. 196)

9. $12 \div 2$ (p. 258)

10. **TEST PREP** Gary has \$2.78 in his pocket and \$3.14 in his bank. He wants to buy a book for \$6.50. How much more does he need? (p. 120)

A \$1.58 **B** \$1.08 **C** \$0.58 **D** \$0.08

LESSON 3

Experiments

> **Quick Review**
>
> 1. $\blacksquare \div 8 = 8$ 2. $\blacksquare \div 4 = 9$
>
> 3. $49 \div 7$ 4. $72 \div \blacksquare = 9$
>
> 5. $24 \div 6$

Learn

TRY IT One way to find out how likely outcomes are is to conduct experiments.

Activity 1

Materials: 4-part spinner pattern

STEP 1

Make a spinner that has four equal parts. Color the parts red, green, blue, and yellow.

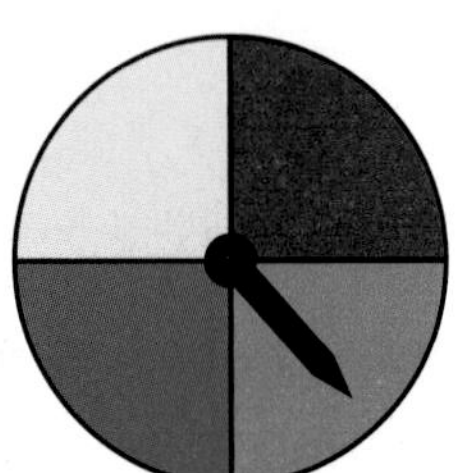

STEP 2

Make a tally table. List all the possible outcomes. Spin 20 times. Record the results in the table.

SPINNER EXPERIMENT	
Color	**Tallies**
red	
blue	
green	
yellow	

STEP 3

Make a bar graph of your data to show the results of your experiment.

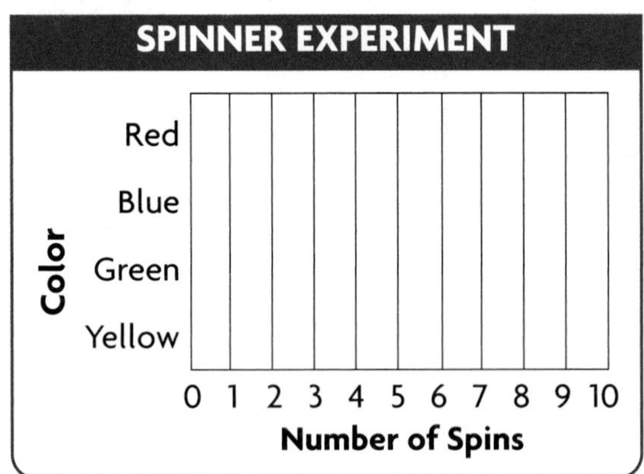

- Compare the graphs from all the experiments in the class. What do the graphs show about the outcomes?
- How would the results of your experiment change if 2 parts of the spinner were red?

Activity 2

Materials: color tiles; paper bag

STEP 1

Put 1 red tile, 3 green tiles, and 6 blue tiles in a paper bag.

STEP 2

Make a tally table. List all the possible outcomes.

STEP 3

Pull one tile, record the color, and put it back in the bag. Make 40 pulls.

STEP 4

Make a bar graph of the data to show the results of your experiment.

Technology Link

More Practice: Harcourt Mega Math Fraction Action, *Last Chance Canyon,* Level D

- Predict the color tile that is most likely to be pulled. Predict which tile is least likely to be pulled. Explain.
- What is the chance that you will pull either a red or a blue tile?

Check

For 1–2, use the spinners.

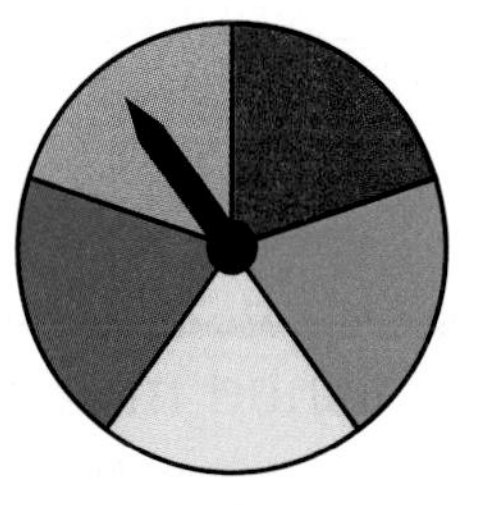

A

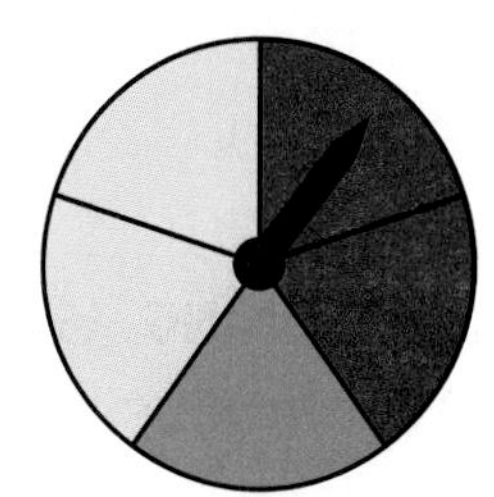

B

1. **Choose** which spinner has equally likely outcomes. Explain.
2. Which spinner has unlikely outcomes? Explain.
3. Draw a spinner on which all of the outcomes are equally likely.
4. Jon pulls color tiles from this bag. Name all the possible outcomes. Which are unlikely? Which are equally likely? Which is most likely?

LESSON CONTINUES

 Extra Practice, page 502, Set B

5. Molly spins the pointer of this spinner. Name all the possible outcomes. Which are unlikely? Which are equally likely? Which is most likely?

6. Keshawn is pulling color tiles from this bag. What is the chance that he will pull a red tile?

7. **USE DATA** Pamela drew the bar graph at the right to show part of the results of an experiment. Predict which color marble she will pull next.

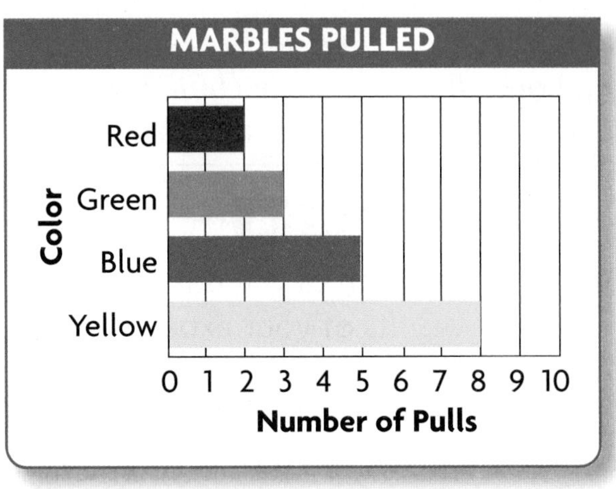

8. Toss a coin 10 times. Record the result of each toss in order. Then repeat the experiment. Is there a pattern in the results? What do you notice?

9. Draw a spinner. Color it so that the chance of spinning red is 2 out of 4, of spinning green is 1 out of 4, and of spinning blue is 1 out of 4.

10. **Vocabulary Power** The prefix *un-* when added to a root word means "the opposite of." *Unhappy* means "not happy." What does *unlikely* mean?

11. Andi started making a spinner at 11:45 A.M. She finished making it 25 minutes later. At what time did Andi finish making her spinner?

12. **Write About It** Explain what a spinner should look like if the three outcomes are all equally likely.

13. **REASONING** Gustavo had 15 cookies. He gave 3 cookies to each of his friends. He kept 3 cookies for himself. With how many friends did he share his cookies?

14. Heather went to the mall and bought 3 tapes. Each tape cost $9. Then she bought lunch for $6. She has $4 left. How much money did Heather start with?

Mixed Review and Test Prep

Add or subtract. (pp. 72, 92, and 96)

15. $\begin{array}{r} 127 \\ +418 \\ \hline \end{array}$ **16.** $\begin{array}{r} 306 \\ -249 \\ \hline \end{array}$ **17.** $\begin{array}{r} 3,485 \\ +2,438 \\ \hline \end{array}$ **18.** $\begin{array}{r} 7,000 \\ -2,463 \\ \hline \end{array}$ **19.** $\begin{array}{r} 3,801 \\ -\ 163 \\ \hline \end{array}$

Find the missing addend. (p. 4)

20. 15 + ■ = 54 **21.** ■ + 212 = 245 **22.** 138 + ■ = 250

23. **TEST PREP** Hank bought a new comb for $1.59. He paid with a $5 bill. How much change should he get? (p. 118)

A $2.41 **C** $3.41
B $2.71 **D** $4.51

24. **TEST PREP** Katya bought a card for $1.85 and ribbon for $0.98. She paid with a $10 bill. How much change should she get? (p. 120)

F $5.71 **H** $7.07
G $6.77 **J** $7.17

Problem Solving  ... to Science

Scientists know that hurricanes most often form in September, October, and November. Hurricanes always have very high-speed winds that travel in circles. They form over warm, tropical ocean waters and then usually move west or northwest. Scientists use this information to predict hurricanes.

1. Which storm was most likely to become a hurricane? Explain.
2. Which storm was most unlikely to become a hurricane? Explain.
3. Which storms were equally likely to become hurricanes?

SUMMER 2001 TROPICAL STORMS

Storm	Circular winds	Warm ocean waters	High-speed winds	September to November	Moving west or northwest
Allison	✓	✓	✓		
Barry	✓	✓	✓		✓
Erin	✓	✓	✓	✓	
Iris	✓	✓	✓	✓	✓
Michelle	✓	✓	✓	✓	

LESSON 4

Predict Outcomes

Quick Review

1. 25¢ = ■ pennies
2. 9 nickels = ■¢
3. ■ dimes = $1.00
4. 4 quarters = ■ pennies
5. 50¢ = ■ nickels

Learn

WEATHER OR NOT Meteorologists are scientists who predict weather. They study weather patterns from around the world to help them.

You can use the results of an experiment to predict what the temperature will be.

HANDS ON

Activity

STEP 1

Take the outdoor temperature every day at the same time for two weeks.

STEP 2

Record each temperature on a line plot. Use a scale:

40's 50's 60's 70's 80's

STEP 3

Use the data to predict the temperature for the next day.

Take the temperature the next day to check your prediction.

- How did you decide on your prediction? Explain.
- What was the temperature the next day? How did it compare with your prediction?

Check

1. Look at the line plot. Tell what you would predict for the next day's temperature. Explain.

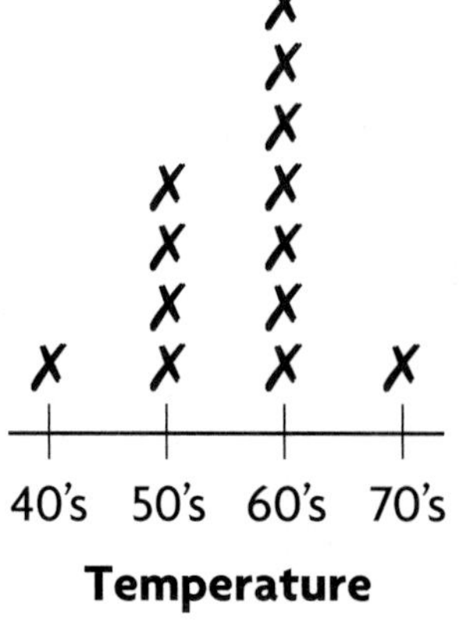

2. **What if** the temperatures for seven days in a row were 46, 48, 52, 55, 46, 48, and 47? What temperature would you predict for the next day? Explain.

Practice and Problem Solving

Extra Practice, page 502, Set C

3. The line plot at the right shows the number of pizzas sold at Annie's Pizza Shop for the last two weeks. Do you predict that more than or less than 50 pizzas will be sold tomorrow? Explain.

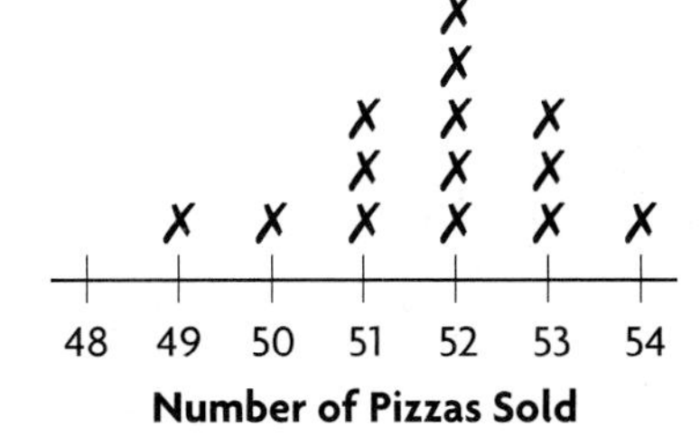

4. This tally table shows the pulls from a bag of tiles. Predict which color is least likely to be pulled next.

EXPERIMENT	
Color	**Tallies**
red	𝍸
blue	𝍸 𝍸 𝍸 ||
green	𝍸 ||
yellow	𝍸 ||||

5. The line plot below shows the results of rolling a number cube. Predict which number you would most likely roll.

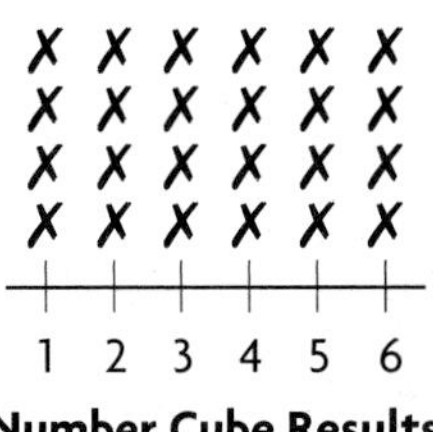

6. **REASONING** Martha rolls a number cube 30 times for an experiment. The number cube is labeled with these numbers: 1, 2, 3, 4, 5, 6. Predict about how many times she will roll an even number.

7. **FAST FACT** • SCIENCE Weather takes place only in the 6 miles of air directly above Earth. There are 5,280 feet in 1 mile. About how many feet are in 6 miles?

8. Jared has a collection of 42 baseball cards. He trades 2 of his cards for 6 other cards. How many cards does he have now?

9. **REASONING** You toss a coin in the air one time. Predict how it will land. Explain.

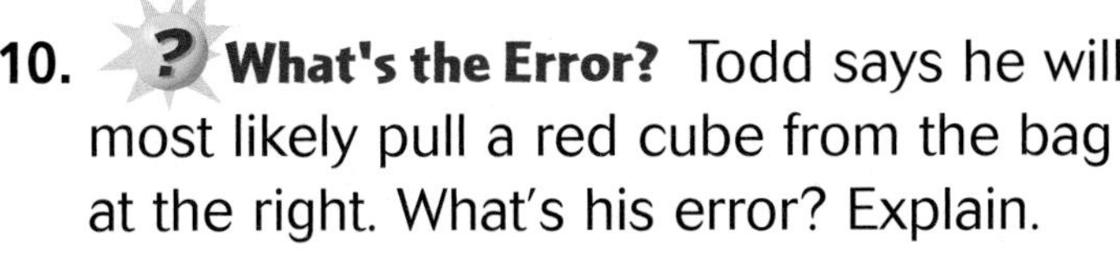

10. **What's the Error?** Todd says he will most likely pull a red cube from the bag at the right. What's his error? Explain.

Mixed Review and Test Prep

Tell the value of the blue digit. (p. 24)

11. 7,593

12. 2,904

13. 8×7 (p. 196)

14. $5\overline{)40}$ (p. 258)

15. TEST PREP Each of 4 students bought 8 packs of cards. How many packs of cards did they buy in all? (p. 178)

A 18 **B** 22 **C** 24 **D** 32

LESSON
5 Combinations

Learn

SWEET COMBINATIONS The third-grade class is having an ice cream sundae party. They have vanilla, chocolate, and strawberry ice cream. The toppings are chocolate syrup and caramel syrup. If each flavor of ice cream has one topping, how many different types of sundaes can they make?

The class made a **tree diagram** to show the possible combinations of ice creams and toppings.

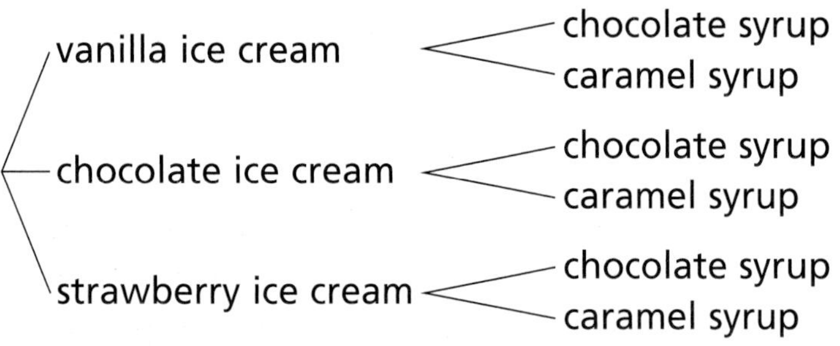

There are 6 possible combinations, or choices of ice cream and topping. So, the third-grade class can make 6 different types of ice cream sundaes.

REASONING Show how you can use the factors 3 and 2 and multiplication to find the number of types of sundaes that can be made.

Quick Review

Complete. Use $<$, $>$, or $=$ for each ●.

1. $6 + 8$ ● 2×7
2. $1 + 1$ ● $13 - 10$
3. $16 - 8$ ● $2 + 4$
4. 3×4 ● $6 + 6$
5. 9×3 ● $14 + 10$

VOCABULARY
tree diagram

Check

1. **Explain** how you can get the same 6 combinations on a tree diagram that lists the toppings first.
2. Mark has a red shirt, a green shirt, and a white shirt. He has tan shorts, blue shorts, and black shorts. Draw a tree diagram to show how many shirt-and-shorts outfits Mark can make.
3. What multiplication sentence can you use to find the total number of shirt-and-shorts outfits Mark can make?

Practice and Problem Solving

Extra Practice, page 502, Set D

For 4–5, make a tree diagram to show all the combinations. Tell how many combinations are possible.

4. yogurt flavors: cherry, blueberry, strawberry, raspberry

sizes: small, large

5. sandwiches: peanut butter, turkey, ham

soups: vegetable, chicken noodle, tomato

6. **What's the Error?** The cafeteria has three types of sandwiches and three types of desserts. Joan says she can make six different combinations of sandwiches and desserts. Describe her error.

7. Olga can practice golf, tennis, or volleyball on Thursday, Friday, Saturday, or Sunday. She chooses a different sport each day. Draw a tree diagram that shows the possible combinations of days and sports.

8. The library has 392 fiction books and 514 nonfiction books. Estimate the total number of fiction and nonfiction books the library has.

9. Jeffrey has 21 marbles. If he gives away 9 marbles, he will have twice as many marbles as Miguel. How many marbles does Miguel have?

10. Chris and Hope play a pattern game. Chris says 3, and Hope says 12. Chris says 4, and Hope says 16. Chris says 5, and Hope says 20. What does Hope say when Chris says 7? Write a rule for the pattern.

11. **What's the Question?** Danielle bought 5 items at the store. She gave the clerk a \$10 bill. Her change was \$5.27. The answer is \$4.73.

Mixed Review and Test Prep

Find the quotient. (p. 274)

12. $8\overline{)48}$ **13.** $6\overline{)42}$

Find the product. (pp. 178, 194)

14. 7×4 **15.** 9×6

16. **TEST PREP** Don's lunch costs \$4.68. He pays with a \$20 bill. How much change should Don get? (p. 118)

A \$24.68 **C** \$15.42

B \$16.42 **D** \$15.32

LESSON 6

Problem Solving Strategy
Make an Organized List

Quick Review

Complete. Use <, >, or = for each ●.

1. 9 ÷ 1 ● 3 × 3
2. 7 × 3 ● 12 + 16
3. 8 + 4 ● 6 + 6
4. 3 + 3 ● 3 × 0
5. 18 ÷ 9 ● 4 ÷ 2

PROBLEM Jake's third-grade class is planning a field day for 25 students. The morning activities are a balloon toss, a tug-of-war, and relay races. How many ways can the activities be arranged?

UNDERSTAND

- What are you asked to find?
- Is there any information you will not use? If so, what is it?

PLAN

- What strategy can you use to solve the problem?

You can make an organized list to show the possible orders of morning activities.

SOLVE

- How can you make a list to solve the problem?

You can select each activity and combine it with each of the other activities.

Then count to find the number of different ways the activities can be arranged.

ACTIVITY 1	ACTIVITY 2	ACTIVITY 3
balloon toss	tug-of-war	relay races
balloon toss	relay races	tug-of-war
tug-of-war	relay races	balloon toss
tug-of-war	balloon toss	relay races
relay races	balloon toss	tug-of-war
relay races	tug-of-war	balloon toss

So, the field day morning activities can be arranged 6 different ways.

CHECK

- Look back. How can you check your answer?

Problem Solving Practice

Make an organized list to solve.

1. How many ways can you arrange the numbers 2, 3, and 4 in a 3-digit number?
2. How many ways can you arrange the letters *A, B, C,* and *D*?
3. How many ways can Josie, Stacey, and Nathalie stand in line?

Strategies

Draw a Diagram or Picture
Make a Model or Act It Out
Make an Organized List
Find a Pattern
Make a Table or Graph
Predict and Test
Work Backward
Solve a Simpler Problem
Write a Number Sentence
Use Logical Reasoning

Problem Solving

Simon is arranging his books on a shelf. He has a book about sports, a book about space, a book about computers, and a book about animals.

4. How many ways can Simon arrange his books?

   A 4 **C** 16
   B 8 **D** 24

5. What is *not* a way Simon can arrange his books?

   F animals, space, computers, sports
   G computers, sports, space, animals
   H space, animals, space, computers
   J sports, space, computers, animals

Mixed Strategy Practice

USE DATA For 6–9, use the table.

PACKS OF PENCILS	COST
2 pencils	\$0.30
3 pencils	\$0.90
4 pencils	\$1.00
5 pencils	\$1.25

6. How much does each pencil cost if you buy a pack of 2 pencils?
7. How much does each pencil cost if you buy a pack of 4 pencils?
8. Is the price for each pencil in the pack of 3 pencils more than the price for each pencil in the pack of 5 pencils? Explain.
9. If you have \$1.20 to spend on 2 packs of pencils, which 2 packs can you buy?
10. A yard of fabric costs \$3. Faye bought 4 yards of fabric and 11 inches of ribbon. How much did she pay for the fabric?
11. Javier writes this number pattern: 4, 12, 20, 28, 36. What are the next three numbers in Javier's pattern?

Extra Practice

Set A (pp. 488–489)

Tell whether each event is *certain* or *impossible*.

1. You will choose a nickel from these coins.

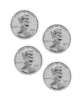

2. You will spin red or blue on this spinner.

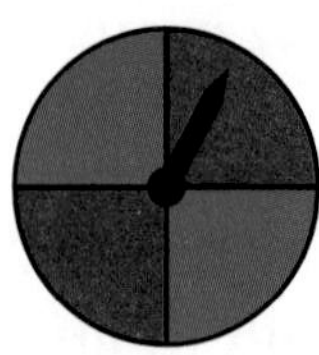

Set B (pp. 492–495)

1. Tenesha pulled animal crackers from the box and put them back. She made the graph below of the outcomes. Which animals are equally likely to be pulled from the box?

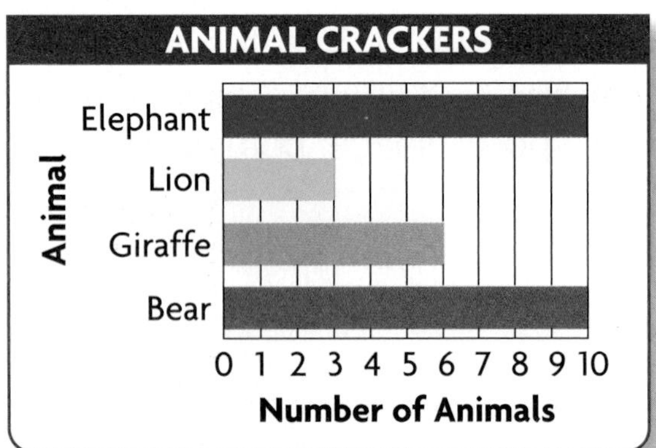

2. Ned pulled marbles from the bag and put them back. He made the graph below of the outcomes. Which color marble is most likely to be pulled from the bag? Which is least likely to be pulled?

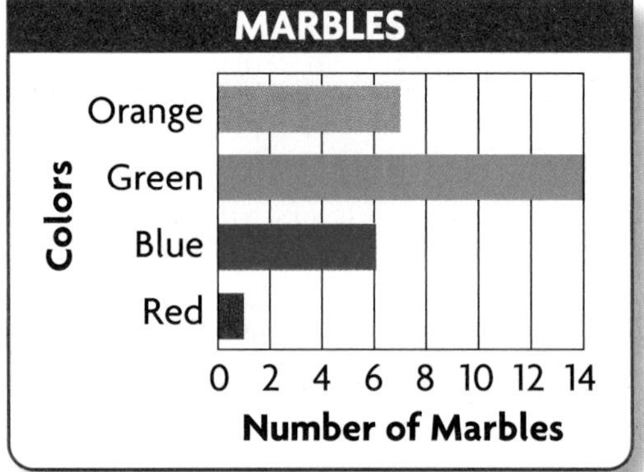

Set C (pp. 496–497)

1. This tally table shows the color tiles that were pulled from a bag. Which color tile is most likely to be pulled?

TILE EXPERIMENT	
green	~~||||~~ |||
blue	|
red	|||
yellow	||

Set D (pp. 498–499)

1. Josh wants frozen yogurt. He can choose chocolate, vanilla, or blueberry. He can order a cup or a cone. Make a tree diagram to show the possible combinations.

2. The deli makes sandwiches with corned beef, pastrami, roast beef, ham, or turkey. It offers American or Swiss cheese. How many types of sandwiches can the deli make with one meat and one cheese?

Review/Test

✓ CHECK VOCABULARY AND CONCEPTS

Choose the best term from the box.

certain
impossible
likely
probability

1. An event that will always happen is __?__. (p. 488)

2. The chance that an event will happen is the __?__ of the event. (p. 488)

Tell whether each event is *certain* or *impossible*.

3. Next year, December 13 will come before December 12. (pp. 488–489)

4. Snow will melt when the temperature is above freezing. (pp. 488–489)

✓ CHECK SKILLS

5. What are the possible outcomes of using this spinner? (pp. 490–491)

6. What outcomes are equally likely when you use this spinner? (pp. 490–491)

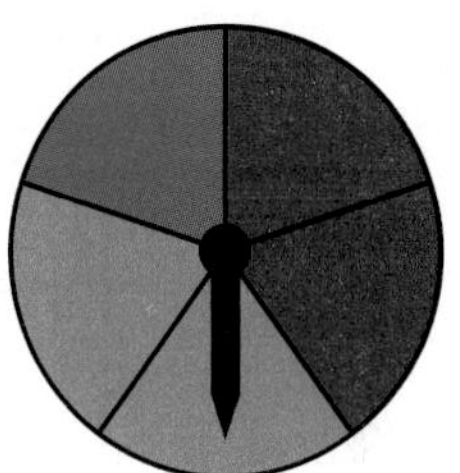

For 7–9, use the spinners. (pp. 492–495)

7. Choose which spinner has equally likely outcomes. Explain.

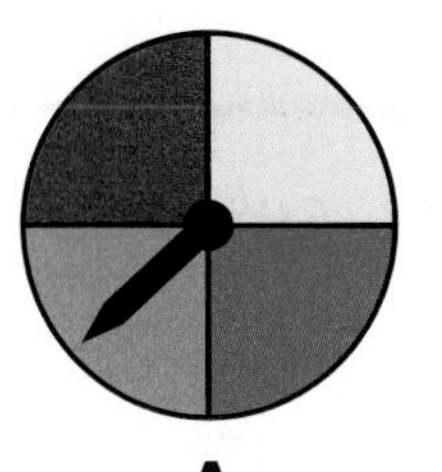

A

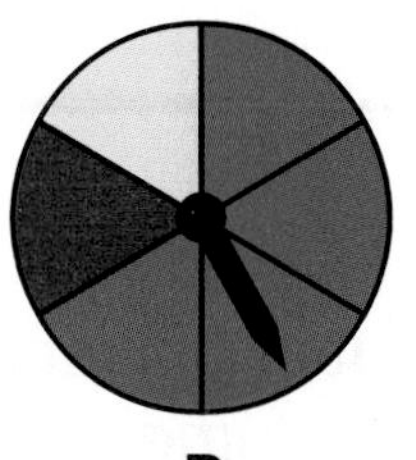

B

8. Name an unlikely outcome for Spinner B.

9. Name the most likely outcome for Spinner B.

✓ CHECK PROBLEM SOLVING

10. How many ways can you arrange the letters X, Y, and Z? Explain. (pp. 500–501)

Standardized Test Prep

NUMBER SENSE, CONCEPTS, AND OPERATIONS

1. Which number has a 7 in the hundreds place?

A 7,563 **C** 5,367
B 6,735 **D** 3,675

TIP **Eliminate choices.** See item 2. The player with the least number of goals must be listed first. So, you can eliminate any choice that does not begin with Cary, since he scored the fewest goals.

2. The table shows the number of goals scored by members of a soccer team.

SOCCER SEASON GOALS	
Player	**Goals Scored**
Emily	23
Cary	18
Danitra	31
Miles	28

Which shows the order of the players from **least** to **greatest** number of goals scored?

F Cary, Emily, Miles, Danitra
G Emily, Danitra, Cary, Miles
H Danitra, Miles, Emily, Cary
J Cary, Miles, Emily, Danitra

3. Explain It Joey scored 28 points in a basketball game. Frederick scored 41 points in the same game. About how many points did Joey and Frederick score in all? Explain your estimate.

MEASUREMENT

4. Donna wants to put a fence around her garden. How many feet of fencing should she buy?

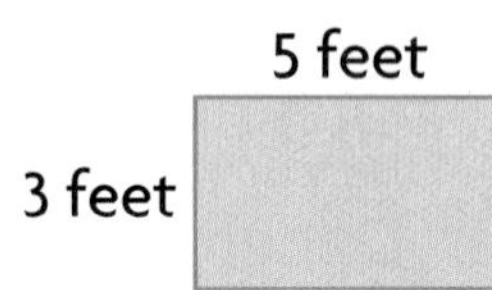

A 8 feet **C** 15 feet
B 11 feet **D** 16 feet

5. At 9:00 A.M., the temperature was 5 degrees less than the temperature shown below. What was the temperature at 9:00 A.M.?

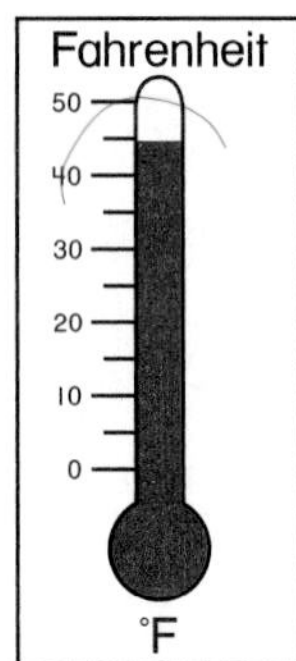

F 30°F **H** 40°F
G 35°F **J** 50°F

6. Explain It Elena estimates that the volume of the rectangular prism below is about 30 cubic units. Do you agree or disagree? Explain your answer.

ALGEBRAIC THINKING

7. Jenny wants to complete this equation.

$72 \div 8 = ■$

Which expression should she use to complete the equation?

A 3×3
B $9 + 1$
C $24 \div 3$
D $15 - 7$

8. Grant collects baseball cards. How many cards are in 6 packs?

Number of Packs	2	4	6	8
Number of Cards	16	32	■	64

F 42
G 48
H 54
J 60

9. **Explain It** Andrew wrote this number pattern.

27, 25, 28, 26, 29, 27, 30

What is the next number in Andrew's pattern? Describe a rule he could have used to make the pattern.

DATA ANALYSIS AND PROBABILITY

10. Abby placed color tiles in a bag. She pulled a tile out of the bag and put it back. She made a bar graph to show the results of 24 pulls. Which color tile is she **least likely** to pull next time?

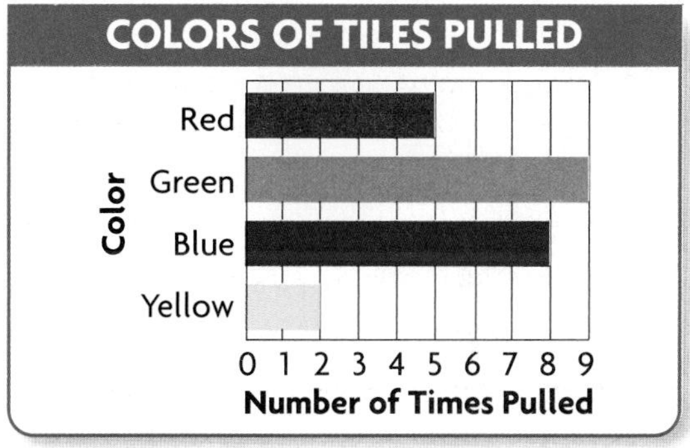

A blue
B red
C yellow
D green

11. The table shows how many cups of lemonade were sold at different times of the day. Use the table to decide what the best time is to sell the most cups of lemonade.

LEMONADE STAND SALES

Time	Number of Cups
12:00–1:00	18
1:00–2:00	7
2:00–3:00	12
3:00–4:00	25

F 12:00–1:00
G 1:00–2:00
H 2:00–3:00
J 3:00–4:00

12. **Explain It** Dustin can wear blue, tan, or black pants. He can wear a white, red, or yellow T-shirt. Make a list of the pants and shirt combinations he can choose. Explain how you made your list.

IT'S IN THE BAG

Probability Clues

PROJECT Match spinners with clues that describe the probability of their outcomes and then test the probability clues.

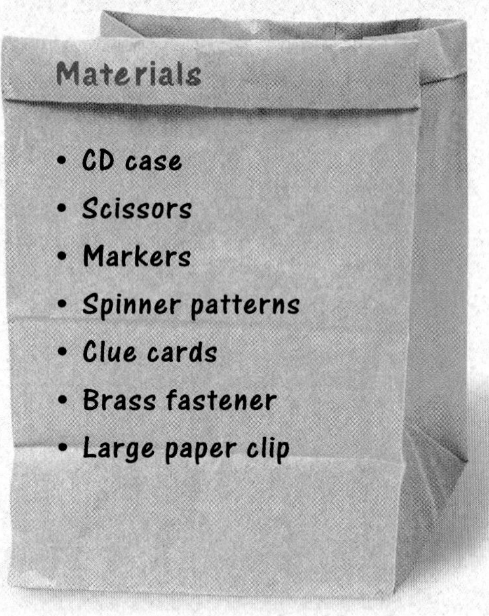

Directions

1. Cut out the pattern for the plain circle. Decorate it with markers, and glue it to the front of your CD case. *(Picture A)*
2. Push a brass fastener through the hole in the CD case, and spread the fastener at the back.
3. Color the spinner patterns according to the labels on each. Cut out each spinner, and place it on your desk. *(Picture B)*
4. Cut apart the clue cards and place each below the spinner that it describes. Cut apart the blank cards, and write a different clue for each spinner.
5. Test the probability clues. Put each spinner in the CD case. Then attach the paper clip to the fastener to use as the pointer. *(Picture C)*

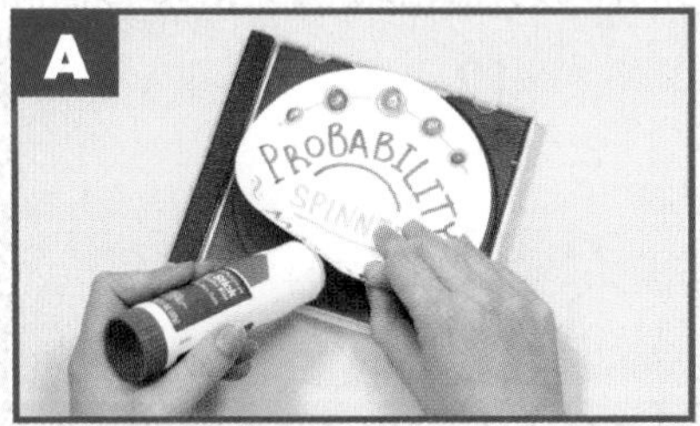

Challenge

Color Patterns

Gina used squares of paper in different colors to make this design. Describe a pattern for her design.

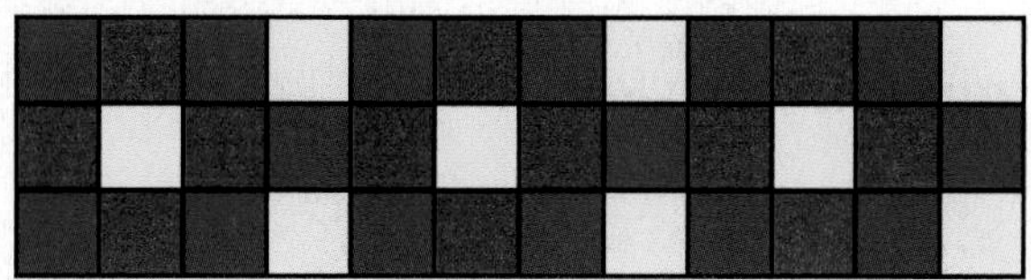

The pattern unit in the first and third rows is *blue, red, blue, yellow*. The pattern unit in the second row is *red, yellow, red, blue*.

Mark used different colors to make this design with paper squares. When he moved it, some squares fell off. What colors are missing?

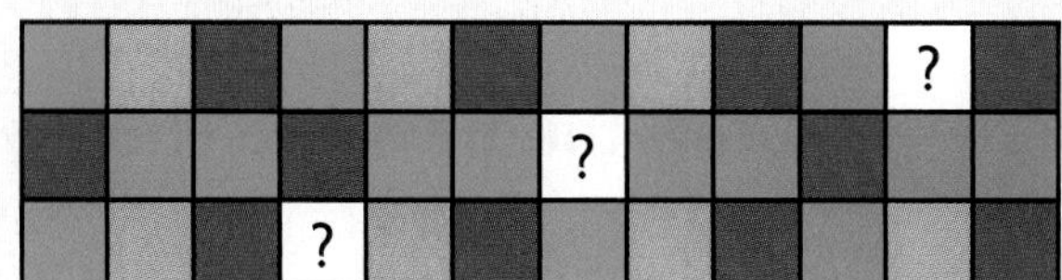

The pattern unit in the first and third rows is *green, orange, purple*. So, the first row is missing orange and the third row is missing green.

The pattern unit in the second row is *purple, green, green*. So, the second row is missing purple.

Try It

1. What colors are missing in the pattern? Describe the pattern unit for each row.

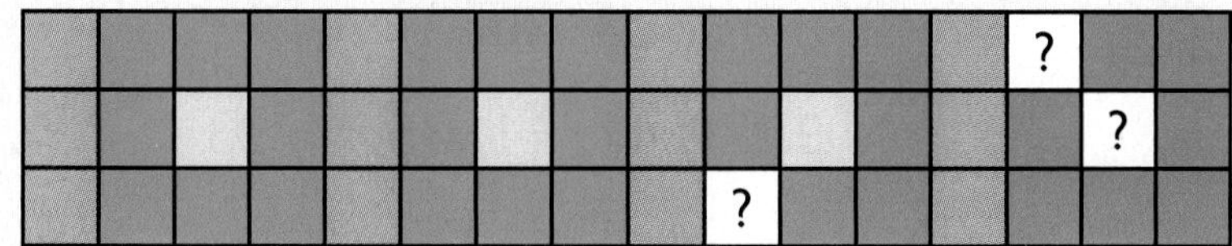

2. Draw a pattern on grid paper using different colors. Ask a classmate to describe your pattern.

Study Guide and Review

VOCABULARY

Choose the best term from the box.

1. The chance that an event will happen is the _?_ of the event. (p. 488)
2. The possible result of an experiment is called an _?_. (p. 490)
3. The probability of an event is _?_ if the event has a good chance of happening. (p. 488)
4. You can _?_ what will happen in an experiment by telling what you think will happen. (p. 490)

certain
likely
probability
predict
outcome

STUDY AND SOLVE

Chapter 23

Find the pattern unit to continue the pattern.

The pattern unit is *circle, rectangle, circle*.

So, the next two shapes are circle, rectangle.

Draw the next two shapes in each pattern. (pp. 470–473)

5. □ ○ • □ ○ • □ ○ • □ _?_ _?_
6. • △ ▽ • △ ▽ • △ ▽ • △ _?_ _?_
7. ○ □ □ ○ □ □ ○ □ □ _?_ _?_

Write a rule for the pattern. Find the missing number.

29, 40, 51, 62, ■, 84

The numbers increase by 11, so a rule for the pattern is *add 11*.

So, the missing number is 73.

Write a rule for each pattern. Then find the missing number. (pp. 476–477)

8. 16, 23, 30, 37, ■, 51
9. 53, 47, 41, 35, ■, 23
10. 114, 123, 132, 141, ■, 159

Chapter 24

Predict outcomes of experiments.

Margo pulled a paper clip from a bag, recorded the color, and put it back. After 10 times she had pulled 1 orange, 3 red, and 6 blue paper clips.

What color paper clip do you predict she will pull next?

Think: Since she pulled a blue paper clip more than half the time, it is most likely that she will pull a blue paper clip next.

List possible combinations.

Make a tree diagram to show the different combinations for pants and shirt outfits with the choices blue pants, tan pants, white shirt, blue shirt.

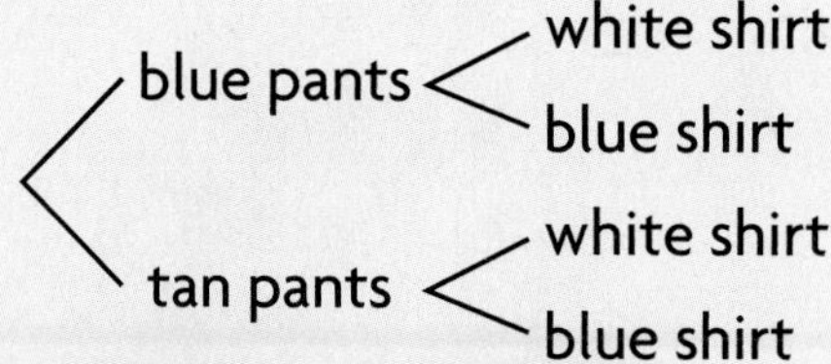

So, there are 4 possible combinations.

For 11–12, use the tally table. (pp. 496–497)

This tally table shows the pulls from a bag of marbles.

OUTCOMES	
Color	**Tallies**
Yellow	||||
Green	~~||||~~ |||
Purple	~~||||~~ |

11. Name the color marble which is least likely to be pulled.

12. Name the color marble which is most likely to be pulled.

Make a tree diagram to solve.

(pp. 498–499)

13. Ashley is buying one sandwich and one drink for lunch. Her sandwich choices are turkey and peanut butter. Her drink choices are milk, juice, and soda. How many different combinations can Ashley buy for lunch?

PROBLEM SOLVING PRACTICE

Solve. (pp. 480–481, 500–501)

14. Dimitri wrote this number pattern. Write a rule to describe the pattern. Then write the next 3 numbers in his pattern.

72, 64, 56, 48, ■, ■, ■

15. Tina needs to write a letter, study, and clean her room. Make a list to find how many different ways these activities can be arranged.

PERFORMANCE ASSESSMENT

TASK A • BASE-TEN BLOCKS ADD UP

Martina used base-ten blocks to make a pattern puzzle for her classmates to solve. She placed a piece of paper over the fourth group of blocks.

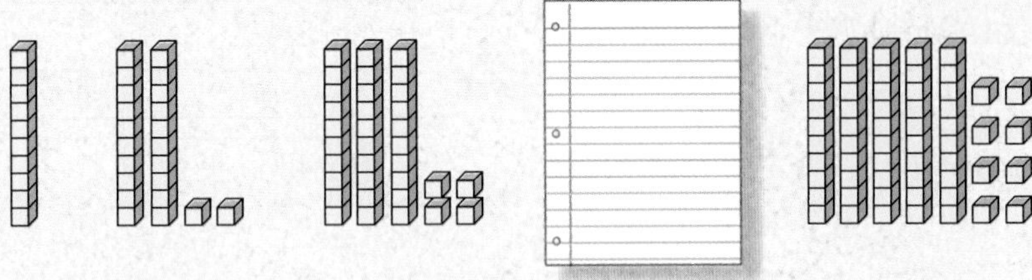

a. Draw a picture of the missing group of blocks. What is a rule for Martina's block pattern?

b. Write a number pattern that shows Martina's pattern. What is a rule for this number pattern?

TASK B • TRY YOUR LUCK

Materials: 8 different markers

You want to make a spinner for a new game. Each section of the spinner will have a different solid color. Two players each choose a color and spin the pointer. If the pointer lands on the chosen color, the player gets one point. The player with more points after 10 spins wins the game.

a. Make a spinner with 8 equal sections. Color each section a different color.

b. List all the outcomes of using the spinner 10 times.

c. Explain why this spinner gives each player the same chance of winning.

Technology Linkup

Make a Graph

Spreadsheet programs can be used to make graphs. The table at the right shows the number of multiplication facts that all of Mr. Spencer's students answered correctly. Make a bar graph of the data in the table.

MULTIPLICATION FACTS	
Quiz	**Number of correct answers**
Quiz 1	10
Quiz 2	13
Quiz 3	15
Quiz 4	18
Quiz 5	21

STEP 1

Enter the data into the spreadsheet program. Highlight all of the data.

STEP 2

Select *Insert Chart* or *Create New Chart*. Choose *bar* or *column* to make a bar graph.

STEP 3

Select *Chart Options*. Type in the title of your graph and a label for each axis.

	A	B
1	Quiz 1	10
2	Quiz 2	13
3	Quiz 3	15
4	Quiz 4	18
5	Quiz 5	21

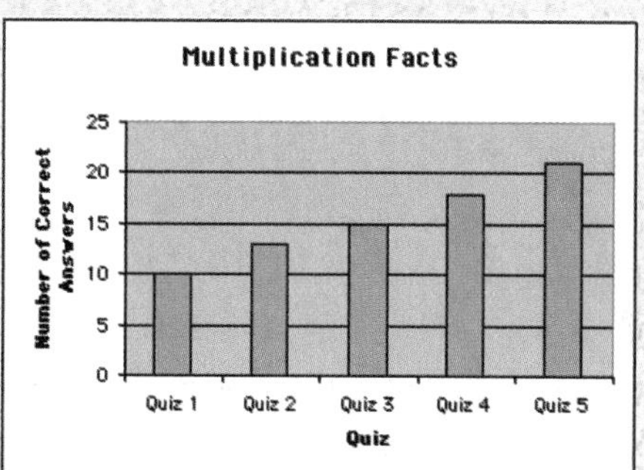

- Describe the trend that you see in the bar graph. Predict the number of multiplication facts that Mr. Spencer's students will answer correctly on Quiz 6.

Practice and Problem Solving

1. Make a spreadsheet showing the number of correct answers on 5 of your spelling tests. Make a bar graph of this data.

GO ON-LINE **Multimedia Math Glossary** **www.harcourtschool.com/mathglossary**

Vocabulary Power Look up *bar graph* and *line graph* in the Multimedia Math Glossary. How are the two types of graphs alike? How are they different?

▲ Cades Cove is a protected area, so visitors must remember to *leave no trace.*

in Tennessee

CADES COVE

Many people look for wildlife when they visit Cades Cove in the Great Smoky Mountains National Park.

The diagram at the right shows the pattern Jillian uses to set up chairs for a slide show at the visitors' center.

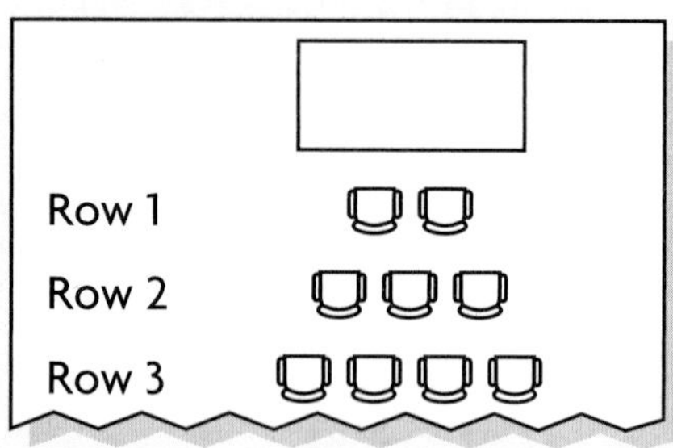

USE DATA For 1–2, use the diagram.

1. Describe the pattern Jillian uses to set up the chairs.
2. How many chairs will Jillian put in the fifth row?
3. **STRETCH YOUR THINKING** Draw a diagram of another pattern that Jillian could use to set up chairs. Describe your pattern.
4. Karen's family plans to visit Cades Cove. They want to see a slide show, go on a hayride, and go on a guided walking tour. Make a list to show all of the possible orders in which they could do these activities.

▼ Smoky Mountain black bears, bobcats, birds, and many other animals live in Cades Cove.

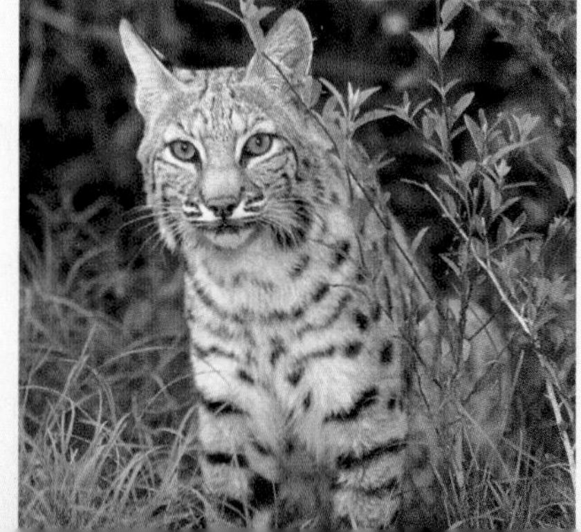

RADNOR LAKE

Radnor Lake State Natural Area, in Nashville, Tennessee, is a wildlife sanctuary. It provides a home for many kinds of birds, reptiles, and mammals, as well as hundreds of kinds of plants.

▲ Hiking, observing nature, and photographing plants and wildlife are the main activities for visitors at Radnor Lake.

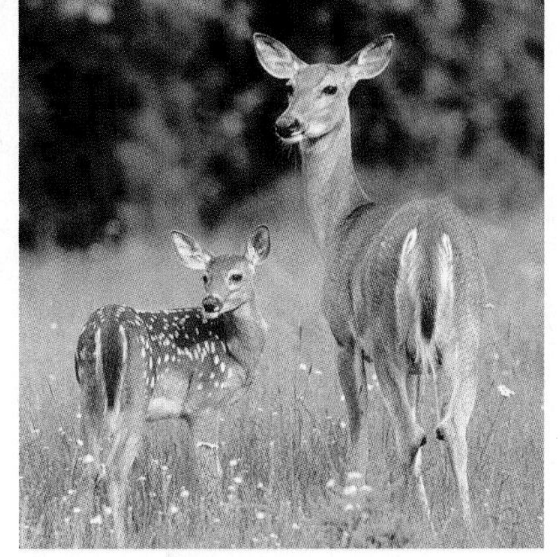

▲ The whitetail deer is the largest mammal that lives at Radnor Lake.

Mrs. Kelly is studying animals at Radnor Lake State Natural Area. The line plot shows the animals that she saw during 3 visits to Radnor Lake.

1. Which animal is Mrs. Kelly most likely to see on her next visit?
2. Which animal is Mrs. Kelly unlikely to see on her next visit?

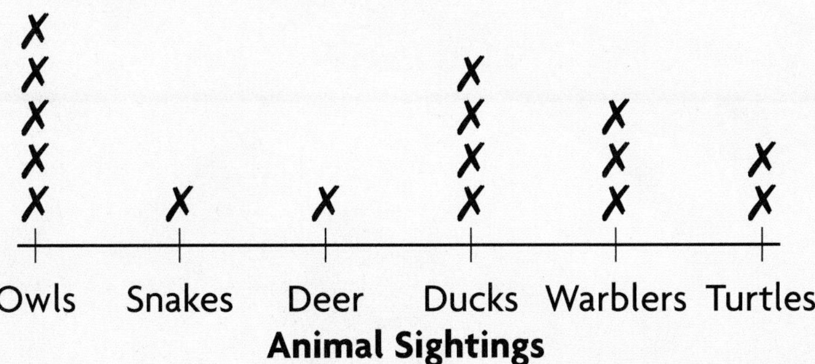

The Tulip Poplar and the Chinquapin Oak are two kinds of trees found at Radnor Lake.

3. **STRETCH YOUR THINKING** The Tulip Poplar can grow to be 200 feet tall. The Chinquapin Oak can grow to be 80 feet tall. Make a bar graph of tree heights using a scale of 20 feet. Include two other kinds of trees.

▲ The Tulip Poplar is Tennessee's state tree.

Understand Fractions

FAST FACT • SCIENCE There are thousands of different kinds of insects in the world. Some are very large. Others are so small that we can't even see them.

PROBLEM SOLVING The table shows some insects and their sizes. Which insect is the smallest? Which is the largest?

SIZES OF INSECTS

Insect	Length
Ant	$\frac{1}{4}$ inch
Mosquito	$\frac{1}{8}$ inch
Grasshopper	2 inches
Goliath beetle	$4\frac{1}{2}$ inches

African Goliath beetle

CHECK WHAT YOU KNOW

Use this page to help you review and remember important skills needed for Chapter 25.

MODEL PARTS OF A WHOLE

Write how many equal parts make up the whole figure. Then write how many parts are shaded.

1. 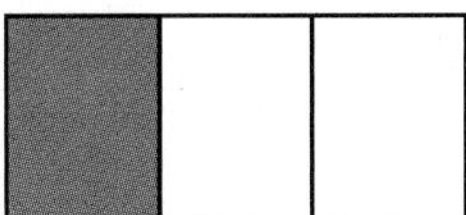

2. 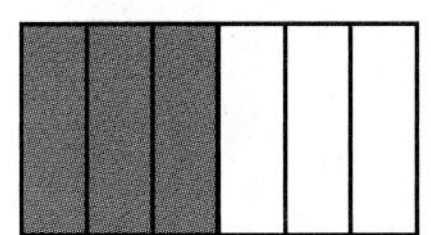

3. 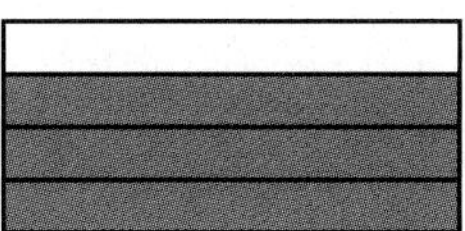

4. 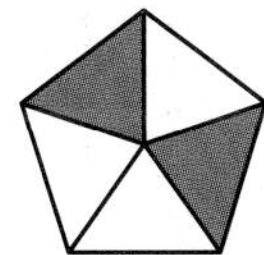

5. 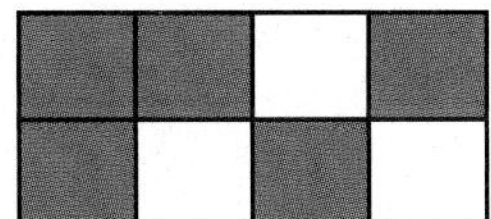

6. 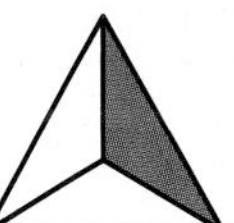

MODEL PARTS OF A GROUP

Write the number in each group. Then write the number in each group that is green.

7. 

8. 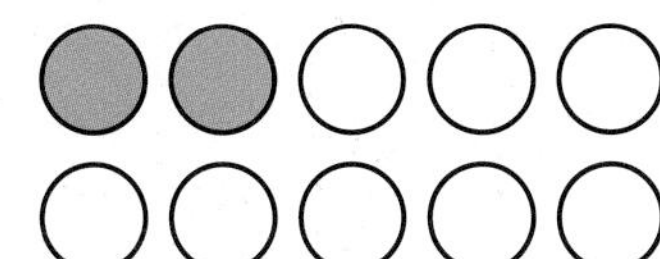

9. 

10. 

11. 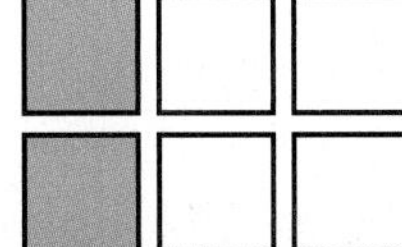

12. 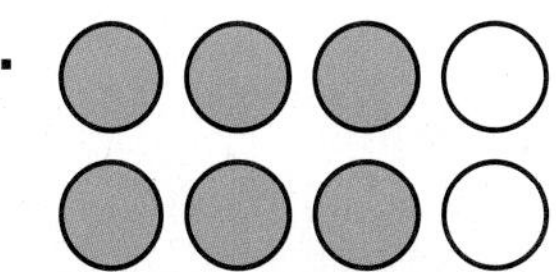

VOCABULARY POWER

REVIEW

fourth [fôrth] *noun*

When there are four equal-sized pieces in one whole, each piece is called one *fourth*. List some things that could be divided into fourths.

PREVIEW

fraction
numerator
denominator
equivalent fractions
mixed number

www.harcourtschool.com/mathglossary

LESSON

Parts of a Whole

Learn

ALL TOGETHER

A number that names part of a whole or part of a group is called a **fraction**.

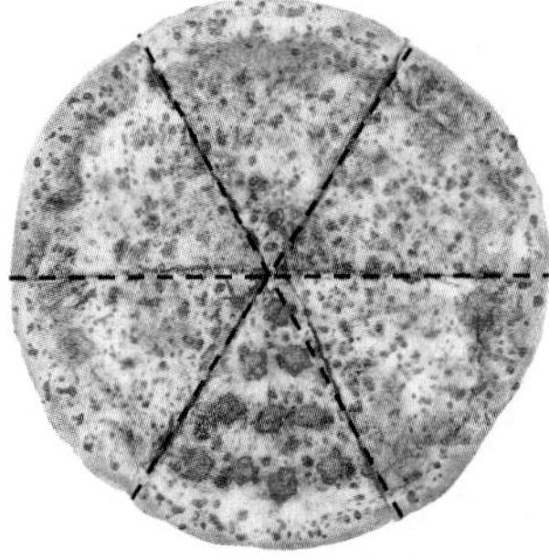

What fraction of this pizza has sausage?

1 part sausage → $\frac{1}{6}$ ← numerator
6 equal parts in all → ← denominator

Read: one sixth **Write:** $\frac{1}{6}$

one part out of six equal parts
1 divided by 6

So, $\frac{1}{6}$ of the pizza has sausage.

The **numerator** tells how many parts are being counted.

The **denominator** tells how many equal parts are in the whole.

- What fraction of the pizza does *not* have sausage? Explain how you know.

Quick Review

Find a rule and the next number in the pattern.

1. 2, 4, 6, 8, ▪
2. 12, 11, 10, 9, ▪
3. 3, 6, 9, 12, ▪
4. 11, 9, 7, 5, ▪
5. 4, 8, 12, 16, ▪

VOCABULARY

fraction
numerator
denominator

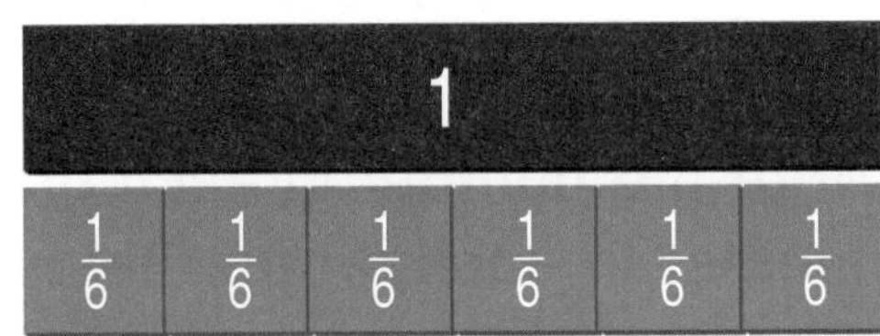

These fraction bars show how a whole can be divided into sixths, or six equal parts.

Examples

A

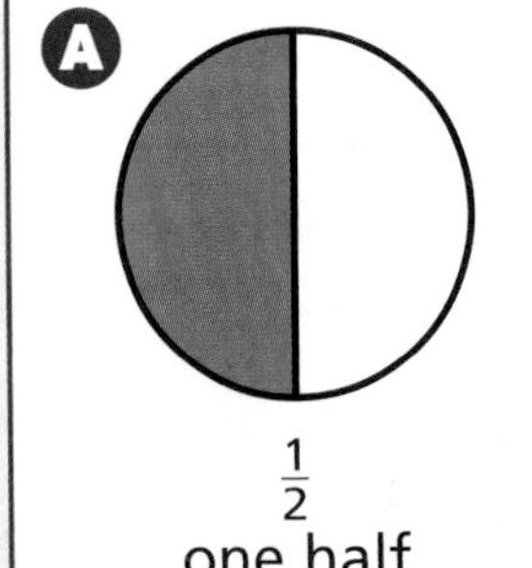

$\frac{1}{2}$
one half

B

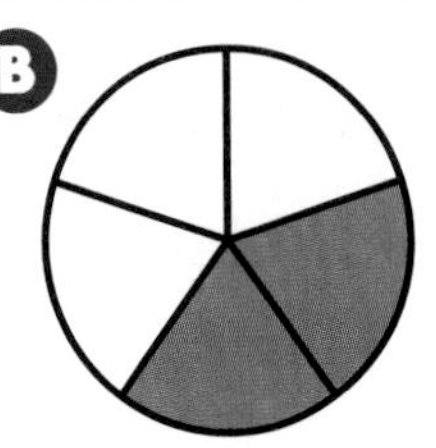

$\frac{2}{5}$
two fifths

C

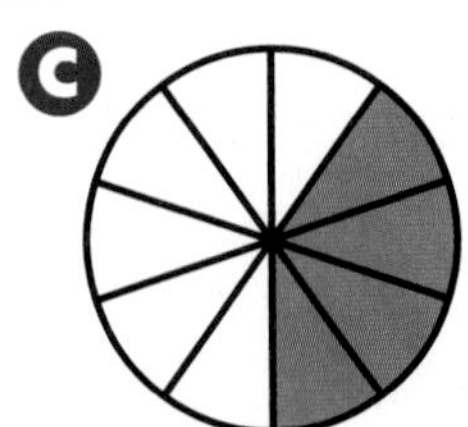

$\frac{4}{10}$
four tenths

D

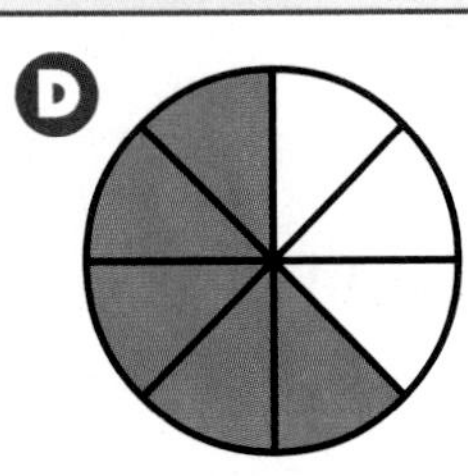

$\frac{5}{8}$
five eighths

Counting Equal Parts

You can count equal parts, such as sixths, to make one whole.

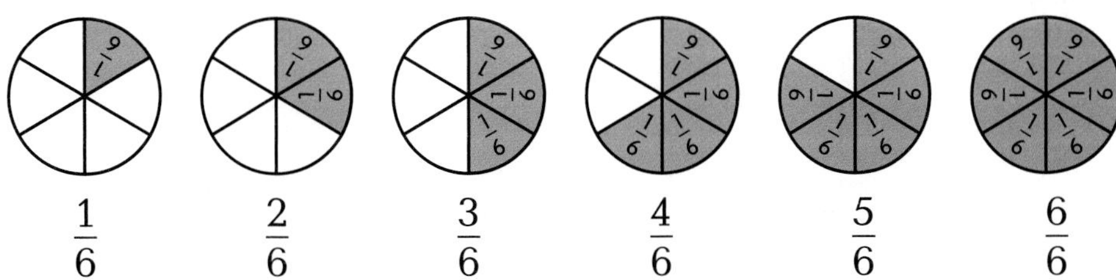

$\frac{6}{6}$ = one whole, or 1

MATH IDEA A number line can show parts of one whole.

The part on a number line from 0 to 1 shows one whole. The line can be divided into any number of equal parts.

This number line is divided into sixths.

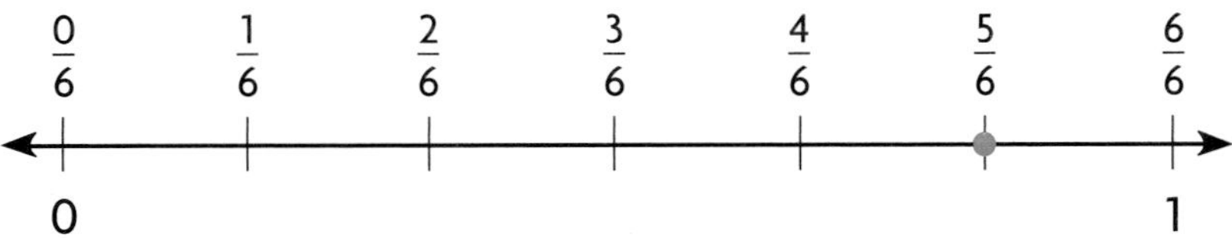

The point shows the location of $\frac{5}{6}$.

Examples

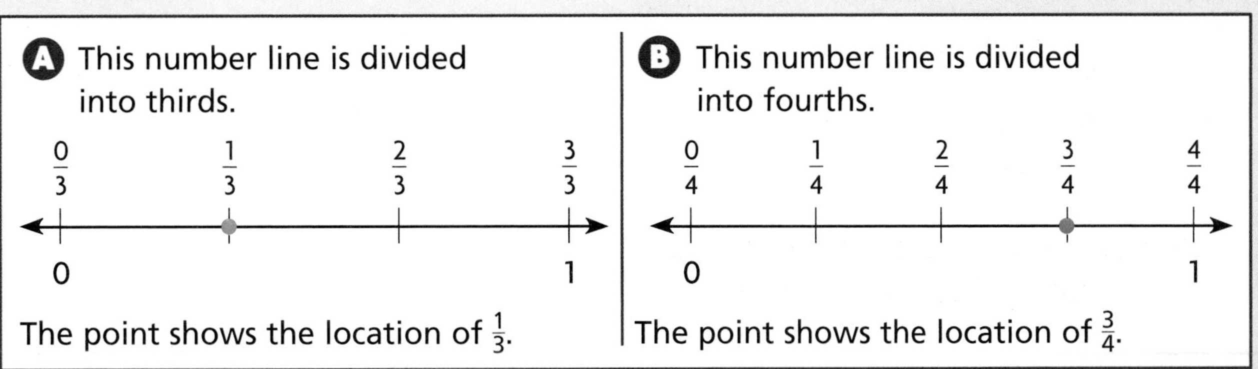

A This number line is divided into thirds.

The point shows the location of $\frac{1}{3}$.

B This number line is divided into fourths.

The point shows the location of $\frac{3}{4}$.

Check

1. Write how to count by eighths to make one whole.

Write a fraction in numbers and in words that names the shaded part.

2.

3. 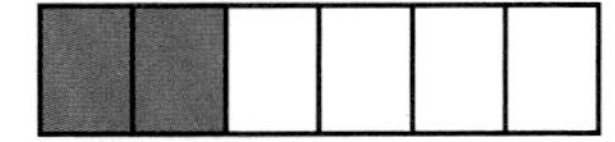

4. 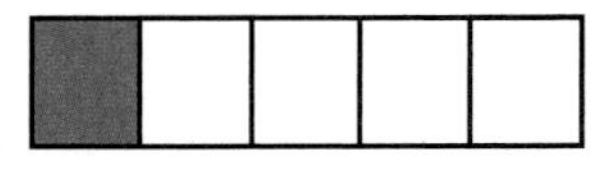

LESSON CONTINUES

Practice and Problem Solving

Extra Practice, page 534, Set A

Write a fraction in numbers and in words that names the shaded part.

5. 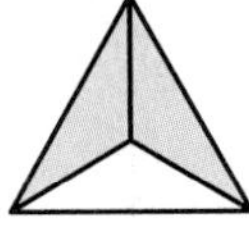

6. 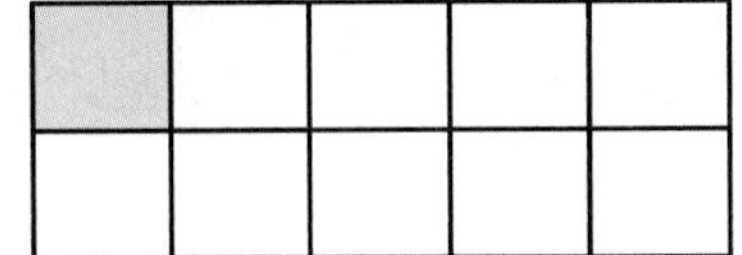

7. 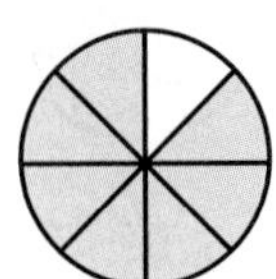

8. 

9. 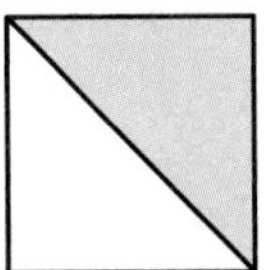

10. 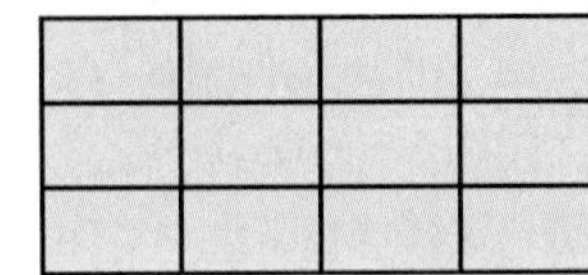

Make a model of each, using fraction circle pieces. Then write the fraction, using numbers.

11. one fourth
12. two out of two
13. six eighths
14. one divided by three
15. three fifths
16. five out of ten

Write a fraction to describe the part of each figure that is shaded.

17. 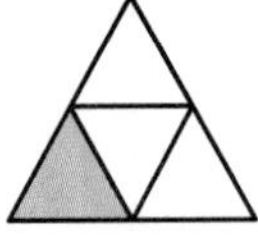  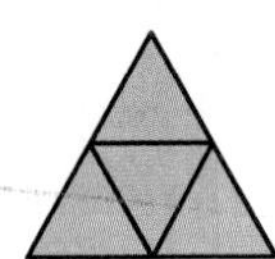

18. 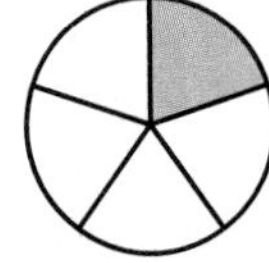 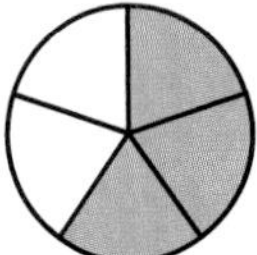 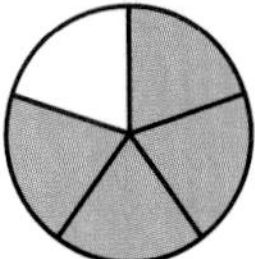 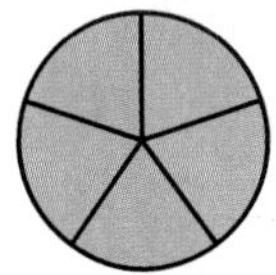

ALGEBRA Write a fraction that names the point for each letter on the number line.

19. 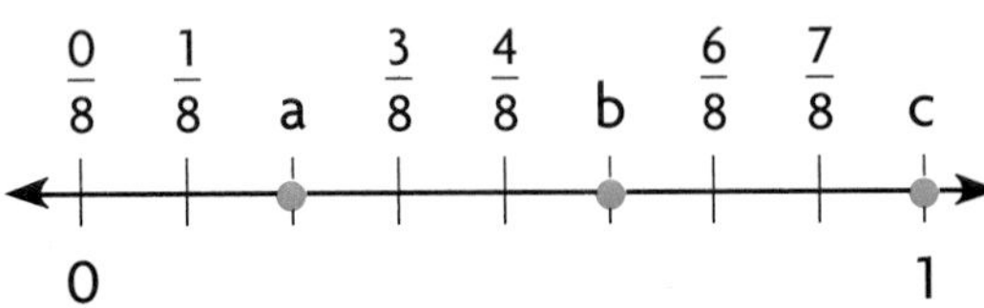

20. 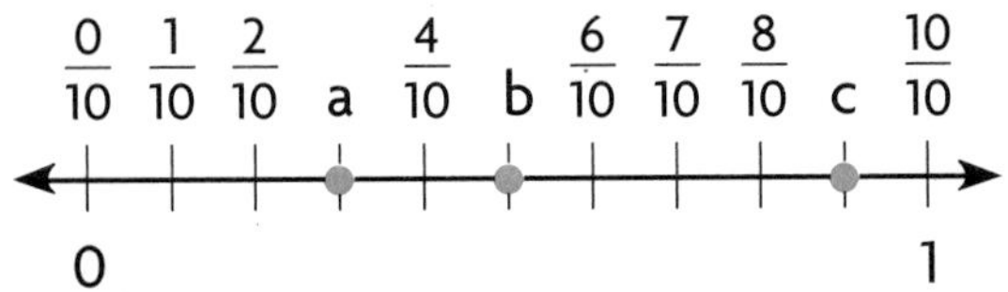

21. **REASONING** There are two pizzas the same size. One is cut into 6 equal pieces. The other is cut into 8 equal pieces. Which pizza has smaller pieces? Explain.

22. **What's the Error?** Lydia said that the fraction $\frac{6}{4}$ names the shaded part of the circle. Explain her error.

23. Suppose you and 4 friends shared equal pieces of a pie. Use fraction circle pieces to model the amount of pie for two people.

24. **REASONING** Mrs. Thomas wants to give $\frac{1}{6}$ of a pie to each visitor. How many whole pies will she need for 6 visitors? 12 visitors?

Mixed Review and Test Prep

Find each difference. (pp. 92, 96)

25. $245 - 152 = \blacksquare$

26. $736 - 379 = \blacksquare$

27. $400 - 118 = \blacksquare$

Find each product.

28. $4 \times 8 = \blacksquare$ (p. 178)

29. $6 \times 6 = \blacksquare$ (p. 194)

30. $7 \times 9 = \blacksquare$ (p. 200)

31. **TEST PREP** Which polygon has 4 sides and 4 angles? (p. 390)

A triangle
B quadrilateral
C pentagon
D hexagon

32. **TEST PREP** Which is the best unit of measure to find the distance between two towns? (p. 342)

F inch
G foot
H yard
J mile

Problem Solving

These alphabet flags are used on ships to send messages in code. For example, if a ship flies the flag for the letter P, that ship is about to sail out of the harbor. Ships carry books that explain the codes in different languages.

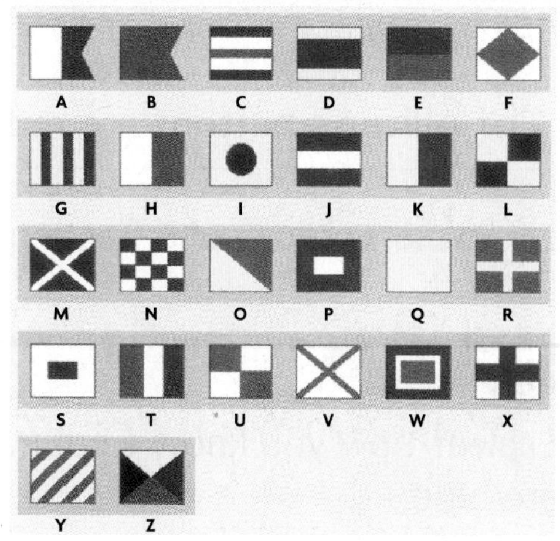

USE DATA For 1–4, use the flags.

1. Look at the flag for the letter G. What fraction names the part of the flag that is yellow?

2. Look at all of the flags. Which of them are divided into four equal parts, or fourths?

3. Look at the flag for the letter N. Into how many equal parts is the flag divided?

4. Write a fraction that names one part of each of these flags: L, O, and T.

LESSON

2 Parts of a Group

Learn

BUYING BUTTONS Allison and Marsha each bought some buttons at the craft store.

What fraction of Allison's buttons are red?

What fraction of Marsha's buttons are red?

Quick Review

Write the next fraction in the counting pattern.

1. $\frac{0}{3}, \frac{1}{3}, \frac{2}{3}, ■$
2. $\frac{1}{5}, \frac{2}{5}, \frac{3}{5}, ■$
3. $\frac{2}{6}, \frac{3}{6}, \frac{4}{6}, ■$
4. $\frac{3}{8}, \frac{4}{8}, \frac{5}{8}, ■$
5. $\frac{3}{10}, \frac{4}{10}, \frac{5}{10}, ■$

Allison's buttons

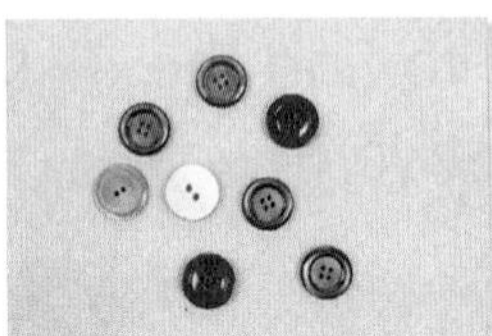

number of red buttons → 2 ← numerator
total buttons → 8 ← denominator

Read: two eighths, or two out of eight

Write: $\frac{2}{8}$

So, $\frac{2}{8}$ of Allison's buttons are red.

Marsha's buttons

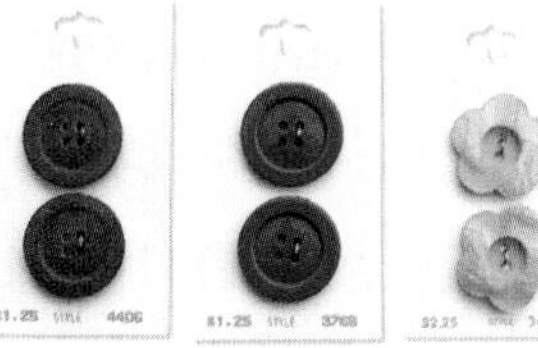

sets of red buttons → 1 ← numerator
total number of sets → 3 ← denominator

Read: one third, or one out of three

Write: $\frac{1}{3}$

So, $\frac{1}{3}$ of Marsha's buttons are red.

MATH IDEA You can use fractions to show parts of a group.

Check

1. **Explain** how you know what fraction of Allison's buttons are blue.

Write a fraction that names the part of each group that is yellow.

2. 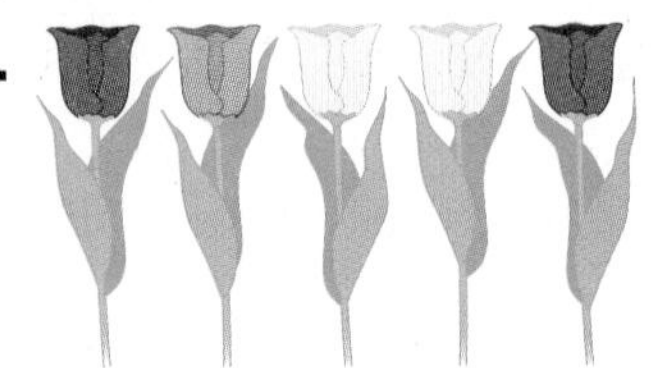

3. 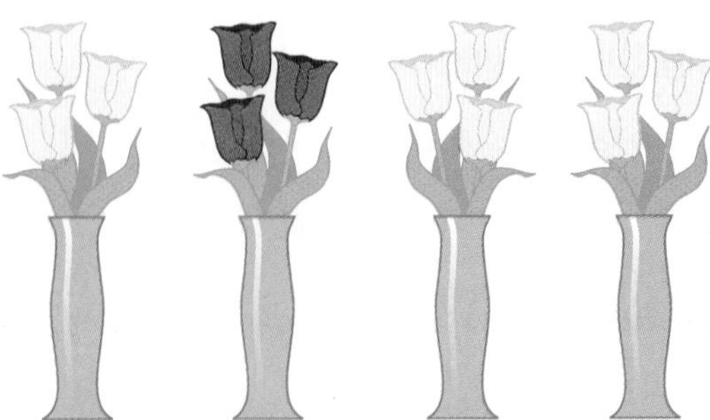

Practice and Problem Solving

Extra Practice, page 534, Set B

For 4–7, write a fraction that names the part of each group that is striped.

4.

5.

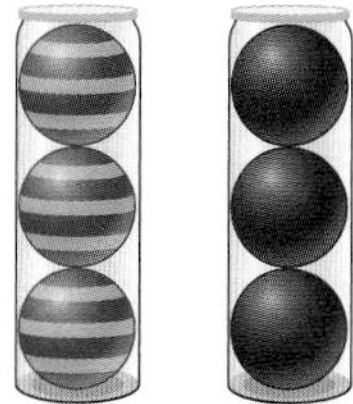

6.

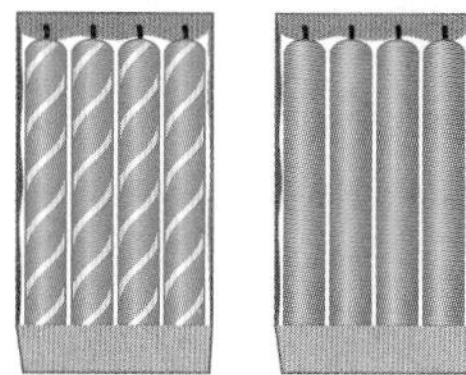

7.

8. Draw 8 squares. Circle $\frac{2}{8}$ of them.

9. Draw 6 triangles. Circle $\frac{5}{6}$ of them.

10. Draw 10 rectangles. Circle $\frac{3}{10}$ of them.

Use a pattern to complete the table.

11.	Model	○○○○○	●○○○○	■	●●●○○	●●●●○	●●●●●
12.	Total number of parts	5	■	5	5	5	5
13.	Number of green parts	0	1	2	■	4	5
14.	Fraction of green parts	$\frac{0}{5}$	$\frac{1}{5}$	$\frac{2}{5}$	$\frac{3}{5}$	$\frac{4}{5}$	■

15. Debra has 12 ribbons. Of those ribbons, $\frac{1}{12}$ are red and $\frac{2}{12}$ are blue. The rest are yellow. How many yellow ribbons does she have?

16. **? What's the Question?** Jonas has 4 blue tiles, 3 green tiles, and 1 yellow tile. The answer is $\frac{7}{8}$.

17. **Write a problem** in which a fraction is used to name part of a group. Tell what the numerator and denominator mean.

Mixed Review and Test Prep

Find each quotient. (p. 262)

18. $4 \div 4 =$ ■

19. $9 \div 1 =$ ■

20. $0 \div 7 =$ ■

21. $8 \div 8 =$ ■

22. **TEST PREP** Find the number that the variable stands for. (p. 242)

$$n \times 7 = 21$$

A 2 **B** 3 **C** 4 **D** 14

LESSON 3

Equivalent Fractions

Learn

EQUAL PARTS Two or more fractions that name the same amount are called **equivalent fractions**.

What other fractions name $\frac{1}{2}$?

Quick Review

Name the fraction for the shaded part.

1. 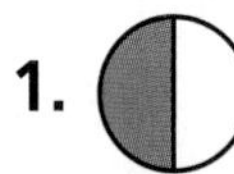
2. 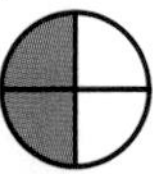
3. 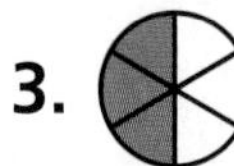
4.  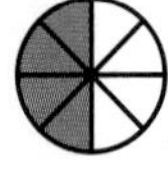
5. 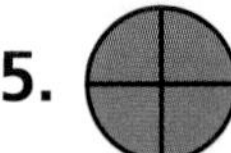

VOCABULARY

equivalent fractions

Activity 1

MATERIALS: sheet of paper, red crayon

STEP 1

Fold a sheet of paper in half. Shade one half of the paper red.

1 out of 2 equal parts is red.

$\frac{1}{2}$ of the paper is red.

STEP 2

Fold the paper in half again.

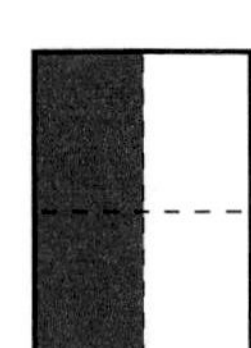

2 out of 4 equal parts are red.

$\frac{2}{4}$ of the paper is red.

STEP 3

Fold the paper in half a third time.

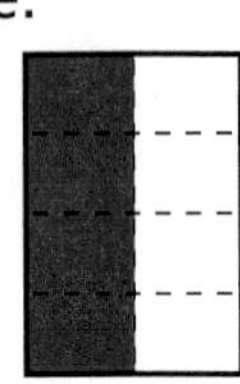
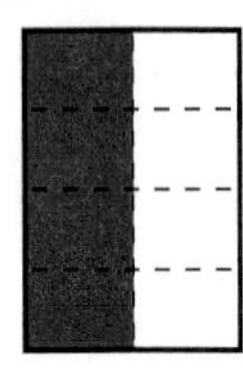

4 out of 8 equal parts are red.

$\frac{4}{8}$ of the paper is red.

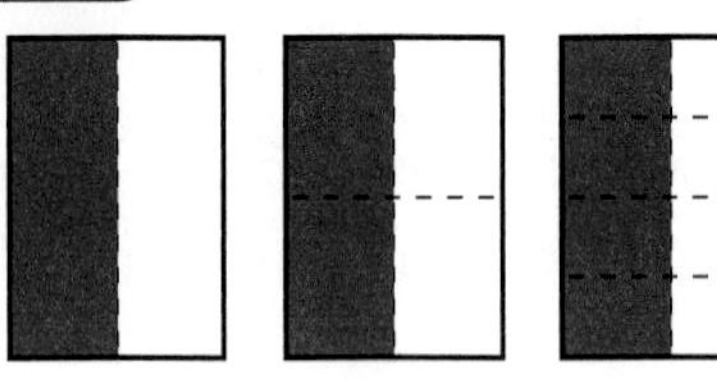

$\frac{1}{2} = \frac{2}{4} = \frac{4}{8}$

So, $\frac{1}{2}$, $\frac{2}{4}$, and $\frac{4}{8}$ are all names for $\frac{1}{2}$.

They are equivalent fractions.

REASONING What pattern do you see in the fractions $\frac{1}{2}, \frac{2}{4}, \frac{4}{8}$?

Activity 2 What fraction is equivalent to $\frac{2}{3}$?

MATERIALS: fraction bars

STEP 1

Start with the bar for 1 whole. Line up two $\frac{1}{3}$ bars for $\frac{2}{3}$.

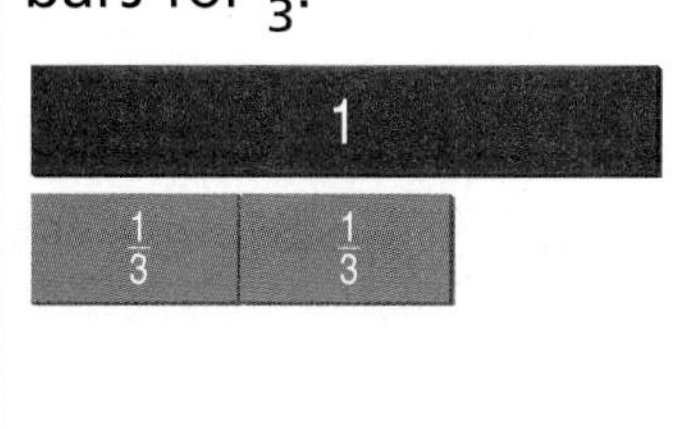

STEP 2

Use $\frac{1}{6}$ bars to match the length of the bars for $\frac{2}{3}$.

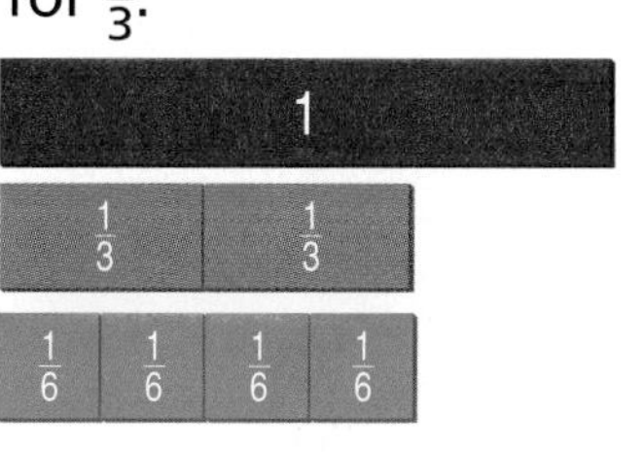

STEP 3

Count the number of $\frac{1}{6}$ bars that make up $\frac{2}{3}$. Write the equivalent fraction.

Count: $\frac{1}{6}$ $\frac{2}{6}$ $\frac{3}{6}$ $\frac{4}{6}$

Write: $\frac{2}{3} = \frac{4}{6}$

- How can you tell that the fraction bars show equivalent fractions?
- Use sixths, eighths, and tenths fraction bars. Find fractions that are equivalent to $\frac{1}{2}$.

Examples Find equivalent fractions.

A

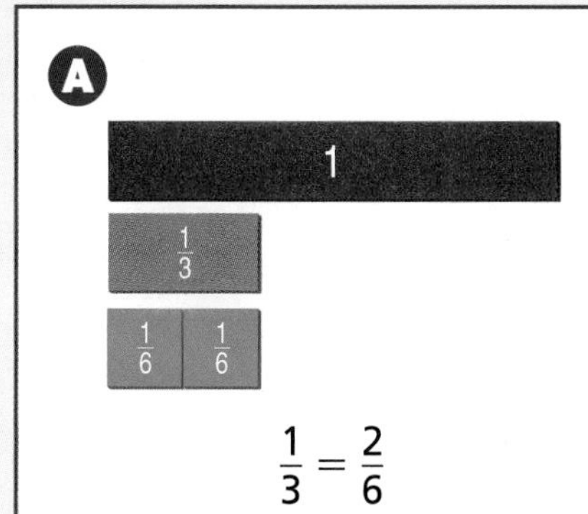

$\frac{1}{3} = \frac{2}{6}$

B

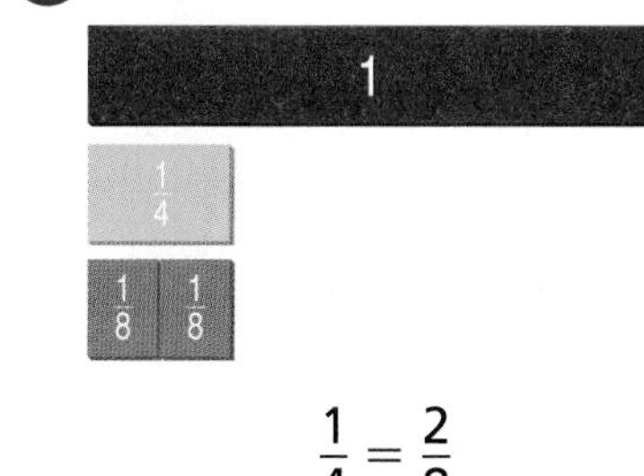

$\frac{1}{4} = \frac{2}{8}$

C

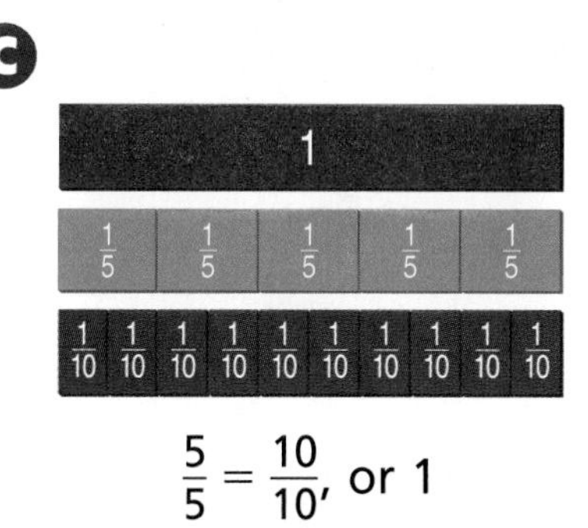

$\frac{5}{5} = \frac{10}{10}$, or 1

Check

1. **Explain** how to use fraction bars to decide if $\frac{2}{4}$ and $\frac{2}{3}$ are equivalent.

Find an equivalent fraction. Use fraction bars.

2.

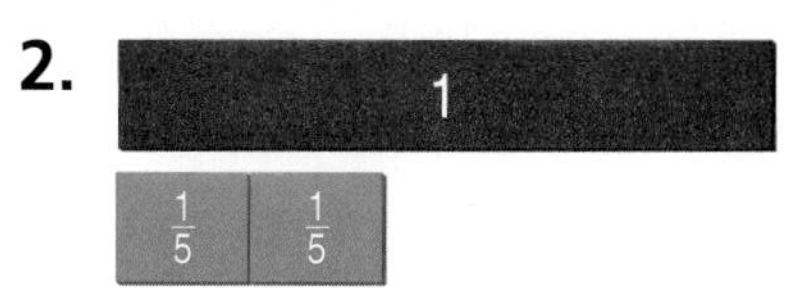

3.

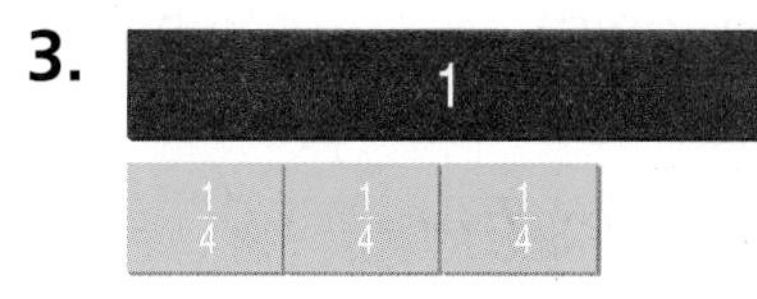

LESSON CONTINUES

Practice and Problem Solving

Extra Practice, page 534, Set C

Find an equivalent fraction. Use fraction bars.

4. 1; $\frac{1}{5}$

5. 1; $\frac{1}{8}$ $\frac{1}{8}$ $\frac{1}{8}$ $\frac{1}{8}$ $\frac{1}{8}$ $\frac{1}{8}$

6. 1; $\frac{1}{10}$ $\frac{1}{10}$ $\frac{1}{10}$ $\frac{1}{10}$ $\frac{1}{10}$

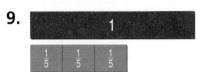

Find the missing numerator. Use fraction bars.

7. 1; $\frac{1}{6}$ $\frac{1}{6}$ $\frac{1}{6}$

$\frac{3}{6} = \frac{■}{2}$

8.

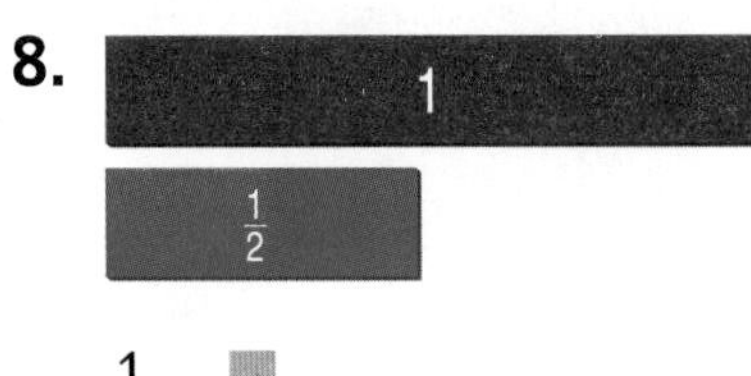

$\frac{1}{2} = \frac{■}{8}$

9. 1; $\frac{1}{5}$ $\frac{1}{5}$ $\frac{1}{5}$

$\frac{3}{5} = \frac{■}{10}$

10. $\frac{3}{9} = \frac{■}{3}$

11. $\frac{1}{2} = \frac{■}{10}$

12. $\frac{2}{4} = \frac{■}{12}$

13. $\frac{1}{4} = \frac{■}{8}$

14. $\frac{2}{6} = \frac{■}{3}$

15. $\frac{3}{5} = \frac{■}{10}$

16. Write the fraction that names the shaded part of each. Then tell which fractions are equivalent.

a. 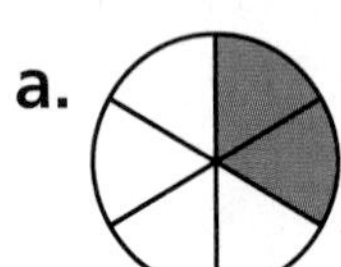

b. 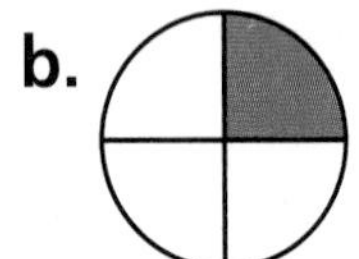

c. 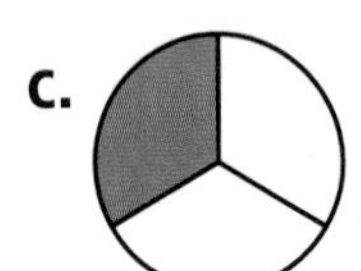

d. 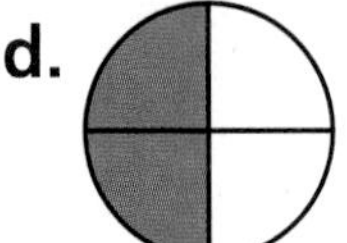

e. 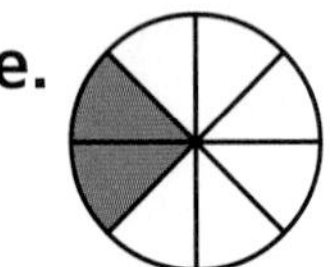

17. Amy's age is an even number between 20 and 29. Her age is a multiple of 3. How old is Amy?

18. **REASONING** Linda used 6 of one kind of fraction bar to show $\frac{1}{2}$. What kind of fraction bars did she use?

19. **ALGEBRA** In his yard, Mr. York has a 42-foot-tall pine tree. The pine tree is 15 feet taller than his oak tree. How tall is his oak tree?

20. There are 8 granola bars in a box. If Lito ate $\frac{1}{4}$ of the granola bars, how many granola bars did he eat? Draw a picture to solve.

21. Jessie has six coins that are worth 71¢ in all. What coins does she have? Explain how you found your answer.

22. There are 12 people having lunch. Each person has $\frac{1}{4}$ of a pizza. How many whole pizzas do they have? Make a model or picture to solve.

Mixed Review and Test Prep

Round to the nearest thousand. (p. 52)

23. 833 **24.** 2,497 **25.** 5,555 **26.** 39,670

Find the quotient. (p. 280)

27. $90 \div 9$ **28.** $56 \div 8$ **29.** $49 \div 7$ **30.** $72 \div 9$

31. TEST PREP Emma left at 11:15 A.M. and returned at 12:35 P.M. For how long was she gone? (p. 134)

A 1 hour 10 minutes
B 1 hour 20 minutes
C 1 hour 40 minutes
D 1 hour 50 minutes

32. TEST PREP Which set is equivalent to 3 quarters? (p. 110)

F 7 nickels, 25 pennies
G 6 dimes, 5 pennies
H 1 quarter, 9 nickels
J 5 dimes, 5 nickels

Problem Solving LINKUP . . . to Science

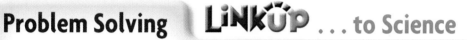

Did you know that there are *thousands* of different kinds of ants in the world?

Not all ants are alike. Different species of ants live in different places, eat different foods, and are different colors and sizes. Here are some interesting facts about three kinds of ants.

Fire ants

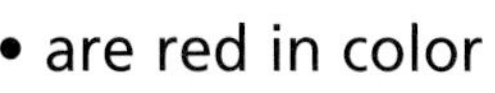

- are red in color
- will sting
- are about $\frac{1}{4}$ inch long

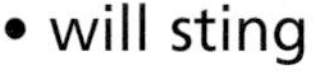

Bulldog ants

- eat meat
- are found in Australia
- are about $\frac{4}{5}$ inch long

Odorous house ants

- are brown or black in color
- smell bad when crushed
- are about $\frac{1}{10}$ inch long

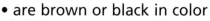

Use fraction bars and the information about the ants to solve.

1. Find an equivalent fraction for the length of:
   a. the fire ant **b.** the bulldog ant
2. Find how many odorous house ants it would take to equal the length of one bulldog ant. Write the equivalent fractions.

LESSON 4

Compare and Order Fractions

Quick Review

Compare. Write <, >, or = for each ●.

1. 27 ● 37
2. 398 ● 399
3. 241 ● 214
4. 4,012 ● 4,012
5. 5,431 ● 5,341

Learn

SIZE IT UP Fraction bars can help you compare parts of a whole.

Examples

A Compare $\frac{1}{4}$ and $\frac{2}{4}$.

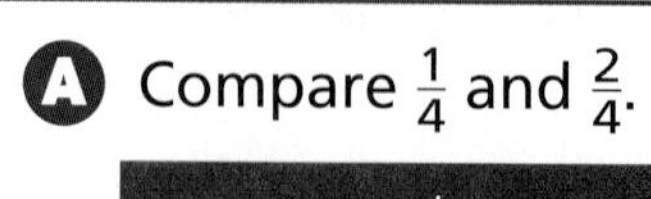

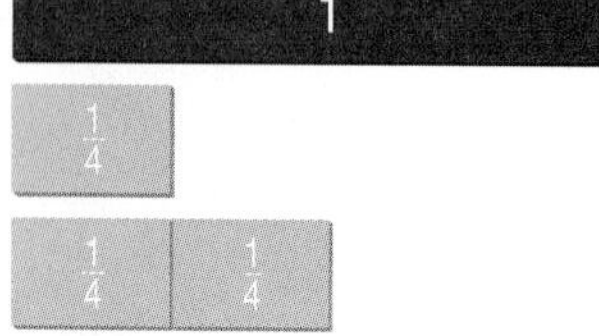

The bar for $\frac{1}{4}$ is shorter than the bars for $\frac{2}{4}$.

So, $\frac{1}{4} < \frac{2}{4}$, or $\frac{2}{4} > \frac{1}{4}$.

B Compare $\frac{1}{3}$ and $\frac{1}{4}$.

The bar for $\frac{1}{4}$ is shorter than the bar for $\frac{1}{3}$.

So, $\frac{1}{4} < \frac{1}{3}$, or $\frac{1}{3} > \frac{1}{4}$.

REASONING When the denominator is greater, is the fraction bar longer or shorter? Why?

Tiles can help you compare parts of a group.

Examples

A Compare $\frac{2}{5}$ and $\frac{3}{5}$.

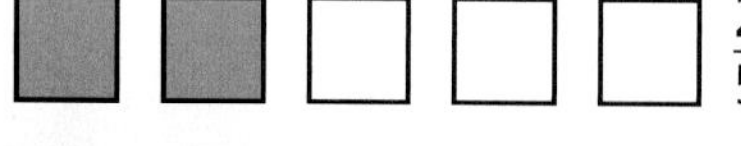

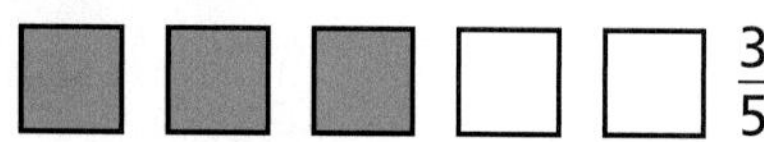

3 green tiles are more than 2 green tiles.

So, $\frac{3}{5} > \frac{2}{5}$, or $\frac{2}{5} < \frac{3}{5}$.

B Compare $\frac{4}{6}$ and $\frac{2}{3}$.

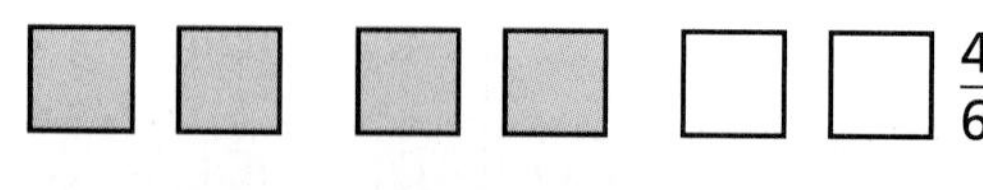

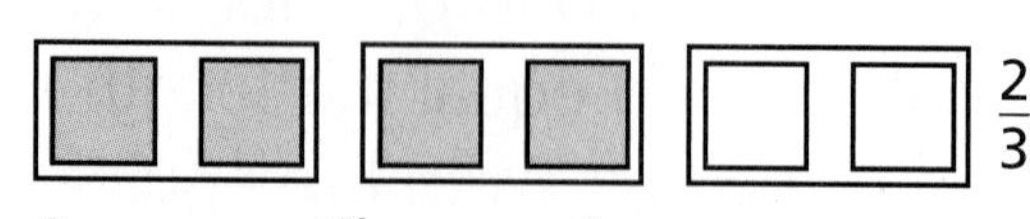

4 orange tiles are the same as 4 orange tiles.

So, $\frac{4}{6} = \frac{2}{3}$.

Ordering Fractions

You can order three or more fractions from least to greatest or from greatest to least.

Cassie needs $\frac{3}{8}$ cup raisins, $\frac{1}{4}$ cup chocolate chips, and $\frac{2}{3}$ cup peanuts to make a trail mix. She wants to know which ingredient she needs the most of. Use fraction bars to order the fractions from greatest to least.

HANDS ON

Activity

MATERIALS: fraction bars

STEP 1

Compare the fractions.

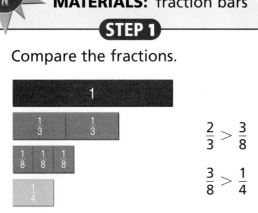

1		
$\frac{1}{3}$	$\frac{1}{3}$	
$\frac{1}{8}$	$\frac{1}{8}$	$\frac{1}{8}$
$\frac{1}{4}$		

$\frac{2}{3} > \frac{3}{8}$

$\frac{3}{8} > \frac{1}{4}$

STEP 2

Order the fractions from greatest to least.

Think: $\frac{2}{3} > \frac{3}{8} > \frac{1}{4}$

Write: $\frac{2}{3}, \frac{3}{8}, \frac{1}{4}$

- Use your models to order the fractions from least to greatest.

Check

1. **Describe** what happens to the size of fraction bars when the denominators become greater, as in $\frac{1}{2}$, $\frac{1}{3}$, and $\frac{1}{4}$.
2. **Describe** what happens to the size of fraction bars when the denominators become smaller, as in $\frac{1}{8}$, $\frac{1}{6}$, and $\frac{1}{4}$.

Technology Link

More Practice: Harcourt Mega Math Fraction Action, *Fraction Flare Up*, Level F

Compare. Write <, >, or = for each ●.

3. 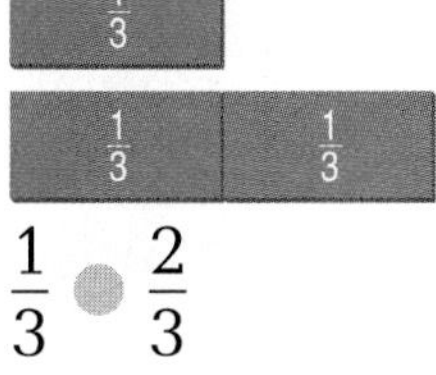

$\frac{1}{3}$ ● $\frac{2}{3}$

4. 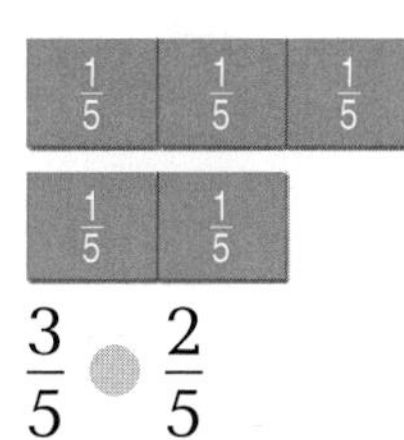

$\frac{3}{5}$ ● $\frac{2}{5}$

5. 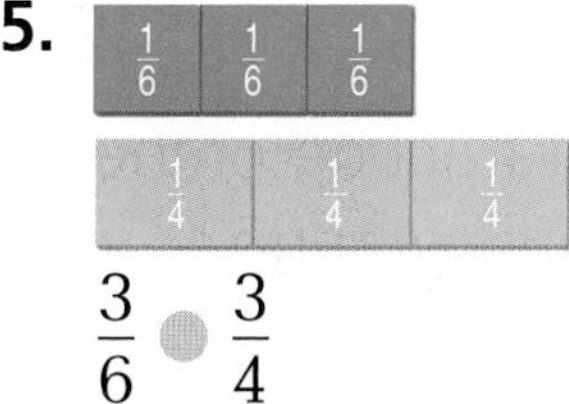

$\frac{3}{6}$ ● $\frac{3}{4}$

LESSON CONTINUES

Practice and Problem Solving

Extra Practice, page 534, Set D

Compare. Write <, >, or = for each ●.

6. 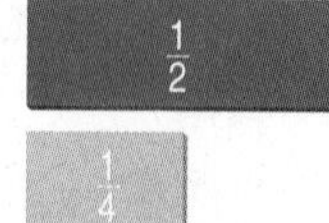

$\frac{1}{2}$ ● $\frac{1}{4}$

7. 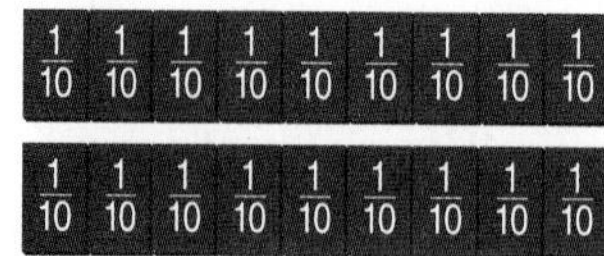

$\frac{9}{10}$ ● $\frac{9}{10}$

8. 

$\frac{3}{12}$ ● $\frac{5}{8}$

9. 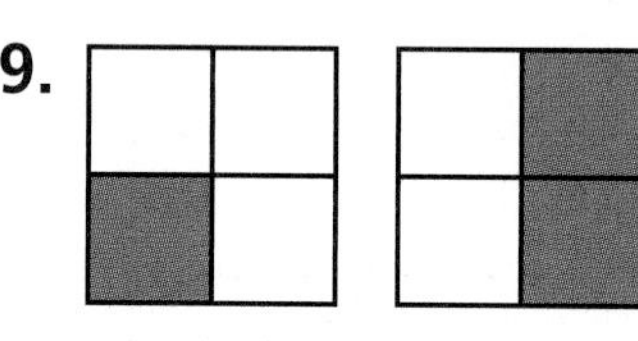

$\frac{1}{4}$ ● $\frac{2}{4}$

10. $\frac{3}{6}$ ● $\frac{1}{3}$

11. 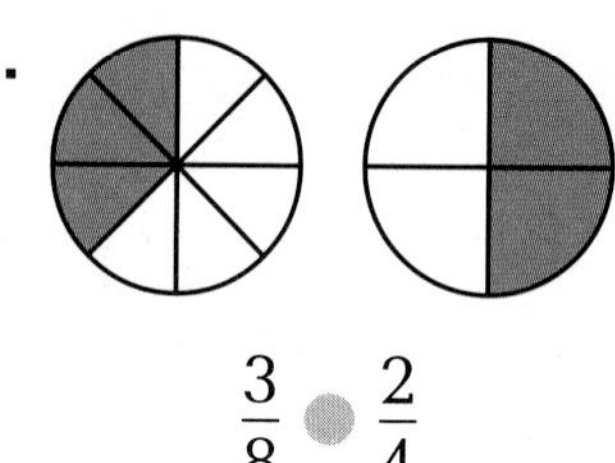

$\frac{3}{8}$ ● $\frac{2}{4}$

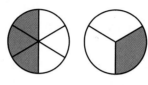

Compare the part of each group that is green.
Write <, >, or = for each ●.

12. 

$\frac{2}{6}$ ● $\frac{3}{6}$

13. 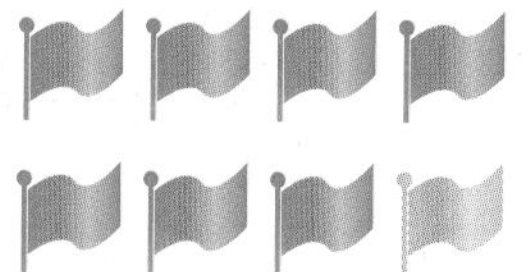

$\frac{4}{4}$ ● $\frac{3}{4}$

14. $\frac{4}{8}$ ● $\frac{4}{8}$

Use fraction bars to compare. Write <, >, or = for each ●.

15. $\frac{2}{2}$ ● 1

16. $\frac{3}{4}$ ● $\frac{1}{2}$

17. $\frac{1}{2}$ ● 1

18. 1 ● $\frac{4}{4}$

19. Order $\frac{1}{3}$, $\frac{1}{6}$, and $\frac{4}{6}$ from greatest to least.

20. Order $\frac{1}{2}$, $\frac{3}{4}$, and $\frac{2}{5}$ from least to greatest.

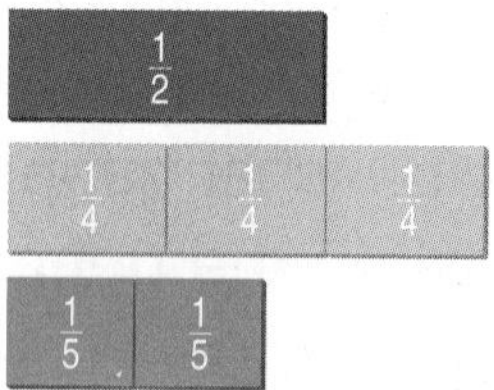

USE DATA For 21–23, use the bar graph.

21. How many leaves did Kevin collect in all?

22. What fraction of the leaves are red? yellow? orange?

23. Order the fractions of leaves from the greatest to the least amount.

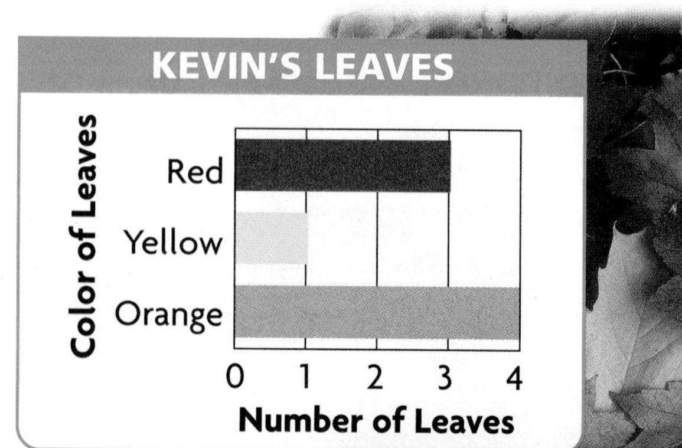

24. **FAST FACT** • SCIENCE In a honeybee colony, the queen bee is about $\frac{3}{4}$ inch long. A worker bee is about $\frac{1}{2}$ inch long. Which bee is longer? Explain how you know.

25. **REASONING** Tom knows that $\frac{2}{4}$ and $\frac{3}{6}$ are equivalent to $\frac{1}{2}$. How can he use $\frac{1}{2}$ as a benchmark to write $\frac{4}{6}$, $\frac{1}{4}$, and $\frac{1}{2}$ in order from least to greatest?

Mixed Review and Test Prep

Order each set of numbers from least to greatest. (p. 46)

26. 110, 111, 101

27. 199, 89, 98

28. 455, 555, 545

Find the number that the variable stands for. (p. 242)

29. $4 \times s = 36$

30. $9 \times r = 45$

31. **TEST PREP** Cheryl bought two markers for $0.55 each and a notebook for $1.79. How much did she spend in all? (p. 120)

A $1.89
B $2.34
C $2.79
D $2.89

32. **TEST PREP** How many feet are in 4 yards? (p. 348)

F 20 feet
G 12 feet
H 9 feet
J 6 feet

Problem Solving LINKUP . . . to Social Studies

At the end of December, some African Americans celebrate Kwanzaa, a 7-day festival that ends with a feast, or "karumu," of healthful foods on December 31. They put a straw mat, called a "mkeka," in the middle of the table. Fresh fruit on the mat represents African harvest festivals.

1. Of the 7 Kwanzaa candles, 3 are red, 1 is black, and the rest are green. What fraction names the part that is green?

2. Clarence takes $\frac{3}{4}$ cup grapes, $\frac{1}{2}$ cup strawberries, and $\frac{1}{4}$ cup blueberries from the mkeka. Use fraction bars to model the amounts of fruit. Write in order from least to greatest.

LESSON 5

Problem Solving Strategy
Make a Model

PROBLEM Three classmates ran a relay in the Spring Sports Day race. George ran $\frac{2}{3}$ mile, Rosa ran $\frac{7}{8}$ mile, and Ben ran $\frac{5}{6}$ mile. Who ran the farthest?

Quick Review

Compare. Write <, >, or = for each ●.

1. $\frac{2}{3}$ ● $\frac{2}{3}$
2. $\frac{4}{6}$ ● $\frac{3}{6}$
3. $\frac{1}{4}$ ● $\frac{2}{4}$
4. $\frac{4}{8}$ ● $\frac{3}{8}$
5. $\frac{2}{6}$ ● $\frac{1}{6}$

UNDERSTAND

- What are you asked to find?
- What information will you use?
- Is there information you will not use? If so, what?

PLAN

- What strategy can you use to solve the problem?

Make a model to show what part of a mile each person ran.

SOLVE

- How can you use the strategy to solve the problem?

Model the problem by using fraction bars.

Line up the fraction bars for $\frac{2}{3}$, $\frac{7}{8}$, and $\frac{5}{6}$.

Compare the lengths of the fraction bars.

Since $\frac{7}{8} > \frac{5}{6} > \frac{2}{3}$, Rosa ran the farthest.

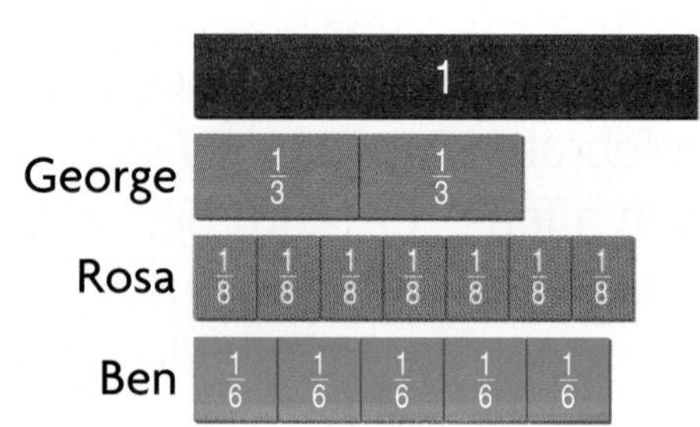

CHECK

- What other strategy could you use to solve the problem?

Problem Solving Practice

For 1–4, use *make a model* to solve.

1. What if George had run $\frac{9}{10}$ mile? Who would have run the farthest?
2. Tina used $\frac{2}{3}$ cup of milk, $\frac{1}{4}$ cup of sugar, and $\frac{1}{2}$ cup of nuts in a recipe. Of which ingredient did she use the most?

Strategies

Draw a Diagram or Picture
Make a Model or Act It Out
Make an Organized List
Find a Pattern
Make a Table or Graph
Predict and Test
Work Backward
Solve a Simpler Problem
Write a Number Sentence
Use Logical Reasoning

Problem Solving

Mr. Collins asked his science class to read a book on insects. By Friday, Alfredo had read $\frac{1}{2}$ of the book. Courtney had read $\frac{2}{5}$ of the book. Sandy had read $\frac{2}{8}$ of the book.

3. Which statement is true?
   - **A** $\frac{2}{8} > \frac{2}{5} > \frac{1}{2}$
   - **B** $\frac{1}{2} > \frac{2}{5} > \frac{2}{8}$
   - **C** $\frac{1}{2} > \frac{2}{8} > \frac{2}{5}$
   - **D** $\frac{2}{5} > \frac{2}{8} > \frac{1}{2}$

4. Who had read the greatest part of the book?
   - **F** Alfredo
   - **G** Courtney
   - **H** Sandy

Mixed Strategy Practice

5. **REASONING** Mohammed folded a sheet of notebook paper in half and then folded it in half again. He unfolded the paper and shaded one of the equal parts red. What fraction shows how many parts are red?
6. Eric had 74 baseball cards. He traded 26 of his cards for 12 of Paul's cards. How many cards does he have now?
7. Arlo has basketball practice from 3:30 P.M. to 5:00 P.M. It takes him a half hour to get home and one hour to do his homework before dinner. At what time does he eat dinner?
8. **REASONING** Kathy is cutting a pie into 8 equal slices. Julie is cutting a pie into 6 equal slices. Kathy says her slices will be larger because 8 is greater than 6. Do you agree? Explain.

LESSON 6

Mixed Numbers

Quick Review

Write a fraction for the shaded part.

1.
2.
3.
4.
5.

VOCABULARY

mixed number

Learn

APPLE FRACTIONS Miss Nell has 6 children in her after-school group. She gave each child $\frac{1}{4}$ of an apple. How many apples did she give to the children in all?

Here are two ways to find the total number of apples.

One Way

You can make a model.

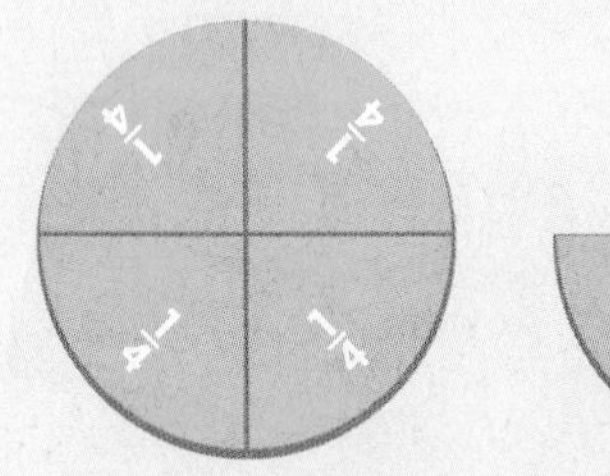

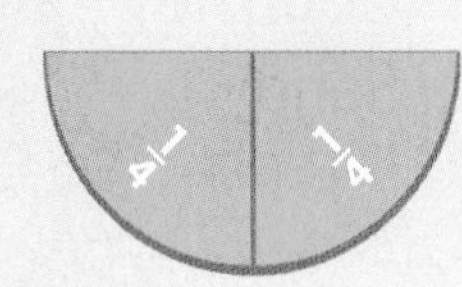

There are $\frac{6}{4}$ in all.
$\frac{4}{4} = 1$ whole

So, $\frac{6}{4} = 1 + \frac{2}{4}$, or $1\frac{2}{4}$.

Another Way

You can use a number line.

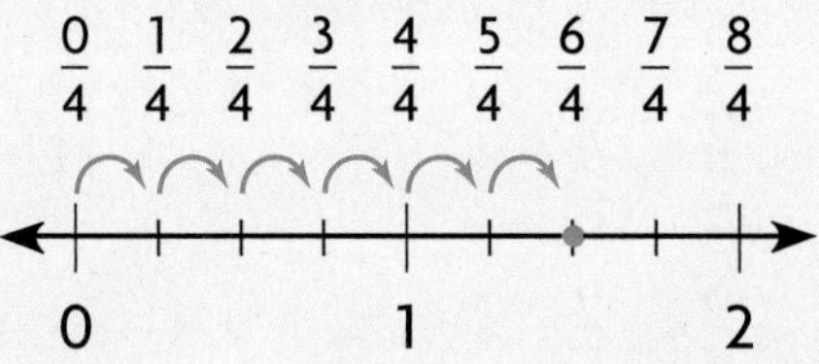

Show one jump for each $\frac{1}{4}$. Six jumps on the number line is two fourths more than 1.

So, $\frac{6}{4} = 1 + \frac{2}{4}$, or $1\frac{2}{4}$.

Read: one and two fourths **Write:** $1\frac{2}{4}$

So, Miss Nell gave the children $1\frac{2}{4}$ apples in all.

The number $1\frac{2}{4}$ is a mixed number. A **mixed number** is made up of a whole number and a fraction.

Check

1. **Explain** how to write $\frac{3}{2}$ as a mixed number.

Write a mixed number for the parts that are shaded.

2. 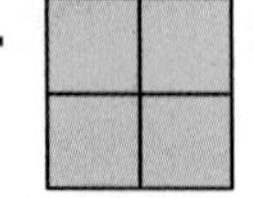 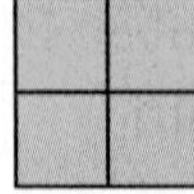 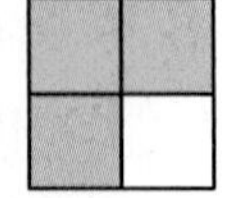

3. 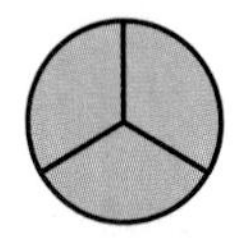 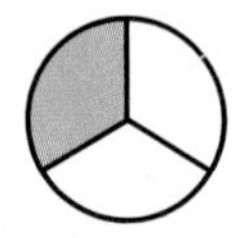

4. 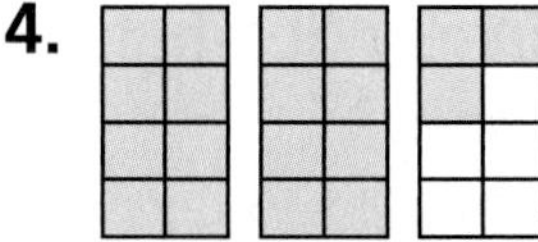

Practice and Problem Solving

Extra Practice, page 534, Set E

Write a mixed number for the parts that are shaded.

5. 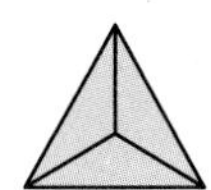 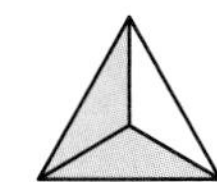

6. 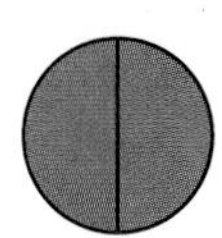

7. 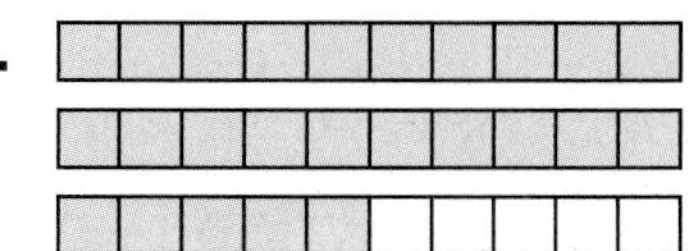

For 8–12, use the number line to write the mixed number.

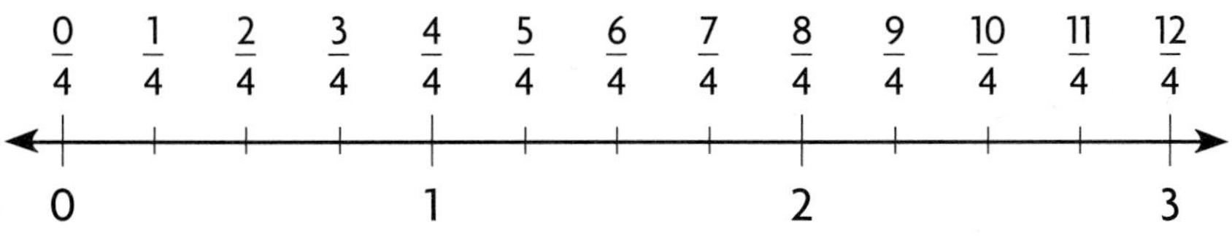

8. $\frac{5}{4}$ **9.** $\frac{7}{4}$ **10.** $\frac{11}{4}$ **11.** $\frac{10}{4}$ **12.** $\frac{9}{4}$

For 13–17, make a model to show the mixed number.

13. $1\frac{5}{8}$ **14.** $2\frac{1}{2}$ **15.** $1\frac{2}{3}$ **16.** $3\frac{3}{4}$ **17.** $1\frac{3}{10}$

18. Oren said that there were $2\frac{1}{2}$ pizzas. If all of the pieces were eighths, how many pieces of pizza were there?

19. Vocabulary Power The word *equivalent* means "equal in value." Write a mixed number that is equivalent to $2\frac{4}{6}$.

20. Each cake has 10 equal slices. If each person eats one slice, how many cakes will 28 people eat? Draw a picture to explain.

21. **Write About It** Explain why a fraction is equal to 1 when the numerator and denominator are equal.

22. Chris is making a model to show $2\frac{3}{6}$. How many sixths will he need for his model?

23. REASONING Since $\frac{2}{2}$ equals 1, what does $\frac{6}{2}$ equal?

Mixed Review and Test Prep

Find the number that the variable stands for. (p. 242)

24. $7 \times r = 35$
$r = \underline{?}$

25. $s \times 4 = 36$
$s = \underline{?}$

26. $24 \div t = 6$
$t = \underline{?}$

27. $u \div 8 = 2$
$u = \underline{?}$

28. **TEST PREP** Jenna has 12 tomato plants in 4 equal rows. Which expression tells how many plants are in each row? (p. 264)

A $12 + 4$
B $12 - 4$
C $12 \div 4$
D 12×4

Extra Practice

Set A (pp. 516–519)

Write a fraction in numbers and in words that names the shaded part.

1. 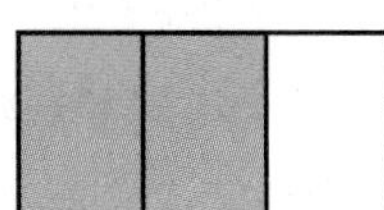
2. 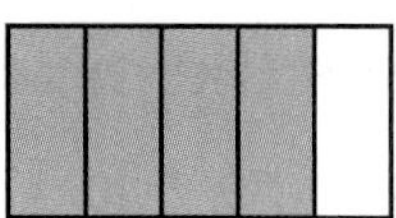
3. 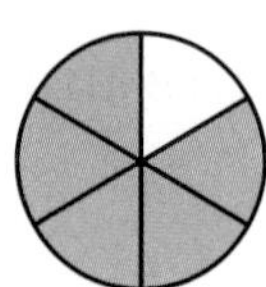

Make a model of each, using fraction circle pieces. Then write the fraction, using numbers.

4. one eighth
5. four out of six
6. two divided by five

Set B (pp. 520–521)

1. Draw 4 nickels. Circle $\frac{3}{4}$ of them.
2. Draw 5 rectangles. Circle $\frac{1}{5}$ of them.
3. Draw 8 triangles. Circle $\frac{5}{8}$ of them.

Set C (pp. 522–525)

Find an equivalent fraction. Use fraction bars.

1. 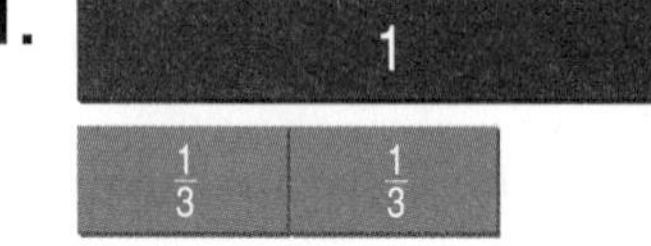

2. 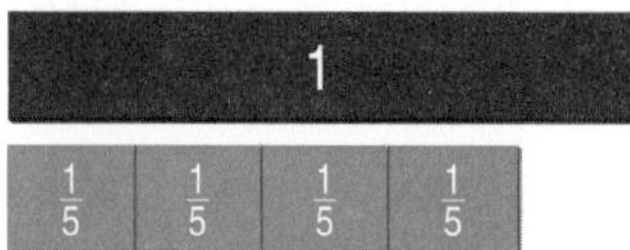

3. 

Set D (pp. 526–529)

Compare. Write <, >, or = for each ●.

1. 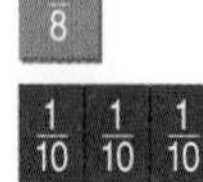

$\frac{1}{8}$ ● $\frac{3}{10}$
2. 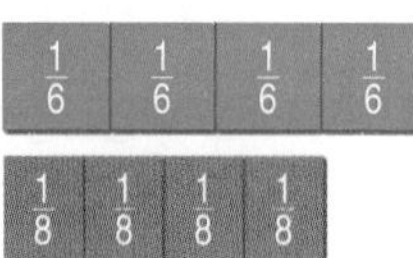

$\frac{4}{6}$ ● $\frac{4}{8}$
3. 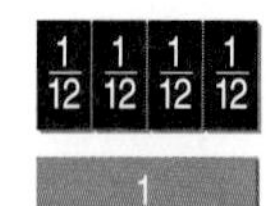

$\frac{4}{12}$ ● $\frac{1}{3}$

4. Use fraction bars to order $\frac{1}{2}$, $\frac{3}{10}$, and $\frac{2}{3}$ from greatest to least.

Set E (pp. 532–533)

Write a mixed number for the parts that are shaded.

1. 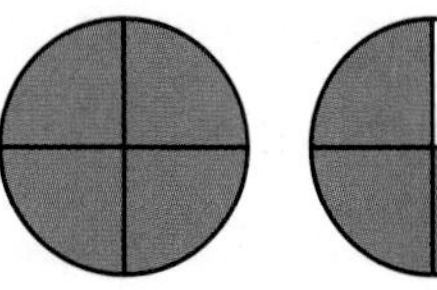
2. 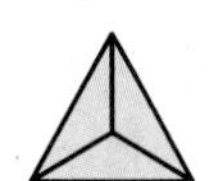 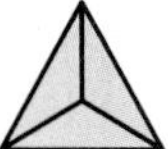 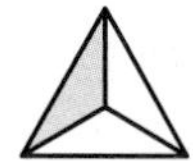
3. 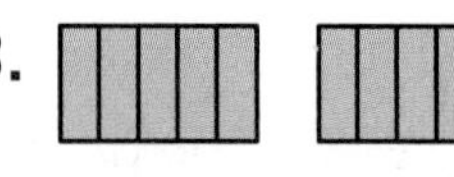 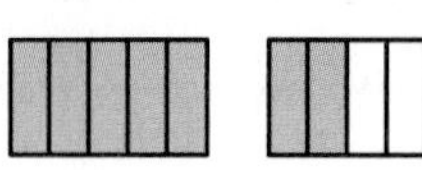

Review/Test

✓ CHECK VOCABULARY AND CONCEPTS

Choose the best term from the box.

fraction
numerator
denominator
mixed number

1. In the fraction $\frac{3}{8}$, the 3 is called the _?_. (p. 516)
2. A number that names part of a whole or part of a group is a _?_. (p. 516)
3. A number that is made up of a whole number and a fraction is called a _?_. (p. 532)

Find the missing numerator. Use fraction bars. (pp. 522–525)

4. 

$\frac{1}{4} = \frac{■}{12}$

5. 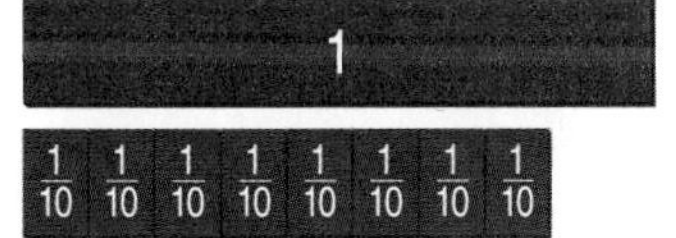

$\frac{8}{10} = \frac{■}{5}$

6. 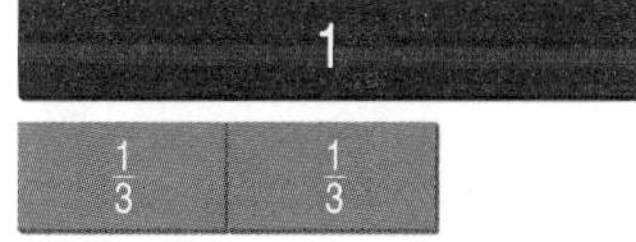

$\frac{2}{3} = \frac{■}{6}$

✓ CHECK SKILLS

Write a fraction in numbers and in words that names the shaded part. (pp. 516–519)

7. 
8. 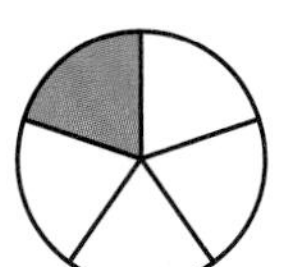
9. 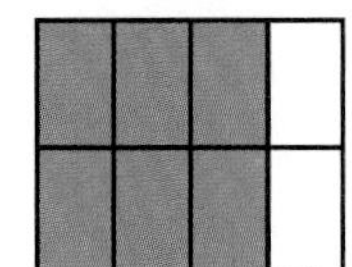
10. 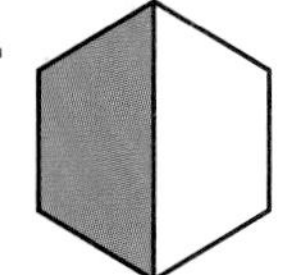

Write a mixed number for the parts that are shaded. (pp. 532–533)

11. 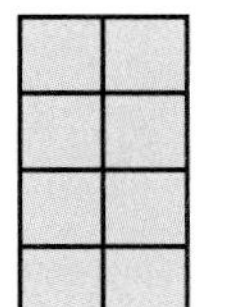
12. 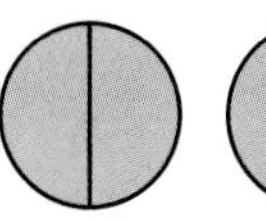 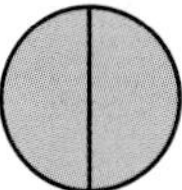 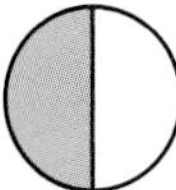
13. 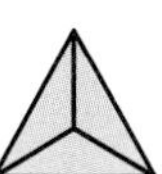 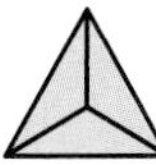 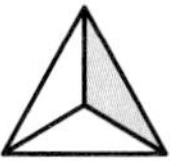

✓ CHECK PROBLEM SOLVING

Use *make a model* to solve. (pp. 530–531)

14. Luke walks $\frac{1}{2}$ mile, Karen walks $\frac{4}{5}$ mile, and Darius walks $\frac{1}{3}$ mile. Who walks the farthest?

15. Katherine has 3 yellow pins, 4 blue pins, and 2 red pins. What fraction of the pins are red?

Standardized Test Prep

NUMBER SENSE, CONCEPTS, AND OPERATIONS

1. Which of the following is forty-two thousand, five hundred nineteen?

A 42,590 **C** 4,259
B 42,519 **D** 42,509

2. Which letter on the number line stands for a fraction that is greater than $\frac{5}{10}$ and less than $\frac{8}{10}$?

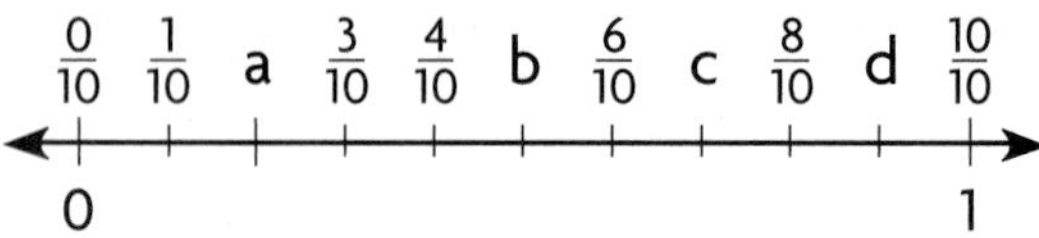

F a **H** c
G b **J** d

3. Nick made this spinner.

Which fraction names the part of the spinner that is blue?

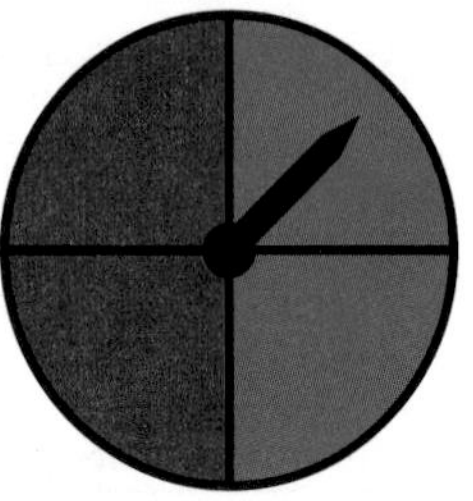

A $\frac{1}{4}$ **C** $\frac{2}{2}$

B $\frac{1}{2}$ **D** $\frac{4}{2}$

4. Explain It At Parkwood School, there are 428 students in the third grade and 371 students in the fourth grade. ESTIMATE how many students are in the third and fourth grades in all. Explain your answer.

MEASUREMENT

> **TIP** **Understand the problem.** See item 5. Each jar holds one pint of soup. So the number of jars the chef needs is equal to the number of pints in 3 quarts.

5. A chef made 3 quarts of soup. He stores all of the soup in jars that hold one pint each. How many jars does he need?

1 quart = 2 pints

F 1
G 2
H 4
J 6

6. At midnight, the temperature was 10°F less than the temperature shown on this thermometer.

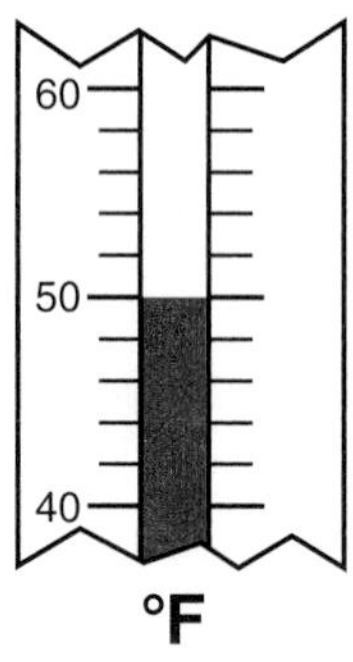

What was the temperature at midnight?

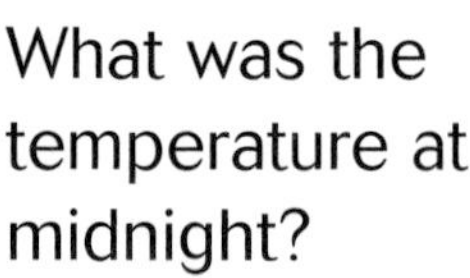

A 40°F
B 45°F
C 50°F
D 60°F

7. Explain It James bought a bookmark for 79¢ and a book for $4.95. About how many dollars did he spend in all? Explain.

ALGEBRAIC THINKING

8. Which figure will be next in this pattern?

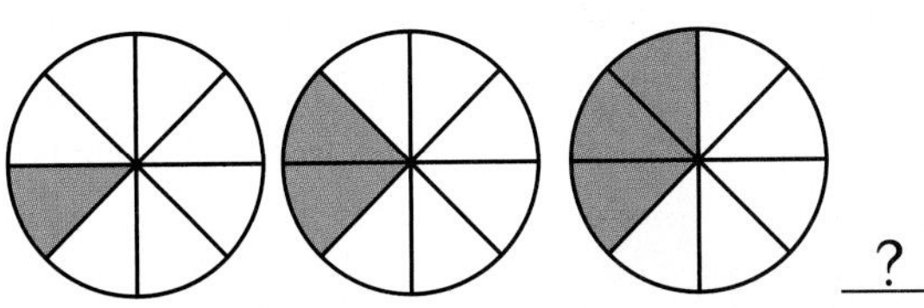

?

F

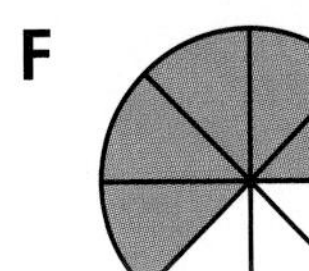

H

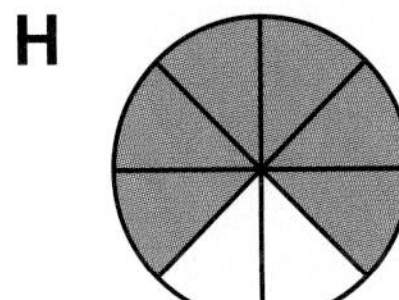

G

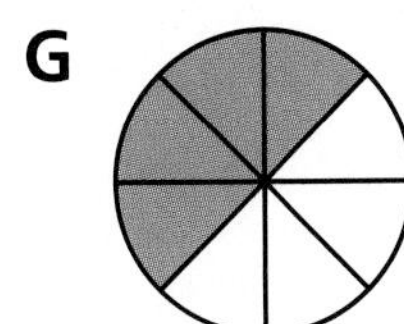

J

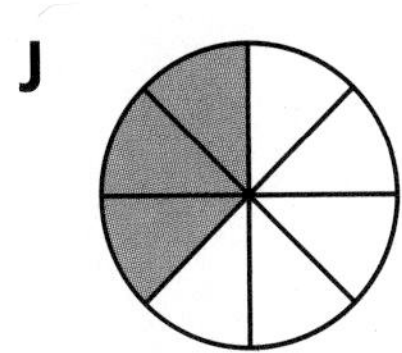

9. Which number completes the equation?

$4 \times 6 = \blacksquare + 13$

A 7
B 10
C 11
D 15

10. Explain It Mr. Warren needs 6 apples to make one pie. He wants to make 3 pies. Does the equation below show how many apples he needs in all? Explain.

$6 + 3 = 9$

DATA ANALYSIS AND PROBABILITY

11. Maria has a bag of marbles. There are 7 red marbles, 2 blue marbles, 4 green marbles, and 5 purple marbles in the bag. Which color is she **most likely** to pull from the bag?

F red
G blue
H green
J purple

12. Miss Kaley's students are writing poems for a class book. The graph shows how many poems some of her students have written.

POEMS

Amy	○ ○ ○ ◖
Matthew	○ ○ ○
Nina	○ ○
Seth	○ ○ ○

Key: Each ○ = 2 poems.

How many poems have these four students written in all?

A 12
B 20
C 21
D 23

13. Explain It Ross is at an ice cream shop. He can choose vanilla, chocolate, or strawberry ice cream. He can choose nuts, sprinkles, or coconut for a topping. How many different combinations of one flavor of ice cream and one topping are there? Explain how you know.

CHAPTER 26

Add and Subtract Like Fractions

FAST FACT • SOCIAL STUDIES Corn bread was a favorite food of early pioneers. It is usually served warm with butter.

PROBLEM SOLVING **This recipe serves 4 people. How can you change the recipe to serve 8 people? Rewrite the recipe.**

Corn Bread

1 cup cornmeal

$\frac{1}{4}$ cup flour

$\frac{1}{2}$ teaspoon baking powder

$\frac{1}{8}$ teaspoon baking soda

$\frac{3}{4}$ teaspoon salt

1 egg

1 tablespoon corn oil

$\frac{3}{4}$ cup buttermilk

Mix dry ingredients. Add egg, oil, and buttermilk. Mix well. Pour batter into a hot iron skillet. Bake at 425° for 20 to 25 minutes.

CHECK WHAT YOU KNOW

Use this page to help you review and remember important skills needed for Chapter 26.

✓ EQUIVALENT FRACTIONS

Find the missing numerator. Use fraction bars.

1. 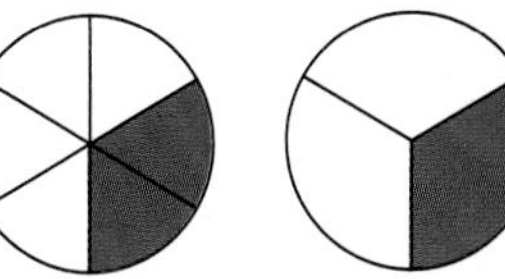

$\frac{2}{6} = \frac{■}{3}$

2. 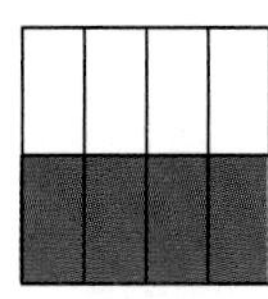

$\frac{4}{8} = \frac{■}{4}$

3. 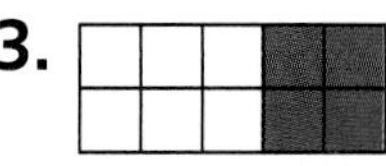 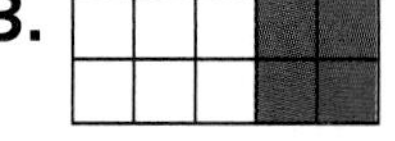 

$\frac{4}{10} = \frac{■}{5}$

✓ COMPARE FRACTIONS

Compare. Write $<$, $>$, or $=$ for each ●.

4. 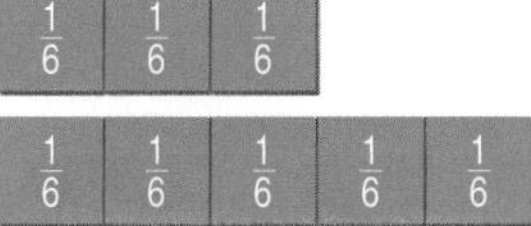

$\frac{3}{6}$ ● $\frac{5}{6}$

5. 

$\frac{4}{5}$ ● $\frac{6}{10}$

6. 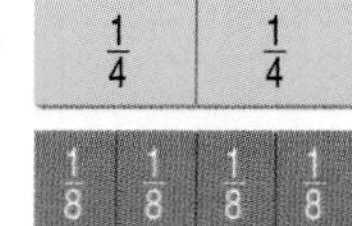

$\frac{2}{4}$ ● $\frac{4}{8}$

VOCABULARY POWER

REVIEW

numerator [no͞o′mə•rā•tər] *noun*

The numerator of a fraction tells how many parts are being counted. *Numerator* comes from the Latin word *enumerate,* which means "count out." In the fraction $\frac{3}{4}$, which number is the numerator?

PREVIEW

like fractions

simplest form

www.harcourtschool.com/mathglossary

LESSON 1

Add Fractions

Quick Review

Name an equivalent fraction.

1. $\frac{4}{6}$ 2. $\frac{2}{8}$ 3. $\frac{2}{4}$

4. $\frac{2}{10}$ 5. $\frac{1}{2}$

VOCABULARY

like fractions

MATERIALS

fraction bars

Explore

Fractions that have the same denominator are called **like fractions**.

A fruit punch recipe says to add $\frac{2}{4}$ cup orange juice and $\frac{1}{4}$ cup pineapple juice. How much juice is needed altogether?

Remember

1 → numerator
2 → denominator

Activity

Use fraction bars to find $\frac{2}{4} + \frac{1}{4}$.

STEP 1

Line up two $\frac{1}{4}$ fraction bars under the bar for 1.

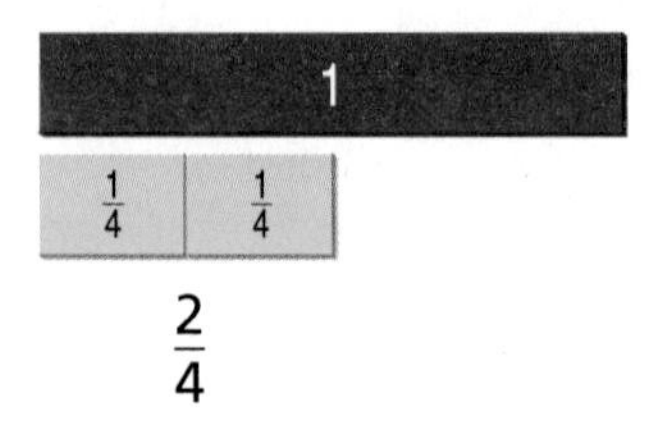

$\frac{2}{4}$

STEP 2

Add one more $\frac{1}{4}$ fraction bar.

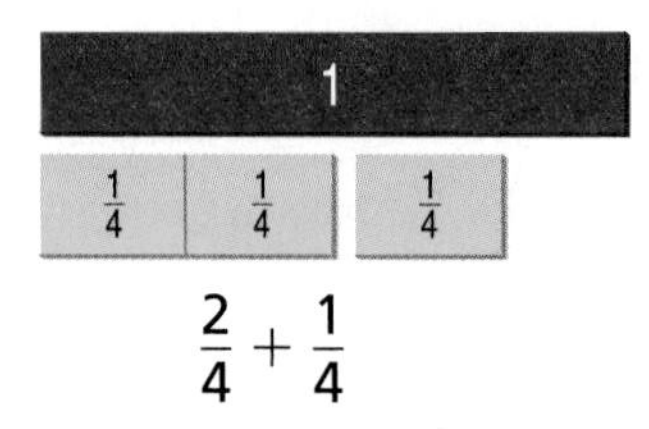

$\frac{2}{4} + \frac{1}{4}$

STEP 3

Count the number of $\frac{1}{4}$ fraction bars.

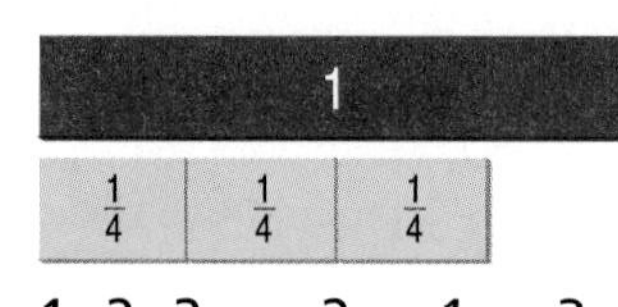

$\frac{1}{4}, \frac{2}{4}, \frac{3}{4}$, or $\frac{2}{4} + \frac{1}{4} = \frac{3}{4}$

So, the recipe calls for $\frac{3}{4}$ cup juice altogether.

- Why doesn't the denominator change when you find the sum?
- Explain how you could use fraction bars to find $\frac{1}{3} + \frac{1}{3}$.

I'm counting the fraction bars to find the sum: $\frac{1}{6}, \frac{2}{6}, \frac{3}{6}$... What comes next?

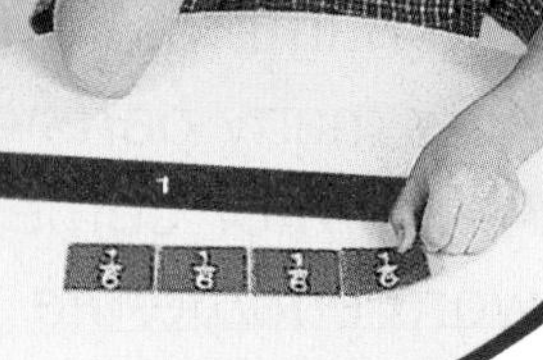

Try It

Use fraction bars to find the sum.

a. $\frac{3}{6} + \frac{1}{6}$ b. $\frac{3}{5} + \frac{2}{5}$

Connect

Add like fractions by adding the numerators.

Example

Tom peeled an orange. It had 8 wedges. He ate 1 wedge, or $\frac{1}{8}$ of it. Then he ate 4 more wedges, or $\frac{4}{8}$ of it. What fraction did he eat in all?

Model

Add the number of $\frac{1}{8}$ wedges that Tom ate.

 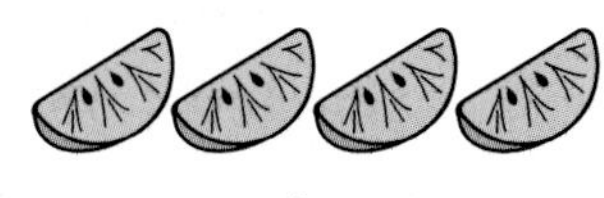

$\frac{1}{8} + \frac{4}{8}$

Record

1 wedge + 4 wedges = 5 wedges

$\frac{1}{8} + \frac{4}{8} = \frac{5}{8}$

So, Tom ate $\frac{5}{8}$ of the orange.

MATH IDEA When you add *like* fractions, you add the numerators, and the denominators stay the same.

Practice and Problem Solving

Find the sum.

1. 

$\frac{1}{5} + \frac{2}{5} = ■$

2. 

$\frac{3}{8} + \frac{3}{8} = ■$

3. 

$\frac{1}{3} + \frac{1}{3} = ■$

Use fraction bars to find the sum.

4. $\frac{2}{5} + \frac{2}{5} = ■$
5. $\frac{1}{6} + \frac{4}{6} = ■$
6. $\frac{4}{10} + \frac{3}{10} = ■$
7. $\frac{3}{8} + \frac{2}{8} = ■$

8. Kris has 6 plums and 2 apples. She buys 2 more apples. What fraction of the fruit are apples?
9. A recipe calls for $\frac{1}{4}$ cup sugar. Celia wants to double the recipe. How much sugar will she need?

Mixed Review and Test Prep

10. $7 \times 9 = ■$ (p. 200)
11. $8 \times 6 = ■$ (p. 196)
12. $72 \div 9 = ■$ (p. 278)
13. 1 foot = ■ inches (p. 342)

14. **TEST PREP** Which figure has four right angles? (p. 396)

A triangle
B rectangle
C circle
D ray

LESSON 2

Add Fractions

Learn

PIECES PLUS When you add fractions, you can show the sum in simplest form. A fraction is in **simplest form** when it uses the largest fraction bars possible.

A whole sub sandwich has 8 pieces. Abby ate 2 pieces. Chris ate 2 pieces. How much of the sandwich did they eat?

$\frac{2}{8} + \frac{2}{8} = ?$

Find $\frac{2}{8} + \frac{2}{8}$ in simplest form.

Quick Review

Compare. Write <, >, or = for each ●.

1. $\frac{5}{8}$ ● $\frac{7}{8}$
2. $\frac{3}{4}$ ● $\frac{1}{4}$
3. $\frac{3}{6}$ ● $\frac{1}{2}$
4. $\frac{6}{10}$ ● $\frac{2}{5}$
5. $\frac{1}{2}$ ● $\frac{4}{8}$

VOCABULARY
simplest form

HANDS ON

Activity

Materials: fraction bars

STEP 1

Line up two $\frac{1}{8}$ fraction bars under the bar for 1.

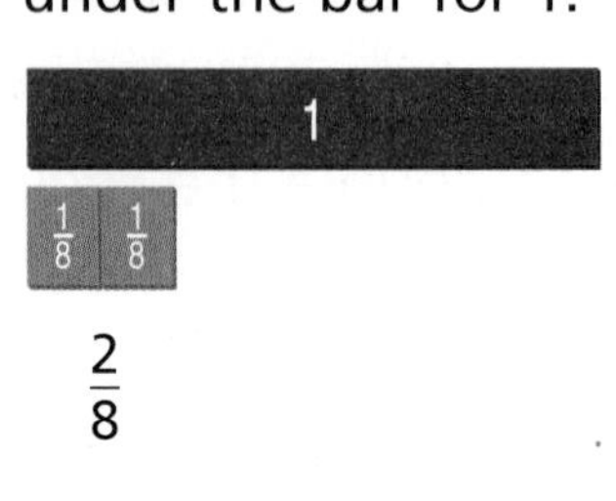

$\frac{2}{8}$

STEP 2

Add two more $\frac{1}{8}$ fraction bars.

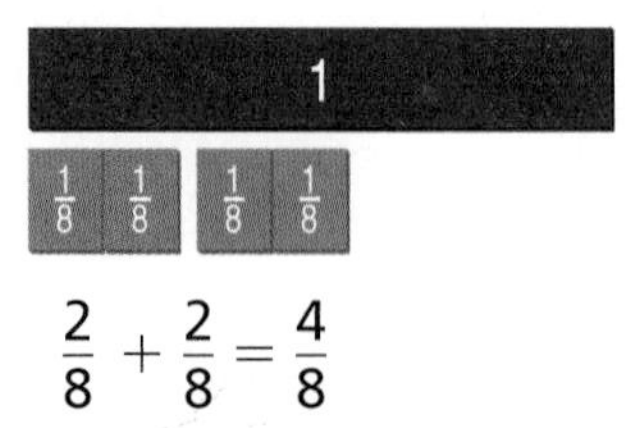

$\frac{2}{8} + \frac{2}{8} = \frac{4}{8}$

STEP 3

Find the largest fraction bar that is equivalent.

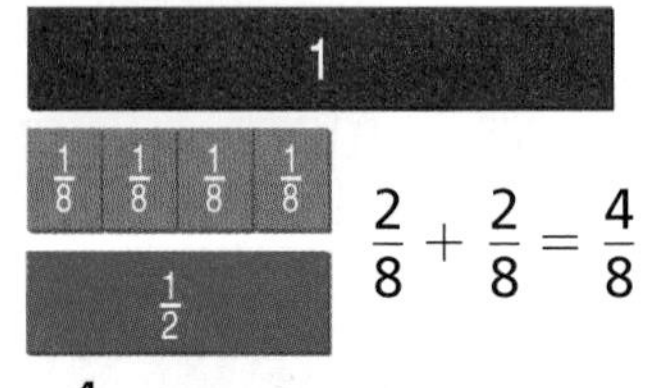

$\frac{2}{8} + \frac{2}{8} = \frac{4}{8}$

$\frac{4}{8}$ in simplest form is $\frac{1}{2}$.

So, Abby and Chris ate $\frac{1}{2}$ of the sub sandwich.

MATH IDEA You can use fraction bars to add fractions and to find the sum in simplest form.

Check

1. **Explain** how to find $\frac{3}{12} + \frac{1}{12}$ in simplest form.

Find the sum. Write the answer in simplest form.

2. 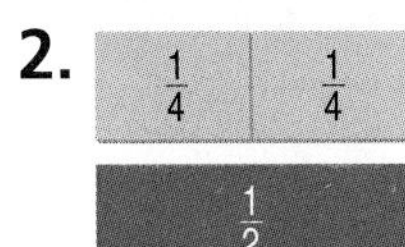

$\frac{1}{4} + \frac{1}{4} = \blacksquare$, or $\blacksquare$

3. 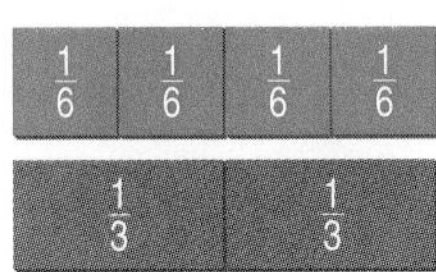

$\frac{2}{6} + \frac{2}{6} = \blacksquare$, or $\blacksquare$

4. 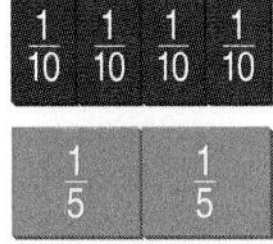

$\frac{2}{10} + \frac{2}{10} = \blacksquare$, or $\blacksquare$

Practice and Problem Solving

Extra Practice, page 552, Set A

Find the sum. Write the answer in simplest form. Use fraction bars if you wish.

5. 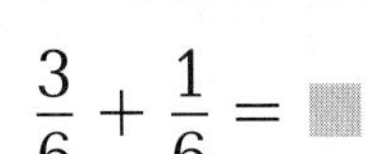

$\frac{3}{6} + \frac{1}{6} = \blacksquare$

6. 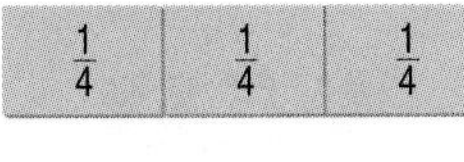

$\frac{2}{4} + \frac{1}{4} = \blacksquare$

7. 

$\frac{4}{8} + \frac{3}{8} = \blacksquare$

8. $\frac{1}{5} + \frac{1}{5} = \blacksquare$

9. $\frac{4}{6} + \frac{1}{6} = \blacksquare$

10. $\frac{5}{10} + \frac{4}{10} = \blacksquare$

11. $\frac{2}{6} + \frac{2}{6} = \blacksquare$

12. $\frac{4}{10} + \frac{4}{10} = \blacksquare$

13. $\frac{1}{3} + \frac{1}{3} = \blacksquare$

14. $\frac{3}{12} + \frac{6}{12} = \blacksquare$

15. $\frac{3}{5} + \frac{1}{5} = \blacksquare$

16. **REASONING** Lamar's mother cut a cake into 12 equal pieces. Lamar's family ate 4 pieces. What fraction, in simplest form, tells how much of the cake was *not* eaten?

17. **? What's the Question?** Sam folded his paper into 8 equal sections. He drew pictures on 3 of the sections. The answer is $\frac{5}{8}$.

Mixed Review and Test Prep

Find the difference.

18. $724 - 182$ (p. 96)

19. $400 - 63$ (p. 92)

20. $1,355 - 628$ (p. 96)

21. $3,742 - 1,281$ (p. 96)

22. **TEST PREP** A box is 4 cubes long, 3 cubes wide, and 2 cubes high. What is the volume of this box? (p. 452)

A 9 cubic units
B 16 cubic units
C 20 cubic units
D 24 cubic units

LESSON 3

Subtract Fractions

Quick Review

Find the difference.

1. 12 – 8 **2.** 15 – 6

3. 18 – 5 **4.** 21 – 8

5. 25 – 11

MATERIALS
fraction bars

Explore

Rebecca's dad has $\frac{7}{8}$ of his pan of corn bread to share with the family. If Rebecca eats $\frac{2}{8}$ of the corn bread, how much of the corn bread is left?

Activity

Use fraction bars to find $\frac{7}{8} - \frac{2}{8}$.

STEP 1

Line up seven $\frac{1}{8}$ fraction bars under the bar for 1.

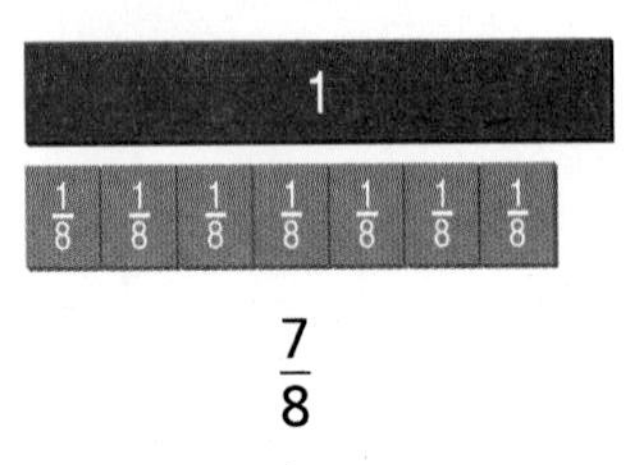

$\frac{7}{8}$

STEP 2

Take away two $\frac{1}{8}$ fraction bars.

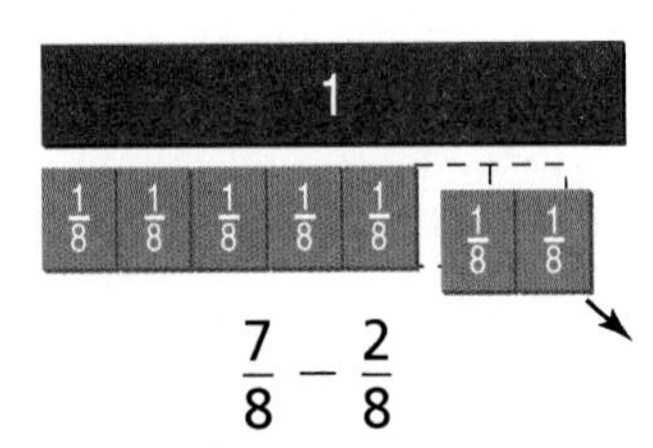

$\frac{7}{8} - \frac{2}{8}$

STEP 3

Count the number of $\frac{1}{8}$ fraction bars left.

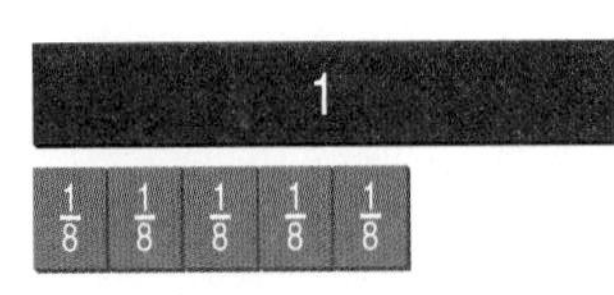

$\frac{7}{8} - \frac{2}{8} = \frac{5}{8}$

So, $\frac{5}{8}$ of the corn bread is left.

- Why doesn't the denominator change when you find $\frac{7}{8} - \frac{2}{8}$?

Try It

Use fraction bars to find the difference.

a. $\frac{3}{6} - \frac{1}{6} = ■$

b. $\frac{5}{8} - \frac{2}{8} = ■$

If I take away one of the $\frac{1}{6}$ bars, how many sixths will be left?

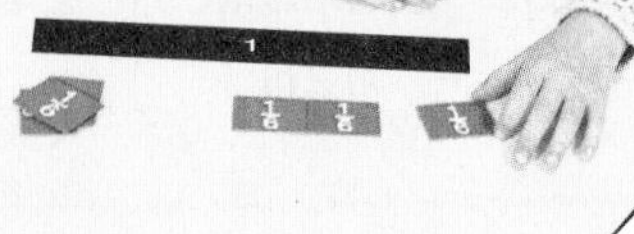

Connect

Subtract like fractions by subtracting the numerators.

Example $\frac{7}{10} - \frac{4}{10} = \blacksquare$

Model

$\frac{1}{10}$	$\frac{1}{10}$	$\frac{1}{10}$	$\frac{1}{10}$	$\frac{1}{10}$	$\frac{1}{10}$	$\frac{1}{10}$

$\frac{7}{10} - \frac{4}{10}$

Record

bars you start with		bars you take away		bars that are left
↓		↓		↓
$\frac{7}{10}$	$-$	$\frac{4}{10}$	$=$	$\frac{3}{10}$

MATH IDEA When you subtract *like* fractions, you subtract the numerators, and the denominators stay the same.

Practice and Problem Solving

Find the difference.

1. | $\frac{1}{8}$ | $\frac{1}{8}$ | $\frac{1}{8}$ | $\frac{1}{8}$ | $\frac{1}{8}$ | $\frac{1}{8}$ | $\frac{1}{8}$ |
   |---|---|---|---|---|---|---|

   $\frac{7}{8} - \frac{4}{8} = \blacksquare$

2. | $\frac{1}{10}$ | $\frac{1}{10}$ | $\frac{1}{10}$ | $\frac{1}{10}$ | $\frac{1}{10}$ | $\frac{1}{10}$ | $\frac{1}{10}$ | $\frac{1}{10}$ |
   |---|---|---|---|---|---|---|---|

   $\frac{8}{10} - \frac{3}{10} = \blacksquare$

3. | $\frac{1}{12}$ | $\frac{1}{12}$ | $\frac{1}{12}$ | $\frac{1}{12}$ | $\frac{1}{12}$ | $\frac{1}{12}$ |
   |---|---|---|---|---|---|

   $\frac{6}{12} - \frac{2}{12} = \blacksquare$

Use fraction bars to find the difference.

4. $\frac{4}{5} - \frac{1}{5} = \blacksquare$
5. $\frac{6}{8} - \frac{3}{8} = \blacksquare$
6. $\frac{9}{10} - \frac{7}{10} = \blacksquare$
7. $\frac{2}{3} - \frac{1}{3} = \blacksquare$
8. $\frac{4}{6} - \frac{2}{6} = \blacksquare$
9. $\frac{11}{12} - \frac{6}{12} = \blacksquare$
10. $\frac{7}{8} - \frac{4}{8} = \blacksquare$
11. $\frac{8}{10} - \frac{7}{10} = \blacksquare$
12. Wilson earned \$30 mowing lawns and \$25 raking leaves. How much more does Wilson need to have a total of \$100?

Mixed Review and Test Prep

Find the sum. (pp. 8, 72)

13. $\begin{array}{r} 73 \\ 86 \\ +95 \\ \hline \end{array}$

14. $\begin{array}{r} 345 \\ 519 \\ +271 \\ \hline \end{array}$

15. $\begin{array}{r} 867 \\ 124 \\ +436 \\ \hline \end{array}$

16. $342 + 139 + 214 = \blacksquare$ (p. 72)

17. **TEST PREP** Malcolm practiced guitar from 11:40 A.M. to 12:55 P.M. How long did he practice? (p. 134)

A 15 minutes
B 1 hour 5 minutes
C 1 hour 15 minutes
D 2 hours 15 minutes

LESSON 4

Subtract Fractions

Quick Review

Find the sum. Write the answer in simplest form.

1. $\frac{3}{12} + \frac{1}{12} = \blacksquare$
2. $\frac{1}{4} + \frac{2}{4} = \blacksquare$
3. $\frac{5}{8} + \frac{1}{8} = \blacksquare$
4. $\frac{3}{10} + \frac{6}{10} = \blacksquare$
5. $\frac{2}{6} + \frac{3}{6} = \blacksquare$

Learn

MANY MORE Kara and Eli shared 10 graham crackers. Kara ate 5 of them. Eli ate 3 of them. What fraction tells how many more of the crackers Kara ate than Eli?

Find $\frac{5}{10} - \frac{3}{10}$ in simplest form.

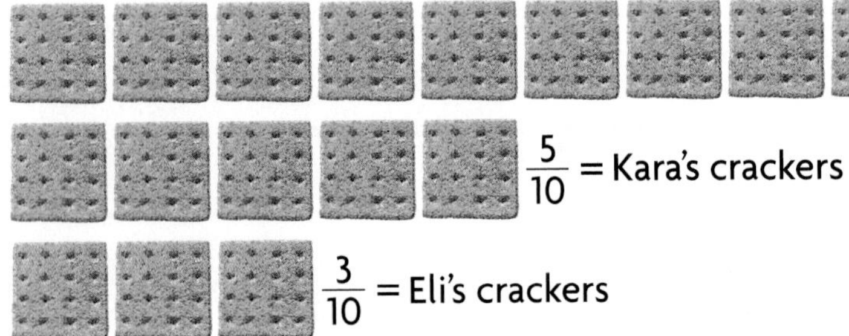

$\frac{10}{10}$ = Total number of crackers

$\frac{5}{10}$ = Kara's crackers

$\frac{3}{10}$ = Eli's crackers

HANDS ON

Activity

Materials: fraction bars

STEP 1

Line up the fraction bars for $\frac{5}{10}$ and $\frac{3}{10}$ under the bar for 1.

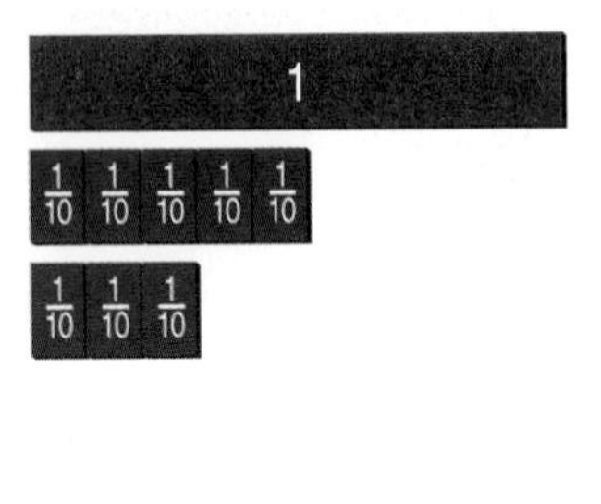

STEP 2

Compare the bars to find the difference.

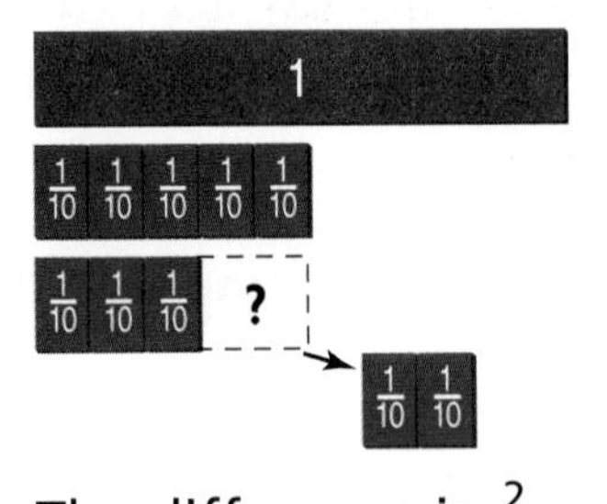

The difference is $\frac{2}{10}$.

STEP 3

Find the largest fraction bar that is equivalent.

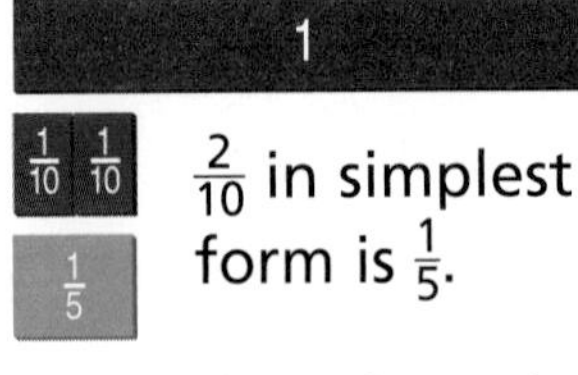

$\frac{2}{10}$ in simplest form is $\frac{1}{5}$.

$\frac{5}{10} - \frac{3}{10} = \frac{2}{10}$, or $\frac{1}{5}$

So, Kara ate $\frac{1}{5}$ more of the crackers than Eli ate.

- How many crackers did Kara and Eli eat altogether? How many are left?

Subtracting Fractions

What if Kara and Eli made 8 peanut butter crackers and ate 4 of the crackers? What fraction of the crackers are left?

Use fraction bars to find $\frac{8}{8} - \frac{4}{8}$ in simplest form.

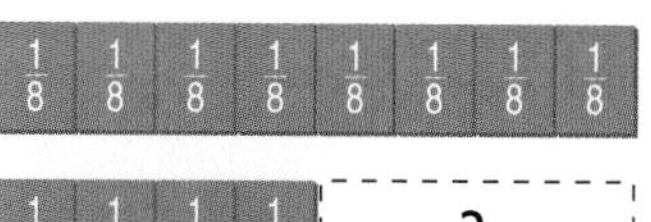

$\frac{8}{8}$ = the total number of crackers

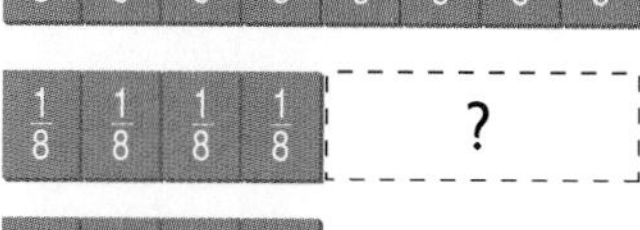

$\frac{4}{8}$ = the 4 crackers they ate

$\frac{4}{8}$ = the crackers that are left

$\frac{4}{8}$ in simplest form is $\frac{1}{2}$.

$\frac{8}{8} - \frac{4}{8} = \frac{4}{8}$, or $\frac{1}{2}$

So, $\frac{1}{2}$ of the crackers are left.

Technology Link

More Practice: Harcourt Mega Math Fraction Action, *Fraction Flare Up*, Level H

MATH IDEA You can compare fraction bars to subtract fractions and to find the difference in simplest form.

Check

1. **Explain** how you can use fraction bars to find $\frac{3}{4} - \frac{1}{4}$ in simplest form.

Compare. Find the difference. Write the answer in simplest form.

2.

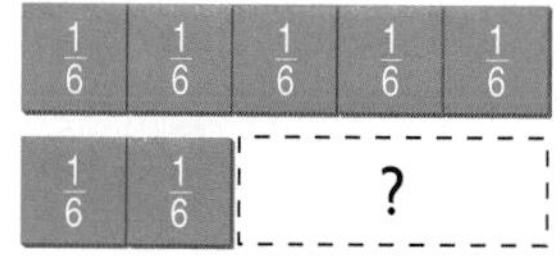

$\frac{5}{6} - \frac{2}{6} = \blacksquare$

3. 1/12 1/12 1/12 1/12 1/12 1/12 — 1/12 1/12 ?

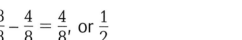

$\frac{6}{12} - \frac{2}{12} = \blacksquare$

4.

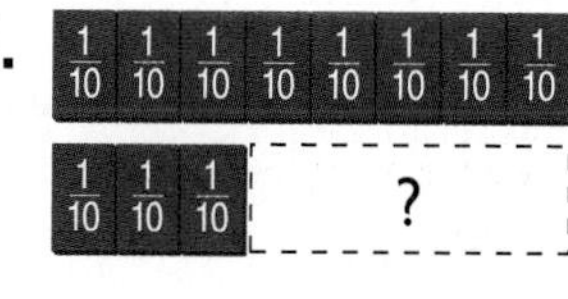

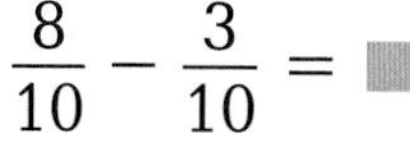

$\frac{8}{10} - \frac{3}{10} = \blacksquare$

5.

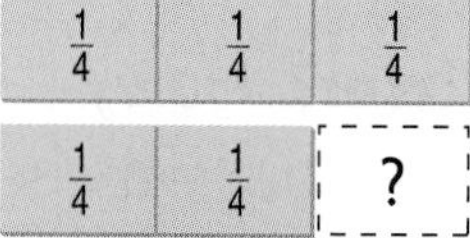

$\frac{3}{4} - \frac{2}{4} = \blacksquare$

6.

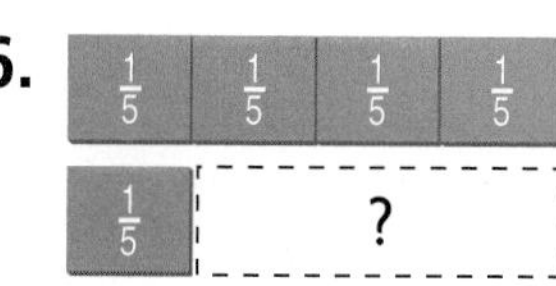

$\frac{4}{5} - \frac{1}{5} = \blacksquare$

7.

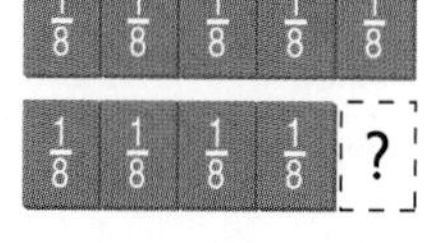

$\frac{5}{8} - \frac{4}{8} = \blacksquare$

LESSON CONTINUES

Practice and Problem Solving

Extra Practice, page 552, Set B

Compare. Find the difference. Write the answer in simplest form.

8. 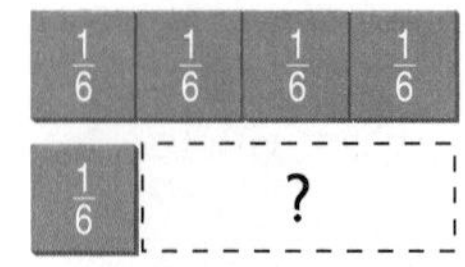

$\frac{4}{6} - \frac{1}{6} = ■$

9. 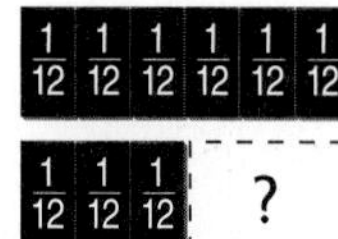

$\frac{6}{12} - \frac{3}{12} = ■$

10. 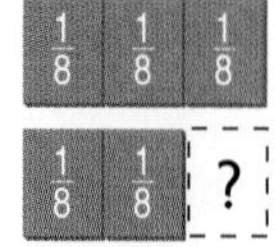

$\frac{3}{8} - \frac{2}{8} = ■$

11. 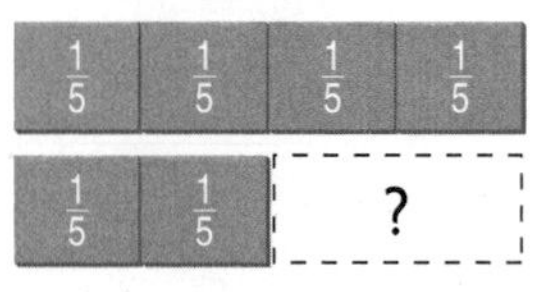

$\frac{4}{5} - \frac{2}{5} = ■$

12. 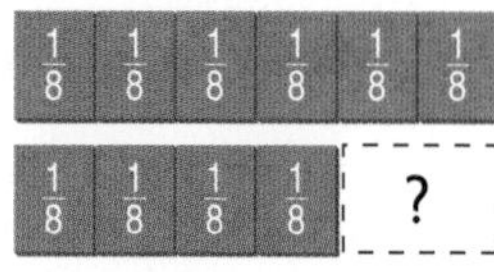

$\frac{6}{8} - \frac{4}{8} = ■$

13. 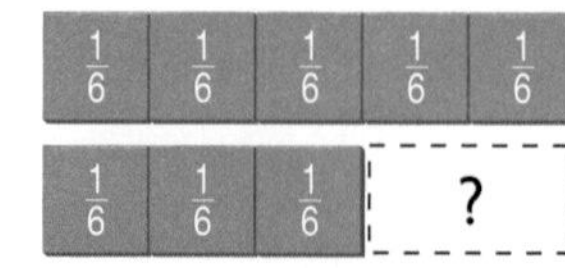

$\frac{5}{6} - \frac{3}{6} = ■$

Find the difference. Write the answer in simplest form. Use fraction bars if you wish.

14. $\frac{2}{3} - \frac{1}{3} = ■$ **15.** $\frac{4}{5} - \frac{1}{5} = ■$ **16.** $\frac{4}{6} - \frac{2}{6} = ■$ **17.** $\frac{5}{6} - \frac{1}{6} = ■$

18. $\frac{7}{10} - \frac{2}{10} = ■$ **19.** $\frac{7}{8} - \frac{5}{8} = ■$ **20.** $\frac{10}{12} - \frac{7}{12} = ■$ **21.** $\frac{6}{8} - \frac{1}{8} = ■$

22. $\frac{11}{12} - \frac{9}{12} = ■$ **23.** $\frac{8}{10} - \frac{5}{10} = ■$ **24.** $\frac{5}{6} - \frac{3}{6} = ■$ **25.** $\frac{6}{8} - \frac{2}{8} = ■$

26. **REASONING** There are 8 letters in the word *Virginia*. The letter *i* is $\frac{3}{8}$ of the word, and the letter *a* is $\frac{1}{8}$ of the word. What fraction of the word, in simplest form, are the vowels?

27. Dana cut an apple pie into 8 equal pieces. She shared the pie with 4 of her friends. Dana and each of her friends ate 1 piece of pie. What fraction of the pie is left?

28. **Vocabulary Power** The *denominator* in a fraction tells how many equal parts in all. Draw a picture to show the fraction two-fifths. Write the fraction and label the denominator.

29. **? What's the Error?** Haley wrote $\frac{5}{12} - \frac{3}{12} = 2$. What was her error?

30. **FAST FACT** • SOCIAL STUDIES Sylvester Graham was born in 1794. In 1829, he invented the graham cracker. How old was he in 1829?

31. **REASONING** An apple was cut into equal-size slices. Kinji ate 3 of them. If 6 slices of apple are left, what fraction of the apple did Kinji eat?

Mixed Review and Test Prep

Find the quotient. (p. 278)

32. $36 \div 9$ **33.** $40 \div 10$

34. $63 \div 9$ **35.** $100 \div 10$

36. $70 \div 10$ **37.** $45 \div 9$

38. $72 \div 9$ **39.** $10 \div 10$

40. $20 \div 10$ **41.** $54 \div 9$

42. $81 \div 9$ **43.** $60 \div 10$

44. **TEST PREP** How many centimeters are in 3 meters? (p. 358)

A 3 C 300
B 30 D 3,000

45. **TEST PREP** Roller-coaster tickets cost $1.50 each. Samantha bought 2 tickets. How much change should she receive from $5.00? (p. 120)

F $2.00 H $3.50
G $3.00 J $4.00

Problem Solving LINKUP... to Geography

You can use what you know about adding and subtracting fractions to find distances on a map. The scale tells you how distances are measured. On this map each unit represents $\frac{1}{10}$ of a mile.

What if you are visiting your friend Carl at his house after school? Use the map to answer the questions.

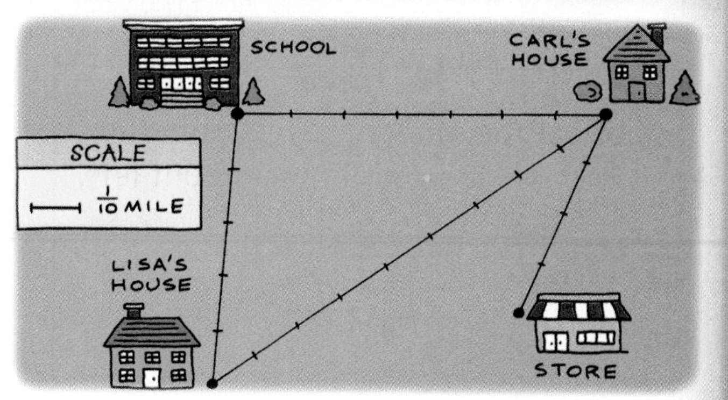

1. How much farther is the school than the store from Carl's house?

2. How far is Lisa's house from the school?

3. Which is farther from Carl's house, Lisa's house or the school? How much farther?

4. **REASONING** Carl says the store is $\frac{1}{2}$ mile from his house. Is he right? Explain your reasoning.

LESSON 5

Problem Solving Skill
Reasonable Answers

UNDERSTAND › PLAN › SOLVE › CHECK

Quick Review

Find the difference.

1. $\frac{8}{12} - \frac{3}{12}$
2. $\frac{9}{10} - \frac{2}{10}$
3. $\frac{5}{6} - \frac{4}{6}$
4. $\frac{7}{8} - \frac{4}{8}$
5. $\frac{2}{3} - \frac{1}{3}$

SOUNDS GOOD Whenever you solve a problem, always check to see that your answer is reasonable and makes sense.

Tanya's mother made a very large chocolate chip cookie. Tanya and Allie each ate $\frac{3}{8}$ of the cookie. What fraction of the cookie was left?

1 whole cookie $= \frac{8}{8}$

Example

STEP 1

Find out what the problem asks.

What fraction of the cookie was left after Tanya and Allie each ate $\frac{3}{8}$ of it?

STEP 2

Add to find how much of the cookie was eaten.

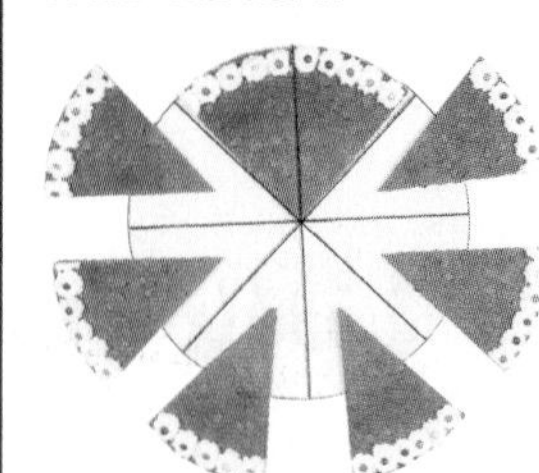

$\frac{3}{8} + \frac{3}{8} = \frac{6}{8}$

STEP 3

Subtract the amount eaten from the whole cookie to find the amount left.

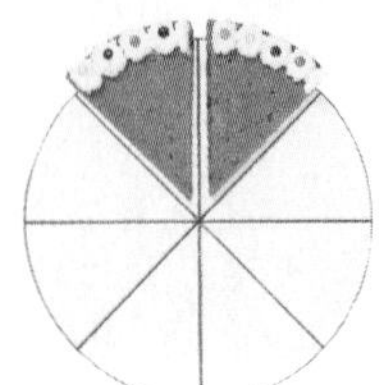

$\frac{8}{8} - \frac{6}{8} = \frac{2}{8}$

So, $\frac{2}{8}$, or $\frac{1}{4}$, of the cookie was left.

STEP 4

Check to see that your answer is reasonable and makes sense.

Think: The girls ate more than $\frac{1}{2}$ of the cookie. So, less than $\frac{1}{2}$ will be left. Since $\frac{2}{8}$ is less than $\frac{1}{2}$, it is a reasonable answer.

Talk About It

- Why is $\frac{8}{8}$ used for the whole cookie?
- Would it be reasonable to decide that $\frac{5}{8}$ of the cookie was left? Explain.

Problem Solving Practice

Problem Solving

Solve. Tell how you know your answer is reasonable.

1. Gil hiked $\frac{2}{5}$ of the mountain trail and rested. Then he hiked another $\frac{1}{5}$ of the trail. How much of the trail does he have left to hike?

2. Clyde opened a new box of cereal. He ate $\frac{1}{3}$ of the cereal in the box. How much cereal was left?

Amy planted $\frac{1}{4}$ of her garden on Monday and $\frac{1}{4}$ of her garden on Tuesday. She planted the rest on Wednesday. How much of the garden did she plant on Wednesday?

3. How can you solve the problem?

   A Compare $\frac{1}{4}$ and $\frac{1}{4}$.

   B Find $\frac{1}{4} + \frac{1}{4}$.

   C Find $\frac{1}{4} + \frac{1}{4}$, and then subtract from $\frac{4}{4}$.

   D Find $\frac{1}{4} - \frac{1}{4}$.

4. What is the answer to the question?

   F $\frac{1}{4}$ **G** $\frac{1}{2}$ **H** $\frac{3}{4}$ **J** $\frac{4}{4}$

Mixed Applications

5. **REASONING** Selma cut a pan of brownies into 3 equal pieces. Then she cut each of those pieces in half. She ate 2 of the pieces. What fraction of the brownies were left? Explain.

6. ALGEBRA The total number of Satoko's apples and pears was 12. She traded each pear for 2 apples. Then she had 15 apples in all. How many of each fruit did Satoko have to begin with?

7. **Write About It** Describe the pattern below. What will the fourteenth shape in the pattern be?

Extra Practice

Set A (pp. 542–543)

Find the sum. Write the answer in simplest form. Use fraction bars.

1. $\frac{2}{4} + \frac{1}{4} = \blacksquare$
2. $\frac{2}{5} + \frac{1}{5} = \blacksquare$
3. $\frac{4}{8} + \frac{1}{8} = \blacksquare$
4. $\frac{4}{10} + \frac{2}{10} = \blacksquare$
5. $\frac{1}{3} + \frac{1}{3} = \blacksquare$
6. $\frac{6}{12} + \frac{1}{12} = \blacksquare$
7. $\frac{3}{6} + \frac{2}{6} = \blacksquare$
8. $\frac{1}{4} + \frac{2}{4} = \blacksquare$
9. $\frac{1}{8} + \frac{2}{8} = \blacksquare$
10. $\frac{6}{10} + \frac{3}{10} = \blacksquare$
11. $\frac{2}{6} + \frac{2}{6} = \blacksquare$
12. $\frac{1}{12} + \frac{1}{12} = \blacksquare$

13. Miles gave $\frac{1}{5}$ of the cake to Molly and $\frac{2}{5}$ to Sarah. What fraction of the cake did Miles give away?

14. Gwen says that the simplest form of $\frac{6}{12}$ is $\frac{3}{6}$. Is she correct? Explain.

Set B (pp. 546–549)

Compare. Find the difference. Write the answer in simplest form.

1. $\frac{1}{5}$ $\frac{1}{5}$ $\frac{1}{5}$ $\frac{1}{5}$ / $\frac{1}{5}$ $\frac{1}{5}$

$\frac{4}{5} - \frac{2}{5} = \blacksquare$

2. 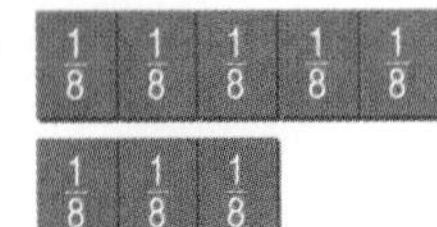

$\frac{5}{8} - \frac{3}{8} = \blacksquare$

3. 

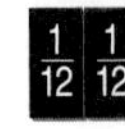

$\frac{8}{12} - \frac{2}{12} = \blacksquare$

Find the difference. Write the answer in simplest form. Use fraction bars.

4. $\frac{2}{3} - \frac{1}{3} = \blacksquare$
5. $\frac{5}{6} - \frac{2}{6} = \blacksquare$
6. $\frac{3}{4} - \frac{2}{4} = \blacksquare$
7. $\frac{5}{10} - \frac{3}{10} = \blacksquare$
8. $\frac{3}{4} - \frac{1}{4} = \blacksquare$
9. $\frac{4}{5} - \frac{1}{5} = \blacksquare$
10. $\frac{7}{8} - \frac{5}{8} = \blacksquare$
11. $\frac{10}{12} - \frac{1}{12} = \blacksquare$

12. Nate and Sam ate a candy bar. Nate ate $\frac{5}{10}$ of the candy, and Sam ate $\frac{5}{10}$ of the candy. How much of the candy bar did the boys eat in all?

13. Valencia and Dora ate some jelly-beans. Valencia ate $\frac{3}{8}$ of them, and Dora ate $\frac{5}{8}$ of them. What fraction tells how much more of the jelly-beans Dora ate than Valencia?

Review/Test

✓ CHECK VOCABULARY AND CONCEPTS

Choose the best term from the box.

like fractions
simplest form
denominator

1. Fractions that have the same denominator are __?__. (p. 540)
2. When a fraction uses the largest fraction bar or bars possible, it is in __?__. (p. 542)

✓ CHECK SKILLS

Find the sum. Write the answer in simplest form. Use fraction bars if you wish. (pp. 542–543)

3. $\frac{2}{4} + \frac{1}{4} = \blacksquare$
4. $\frac{3}{5} + \frac{1}{5} = \blacksquare$
5. $\frac{2}{8} + \frac{4}{8} = \blacksquare$
6. $\frac{3}{12} + \frac{2}{12} = \blacksquare$
7. $\frac{2}{6} + \frac{1}{6} = \blacksquare$
8. $\frac{3}{8} + \frac{2}{8} = \blacksquare$
9. $\frac{2}{10} + \frac{7}{10} = \blacksquare$
10. $\frac{1}{3} + \frac{2}{3} = \blacksquare$

Find the difference. Write the answer in simplest form. Use fraction bars if you wish. (pp. 546–549)

11. $\frac{4}{6} - \frac{2}{6} = \blacksquare$
12. $\frac{7}{10} - \frac{3}{10} = \blacksquare$
13. $\frac{6}{8} - \frac{4}{8} = \blacksquare$
14. $\frac{5}{5} - \frac{3}{5} = \blacksquare$
15. $\frac{10}{12} - \frac{7}{12} = \blacksquare$
16. $\frac{2}{4} - \frac{1}{4} = \blacksquare$
17. $\frac{8}{10} - \frac{5}{10} = \blacksquare$
18. $\frac{8}{12} - \frac{4}{12} = \blacksquare$

✓ CHECK PROBLEM SOLVING

Solve. Tell how you know your answer is reasonable.

(pp. 550–551)

19. Joe gave $\frac{1}{8}$ of his football cards to Pete and $\frac{3}{8}$ of his cards to Ron. What fraction of his cards did he keep for himself?

20. On Monday Raquel read $\frac{1}{10}$ of her library book. On Tuesday she read $\frac{1}{10}$ of her book. What fraction of her book does she have left to read?

Standardized Test Prep

NUMBER SENSE, CONCEPTS, AND OPERATIONS

1. Aaron and Lana ordered a pizza. Aaron ate $\frac{2}{8}$ of the pizza. Lana ate $\frac{3}{8}$ of the pizza. How much of the pizza did Aaron and Lana eat?

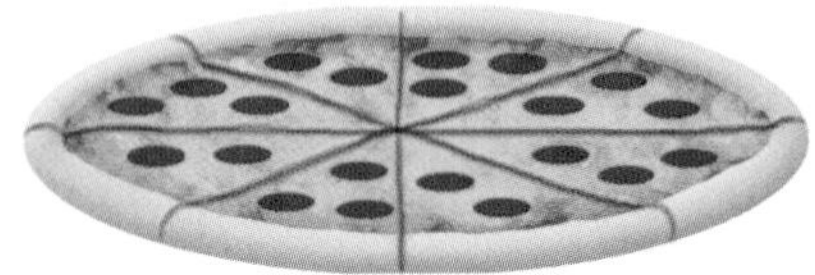

A $\frac{2}{8}$

B $\frac{3}{8}$

C $\frac{5}{8}$

D $\frac{7}{8}$

2. Sabrina is baking cookies. The cookie sheet has 6 rows with 7 cookies in each row. How many cookies are there in all?

F 13

G 36

H 42

J 48

3. **Explain It** The table shows how many tickets the drama club sold from Thursday through Saturday. About how many more tickets were sold on Saturday than on Friday? Tell how you estimated.

DRAMA CLUB TICKET SALES	
Day	**Number of Tickets**
Thursday	515
Friday	628
Saturday	846

MEASUREMENT

TIP **Understand the problem.** See item 4. Decide whether the temperature shown on the thermometer is cold, hot, or in between. Then select the clothing that fits the temperature.

4. What should Tanya wear outside if her outdoor thermometer looks like this?

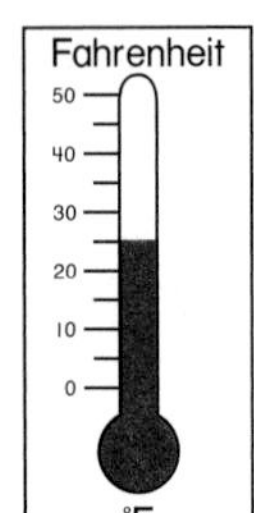

A coat, hat, and gloves

B bathing suit and sandals

C shorts and T-shirt

D sweater and jeans

5. Alfred wants to measure the length of a calculator. Which unit of measure should he use?

F inch

G foot

H yard

J mile

6. **Explain It** Karen put this money in her wallet. About how much money is this? Explain how you estimated.

GEOMETRY AND SPATIAL SENSE

7. How many lines of symmetry does the figure have?

A 0
B 1
C 2
D 3

8. Which angle is a right angle?

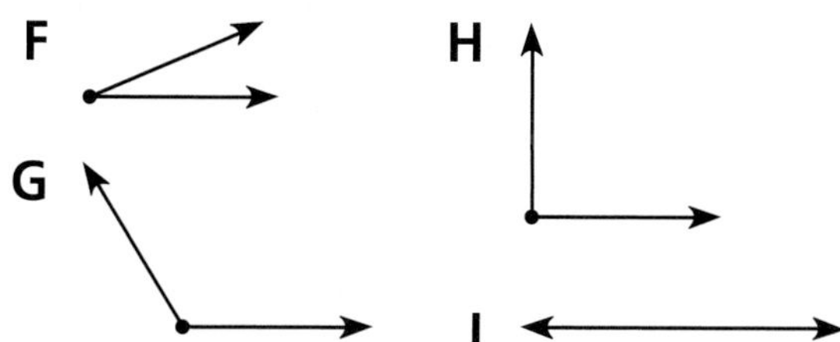

9. Which solid figure does a soup can look like?

A cube
B cylinder
C sphere
D rectangular prism

10. Explain It Ken said these lines are perpendicular.

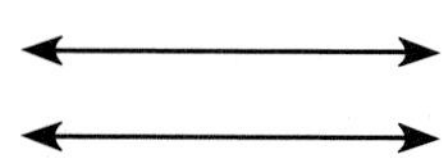

Do you agree or disagree with him? Explain your answer.

DATA ANALYSIS AND PROBABILITY

11. Which color is the pointer of the spinner **most likely** to land on?

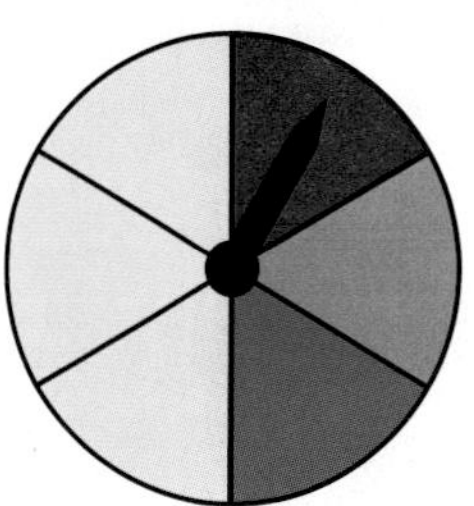

F red
G blue
H green
J yellow

12. The line plot shows the test scores in Kevin's class.

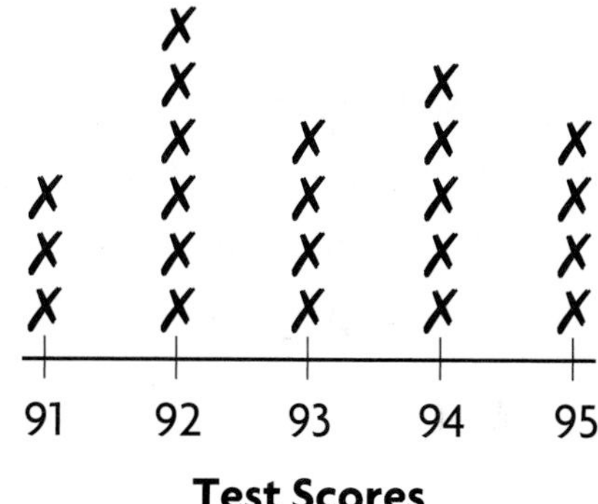

What is the median of this data?

A 92
B 93
C 94
D 95

13. Explain It At the Pizza Palace, you can choose cheese, sausage, or pepperoni pizza. You can choose bottled water, juice, or milk to drink. List all of the different pizza and drink combinations you can make. Then explain how you found your answer.

CHAPTER 27 Fractions and Decimals

FAST FACT • SOCIAL STUDIES
The 1,000-meter race is one of many speed skating events in the Winter Olympics. Skaters race on a 400-meter oval track. Race times are in decimals to show 100 parts of one second.

PROBLEM SOLVING Use the table to find which skater finished the race first.

2002 WINTER OLYMPICS MEN'S 1,000 METERS - FINAL	
Skater	**Time**
Joey Cheek	67.61 seconds
Jan Bos	67.53 seconds
Gerard van Velde	67.18 seconds
Kip Carpenter	67.89 seconds

CHECK WHAT YOU KNOW

Use this page to help you review and remember important skills needed for Chapter 27.

NAME THE FRACTION

Write a fraction for the shaded part.

1. 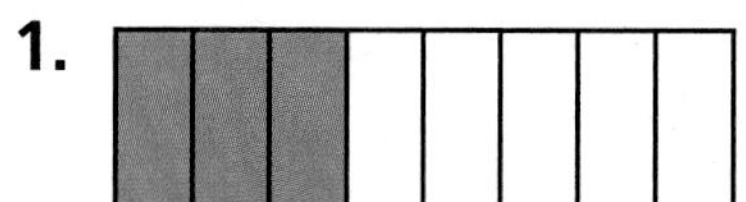

2. 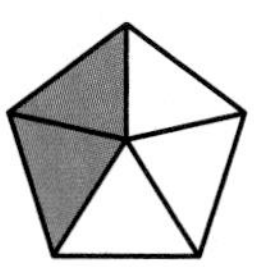

3. 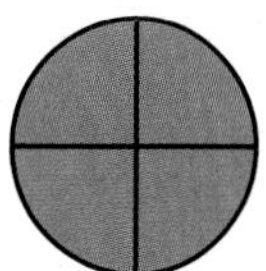

Write a fraction that names the part of each group that is shaded.

4. 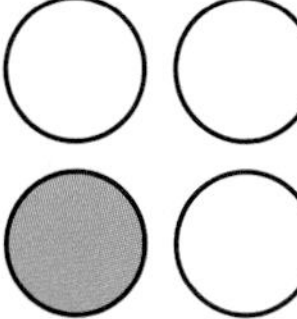

5. 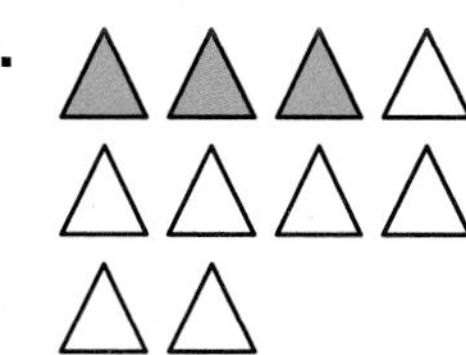

6. 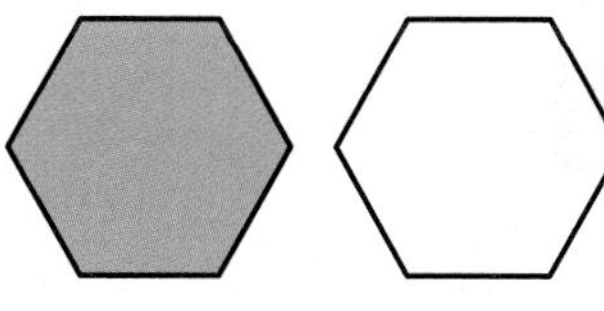

MIXED NUMBERS

Write a mixed number for the parts that are shaded.

7. 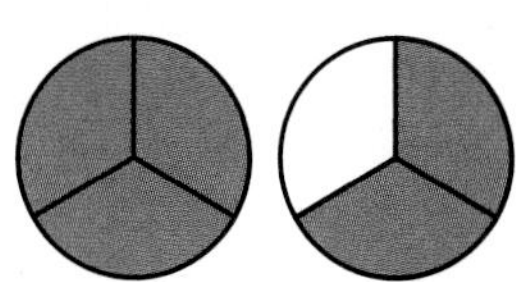

8. 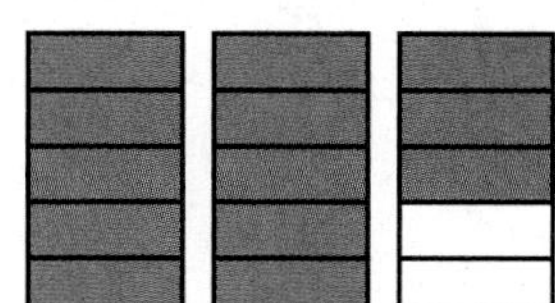

9. 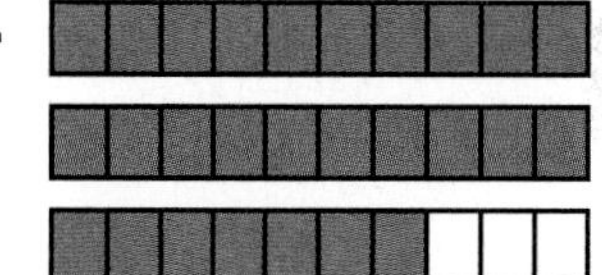

VOCABULARY POWER

REVIEW

digit [di′jət] *noun*

The word *digit* can mean "a finger or a toe." What is the meaning of *digit* in your math book? Write a sentence to describe the math meaning of *digit*.

PREVIEW

decimal

tenth

hundredth

www.harcourtschool.com/mathglossary

LESSON 1

Fractions and Decimals

Quick Review

Write each fraction in words.

1. $\frac{1}{3}$
2. $\frac{2}{5}$
3. $\frac{2}{10}$
4. $\frac{3}{8}$
5. $\frac{1}{2}$

VOCABULARY

decimal
tenth

Learn

FAIR SHARE A **decimal** is a number with one or more digits to the right of the decimal point. A decimal uses place value to show values less than one, such as tenths.

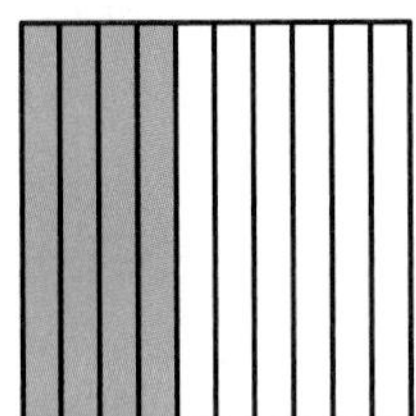

This square has 10 equal parts. Each equal part is one **tenth**.

Fraction	**Decimal**
Write: $\frac{4}{10}$	**Write:** 0.4 (↑ decimal point)
Read: four tenths	**Read:** four tenths

The fraction $\frac{4}{10}$ and the decimal 0.4 name the same amount.

MATH IDEA You can use a fraction or a decimal to show values in tenths.

Examples

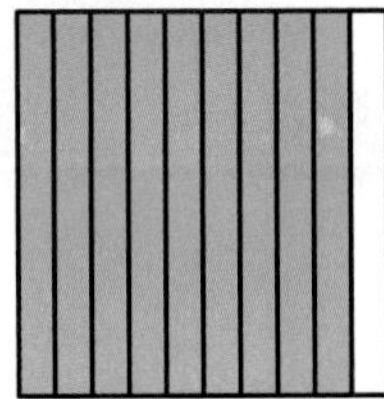

Fraction: $\frac{9}{10}$
Decimal: 0.9
Read: nine tenths

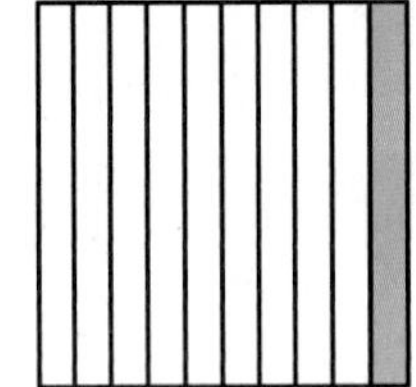

Fraction: $\frac{1}{10}$
Decimal: 0.1
Read: one tenth

C

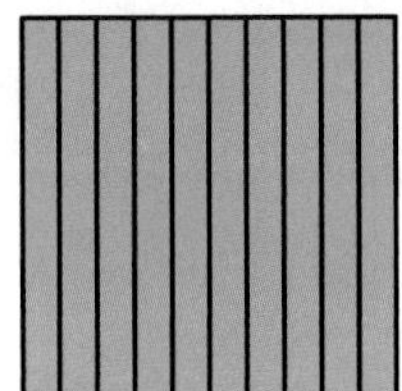

Fraction: $\frac{10}{10}$
Decimal: 1.0, or 1
Read: ten tenths, or one

- How many parts on the square would you shade to show 0.3?

Check

1. **Write** a fraction that shows the amount of crispy treats that are left. Then write the same amount as a decimal.

Write the fraction and decimal for the shaded part.

2. 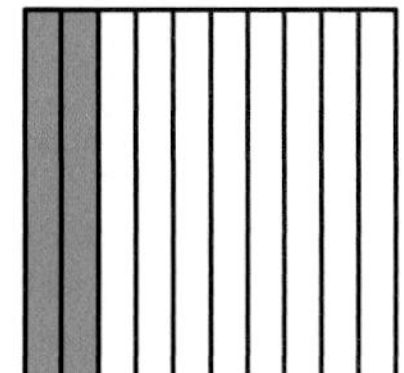

3. 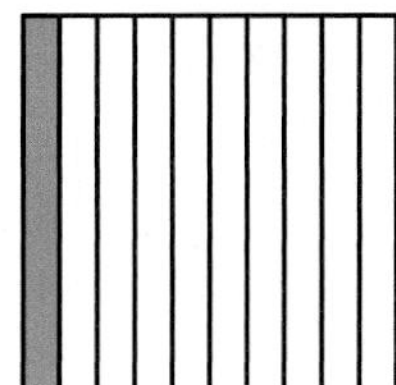

4. 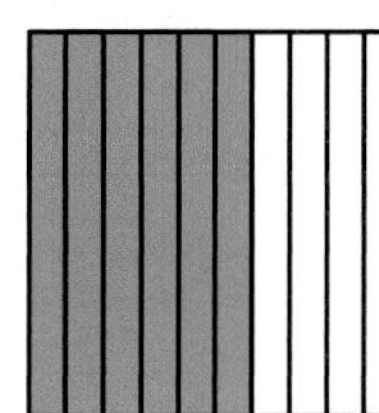

Practice and Problem Solving

Extra Practice, page 570, Set A

Write the fraction and decimal for the shaded part.

5. 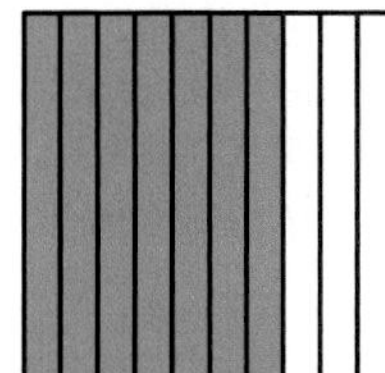

6. 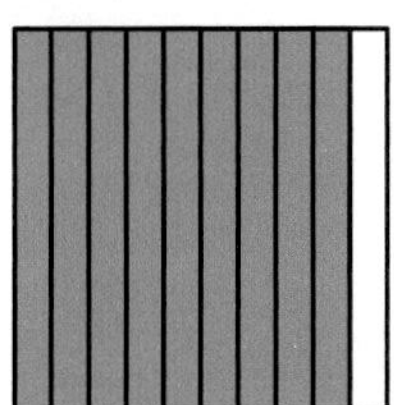

7. 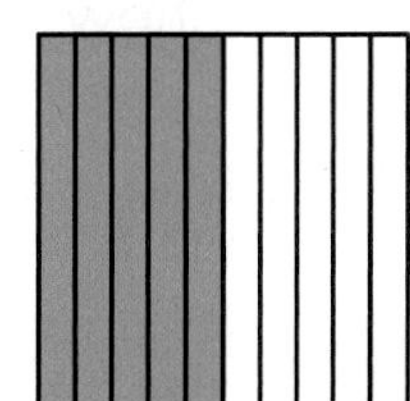

8. 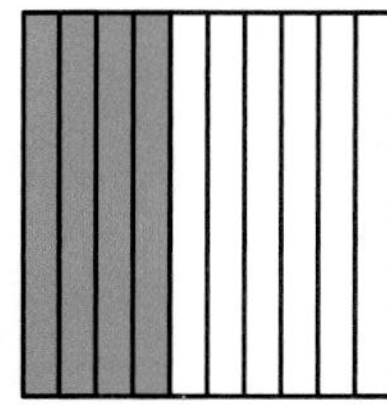

9. ***FAST FACT*** • SCIENCE In 2002, a new kind of centipede was identified. It was found in Central Park in New York. It has 82 legs and is four tenths of an inch long. Write this length as a decimal.

10. **REASONING** Look at the decimal model in Exercise 8 above. How could subtraction be used to find the decimal amount that is NOT shaded?

11. **Write About It** Look at the fraction bars at the right. Explain why 0.5 is the same as $\frac{1}{2}$.

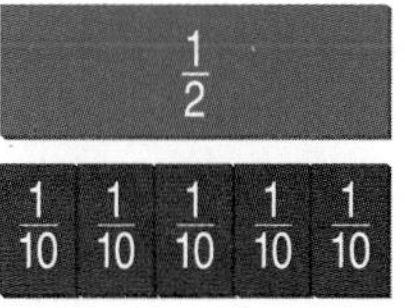

Mixed Review and Test Prep

Find the quotient. (p. 274)

12. $49 \div 7 = \blacksquare$

13. $63 \div 7 = \blacksquare$

14. $42 \div 6 = \blacksquare$

15. $32 \div 8 = \blacksquare$

16. **TEST PREP** Frieda puts 5 beads on each of 9 necklaces. How many beads does she use? (p. 160)

A 45 **B** 54 **C** 72 **D** 81

LESSON 2

Tenths

Quick Review

Write each fraction in words.

1. $\frac{2}{10}$
2. $\frac{5}{10}$
3. $\frac{1}{10}$
4. $\frac{4}{10}$
5. $\frac{7}{10}$

MATERIALS
decimal models
markers

Explore

You can use a decimal model to show part of a whole. This model shows six tenths.

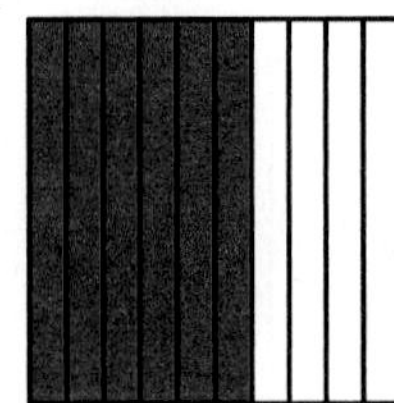

Write: 0.6, or $\frac{6}{10}$

Activity

Use a decimal model to show 0.2, or $\frac{2}{10}$.

STEP 1

Shade the decimal model to show two tenths.

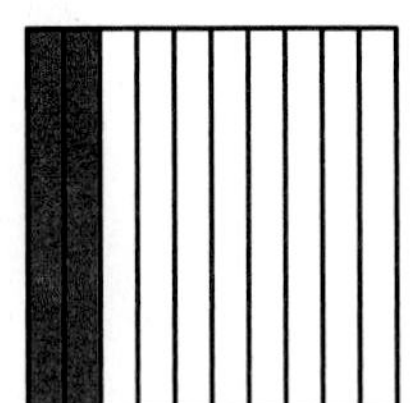

STEP 2

Below your decimal model, write the fraction and decimal amount you have shown.

Technology Link
More Practice: Harcourt Mega Math Fraction Action, *Fraction Flare Up*, Level L

- Use a new decimal model. Shade and label the decimal model to show 0.8, or $\frac{8}{10}$.

Try It

Shade and label decimal models to show each amount.

a. 0.9, or $\frac{9}{10}$ **b.** 0.5, or $\frac{5}{10}$

c. 0.7, or $\frac{7}{10}$ **d.** 0.1, or $\frac{1}{10}$

We shaded 9 out of 10 equal parts on a decimal model. What decimal does this show?

Connect

You can show tenths in different ways.

Use a model.

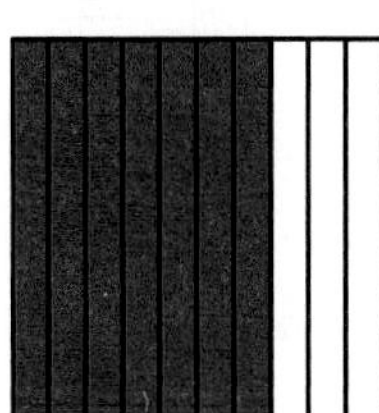

Use a fraction.

$\frac{7}{10}$

Use a place-value chart.

ONES	.	TENTHS
0	.	7

Write: 0.7

Read: seven tenths

Practice and Problem Solving

Use decimal models to show each amount. Then write each fraction as a decimal.

1. $\frac{3}{10}$ **2.** $\frac{8}{10}$ **3.** $\frac{4}{10}$ **4.** $\frac{6}{10}$

Write each decimal as a fraction.

5. 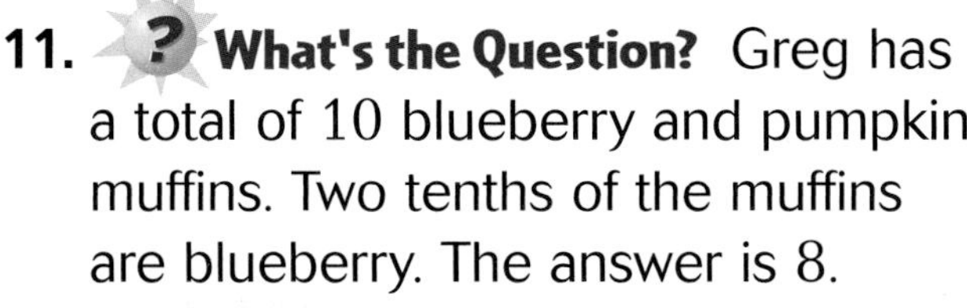

ONES	.	TENTHS
0	.	2

6. 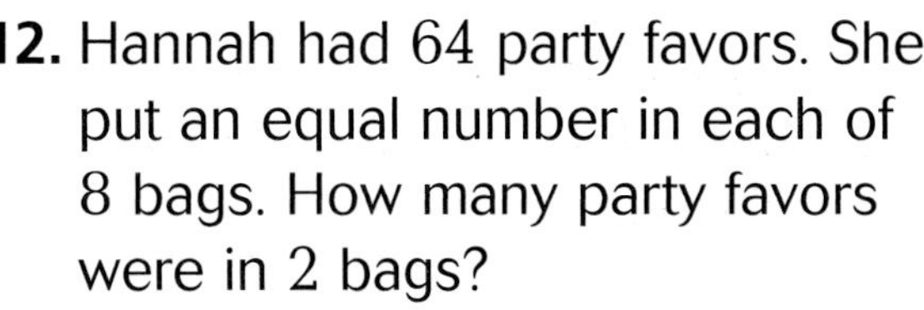

ONES	.	TENTHS
0	.	9

7. 0.5 **8.** 0.4 **9.** 0.3 **10.** 0.1

11. **? What's the Question?** Greg has a total of 10 blueberry and pumpkin muffins. Two tenths of the muffins are blueberry. The answer is 8.

12. Hannah had 64 party favors. She put an equal number in each of 8 bags. How many party favors were in 2 bags?

Mixed Review and Test Prep

Write <, >, or = for each ●. (p. 202)

13. 4×9 ● 36

14. 9×7 ● 8×8

15. 3×6 ● 9×2

16. 8×7 ● 9×6

17. **TEST PREP** Sara had \$4.08. She bought a sticker for \$0.29. How much money did she have left? (p. 120)

A \$3.89 **C** \$3.79
B \$3.81 **D** \$3.70

LESSON 3

Hundredths

Quick Review

Write each fraction as a decimal.

1. $\frac{1}{10}$ **2.** $\frac{3}{10}$ **3.** $\frac{6}{10}$

4. $\frac{9}{10}$ **5.** $\frac{2}{10}$

VOCABULARY

hundredth

MATERIALS

decimal models

markers

Explore

Each of these decimal models has 100 equal parts. Each equal part is one **hundredth**.

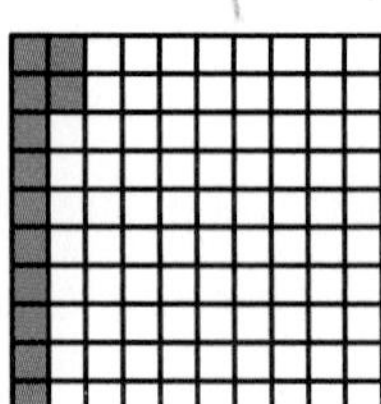

Write: 0.12, or $\frac{12}{100}$

Read: twelve hundredths

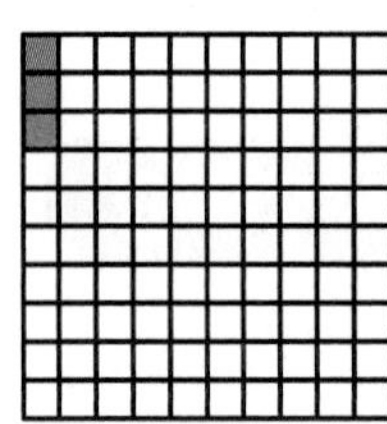

Write: 0.03, or $\frac{3}{100}$

Read: three hundredths

Activity

Use a decimal model to show 0.05, or $\frac{5}{100}$.

STEP 1

Shade the decimal model to show five hundredths.

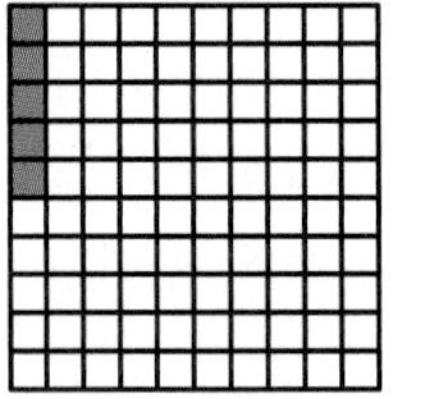

STEP 2

Below your model, write the fraction and decimal you have shown.

- Use a new decimal model. Shade and label the decimal model to show 0.13, or $\frac{13}{100}$.
- **REASONING** How many hundredths would be shaded on a decimal model to show 1.00?

Technology Link

More Practice: Harcourt Mega Math Fraction Action, *Number Line Mine,* Level M

Try It

Use decimal models to show:

a. 0.06 **b.** 0.60

Connect

You can show hundredths in different ways.

Use a model.

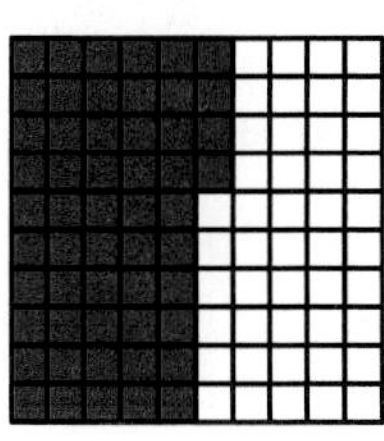

Use a fraction.

$\frac{54}{100}$

Use a place-value chart.

ONES	.	TENTHS	HUNDREDTHS
0	.	5	4

Write: 0.54
Read: fifty-four hundredths
Expanded form: $0.5 + 0.04$

Practice and Problem Solving

Use decimal models to show each amount. Then write each fraction as a decimal.

1. $\frac{8}{100}$ **2.** $\frac{10}{100}$ **3.** $\frac{24}{100}$ **4.** $\frac{22}{100}$ **5.** $\frac{83}{100}$

Write each decimal as a fraction.

6.

ONES	.	TENTHS	HUNDREDTHS
0	.	1	5

7.

ONES	.	TENTHS	HUNDREDTHS
0	.	6	7

Write each decimal as a fraction and in expanded form.

8. 0.31 **9.** 0.56 **10.** 0.20 **11.** 0.02 **12.** 0.15

13. **What's the Error?** Sean said that this model shows 0.90. Describe his error. Write the correct decimal.

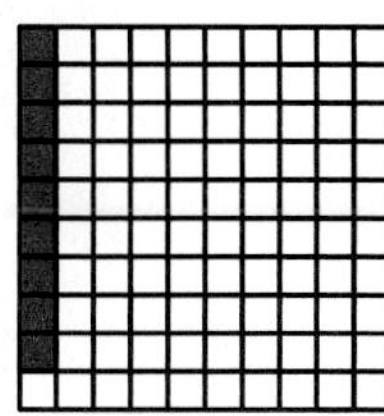

14. Janet and Kim are sharing a pizza. If Janet eats $\frac{3}{8}$ of the pizza, and Kim eats $\frac{2}{8}$, what fraction of the pizza will be left?

Mixed Review and Test Prep

15. $3{,}921 + 765 = ■$ (p. 72)

16. $593 + 1{,}421 = ■$ (p. 72)

17. $3{,}843 - 258 = ■$ (p. 96)

18. $706 - 55 = ■$ (p. 92)

19. **TEST PREP** Jacob's photo is 5 inches wide and 7 inches long. What is its perimeter? (p. 444)

A 12 inches
B 24 inches
C 26 inches
D 35 inches

LESSON

Decimals Greater Than One

Learn

CUT THE CAKE Greg went to a party. There were 2 large cakes. Each cake was cut into 100 equal pieces. If 135 pieces were eaten, what decimal shows how much was eaten?

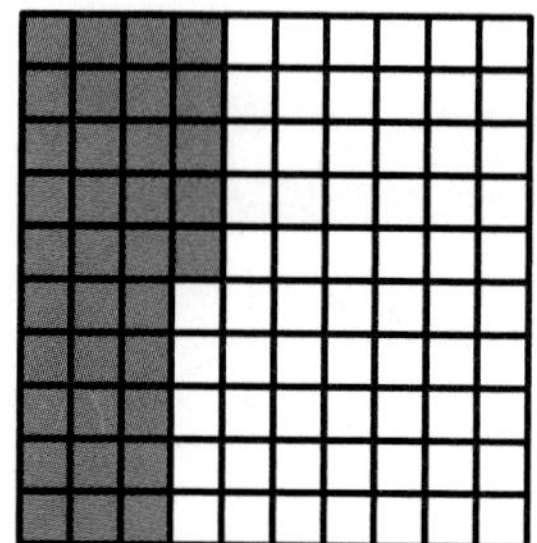

ONES	.	TENTHS	HUNDREDTHS
1	.	3	5

Write: 1.35 **Read:** one and thirty-five hundredths

So, 1.35 cakes were eaten.

You can also show a decimal in expanded form.

expanded form: $1 + 0.3 + 0.05$

1.35 is the same as 1 one 3 tenths 5 hundredths.

Example

Write 2.46 in different ways.

ONES	.	TENTHS	HUNDREDTHS
2	.	4	6

standard form: 2.46

word form: two and forty-six hundredths

expanded form: $2 + 0.4 + 0.06$

2.46 is the same as 2 ones 4 tenths 6 hundredths.

- **REASONING** What is the expanded form for 3.08?

Quick Review

Write each number in standard form.

1. $400 + 50 + 3$
2. $100 + 70 + 6$
3. $300 + 0 + 3$
4. $900 + 20 + 1$
5. $200 + 40 + 9$

Remember

A mixed number is made up of a whole number and a fraction.

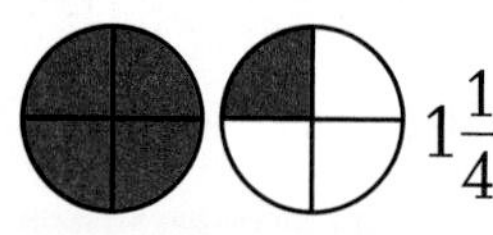

Check

1. Write the standard form for one and fifty-two hundredths.

Write the word form and expanded form for each decimal.

2.

ONES	.	TENTHS	HUNDREDTHS
4	•	6	2

3.

ONES	.	TENTHS	HUNDREDTHS
3	•	5	5

Practice and Problem Solving

Extra Practice, page 570, Set B

Write the word form and expanded form for each decimal.

4.

ONES	.	TENTHS	HUNDREDTHS
2	•	7	4

5.

ONES	.	TENTHS	HUNDREDTHS
5	•	0	3

6.

ONES	.	TENTHS	HUNDREDTHS
4	•	5	0

7.

ONES	.	TENTHS	HUNDREDTHS
1	•	2	9

Write the missing numbers.

8. $3.14 = 3 + \blacksquare + 0.04$

9. $6.75 = 6 + 0.7 + \blacksquare$

10. $4.28 = \blacksquare + 0.2 + 0.08$

11. $\blacksquare = 2 + 0.3 + 0.01$

12. $9.02 = \blacksquare$ ones 0 tenths $\blacksquare$ hundredths

13. $2.28 = 2$ ones $\blacksquare$ tenths $\blacksquare$ hundredths

14. Mrs. Lightfoot displayed her students' drawings. She had 4 rows of 5 drawings on one wall, and 3 rows of 7 drawings on another wall. How many were displayed in all?

15. Raul says that 4 tenths is the same as 40 hundredths. Do you agree? Explain. Use this decimal model to help.

Mixed Review and Test Prep

Find the number that the variable stands for. (p. 242)

16. $a \times 4 = 32$

17. $7 \times b = 21$

18. $8 \times c = 40$

19. $d \times 5 = 30$

20. TEST PREP Pilar put 6 olives on each pizza. If she made 8 pizzas, how many olives did she use? (p. 194)

A 14
B 24
C 40
D 48

LESSON

5 Compare and Order Decimals

Quick Review

Compare. Use <, >, or = for each ●.

1. 35 ● 53
2. 901 ● 1,093
3. 1,243 ● 1,423
4. 30 + 5 ● 25 + 10
5. 45 + 6 ● 55 − 5

Learn

TAKE YOUR PLACE A place-value chart can help you compare tenths.

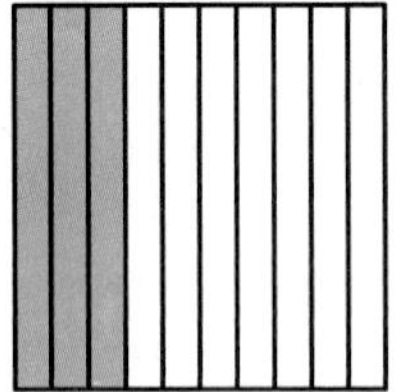
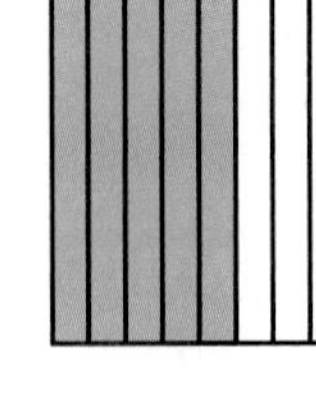

0.3 < 0.5

ONES	.	TENTHS
0	•	3
0	•	5

- Compare ones.
- Compare tenths. 0.3 is less than 0.5.

You can also compare decimals with hundredths.

Swimmers and other athletes compare their times written in hundredths of seconds.

ONES	.	TENTHS	HUNDREDTHS
4	•	7	9
4	•	5	1

4.79 > 4.51

- Begin with the digit in the greatest place value.
- Compare the ones. 4 ones = 4 ones.
- Compare the tenths. 7 tenths > 5 tenths. So, 4.79 seconds is greater than 4.51 seconds.

You can use a number line to order decimals.

Example

Write 0.7, 0.3, and 0.9 in order from least to greatest.

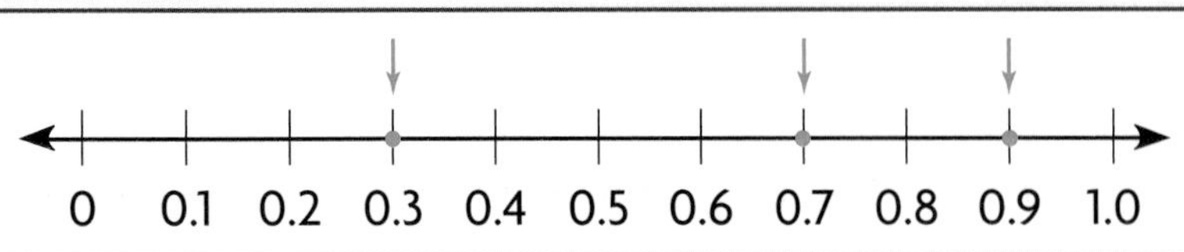

The numbers from least to greatest are 0.3, 0.7, 0.9.

- How could you use the number line to compare 0.5 and 0.8?

Check

1. **Explain** how to compare 3.54 and 3.52.

Compare. Write < or > for each ●.

2. 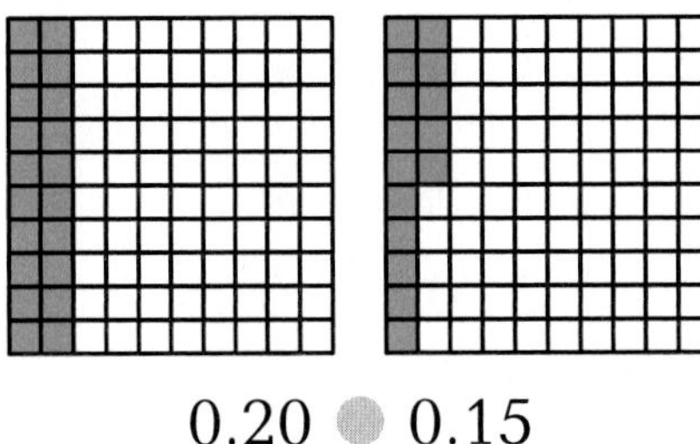

0.20 ● 0.15

3.

ONES	.	TENTHS
4	•	1
4	•	6

4.1 ● 4.6

Practice and Problem Solving

Extra Practice, page 570, Set C

Compare. Write < or > for each ●.

4.

ONES	.	TENTHS
1	•	5
2	•	6

1.5 ● 2.6

5.

ONES	.	TENTHS	HUNDREDTHS
2	•	5	1
2	•	3	9

2.51 ● 2.39

6. 2.4 ● 2.1
7. 3.5 ● 2.6
8. 0.22 ● 0.25
9. 1.67 ● 1.76

For 10–15, order the decimals from least to greatest. For 10–13, use the number line.

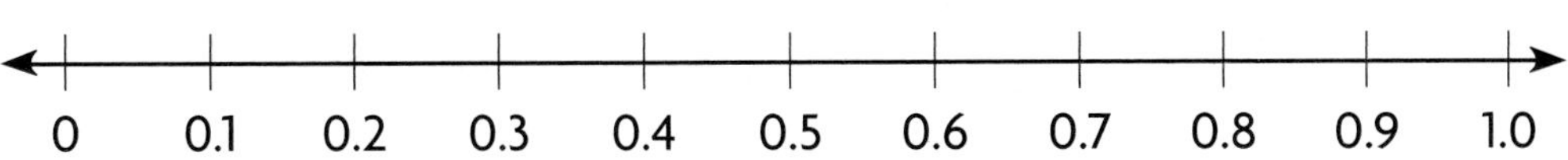

10. 0.5, 0.2, 0.1
11. 0.6, 0.5, 0.8
12. 0.1, 0.3, 0.2
13. 0.4, 0.9, 0.3
14. 0.13, 0.09, 0.2
15. 0.11, 0.3, 0.04
16. **Vocabulary Power** The *place*, or position, of a digit, decides the *value* of that digit in a number. What is the *place value* of each digit in 3.65?
17. Silvia had 47 stickers. She gave the same number of stickers to each of 4 friends, and kept 11. How many did each friend get?

Mixed Review and Test Prep

Find the sum or difference. (pp. 72, 96)

18. 132 + 65
19. 4,209 + 2,371
20. 700 − 132
21. 4,082 − 1,536

22. **TEST PREP** 72 ÷ 9 = ■ (p. 278)

A 8
B 7
C 6
D 5

LESSON 6

Problem Solving Skill
Too Much/Too Little Information

UNDERSTAND | PLAN | SOLVE | CHECK

Quick Review

Compare. Write $<$ or $>$ for each ●.

1. 0.3 ● 0.5

2. 1.2 ● 0.5

3. 0.8 ● 0.09

4. 2.0 ● 1.1

5. 0.57 ● 0.62

FIND THE INFORMATION Mr. Dixon went to the store. He bought 3.4 pounds of grapefruit and 1.7 pounds of oranges. He also bought 2.8 pounds of apples and 2 pounds of sugar. List the weights of the fruit that he bought in order from least to greatest.

STEP 1

Find what the problem asks.

- List the weights of the fruit Mr. Dixon bought in order from least to greatest.

STEP 2

Find the information that you need to solve the problem.

- Look for the weights of the fruit:
  3.4 pounds of grapefruit
  1.7 pounds of oranges
  2.8 pounds of apples

STEP 3

Look for extra information.

- Look for any items that are not fruit:
  2 pounds of sugar

STEP 4

Solve the problem.

- Compare the weights of the fruit. List them in order from least to greatest.
  $1.7 < 2.8 < 3.4$

So, the order is 1.7 pounds of oranges, 2.8 pounds of apples, and 3.4 pounds of grapefruit.

Talk About It

- Read the problem below. Is there too much, too little, or the right amount of information? Explain.

Jim and his friends shared a pizza. They each ate 2 slices. There were 2 slices left over. How many slices were in the whole pizza?

Problem Solving Practice

For 1–4, write *a*, *b*, or *c* to tell whether the problem has

a. too much information.

b. too little information.

c. the right amount of information.

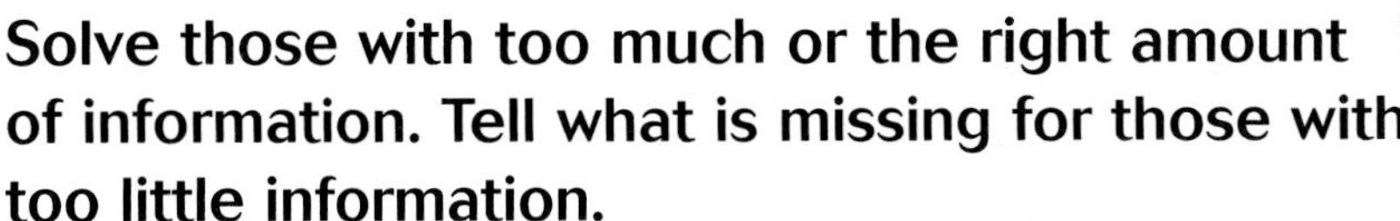

Solve those with too much or the right amount of information. Tell what is missing for those with too little information.

1. Mrs. Brody made a birthday cake and cut it into equal-size pieces. She gave 8 pieces to Robert and his friends. How many pieces were left?

2. Mrs. Brody bought 10 party hats and 20 noisemakers. She gave 8 hats to Robert and his friends. What fraction of the hats were NOT used?

3. Mr. Grant bought two shirts and a tie. Each shirt cost $19. He gave the clerk $60. What was his change?

4. At practice, Jill ran 3.2 miles. Betty ran 2.9 miles, and Trish ran 3.1 miles. Who ran the farthest?

Mixed Applications

5. Ms. Cortez built a fence around her garden. The length of the garden is 4 feet and the width is 3 feet. What is the perimeter of her fence?

6. Mia baked 30 cookies. She gave 6 cookies to each of 4 teachers. Then she gave half of the rest of the cookies to her sister. How many cookies did Mia keep?

USE DATA **For 7–9, use the graph.**

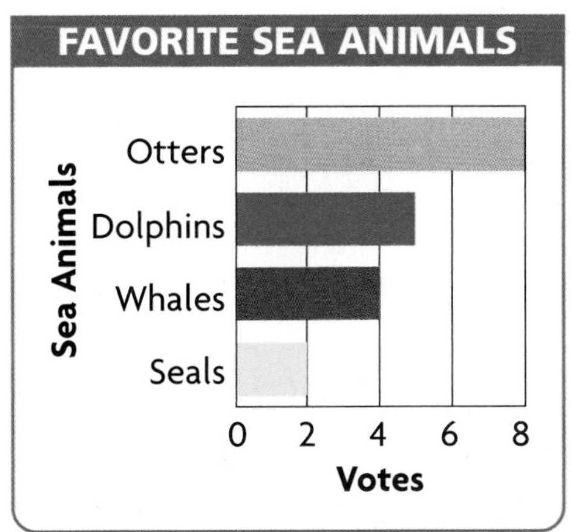

7. How many more students voted for otters and seals than voted for whales and dolphins?

8. How many students did NOT vote for dolphins?

9. **Write a problem** using the data in the bar graph. Then explain how to solve the problem.

Extra Practice

Set A (pp. 558–559)

Write the fraction and decimal for the shaded part.

1. 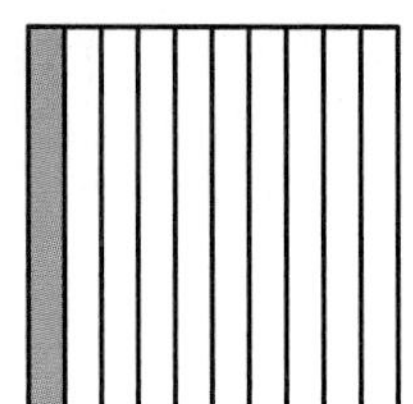

2. 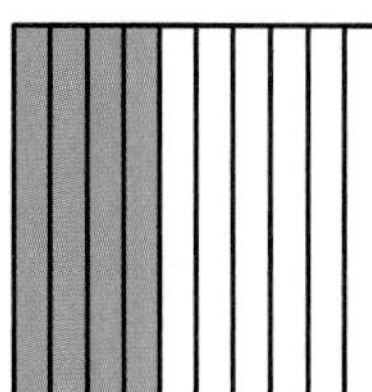

3. 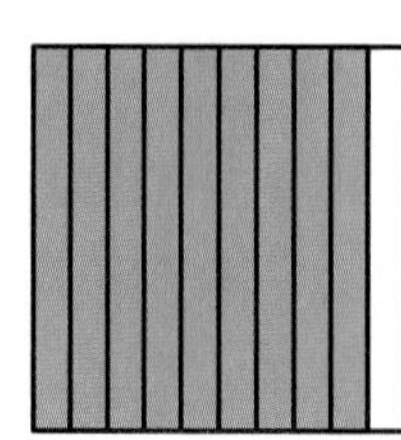

4. 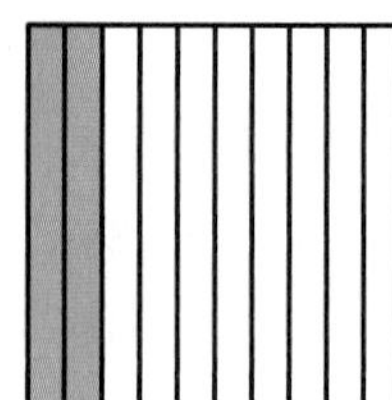

5. What decimal names the amount in Exercise 1 that is NOT shaded?

6. How many more parts would you shade in Exercise 2 to show 0.6?

Set B (pp. 564–565)

Write the word form and expanded form for each decimal.

1.

ONES	.	TENTHS	HUNDREDTHS
2	.	1	8

2.

ONES	.	TENTHS	HUNDREDTHS
1	.	3	3

Write the missing numbers.

3. $3.67 = 3 + ■ + 0.07$

4. $1.25 = 1 + 0.2 + ■$

Set C (pp. 566–567)

Compare. Write < or > for each ●.

1.

ONES	.	TENTHS
2	.	2
2	.	4

2.2 ● 2.4

2.

ONES	.	TENTHS	HUNDREDTHS
1	.	0	9
1	.	0	3

1.09 ● 1.03

3. 2.31 ● 1.32

4. 5.1 ● 1.5

5. 0.09 ● 0.90

6. 1.10 ● 0.10

For 7–10, use the number line to order the decimals from least to greatest.

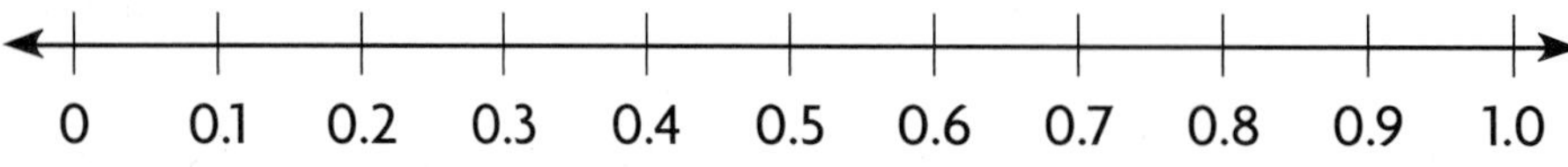

7. 0.2, 0.1, 0.3

8. 0.7, 0.1, 0.4

9. 0.9, 0.6, 0.3

10. 0.4, 0.2, 0.6

Review/Test

✓ CHECK VOCABULARY AND CONCEPTS

Choose the best term from the box.

decimal
product

1. A number with one or more digits to the right of the decimal point is a __?__ . (p. 558)

Write each decimal as a fraction. (pp. 560–561, 562–563)

2. 0.3
3. 0.81
4. 0.03

✓ CHECK SKILLS

Write the fraction and decimal for the shaded part. (pp. 558–559)

5. 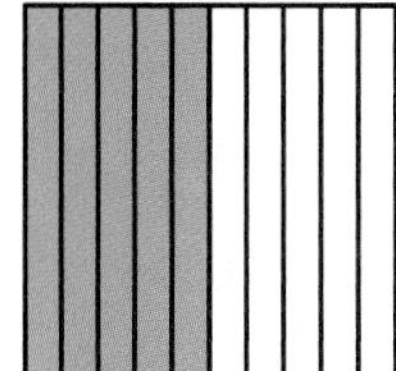
6. 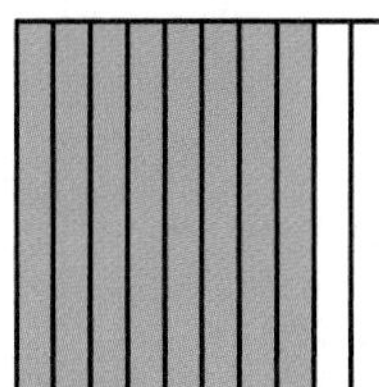
7. 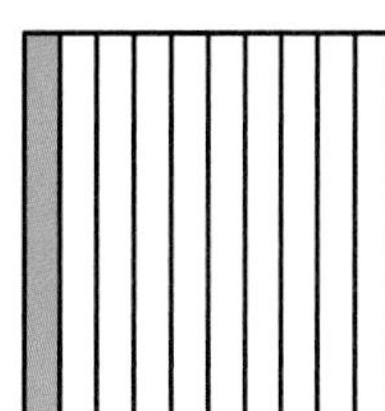
8. 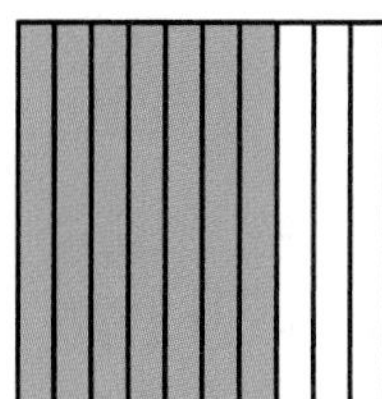

Write the missing numbers. (pp. 564–565)

9. $5.11 = 5 + ■ + 0.01$
10. $2.83 = 2 + 0.8 + ■$

Compare. Write < or > for each ●. (pp. 566–567)

11. 1.9 ● 1.1
12. 3.42 ● 3.41
13. 0.13 ● 0.31

✓ CHECK PROBLEM SOLVING

Write *a*, *b*, or *c* to tell whether the problem has

a. too much information.
b. too little information.
c. the right amount of information.

Solve those with too much or the right amount of information. Tell what is missing for those with too little information. (pp. 568–569)

14. Mark paid \$6.25 for a book, \$4.50 for a sandwich, and \$1.00 for crackers. How much did he spend on food in all?

15. Tia made a salad with 1.2 pounds of lettuce, 0.3 pound of cucumber, and some carrots. Of which vegetable did she use the least amount?

Standardized Test Prep

NUMBER SENSE, CONCEPTS, AND OPERATIONS

1. Luke has 2 quarters and 3 nickels. What is the total value of his coins?

A \$0.80
B \$0.65
C \$0.50
D \$0.23

2. Which number has the same value as this expression?

$3{,}000 + 700 + 2$

F 372
G 3,072
H 3,702
J 3,720

3. Which of the following is **true**?

A $4{,}889 < 4{,}898$
B $359 > 395$
C $2{,}794 < 2{,}793$
D $5{,}215 > 5{,}220$

4. Max has 3 toy cars on each shelf. If he has 5 shelves, how many cars does he have in all?

F 7 **H** 12
G 8 **J** 15

5. Explain It Sue puts 55 trading cards into 6 stacks. Each stack has about the same number of cards in it. About how many cards does Sue put into each stack? Explain your answer.

GEOMETRY AND SPATIAL SENSE

6. On which clock do the hour and minute hands form a right angle?

A

C

B

D

TIP **Understand the problem.** See item 7. A line of symmetry divides a figure in half. You must find how many different lines can be drawn on the figure to form two matching halves.

7. How many lines of symmetry does this figure have?

F 0 **H** 2
G 1 **J** 3

8. Explain It Write the ordered pair that names the location of Point *x* on the grid. Explain.

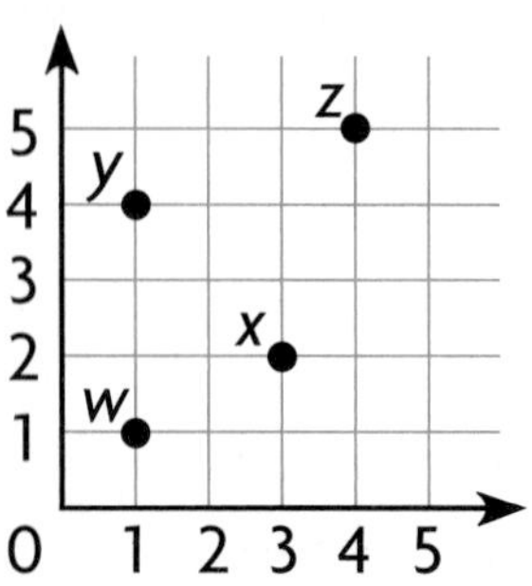

ALGEBRAIC THINKING

9. Mary drew this pattern as a border for her poster. What are the next two figures in Mary's pattern?

A □△

B ▽□

C △□

D □▽

10. George is 45 years old. He has four sisters. Donna is 41 years old. Kim is 43 years old. Jenna is 42 years old, and Carol is 48 years old. Which of his sisters is older than George?

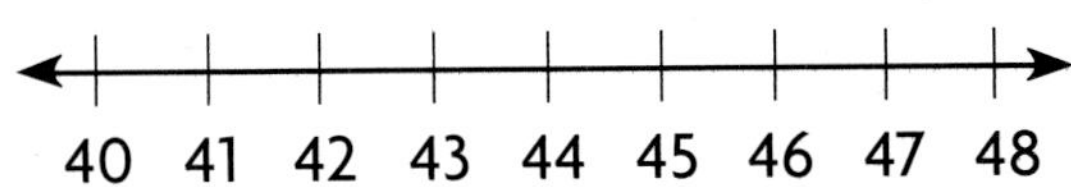

F Donna
G Carol
H Kim
J Jenna

11. **Explain It** Write a problem that can be solved by using this equation.

$35 \div 7 = \blacksquare$

Explain why this equation will solve the problem.

DATA ANALYSIS AND PROBABILITY

12. The bar graph shows the number of hours Mrs. Fields worked in five days. How many hours did she work in all?

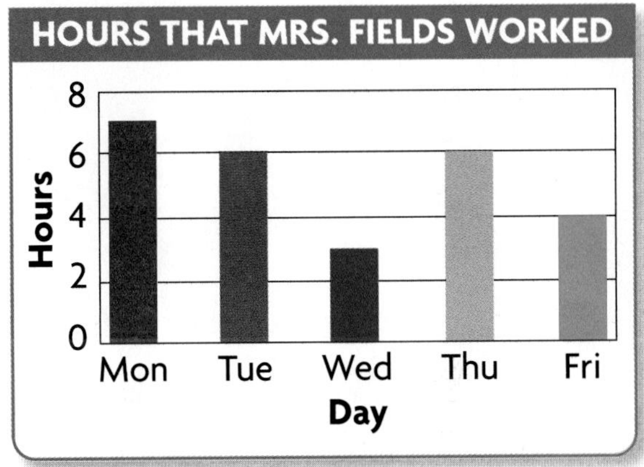

A 18 hours
B 23 hours
C 26 hours
D 29 hours

13. José used cubes to record the number of birds he saw each day.

What is the mean of the data?

F 2
G 3
H 5
J 10

14. **Explain It** Rhonda looked at the shirts that her classmates were wearing. She saw 3 striped shirts, 10 solid shirts, and 5 shirts with writing on them. Should she display this data in a bar graph, pictograph, or tally table? Explain your choice, and describe what the data will look like.

CHAPTER 28

Decimals and Money

FAST FACT • SOCIAL STUDIES In 1999 the U.S. Mint began its ten-year 50 State Quarters® Program. Each year 5 state quarters are minted. The Tennessee quarter was minted in 2002. The musical instruments on the back stand for the types of music Tennessee is known for.

PROBLEM SOLVING Use the map. By the end of 2004, how many state quarters will not yet be minted?

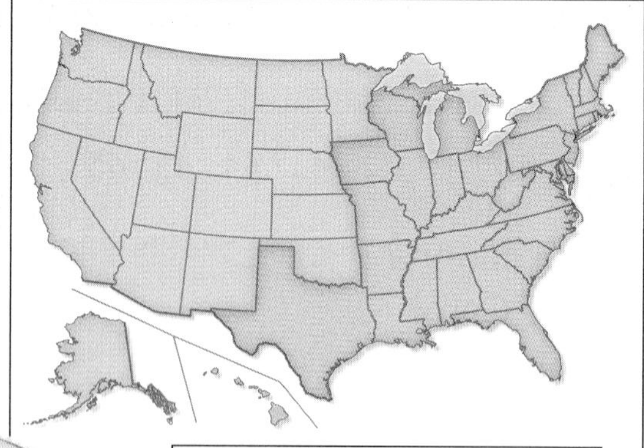

CHECK WHAT YOU KNOW

Use this page to help you review and remember important skills needed for Chapter 28.

USE MONEY NOTATION

Write the amount, using a dollar sign and decimal point.

1.     

2.   

3. 

4. 

NAME THE DECIMAL

Write each as a decimal.

5. $\frac{1}{10}$ 6. $\frac{7}{10}$ 7. $2\frac{6}{10}$ 8. $\frac{2}{10}$ 9. $\frac{5}{10}$

10. $1\frac{65}{100}$ 11. $\frac{4}{100}$ 12. $\frac{30}{100}$ 13. $\frac{3}{100}$ 14. $\frac{10}{100}$

15. eight tenths 16. fourteen hundredths 17. six and nine hundredths

VOCABULARY POWER

REVIEW

decimal [de′sə•məl] *noun*

The word *decimal* comes from the Latin word *decimus*, which means "tenth." How many tenths are in 0.5?

www.harcourtschool.com/mathglossary

LESSON 1

Fractions and Money

Quick Review

Write each decimal as a fraction.

1. 0.9 **2.** 0.1

3. 0.09 **4.** 0.75

5. 0.50

Learn

MILK MONEY Jesse needs half a dollar for milk at school. How many quarters does Jesse need?

4 quarters = 1 dollar = $\$1.00$

\$0.25 \$0.25 \$0.25 \$0.25

2 quarters are $\frac{2}{4}$ of a dollar. $\frac{2}{4} = \frac{1}{2}$

$\frac{1}{2}$ of a dollar = $\$0.50$, or 50 cents

So, Jesse needs 2 quarters.

\$0.25 \$0.25 \$0.25 \$0.25

Three quarters are $\frac{3}{4}$ of a dollar, or $\$0.75$.

$\frac{3}{4}$ of a dollar = $\$0.75$, or 75 cents

\$0.25 \$0.25 \$0.25 \$0.25

One quarter is $\frac{1}{4}$ of a dollar, or $\$0.25$.

$\frac{1}{4}$ of a dollar = $\$0.25$, or 25 cents

Example

Write the amount of money shown. Then write the amount as a fraction of a dollar.

\$0.25, or $\frac{1}{4}$ of a dollar

Check

1. **Tell** how much money Anna will have left if she spends $\frac{3}{4}$ of a dollar on a frozen fruit bar.

Anna's money

Write the amount of money shown. Then write the amount as a fraction of a dollar.

2. 

3. 

Practice and Problem Solving

Extra Practice, page 586, Set A

Write the amount of money shown. Then write the amount as a fraction of a dollar.

4. 

5. 

6. 

7. 

8. ***FAST FACT*** • SOCIAL STUDIES All quarters minted since 1932 carry a portrait of George Washington to honor the 200th anniversary of his birth. In what year was he born?

9. Anthony and Jacob each have $\frac{3}{4}$ of a dollar, but they have different coins. Draw a picture that shows 2 different sets of coins the boys could have.

Mixed Review and Test Prep

Add or subtract.

10. $\frac{3}{8} + \frac{2}{8}$ (p. 542)

11. $\frac{9}{10} - \frac{2}{10}$ (p. 546)

12. $\frac{5}{6} - \frac{5}{6}$ (p. 546)

13. $\frac{7}{8} - \frac{2}{8}$ (p. 546)

14. **TEST PREP** Leroy has a scrapbook with 8 pages. Each page has 7 stickers. How many stickers does he have in all? (p. 196)

A 52 **B** 54 **C** 56 **D** 64

Decimals and Money

Quick Review

Write in expanded form.

1. 0.21
2. 0.45
3. 0.72
4. 0.53
5. 2.87

MATERIALS play money: 100 pennies, 10 dimes

 = 

100 pennies = 1 dollar

 $= \frac{1}{100}$, or 0.01, of a dollar

 = 

10 dimes = 1 dollar

 $= \frac{1}{10}$, or 0.1, of a dollar

Use play money to connect money and decimals.

Activity

Copy Tables A and B.

STEP 1

Use pennies to show $\frac{31}{100}$, or 0.31, of a dollar. Then show $\frac{2}{100}$, or 0.02, of a dollar. Record the number of pennies you used.

TABLE A

Decimal	Number of Pennies
0.31	■
0.02	■

STEP 2

Use dimes and pennies to show $\frac{31}{100}$, or 0.31, of a dollar. Use as few coins as possible. Then show $\frac{2}{100}$, or 0.02, of a dollar. Record the coins you used.

TABLE B

Decimal	Number of Dimes	Number of Pennies
0.31	■	■
0.02	■	■

Try It

a. Write 53¢, or $\frac{53}{100}$ of a dollar, as a decimal.

b. What coins would you use to show 0.12 of a dollar?

Connect

You can think of dimes as tenths and pennies as hundredths.

0.49			
Ones	.	Tenths	Hundredths
0	.	4	9

0.49 = 49 hundredths

0.49 = 4 tenths 9 hundredths

\$0.49			
Dollars	.	Dimes	Pennies
0	.	0	49
0	.	4	9

\$0.49 = 49 pennies = 49 hundredths of a dollar

\$0.49 = 4 dimes 9 pennies = 4 tenths 9 hundredths of a dollar

Practice and Problem Solving

Write the money amount for each fraction of a dollar.

1. $\frac{59}{100}$ **2.** $\frac{3}{100}$ **3.** $\frac{13}{100}$ **4.** $\frac{20}{100}$ **5.** $\frac{10}{100}$

Write the money amount.

6. 3 hundredths of a dollar

7. 24 hundredths of a dollar

8. 19 hundredths of a dollar

Write the missing numbers. Use the fewest coins possible.

9. \$0.52 = ■ dimes ■ pennies \$0.52 = ■ tenths ■ hundredths of a dollar

10. \$0.80 = ■ dimes ■ pennies \$0.80 = ■ tenths ■ hundredths of a dollar

11. \$0.06 = ■ dimes ■ pennies \$0.06 = ■ tenths ■ hundredths of a dollar

12. **Write About It** You know that 1 dime is 0.1, or 1 tenth, of a dollar. Is 1 dime also 0.10, or 10 hundredths, of a dollar? Explain.

13. Juan has \$1.50 to spend. He spends $\frac{3}{4}$ of a dollar on a hot dog and $\frac{1}{2}$ of a dollar on a drink. Draw a picture that shows how much money he has left over.

Mixed Review and Test Prep

Subtract 352 from each number. (p. 96)

14. 556 **15.** 398

16. 409 **17.** 500

18. **TEST PREP** How many sides does a rectangle have? (p. 390)

A 1 **C** 3

B 2 **D** 4

LESSON 3

Add and Subtract Decimals and Money

Quick Review

1. $\frac{1}{10} + \frac{3}{10}$
2. $\frac{2}{10} + \frac{5}{10}$
3. $\frac{5}{10} - \frac{1}{10}$
4. $\frac{7}{10} - \frac{4}{10}$
5. $\frac{9}{10} - \frac{3}{10}$

Learn

MOVING RIGHT ALONG Gary walked to Dan's house and then went to the playground. How far did Gary walk in all?

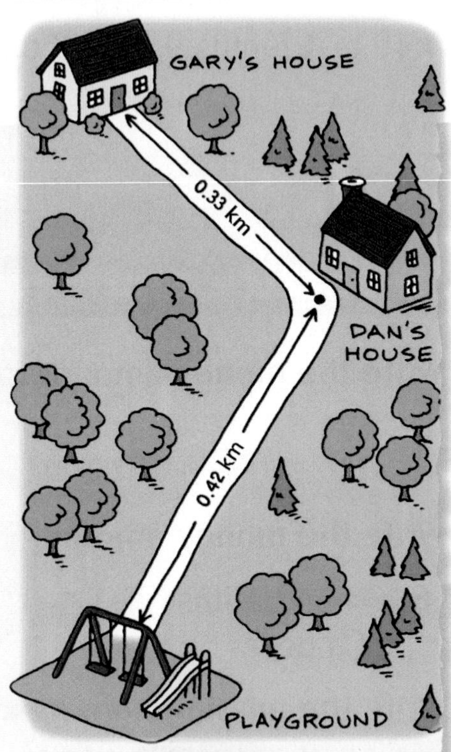

Example

One Way Use decimal models to add.

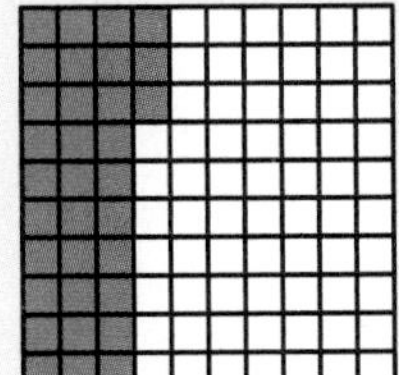

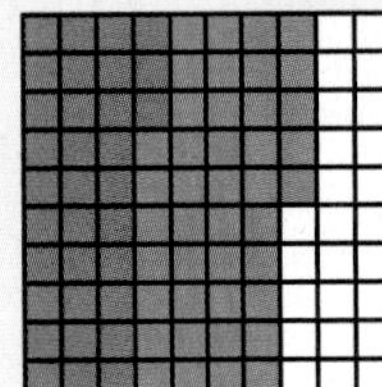

Shade 0.33 and 0.42. Add the shaded squares.

$0.33 + 0.42 = 0.75$

So, Gary walked 0.75 kilometer.

Another Way Use paper and pencil to add.

STEP 1

Line up the decimal points.

decimal point ↓

$$\begin{array}{r} 0.33 \\ +0.42 \\ \hline \end{array}$$

STEP 2

Add decimals like whole numbers. Regroup if necessary.

$$\begin{array}{r} 0.33 \\ +0.42 \\ \hline 0\ 75 \end{array}$$

STEP 3

Write the decimal point in the sum.

$$\begin{array}{r} 0.33 \\ +0.42 \\ \hline 0.75 \end{array}$$

Technology Link

More Practice: Harcourt Mega Math The Number Games, *Buggy Bargains,* Level I; *Tiny's Think Tank,* Level L

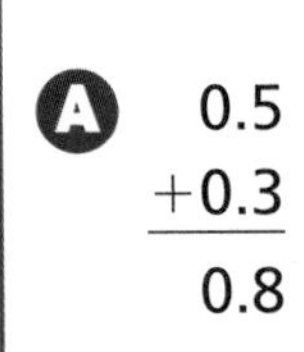

More Examples

A

$$\begin{array}{r} 0.5 \\ +0.3 \\ \hline 0.8 \end{array}$$

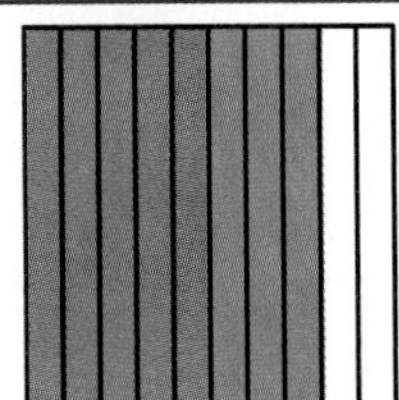

B

$$\begin{array}{r} ^{1}\ \ \ \ \\ 1.49 \\ +0.06 \\ \hline 1.55 \end{array}$$

C

$$\begin{array}{r} ^{1}\ \ \ \ \\ \$2.17 \\ +\$3.58 \\ \hline \$5.75 \end{array}$$

Example

One Way Use decimal models to subtract.

Find 0.73 − 0.50.

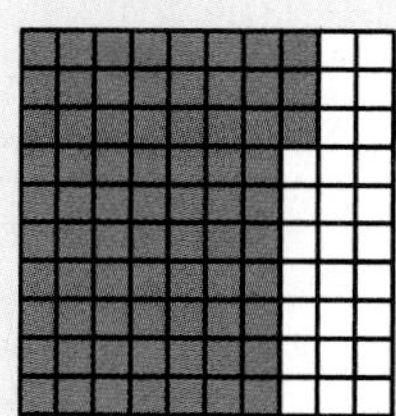

Shade 0.73 of a decimal model.

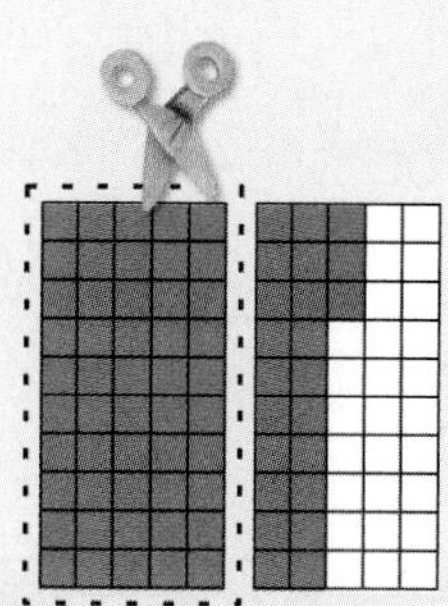

Take away 50 shaded squares. 23 shaded squares are left. So, 0.73 − 0.50 = 0.23.

Another Way Use paper and pencil to subtract.

STEP 1

Line up the decimal points.

decimal point ↓

$$\begin{array}{r} 0.71 \\ -0.38 \\ \hline \end{array}$$

STEP 2

Subtract decimals like whole numbers.

$$\begin{array}{r} {}^{6\ 11} \\ 0.\not{7}\not{1} \\ -0.38 \\ \hline 0\ 33 \end{array}$$

STEP 3

Write the decimal point in the difference.

$$\begin{array}{r} {}^{6\ 11} \\ 0.\not{7}\not{1} \\ -0.38 \\ \hline 0.33 \end{array}$$

More Examples

A

$$\begin{array}{r} 0.9 \\ -0.5 \\ \hline 0.4 \end{array}$$

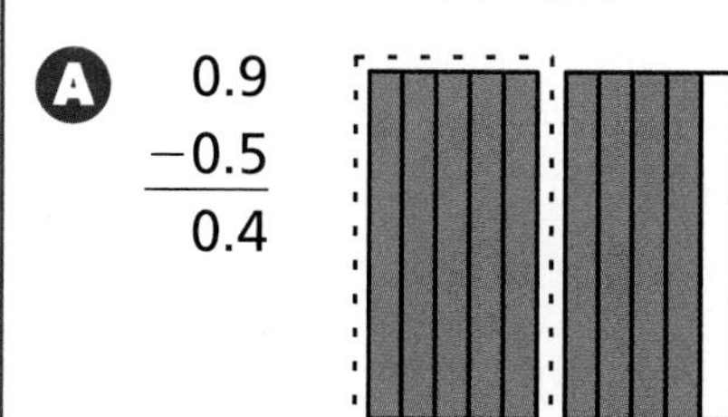

B

$$\begin{array}{r} 2.75 \\ -1.33 \\ \hline 1.42 \end{array}$$

C

$$\begin{array}{r} {}^{4\ 14} \\ \$3.\not{5}\not{4} \\ -\$0.05 \\ \hline \$3.49 \end{array}$$

You can also use a calculator to find a sum or difference.

0.83 + 0.39 = ■

0.71 − 0.28 = ■

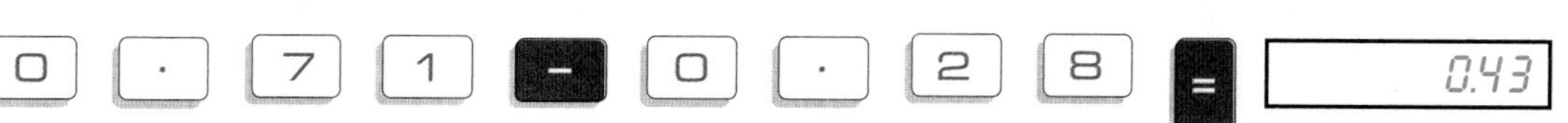

LESSON CONTINUES

Check

1. Explain why you write a 4 above the 5 tenths in Example C.

Add or subtract.

2. $\begin{array}{r} 0.46 \\ +0.19 \\ \hline \end{array}$

3. $\begin{array}{r} 0.75 \\ -0.56 \\ \hline \end{array}$

4. $\begin{array}{r} 0.29 \\ +0.33 \\ \hline \end{array}$

5. $\begin{array}{r} 0.63 \\ -0.48 \\ \hline \end{array}$

Practice and Problem Solving

Extra Practice, page 586, Set B

Add or subtract.

6. $\begin{array}{r} \$7.73 \\ -\$4.55 \\ \hline \end{array}$

7. $\begin{array}{r} \$0.39 \\ +\$0.46 \\ \hline \end{array}$

8. $\begin{array}{r} 5.5 \\ -1.3 \\ \hline \end{array}$

9. $\begin{array}{r} 0.80 \\ -0.53 \\ \hline \end{array}$

10. $\begin{array}{r} 2.3 \\ -1.1 \\ \hline \end{array}$

11. $\begin{array}{r} 2.35 \\ +6.19 \\ \hline \end{array}$

12. $\begin{array}{r} \$0.13 \\ +\$2.41 \\ \hline \end{array}$

13. $\begin{array}{r} 0.73 \\ -0.32 \\ \hline \end{array}$

14. $\begin{array}{r} \$3.33 \\ -\$0.25 \\ \hline \end{array}$

15. $\begin{array}{r} 0.5 \\ +0.4 \\ \hline \end{array}$

16. $\begin{array}{r} 1.6 \\ -1.2 \\ \hline \end{array}$

17. $\begin{array}{r} 0.79 \\ +0.12 \\ \hline \end{array}$

18. **? What's the Error?** Gina wrote 0.20 + 0.07 = 0.90. Describe her error. Find the correct sum.

19. **REASONING** Do you have to regroup to find 0.64 – 0.27? Explain.

20. **Vocabulary Power** *Cent* comes from a Latin word which means any collection of 100 items. Find out what the word *centi*pede means.

21. Rhea lives 0.92 kilometer from school. She has walked 0.38 kilometer so far this morning. How much farther must she walk to get to school?

22. **ALGEBRA** Use the price list. Conner bought popcorn and one other item with a $5 bill. His change was $4.05. What was the other item?

23. **Write a problem** about adding or subtracting money amounts. Use the price list. Trade with a partner and solve.

PRICE LIST	
Item	**Cost**
Popcorn	$0.50
Juice	$0.45
Trail mix	$0.39

24. David went to the store with $\$10.00$. He bought milk, apples, and eggs. He had $\$4.78$ when he left the store. The milk was $\$2.89$, and the eggs were $\$0.89$. How much were the apples?

Mixed Review and Test Prep

Find each missing factor. (p. 186)

25. ■ $\times 8 = 32$ **26.** $8 \times$ ■ $= 48$

27. ■ $\times 4 = 28$ **28.** $7 \times$ ■ $= 21$

Find each quotient. (p. 274)

29. $12 \div 6 =$ ■ **30.** $54 \div 6 =$ ■

31. $24 \div 8 =$ ■ **32.** $49 \div 7 =$ ■

33. **TEST PREP** Find $309 - 87$. (p. 92)

A 396 **C** 241
B 322 **D** 222

34. **TEST PREP** Lori had 5 carrots. She cut each carrot into 3 pieces. Then she ate 2 pieces. How many pieces of carrot did she have left? (p. 222)

F 10 **G** 12 **H** 13 **J** 15

Problem Solving LINKUP . . . to Reading

STRATEGY • MAKE PREDICTIONS You can use a graph to help you make a prediction. A prediction is a guess that is based on information.

USE DATA Emmett's sunflower should grow to be about 1 meter tall. Using the graph, predict whether the flower will be taller than 0.65 m at the end of the fifth week.

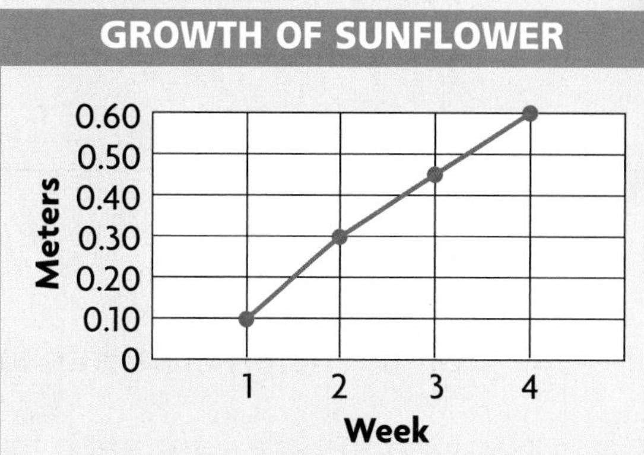

- By the end of week 2 the flower grew 0.20 meter.
- By the end of week 3 it grew 0.15 meter.
- By the end of week 4 it grew 0.15 meter.

The sunflower has grown at least 0.15 m each week. It was 0.60 m tall at the end of the fourth week.

$$0.60 \text{ m} + 0.15 \text{ m} = 0.75 \text{ m}$$

So, the sunflower will probably be taller than 0.65 m at the end of the fifth week.

1. Predict whether the sunflower will be taller than 0.75 m at the end of the sixth week. Explain.

2. Between which two weeks was the sunflower 0.35 m tall?

Problem Solving Strategy
Solve a Simpler Problem

Quick Review

1. 0.24 + 0.24
2. 0.3 + 0.3
3. 0.46 + 0.46
4. 0.2 + 0.2
5. 0.39 + 0.39

PROBLEM Alma has $5 to buy fruit. If she buys 1 pound of grapes and 2 pounds of bananas, how much money will she have left?

UNDERSTAND

- What are you asked to find?
- What information will you use?
- Is there information you will not use? If so, what?

PLAN

- What strategy can you use to solve the problem?

  You can *solve a simpler problem.*

SOLVE

- How can you use the strategy to solve the problem?

  Break the problem into simpler parts.

Find the price for each fruit.
1 lb of grapes: $0.98
2 lb of bananas: $0.45 + $0.45

Add to find the total cost.

grapes:	$0.98
bananas:	+$0.90
	$1.88

Subtract the total cost of the fruit from $5.

$$\begin{array}{r} \$5.00 \\ -\$1.88 \\ \hline \$3.12 \end{array}$$

So, Alma will have $3.12 left.

CHECK

- Look at the Problem. Does your answer make sense for the problem? Explain.

Problem Solving Practice

Use the prices on page 584. *Solve a simpler problem* to solve.

1. **What if** Alma buys 2 pounds of grapes and 1 pound of bananas? How much change will she receive from $5?
2. Brandon has $3. Does he have enough money to buy 2 apples and 2 pounds of grapes? Explain.

Strategies

- Draw a Diagram or Picture
- Make a Model or Act It Out
- Make an Organized List
- Find a Pattern
- Make a Table or Graph
- Predict and Test
- Work Backward
- **Solve a Simpler Problem**
- Write a Number Sentence
- Use Logical Reasoning

Problem Solving

Maddie bought 3 apples and 1 pound of grapes. She gave the clerk $2. How much change did she get? Use the prices on page 584.

3. Which number sentence could help you solve a simpler problem?
   - **A** $0.24 + $4 = $4.24
   - **B** $0.24 + $0.61 = $0.85
   - **C** $0.24 + $0.24 + $0.24 = $0.72
   - **D** $0.98 + $0.98 = $1.96
4. Which answers the question?
   - **F** $0.30
   - **G** $0.75
   - **H** $0.99
   - **J** $1.55

Mixed Strategy Practice

5. On Wednesday, Emily had $24.75. She earned $5.50 on Thursday. Then she spent $6.25. How much money does she have now?
6. Norm biked $\frac{7}{10}$ of a mile one Saturday. Joel biked $\frac{9}{10}$ of a mile. How much farther did Joel bike?
7. Mark is 1 year younger than Rick. Jaime is twice as old as Rick. Jaime is 12 years old. How old are Mark and Rick?
8. **? What's the Question?** The perimeter of Kiyo's rectangular rabbit pen is 20 ft. The length is 6 ft. The answer is 4 ft.
9. Shelly worked on her science project for 45 minutes on Monday and for 1 hour and 20 minutes on Tuesday. How much time did she work on her project in the two days?
10. Toni baby-sat from 4:30 P.M. until 8:30 P.M. She earned $3 per hour. How long did she baby-sit? How much did she earn?

Extra Practice

Set A (pp. 576–577)

Write the amount of money shown. Then write the amount as a fraction of a dollar.

1. 

2. 

3. 

4. 

5. Ian had 2 quarters, 2 dimes, and 5 pennies. He gave $0.50 to Lucia. What fraction of a dollar does he have left?

6. Draw two examples of how you could show $\frac{1}{4}$ of a dollar using dimes, nickels, and pennies.

Set B (pp. 580–583)

Add or subtract.

1. 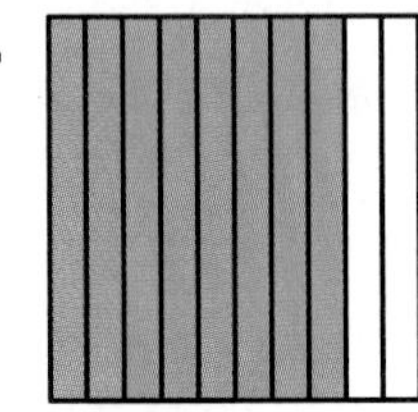
$$\begin{array}{r} 0.2 \\ +0.6 \\ \hline \end{array}$$

2. 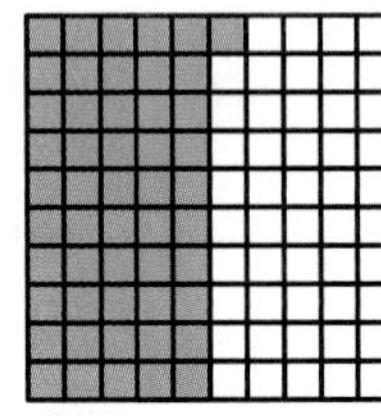
$$\begin{array}{r} 0.30 \\ +0.21 \\ \hline \end{array}$$

3. 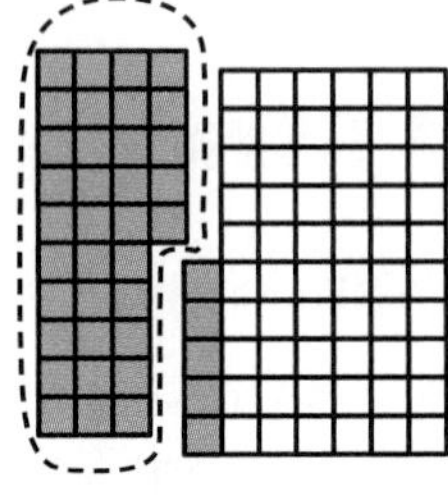
$$\begin{array}{r} 0.40 \\ -0.35 \\ \hline \end{array}$$

4. $\begin{array}{r} 0.1 \\ +0.6 \\ \hline \end{array}$

5. $\begin{array}{r} 3.09 \\ +2.51 \\ \hline \end{array}$

6. $\begin{array}{r} 1.7 \\ -0.2 \\ \hline \end{array}$

7. $\begin{array}{r} \$0.70 \\ -\$0.54 \\ \hline \end{array}$

8. $\begin{array}{r} 0.88 \\ +0.01 \\ \hline \end{array}$

9. $\begin{array}{r} \$4.56 \\ -\$2.38 \\ \hline \end{array}$

10. $\begin{array}{r} 0.5 \\ +0.3 \\ \hline \end{array}$

11. $\begin{array}{r} 8.43 \\ -7.22 \\ \hline \end{array}$

12. Mrs. Saguchi is training for a bike race. She rode 2.5 kilometers on Tuesday and 2.7 kilometers on Thursday. How far did she ride on those two days?

Review/Test

CHECK CONCEPTS

Write the money amount for each fraction of a dollar. (pp. 578–579)

1. $\frac{20}{100}$ **2.** $\frac{7}{100}$ **3.** $\frac{44}{100}$ **4.** $\frac{75}{100}$

Write the money amount. (pp. 578–579)

5. 14 hundredths of a dollar
6. 10 hundredths of a dollar
7. 54 hundredths of a dollar

CHECK SKILLS

Write the amount of money shown. Then write the amount as a fraction of a dollar. (pp. 576–577)

8. 

9. 

10. 

Add or subtract. (pp. 580–583)

11. $\begin{array}{r} 0.6 \\ +0.2 \\ \hline \end{array}$ **12.** $\begin{array}{r} 2.5 \\ +7.4 \\ \hline \end{array}$ **13.** $\begin{array}{r} 0.06 \\ +0.19 \\ \hline \end{array}$ **14.** $\begin{array}{r} \$3.52 \\ +\$4.16 \\ \hline \end{array}$

15. $\begin{array}{r} 0.9 \\ -0.6 \\ \hline \end{array}$ **16.** $\begin{array}{r} 2.8 \\ -0.1 \\ \hline \end{array}$ **17.** $\begin{array}{r} \$1.70 \\ -\$0.05 \\ \hline \end{array}$ **18.** $\begin{array}{r} 0.61 \\ -0.59 \\ \hline \end{array}$

PROBLEM SOLVING

Solve. (pp. 584–585)

19. Felix bought a notebook for \$1.29 and 2 pens for \$0.41 each. He gave the clerk \$5.00. How much change did he receive?

20. Ginger wants to buy 2 pears for \$0.35 each and 1 cookie for \$1.05. She has \$2.00. Will she have enough money? Explain.

Standardized Test Prep

NUMBER SENSE, CONCEPTS, AND OPERATIONS

1. Kira cut a pie into 8 pieces. She ate 1 piece. Kira's sister Kaylee ate 2 pieces.

Which fraction shows how much of the pie is left?

A $\frac{1}{4}$ **C** $\frac{3}{8}$

B $\frac{1}{8}$ **D** $\frac{5}{8}$

2. Keith has 31 hundredths of a dollar in his pocket. Which shows how much money Keith has?

F \$3.10
G \$3.01
H \$0.31
J \$0.03

3. **Explain It** The box has 10 apples in it.

About how many apples can be put in the box? Explain how you know.

GEOMETRY AND SPATIAL SENSE

4. Rashid drew the figure below.

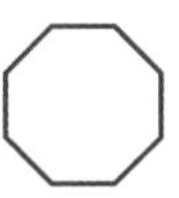

Which figure is similar to the one Rashid drew?

A **C**

B **D**

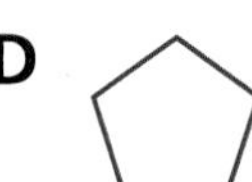

TIP **Understand the problem.** See item 5. To name a point on a grid, always start at 0 and move right first. Then move up.

5. Which ordered pair names the location of the star?

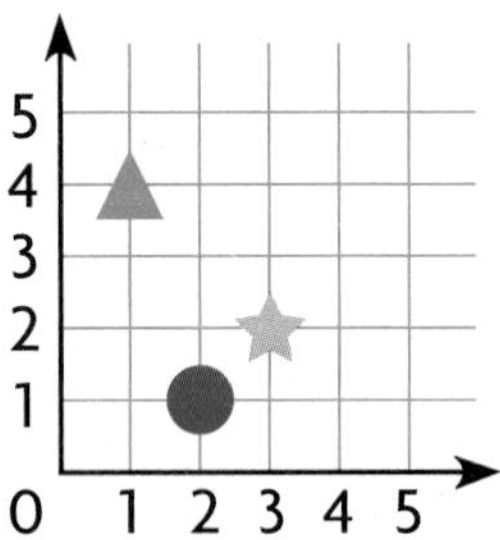

F (3, 2) **H** (2, 1)
G (1, 4) **J** (2, 3)

6. **Explain It** Ryan has a garden that is 6 feet wide and 8 feet long. Find the area and the perimeter of Ryan's garden. Explain the difference between area and perimeter.

ALGEBRAIC THINKING

7. Zach wrote this number pattern. Which number is missing?

15, 30, 45, ■, 75

A 55 **C** 65
B 60 **D** 70

8. This week, Curtis delivers papers on Sunday, Wednesday, and Saturday. If this pattern continues, on which days will Curtis deliver newspapers next week?

October						
Sun	Mon	Tue	Wed	Thu	Fri	Sat
		1	2	3	4	5
6	7	8	9	10	11	12
13	14	15	16	17	18	19
20	21	22	23	24	25	26
27	28	29	30	31		

F Monday and Thursday
G Tuesday and Saturday
H Wednesday and Friday
J Tuesday and Friday

9. Jade created the table below to show how much money she earned.

Hours Worked	1	2	3	4
Money Earned	\$8	\$16	\$24	\$32

Which rule describes the pattern in her table?

A Subtract \$7. **C** Add \$7.
B Multiply by \$8. **D** Divide by \$4.

10. Explain It Brenna wrote the number sentence below. Is this a true equation? Explain your answer.

$22 + 33 = 8 \times 7$

DATA ANALYSIS AND PROBABILITY

11. The line graph shows the estimated number of Florida panthers living in southern Florida.

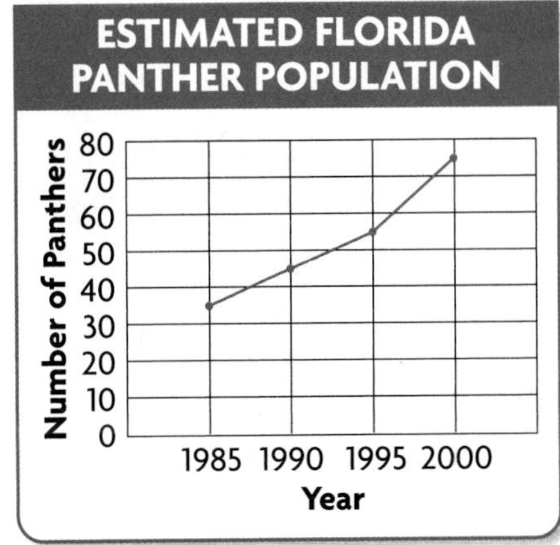

Which statement is true?

F There were fewer Florida panthers in 2000 than in 1990.
G There were more Florida panthers in 1990 than in 1995.
H There were more Florida panthers in 1995 than in 1985.
J There will likely be more than 400 Florida panthers by 2010.

12. Explain It The bar graph shows the results of Connor's survey. Write 3 different statements to describe the results of his survey.

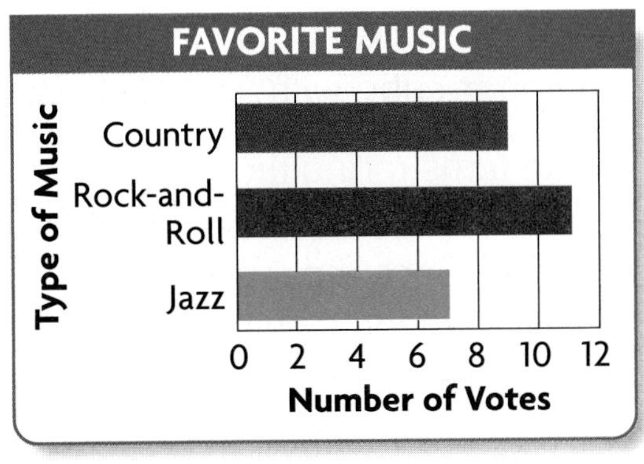

IT'S IN THE BAG

Fraction Trade Game

PROJECT Make a game to practice adding like fractions and finding equivalent fractions for the sums.

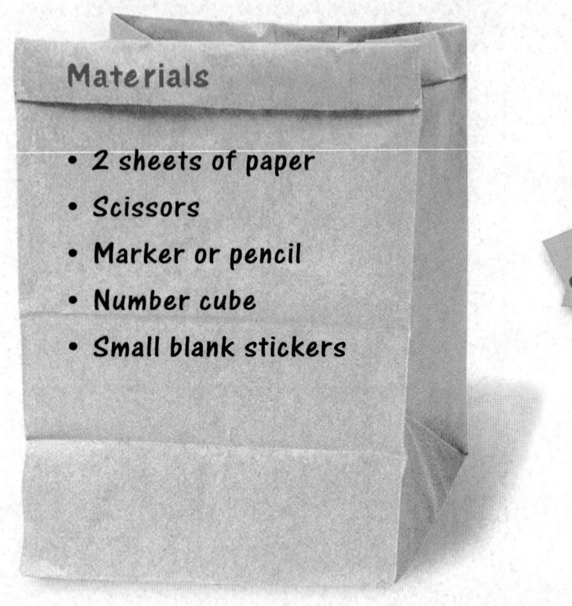

Materials
• 2 sheets of paper
• Scissors
• Marker or pencil
• Number cube
• Small blank stickers

Directions

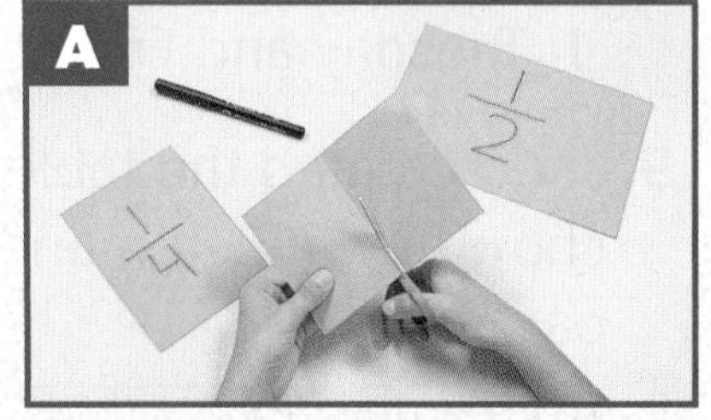

1. Fold a sheet of paper in half. Cut along the fold. Write $\frac{1}{2}$ on one of the two pieces. Fold the other piece in half, and cut along the fold. Write $\frac{1}{4}$ on one of the two pieces. Take the other piece, fold it in half, and cut along the fold. Write $\frac{1}{8}$ on each of these pieces. *(Picture A)*

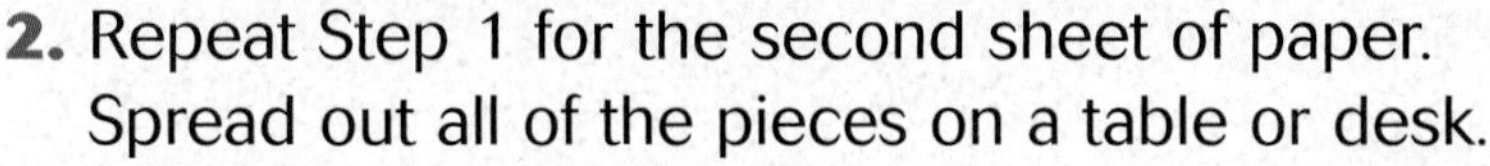

2. Repeat Step 1 for the second sheet of paper. Spread out all of the pieces on a table or desk.

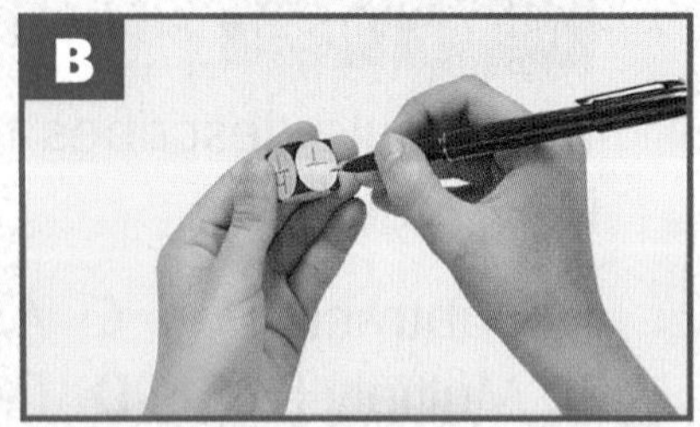

3. Use the stickers to label the six sides of the number cube with $\frac{1}{4}$, $\frac{1}{4}$, $\frac{1}{4}$, $\frac{1}{8}$, $\frac{1}{8}$, and $\frac{1}{8}$. *(Picture B)*

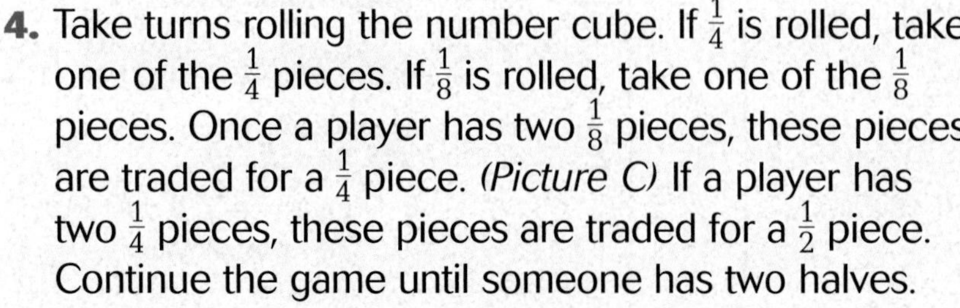

4. Take turns rolling the number cube. If $\frac{1}{4}$ is rolled, take one of the $\frac{1}{4}$ pieces. If $\frac{1}{8}$ is rolled, take one of the $\frac{1}{8}$ pieces. Once a player has two $\frac{1}{8}$ pieces, these pieces are traded for a $\frac{1}{4}$ piece. *(Picture C)* If a player has two $\frac{1}{4}$ pieces, these pieces are traded for a $\frac{1}{2}$ piece. Continue the game until someone has two halves.

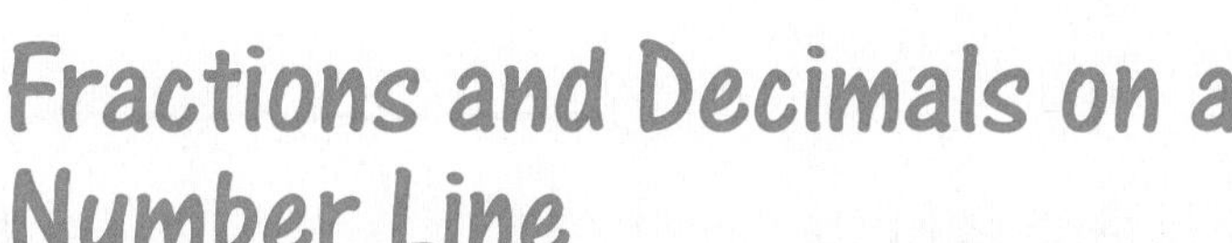

Fractions and Decimals on a Number Line

You can use decimal models and a number line to help you understand fractions and decimals.

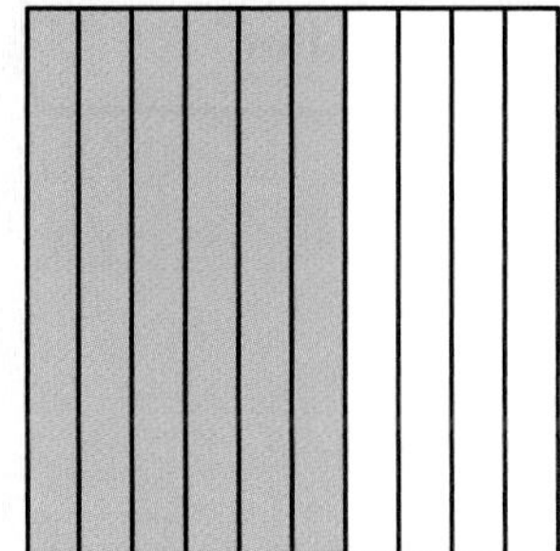

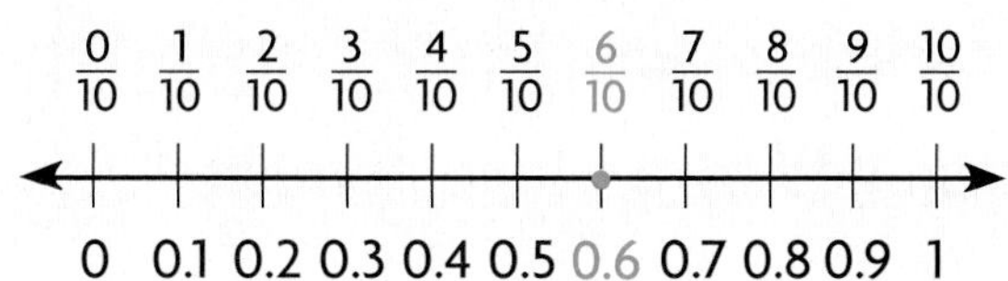

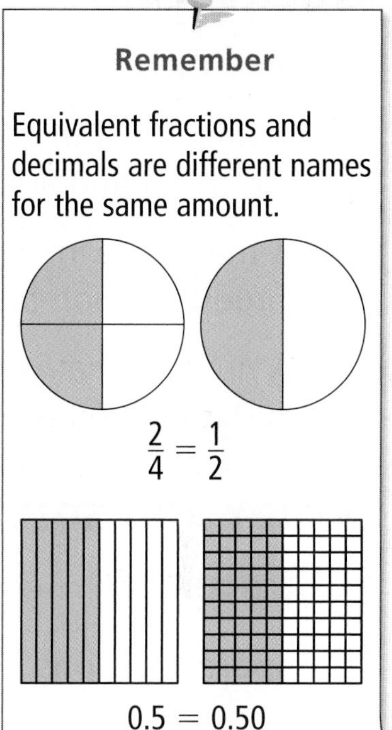

Remember
Equivalent fractions and decimals are different names for the same amount.
2/4 = 1/2
0.5 = 0.50

Since 0.6 and $\frac{6}{10}$ name 6 parts out of 10, they name the same amount, or are equivalent.

One whole can be divided into 100 equal parts on a number line.

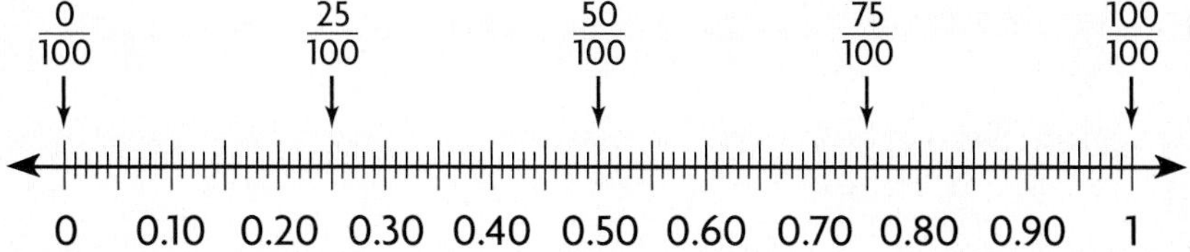

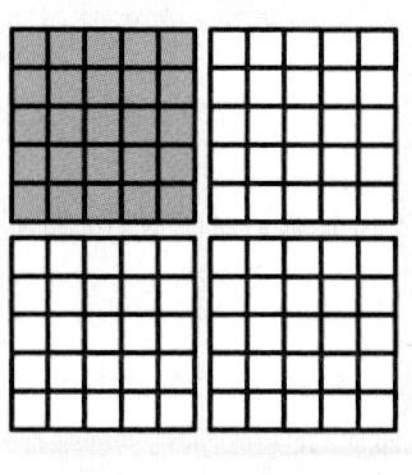

$\frac{25}{100} = \frac{1}{4}$

Try It

1. Find the point on the number line that is halfway between 0 and 1. Write a fraction name and a decimal name for that point.
2. Find the point on the number line that is one fourth of the way from 0 to 1. Write a fraction name and a decimal name for that point.

Use the number line. Write each as a fraction.

3. 0.30 **4.** 0.45 **5.** 0.75 **6.** 0.99

UNIT 8

Study Guide and Review

VOCABULARY

Choose the best term from the box.

1. A number with one or more digits to the right of the decimal point is a _?_. (p. 558)
2. A fraction is in _?_ when a model of it uses the largest fraction bars possible. (p. 542)
3. A number that is represented by a whole number and a fraction is a _?_. (p. 532)

decimal
fraction
equivalent fractions
simplest form
mixed number

STUDY AND SOLVE

Chapter 25

Compare fractions.

Compare $\frac{1}{2}$ and $\frac{3}{5}$.

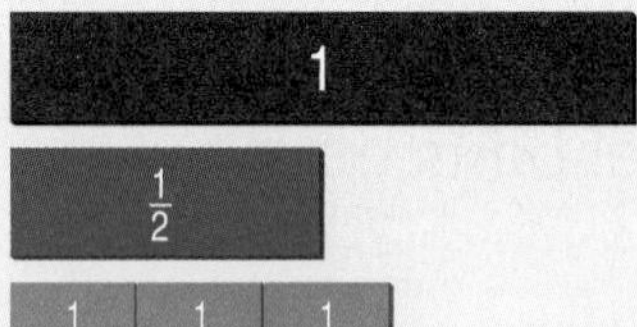

The bar for $\frac{1}{2}$ is shorter than the bars for $\frac{3}{5}$.

So, $\frac{1}{2} < \frac{3}{5}$ or $\frac{3}{5} > \frac{1}{2}$.

Compare. Write <, >, or = for each ●. (pp. 526–529)

4. 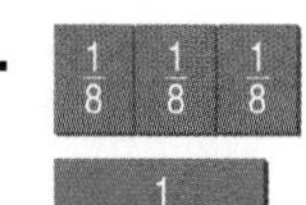

$\frac{3}{8}$ ● $\frac{1}{3}$

5. 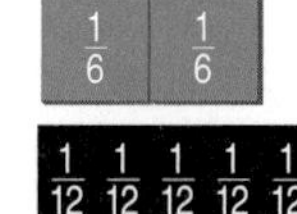

$\frac{2}{6}$ ● $\frac{5}{12}$

Chapter 26

Add and subtract like fractions.

Write the answer in simplest form.

$\frac{3}{8} + \frac{1}{8} = \frac{4}{8}$

$\frac{4}{8}$ in simplest form is $\frac{1}{2}$.

$\frac{4}{6} - \frac{2}{6} = \frac{2}{6}$

$\frac{2}{6}$ in simplest form is $\frac{1}{3}$.

Use fraction bars to find the sum or difference in simplest form. (pp. 540–549)

6. $\frac{1}{8} + \frac{1}{8} = \blacksquare$
7. $\frac{2}{4} + \frac{1}{4} = \blacksquare$
8. $\frac{1}{6} + \frac{3}{6} = \blacksquare$
9. $\frac{9}{12} - \frac{5}{12} = \blacksquare$
10. $\frac{2}{5} - \frac{1}{5} = \blacksquare$
11. $\frac{4}{10} - \frac{2}{10} = \blacksquare$

Chapter 27

Relate fractions and decimals.

Write the fraction and the decimal for the shaded part.

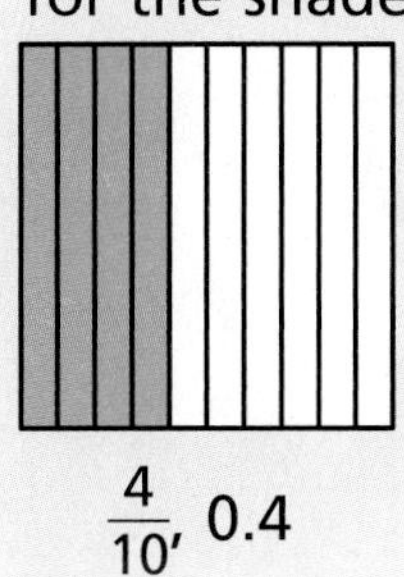

$\frac{4}{10}$, 0.4

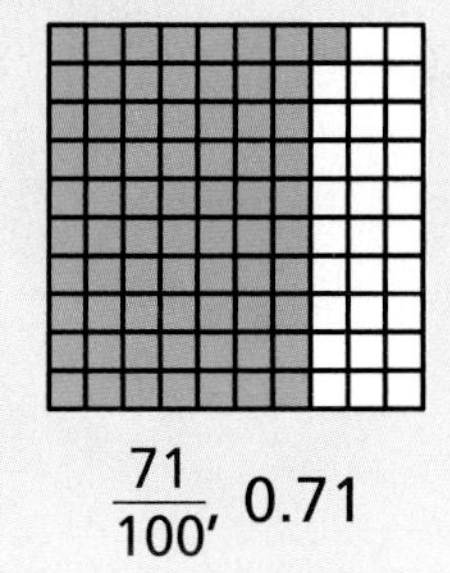

$\frac{71}{100}$, 0.71

Write the fraction and the decimal for the shaded part. (pp. 562–563)

12. 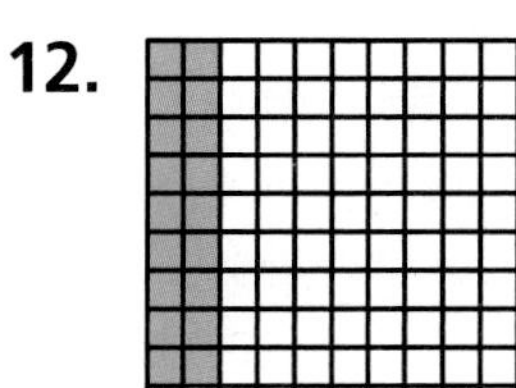

Write each fraction as a decimal. (pp. 560–563)

13. $\frac{6}{10}$ **14.** $\frac{12}{100}$ **15.** $\frac{55}{100}$

Chapter 28

Add and subtract decimals.

Subtract. $0.83 − $0.56

$$\begin{array}{r} \scriptstyle 7\ 13 \\ \$0.8\not{3} \\ -\$0.56 \\ \hline \$0.27 \end{array}$$

- Line up the decimal points.
- Subtract. Regroup if necessary.
- Write the decimal point in the difference.

Remember to write the dollar sign in your answer when you are adding or subtracting money amounts.

Find the sum or difference. (pp. 580–583)

16. $\begin{array}{r} \$0.23 \\ +\$0.44 \\ \hline \end{array}$ **17.** $\begin{array}{r} 0.78 \\ +0.04 \\ \hline \end{array}$

18. $\begin{array}{r} \$0.64 \\ +\$0.29 \\ \hline \end{array}$ **19.** $\begin{array}{r} 0.5 \\ -0.4 \\ \hline \end{array}$

20. $\begin{array}{r} \$0.72 \\ -\$0.19 \\ \hline \end{array}$ **21.** $\begin{array}{r} \$0.19 \\ -\$0.12 \\ \hline \end{array}$

PROBLEM SOLVING PRACTICE

Solve. (pp. 550–551, 584–585)

22. Cole and Jon are sharing a pizza. If they each eat $\frac{1}{3}$ of the pizza, is it reasonable to say that $\frac{1}{2}$ of the pizza will be left? Explain.

23. Mr. Jackson is training for a race. Last week, he ran 1.25 miles on each of two days. He ran 1.1 miles on each of two other days. How far did Mr. Jackson run last week?

PERFORMANCE ASSESSMENT

TASK A • Mmmm . . . BROWNIES!

Jeff made a pan of brownies to share with Carla and Keith. The brownies were cut into equal pieces. The three friends each ate a different number of brownies.

a. Make a drawing of the pan of brownies. Mark each piece with J, C, or K to show which child ate it.

b. Write each child's name and tell what fraction of the brownies he or she ate.

c. Who ate the most brownies?

d. Write a fraction in simplest form that tells what part of the brownies Jeff and Keith ate altogether.

TASK B • SCHOOL FAIR

Colton, Erica, and Whitney each have 100 tickets to sell for the school fair. Colton sold 45 tickets, and Whitney sold 70 tickets. Erica sold more tickets than Colton but fewer tickets than Whitney.

a. Shade the decimal model to show the part of her 100 tickets that Erica may have sold.

b. Write a decimal and a fraction for the part of the model that you shaded.

c. Each ticket for the fair costs $\frac{1}{4}$ of a dollar. Erica's brother has $2.00. Can he buy 5 tickets and still have $\frac{1}{2}$ of a dollar left to buy a pretzel?

Technology Linkup

Fractions and Decimals

Marcus and Tyler were painting a fence. Marcus painted $\frac{3}{10}$ of the fence. Tyler painted $\frac{2}{5}$ of the fence. Name these amounts as decimals. Compare the decimals to decide who painted more of the fence.

STEP 1

Use a calculator to name $\frac{3}{10}$ as a decimal. $\frac{3}{10}$ is the same as 3 divided by 10. Press:

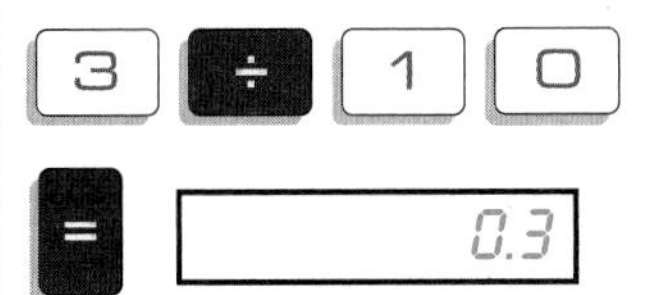

STEP 2

Use a calculator to name $\frac{2}{5}$ as a decimal. $\frac{2}{5}$ is the same as 2 divided by 5. Press:

STEP 3

Compare the decimals.
$0.3 < 0.4$

Since $0.3 < 0.4$, $\frac{3}{10} < \frac{2}{5}$.

So, Tyler painted more of the fence than Marcus.

Practice and Problem Solving

Use a calculator to name each fraction as a decimal. Then compare the decimals using <, >, or =.

1. $\frac{1}{4}$ ● $\frac{1}{5}$ **2.** $\frac{4}{10}$ ● $\frac{2}{5}$ **3.** $\frac{1}{2}$ ● $\frac{7}{10}$ **4.** $\frac{30}{100}$ ● $\frac{3}{4}$

5. $\frac{75}{100}$ ● $\frac{3}{4}$ **6.** $\frac{8}{10}$ ● $\frac{3}{5}$ **7.** $\frac{6}{10}$ ● $\frac{2}{4}$ **8.** $\frac{4}{5}$ ● $\frac{9}{10}$

GO ON-LINE **Multimedia Math Glossary** www.harcourtschool.com/mathglossary

Vocabulary Power Look up *decimal* in the Multimedia Math Glossary. Choose any three decimals that you used in Exercises 1–8. Write each decimal in word form.

▲ There are many beautiful views along Skyline Drive.

in Virginia

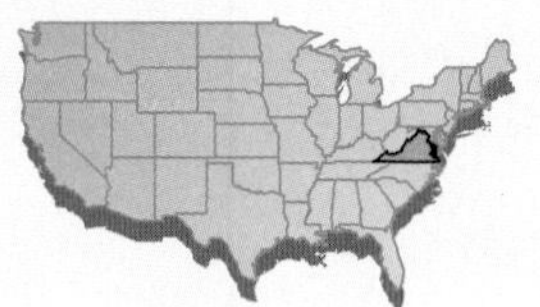

SHENANDOAH NATIONAL PARK

Shenandoah National Park in the Blue Ridge Mountains is a popular place for hiking and camping. Skyline Drive is a 105-mile-long road through the park. While in the park, be sure to visit Luray Caverns in Luray, Virginia.

USE DATA For 1–3, use the table.

1. What is the difference between the greatest amount and the least amount of average monthly rainfall in Luray, Virginia?
2. What is the average rainfall for the month of May? Write this decimal in word form and in expanded form. Then write this decimal as a mixed number.
3. What is the total average rainfall for the first six months of the year?
4. **STRETCH YOUR THINKING** The Luray Singing Tower has 47 bells. The largest bell weighs 7,640 pounds, and the smallest bell weighs $12\frac{1}{2}$ pounds. What is the difference in the weight of the largest and the smallest bells?

Average Rainfall in Luray

Month	Inches
January	2.5
February	2.5
March	3.1
April	2.7
May	3.9
June	3.4
July	3.7
August	4.2
September	3.5
October	3.5
November	3.2
December	2.7

HIKING IN SHENANDOAH NATIONAL PARK

All hiking trails in the park have blazes, which are marks painted on trees to give information. Different colors of paint mean different things. For example, yellow blazes mean that the trail is open to hikers and horseback riders.

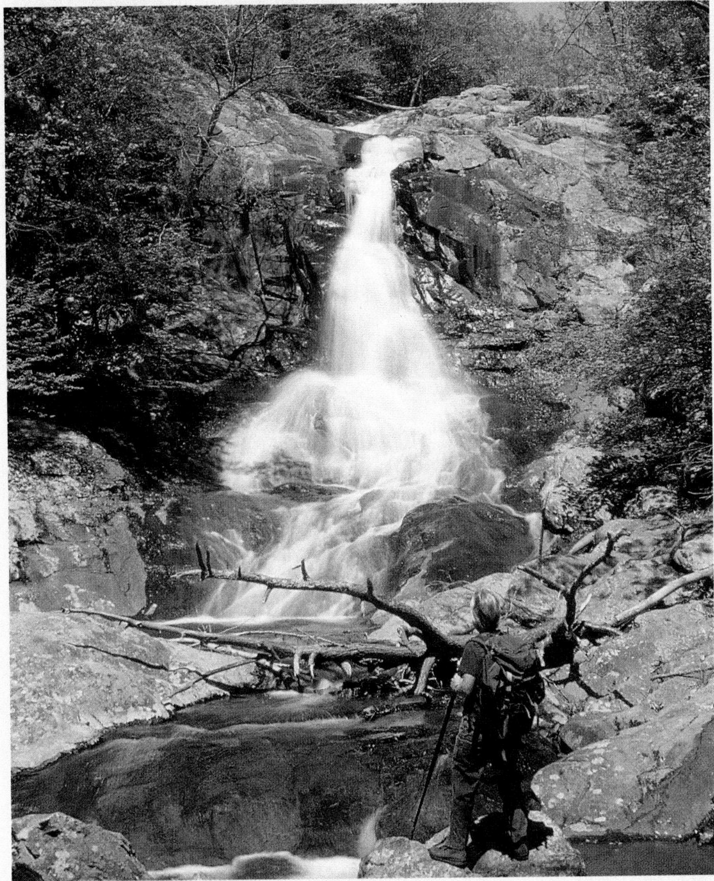

▲ Hiking trails may lead to waterfalls, deep canyons, or high summits.

▲ The park has more than 500 miles of trails.

▲ While in the park, look for the different kinds of wildflowers that grow there.

1. Carla is hiking to the viewpoint at Chimney Rock. The trail is 3.4 miles round-trip. If she has hiked 1.9 miles already, how much farther does she have to go to finish hiking the trail?
2. Michael spends $12.95 on a guidebook and $6.25 on postcards. How much does he spend in all?
3. Emma took a camera along on her hike. She took 6 photographs of wildflowers and 2 photographs of insects. What fraction of her photographs were of wildflowers?
4. Theo hiked $\frac{1}{4}$ of a mile. Use fraction bars to find two fractions that are equivalent to this fraction.

CHAPTER 29

Multiply by 1-Digit Numbers

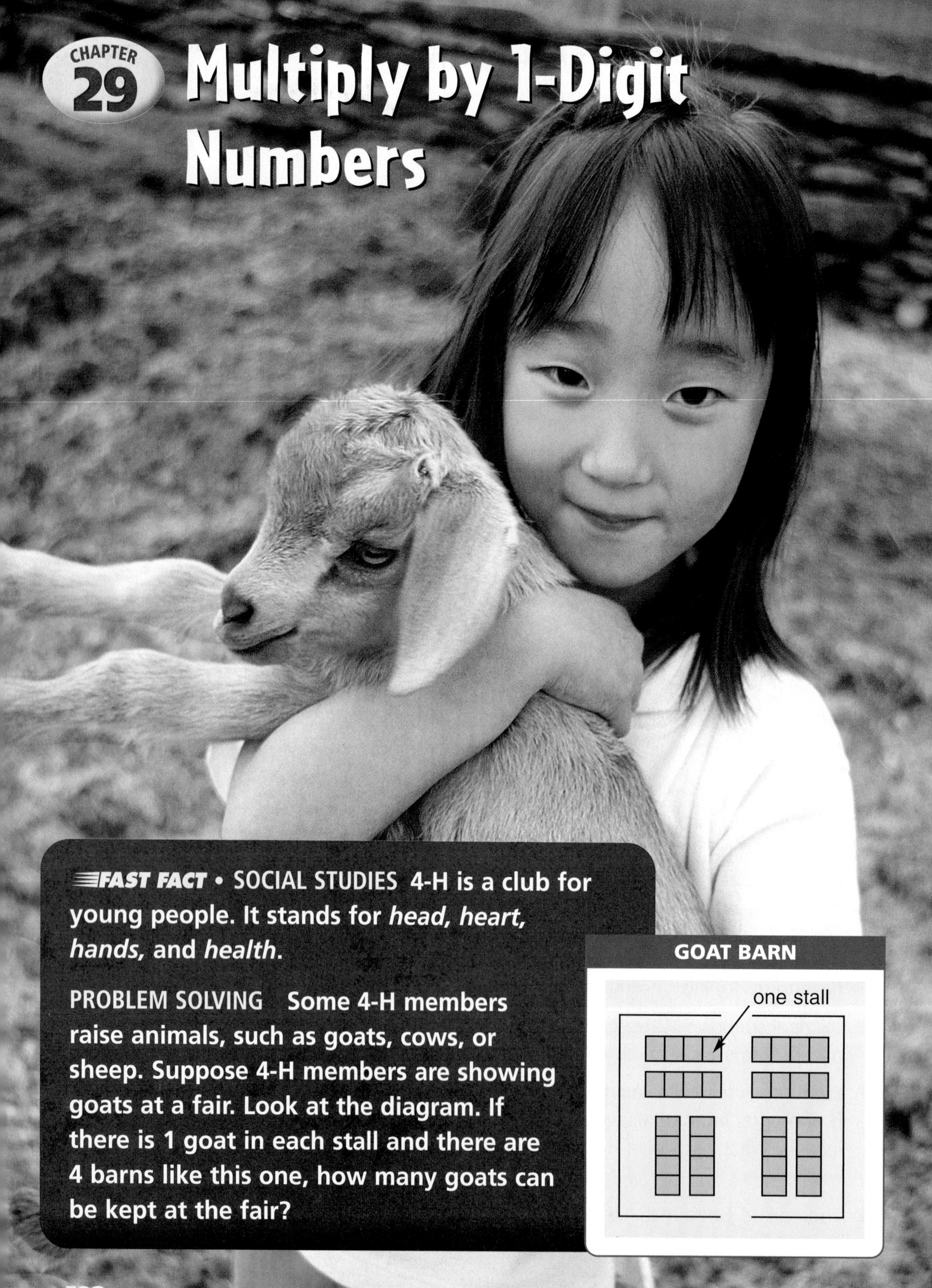

FAST FACT • SOCIAL STUDIES **4-H is a club for young people. It stands for *head, heart, hands,* and *health*.**

PROBLEM SOLVING **Some 4-H members raise animals, such as goats, cows, or sheep. Suppose 4-H members are showing goats at a fair. Look at the diagram. If there is 1 goat in each stall and there are 4 barns like this one, how many goats can be kept at the fair?**

GOAT BARN

one stall

CHECK WHAT YOU KNOW

Use this page to help you review and remember important skills needed for Chapter 29.

ADDITION

Find the sum.

1. $\begin{array}{r} 47 \\ +64 \\ \hline \end{array}$
2. $\begin{array}{r} 29 \\ +81 \\ \hline \end{array}$
3. $\begin{array}{r} 52 \\ +119 \\ \hline \end{array}$
4. $\begin{array}{r} 28 \\ +253 \\ \hline \end{array}$
5. $\begin{array}{r} 88 \\ +93 \\ \hline \end{array}$
6. $\begin{array}{r} 346 \\ +389 \\ \hline \end{array}$
7. $\begin{array}{r} 284 \\ +172 \\ \hline \end{array}$
8. $\begin{array}{r} 314 \\ +726 \\ \hline \end{array}$
9. $\begin{array}{r} 672 \\ +361 \\ \hline \end{array}$
10. $\begin{array}{r} 521 \\ +229 \\ \hline \end{array}$

MULTIPLICATION FACTS

Find the product.

11. $6 \times 7 = \blacksquare$
12. $5 \times 5 = \blacksquare$
13. $\blacksquare = 9 \times 4$
14. $9 \times 1 = \blacksquare$
15. $7 \times 10 = \blacksquare$
16. $\blacksquare = 8 \times 6$
17. $5 \times 9 = \blacksquare$
18. $\blacksquare = 2 \times 3$
19. $\blacksquare = 4 \times 5$
20. $4 \times 8 = \blacksquare$
21. $\blacksquare = 0 \times 6$
22. $8 \times 7 = \blacksquare$
23. $\begin{array}{r} 5 \\ \times 7 \\ \hline \end{array}$
24. $\begin{array}{r} 8 \\ \times 4 \\ \hline \end{array}$
25. $\begin{array}{r} 4 \\ \times 9 \\ \hline \end{array}$
26. $\begin{array}{r} 10 \\ \times\ 3 \\ \hline \end{array}$
27. $\begin{array}{r} 8 \\ \times 8 \\ \hline \end{array}$

VOCABULARY POWER

REVIEW

multiple [mul′tə•pəl]

Part of the word *multiple* is *multi,* which means "many times over." Look in a dictionary and find another word that begins with *multi*. What does the word mean?

www.harcourtschool.com/mathglossary

LESSON 1

Algebra: Multiply Multiples of 10 and 100

Quick Review

1. $2 \times 4 = \blacksquare$
2. $5 \times 7 = \blacksquare$
3. $\blacksquare = 2 \times 10$
4. $10 \times 7 = \blacksquare$
5. $\blacksquare = 6 \times 10$

MATERIALS
base-ten blocks

Explore

You can use models or drawings to find multiples. A multiple is the product of a given whole number and another whole number.

$3 \times 2 = \mathbf{6} \leftarrow$ 6 is a multiple of 3 and 2.

HANDS ON

Activity 1

Model or draw the first nine multiples of 10 and 100. The first three are shown.

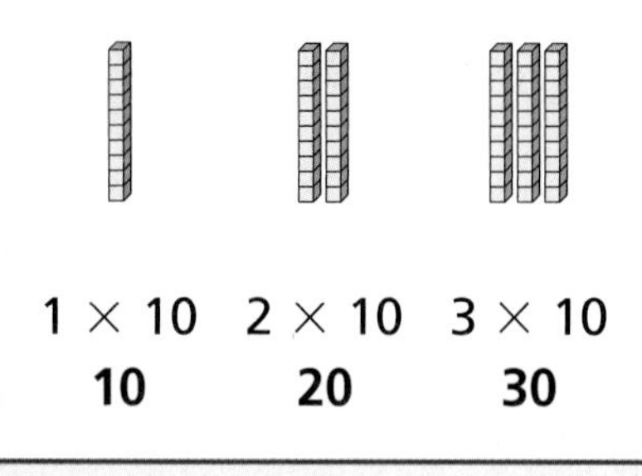

1×10	2×10	3×10
10	**20**	**30**

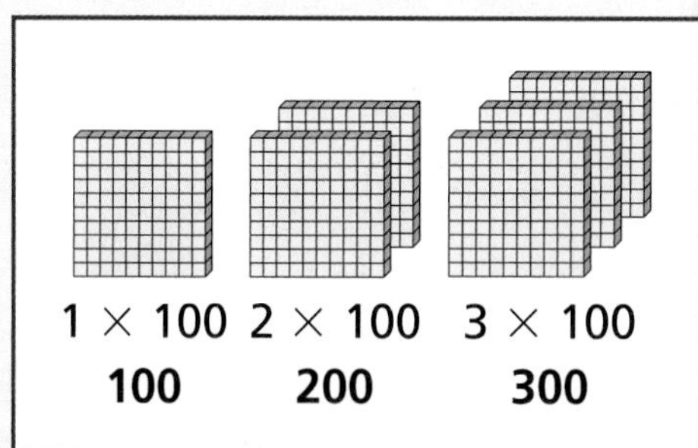

1×100	2×100	3×100
100	**200**	**300**

- What are the first nine multiples of 10? the first nine multiples of 100?

Activity 2 You can multiply by multiples of 10 and 100. Find 4×30.

STEP 1

Model 4 groups of 30.

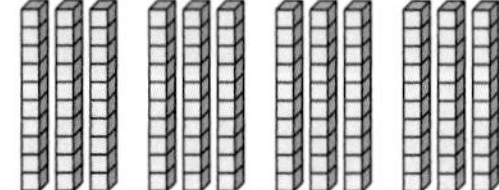

STEP 2

Combine the tens. Regroup 12 tens as 1 hundred 2 tens.

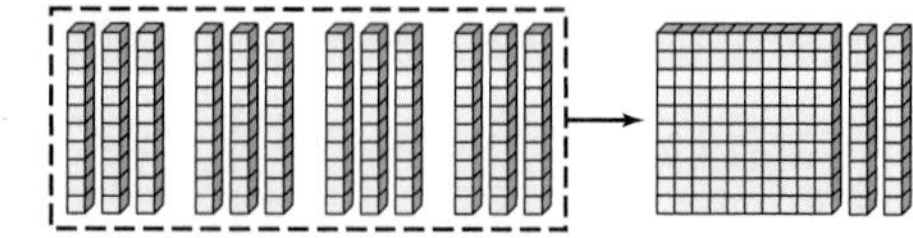

So, $4 \times 30 = 120$.

Try It

Use base-ten blocks to find each product.

a. $5 \times 20 = \blacksquare$ **b.** $4 \times 200 = \blacksquare$ **c.** $6 \times 30 = \blacksquare$

Connect

You can use multiplication facts and patterns to help you multiply multiples of 10 and 100.

Examples Use a basic fact. Then use a pattern.

$3 \times 2 = 6$ $3 \times 20 = 60$ $3 \times 200 = 600$	The product has the same number of zeros as the factor.
$2 \times 5 = 10$ $2 \times 50 = 100$ $2 \times 500 = 1{,}000$	When a basic fact has a zero in the product, all products in the pattern have an additional zero.

Practice and Problem Solving

Copy and complete. Use patterns and mental math to help.

1. $6 \times 1 = \blacksquare$ $\quad 6 \times 10 = \blacksquare$ $\quad 6 \times 100 = \blacksquare$

2. $4 \times 5 = \blacksquare$ $\quad 4 \times 50 = \blacksquare$ $\quad 4 \times 500 = \blacksquare$

Use mental math and basic facts to find the product.

3. $2 \times 70 = \blacksquare$ **4.** $\blacksquare = 6 \times 400$ **5.** $4 \times 800 = \blacksquare$

6. $\blacksquare = 5 \times 300$ **7.** $5 \times 60 = \blacksquare$ **8.** $\blacksquare = 3 \times 90$

9. USE DATA Emilio wants to save money for a new bicycle. How many dollars does he need to save? Use the table.

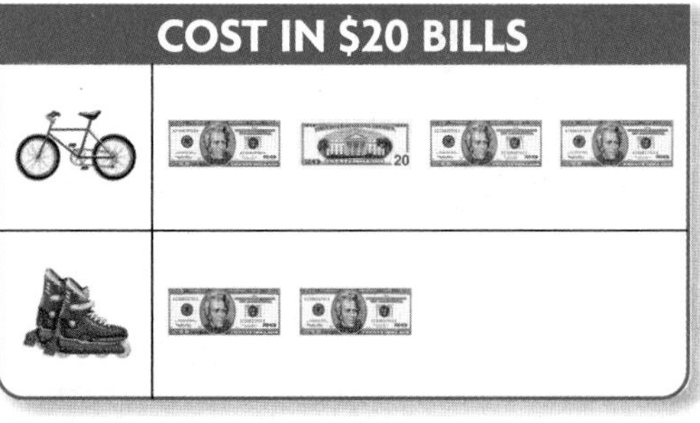

10. REASONING Tom adds a number to itself and then subtracts 13. The answer is 37. What is Tom's number?

11. **? What's the Question?** A case of popcorn contains 80 boxes. The answer is 480 boxes.

Mixed Review and Test Prep

For 12–14, divide. (p. 280)

12. $4\overline{)32}$ **13.** $7\overline{)28}$ **14.** $5\overline{)40}$

15. $5.2 + 3.1$ (p. 580) **16.** $4.9 + 5.8$ (p. 580)

17. TEST PREP The parking lot can hold 132 cars. There are 84 cars in the lot. How many more cars can park in the lot? (p. 90)

A 36 **B** 46 **C** 48 **D** 58

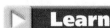

LESSON 2

Multiply 2-Digit Numbers

Learn

Students in the school chorus stand in 4 rows of 16. How many students are in the chorus?

$4 \times 16 = \blacksquare$

Quick Review

1. $6 \times 5 = \blacksquare$
2. $\blacksquare = 4 \times 3$
3. $10 \times 6 = \blacksquare$
4. $\blacksquare = 6 \times 8$
5. $4 \times 10 = \blacksquare$

One Way Build arrays with base-ten blocks to model the problem. Find the product.

STEP 1

Use 1 ten 6 ones to show 16. Make 4 rows of 16 to show 4×16.

STEP 2

Combine the ones and the tens to find the product.

$4 \times 10 = 40$ $\quad$ $4 \times 6 = 24$

$40 + 24 = 64$

$4 \times 16 = 64$

So, 64 students are in the chorus.

- How did you combine the ones and tens to find the product?

Another Way Draw arrays on grid paper to model the problem.

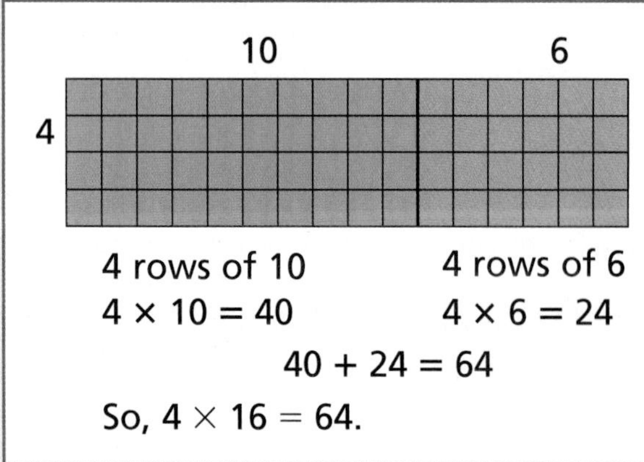

4 rows of 10 $\quad$ 4 rows of 6

$4 \times 10 = 40$ $\quad$ $4 \times 6 = 24$

$40 + 24 = 64$

So, $4 \times 16 = 64$.

- How could you find 3×17 using grid paper?

Record Multiplication

For the field trip, there are 5 buses with 23 people on each bus. How many people in all are going on the field trip?

$5 \times 23 = \blacksquare$ or $\begin{array}{r} 23 \\ \times\ 5 \\ \hline \end{array}$

STEP 1

Model 5 groups of 23. Multiply the ones.

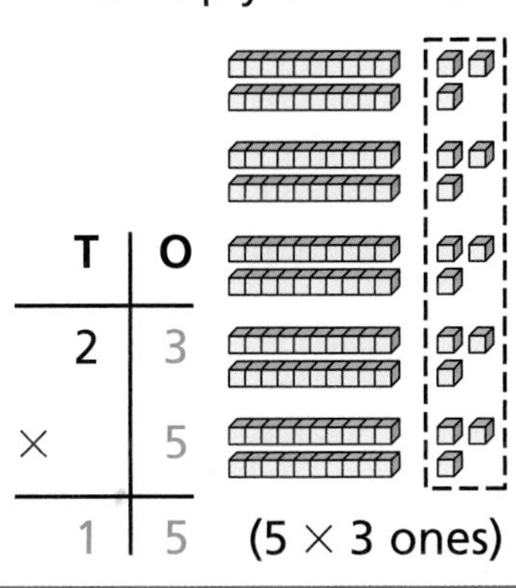

	T	O
	2	3
×		5
	1	5

(5 × 3 ones)

STEP 2

Multiply the tens.

	H	T	O
		2	3
×			5
		1	5
	1	0	0

(5 × 2 tens)

STEP 3

Add to find the product.

	H	T	O
		2	3
×			5
		1	5
+	1	0	0
	1	1	5

So, 115 people are going on the field trip.

- How does knowing 5×2 help you multiply 5×20?

Examples

A

$$\begin{array}{rl} 32 & \\ \times\ 4 & \\ \hline 8 & (4 \times 2 \text{ ones}) \\ +120 & (4 \times 3 \text{ tens}) \\ \hline 128 & \end{array}$$

B

$$\begin{array}{rl} 51 & \\ \times\ 3 & \\ \hline 3 & (3 \times 1 \text{ one}) \\ +150 & (3 \times 5 \text{ tens}) \\ \hline 153 & \end{array}$$

C

$$\begin{array}{rl} 73 & \\ \times\ 5 & \\ \hline 15 & (5 \times 3 \text{ ones}) \\ +350 & (5 \times 7 \text{ tens}) \\ \hline 365 & \end{array}$$

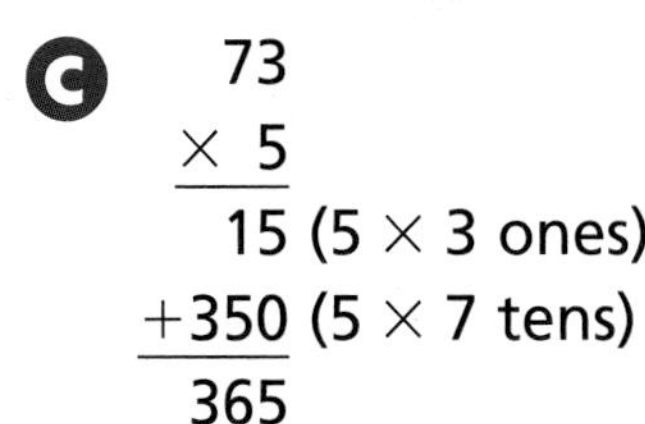

Check

1. **Model** 5×18 with base-ten blocks or grid paper. Use paper and pencil to record what you did.

Technology Link

More Practice: Harcourt Mega Math The Numbers Game, *Up, Up, and Array*, Level J

Find the product.

2. 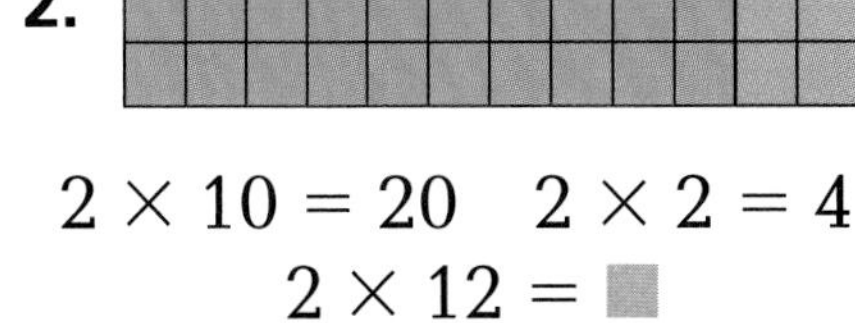

$2 \times 10 = 20 \quad 2 \times 2 = 4$

$2 \times 12 = \blacksquare$

3. $\begin{array}{r} 24 \\ \times\ 3 \\ \hline \end{array}$

4. $\begin{array}{r} 38 \\ \times\ 2 \\ \hline \end{array}$

Practice and Problem Solving

Extra Practice, page 612, Set A

Find the product.

5. $3 \times 10 = 30 \quad 3 \times 4 = 12$

$3 \times 14 = ■$

6. 22×4

7. 47×2

Find the product. You may wish to use base-ten blocks or grid paper.

8. 18×3 **9.** 31×5 **10.** 40×6 **11.** 19×8

12. 18×2 **13.** 41×3 **14.** 17×3 **15.** 52×5

16. 14×9 **17.** 21×4 **18.** 28×4 **19.** 15×5

ALGEBRA For 20–23, use base-ten blocks to find the missing factor.

20. $6 \times ■ = 132$ **21.** $■ \times 25 = 100$ **22.** $■ \times 21 = 63$ **23.** $4 \times ■ = 56$

24. **Write a problem** There are 24 hours in a day. There are 7 days in a week. Write a multiplication problem using this information. Solve your problem.

25. **What's the Error?** Lori says that the product 3×16 is the same as the sum $16 + 16$. Describe Lori's error and then find the product.

26. Tanya bought 2 pairs of jeans for \$18 each, a shirt for \$12, and a sweatshirt for \$8. How much did Tanya spend?

27. **REASONING** The sum of two numbers is 20. The product of the two numbers is 75. What are the numbers?

28. **USE DATA** How many bagels were sold on Wednesday? What was the total number of bagels sold in the three days?

NUMBER OF BAGELS SOLD

Monday	◯ ◯ ◯ ◯
Tuesday	◯ ◯ ◯
Wednesday	◯ ◯ ◯ ◯ ◯ ◯

Key: Each ◯ = 12 bagels.

Mixed Review and Test Prep

Find the number that the variable stands for. (p. 242)

29. $2 \times a = 8$
30. $b \times 3 = 18$
31. $c \times 4 = 16$
32. $8 \times d = 56$
33. $5 \times a = 35$
34. $b \times 7 = 63$
35. $c \times 6 = 42$
36. $d \times 9 = 81$

37. **TEST PREP** Choose the unit you would use to measure the length of your finger. (p. 342)

A foot **C** inch
B yard **D** mile

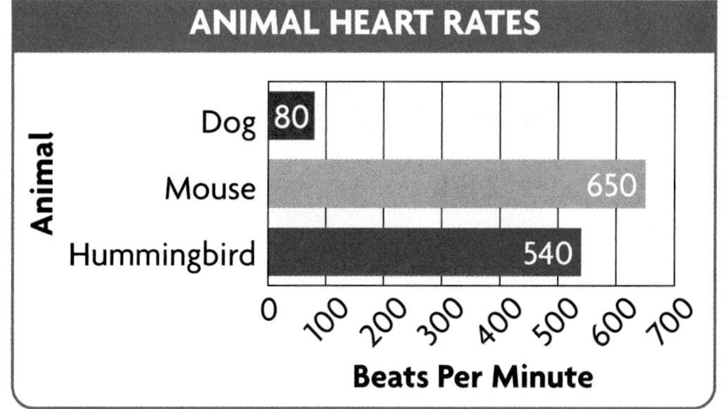

38. **TEST PREP** How many more beats per minute does a hummingbird's heart beat than a dog's heart? (p. 324)

F 460 **G** 505 **H** 585 **J** 595

Problem Solving LINKUP . . . to Art

Dr. John Biggers is known for his murals about African American and African culture. He visited Africa in 1957. While there he studied the traditions, culture, and people. In 1997 an exhibit showed almost 100 of John Biggers' drawings, prints, sculptures, paintings, and murals. The exhibit traveled to different art museums.

John Thomas Biggers *Starry Crown* 1987. Acrylic mixed media on masonite Dallas Museum of Art. Museum League Purchase Fund.

Starry Crown **is one of John Biggers' most famous works of art.**

1. **What if** 35 people see the John Biggers exhibit every hour? How many people see it in 8 hours?
2. A school field trip brings 3 buses with 57 students in each bus to the museum to see the exhibit. How many students are there in all?
3. Suppose the museum sells prints of John Biggers' paintings for \$13 each. How much would 7 prints cost?
4. Suppose the museum sells John Biggers T-shirts for \$19 each. How much would it cost to buy 5 T-shirts?

LESSON 3

Problem Solving Skill
Choose the Operation

UNDERSTAND › PLAN › SOLVE › CHECK

Quick Review

1. $\begin{array}{r} 15 \\ \times\ 6 \\ \hline \end{array}$
2. $\begin{array}{r} 72 \\ \times\ 8 \\ \hline \end{array}$
3. $\begin{array}{r} 232 \\ +125 \\ \hline \end{array}$
4. $\begin{array}{r} 495 \\ -208 \\ \hline \end{array}$
5. $18 \div 9 = \blacksquare$

GRAND CHAMP Steve will work 28 hours each week to get his cattle ready for the State Fair. The fair is in 4 weeks. How many hours will Steve work to get his cattle ready?

This chart can help you decide which operation to use.

Add	• Join groups of different amounts.
Subtract	• Take away. • Compare amounts.
Multiply	• Join equal groups.
Divide	• Separate into equal groups. • Find the number in each group.

Since you are joining equal groups, you multiply.

number of weeks worked ↓	×	number of hours worked per week	=	total number of hours
4	×	28	=	■

or $\begin{array}{r} 28 \\ \times\ 4 \\ \hline 112 \end{array}$

So, Steve will work 112 hours to get his cattle ready.

MATH IDEA Before you solve a problem, decide what operation to use.

Talk About It

- What other operation could you use to solve the problem? Explain.
- **What if** Steve will work 8 more hours during the week before the fair? How many hours will he work to get ready?

Problem Solving Practice

Write whether you would *add, subtract, multiply,* or *divide.* Then solve.

1. Tamara spends 30 minutes each day grooming her horse. How many minutes does she spend grooming her horse in 5 days?

2. Drew paid $12.99 for a state fair T-shirt and $10.95 for a cap. How much more did the T-shirt cost than the cap?

Mieko bought 3 flowers for 75¢ each. How much did she spend for the flowers?

3. Which is the best number sentence to use to solve the problem?
   A 75¢ + 3¢ = ■
   B 75¢ − 3¢ = ■
   C 3 × 75¢ = ■
   D 75¢ ÷ 3 = ■

4. How much did Mieko spend for the flowers?
   F 25¢
   G 75¢
   H $1.50
   J $2.25

Mixed Applications

USE DATA For 5–9, use the table.

ANIMAL CONTEST ENTRIES	
Animals	**Number of Entries**
Horses	60
Hogs	55
Sheep	50
Rabbits	30

5. Six rabbits were entered in a special contest. The others were put into 3 equal groups for the Largest Rabbit Contest. How many rabbits were in each of the 3 groups?

6. The horses are shown in groups of 6. How many groups of horses will there be?

7. Make a bar graph using the data in the table. Be sure to write a title and labels.

8. Llamas were added to the contest. They were put into 2 equal groups. Do you have enough information to find the number of llamas in each group? Explain.

9. **? What's the Question?** The answer is 10 more animals. What is the question? What operation would you use?

LESSON 4

Choose a Method

Quick Review

Find each product.

1. $\begin{array}{r} 3 \\ \times 8 \\ \hline \end{array}$
2. $\begin{array}{r} 5 \\ \times 6 \\ \hline \end{array}$
3. $\begin{array}{r} 6 \\ \times 4 \\ \hline \end{array}$
4. $\begin{array}{r} 4 \\ \times 7 \\ \hline \end{array}$
5. $\begin{array}{r} 6 \\ \times 3 \\ \hline \end{array}$

Learn

You can find a product by using paper and pencil, a calculator, or mental math.

LUNCH TIME The airline catering service is preparing lunches for 2 flights. There are 98 passengers on each flight. How many lunches will the service prepare?

$2 \times 98 = \blacksquare$

Estimate. $2 \times 100 = 200$

Use Paper and Pencil The problem involves regrouping. So, paper and pencil is a good choice.

One Way You can multiply and regroup.

STEP 1

Multiply the ones.

2 × 8 ones = 16 ones

Regroup 16 ones as 1 ten 6 ones.

	Hundreds	Tens	Ones
		1	
		9	8
×			2
			6

STEP 2

Multiply the tens.

2 × 9 tens = 18 tens

18 tens + 1 ten = 19 tens

Regroup 19 tens as 1 hundred 9 tens.

	Hundreds	Tens	Ones
		1	
		9	8
×			2
	1	9	6

Another Way You can multiply ones, multiply tens, and then add.

$$\begin{array}{rl} 98 & \\ \times\ 2 & \\ \hline 16 & \text{Multiply the ones. } (2 \times 8 \text{ ones}) \\ +180 & \text{Multiply the tens. } (2 \times 9 \text{ tens}) \\ \hline 196 & \end{array}$$

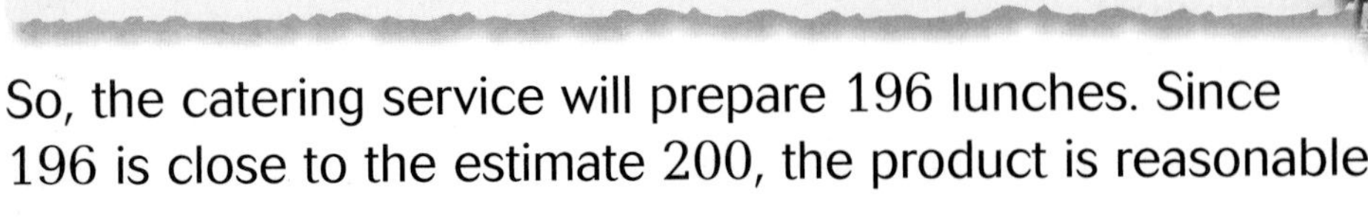

So, the catering service will prepare 196 lunches. Since 196 is close to the estimate 200, the product is reasonable.

Use a Calculator

$7 \times 97 = \blacksquare$

The product will be large. The problem involves regrouping. So, a calculator is a good choice. Estimate first. $7 \times 100 = 700$

So, 679 is probably correct.

Use Mental Math

$7 \times 31 = \blacksquare$

Since there is no regrouping, mental math is a good choice.

Think: Multiply the tens. 7 times 3 tens, or $7 \times 30 = 210$.
Multiply the ones. 7 times 1 one, or $7 \times 1 = 7$.
So, $31 \times 7 = 210 + 7$, or 217.

More Examples

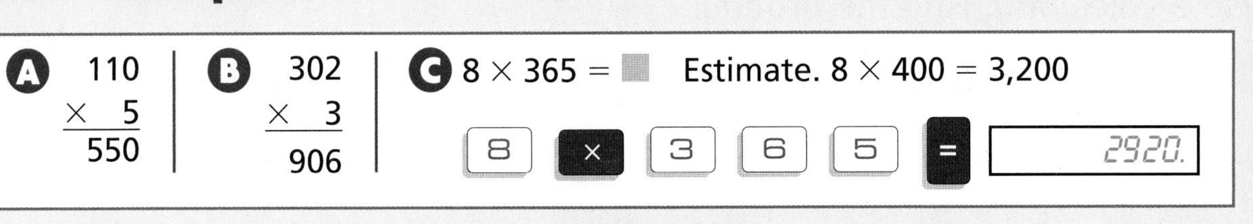

A $\begin{array}{r} 110 \\ \times \quad 5 \\ \hline 550 \end{array}$

B $\begin{array}{r} 302 \\ \times \quad 3 \\ \hline 906 \end{array}$

C $8 \times 365 = \blacksquare$ Estimate. $8 \times 400 = 3{,}200$

• Which problems can you solve by using mental math? Explain.

MATH IDEA You can find a product by using paper and pencil, a calculator, or mental math. Choose the method that works best with the numbers in the problem.

Check

1. **Explain** what method you would use to multiply 142 by 2.

Find the product. Tell what method you used.

2. $\begin{array}{r} 24 \\ \times \ 3 \\ \hline \end{array}$

3. $\begin{array}{r} 75 \\ \times \ 4 \\ \hline \end{array}$

4. $\begin{array}{r} 46 \\ \times \ 5 \\ \hline \end{array}$

5. $\begin{array}{r} 54 \\ \times \ 2 \\ \hline \end{array}$

6. $\begin{array}{r} 63 \\ \times \ 2 \\ \hline \end{array}$

LESSON CONTINUES

Practice and Problem Solving

Extra Practice, page 612, Set B

Find the product. Tell what method you used.

7. 203×2
8. 41×9
9. 38×3
10. 48×5
11. 36×4
12. 87×3
13. 22×7
14. 123×3

Use mental math. Find the product.

15. 202×4
16. 41×3
17. 20×6
18. 112×4
19. 21×8
20. 131×3
21. 40×4
22. 24×5

Use a calculator. Find the product.

23. $4 \times 45 = $ ■
24. $2 \times 99 = $ ■
25. ■ $= 6 \times 322$
26. $3 \times 279 = $ ■
27. $5 \times 118 = $ ■
28. ■ $= 4 \times 421$
29. $8 \times 123 = $ ■
30. ■ $= 2 \times 391$

USE DATA For 31–34, use the table.

31. Diesta and her family took a train to Washington, D.C. How many seats were on the train in all?
32. How many deluxe seats are there on 4 trains?
33. **What's the Question?** The answer is 192 seats.
34. Claudia orders 2 pillows for each seat in the sleeper car and in the deluxe car. How many pillows does she order?
35. **FAST FACT • SOCIAL STUDIES** The oldest railroad bridge in use is the Carrollton Viaduct in Baltimore, Maryland. It was built in 1829. How old is it?

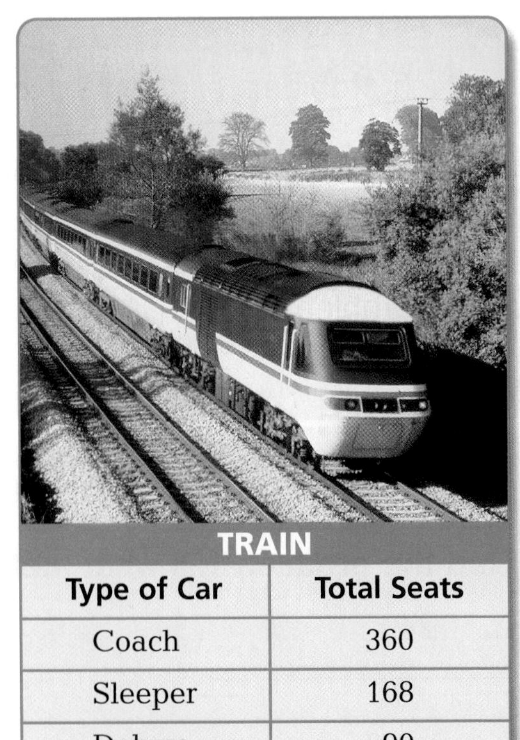

TRAIN

Type of Car	Total Seats
Coach	360
Sleeper	168
Deluxe	90

36. **Vocabulary Power** One meaning of *product* is "a result of something." A cake is the result of ingredients baked in an oven. What is the product in multiplication the result of?

37. Marla bought 2 pounds of apples for $1.29 per pound. She paid with a $5 bill. How much change did she receive?

Mixed Review and Test Prep

Find the sum or difference.

38. $\begin{array}{r} 275 \\ +376 \\ \hline \end{array}$ (p. 70)

39. $\begin{array}{r} 382 \\ -158 \\ \hline \end{array}$ (p. 90)

40. $\begin{array}{r} 822 \\ -568 \\ \hline \end{array}$ (p. 90)

41. $\begin{array}{r} 936 \\ +826 \\ \hline \end{array}$ (p. 70)

42. $\frac{1}{5} + \frac{2}{5} = \blacksquare$ (p. 540)

43. $\frac{9}{10} - \frac{7}{10} = \blacksquare$ (p. 544)

44. TEST PREP What is the perimeter of a square when one side is 3 cm? (p. 444)

A 3 cm　　**C** 9 cm
B 6 cm　　**D** 12 cm

45. TEST PREP What is 5,976 rounded to the nearest thousand? (p. 52)

F 5,000　　**H** 5,980
G 5,900　　**J** 6,000

Problem Solving LINKUP . . . Math History

Lattice multiplication was used in Europe during the fourteenth and fifteenth centuries. You can use basic multiplication facts and a grid to find 7 × 89.

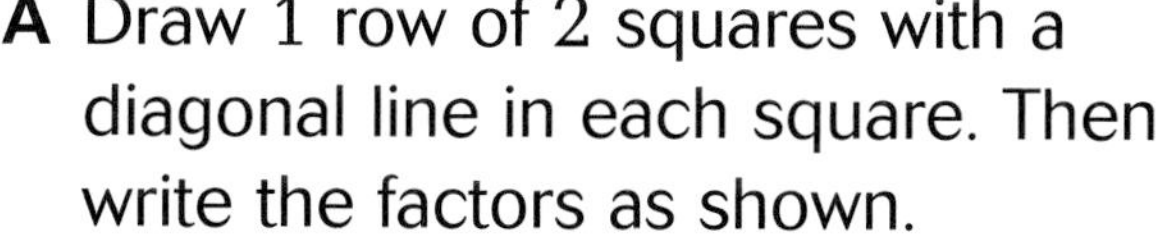

A Draw 1 row of 2 squares with a diagonal line in each square. Then write the factors as shown.

B Multiply each pair of digits.

$7 \times 9 = 63$
$7 \times 8 = 56$

Write each product as shown.

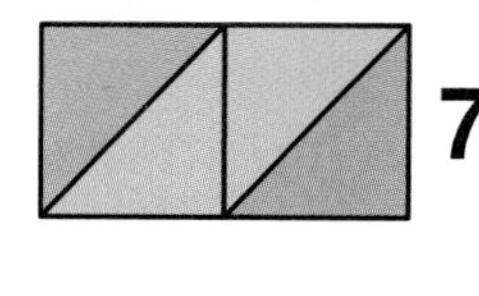

C Start at the right. Add the digits in each diagonal. Regroup if needed.

So, $7 \times 89 = 623$.

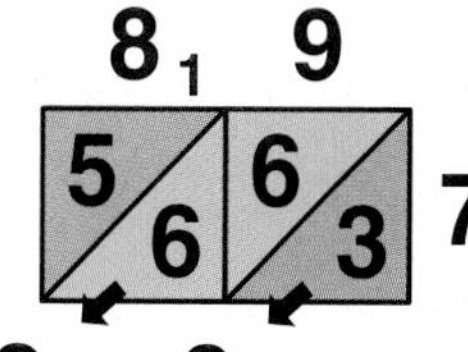

Use a grid to find the product.

1. $6 \times 72 = \blacksquare$　**2.** $8 \times 46 = \blacksquare$　**3.** $4 \times 96 = \blacksquare$　**4.** $3 \times 85 = \blacksquare$

Extra Practice

Set A (pp. 602–605)

Find the product.

1. $\begin{array}{r} 15 \\ \times\ 3 \\ \hline \end{array}$

2. $2 \times 10 = 20 \quad 2 \times 8 = 16$

$2 \times 18 = ■$

Find the product.

3. $\begin{array}{r} 16 \\ \times\ 2 \\ \hline \end{array}$ **4.** $\begin{array}{r} 32 \\ \times\ 3 \\ \hline \end{array}$ **5.** $\begin{array}{r} 13 \\ \times\ 6 \\ \hline \end{array}$ **6.** $\begin{array}{r} 25 \\ \times\ 5 \\ \hline \end{array}$ **7.** $\begin{array}{r} 47 \\ \times\ 4 \\ \hline \end{array}$

8. $\begin{array}{r} 34 \\ \times\ 8 \\ \hline \end{array}$ **9.** $\begin{array}{r} 73 \\ \times\ 2 \\ \hline \end{array}$ **10.** $\begin{array}{r} 23 \\ \times\ 7 \\ \hline \end{array}$ **11.** $\begin{array}{r} 45 \\ \times\ 5 \\ \hline \end{array}$ **12.** $\begin{array}{r} 99 \\ \times\ 3 \\ \hline \end{array}$

13. $6 \times 15 = ■$ **14.** $9 \times 21 = ■$ **15.** $7 \times 33 = ■$ **16.** $4 \times 51 = ■$

17. Jill has 3 boxes of nature magazines. There are 28 magazines in each box. How many nature magazines does Jill have in all?

Set B (pp. 608–611)

Find the product. Tell what method you used.

1. $\begin{array}{r} 21 \\ \times\ 4 \\ \hline \end{array}$ **2.** $\begin{array}{r} 23 \\ \times\ 9 \\ \hline \end{array}$ **3.** $\begin{array}{r} 38 \\ \times\ 5 \\ \hline \end{array}$ **4.** $\begin{array}{r} 44 \\ \times\ 3 \\ \hline \end{array}$ **5.** $\begin{array}{r} 33 \\ \times\ 3 \\ \hline \end{array}$

Find the product.

6. $\begin{array}{r} 14 \\ \times\ 6 \\ \hline \end{array}$ **7.** $\begin{array}{r} 29 \\ \times\ 5 \\ \hline \end{array}$ **8.** $\begin{array}{r} 37 \\ \times\ 7 \\ \hline \end{array}$ **9.** $\begin{array}{r} 18 \\ \times\ 2 \\ \hline \end{array}$ **10.** $\begin{array}{r} 22 \\ \times\ 3 \\ \hline \end{array}$

11. $\begin{array}{r} 38 \\ \times\ 4 \\ \hline \end{array}$ **12.** $\begin{array}{r} 25 \\ \times\ 8 \\ \hline \end{array}$ **13.** $\begin{array}{r} 72 \\ \times\ 7 \\ \hline \end{array}$ **14.** $\begin{array}{r} 49 \\ \times\ 8 \\ \hline \end{array}$ **15.** $\begin{array}{r} 53 \\ \times\ 9 \\ \hline \end{array}$

16. $9 \times 19 = ■$ **17.** $4 \times 91 = ■$ **18.** $3 \times 12 = ■$ **19.** $8 \times 88 = ■$

20. Angelo sells hot dogs for \$3 each. If he sells 56 hot dogs, how much money will he make?

Review/Test

CHECK CONCEPTS

Use the array to help find the product. (pp. 602–605)

1\.

$2 \times 10 = 20 \qquad 2 \times 7 = 14$

$2 \times 17 = ■$

2\. 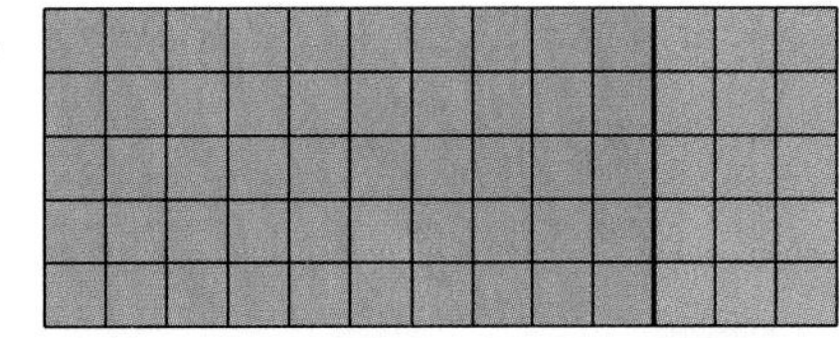

5 rows of 10   5 rows of 3

$5 \times 10 = 50 \qquad 5 \times 3 = 15$

$5 \times 13 = ■$

CHECK SKILLS

Find the product. (pp. 602–605; 608–611)

3\. 18×4 4. 34×3 5. 40×7 6. 12×6 7. 27×5

8\. 14×2 9. 27×3 10. 36×6 11. 20×4 12. 56×8

13\. $9 \times 40 = ■$ 14. $4 \times 35 = ■$ 15. $7 \times 83 = ■$ 16. $6 \times 18 = ■$

CHECK PROBLEM SOLVING

Write whether you would *add, subtract, multiply,* or *divide*. Then solve. (pp. 606–607)

17\. Caitlin practices the flute for 45 minutes each day. How many minutes does she practice in 4 days?

18\. Manny paid $2.99 for a magazine and $1.09 for a bottle of apple juice. How much money did he spend?

19\. Eva sold 7 plates of cookies at a bake sale. There were 18 cookies on each plate. How many cookies did she sell?

20\. Lee has 64 photos in an album. There are 8 pages with the same number of photos on each page. How many photos are on each page?

Standardized Test Prep

NUMBER SENSE, CONCEPTS, AND OPERATIONS

1. Jon saw these kites. What fraction of the kites are striped?

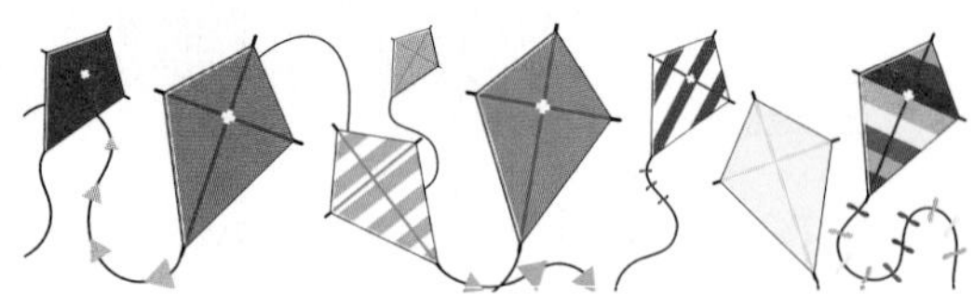

A $\frac{1}{3}$ C $\frac{3}{8}$

B $\frac{3}{5}$ D $\frac{5}{8}$

2. Ariel drew this figure.

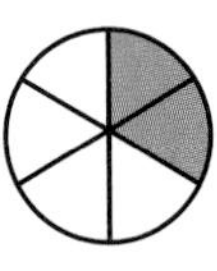

Which figure has a shaded part equivalent to the one Ariel drew?

F 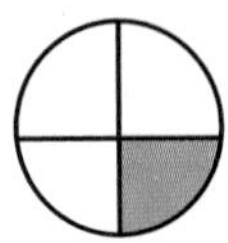

H 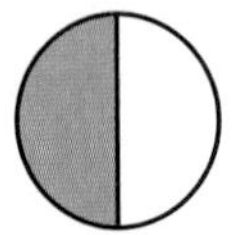

G 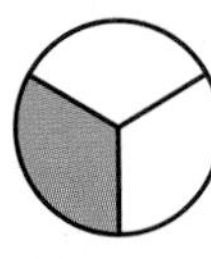

J 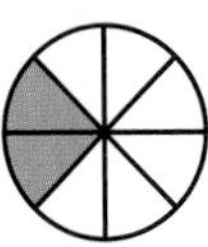

3. Each of the 3 third-grade classes at Blue Hill School collected 1,000 aluminum cans. How many cans did the classes collect?

A 30 C 300
B 100 D 3,000

4. **Explain It** Christy has 8 packs of stickers. Each pack contains 36 stickers. Tell how to ESTIMATE the total number of stickers.

MEASUREMENT

TIP **Understand the problem.** See item 5. The word *about* shows that you should estimate the total cost of the items.

5. Lynn bought a book that cost $3.89 and a bookmark that cost $1.09. About how much money did Lynn spend?

F $3.00
G $4.00
H $5.00
J $6.00

6. Soccer practice ended at 3:45 P.M. The team had practiced for one hour. At what time did soccer practice begin?

A 4:45 P.M. C 3:00 P.M.
B 3:15 P.M. D 2:45 P.M.

7. Lee jogged all around the edge of this square field.

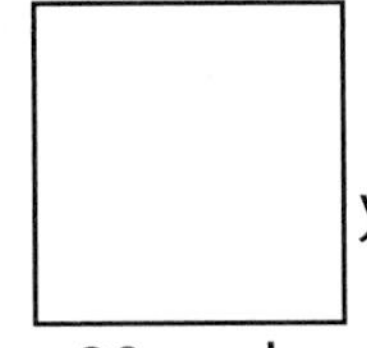

How far did Lee jog?

F 116 yards H 112 yards
G 124 yards J 164 yards

8. **Explain It** Sue has $2.25 and Bev has $4.85. About how much money do the girls have altogether? Explain how you found your answer.

ALGEBRAIC THINKING

9. Logan drew this pattern.

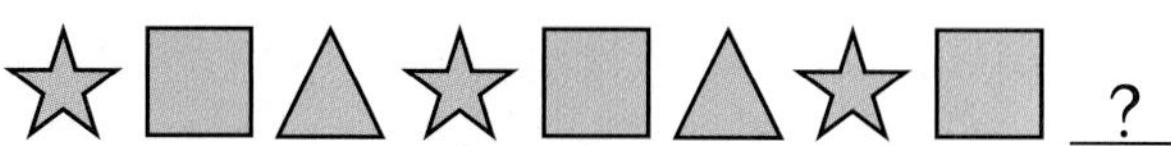

What is the next figure in her pattern?

A ☆
B ▢
C △
D ▭

10. Kira is making bracelets. What rule tells the number of beads Kira used for each bracelet?

KIRA'S BRACELETS	
Bracelets	Beads
1	8
2	16
3	24
4	32

F The number of beads is 8 times the number of bracelets.
G The number of beads is 7 more than the number of bracelets.
H The number of bracelets is 8 times the number of beads.
J The number of bracelets is half the number of beads.

11. **Explain It** Tell how you can use the table above to find the number of beads Kira will use to make 9 bracelets.

DATA ANALYSIS AND PROBABILITY

12. On which of the following numbers is the pointer most likely to land?

A 1
B 2
C 3
D 4

13. Julie packed an orange, a blue, a green, and a yellow shirt. She also packed blue shorts and green shorts.

How many different shirt-and-shorts outfits can Julie wear?

F 4
G 6
H 8
J 10

14. **Explain It** This table shows the number of movie tickets sold during 5 days.

NUMBER OF TICKETS SOLD	
Day	Tickets Sold
Wednesday	112
Thursday	109
Friday	298
Saturday	324
Sunday	307

Look at the data. Describe a trend you see.

CHAPTER 30

Divide by 1-Digit Numbers

FAST FACT • SOCIAL STUDIES Soccer is the world's most popular sport. A game like soccer was played in China about 2,500 years ago.

PROBLEM SOLVING Suppose a soccer coach orders 4 pairs of shin guards. How much does 1 pair of shin guards cost? Explain how to find the answer.

SOCCER SUPPLIES

Item	Quantity	Cost
Corner flags	8	$64
Goal nets	4	$120
Soccer balls	3	$48
Air pumps	3	$60
Shin guards	4 pairs	$48

CHECK WHAT YOU KNOW

Use this page to help you review and remember important skills needed for Chapter 30.

SUBTRACTION

Find the difference.

1. $\begin{array}{r} 9 \\ -7 \\ \hline \end{array}$
2. $\begin{array}{r} 41 \\ -\ 4 \\ \hline \end{array}$
3. $\begin{array}{r} 34 \\ -\ 8 \\ \hline \end{array}$
4. $\begin{array}{r} 52 \\ -\ 6 \\ \hline \end{array}$
5. $\begin{array}{r} 75 \\ -\ 8 \\ \hline \end{array}$
6. $\begin{array}{r} 92 \\ -63 \\ \hline \end{array}$
7. $\begin{array}{r} 64 \\ -29 \\ \hline \end{array}$
8. $\begin{array}{r} 73 \\ -55 \\ \hline \end{array}$
9. $\begin{array}{r} 43 \\ -26 \\ \hline \end{array}$
10. $\begin{array}{r} 95 \\ -52 \\ \hline \end{array}$

MULTIPLICATION AND DIVISION FACTS

Find the product.

11. $6 \times 6 = \blacksquare$
12. $\blacksquare = 3 \times 9$
13. $6 \times 8 = \blacksquare$
14. $7 \times 3 = \blacksquare$
15. $6 \times 7 = \blacksquare$
16. $5 \times 5 = \blacksquare$
17. $\blacksquare = 2 \times 9$
18. $8 \times 8 = \blacksquare$
19. $\blacksquare = 9 \times 7$
20. $6 \times 4 = \blacksquare$
21. $5 \times 6 = \blacksquare$
22. $\blacksquare = 9 \times 9$

Find the quotient.

23. $8\overline{)56}$
24. $9\overline{)45}$
25. $4\overline{)32}$
26. $7\overline{)49}$
27. $6\overline{)54}$
28. $5\overline{)40}$
29. $6\overline{)42}$
30. $8\overline{)48}$

VOCABULARY POWER

REVIEW

divisor [di • vī′ zər] *noun*

In a division problem, the *divisor* is the number being used to divide another number, called the dividend. What is the answer in a division problem called?

PREVIEW

remainder

www.harcourtschool.com/mathglossary

LESSON 1

Divide with Remainders

Quick Review

1. $3\overline{)9}$
2. $6\overline{)12}$
3. $4\overline{)24}$
4. $5\overline{)35}$
5. $7\overline{)28}$

VOCABULARY
remainder

MATERIALS
counters

Explore

Noah collected all 19 dinosaur toys from Crispy Crunch cereal. He wants to keep an equal number of toys in each of 3 shoe boxes. Can Noah divide them equally among the 3 boxes? Why or why not?

Remember

30	÷	6	=	5
↑		↑		↑
dividend		*divisor*		*quotient*

Activity

Use counters to find 19 ÷ 3.

STEP 1

Use 19 counters. Draw 3 circles.

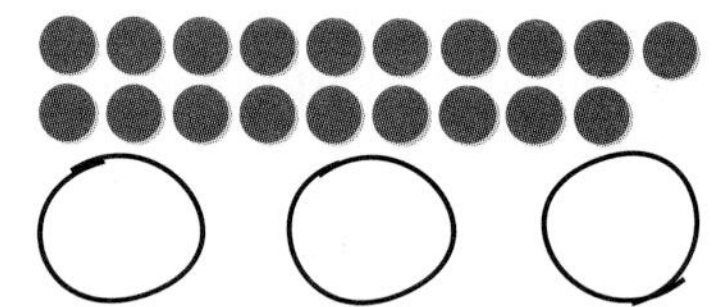

STEP 2

Divide the 19 counters into 3 equal groups by putting them in the circles.

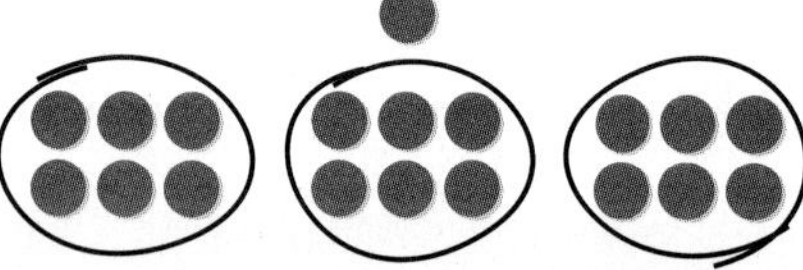

No, Noah cannot divide the toys equally because there will be 6 toys in each shoe box, with 1 toy left over.

I'm putting 11 counters into 2 equal groups. Will there be any left over?

Try It

Use counters to make equal groups. Draw a picture of the model you made.

a. 11 ÷ 2 **b.** 15 ÷ 4 **c.** 26 ÷ 3

Connect

In division, the amount left over when a number cannot be divided evenly is called the **remainder**.

Technology Link

More Practice: Harcourt Mega Math The Number Games, *Up, Up and Array,* Level L

Activity

Find 20 ÷ 6.

STEP 1

Use 20 counters. Draw 6 circles.

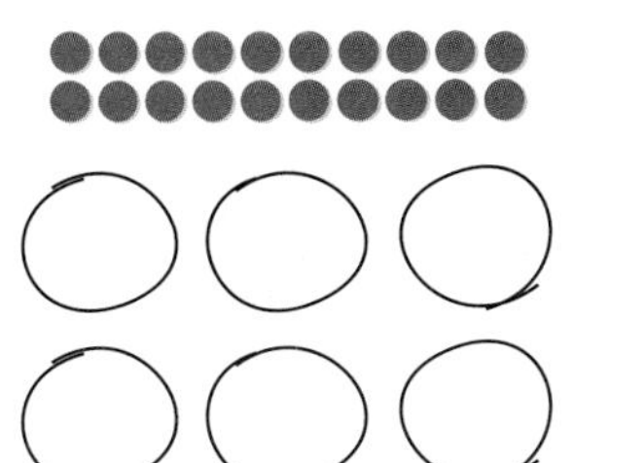

STEP 2

Divide the 20 counters into 6 equal groups.

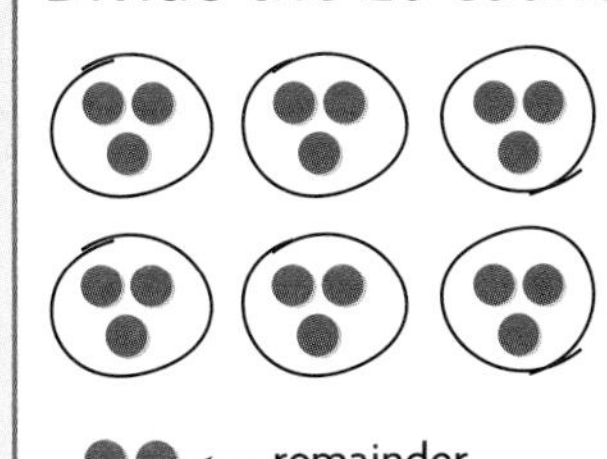

The quotient is 3.
The remainder is 2.

Practice and Problem Solving

Use counters to find the quotient and remainder.

1. $9 \div 2 = \blacksquare$
2. $17 \div 4 = \blacksquare$
3. $10 \div 3 = \blacksquare$
4. $20 \div 3 = \blacksquare$
5. $4\overline{)18}$
6. $5\overline{)19}$
7. $5\overline{)27}$
8. $6\overline{)21}$

Find the quotient and remainder. Use counters or draw a picture to help.

9. $16 \div 3 = \blacksquare$
10. $21 \div 5 = \blacksquare$
11. $2\overline{)15}$
12. $4\overline{)22}$
13. Tom has 3 letter cards—A, E, and T. List all of the 3-letter combinations he can make using each letter once. How many combinations are words?
14. **? What's the Question?** Darnell has 14 Beastie Buddies in his collection. He puts 4 of them in each of 3 drawers. The answer is 2 Beastie Buddies.

Mixed Review and Test Prep

Multiply. (p. 602)

15. $2 \times 13 = \blacksquare$
16. $3 \times 16 = \blacksquare$
17. $5 \times 14 = \blacksquare$
18. $4 \times 19 = \blacksquare$
19. **TEST PREP** Judy has 2 rolls of pennies with 50 pennies in each roll. She also has 4 dimes and 1 quarter. How much money does she have in all? (p. 110)

A \$1.65 **B** \$1.40 **C** \$1.00 **D** \$0.65

LESSON 2

Divide 2-Digit Numbers

Quick Review

1. 16 ÷ 4 = ■
2. 14 ÷ 7 = ■
3. 15 ÷ 3 = ■
4. 32 ÷ 4 = ■
5. 18 ÷ 6 = ■

Learn

COOL COLLECTIONS Suppose you have a collection of 63 hockey cards. You display an equal number of cards on each of 5 shelves. How many cards are on each shelf? How many cards are left over?

Activity

63 ÷ 5 = ■ 5)63

Materials: base-ten blocks

STEP 1

Model 63 with base-ten blocks. Put an equal number of tens in each of 5 groups.

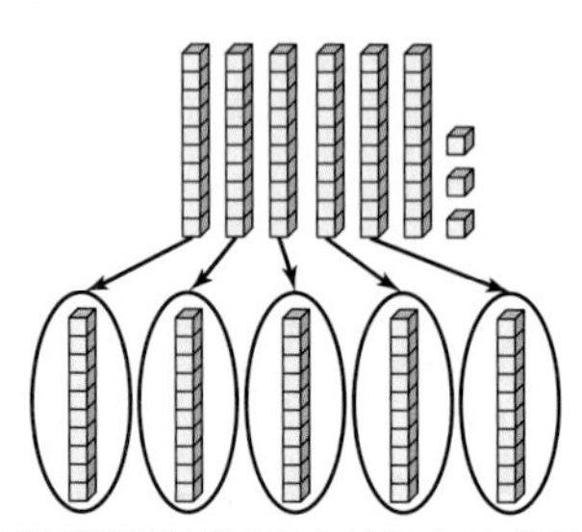

STEP 2

One ten is left. Regroup it as 10 ones. Put an equal number of ones in each of 5 groups.

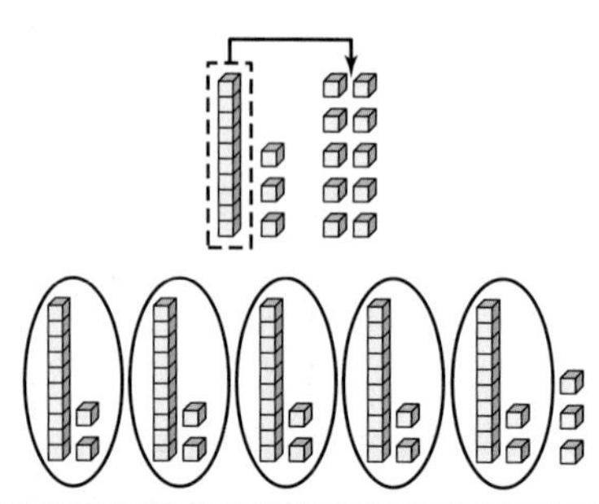

STEP 3

Use the letter *r* to show the remainder.

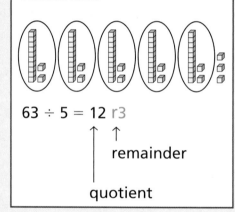

63 ÷ 5 = 12 r3

↑ quotient ↑ remainder

So, there are 12 cards on each shelf. There are 3 cards left over.

- In Step 2, why was the 1 ten regrouped into 10 ones?

Examples

A

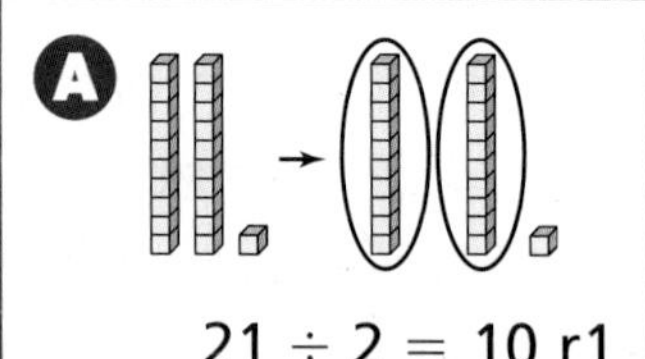

21 ÷ 2 = 10 r1

B

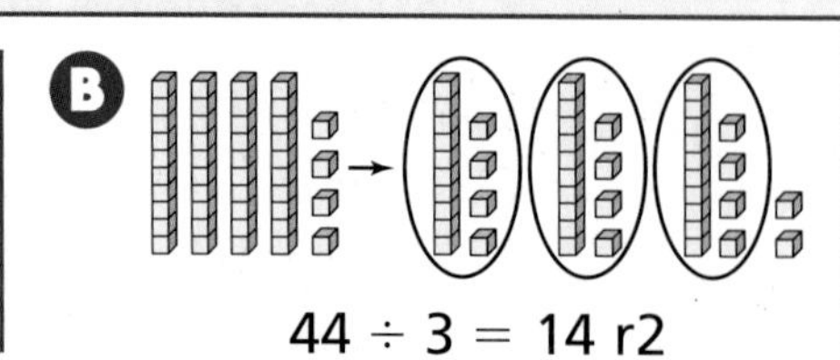

44 ÷ 3 = 14 r2

Recording Division

MATH IDEA The steps to record division are *divide, multiply, subtract, compare.*

Example 1

Find 58 ÷ 3 = ■. **Read:** 58 divided by 3 **Write:** $3\overline{)58}$

STEP 1

Divide the 5 tens first. $3\overline{)5}$

Think: $3 \times 1 = 3$

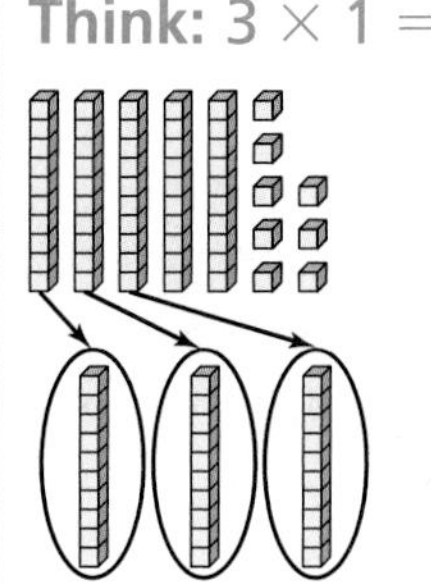

1 ten in each group.

$$\begin{array}{r} 1 \\ 3\overline{)58} \\ -3 \\ \hline 2 \end{array}$$

Divide. $3\overline{)5}$
Multiply. 3×1
Subtract. $5 - 3$
Compare. $2 < 3$

The difference, 2, must be less than the divisor, 3.

STEP 2

Bring down the 8 ones.

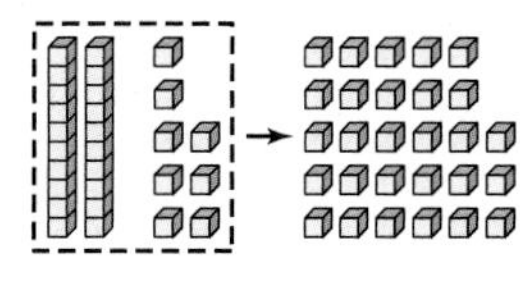

$$\begin{array}{r} 1 \\ 3\overline{)58} \\ -3\downarrow \\ \hline 28 \end{array}$$

Regroup 2 tens 8 ones as 28 ones.

STEP 3

Divide the 28 ones. $3\overline{)28}$ Think: $3 \times 9 = 27$

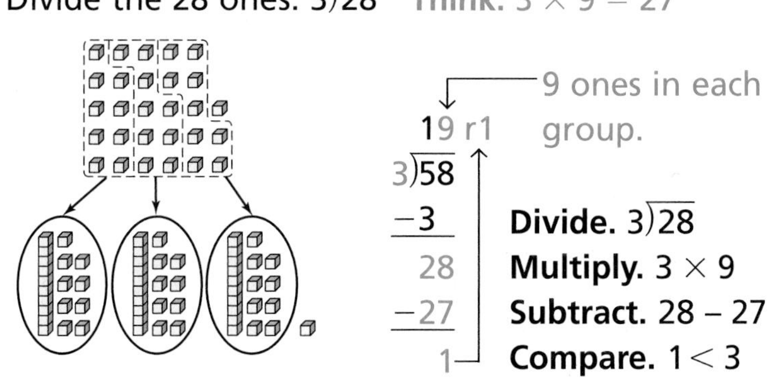

9 ones in each group.

$$\begin{array}{r} 19 \text{ r1} \\ 3\overline{)58} \\ -3 \\ \hline 28 \\ -27 \\ \hline 1 \end{array}$$

Divide. $3\overline{)28}$
Multiply. 3×9
Subtract. $28 - 27$
Compare. $1 < 3$

STEP 4

Multiply to check your answer.

$$\begin{array}{r} 19 \\ \times\ 3 \\ \hline 57 \end{array}$$

19 ← quotient
× 3 ← divisor

$$\begin{array}{r} 57 \\ +\ 1 \\ \hline 58 \end{array}$$

+ 1 ← Add the remainder.
58 ← This should equal the dividend.

Example 2

Find 35 ÷ 4 = ■. **Read:** 35 divided by 4 **Write:** $4\overline{)35}$

STEP 1

Since there are not enough tens to divide, start with ones.

$4\overline{)35}$ $4 > 3$, so place the first digit in the ones place.

STEP 2

Divide the 35 ones.

$$\begin{array}{r} 8 \text{ r3} \\ 4\overline{)35} \\ -32 \\ \hline 3 \end{array}$$

Divide. $4\overline{)35}$
Multiply. 4×8
Subtract. $35 - 32$
Compare. $3 < 4$

STEP 3

Multiply to check.

$$\begin{array}{r} 8 \\ \times 4 \\ \hline 32 \end{array}$$

8 ← quotient
×4 ← divisor

$$\begin{array}{r} 32 \\ +\ 3 \\ \hline 35 \end{array}$$

+ 3 ← Add the remainder.

LESSON CONTINUES

Check

1. **Explain** why $63 \div 5$ has a remainder.

Use the model. Write the quotient and remainder.

2. $43 \div 2$

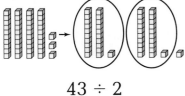

3. $38 \div 3$

Divide. You may use base-ten blocks to help.

4. $31 \div 2 = \blacksquare$
5. $86 \div 3 = \blacksquare$
6. $29 \div 4 = \blacksquare$
7. $32 \div 4 = \blacksquare$

Practice and Problem Solving

Extra Practice, page 630, Set A

Use the model. Write the quotient and remainder.

8. $62 \div 4$

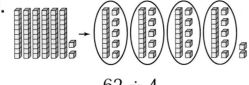

9. $71 \div 5$

Divide. Use base-ten blocks to help.

10. $23 \div 2 = \blacksquare$
11. $25 \div 2 = \blacksquare$
12. $39 \div 3 = \blacksquare$
13. $43 \div 4 = \blacksquare$
14. $4\overline{)77}$
15. $6\overline{)52}$
16. $5\overline{)73}$
17. $3\overline{)66}$

Divide and check.

18. $5\overline{)48}$
19. $2\overline{)71}$
20. $7\overline{)92}$
21. $9\overline{)89}$
22. $2\overline{)87}$
23. $7\overline{)34}$
24. $8\overline{)99}$
25. $6\overline{)39}$

26. **What's the Error?** Lou began to solve this problem. What is his error? Solve the problem.

$$\begin{array}{r} 1 \\ 2\overline{)53} \\ \underline{2} \\ 3 \end{array}$$

27. **ALGEBRA** Find the missing digit.

$$\begin{array}{r} 15 \text{ r2} \\ 3\overline{)4\blacksquare} \end{array}$$

28. **REASONING** Alyssa divided 79 jelly beans equally into 6 jars. She kept 1 jar and the leftover jelly beans. How many jelly beans did she keep?

29. **FAST FACT • SOCIAL STUDIES** Strawberries have been grown in the United States since 1834. Today every state in the United States grows strawberries. In how many states are strawberries not grown?

30. It takes Grant 12 minutes to get to his friend's house. It takes him 4 times as long to get to his uncle's house. How long does it take Grant to get to his uncle's?

Mixed Review and Test Prep

Find the product. (p. 602)

31. $\begin{array}{r} 21 \\ \times\ 2 \\ \hline \end{array}$ **32.** $\begin{array}{r} 34 \\ \times\ 4 \\ \hline \end{array}$ **33.** $\begin{array}{r} 55 \\ \times\ 3 \\ \hline \end{array}$

34. TEST PREP Mrs. Martin kept a lunch box she bought in 1971. She was 9 years old when she bought the lunch box. How old was she in 2000? (p. 98)

A 38 **B** 28 **C** 19 **D** 9

Compare. Write <, >, or = for each ●.

35. 3×4 ● 6×2 (p. 182)

36. $54 \div 9$ ● $18 \div 2$ (p. 280)

37. TEST PREP Elise cut a pie into 8 equal pieces. She gave 2 pieces to her teacher. Elise ate 1 piece. What fraction of the pie was left? (p. 546)

F $\frac{5}{8}$ **G** $\frac{3}{8}$ **H** $\frac{2}{8}$ **J** $\frac{1}{8}$

Problem Solving LINKUP . . . to Reading

STRATEGY • USE GRAPHIC AIDS
The steps for making crayons have not changed much since 1903. Wax in different colors is heated to 240°F. Workers pour the hot wax across crayon molds. In $7\frac{1}{2}$ minutes, the wax cools into 72 rows of 8 crayons.

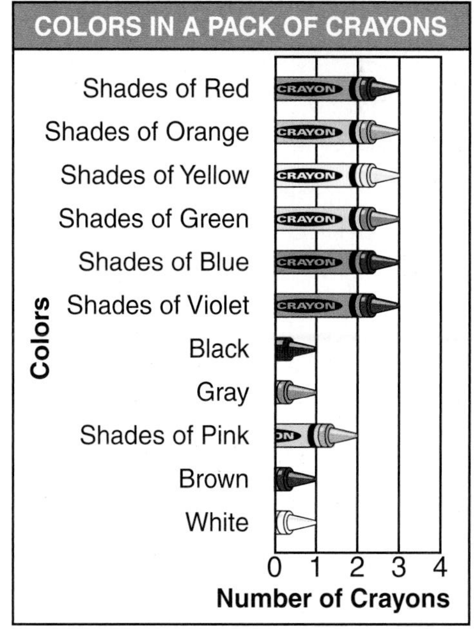

USE DATA For 1–2, use the bar graph.

1. How many crayons are in the pack shown in the bar graph?
2. **Write a problem** about the bar graph. Use division. Trade with a partner and solve.
3. How many crayons are made in each mold of 72 rows of 8 crayons?
4. The pack of 64 crayons has 4 equal rows. How many crayons are in each row?

LESSON 3

Problem Solving Skill
Interpret the Remainder

UNDERSTAND | PLAN | SOLVE | CHECK

Quick Review

1. $3\overline{)55}$
2. $4\overline{)18}$
3. $2\overline{)61}$
4. $5\overline{)60}$
5. $7\overline{)32}$

PICNIC PLANS Clare needs to take 50 cans of juice to the picnic. The juice is sold in packages of 6 cans. How many packages must she buy?

Since you need to know how many groups of 6 are in 50, you divide.

Find $50 \div 6$.

$$\begin{array}{r} 8 \text{ r}2 \\ 6\overline{)50} \\ -48 \\ \hline 2 \end{array}$$

The 8 packages of juice will have only 48 cans.

If Clare buys 8 packages of juice, she will still need 2 more cans of juice. So, Clare must buy 9 packages of juice.

Rico is making crispy treats for the picnic. He needs 2 cups of cereal for each pan of treats. If he has 13 cups of cereal, how many pans of treats can he make?

Find $13 \div 2$.

$$\begin{array}{r} 6 \text{ r}1 \\ 2\overline{)13} \\ -12 \\ \hline 1 \end{array}$$

Making 6 pans of treats uses 12 cups of cereal.

If Rico makes 6 pans of treats, he will have only 1 cup of cereal left. This is not enough for another pan of treats. So, he can make 6 pans of treats.

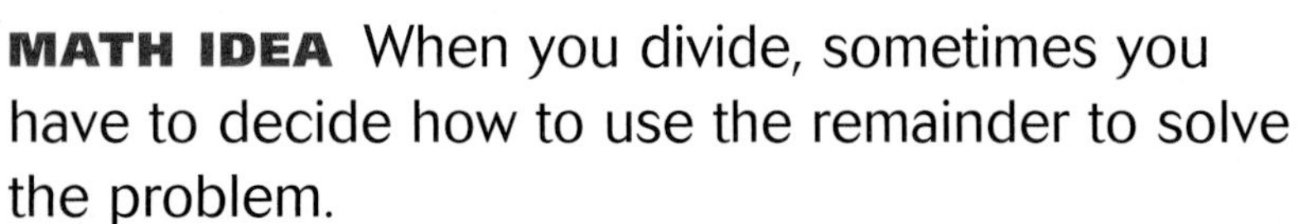

MATH IDEA When you divide, sometimes you have to decide how to use the remainder to solve the problem.

Problem Solving Practice

1. **What if** Clare had to take 56 cans of juice to the picnic? If there are 6 cans in each package, how many packages would she need to buy?

2. Simon has 63 bird stamps in a collection. He can fit 8 stamps on a page. How many pages does he need?

3. Beth is making bows to decorate a float in a parade. It takes 5 feet of ribbon to make a bow. She has 89 feet of ribbon. How many bows can Beth make?

4. Dimitri worked on a math puzzle for 32 minutes. If each part of the puzzle took 5 minutes to solve, how many parts did he solve?

A class of 28 students is going on a field trip. Each van can hold 8 students. How many vans does the class need?

5. Which number sentence can help solve the problem?

   A $28 - 28 = 0$
   B $28 \times 8 = 224$
   C $28 \div 8 = 3 \text{ r}4$
   D $8 \div 8 = 1$

6. How many vans does the class need?

   F 3 vans
   G 4 vans
   H 8 vans
   J 28 vans

Mixed Applications

USE DATA For 7–9, use the price list.

7. Tomas bought 1 pound of peanuts and 1 pound of cashews. He paid with $5. How much change did he get?

8. Sheila has $5.36. Does she have enough to buy 1 pound of raisins, 1 pound of peanuts, and 1 pound of cashews? Explain.

9. Cole bought 2 pounds of raisins. The checker charged him $1.19. Is this price reasonable? Explain.

PRICE LIST	
Raisins	$0.85 per lb
Peanuts	$1.99 per lb
Cashews	$2.50 per lb

LESSON 4

Divide 3-Digit Numbers

Quick Review

1. $56 \div 7$
2. $45 \div 5$
3. $24 \div 6$
4. $72 \div 9$
5. How many twos are in 15? What is left over?

Learn

FAIR TRADE Roger and his sister have 358 trading cards. They want to divide them evenly. How many cards does each one get?

Example

Divide. $358 \div 2 = \blacksquare$ or $2\overline{)358}$

STEP 1

Decide where to place the first digit in the quotient.

$$\begin{array}{r} \blacksquare \\ 2\overline{)358} \end{array}$$

$3 > 2$, so divide the hundreds.

STEP 2

Divide 3 hundreds by 2.

$$\begin{array}{r} 1 \\ 2\overline{)358} \\ -2 \\ \hline 1 \end{array}$$

Multiply.
Subtract.
Compare.
$1 < 2$

STEP 3

Bring down the 5 tens. Divide 15 tens.

$$\begin{array}{r} 17 \\ 2\overline{)358} \\ -2\downarrow \\ \hline 15 \\ -14 \\ \hline 1 \end{array}$$

Multiply.
Subtract.
Compare.
$1 < 2$

STEP 4

Bring down the 8 ones. Divide 18 ones.

$$\begin{array}{r} 179 \\ 2\overline{)358} \\ -2 \\ \hline 15 \\ -14\downarrow \\ \hline 18 \\ -18 \\ \hline 0 \end{array}$$

Multiply.
Subtract.
Compare.
$0 < 2$

So, each one gets 179 trading cards.

- In Step 1, where would you place the first digit if the divisor was 4 instead of 2? Explain.

More Examples

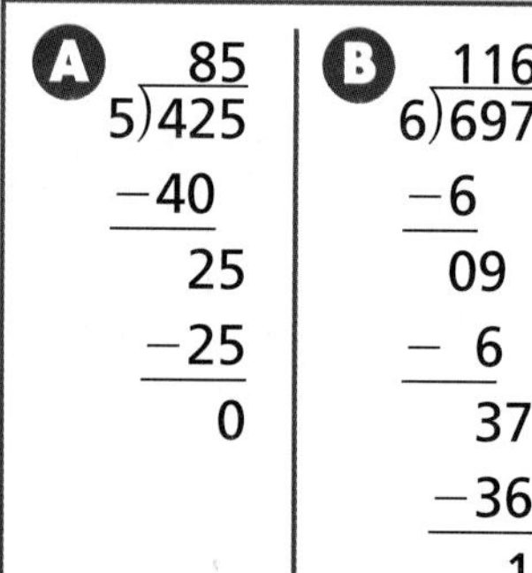

A

$$\begin{array}{r} 85 \\ 5\overline{)425} \\ -40 \\ \hline 25 \\ -25 \\ \hline 0 \end{array}$$

B

$$\begin{array}{r} 116 \text{ r1} \\ 6\overline{)697}\phantom{\text{ r1}} \\ -6\phantom{\text{ r1}} \\ \hline 09\phantom{\text{ r1}} \\ -\ 6\phantom{\text{ r1}} \\ \hline 37\phantom{\text{ r1}} \\ -36\phantom{\text{ r1}} \\ \hline 1\phantom{\text{ r1}} \end{array}$$

C You can also use a calculator to divide greater numbers.

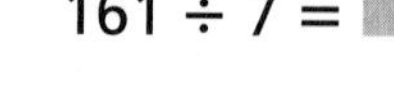

$161 \div 7 = \blacksquare$

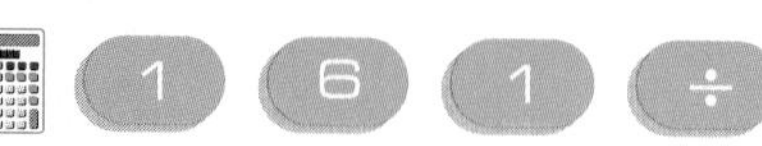

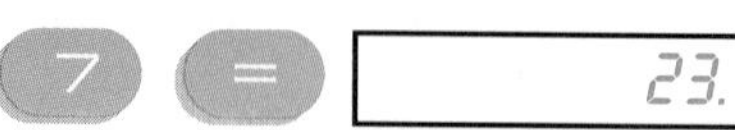

Check

1. **Explain** how you can decide where to place the first digit in this problem. $3\overline{)216}$

Divide.

2. $5\overline{)365}$ **3.** $3\overline{)354}$ **4.** $4\overline{)156}$ **5.** $6\overline{)138}$

Practice and Problem Solving

Extra Practice, page 630, Set B

Divide.

6. $5\overline{)155}$	**7.** $2\overline{)384}$	**8.** $3\overline{)844}$	**9.** $4\overline{)472}$
10. $8\overline{)680}$	**11.** $4\overline{)136}$	**12.** $7\overline{)294}$	**13.** $5\overline{)757}$
14. $3\overline{)726}$	**15.** $4\overline{)475}$	**16.** $9\overline{)819}$	**17.** $6\overline{)294}$
18. $7\overline{)158}$	**19.** $2\overline{)784}$	**20.** $5\overline{)905}$	**21.** $9\overline{)558}$

22. Write a problem in which the dividend has 3 digits and the first digit of the quotient is in the tens place.

23. **Vocabulary Power** The word *remainder* means "something left over." Use $26 \div 4$ and explain what a remainder is in division.

24. Bonnie has \$2.35 in pennies. John has \$1.20 less than Bonnie. How much money do they have altogether?

25. **REASONING** Julie bought cards for \$3.00. She paid for them with the same number of dimes as nickels. She received no change. How many of each coin did she use?

Mixed Review and Test Prep

What time does each clock show? (p. 128)

26.

27.

28.

29.

30. **TEST PREP** Max's team had practice 3 days a week for 9 weeks. Max missed 2 practices. How many practices did he go to? (p. 222)

A 3 **B** 24 **C** 25 **D** 27

LESSON

5 Estimate Quotients

Quick Review

1. $700 \div 7$
2. $90 \div 3$
3. $200 \div 4$
4. $180 \div 2$
5. $120 \div 3$

Learn

PUNCH LINE Mrs. Allison is making 135 cups of punch. If she divides the punch evenly among 3 punch bowls, about how many cups will be in each bowl?

When you do not need an exact answer, you can *estimate* to find the quotient.

Example

Estimate. $135 \div 3$ or $3\overline{)135}$

STEP 1

Look at the first two digits.

$135 \div 3 = \blacksquare$

STEP 2

Think of a basic fact that is close to $13 \div 3$.

$12 \div 3 = 4$

STEP 3

Then use a pattern to estimate.

$12 \div 3 = 4$

$120 \div 3 = 40$

So, about 40 cups of punch will be in each bowl.

- Will the exact answer be more than or less than 40 cups? Explain.

Check

1. Tell what estimate you would get if you used $15 \div 3 = 5$ as the basic fact to find the number of cups of punch.

Estimate each quotient. Write the basic fact you used to find the estimate.

2. $181 \div 2 = \blacksquare$
3. $501 \div 5 = \blacksquare$
4. $374 \div 6 = \blacksquare$
5. $8\overline{)490}$
6. $3\overline{)268}$
7. $7\overline{)223}$

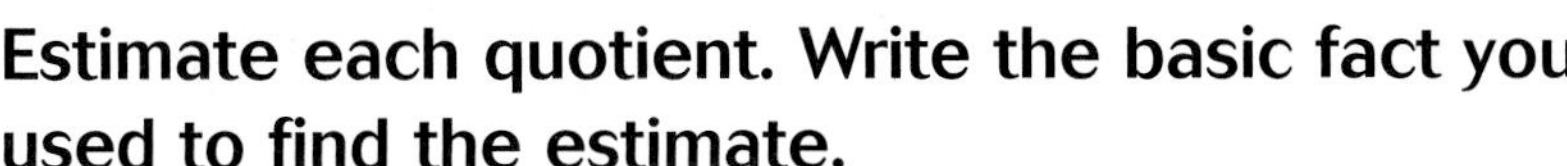

Practice and Problem Solving

Extra Practice, page 630, Set C

Estimate each quotient. Write the basic fact you used to find the estimate.

8. $143 \div 5 = ■$ **9.** $174 \div 9 = ■$

10. $161 \div 2 = ■$ **11.** $253 \div 6 = ■$

Estimate the quotient.

12. $365 \div 5 = ■$ **13.** $116 \div 4 = ■$ **14.** $493 \div 8 = ■$

15. $618 \div 6 = ■$ **16.** $784 \div 2 = ■$ **17.** $407 \div 4 = ■$

18. $3\overline{)876}$ **19.** $7\overline{)644}$ **20.** $9\overline{)716}$

21. $5\overline{)442}$ **22.** $8\overline{)331}$ **23.** $8\overline{)552}$

For 24–26, find an estimate to solve each problem.

24. The students raised $226 to buy 3 new trees for their school. About how much can they spend for each tree?

25. Kathy put 102 photos into her album. She put 3 photos on each page. About how many pages have photos?

26. There are 4 large tables at the sports banquet. There are 163 team members. About how many team members will be at each table?

27. **REASONING** Masao thought of this number pattern. What is his rule? What is the next number?

2, 6, 18, 54, ■

28. **? What's the Error?** A clerk has 196 shirts to display on 6 racks. She wants to display about the same number of shirts on each rack. She says she can put about 20 shirts on each rack. What's her error?

Mixed Review and Test Prep

Complete. (p. 242)

29. $■ \times 3 = 30 \div 5$

30. $24 \div ■ = 4 \times 2$

31. $2 \times 2 = ■ \div 4$

32. $14 \div 2 = 1 \times ■$

33. **TEST PREP** Tara's quilt is 3 feet long and 4 feet wide. What is the perimeter of her quilt? (p. 444)

A 16 feet
B 14 feet
C 12 feet
D 10 feet

Extra Practice

Set A (pp. 620–623)

Use the model. Write the quotient and remainder.

1. 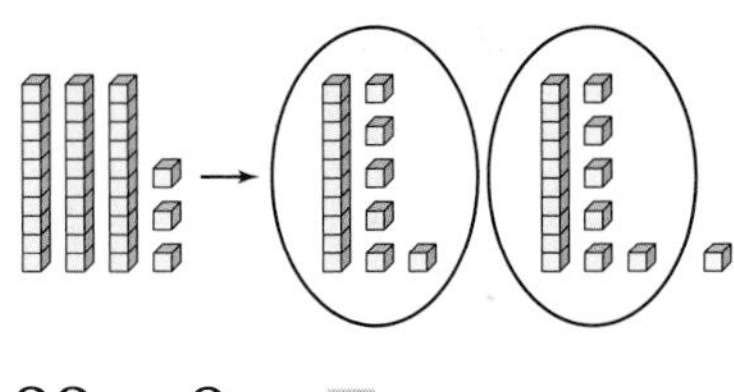

$33 \div 2 = $ ■

2. 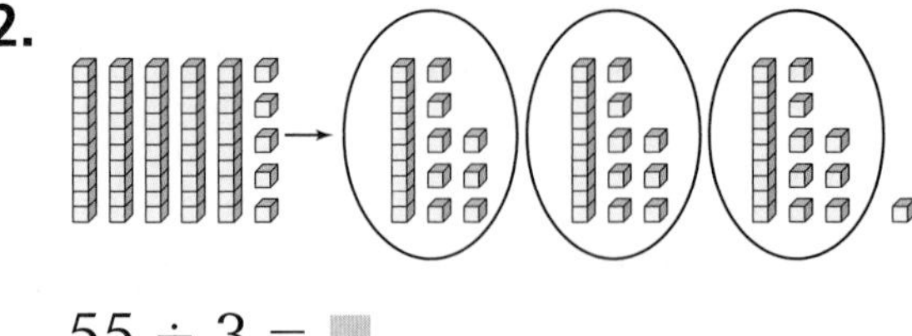

$55 \div 3 = $ ■

Divide and check.

3. $9\overline{)16}$
4. $8\overline{)74}$
5. $5\overline{)70}$
6. $4\overline{)89}$
7. $3\overline{)56}$
8. $9\overline{)32}$
9. $3\overline{)47}$
10. $2\overline{)27}$
11. Ms. Payne divides 65 crayons equally among 9 students. How many crayons does each student get? How many are left over?
12. Jackie has 35 crackers. She divides them equally among 5 plates. How many crackers are on 2 plates?

Set B (pp. 626–627)

Divide.

1. $2\overline{)684}$
2. $3\overline{)108}$
3. $5\overline{)250}$
4. $9\overline{)279}$
5. $6\overline{)552}$
6. $4\overline{)298}$
7. $7\overline{)119}$
8. $8\overline{)629}$
9. $2\overline{)200}$
10. $4\overline{)128}$
11. $6\overline{)672}$
12. $3\overline{)549}$
13. $5\overline{)495}$
14. $9\overline{)369}$
15. $8\overline{)896}$
16. $7\overline{)623}$
17. The product of 7 and a certain number is 238. What is the other number?
18. Marian has 516 sunflower seeds. How many seeds can she put in each of 3 bags?

Set C (pp. 628–629)

Estimate each quotient. Write the basic fact you used to find the estimate.

1. $155 \div 3 = $ ■
2. $639 \div 7 = $ ■
3. $374 \div 6 = $ ■
4. $318 \div 4 = $ ■

Estimate the quotient.

5. $5\overline{)212}$
6. $2\overline{)801}$
7. $3\overline{)291}$
8. $8\overline{)653}$

Review/Test

✓ CHECK VOCABULARY AND CONCEPTS

Choose the best term from the box.

divisor
remainder

1. In division, the amount left over is called the __?__. (p. 619)

Find the quotient and remainder. Use counters or draw a picture to help. (pp. 618–619)

2. $11 \div 2 =$ ■
3. $26 \div 4 =$ ■
4. $38 \div 5 =$ ■
5. $14 \div 5 =$ ■

✓ CHECK SKILLS

Use the model. Write the quotient and remainder. (pp. 620–623)

6. $27 \div 2 =$ ■

7. 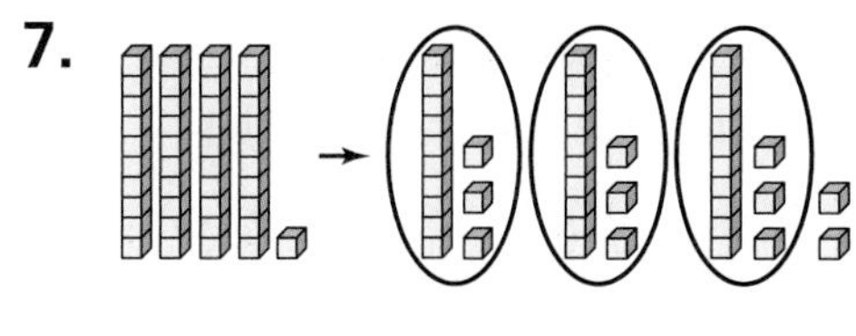

$41 \div 3 =$ ■

Divide. (pp. 618–623, 626–627)

8. $2\overline{)24}$
9. $5\overline{)72}$
10. $3\overline{)94}$
11. $6\overline{)39}$
12. $8\overline{)68}$
13. $2\overline{)186}$
14. $3\overline{)213}$
15. $5\overline{)255}$
16. $4\overline{)253}$
17. $9\overline{)747}$
18. $3\overline{)744}$
19. $6\overline{)678}$

Estimate the quotient. (pp. 628–629)

20. $5\overline{)240}$
21. $8\overline{)497}$
22. $3\overline{)268}$
23. $9\overline{)362}$

✓ CHECK PROBLEM SOLVING

Solve. (pp. 624–625)

24. A class of 33 students is going to the science museum. If each van holds 9 students, how many vans does the class need?

25. Caroline needs 4-inch pieces of yarn for an art project. She has 58 inches of yarn. How many 4-inch pieces can she make?

Standardized Test Prep

NUMBER SENSE, CONCEPTS, AND OPERATIONS

1. Karen made this model. What division sentence does it show?

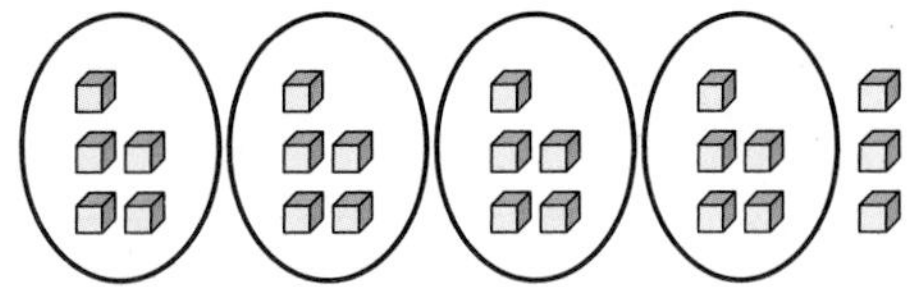

A $18 \div 4 = 4$ r2
B $20 \div 3 = 6$ r2
C $20 \div 4 = 5$
D $23 \div 4 = 5$ r3

2. Tim has 91 coins. He puts an equal number of coins into 7 albums. How many coins does Tim put in each album?

F 38
G 21
H 13
J 7

3. Tao wants to take 30 hot dogs to a picnic. The hot dogs are sold in packages of 8. How many packages of hot dogs should she buy?

A 5 **C** 3
B 4 **D** 2

4. **Explain It** Rita bought 4 boxes of straws for a school fair. Each box holds 196 straws. About how many straws did Rita buy? Tell how you found your answer.

MEASUREMENT

TIP **Understand the problem.** See item 5. Before you can compare the amounts, you must rename them using the same unit of capacity.

5. Brooke has 5 cups of juice. Carly has 3 pints of juice. Lois has 1 quart of juice. List the amounts of juice from **least** to **greatest**.

F 1 quart, 3 pints, 5 cups
G 1 quart, 5 cups, 3 pints
H 5 cups, 3 pints, 1 quart
J 3 pints, 1 quart, 5 cups

6. Yara measured the length of her thumb. She wrote 6 but forgot to record the unit of measure. What unit should Yara write?

A inches **C** feet
B centimeters **D** meters

7. **Explain It** This is what an outdoor thermometer showed at noon.

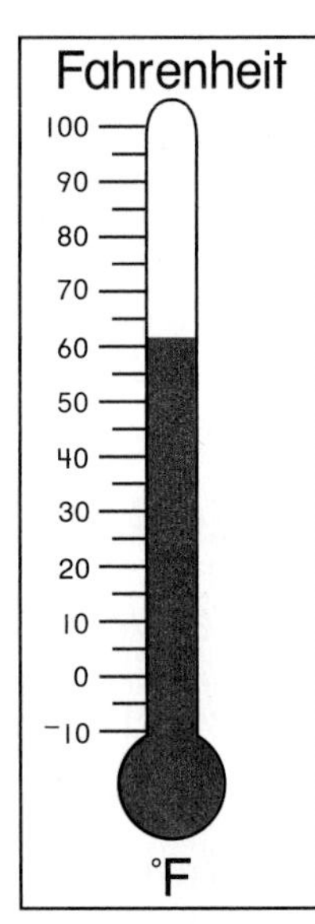

At 4:00 P.M., the temperature was about 10 degrees lower. About what was the temperature at 4:00 P.M.? Explain how you found your answer.

GEOMETRY AND SPATIAL SENSE

8. Lisa drew this figure.

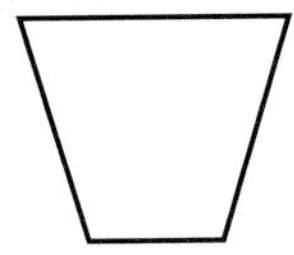

Which figure below appears to be congruent to Lisa's figure?

F 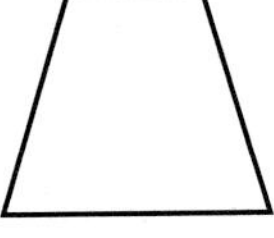

H 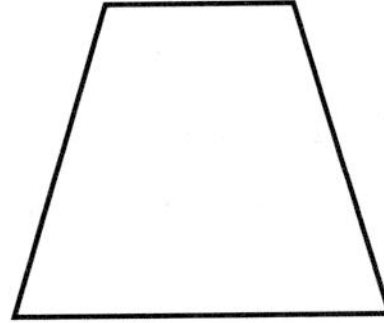

G 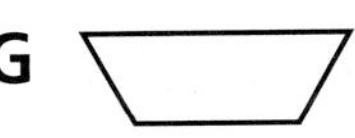

J

9. Carl flipped this triangle over the line.

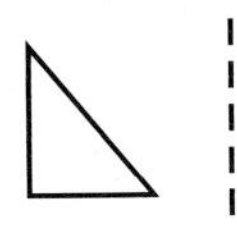

Which figure below did he see?

A 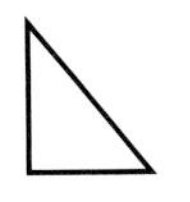

C 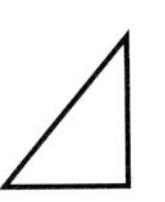

B 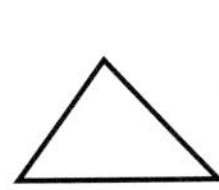

D 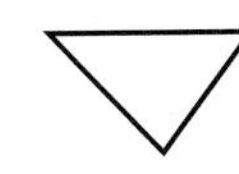

10. Explain It Elisa says that this log looks like a cube.

Do you agree with Elisa? Explain why or why not.

ALGEBRAIC THINKING

11. Susan wrote this pattern. Which are the next two numbers in her pattern?

12, 24, 36, 48, ■, ■

F 54, 66
G 58, 68
H 60, 72
J 62, 74

12. Greg wrote this pattern. Which rule could he have used?

7, 12, 17, 22, 27

A Add 10.
B Subtract 10.
C Multiply by 2.
D Add 5.

13. Which of the following could Cammie write to complete the equation?

$54 - 18 = $ ■

F $40 - 8$
G 5×7
H $30 + 8$
J 6×6

14. Explain It Beth had 47 pennies. Carlos gave Beth more pennies. Now Beth has 61 pennies. Tell how you can find how many pennies Carlos gave to Beth. Then write an equation to solve the problem.

IT'S IN THE BAG

Multiply and Divide Start to Finish

PROJECT Make a board game to practice multiplication and division of 2-digit numbers

Materials

- 1 file folder
- Construction paper
- Path pattern
- Markers, crayons, or color pencils
- Scissors
- Card stock
- Paper and pencil
- Dot cube or number cube
- Game pieces

Directions

1. Think of a theme for your game. Decorate the front of the file folder to match the theme. *(Picture A)*
2. Use the pattern and cut the path out of construction paper. Glue it onto the inside of the folder. Mark the beginning of the path with the word *Start* and the end of the path with *Finish*. Draw a rectangle somewhere on the board to hold the cards. Decorate the folder around the path. *(Picture B)*
3. Cut $1\frac{1}{2}$ in. $\times$ 2 in. pieces of cardstock. Write a 2-digit multiplication or division problem on each card. Place these cards on the rectangle. *(Picture C)*
4. Write the directions for playing your game. Glue the directions on the back of the folder. Be sure each person has paper and pencil to solve the problems.

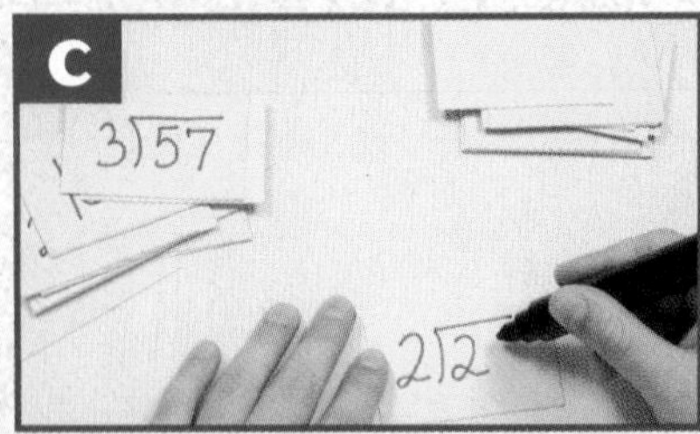

Challenge

Multiply 3-Digit Numbers

Brook Elementary School is presenting a play. There will be 4 shows, and 185 people can attend each show. How many people can attend all of the shows?

$4 \times 185 = ■$

Estimate. $4 \times 200 = 800$

STEP 1

Multiply the ones.
4 × 5 ones = 20 ones
Regroup 20 ones as 2 tens 0 ones.

Hundreds	Tens	Ones
	2	
1	8	5
×		4
		0

STEP 2

Multiply the tens.
4 × 8 tens = 32 tens
32 tens + 2 tens = 34 tens
Regroup 34 tens as 3 hundreds 4 tens.

Hundreds	Tens	Ones
3	2	
1	8	5
×		4
	4	0

STEP 3

Multiply the hundreds.
4 × 1 hundred = 4 hundreds
4 hundreds + 3 hundreds = 7 hundreds

Hundreds	Tens	Ones
3	2	
1	8	5
×		4
7	4	0

So, 740 people can attend the play. Since 740 is close to 800, the product is reasonable.

Talk About It

- Why can you regroup 34 tens as 3 hundreds 4 tens?

Try It

Find the product.

1. $5 \times 194 = ■$ **2.** $3 \times 216 = ■$ **3.** $2 \times 823 = ■$ **4.** $4 \times 275 = ■$

Study Guide and Review

VOCABULARY

Choose the best term from the box.

array
divisor
remainder

1. In division, the amount left over is called the ? .
(p. 618)

STUDY AND SOLVE

Chapter 29

Multiply multiples of 10 and 100.

Find the product. $4 \times 800 = \blacksquare$

- $4 \times 8 = 32$ • Use a basic fact.
- $4 \times 80 = 320$ • Then use a pattern.
- $4 \times 800 = 3{,}200$ • The product and the factor have the same number of zeros.

Use mental math and basic facts to find the product. (pp. 600–601)

2. $2 \times 60 = \blacksquare$ **3.** $3 \times 90 = \blacksquare$

4. $4 \times 200 = \blacksquare$ **5.** $6 \times 300 = \blacksquare$

6. $8 \times 20 = \blacksquare$ **7.** $7 \times 400 = \blacksquare$

8. $5 \times 90 = \blacksquare$ **9.** $9 \times 500 = \blacksquare$

10. $3 \times 700 = \blacksquare$ **11.** $4 \times 70 = \blacksquare$

Multiply 2-digit numbers by 1-digit numbers.

Find the product. $9 \times 36 = \blacksquare$

$$\begin{array}{r} {}^{5}\\ 36 \\ \times\ 9 \\ \hline 324 \end{array}$$

- Multiply the ones. Regroup into tens and ones.
- Multiply the tens. Add the regrouped tens.
- Regroup the tens as hundreds and tens.

So, $9 \times 36 = 324$.

Find each product. (pp. 602–605, 608–611)

12. $\begin{array}{r} 15 \\ \times\ 2 \\ \hline \end{array}$ **13.** $\begin{array}{r} 26 \\ \times\ 5 \\ \hline \end{array}$

14. $\begin{array}{r} 38 \\ \times\ 4 \\ \hline \end{array}$ **15.** $\begin{array}{r} 42 \\ \times\ 8 \\ \hline \end{array}$

16. $\begin{array}{r} 67 \\ \times\ 6 \\ \hline \end{array}$ **17.** $\begin{array}{r} 88 \\ \times\ 9 \\ \hline \end{array}$

18. There are 24 hours in a day. How many hours are there in 9 days?

Chapter 30

Divide 2-digit dividends.

Divide and check. $97 \div 8 = ■$

$$\begin{array}{r} 12 \text{ r1} \\ 8\overline{)97} \\ -8\downarrow \\ \hline 17 \\ -16 \\ \hline 1 \end{array}$$

- Divide the 9 tens.
- Bring down the 7 ones.
- Divide the 17 ones.
- Write the remainder beside the quotient.

So, $97 \div 8 = 12$ r1.

Check: $8 \times 12 = 96$; $96 + 1 = 97$

Divide and check. (pp. 620–623)

19. $54 \div 6 = ■$

20. $17 \div 5 = ■$

21. $25 \div 4 = ■$

22. $42 \div 3 = ■$

23. $2\overline{)37}$

24. $6\overline{)90}$

25. $4\overline{)45}$

26. $5\overline{)74}$

27. $3\overline{)99}$

28. $8\overline{)67}$

Divide 3-digit dividends.

$147 \div 3 = ■$

$$\begin{array}{r} 49 \\ 3\overline{)147} \\ -12\downarrow \\ \hline 27 \\ -27 \\ \hline 0 \end{array}$$

So, $147 \div 3 = 49$.

$318 \div 2 = ■$

$$\begin{array}{r} 159 \\ 2\overline{)318} \\ -2\downarrow \\ \hline 11 \\ -10\downarrow \\ \hline 18 \\ -18 \\ \hline 0 \end{array}$$

So, $318 \div 2 = 159$.

Divide. (pp. 626–627)

29. $2\overline{)166}$

30. $3\overline{)291}$

31. $5\overline{)\$2.45}$

32. $7\overline{)434}$

33. $6\overline{)306}$

34. $8\overline{)736}$

35. $4\overline{)\$4.68}$

36. $8\overline{)544}$

37. $9\overline{)801}$

38. $3\overline{)\$7.23}$

PRACTICE AND PROBLEM SOLVING

Solve. (pp. 606–607, 624–625)

39. At a garage sale, Paul bought 3 toy cars for 49¢ each. He had a $5 bill. What operations would you use to find out how much change Paul received? What was Paul's change?

40. Mrs. Ramsey bakes pies at a bakery. She has 52 cups of apples. If 6 cups of apples are needed for one pie, how many pies can she make? Explain.

PERFORMANCE ASSESSMENT

TASK A • TABLETOP TILES

Evan has 90 square tiles to make a rectangular design for a tabletop. So far, his design has 4 rows with 18 tiles in each row.

a. How many tiles has Evan used so far? Draw a model and write a multiplication sentence to show that your answer is correct.

b. How many rows of 18 tiles can Evan make with 90 tiles?

c. Draw a model and write a multiplication sentence to show a different way to use 90 tiles to make a rectangular design.

TASK B • SHELL ART

The table shows the number of shells Jarrod, Gina, and Tim have collected. They will use the shells to make flower pictures. It takes 4 shells to make a small flower and 8 shells to make a large flower.

SHELLS WE COLLECTED	
Jarrod	62
Gina	45
Tim	60

a. Jarrod wants to make all large flowers. Draw a model to show how he can use his shells. How many large flowers can he make? How many shells will he have left over?

b. Gina wants to make all small flowers. Draw a model to show how she can use her shells. How many small flowers can she make? How many shells will she have left over?

c. Tim wants to use all of his shells to make some large flowers and some small flowers. Draw a model to show how he can use his shells. How many large flowers and how many small flowers can he make?

Technology Linkup

Multiply and Divide

Craig is a helicopter pilot. He gives helicopter tours. On each tour in his helicopter he can take 5 passengers.

Examples

A Craig can give 42 tours each week. How many passengers can Craig take each week?
Use a calculator to multiply.

So, Craig can take 210 passengers each week.

B A group of 95 people want to take helicopter tours. How many tours must Craig give to serve the whole group?
Use a calculator to divide.

So, Craig must give 19 tours to serve the whole group.

Practice and Problem Solving

Use a calculator to multiply or divide.

1. 94×6 **2.** 527×3 **3.** 434×9

4. $96 \div 4$ **5.** $185 \div 5$ **6.** $312 \div 6$

7. Austin has 8 days to read 176 pages. He wants to read the same number of pages each day. How many pages should Austin read each day?

8. Claire walks 14 blocks to school and back every day. How many blocks does she walk in 5 days? How many blocks does she walk in 30 days?

GO ON-LINE **Multimedia Math Glossary** www.harcourtschool.com/mathglossary

Vocabulary Power Look up *remainder* in the Multimedia Math Glossary. Write three examples of division problems that have remainders.

▲ More than 750,000 people visit the fair every summer.

at the Indiana State Fair

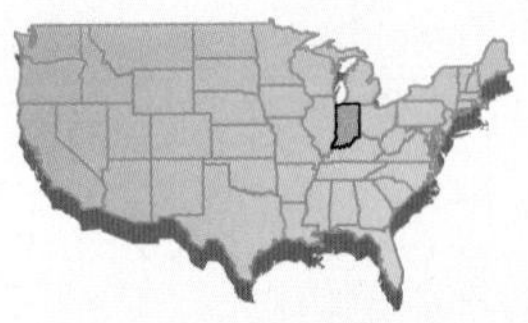

The Indiana State Fair is held in Indianapolis every summer. At the fair, you can munch on a corn dog, ride on a roller coaster, listen to country music, or watch marching bands.

1. The Indiana State Fairgrounds opened for the first time on September 19, 1892. For how many years has there been a state fair at the fairgrounds?
2. The National City Band Day Competition is held every year at the state fair. A large band with 225 members marched in the parade. The drum major marched in front of the band. The rest of the band marched in rows of 7. How many rows of band members were there?
3. The Ferris wheel has 20 gondolas. Each gondola can hold up to 6 people. What is the greatest number of people that can ride the Ferris wheel at one time?
4. During the state fair about 14,285 pounds of hot dogs were eaten. To the nearest thousand, how many pounds of hot dogs were eaten at the fair?

▲ High school bands from all over Indiana come to the fair to march in the Band Day contest.

FAMILY FUN AT THE INDIANA STATE FAIR

Children and their families are special guests at the Indiana State Fair. They can visit the livestock nursery, go on a barn tour, and watch dog teams at the Fun Park.

1. Addison's family wants to visit the Pioneer Village, go on the Barn Tour, see the Livestock Nursery, and go through the Exhibit Hall. How many different orders of activites can the family choose? Make a list to show your answer.

2. Children from 3 to 12 can be a farmer for a day at the Little Hands on the Farm exhibit. They can plant seeds, harvest farm products, and exchange products for money to buy food at the grocery story. If the children in Todd's group planted 6 corn packets and there were 35 seeds in each packet, how many corn seeds did they plant?

3. Each year, visitors eat about 4,350 pounds of popcorn at the fair. To the nearest hundred, about how many pounds of popcorn are eaten at the fair?

▼ **Families can visit the Livestock Nursery to see chicks and calves and to try milking dairy cows.**

▲ **At Pioneer Village, families can see grain threshing, corn shelling, and other farm chores of years ago. They can also see old farm equipment such as the steam engine tractor pictured above.**

STUDENT HANDBOOK

Troubleshooting H2

PREREQUISITE SKILLS REVIEW Do you have the math skills needed to start a new chapter? Use this list of skills to review and remember your skills.

Skill	Page
Ordinal Numbers	H2
Place Value: 2-Digit Numbers	H2
Model 3-Digit Numbers	H3
Compare 2- and 3-Digit Numbers	H3
Order Numbers	H4
Addition Facts	H4
2-Digit Addition	H5
Subtraction Facts	H6
2-Digit Subtraction	H6
Count Coins	H7
Same Amounts	H7
Tell Time	H8
Calendar	H8
Skip-Count	H9
Equal Groups	H9
Column Addition	H10
Arrays	H10
Find Missing Factors	H11
Multiplication Facts	H11
Make Equal Groups	H12
Multiplication Facts Through 5	H12
Skip-Count by Tens	H13
Model Division	H13
Model Multiplication	H14
Multiplication Facts Through 10	H14
Fact Families	H15
Division Facts Through 5	H15
Commutative Property of Multiplication	H16
Missing Factors	H16

Skill	Page
Read a Table	H17
Use a Tally Table	H17
Use Symbols	H18
Identify Parts of a Whole	H18
Compare Parts of a Whole	H19
Use a Rule	H19
Read a Thermometer	H20
Multiplication Facts	H20
Addition	H21
Subtraction	H21
Multiplication and Division Facts	H22
Identify Solid Figures	H23
Identify Plane Figures	H23
Sides and Vertices	H24
Equivalent Fractions	H24
Same Size, Same Shape	H25
Mixed Numbers	H25
Measure to the Nearest Inch	H26
Find a Rule	H27
Use a Metric Ruler	H27
Measure to the Nearest Centimeter	H28
Model Parts of a Whole	H28
Model Parts of a Group	H29
Name the Fraction	H29
Compare Fractions	H30
Use Money Notation	H30
Name the Decimal	H31
Compare and Order Decimals	H31

Sharpen Your Test-Taking Skills H32

Before a test, sharpen your test-taking skills by reviewing these pages. Here you can find tips such as how to get ready for a test, how to understand the directions, and how to keep track of time.

Basic Facts Tests H36

Review addition, subtraction, multiplication, and division facts by taking the basic facts tests throughout the year to improve your memorization skills.

Table of Measures H41

All the important measures used in this book are in this table. If you've forgotten exactly how many feet are in a mile, this table will help you.

Glossary H42

This glossary will help you speak and write the language of mathematics. Use the glossary to check the definitions of important terms.

Index H55

Use the index when you want to review a topic. It lists the page numbers where the topic is taught.

TROUBLESHOOTING

✓ ORDINAL NUMBERS

Ordinal numbers tell order or position.

★ first ★ second ★ third ★ fourth ★ fifth ★ sixth ★ seventh ★ eighth ★ ninth ★ tenth

Example

Write the position of the yellow marble.

   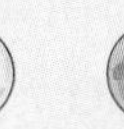 

The yellow marble is second.

▶ Practice

Write the position of each marble.

1. purple **2.** white **3.** red **4.** green

✓ PLACE VALUE: 2-DIGIT NUMBERS

Look at the position of each digit to find the value of a number.

Example

Find the value of each digit in 34.

3 4

tens place ones place

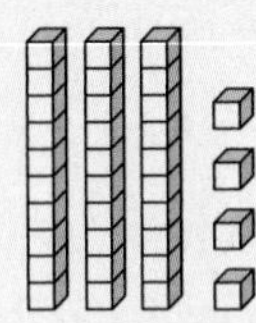

3 tens 4 ones = 34

The 3 has a value of 3 tens, or 30.
The 4 has a value of 4 ones, or 4.

▶ Practice

Write the value of the underlined digit.

1. $\underline{2}8$ **2.** $5\underline{3}$ **3.** $4\underline{5}$ **4.** $\underline{7}6$

5. $\underline{9}1$ **6.** $3\underline{8}$ **7.** $\underline{1}7$ **8.** $\underline{6}0$

✓ MODEL 3-DIGIT NUMBERS

You can use base-ten blocks to model numbers.

Examples

A

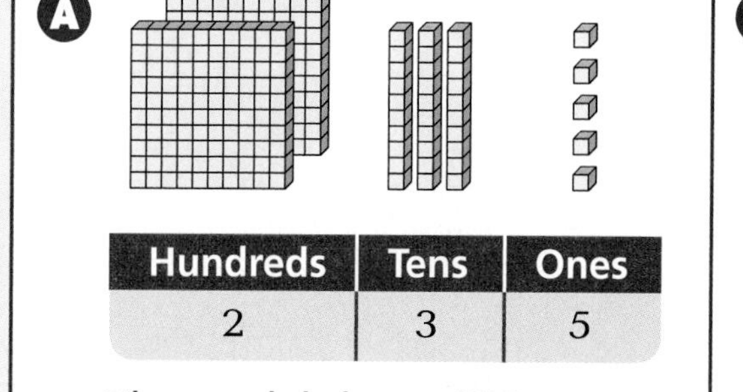

Hundreds	Tens	Ones
2	3	5

The model shows 235.

B

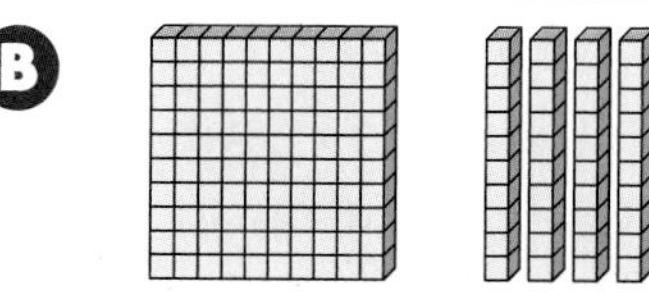

Hundreds	Tens	Ones
1	4	2

The model shows 142.

▶ Practice

Write the number that matches the model.

1.

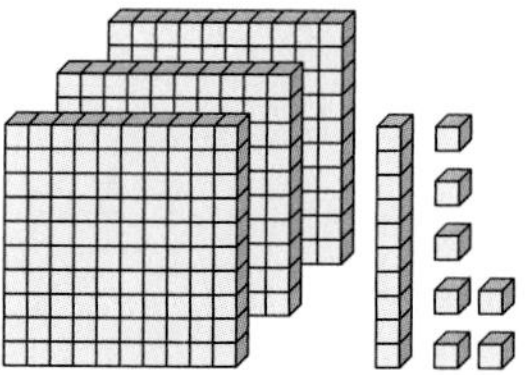

2.

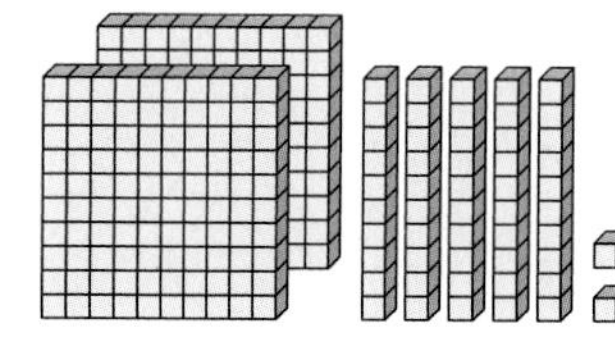

✓ COMPARE 2- AND 3-DIGIT NUMBERS

Compare numbers, beginning with the greatest place value.

Examples

A

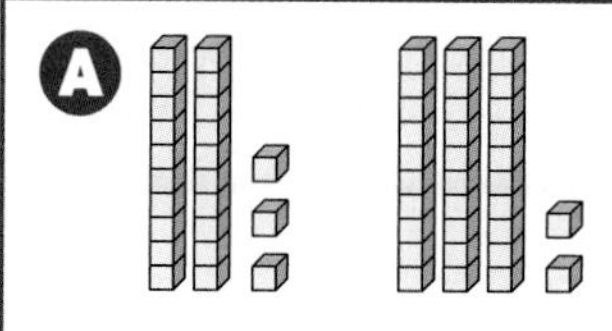

23 ● 32

Compare tens.
2 tens is less than 3 tens.
So, 23 < 32.

B

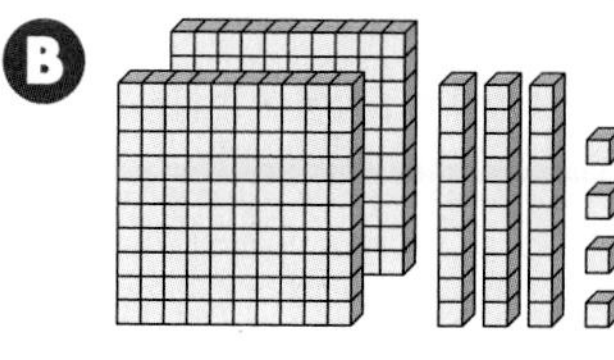

234 ● 215

Compare hundreds.
2 hundreds = 2 hundreds
Compare tens. 3 tens is greater than 1 ten.
So, 234 > 215.

▶ Practice

Write < or > for each ●.

1. 45 ● 63 **2.** 72 ● 71 **3.** 487 ● 456

TROUBLESHOOTING

ORDER NUMBERS

You can use a number line to order numbers. As you move from left to right, the numbers increase in value.

Example

Find 278, 283, and 276 on the number line. Then write in order from least to greatest.

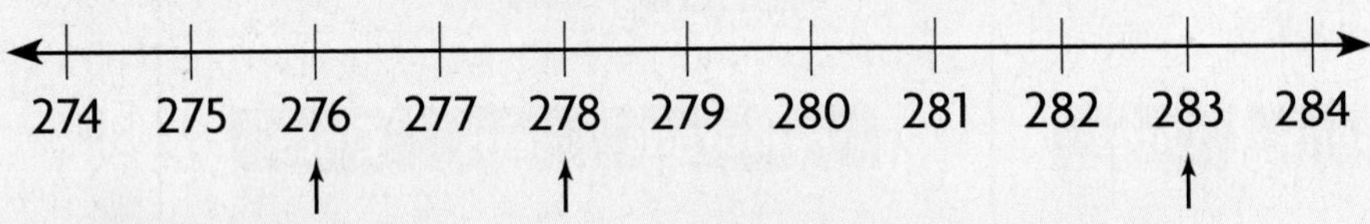

So, the numbers from least to greatest are:

276, 278, 283

▶ **Practice**

Write the numbers in order from least to greatest.

1. 279, 277, 281

2. 284, 280, 275

3. 282, 278, 279

4. 276, 275, 278

ADDITION FACTS

The answer to an addition problem is the **sum**. If you do not remember a fact, you can think about how to **make a ten** to help find the sum.

Example Find 7 + 5.

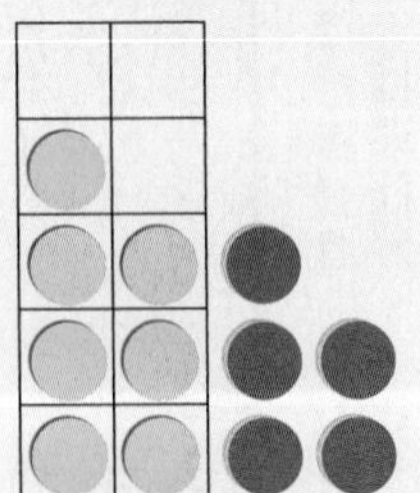

Show 7 + 5.

Move 3 counters to fill the ten frame. 7 + 3 = 10

There are 2 more counters to add. 10 + 2 = 12

So, 7 + 5 = 12.

▶ **Practice**

Add. You may wish to make a ten.

1. $5 + 6$

2. $8 + 5$

3. $6 + 4$

4. $7 + 7$

5. $9 + 6$

2-DIGIT ADDITION

Sometimes you must regroup when adding 2-digit numbers.

Find 24 + 17.

STEP 1

Add the ones.
4 + 7 = 11

tens	ones
2	4
+ 1	7

STEP 2

Regroup.
11 ones = 1 ten 1 one

tens	ones
1	
2	4
+ 1	7
	1

STEP 3

Add the tens.
1 + 2 + 1 = 4

tens	ones
1	
2	4
+ 1	7
4	1

So, 24 + 17 = 41.

▶ Practice

Add.

1.

tens	ones
3	5
+ 1	8

2.

tens	ones
1	6
+ 5	7

3.

tens	ones
6	0
+ 2	4

4.

tens	ones
3	7
+ 2	8

5. $23 + 59$

6. $42 + 37$

7. $27 + 24$

8. $14 + 36$

9. $62 + 23$

10. $31 + 49$

11. $58 + 18$

12. $73 + 17$

TROUBLESHOOTING

✓ SUBTRACTION FACTS

The answer to a subtraction problem is the **difference**. If you do not remember a fact, you can **count back** or **count up** to help find the difference.

Example

Find 7 − 2.

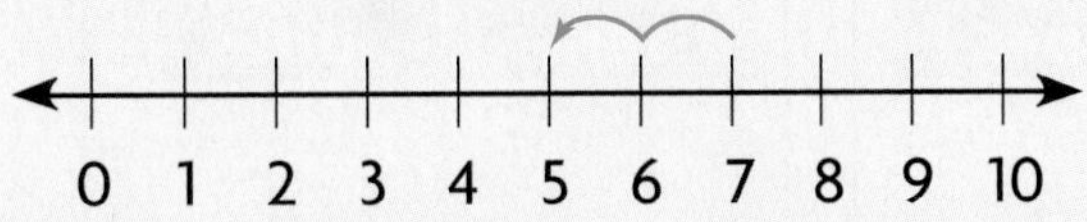

Say 7. Count back 2.

6, 5

The difference is 5. So, 7 − 2 = 5.

▶ Practice

Subtract.

1. $11 - 2$
2. $11 - 5$
3. $13 - 7$
4. $15 - 8$
5. $18 - 9$

✓ 2-DIGIT SUBTRACTION

Sometimes you must regroup when subtracting 2-digit numbers.

Find 32 − 15.

STEP 1

Since 5 > 2, you must regroup.

tens	ones
3	2
− 1	5

STEP 2

Regroup.
3 tens 2 ones = 2 tens 12 ones
Subtract the ones.

tens	ones
2	12
~~3~~	~~2~~
− 1	5
	7

STEP 3

Subtract the tens.

tens	ones
2	12
~~3~~	~~2~~
− 1	5
1	7

So, 32 − 15 = 17.

▶ Practice

Subtract.

1. $57 - 22$
2. $73 - 34$
3. $66 - 18$
4. $31 - 17$
5. $80 - 27$

COUNT COINS

half-dollar = 50¢ quarter = 25¢ dime = 10¢ nickel = 5¢ penny = 1¢

Count on to find the value of a group of coins.

Example

Count and write the amount.

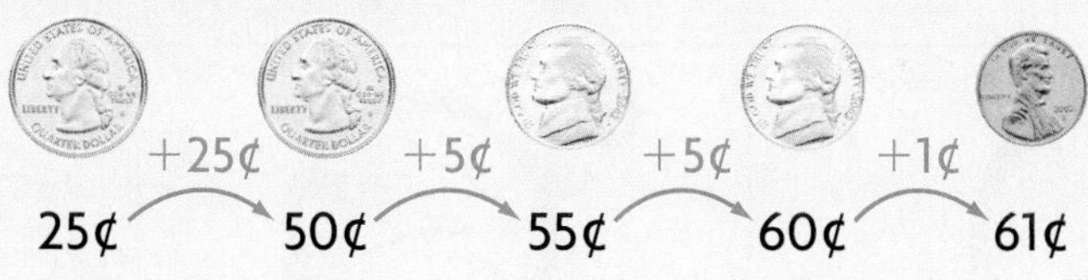

So, the value of the coins is 61¢.

▶ Practice

Count and write the amount.

1.      

2.  

SAME AMOUNTS

You can show the same amount of money in different ways.

Example

Show 35¢ in two ways.

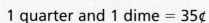

1 quarter and 1 dime = 35¢

3 dimes and 1 nickel = 35¢

▶ Practice

Show the amount of money in a different way.
Draw and label each coin.

1.    

2.    

TROUBLESHOOTING

TELL TIME

The short hand on a clock is the **hour hand**. The long hand on a clock is the **minute hand**.

You can **count by fives** to find the minutes after the hour.

This clock shows 9:35.

Examples

Write the time.

A 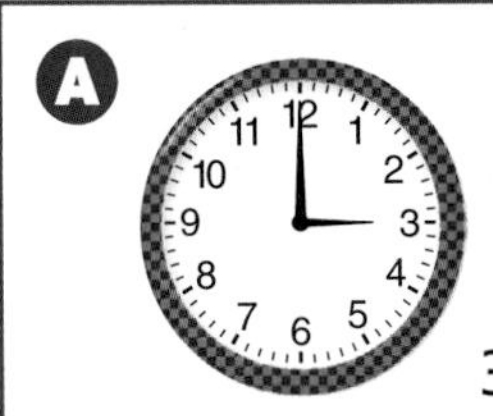 3:00

B  3:30

C  3:45

▶ **Practice**

Write the time.

1. 

2. 

3. 

CALENDAR

You can use a calendar to keep track of days, weeks, and months.

There are 5 Wednesdays in October. The third Friday in this month is October 18.

OCTOBER						
Sun	Mon	Tue	Wed	Thu	Fri	Sat
		1	2	3	4	5
6	7	8	9	10	11	12
13	14	15	16	17	18	19
20	21	22	23	24	25	26
27	28	29	30	31		

▶ **Practice**

Use the calendar.

1. The second Tuesday in October is _?_.
2. The last day in October is a _?_.
3. There are _?_ Mondays in October.
4. The fifth Wednesday in October is _?_.

SKIP-COUNT

To skip-count, start with any number and add or subtract the same number.

Example

Skip-count to find the missing numbers. 6, 9, 12, ■, ■

Think: $6 + 3 = 9$ $9 + 3 = 12$

So, skip-count by threes to find the missing numbers.

$12 + 3 = 15$ $15 + 3 = 18$

So, the numbers are 6, 9, 12, 15, 18.

▶ Practice

Skip-count to find the missing numbers.

1. 8, 10, 12, ■

2. 25, 30, 35, ■

3. 100, 90, 80, ■, ■

4. 36, 38, 40, ■

5. 12, 15, 18, ■

6. 35, 40, 45, ■, ■

EQUAL GROUPS

When you have **equal groups**, you can skip-count to find how many in all.

Example

Write how many there are in all.

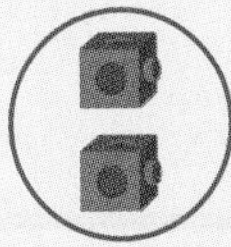

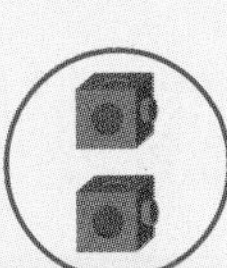
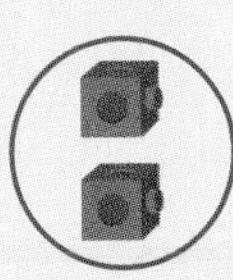

Think: Since there are 2 in each group, you can skip-count by twos: 2, 4, 6, 8.

So, 4 groups of $2 = 8$.

▶ Practice

Write how many there are in all.

1.

3 groups of 2 = ■

2.

5 groups of 3 = ■

3.

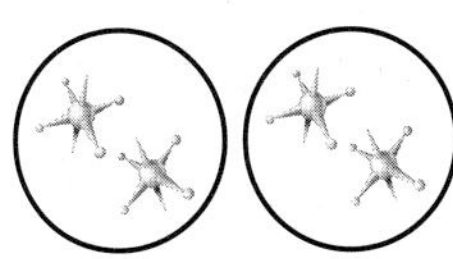

2 groups of 2 = ■

TROUBLESHOOTING

✓ COLUMN ADDITION

To add more than two numbers, choose two numbers to add first. Look for facts you know.

Example

$\begin{array}{r} 2 \\ 5 \\ +\ 8 \\ \hline 15 \end{array}$ $2 + 8 = 10$, $10 + 5 = 15$	$\begin{array}{r} 2 \\ 5 \\ +\ 8 \\ \hline 15 \end{array}$ $2 + 5 = 7$, $7 + 8 = 15$	$\begin{array}{r} 2 \\ 5 \\ +\ 8 \\ \hline 15 \end{array}$ $5 + 8 = 13$, $13 + 2 = 15$

▶ Practice

Find the sum.

1. $\begin{array}{r} 4 \\ 4 \\ +\ 2 \\ \hline \end{array}$ **2.** $\begin{array}{r} 6 \\ 2 \\ +\ 3 \\ \hline \end{array}$ **3.** $\begin{array}{r} 9 \\ 1 \\ +\ 2 \\ \hline \end{array}$ **4.** $\begin{array}{r} 7 \\ 3 \\ +\ 5 \\ \hline \end{array}$ **5.** $\begin{array}{r} 2 \\ 7 \\ +\ 4 \\ \hline \end{array}$ **6.** $\begin{array}{r} 1 \\ 8 \\ +\ 1 \\ \hline \end{array}$

✓ ARRAYS

You can use arrays to model multiplication.

Example

3 rows of 4 = 12
$3 \times 4 = 12$

There are 3 rows, or groups, of 4.
You can skip-count by 4s: 4, 8, 12
You can use repeated addition: $4 + 4 + 4 = 12$
You can multiply: $3 \times 4 = 12$

▶ Practice

Find the product.

1. 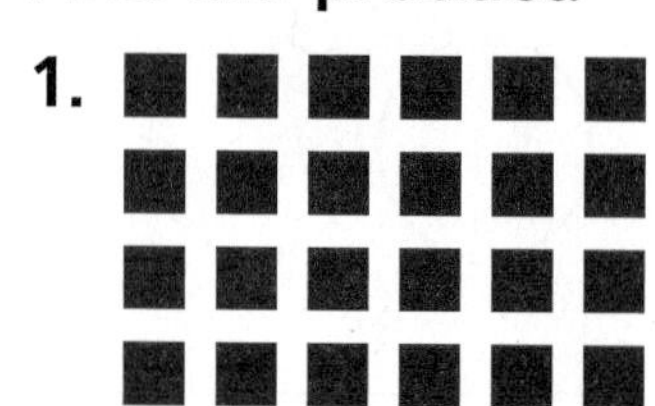

4 rows of 6 = ■
$4 \times 6 =$ ■

2.

3 rows of 3 = ■
$3 \times 3 =$ ■

3. 

3 rows of 5 = ■
$3 \times 5 =$ ■

FIND MISSING FACTORS

You can use a multiplication table to find missing factors.

Example

Find the missing factor.

6 × ▇ = 42

Start on the row for 6.
Look right for the product, 42.
Look up the column from 42.
So, the missing factor is 7.

×	0	1	2	3	4	5	6	7	8	9
0	0	0	0	0	0	0	0	0	0	0
1	0	1	2	3	4	5	6	7	8	9
2	0	2	4	6	8	10	12	14	16	18
3	0	3	6	9	12	15	18	21	24	27
4	0	4	8	12	16	20	24	28	32	36
5	0	5	10	15	20	25	30	35	40	45
6	0	6	12	18	24	30	36	42	48	54
7	0	7	14	21	28	35	42	49	56	63
8	0	8	16	24	32	40	48	56	64	72
9	0	9	18	27	36	45	54	63	72	81

▶ Practice

Find the missing factor.

1. $3 \times$ ▇ $= 24$ **2.** $4 \times$ ▇ $= 16$ **3.** $8 \times$ ▇ $= 48$ **4.** $7 \times$ ▇ $= 28$

MULTIPLICATION FACTS

The answer to a multiplication problem is the **product**.

Examples

A Find 2 × 6.

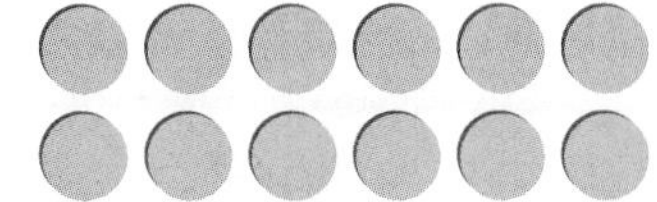

2 rows of 6 = 12
So, 2 × 6 = 12.

B Find 3 × 5.

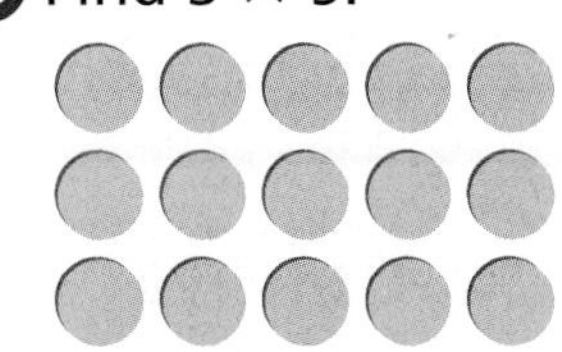

3 rows of 5 = 15
So, 3 × 5 = 15.

▶ Practice

Find the product.

1. $2 \times 2 =$ ▇ **2.** $4 \times 3 =$ ▇ **3.** $5 \times 2 =$ ▇

4. ▇ $= 5 \times 5$ **5.** $3 \times 2 =$ ▇ **6.** ▇ $= 5 \times 9$

7. $8 \times 3 =$ ▇ **8.** ▇ $= 7 \times 5$ **9.** $3 \times 7 =$ ▇

TROUBLESHOOTING

✓ MAKE EQUAL GROUPS

When you multiply, you join equal groups.

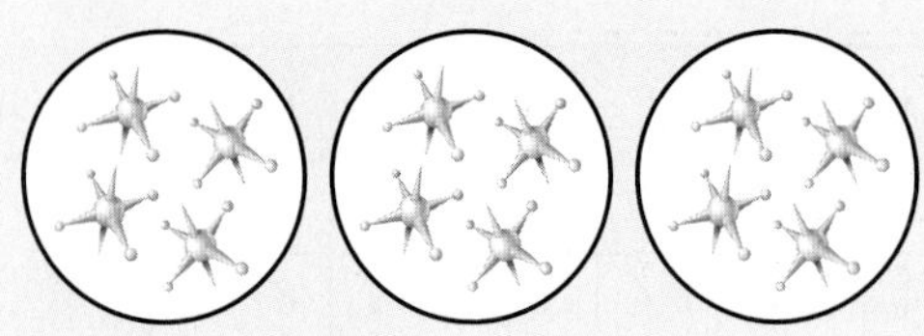

There are 3 groups of jacks.
There are 4 jacks in each group.
There are 12 jacks in all.

▶ Practice

Complete.

1. 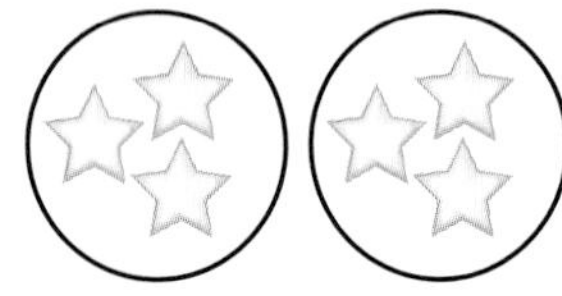

■ groups of stars
■ stars in each group
■ stars in all

2. 

■ groups of ladybugs
■ ladybugs in each group
■ ladybugs in all

✓ MULTIPLICATION FACTS THROUGH 5

When one of the factors of a problem is even, you can double a fact you already know.

Example

Find 4×7.

Think: To find a 4s fact, you can double a 2s fact.

- First find the 2s fact. $\mathbf{2 \times 7 = 14}$
- Double the product. $\mathbf{14 + 14 = 28}$

So, $4 \times 7 = 28$.

▶ Practice

Find the product.

1. $8 \times 2 =$ ■ **2.** $4 \times 4 =$ ■ **3.** $4 \times 6 =$ ■

4. $6 \times 5 =$ ■ **5.** $3 \times 6 =$ ■ **6.** ■ $= 4 \times 7$

7. $9 \times 4 =$ ■ **8.** $7 \times 6 =$ ■ **9.** $8 \times 3 =$ ■

10. $4 \times 5 =$ ■ **11.** ■ $= 6 \times 2$ **12.** $8 \times 4 =$ ■

SKIP-COUNT BY TENS

You can use a pattern to skip-count by tens.

Example

Skip-count by tens to find the missing numbers.

18, 28, 38, ■, ■, 68

38 + **10** = 48
48 + **10** = 58

So, the numbers are 18, 28, 38, 48, 58, 68.

1	2	3	4	5	6	7	8	9	10
11	12	13	14	15	16	17	18	19	20
21	22	23	24	25	26	27	28	29	30
31	32	33	34	35	36	37	38	39	40
41	42	43	44	45	46	47	48	49	50
51	52	53	54	55	56	57	58	59	60
61	62	63	64	65	66	67	68	69	70

▶ Practice

Skip-count by tens to find the missing numbers.

1. 15, 25, 35, 45, ■, 65

2. 11, 21, 31, ■, 51, 61

3. 54, 44, 34, ■, ■

4. 16, 26, 36, ■, 56, ■

MODEL DIVISION

You can use arrays to model division.

There are 18 tiles in all.
The tiles are in 3 equal rows.
There are 6 tiles in each row.

18	÷	3	=	6
tiles in all		equal rows		tiles in each row

▶ Practice

Copy and complete.

1.

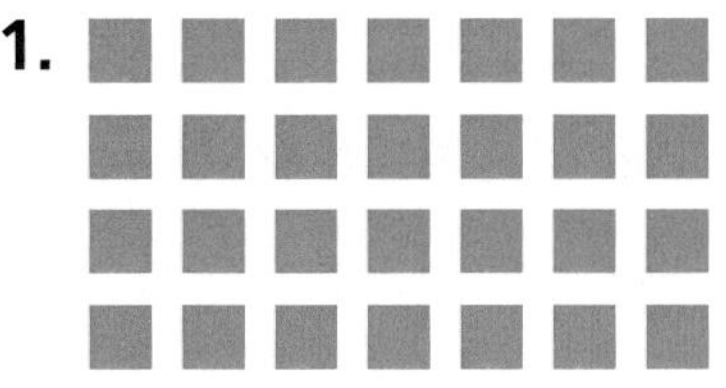

4 rows of ■ = 28
28 ÷ 4 = ■

2.

3 rows of ■ = 15
15 ÷ 3 = ■

TROUBLESHOOTING

✓ MODEL MULTIPLICATION

When you multiply, you add equal groups.

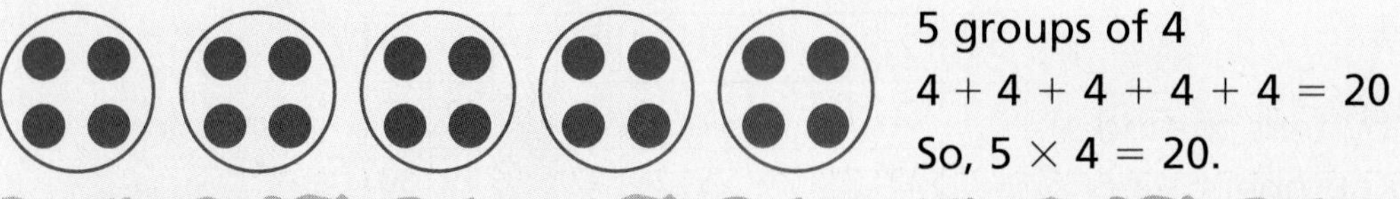

5 groups of 4

4 + 4 + 4 + 4 + 4 = 20

So, 5 × 4 = 20.

▶ Practice

Copy and complete.

1.

a. ■ groups of ■

b. ■ + ■ + ■ = ■

c. ■ × ■ = ■

2.

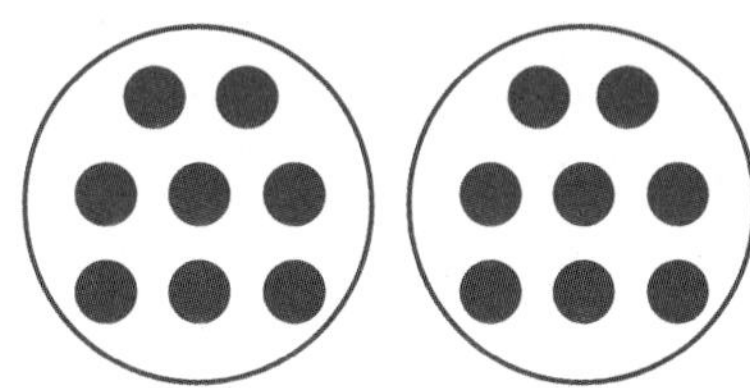

a. ■ groups of ■

b. ■ + ■ = ■

c. ■ × ■ = ■

✓ MULTIPLICATION FACTS THROUGH 10

You can use an array to find a multiplication fact.

Examples

A Multiply. 5 × 9 = ■

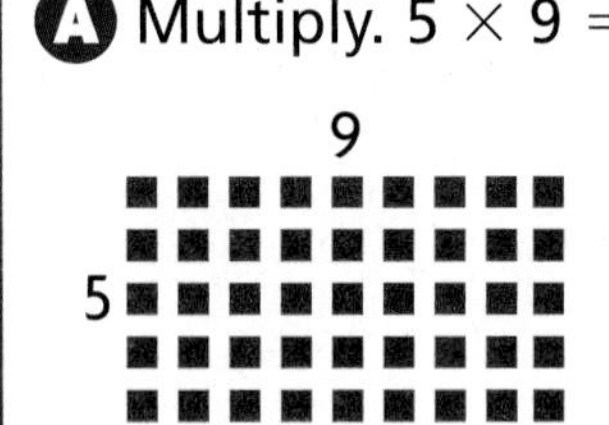

So, 5 × 9 = 45.

B Multiply. 4 × 6 = ■

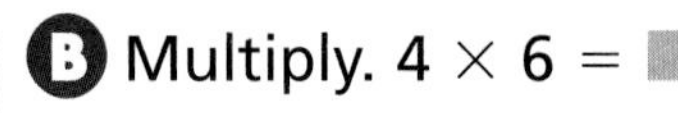

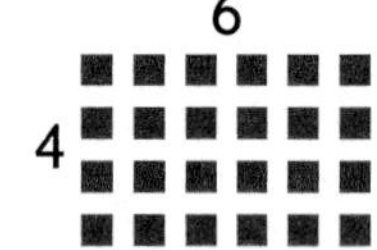

So, 4 × 6 = 24.

▶ Practice

Find the product.

1. 9 × 7 = ■ **2.** 8 × 10 = ■ **3.** 6 × 9 = ■ **4.** 5 × 9 = ■

5. 10 × 7 = ■ **6.** 9 × 9 = ■ **7.** 7 × 7 = ■ **8.** 10 × 6 = ■

9. 9 × 6 = ■ **10.** 3 × 8 = ■ **11.** 3 × 10 = ■ **12.** 6 × 8 = ■

13. 9 × 8 = ■ **14.** 9 × 4 = ■ **15.** 9 × 10 = ■ **16.** 8 × 8 = ■

FACT FAMILIES

A **fact family** is a set of related multiplication and division sentences.

Examples

A Fact family for 2, 3, and 6:		**B** Fact family for 4, 5, and 20:	
$2 \times 3 = 6$	$6 \div 3 = 2$	$4 \times 5 = 20$	$20 \div 5 = 4$
$3 \times 2 = 6$	$6 \div 2 = 3$	$5 \times 4 = 20$	$20 \div 4 = 5$

▶ Practice

Write the fact family for each group of numbers.

1. 3, 4, 12 **2.** 2, 8, 16 **3.** 6, 3, 18 **4.** 4, 6, 24

DIVISION FACTS THROUGH 5

The answer in a division problem is the **quotient**. You can make equal groups to find a quotient.

Example

Find $3\overline{)15}$.

Read: 15 divided by 3
Write: 15 ÷ 3 = ■

Think: 15 counters in 3 groups
How many in each group?

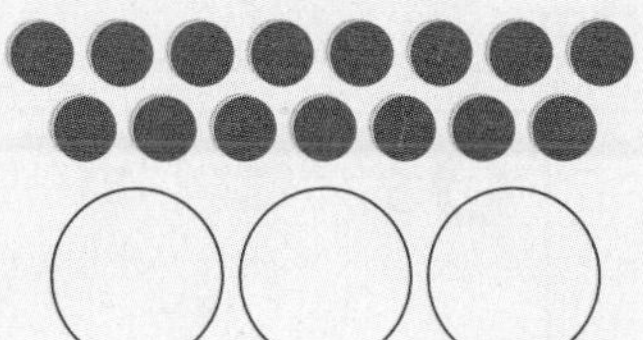

5 in each group

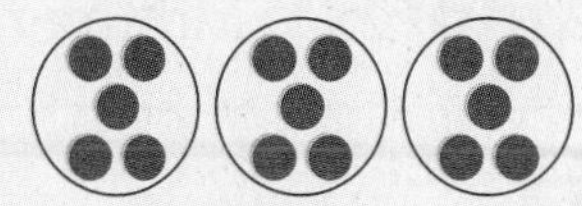

So, 15 ÷ 3 = 5, or $\begin{array}{r} 5 \\ 3\overline{)15} \end{array}$.

▶ Practice

Find the quotient.

1. 25 ÷ 5 = ■ **2.** 30 ÷ 5 = ■ **3.** 24 ÷ 3 = ■

4. 14 ÷ 2 = ■ **5.** 40 ÷ 5 = ■ **6.** 36 ÷ 4 = ■

7. 28 ÷ 4 = ■ **8.** 45 ÷ 5 = ■ **9.** 18 ÷ 3 = ■

10. 16 ÷ 2 = ■ **11.** 21 ÷ 3 = ■ **12.** 24 ÷ 4 = ■

TROUBLESHOOTING

✓ COMMUTATIVE PROPERTY OF MULTIPLICATION

Two numbers can be multiplied in any order. The product will be the same.

Example

3 groups of 5 = 15
So, $3 \times 5 = 15$.

5 groups of 3 = 15
So, $5 \times 3 = 15$.

If you can't remember 3×5, try thinking of 5×3.

So, $3 \times 5 = 5 \times 3$.

▶ Practice

Use the Commutative Property of Multiplication to help you find each product.

1. $4 \times 5 = \blacksquare$ **2.** $8 \times 4 = \blacksquare$ **3.** $7 \times 8 = \blacksquare$

4. $9 \times 6 = \blacksquare$ **5.** $7 \times 3 = \blacksquare$ **6.** $6 \times 3 = \blacksquare$

✓ MISSING FACTORS

You can use division to find a missing factor.

Examples Find the missing factor.

A $4 \times \blacksquare = 36$

Think: $36 \div 4 = 9$

So, the missing factor is 9.
$4 \times 9 = 36$

B $5 \times \blacksquare = 40$

Think: $40 \div 5 = 8$

So, the missing factor is 8.
$5 \times 8 = 40$

▶ Practice

Find the missing factor.

1. $\blacksquare \times 3 = 18$ **2.** $4 \times \blacksquare = 20$ **3.** $3 \times \blacksquare = 24$

4. $\blacksquare \times 4 = 32$ **5.** $\blacksquare \times 5 = 15$ **6.** $4 \times \blacksquare = 16$

7. $4 \times \blacksquare = 40$ **8.** $\blacksquare \times 5 = 35$ **9.** $\blacksquare \times 3 = 27$

READ A TABLE

A table is used to organize information.

FAVORITE BREAKFAST	
Type	**Votes**
Cereal	12
Pancakes	6
Eggs	7
Fruit	3

← Title

The data show the number of students who voted for each type of breakfast food.

This table shows that:

- Cereal had the most votes.
- 7 students voted for eggs.
- 28 students voted in all.

▶ Practice

For 1–3, use the information in the table above.

1. Which breakfast food had the fewest votes?
2. How many students voted for pancakes?
3. How many students in all voted for cereal or eggs?

USE A TALLY TABLE

A **tally table** has tally marks to record data.
Tally marks are grouped by fives. (卌 = 5)

FAVORITE SPORT	
Sport	**Tally**
Baseball	卌 I
Basketball	卌 卌
Hockey	IIII
Soccer	卌 IIII

Baseball: ← 6 students chose baseball.

Soccer: ← 9 students chose soccer.

▶ Practice

For 1–2, use the tally table.

1. How many students chose basketball as their favorite sport?
2. How many students did NOT choose soccer as their favorite sport?

TROUBLESHOOTING

✓ USE SYMBOLS

A **pictograph** shows data by using symbols.

The **key** in this pictograph shows that each ◆ equals 2 votes.

FAVORITE JUICE	
Orange	◆◆
Apple	◆◆◆
Grape	◆◆◆◆
Cranberry	◆
Key: Each ◆ = 2 votes.	

▶ Practice

Use the value of the symbol to find the missing number.

1. If ✱ = 2, then
✱ + ✱ + ✱ = ■.

2. If ❋ = 4, then
❋ + ❋ = ■.

3. If ★ = 10, then
★ + ★ + ★ + ★ = ■.

4. If ✿ = 5, then
✿ + ✿ + ✿ = ■.

✓ IDENTIFY PARTS OF A WHOLE

A **fraction** names a part of a whole.

The top number tells how many parts are being used.

The bottom number tells how many equal parts are in the whole.

$\frac{3}{8}$ of the spinner is red.

▶ Practice

Write a fraction that names the red part of the spinner.

1. 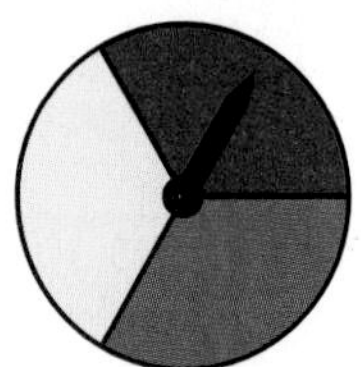

2. 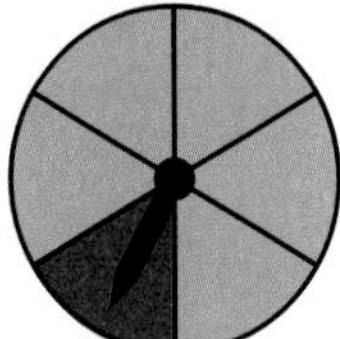

3. 

4. 

COMPARE PARTS OF A WHOLE

You compare fractions by comparing parts of a whole.

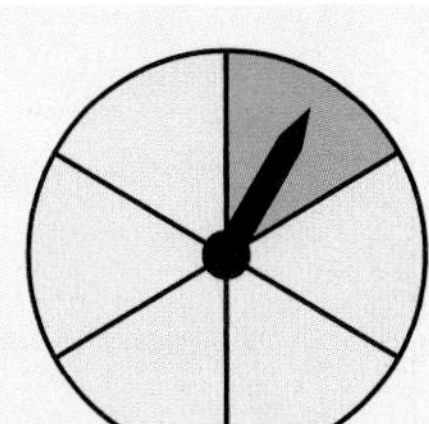

$\frac{1}{6}$ of the spinner is blue.

$\frac{5}{6}$ of the spinner is yellow.

The greater part of the spinner is yellow.

▶ Practice

Write the color shown by the greater part of each spinner.

1. 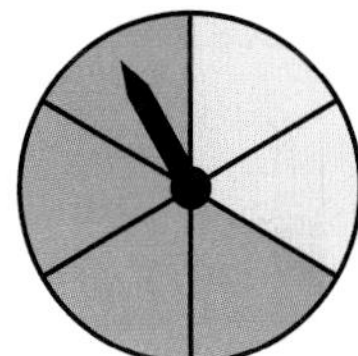

2. 

3. 

4. 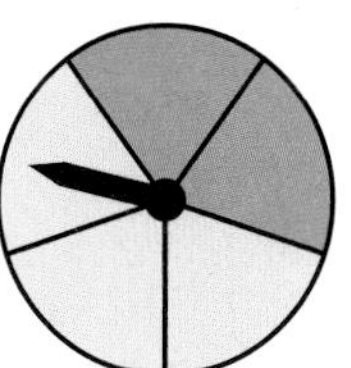

USE A RULE

Some tables of data are made by using a rule.

Example

Rule: Multiply the number of nickels by 5.

Nickels	2	3	4	5	6
Pennies	10	15	20	25	30

$3 \times 5 = 15$

▶ Practice

Copy and complete each table.

1.

Teams	3	4	5	6	7
Players	30	40	50	■	70

Rule: Multiply the number of teams by 10.

2.

Tables	1	2	3	4	5
Chairs	4	■	12	16	■

Rule: Multiply the number of tables by 4.

TROUBLESHOOTING

✓ READ A THERMOMETER

Only some lines on a thermometer are labeled. Use the scale like a number line that does not have all of the marks labeled.

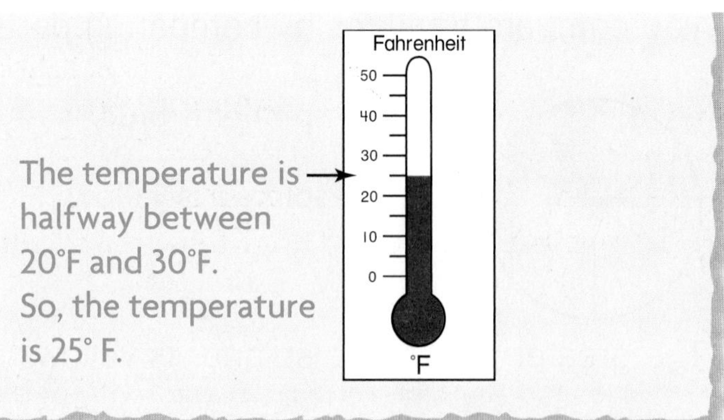

▶ Practice

Write the temperature.

1. 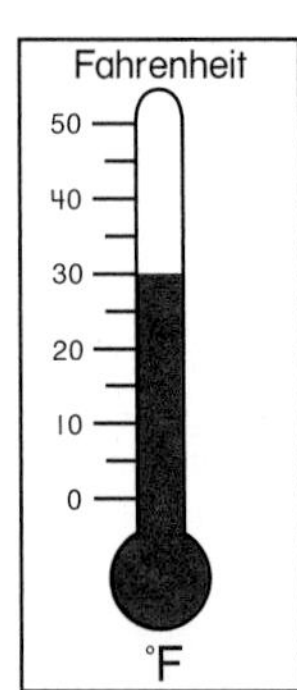

2. 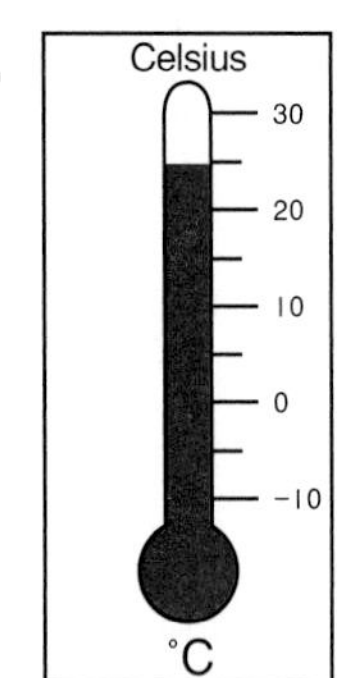

3. 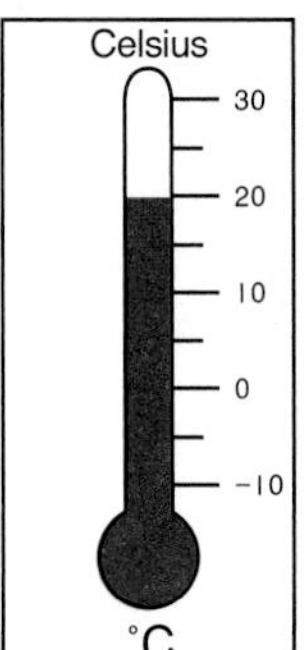

✓ MULTIPLICATION FACTS

There are many ways to remember multiplication facts.

Example

Find 4×9.

- Skip-count by equal groups.
- Use an array.
- Break apart an array.
- If one of the factors is even, use doubling.

So, $4 \times 9 = 36$.

▶ Practice

Find the product.

1. $6 \times 8 = \blacksquare$ **2.** $3 \times 9 = \blacksquare$ **3.** $5 \times 7 = \blacksquare$ **4.** $6 \times 7 = \blacksquare$

5. $3 \times 5 = \blacksquare$ **6.** $7 \times 7 = \blacksquare$ **7.** $5 \times 8 = \blacksquare$ **8.** $2 \times 9 = \blacksquare$

ADDITION

When adding, begin with the ones. Regroup when needed.

Find 64 + 159.

STEP 1

Add the ones.
$4 + 9 = 13$
Regroup.
13 ones = 1 ten 3 ones

$$\begin{array}{r} ^{1} \\ 64 \\ +\ 159 \\ \hline 3 \end{array}$$

STEP 2

Add the tens.
$1 + 6 + 5 = 12$
Regroup.
12 tens = 1 hundred 2 tens

$$\begin{array}{r} ^{1\,1} \\ 64 \\ +\ 159 \\ \hline 23 \end{array}$$

STEP 3

Add the hundreds.
$1 + 1 = 2$

$$\begin{array}{r} ^{1\,1} \\ 64 \\ +\ 159 \\ \hline 223 \end{array}$$

So, $64 + 159 = 223$.

▶ Practice

Find the sum.

1. $\begin{array}{r} 35 \\ +\ 225 \\ \hline \end{array}$ **2.** $\begin{array}{r} 104 \\ +\ 730 \\ \hline \end{array}$ **3.** $\begin{array}{r} 82 \\ +\ 457 \\ \hline \end{array}$ **4.** $\begin{array}{r} 126 \\ +\ 538 \\ \hline \end{array}$

SUBTRACTION

When subtracting, begin with the ones. Regroup when needed.

Find 43 − 17.

STEP 1

Since $7 > 3$, regroup.
4 tens 3 ones = 3 tens 13 ones
Subtract the ones.

$$\begin{array}{r} ^{3\ 13} \\ \not{4}\,\not{3} \\ -\ 17 \\ \hline 6 \end{array}$$

STEP 2

Subtract the tens.

$$\begin{array}{r} ^{3\ 13} \\ \not{4}\,\not{3} \\ -\ 17 \\ \hline 26 \end{array}$$

So, $43 - 17 = 26$.

▶ Practice

Find the difference.

1. $\begin{array}{r} 56 \\ -\ 19 \\ \hline \end{array}$ **2.** $\begin{array}{r} 12 \\ -\ \ 4 \\ \hline \end{array}$ **3.** $\begin{array}{r} 27 \\ -\ \ 5 \\ \hline \end{array}$ **4.** $\begin{array}{r} 49 \\ -\ 12 \\ \hline \end{array}$ **5.** $\begin{array}{r} 34 \\ -\ 19 \\ \hline \end{array}$

TROUBLESHOOTING

✓ MULTIPLICATION AND DIVISION FACTS

Fact families can help you remember multiplication and division facts.

Examples

A Find 21 ÷ 3.	**B** Find 4 × 6.
Think of a related multiplication fact.	Think of a related division fact.
3 × ■ = 21	■ ÷ 4 = 6
If you know 3 × 7 = 21, then you know 21 ÷ 3 = 7.	If you know 24 ÷ 4 = 6, then you know 4 × 6 = 24.

▶ **Practice**

Find the product or quotient.

1. 6 × 7 = ■

2. 9 × 3 = ■

3. 56 ÷ 7 = ■

4. $\begin{array}{r} 6 \\ \times\, 6 \\ \hline \end{array}$

5. 45 ÷ 5 = ■

6. $\begin{array}{r} 3 \\ \times\, 8 \\ \hline \end{array}$

7. 42 ÷ 6 = ■

8. 72 ÷ 9 = ■

9. 5 × 4 = ■

10. 81 ÷ 9 = ■

11. 10 × 3 = ■

12. 16 ÷ 8 = ■

13. $\begin{array}{r} 6 \\ \times\, 3 \\ \hline \end{array}$

14. 42 ÷ 7 = ■

15. $\begin{array}{r} 8 \\ \times\, 7 \\ \hline \end{array}$

16. 36 ÷ 9 = ■

17. 8 × 8 = ■

18. 32 ÷ 4 = ■

19. $\begin{array}{r} 7 \\ \times\, 4 \\ \hline \end{array}$

20. 35 ÷ 5 = ■

21. $\begin{array}{r} 3 \\ \times\, 5 \\ \hline \end{array}$

22. 40 ÷ 10 = ■

23. 9 × 10 = ■

24. 5 × 8 = ■

IDENTIFY SOLID FIGURES

These are solid figures.

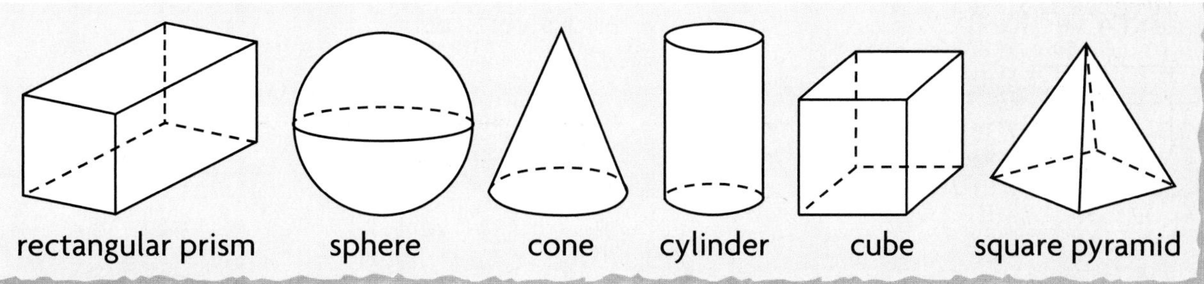

▶ Practice

Write the name of each solid figure.

1. 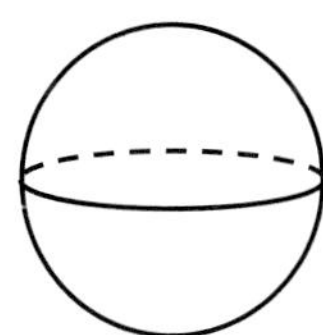

2. 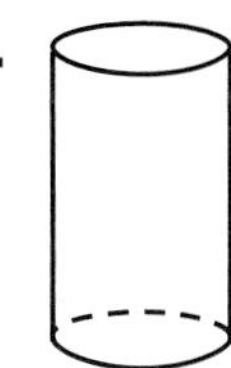

3. 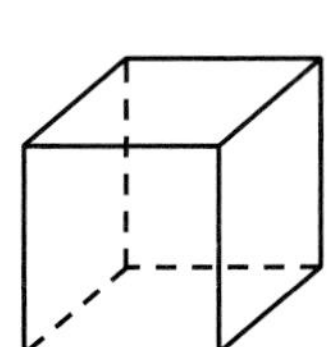

4. 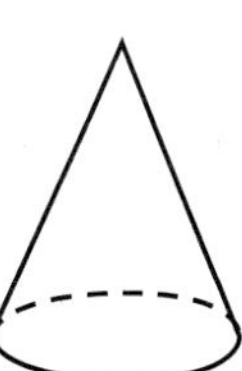

IDENTIFY PLANE FIGURES

These are plane figures.

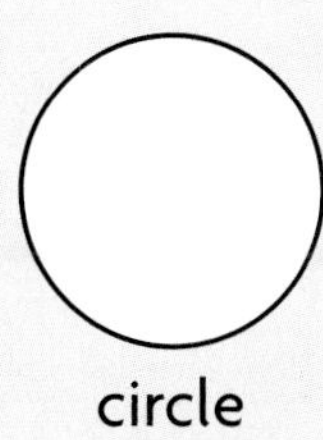
circle

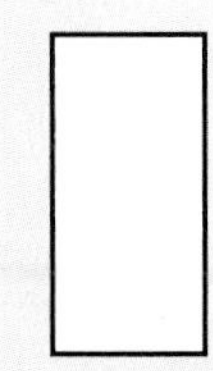
rectangle

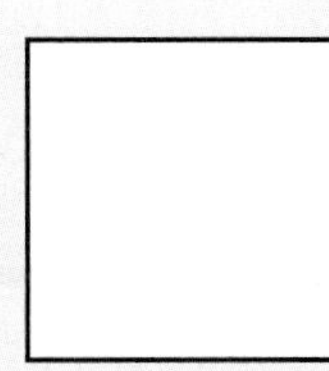
square

triangle

▶ Practice

Write the name of each plane figure.

1. 

2. 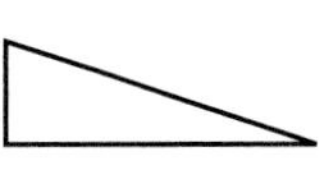

3. 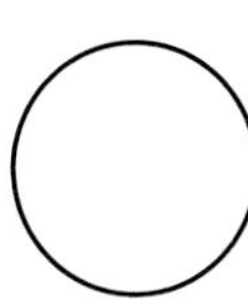

4. 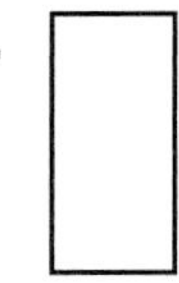

TROUBLESHOOTING

SIDES AND VERTICES

A rectangle has 4 sides and 4 vertices.

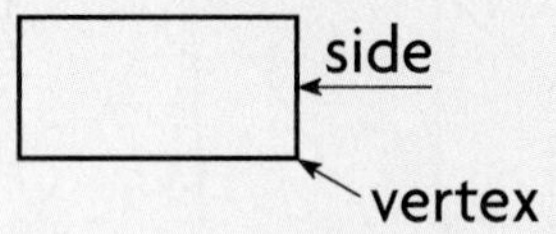

A triangle has 3 sides and 3 vertices.

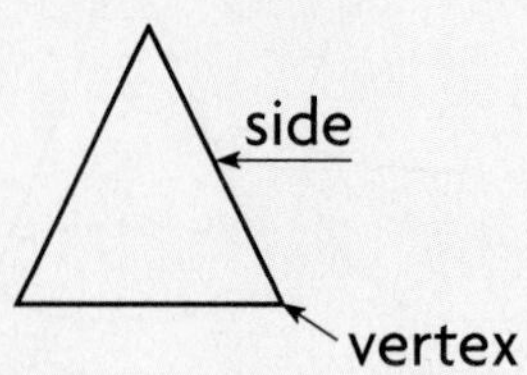

▶ Practice

Write the number of sides and vertices in each figure.

1. 

2. 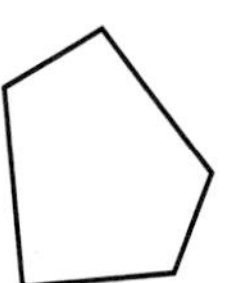

3. 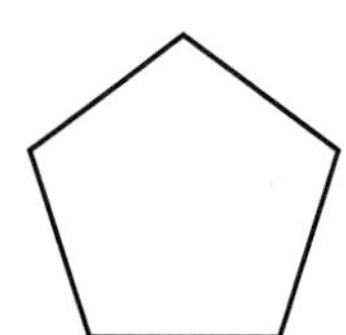

4. 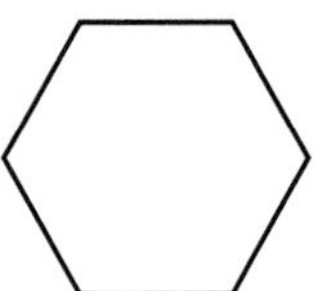

EQUIVALENT FRACTIONS

Fractions that name the same amount are **equivalent**.

Example

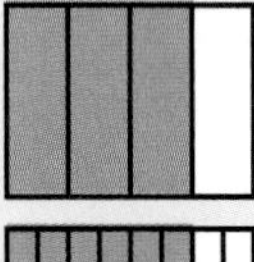

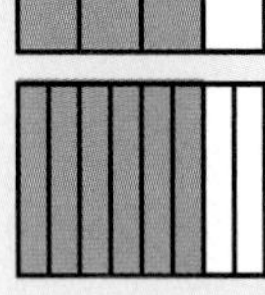

Compare the shaded areas of the rectangles.

The shaded areas of the rectangles are equal. So, the fractions that name the shaded areas are equivalent fractions.

$\frac{3}{4} = \frac{6}{8}$

▶ Practice

Find the missing numerator to show equivalent fractions.

1. 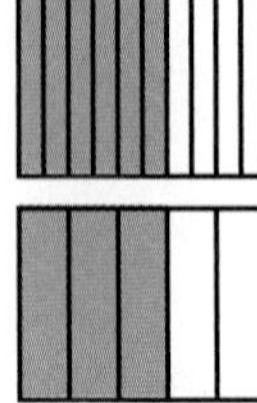

$\frac{6}{10} = \frac{■}{5}$

2. 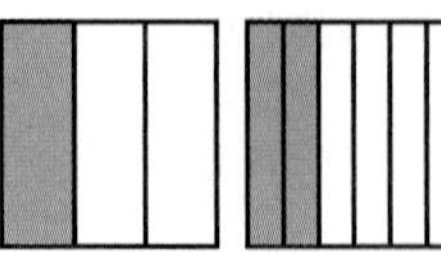

$\frac{1}{3} = \frac{■}{6}$

3. 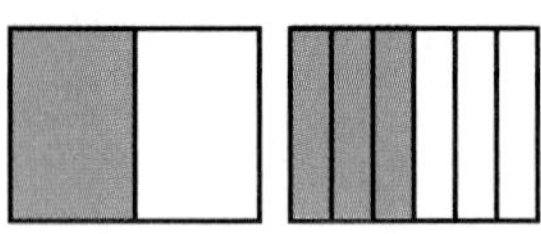

$\frac{1}{2} = \frac{■}{6}$

SAME SIZE, SAME SHAPE

Figures that are the same size and shape are **congruent**.

These figures have the same size and shape. They are **congruent**.

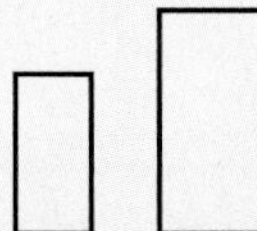

These figures have the same shape, but they are not the same size. They are **not congruent**.

▶ Practice

Tell whether the two figures are congruent. Write *yes* or *no*.

1. 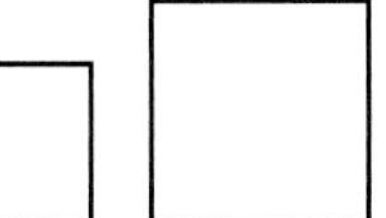

2. 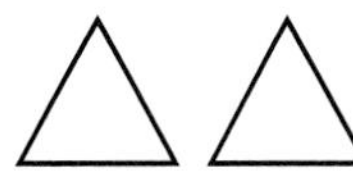

3. 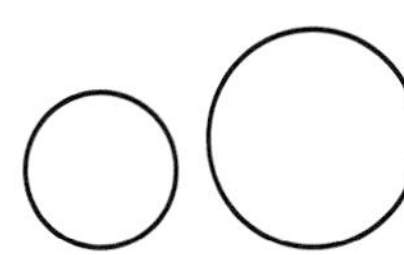

4. 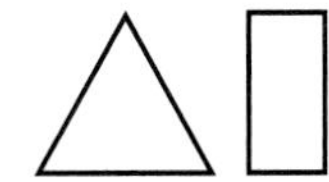

5. 

6.

MIXED NUMBERS

A **mixed number** is made up of a whole number and a fraction.

Example

Write a mixed number for the amount that is shaded.

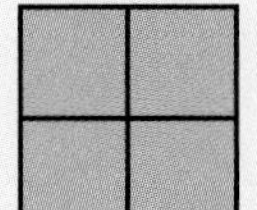

1 whole

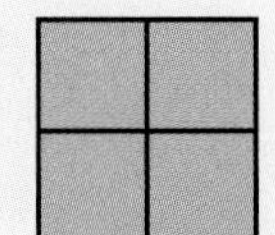

1 whole

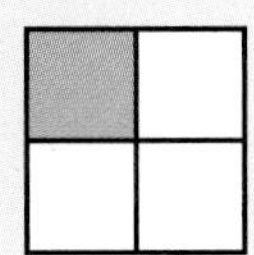

$\frac{1}{4}$

2 whole figures are shaded.

$\frac{1}{4}$ of a whole is shaded.

So, $2\frac{1}{4}$ names the amount that is shaded.

▶ Practice

Write a mixed number for the amount that is shaded.

1. 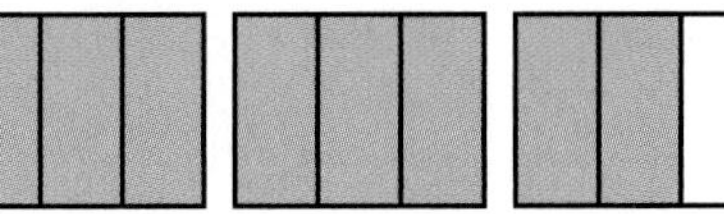

2. 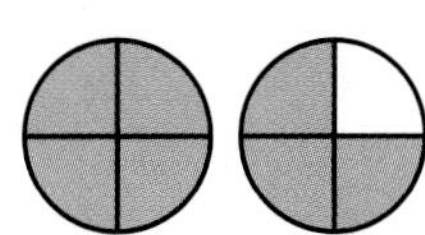

3. 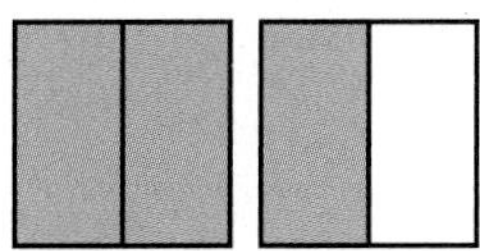

TROUBLESHOOTING

✓ MEASURE TO THE NEAREST INCH

An **inch (in.)** is used to measure length.

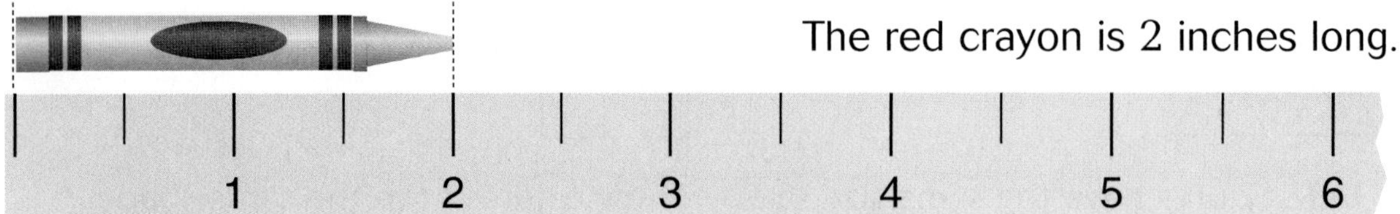

The red crayon is 2 inches long.

Example

Write the length to the nearest inch.

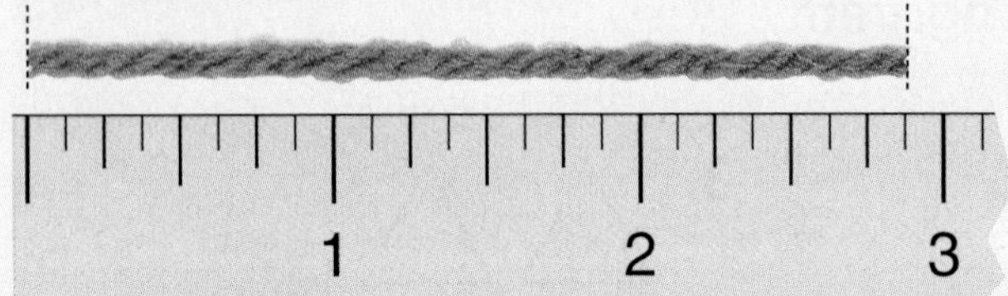

To measure to the nearest inch:

- Line up one end of the object with the zero mark of the ruler.
- Find the inch mark nearest the other end of the object.

The yarn is 3 inches long to the nearest inch.

▶ Practice

For 1–2, use the drawing below.

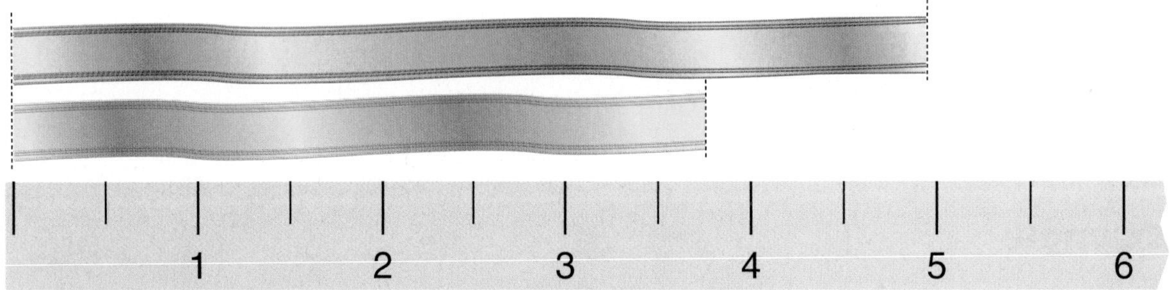

1. Which ribbon is about 5 inches long?

2. Which ribbon is between 3 and 4 inches long?

Write the length to the nearest inch.

3.

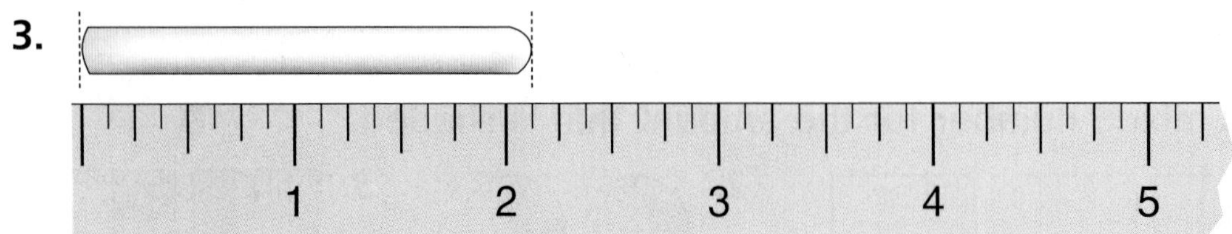

FIND A RULE

You can write a rule to describe a number pattern.

Example

Write a rule for the table. Then complete the table.

Tricycles	1	2	3	4	5	6
Wheels	3	6	9	12	■	■

Pattern: The number of wheels equals the number of tricycles times 3.

Rule: Multiply the number of tricycles by 3.

So, the missing numbers are 15 and 18.

▶ Practice

Write a rule for the table. Then complete the table.

1.

Packs	1	2	3	4	5	6
Cookies	6	12	18	24	■	■

2.

Chairs	3	6	2	5	1	4
Legs	12	24	8	20	■	■

USE A METRIC RULER

A **centimeter (cm)** is a metric unit used to measure length.

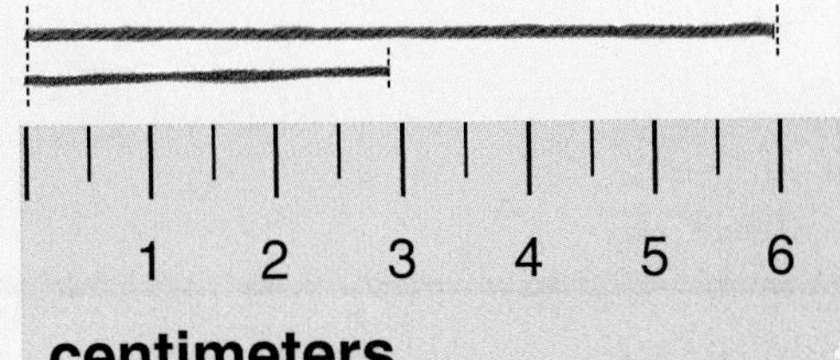

- The blue string is about 6 cm long.
- The red string is about 3 cm long.

▶ Practice

For 1–3, use the drawing below.

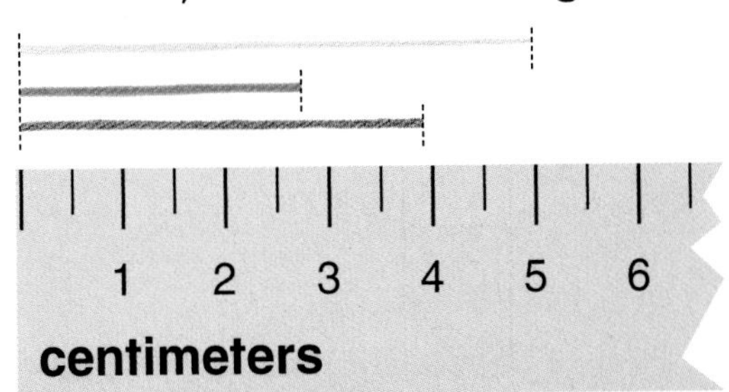

1. Which string is about 5 cm long?
2. Which string is about 1 cm longer than the pink string?
3. Which string is less than 3 cm long?

TROUBLESHOOTING

✓ MEASURE TO THE NEAREST CENTIMETER

To measure to the nearest centimeter:

- Line up one end of the object with the zero mark of the ruler.
- Find the cm mark nearest the other end of the object.

Example

Write the length to the nearest centimeter.

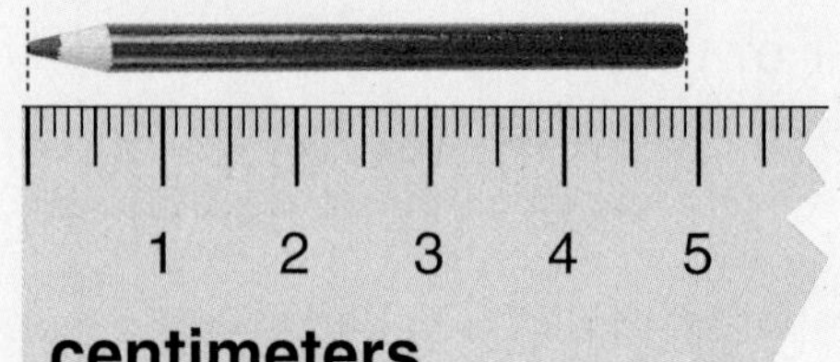

The pencil is 5 centimeters long to the nearest centimeter.

▶ Practice

Write the length to the nearest centimeter.

1.

1 2 3 4
centimeters

2.

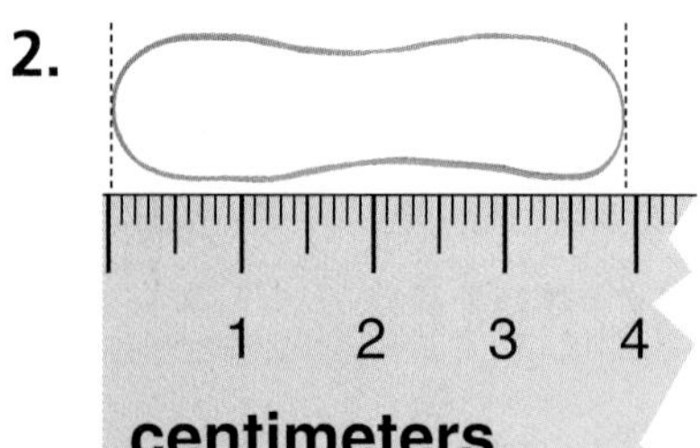

✓ MODEL PARTS OF A WHOLE

This figure has 5 equal parts.

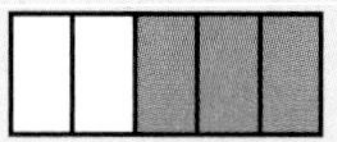

- 3 equal parts are shaded.
- 2 equal parts are *not* shaded.

▶ Practice

Write how many equal parts are in the whole figure. Then write how many parts are shaded.

1. 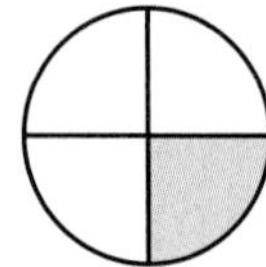

2. 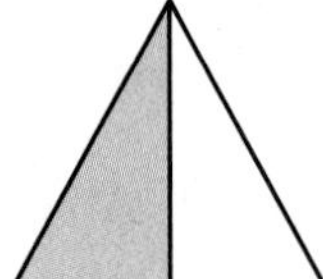

3. 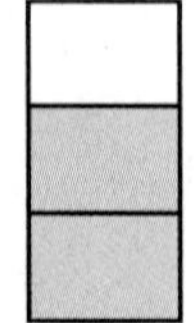

MODEL PARTS OF A GROUP

This group has 6 squares.

- 1 square is yellow.
- 5 squares are *not* yellow.

▶ Practice

Write the number in each group. Then write the number that are *not* yellow in each group.

1. 

2.

3.

NAME THE FRACTION

A number that names part of a whole or part of a group is called a **fraction**.

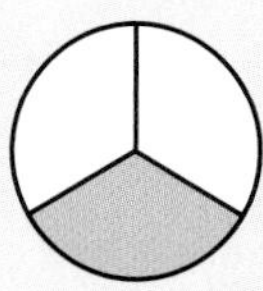

- 1 part is shaded.
- There are 3 parts in all.

So, $\frac{1}{3}$ of the circle is shaded.

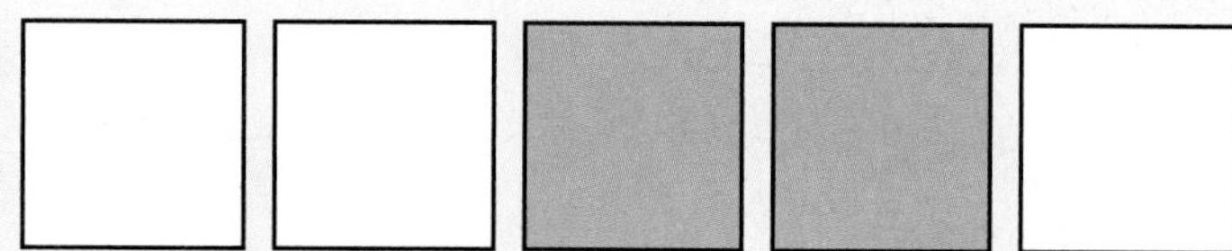

- 2 squares are blue.
- There are 5 squares in all.

So, $\frac{2}{5}$ of the squares are blue.

▶ Practice

Write the fraction for the part that is shaded.

1. 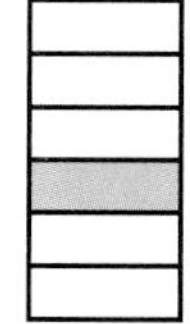

2. 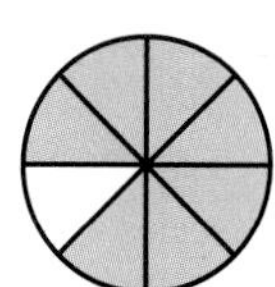

3. 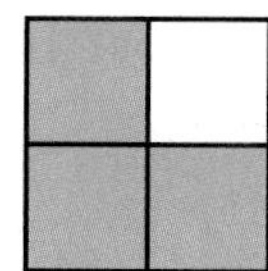

Write the fraction for the part that is blue.

4. 

5. 

6. 

TROUBLESHOOTING

✓ COMPARE FRACTIONS

As you compare fractions, remember the symbols you have used.

$<$ means *is less than*.
$1 < 3$

$>$ means *is greater than*.
$3 > 1$

Examples

A Compare $\frac{2}{4}$ and $\frac{3}{4}$.

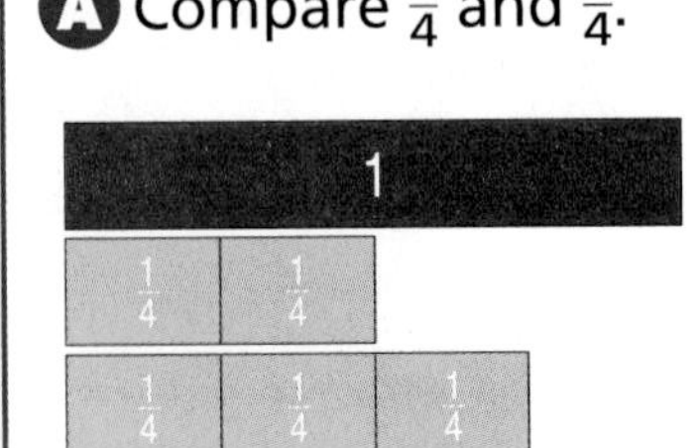

$\frac{2}{4} < \frac{3}{4}$ or $\frac{3}{4} > \frac{2}{4}$

B Compare $\frac{3}{5}$ and $\frac{4}{10}$.

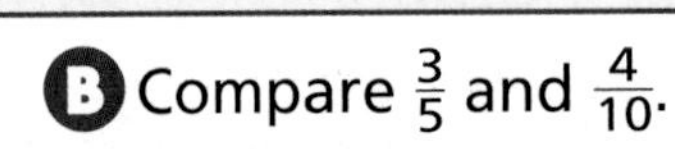

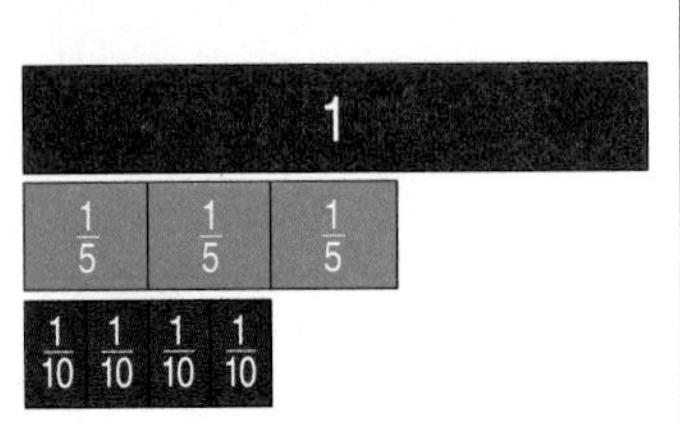

$\frac{3}{5} > \frac{4}{10}$ or $\frac{4}{10} < \frac{3}{5}$

▶ Practice

Compare. Write $<$ or $>$ for each ●.

1. 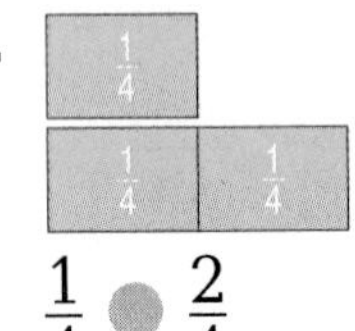

$\frac{1}{4}$ ● $\frac{2}{4}$

2. 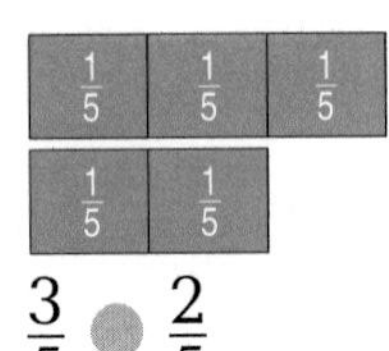

$\frac{3}{5}$ ● $\frac{2}{5}$

3. 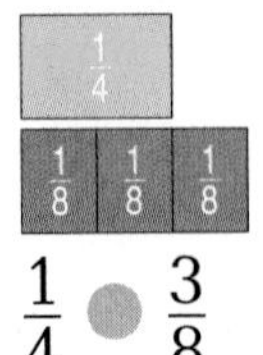

$\frac{1}{4}$ ● $\frac{3}{8}$

✓ USE MONEY NOTATION

Use a **dollar sign** and a **decimal point** to write money amounts.

Example

Count and write the amount.

$0.25

$0.35

$0.40

$0.45

$0.46

$0.46
↑ dollar sign ↑ decimal point

So, the value of the coins is $0.46.

▶ Practice

Count and write the amount.

1.    

2.     

✓ NAME THE DECIMAL

You can use decimals to show tenths and hundredths.

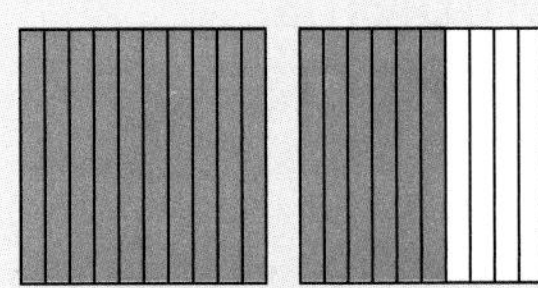

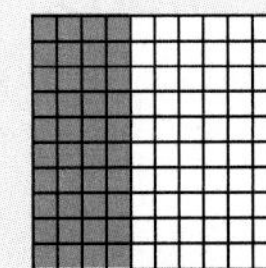

Mixed number: $1\frac{6}{10}$

Decimal: 1.6

Fraction: $\frac{40}{100}$

Decimal: 0.40

▶ Practice

Write each fraction or mixed number as a decimal.

1. $\frac{3}{10}$ **2.** $\frac{9}{10}$ **3.** $\frac{45}{100}$ **4.** $1\frac{5}{10}$

5. $\frac{2}{100}$ **6.** $\frac{50}{100}$ **7.** $1\frac{7}{10}$ **8.** $1\frac{75}{100}$

✓ COMPARE AND ORDER DECIMALS

Use a number line to compare and order decimals.

Example

Write 0.9, 0.5, and 0.8 in order from least to greatest.

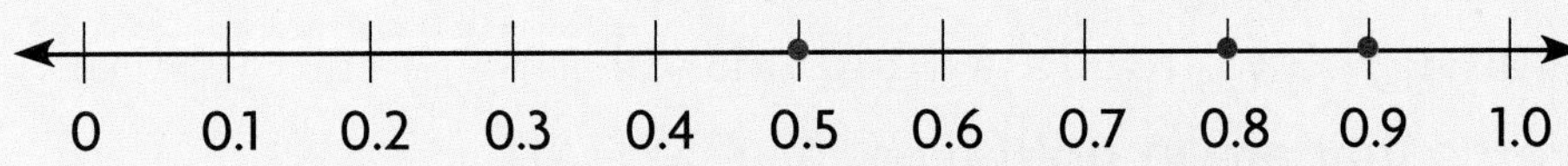

0.5 is to the left of 0.8 0.8 is to the left of 0.9

So, the numbers from least to greatest are 0.5, 0.8, 0.9.

▶ Practice

Use the number line above. Write $<$ or $>$ for each ●.

1. 0.6 ● 0.5 **2.** 0.3 ● 0.6 **3.** 0.7 ● 0.4 **4.** 0.9 ● 1.0

Use the number line to order the decimals from least to greatest.

5. 0.1, 0.7, 0.4 **6.** 1.0, 0.2, 0.1 **7.** 0.9, 0.8, 0.7 **8.** 0.8, 0.4, 1.0

Use the number line to order the decimals from greatest to least.

9. 0.4, 0.9, 0.2 **10.** 0.1, 0.8, 1.0 **11.** 0.7, 0.3, 0.5 **12.** 0.6, 0.2, 0.8

Tips for Taking Math Tests

Being a good test-taker is like being a good problem solver. When you answer test questions, you are solving problems. Remember to **UNDERSTAND, PLAN, SOLVE,** and **CHECK.**

UNDERSTAND

Read the problem.

- Look for math terms and recall their meanings.
- Reread the problem and think about the question.
- Use the details in the problem and the question.

1. The sum of the digits of a number is 14. Both the digits are odd. The ones digit is 4 less than the tens digit. What is the number?

A 59 **C** 86

B 77 **D** 95

TIP! **Understand the problem.** Remember the meanings of *sum, digits,* and *odd*. Reread the problem to compare the details to the answer choices. Since all choices have a sum of 14, look for the odd digits. Then look for a ones digit that is 4 less than the tens digit. The answer is **D**.

- Each word is important. Missing a word or reading it incorrectly could cause you to get the wrong answer.
- Pay attention to words that are in **bold** type, all CAPITAL letters, or *italics*.
- Some other words to look for are <u>round</u>, <u>about</u>, <u>only</u>, <u>best</u>, or <u>least to greatest</u>.

2. Mr. Karza drew a diagram of 8 squares. He made 3 squares red, 2 squares blue, 2 squares yellow, and 1 square green. What fraction of the squares was NOT green?

F $\frac{7}{8}$ **H** $\frac{1}{2}$

G $\frac{5}{8}$ **J** $\frac{1}{8}$

TIP! **Look for important words.** The word **NOT** is important. Without the word **NOT**, the answer would be $\frac{1}{8}$. Find the number of squares that were **NOT** green. The answer is **F**.

PLAN

Think about how you can solve the problem.

- See if you can solve the problem with the information given.
- Pictures, charts, tables, and graphs may have the information you need.
- You may need to think about information you already know.
- The answer choices may have information you need.

3. Soccer practice started at 12:00. The clock shows the time practice ended. How long did soccer practice last?

A 10 minutes **C** 35 minutes

B 20 minutes **D** 50 minutes

TIP! **Get the information you need.** Use the clock to find how long soccer practice lasted. You can find out how much time passed by counting by fives. The answer is **D**.

- You may need to write a number sentence and solve it.
- Some problems have two steps or more.
- In some problems you need to look at relationships instead of computing an answer.
- If the path to the solution isn't clear, choose a problem solving strategy and use it to solve the problem.

4. June always has 30 days. Mary takes swimming lessons every three days in June, starting on June 3. How many times will she have lessons?

F 5 **H** 12

G 10 **J** 30

TIP! **Decide on a plan.** Lessons every three days sounds like a pattern. Use the strategy *find a pattern*. Count by 3 beginning with June 3 until you reach 30. You need to count 10 numbers, so the answer is **G**.

SOLVE

Follow your plan, working logically and carefully.

- Estimate your answer. Look for unreasonable answer choices.
- Use reasoning to find the most likely choices.
- Solve all steps needed to answer the problem.
- If your answer does not match any answer choice, check your numbers and your computation.

5. The cafeteria served 76 lunches each day for a week. How many lunches were served in 5 days?

A 76 **C** 380
B 353 **D** 1,380

TIP!

Estimate the product (5 × 80). The only reasonable answers are B and C. Since 5 times the ones digit 6 is 30, the answer must end in zero. If you are still not certain, multiply and check your answer against B and C. The answer is C.

- If your answer still does not match, look for another form of the number, such as a decimal instead of a fraction.
- If answer choices are given as pictures, look at each one by itself while you cover the other three.
- Read answer choices that are statements and relate them to the problem one by one.
- If your strategy isn't working, try a different one.

6. Mr. Rodriguez is putting a wallpaper border around a room. The room is 9 feet wide and 12 feet long. How many feet of border does he need?

F 21 feet **H** 84 feet
G 42 feet **J** 108 feet

TIP! **Choose the answer.**

The border goes around all four walls, two that are 9 feet and two that are 12 feet. Add the lengths of the four walls (9 + 9 + 12 + 12). Find the answer choice that shows this sum. The answer is G.

CHECK

Take time to catch your mistakes.

- Be sure you answered the question asked.
- Check for important words you might have missed.
- Did you use all the information you needed?
- Check your computation by using a different method.
- Draw a picture when you are unsure of your answer.

7. Katy is buying 3 books. Their prices are $4.95, $3.25, and $7.49. What is the total cost of the books?

A $14.59 **C** $15.59

B $14.69 **D** $15.69

TIP! Check your work. To check column addition, write the numbers in a different order. Then you will be adding different basic facts. For example, add $7.49 + $3.25 + $4.95. The answer is **D**.

Don't Forget!

Before the test

- Listen to the teacher's directions and read the instructions.
- Write down the ending time if the test is timed.
- Know where and how to mark your answers.
- Know whether you should write on the test page or use scratch paper.
- Ask any questions you may have before the test begins.

During the test

- Work quickly but carefully. If you are unsure how to answer a question, leave it blank and return to it later.
- If you cannot finish on time, read the questions that are left. Answer the easiest ones first. Then answer the others.
- Fill in each answer space carefully. Erase completely if you change an answer. Erase any stray marks.
- Check that the answer number matches the question number, especially if you skip a question.

ADDITION FACTS TEST

	K	L	M	N	O	P	Q	R
A	3 + 2	0 + 6	2 + 4	5 + 9	6 + 1	2 + 5	3 + 10	4 + 4
B	8 + 9	0 + 7	3 + 5	9 + 6	6 + 7	2 + 8	3 + 3	7 + 10
C	4 + 6	9 + 0	7 + 8	4 + 10	3 + 7	7 + 7	4 + 2	7 + 5
D	5 + 7	3 + 9	8 + 1	9 + 5	10 + 5	9 + 8	2 + 6	8 + 7
E	7 + 4	0 + 8	3 + 6	6 + 10	5 + 3	2 + 7	8 + 2	9 + 9
F	2 + 3	1 + 7	6 + 8	5 + 2	7 + 3	4 + 8	10 + 10	6 + 6
G	8 + 3	7 + 2	7 + 0	8 + 5	9 + 1	4 + 7	8 + 4	10 + 8
H	7 + 9	5 + 6	8 + 10	6 + 5	8 + 6	9 + 4	0 + 9	7 + 1
I	4 + 3	5 + 5	6 + 4	10 + 2	7 + 6	8 + 0	6 + 9	9 + 2
J	5 + 8	1 + 9	5 + 4	8 + 8	6 + 2	6 + 3	9 + 7	9 + 10

SUBTRACTION FACTS TEST

	K	L	M	N	O	P	Q	R
A	9 − 1	10 − 4	7 − 2	6 − 4	20 − 10	7 − 0	8 − 3	13 − 9
B	9 − 9	13 − 4	7 − 1	11 − 5	9 − 7	6 − 3	15 − 10	6 − 2
C	10 − 2	8 − 8	16 − 8	6 − 5	18 − 10	8 − 7	13 − 3	15 − 6
D	11 − 7	9 − 5	12 − 8	8 − 1	15 − 8	18 − 9	14 − 10	9 − 4
E	9 − 2	7 − 7	10 − 3	8 − 5	16 − 9	11 − 9	14 − 8	12 − 6
F	7 − 3	12 − 10	17 − 9	6 − 0	9 − 6	11 − 8	10 − 9	12 − 2
G	15 − 7	8 − 4	13 − 6	7 − 5	11 − 2	12 − 3	14 − 6	11 − 4
H	7 − 6	13 − 5	12 − 9	10 − 5	13 − 8	11 − 3	16 − 10	14 − 7
I	5 − 0	10 − 8	11 − 6	9 − 3	14 − 5	5 − 4	7 − 7	14 − 9
J	15 − 9	9 − 8	13 − 7	8 − 2	7 − 4	13 − 10	10 − 6	16 − 7

MULTIPLICATION FACTS TEST

	K	L	M	N	O	P	Q	R
A	2 × 7	0 × 6	6 × 6	9 × 2	8 × 3	3 × 4	2 × 8	6 × 1
B	7 × 7	5 × 9	2 × 2	7 × 5	2 × 3	10 × 8	4 × 10	8 × 4
C	4 × 5	5 × 1	7 × 0	6 × 3	3 × 5	6 × 8	7 × 3	9 × 9
D	0 × 9	6 × 4	6 × 10	1 × 6	9 × 8	4 × 4	3 × 2	9 × 3
E	0 × 7	9 × 4	1 × 7	9 × 7	2 × 5	7 × 9	5 × 6	5 × 8
F	4 × 3	6 × 9	1 × 9	7 × 6	7 × 10	6 × 0	2 × 9	10 × 3
G	5 × 3	1 × 5	7 × 1	3 × 8	3 × 6	8 × 10	3 × 9	6 × 7
H	7 × 4	7 × 2	3 × 7	2 × 4	7 × 8	4 × 7	5 × 10	8 × 6
I	4 × 6	5 × 5	5 × 7	3 × 3	9 × 6	8 × 0	4 × 9	8 × 8
J	8 × 9	6 × 2	4 × 8	9 × 5	5 × 4	0 × 5	10 × 6	9 × 10

DIVISION FACTS TEST

	K	L	M	N	O	P	Q	R
A	$1\overline{)1}$	$3\overline{)9}$	$2\overline{)6}$	$2\overline{)4}$	$1\overline{)6}$	$3\overline{)12}$	$5\overline{)15}$	$7\overline{)21}$
B	$6\overline{)24}$	$8\overline{)56}$	$5\overline{)40}$	$6\overline{)18}$	$6\overline{)30}$	$7\overline{)42}$	$9\overline{)81}$	$5\overline{)45}$
C	$5\overline{)30}$	$2\overline{)16}$	$3\overline{)21}$	$7\overline{)35}$	$3\overline{)15}$	$9\overline{)9}$	$8\overline{)16}$	$9\overline{)63}$
D	$4\overline{)32}$	$9\overline{)90}$	$4\overline{)8}$	$8\overline{)48}$	$9\overline{)54}$	$3\overline{)18}$	$10\overline{)50}$	$6\overline{)48}$
E	$7\overline{)28}$	$3\overline{)0}$	$5\overline{)20}$	$4\overline{)24}$	$7\overline{)14}$	$3\overline{)6}$	$5\overline{)50}$	$10\overline{)60}$
F	$9\overline{)18}$	$4\overline{)36}$	$5\overline{)25}$	$7\overline{)63}$	$1\overline{)5}$	$8\overline{)32}$	$9\overline{)45}$	$6\overline{)54}$
G	$2\overline{)14}$	$8\overline{)24}$	$4\overline{)4}$	$5\overline{)40}$	$3\overline{)9}$	$4\overline{)12}$	$7\overline{)56}$	$8\overline{)72}$
H	$5\overline{)35}$	$1\overline{)4}$	$8\overline{)64}$	$5\overline{)10}$	$8\overline{)40}$	$2\overline{)12}$	$6\overline{)42}$	$10\overline{)70}$
I	$7\overline{)49}$	$9\overline{)27}$	$10\overline{)90}$	$3\overline{)27}$	$9\overline{)36}$	$4\overline{)20}$	$9\overline{)72}$	$8\overline{)80}$
J	$8\overline{)0}$	$4\overline{)28}$	$2\overline{)10}$	$7\overline{)70}$	$1\overline{)3}$	$10\overline{)80}$	$6\overline{)60}$	$10\overline{)100}$

MULTIPLICATION AND DIVISION FACTS TEST

	K	L	M	N	O	P	Q	R
A	$2\overline{)18}$	8×4	$5\overline{)15}$	10×6	8×1	$3\overline{)24}$	$6\overline{)12}$	5×8
B	8×2	$7\overline{)56}$	$9\overline{)81}$	4×10	7×9	$1\overline{)6}$	$8\overline{)80}$	4×9
C	$6\overline{)36}$	8×5	7×7	$10\overline{)90}$	$5\overline{)45}$	6×7	$8\overline{)16}$	9×9
D	10×2	$4\overline{)32}$	$9\overline{)54}$	7×8	9×3	$9\overline{)90}$	$6\overline{)54}$	9×4
E	8×10	7×6	$8\overline{)64}$	$2\overline{)20}$	9×0	10×10	$3\overline{)36}$	$10\overline{)100}$
F	$4\overline{)40}$	8×3	8×6	9×6	$7\overline{)49}$	$9\overline{)45}$	10×3	9×7
G	$8\overline{)48}$	$6\overline{)60}$	9×2	5×9	$7\overline{)42}$	$4\overline{)36}$	5×10	9×8
H	6×5	8×8	$9\overline{)72}$	$5\overline{)50}$	6×9	8×5	$9\overline{)36}$	$7\overline{)63}$
I	$8\overline{)56}$	$10\overline{)80}$	7×8	10×9	$5\overline{)50}$	9×5	10×8	$10\overline{)70}$
J	6×8	10×9	$4\overline{)40}$	$7\overline{)35}$	3×6	$8\overline{)56}$	9×8	7×5

TABLE OF MEASURES

METRIC	CUSTOMARY
Length	
1 decimeter (dm) = 10 centimeters	1 foot (ft) = 12 inches (in.)
1 meter (m) = 100 centimeters	1 yard (yd) = 3 feet, or 36 inches
1 meter (m) = 10 decimeters	1 mile (mi) = 1,760 yards, or 5,280 feet
1 kilometer (km) = 1,000 meters	
Mass/Weight	
1 kilogram (kg) = 1,000 grams (g)	1 pound (lb) = 16 ounces (oz)
Capacity	
1 liter (L) = 1,000 milliliters (mL)	1 pint (pt) = 2 cups (c)
	1 quart (qt) = 2 pints
	1 gallon (gal) = 4 quarts

TIME

1 minute (min) = 60 seconds (sec)
1 hour (hr) = 60 minutes
1 day = 24 hours
1 week (wk) = 7 days
1 year (yr) = 12 months (mo), or about 52 weeks
1 year = 365 days
1 leap year = 366 days

MONEY

1 penny = 1 cent (¢)
1 nickel = 5 cents
1 dime = 10 cents
1 quarter = 25 cents
1 half dollar = 50 cents
1 dollar ($) = 100 cents

SYMBOLS

< is less than
> is greater than
= is equal to
≠ is not equal to
°F degrees Fahrenheit
°C degrees Celsius
(2,3) ordered pair

GLOSSARY

Pronunciation Key

a	add, map	f	fit, half	n	nice, tin	p	pit, stop	yōō	fuse, few
ā	ace, rate	g	go, log	ng	ring, song	r	run, poor	v	vain, eve
â(r)	care, air	h	hope, hate	o	odd, hot	s	see, pass	w	win, away
ä	palm, father	i	it, give	ō	open, so	sh	sure, rush	y	yet, yearn
b	bat, rub	ī	ice, write	ô	order, jaw	t	talk, sit	z	zest, muse
ch	check, catch	j	joy, ledge	oi	oil, boy	th	thin, both	zh	vision, pleasure
d	dog, rod	k	cool, take	ou	pout, now	t̶h̶	this, bathe		
e	end, pet	l	look, rule	ŏŏ	took, full	u	up, done		
ē	equal, tree	m	move, seem	ōō	pool, food	û(r)	burn, term		

ə the schwa, an unstressed vowel representing the sound spelled *a* in above, *e* in sicken, *i* in possible, *o* in melon, *u* in circus

Other symbols:
- • separates words into syllables
- ′ indicates stress on a syllable

A

acute angle [ə•kyōōt′ ang′gəl] An angle that has a measure less than a right angle (p. 385)
Example:

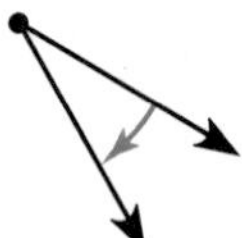

Word History

When the letter "g" is replaced with the letter "k" in the word *angle*, the word becomes *ankle*. Both words come from the same Latin root, *angulus*, which means "a sharp bend."

acute triangle [ə•kyōōt′ trī′ang•gəl] A triangle that has three acute angles (p. 393)

addend [a′dend] Any of the numbers that are added (p. 4)
Example: 2 + 3 = 5
↑ ↑
addend addend

addition [ə•dish′ən] The process of finding the total number of items when two or more groups of items are joined; the opposite operation of subtraction (p. 2)

A.M. [ā em] The hours between midnight and noon (p. 132)

angle [ang′gəl] A figure formed by two rays or line segments that share an endpoint (p. 384)
Example:

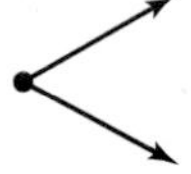

area [âr′ē•ə] The number of square units needed to cover a flat surface (p. 448)
Example:

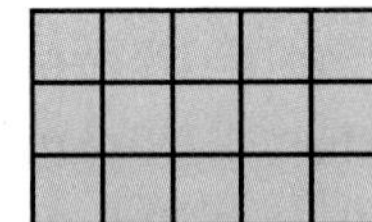

area = 15 square units

array [ə•rā′] An arrangement of objects in rows and columns (p. 162)
Example:

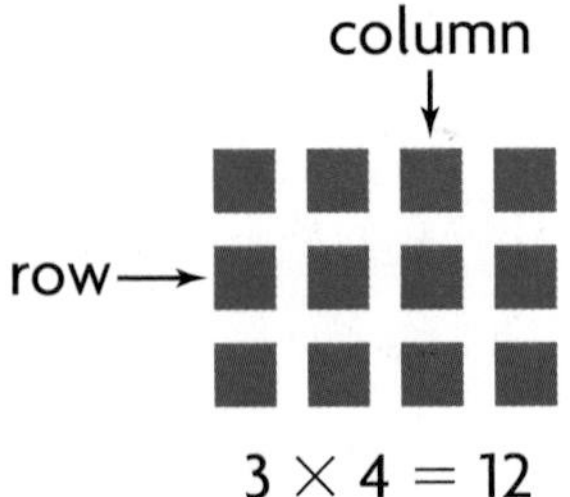

Associative Property of Addition
See Grouping Property of Addition.

Associative Property of Multiplication [a•sō′shē•ā•tiv prä′pər•tē əv mul•tə•plə•kā′shən] The property that states that when the grouping of factors is changed, the product remains the same (p. 218)
Example:
$(3 \times 2) \times 4 = 24$
$3 \times (2 \times 4) = 24$

bar graph [bär graf] A graph that uses bars to show data (p. 324)
Example:

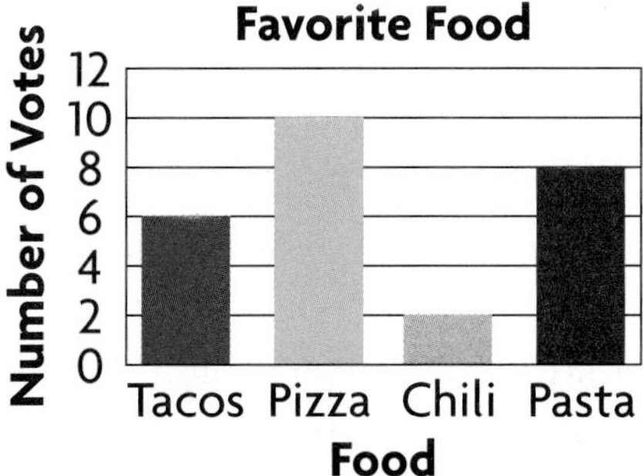

benchmark numbers [bench′märk num′bərz] Numbers that help you estimate the number of objects without counting them, such as 25, 50, 100, 1,000 (p. 40)

calendar [ka′lən•dər] A chart that shows the days, weeks, and months of a year (p. 138)

capacity [kə•pa′sə•tē] The amount a container can hold (p. 344)

center [sen′tər] A point in the middle of a circle that is the same distance from anywhere on the circle (p. 435)
Example:

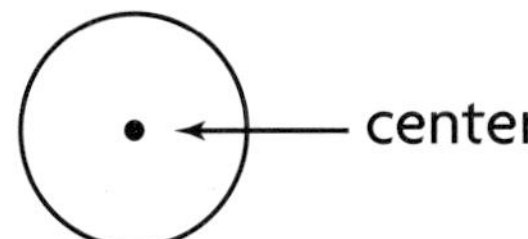

centimeter (cm) [sen′tə•mē•tər] A me that is used to measure length or distance (p. 358)
Example:

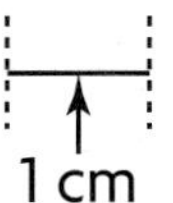

certain [sûr′tən] An event is certain if it wi always happen. (p. 488)

circle [sər′kəl] A closed figure made up of points that are the same distance from the center (p. 435)

circle graph [sər′kəl graf] A graph in the shape of a circle that shows data as a whole made up of different parts (p. 313)
Example:

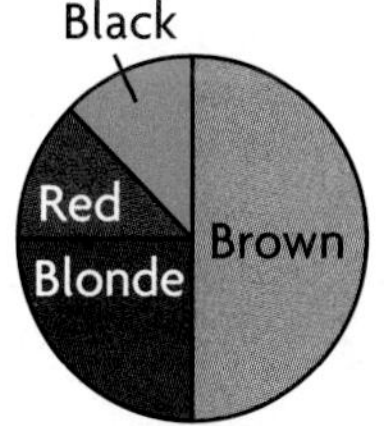

classify [kla′sə•fī] To group pieces of data according to how they are the same; for example, you can classify data by size, color, or shape. (p. 306)

clockwise [klok′wīz′] In the same direction in which the hands of a clock move (p. 131)

closed figure [klōzd fi′•gyər] A shape that begins and ends at the same point (p. 390)
Examples:

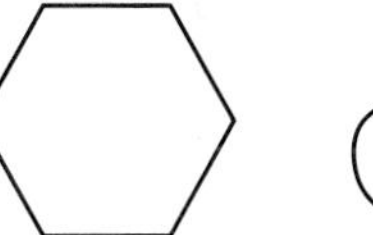

Commutative Property of Addition
See Order Property of Addition.

Commutative Property of Multiplication [kə•myo͞o•tə•tiv prä′pər•tē əv mul•tə•plə•kā′shən] The property that states that you can multiply two factors in any order and get the same product (p. 163)
Examples: $2 \times 4 = 8$
$4 \times 2 = 8$

compare [kəm•pâr′] To describe whether numbers are equal to, less than, or greater than each other (p. 42)

n] A solid, pointed figure that has round base (p. 424)
ple:

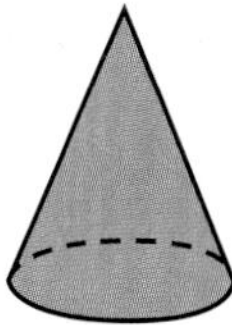

ngruent [kən•grōō′ənt] Figures that have the same size and shape (p. 408)
Example:

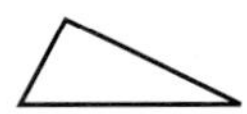 

counterclockwise [koun′tər•klok′wīz′] In the opposite direction in which the hands of a clock move (p. 131)

counting back [koun′ting bak] A way to find the difference when you subtract 1, 2, or 3
Example: 8 − 3 = ■ Count: 8 . . . 7, 6, 5

counting on [koun′ting on] A way to find the sum when one of the addends is 1, 2, or 3
Example: 5 + 2 = ■ Count: 5 . . . 6, 7

counting up [koun′ting up] A way to find the difference by beginning with the smaller number
Example: 7 − 4 = ■

Count: 4 . . . 5, 6, 7 ← 3 is the difference.

cube [kyōōb] A solid figure with six congruent square faces (p. 424)
Example:

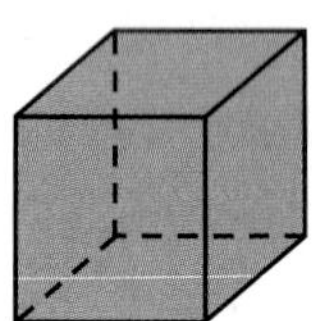

cubic unit [kyōō′bik yōō′nət] A cube with a side length of one unit; used to measure volume (p. 452)

cup (c) [kup] A customary unit used to measure capacity (p. 344)

cylinder [sil′in•dər] A solid or hollow object that is shaped like a can (p. 424)
Example:

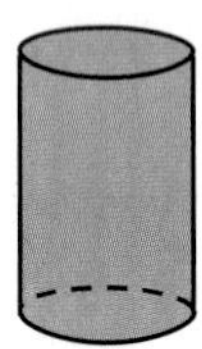

D

data [dā′tə] Information collected about people or things (p. 302)

decimal [de′sə•məl] A number with one or more digits to the right of the decimal point (p. 558)

decimal point [de′sə•məl point] A symbol used to separate dollars from cents in money and to separate the ones place from the tenths place in decimals (p. 110)
Example: 4.5
↑decimal point

decimeter (dm) [de′sə•mē•tər] A metric unit that is used to measure length or distance; 1 decimeter = 10 centimeters (p. 358)

degree (°) [di•grē′] The unit used to measure angles and temperature (p. 385)

degree Celsius (°C) [di•grē′ sel′sē•əs] A metric unit for measuring temperature (p. 368)

degree Fahrenheit (°F) [di•grē′ far′ən•hīt] A customary unit for measuring temperature (p. 368)

denominator [di•nä′mə•nā•tər] The part of a fraction below the line, which tells how many equal parts there are in the whole or in the group (p. 516)
Example: $\frac{3}{4}$ ←denominator

difference [dif′rən(t)s] The answer in a subtraction problem (p. 10)
Example: 6 − 4 = 2
↑difference

digits [di′jəts] The symbols 0, 1, 2, 3, 4, 5, 6, 7, 8, and 9 (p. 22)

Word History

The word *distributive* comes from the Latin word *distribuere* which means "to divide up." When you use the Distributive Property, you *divide up* one factor and multiply each part by the other factor.

Distributive Property [di•strib′yə•tiv prä′pər•tē] The property that states that multiplying a sum by a number is the same as multiplying each addend by the number and then adding the products (p. 220)
Examples:
$3 \times (4 + 2) = (3 \times 4) + (3 \times 2)$
$3 \times 6 = 12 + 6$
$18 = 18$

divide [di•vīd′] To separate into equal groups; the opposite operation of multiplication (p. 238)

dividend [di′və•dend] The number that is to be divided in a division problem (p. 242)
Example: 35 ÷ 5 = 7
↑dividend

divisor [di•vī′zər] The number that divides the dividend (p. 242)
Example: 35 ÷ 5 = 7
↑divisor

edge [ej] A line segment formed where two faces meet (p. 424)
Example:

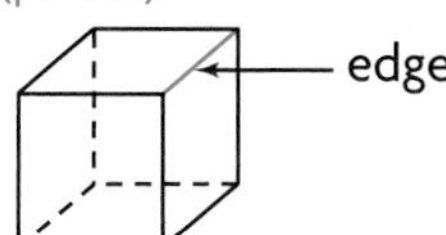

elapsed time [i•lapst′ tīm] The amount of time that passes from the start of an activity to the end of that activity (p. 134)

equal sign (=) [ē′kwəl sīn] A symbol used to show that two numbers have the same value (p. 42)
Example: 384 = 384

equal to (=) [ē′kwəl to͞o] Having the same value (p. 42)
Example: 4 + 4 is equal to 3 + 5

equally likely [ē′kwəl•lē lī′klē] Having the same chance of happening (p. 490)

equation [i•kwā′zhən] A number sentence that uses the equal sign to show that two amounts are equal (p. 242)
Examples:
$3 + 7 = 10$
$4 - 1 = 3$
$12 + n = 21$

equilateral triangle [ē•kwə•lat′ər•... A triangle that has three equa...
Examples:

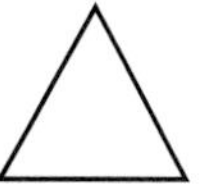

equivalent [ē•kwiv′ə•lənt] Two or mor... that name the same amount (p. 111)

equivalent fractions [ē•kwiv′ə•lənt frak′shən... Two or more fractions that name the sam... amount (p. 522)
Example:

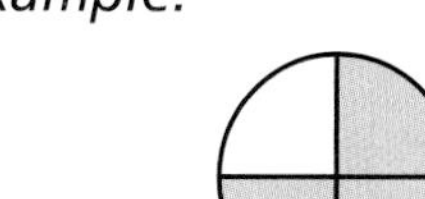
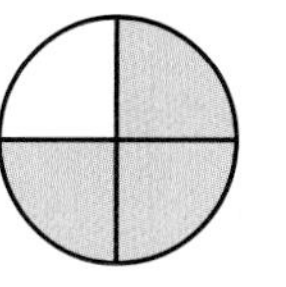
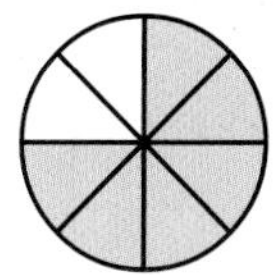

$\frac{3}{4} = \frac{6}{8}$

estimate [es′tə•māt] *verb*: To find about how many or how much (p. 68)

estimate [es′tə•mit] *noun*: A number close to an exact amount (p. 68)

even [ē′vən] A whole number that has a 0, 2, 4, 6, or 8 in the ones place (p. 20)

event [i•vent′] Something that happens (p. 488)

expanded form [ik•spand′id fôrm] A way to write numbers by showing the value of each digit (p. 22)
Example: 7,201 = 7,000 + 200 + 1

experiment [ik•sper′ə•mənt] A test that is done in order to find out something (p. 492)

expression [ik•spre′shən] The part of a number sentence that combines numbers and operation signs, but doesn't have an equal sign (p. 80)
Example: 5×6

face [fās] A flat surface of a solid figure (p. 424)
Example:

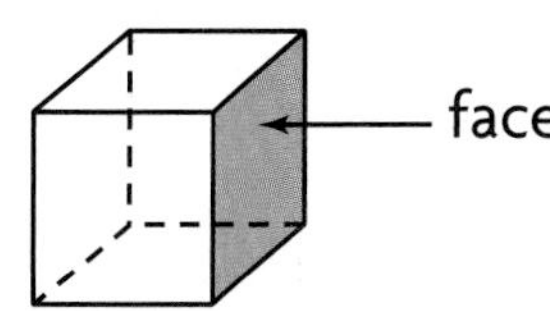

ly [fakt fam′ə•lē] A set of related on and subtraction, or multiplication division, number sentences (pp. 2, 246)
nple:

4 × 7 = 28   28 ÷ 7 = 4
7 × 4 = 28   28 ÷ 4 = 7

or [fak′tər] A number that is multiplied by nother number to find a product (p. 160)
xample: 3 × 8 = 24

↑ ↑
factor factor

lip [flip] A movement of a figure to a new position by flipping the figure over a line (p. 414)
Example:

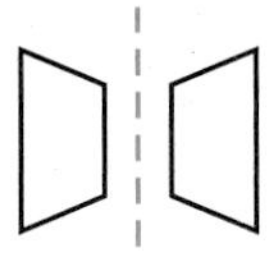

foot (ft) [fo͝ot] A customary unit used to measure length or distance;
1 foot = 12 inches (p. 342)

fraction [frak′shən] A number that names part of a whole or part of a group (p. 516)
Example:

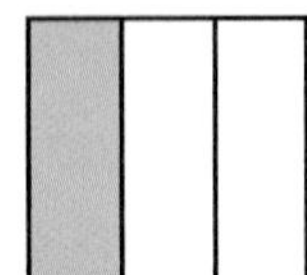

$\frac{1}{3}$

Word History

A *fraction* is a part of a whole, or a whole that is broken into pieces. *Fraction* comes from the Latin word *frangere,* which means "to break".

frequency table [frē′kwen•sē tā′bəl] A table that uses numbers to record data (p. 302)
Example:

FAVORITE COLOR	
Color	**Number**
blue	10
red	7
green	8
yellow	4

front-end estimation [frunt-end es•tə•mā′shən] A method of estimating a sum or difference by using the front digit of the number and adding zeros for the other digits (p. 68)
Example:

4,496 → 4,000
+3,745 → +3,000
7,000

G

gallon (gal) [ga′lən] A customary unit for measuring capacity; 1 gallon = 4 quarts (p. 344)

gram (g) [gram] A metric unit that is used to measure mass (p. 366)

greater than (>) [grā′tər t͟han] A symbol used to compare two numbers, with the greater number given first (p. 42)
Example: 6 > 4

grid [grid] Horizontal and vertical lines on a map (p. 328)

Grouping Property of Addition [gro͞o′ping prä′pər•tē əv ə•dish′ən] A rule stating that you can group addends in different ways and still get the same sum (p. 6)
Example:

4 + (2 + 5) = 11 and
(4 + 2) + 5 = 11

Grouping Property of Multiplication [gro͞o′ping prä′pər•tē əv mul•tə•plə•kā′shən] The property that states that when the grouping of factors is changed, the product remains the same (p. 218)
Example:

3 × (4 × 1) = 12 and
(3 × 4) × 1 = 12

H

half hour [haf our] 30 minutes (p. 129)
Example: Between 4:00 and 4:30 is one half hour.

hexagon [hek′sə•gän] A polygon with six sides (p. 390)
Examples:

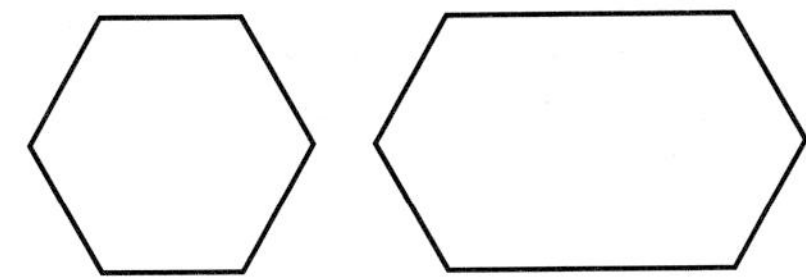

horizontal bar graph [hôr•ə•zän′təl bär graf] A bar graph in which the bars go from left to right (p. 324)

hour (hr) [our] A unit used to measure time; in one hour, the hour hand on a clock moves from one number to the next;
1 hour = 60 minutes (p. 129)

hour hand [our hand] The short hand on an analog clock (p. 128)

hundredth [hun′drədth] One of one hundred equal parts (p. 562)
Example:

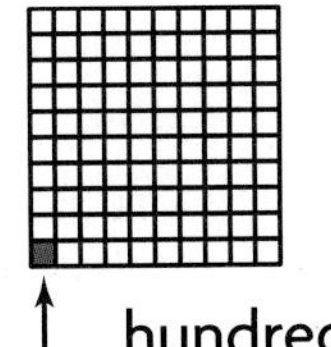

Identity Property of Addition [ī•den′tə•tē prä′pər•tē əv ə•dish′ən] The property that states that when you add zero to a number, the result is that number (p. 6)
Example: 24 + 0 = 24

Identity Property of Multiplication [ī•den′tə•tē prä′pər•tē əv mul•tə•plə•kā′shən] The property that states that the product of any number and 1 is that number (p. 220)
Example: $5 \times 1 = 5$
$1 \times 8 = 8$

impossible [im•pä′sə•bəl] An event that will never happen (p. 488)

inch (in.) [inch] A customary unit used for measuring length or distance (p. 338)
Example:

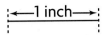

intersecting lines [in•tər•sek′ting līnz] Lines that cross (p. 388)
Example:

inverse operations [in′vərs ä•pə•rā′shənz] Opposite operations, or operations that undo each other, such as addition and subtraction or multiplication and division (pp. 2, 242)

isosceles triangle [ī•sos′ə•lēz trī′ang•gəl] A triangle that has two equal sides (p. 393)
Example:

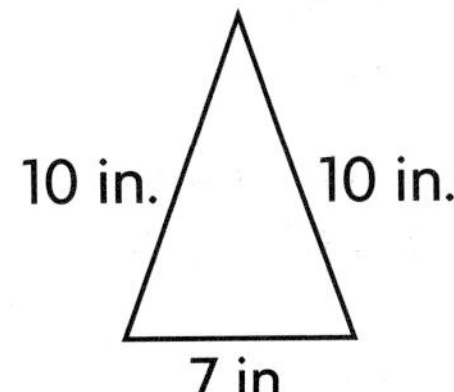

kilogram (kg) [kil′ə•gram] A metric unit for measuring mass;
1 kilogram = 1,000 grams (p. 366)

kilometer (km) [kə•lä′mə•tər] A metric unit for measuring length or distance;
1 kilometer = 1,000 meters (p. 358)

less than (<) [les t͟han] A symbol used to compare two numbers, with the lesser number given first (p. 42)
Example: $3 < 7$

like fractions [līk frak′shənz] Fractions that have the same denominator (p. 540)
Example: $\frac{3}{8}$ and $\frac{7}{8}$

likely [līk′lē] An event is likely if it has a good chance of happening (p. 488)

line [līn] A straight path extending in both directions with no endpoints (p. 384)
Example:

Word History

The word *line* comes from *linen,* a thread spun from the fibers of the flax plant. In early times thread was held tight to mark a straight line between two points.

line graph [līn graf] A graph that uses a line to show how data change over time (p. 330)
Example:

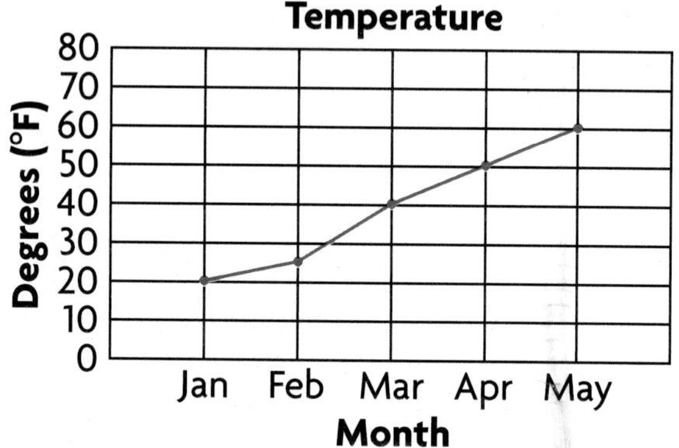

line of symmetry [līn əv sim′ə•trē] An imaginary line on a figure that when the figure is folded on this line, the two parts match exactly (p. 410)
Example:

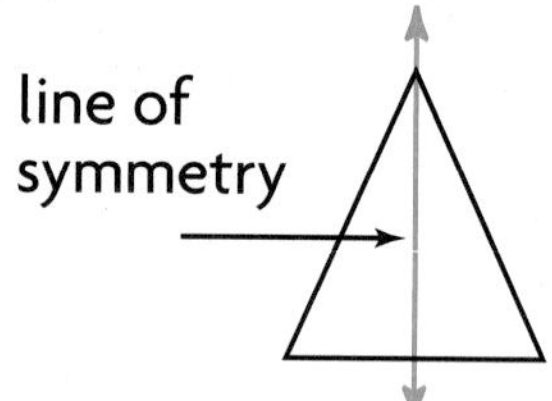

line plot [līn plöt] A graph that records each piece of data on a number line (p. 310)
Example:

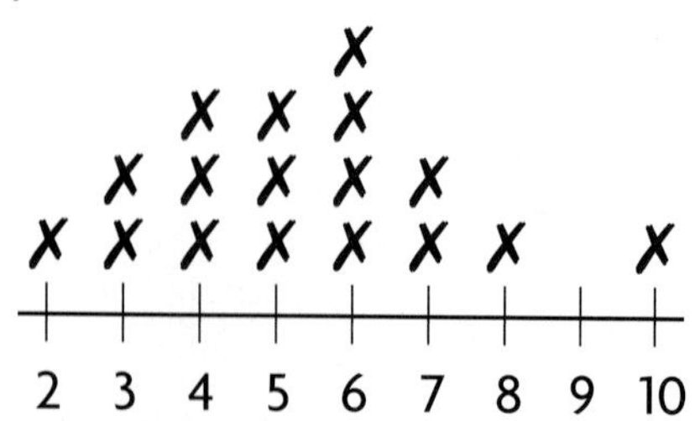

line segment [līn seg′mənt] A part of a line that includes two points, called endpoints, and all of the points between them (p. 384)
Example:

liter (L) [lē′tər] A metric unit for measuring capacity; 1 liter = 1,000 milliliters (p. 364)

M

mass [mas] The amount of matter in an object (p. 366)

mean [mēn] The number found by dividing the sum of a set of numbers by the number of addends (p. 314)
Example:
Find the mean for: 2, 3, 5, 5, 6, and 9
$2 + 3 + 5 + 5 + 6 + 9 = 30$
$30 \div 6 = 5$
The mean is 5.

median [mē′dē•ən] The middle number in an ordered list of numbers (p. 314)

1, 3, 4, 6, 7
↑ median

meter (m) [mē′tər] A metric unit for measuring length or distance; 1 meter = 100 centimeters (p. 358)

midnight [mid′nīt] 12:00 at night (p. 132)

mile (mi) [mīl] A customary unit for measuring length or distance; 1 mile = 5,280 feet (p. 342)

milliliter (mL) [mi′lə•lē•tər] A metric unit for measuring capacity (p. 364)

minute (min) [min′it] A unit used to measure short amounts of time; in one minute, the minute hand moves from one mark to the next (p. 128)

minute hand [mi′nət hand] The long hand on an analog clock (p. 128)

mixed number [mikst num′bər] A number represented by a whole number and a fraction (p. 532)
Example: $4\frac{1}{2}$

mode [mōd] The number or item found most often in a set of data (p. 310)

multiple [mul′tə•pəl] A number that is the product of a given number and a whole number (p. 178)
Example:

$$\begin{array}{cccc} 10 & 10 & 10 & 10 \\ \times 1 & \times 2 & \times 3 & \times 4 \\ \hline 10 & 20 & 30 & 40 \end{array} \leftarrow \text{multiples of } 10$$

multiply [mul′tə•plī] When you combine equal groups, you can multiply to find how many in all; the opposite operation of division. (p. 158)

multistep problem [mul′tē•step prä′bləm] A problem with more than one step (p. 222)

noon [no͞on] 12:00 in the day (p. 132)

not equal to (≠) [not ē′kwəl to͞o] A number or set of numbers that is not equal to another number or set of numbers (p. 80)
Examples:

$$4 \neq 5$$
$$3 + 3 \neq 3 + 8$$
$$217 \neq 271$$

number sentence [num′bər sen′təns] A sentence that includes numbers, operation symbols, and a greater than or less than symbol or an equal sign (p. 80)
Example:
$5 + 3 = 8$ is a number sentence.

numerator [no͞o′mə•rā•tər] The part of a fraction above the line, which tells how many parts are being counted (p. 516)
Example: $\frac{3}{4}$ ←numerator

obtuse angle [əb•t(y)o͞os′ ang′gəl] An angle that has a measure greater than a right angle (p. 385)
Example:

obtuse triangle [əb•t(y)o͞os′ trī′ang•gəl] A triangle that has 1 obtuse angle (p. 393)

octagon [äk′tə•gän] A polygon with eight sides (p. 390)
Example:

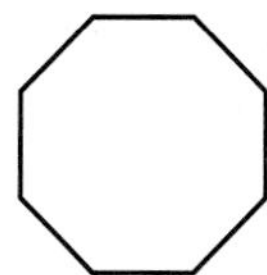

odd [od] A whole number that has a 1, 3, 5, 7, or 9 in the ones place (p. 20)

open figure [ō•pən fi′•gyər] A figure that does not begin and end at the same point (p. 390)
Examples:

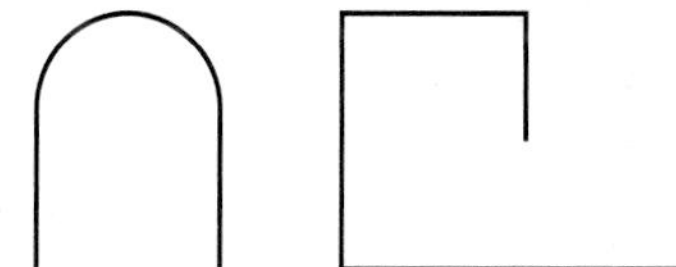

Order Property of Addition [ôr′dər prä′pər•tē əv ə•dish′ən] The property that states that you can add two numbers in any order and get the same sum (p. 6)
Example: $6 + 7 = 13$
$7 + 6 = 13$

Order Property of Multiplication [ôr′dər prä′pər•tē əv mul•tə•plə•kā′shən] The property that states that you can multiply two factors in any order and get the same product (p. 163)
Example: $4 \times 2 = 8$
$2 \times 4 = 8$

ordered pair [ôr′dərd pâr] A pair of numbers that names a point on a grid (p. 328)
Example: **(3,4)**

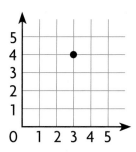

ounce (oz) [ouns] A customary unit for measuring weight (p. 346)

outcome [out′kum′] A possible result of an experiment (p. 490)

parallel lines [par′ə•lel līnz] Lines that never cross; lines that are always the same distance apart (p. 388)
Example:

parallelogram [par•ə•lel′ə•gram] A quadrilateral with 2 pairs of parallel sides and 2 pairs of equal sides (p. 397)
Example:

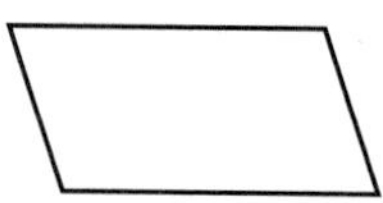

pattern [pat′ərn] An ordered set of numbers or objects; the order helps you predict what will come next. (p. 30)
Examples:
2, 4, 6, 8, 10

pattern unit [pat′ərn yo͞o′nət] The part of a pattern that repeats (p. 470)
Example:

pentagon [pen′tə•gän] A polygon with five sides (p. 390)
Example:

perimeter [pə•ri′mə•tər] The distance around a figure (p. 444)
Example:

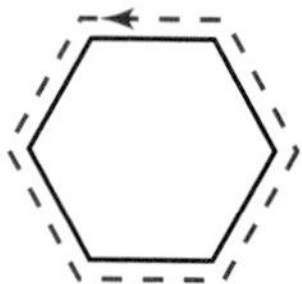

perpendicular lines [pûr•pən•dik′yə•lər līnz] Lines that intersect to form right angles (p. 388)
Example:

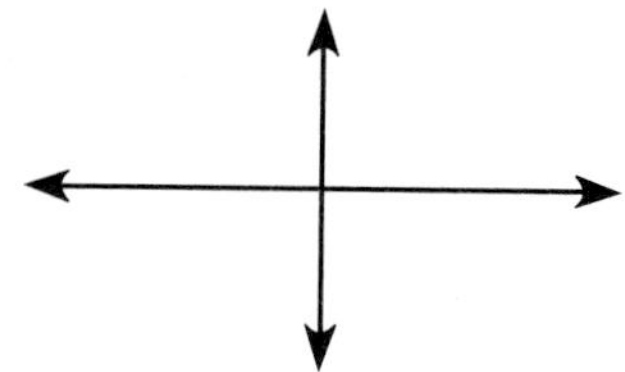

pictograph [pik′tə•graf] A graph that uses pictures to show and compare information (p. 198)
Example:

HOW WE GET TO SCHOOL

Walk	❊ ❊ ❊
Ride a Bike	❊ ❊ ❊ ❊
Ride a Bus	❊ ❊ ❊ ❊ ❊ ❊
Ride in a Car	❊ ❊

Key: Each ❊ = 10 students.

pint (pt) [pīnt] A customary unit for measuring capacity; 1 pint = 2 cups (p. 344)

place value [plās val′yo͞o] The value of each digit in a number, based on the location of the digit (p. 22)

plane [plāne] A flat surface that goes on and on
Example:

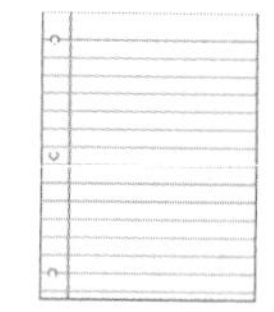
part of a plane

plane figure [plāne fi′•gyər] A closed figure in a plane that is formed by lines that are curved, straight, or both (p. 390)
Example:

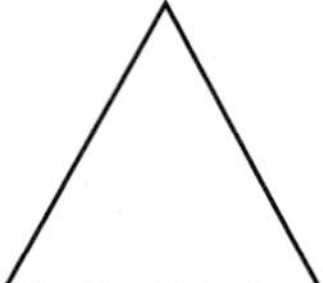

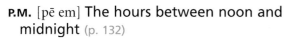

P.M. [pē em] The hours between noon and midnight (p. 132)

point [point] An exact position or location (p. 384)

polygon [pol′ē•gän] A closed plane figure with straight sides that are line segments (p. 390)
Examples:

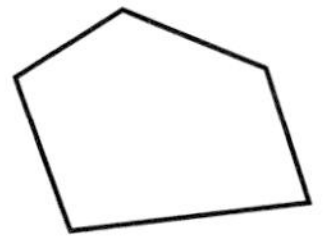

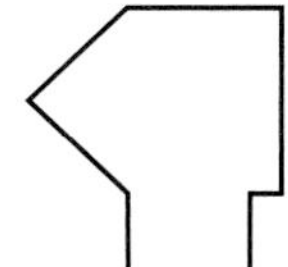

Word History

Did you ever notice that a *polygon* looks like a bunch of knees that are bent? This is how the term got its name. *Poly-* is from the Greek root, *poli*, that means "many". The ending *-gon* is from the Latin, *gonus*, which means "to bend the knee".

possible outcome [pos′ə•bəl out′kəm] Something that has a chance of happening (p. 490)

pound (lb) [pound] A customary unit for measuring weight; 1 pound = 16 ounces (p. 346)

predict [pri•dikt′] To make a reasonable guess about what will happen (p. 490)

probability [prä•bə•bi′lə•tē] The chance that a given event will occur (p. 488)
Example:

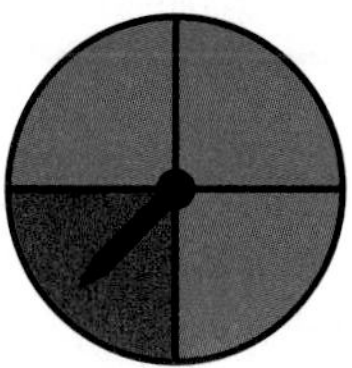

probability of red = one out of four

product [prä′dəkt] The answer in a multiplication problem (p. 160)
Example: 3 × 8 = 24
↑product

Q

quadrilateral [kwa•drə•lat′ər•əl] A polygon with four sides (p. 390)
Example:

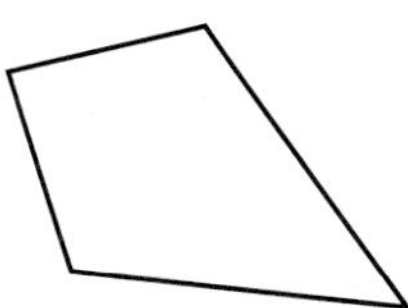

quart (qt) [kwôrt] A customary unit for measuring capacity; 1 quart = 2 pints (p. 344)

quarter hour [kwôr•tər our] 15 minutes (p. 129)
Example: Between 4:00 and 4:15 is one quarter hour.

quotient [kwō′shənt] The number, not including the remainder, that results from division (p. 242)
Example: 8 ÷ 4 = 2
↑quotient

R

range [rānj] The difference between the greatest number and the least number in a set of data (p. 310)

ray [rā] A part of a line, with one endpoint, that is straight and continues in one direction (p. 384)
Example:

rectangle [rek′tang•gəl] A quadrilateral with 2 pairs of parallel sides, 2 pairs of equal sides, and 4 right angles (p. 397)
Example:

rectangular prism [rek•tan′gyə•lər pri′zəm] A solid figure with six faces that are all rectangles (p. 424)
Example:

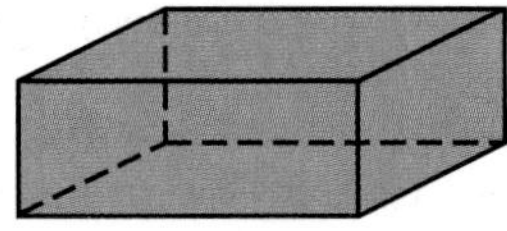

regroup [rē•grōōp′] To exchange amounts of equal value to rename a number (p. 8)
Example: 5 + 8 = 13 ones or 1 ten 3 ones

remainder [ri•mān′dər] The amount left over when a number cannot be divided evenly (p. 618)

results [ri•zults′] The answers from a survey (p. 304)

rhombus [räm′bəs] A quadrilateral with 2 pairs of parallel sides and 4 equal sides (p. 397)
Example:

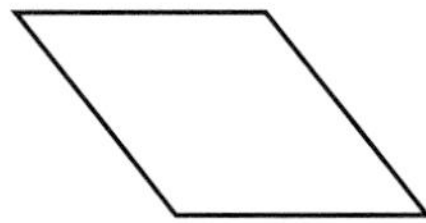

right angle [rīt ang′gəl] A special angle that forms a square corner; a right angle measures 90° (p. 384)
Example:

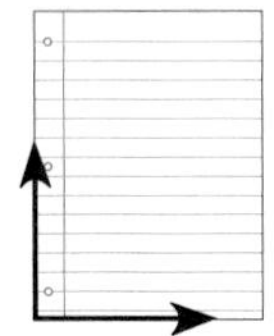

right triangle [rīt trī′ang•gəl] A triangle with one right angle (p. 393)
Example:

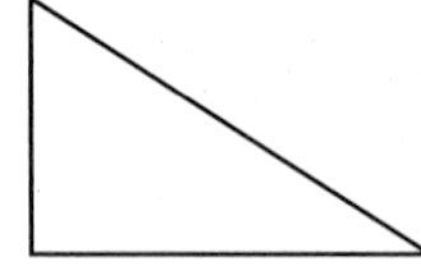

rounding [roun′ding] Replacing a number with another number that tells about how many or how much (p. 50)

scale [skāl] The numbers on a bar graph that help you read the number each bar shows (p. 324)

scalene triangle [skā′lēn trī′ang•gəl] A triangle in which no sides are equal (p. 393)
Example:

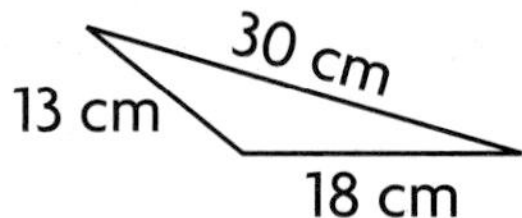

schedule [ske′•jōōl] A table that lists activities or events and the times they happen (p. 136)

sequence [sē′kwəns] To write events in order (p. 142)

similar [si′mə•lər] Having the same shape and the same or different size (p. 412)
Example:

simplest form [sim′pləst fôrm] When a fraction is modeled with the largest fraction bar or bars possible (p. 542)

slide [slīd] A movement of a figure to a new position without turning or flipping it (p. 414)
Example:

sphere [sfir] A solid figure that has the shape of a round ball (p. 424)
Example:

square [skwâr] A quadrilateral with 2 pairs of parallel sides, 4 equal sides, and 4 right angles (p. 397)
Example:

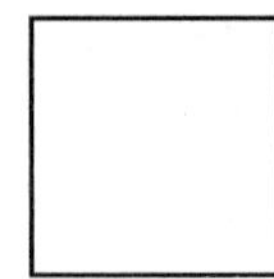

square pyramid [skwâr pir′ə•mid] A solid, pointed figure with a flat base that is a square (p. 424)
Example:

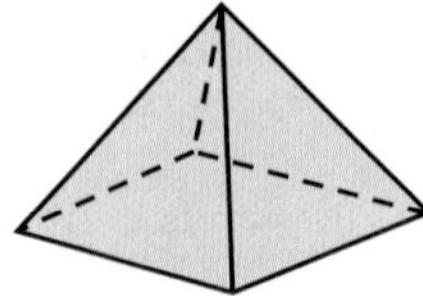

square unit [skwâr yo͞o′nət] A square with a side length of one unit; used to measure area (p. 448)

standard form [stan′dərd fôrm] A way to write numbers by using the digits 0–9, with each digit having a place value (p. 22)
Example: 345 ← standard form

subtraction [səb•trak′shən] The process of finding how many are left when a number of items are taken away from a group of items; the process of finding the difference when two groups are compared; the opposite operation of addition (p. 10)

sum [sum] The answer to an addition problem (p. 4)

survey [sər′vā] A method of gathering information (p. 304)

symmetry [sim′ə•trē] A figure has symmetry if it can be folded along a line so that the two parts match exactly; one half of the figure looks like the mirror image of the other half (p. 410)

tally table [ta′lē tā′bəl] A table that uses tally marks to record data (p. 302)
Example:

FAVORITE SPORT	
Sport	**Number**
Soccer	𝍸 III
Baseball	III
Football	𝍸
Basketball	𝍸 I

tenth [tenth] One of ten equal parts (p. 558)
Example:

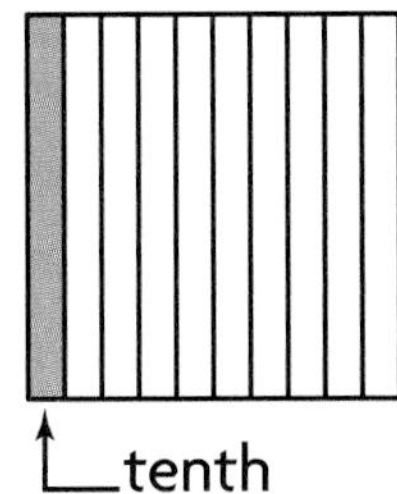

tessellate [tes′ə•lāt] To combine plane figures so they cover a surface without overlapping or leaving any space between them (p. 430)

tessellation [te•sə•lā′shən] A repeating pattern of closed figures that covers a surface with no gaps and no overlaps (p. 430)
Example:

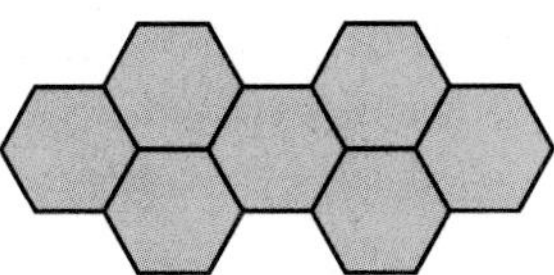

time line [tīm līn] A drawing that shows when and in what order events took place (p. 142)

trapezoid [trap′ə•zoid] A quadrilateral with one pair of parallel sides (p. 396)
Example:

tree diagram [trē dī′ə•gram] An organized list that shows all possible outcomes of an event (p. 498)
Example:

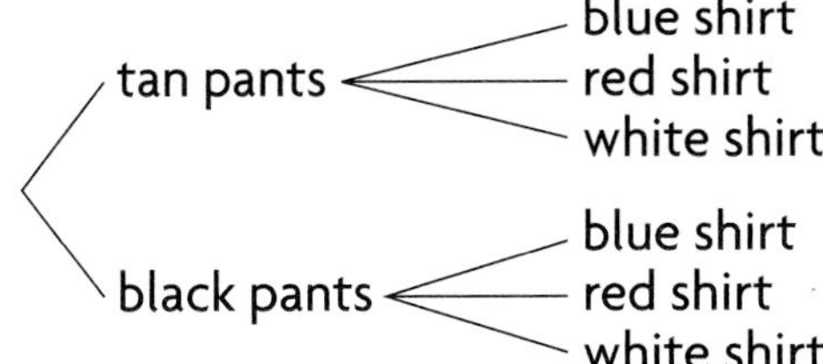

trends [trendz] Areas on a graph where data increase, decrease, or stay the same over time (p. 330)

triangle [trī′ang′gəl] A polygon with three sides (p. 392)
Examples:

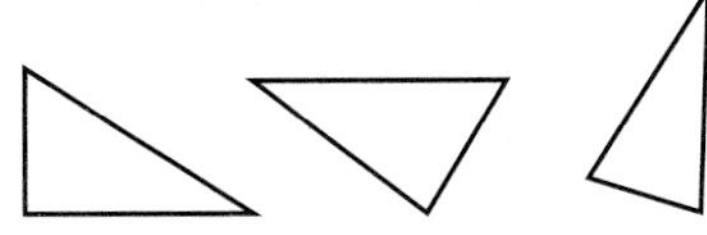

turn [tûrn] A movement of a figure to a new position by rotating the figure around a point (p. 414)
Example:

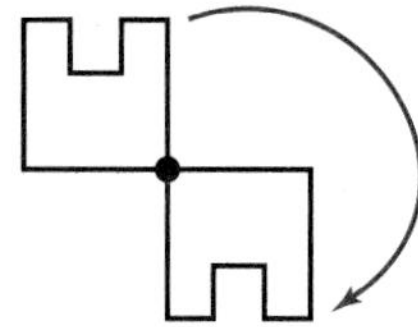

unit cost [yōō′nit kôst] The cost of one item when several items are sold for a single price (p. 297)

unlikely [ən•līk′lē] An event is unlikely if it does not have a good chance of happening. (p. 488)

variable [vâr′ē•ə•bəl] A symbol or a letter that stands for an unknown number (p. 243)

Word History

Variable The word *vary* comes from the Latin, *variabilis,* meaning "changeable." At first the word applied to changes of color, as in the speckled fur of animals. Eventually the word was used for things that involve change of any kind.

Venn diagram [ven dī′ə•gram] A diagram that shows relationships among sets of things (p. 400)
Example:

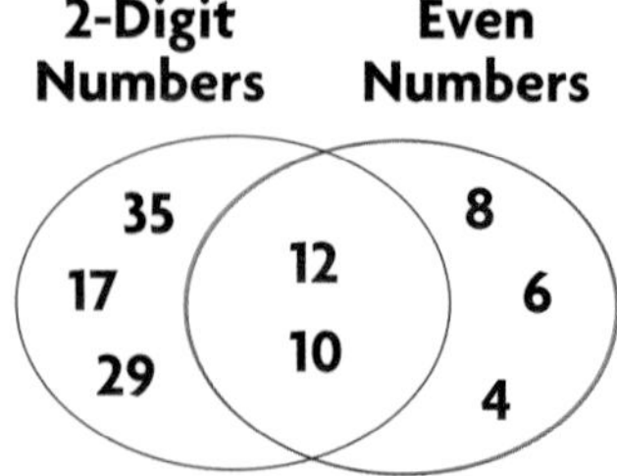

vertex [vûr′teks] The point at which two or more line segments meet in a plane figure or where three or more edges meet in a solid figure (p. 424)
Examples:

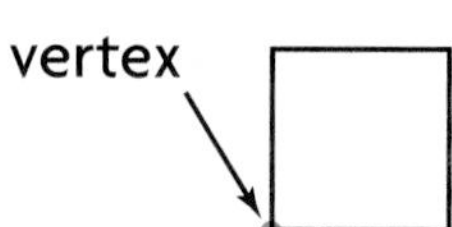

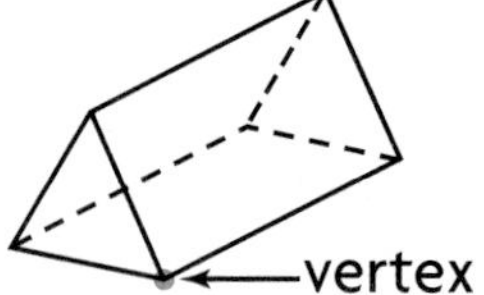

vertical bar graph [vûr′ti•kəl bär graf] A bar graph in which the bars go up from bottom to top (p. 324)

volume [väl′yəm] The amount of space a solid figure takes up (p. 452)

whole number [hōl nəm′bər] One of the numbers 0, 1, 2, 3, 4, ... The set of whole numbers goes on without end.

word form [wûrd form] A way to write numbers by using words (p. 22)
Example: The word form of 212 is two hundred twelve.

yard (yd) [yärd] A customary unit for measuring length or distance; 1 yard = 3 feet (p. 342)

Zero Property of Multiplication [zir′ō prä′pər•tē əv mul•tə•plə•kā′shən] The property that states that the product of zero and any number is zero (p. 220)
Example: $0 \times 6 = 0$

A

A.M., 132–133
Acute angle, 385–386
Acute triangle, 393–395
Addends, 1, 4–5, 68, 69
- missing, 73, 78, 94

Addition
- to check subtraction, 94, 98
- column addition, H10
- estimating sums, 68–69, 72–73
- fact families, 2–3
- facts, H4
- four-digit numbers, 72–73
- fractions, 540–541, 542–543
- greater numbers, 72–73
- grouping addends, 68
- Grouping Property of, 6–7, 68–69
- Identity Property, 6–7
- inverse operation of subtraction, 2–3
- mental math and, 77
- modeling for
  - simple fractions, 540
  - whole numbers, 70
- of money, 120–121, 580–583
- of more than two addends, 68–69
- and multiplication, 158–159
- of one-digit numbers, 68–69, 158–159, 175
- order of addends, 68
- Order Property of, 6–7
- properties of, 6–7
- regrouping, 70–73, 76–79
- repeated, 158–159
- three-digit numbers, 70–73, H21
- three or more addends, 68–69
- two-digit numbers, 8–9, 69, H5

Addition strategies
- predicting and testing, 74–75

Algebra
- add/subtract money, 120–121
- addition of like fractions, 540–543
- connecting addition and multiplication, 158–159
- equations, 264–266
- expressions, 80–81, 264–265
  - comparing, 121, 263
  - evaluating, 197, 204, 446, 454, 551, 582
  - writing, 80–81, 264–265
- extending linear pattern by its rules, 180–181, 212–213, 216–217, 259, 261
- fact families, 2–3, 246–249
- find a rule, 216–217
- find the cost, 284–285
- functional relationships, 113, 276, 284–285
- inequalities, 44, 47–49, 201, 263, 282
- inverse operations of addition and subtraction, 2–3
- inverse operations of multiplication and division, 242–248
- missing addend, 4–5, 73, 78, 94, 276
- missing digit, 261, 276, 622
- missing factors, 186–187, 195, 201, 204, 211, 213, 219, 221, 244, 248, 259, 261, 274, 276, 281, 604, H11, H16
- missing operation symbol, 241, 279
- multiply with three factors, 218–219
- number sentences, 80–81, 622
- patterns, 216–217, 470–473, 474–475, 476–477, 478–479, 480–481, 518
- practice the facts, 202–205
- recording division of two-digit numbers, 621–623
- recording multiplication of two-digit numbers, 603–605
- relating multiplication and division, 242–243
- solving unit cost problems, 284–285
- subtraction of greater numbers, 98–101, 104
- subtraction of like fractions, 544–549

Angles, 384–385
- acute, 385, 386, 387
- measured in degrees, 385
- naming, 385
- obtuse, 385, 386, 387
- in polygons, 390–391
- in quadrilaterals, 396–399
- right, 384–389, 392–395
  - identify in polygons, 386, 390–391
- sorting triangles by, 392–395

Area
- estimate, 448
- find, 448–449, 450–451

Arrangements, 500–501
Arrays, 162–163, 602
- dividing through tens, 278–279, 280–283
- in division, 242–243, 275, 276, 280
- to find products, 182–184, 194–201, 196, 202, 205, 207, 218, 242–243, 602–603
- to find quotients, 242–243, 275–276, 280
- and multiplication, 162–163, 200, 242–243, 602–604, H10

Assessment
- Chapter Review/Test, 15, 35, 55, 83, 105, 123, 145, 171, 189, 207, 225, 253, 269, 289, 317, 333, 353, 371, 403, 419, 439, 457, 483, 503, 535, 553, 571, 587, 613, 631
- Check What You Know, 1, 19, 39, 67, 87, 109, 127, 157, 175, 193, 211, 237, 257, 273, 301, 321, 337, 357, 383, 407, 423, 443, 469, 487, 515, 539, 557, 575, 599, 617
- Mixed Review and Test Prep, 3, 5, 7, 9, 11, 21, 23, 27, 31, 33, 41, 45, 47, 51, 53, 69, 71, 73, 79, 81, 89, 91, 95, 97, 101, 113, 117, 119, 121, 131, 133, 135, 137, 141, 159, 161, 163, 167, 177, 179, 185, 187, 195, 197, 201, 205, 215, 217, 219, 221, 239, 241, 245, 249, 259, 261, 263, 265, 277, 279, 283, 285, 303, 305, 307, 313, 315, 325, 327, 329, 331, 341, 343, 345, 347, 349, 361, 365, 367, 369, 387, 389, 391, 395, 399, 409, 411, 413, 415, 427, 429, 431, 447, 449, 455, 473, 475, 477, 479, 489, 491, 519, 521, 525, 529, 533, 541, 543, 545, 549, 559, 561, 563, 565, 567, 577, 579, 583, 601, 605, 611, 619, 623, 627, 629
- Performance Assessment, 62, 152, 232, 296, 378, 464, 510, 594, 637
- Standardized Test Prep, 16–17, 36–37, 56–57, 84–85, 106–107, 124–125, 146–147, 172–173, 190–191, 208–209, 226–227, 254–255, 270–271, 290–291, 318–319, 334–335, 354–355, 372–373, 404–405, 420–421, 440–441, 458–459, 484–485, 504–505, 536–537, 554–555, 572–573, 588–589, 614–615, 632–633
- Study Guide and Review, 60–61, 150–151, 230–231, 294–295, 376–377, 462–463, 508–509, 592–593, 636–637

Associative Property
- *See* Grouping Property

B

Bar graph, 48–49, 55, 94, 166, 278, 324, 325, 326, 327, 343, 395, 447, 492, 494, 528, 569, 605, 623
- horizontal, 324–325, 326, 327
- making, 326–327
- reading, 324–325
- vertical, 324–325, 327

Base-ten blocks, 19, 22–26, 30–31, 42, 43, 70, 71, 90, 91
- in addition, 70–71

in division, 620–621
in multiplication, 602–604
in subtraction, 90–91
Basic Facts tests, H36–H40
Benchmark numbers, 40–41
in estimation, 40–41
Bills, counting, 109–113, 118–119
Break Problems into Simpler Parts strategy, 584–585

C

Calculator, 63, 76, 98, 581, 609
Calendar, 127, 138–141
Capacity
customary, 344–345
estimating, 344–345
metric, 364–365
Celsius temperature, 368–369
Centimeter, 358–363
Certain events, 488–489
Challenge, 59, 149, 229, 293, 375, 461, 507, 591, 635
Change, making, 118–119
Chapter Review/Test, 15, 35, 55, 83, 105, 123, 145, 171, 189, 207, 225, 253, 269, 289, 317, 333, 353, 371, 403, 419, 439, 457, 483, 503, 535, 553, 571, 587, 613, 631
Check What You Know, 1, 19, 39, 67, 87, 109, 127, 157, 175, 193, 211, 237, 257, 273, 301, 321, 337, 357, 383, 407, 423, 443, 469, 487, 515, 539, 557, 575, 599, 617
Choose a Method, 76–79, 98–101, 608–611
Choose the operation, 12–13, 266–267, 606–607
Circle, 383, 390, 435, 436, 437
Circle graphs, 313, 375
Classify, 306
data, 306–307
polygons, 390–391
quadrilaterals, 390–391
triangles, 390–391
Clocks
analog, 127, 128, 129, 132, 133, 145, 277
digital, 128, 129, 131, 133, 144, 145
Clockwise, 131
Closed figures, 390
Coins
counting, 109–113, 118–119
dimes, 109–113, 118–119
half dollars, 110–112, 576
nickels, 109–113, 118–119
pennies, 109–113, 118–119
quarters, 109–113, 118–119
Combinations, 498–499
Combining solid figures, 428–429
Commutative Property of Addition, 6–7
See also Order Property of Addition
Commutative Property of Multiplication, 162–167, 175, 182, 183, 202
Compare, 42
and contrast, 455
data, 313
decimals, 566–567
fractions, 526–529, 539, 546–547
graphs, 324–325
money amounts, 116
on number line, 42, 43
numbers, 42–45, H3
parts of a whole, 487, 526–529, 530–531
Computer Software
Harcourt Mega Math, 2, 8, 22, 25, 43, 70, 77, 91, 111, 119, 158, 162, 182, 200, 213, 216, 242, 247, 261, 274, 281, 311, 325, 330, 489, 493, 547, 580, 603, 619
Cone, 423, 424, 425, 428
Congruent figures, 408–409, H25
Convert units, 348–349
Counterclockwise, 131
Counting
bills and coins, 110–115
change, 118–119
money, 110–115, 116–117, 118–119
skip-counting
by fives, 21, 157
by fours, 321
by tens, 21, 157, 211, 212, H13
by threes, 157, 164–167, 182, 321
by twos, 21, 157, 321
Cross-Curricular Connections
Art, 395, 605
Geography, 549
Math History, 611
Reading, 215, 277, 313, 399, 455, 583, 623
Science, 95, 495, 525
Social Studies, 113, 435, 447, 519, 529
Cube, 423, 424–427, 428
and rectangular prism, 427, 436
Cubic unit, 452–455
Cup, 344–345
Customary units
of capacity, liquid measure
cups, 344–345
gallons, 344–345
pints, 344–345
quarts, 344–345
changing units in, 348–349
of length
feet, 342–343
inches, 338–341, 342–343
miles, 342–343
yards, 342–343
of weight
ounces, 346–347
pounds, 346–347
Cylinder, 423, 424, 425, 428–429, 436

D

Data, 302
analyzing and interpreting bar graphs, 48–49, 55, 94, 108, 166, 278, 325, 326, 327, 343, 351, 401, 437, 447, 492, 494, 528, 569, 623
analyzing and interpreting charts and tables, 11, 22, 49, 51, 53, 75, 78, 100, 103, 115, 121, 122, 143, 158, 169, 199, 204, 272, 300, 307, 327, 351, 356, 501, 601, 607, 610
circle graphs, 313, 375
classifying, 306–307
collecting and organizing responses, 302–303
diagrams, 394, 400–401
display, 322–323, 326–327, 511
generate questions, 240
in identifying relationships, 49
line graphs, 330–331, 583
line plots, 310–312, 417
make graphs, 322–323, 326–327, 511

money, 121
ordering numbers, 46–47
pictographs, 2, 13, 18, 26, 29, 79, 140, 156, 174, 181, 198, 207, 210, 223, 267, 320–321, 322–323
price list, 285, 287, 625
schedules, 136, 137, 145
survey, 304–305, 311
tally table, 302–305, 308
understanding, 304–305
Days, 138, 139
Decimal point, 558
Decimals
adding, 580–583
comparing, 566–567, H31
equivalent fractions and, 591
forms of, 564–565
fractions and, 558–559
greater than one, 564–565
hundredths, 562–563
models, 560, 561
money amounts, 576–577
money and, 578–579, 580–583
naming, H31
number line, 566–567, 591
ordering, 566–567, H31
place value in, 558
subtracting, 580–583
tenths, 558–561
Decimeter, 358–360
Degrees
Celsius, 368–369
Fahrenheit, 368–369
measure angles with, 385, 461
Denominator, 516–519, 540
Differences. *See* Subtraction
Digits, 22–33
place in quotient, 626–627
place value of, 42–49
Dime, 109–113, 118
Dividend, 242, 258, 618
three-digit, 609–610
two-digit, 280–283
Division
divisor, 242, 258, 618
by eleven and twelve, 293
estimate quotients, 628–629
fact families, 246–249, 280–282, H15
facts through five, 256–270, H15
facts through ten, 272–290, H22
as inverse of multiplication, 238, 242–245, 626
meaning of, 238–239
model, H13
of money amounts, 284–285
by nine and ten, 278–279
by one, 262–263
placing first digit in quotient, 626–627
practice, 280–281
quotient, 242, 280–281
recording, 621
relating to subtraction, 240–241, 280
with remainders, 618–619, 624–625
by six, seven, and eight, 274–277
by three and four, 260–261
of three-digit numbers, 626–627
by two and five, 258–259
of two-digit numbers, 620–621
writing a number sentence, 250–251
zeros in, 262–263
Divisor, 242
Dollar, 110–117, 118–119
Doubles (doubling)
even factors, 202, 203
to find products, 182–183
using to multiply, 194, 202, 203
Draw a Diagram strategy, 400–401
Draw figures, 432–435

E

Edge, 424, 433
Elapsed time, 134–135, 138, 145
Endpoints, 384–385
Equal groups, 157–161, 165, 175, 176, 182, 193, 237, 238–239, 275, 280, H9, H12, H15
to find quotient, 275, 281
Equal to, 42
symbol for, 42
Equally likely events, 490–491
Equilateral triangle, 393–395
Equivalent forms of numbers
decimals, 591
fractions, 522–525, 539
identify, 22–27
model, 22, 28–29, 42–45, 540–545, 558–565
whole numbers, 22–27
Equivalent sets, 110–113, 122
Estimate or Exact Answer, 102–103
Estimate or Measure, 350–351
Estimation
add/subtract money, 121,122
benchmark numbers, 40–41
of capacity, 344–345
to check reasonableness of answer, 72, 88, 98, 99, 121, 122, 306, 608, 609
of differences, 88–89
front-end, 68–69, 88–89, 628–629
of measurement, 338
perimeter, 444–447
quotients, 628–629
and rounding, 50–53, 68, 88
of sums, 68–69
of temperature, 368–369
three- and four-digit numbers, 72–73, 97
of time, 129
using a number line, 50–53
volume, 452–455
weight, 346
Estimation strategies
benchmark numbers, 40–41
choose, 88
describe, 89, 628
explain, 68
front-end, 68–69, 88–89, 628–629
rounding, 50–53, 68, 88
Even numbers, 20–21
Event, 488
Events, sequencing, 142–143
Expanded notation, 22, 25, 26, 28, 29, 32, 33, 563, 564, 565
Experiments, in probability, 492–495
Explain, *Opportunities to explain are contained in every exercise set. Some examples are* 3, 5, 7, 9, 10, 22, 25, 30, 33, 41, 43, 46, 51, 53, 69, 73, 77, 89, 93, 97, 99, 111, 117, 121, 129, 136, 139, 158, 165, 177, 178, 183, 187, 195, 197, 200, 203, 213, 216, 221, 241, 243, 247, 258, 260, 263, 275, 281, 284, 304, 306, 311, 325, 329, 330, 341, 351, 359, 388, 390,

398, 411, 428, 430, 433, 445, 449, 453, 471, 474, 476, 488, 498, 520, 523, 532, 543, 547, 567, 582, 622, 627
Explain It, 16–17, 36–37, 56–57, 84–85, 106–107, 124–125, 146–147, 172–173, 190–191, 208–209, 226–227, 254–255, 270–271, 290–291, 318–319, 334–335, 354–355, 372–373, 404–405, 420–421, 440–441, 458–459, 484–485, 504–505, 536–537, 554–555, 572–573, 588–589, 614–615, 632–633
Expression, 80–81, 264–265
evaluating, 80, 81
writing, 264–265
Extra Practice, 14, 34, 54, 82, 104, 122, 144, 170, 188, 206, 224, 252, 268, 288, 316, 332, 352, 370, 402, 418, 438, 456, 482, 502, 534, 552, 570, 587, 612, 630

F

Faces, 424
of solid figures, 424–426, 433, 436
tracing and naming, 425
Fact family, 2–3, 246–249
addition and subtraction, 2, 3
division, 280, 281
multiplication, 246–247
multiplication and division, 246–247, 280, 281
Facts tests, H36–H40
Factors, 160, 178
in arrays, 162–163, 280–281
missing, 186–187, 195, 201, 204, 211, 213, 219, 221, 244, 248, 259, 260, 274–276, 281, 604, H11, H16
Fahrenheit temperature, 368–369
Fast Facts, xxvi, 5, 18, 23, 38, 53, 66, 86, 97, 108, 113, 126, 141, 156, 161, 174, 179, 192, 195, 210, 214, 236, 245, 265, 272, 277, 300, 307, 320, 323, 336, 340, 356, 360, 382, 387, 406, 411, 422, 434, 442, 454, 468, 477, 486, 497, 514, 529, 538, 549, 556, 559, 574, 577, 598, 610, 616, 622
Feet, 342–343
Figures
closed, 390
congruent, 408–409
draw, 433–435
open, 390
patterns with, 470–475, 478–479
plane, 448–449
similar, 412–413
slides, flips, and turns, 414–415
solid, 424–429
that tessellate, 430–431
Find a Pattern strategy, 180–181, 480–481
Flip, 414–415
Foot, 342–343
Fraction bars
to add fractions, 540–543
and equivalent fractions, 523, 524
model making, 525, 530
to order fractions, 527–528
and parts of a whole, 516–520
to subtract fractions, 544–549
Fractions
adding, 540–541, 542–543
comparing, 526–529, 539, 557, H30
concept of, 516–519, H18, H19
decimals and, 558–559, 575
denominator, 516–519, 520–521, 540
equivalent, 522–525, H24
like, 540
in measurements, 339–340
in mixed numbers, 532–533, H25
modeling
with fraction bars, 516, 523, 524, 526, 527, 530, 539, 542, 543, 546
on number line, 517
as part of group, 520–521, H28
as part of whole, 516–519, H29
with tiles, 526
and money, 576–577
naming, 557, H29
on number line, 591
numerator, 516, 540
ordering, 526–529
simplest form of, 542–543, 553
subtracting, 544–549
Frequency table, 302, 305, 327

G

Gallon, 344
Geometry
angles, 384–389
classifying, 384–387
in plane figures, 390–391
in quadrilaterals, 396–399
area, concept of, 448–449
classifying
angles, 384–387
plane figures, 390–391
polygons, 390–391
solid figures, 424–427, 428–429
triangles, 392–395
closed figures, 390
congruent figures, 408–409
curves in plane figures, 390–391
draw figures, 432–435
faces of solids, 424
line of symmetry, 410–411
lines, 384–387
angle relationships and, 384–387, 392–395
intersecting, 388–389
parallel, 388–389
perpendicular, 388–389
ray, 384–385
segment, 384–385
making complex solid forms from simpler solids, 428–429
one-dimensional figures, 384–387
open figures, 390
patterns, 470–473
perimeter of polygons, 444–445
plane figures, 390–391
circles, 383, 390, 436, 437
combine, 430–431
hexagons, 390–391, 430
octagons, 390–391
parallelograms, 396–399
pentagons, 390–391
polygons, 390–391
quadrilaterals, 496–499
rectangles, 397–399, 449
squares, 397–399
triangles, 390–391, 392–395, 430–431
point, 384
polygons, 390–399
quadrilaterals, 390–391, 396–399
solid figures, 424–427
combine, 428–429

cones, 423, 424, 425, 428, 436–437
cubes, 423–428, 436–437
cylinders, 423–428
edges, 424–427, 436–437
faces, 424–427
rectangular prisms, 423–428, 436–437
spheres, 423–426, 436–437
square pyramids, 423, 424–429, 436–437
vertices, 424
symmetry, 410–411
tessellation, 430–431
three-dimensional figures, 423–429
triangle
acute, 392–395
equilateral, 392–395
isosceles, 392–395
obtuse, 392–395
right, 392–395
scalene, 392–395
two-dimensional figures, 390–399
volume, 452–456
Glossary, H42–H54
Gram, 366–367
Graphic aids, 313, 399, 623
Graphs
bar, 49, 55, 94, 108, 166, 278, 325, 326, 327, 343, 351, 401, 437, 447, 492, 494, 528, 569, 623
circle, 313, 375
data labels on, 326
and frequency table, 327
identifying parts of, 322
key of, 267, 322–323
kinds of, 322–327
line, 330–331
line plots, 310–313
making, 322–323, 326–327, 511
pictographs, 2, 13, 18, 26, 29, 79, 140, 156, 174, 181, 198, 207, 210, 223, 267, 320–321, 322–323
as problem solving skill, 48–49, 198–199
as problem solving strategy, 322–323
scale and, 324, 326–327
Greater than, 42–45
symbol for, 42
Grid, 328
locating points on, 328–329
ordered pairs, 328–329
Grouping Property
of Addition, 6
of Multiplication, 218–219, 220–221

H

Half dollar, 110–115, 576
Hands On
add fractions, 540–541, 542–543
addition with regrouping, 70–71
add three-digit numbers, 70–71
area of plane figures, 448–449
arrays, 162–163
capacity, 344–345
liters and milliliters, 364–365
collect data, 302–303
congruent figures, 408–409
decimals and money, 578–579
divide two-digit numbers, 620–621
divide with remainders, 618–619
draw figures, 432–435
draw polygons, 432
elapsed time, 134–135
equivalent fractions, 522–525
estimating length, 338
even and odd, 20–21
fact families, 246–249
Fahrenheit and Celsius, 368–369
hundredths, 562–563
length, 338–341, 358–361
make bar graphs, 326–327
make change, 118–119
make equivalent sets, 110–113
make line plots, 311
make patterns, 478–479
mass: grams and kilograms, 366–367
mean and median, 314–315
meaning of division, 238–239
measure temperature, 368–369
multiply multiples of ten and one hundred, 600–601
number patterns on a hundred chart, 20–21
ordering fractions, 527
perimeter, 444, 447
place value with four-digit numbers, 24–27
plane and solid figures, 425
possible outcomes, 490–491, 492–495, 496–497
relate decimals and money, 578–579
relating units, 359
similar figures, 412–413
slides, flips, and turns, 414–415
solid figures, 424–427
subtract fractions, 544–545, 546–547
subtraction with regrouping, 90–91
symmetry, 410–411
tenths, 560–561
volume, 452
weight, 346–347
Harcourt Mega Math, 2, 8, 22, 25, 43, 70, 77, 91, 111, 119, 158, 162, 182, 200, 213, 216, 242, 247, 261, 274, 281, 311, 325, 330, 489, 493, 547, 580, 603, 619
Hexagons, 390–391, 430
Horizontal bar graph, 324
Hour, 126, 127, 128–135
Hundred chart, 28–29
patterns in, 20–21, 185
Hundred thousands, 32–33
Hundreds, place value and, 22–23
Hundredths
adding and subtracting, 580–583
relating fractions and decimals, 562–563

I

Identify relationships, 436–437
Identity Property of Addition, 6–7
Identity Property of Multiplication, 176–177
Impossible event, 488
Inch(es), 338–341, 342–343
Inequalities
solve problems involving, 42–49, 201, 204, 263, 282
Information, too much/too little, 168–169
Interpret remainder, 624–625
Intersecting lines, 388
Inverse operations
addition and subtraction, 2–3
multiplication and division, 242–243, 246–247
Isosceles triangle, 393–395
It's in the Bag, 58, 148, 228, 292, 374, 460, 506, 590, 634

K

Key, 322–323
Kilogram, 366–367
Kilometer, 358–360, 363

L

Lattice multiplication, 611
Length. *See* Measurement
Less than, 42–45, 121
symbol for, 42
Like fractions, 540–541
addition of, 540–543, 553
subtraction of, 544–549
Likely events, 488–489
Line graphs, 330–331, 583
reading, 330–331
Line of symmetry, 410–411
Line plots, 310–313, 496, 497
Lines, 384
intersecting, 388–389
parallel, 388–389, 396–399
perpendicular, 388
segments, 384–387
types of, 388–389
Linkup
Art, 395, 605
Geography, 549
Math History, 611
Reading Strategies
analyze information, 455
choose important information, 277
classify and categorize, 215
make predictions, 283, 583
use graphic aids, 313, 399, 623
Science, 95, 495, 525
Social Studies, 113, 435, 447, 519, 529
Liters, 364–365

M

Make a graph, 511
Make a Model strategy, 416–417, 530–531
Make a Table strategy, 114–115, 308–309, 362–363
Make an Organized List strategy, 500–501
Make Generalizations, 450–451
Manipulatives and visual aids
arrays, 162, 163, 280, 281
balance, 346, 366
base-ten blocks,19, 22–26, 42, 43, 70, 71, 90, 91, 602–604, 620–621
centimeter ruler, 358–361, 446
clock dials, 127–129, 133–135
connecting cubes, 20, 314, 452–454
counters, 160, 238, 239, 275, 276, 280–282, 618, 619
decimal models, 560–563, 580, 581
dot paper, 432, 433, 434, 438, 472
fact cards, 246, 249
fraction bars, 516, 523, 528, 530, 531, 539–542, 544–548, 553, 557, 559
geometric wood solids, 425–426, 436–437
grid paper, 412–413, 448, 451, 602
hundred chart, 21, 215
multiplication tables, 178, 280, 281
number cards, 79
number cube, 309
number lines, 164–166, 240, 311, 517, 532–533, 566, 567
pattern blocks, 408–409, 410, 414–415, 416–417, 470, 478–479
place-value chart, 24, 32, 43, 566, 567
play money, 109–113, 116–119, 575–578
ruler, 338–341, 358–361, 445, 446
scale, 346
spinners, 308, 488, 491, 492–494
tiles, 162–163, 182–184, 194, 196, 200, 201–202, 218, 242, 243, 275, 276, 280–282, 448, 493, 494
time line, 142
yardstick, 342
Mass, 366–367
Mean, 314–315
Measurement
of angles in degrees, 385, 461
area, 448–449
capacity, 344–345
changing units, 348–349
choosing a reasonable unit, 348–349, 358, 359, 364–367
choosing an appropriate measuring tool, 338, 348–349, 358, 359, 364–367
customary units
cups, 344–345
feet, 339–343
gallons, 344–345
inches, 337–343
miles, 342–343
ounces, 346–347
pints, 344–345
pounds, 346–347
quarts, 344–345
yards, 342–343
degrees Celsius, 368–369
degrees Fahrenheit, 368–369
estimating
capacity, 364–365
length, 340–341
volume, 350–351, 452–453
weight/mass, 346–347, 366–367
half inch, 339
length, 338–343, 358–361
liquid volume, 344–345, 364–365
mass, 366–367
metric units
centimeters, 358–361
decimeters, 358–361
grams, 366–367
kilograms, 366–367
kilometers, 358–361
liters, 364–365
meters, 358–361
milliliters, 364–365
to nearest centimeter, H28
to nearest half inch, 339–340
to nearest inch, 337–341, H26
in nonstandard units, 338, 346, 365, 366, 444
perimeter of polygon, 444–445
relating units, 359
square units, 448
Table of Measures, 342, 348, 359
temperature, 368–369
time
day, 138, 139
hour, 128–135
minute, 128–135

month, 138, 139
week, 138, 139
year, 138
unit conversions, 348–349, 362–363
using rulers, 337–341, 358–361
volume of solid figure, 452–455
weight, 346–347
Median, 314–315
Mental math
choose a method, 76–79, 98–101, 608–611
Meter, 358–363
Metric system
capacity
liters, 364–365
milliliters, 364–365
changing units in, 362–363
length
centimeters, 358–363
decimeters, 358–363
kilometers, 358–363
meters, 358–363
relationship of units, 359
use a metric ruler, 358–361, H27
mass
grams, 366–367
kilograms, 366–367
Midnight, 132–133
Mile, 342–343
Milliliter, 364–365
Minute, 128–135
Mixed Applications, 13, 49, 103, 143, 169, 199, 223, 267, 351, 437, 451, 551, 569, 607, 625
Mixed numbers, 532–533, H25
decimals and, 575
fractions and, 575
Mixed Review and Test Prep, 3, 5, 7, 9, 11, 21, 23, 27, 31, 33, 41, 45, 47, 51, 53, 69, 71, 73, 79, 81, 85, 89, 91, 95, 97, 101, 113, 117, 119, 121, 131, 133, 135, 137, 141, 159, 161, 163, 167, 177, 179, 185, 187, 195, 197, 201, 205, 215, 217, 219, 221, 239, 241, 245, 249, 259, 261, 263, 265, 277, 279, 283, 285, 303, 305, 307, 313, 315, 325, 327, 329, 331, 341, 343, 345, 347, 349, 361, 365, 367, 369, 387, 389, 391, 395, 399, 409, 411, 413, 415, 427, 429, 431, 447, 449, 455, 491, 519, 521, 525, 529, 533, 541, 543, 545, 549, 559, 561, 563, 565, 567, 577, 579, 583, 601, 605, 611, 619, 621, 623, 627, 629
Mixed Strategy Practice, 29, 75, 115, 181, 251, 287, 309, 323, 363, 401, 417, 481, 501, 531, 585
Mode, 310
Modeling
adding fractions, 540–543
decimals, 558–565
subtracting fractions, 544–548
whole numbers, 22–27, 42–45
Models
addition with regrouping, 70–71
division, 238–239, 242, 618–622
to find sum, 70–71
fractions, 516–529
hundredths, 562–565
mixed numbers, 532–533
multiplication, 600, 602–604
problem solving strategy, 416–417, 530–531
solid figures, 424
subtraction with regrouping, 90–92
Money
adding, 120–121, 580–583
amounts to one hundred dollars, 149
comparing and ordering amounts of, 116–117
count coins, H7
counting bills and coins, 110–113, 118–119
and decimal notation, 109–112, 575–585, H30
dividing amounts of, 545
dollar-and-cent notation, 109–112
equivalent sets, 110–113, H7
estimating with, 121, 122
find the cost, 284–285
fractions and, 576–577
making change, 118–119
subtracting, 120–121, 580–583
Multimedia math glossary, 1, 19, 39, 63, 67, 87, 109, 127, 153, 157, 175, 193, 211, 233, 237, 257, 273, 297, 301, 321, 337, 357, 379, 383, 407, 423, 443, 465, 469, 487, 511, 515, 539, 557, 575, 595, 599, 617, 639
Multiple, 178, 600–601
Multiplication
and addition, 158–159
Associative Property of, 218–219, 220–221
checking division with, 258–259
Commutative Property of, 162–167, 182–183, 202–203, 220–221, H16
Distributive Property of, 220–221
and division, 242–245
fact families, 246–249, H15
factors, 160
zero, 176–177
one, 176–177
two, 160–161
three, 164–165
four, 178–179
five, 160–161
six, 194–195
seven, 200–201
eight, 196–197
nine 212–213
ten, 212–213
eleven, 229
twelve, 229
facts, Troubleshooting, H11, H12, H14, H20, H22
Grouping Property of, 218–219, 220–221
Identity Property of, 220–221
as inverse of division, 242–243, 626
model, 158–159, 160–161, 162–163, 164–165, 176, 182–183, 194, 196, 200, 202, 218, 220, H14
multiples of ten and one hundred, 600–601
Order Property of, 162–167, 182–183, 202–203, 220–221, H16
product, 160
Property of One, 220–221
skip-counting in, 157, 182–185, 212
three-digit numbers, 635
with three factors, 218–219
two-digit numbers, 602–605, 608–611
Zero Property, 220–221
Multiplication facts, 156–235
through eleven and twelve, 229
through five, 174–175, 193
through ten, 212–215
Multiplication table, 178–179
to find missing factor, 186, 281
to five, 258
to nine, 178, 183, 186, 202, 260
to six, 247
to ten, 212, 281
Multistep problems
At least one multistep problem is provided in every exercise set. Some examples are 8, 9, 10, 11, 20, 46, 48, 69, 70, 71, 72, 76, 90, 91, 92, 93, 94, 95, 98, 100, 101, 120, 121, 122, 159, 179, 184, 185, 187, 194, 195, 197, 200, 201, 202,

212–215, 222–223, 238, 246–248, 258–261, 266, 274–285, 302–303, 314, 326–327, 338, 344, 346, 358, 359, 361, 363, 364, 365, 366, 368, 425, 432, 433, 444, 448, 449, 450, 452, 490, 492, 493, 496, 522, 523, 527, 540, 542, 544, 550, 560, 561, 568, 569, 578, 580, 581, 606–607, 608–609, 619, 620, 621, 622, 623, 626

N

Nickel, 109–113, 118–119
Noon, 132
Not equal to, 80–81
symbol for, 80
Number
benchmark, 40–41
comparing, 42–45
even or odd, 20–21
expanded form, 22–23, 25, 26, 32–33, 564, 565
hundred thousands, 32–33
mixed, 532–533
ordering, 42, 46–47
patterns, 30–31, 476–477, 478–479, 480–481
rounding, 50, 52
sentences, 80–81, 250–251
size of, 40–41
standard form, 22–23, 25–26, 32–33
to ten thousand, 32–33
word form, 22–24, 32–33
Number line
comparing numbers on, 42, 43
decimals on, 566–567, 570, 591
to find product, 164–166
finding a pattern on, 180
fractions on, 516–519, 591
mixed numbers on, 532–533
multiplication, 164–165
ordering numbers, 39, 42, 46–47, 566–567
patterns on, 180
in rounding, 50, 52
skip-counting on, 182, 212
Number Sense
adding
decimals, 580–585
fractions, 540–541, 542–543
multidigit whole numbers, 68–81
benchmarks, 40–41
checking division with multiplication, 258, 278, 626
comparing and ordering
decimals, 566–567
fractions, 526–531
whole numbers, 42–47, 48–49
connecting addition and multiplication, 158–159
counting whole numbers, 20–29
dividing multidigit numbers, 618–622, 626–629
estimation, 68–69, 88–89, 96–97, 102–103
Grouping, or Associative, Property of Multiplication, 220–221
Grouping Property of Addition, 2–3, 68–69
identify place value, 19, 22–23, 24–26, 32–33, 46–47, 50–53
Identity Property of Addition, 6–7
Identity Property of Multiplication, 176–177, 220–221
inverse, 2–3, 242–248, 258–261, 274–279, 281, 622
memorize division facts, 258–263, 274–283
memorize multiplication facts, 158–167, 176–179, 182–187, 194–197, 200–205, 212–215, 218–219, 220–221
modeling fractions, 516–519, 520–525
money, 110–121, 580–585
multiply multidigit numbers, 602–607, 608–611
Order, or Commutative, Property of Multiplication, 162–163, 164–165, 202
Order Property of Addition, 6–7
reading and writing
decimals, 558–568
fractions, 516–519, 520
whole numbers, 20–27
relating addition and multiplication, 158–159
relating decimals and money, 578–579
relating fractions and money, 576–577
relating multiplication and division, 242–246
relating subtraction and division, 240–241
relating whole numbers, fractions, and decimals, 516–531, 558–565
rounding, 50–53, 68–69
subtracting
decimals, 580–585
fractions, 544–549
multidigit whole numbers, 90–101
unit cost, 284–285
using expanded notation, 22–23, 25, 26–33, 564–565
Zero Property, 176–177, 204, 262, 263
Number sentence
expressions in, 264
as problem solving strategy, 250–251
true/false, 80, 81
writing, 250–251
Numerator, 516–519, 520–521, 539

O

Obtuse angle, 385–386
Obtuse triangle, 393–395
Octagons, 390–391
Odd numbers, 20–21
Ones
division by, 262–263
multiplying by, 176–177
place value and, 19
Open figure, 390
Operation
choosing, 266–267, 606–607
symbols for, 80–81, 264–265
Order Property of Addition, 6–7
Order Property of Multiplication, *See* Commutative Property of Multiplication
Ordered pair, 328–329
Ordering
decimals, 566–567
fractions, 527–529
on number line, 39, 42, 46–47, 566–567
numbers, 42, 46–47, 48–49, H4
Ordinal numbers, H2
Ounce, 346–347
Outcomes
possible, 490–491
predicting, 490–491, 496–497
recording, 490–491, 492–494

P

P.M., 132–133
Parallel lines, 388–389, 396–399
Parallelogram, 396–399
Parts of a group, 520–521, H29

Parts of a whole, 516–519, H28
Pattern Finding strategy, 180–181, 480–481
Patterns
color, 507
create, 478–479
describe, 180–181, 216–217, 470–481
even/odd numbers, 21
extend, 180–181, 216–217, 470–477, 478–479
finding, 180–181, 216–217, 480–481
geometric, 470–472
identify missing parts in, 470, 476, 480
make, 478–479
with multiples, 194, 196, 212, 600–601
number, 30–31, 476–481
with number line, 180
with pattern blocks, 470, 478–479
place value, 30–31
plane figures, 430–431, 470–472
in problem solving, 180–181, 480–481
repeating, 180–181, 216–217
and tessellation, 430–431
translating, 471
units, 470–472
visual, 473, 474–475
write a rule, 216–217, 474–481
Penny, 109–115, 118–119
Pentagons, 390–391
Performance Assessment, 62, 152, 232, 296, 378, 464, 510, 594, 638
Perimeter
estimate, 444
find, 442, 444–447
Permutations, *See* Arrangements
Perpendicular lines, 388
Pictographs, 2, 13, 18, 26, 29, 79, 140, 156, 174, 181, 198, 207, 210, 223, 267, 320–321, 322–323, H18
Pint, 344–345
Place value
chart, 22, 24, 32, 43–44
comparing numbers, 44
decimal use of, 558–559
five- and six-digit numbers, 32–33
four-digit numbers, 24–25
hundreds, 22–23
in hundred thousands, 32–33
multiply nine and ten, 212–215
ordering numbers, 46–47
patterns, 30–31
ten thousands, 32–33
thousands, 24–27
three-digit numbers, 22–23
two-digit numbers, H2
Plane figures, 390–391
area of, 448–449, 450–451
combine, 430–431
identifying, 390–391, 392–395, 396–399, 425, H23
patterns with, 470–472
sides and vertices, H24
Points, 384
end point, 384
on grid, 328–329
Polygons, 390–401
classifying, 386, 390, 391, 392–395, 396–399, 400–401
describing, 390, 391, 396–399
draw, 432–435
hexagons, 390–391
identify right angles in, 384–386, 392–401
identifying, 390–391, 392–395, 396–399
octagons, 390–391
pentagons, 390–391
quadrilaterals, 390–391, 396–399
rectangles, 396–399
rhombuses, 396–399
squares, 396–399
trapezoids, 396–399
triangles, 390–395
Possible outcome, 490–491
Pound, 346–347
Predict, 490
Predict and Test strategy, 74–75
Predict relative size of a solution, 68–69, 74–75, 88–89, 102–103, 350–351, 550–551, 628–629
Predictions, 490
of certain events, 488–489
in experiments, 492–495
of impossible events, 488–489
of likely or equally likely events, 490–494
of possible outcomes, 490–491, 492–497, 583
of unlikely events, 493
Prisms, rectangular, 424–429, 436–437
Probability
arrangements, 500–501
certain events, 488–489
combinations, 498–499
equally likely, 490–491
impossible, 488–489
likely events, 488–489
outcomes, 490–491
possible events, 490–491, 583
predictions, 490, 496–497, 583
recording possible outcomes, 490–495
summarizing and displaying results of experiments, 492–495
unlikely events, 488–489
Problem solving, *See* Linkup, Problem Solving on Location, Problem solving skills, Problem solving strategies, Thinker's Corner
Problem Solving on Location, 64–65, 154–155, 234–235, 298–299, 380–381, 466–467, 512–513, 596–597, 640–641
Problem solving skills
choose the operation, 12–13, 266–267, 606–607
estimate or exact answer, 102–103
estimate or measure, 350–351
identify relationships, 436–437
interpret remainder, 624–625
make generalizations, 450–451
multistep problems, 222–223
reasonable answers, 550–551
sequence events, 142–143
too much/too little information, 168–169, 568–569
use a bar graph, 48–49
use a pictograph, 198–199
Problem solving strategies
draw a diagram, 400–401
find a pattern, 180–181, 480–481
make a graph, 322–323
make a model, 416–417, 530–531
make a table, 114–115, 308–309, 362–363
make an organized list, 500–501
predict and test, 74–75
solve a simpler problem, 584–585
use logical reasoning, 28–29
work backward, 286–287
write a number sentence, 250–251
Product, 160–161. *See also* Multiplication
Projects, 58, 148, 228, 292, 374, 460, 506, 590, 634
Properties
Associative, or Grouping, Property of Addition, 6–7

Associative, or Grouping, Property of Multiplication, 218–219, 220–221
Commutative, or Order, Property of Addition, 6–7
Commutative, or Order, Property of Multiplication, 162–167, 182–183, 202–203, 220–221
Identity Property of Addition, 6–7
Identity Property of Multiplication, 176–177, 220–221
Zero Property of Multiplication, 176–177, 220–221
Pyramids
square, 424–429, 436–437

Q

Quadrilaterals, 390–391, 396–399
attributes of, 390–391, 396–399
classifying, 396–399
identify right angles in, 396–399
naming, 396–399
parallelograms, 396–399
rectangles, 396–399
rhombuses, 396–399
sorting, 396–399
squares, 396–399
Quart, 344–345
Quarter, 109–115, 118–119
Quotient, 242
estimating, 628–629
finding, 242–251, 258–265, 274–283
placing first digit in, 626–627
use of multiplication table to find, 258, 260, 281

R

Range, 310
Ray, 384, 385
Reading strategies
analyze information, 455
choose important information, 277
classify and categorize, 215
compare, 45
make predictions, 583
use graphic aids, 313, 399, 623
Reasonable answers, 550–551
Reasoning
applying strategies from simpler problem to solve more complex problem, 584–585
breaking problem into simpler parts, 584–585
estimating, 68–69, 88–89, 608, 628–629
evaluate reasonableness, 28–29, 72–73, 76, 96–97, 98–99, 120, 446–451, 562–569, 584, 627
generalizing beyond a particular problem to other situations, 450–451
identifying relationships among numbers, 2–3, 158–159, 240–241, 242–245, 246–247
note method of finding solution, 76–79, 98–101, 608–611
observing patterns, 21, 30, 180–181, 217, 470–471, 520–521
Opportunities to explain reasoning are contained in every exercise set. Some examples are 5, 7, 9, 20, 21, 23, 26, 47, 51, 69, 84–85, 91, 94, 103, 116, 119, 129, 137, 139, 159, 161, 164, 176, 177, 181, 184, 186, 197, 201, 203, 212, 217, 219, 221, 236, 239, 241, 243, 244, 246, 247, 248, 259, 261, 262, 263, 276, 279, 282, 285, 307, 309, 315, 323, 325, 329, 347, 351, 360, 365, 387, 388, 389, 415, 424, 425, 426, 432, 444, 445, 449, 451, 470, 471, 472, 479, 488, 489, 494, 497, 498, 519, 522, 529, 531, 533, 543, 549, 559, 563, 577, 582, 601, 604, 622, 627
recognizing relevant and irrelevant information, 168–169, 277
sequencing and prioritizing, 140–141, 142–143
in Thinker's Corner, 27, 79, 101, 167, 185, 205, 249, 341, 361, 387, 427
use of estimation to verify reasonableness of an answer, 68–69, 88–89, 608, 628–629
Recording
data, 302–303, 308–309, 310–312
division of two-digit numbers, 621–623
multiplication of two-digit numbers, 603–605
outcomes of experiments, 490, 492–494
Rectangle, 396–399
Rectangular prism, 423, 424, 426, 436–437
Regrouping
in addition, 70–73, 76–78
in division, 620–623, 626–627
in multiplication, 603–605, 608–611
in subtraction, 90–95, 96–101
Remainder, 618–619
division with, 618–623
interpreting, 624–625
use of, 624
Repeated subtraction, 240–241
Results of a survey, 302–305
Results of probability experiments
display and summarize, 492–494, 496–497
Review Test, *See* Chapter Review/Test
Rhombus, 396–399
Right angles, 384–387, 392–395
defined, 384
in quadrilaterals, 396–399
in triangles, 392–395
Right triangle, 393–395
Roman Numerals, 59
Rounding, 50
estimate differences, 88–89
estimate sums, 68–69
to nearest hundred, 50–51
to nearest ten, 50–51
to nearest thousand, 52–53
rules for, 52
using number line, 50–51, 52
Rule
finding, 216–217, H27
for patterns, 474–475, 476–477
Rulers
using customary, 337–341
using metric, 358–361, 445–446

Scale of a graph, 324–327
Scale, measuring weight, 346
Scalene triangle, 393–395
Schedules, 136–137
Sequence events, 140–141, 142–143
Sharpen Your Test-Taking Skills, H32–H35
Sides
and angles, 390–391
of polygons, 390–391, 396–399
sorting triangles by, 392–395
Similar figures, 412–413
Simplest form of fraction, 542–543, 546–548
Skip-count
by fives, 21, 157
by fours, 321

by tens, 21, 157, 211, 212, H13
by threes, 157, 164–167, 182, 321
by twos, 21, 157, 321
on hundred chart, 21
Slide, 414–415
Solid figures
combining, 428–429
identifying, 424–427, H23
Solve a Simpler Problem strategy, 584–585
Sphere, 424–426, 436
Square pyramid, 424–429, 436–437
Square unit, 448–449, 450–451
Squares, 396–399
Standard form, 22–26, 564, 565
Standardized Test Prep, 16–17, 36–37, 56–57, 84–85, 106–107, 124–125, 146–147, 172–173, 190–191, 208–209, 226–227, 254–255, 270–271, 290–291, 318–319, 334–335, 354–355, 372–373, 404–405, 420–421, 440–441, 458–459, 484–485, 504–505, 536–537, 554–555, 572–573, 588–589, 614–615, 632–633
Statistics
bar graph, 49, 55, 94, 108, 166, 278, 325, 326, 327, 343, 351, 401, 437, 447, 492, 494, 528, 569, 623
line graph, 330–331
line plot, 310–313
pictograph, 2, 13, 18, 26, 29, 79, 140, 156, 174, 181, 198, 207, 210, 223, 267, 320, 322–323
survey, 302–305, 311
Student Handbook, H1–H67
Study Guide and Review, 60–61, 150–151, 230–231, 294–295, 376–377, 462–463, 508–509, 592–593, 636–637
Subtraction
across zeros, 92–95
addition and, 2–3, 94, 96, 98, 100
basic facts, 10–11, H6
decimals, 580–583
and division, 240–241
estimation and, 88–89
fact families, 2–3
fractions, 544–549
greater numbers, 96–101
inverse operation of addition, 2–3
with money, 120–121
regrouping, 90–91, 92–97, 98–100
repeated, 240–241, 280–282
three- and four-digit numbers, 90–95, 96–97
two-digit numbers, 10–11, H6, H21
Sum, *See* Addition
Survey, 304–305, 311–312, 327
Symbols
equal to, 42–43
finding missing operation symbol, 80–81, 104–105, 265, 279
greater than, 42–43
less than, 42–43
not equal to, 80–81
Symmetry, 410–411
line of, 410–411

T

Table of Measures, 139, 342, 348, 359, H41
Tables and charts
analyzing data from, 11, 22, 49, 51, 53, 75, 78, 100, 103, 115, 121, 122, 143, 158, 169, 199, 204, 272, 300, 307, 327, 351, 356, 501, 601, 607, 610
bar graphs from, 327
classifying data from, 306–307
completing, 9, 11, 73, 119, 195, 197, 201, 214, 217, 426, 526
division, 259, 261, 275, 276, 278, 279
frequency, 302, 305
grouping data in, 342, 358, 444, 578
making, 275, 276, 306, 348
as problem solving strategy, 114–115, 308–309, 362–363
multiplication, 202, 212, 239, 276, 278, 279
read, H17
schedules, 136–137
tally, *See* Tally table
use a rule, H19
writing rules, 216, 217
Tally table, 302, 303, 304, 305, 308, 310, 311, 321, 487, 490, 492, 497, H17
Technology Link
Harcourt Mega Math, 2, 8, 22, 25, 43, 70, 77, 91, 111, 119, 158, 162, 182, 200, 213, 216, 242, 247, 261, 274, 281, 311, 325, 330, 489, 493, 547, 580, 603, 619
Technology Linkup, 63, 153, 233, 297, 379, 465, 511, 595, 639
Temperature
degrees Celsius, 368–369
degrees Fahrenheit, 368–369
measuring, 368–369
read a thermometer, H20
Ten thousand
numbers to, 24–29
understanding, 32–33
Tens, place value and, 20
Tenths
adding and subtracting, 580–583
modeling, 560–561
relating fractions and decimals, 558–559
Tessellation, 430–431
Thinker's Corner, 27, 45, 79, 101, 131, 141, 167, 185, 205, 245, 249, 283, 341, 361, 387, 427, 473
Thousands
comparing, 43
multiples of, 24–28
numbers to, 24–29
place value of, 24, 28
rounding, 52–53
understanding, 25
Three-digit numbers
adding, 70–73
division of, 626–627
estimating with, 88–89
modeling, H3
multiplying, 600–611
rounding, 50
subtracting, 90–93
Three-dimensional figures
See Solid figures
Time
A.M., 132–133
analog clocks, 128–131, 132–133, 134–135, H8
calendars, 127, 138–140, H8
days, 138, 139, 140
digital clocks, 128, 129, 131, 133
elapsed, 134–135, 136–137, 138–140
hour, 128
midnight, 132
minute, 128
months, 138, 139
noon, 132
P.M., 132–133
schedules, 136–137

telling, 128–130, H8
units of, 139
weeks, 138–140
years, 138–139
Time line, 142, 143
Too Much/Too Little Information, 168–169, 568–569
Trapezoid, 396–398
Tree diagram, 498–499
Trend, 330–331
Triangles
acute, 392–395
attributes of, 392–395
classifying, 392–395
equilateral, 392–395
as face of solid figure, 424–427
isosceles, 392–393
naming, 392–393
obtuse, 392–395
right, 392–395
scalene, 392–395
sorting, 392–395
Troubleshooting, H2–H31
Turn, 414–415
Two-digit numbers
addition, 8–9, 36, 69
multiplication with, 600–611
record division of, 621–623
subtraction, 10–11, 87
Two-dimensional figures
See Plane figures

Unit cost, finding, 284–285
Units, changing, 348–349
Unlikely events, 488–489, 492–495
Use Logical Reasoning strategy, 28–29

Variable, 243–244
Venn diagram, 400–401
Vertex (vertices), 383, 424–426, 433
Vertical bar graph, 324
Visual patterns, 474–475
Vocabulary Power, 1, 3, 19, 23, 39, 47, 67, 78, 87, 100, 109, 112, 127, 141, 157, 167, 175, 193, 211, 219, 237, 244, 257, 265, 273, 279, 301, 312, 321, 325, 337, 340, 357, 369, 383, 395, 407, 411, 423, 429, 443, 454, 469, 472, 487, 494, 515, 533, 539, 548, 557, 567, 575, 582, 599, 611, 617, 627
Volume
estimate, 452
find, 452–455

Weeks, 138, 139
Weight/Mass
customary units, 346–347
metric units, 366–367
What's the Error?, 5, 33, 47, 78, 94, 97, 117, 133, 166, 181, 184, 197, 214, 249, 259, 287, 305, 329, 349, 361, 398, 435, 454, 477, 497, 518, 548, 563, 582, 604, 622
What's the Question?, 13, 31, 44, 73, 103, 119, 135, 169, 187, 201, 223, 244, 267, 276, 309, 323, 389, 351, 365, 389, 394, 437, 449, 475, 499, 521, 543, 561, 585, 601, 607, 610, 619
Whole numbers
benchmark, 40
comparing, 22–23, 42–45
expanded form of, 22–23, 25–33
ordering, 46–47
place value of, 22–23, 24–27, 32–33
rounding, 50–53
standard form, 22–23, 25–33
word form, 22–23, 25–33
Word form, 22–23, 25–33, 564–565
Work Backward strategy, 286–287
Write a Number Sentence strategy, 250–251
Write a Problem, 3, 29, 31, 41, 51, 89, 100, 121, 140, 143, 159, 166, 181, 199, 223, 251, 265, 282, 303, 347, 411, 427, 437, 451, 477, 521, 582, 604, 627
Write About It, 3, 26, 44, 49, 53, 115, 135, 137, 163, 177, 187, 195, 239, 261, 279, 305, 312, 313, 315, 331, 343, 351, 360, 367, 386, 389, 391, 398, 409, 413, 415, 426, 431, 446, 454, 475, 494, 533, 551, 559, 579
Writing in Math, *Opportunities to write in math are contained in every exercise set. See also* What's the Question?, Write About It, Write a Problem, and What's the Error?

Yard, 342–343
Year, 138, 139

Zero
addition with, 6–7
in division, 262–263
multiply with, 176–177, 220–221
subtraction across, 92–94
Zero Property, 220–221

Photography Credits
Page placement key: (t) top, (c) center, (b) bottom, (l) left, (r) right, (bg) background, (i) inset.
v Laurie Campbell/Stone; xii Stephen J. Krasemann/DRK; xiv Mike Severn/Stone; xix Bill Bachmann/PhotoEdit; xx Tony Freeman/PhotoEdit; 1 Buzz Binzen/International Stock Photography; 4 (b) Larry Lefever/Grant Heilman Photography; 16 Darrell Gulin/Dembinsky Photo Associates; 18 (b) Mugshots/The Stock Market; 23 John Elk III/Bruce Coleman, Inc.; 24 Jeff Greenberg/Photri; 26 Ric Ergenbright/Corbis; 28 AFP/Corbis; 29 Kevin Schafer; 30 Joe McDonald/PictureQuest; 31 Ronn Maratea/International Stock; 34 Lawrence Migdale/Photo Researchers; 36 JC Carton/Bruce Coleman, Inc.; 37 (t) Orion/International Stock; 37 (b) Patricia Doyle/Stone; 38 Index Stock; 45 John Daniels/Bruce Coleman, Inc.; 52 D. Muench/H. Armstrong Roberts; 54 Luiz C. Marigo/Peter Arnold, Inc.; 55 Fred Bavendam/Peter Arnold, Inc.; 58 Doug Perrine/Innerspace Visions; 59 Mike Severns/Stone; 61 Ingrid Visser/Innerspace Visions; 62 Superstock; 63 Bob Burch/Bruce Coleman, Inc.; 64 Mark E. Gibson; 66 David Young Wolff/Stone; 68 Jackie Pirret; 69 Steven Needham/Envision; 77a (b) Scott Barrow, Inc.; 77b (b) June Evelyn Atwood/Contact Photos/PictureQuest; 78 J. Scott Applewhite/AP/Wide World Photos; 89 (t) Patricia Doyle/Stone; 89 (b) Hans Reinhard/Stone; 92 R. Kord/H. Armstrong Roberts; 101 Mark Newman/International Stock Photography; 105 Mark E. Gibson; 109 (tr) Myrleen Ferguson/PhotoEdit; 109 (bl) Robert Rubic, Photographer/New York Public Library; 109 (br) NASA; 109 (tl) The Granger Collection, New York; 113a (t) Jean Higgins/Envision; 113b (t) Jim Pickerell/Stock Connection/PictureQuest; 113b (b) National Gallery of Art Credit Mark C. Burnett/Stock, Boston/PictureQuest; 114 Thayer Syme/FPG International; 118 (t) Don Mason/The Stock Market; 118 (b) Charles D. Winters/Photo Researchers; 118 (bl) Carolina Biological Supp/Phototake; 118 (bc) Stephen J. Krasemann/Photo Researchers; 118 (br) Kelvin Aitken/Peter Arnold, Inc.; 130 Dan Feicht/Cedar Point; 132 Comstock; 133 Vicki Silbert/PhotoEdit; 138 Chuck Mason/International Stock; 139 Chris Sorensen; 146 John Troha/Black Star/Harcourt; 148 Myrleen Ferguson/PhotoEdit; 150 Chromo Sohm/Sohm/Visions of America; 156 Tony Freeman/PhotoEdit; 157 Bill Bachmann/PhotoEdit; 162 Kim Heacox/Peter Arnold, Inc.; 164 Pat & Tom Leeson/Photo Researchers; 167 Zefa/The Stock Market; 181A Bob Krist/Corbis; 181b (t) S. J. Krasemann/Peter Arnold, Inc.; 181B (b) Steve Gettle/ENP Images; 182 Mug Shots/The Stock Market; 191 H. Mark Weidman; 200 Charles Gupton/The Stock Market; 210 Len Rue Jr./Photo Researchers; 211 Laurie Campbell/Stone; 214 Paul Chauncey/The Stock Market; 225 Ted C. Hilliard; 237A Kelly-Mooney Photography/Corbis; 237B Churchill & Klehr; 238 AP/Wide World Photos; 238 (inset) AFP/Corbis; 242 Bob Firth/International Stock; 243 Bill Tocker/International Stock; 250 Mark J. Thomas/Dembinsky Photo Associates; 253 David Stoecklein/The Stock Market; 254 Erwin & Peggy Bauer/Bruce Coleman, Inc.; 255 Robert Winslow/Animals Animals; 256 (t) Anup Shah/DRK; 257 Stephen J. Krasemann/DRK; 260 (b) Orion Press/Stone; 261 Barbara Kreye/International Stock; 262 Christoph Burki/Stone; 263 David Northcott/DRK; 264 Curt Maas/AGStock USA; 268 Terry Donnelly/Dembinsky Photo Associates; 279 NASA/Peter Arnold, Inc.; 291a Effigy Mounds State Park, Iowa; 291b (t) Scott Leonhart/Positive Images; 291b (b) Effigy Mounds State Park, Iowa; 292 Paula Lerner/Woodfin Camp & Associates; 294 (bl) Dick Durrance/Woodfin Camp & Associates; 296 #6 Dick Durrance/Woodfin Camp & Associates; 296 #9 Robert Stottlemeyer/International Stock; 298 Tom McCrathy/Unicorn Stock Photography; 312 (bg) Jose L. Pelaez/The Stock Market; 312 (i) Aneal Vohra/Unicorn Stock Photos; 312 (i) Jim Shippe/Unicorn Stock Photos; 312 (i) Aneal Vohra/Unicorn Stock Photos; 319 Eric A. Wessman/Stock, Boston; 324 Cordon Art-Baarn-Holland; 330 Stephen Frink/Waterhouse Stock Photo; 349A Sandy Felsentha/Corbis; 349B Richard A. Cooke/Corbis; 350 NASA; 357 (c) J H. Robinson/Photo Researchers; 370 Larry Ulrich/DRK; 381 (t) Tetsu Yamazaki/International Stock Photography; 381 (#3) Oliver Strewe/Tony Stone Images; 384 ({no}9) Rod Planck/Tony Stone Images;385 Peter Vadnai/The Stock Market; 386 Lefever/Grushow/Grant Heilman Photography; 393 (b) R. Lautman/Poplar Forest; 409 A American Maze Company's Amazing Maize Maze at Lebanon Valley College, Annville, PA 1993 *www.AmericanMaze.com* Maze design Team; Don Frantz, Ian Marshall, Adrian Fisher, and Rich Whorl; 409B (l) American Maze Company's Amazing Maize Maze at Mountain Creek, Vernon, NJ 2000 *www.AmericanMaze.com* Maze design Team; Don Frantz, Ian Marshall, Adrian Fisher, and Rich Whorl; 409B (r) American Maze Company's Amazing Maize Maze at Cherry-Crest Farm, Paradise, PA 1996 *www.AmericanMaze.com* Maze design Team; Don Frantz, Ian Marshall, Adrian Fisher, and Rich Whorl; 410 Bruce Davidson/Animals Animals/Earth Scenes; 416 M. Gibbs/Animals Animals; 417 (l) B. Von Hoffmann/H. Armstrong Roberts, Inc.; 417 (r) Carolyn A. McKeone/Photo Researchers; 421 (t) Robert & Linda Mitchell; 421 (c) Norman Owen Tomalin/Bruce Coleman, Inc.; 421 (b) Dwight R. Kuhn; 424 Wes Thompson/The Stock Market; 425 Steven Needham/Envision; 432 Index Stock Photography; 447 Superstock; 450 VCG/FPG International; 460 Ryan Williams/International Stock; 462 Nancy Sheehan/PhotoEdit; 466 Nicholas DeVore/Stone; 475 Scott Nielsen/Bruce Coleman, Inc.; 485a Daniel Waggoner/Envision; 485b (b) Steve Bly/Dave G. Houser; 486 Scott Smith/Animals Animals Earth Scenes; 490 Gail Mooney/Kelly/Mooney Photography; 493 John Thomas Biggers, Starry Crown 1987. Acrylic, mixed media on masonite. Dallas Museum of Art. Museum League Purchase Fund; 497 Ed Harp/ Unicorn Stock Photos; 500 TravelPix/FPG International; 506 R. Hutchings/PhotoEdit; 507 Richard Hutchings/Photo Researchers; 516 Kevin Horan/Stock, Boston; 522 Ron Kimball; 523 Barbara Reed/Animals Animals; 524 Chris Sorensen; 526 Chris Kapolka/Stone; 534 Rudi Von Briel/PhotoEdit; 540 Myrleen Ferguson Cate/PhotoEdit; 541 American Images, Inc./FPG International; 542 D. Young-Wolfe/ PhotoEdit; 546 Rudi Von Briel/PhotoEdit; 554 George Lepp/Corbis; 555a (l) Lynn M. Stone; 555a (r) Ted Levin; 555b Francis & Donna Caldwell/Affordable Photo Stock.

Problem Solving On Location Credits:
Page 380(tl), 380(tr), Tom & Susan Bean, Inc.; 380(c), Johnny Johnson/Animals Animals; 380(b), Thomas Kitchin/Tom Stack & Associates; 381(l), Wayne Nelson/Earth Images; 381(tr), Thomas Kitchin/Tom Stack & Associates; 381(cr), Alan G. Nelson/Animals Animals; 381, Jim Roetzel/Dembinsky Photo Associates; 512(t), Pat & Chuck Blackley; 512(b), Adam Jones/Photo Researchers, Inc.; 513(t), Bruce Clarke/Transparencies, Inc.; 513(c), Skip Moody/Dembinsky Photo Associates; 513(b), Ed Kanze/Dembinsky Photo Associates; 596, Montage Stock Photography/Pictures, Inc.; 597(all), Pat & Chuck Blackley; 638-639(all), Indiana State Fair.

All other photographs by Harcourt photographers listed below,
© Harcourt: Weronica Ankarorn, John Bateman, Victoria Bowen, Ken Kinzie, Ron Kunzman, Allan Maxwell, Sheri O'Neal, Quebecor Digital Imaging, Sonny Senser, Terry Sinclair.

Chapter Opener Photography Credits by Chapter: 1 Peter Adams/FPG/Getty Images; 2 Buzz Binzen/International Stock Photography; 3 Ed Simpson/Stone/Getty Images; 4 Lawrence Migdale/Photo Researchers; 5 Paul Harris/Stone/Getty Images; 6 J. Scott Applewhite/Wide World Photos; 7 Travel Pix/FPG International; 8 Dan Feicht/Cedar Point; 9 Thayer Syme/FPG International; 10 Gary Conner/Photo Edit; 11 Kim Heacox/Peter Arnold, Inc.; 12 Harrison Shull/shullphoto.com; 13 Carl & Ann Purcell/Corbis; 14 Paul Chauncey/The Stock Market; 15 AP/Wide World Photos; 16 Mark J. Thomas/Dembinsky Photo Associates; 17 NASA; 18 Karl Weatherly/Corbis; 19 Jose L. Pelaez/The Stock Market; 20 Stephen Frink/Waterhouse Stock Photo; 21 Pat & Chuck Blackley; 22 Lefever/Grushow/Grant Heilman Photography; 23 Miniature Pima Baskets by Rikki Francisco, Photographed by Erik Ostling, Courtesy of Salt River Pima-Maricopa Indian Community; 23(inset) Jerry Jacka Photography; 24 Jeff Vanuga/Corbis; 25 Bruce Davidson/Animals Animals/Earth Scenes; 26 Index Stock Photography; 27 AP Photo/Itsu Inouye; 28 Joseph Allen; 29 Shelley Rotner/Omni Photo Communications, Inc.; 30 Rudi Von Briel/Photo Edit.

ST. JOHN THE BAPTIST SCHOOL
504 S. BROADWAY